ALLIES OF A KIND

CHRISTOPHER THORNE

Allies of a Kind

The United States, Britain
and the war against Japan, 1941–1945

OXFORD UNIVERSITY PRESS
NEW YORK

First published in Great Britain 1978
by Hamish Hamilton Ltd
90 Great Russell Street London WC1B 3PT

Copyright © 1978 by Christopher Thorne

Published in the U.S.A. by
Oxford University Press
New York

ISBN 0 19 520034 9

Printed in Great Britain by
Western Printing Services Ltd, Bristol

To
ALISON and STEPHANIE
For their companionship

CONTENTS

List of Maps

PREFACE

THIS BOOK is in many respects a sequel to my study of the West and the
Far Eastern crisis of 1931 to 1933, *The Limits of Foreign Policy*, although it
can be read quite independently of that work.[1] It marks a further step, in
other words, in what has so far been a nine-year search for an understanding
of Western policies, actions and interactions in the Far East following the
Japanese attack in Manchuria. As was the case with that earlier volume, the
largest area where publications have been lacking in respect of the West and
the 1941–1945 war against Japan is the one involving the policies of Great
Britain. Yet, as for 1931–1933, it did not take long to decide that it would be
highly unsatisfactory to attempt to divorce the British side of things from
that of the United States above all, and of other Western states. I was
encouraged to expand the study in that direction by being able to obtain
access to newly-released material in American archives; in addition, I believe
that one's understanding of United States Far Eastern policies and actions
can be enhanced by placing them within a wider, comparative setting.

In other ways, too, the scope of the study required enlarging, it seemed,
however daunting the size of the undertaking that might result. Geographically, therefore, it embraces not only the United States and Great Britain but
also France, the Netherlands, Australia and New Zealand, all in various
ways involved in the Far Eastern war and in the accompanying problems
that Western states encountered among themselves during those years.
Again, I was prompted to pursue this course by being able to obtain access
to extensive, unpublished archive material in the Netherlands and Australia.
(In France, alas, such documents are as yet unavailable to researchers.)
Besides this, and as was done in the survey of the 1931–1933 crisis, I have
attempted to place the central period of 1941–1945 within a wider setting,
chronologically, in the belief that a full understanding of, say, the separate
policies followed by Britain and the United States during the war, and the
interactions between them, can be achieved only if much earlier developments, stretching back into the nineteenth century, and even to 1776, are
borne in mind. Similarly, I have tried to indicate, in the broadest of ways
only, something of the international aftermath and consequences of the
war against Japan.

The study has become an extensive one in two other respects. First,
unlike, for example, the British official histories of the war, it attempts to
bring together both strategic and military developments on the one hand,

and on the other the more strictly 'political' affairs of bodies like the State Department or Britain's India Office, the Australian Department of External Affairs or the Netherlands Council of Ministers. There is of course something to be gained from keeping such subjects distinct from one another, and I have obviously not sought to provide, for instance, the kind of detailed material on strategic matters or military operations that can be found in books like the British *Grand Strategy* series, Captain Roskill's *War at Sea* volumes, or S. E. Morison's huge survey of U.S. naval warfare against Japan. Nevertheless, a separation of the war-time affairs of foreign offices from those of military staffs and their commanders in the field is essentially an artificial one, and I have sought to bring the two elements together in respect of all the countries concerned.

The second wider aspect of this book involves the setting of Anglo-American relations in their entirety, within which the Allies conducted the conflict in the Far East. Again, the subject of the war-time partnership of Britain and the United States is one which deserves separate treatment, running, indeed, to several volumes. But just as an analysis of the American involvement in China can be enhanced by placing it within a broad setting encompassing both Asia and the West as a whole, so, too, Anglo-American relations concerning that part of the world lying between Suez and thence eastwards to the coast of California can be appreciated far more fully in the light of the association of the two countries with each other on a global scale. In turn, moreover, their mutual dealings in the Far East made their own impact upon the nature and course of the entire partnership, as I have tried to demonstrate.

The result of including these various additional aspects is an undertaking the scope of which could well be thought to be excessive or to require a team of historians to do it justice. While acknowledging the force of such suggestions, however, I continue to believe that there is in this whole subject a synthesis of topics and themes which it is worth attempting; I would also argue that the lone student is in some ways better suited than a group to a task of this kind, even though he may be in danger of flagging as he makes his way to one more country and yet another archive. In any case, I enjoy working that way.

The size and complexity of the study as it stands is one reason why I have put aside the idea of attempting to draw from it conclusions relating to the analysis of alliances in general—a question explored by, for example, George Liska in his *Nations In Alliance*,[2] and, in terms of a particular case, by Roger Morgan in his *United States and West Germany, 1945–1973*.[3] The other reason for not pursuing the subject in this direction is that the Anglo-American war-time alliance (or, more correctly, quasi-alliance) was in so many ways *sui generis* that one would have to make numerous qualifications and reservations when offering it as material for the student of alliance-politics as a whole. As for other, so-called 'scientific' approaches to the study of international relations, I remain, as I confessed in the Preface to *The Limits of Foreign Policy*, sceptical of the value of some of the work done and claims made in this field. Nevertheless, I also continue to believe that the international historian can learn much from the political scientist or the social psychologist. And in setting about an examination of policies during the Pacific war of 1941–45, I have tried to benefit from works concerning foreign policy analysis in general. As in *The Limits of Foreign Policy*, I have dismantled the analytical scaffolding itself before presenting the final study. Readers who are interested in knowing what was involved in that framework may care to refer to Professor Brecher's work, *The Foreign Policy System of Israel*,[4] the scheme of enquiry in which is close to the one I developed for my own purposes before writing the volume on the 1931–33 crisis.

It may be helpful, however, to set out here in brief the shape of the present work. Where both the Anglo-American setting and Far Eastern policies and relationships are concerned, there was obviously a great deal of continuity between Pearl Harbour and the Japanese surrender. Yet there were also important changes which occurred during certain stages of the war, and for this reason, as well as in order to make the study a more manageable one, the 1941–45 period is divided into four sections. Exactly where such dividing lines should be drawn could be argued at length, and would differ according to the specific subject that was being explored. In various ways, however, each of the occasions chosen here was of considerable significance: Pearl Harbour; the Casablanca Conference (where the strategy of 'Germany first' was reaffirmed and the policy of unconditional surrender announced); the Cairo Conference (when China reached the height of her position within Allied circles and at which a declaration was issued over the future of a number of Far Eastern territories; when Britain's decline in strength relative to the U.S.A. was becoming clear, and after which the Anglo-American relationship was to deteriorate in certain respects); the Second Quebec Conference (at which American dominance and Britain's dependence on the U.S.A. for financial and material aid were made more apparent than ever, and where major issues concerning Britain's role in the war against Japan were dealt with); and, finally, the surrender of Japan (not the only possible date at which to terminate the study—one could, for example, carry it on to include the return of the European powers to their Southeast Asian colonial territories, which I have chosen to leave to a subsequent chapter—but one which scarcely needs justifying).

Each of the resulting periods begins with a broad survey of developments in the Second World War as a whole, and in the field of Anglo-American relations in particular. This is followed by a summary of strategic and military aspects of the war against Japan, together with a review of broad themes emerging from that Far Eastern conflict, such as its racial and commercial features, and above all relations between Britain and the United States in that context. Thereafter, these themes, together with others such as the question of the future of colonies or of the post-war international structure to be created in the Pacific and East Asia, are developed within a series of geographical settings: China; Southeast Asia; India; Australasia and the Pacific, and Japan herself. Obviously, a considerable degree of overlapping is involved: to give merely one illustration of this, the strategic and military aspects of the China Theatre were bound up with those of Southeast Asia. For this reason, it has been impossible to avoid having to look at a single topic on more than one occasion, but I have endeavoured to compress material where an element of repetition has been essential. Similarly, in view of the degree of continuity which is to be found where various subjects are concerned, and of the somewhat complex nature of the study as a whole, I have, at the risk of irritating him, tried to be of assistance to the reader by including a fair number of signposts of the 'as-will-be-seen-below' variety.

One further point may be worth making at the outset, this time concerning some of the arguments and judgments that are put forward in the body of the work. No one can explore the history of the war-time years—and this is perhaps all the more so if the student himself lived through that dramatic period—without being aware of the strong emotions which, to this day, can be aroused, particularly among older generations, by such figures as Roosevelt and Churchill, by the contribution that was made to the struggle by one's own nation, or by the achievements of the Anglo-American partnership as a whole between 1939 and 1945. In consequence, I have little doubt that some of the opinions and items of evidence which are proffered in the pages that follow will give rise to not only disagreement but even resentment on the part of certain readers. (I have already encountered this phenomenon where Australia is concerned, when articles that I based on hitherto-unpublished material from numerous American archives revealed that General MacArthur and various other prominent U.S. military and political figures had not always thought very highly of the Australian people or their much-prized Army.)[5]

Therefore I will summarize here three judgments that I hope will in any case emerge clearly enough in the remainder of the book: that, in common with many before me, I believe Franklin Roosevelt to have been a politician of enormous stature and that his friendship for Great Britain was invaluable to her, above all in 1940–41; that there is complete justification for the belief common in Britain and elsewhere in the West that Winston Churchill was a man of greatness, and an incomparable war leader who contributed more than anyone else could have done to the saving of his country in 1940; and that the Anglo-American partnership during the Second World War was a remarkable achievement on the part of two sovereign states. Yet there is, obviously, more to be said than this on these subjects, and in the chapters that follow I shall attempt in that connection to substantiate judgments which may perhaps lead some readers to take a second look at their own views regarding those war-time years.

As was the case when preparing the preceding volume, I have been fortunate enough to be able to supplement the extensive archive material now available by interviews and/or correspondence with various individuals who were involved in the events in question. As usual, it has sometimes transpired that the passage of time has rather narrowed the memory, and in certain instances my own interpretation of developments has come to diverge to a significant extent from the one offered to me by a participant. Nor have I relied upon oral testimony for a major point without having obtained satisfactory documentary support in that respect; where I have only the oral record but feel that the substance of that is of value, I have usually included it as a footnote.

Nevertheless, I believe that my 'feel' for the subject has been much enhanced by those who have helped me in this way, and I am most grateful for the many hours which they have given up to talking or writing to me, often both. My warm thanks therefore go to the following, whose relevant war-time positions are indicated in each case:

Australia

W. D. Forsyth, Head of the Postwar Planning Section of the Australian Ministry of External Affairs.

Sir Robert Menzies, Prime Minister of Australia and subsequently Leader of the Opposition.

General Sir Sydney Rowell, Commander of the Australian forces in New Guinea in 1942.

Sir Alan Watt, Counsellor of the Australian Legation in Washington.

France

M. René Massigli, Commissioner for Foreign Affairs on the French Committee of Liberation; subsequently French Ambassador in London.

Netherlands

Mr. J. G. Kist, Secretary to the Government of the Netherlands East Indies in Australia.

Dr. E. N. van Kleffens, Netherlands Minister for Foreign Affairs.

Mr. den Hollander, Attaché to the Netherlands Senior Naval Officer in Melbourne; subsequently attached to the staff of General MacArthur.

Dr. J. E. van Hoogstraten, Chairman of the Netherlands Indies Commission in Australia; subsequently Director of Economic Affairs for the Government of the East Indies.

United Kingdom

Eric Battersbee, A.D.C. to the Governor of Burma.

Sir Isaiah Berlin, attached to the British Embassy in Washington.

Sir Ronald Campbell, Minister of the British Embassy in Washington; subsequently Assistant Under Secretary of State in the Foreign Office.

Sir Olaf Caroe, Secretary of the External Affairs Department of the Government of India.

Sir Ashley Clarke, Head of the Far East Department of the Foreign Office.

Lord Coleraine, as Richard Law, M.P., Parliamentary Under Secretary of State and then Minister of State at the Foreign Office.

Major General R. H. Dewing, Commander of the U.K. Army and Air Force Liaison Staff in Australia, 1942.

The late Sir Reginald Dorman-Smith, Governor of Burma.

Sir Berkeley Gage, First Secretary of the British Embassy in Chungking; member of the British delegations to the Dumbarton Oaks and San Francisco Conferences.

Lord Gladwyn, Head of the Economic and Reconstruction Department of the Foreign Office.

Leo Handley-Derry, member of 204 Military Mission in Burma and China.

Sir William Hayter, First Secretary of the British Embassy in Washington.

Sir John Keswick, representative of Special Operations Executive in Chungking; subsequently Counsellor of Embassy in Chungking, representing the Supreme Allied Commander, South East Asia.

Philip Mason, Secretary of the Chiefs of Staff Committee, India; subsequently Head of the Conference Section, South East Asia Command.

Earl Mountbatten of Burma, Supreme Allied Commander, South East Asia Command.

Dr. Joseph Needham, Director of the British Council Cultural Scientific Office in China and Scientific Counsellor of the British Embassy in Chungking.

Dame Margery Perham, student of colonial affairs, also involved in the training of colonial administrators.

A. D. C. Peterson, Head of the Political Warfare Section of Force 136, S.O.E., and Deputy Director of Psychological Warfare, South East Asia Command.

Sir Horace Seymour (with Lady Seymour), British Ambassador to China.

The late Sir John Wheeler-Bennett, Personal Assistant to the British Ambassador in Washington; subsequently Head of the New York Office of the British Political Warfare Mission to the U.S.A.

United States

Dr. Dorothy Borg, member of the Secretariat of the Institute of Pacific Relations.

John Paton Davies, American Foreign Service Officer in China; Political Adviser to General Stilwell; one of the American officials to visit Yenan.

Professor J. K. Fairbank, involved in the American cultural relations programme in China, and in work there for the Office of Strategic Services.

W. Averell Harriman, special representative of President Roosevelt in London; subsequently U.S. Ambassador in Moscow.

Professor Konrad Hsu, recruited by British Intelligence to assist in setting up information networks in Japanese-occupied China.

George F. Kennan, Counsellor of the U.S. Embassy in London; subsequently Minister-Counsellor of the U.S. Embassy in Moscow.

Professor Owen Lattimore, Personal Adviser to Generalissimo Chiang Kai-shek; Director of Pacific Operations for the U.S. Office of War Information; member of the Wallace mission to China, 1944; delegate at the conferences of the Institute of Pacific Relations, 1942 and 1945.

H. Freeman Matthews, Counsellor of the U.S. Embassy in London; sub-
  sequently Chief of the Division of European Affairs and Director of the
  Office of European Affairs, Department of State; member of the U.S.
  delegation to the Yalta Conference.
John S. Service, American Foreign Service officer in China; member of the
  American mission to Yenan.

To this list I would add three brief comments. First, I hope that those
concerned will not take it amiss that I have referred to them in the text in the
style usually accorded to historical figures. Second, in the case of Lord
Mountbatten, I am additionally beholden to him for allowing me to see—
though not to quote or cite—certain private papers of his. Finally, as an
example of the pleasure, as well as knowledge, which I have obtained from
such discussions, I would single out my meetings and correspondence with
John Davies, during which an initial relationship of student and participant
has become one of valued friendship—to which I can happily add that, as
will be seen below, this friendship has not inhibited me from directing a few
brickbats, along with some bouquets, at the historical personage of that
remarkable diplomat.

In undertaking the research for this book I have received generous assistance from numerous individuals and institutions. In particular, drs. Albert
Kersten provided invaluable help within the various archives in The Hague,
guiding me through the files and rendering for me key portions of the
relevant documents; the translations from Dutch that appear below are his,
and I am most grateful for the enjoyable partnership which, thanks to him,
we achieved and have continued to this day. I am also once more indebted
to Dr. Theo Alkema, Chief of the Research and Documentation Branch of
the Netherlands Foreign Ministry, who again opened the way for me into
his archives, as well as making me welcome in his own home. Dr. Marius
Meijer was, as before, another kind and informative contact in The Hague.
In Canberra, Mrs. Nicola Feakes was good enough to help me obtain photo-
copies of documents in the Commonwealth Archives.

I am also grateful to the various academic institutions which have invited
me to give seminar papers to faculty and students on certain aspects of my
research over the years, thus providing me with opportunities for debating
my findings. My thanks in this respect go to the Nederlandsch Genootschap
voor Internationale Zaken; the University of California at Los Angeles; the
Southern California Japan Society; Rutgers University; the Fletcher School
of Law and Diplomacy; Yale University—at whose invitation I participated
in the 1974 Mount Kisco Conference on Far Eastern history; the Australian
National University; St. Antony's College, Oxford; and the London School
of Economics. Above all I am indebted to the Council of Trinity College,
Cambridge, for honouring me with an invitation to deliver the Lees-
Knowles lectures to the University in 1976–77, on the subject of my recent
research.

Discussions with individual scholars working in overlapping and adjoining fields of study have also been of considerable value, and in this respect I would mention and thank especially Professor S. van der Wal of the University of Utrecht, Professor Roger Louis of the University of Texas, Professor Robert Dallek of U.C.L.A., Dr. Richard Storry of St. Antony's College, Oxford, Professor Donald Watt of the L.S.E., Dr. Peter Lowe of Manchester University, and Professor Gregory Sevostyanov of the Soviet Institute of General History. The many librarians and archivists involved in my research have also been uniformly helpful; they will forgive me if I do not name them all, but I should like to thank in particular the staff of what was the Portugal Street branch of the Public Record Office in London, those of the manuscript room of the Library of Congress and of the Franklin D. Roosevelt Memorial Library, and above all Mrs. Pat Dowling, whose warm welcome and highly skilled advice make the National Archives in Washington such a pleasure to work in for the peripatetic student of American diplomacy.

It would have been impossible to undertake this programme of world-wide research without the generous assistance of a number of institutions. I wish to record my gratitude, therefore, to the Social Science Research Council, whose grant met the costs of my overseas travel; to the Nuffield Foundation, which awarded me a Social Science Research Fellowship that freed me from teaching and administrative duties for two terms; to the Australian National University, and in particular Professor Bruce Miller, who made me welcome as a Visiting Fellow in the Department of International Relations, Research School of Pacific Studies; and to my own University of Sussex, which provided help towards the costs of travel within the U.K., and which kindly granted me leave during which to complete the final draft of the book.

Extracts from Crown-copyright material in the Public Record Office, London, appear by permission of the Controller of H.M. Stationery Office, while for their permission to quote from various private papers or to record their verbal testimony I am beholden to Mrs. Anna Chennault; Lord Coleraine; the Librarian of Columbia University; Major General R. H. Dewing; Sir Reginald Dorman-Smith; Mrs. Nancy Stilwell Easterbrook; the Reverend E. Eggleston; the English Speaking Union; Lady Beatrix Evison; Mr. Michael Forrestal; Lord Halifax; the Curator of Manuscripts at the Houghton Library, Harvard; Lady Ismay; Professor Owen Lattimore; Admiral William H. Leahy, U.S.N. (Ret.); the Liddell Hart Centre for Military Archives at King's College, London; the late Walter Lippmann; the Librarian of the London School of Economics; the Librarian of Princeton University; the Archivist of the Royal Institute of International Affairs; Eric Sevareid; Commander John Somerville; Dr. Rupert Wilkinson, together with Mrs. Mariana Berry; and Yale University Library. Should there be others whose permission I should have sought—and I have not in every case been able to trace possible literary executors—I ask them to forgive the oversight involved.

*

Finally, it is a great pleasure to be able to thank publicly those friends who have been of special assistance. Captain Stephen Roskill of Churchill College, Cambridge, has continued to provide encouragement which I value highly. As for the labour of reading and commenting on the typescript, this was undertaken by three other scholars who have long been companions of mine on the journey of enquiry into contemporary international history: Peter Calvocoressi, Professor Lloyd Gardner, and Professor Akira Iriye. Their advice has been of very great help, although I must duly add that for the errors and shortcomings that remain I alone am responsible.

Two other friends and their families, Professor Robert Webb and Professor Gordon Wright, did much to sustain me when ill-health interfered with my labours in the United States, while E. K. and Philippa Martin, who have taken an interest in my work for many years, once more made available a rural retreat in which I could revise the final draft of the book without interruption. I also owe a great deal to my former secretary, Barbara Wilczynska, who, having helped arrange my research tours, has gone on to type the final text with a remarkable combination of stamina, enthusiasm and care. Christopher Sinclair-Stevenson of Hamish Hamilton, for his part, has continued to be the ideal publisher, ever-encouraging, yet patient.

Above all, the understanding and support of my family have again formed a central element in the enterprise. Over the years, for example, my two daughters have not only come to accept the inconveniences involved in having a member of the household who studies the history of international relations, but have helped to lighten his task by despatching a stream of letters after him during his assaults on far-flung archives. It is to them, therefore, as they now come near to departing on their own, individual travels, that this book is lovingly and gratefully dedicated.

CHRISTOPHER THORNE
Henfield, Sussex, 1972–77

Notes to Preface

1 C. Thorne, *The Limits of Foreign Policy: The West, the League and the Far Eastern Crisis of 1931–1933* (London and New York, 1972).
2 G. Liska, *Nations In Alliance* (Baltimore, 1962).
3 R. Morgan, *The United States and West Germany, 1945–73: A Study In Alliance Politics* (London, 1974).
4. M. Brecher, *The Foreign Policy System of Israel* (London, 1972).
5 See, e.g., C. Thorne: 'MacArthur, Australia and the British', in *Australian Outlook*, April and August 1975; 'Australia and the Americans: Letters From The Minister', in *The Age* (Melbourne), 8 and 9 Jan. 1975; 'Evatt, Curtin and the United States', in *The Age* (Melbourne), 30 June and 1 July 1974. Also *New York Herald Tribune*, 18 June 1974 and correspondence in *The Australian*, 26 June 1974.

Notes on Abbreviations, References, etc.

Abbreviations used in the text.

A.B.D.A.	American, British, Dutch and Australian Command.
A.F.P.F.L.	Anti-Fascist People's Freedom League (Burma).
A.O.C.	Air Officer Commanding.
A.V.G.	American Volunteer Group (air arm in China).
B.A.A.G.	British Army Aid Group (China).
B.N.A.	Burma National Army.
B.S.C.	British Security Coordination (in U.S.A.).
C.B.I.	China–Burma–India Command (U.S. Army).
C.C.S.	Combined Chiefs of Staff (U.S. and G.B.).
C.E.R.	Chinese Eastern Railway.
C. in C.	Commander in Chief.
C.I.G.S.	Chief of the Imperial General Staff (G.B.).
C.N.O.	Chief of Naval Operations (U.S.).
C.O.S.	Chiefs of Staff Committee (G.B.).
D.G.E.R.	Direction Générale des Études et Recherches.
E.A.M.	National Liberation Front (Greece).
E.L.A.S.	People's Liberation Army (Greece).
F.B.I.	Federal Bureau of Investigation.
F.E.	Far Eastern Division/Office, Department of State.
F.O.R.D.	Foreign Office Research Department.
F.R.P.S.	Foreign Research and Press Service (G.B.).
F.S.M.	Free Siamese Movement.
G.O.C.	General Officer Commanding.
I.C.I.	Imperial Chemical Industries.
I.P.R.	Institute of Pacific Relations.
I.R.R.C.	International Rubber Regulating Committee.
J.C.S.	Joint Chiefs of Staff (U.S.).
J.I.C.	Joint Intelligence Committee (G.B.).
K.M.T.	Kuomintang.
M.O.I.	Ministry of Information (G.B.).
M.P.A.J.A.	Malayan People's Anti-Japanese Army.
M.P.A.J.U.	Malayan People's Anti-Japanese Union.
O.S.S.	Office of Strategic Services (U.S.).
O.W.I.	Office of War Information (U.S.).
P.W.J.C.	Political Warfare Against Japan Committee (G.B.).

R.A.F.	Royal Air Force.
R.I.I.A.	Royal Institute of International Affairs.
R.N.	Royal Navy.
S.A.C.S.E.A.C.	Supreme Allied Commander, South East Asia Command.
S.E.A.C.	South East Asia Command.
S.I.S.	Secret Intelligence Service (G.B.).
S.M.R.	South Manchurian Railway.
S.O.E.	Special Operations Executive (G.B.).
S.W.N.C.C.	State–War–Navy Coordinating Committee (U.S.).
S.W.P.A.	South West Pacific Area.
U.A.C.F.	United Aid To China Fund (G.B.).
U.N.R.R.A.	United Nations Relief and Rehabilitation Administration.

Abbreviations used in references.

AAWC	Australian Advisory War Council minutes, Commonwealth Archives, Canberra.
ADEA	Australian Department of External Affairs files, Commonwealth Archives, Canberra.
ADOD	Australian Department of Defence files, Commonwealth Archives, Canberra.
APMD	Australian Prime Minister's Department files, Commonwealth Archives, Canberra.
APW	Armistice and Post-War Cabinet Committee, London.
AWC	Australian War Cabinet minutes, Commonwealth Archives, Canberra.
BM	British Museum manuscript collection.
BO	Burma Office records, India Office Library, London.
BWP	*The British Way And Purpose*, Directorate of Army Education, London.
CAB	Records of the Cabinet; Cabinet Committees; Chiefs of Staff Committee; Combined Chiefs of Staff Committee; Joint Planning Sub-Committee; Combined Staff Planning Committee; Commonwealth meetings; inter-Allied conferences; Pacific War Council (London); Far Eastern Committee; Cabinet Office. All Public Record Office, London.
Cab	War Cabinet, London.
CCS	Combined Chiefs of Staff Committee records, Public Record Office, London.
CO	Colonial Office records, Public Record Office, London.
COS	Chiefs of Staff Committee records, Public Record Office, London.
CP	War Cabinet memoranda (1945), London.

Ch.A.	China Association records, China Association, London.
CSP	Combined Staff Planners.
DBFP	*Documents on British Foreign Policy, 1919–39*, second and third series.
DC(Ops.)	War Cabinet Defence Committee (Operations), London.
DGFP	*Documents on German Foreign Policy, 1918–45*, series D.
DNZ	*Documents Relating To The New Zealand Participation In The Second World War.*
DO	Dominions Office records, Public Record Office, London.
DS	Department of State decimal and other files, National Archives, Washington, D.C.
FDR	Franklin D. Roosevelt.
FEC	Far Eastern Committee, London.
FE(M)C	Far Eastern (Ministerial) Committee, London.
FO	Foreign Office files, Public Record Office, London.
FRUS	*Foreign Relations of the United States.*
Hansard, H.C. Deb.	*Hansard, House of Commons Debates, 5th series.*
HST	Harry S. Truman.
IMTFE	International Military Tribunal for the Far East, mimeographed records, Imperial War Museum, London.
IO	India Office records, India Office Library, London.
IPR	Institute of Pacific Relations papers, Columbia University, New York.
JCS	Joint Chiefs of Staff Committee and records, National Archives, Washington D.C.
JIC	Joint Intelligence Committee, London.
JPS	Joint Planning Staff, London.
JSM	Joint Staff Mission (of G.B. in U.S.).
MR	Map Room files, Roosevelt Papers, Roosevelt Library, Hyde Park, N.Y.
NCM	Netherlands Council of Ministers minutes, Notulen Ministerraad, 1940–45, Algemeen Rijksarchief, The Hague.
NCol.M	Netherlands Colonial Ministry records, Departement van Koloniën, Ministerie van Binnenlandse Zaken, The Hague.
NFM	Netherlands Foreign Ministry files, Ministerie van Buitenlandse Zaken, Bureau Der Rijkscommissie Voor Vaderlandse Geschiedenis, The Hague.
OPD	Operational Plans Division (U.S. Army) records, National Archives, Washington, D.C.

OSS	Office of Strategic Services, Research and Analysis reports, National Archives, Washington, D.C.
PP	M. Gravel (ed.), *The Pentagon Papers* (Boston, 1971).
PPF	President's Personal Files, Roosevelt Papers.
PREM	Prime Minister's Office files, Public Record Office, London.
PSF	President's Secretary's files, Roosevelt Papers.
PWC(L)	Pacific War Council, London.
PWC(W)	Pacific War Council, Washington, D.C.
RIIA	Royal Institute of International Affairs records, Chatham House, London.
SEAC	South East Asia Command papers, National Archives, Suitland, Maryland.
SWNCC	State–War–Navy Coordinating Committee records, National Archives, Washington, D.C.
UCR	United China Relief, Inc., records, Princeton University Library.
USNOA	United States Navy Operational Archives, Navy Yard, Washington, D.C.
WP	War Cabinet memoranda (1939–45), Public Record Office, London.
WSC	Winston S. Churchill.

Further notes.

Unless otherwise stated, numbers in references are to pages. In order to reduce the length of references a little, I have included full details of sender, recipient and date only when such information appeared to be of immediate value to the reader; elsewhere, only the document and/or file or volume number is given. Where no file or box number appears, it indicates the absence of any permanent classification scheme at the time of my research. Where I have used archive material that has also been published, I have given the latter reference unless compression is involved in the published version.

I have given Japanese names in the text in their native version, that is with the surname before the given name; on the other hand I have omitted Japanese accents, which would be meaningless to the great majority of readers and which to the remainder will be obvious in their absence. The *Times* refers to the London paper, the *New York Times* being named in full. For the sake of brevity, I have generally used the term 'the Far East' as including all those parts of East Asia, Southeast Asia, Australasia and the Western Pacific that were involved in the war with Japan; when dealing with any one of these constituent areas separately I have named it in the more usual fashion.

Although the Soviet Union lies to the West of Japan, it is not included within my use of the term, 'the West'. On the other hand, Australia and New Zealand, situated in the Southern Pacific, are so included. Where the alternatives, 'Thailand' or 'Siam' are concerned, in order to avoid any confusion I have used 'Siam' throughout, largely because the self-styled 'Free Siamese Movement' also figures in the study. All times and dates are local unless otherwise stated.

C.G.T.

PRESIDENT ROOSEVELT: 'I do not want to be unkind or rude to the British, but in 1841, when you acquired Hongkong, you did not acquire it by purchase.'
OLIVER STANLEY (Colonial Secretary): 'Let me see, Mr. President, that was about the time of the Mexican War, wasn't it?'

—Conversation of January 1945

'Each of our friends has his defects so markedly that to continue to love him we are obliged to seek consolation for these defects—in the thought of his talent, his goodness, his affection for ourself—or rather to leave them out of account, and for that we need to display all our goodwill. Unfortunately our obliging obstinacy in refusing to see the defect in our friend is surpassed by the obstinacy with which he persists in that defect . . .'

—MARCEL PROUST, *A la Recherche du Temps Perdu*
(Trans. C. K. Scott Moncrieff, 1969 edition, vol. 4, 56.)

'If the American way of life is to prevail in the world, it must prevail in Asia.'
—PEARL BUCK, speech of February 1942

'Why be apologetic about Anglo-Saxon superiority [to other races]? We are superior.'
—WINSTON CHURCHILL, conversation of May 1943

'The instinct to create myth, to colonize reality with the emotions, remains. The myths become tyrannies until they are swept away, when we invent new tyrannies to hide our suddenly perceived nakedness. Like caddis-worms or like those crabs which dress themselves with seaweed, we wear belief and custom.'

—'PALINURUS', *The Unquiet Grave* (1951 edition, 104.)

PART ONE

The Setting before Pearl Harbour

CHAPTER ONE

THE WEST AND THE FAR EAST, TO SEPTEMBER 1939

THE AMERICAN people, together with others in the West, were astounded by the blows which Japan struck at Pearl Harbour, Malaya and elsewhere in December 1941. Yet it was only in immediate and local terms that these blows fell from a clear sky. In the context of international relations in the Far East, this was far from being the case. Since the early 1930s, and especially since the outbreak of undeclared war between Japan and China in 1937, it had been impossible to ignore the growing threat to the Far Eastern possessions and interests of the West. Both the British and American Ambassadors in Tokyo, for example, had repeatedly warned of the possibility of a sudden attack.

Nevertheless, there were those in high places who had not brought themselves to believe that the Japanese would be so foolish as to challenge the potential might of the United States and Britain. 'Japan has historically shown', wrote the American Secretary of War and former Secretary of State, Henry Stimson, in 1940, 'that when the United States indicates by clear language and bold actions that she intends to carry out a clear and affirmative policy in the Far East, Japan will yield to that policy, even though it conflicts with her own Asiatic policy and conceived interests.'[1] Earlier, in March 1939, Winston Churchill had expressed broadly similar sentiments in a memorandum to the then-Prime Minister, Neville Chamberlain:

'Consider how vain is the menace that Japan will send a fleet and army to conquer Singapore. It is as far from Japan as Southampton is from New York . . . To send such a large part of their strictly limited naval forces on such a wild adventure . . . will never commend itself to them until England has been decisively beaten, which will not be the case in the first year of the war . . . Do not therefore let us worry about this bugbear. . . . You may be sure that provided [Singapore] is fully armed, garrisoned and supplied, there will be no attack in any period which our foresight can measure.'[2]

At the end of 1941, of course, Singapore was not to be 'fully armed, garrisoned and supplied'; nor was it, as Churchill had supposed, 'a fortress . . . with cannon which can hold any fleet at arm's length.' But Churchill's general line of reasoning remains instructive, based in part as it was on the notion that the Japanese were 'an extremely sensible people' who 'would not run such a risk.' Indeed, when the immediate situation in the Far East was far more ominous, in the autumn of 1941, the Prime Minister (as Churchill had by then become) persisted in the same way of thinking. On 20 October 1941, for example, he told the Cabinet's Defence Committee that 'he did not foresee an attack in force on Malaya',[3] while four days before Pearl Harbour he was describing the idea of Japan commencing hostilities as 'a remote contingency.'[4] Like Stimson, Churchill believed that a flexing of Anglo-Saxon muscle would keep the Japanese in their place: therefore, against the wishes of the Admiralty and through a process of illogical reasoning,* he sent the *Prince of Wales* and *Repulse* to their rapid destruction in the belief that their mere presence in the Far East would restrain 'Japanese foreign policy.'

This belief that the Japanese would not act rashly and risk almost certain defeat—an assumption wholly at odds with the actual situation as recorded in the proceedings of Japan's Liaison and Imperial Conferences in 1941[5]—was to be found not merely far from the scene of impending action, in Washington or London. Examples abound of complacency, even scorn, among those who were maintaining the position of the West in the Far East. The Australian Minister to China, for example, en route to his post in 1941, found Dutch officials in the Netherlands East Indies impressive men, but 'they were very satisfied that they had beaten the Japanese [over the latter's demands for massive increases in oil supplies] and were full of contempt for them.'[6] Likewise, the views of Britain's Malaya Command were, in the words of the official war historian, 'out of touch with reality', involving a 'consistent underrating of the efficiency and skill of the Japanese.' For their part, when the garrison of Hongkong found themselves being accurately strafed by Japanese planes, they had been so nourished on tales of the yellow man's ineptitude in the air that they were convinced that German pilots must have come out to undertake the assault.[7] (In this context, one recalls the British Naval Attaché in Tokyo informing the Admiralty in 1935 that the Japanese 'have peculiarly slow brains', and the C. in C. China in 1937 dismissing both Chinese and Japanese as 'these inferior yellow races.')[8] On the American side, the element of insouciance which was present in the Pearl Harbour disaster is well known, followed as it was by what the official American naval historian calls the 'completely incomprehensible' behaviour of General MacArthur in the Philippines, in allowing his planes to present

---

* To the Defence Committee on 17 October (CAB 69/2), Churchill argued for the presence of 'one modern capital ship in Far Eastern waters' by using the analogue of Germany's *Tirpitz*, which was tying down a greatly superior force of British ships. Yet he went on to justify the weakening of the Home Fleet which would be entailed in despatching the *Prince of Wales* by stressing that, if *Tirpitz* did break out in the meanwhile, she would be vulnerable to air strikes—the very weapon that was to spell doom for the *Prince of Wales*. The final decision to send the *Prince of Wales* and *Repulse* on from Cape Town to Singapore is not to be found in the archives, but Churchill's impulsion (with the support of the Foreign Office) and the Admiralty's reluctance are clear. (See S. W. Roskill, *The War At Sea*, vol. I (London, 1954), 557.)

sitting targets on the ground eight or nine hours after learning of the first Japanese attack on Hawaii.[9]

Such Western complacency and underrating of Japan calls for an explanation which stretches back, beyond the immediate pre-war years, and applies to an area wider than that of Japan alone. Obviously, one must allow something for the temptation which in 1941 must have faced men in London, say, or Singapore, lacking as they did adequate means to defend the over-stretched British Empire, to believe that devastation was not at hand, just as their predecessors in 1933, helpless in the face of Japan's seizure of Manchuria, had eagerly and comfortingly assumed that she would somehow suffer from her new gains.[10] More significant than such immediate temptations, however, were the assumptions which had been built up in the eighteenth and nineteenth centuries by many Europeans who arrived in various parts of Asia, that they came as 'the lords of human kind.'[11] Equally significant was the long history of Western misconceptions about East Asia among other areas:[12] the belief, for example, bolstered by a temporary scientific and technological superiority, that Western notions of religion, law, economics and the ordering of society were of universal validity; that, as Henry Stimson put it in the case of China, Christianity, 'American idealism' and 'our economic civilization' were the key to that country's development 'along the pathway of modern civilization.'[13]

There were thus at least two strands among Western attitudes towards Asia and the Far East in particular which, although somewhat contradictory, helped to provide comfort amid the perils before Pearl Harbour. One was a tendency to assume that the Japanese would ultimately make their decisions on the basis of an idealized process of Western rationality, weighing up the prospects of gain and loss, pleasure and pain, as would, in Churchill's phrase, 'sensible people.' The present writer's *Limits of Foreign Policy* has attempted to show how deeply embedded were such assumptions during the Far Eastern crisis of 1931–33, when Lord Cecil and others on both sides of the Atlantic believed that the Japanese would bow to 'world opinion', as a John Stuart Mill might have done, or shrink from the prospect of economic deprivation as would, perhaps, a true Benthamite.

If this line of thinking in a way 'elevated' the Japanese, or at least Japan's political and military leaders, to the status of honorary Westerners, there existed at the same time, however, a pervasive racial arrogance—explicit or implicit; sometimes confident, sometimes defensive—which relegated not only the Japanese but all Asians to the second class or lower. There are many examples of this, British and American, high and low, both before and during the war, and the subject will be covered more fully in later stages of the book. But at the outset it is the long-term historical setting which has to be borne in mind when one hears Churchill, for example, talking of India, 'launch into a most terrible attack on the "baboos", saying that they were gross, dirty and corrupt';[14] when observing the Prime Minister refer to the Chinese as 'Chinks' or 'pigtails',[15] or talk of 'not letting the Hottentots by popular vote throw the white people into the sea',[16] or—trivial but again instructive—choose as his topic of conversation with a Chinese political mission to London the game of mah-jong.[17] 'To President [Roosevelt]', noted Churchill's doctor in 1943, 'China means four hundred million people who are going to count in the world of tomorrow, but Winston thinks only of the colour of their skins; it is when he talks of India or China that you remember he is a Victorian.' 'Little yellow men' was one phrase with which he was wont to refer to the Chinese[18] (Halifax wrote of them in his diary as 'Chinks'),[19] while his close adviser, Lord Cherwell, was, in his biographer's words, 'filled with physical repulsion' by non-white people.[20]

It is not enough simply to dismiss Cherwell as the emotional cripple which he was,[21] or to make an exception of Churchill as having been a notable but idiosyncratic racist.* Nor is it merely a matter of finding strong racial prejudices in other Allied leaders—in Stimson, for example, who believed that 'social equality [between white and black in the United States] . . . was basically impossible . . . because of the impossibility of race mixture by marriage', and who would accept only that Negroes made 'fairly good soldiers when they are officered by white men'.[22] Or in General Stilwell, who, when passing through Africa, wrote in his diary of 'niggers' and 'fuzzy wuzzies'.[23] Or in the patronizing remarks of Roosevelt himself—the champion of colonial peoples—about the inhabitants of Burma. ('I have never liked the Burmese', he wrote to Churchill, 'and you people must have had a terrible time with them for the last fifty years. Thank the Lord you have He-Saw, We-Saw, You-Saw [i.e., U. Saw, the Prime Minister of Burma who had been in touch with the Japanese] under lock and key. I wish you could put the whole bunch of them into a frying pan with a wall around it and let them stew in their own juice.')[24]

This phenomenon of a sense of white racial superiority goes much wider and deeper than a few eminent men such as these. It embraces, for example, the attitude of many American troops in India and Burma, where, despite their country's scorn for British imperialism, they were wont to refer to Indians as 'wogs' and to Chinese as 'slopeys', and where one serving American journalist felt bound to admit that 'British color prejudice seemed much less violent than our own.'[25] In terms of Japan during the war, also, the very word 'Japs' helped inculcate the idea that the West was fighting a different species—as did the unspeakable atrocities committed by the

---

* That Churchill was a racist, which seems quite apparent from the written evidence presented throughout this book, has been confirmed for the writer by conversations with, for example, Sir Reginald Dorman-Smith, who, as Governor of Burma during the war, had to try to communicate with the Prime Minister on related subjects. In using the term 'racist', for which there is not as yet an agreed definition, I follow Professor Hugh Tinker in his *Race, Conflict, and the International Order* (London, 1977), when he suggests: 'We have a *racial* factor when one group of people, united by their own perception of inherited and distinctive qualities, are set apart from another group with (supposedly) separate inherited and distinctive qualities. We have a *racist* factor when one group claims a dominant position, justified by the supposed inferiority of the other group.' On Churchill's child-like, black-or-white, stereotyped images of other peoples, see R. W. Thompson (ed.), *Churchill and Morton* (London, 1976), 194.

enemy.[26] It will be suggested below that there is a connection between such war-time features and the American attitude towards Vietnamese 'gooks' in the 1960s; likewise there is a clear link between Washington and London's false calculations about Japan in 1941 and 'the mistakes of political judgment which stemmed from ignorance, which was the base of American policy in Vietnam . . .: ignorance not so much of current facts as of their significance in terms of an unfamiliar cultural framework.'[27]

In one of its vital aspects, the Pacific war of 1941 to 1945 was a racial war, and needs to be seen as such within a perspective of a hundred years or more. That is not to say that the immediate causes of the conflict were essentially racial ones. They were not. As we shall see below, the Japanese struck at Pearl Harbour in 1941 in the belief that only thus could they establish and protect the self-sufficiency, safety and independence of their country, and that dominance over extensive areas of East and Southeast Asia was vital in these respects. As for Britain and the United States, each in its different way had interests in those same parts of the world that it was not prepared to surrender, and saw a further extension of Japan's power and conquests as a major threat. In these terms, the colour of the skins of those involved was not a matter of primary significance. And yet, in its wider setting, the war between Japan and the West did bring sharply into focus tensions of a racial nature that had long existed, with that aspect achieving much greater prominence once battle had been joined. Time and again, as will be seen, it was the threat to Western, white prestige that troubled those in power in Washington and London. When Churchill, for example, read a report of September 1942 by the Netherlands Prime Minister on the situation in the now-occupied Dutch East Indies, what he singled out was 'the interesting conclusion that the natives were looking to Europeans for their future, and were not making common cause with their fellow-Asiatics. This augured well.'[28]* Again, where the threat to Australia and New Zealand was concerned, a similar line of reasoning is to be found in both London and Washington, despite their differences in other respects. 'We could never stand by', Churchill told the Cabinet, 'and see a British Dominion overwhelmed by a yellow race';[29] likewise, we shall see that Admiral Ernest King, the United States Chief of Naval Operations and no lover of things British, argued that Australia and New Zealand must be saved because they were ' "white men's countries".'[30] In Australia itself during the war, officials

* Such an assumption, startling as it is in retrospect, was by no means uncommon at the time. A senior official of the Netherlands Indies administration, for example, has confirmed to the author what the archives in The Hague suggest: that until the return to Java in the late summer of 1945, there was no awareness of the extent to which Indonesian nationalism had taken hold of the population. Similarly, with the paternalist designs of de Gaulle's administration towards the end of the war bearing no relation to the situation in Indochina, 'Beaucoup trop de Français', in the words of one of the French officials concerned, 's'imaginent que les Indochinois attendent notre retour avec impatience et s'apprêtent à nous recevoir à bras ouverts.' (J. Sainteny, *Histoire d'Une Paix Manquée* (Paris, 1953), 47; interview with Dr. van Hoogstraten; see also D. B. Marshall, *The French Colonial Myth and Constitution Making In The Fourth Republic* (New Haven, 1973), 137.)

anxiously contemplated the future position of the white man in Asia and the Pacific, seeking new arguments with which to justify their 'White Australia' policy—euphemistically changed in official documents to 'the established Australian immigration policy'—against a background of antipathy to idealistic pronouncements on the world stage concerning the brotherhood of man. 'Don't get led into inviting Wendell Willkie to Australia', wrote W. S. Robinson, a prominent businessman, international negotiator and companion of the Minister for External Affairs, Dr. H. V. Evatt, to the latter: 'he can do no good and . . . I can't see his attitude towards the 1,100 million coloured people in the vicinity of Australia appealing very much to the 7 million Australians.'[31] Even the arrival of American Negro troops in Australia caused a flurry of trouble.[32]

The Australian Minister in Chungking, writing in 1943, saw an even more disquieting possibility,

'namely, that the Asiatic peoples might band together [after the war] to forward their mutual interests; in fact, a Pan-Asiatic movement. India might be able to come to an arrangement with Japan; China might then join in and with her millions she would be a tremendous asset to the combination . . . The idea has an attraction to the Asiatic mind and I feel it must be watched. In my opinion the possibility is such that we should do our best to come to a working arrangement both with China and India before the [peace] conference.'[33]

Others shared this concern. Churchill, for example, uneasy at the possible consequences of Chiang Kai-shek's visit to New Delhi in 1942, foresaw 'a pan-Asian malaise [spreading] through all the bazaars of India.'[34] In the State Department, the very case of India, and of Britain's refusal to grant her immediate independence, was seen in similar terms: India might be overrun, and 'psychologically, Japan might well obtain such a secure place as the leader of the Asiatic races, if not the colored races of the world, that Japan's defeat by the United Nations might not be definitive.'[35] Netherlands officials in Australia talked anxiously with General MacArthur in similar terms, about how to avoid 'a racial war in Southeast Asia.'[36] Away in South Africa, Jan Smuts felt the same currents to be at work: 'I have heard Natives saying', he wrote, '"Why fight against Japan? We are oppressed by the whites and we shall not fare worse under the Japanese."'[37] Fears such as these, indeed, were often greater in Western circles than were fears of Communism, at least until the later stages of the war. Roosevelt provides one more illustration of this, believing as he did in the vital necessity of keeping China out of a pan-Asiatic movement and within the Western (above all, American) camp, while in private he was burbling away in his hare-brained fashion about the possibility of bringing about a cross-breeding of European and various Asian races in the Far East in order to produce a stock less delinquent than the Japanese, whose skull pattern, he suspected, being less developed than that of the Caucasians, might be responsible for their aggressive behaviour.[38] There would appear to be a similarity between such a way of thinking and the approaches adopted by others during the war. The President's notions, of course, were totally removed from anything in the nature of genocide; and yet, the kind of assumptions which, it seems, he was ready to make suggest that the Germans were not alone at this time in thinking of fellow human-beings as *Untermenschen*. We shall later observe Leo Amery, the British Secretary of State for India, making a proposal that carried similar implications.

Moreover, the State Department's reference to 'all the colored races of the world' also serves as a reminder that racial aspects of the war could have explosive implications for the United States within her own borders. Indeed, even early in the twentieth century not only had there been fierce outcries against the amount of yellow and other non-white immigrants in the U.S.A.,* but the fear had been expressed that an expansionist Japan might find sympathizers among America's Negroes.[39] Now, not only was the National Association for the Advancement of Colored People championing the cause of Indian independence, but in 1942–43 small pro-Japanese Negro cults were unearthed in a few American cities. 'Write on my tomb', one Negro draftee was said to have declared, 'Here lies a black man, killed fighting a yellow man for the protection of a white man.' Writing in 1942, Gunnar Myrdal observed: 'In this war there was a "coloured" nation on the other side—Japan. And that nation had started out by beating the white Anglo-Saxons on their own ground ... Even unsophisticated Negroes began to see vaguely a colour scheme in world events.'[40] 'I venture to think', declared Gandhi to Roosevelt in the same year, 'that the Allied declaration that [they] are fighting to make the world safe for freedom of the individual sounds hollow, so long as India, and for that matter, Africa, are exploited by Great Britain, and America has the Negro problem in her own home.'[41]

Gandhi's warning was merely one sign of the extent to which, on the Asian side, the war was being seen in racial and colour terms. The fact that Japan's Great East Asia Coprosperity Sphere failed to mask the reality of Japanese imperialism and domination did not vitiate the appeal of Tokyo's call to fellow-Asians to throw off the domination of the alien West.[42] In Indonesia, for example, as we shall see, Japan's fostering of anti-Dutch nationalism met with a considerable response; even in the Philippines, so eternally and unswervingly loyal to America in the latter's mythology, a collaborationist native regime was found and in 1943 given its 'independence.'[43] In Burma, politicians like Ba Maw and guerilla leaders like Aung San worked with the Japanese to ensure the ending of British rule;[44] in Malaya, there was some stirring of pan-Malay ideas involving possible links with Indonesia,[45] while it seems that at the outset 'the bulk of the Malays were not particularly hostile to the Japanese occupation.'[46]

* Woodrow Wilson, for example, running for President in 1912, declared: 'I stand for the national policy of exclusion. The whole question is one of assimilation of diverse races. We cannot make a homogeneous population of a people who do not blend with the Caucasian race.' See R. F. Weston, *Racism in U.S. Imperialism* (Columbia, South Carolina, 1972).

There remained, it is true, great tensions and animosities among the various societies which made up a country like Burma and Malaya, as well as divisions within what were to become Indonesia and Vietnam. This factor, together with mounting anti-Japanese sentiments (in Ba Maw's words, 'the [racial] polarity was complete from the beginning')[47], made the notion of a lasting pan-Asianism as impracticable as, say, pan-Slavism or pan-Africanism. Yet Ba Maw, then head of the 'independent' Burmese Government, was also correct when he described the Great East Asia Conference, held in Tokyo in November 1943, as having been dominated by 'a new Asian spirit.'[48] 'The Pacific War', writes a former official in Malaya and distinguished historian of the region, 'created an entirely new pattern in Southeast Asian politics—so much so that the observer who was fairly closely in touch with the situation in 1940 would, if he did not return to Southeast Asia until 1948 and had not kept himself up to date with a close study of reports, find himself unable to recognize what he saw.'[49]

Even earlier, writing in 1942 amid the shock of Japan's initial triumphs, Dr Margery Perham had drawn attention in *The Times* to the change that was taking place:

'Japan's attack in the Pacific has produced a very practical revolution in race relationships. An Asiatic people has for the moment successfully challenged the ascendancy there of three great white imperial powers. Indian troops, towards whom a changed India may develop a more direct connexion, are fighting for our colonial empire; Chinese, Indonesian and Filipino soldiers, as well as American and Dutch, are all in the same battle. Will our colonies, saved from Japanese conquest by this alliance in arms, revert to the same status of imperial possessions with all their links gathered exclusively to Whitehall? Yet if the alliance in arms is to develop into a Far Eastern cooperation for defence and development, what an energetic exercise in racial understanding with Asiatic Powers, including Russia, must be built up almost from nothing in the next few years!'[50]

In this perspective, the assault launched by Japan at Pearl Harbour can be seen as only one aspect of a widespread Asian revolt, both spiritual and material, racial in outline and directed against an Occidental world order—political, economic and cultural. 'The central fact of modern East Asian history', writes Professor Fairbank, 'and of [American] relations there is that the intrusion of the West into Asia by sea during the past five centuries has produced a conflict of cultures which in the case of China still goes on.'[51] The Asian revolt had left other notable landmarks, such as the 4 May (1919) movement in China, and, as Professor Fairbank observes, is still a potent force at the time of writing.* In 1941, it threw light upon, amongst other things, those means of superior force which had been employed initially by

* 'Independence to the East Asian mind', writes Richard Harris in *The Times* of 13 December 1974, 'means first the removal from the totality of East Asian civilisation of all Western intrusions and the complete fulfilment of an acquired nationalism.'

various Western powers themselves in winning the position they still held in Asia on the eve of Pearl Harbour. This, indeed, was one of the contextual questions which was raised by an Asian member of the International Military Tribunal for the Far East in Tokyo after the war, Mr. Justice Pal of India, whose observations (which will be set out in a later chapter) on the enjoyment by the Western powers before 1941 of a privileged position did not make comfortable listening for those who now proclaimed their cause to be that of peace and justice.[52]

This potential embarrassment existed, even though many on the Western side did not see it, understandably regarding their fight against Japanese cruelty and aggression as being undertaken for the highest ends. 'If ever an army [i.e. the British Fourteenth Army in Burma] fought in a just cause', wrote Field Marshal Slim later, 'ours did. We coveted no man's country; we wished to impose no form of government on any nation. We fought for the clean, the decent, the free things of life . . .'[53] Likewise, few had the time, or inclination, to reflect on another aspect of the setting which Pal was to emphasize during the war-crimes trial, namely the predominantly Anglo-American economic world order which Japan had faced as she developed in the late nineteenth century, together with the rapid shutting of commercial doors against her by the West when she became all-too competitive in various fields during the inter-war period.[54]

The economic factor within Western policies during the war itself will figure prominently in this study—bullish American expansionism, for example, and the desperate hopes entertained in London of somehow being able to cobble together again the position which had been lost. This does not mean that the driving force of economic imperialism is being advanced as the sole key to Western policies: men and governments were moved by a variety of motives. In addition, even within business and expatriate communities themselves one can find an acceptance that there would have to be a new economic order in the Far East after the war. 'The people will never stand for a mere restoration of the past', an Englishman whose family had been living in Malaya for a hundred years wrote to a senior Colonial Office official. 'They have suffered too great a shock and too great a disillusionment . . . After all, it never was right to run a country in the interests of capitalists at home rather than in the interests of those whose homes it was and who indeed knew no other home.'[55] A *Times* leader of March 1942 likewise recognized that

'the defect of the British Colonial system, and the essence of the challenge which it has to meet, is that it has been too long and too deeply rooted in the traditions of a bygone age, and that it has retained too much of that "stratified" spirit of inequality and discrimination whose last strongholds are now being rapidly attacked and eliminated in our contemporary society.'[56]

Enthusiasm for Empire in Britain had long since passed its zenith, and Empire itself, in the words of A. P. Thornton, had become 'the narrowest world of all—the world of the clubs and the shooting boxes of a colonised Scotland.'[57]

Whatever the qualifications that have to be made, however, it remains essential to view the Far Eastern war of 1941–45 in wide perspective, not least in terms of underlying Western attitudes, assumptions and aspirations, and of the means that had been adopted to establish the Western presence in Asia and the Far East in particular; of the forces that were rising up against that presence, and of the particular interests that were seen as being at stake. Indeed, if one takes as a starting point the very beginning of the age of Western dominance in Asia, with the arrival of Vasco da Gama at the end of the fifteenth century,[58] then it can be suggested that in one sense, despite their eventual surrender in 1945, the Japanese had already won their war. Some contemporaries, even, realized as much. One French observer, for example, who had spent the war in Batavia, drew up a report towards the end of 1945, as the Japanese-sponsored Indonesian nationalists resisted the reimposition of colonial rule, in which he concluded that, 'though defeated in a general sense, Japan has "won the war" in this corner of Asia.'[59]

True, the Asian position of the European powers was being slowly undermined even before 1941; true, there was still to come in the Far East the full manifestation of American power and arrogance of spirit. But the Japanese victories of 1941–42 meant that the position of the white man in Asia—Americans as well as Europeans—could never be the same again. Brutally, yet in a way mercifully, they set a far shorter term than would otherwise have been the case to the European empires; and although in the short run they opened the way for the attempted realization of the belief, held by Stimson and others, that the United States should 'police the world',[60] they also increased the futility of the accompanying assumption, as expressed by MacArthur, that 'the future, and indeed the existence of America, were irrevocably entwined with Asia and its island outposts, . . . Western civilization's last earth frontier.'[61]

At the same time, developments during the war between Asia and the West are not the only ones which need to be seen within a perspective reaching well back from 1941. The same is true, even if the time-scale involved is somewhat less, of war-time relations among Western states themselves. To give an obvious example, one needs to bear in mind amongst other things the revolt of the American colonies at the end of the eighteenth century as well as the paternalism of America towards China from the early twentieth century, when reading the following message to President Truman, written in May 1945 by the American Ambassador to China:

'Should Lord Louis [Mountbatten] or any other British Admiral or General receive this appointment [as Commander of United Nations forces in China] in preference to an American, it would constitute an overwhelming victory for the hegemony of the imperialist nations and the principles of colonial imperialism in Asia . . . In fact we have found evidence that some of Great Britain's agents were actually endeavouring to keep China divided against herself . . . The question is, will we now permit British, French and Dutch imperialists to use the resources of America's democracy to reestablish imperialism in Asia . . .'[62]

There were times, of course, when some of those involved in the international politics of the war did provide their own long-term analyses of what was taking place. On the British side, for example, one could scarcely remain unaware of the great change that had taken place within only a decade in the relative positions of Britain and of the United States in the affairs of China. Thus, the Foreign Office's adviser on China, describing for the inter-departmental Far Eastern Committee in December 1944 how 'the American position in China . . . has developed, as it were at one step, into a general and practically overwhelming predominance', quoted a note on the subject written by his counterpart in the British Embassy in Chungking:

'Comparing China's foreign policy in 1943 with her attitude of ten years earlier', Sir Eric Teichman had observed, 'nothing is more striking than her dependence on America and her acceptance of American leadership in her affairs. Signs of this meet one at ever turn, alike in the cultural, diplomatic, economic, financial and military fields . . . On our side, because we are not in a position to do otherwise, we have accepted this condition and have abdicated from the position of leadership which we have occupied in China for the past hundred years. China is by agreement regarded as in the American theatre of war, a decision the consequences of which seem to become more far-reaching every day; we are not in a position to keep pace with the United States in the furnishing of financial, economic and military assistance to the Chinese and their Government; and in the diplomatic sphere, where ten years ago we naturally took the lead, we now wait anxiously to see what the American Government may do.'[63]

In short, without going back in detail to the Western arrival on the Asian scene in the late fifteenth century, it is as well to recall various antecedents of the Pacific war in order to obtain a fuller appreciation of the tumultuous and tangled developments of 1941–45. Both the events and the underlying themes which are involved are already the subject of numerous works, including the predecessor to the present volume, and only a brief and selective survey will be provided here.[64] For example, for the Chinese during the Second World War it was a matter of considerable importance to put an end to the system of treaty ports and the extraterritorial legal and financial privileges which Western states, led by Britain, had forcibly extracted from China from 1842 onwards.* Where Japan is concerned, her assault on the West needs to be seen in the context of her rapid development as a modern

* It is interesting to note in passing that, exactly a century before Pearl Harbour, there occurred at Canton resistance to a British invading force, resistance which some historians have seen as the first evidence of a modern spirit of nationalism among the Chinese masses. (See Reischauer, Fairbank and Craig, *East Asia: The Modern Transformation*, 143.)

power—absorbing Western technology and techniques in part in order to
resist the West—after having concessions forced from her by Commodore
Perry and his American warships in the 1850s.

For Japan, indeed, unlike China, the extraterritorial privileges obtained
by the West had been set aside before the end of the nineteenth century, by
which time Japan had already inflicted defeat upon China in battle (1894–5),
and was on the verge of two even greater achievements, the securing of an
alliance with Britain in 1902 and the defeat of a major white power, Russia,
in 1904–5. The repercussions throughout Asia of this last triumph were
considerable, and can be linked with Japan's later victories of 1941–42 as
irreversible setbacks to the entire position of the West in that continent.
'The defeat of Russia', writes a historian of nationalist opposition in
British India, 'had freed the minds . . . of the young men of India . . . from
the spell of European invincibility',[65] while a Japanese contemporary
declared that 'the war proves that there is nothing that Westerners do
which Asians cannot do, or that there is nothing Westerners try that Asians
cannot also try.'[66] Japan's growing strength was also apparent during the
First World War, as she seized Germany's Far Eastern territories and
pressed for further concessions from China, in the shape of the Twenty-One
Demands of 1915. At the Paris peace conference Japan failed to obtain the
lasting benefits to which she felt entitled; but the Washington Conference of
1921–22, by freezing work on the fortified bases of Britain and the U.S.A.,
as well as of Japan, in the Western Pacific, did implicitly recognize and help
to preserve what was to be a vital factor in 1941: an immense Japanese
military superiority in local terms. Any Western doubts on this score should
have been removed in 1931–33, when Japan seized Manchuria from China,
creating there the puppet state of Manchukuo. The West might protest
discreetly or through the League of Nations, and eager internationalists
might believe that economic sanctions would bring about a speedy Japanese
withdrawal. In essence, however, the choice for the United States, Britain,
France and others lay between what amounted to a humiliating acquiescence,
and the high risk of a major war in which Japan, for all her long-term
vulnerability, would start with very great advantages. The West chose
passivity; Japan, unrepentant, left the League of Nations.

This Manchurian crisis, ten years before Pearl Harbour, did not directly
involve the Soviet Union. Nevertheless, the Russian/Soviet presence in the
Far East had long been of great potential significance, a factor which was
also to be of growing concern to both Western and Japanese officials as the
Pacific war approached its closing stages. Russia, too, had demanded and
obtained concessions from China—more substantial ones, indeed, than the
West's—in the shape of the Maritime Provinces situated between the Ussuri
River and the Pacific, ceded by China in 1860. And although the defeat at
the hands of Japan in 1904–5 was a substantial setback to further Russian
ambitions in the Far East (notably in Korea and Manchuria), her presence,
centred upon Vladivostok and sustained by the Trans-Siberian Railway,
remained a formidable one. Moreover, there was to be a broad continuity

of policies from the Tsarist to the Soviet regimes, each seeking to dominate Northern Manchuria through control of its main communication system, the Chinese Eastern Railway. In the 1920s, Moscow offered encouragement to the forces of anti-Western nationalism in China, but this did not prevent her from delivering a sharp military rebuff to those same forces in 1929 when they resulted in a Chinese attempt to loosen the Soviet hold on the C.E.R. Japan, the old enemy, presented Moscow with a more formidable challenge, however, and when she took over Northern Manchuria in 1932 the Soviet Union acquiesced, even to the point of selling her C.E.R. rights to the Manchukuo regime in 1935. Even so, the Soviet interest in dominating the communications of the vital area north of the Great Wall remained, as Stalin was to demonstrate in the demands he made upon China in 1945.

Meanwhile the United States, although lacking Russia's firm and extensive territorial base in the area, had become more closely involved in East Asian affairs since the days when she had followed Britain in securing extraterritorial privileges from China and had led the way in 'opening up' Japan. Notably, in 1898 she obtained the Philippines as a result of war with Spain, thereafter crushing a native nationalist movement whose declaration of independence, ironically, was the first of several such documents for which Asians took America's own declaration of 1776 as a model. Thus, by the turn of the century it seemed that 'Manifest Destiny' had moved on westwards from the New World to give the United States a chain of possessions—however slender and overstretched in strategic terms—from the Hawaiian Islands, through Guam and other small ones in the mid and Western Pacific, to a Philippine base which some regarded as a vital springboard from which to make commercial and political advances into the mainland of Asia itself. No further territorial acquisitions followed, but the inclination towards expansion found expression in, for example, attempts through dollar-diplomacy to secure an interest in Manchurian railway development. At the same time, although no intervention on the ground occurred, the self-appointed role of mentor and guardian of China—happily, in American eyes, Republican China since 1912—was beginning to find expression. In this context, the major success achieved before 1931 appeared to be the Washington Conference of 1921–22, for which the United States supplied the main impetus and where nine powers, including Japan, joined in a reaffirmation of China's sovereign independence and pledged their respect for her territorial and administrative integrity.

Woven in among these and other events which were helping to shape the Far Eastern international scene in the 1930s, there were developments and themes—like those in the field of racial conflict, mentioned earlier—which were also to be of significance during the Pacific war. Where the various Western powers were concerned, for example, the essential dependence of the French and Dutch positions in the Far East upon that of Britain can be seen long before 1941; so, too, can the growing attraction of their colonial resources, above all those of the Netherlands East Indies, for a Japan that was greatly reliant on external supplies of certain raw materials, such as oil.

Or again, there were the long-standing differences (although not necessarily noticed by people living under colonial rule) between the imperial philosophies of France and of Britain, differences which made it more likely that, ultimately, London would hand over independence to a distinct and separate Burma, say, whilst Paris would struggle on to Dien Bien Phu in its desire to preserve in Indochina the indivisible body of France.*

The war with Japan, as noted already, was to raise acutely this issue of the future of the European empires. Long before this, however, Britain had herself placed a question mark over her presence in India and elsewhere, however reluctant and inadequate the process of abdication appeared in the eyes of local nationalists, and however far-distant or unthinkable, even, in practical terms, the day of departure might seem to many of those engaged in administering the overseas territories. Moreover, although by 1921 Britain's empire had attained even larger proportions than before the First World War, at home there had also been an increase in anti-imperialism, and a marked decline of what has been termed 'the sense of a moral basis for imperial rule.'[67] In this respect, Churchill's fiercely negative stance during the Second World War was to be anachronistic, in terms not only of the society of the time but of British history well before 1939. During his fight to prevent the Government of India Act being passed in 1935, this had not mattered so much, except that it helped to weaken his position when he came to warn against the threat from Nazi Germany.[68] After 1940, however, it was easy for the world to assume that Churchill spoke for Britain, and easy for anti-British and anti-imperialist sentiment in the United States, for example, to be reinforced thereby. Nor was it Americans and Asian nationalists alone who found unacceptable, during a war fought in the name of freedom, an imperial outlook which reflected the Prime Minister's experiences as a cavalry subaltern in India around the turn of the century. It was his own Secretary of State for India, the scarcely-radical Leo Amery, who in 1943 wrote in despair to the Governor of Burma about Churchill:

'The thing is that he has an instinctive hatred of self-government in any shape or form and dislikes any country or people who want such a thing or for whom such a thing is contemplated. So far from being pleased with the thought of continued direct rule for a period of years [in Burma, for reconstruction purposes], all he sees in it is that we are to spend money in order to be, as he puts it, kicked out by the Burmese afterwards.'[69]

Yet whatever the long-term uncertainties, India before 1941 still stood at the heart of Britain's position in Asia as a whole. Further east still, there also remained major and automatic defence commitments involving the Dominions of Australia and New Zealand. This was so, despite the evolution of such Dominions towards both a legal equality of status as eventually

* In addition to differences between philosophies of empire, there also existed, of course, considerable variations in the nature of the European presence and the pattern of relations between invaders and natives. See P. Mason, *Patterns of Dominance* (London, 1971), cap. VI.

embodied in the Statute of Westminster of 1931, and a greater independence in international politics, as manifested during the Chanak crisis of 1922, when Britain's assumption that Commonwealth support would be readily forthcoming if war came about with Turkey was proved to be largely unfounded. Here, too, and especially as regards her relations with Australia, the Pacific war was to throw into much sharper focus a problem for Britain which had already been developing for some years.

As for Britain's other interests in the Far East together with Southeast Asia, in material terms, even as late as 1931, they far exceeded those of the United States: British investments in China alone, for example, amounted then to £244 million, representing 5·9 per cent of her foreign total, whereas the same figures for the U.S.A. were around $200 million and 1·3 per cent respectively. The entrepôt trade of Hongkong dwarfed that of the Philippines, and in services like insurance Britain remained pre-eminent. A group of dependencies like Malaya produced far more in the way of valuable raw materials—and hence foreign exchange earnings—than did any outposts of the United States, who herself derived about 90 per cent of her crude rubber and 75 per cent of her tin from Malaya and the Netherlands East Indies. In the latter territory, one could also cite as a European/American contrast the fact that the investment there of the Royal Dutch Shell Company alone was greater than that of all American firms in Japan and China combined.[70]

In China, indeed, Britain's concern was essentially commercial. In this respect the 'open door' policy of desiring equal and unrestricted trading and financial opportunities in that country had been developed above all by the British in the nineteenth century; and if the term is to be used in this strictly practical sense, it remained more appropriate as a description of British policy than that of the United States, for whom, as we shall see, 'the open door' became a phrase that was overlaid with aspirations of a more cloudy and less measurable kind. There were British missionaries in China, it is true, while a man like Curzon liked to talk grandly about the country's task, under Providence, in the East as a whole; London also, like other Western capitals, demanded from the Chinese an acceptance of Western standards and practices of law before extraterritoriality could be surrendered. In general, however, there was little sense of mission about the attitudes and policies of the British people or their governments where the Far East was concerned. If one seeks the notion of 'civilising' and 'uplifting', of helping to create order and leading the local people into the modern world, then such echoes of the evangelicalism of Empire in India are to be found, for the Far East, in America, rather: in President McKinley's decision not only to annex the Philippines but to 'uplift, civilise and Christianise them'; in President Wilson's delight at the 'awakening' of China herself to Christianity; in the visions, already cited, of Stimson, MacArthur and others less notable in American history.

Among the relatively small proportion of British who were involved in or cared about Chinese affairs, wariness, indifference, cynicism or a grudging respect were more likely to be found than an expectation of finding eager and grateful disciples. True, some officials and businessmen in Britain tended to share with their American counterparts the idea of China as a market with a vast potential for expansion[71]—far greater than that of Japan, with whom Britain's trade was roughly equal to that with China in the early 1930s. The hope of seeing a settled, orderly China was likewise entertained in London, and indeed by 1931 it was Britain, rather than the United States, who was taking the lead in negotiating with the new Chinese National Government terms for the gradual surrender of extraterritorial rights. The main aims, however, were to secure conditions that were good for business and to avoid international conflict, rather than to achieve a leap forward in the political and spiritual progress of mankind. With fewer aspirations clustered around them, British pre-war policies in China were essentially pragmatic. There was thus to be a certain continuity of approach and style, as well as an awareness of relative powerlessness to affect the situation, behind London's fairly cool appraisal of, say, the advance of Communism in China during our war-time period, in contrast to the more feverish reactions, both for and against, in American circles.

Nevertheless, there had been much alarm in London after the Great War at the rapid decline in Britain's export trades in the Far East, a special Foreign Office and Board of Trade mission forecasting 'bankruptcy and disaster at home' should the trend continue. Japan in particular was proving far too effective a competitor, in China and Malaya and even in India and Australia. (In India, for example, the British share of imported textile goods fell from 75·2 per cent in 1928–9 to 48·7 per cent in 1932–3, while the Japanese share rose from 18·4 per cent to 47·3 per cent.)[72] Faced with this situation, 'open doors' into one's own territories began to look decidedly less attractive than those giving access to a country like China. As it was, Britain at the end of the Second World War would be faced with the task of recreating a commercial presence in Asia which had become severely threatened even before Japan's armed attack.

Likewise, the rapid military collapse of Britain in the Far East under those initial blows of 1941–42 sprang from conditions which went back far beyond, and were wider than, the complacency and incompetence of some of those responsible at the time—indeed, which antedated even those governments and electorates which were slow to rearm in the 1930s.[73] Britain's relative decline as a military and industrial power, it is now well known, can be traced back to at least the 1870s, and even before the First World War her Empire was stretched well beyond the limits of her resources to guard and control it. In such a situation, it is often the Chancellor of the Exchequer, as much as or more than the Foreign Secretary, whose policies and influence illuminate the process of decline: Sir Michael Hicks Beech, urging retrenchment in the Far East, prompting the Admiralty to appreciate the value of Japanese cooperation, and thus helping to bring about the Anglo-Japanese alliance of 1902;[74] Winston Churchill in the mid 1920s, pouring scorn on the warnings of Admiral Beatty and others concerning Britain's vulnerability to a possible Japanese attack (there was not, wrote

Churchill, 'the slightest chance of it in our lifetime') and fighting the Admiralty's estimates accordingly;[75] Neville Chamberlain, leading the search for a rapprochement with Japan in the mid-1930s.[76] In 1905, as part of the fruits of the alliance with Japan, Britain's China-Station battleships had sailed away; even so, within a few years the Committee of Imperial Defence was pointing out the danger to Australia and New Zealand should the country's newly-found Far Eastern friend become an enemy.[77] Yet such was the degree of Britain's over-commitment on a world scale once major trouble occurred in the European arena, that during the Great War London had to ask Tokyo for naval assistance, not merely in the Pacific but in the Indian Ocean and Mediterranean as well.[78]

The dangers which could arise if Britain were to drift apart from or alienate Japan were appreciated in some political quarters as well as in naval circles. Curzon, for example, together with the Australian delegates and others, argued strongly in these terms at the Imperial Conference of 1921, when urging that the alliance should be renewed.[79] (That so expansive and confident a believer in Empire should think in such a fashion is but one, ironic illustration of the essential defensiveness of British policies in and approaches to the Far East in the twentieth century.) Yet continued partnership with Japan did not provide an easy answer to the problem. Already, before and during the Great War, Tokyo's rapacious behaviour in China and the Western Pacific, her hard bargaining as an ally and her tendency to flirt with Germany, had alienated a good many in British official circles.[80] More important still, in the long run, was the dilemma which was to continue even after the alliance had been brought to an end at the Washington Conference: how to maintain friendship with Japan while at the same time seeking to increase cooperation with the United States in both naval and Far Eastern matters, and this against a background of mounting Japanese-American tension.[81] The 1911 renegotiation of the alliance had given Britain the opportunity to remove the possibility of becoming involved, through Japan, in war against the United States. But this did not solve, for example, the question of a naval-limitation agreement, much needed by a financially hard-pressed and disarmament-minded Britain after 1918; nor did it provide a basis for harmonizing foreign business activities in China. Within the Foreign Office, the possibility was aired of replacing the alliance with a three-way entente that would bring in the United States, but in the end the Washington Conference produced as a substitute merely an anodyne treaty in which the U.S.A., Japan, Britain and France agreed to respect the status quo and to confer over any threats to their insular possessions in the Pacific. At the same time, Japan reluctantly accepted a capital-ship ratio of 3.5.5. for herself, Britain and the U.S.A. respectively, while maintaining her superiority in the Western Pacific through the fortification standstill already mentioned.[82]

The Washington Conference demonstrated that, if forced to choose between Japan and the United States, Britain would almost certainly lean towards the latter. Arguments of kinship, history and mutual interests

were among those which could be adduced to this end, quite apart from the
need to stay close to a country to which one was now in debt and which had
the potential to outbuild by far her rivals in a naval free-for-all. In the
specific context of China, too, Anglo-American collaboration was seen in
London as being highly desirable—as was to be the case between 1941 and
1945—and was symbolized in the early 1920s by the establishment of an
International Consortium to coordinate financial and commercial activities
there. 'The closer our cooperation with America', observed a Foreign
Office official, 'the wider the open door.'[83]

Yet could America be regarded as a reliable friend in the Far East, let
alone elsewhere? Would it not be 'a fatal policy', in Lloyd George's words,
to put oneself 'at the mercy of the United States'?[84] If the interests of the
two countries were indeed similar, the message did not appear to have
penetrated naval circles, where the admirals of the United States tended to
look upon the Royal Navy in a spirit of intense rivalry,[85] and where Captain
Roskill has entitled the years 1919 to 1929 'the period of Anglo-American
antagonism.'[86] The existence of Anglo-Saxon elites on both sides of the
Atlantic, with many connections between them,[87] did not outweigh either
the latent strength of anglophobia in the United States* or the widespread
distrust of that country which existed in Whitehall. Disagreements over
debts, tariff barriers, disarmament and the wide issues involved in the
search for international peace and security all helped to create a relationship
that was far removed from that 'hands-across-the-sea' version that was later
to be projected outwards from the temporary alliance in arms of 1941 to
1945. More typical of the views of British officials in 1931 was the observation of Sir Robert Vansittart, Permanent Under Secretary at the Foreign
Office:

> 'We shall doubtless continue to hear much about idealism from across the
> Atlantic and to be furnished with many facile but impractical recipes for
> expediting the arrival of the millennium; but we must recognise that there
> will be no . . . activity which by any stretch of the imagination could be
> described as the assumption of an obligation or a responsibility.' 'The
> Americans', he wrote a year later, 'have often let us down.'[88]

Vansittart's reference to 'facile recipes' reflected a widespread and often
patronizing British weariness with American idealism and moralizing over
international relations which was matched in the opposite direction by a
belief in the ineradicably corrupt and war-engendering nature of European
politics. In a Far Eastern context, too, there had long been a tendency in

---

* It is important to note, since it is a phenomenon that will be encountered again during
the Pacific war, that in some Americans a strong antipathy towards Britain and towards
European entanglements generally, amounting to 'isolationism' in that direction, could
and did coexist with expansionist inclinations westwards, across the Pacific. Senator
Albert J. Beveridge, for example, who was to be a fierce critic of European involvement
for the U.S.A., also believed that 'the Power that rules the Pacific is the Power that rules
the World. And with the Philippines, that Power is, and will forever be, the American
people.' (See e.g. S. Adler, *The Isolationist Impulse* [New York, 1960].)

the United States to assume that American motives and behaviour were on a plane far above that of the self-seeking European states.[89] Late in developing precise Far Eastern policies of her own, the United States in the nineteenth century had been happy to demand and share in all the extra-territorial benefits of the unequal-treaty system, in the wake of Britain and others. Yet the fact that it had been British ships and guns which had led the way and which for many years upheld the resulting structure of Western privileges fostered the growth of a myth which we shall find still flourishing during the Second World War. It was easy to overlook the involvement of Americans in the opium trade into China, or the importing of Chinese coolie labour into the U.S.A.;[90] easy to ignore the essential similarity of all Western barbarians and their intrusions in East Asian eyes. In Professor Fairbank's words: 'The American self-image in the nineteenth century heightened this myopia, for the Americans set themselves apart from the Old World, claiming and proclaiming a new vision of man and society, and inveighing against all empires, at the very same time that they found it necessary and desirable to accept the treaty system with all its imperial privileges . . . This was an accident of history: that we Americans could enjoy the East Asia treaty privileges, the fruits of European aggression, without the moral burden of ourselves committing aggression. It gave us a holier-than-thou attitude, a righteous self-esteem, an undeserved moral grandeur in our own eyes that was built on self-deception and has lasted into our own day until somewhat dissipated by our recent record in Vietnam.'[91]

This comfortable view also entailed the overlooking of aggressive American actions nearer home, another irritation for Europeans to whom the usual lessons were preached. 'I do not want to be unkind or rude to the British', observed President Roosevelt to the British Colonial Secretary, Oliver Stanley, in January 1945, 'but in 1841 [sic], when you acquired Hong Kong, you did not acquire it by purchase.' 'Let me see, Mr. President', replied Stanley, 'that was about the time of the Mexican War, wasn't it?'[92]* Likewise, there was to be nothing new about American protestations during the Second World War that their determination to acquire new island strongholds in the Pacific was essentially disinterested and unselfish. Theodore Roosevelt, for example, who had thoroughly enjoyed helping to drive the Spaniards from Cuba with his Rough Riders, and for whom 'no triumph of peace [was] so great as the supreme triumph of war', could nevertheless state at the turn of the century 'that there is nothing even

---

* In addition to recalling American imperialism in action in Puerto Rico, Haiti, the Dominican Republic and elsewhere, it is also important to note that, to a significant extent, assumptions of racial superiority that were present among those in favour of such extensions of U.S. power around the turn of the century were shared by opponents who feared lest constitutional rights and Congressional representation would eventually have to be accorded to the lesser breeds in newly-acquired territories—with implications for the position of the many Negroes in southern states who were already being denied such rights and representation, despite the 14th and 15th amendments to the Constitution. See Weston, *Racism in U.S. Imperialism*, 260.

remotely resembling "imperialism" or "militarism" involved in the present development of that policy of expansion which has been part of the history of America from the day when she became a nation.'

Historians do remain greatly divided, of course, over the subject of American expansion in the Far East in Roosevelt's time. How much emphasis, for example, should be placed upon individuals like Roosevelt and Alfred Mahan, 'neo-Hamiltonians' as they have been called, who argued in terms of power and the national interest, albeit suitably clothed in the language of universal moral values? Or again, when John Hay, as Secretary of State, issued his celebrated 'Open Door' notes on the involvement of the Powers in China, was this part of a wider expansionist drive by the United States? And did such an expansionist impulse derive mainly from the nature of America's domestic economic system, the vital needs of which, in terms of overseas markets, had long been proclaimed by her agricultural lobbies, as well as, at the time of Cuba and the Philippines, by publicists, politicians and intellectuals?[93]

When considering questions such as these, whether in relation to the turn of the century or to the Second World War, a distinction must obviously be made between what the needs of the American economy did in fact require, and what they were thought to require. Similarly, when looking at American trade with the Far East, what was believed to be its potential should be set alongside the actual statistics of the time. (From the latter one discovers, for instance, that in the first half of the 1930s, the Far Eastern trade of the U.S.A. was only half the value of its trade with Europe; that an adverse balance in the Far East contrasted with a positive balance with Europe; and that within the Far Eastern total, trade with Japan from the turn of the century to the end of the 1930s became more valuable than that with China.)[94]

Neither actual nor potential material interests, however, are sufficient to account for the peculiarly cloudy and unstable attitudes and beliefs with which many Americans, both within and outside official circles, were often to approach questions involving policy towards China. Behind the statements quoted earlier, about China 'awakening' to civilization, Christianity and democracy, there lay among other factors the repercussions of the American missionary effort in that country in the nineteenth and twentieth centuries.[95] With American help (and again, as in commercial matters, the Philippines were to appear attractive as a base for the enterprise, having already received the Christian message and being, as Stimson saw it, 'the interpreters of American idealism to the Far East'),[96] a spiritual and moral regeneration would take place in China which would alter the course of the history of mankind. During the Far Eastern war, such hopes were to become particularly precious. 'How many have considered', demanded the *Christian Science Monitor* in July 1942, 'what a different balance the world might have today were not the Generalissimo [Chiang Kai-shek] a Christian and his wife American-educated?'[97] For Franklin Roosevelt, writing not for the purposes of publicity but privately to General Marshall in March 1943,

Chiang Kai-shek's achievement in China had been more than simply a political one: above all it was that of an enlightened modernizer who had become 'the undisputed leader of 400 million people' and 'created in a very short time throughout China what it took us a couple of centuries to attain . . .'[98] And even if Chiang Kai-shek proved, in the event, to be a little less than George Washington and John the Baptist combined in one, there were those Americans who came to believe that they had discovered their regenerated Chinese man, not amid the corruption of Chungking but in the asceticism and rural democracy of Yenan. 'China needs more of the Puritan spirit', wrote Stilwell's political adviser, the diplomat John Paton Davies, in 1943, and in the Communist north-west that spirit was to be found. Neither Davies nor his principal colleague in Yenan, John Stewart Service (who shared his high, and in many ways correct, estimate of Mao Tse-tung and his men), was himself a Communist. It is worth noting, however, that both were the sons of missionary parents in China.

If the legacies of religious endeavour were not divorced from political analysis, nor were they from commercial aspirations. In one breath, for example, Henry Stimson, as Secretary of State in 1932, urged upon Britain's Sir John Simon both the moral issue at stake over Japan's attack on China at Shanghai, and 'the very real direct cash value to all of us in the policy towards China.'[99] It was this singular blend of evangelicalism, political calculation, benevolent paternalism and crude self-interest which came to surround the American use of the term, 'the Open Door'. Whatever may have been the motives behind Hay's original notes on the subject, this cloudy mixture of interests and aspirations was what was involved when men like Stimson spoke of 'the real nobility of the traditional . . . American doctrine towards China of the "Open Door."'[100] It meant that the requirements of morality and of profit happily coincided; that Chinese nationalism could be welcomed as a force which would resist the incursions of Japan and of Europe, but not of the United States; that in China one could find and build up an ally who would also, in the widest sense, be loyal to the American way of life.

Yet here, too, as with the lure of the China market, there was another myth in the making, and one which, in terms of first its power and then its essential hollowness, was to exercise considerable influence during the Second World War: the myth that the American people as a whole cared steadily, deeply and resolutely for and about China.[101] The reality was very different: a spasmodic attention which rested on projected and idealized images of oneself more than on a knowledge of the real China,[102] and which goes far to explain the emotional and unstable shifts of opinion between 1941 and 1945; a general sympathy that did not take precedence over self-interest, even at China's expense, and which fell far short of a readiness to make major sacrifices in order to defend China's interests as she herself saw them. 'No large segment of the American public', writes Professor Varg of the period around the turn of the century, 'took China as seriously as the very vocal and enthusiastic missionaries and scholars . . . Their image of China was not greatly shared.'[103] The same conclusion is reached by Professor Cohen, in a remark which could also be applied to the 1920s and much of the 1930s: 'Despite the importance that businessmen and missionaries attached to their activities in China, neither the people nor the government of the United States could long focus on Asian affairs. There were more important problems to be dealt with at home. And for those less provincial, the problems of Europe were obviously of greater significance.'[104]

Certainly, Americans in general had long displayed little love for their Asian brothers when brought into closer contact with them at home. Chinese labour, imported into the United States in the nineteenth century, often received brutal treatment, and was left to live in squalid conditions;[105] pressure to exclude such Chinese immigrants altogether built up to a successful conclusion, whilst Japanese who had gone to live in California likewise found themselves unwelcome and the object of discriminatory legislation. Meanwhile Hay's Open Door notes did not involve the United States in any surrender of her extraterritorial privileges in China, or prevent her demanding new concessions. They did not remove American forces from that country (there were 5,000 U.S. troops and marines in the Shanghai and Peking-Tientsin regions by the beginning of 1928), or, in extreme cases, prevent the use of American force against Chinese, as happened at Nanking in 1927. Secretaries of State Frank Kellogg in the late 1920s and Henry Stimson in the early 1930s did pronounce their genuine desire to work closely with the Chinese Republic and its new National Government, but as Britain and China slowly approached agreement over extraterritoriality in 1931, the intention in Washington was to try to exclude Shanghai, Tientsin, Canton and Hankow from any such surrender of privileges.[106] During the Japanese attack on the Chinese portion of Shanghai in 1932, no less a person than Stanley Hornbeck himself, Chief of the State Department's Far Eastern Division and zealous upholder of the doctrine of America's political purity in the Far East, suggested that advantage might be taken of the desperate situation the Chinese were in to 'smooth off' some of the problems being created by those Chinese for the working of the International Settlement.[107]

Moreover, this last episode of the attacks on Manchuria and Shanghai by Japan brought forth no retaliation from the United States beyond a flood of words and a declaration of non-recognition of the new state of Manchukuo. This was in keeping with America's failure to act forcefully in 1915, when Tokyo presented Peking with the Twenty-One Demands, and did not contravene the letter of the much-publicized Washington Nine-Power Treaty, which involved no pledge to act in defence of China's integrity. Legalistic approaches and pronouncements were, indeed, within the American tradition: Hay, Root and Knox, all lawyers before becoming Secretaries of State,[108] had set an example which stretched ahead to Stimson and Dulles. But armed action on behalf of China was tacitly or openly acknowledged to be out of all proportion to the tangible American interests which existed in the area, however much verbiage might be piled on top of them: the country, Secretary of State Hughes told his delegation to the

Washington Conference, 'would never go to war over any aggression on the part of Japan in China.' In any event, after that same Washington Conference action in the Western Pacific on a major scale was beyond the resources of the American forces and the bases at their disposal—not that this prevented the myth of United States power and of her protection of China from being preserved in the shape of the Navy's War Plan Orange, which envisaged a dash across the Pacific by the fleet in order to operate against Japan from the Philippines.[109]

The U.S. Navy in the inter-war years needed to preserve its bold trans-Pacific plans as a lever with which to try to extract more resources from a reluctant Congress; however, the confusion, ambivalence and ambiguity[110] surrounding America's Far Eastern policies were only heightened thereby. We shall see that such confusion was not to end with the coming of war in 1941. When that moment arrived, some, perhaps many, Americans were able to delude themselves into believing that—at last—their country had taken up arms primarily in order to defend China. This was not so. Moreover, in the years which followed, the refusal of Roosevelt and General Marshall to commit substantial American land forces in Asia continued the tradition of limited action only. True, an eager press and public were by then demanding a substantial increase in aid of various kinds to the Chungking Government. (The making of such demands may have helped to ease a sense of guilt, arising from America's past neglect of China; that same sense of guilt could also be assuaged by setting the United States apart from Great Britain who, however splendid in terms of 1940 and Europe, could readily and traditionally be thought of as corrupt and Machiavellian in her attitude towards China.) Yet there was to remain during the 1941–45 war a considerable gap between, on the one hand, the restricted amount of American financial, material and military assistance given to China, and on the other the lofty aspirations and rhetoric which looked towards the emergence of China as a modernized Great Power. Moreover, this gap between means and end was inherent in the end itself. A powerful, friendly and grateful China was needed as America's proxy in the Far East precisely because the United States herself was not, in fact, a genuine Far Eastern power, either geographically, or in terms of sustained interest, or in her degree of readiness to make the necessary sacrifices. The contrast with Japan and the Soviet Union, each a true Far Eastern power, is obvious enough.

Japan had attained this status by 1905, if not earlier. And Japan, which as late as the 1890s had been widely regarded by American opinion as a protégé, a modernizing force to be contrasted with China's stubborn backwardness,[111] was seen by many by the end of the first decade of the twentieth century as constituting a growing threat. It is important to note that, in fact, expansionist ideas in Japan in this early part of the century were by no means entirely militaristic and territorial in nature: considerable emphasis was also placed upon emigration and the peaceful extension of commerce.[112] Successful wars against China and Russia, however, together with the gains made in 1914–18, helped to develop in Japan an outlook that would not meekly accept the frustration of what was seen as the country's vital need for expansion of some kind or other, nor pass over such humiliations as the rejection of a racial-equality clause for the Covenant of the new League of Nations[113] and the enactment of the blatantly anti-Japanese American Immigration Bill of 1924. Japan did, indeed, become a member of the League, though less wholeheartedly than Western enthusiasts liked to think;[114] she also joined Britain and the United States in short-lived endeavours in the 1920s to develop a basis of understanding and even cooperation over Far Eastern affairs.[115] By 1931, however, with the repercussions of the Depression biting deeply into Japanese society, the proponents of peace and international understanding were on the defensive against those who argued that the country's problems must be solved by herself alone, and, ultimately, by force.

The Japanese attack in Manchuria in 1931 did not suddenly destroy an established international system in the Far East: it demonstrated—more savagely and finally than any other previous event, it is true—that no such viable system had been created. The intention of some of those, especially on the American side, who had worked to bring about the Washington Conference of 1921–22, had been to lift international relations on to a new plane, where commercial development (exploitation, a Chinese nationalist would have called it) on an Open Door basis, linked to arms limitation and a respect for China, would replace the earlier race for naval bases and exclusive spheres of influence.[116] The Conference, however, did not put an end to extraterritoriality or in other ways meet the demands of a swelling Chinese nationalism; nor did it include in its discussions and agreements the Soviet Union, to whom Sun Yat-sen now turned for assistance, disillusioned as he was by the modest proposals of the West. The ensuing alliance between the Kuomintang and Communists in China, although enjoying only a short existence before being brutally ended by Chiang Kai-shek in 1927, marked a turning away by Chinese revolutionaries from Western inspiration in a general sense, as well as a rejection of the gradualist temper and limited political assumptions made at Washington.[117] The fear that Communism itself might be spread by Moscow throughout Asia, voiced within the British Foreign Office and in the United States by President Hoover among others, could be partly offset by a comforting belief that such a political doctrine was fundamentally alien to the Chinese character.[118] Even so, by 1931 Asian nationalisms in general had pushed the West on to the defensive. And in China itself, meanwhile, the Western powers had reverted to seeking bilateral agreements with that country, rather than acting on a joint basis that would include Japan. In Professor Iriye's words, 'they were unwittingly putting an end to one act of the Far Eastern drama and ushering in the next.'[119]

As we shall see later, the problem of creating a durable international system for that part of the world was to remain a major one, with which Western officials were wrestling as the Pacific war drew to a close. We shall also observe in that context a feature which had again been present before

1941: that is, the tendency for Western approaches to the international politics of the Far East to be strongly influenced by developments in Europe. Where Britain, France and the Netherlands were concerned, this is only to be expected. For the United States too, however, notwithstanding those who clamoured for a new frontier and a new appointment with destiny in the Pacific and Asia, and despite those who rejected the Old World, it was often transatlantic, rather than trans-Pacific, issues which carried the greater weight. They plunged the nation, 'too proud to fight', into war in 1917. Between 1939 and 1941 they, more than China's peril, drew it back towards war again. In 1945, they were to help produce a marked change in the attitudes of the United States towards the position of her European allies in Asia. This point will be developed a little more, in terms of the 1930s, in a moment.

Meanwhile, before Japan's act of open defiance in 1931, there had emerged in various quarters an awareness of the racial tensions underlying various Far Eastern issues. In Japan and the United States during the early years of the century, for example, one can see the growth of what Professor Iriye has called 'strikingly similar ideas . . ., [with] each country's expansion manifesting self-consciousness about civilization and race.'[120] An individual like Theodore Roosevelt saw in the Japanese certain failings by American standards, failings that were of an inherent and racial character,[121] just as Sir Alexander Cadogan was to pronounce from the British Embassy in Nanking in the 1930s that 'what was wrong with China was that there was something wrong with the Chinese—something at least that made them unable properly to adjust to Western standards.'[122] Of China's attempt to enlist American help in Manchuria around 1910, Dr. Hunt writes: 'Her overtures miscarried [partly] because of the condescension and disdain which Americans felt for the "poor Chinks." The American response . . . was burdened by racial stereotypes, ignorance and misinformation.'[123] Later, in the inter-war years, officials in London did recognize at times that latent racial antagonism was a major problem to be reckoned with in the Far East;[124] yet in both London and Washington, it was Western standards and concepts of law and society that were set up as being those by which China's progress towards the status of a worthy member of the comity of nations would be judged. (The present writer has described this elsewhere as 'cultural aggression', others as 'cultural imperialism.')[125] We shall also hear strong echoes between 1941 and 1945 of the inter-war argument of an American Governor of the Philippines, that his country should retain that colony in order to sustain 'Anglo-Saxonism in the Western Pacific, in the Far East, [and] in India.'

Crude and condescending images were not, it should be emphasized, the exclusive property of people in the West. Japanese, too, often looked at China in such a fashion, and in Japan, as well as in the United States, there was developing from the early part of the century the notion of a special mission in Asia, with particular reference to the reform and enlightenment of China.[126] Japan also contributed to another feature of the Far Eastern setting: the widespread sense of economic rivalry and dangers. As early as the latter part of the nineteenth century the teachings of Malthus on population and resources had helped to create a widespread belief in Japan that the country would soon have too many people and too little food—an idea which was among those which led to the seizure of Manchuria in 1931.[127] Meanwhile in Britain, as we have seen, officials and merchants in the inter-war years came to foresee the direst consequences if the country's Asian trade was not pulled out of its downward slide. Similarly, amid the wreckage of the Depression in the United States, loud protests by manufacturers against cheap Japanese competition found a ready audience, and helped to lead to the 1930 Hawley-Smoot tariff act which was widely seen as 'a virtual declaration of economic war on the rest of the world.'[128] More positively, there remained for some Americans the hope that, in the words of an Ambassador to Japan, 'an orderly China would be a tremendous field for foreign salesmanship—bringing back to the world, perhaps, good times.'[129]

The severe curtailing of other nations' trading opportunities by the United States in 1930 (and Britain was soon to follow suit with the Ottawa tariffs and other measures) was taken by fervent Japanese nationalists as further proof of Western hypocrisy and selfishness. Japan, they could argue, had learned from the West the game of imperial power-politics in East Asia, but on defeating China in 1895 had had her spoils in Manchuria denied her by the intervention of Germany, France and Russia—only to see Russia then take them for herself. After the First World War, standards of self-denial had been demanded of her which the Western powers, with their existing areas of special interest like Central America and Egypt, were not ready to live up to themselves. Then, when Japanese commercial competition, perfectly allowable under the new 'rules' of the League and the Washington Conference, became too successful, doors which Japan had to help keep open in China were shut in her face elsewhere.[130] The answer thus appeared to be the seizure of her own, privileged zone, of which Manchukuo was the start and the Greater East Asia Coprosperity Sphere the culmination.

That war on a major scale would come to the Western Pacific was in itself no new idea. Social Darwinist notions; the teachings of Mahan that the healthy nation had to expand and to seek its destiny without flinching from conflict; the belief—again of Mahan among others—that mankind stood 'at the opening of a period when the question is to be settled decisively, though the issue may be long delayed, whether Eastern or Western civilisation is to dominate the earth and to control its future':[131] all these had found their adherents in Japan. As a consequence, there existed in various quarters on both sides of the Pacific, even thirty years or more before Pearl Harbour, an accompanying belief—one which the Japanese and American navies held on to after 1918, and which came to be accepted by Stimson, as well as by Japanese 'double patriots' during the Manchurian crisis: the belief, that is, that war between Japan and the United States was 'inevitable.' Indeed, in the view of one scholar, this sense of impending conflict had been more marked on the American side of the water during the early years of the

century. 'Whereas the Japanese regarded the United States and its possessions primarily as spheres for peaceful, economic activity', writes Professor
Iriye, 'America believed with equal firmness in the likelihood of military
confrontation. All factors—political, economic, racial and cultural—
combined to create a particular attitude towards Japanese expansion which
was never to leave American consciousness until the end of World War
Two.'[132]

It is worth noting that during these same years of the early twentieth
century, there had flourished in Europe, too, 'a new literature of anxiety and
belligerent nationalism', and that there, too, there was frequent talk of an
inevitable war, this time usually centred upon Anglo-German rivalry.[133]
And in both contexts, European and trans-Pacific, the question arises of
whether such warnings may not have to some extent become self-fulfilling
prophecies.

The Far Eastern crisis of 1931–33, when Japan seized Manchuria, created
the puppet state of Manchukuo and left the League of Nations, did not, as
has often been claimed subsequently, 'cause' the series of international
crises which followed in Europe and the Mediterranean. Nor did it 'cause'
the failure of the League, but rather exposed its inherent limitations. Even
regarding the Far East itself, it would be too much to say that a major war
was now inevitable: the course pursued by Japan thereafter was not a
simple one leading directly to Pearl Harbour, and developments in Europe
continued to exercise considerable influence on events on the other side of
the world.[134] Nevertheless, Japan's brutal success did represent the greatest
blow yet struck against the post-1918 settlement and the accompanying
hopes for the peaceful resolving of international disputes. It revealed Japan's
alienation from a Western-orientated League of Nations and its surrounding
rules of international behaviour, her disillusionment with the notional
Washington Conference system of cooperation in the Far East, and the
unstable and ineffectual nature of her own civilian policy-making institutions, overshadowed as they were by the actions and wishes of the Army.

The crisis also threw a harsh new light on the extent of the West's vulnerability in China and the Western Pacific. For Britain, as for the United
States, each preoccupied with major economic and political troubles at
home, not only was the will lacking to force Japan to back down, but so
were the means. The choice lay between, on the one hand verbal protest and
acquiescence in practice, and on the other the risk of having to take a huge
step up, possibly via an attempt to impose economic sanctions, on to the
plane of direct confrontation and war. And in such a war, as the navies of
both countries eventually made clear to those responsible for foreign
policy,[135] Japan could plunder Western possessions in her part of the world
and down into Southeast Asia before being checked in a long-term contest.
Without adequate fortified bases and air-cover, the U.S. Navy's planned
trek to the Philippines would be folly; so, too, would the Royal Navy's
intended move from home waters or the Mediterranean to a Singapore

which was almost devoid of defences. Once it was accepted that, within this strategic framework, Japan regarded Manchuria as a vital interest—which for the West it plainly was not—then humiliation was bound to follow.

Throughout the 1931–33 crisis, Britain and the United States had a common interest in seeking to preserve the principles of conciliation and peaceful change in the Far East: idealism apart, the future safety of their own possessions in the area clearly demanded it. And although the United States remained outside the League, within which Britain was inclined to take shelter among numbers, each felt itself to be dependent on the other: Britain, obviously, on the United States for the latter's economic strength and military potential; but also, as became clear during the local crisis at Shanghai in the early part of 1932, the United States on Britain for moral solidarity in the face of wrongdoing, as well as, perhaps, for the aid of the Royal Navy.[136] Yet in immediate and practical terms, Britain had too much at stake within Japan's reach, and the United States too little, to make major risks acceptable to either. The result was a broad, underlying similarity between the cautious policy pursued during the crisis by the Government and Foreign Office in London, and the limits to American action set by President Hoover in Washington.

This degree of similarity, however, did not prevent the development of further mutual distrust and recrimination, both during the crisis and afterwards. Stanley Baldwin, for example, voiced a common—and correct—assumption among his colleagues when he observed: 'You will get nothing out of Washington but words. Big words, but only words.' To Henry Stimson on the other hand, it was Britain, and in particular her Foreign Secretary, Sir John Simon, who had 'let America down.' Stimson's own book, *The Far Eastern Crisis*, which appeared in 1936, helped to prolong the ensuing controversy, being rebutted in its turn by Sir John Pratt, formerly of the Foreign Office, in a letter to *The Times* in 1938 and in his own book, *War and Peace in China*. The truth of the matter[137] became less significant than the widely-accepted notion in the United States that Britain had indeed been pusillanimous and disloyal. It was a version of events whose growth was encouraged by the existence of the wider, yet equally erroneous, belief that in 1931–32, not only could Japan easily have been halted, but the whole succeeding descent into world war prevented at small cost.[138] On the British side, too, helped no doubt by the unlovable and sinuous personal qualities of Simon, there was a readiness to look back with contrition. When Stimson, now Secretary of War, came to London in July 1943, for example, his opposite number, Sir P. J. Grigg, together with Churchill, expressed themselves as 'very much against Simon on that affair, ... condemning the Foreign Secretary decidedly.'[139] Even when the Stimson version was rejected, as it was within the Foreign Office, the memory of the episode lingered on as a warning not to risk similar accusations being made during later Far Eastern episodes.

The breach between the United States and Britain during the Manchurian crisis was fostered in part by the need, in an age of Covenants and Kellogg

Pacts, to idealize their respective policies for domestic and international consumption while pursuing in fact a course that was less than bold and noble, even if realistic. Yet tension also sprang from the contrasts between their respective approaches to Far Eastern affairs which have already been noted, and which were to occur again during the Second World War. In London, while there was some genuine concern for China (as well as distaste for assertive Chinese nationalism), there was also an overpowering anxiety to avoid a clash with Japan and to 'keep her in play' with a view to re-establishing a framework of Far Eastern relations when the crisis had passed. This approach was pragmatic and defensive, but it was practical as well, as illustrated by the crucial role played by Sir Miles Lampson, the British Minister to China, in bringing about a Sino-Japanese agreement whereby the latter withdrew from its savage incursion into Chinese territory around Shanghai. In contrast, Stimson's celebrated public pronouncements on the non-recognition of Japan's gains reflected that legalistic and moralizing approach which we have seen before in American Far Eastern policies, and one which, as before, did nothing whatever to assist China in practical terms. Fundamental to Stimson's reactions, however, vacillating and emotional though they were, was a firm belief in America's destiny in China, leading to the eventual conclusion that 'during the course of . . . rivalry [with Japan over the Open Door] it is, in my opinion, almost impossible that there should not be an armed clash between two such different civilizations.'[140] At the same time, he began to believe in something which, in retrospect, can be seen as pointing ahead, past 1941–45, to Korea and Vietnam: that, given the weakness of the League and the decline of Britain, the United States might well have to 'police the world.'

Developments between Japan's departure from the League in 1933 and the onset of European war in 1939 served only to underline the unstable nature of the international setting in the Far East. Within Japan itself, there was a patent fragility about the entire process of government in the face of political assassinations and the increasing assertiveness of the military and Navy.[141] Externally, Japanese pressure upon China continued: in 1934, for example, with the Amau statement, in which a Tokyo official declared that his country alone bore responsibility for maintaining peace in Asia; in 1935 by an overt extension of control and influence in North China; and finally in 1937, following a clash between Japanese and Chinese troops at the Marco Polo bridge, by war itself. From 1938 to 1944, the fighting in China was to diminish for the most part into skirmishes around a belt of no-man's-land running down the middle of the country; but the National Government of Chiang Kai-shek had already been driven out of Eastern China, with its vital ports, and forced to find refuge in Chungking. Moreover, Japan's successes also showed up divisions within China itself. In 1936, Chiang Kai-shek had been forcibly persuaded that in the face of the external threat to the country he should suspend his campaign against Mao Tse-tung and the Communists, now installed in Yenan in the north-west after their successful Long March; however, the fundamental incompatibility of the two regimes remained. Within the ruling Kuomintang, too, division and intrigue continued, and at the end of 1938 one of the party's leading figures, Wang Ching-wei, defected from Chungking to begin negotiations with the Japanese for the setting up of a puppet government in occupied territory. (Such a government was eventually inaugurated in Nanking in March 1940.)[142] Chiang Kai-shek himself not only made frequent appeals for help from the United States and Britain, but began to allow the shadowy threat to emerge that unless he received such aid he might come to terms with Tokyo in order to pursue the cause of Asia for the Asians.[143]

Towards the West, too, Japan maintained during these years of 1933–39 a predominantly intransigent and sometimes menacing attitude. At the beginning of 1936 she withdrew from the London Naval conference which was attempting to find a replacement for the expiring Washington agreement.[144] Later in the same year, she signed with Nazi Germany the Anti-Comintern Pact, which, for all its overtly anti-Soviet orientation, entailed implicitly a major threat to the position of Britain above all, particularly when Italy adhered to the pact in 1937. Japan's war with China also brought with it direct harassment of Western people and possessions, notably in 1937 when Japanese forces shelled two British gunboats and sank the U.S.S. *Panay*. Pressure was also brought to bear on the International Settlement in Shanghai and on the largely British-staffed Chinese Maritime Customs Administration, while in 1939 the Japanese blockaded the British Concession at Tientsin, the issues there being the circulation of National Government currency, the existence in the Concession of Chinese silver reserves, and the alleged anti-Japanese activities carried out from the Concession by Chinese guerillas.[145]

The verdict rendered by the International Military Tribunal for the Far East after Japan's defeat in 1945, that these and other moves in the 1930s had been part of a single, long-planned conspiracy, has been shown to have been a considerable over-simplification. It is now known, for example, that neither the Government in Tokyo nor the Kwantung Army on the spot sought to bring about the 1937 incident that led to full-scale war with China, and that the Army's General Staff were even thinking of reducing their efforts to combat defiant nationalism in North China. It is known also that, within the Japanese Foreign Office, Army and Navy there existed considerable differences of opinion over policy, and that the 1936 pact with Germany was deliberately framed in such a way as not to tie Japan's hands; that several Ministers and officials remained anxious to reach an agreement with Britain and that as late as 1939, the Army continued to believe that war with the United States could and should be avoided, while the Navy for its part had still not committed itself in an anti-British direction.

Yet when all the necessary qualifications and revisions have been made, the trend in Japan towards aggression and authoritarianism remains clear. So, too, does the belief in the need to dominate China, and a growing acceptance that eventually the country's survival and independence could be secured only through conflict with both the Soviet Union to the west and north, and the Western powers to the east and south.* The very fragmentation of the policy-making system assisted these developments, as did a tendency to avoid a thorough exploration of various policy options and their possible consequences. The influence exerted by middle-ranking Service officers also led in the same direction. If there was ultimately to be a lashing-out against what was increasingly seen as the country's encirclement, then there still remained the question, China apart, of which way to aim the blow. In the event, the choice between a move against the Soviet Union or one against the European powers was still being debated at the highest levels in 1941.[146] Already, in the 1930s, however, there was a strong argument for moving southwards in the shape of the raw materials—oil above all, but also tin, rubber and other commodities—of the Netherlands East Indies and various British territories. Moreover, it was Britain which at this stage was frequently seen as being the main obstacle to Japan's requirements and ambitions. (A book written by a retired Japanese naval officer, *The Certainty Of An Anglo-Japanese War*, sold over a million copies in the middle 'thirties.) 'Up to the beginning of the pre-Pearl Harbour negotiations in Washington', writes a Japanese scholar, 'Japan regarded Britain rather than the United States as its hypothetical enemy, and endeavoured not to involve the United States in any conflict with Britain.'[147] Even aside from the resources of Southeast Asia, it was the aid which China was receiving from Britain, rather than from the United States, that aroused Tokyo's anger during this period.[148]

In the light of what was to follow between 1941 and 1945, this focus of Japan's upon Britain may at first sight appear surprising. So cast into America's shade was Britain during the Far Eastern war, that by its end there were many on both sides of the Atlantic who regarded her presence in that area as little more than a token one, or a pretence. Even in the 1930s, the rapidly mounting threat of Germany and Italy, far more direct for Britain than for the United States, might have been expected to take London, rather than Washington, out of play, so to speak, as regards affairs on the other side of the world.

A comparison of British and American roles between 1933 and 1939, however, leads to conclusions which in some cases are not only instructive but also ironic in view of the widespread American assumption after 1941 that Britain's stance vis-à-vis Japan was a feeble one, and that her attitude towards China was one of contempt and indifference. It is true that in the 1930s London was more anxious than was Washington to find some basis for an international settlement or understanding that would involve Japan. This is hardly surprising in that, as already indicated, within the area which Japan could threaten, British territories, Dominions, money† and raw

---

* Japan's military expenditure, as a proportion of her Gross National Product, rose from 6·8 per cent in each of the years 1932–36 to 17·4 per cent in 1938. See A. S. Milward, *War, Economy and Society, 1939–1945* (London, 1977), 30ff.

† It is true that only 2 per cent of Britain's overseas trade at this time was with China.

materials were at risk to an extent that jeopardized her very stature and existence as a world power. By contrast, the United States still had less financial and other material interests at stake. She was also pledged, after 1934, to grant the Philippines their independence in the near future, and can be said to have been 'vitally' concerned only in the matter of a few commodities, especially crude rubber, which, as we have seen, she obtained from European possessions in Southeast Asia.

For Britain, the 1932 crisis at Shanghai had been a particular shock. It led the Chiefs of Staff to warn that 'the whole of our territory in the Far East, as well as the coastline of India and the Dominions and our vast trade and shipping lies open to attack . . .',[149] and it precipitated the withdrawal of the assumption, for the purposes of defence planning, that at any given date there would be no major war for ten years. In 1934 the Defence Requirements Sub-Committee of the Committee of Imperial Defence was again urging that, while Germany represented 'the ultimate potential enemy', the immediate danger came from Japan, before whom British interests still lay wide open. In this ominous situation, work that had been so often postponed was at last put in hand to develop the defences and facilities of Singapore, and the base was eventually believed to be adequate, though not fully ready, for a major conflict in 1938.[150] Yet the threat from Italy and Germany was also growing meanwhile, and in the words of the Chiefs of Staff in 1937, 'We cannot foresee the time when our defence forces will be strong enough to safeguard our territory, trade and vital interests against Germany, Italy and Japan simultaneously.'[151]

The struggle of the Services to increase their strength during this period, in the face of the Treasury's stringency, the public's lack of realism and the caution of politicians, is now too well-known to need summarizing here.[152] Although the Navy was not especially hard done by, its world-wide commitments were far greater than its resources. 'We literally have not got the income to keep up a first-class Navy', wrote the First Sea Lord privately in 1933.[153] Thus, during the international naval negotiations of 1934–36, the British side were faced with a complex and closely-interlocking series of problems,[154] while during the Abyssinian crisis of 1935–36 it was the need to preserve intact the Mediterranean route to the Far East which as much as anything prompted a policy of avoiding a confrontation with Italy.[155] By the end of 1939, with the Germans preparing ships such as the *Bismarck* and *Scharnhorst*, the composition of the British fleet which, it was judged, would have to remain in home waters in the event of trouble in the Far East had had to be increased accordingly,[156] while, crises apart, the most that the Admiralty could offer the Foreign Office was the 'hope' that one battleship could be sent out to Singapore in 1942. Even in an emergency, the time which was allowed for the Fleet to reach and relieve Singapore was now put

Nevertheless, the possibility of losing that trade—let alone investments in China—aroused considerable apprehension. (See A. Trotter, *Britain and East Asia, 1933–1937* [Cambridge, 1975; hereafter, *Trotter*], 130.)

at 180 days, as compared to 38 in 1932. In 1942 the Japanese were to capture the base in 70 days.[157]

Thus, long before the outbreak of war in Europe, there was a large element of unreality about the plans of the Royal Navy, as there was about those of the U.S. Navy, for war with Japan. By the same token, the assurances given to Australia and New Zealand at the Imperial Conference of 1937 (even if Germany and Italy were to join in a war against Britain, they were told, 'no anxieties or risks in the Mediterranean . . . can be allowed to interfere with the despatch of a fleet to the Far East'), and again in 1939 ('it is our full intention to despatch to the Far East a fleet of sufficient strength to make the position of any Japanese major expedition precarious') were, to put it mildly, less than frank.[158] One reason for this, perhaps, was that the Chiefs of Staff, as Captain Roskill has pointed out, still underestimated 'to a staggering degree' the scale of forces that would be needed to defend the country's interests against Japan.[159] Moreover, Commonwealth preparedness in general was also handicapped by the lack of a closely coordinated defence policy.[160] In addition, it was strongly felt in London that the Dominions could take a far greater share of the financial burden of defence than they were doing—a complaint to be heard again towards the end of the Pacific war.* In their turn the Dominions, and more particularly from our point of view, the Labour Party in Australia, continued to develop a more independent, even isolationist, line.[161] In Australia also (as well as, more obviously, in Canada), there were already those who were looking to the United States, rather than to Britain, for ultimate security.[162] Meanwhile in Malaya, Singapore and other British areas there were instances of a serious lack of inter-Service coordination,[163] just as there were still glaring deficiencies in matériel and training.[164] Native populations remained 'generally indifferent and apathetic', and were seldom involved in civil-defence measures of any kind. Expatriate communities, too, were often ignorant of the true and perilous nature of the situation facing the Eastern Empire in which they occupied a privileged place.[165]

Small wonder, then, that in such a strategic setting the idea of seeking some political means of easing the Far Eastern situation, and in particular of bringing about a rapprochement with Japan, was eagerly looked at in London. Such notions were particularly in evidence in 1934, when Neville Chamberlain, as Chancellor of the Exchequer, together with Simon, put forward the idea of seeking some form of non-aggression pact with Tokyo.[166] Indeed, the Treasury at this time was beginning to develop its own, emphatic line over Far Eastern policy, thereby greatly discomforting the Foreign Office.[167] There also existed in some quarters a measure of sympathy for Japan's economic problems and her apparent need to find outlets for emigration, for example;[168] moreover, in 1937 it was generally (and as we

---

* India, however, was given in 1939 a more favourable financial basis for defence expenditure, as between her and the United Kingdom. This settlement was to have serious repercussions for the latter's sterling debts during the war. (See e.g. Kirby, *The War Against Japan*, vol. I, 39.)

now know, correctly) accepted in the Foreign Office that Japan had not instigated the new outbreak of fighting in China,[169] while the Chinese themselves were often seen as exasperatingly wayward and unruly. Above all, there were the evident dangers involved in risking any serious confrontation with the Japanese, given Britain's existing state of unpreparedness. Whether the occasion was a direct, bilateral affair, as at Tientsin, or a broader, international one, as during the 1937 Brussels Conference called to consider the Sino-Japanese conflict, or an indirect matter such as a possible loan to China, great caution was usually the order of the day.[170] In particular, the possibility of applying economic sanctions against Japan, which for a while hovered around the Brussels talks and was raised privately on another occasion by Henry Morgenthau Jr., the American Secretary of the Treasury, was regarded with much distaste in London, notably by Chamberlain as Prime Minister (from 1937) and by the Permanent Under Secretary at the Treasury, Sir Warren Fisher.[171] Moreover on two occasions, one involving the Chinese Customs and the other concerning the role of Japan in maintaining order in China, the British Government retreated in the face of Japanese intransigence.[172]

Yet by no means all was timidity and acquiescence. There are a good many examples to be found, for instance, of a certain lofty belief that in the end the natural order of things was bound to reassert itself and that Japan would then become less tiresome: as one Foreign Office official rather grandly put it, 'The point that we are a much greater Asiatic Power than Japan is one that might well be made to the Japanese when they become over-insistent on their claim to a leading role in Asiatic affairs.'[173] Accompanying this belief, there was also at times an implicit or explicit assumption, no doubt bred originally in India, that in dealing with Asiatics, Japanese or otherwise, 'consistent firmness . . . is unquestionably the policy to adopt.' What was needed, wrote Eden in a telling phrase early in 1938, was to 'effectively assert white-race authority in the Far East.'[174] Chamberlain, too, for all his desire for a political and military rapprochement with Japan, had no hesitation about supporting the claims of the Lancashire textile industry by encouraging New Delhi to restrict severely the entry of such Japanese goods into India, and crowed in private when the Japanese yielded the point.[175]

In addition, the Foreign Office tended to believe that China, for her part, would ultimately and successfully resist Japanese aggression—for aggression was what it was seen as being, whatever might be the details of the 1937 incident. It was plainly in Britain's interest that this should be so (that a triumphant China might herself come to pose a threat seemed so far off as to be scarcely worth considering), and it was generally accepted that China should be helped whenever possible—that is, when the resources were available and the risk of provoking Japan was not too great. In the words of one historian, 'Britain generally tended to view China as the Empire's first line of defence.'[176] Thus, despite the Treasury's desire to harmonize relations with Japan, it also despatched the Leith-Ross mission to the Far

East in 1935, one of its aims being to help improve China's economy. In the same year, China's switch from a silver standard to a managed, paper currency was also assisted by Britain.[177]

At the end of 1937 in particular, and in marked contrast to the direction her policies were taking in Europe, Britain's attitude towards Japan was firm rather than yielding. In the Foreign Office, the suggestions of Sir Robert Craigie, Ambassador in Tokyo, that improved relations with Japan should be sought, if necessary, at China's expense, were regarded as quite unacceptable. In December 1938, when the Burma Road was completed, it was used to carry vital supplies to the Chungking regime, while it was agreed in principle to reinforce the link by building a railway from Burma to Yunnan. Loans, export credits and assistance in stabilizing her currency were also given to China during these years, even though such aid fell far short of what the Chinese themselves desired.[178] (A senior American adviser to Chiang Kai-shek's Government has subsequently noted of this period that the British authorities in Hongkong were always cooperative towards China.)[179] Over the Tientsin blockade, too, there was a strong inclination in the Foreign Office not to yield to such Japanese pressure, while public opinion, probably entirely ignorant of the military situation, clearly inclined towards a show-down over the issue, either through applying economic sanctions or even by going to war.[180]

Meanwhile, where the political position within China was concerned, it was generally believed in London that Chiang Kai-shek was and would be for the foreseeable future the country's indispensable leader, whose good-will was 'of essential importance to our [own] position in [that] country in the future.'[181] The Chinese Communists were greatly underrated, both by British diplomats on the spot and in the Foreign Office, and this despite the fact that more could now be learned about them through the writings of Agnes Smedley and Edgar Snow.* As will be seen later, Britain's idiosyncratic but influential Ambassador to China during the latter part of this period, Sir Archibald Clark Kerr, was one of those who subscribed to the view that Mao Tse-tung and his comrades were not really Communists at all, but 'agrarian radicals' of a fairly mild political colour.[182]

Thus, to return to the formulation of Britain's Far Eastern policies up to 1939, it was believed that Japan had to be treated with caution and brought back into a cooperative relationship if possible, but should not be pandered to over her expansionist course or her pretensions regarding the creation of a new order in the Far East. At the same time, however, there was no getting away from the formidable nature of the problem which she presented. (Britain, wrote Sir George Sansom, scholar and Commercial Attaché at the Tokyo Embassy, 'did not have any really useful friends in Japan. All Japanese want a "new order" in Asia, and a "new order" involves the ultimate displacement of Great Britain in the Far East.')[183] Britain alone could not tame the miscreant. Given that the idea of Soviet intervention in

* It was, however, recognized in London that the Japanese invasion was helping to enhance the influence of the Communists in China.

the area was regarded with distaste and distrust,[184] this meant, for London, a strong and continuing sense of dependence upon the policies and responses of the United States.

Yet, as we have seen for earlier years, a good many British officials and politicians had been taught by experience that there was little enough to be expected from that quarter. 'It is always best and safest', wrote Chamberlain, 'to count on nothing from the Americans but words.' Again, moreover, even these 'words' were often listened to with a blend of scorn and despair, as when the Ambassador in Washington—sympathetic to the United States and keen for cooperation with her—described President Roosevelt's musings at the end of 1937 about possible forms of pressure on Japan as 'the utter-ances of a hare-brained statesman or an amateur strategist.'[185] More abrasively, Sir Warren Fisher, in the context of the conflicting naval desiderata of the two countries, quoted with approval the warning of a scholar from before the Great War:

'Now we know how the Americans—represented by their Government—have always dealt with us since they have been an independent State. They must always prevail and never concede; they enjoy the flouting of an older community as proof of their superiority; and they esteem a good bargain, even if gained by dishonourable means, to mark the highest form of ability. The United States cannot engage in any form of competition with us, from athletics to diplomacy, without using foul play.'[186]

Nevertheless, there were other politicians and officials who chose to place their emphasis in a different direction. Eden and Vansittart, for example, were among those who, although greatly exasperated on occasions, stressed the need to continue to strive for Anglo-American cooperation. Even if arguments of history and kinship were ignored, the strategic situation was very persuasive in this respect. As Vansittart had observed during the Manchurian crisis, until the United States could be persuaded to stand by her, Britain 'must eventually be done for in the Far East.'[187] In the words of another Foreign Office minute, this time in 1939: 'There is much in the American attitude which strikes us as unfair, illogical, even perverse. But the rules of American conduct of foreign affairs are fairly well known to us now; and our need of American support is such that we are bound to shape our own action according to those rules.'[188] Britain, wrote Lord Lothian after becoming Ambassador in Washington, 'is really dependent on the United States for security in the Pacific.'[189] It was a situation long foreshadowed, and one that was to be made plain for all to see during the Second World War.

As Japan's intransigence increased during the 1930s, therefore, a series of suggestions passed from London to Washington, seeking joint action of various kinds in order to hold the situation and perhaps construct some-thing more stable in its place. The details of these approaches and their reception can be read elsewhere.[190] The occasions included Japan's renewed pressure on North China in 1935, the prelude to the London Naval Conference, the outbreak of fighting in 1937, and the attacks on the *Panay* and H.M.S. *Ladybird*. The possible courses of action which were considered ranged from some form of Anglo-American alliance to joint protests, synchronized naval movements, coordinated financial aid to China, and even economic measures against Japan.

Some of these proposals, it is true, were put forward with certain reservations in mind. For example, although in 1937 London informed Washington that they would go as far as the latter in any moves to deter Japan, it remains very doubtful whether, in the event, they would have followed an American initiative on economic sanctions. At the same time, Washington did on occasions respond in such a way that something was achieved. Anglo-American differences over naval armaments were sufficiently resolved, for example, for a treaty on the subject to be signed in March 1936 (although Japan's absence threatened to undermine the whole exercise),[191] while staff talks held early in 1938 between the Admiralty and a member of the U.S. Navy's War Plans Division, though entailing no binding commitments on either side, did at least help to diminish the suspicion and coldness which had long tended to surround relations in that sphere.[192]

Nevertheless, as far as action or joint protests in East Asia were concerned, the predominant pattern was one of tentative British proposals and firm American rejections—those rejections sometimes being accompanied by a warning that London should not endanger relations by revealing publicly that it was Washington which was dragging its feet. (This desire to preserve the façade of American righteousness in the Far East was to make itself felt again in 1940, when Cordell Hull, as Secretary of State, after privately indicating that he understood why Britain had to close the Burma Road in the face of Japanese pressure and in the absence of American support, nevertheless felt obliged to deprecate the move publicly.) The outcome was that those in London who already dismissed the idea of fruitful Anglo-American cooperation were strengthened in this belief; those who still hoped to find such a way out of Britain's dilemma, downcast. 'It is a poor performance', wrote Sir Alexander Cadogan, now Permanent Under Secretary of State at the Foreign Office, of the American refusal to allow government ships to carry munitions to either China or Japan, 'and a warning to us—if such were needed—of what to expect from them.'[193]

Thus, by the summer of 1939 the United States had done nothing to ease the overwhelming danger which faced Britain as a power with world-wide interests and greatly inadequate resources. As the Tientsin crisis became more acute and a commitment was entered into to defend Poland against Germany, no solution had yet been found to the interlocking problems involving the threat from the three main anti-Comintern powers. Might not Japan strike first, leaving Germany and Italy to act against Britain the moment the Royal Navy had been weakened by the despatch of major units to Singapore? Could the Mediterranean route be preserved by a sudden, knock-out blow against Italy? If a humiliatingly meek line were adopted vis-à-vis Tokyo, would not the European dictators derive encouragement from this, and would not that vital commodity, prestige, be drained away from Britain's Asian Empire?[194] Only an American commitment, it seemed, could offer a solution, and in 1939 that appeared almost as remote a possibility as ever.

Almost as remote, rather than as remote. There were some signs in 1939 which pointed in the direction of a possible development of the American role in checking Japan. During that year, a 'moral embargo' was placed on sending aeroplanes and spare parts to Japan, credits for her were brought to an end, and, in response to strong domestic pressure, Tokyo was notified in July that in six months' time the commercial treaty between the two states would be terminated. The war in China from 1937 onwards had heightened American sympathies for that country, and by the spring of 1939 the over-whelming majority favoured an embargo on supplies which could assist Japan in her aggression.[195] Individual Americans in China itself were also endeavouring to help in the strengthening of national life and resistance.[196] Within official circles, moreover, there were those who already inclined towards a more forward policy in the Far East. The U.S. Navy, for example, whose strength was being built up again under the Roosevelt Administration, 'regarded war with Japan as practically inevitable some day', and tended to stiffen the overall American approach towards that country.[197] At the Treasury, Morgenthau not only felt that more should be done for China, but believed that Japan could be defeated by economic measures alone.[198] Even within the mainly cautious State Department, Hornbeck, especially, carried on the Stimsonian belief that China's good-will towards the United States represented 'both a moral and a business asset'; as the Japanese attacks continued, he also began to move towards a belief in the likelihood of a confrontation taking place, with war itself to be avoided only by the United States taking a firm stand.[199] In addition, Hornbeck embodied a tendency to see the Sino-Japanese conflict in terms of good and evil, of a threat to world-wide principles of international relations—a belief which, if acted upon, would tend to preclude some form of modus vivendi being arrived at with Japan.[200]

The American Army, it is true, were displaying little enthusiasm for the notion of having China as a ward and potential ally. In the Philippines, however, General Douglas MacArthur, as adviser to the Government of those islands, was beginning to develop the idea (one which stood in contrast to the predominant, and correct, military opinion) that the colony could, after all, be defended successfully against Japanese attack.[201] More-over, while the pledge of Philippines independence—reflecting in part, as it did, the anti-imperial tradition in American life—appeared in one respect to emphasize United States desires not to become entangled in the Western Pacific, the commercial and financial dependence of the Philippines on the parent country, which Washington's policies fostered, could be seen as a symbol of continuing American expansionist tendencies. And those tend-encies could involve a collision with Japan.[202]

Yet throughout the period 1933–39, United States policies suggested little desire for such a collision. Despite an increase in naval construction, the basic unreality of War Plan Orange became even more marked, and both the Army's planners and the commanders on the spot were ready, as the Navy were not, to face the fact that a fleet could not reach the Philippines in time to forestall the Japanese there, and that the resources to do the job by air power instead were not available.[203] The Navy for its part continued to press for better and more widespread base facilities; and indeed, in a high-handed move which foreshadowed some of his actions during the war, Roosevelt himself, in 1938, ordered the occupation of the Canton and Enderbury Islands whose ownership was in dispute with Great Britain.[204] When it came to the risk of provoking Japan, however, matters were different, and when, for example, Congress, at the instigation of the State Department and President, turned down a proposal to build a major base on the American West Pacific island of Guam, it was part of a general pattern.[205] Whether the issue was the protection of American nationals in the war-zones of China, the silver problem in that country, or the continuing shipment of vital raw materials like oil and scrap metal to Japan, the policy pursued was that of minimum provocation.[206] From Tokyo, Joseph Grew, as Ambassador, warned that the United States should prepare 'a big stick', but he also believed that, by 'speaking softly' at the same time, a way could be found of avoiding a conflict between the two countries.[207] Hull himself shaped his course, as Dr. Borg has put it, by the profound conviction 'that most of the basic problems of international relations could be solved by moral education', a field in which he tended to find Great Britain somewhat lacking and unduly sceptical.[208]

Even if the danger of clashing with Japan were not a sufficient deterrent for the American Administration, there existed also the powerful desire of their own electorate to keep out of entanglements and wars, a desire symbolized by the Neutrality Acts of 1935 and 1936. Roosevelt did in fact take advantage of Japan's failure to declare war formally on China by not invoking those neutrality laws, but little practical assistance flowed to China as a result. In general, indeed, it has been suggested that the President was even more cautious than the actual strength of isolationist opinion required.[209] The position which he instructed his delegation to the Brussels Conference to adopt, that the United States must not 'be pushed out in front as the leader in or suggester of future action' was, in essence, maintained throughout. Even Roosevelt's celebrated 'quarantine' speech of October 1937 (in which he declared that 'when an epidemic of physical disease starts to spread, the community approves and joins in a quarantine of the patients in order to protect the health of the community . . .') was far from being intended as a prelude to taking stern measures against Japan: 'sanction', he emphasized soon afterwards, was 'a terrible word' which should be thrown out of the window.[210] Nor was the termination of America's commercial treaty with Japan carried out with the likelihood of sanctions in mind.[211]

While Japan was thus being approached with great caution, China was receiving little substantial assistance from the United States. No help was forthcoming, for example, to prevent China being forced off the silver standard in 1935: the problem, declared Roosevelt privately, was 'China's business and not ours.'[212] Meanwhile American salesmen on the spot were happy enough to deal with the new regime in Manchukuo,[213] and when the business community as a whole was called upon in the mid-1930s to assist China in her economic growth, the response was lukewarm.[214] Before 1937 especially, there is little evidence of that widespread and sustained concern for China among the public which American mythology would suggest.[215] Even after the fighting had broken out in 1937, few war materials were sent to China, and even an individual like Hornbeck, so concerned for America's destiny in that country, spent much of this post-1933 period subordinating the requirements of aid to those of avoiding war with Japan.[216] 'The Roosevelt years', writes Professor Cohen, 'demonstrate that American policy was designed to serve American interests without particular regard for China.'[217] Moreover, by 1938 the belief was already beginning to exist in official circles that Chiang Kai-shek had virtually stopped fighting the Japanese in order to conserve his strength for the domestic struggle against the Communists*—a belief which, as we shall see, was to find fuller and more bitter expression by 1944.[218]

Above all, the 1930s saw no clarification of American Far Eastern policy as a whole, no reconciliation of cloudy, expansive aspirations with limited tangible interests, restricted means, and small readiness for sacrifice. As the Joint Army–Navy Planning Committee plaintively observed in 1939: '[We have] frequently had to work in the dark with respect to what national policy is with respect to a specific problem, or what it may be expected to be.'[219] Hence, lacking clear guidelines, individuals and branches of government were left to formulate their own ideas on the subject, thus adding to the confusion. (The U.S. Navy, for example, tended to go back to Mahan and Theodore Roosevelt as a basis for a tough-minded, expansionist outlook which happily chimed with a professional desire for more ships and men.)[220]

As in earlier periods, this shapeless and ambiguous quality about American Far Eastern policy did not assist relations with Britain. Within the State Department, it is true, there was some desire in principle to foster cooperation or work for parallel action by the two countries, especially

---

* In Washington, as in London, knowledge and appreciation of the Chinese Communist movement remained seriously inadequate. Roosevelt, however, was from 1937 onwards receiving reports from Captain Evans F. Carlson of the U.S. Marines, who was journeying in the Communist-held territories of the north-west. 'The Chinese Communist group (so-called)', wrote Carlson in March 1938, 'is not Communistic in the sense that we are accustomed to use the term. Its economic program does not include the communization of land and redistribution of property. I would call them a group of Liberal Democrats, perhaps Social Democrats . . . They seek equality of opportunity and honest government.' Roosevelt Papers, PPF 4951; see *Shewmaker*, 102. In 1940, however, Edgar Snow was emphasizing Mao Tse-tung's own insistence that the Chinese Communists were indeed Marxist revolutionaries. E. Snow, *Journey To The Beginning* (London, 1959), 239.

when Japan began to be identified with the European dictatorships as a threat to the entire basis of international relations.[221] Often, however, as already indicated, reasons were found why, in the event, reactions to Japanese moves should not be placed on such a basis.[222] Within the U.S. Treasury, moreover, there existed deep suspicions of British financial and commercial manoeuvrings in China. As seen by Morgenthau, Far Eastern politics were a contest, not simply between Japan and the United States, but between the yen bloc, the sterling bloc, and the burgeoning dollar: 'It's an international battle between Great Britain, Japan and ourselves, and China is the bone in the middle, see?'[223] Such a sense of rivalry for the wealth of the East, coupled with the belief in America's superior understanding of and care for the Chinese, did not augur well, on the United States side, for war-time collaboration. Between individuals on the spot there could exist, of course, friendship and accord: even Agnes Smedley, for example, champion of Mao Tse-tung's Yenan regime and supporter of Indian nationalism against British imperialism, found Britons in Hongkong who were zealous on China's behalf after 1937, Clark Kerr himself proving an understanding and helpful Ambassador.[224] (Major Carlson reported to Roosevelt that Clark Kerr was 'very sympathetic with China and desirous of aiding the Chinese cause.')[225]

In general, however, there already existed the makings of the tension and misunderstanding which were to mark the war-time years, when the Australian Minister to China was to observe 'two nations of such out-standing achievements standing and glaring at each other . . .'[226] In the greater emotionalism and lesser practicality and pragmatism of the American approach to China, there lay also a key to another comment made by the same shrewd and by no means uncritically pro-British diplomat, Sir Frederick Eggleston, in 1942: that there was 'far greater personal hostility to the Chinese and criticism of their inefficiency among American diplomats and military officials and journalists than among the British.'[227]

One final aspect of these years leading up to 1939, which should be borne in mind in terms of the war that followed, concerns the relative positions of Far Eastern policies and of those centred upon Europe. The interaction of developments in the two spheres, for both Japan and Britain, has already been indicated. As for the United States, it is evident that caution, passivity and 'appeasement' were the predominant characteristics of her 1930s policies with regard to Europe, as well as to the Far East.[228] Over European affairs, too, there existed considerable American distrust of the British.[229] In return, Chamberlain, who was far less anxious for American intervention in Europe than in the Far East, handled in a negative and insensitive fashion Roosevelt's proposal, early in 1938, that he should address the Washington Diplomatic Corps on the subject of 'essential principles' for the conduct of international relations. There is no evidence to suggest, however, that any-thing substantial would have come of the idea in terms of checking Germany, and Churchill's subsequent magnification of the opportunity thus lost is merely one example of his crudity as a historian and his tendency to make exaggerated, hands-across-the-sea assumptions about the United States in relation to Great Britain.[230]

Of greater interest for our purpose, however, are the degrees of concern shown in both Britain and the United States over European, as compared to Far Eastern, affairs. In Britain's case, as already indicated, it is in no way surprising that developments and threats nearer home should weigh the more heavily (even though one can find Halifax in August 1939 telling the Cabinet that 'the position in the Far East was now causing him more anxiety than the position in any other part of the world').[231] And so it was to be during the war itself. Yet it is also apparent that, beneath all the periodic outbursts of emotion about China and the Far East, American concern, too, tended to lie more strongly in a European direction. In July 1939, for example, a major lobbying effort in Washington on behalf of China and of sanctions against Japan failed, in the words of one of those taking part, because 'everyone seems more concerned with the Neutrality Bills and Europe.'[232] Between 1931 and 1941, writes a leading student of the subject, 'American Congressmen and political party leaders . . . generally gave less priority to relations with Japan and East Asia than to relations with European states, and considered Nazi Germany and Fascist Italy more dangerous than Japan.'[233] Even the growing hostility towards Japan which did develop owed a considerable amount to her proclaimed closeness to the European dictatorships, first in the Anti-Comintern Pact and then, more boldly, in the Tripartite Pact of 1940—this in turn bestowing upon China in some sense the status of a Western democracy, fighting with Britain and France in a common cause.[234]

This association of Japan with Germany and Italy also had its effect upon American strategic thinking. At the outbreak of war in Europe, it is true, the main emphasis was still on the Pacific as a likely theatre of operations. However, the much-amended War Plan Orange against Japan had already been supplemented by a series of numbered 'Rainbow' plans, which envisaged war against a coalition of the dictatorships; and the fifth of these Rainbow plans, which placed its emphasis upon transatlantic operations, was to become the basis of American strategy during the Second World War.[235] Given the high-flown talk about the country's Far Eastern destiny, such a strategy was bound to provoke domestic controversy, and doubly so after the shock and humiliation of Pearl Harbour. This in turn would help ensure that, however realistic a strategy of concentrating upon Germany first might be, its formal adoption would not prevent tension continuing to arise between the United States and Britain over war-time global priorities.

Thus, at the time when Britain became involved in war against Hitler's Germany, there were aspects of United States policies which held out some hope that the threatening situation in the Far East might be improved. And yet, as we shall see, even the development between 1939 and 1941 of close Anglo-American ties where the European war was concerned was not to produce, until the very last moment, a guarantee by Washington that if

Japan struck at Britain's vulnerable possessions in the Far East, American armed assistance would be forthcoming. In addition, moreover, there existed in 1939, and were still to exist in 1941, a variety of factors which were to ensure that when the time did come to fight Japan together, it would not be on a basis of mutual understanding or complete trust.

Notes to Chapter One

1 Thorne, *The Limits of Foreign Policy* (hereafter, *Thorne*), 390.
2 WSC to Chamberlain, 25 March 1939, PREM 1/345.
3 CAB 69/8.
4 CAB 69/2. See also his reassurances to Sir Earle Page of Australia in the Cabinet of 12 Nov. 1941 concerning 'possible but unlikely dangers' from Japan. CAB 65/24.
5 N. Ike, *Japan's Decision For War* (Stanford, 1967).
6 Eggleston Papers, 423/9/395.
7 S. W. Kirby, *The War Against Japan* (hereafter, *Kirby*, I, etc.) vol. I (London, 1957), 147, 166, 184.
8 S. W. Roskill, *Naval Policy Between The Wars*, vol. II (London, 1976), 188.
9 S. E. Morison, *The Two-Ocean War* (Boston, 1963), 78. On Pearl Harbour, see R. Wohlstetter, *Pearl Harbor: Warning and Decision* (Stanford, 1962).
10 *Thorne*, cap. 10.
11 V. G. Kiernan, *The Lords of Human Kind* (Harmondsworth, 1972).
12 See the relevant essays in J. Needham, *Within The Four Seas* (London, 1969).
13 *Thorne*, 55.
14 R. A. Butler, *The Art of the Possible* (London, 1971), 111.
15 Memo. of 16 Jan. 1945, Taussig Papers, box 49.
16 Memo. of 17 Dec. 1942, ibid, box 46.
17 See below, 446, note 17.
18 Lord Moran, *Churchill: The Struggle For Survival, 1940–1965* (London, 1966), (hereafter, *Moran*), 131, 559. See H. Pelling, *Winston Churchill* (London, 1974), 267.
19 Halifax Diary, e.g. 27 Nov. 1941.
20 Lord Birkenhead, *The Prof In Two Worlds* (London, 1961), 23.
21 See ibid, e.g. 51.
22 Stimson Diary, 24 Jan. 1942, 12 May 1942.
23 Stilwell Diary, 18 and 21 Feb. 1942.
24 FDR to WSC, 16 April 1942, PREM 3, 152/1.
25 H. R. Isaacs, *No Peace For Asia* (New York, 1947), 10ff.; E. Taylor, *Richer By Asia* (London, 1948), 84, 96.
26 See IMTFE passim, a record of savagery beside which even the Nuremberg-trial evidence seems pale at times.
27 R. Smith, *Vietnam And The West* (Ithica, N.Y., 1968), 177; D. Halberstam, *The Best And The Brightest* (New York, 1972); A. Lake (ed.), *The Legacy of Vietnam* (New York, 1976).
28 PWC(L), 21 Oct. 1942, CAB 99/26.
29 Cab, 8 Aug. 1940, CAB 65/8.
30 See below, 259.
31 Robinson to Evatt, 12 Nov. 1942, Evatt Papers, Robinson file. On immigration policy, see ADEA, file A989/44/655/37.
32 E.g. Johnson to Hornbeck, 8 and 20 Jan. 1942, Hornbeck Papers, box 262.
33 'The Outlines of a Constructive Peace in the Pacific', 2 Feb. 1943, ADEA, A989/44/655/25.
34 WSC to Linlithgow, 3 Feb. 1942, PREM 4, 45/3.
35 Hamilton memo., 17 June 1942, FRUS, 1942, China, 71.

36 van der Plas memo., 19 Aug. 1944, NFM, Brandkast la 13.
37 Smuts to Gillett, 7 June 1942, in J. van der Poel (ed.), *Selections From The Smuts Papers*, vol. VI (Cambridge, 1973).
38 Campbell to Cadogan, 6 Aug. 1942, PREM 4, 42/9. See below, 158–9 and 167–8.
39 A. Iriye, *Pacific Estrangement* (Cambridge, Mass., 1972), 159.
40 G. Myrdal, *An American Dilemma*, vol. II (New York, 1944), 1006.
41 FRUS, 1942, I, 677.
42 See in general W. L. Holland (ed.), *Asian Nationalism And The West* (New York, 1953).
43 See J. Friend, *Between Two Empires* (New Haven, 1965), 211ff. and, on Quezon's 'thoroughly ambiguous' stance between the U.S.A. and Japan in the 1930s, ibid, 183.
44 See e.g. Thakin Nu, *Burma Under The Japanese* (London, 1954) and Ba Maw, *Breakthrough In Burma* (New Haven, 1968).
45 J. Kennedy, *A History of Malaya* (London, 1970), 260.
46 V. Purcell, *The Chinese In Southeast Asia* (Oxford, 1965), 311.
47 Ba Maw, *Breakthrough In Burma*, 179ff.
48 Ibid, 336ff. Besides Ba Maw and Tojo for Japan, the principal participants were President Wang Ching-wei of the puppet regime in Nanking, Prince Wan Waithaya-kon of Siam, Chang Ching-hu of Manchukuo, President Laurel of the Philippines, and Subhas Chandra Bose, Head of Azad Hind, the Government of 'Free India'.
49 Purcell, *The Chinese In Southeast Asia*, 155.
50 *Times*, 13 and 14 March 1942, and quoted in M. Perham, *Colonial Sequence, 1930–1949* (London, 1967), 225.
51 J. K. Fairbank, '"American China Policy" to 1898: A Misconception', *Pacific Historical Review*, Nov. 1970. For a stimulating essay on the relationship between imperial attitudes and domestic class-consciousness, see P. Mason, *Prospero's Magic* (London, 1962).
52   See below, 728.
53 W. Slim, *Defeat Into Victory* (London, 1960), 139.
54 On this and related points, see *Thorne*, 417–9.
55 Braddell to Gent, 27 Nov. 1942, CO 865/1. See S. Rose, *Britain and Southeast Asia* (London, 1962), 66.
56 *Times*, 14 March 1942.
57 A. P. Thornton, *The Imperial Idea And Its Enemies* (London, 1966), 306 and passim. See also J. Bowle, *The Imperial Achievement: The Rise and Transformation of the British Empire* (London, 1974), books 4 and 5.
58 See K. M. Panikkar, *Asia And Western Dominance* (London, 1953).
59 FO 371, F 11097/6390/61. See H. Kahn, *The Emerging Japanese Superstate* (London, 1971).
60 *Thorne*, 57, 246.
61 D. MacArthur, *Reminiscences* (London, 1964), 32.
62 Hurley to HST, 20 May 1945, FRUS, 1945, VII, 107.
63 FEC, 21 Dec. 1944, CAB 96/5.
64 See e.g. *Thorne*; E. Reischauer, J. Fairbank and A. Craig, *East Asia: The Modern Transformation* (London, 1965); W. L. Neumann, *America Encounters Japan* (Baltimore, 1963); A. Iriye, *Across The Pacific* (New York, 1967) and *Pacific Estrangement*; W. R. Fishel, *The End of Extraterritoriality in China* (Berkeley, 1952); W. Cohen, *America's Response To China* (New York, 1971; hereafter, *Cohen*); E. May and J. Thomson (eds.), *American-East Asian Relations* (Cambridge, Mass., 1972; hereafter, *May and Thomson*); G. F. Hudson, *The Far East In World Politics* (London, 1939); P. S. Tang, *Russian and Soviet Policy In Manchuria and Outer Mongolia, 1911–1931* (Durham, N. C., 1959); M. H. Hunt, *Frontier Defense and the Open Door* (New Haven, 1973).
65 B. N. Pandey, *The Break-Up of British India* (London, 1969), 68; see also Panikkar, *Asia and Western Dominance*.
66 Iriye, *Pacific Estrangement*, 98.

67 M. Beloff, *Imperial Sunset*, vol. I (London, 1969), 347–8; Thornton, *The Imperial Idea And Its Enemies*, passim.
68 See R. R. James, *Churchill, A Study In Failure* (Harmondsworth, 1973), part five; M. Gilbert, *Winston S. Churchill*, vol. V (London, 1976), 356–619, passim, makes clear not only Churchill's anachronistic belief in what could be achieved by a re-assertion of Britain's 'will to rule', but his complete misjudgment of the attitude of the British as a whole towards India.
69 Amery to Dorman-Smith, 15 April 1943, Dorman-Smith Papers, E 215/3.
70 *Thorne*, 49ff.
71 Ibid, 49, and W. R. Louis, *British Strategy In The Far East, 1919–1939* (Oxford, 1971), 26.
72 *Thorne*, 42.
73 On Britain's inter-war armament and defence problems, see N. Gibbs, *Grand Strategy*, vol. I (London, 1976).
74 I. Nish, *The Anglo-Japanese Alliance* (London, 1966), 175–6.
75 S. W. Roskill, *Naval Policy Between The Wars*, vol. I (London, 1968), 420, 445; S. W. Roskill, *Hankey, Man Of Secrets*, vol. II (London, 1972), 403; Gilbert, *Churchill*, vol. V, 76, 105.
76 *Thorne*, 392ff.
77 I. Nish, *Alliance In Decline* (London, 1972), 61.
78 Ibid, 118, 173, 203.
79 Louis, *British Strategy*, 81.
80 Ibid, 37; Nish, *Alliance In Decline*, 256.
81 E. g. Nish, *Alliance In Decline*, 72, 216.
82 On the Washington Conference, see e.g. ibid; Louis, *British Strategy*, 50ff.; Roskill, *Naval Policy*, I, 300ff.; Roskill, *Hankey*, II, 238ff.
83 Louis, *British Strategy*, 28.
84 Ibid, 55.
85 See H. and M. Sprout, *Towards A New Order of Sea Power* (London, 1943).
86 Roskill, *Naval Policy*, vol. I.
87 See e.g. D. C. Watt, *Personalities and Policies* (London, 1965).
88 *Thorne*, 123.
89 See e. g. S. K. Hornbeck, *The United States In The Far East* (Boston, 1942).
90 A. T. Steele, *The American People And China* (New York, 1966), 13.
91 Fairbank, in *Pacific Historical Review*, Nov. 1970.
92 Taussig memo., 16 Jan. 1945, Taussig Papers, box 48.
93 S. P. Huntington, *The Soldier And The State* (New York, 1957), cap. 10; W. A. Williams, *The Roots of the Modern American Empire* (New York, 1969); M. Young, 'The Quest For Empire', in *May and Thomson*; R. Hofstadter, *The Paranoid Style in American Politics* (New York, 1967).
94 *Thorne*, 50–1; *May and Thomson*, xiv.
95 See P. Varg, *Missionaries, Chinese and Diplomats* (Princeton, 1958). By 1920 there were over 3,000 American missionaries in China with a capital investment of around $12 million.
96 *Thorne*, 55.
97 *Christian Science Monitor*, 25 July 1942.
98 FDR to Marshall, 8 March 1943, Roosevelt Papers, MR box 165.
99 *Thorne*, 236.
100 Ibid, 57.
101 See e.g. *Cohen*, 102.
102 In general, see Iriye, *Across The Pacific*.
103 P. Varg, *The Making of a Myth: The United States And China, 1897–1912* (East Lansing, Michigan, 1968), 117. On the general question of people's focus of attention and attitude changes, see the relevant material in H. C. Kelman, *International Behavior* (New York, 1966).
104 *Cohen*, 65, 110, 150.

48   PART ONE: THE SETTING BEFORE PEARL HARBOUR

105 Ibid, 37; Steele, *The American People And China*, 13.
106 *Thorne*, 51.
107 Ibid, 236.
108 See e.g. Hunt, *Frontier Defense*, passim.
109 *Thorne*, 64ff.
110 See the essay by Neumann in A. De Conde (ed.), *Isolation and Security* (Durham, N.C., 1957).
111 Neumann, *America Encounters Japan*, 104ff.; *Cohen*, 41.
112 Iriye, *Pacific Estrangement*, passim.
113 See Nish, *Alliance In Decline*, 269.
114 *Thorne*, 22.
115 See A. Iriye, *After Imperialism* (Cambridge, Mass., 1965).
116 *Thorne*, 27–32; Iriye, *After Imperialism*.
117 See C. P. Fitzgerald, *The Birth of Communist China* (Harmondsworth, 1964), 58.
118 E.g. Louis, *British Strategy*, 12; K. E. Shewmaker, *Americans And Chinese Communists, 1927–1945* (Ithica, N.Y., 1971; hereafter *Shewmaker*), 31.
119 Iriye, *After Imperialism*, 87.
120 Iriye, *Pacific Estrangement*, 49.
121 Ibid, 111.
122 Louis, *British Strategy*, 234.
123 Hunt, *Frontier Defense*, 245, 251. See H. R. Isaacs, *Scratches On Our Minds* (New York, 1963).
124 Louis, *British Strategy*, 46, 77, 95.
125 *Thorne*, 46, 56; see Fairbank in *Pacific Historical Review*, Nov. 1970.
126 Iriye, *Pacific Estrangement*, 98.
127 Ibid, 18.
128 *Thorne*, 52.
129 Ibid, 227.
130 Ibid, 419.
131 Iriye, *Pacific Estrangement*, 31, 44; see R. Storry, *The Double Patriots* (London, 1957).
132 Iriye, *Pacific Estrangement*, 151.
133 I. F. Clarke, *Voices Prophesying War, 1763–1984* (Oxford, 1966), 44.
134 *Thorne*, 404ff.
135 E.g. ibid, 241, 246.
136 Ibid, 225ff.
137 Ibid, 247ff.
138 Ibid, 8, 404.
139 Stimson Diary, 14 July 1943.
140 *Thorne*, 268.
141 E.g. Storry, *The Double Patriots*; D. Borg and S. Okamoto (eds.), *Pearl Harbor As History* (New York, 1973; hereafter, *Borg and Okamoto*); *Thorne*, 373ff.; J. Crowley, *Japan's Quest For Autonomy* (Princeton, 1966); M. Maruyama, *Thought And Behaviour In Modern Japanese Politics* (London, 1963).
142 J. H. Boyle, *China And Japan At War, 1937–1945* (Stanford, 1972); T. A. White and A. Jacobee, *Thunder Out Of China* (London, 1947).
143 Boyle, *China and Japan*, 222.
144 See DBFP, Second Series, XIII.
145 E.g. B. A. Lee, *Britain and the Sino-Japanese War, 1937–1939* (Stanford, 1973; hereafter, *Lee*), cap. 7.
146 See Ike, *Japan's Decision For War*, and J. W. Morley (ed.), *Deterrent Diplomacy: Japan, Germany and the U.S.S.R., 1935–1940* (New York, 1977).
147 *Borg and Okamoto*, 598.
148 E.g. D. Borg, *The United States and the Far Eastern Crisis of 1933–1938* (Cambridge, Mass., 1964; hereafter, Borg, *The United States*), 137.
149 *Thorne*, 266.
150 Ibid, 394.

151 *Lee*, 80.
152 See e.g. Gibbs, *Grand Strategy*, I; K. Middlemas and J. Barnes, *Baldwin* (London, 1969); Roskill, *Hankey, Man of Secrets*, vol. III (London, 1974); M. Howard, *The Continental Commitment* (Harmondsworth, 1974); K. Middlemas, *The Diplomacy of Illusion* (London, 1972); K. Hancock and M. Gowing, *British War Economy* (London, 1949; hereafter, *Hancock and Gowing*).
153 *Thorne*, 395, note.
154 See DBFP, Second Series, XIII.
155 A. Marder, 'The Royal Navy and the Ethiopian Crisis of 1935–6', *American Historical Review*, vol. LXXV No. 5, 1970.
156 *Thorne*, 395, note.
157 Ibid, 395.
158 Roskill, *Hankey*, III, 280, 287.
159 Ibid, 395; Roskill, *Navy Policy*, II, 349, 352, 436; PREM 1/309 and 314.
160 See e.g. Watt, *Personalities and Policies*, essay 7.
161 P. Hasluck, *The Government And The People, 1939–1941* (Canberra, 1952; hereafter, *Hasluck*, I), 29, 223; see A. Watt, *The Evolution of Australian Foreign Policy, 1938–1965* (Cambridge, 1967), 25.
162 *Thorne*, 398.
163 E.g. *Kirby*, I, 31; Dreyer to Chatfield, 23 Jan. 1935, Chatfield Papers.
164 *Kirby*, I, 21.
165 Ibid, 22.
166 *Thorne*, 396.
167 *Trotter*, passim.
168 Louis, *British Strategy*, 215.
169 *Lee*, 26.
170 E.g. ibid, 55, 63, 70, 72, 92, 136, 142.
171 *Thorne*, 398, note.
172 *Lee*, 119, 195.
173 Ibid, 46.
174 Ibid, 94; see *Trotter*, cap. 9.
175 *Thorne*, 400.
176 *Lee*, 18, 47–8.
177 Ibid, 10ff.
178 Ibid, 85, 162–3, 193.
179 A. W. Young, *China And The Helping Hand, 1937–1945* (Cambridge, Mass., 1963; hereafter, *Young*), 49.
180 *Thorne*, 380, note.
181 *Lee*, 128, 155.
182 Ibid, 129, 214; see *Shewmaker*, and E. Snow, *Red Star Over China* (Harmondsworth, 1973).
183 *Lee*, 199. In retrospect, however, Sansom's verdict can be seen as implying a clearer conception on the part of the Japanese of what a 'new order' entailed than was actually the case.
184 Ibid, 32.
185 Ibid, 91.
186 DBFP, Second Series, XIII, 927.
187. *Thorne*, 247.
188 *Lee*, 208.
189 Ibid, 204.
190 E.g. *Thorne*, 401–2; *Lee*, passim; Borg, *The United States*, passim; *Trotter*, passim; S. L. Endicott, *Diplomacy and Enterprise: Britain's China Policy, 1933–1937* (Cambridge, 1975).
191 DBFP, Second Series, XIII, No. 718.
192 Roskill, *Naval Policy*, II, 367; L. Pratt, 'The Anglo-American Conversations on the Far East of January 1938', *International Affairs*, Oct. 1971.

193 *Lee*, 42.
194 See e.g. R. J. Pritchard, 'The Far East As An Influence On The Chamberlain Government's Pre-War European Policies', *Millennium*, vol. 11, No. 3, 1973–4, and J. Harvey (ed.), *The Diplomatic Diaries of Oliver Harvey, 1937–1940* (London, 1970), entry for 24 June 1939.
195 *Cohen*, 146; Steele, *The American People*, 21.
196 See *Young*, passim.
197 W. H. Heinrichs, 'The Role of the United States Navy', in *Borg and Okamoto*.
198 L. C. Gardner, 'The Role of the Commerce and Treasury Departments', in ibid.
199 J. C. Thomson, 'The Role of the Department of State', in ibid.
200 Ibid, 126.
201 Ibid, 175.
202 Friend, *Between Two Empires*, 6.
203 L. Morton, 'War Plan Orange', *World Politics*, Jan. 1959; *Thorne*, 390.
204 *Borg and Okamoto*, 216.
205 Borg, *The United States*, 251.
206 E.g. ibid, 154, 334; Neumann, *America Encounters Japan*, 222.
207 E.g. Borg, *The United States*, 115.
208 Ibid, 96.
209 Ibid, 334ff.; *Cohen*, 144.
210 Borg, *The United States*, 369ff.
211 *Cohen*, 148.
212 Ibid, 140; see Borg, *The United States*, 121ff.
213 *Thorne*, 225.
214 Borg, *The United States*, 274.
215 E.g. ibid, 89.
216 Ibid, 193.
217 *Cohen*, 163.
218 Ibid, 156.
219 *Thorne*, 391.
220 *Borg and Okamoto*, 201.
221 Borg, *The United States*, 131, 510.
222 E.g. ibid, 294.
223 *Borg and Okamoto*, 264, 274.
224 A. Smedley, *Battle Hymn of China* (London, 1943), 149, 159.
225 Carlson to Le Hand, 13 June 1939, Roosevelt Papers, PPF 4951.
226 Eggleston Papers, 423/9/1148.
227 Ibid.
228 See A. Offner, *American Appeasement* (Cambridge, Mass., 1969).
229 E.g. ibid, 213.
230 Ibid, 231, 271; Roskill, *Hankey III*, 298–302.
231 *Lee*, 198.
232 *Cohen*, 148.
233 W. S. Cole, 'The Role of the U.S. Congress and Political Parties', in *Borg and Okamoto*.
234 *Borg and Okamoto*, 15; Borg, *The United States*, 518.
235 *Borg and Okamoto*, 177; L. Morton, *Strategy And Command: The First Two Years* (Washington D.C., 1962); M. Matloff and E. Snell, *Strategic Planning For Coalition Warfare, 1941–42* (Washington D.C., 1953; hereafter, *Matloff and Snell*).

CHAPTER TWO

THE UNITED STATES,
BRITAIN AND THE FAR EAST, 1939–1941

DURING THE two years following the outbreak of war over Poland in
September 1939, developments in Europe tended to promote the idea in
Japan that she, too, should resort to arms. It was by no means a case, how-
ever, of Tokyo's slavishly fitting in with the policies and promptings of
Berlin. Germany's signing of the Molotov–Ribbentrop agreement in August
1939 had come as a severe shock to Japan's leaders, more steadfastly wedded,
as they were, to the Anti-Comintern Pact. Conversely, Japan signed her own
Non-Aggression Pact with the Soviet Union in 1941—an ominous development for her other potential enemies to the south and east—and ignored
German suggestions thereafter that she should seize Soviet Far Eastern
territories as a complementary move to Hitler's advance towards Moscow
and the Caucasus.[1] As was also to be the case after Pearl Harbour, Berlin
and Tokyo each sought to use the other rather than to collaborate closely
in a common cause.

At the same time, confusion and faction-fighting continued to characterize
the policy-making process within Japan, with middle-ranking army officers,
for example, often exercising a greater influence than did their nominal
superiors.[2] Schemes and assumptions were still made without their possible
consequences being fully explored,[3] while it was only in 1941 that a conflict
with the European powers was accepted as being likely to involve war with
the United States as well. In July 1940, the Cabinet had aimed to solve both
the struggle in China and the need to obtain raw materials from Southeast
Asia without becoming involved in a new conflict;[4] in September 1940, the
Navy was still emphasizing that 'every conceivable measure will be taken to
avoid war with the United States', and that 'the Southward advance will be
attempted as far as possible by peaceful means';[5] it was late June to early
July, 1941, before it was decreed that 'preparations for war with Great
Britain and the United States will be made', and it was accepted that such a
price would be paid if necessary in order to achieve Japan's designs in Southeast Asia.[6]

Nevertheless, the drift towards a violent solution of Japan's perceived
problems was clearly quickening, involving an alignment in spirit, if not in
terms of practical collaboration, with the apparently invincible Germans.
The Nazi victories in Europe in the summer of 1940 left the French and

Netherlands empires in the East more exposed than ever, and further reduced the once-imposing stature of Britain; Tokyo and Berlin were still looking askance at each other, but Ribbentrop was already encouraging the Japanese to expand into Southeast Asia.[7] In September 1940 the direction that developments were taking was made clear when Japan signed a Tripartite Pact with Germany and Italy. In it, Japan 'recognised and respected the leadership of Germany and Italy in the establishment of a new order in Europe'; Hitler and Mussolini in return acknowledged Tokyo's leadership in bringing about 'a new order in Greater East Asia.' Mutual assistance was pledged (though in a secret exchange of letters, Tokyo reserved its own freedom of decision) should one of the signatories find itself attacked 'by a power at present not involved in the European war or in the Sino-Japanese conflict'—a move clearly intended to deter the United States from intervening whilst Japan was creating a new sphere of dominance in what her Foreign Minister, when defining 'Greater East Asia', had described as 'the countries of East Asia and the regions of the South Seas'.[8] According to more detailed and secret Japanese blueprints, the areas marked out for eventual conquest comprised the Philippines, Indochina, Siam, Malaya, Burma, Borneo, the Netherlands East Indies, Australia, New Zealand and possibly also India—although she might come under Germany's sway instead. Singapore, because of its vital strategic situation, would remain under direct Japanese rule, but 'independence' of a kind would be granted to an 'Indonesian Federation', Indochina (centring upon Annamite nationalists) and the Philippines, with autonomy for Burma. Nevertheless, Japan's predominant position would be maintained, as it had been in the case of Manchukuo, with ultimate military and political control of the so-called independent states residing in Tokyo.[9]

Meanwhile in the short run, and in her 'quest for autonomy', Japan needed above all to obtain secure oil supplies. And oil, in General Tojo's words, 'in the end comes down to the matter of the Netherlands East Indies.'[10] From 1940 to June 1941, strong pressure was brought to bear on the Government of the Indies for a privileged economic position to be granted to Japan in those islands, together with massive guaranteed supplies of oil and other vital raw materials such as tin, rubber and bauxite. Despite a lack of unequivocal support from the major Western powers, the Dutch delayed and ultimately refused to meet the main wishes of the Japanese, who then broke off negotiations. Meanwhile, Tokyo was having more to show for its pressure upon the Vichy French Government of Indochina, that springboard to the South. The Japanese obtained military facilities there in August 1940; in the following month they occupied the province of Tonkin; and in the spring of 1941 forcibly mediated in a border dispute between Indochina and Siam. Finally, in July 1941, they seized key points in Southern Indochina.

At the time when this last, and menacing, move took place, Japan and the United States were engaged in a series of diplomatic discussions, which will be referred to in more detail later in this chapter.[11] Nevertheless, at an

Imperial Conference in Tokyo on 6 September 1941 the decision was taken to complete preparations for war with the U.S.A., Britain and the Netherlands. On 5 November, the country's final negotiating positions were adopted, failing the acceptance of which by Washington Japan would resort to force early in December.[12] Complete military victory in the long run could not be anticipated: as a document prepared for the conference of 6 September put it, 'it would be well-nigh impossible to expect the surrender of the United States.' The hope was, rather, that initial Japanese successes, together with the triumphs of Germany in Europe, would condition the American public to accept a compromise peace which would leave Japan with a strategically and economically secure sphere of influence in East Asia and the South. In any event, the alternatives were increasingly seen as being stark and simple: to accept growing United States dictation, backed by her control of raw materials, or to fight. In the words of one member of the conference of 5 November, 'A war against the United States and Britain is inevitable if Japan is to survive.' Berlin, too, was urging Tokyo on throughout 1941—to make a surprise attack on Singapore, to expand southwards generally, and to adopt an unyielding position in the negotiations with Washington. Hitler himself promised in April that if Japan became involved in war with the United States, Germany would come to her assistance.[13]

Tokyo's final negotiating position vis-à-vis Washington was rigid over what were held to be essentials:[14] although the possibility was suggested of a withdrawal of Japanese troops in the foreseeable future from Indochina and central and southern China, a secure supply of raw materials must be obtained; moreover, the 'China incident' must be settled without outside interference and on terms which, for Tokyo, would entail a Japanese military presence in North China, Inner Mongolia and Hainan island for at least twenty-five years. A foretaste of such a settlement was already to be had in the shape of the treaty signed in November 1940 between Japan and Wang Ching-wei's puppet regime in Nanking.[15] More generous terms, however, might have been accorded to Chiang Kai-shek had he agreed to seek an accommodation with the invader, and it obviously paid Chiang, clamouring for financial and material aid, and once more in open conflict with the Chinese Communists,* to allow such a possibility to weigh upon the minds of Western policy-makers. Even without this additional burden, those policy-makers already had much to worry them, especially in London.

For Britain, Far Eastern developments between 1939 and 1941 were inevitably seen within the overriding context of the desperate struggle for survival against Germany. No reading of her policies towards Japan and China in these years can be adequate without constantly bearing in mind the effects of fluctuating circumstances nearer home: the fall of France and the entry of Italy into the war in the summer of 1940, for example, with a consequent severe worsening of the naval balance against Britain and hence an

---

* In January 1941, Nationalist troops fought a major battle with the Communist New Fourth Army. (See, e.g., Snow, *Journey To The Beginning*, 235ff.)

increased vulnerability in the Far East; the threat of invasion which followed; the easing of the situation when Hitler turned against the Soviet Union in the summer of 1941.

Likewise, all estimates of what was at stake for Britain in the Far East were dominated by the requirements of war. Australia and New Zealand headed a list of interests prepared by the Chiefs of Staff in July 1940. The document[16] needed little gloss, but it noted that the gains Japan had already made had cut into the country's commercial interests in China, trade with whom, only two per cent of the country's total, could cease without 'seriously affecting the ability of the Empire to carry on the war.' When it came to Malaya, Burma and the Netherlands East Indies, however, supplies of raw materials like tin and rubber were involved which were essential to the continuation of Britain's struggle;* her 'dependence upon the economic weapon to defeat Germany' also increased the importance of controlling these sources, while the sale of such materials earned desperately needed dollars, with which to buy resources from the United States.[17]†

Although the British public in general became interested in Far Eastern affairs only at times of crisis ('The British called it a "world war" ', writes Calder, 'yet thought of it essentially as a European squabble in which the Japs had irrelevantly intervened'),[18] in official circles there was often considerable alarm over Japan's likely moves. True, in March 1940 the Chiefs of Staff, with the Tientsin episode now behind them, thought that the risk of war had 'considerably receded'[19], while in April 1941 the Cabinet's Defence Committee (Operations) were generally in agreement with the Prime Minister in welcoming 'a slackening of tension in the Far East.'[20] By the following July, however, the inter-departmental Far Eastern Committee were acknowledging that the signs pointed to 'a policy of southward expansion' by Japan,[21] and at the end of September Anthony Eden, as Foreign Secretary, warned the Cabinet of the possible consequences of the embargo now being enforced by the West on supplies of raw materials to Japan: 'The time must come before very long when she must begin to draw upon her war stocks. When Japan reaches the conclusion that that moment is in sight, she must either come to an understanding with the United States and ourselves or break out, at the risk of war with us both, in order to escape economic strangulation.'[22]

This perception of Japan's vulnerability to economic pressure had for some time provided a much-needed source of comfort in London. In August

* In July 1941 the Foreign Office estimated that Britain had seven months stocks of rubber and only two months reserves of tin; meanwhile over ninety per cent of U.S. supplies of these commodities were coming from the area threatened by Japan. (FO 371, file 27860.)

† Investments in Southeast Asia before the Second World War totalled something over £200 million, only three-to-four per cent of long-term overseas investments. A high proportion of this money, however, was direct, entrepreneurial and not rentier investment. Southeast Asian trade, which was declining, amounted to only about five per cent of Britain's total, but obviously the qualitative importance of e.g. tin and rubber was high. See in general S. Rose, *Britain And Southeast Asia* (London, 1962).

1940, for example, the Chiefs of Staff had estimated that, even if Japan held the Netherlands East Indies, a rigorous Anglo-American embargo on raw materials 'might bring about her commercial ruin at the end of twelve months.'[23] In addition, one could choose to believe, as did Churchill himself, that a token gesture of power and resolution by Britain could do much to stabilize the situation: thus, R. A. Butler, in his not-altogether happy role as Parliamentary Under Secretary at the Foreign Office, felt that the moving of a battle-cruiser and an aircraft carrier to Ceylon would stimulate morale in Indochina, Siam, the Netherlands Indies, Burma, Malaya, Australia and New Zealand, and 'also [among] the people of China.'[24] Moreover, as suggested earlier, there existed a widespread tendency to believe that such intrinsically inferior beings as the Japanese—'dwarf slaves', the Permanent Under Secretary at the Foreign Office called them in his diary[25]—would not dare to strike at British and Dutch possessions, especially whilst the U.S. Pacific Fleet was in being.[26] The Joint Planning Staff in London, like the C. in C. Far East, dismissed the capacity of the Japanese for aerial warfare as likely to be no more formidable than that of the Italians,[27] while the Royal Navy estimated the efficiency of the Japanese Navy as being about eighty per cent of its own.[28]

In Singapore, meanwhile, visitors such as senior Australian diplomats found 'a vast complacency' among the leading citizens and, in September 1941, 'a determination [among officials] that the war would not take place.'[29] Two American newspaper correspondents reported to the local American air-force commander that 'the organization at Singapore is confused to the last degree', with Admiral Layton, the C. in C. China, according to them openly making fun of the Commander in Chief, Far East, Air Chief Marshal Sir Robert Brooke-Popham, and calling him 'old Pop-off' on account of his frequent tours. (Layton himself, the correspondents added, 'appears to be a fool.')[30] Likewise the Chancellor of the Duchy of Lancaster, Duff Cooper, who was on a mission from the Cabinet in London and was resented by certain of the locals, who referred to him as 'tough snooper', found the Governor of Singapore, Sir Shenton Thomas, together with some senior aides, inadequate for the situation, and General Percival, the Army Commander, 'a nice, good man' but 'not a leader.'[31]* (When the outbreak of war came, for example, no scheme for the conscription or control of local labour in such an emergency existed in Malaya.) To the Australian Advisory War Council in the middle of October 1941, Brooke-Popham confidently averred that 'for the next three months Japan would not be able to undertake a large-scale attack in the South.'[32] A similar complacency on the part of the

* For *The Times*' correspondent's impressions of the Governor and Percival, see Morrison, I., *Malayan Postscript* (London, 1942), 157-9. In his *Singapore, 1941-1942*, (London, 1977), Louis Allen demonstrates that various officers (including Percival), together with the civilian Secretary of Defence of the Colony, C. A. Vlieland, had urged before 1941 that in order to protect Singapore the entire peninsula would have to be defended. (Allen, appendices II and III.) Levelling criticisms at the official military history, Allen also seeks, not entirely convincingly, to defend the Governor's record in certain respects (198ff. and 212ff.).

Hongkong administration was later reported by men who escaped from Japanese captivity following the fall of the Colony.[33] (It may have been an exaggeration to write, as one officer did, of a Government 'rotten to the core' and of a mentality of 'apathy, inertia and self-complacency.' Unfortunately, the Colonial Office file containing the correspondence of the Governor on defence matters in 1941 is closed for fifty, rather than the usual thirty, years, although the summary in the register reads: 'Sir Mark Young satisfied with defence preparations.')[34]

Officials on the spot could have been forgiven if they had claimed that they were but reflecting the confidence of the Prime Minister himself. Churchill's problems, of course, were infinitely greater than theirs, as he sought to wage a war beyond Britain's capacity to win. In such a situation, as he observed, risks had to be run and scarce resources not frittered away by seeking to guard against all contingencies. Yet it remains the case that he consistently played down the likelihood of a Japanese attack, and resisted professional advice over strengthening the Singapore garrison, for example, as he did over the despatch of the *Prince of Wales* and *Repulse*.[35] Mistakenly continuing to believe that Singapore was 'a fortress', he repeated in November 1939 that the Japanese would not embark upon the 'mad enterprise' of trying to take it.[36] Japan would surely not declare war, he assured the Prime Ministers of Australia and New Zealand in August 1940, 'unless Germany can make a successful invasion of Britain'—a belief that he reiterated to the Defence Committee in April 1941.[37] 'As for a Japanese attack on Singapore', he told the Cabinet in the following July, 'he did not believe that anything of the sort was contemplated', and again to the Australian and New Zealand Prime Ministers in September: 'I cannot believe the Japanese will face the combination now developing around them.'[38] In October it was the same: 'he did not believe that the Japanese would go to war with the United States and ourselves', and he now found a new condition that would need to be satisfied before she might do so: the 'decisive breaking' of the Soviet Union.[39] 'Possible but unlikely dangers' were what he was seeing on 12 November, a time when the Ambassador in Tokyo, Sir Robert Craigie, was warning of a 'serious danger of [Japan] starting a war.'[40]*

In retrospect (and historian and reader alike can be thankful that they will never be called upon to shoulder the burdens carried by Churchill in 1940–41), it can be said that the risks the Prime Minister advocated taking over a possible Japanese attack were justified in the early part of the war, in that no such attack materialized. On the other hand, an adequate defence of Malaya and Singapore could not be created in a matter of days or even months, and Churchill's continuing confidence did not help to impart the sense of urgency and the reforming zeal that were needed in many military and official quarters in Britain's Far Eastern Empire. By 1941, as the official historian has observed, the Prime Minister was 'heart and soul in the war in the Middle

* It should be added that Craigie's own estimate was also at fault, in that he believed that Japan would arrive at such a point only 'through having miscalculated the strength of the United States reaction to a given movement by herself.'

East', where he could strike at the enemy; by comparison, waiting to be struck oneself in the Far East was small beer.[41] Not only did he, in consequence, continue to misperceive the military nature of Singapore, but he overrode his professional advisers in the matter of defence preparations. Again, however, it must be emphasized that he was bearing responsibilities far beyond the capacity of any one man, however gifted, to fulfil in every respect; that he was engaged, in 1940 especially, in saving his country and ultimately the freedom of Western Europe; and that such were Britain's resources compared to her commitments in these years that a successful defence against Japan's initial assault in the Far East were almost certainly beyond her.

The actual military situation, the details of which can be read in official studies,[42] was indeed grim. Apart from the mounting problem of finding a naval force to send out to the Far East without at the same time running unacceptable risks in waters nearer home (and there was, for example, the speed of the Japanese fleet to consider, for it was such as to make it hazardous to despatch ageing Royal Navy units like the four 'R' class battleships),[43] there was also a paucity of first-class air cover. The largest source of additional manpower for the land forces, the Indian Army, would need much time to produce substantial numbers of front-line units in addition to those already engaged in the Middle East. Inadequate coordination between Services in the Far East continued to make things worse than they need have been, and the appointment of an over-all Commander in Chief in October 1940—even then, the Navy was excluded from the arrangement—tended to complicate rather than to streamline affairs. (The C. in C. himself privately deplored the 'lack of interest of Singapore in war problems' and the 'latent hostility between the Central Government, the Services and the civilian community.' For his own part, unfortunately, he tended to fall asleep during meetings that he was chairing, which cannot have improved the general atmosphere.)[44] Hongkong, where Japanese forces were already in control of the neighbouring Chinese mainland, was bound to fall, and this was accepted in London; its defence would be conducted essentially for reasons of prestige. But the belated attempt to reorientate the defences of Singapore, not simply against direct, sea-borne assault, but on the basis of defending the whole of Malaya, was not promising well either, while Burma, whose invasion had long been regarded by the C.O.S. as only a remote possibility, was in the autumn of 1941, as the official historian has put it, 'practically without the means of defending herself.'[45]

Inadequate liaison on the military side was matched by the complex and confused nature of the lines of responsibility which joined the Far Eastern Commonwealth and Empire to London. The separate interests of the Foreign Office, Dominions Office, Colonial Office, India Office and Burma Office had not been coordinated before the war; after September 1939 these departments were joined by others such as the Ministry of Information, Ministry of Economic Warfare and Ministry of War Transport to produce a system involving fragmentation, duplication and at times self-contradiction. (For example, the representative of the M.O.I. in Singapore was busy pouring scorn on the Vichy regime in Saigon at the same time as the Navy's C. in C. China was trying to retain Saigon's sympathy and to promote a reconciliation with the local Free French.) The long-term solution proposed in October 1941 by Duff Cooper was the establishment of a Far Eastern Department of State and a single Far Eastern Service; for the moment, however, he believed that the situation might be improved by the appointment of a 'Commissioner General for the Far East.'[46]

Duff Cooper prefaced his report with a survey of wider considerations that, in his view, were going to demand a drastic revision of British policies and practices:

'The Far East', he wrote, 'seems likely to play a part of increased and increasing importance both in the present war and in the future of the World. This new importance is due principally to two causes . . . . The first is the revolution that has recently taken place in the ease and speed of communications; the second is the change in the mental attitude of the oriental populations . . . We are now faced by vast populations of industrious, intelligent and brave Asiatics who are unwilling to acknowledge the superiority of Europeans or their right to special privileges in Asia . . . . According to all observers the Chinese people are more united as a nation today than they have ever been before, an event which, remembering that they consist of over 440 millions of the hardest working and most intelligent people in Asia, may have far greater consequences than it is possible to foresee. The Dutch East Indies also contains a population half as great again as that of Great Britain, among whom the rumbling of nationalist aspirations begins to be audible . . .'

Cooper was by no means alone in discerning the increasing pressure which, even before the Japanese struck, was bearing down on Imperial territories in the Far East and elsewhere. Deploring the neglect of colonial issues displayed by Parliament, Margery Perham, for example, had written in the *Spectator* in October 1939:

'Suppression is becoming, for the British, an impracticable weapon . . . This is mainly because we have lost faith in it ourselves. We have, especially in recent months, solemnly declared . . . that not only the Commonwealth but also the Colonial empire is based upon respect for freedom and leads, however gradually, towards self-government for the peoples. With whatever qualifications when applied to our heterogeneous possessions, such statements must mean something, and war is an occasion when we may be asked by subject peoples exactly what they do mean.'[47]

'Is this an *Imperialist* war?' demanded Harold Laski in a Labour Party pamphlet, while the Party's National Executive, in a declaration of February 1940 on 'Labour, The War and the Peace', asserted that 'colonial peoples everywhere should move forward as speedily as possible towards self-government. In the administration of Colonies not yet ready for self-government, the interests of the native population should be paramount and should be safeguarded through an extension and strengthening of the Mandate system. There must be equal opportunity of access for all peaceful peoples to raw materials and markets in Colonial territories.'*

Meanwhile, however, whatever people's plans for the future, the situation in the territories facing a possible Japanese advance was not such as to produce a solid resistance to the invader. This is not to dismiss the positive benefits which British rule had brought to, say, Malaya,[48] nor to suggest that there were easy solutions to the immense problems of plural societies like that of the Chinese and Malays in Malaya, or the Burmese, Indians, Chinese, Karens and others in Burma.[49] In addition, there can be little doubt that, had Britain done more during the inter-war years to organize her colonial peoples on a military basis, she would have incurred much odium, both domestically and internationally.

Yet however benevolent British rule might be, it could not prevent a rising feeling of resentment among the colonial peoples of Southeast Asia against what they saw as exploitation. To proud people, paternalism could be 'an intolerable attitude.'[50] The British themselves had helped to bring about the plural societies of the region, and whilst in the Malaya of 1941 this meant the existence of a staunchly anti-Japanese Chinese community, it also helped to ensure that 'to begin with, the bulk of the Malays were . . . not particularly hostile to the Japanese occupation, and many indeed welcomed the change, since it promised to put an end to the economic and political encroachment of the Chinese.'[51] It was also British tin and rubber magnates in Malaya who had held down wages in 1940–41, despite a boom in their industries. Moreover, in only one country in the region, Burma, had a clear move been made by 1941 towards ultimate self-government, with a native administration elected by a franchise of about one-third of the adult male population. Even there, however, the powers reserved to the Governor in such matters as defence, foreign policy and finance were increasingly resented, and in 1940–41 the Burmese Prime Minister, U Saw, was calling strongly for Dominion status. 'What Burma wants to know', he wrote to *The Times* in October 1941, 'is whether in fighting with many other countries for the freedom of the world, she is also fighting for her own freedom . . . The demand for complete self-government is a unanimous demand of the Burmese people, and it was made incessantly long before the Atlantic Charter.'[52]

Reporting on the Burmese scene in 1941, the Agent there of the Government of India wrote back to Sir Gilbert Laithwaite in New Delhi: 'The

* The Labour Party's own Advisory Committee on Imperial Questions was surveying these issues in more detail both before and during the war. Its secretary, Leonard Woolf, believed in September 1941 that 'nearly all the Colonies outside Africa are . . . ripe for full self-government or at any rate for a very large measure of self-government.' Both Woolf and the Committee as a whole, however, were convinced of the need for the continuation of British administration in many areas, on a trusteeship basis. Even for Burma, they recommended that while Dominion status should be granted immediately after the war, defence and foreign affairs matters should continue to be reserved for the Governor. (Leonard Woolf Papers, boxes 35, 40; see Hansard H.C. Deb., 376, col. 513ff.)

Burmese people have I am convinced no loyalty to Britain or the Empire. Their policy for the future is purely opportunist and hostile to Europeans generally . . . My own view is that the Burmans and the Burman Ministry are not to be relied on at all if we are attacked by Japan.'[53] This thesis appeared to be confirmed early in 1942 when U Saw himself was arrested for having been in touch with the Japanese earlier with a view to cooperating with them in Burma; the inherent strength of the Thakin Party and other groups in the Freedom Bloc remained intact,[54] however, despite this arrest, reflecting a disenchantment with British rule which was to result in aid of various kinds—including activities by the Burma Independence Army—being given to the Japanese when they arrived. 'At the time [of the invasion]', wrote a post-war Burmese Premier, 'Burmans had such faith in the Japanese that when the Japanese bombers came they would not take cover in the shelters. Some tore off their shirts and waved a welcome.'[55] 'It is quite significant how the Japanese are employing Burmese to fight', wrote the Governor of Burma to the Viceroy of India in March 1942. 'They are undoubtedly receiving a lot of help. It is an interesting study. Why should the Burmese show greater fighting qualities when led by the Japanese than when led by us? I leave you to work out the answer.'[56]*

These were not the kinds of questions to which the Prime Minister in London was ready to devote much attention. Indeed, he was to cut short abruptly—'Young man, you had better leave'—a weekend visit to Chequers by that same Governor of Burma, Sir Reginald Dorman-Smith, a former Conservative Minister of Agriculture, when the latter had the temerity to raise them and to argue that plans should be drawn up for a transfer of power within the not-too-distant future. (During this visit to Britain, Dorman-Smith, talking to the Prime Minister at 10 Downing Street, was told by him, with reference to the coloured populations of the Empire, that 'what those people need is the sjambok', and that Britain could well do without the Indian Army.)[57] Constitutional issues, Churchill told U Saw, could wait until the war had been won.[58] That maxim applied strongly, in his view, to the major case of India, whatever might be the demands of the Congress Party, backed by a civil disobedience movement, for a declaration of post-war independence and for a greater share in the war-time government of the country.[59] The farthest that London would go was to give a promise in August 1940 that Dominion status for India was Britain's objective and that a representative body to devise her constitution would be set up as soon as possible after the war. This was coupled, however, with assurances to the Muslim League that power would not be transferred to a system of government that was opposed by large sections of the community. For Congress,

* One person who supplied his own answers over the case of Hongkong was a former press secretary to Clark Kerr as Ambassador, the Marxist, James Bertram, who was captured in the fighting for the colony. 'Nobody really cared enough about Hongkong', he wrote later, 'to rally to its defence that last reserve of human spirit that has, at certain moments in history, enabled men to hold out against impossible odds . . . And the one main group that might have defended Hongkong with real passion, the Chinese, was never called upon.' (J. Bertram, *The Shadow of a War* [London, 1947], 120.)

this was unacceptable, and the party's ministries in several provinces resigned.

Nevertheless, some of Churchill's colleagues were inclined to go further. 'I must confess', wrote Ernest Bevin, Minister of Labour, to Leo Amery in September 1941, 'that leaving the settlement of the Indian problem until after the war fills me with alarm . . . It seems to me that the time to take action to establish Dominion status is now . . .'[60] Stafford Cripps, for his part, had close links with Congress leaders. As for Clement Attlee, leader of the Labour Party and Lord Privy Seal, although he was by no means consistently bold over Indian issues (Amery complained privately that in Cabinet he received no support from Attlee when it came to attacking Churchill's ignorant and reactionary stand),[61] he was nevertheless to point out to the Prime Minister in February 1942: 'The fact that we are now accepting Chinese aid in our war against the Axis powers and are necessarily driven to a belated recognition of China as an equal and of Chinese as fellow fighters for civilisation against barbarism, makes the Indian ask why he too cannot be master in his own home.'[62]

Earlier, in August 1941, Attlee had also raised the related issue of how to interpret the Atlantic Charter, signed by Churchill and Roosevelt on the 12th of that month, and article three of which declared their respect for 'the right of all peoples to choose the form of government under which they will live.' The Charter, Attlee told an audience of West African students in London, 'applied to all peoples of the world . . . [and] all the races of mankind.' To a worried Amery, Churchill responded that he was sure that the Lord Privy Seal had not meant 'e.g. that the natives of Nigeria or of East Africa could by a majority vote choose the form of government under which they live . . . It is evident', he added, 'that prior obligations require to be considered and respected and that circumstances alter cases.'[63] To the Viceroy, Amery himself commented on the Charter's 'meaningless platitudes and dangerous ambiguities'; article three, he concluded in remarkable fashion, 'was inserted primarily as reassurance that we are not out to democratise countries that prefer a different form of government . . . and [it] had already given substantial comfort to Salazar in Portugal and to friendly dictators elsewhere.'[64] In September 1941 Amery could take heart all the more when the Prime Minister publicly affirmed that developments within the British Empire were not affected by the Charter, and that he and the President had 'had in mind primarily the restoration of the sovereignty, self-government and national life of the states and nations now under the Nazi yoke.'[65] He was to maintain this line, as we shall see, against subsequent pressure from Roosevelt. Even so, as a Colonial Office official anxiously observed, the Charter had at least by implication publicly committed Britain to develop self-government throughout the Empire.

As for the particular case of India, so important for both the material and ideological conduct of any Far Eastern war on Britain's part, Churchill's reactionary stand dismayed even Amery. 'The real trouble is', the latter wrote in November 1941, 'that in the world of political ideas he has never really advanced beyond the mid-Victorian period . . . He has never really sympathised with the developments of self-government in the Empire, even in the European Dominions, and as regards India has never got beyond the early Kipling stage.'[66] From the first months of the war, Churchill had been warning against embarking upon 'the slippery slope of concessions', and unhesitatingly welcomed 'the Hindu/Moslem feud' as 'a bulwark of British rule in India', which, if ended, would be followed by 'the united communities joining in showing us the door.'[67] In taking this stand, the Prime Minister was encouraged by the Viceroy, Lord Linlithgow, who valued the Muslim League as a counterweight to Congress, and for whom the rule of force, rather than of consent and loyalty, was inherent in the Imperial situation. India and Burma, he declared, had

'no natural association with the Empire, from which they are alien by race, history and religion, and for which as such neither of them have any natural affection, and both are in the Empire because they are conquered countries which had been brought there by force, kept there by our controls, and which hitherto it has suited to remain under our protection. I suspect that the moment they think that we may lose the war or take a bad knock, their leaders would be much more concerned to make terms with the victor at our expense than to fight for the ideals to which so much lip-service is given . . . . What we have to decide, however, is whether in such circumstances, whatever the feeling of India, we intend to stay in this country for our own reasons . . .'[68]

Another pessimist and reactionary was Sir James (P.J.) Grigg, a former Personal Private Secretary of Churchill's at the Exchequer, Finance Member of the Indian Government in the 1930s, now Permanent Under Secretary at the War Office and soon, in February 1942, to be elevated to the post of Secretary of State for War. Grigg, too, believed that Britain could not depend upon Indian loyalty, and felt that even Linlithgow was too accommodating towards Congress. In his eyes, The Atlantic Charter was 'great poppycock.'[69]

Meanwhile, if unresolved questions of Empire hung over Britain's degree of preparedness for a major Far Eastern conflict, so, too, did issues involving relations between Britain and the Dominions.[70] In one way, the Commonwealth between 1939 and 1941 was being drawn closer together on the fields of battle; yet at the same time the war was throwing into sharper relief than before various underlying questions, which in some cases involved the association's very future existence. Smuts, for example, had been able to bring South Africa into the war by only thirteen votes against Hertzog and his supporters, and continued to have to fight on the domestic front thereafter.[71] For Canada, there remained not only those sections of opinion that were cool towards Britain, but also the ever-present need to avoid any suggestion of a Commonwealth line-up against the U.S.A.[72] In both military and political spheres, the war also raised questions concerning consultation and liaison which had not been solved by the time Japan attacked[73]— although where Australia, especially, remained dissatisfied, the Canadian

Prime Minister, happy with a looser form of relationship, felt that it would be 'difficult if not impossible to improve upon existing machinery for Commonwealth consultation.'[74] In the field, too, the Dominions were demanding that Britain should recognize the separate identity of their units. (In the Middle East in 1942, even the commander of troops from that most loyal and cooperative of countries, New Zealand, would be protesting that British senior officers 'are prone to look upon us as just another British division . . . [and] want to stop any candid account from me being sent [to Wellington] after the battle.')[75]

In London, there was an awareness of such problems in some quarters, and vain proposals were made in 1940 for an Imperial conference, and in the summer of 1941 for a conference of Commonwealth Prime Ministers.[76] Various members of the British Government and others had personal ties of their own with Commonwealth friends, ties which were an important part of relations on a non-official basis.[77] Yet there also existed an impatience with and even indifference to the separate anxieties and claims of Dominions: Cadogan at the Foreign Office, for example, privately dismissed the High Commissioners in London as 'undependable busybodies . . . [with not] really enough to do.' 'What irresponsible rubbish these Antipodeans talk', he noted after a meeting with the Australian Prime Minister and High Commissioner early in 1941.[78] As for Churchill, he was glad to exchange private telegrams with Menzies and other Prime Ministers,[79] but only one such relationship carried real weight with him: that with Smuts. On the latter's advice and companionship he was glad to lean, 'rejoicing that we are once again on commando together.'[80] For the rest, his concept of the Commonwealth was one which accorded to Britain and to himself a more paternal position and authority than changing circumstances allowed.

This lack of sensitivity on Churchill's part was keenly felt in Australia, even before the Labour Government of John Curtin, with its strongly isolationist and anti-imperialist background, came into power in October 1941.* That most British-orientated of Australians, Robert Menzies, who was then Prime Minister, told his Advisory War Council on his return from London in May 1941 that 'Mr Churchill has no conception of the British Dominions as separate entities. Furthermore, the more the distance from the heart of the Empire, the less he thinks of it.'[81] General Blamey, the Australian Commander in Chief, was reporting in similar vein as regards his own sphere: 'There was a curious element in the British make-up', he suggested, 'which led them to look upon the Dominions as appendages of Great Britain. They had difficulty in recognising the independent status of the Dominions.'[82] Menzies also judged that Churchill had too many 'yes-men' around him, and that the British Cabinet was not exercising a sufficiently critical or restraining function. Attlee, Bevin and Cranborne were able, he informed his Advisory War Council, but the first-named was not forceful enough and the second was

* The nature of Australian politics did not make a National Government a feasible war-time development. No more was the new emergency likely to remove militant labour unrest, in New South Wales especially. (See *Hasluck*, I, 564, 603ff.)

wholly absorbed in his work at the Ministry of Labour. As for Eden, he was 'a lightweight who had not developed in recent years', while the Foreign Office as a whole merited 'the lowest opinion' for its negative, drifting approach to affairs.

Churchill's handling of military operations in the Middle East and Mediterranean, where Australian troops were involved, was also giving rise to much concern and sometimes offence in Canberra in 1941.[83] In this situation, the desire arose for the creation of a full, Imperial War Cabinet in London; failing that—and there seemed no chance of obtaining Britain's agreement to it—there should be Australian representation on Churchill's own War Cabinet. The most that the Prime Minister would concede, however, was that an Australian Minister could sit with the Cabinet whenever matters affecting that country were under consideration.[84] For this purpose, Sir Earle Page arrived in London at the end of October 1941. After much struggling, he felt by the end of the year that he had found means of inserting Australian views into the complex Whitehall machinery, the problem having been in many ways most difficult to solve at levels below that of the Cabinet.[85] We shall see later, however, that even where Cabinet business was concerned, the arrangement quickly crumbled away in 1942, and was resented by Churchill.

What Paige and successive Australian Governments wished to convey above all was their alarm at the danger from Japan, and the urgent need, as they saw it, to increase defence preparations in Singapore and the Netherlands East Indies.[86]* As regards the other European powers in the area, two secondary aspects of Australia's external relations during the Pacific war were already being foreshadowed during this period of 1939 to 1941: support by Canberra for the Free French cause in New Caledonia and elsewhere;† and a certain tension between Australia and the Netherlands Government

---

* At one point, in May 1941, the leader of the Australian Labour Party and future Prime Minister, Curtin, even suggested in the Advisory War Council that Britain should 'evacuate the Mediterranean by the transfer of the Mediterranean Fleet to the Atlantic [and thus] bottle up the enemy fleet in the Mediterranean [with] . . . better prospects of a British fleet based on Singapore, immediately relieving Australia and the Empire of the danger of Japanese entry into the war.' Under challenge, however, Curtin fumblingly made his somewhat muddled idea dependent on the entry of the U.S.A. into the war. (AAWC, 8 May 1941, A2682, vol. I.)

† While French Oceania, French India, the New Hebrides and New Caledonia went over to de Gaulle in September 1940, there was a strong tendency for colonial officials to continue to obey the Government in power in metropolitan France. Thus in French Indochina, Admiral Decoux maintained an allegiance to Vichy. On this, see P. Devilliers, *Histoire du Viêt-Nam, 1940–1952* (Paris, 1952), 81ff. The Vichy regime itself had visions of building up its overseas empire as some compensation for its restricted position in Europe, while the Gaullists likewise believed 'that the colonies offered an invaluable means of regenerating France and restoring her to a position of greatness among the nations of the world.' On this, see R. O. Paxton, *Vichy France: Old Guard and New Order, 1940–1944* (New York, 1972), 57; D. B. Marshall, *The French Colonial Myth and Constitution-Making in the Fourth Republic* (New Haven, 1973), 76. During the Pacific war, much tension between the French on the one hand and both Britain and the United States on the other was to centre around these visions of the role of overseas France.

over the prospect of an increasing interest on the part of the former in the affairs of the East Indies.[87]

Another, and larger, feature of the Far Eastern scene that concerned Australian leaders was the situation in China and the need to sustain her struggle against Japan, if only for the obvious reason that this would help to keep the latter's hands tied. An Australian Minister to the Chungking Government was appointed in the summer of 1941, to match the one who was already established in Tokyo, while in September Canberra, not for the first time, was urging London that 'every possible assistance should be given to China ... [and] our own action should not be delayed merely on account of any American hesitancy to take action.'[88] Chiang Kai-shek, needless to say, supported by British officials and private citizens in China, was being most pressing in the same sense.[89]

From the standpoint of London before the Pacific war, however, there existed some grounds for looking with a certain coolness in China's direction. The selection of a new Chinese Ambassador to Britain, Wellington Koo, did not help matters, in that the Foreign Office found him 'an unpleasant character', and Eden himself 'did not like or trust him.'[90] A more substantial obstacle to close liaison with Chungking, and one which was to remain throughout the war, was the conviction that 'anything of a confidential nature, if communicated to the Chinese Government, would reach the Japanese shortly afterwards.'[91] In addition, fresh evidence of the confusion, inefficiency and downright corruption that surrounded Chiang Kai-shek's regime* was being supplied at the end of 1941 by Sir Otto Niemeyer of the Treasury, as he vainly attempted, on the spot, to have fundamental reforms adopted which would assist the currency and check the raging inflation from which China was now suffering. In this general context, the Ambassador, Clark Kerr, fiercely criticised in reports to London Dr. H. H. Kung, the Finance Minister, who was married to a sister of Madame Chiang Kai-shek. Kung was, in the opinion of Clark Kerr (and of many others, then and since), 'a cancer in the belly of China. His mischievous hand', continued the Ambassador, 'may be detected everywhere. His varlets are in every post. It is probably fair to say that many of the acutest of China's present financial and economic problems are due to his ignorance, his cocksureness and his preference for his own interests over those of his country.'[92]

With men like Kung established in high places, it was not difficult to discount talk of a new spirit that was pervading China; nor is it surprising to find that some of the long-established British firms with commercial and financial interests in China were still approaching a subject like that of extraterritorial privileges with the belief that Britain, in the words of Messrs. Butterfield and Swire, must seek to 'retain the substance and give away only

---

* It seems quite possible that Chiang Kai-shek, unlike many of those around and related to him, was not personally corrupt in a financial way; it should also be remembered that his position cannot be compared to that of a Hitler in terms of dictatorial power, in that he endlessly had to balance and manoeuvre among rival Kuomintang factions, local warlords, etc.

the shadow.'[93] Further afield, officials in British colonies in Southeast Asia, like some of their colleagues in London, were also looking warily at the activities of the Kuomintang among expatriate Chinese communities. A Foreign Office official, for example, warned in September 1941: 'We must not let our present policy of helping China blind us to the fact that our Far Eastern possessions are quite as much menaced by Chinese disruption from within as by Japanese aggression from without.'[94] There also existed in the Foreign Office a weary awareness that, especially after Britain's temporary closing of the Burma Road at Japan's bidding in 1940,* the Chinese were making her a target for their resentment at not receiving greater assistance from the West.[95]

Yet even though the attention of the great majority of British officials and their public was obviously focussed on events nearer home, there continued to be concern in the country for China's plight, as there had been at earlier stages of Japanese aggression in the 1930s.[96] Gilbert Murray, H. G. Wells, Harold Laski and J. B. Priestley were among those who wrote publicly in support of her cause.[97] Moreover, within the Foreign Office it was admitted that China's resentment against Britain was not without justification. 'We can hardly blame the Chinese', wrote Sir John Brenan, formerly Consul-General in Shanghai, 'for believing that the British and Americans are content so long as Japan continues to attack China and does not move southwards or northwards.' 'No indeed', added the Head of the Far Eastern Department.[98] 'Our attitude towards Japan has been so consistently cautious', observed Brenan in April 1941, 'that the Chinese are not un-justified in suspecting that we are deliberately keeping the way open for a deal with Japan at China's expense . . . Concrete evidence [of our support for China] has been forcibly limited, while our various concessions to the Japanese have had a cumulative effect in Chungking.'[99]

The value to Britain of continued Chinese opposition to Japan was obvious enough—doubly so at a time when the Soviet–Japanese pact might encourage Tokyo to move southwards. 'The collapse of Chiang Kai-shek's resistance', wrote Brenan, 'will be a very serious blow to our world position.' In September 1939, indeed, the Chiefs of Staff had described the situation in a still more stark and self-interested fashion: 'From the strictly military point of view', they had observed, 'the prolongation of the Sino-Japanese conflict was to the advantage of this country.'[100] 'It is more important than ever that the Chinese should be kept going', wrote Halifax as Foreign Secretary in the autumn of 1940, when arguing for the reopening of the Burma Road.[101] Churchill himself put the matter in terms closer to those of the Chiefs of Staff: 'Don't you think', he asked Halifax in July 1940, 'that we might go slow on all this general and equitable, fair and honourable peace business between China and Japan? . . . I am sure that it is not in our interest that the Japanese should be relieved of their preoccupation.'[102]

* Interestingly, however, Chiang Kai-shek later told Owen Lattimore that he understood why Churchill had had to close the Road, and that he still knew him to be 'a fighter', and in that sense trusted him. (Interview with Professor Lattimore.)

Indeed, in some quarters of Whitehall during the early stages of the European war, faint hopes of arriving at 'a comprehensive agreement with Japan' with regard to the position in China and the Far East as a whole had lingered on.[103] The same notion was to be found in Canberra ('Japan was still susceptible to a face-saving arrangement', argued Curtin in August 1941, 'and Government should talk to Government in a frank manner to ascertain if a solution was possible'), despite the need to safeguard the White Australia policy.[104] Nevertheless, the belief was stronger and more lasting that Japan would continue to constitute a major threat to the British position in that part of the world. 'Japan's ultimate aims', as the Chiefs of Staff saw them in July 1940, 'are the exclusion of Western influence from the Far East and the control of Far Eastern resources of raw materials. Japan cannot be sure of securing these aims unless she captures Singapore . . . Japan's immediate aim, in accordance with her traditional step-by-step policy, is likely to be the exclusion of British influence from China and Hong Kong . . .'[105]

Churchill too, for all his belief that Japan would not join in the existing conflict, looked ahead to an eventual confrontation. 'At the end of the war', he informed his Cabinet colleagues in October 1940, 'we should be faced with the formidable task of clearing up the situation in the Far East, and we should be unequal to the task if we fall behind in capital-ship construction . . . The potentialities of capital ships for altering a military situation were very great indeed.'[106] Moreover, he added in the following month, one could hope to obtain the help of others who were menaced by Japan, in which context 'the advantage of China's friendship to us after the war might be very great indeed.'[107] The Prime Minister was thus not devoid of sincerity when, in a fulsome exchange of salutes with Chiang Kai-shek in May 1940, he proclaimed that 'in our different spheres our two countries are both fighting in the ranks of freedom against tyranny and aggression. Your cause, too, is that of democracy. Have no doubt, therefore, that we shall do all we can to help China to maintain her independence.'[108] The same sentiment had been expressed during Cabinet discussions in September 1939: 'General Chiang Kai-shek represented a new spirit in the Chinese nation . . . [and] it might well be that, given time, he might defeat the Japanese. Further, his struggle was in effect the same as ours.'[109]

Estimates drawn up by British officials in both Chungking and London continued to point in this cautiously hopeful direction, even though accompanied by warnings that things could easily go wrong. There was no intrinsic reason, it was believed, why Chinese resistance should not continue, provided that morale could be sustained. In this sphere of morale, Britain and the United States had an important role to play, and in Foreign Office eyes it was important that the latter should not be left to sustain it alone. Above all else, the vital factor was seen as being the position of Chiang Kai-shek. 'The chiefest of our concerns', wrote Clark Kerr in his final review on leaving the Chungking Embassy, 'should be to hold the confidence of the Generalissimo, for in him we have a tower of strength, and with his confidence we have that of the mass of the Chinese people. It is remarkable, in these days when dictators are execrated, that a man who is so completely a dictator should command the unquestioning faith and affection of the millions he rules.'[110]

The Ambassador was prepared to acknowledge in 1941 that 'the differences between the Central Government and the Communists have certainly not been settled', and that it was 'impossible to foretell what developments may occur.'[111] His own approach, however, resting as it did on a major misreading of the nature of the Yenan regime, tended to play down the problem. Mao Tse-tung and his colleagues, he averred in 1941, 'were not Communists but agrarian reformers', and he expressed 'some admiration for [them]' to the Australian Minister.[112] To the Foreign Secretary, he deplored the increasing intransigence that was being displayed in this connection by Chiang Kai-shek—a result, he thought, of the influence exerted by Tai Li, head of the Chinese secret police, who had 'an inordinate fear of the mild radicalism that in China is called Communism.' (In a separate paper, Clark Kerr nevertheless recalled that 'although I disapproved of nearly everything Tai Li did . . . [as] the Himmler of China . . . he was one of my warmest friends.')[113]

Clark Kerr had impressed even the most anti-imperialist of Americans in China with his concern for the well-being of that country. He took a considerable interest, for example, in the Industrial Cooperatives movement being developed by the New Zealander, Rewi Alley, and he counted Madame Sun Yat-sen among others as a special friend. Stafford Cripps, who visited the country during the early stages of the European war, was another who, while dismissing the Communist issue, wrote and spoke enthusiastically of the new China, and was anxious to see her receive more help from Britain.[114] (He and his wife were to play a major part in that cause in the years ahead.) Even within the cooler atmosphere of the Foreign Office, it was accepted that Britain should be prepared to surrender her extraterritorial rights and concessions in China without seeking a substantial quid pro quo. London's readiness to negotiate over this 'when peace is restored in the Far East' was formally conveyed to the Chinese Foreign Minister in July 1941.[115]

The outcome of these various considerations was what one Foreign Office official described as a 'fumbling' Far Eastern policy on Britain's part before Pearl Harbour. 'The overriding consideration', as the Chiefs of Staff put it, was the need to avoid war with Japan.[116] For this reason, Churchill accepted the argument of the C.O.S. that 'we are not in a position to stand fast on all Japanese demands', when he agreed in July 1940 that the Burma Road, which carried war materials to China, must be closed as Tokyo insisted, though only for three months. (The Prime Minister 'thought that the responsibility for the decision should be placed where it ought to be, namely, with the United States'; Cadogan's private and realistic comment was that 'it's hopeless to try to put the U.S. on the spot. They simply won't stand there.') Halifax and the Foreign Office, on the other hand, with the support of Amery but not of the Labour Party members of the Cabinet, urged that the closure would be 'a material and moral blow' to Chiang Kai-shek, might open the way to increased Soviet influence in China, and would certainly diminish Britain in American eyes. Halifax in particular appeared anxious to avoid any suggestion of another Munich: 'He believed that there was a big element of bluff in [the Japanese] attitude . . . and that in the long run we should lose less by standing up to Japanese blackmail than by relinquishing our principles.'[117] This approach—which helped to ensure that the Burma Road was reopened in the autumn of 1940—was continued by Eden as Halifax's successor. 'I suggest', he put it to the Cabinet in September 1941, 'that a display of firmness is more likely to deter Japan from war than to provoke her to it.'[118]

In similar vein, and with Australian support, the idea was developed in London during the late summer of 1941 of giving Japan a blunt warning against any further encroachments to the south—although, as will be seen below, a parallel warning by the United States was regarded as being an essential prerequisite.[119] Meanwhile, in the autumn of 1940, an inter-departmental Far Eastern Committee was established 'to concert measures of precaution or pressure against Japan; to facilitate resistance to her, and to diminish her war potential, while bearing in mind the great importance of avoiding action likely to provoke Japan into aggression against our own possessions in the Far East or the Netherlands East Indies.'[120] A system of licensing control was soon established throughout the Empire, enabling 'the screw . . . to be applied more or less firmly in proportion as the Japanese control their wayward tendencies, or as our hand grows stronger in Europe and the Middle East, or as the United States Administration interests itself more in the Far East.' By February 1941, the Committee's Chairman, R. A. Butler, was talking of the need to 'bring strong pressure to bear on the Americans' to cooperate in turning the screw hard.[121]

More positively, although again within the limitations set by the strained position regarding Britain's resources and, above all, by the desire not to precipitate war with Japan, some further help was given to China during this period. Financial assistance was announced in December 1940, £5 million going to China's stabilization fund, with £5 million—a grant repeated in June 1941—for export credits. (Arthur Young, an American financial adviser to the Chinese Government, wrote to his wife on the eve of Pearl Harbour that, as regards the country's monetary problems, 'I have to say that on the whole the British have held up their end best.')[122] Expenditure on the Burmese section of a Burma–China railway was also approved.[123] More reluctantly—and both London and Washington were tying to cover themselves against the possibility of a hostile Japanese reaction—it was agreed that 100 American-made Tomahawk planes, originally earmarked for Britain, should go to China instead, while an American company was allowed to assemble planes for China in Burma and India, following the bombing of its factories in Yunnan. Chinese pilots were also permitted to practise in Burma, where the Governor, Dorman-Smith, got his Prime Minister, U Saw, to agree that planes en route for Colonel Chennault's American Volunteer Group in China could be armed before departure. Collaboration over intelligence matters was also established between Chennault's unit and the R.A.F., the former writing at the time to thank the British A.O.C. Far East for his 'unfailing cooperation' and recalling later that 'the British authorities were extraordinarily helpful and stretched their policy to its limits to provide the A.V.G. with what it needed.'[124]

All this, it is true, was little enough help for a country in its fourth year of war with Japan, and nothing of substance was added either by Whitehall's instructions that an attempt should be made to improve local relations with the Chinese in Malaya, or by Eden's statement in the Commons in May 1941 that China's struggle had a 'natural appeal' for Britain, who, like her, was resisting foreign domination.[125] Militarily, too, it was a case of 'jam tomorrow' rather than today, with Major General Dennys, as Military Attaché in Chungking, preparing a scheme whereby British teams would train and lead Chinese guerilla parties in operations behind the Japanese lines in China. (5 cadre battalions, each of 150 men, were established in readiness for this '204 Mission' before Pearl Harbour; in the event, however, only 3 cadres, each of 50 men, went into China in January 1942.)[126]

Nevertheless, the desire to help was there, and by the autumn of 1941, faced with increasing appeals from Chungking, Churchill was changing his position on the question of allowing volunteer Commonwealth air crews to go to fight in China, a move which he had ruled out during the summer. At the beginning of November the Generalissimo warned Churchill of the likelihood of a Japanese attack in Yunnan, aimed at cutting the Burma Road; in turn the Prime Minister urged Roosevelt to increase China's air-power, and declared his willingness to send British planes and pilots as well. Despite the President's 'somewhat negative' response, moreover, Churchill pushed ahead on his own, and by the time Pearl Harbour came a scheme was in hand for the despatch of one Blenheim and one Buffalo squadron to join Chennault, manned by volunteer Commonwealth crews (Australia and New Zealand had given their consent).[127] It was also in keeping with this sense of urgency when Churchill in November 1941 stressed in Cabinet his belief that the United States 'would not abandon the cause of China'; moreover, it was the Prime Minister's forceful reminder to Roosevelt on 25 November that helped to ensure the demise of Cordell Hull's tentative idea for a stand-still agreement with Japan, a *modus vivendi* which might hold the situation in the Far East for another three months.[128] 'Of course, it is up to you to handle this business', cabled Churchill, 'and we certainly do not want an additional war. There is only one point that disquiets us. What about Chiang Kai-shek? Is he not having a very thin diet? Our anxiety is about China. If they collapse our joint dangers would enormously increase . . .'[129]* It was to be one of the ironies of the Pacific war that American involvement, by swamping Britain's own efforts in China and by reducing her need to voice her concern over the fortunes of that country, would facilitate the American belief that Britain had never cared for the cause of China in the first place.

* In addition, Chiang's own strong cable of protest against a *modus vivendi* was later claimed by Clark Kerr to have been drafted by him. (Eggleston Papers, 423/9/1642.)

If London's response to Britain's future Asiatic ally was a limited one in 1940–41, this was also the case where a fellow white imperial power was concerned. The Foreign Office and Eden repeatedly argued that one could not and should not decline to align oneself with the Netherlands in the Far East, where the fate of the East Indies was crucial, when one was already in partnership with the Dutch in a European context. Churchill himself at first believed 'that an attack on the Netherlands East Indies by Japan is an even greater menace to our safety and interests than an attack on Hong Kong, when it is admitted that we should have to fight.'[130] The First Sea Lord, however, had from the outset been adamant that no automatic commitment concerning the East Indies could be entered into,[131] and the Prime Minister, in the light of the slender resources at his disposal, came to agree. 'Even if Japan encroached on the Dutch East Indies', he observed in July 1941, 'it might well be . . . that the right policy would be that we should not make an immediate declaration of war on Japan.' In November he was maintaining the same veto on any pledge to the Dutch, saying that 'we should not run the risk of finding ourselves at war with Japan without American support.'[132] Likewise, there could be no British guarantee for Siam, even though the defence of Malaya might be greatly affected by a Japanese invasion of that country. As the Vice Chief of Naval Staff put it to the Cabinet's Defence Committee in August 1941, 'since the outbreak of war we had readjusted our ideas as to what was vital to us; the Isthmus of Kra was not.'[133] There could thus be no bolstering of the Anglo-Siamese Non-Aggression Treaty of June 1940, and no substantial encouragement for those liberal elements in Siamese politics who, in the words of the British Minister in Bangkok, were 'in sympathy with the democracies in their struggle against the authoritarian powers, including Japan', but who were for the present overshadowed by the military dictatorship of Luang Pibul.[134]

Wherever one looked, in other words, Britain's Far Eastern position in 1940–41 was one that she could not sustain on her own. Indirect assistance from the Soviet Union was not only an unlikely but an unwelcome prospect, even though the possibility of a Japanese attack upon the U.S.S.R. was also viewed with alarm.[135] Everything thus depended upon Washington. As the Chiefs of Staff put it in May 1940, when envisaging an Italian entry into the European war, 'we must rely on the United States of America to safeguard our interests in the Far East.' A month later, as France plunged towards defeat, they repeated that 'it will be vital that the United States should publicly declare her intention to regard any alteration of the status quo in the Far East as a casus belli.'[136] In Australia, also, the same conclusion was being reached, and means were anxiously sought to increase the ties which would link Americans to their fellow-whites—American blacks were for the present disregarded as an unfortunate complication—in the Southwest Pacific: local bases for the U.S.A., perhaps, or at least an aroused concern on her part.[137] In the summer of 1940, indeed, the fostering of an American belief in 'common interest and close ideological ties with the peoples of Australasia' was regarded by the Australian Department of Information as being 'an Australian defence measure of the first importance.' 'I want to get [Americans] used to seeing the name "Australia" in their papers', wrote Richard Casey, the Australian Minister in Washington, 'to foster the picture of a young and virile nation composed of people like themselves, developing a land the size of their own, and at the same time defending their freedom and independence against the forces of aggression.' Menzies, as Prime Minister, also emphasized the need to attract more American capital to Australia, and to look farther ahead still, in a direction that was to lead eventually, through MacArthur's arrival as the saviour of Australia in 1942, to the ANZUS Pact of 1951. 'In the long run', he told his Advisory War Council in November 1940, 'the United Kingdom might be defeated in the war, and a regrouping of the English-speaking peoples might arise.'[138]

Meanwhile, what both London and Canberra wanted to hear was an unequivocal American declaration warning Japan to respect the status quo or risk war. The possibility of joint or parallel declarations in some such sense was raised with Washington on several occasions, and was pressed upon Roosevelt by Churchill in person at their meeting in Placentia Bay in August 1941.[139] Whilst awaiting such a happy eventuality, nothing must be done that would discourage the idea of American leadership against Japan—a position which would be all too thoroughly assumed by Washington during the war itself. 'It was most important', Churchill stressed at the end of 1940, 'that the attitude to be adopted by our delegation [to the Anglo–American staff talks] in the discussions on naval strategy should be one of deference to the views of the United States in all matters concerning the Pacific theatre of war . . . Our delegation should open the discussion by saying that they recognized that the United States Navy would be in charge in the Pacific, and that American views on strategy in that theatre must prevail.'[140] Likewise, London acquiesced when the crucial American–Japanese diplomatic talks in 1941 were conducted with little regard for Britain—conducted so independently, indeed, that Halifax in October 1941 sourly rejected a Foreign Office proposal to send a Far Eastern expert to his Embassy in order to work full-time on such matters, on the grounds that it would only 'encourage the State Department to pursue their already existing tendency to feel that all Far Eastern policy, British as well as American, should be laid down by Washington.'[141]

Time and again, in the agitated search for some way forward in the Far East, Cabinet discussions in London came round to the importance of not antagonizing the United States over that part of the world, and of encouraging every initiative she might take against Japan. 'I cannot conceal from my colleagues', wrote Eden in a Cabinet memorandum of July 1941, 'the dangers inherent in our lagging behind the United States Government in dealing with Japan, *a fortiori* in our actually attempting to dissuade them from firm action. The risk of another Simon-Stimson incident and of seriously weakening the ties between us and America is real.' Halifax had argued for increased aid to China on similar grounds,[142] while the Far Eastern Committee pointed out that it would be 'economically futile and politically dangerous' to adopt economic measures against Japan without United States cooperation. In return, the Committee were told by the Cabinet in July 1941 that 'we must not on any account discourage any action which the United States may wish to take in [putting] pressure on Japan and we must as far as possible match our actions to theirs'—though it was recognized at the same time that Britain should not seem to 'force the issue' and in that way, too, risk antagonizing the American public.[143] 'Keep in step' was the dominant thought during that vital month of July 1941 when Japan moved south into Indochina and American sanctions were increased as a result.[144] In a broadcast in the following month, Churchill also made public Britain's involvement alongside the United States in seeking to check Japan, while in a speech in November he pledged that Britain would declare war 'within the hour' should Japan attack the U.S.A. Privately, Washington was told: 'We are prepared to support any action, however serious, which the United States may decide to take.'[145]

Thus, if there existed any faint hopes of an American–Japanese understanding being reached in the final period before Pearl Harbour, they received little encouragement from London. The reason for this, of course, lay as much in Europe as in Britain's exposed position in the Far East. What was desired above all was an American entry into the war—the current, German war—and if a show-down with Japan would provide that supreme blessing in addition to its direct, Asian benefits, then so much the better. 'I suppose', wrote an Assistant Under Secretary at the Foreign Office in August 1941, 'that the chief objective at the present moment in our foreign policy is to get America fully into the war.'[146] The Prime Minister's own anxiety to see such an outcome had long been evident; together with his colleagues, he entirely rejected the idea, occasionally to be heard, that the United States could be of more help to Britain if she remained a non-combatant. How to influence American opinion in the direction of participation in the war, without thereby provoking an anti-British reaction, was a major concern of the Cabinet and Defence Committee during the summer of 1941.[147] Roosevelt's attitude at his August meeting with Churchill was encouraging: 'He was obviously determined that they should come in', reported the latter, ' . . . [But] if he were to put the issue of peace and war to Congress, they would debate it for three months. The President had said that he would wage war but not declare it, and that he would become more and more provocative. If the Germans did not like it, they could attack American forces . . . Everything was to be done to force an "incident".'

Yet American opinion was felt in London at the end of August to be still 'rather static, and failing some new development, the position in regard to supplies to this country might not develop favourably.' Churchill warned the President's confidant, Harry Hopkins, of 'a wave of depression through the Cabinet and other informed circles here about the President's many assurances about no commitments, no closer to war, etc . . . If 1942 opens', he continued, 'with Russia knocked out and Britain left again alone, all kinds of dangers may arise.' At least it seemed, however, as Attlee comfortingly reported on his return from a visit to the United States in November, that 'the feeling [there] against Japan is very strong and intervention in the Far East would meet with little opposition.'

There appeared to be every reason, therefore, to let Washington take the lead in tangling with Tokyo. 'The Far Eastern situation had undoubtedly changed', observed Churchill to the Cabinet on 16 October 1941, 'and the United States Government was nearer to a commitment than they had been in the past. We ought to regard the United States as having taken charge in the Far East. It was for them to take the lead in this area, and we would support them.'[148] This involved, in effect, as Halifax observed in his diary on 26 November, handing over Britain's Far Eastern diplomacy (within which the Ambassador saw a greater inclination to take a stiff line with Japan than existed in Washington) to the United States.[149] It meant, as already noted, accepting an inadequate amount of information from the Americans regarding the talks between Hull and the Japanese negotiator, Nomura. In this last context, Churchill did appreciate the need to win time, writing to Eden on 23 November, in connection with a question received from the American Secretary of State:

'My own feeling is that we might give Hull the latitude he asks. Our major interest is: no encroachment and no war, as we have already enough of the latter . . . We ought not to agree to any veto on America or British help to China . . . [But] I must say that I should feel pleased if I read that an American–Japanese agreement had been made by which we were to be no worse off three months hence in the Far East than we are now.'[150]

Nevertheless, the Prime Minister also warned Roosevelt that, in the Washington talks, the Japanese would, of course, 'double-cross him and would try to attack China or cut Burma communications.'[151]

Britain's potential degree of influence over Japanese–American relations at this crucial juncture was thus severely limited by her own desire to be seen as following an American lead. One senior diplomat who greatly regretted this state of affairs, and who believed that the chance to exercise a moderating influence on trans-Pacific exchanges had thereby been thrown away, was Sir Robert Craigie, the Ambassador in Tokyo. After his eventual repatriation to Britain, he was to write an explosive account[152] of the final pre-war period, in which he strongly condemned the rigidity and insensitivity of the American handling of the situation. Japan's final compromise proposal of November 1941 could, he declared, have opened up the possibility of a modus vivendi, as might Hull's initial and unused draft response. 'I consider', wrote Craigie, 'that had it been possible to reach a compromise with Japan in December 1941 involving the withdrawal of Japanese troops from South Indo-China, war with Japan would not have been inevitable.' As it was, the United States' final proposal in the negotiations had not had the slightest chance of acceptance, and must have been based on either a total misreading of the situation in Japan, or a readiness for war.

Craigie's 'Final Report', in which these opinions were expressed and which chimed in many respects with the views of his American colleague in Tokyo, Joseph Grew,[153] was held up for a long time by an embarrassed Foreign Office; eventually it was expurgated by him at the request of Cadogan, who found it 'a pretty sweeping indictment of U.S. policy.' Even so, in its final version, dated February 1943, the Report was accompanied by a Far Eastern Department memorandum which gave a very different interpretation of events, laying the blame for war firmly at the door of Japan. Officials who had been in Washington and London at the time did agree that Hull had been prickly over British advice, that he had given Halifax only 'a general idea from time to time' of his talks with Nomura, and that only belatedly had Britain been informed of the final and obviously unacceptable proposal that was put to Japan on 26 November (a copy of the document itself was not formally given to Halifax until 2 December). Some officials also accepted that, in presenting Japan with such an unacceptable offer, 'the President and Mr Hull were . . . fully conscious of what they were doing.' Nevertheless, the crucial objections to any *modus vivendi* were held by the Foreign Office to have been those of China, Hull's subsequent blaming of Britain over this being put down to his bad temper and his need to find a scapegoat.

In any event, and despite the extent to which it is possible to argue that Washington pushed Tokyo into a corner, Japan's momentum towards war was by then almost certainly too great to be checked. One can add that, even if Britain had been invited by Washington to play a part in the talks, the general stance of the Foreign Office and of Churchill at the time makes it unlikely that a softening of the Western approach would have resulted.[154]

On the Prime Minister's orders, the few copies of Craigie's Report which had been circulated among Ministers and officials in 1943 were hastily recalled. Churchill's own comment on the paper might have been expected:

'It is a very strange document', he wrote in September 1943, 'and one which should be kept most scrupulously secret. A more one-sided and pro-Japanese account of what occurred I have hardly ever read. The total lack of all sense of proportion as between British and American slips on the one hand and the deliberate scheme of war eventuating in the outrage of Pearl Harbour on the other shows a detachment from events and from his country's fortunes. He also writes of the breach with Japan as if it were an unmitigated disaster . . . It was [in fact] a blessing that Japan attacked the United States and thus brought America wholeheartedly into the war. Greater good fortune has rarely happened to the British Empire than this event which has revealed our friends and foes in their true light and may lead, through the merciless crushing of Japan, to a new relationship of immense benefit to the English-speaking countries and to the whole world.'

However great the blessing for Britain that arrived on 7 December 1941— and Churchill was obviously correct in so describing it, just as he was in his immediate thought: 'So we had won after all!'[155]*—it seemed a long time in

* William Hayter, a First Secretary in the British Embassy in Washington, telephoned

coming to those responsible for the Empire's overstretched defences. In the summer of 1940, for example, no useful response had been obtained from Washington when, faced with Japan's demand that she must close the Burma Road, Britain had suggested either a joint and strong Anglo-American response or a combined search for a comprehensive settlement in the Far East. Nor had help been forthcoming in September 1940 over Japan's designs on northern Indochina.[156] From time to time, indeed, there was exasperation in London over the sactimonious attitude of Hull and others as the United States urged upon Britain a 'correct' policy, without at the same time pledging any support.[157] And although, after a moment's hesitation over the drastic nature of the move, it was decided that Britain should follow the United States when in 1941 the latter applied such sanctions as the freezing of Japanese assets and an embargo on vital raw materials, the Far Eastern Committee found it difficult to obtain from Washington a clear statement of American policy and its implementation.[158] As Halifax observed and as the Pacific war itself was to bring out more fully, there was a tendency on the part of the U.S. Administration to accord a low priority to obtaining coordinated Western action in the Far East. As an Assistant Secretary of State in Washington, Dean Acheson was himself in September 1941 regretting this feature of American policy towards Japan: British and Dutch restrictions against that country, he wrote, 'are in advance of ours in many respects. Our own policy . . . is obscure and not fully developed . . . Unless we give the British and Dutch a clear statement of our policy, and take immediate and decisive action on the questions now before us, the whole program of concerted action against Japan will be seriously imperilled.'[159]

Above all, no American commitment to declare war on Japan if she moved southwards was forthcoming until the very last days of peace in the Far East. Sometimes there were hints that all would be well.[160] At their meeting in Placentia Bay in August 1941, the President himself agreed to Churchill's proposal for parallel private warnings to Japan that further advances on her part would call forth countermeasures, even at the risk of war. 'I am confident', the Prime Minister told the Cabinet, 'that the President will not tone it down.' But tone it down he did, at the instigation of Hull, both the word 'war' and references to Britain being omitted from the eventual American communication.[161] For the rest, it remained the case, as Halifax had observed in June 1940, that 'they would certainly give no answer to the flat question of whether they would be prepared to go to war.'[162]

Churchill, it is true, did frequently voice the belief that one could count on the United States coming in if Japan attacked European possessions. (In a directive to the Service Departments in April 1941, for example, in which he

the Foreign Office with the stunning news of Pearl Harbour, requesting that it be passed immediately to the Prime Minister. ' "What was that place?" asked the Resident Clerk in London. "Would you spell it?" He did not seem at all sure,' recalls Hayter, 'that the Prime Minister would be interested.' (W. Hayter, *A Double Life* (London, 1974), 67.)

minimized the likelihood of a Japanese attack, he held it to be 'almost certain that the entry of Japan into the war would be followed by the immediate entry of the United States on our side.')[163] Washington was also, with a delay of some days, sending London its 'Magic' decodings of Japanese communications, while Churchill learned in secret on 27 November, from Roosevelt and via the British intelligence service in the U.S.A., that American–Japanese negotiations had been broken off and that the United States Services 'expect action within two weeks.'[164] Yet as late as 1 December 1941, the Prime Minister felt bound to inform the Cabinet, Chiefs of Staff and senior Australian officials that 'he did not share the view of the Australian Government that the outbreak of Anglo-Japanese hostilities would precipitate the American entry into the war.'[165]

On that same day, 1 December, however, Roosevelt, talking to Halifax and Hopkins, made the vital commitment. It was done in typically casual fashion, when he 'threw in an aside', as Halifax reported it, 'that in the case of direct attack on ourselves or the Dutch, we should obviously all be together.' For the Prime Minister and the Cabinet this was the decisive moment, and two days later Roosevelt confirmed that armed support would be forthcoming if Britain clashed with Japan over a move by the latter into Siam. At last London could now prepare in its turn a guarantee of support for the Dutch as regards the Netherlands East Indies; Siam, too, could be assured of British help and a more forward policy could be adopted over the Kra Isthmus.[166]

Even before this final moment of reassurance, Britain had obtained one other very important, if unofficial, understanding in the field of grand strategy. This was distinct from specific military moves to be undertaken in the face of Japan's advance, for which an agreed and coordinated basis had for the most part not been found. (For example, a complicated scheme favoured by Stimson, whereby ships of the American Pacific Fleet would shift to the Atlantic, thereby enabling Royal Navy units to move to the Far East, fizzled out, although initially welcomed by Churchill.[167] The U.S. Navy also declined an invitation to send major units to Singapore, partly due to the inadequate facilities of the base there, partly for political reasons.[168] In addition, staff talks held between British, American and Dutch officers in Singapore in the spring of 1941, aimed at drawing up a plan for local defence, failed to produce an agreement that could be endorsed by the U.S. Joint Chiefs of Staff. The J.C.S. looked more coolly than did London at the need to defend Singapore and the Malay barrier; urged on by MacArthur and encouraged by the potential of the B17 bomber, they were now thinking, rather, of the possibility of making the Philippines defensible, and of getting more aid to China.)[169] Nevertheless, secret Anglo-American staff talks held in Washington between January and March 1941[170] did lead to the plan known as ABC-1: in this it was recognized that, should the two powers become involved in a war that spanned both Europe and the Far East, their principal effort should be made in the former sphere. This decision, fundamental to Allied strategy after December 1941, was to be the cause of much resentment in China, Australia, and among those American circles which wished above all to avenge Pearl Harbour. It is important to emphasize again, therefore, that this ABC-1 agreement, although not formally endorsed by either Roosevelt or the British Government, was not thrust upon an unwilling United States by a machiavellian Britain, but was entirely in line with the contingency strategic outlines known as the Rainbow 5 plan and 'Plan Dog' which had already been drawn up in Washington. As the American official naval historian puts it, 'naturally the decision pleased the British, but the Americans initiated it.'*

In other words, despite American rhetoric about the cause of China, the defence of Britain appeared to her planners to be far more important in 1940–41. ('It is desirable that large Japanese forces be kept involved in China', declared a U.S. War Department memorandum of November 1941. 'However, from the larger viewpoint, prospective Chinese defeat would not warrant involvement of the United States, at this time, in war with Japan.')[171] This did not mean, however, that the interests of the two Western powers were now seen in Washington, as they tended to be viewed by Churchill, as being one and the same. Already, in fact, there existed a wariness on the American side concerning what was thought to be an inbred British skill at manoeuvring and self-seeking. Thus, for example, Presidentially-approved instructions to the American representatives at the 1941 Washington staff talks stated: 'It is believed that we cannot afford, nor do we need, to entrust our national future to British direction . . . It is to be expected that proposals of the British representatives will have been drawn up with chief regard for the British Commonwealth. Never absent from British minds are their postwar interests, commercial or military. We should likewise safeguard our own eventual interests.'[172] In a similar spirit, William Bullitt, diplomat and intriguer, was soon warning Roosevelt not to let Churchill entangle him in treaties any more specific than the Atlantic Charter, while the President himself was agreeing with the financier and éminence grise, Bernard Baruch, on the need to beware of the wiles of Lord Keynes. For similar reasons, Stimson wanted to keep Roosevelt away from Churchill during the negotiations with Japan.[173]

Thus, with some sidelong glances at each other, the future partners moved towards war in the Far East.

'The key to our entire future is the survival of Great Britain.'[174] So wrote a leading member of the Committee to Defend America by Aiding the Allies in the autumn of 1940; aid to China, therefore, however important, must be seen within that context. The Tripartite Pact, by linking Japan to public enemy number one, Germany, had probably done more than anything else to rouse Americans on China's behalf, but it was the war in Europe which, from 1939 to Pearl Harbour, captured the attention of the bulk of the

* It is also worth noting that the Japanese Embassy in Washington was aware of the 'Germany-first' line of thought which was developing. Berlin was informed accordingly. (DGFP, XI, No. 210.)

American people and the greater number of pressure groups.[175] It can also be argued that during this period European factors often played a major part in shaping the Far Eastern policies of the United States. At times, this resulted in a greater degree of caution, as when Roosevelt refrained from cutting off Japan's oil supplies lest she should be driven thereby to attack the Netherlands East Indies.[176] 'I simply have not got enough Navy to go round', he told Harold Ickes, his Secretary of the Interior, 'and every little episode in the Pacific means fewer ships in the Atlantic.'[177] In the long run, however, European considerations strengthened rather than weakened the American stance vis-à-vis Japan. In his private correspondence with officials, the President repeatedly emphasized that the trade and resources of the Far East were of major importance for Britain's survival in her fight against Germany, and must therefore be defended with American assistance.[178] In Tokyo, Joseph Grew agreed, even though he believed that war with Japan could be avoided. 'It would be senseless for us', he wrote to a British former colleague, 'to continue to supply Britain with the sinews of war and at the same time to stand complacently by while Japan proceeded to cut Britain's life-line from the East.'[179] 'We are acting as stabilizers in the Far East and Pacific', wrote the U.S. Military Attaché in London, 'and that is more to the interests of the French and British than to ours.'[180]

The U.S. Navy Department likewise argued in European-orientated terms which would have seemed strange only a few years later, when assessing the strategic significance of French Indochina in July 1941: if Japan were to occupy that territory, it was decided, it would constitute a threat to Singapore and the Netherlands East Indies, and hence to the British Isles themselves; therefore the United States should strive to preserve the status quo.[181] Others, like the Chief of Naval Operations, Admiral Stark, in his 'Plan Dog', emphasized the economic damage likely to be done to the United States herself if the British Empire and its trade were to be disrupted, while Ickes wrote in his diary in October 1941: 'For a long time I have believed that our best entrance into the war would be by way of Japan . . . [which] will inevitably lead us into war against Germany.'[182]

'We have not in this Department a Far Eastern mentality', noted a senior State Department official in his diary at the end of 1941, while at least one of his colleagues was pointing out that American interests, commercial and political, were far less significant in the Far East than they were in Europe and South America.[183] 'When we Americans direct our political thought towards Africa or Asia', complained Owen Lattimore later (a former editor of the Institute of Pacific Relations' journal, *Far East Survey*, he served from 1941 to 1943 as Personal Adviser to Chiang Kai-shek, and then as Director of Pacific Operations for the Office of War Information), 'we are still in the habit of routing it via Europe.'[184] He himself, in a letter which is of interest in the light of his subsequent hostility towards the British Empire in Asia, had written in June 1940 that 'the British and Dutch and French Empires in the Far East are in desperate danger, and America alone would have a tough time saving them. And if they go, our position will be badly impaired. For saving British, Dutch, French and American interests in the Far East, the best ally in sight is China.'[185]

Yet despite this widespread concern, American policy vis-à-vis European Far Eastern interests remained blurred in 1941, the military planners, for example, lacking 'even a hypothetical exploration of the politically explosive question of sending U.S. Army forces to defend European colonial possessions in the Far East.'[186] On 28 November, Stimson, now Secretary of State for War, who preferred 'to fight [Japan] at once', agreed with his professional advisers that Japanese landings in Siam 'must not be allowed', and that 'if the British fought, we would have to fight.'[187] Yet Hull, for his part, admitted later to Admiral Stark that, had Japan avoided attacking America's possessions in December 1941, the latter might not have fought there and then—although the Secretary of State may well have been ignorant, when he said that, of Roosevelt's casual pledge to Halifax on 1 December.[188]

As for the case of China, even there—amazingly, if looked at from the standpoint of, say, 1945—there was a tendency to see Britain's interests as being greater than America's. 'Although the War Department wanted Japan to be contained in China', write two of the American official military historians, 'the British Commonwealth with its vast holdings in the Orient was considered to have a predominant interest in maintaining China as a belligerent.'[189] Indeed, as the Australian Minister in Chungking was to observe in 1943, the very smallness of America's past commercial involvement in China, compared to that of Britain, made it easier for the former to assume a harmony of interests with Chiang Kai-shek's resentfully nationalistic country, just as, conversely, the United States benefited from the greater number of American-educated, as opposed to British-educated, Chinese now occupying official positions.[190]

As it was, America's own military mission to China at this time had only a very limited brief, and no staff talks were held on Sino–American cooperation in the event of a Pacific War. Several members of the mission also became greatly disillusioned by the corruption and incompetence that they encountered in China. (As regards the Burma Road in the summer of 1941, for example, it was estimated that to get 5,000 tons of supplies through to Kunming in China, 14,000 tons had to be loaded at Lashio, at the Burmese end of the run.)[191] Again, where American Lend Lease priorities were concerned, China came a poor third behind Britain and the Soviet Union, China's share in 1941 being only 1·7 per cent of the total distributed,[192] while at the Treasury, Morgenthau, although still anxious to aid China, now resented the pressures that were being brought to bear by what he saw as a possibly dishonest Chiang Kai-shek regime in its quest for more American money.[193] As for the American public, a substantial proportion of it remained opposed to any risk of war with Japan in order to save China from being overrun. China's continuing struggle had not brought about an amending of the American immigration laws, nor a wider knowledge of Asia (four months after Pearl Harbour, 60 per cent of a national sample poll would be unable to locate China or India on an outline map of the world).

Meanwhile the American branch of the Institute of Pacific Relations, which sought to increase understanding of that area, and which was to be blown up to giant and sinister proportions during post-war, anti-Communist witch hunts, remained a small body, working from ramshackle offices and on a very restricted budget.[194]

Nevertheless, American aid to China was increasing during this final pre-war period, a $20 million credit being given in April 1940, for example, and $100 million-worth in the following autumn, together with Lend Lease aid after May 1941 as a result of Roosevelt's declaration that China was vital to the defence of the U.S.A.[195] Some attempt was also made to help stabilize the rapidly deteriorating Chinese currency. (Prices in China increased about twenty times between 1937 and the end of 1941.) The last endeavour, however, was severely handicapped by faction-fights within the Chinese administration—the Finance Minister, H. H. Kung, versus T. V. Soong, who was doing the negotiating, for example.* There was also a lack of harmony between the U.S.A. and Britain on the currency issue, over which Washington had declined to join forces in the crucial period of 1938 to 1940. A Stabilization Board was set up, with a British and an American representative on it, but friction and at times a sense of hopelessness continued to attend its activities.[196] Manuel Fox, working in China on behalf of the U.S. Treasury, was particularly hostile to the British role there, and to the efforts of Sir Otto Niemeyer; Fox in turn was regarded by British officials as a menace and a toady of Kung's.[197]

Besides Fox, other individual Americans were occupying a variety of significant positions in China before Pearl Harbour: Chennault, for example, commanding the volunteer pilots of the A.V.G., known as 'the Flying Tigers'; Lattimore, as Chiang Kai-shek's Personal Adviser, who had a direct line to the President through the latter's aide, Laughlin Currie (thus further undermining the position of Clarence Gauss as Ambassador in Chungking),† and who urged in November 1941 that 'the faintest rumour of a "modus vivendi" [between the U.S.A. and Japan] would be more disastrous for Chinese belief in America than was the closing of the Burma Road, which permanently destroyed British prestige [in China].'[198] As a biographer of Roosevelt has observed, 'Its very failure to aid China made the Administration all the more sensitive to any act that might break Kuomintang morale.'[199] Indeed, a guilty conscience over China was to contribute significantly to the confused nature of American policy towards that country during the Pacific war, and to exacerbate friction with the British in that same part of the world.

* Kung's background was that of a long-established, traditional Chinese banking family, Soong, on the other hand, was American-educated, and had a modern business approach—combining public office and money making, of course. Chiang Kai-shek remarked to Owen Lattimore that he distrusted Soong, who 'thought like an American.' (Interview with Professor Lattimore.)

† Two special code books were kept: one by Currie in Washington, the other by Madame Chiang Kai-shek in Chungking, through whom all Lattimore's messages thus had to pass. (Interview with Professor Lattimore.)

Meanwhile, those Americans in China who wanted to see Washington take a stronger line against Japan were matched by men holding important positions within the Administration itself: Morgenthau for one; the dour Ickes at the Department of the Interior; and two Republicans brought in by Roosevelt in the summer of 1940 to help broaden the basis of his Government, Henry Stimson and Frank Knox at the War and Navy Departments respectively. In Congress, too, opposition to the economic coercion of Japan had already dwindled, despite the occasional voice which—significantly for the 1944–45 period ahead—was still raised in not only an isolationist but also an anti-British sense. (If the United States fought Japan, warned Senator Wheeler, it would simply be 'undertaking to preserve the British domination of Asia.') It was thus possible, and indeed in the minds of some of his colleagues it was long overdue, for the President to increase the pressure on Japan by denying her vital raw materials, notably scrap metal in the autumn of 1940 and above all oil at the end of July 1941.[200]

Not that there was any simple and consistent division within official American circles between bodies seeking a showdown with Japan and those advocating a more patient policy. Both the Army and the Navy, for example, were divided at the highest levels. If Stimson was a hard-liner—partly because of his confidence that the Japanese would ultimately back down—his Chief of Staff, General George Marshall, together with the Chief of Naval Operations, Admiral 'Betty' Stark, was still urging in November 1941 that no ultimatum should be delivered to Tokyo, and that time for improving her military preparations was what the United States needed above all.[201] Within the Treasury meanwhile, despite the aggressiveness of Morgenthau (and even, surprisingly enough, with the Secretary's blessing), a senior official, Harry Dexter White, drew up in June and November 1941 a draft basis for a possible settlement with Japan, one which would involve considerable financial, economic and military concessions on the part of the United States in return for a withdrawal of Japanese troops from China and Indochina.[202]* In addition, there existed sharp differences of opinion among State Department officials and overseas diplomats: between the European and Far Eastern Divisions, for example;[203] between those who still sought to keep the United States clear of entanglements and war, and those who saw America's fate as being linked with that of Britain; and, over Far Eastern affairs in particular, between those like Hornbeck who defined the issues in terms of universal moral principles, and those like Eugene Dooman, Grew's Counsellor in Tokyo, who accepted that there were such things as 'spheres of interest', and that Japan must be expected to have hers.

This latter group (although that term gives too organized an impression) were to come into greater prominence in the later stages of the war. In 1940–41, however, it was the Hornbeck approach which gradually came to pre-

* Interestingly enough, the White plan also required Britain to 'give Hong Kong back to China', and called for the placing of Indochina under 'a joint British, French, Japanese, Chinese and American Commission'—a body whose composition would surely have led it into disarray before long.

dominate. Until late in the day, Roosevelt himself, like Hornbeck, seems to have been confident that Japan would not risk fighting the U.S.A. and the British Empire simultaneously.[204] Hull, for his part, was inclined to be far more cautious and patient than Hornbeck, nor did he share the latter's exhilarated confidence at the end of November 1941: while Hornbeck offered on paper to take bets that 'the Japanese Government does not desire or intend or expect to have forthwith armed conflict with the United States',* Hull spoke sourly to various people, including Halifax and Stimson, to the effect that he had 'washed his hands' of relations with Japan, which were now 'in the hands of . . . the Army and the Navy.'[205] Yet by that time, Hull, too, had helped to ensure by his own rigidity that negotiations reached deadlock —and this despite his having had the inestimable advantage of knowing in advance the position his Japanese interlocutors would adopt, thanks to the United States success in breaking the main Japanese diplomatic code. (Amazingly enough, the German Embassy in Washington had obtained reliable information concerning this American achievement; yet Berlin either failed to pass on the vital news to Tokyo, or the latter failed to heed the warning.)[206]

Where only step-by-step, practical bargaining might just conceivably have succeeded, Hull based his approach in 1941 on sweeping general principles, admirable in themselves, but inappropriate if the aim were to secure a *modus vivendi*.† Under Hull, and with Hornbeck in the van, the State Department helped ensure that Roosevelt declined the offer made in August 1941 by Prince Konoye, the Japanese Prime Minister at the time, to meet him in order to try to reach a settlement. The Department also emasculated the White proposals; in addition, it quickly abandoned, in the face of Chinese objections (seconded by Churchill), a scheme for an easing of the embargo against Japan in return for a reduction of her forces in Indochina, and drew up instead a final proposal which was presented to the Japanese on 26 November and which it was inevitable they would reject.‡ (Already, on the 25th, Stimson was noting in his diary the President's warning 'that we were likely to be attacked, perhaps by next Monday . . . The question was how we should manoeuvre them into the position of firing the first shot without allowing too much danger to ourselves.' On 2 December, Stimson also advised T. V. Soong to tell Chiang Kai-shek 'to have just a little more

---

* This is one of the more supple passages of Hornbeck's prose; later examples will demonstrate more fully his talent, amounting to near-genius, for murdering the English language by slow strangulation.

† In April 1941, Hull presented the Japanese negotiators with four basic principles to which Japan must subscribe: '(1) Respect for the territorial integrity and sovereignty of each and all nations; (2) support of the principle of noninterference in the internal affairs of other countries; (3) support of the principle of equality, including equality of commercial opportunity [racial equality was not specifically mentioned, it should be noted]; (4) nondisturbance of the status quo in the Pacific except as the status quo may be altered by peaceful means.'

‡ Hull's four principles were reiterated; a non-aggression pact was proposed for the Far East; Japan was to withdraw all her forces from China and Indochina. (See FRUS, Japan, 1931–1941, II, 768, and C. Hull, *Memoirs*, vol. II (London, 1948), 1077ff.)

patience, and then I think all things will be well.') To this extent, Washington can be said to have helped bring Tokyo to the point of deciding to strike, although it would be far too one-sided an interpretation to conclude from that that the United States, rather than Japan, was the party more responsible for the outbreak of war.

Roosevelt's own switch on 1 December, when he suddenly assured Halifax that armed American assistance would be forthcoming, has already been noted. Until then, not only the British but the Dutch and French as well had had to go without any such comfort while facing great pressure from Japan. Indeed, the Vichy French regime in the spring of 1942, stung by a slighting reference of the President's on the radio to their surrender of Indochina to Japan, were to present the State Department with a bitter recital of the numerous occasions when American help over Indochina had been sought and refused.[207] (The Gaullists were also to keep such potentially embarrassing material ready to hand, as a weapon which might have to be used against Roosevelt in connection with his desire to take Indochina away from France.) This refusal on the American part to form a solid Western front against Japan can, of course, be attributed in part to the country's deep dislike of 'entanglements' and secret pledges, to the substantial proportion of the public that was still unwilling to become involved in war, and to the Congressional troubles which an open commitment would have entailed, at a time when Lend Lease and other delicate matters were already having to be nursed through the legislature. In addition, however, America's refusal reflected the continuing confusion that underlay her Far Eastern policies, a confusion that was to create great difficulties for both the United States and her allies during the Pacific war itself.

There existed, for example, a lack of clarity over the immediate matter of the confrontation with Japan, in which, as a leading student of the Pearl Harbour episode has pointed out, one is faced time and again on the American side 'by the paradox of pessimistic realism coupled with loose optimism in practice.'[208] Uncertainty and misjudgement, however, went beyond a complacent belief in American might and an underestimating of the Japanese. As the same writer has concluded, the main confusion and ignorance among American officials in 1940–41 concerned, not so much the intentions of the Japanese as what was the policy of their own country in the Far East.[209] Moreover, this confusion was to be found at the highest levels. In Dr. Feis's words, 'not only did the British not know what we would do . . . if Japan attacked Singapore or the Dutch East Indies . . . but neither did Roosevelt or Hull know.'[210]* How far would the United States go in order to defend

* In 1932, the newly appointed American Ambassador to Japan, Grew, had gone round the senior members of the Washington Administration, asking what the country's policy was in the Far East. No two men gave him the same answer. (See *Thorne*, 88.) In the 1960s, as we shall see later, a special adviser to the American Government on counter-insurgency in Vietnam was to undergo the same experience. This was not a mere coincidence. As for 1941, when Lattimore was nominated by Roosevelt to be Personal Adviser to Chiang Kai-shek he was summoned to see the President before leaving. They had not met before, but Roosevelt ('Come in, Owen! Good to see you, Owen!') said nothing about

European possessions? What future role did she seek for herself in the area? Was China, in truth, vital to her defence? Was the United States moving to challenge Japan in order to preserve the existing balance of power in the Far East, or to uphold certain fundamental principles of international relations, or both?

Even the forthcoming Japanese attack would not provide clear answers to such questions. As the war progressed, they hovered still over America's relations with China, over her attitude towards the European colonial empires in Asia, and over the structure to be created in the Far East when victory had been achieved. Pearl Harbour would, of course, supply the immediate and unambiguous aim of obtaining revenge by defeating Japan; it would enhance feelings of paternalism and guilt towards China; it would bring about a partnership of a kind with Britain in the Far East. Above all, it would lead eventually to a massive increase in American power in the Western Pacific. Yet it would not clarify the purposes for which that power should be used. Nor would it wipe away American suspicions of Britain in a Far Eastern context, suspicions which, as we have seen, derived not merely from the experiences of the 1930s, but from the nineteenth century and even from the American Revolution itself. Japan's act of aggression was to cement the Anglo–American war-time partnership in global terms. Paradoxically, however, it was also to open the way for some of the most severe strains that partnership had to undergo.

U.S. China policies, only briefly asking his visitor whether he thought that the U.S.S.R. would hold the German attack. Lattimore never saw the President again.

Notes to Chapter Two

1 See DGFP, XIII, Nos. 35, 53, 239.
2 E.g. *Borg and Okamoto*, 191; R. J. Butow, *Tojo and the Coming of War* (Princeton, 1961).
3 E.g. *Borg and Okamoto*, 195, 250, 254; Maruyama, *Thought and Behaviour in Modern Japanese Politics.*
4 E.g. H. Feis, *The Road To Pearl Harbor* (Princeton, 1971), 85.
5 N. Ike, *Japan's Decision For War* (Stanford, 1967; hereafter, *Ike*), 13.
6 Ibid, 78.
7 DGFP, VIII, Nos. 29, 32, 61, 132.
8 DGFP, XI, No. 118; Morley, *Deterrent Diplomacy*, 187.
9 W. H. Elsbree, *Japan's Role in Southeast Asian Nationalist Movements* (Cambridge, Mass., 1953), caps. 1 and 2.
10 *Ike*, 11.
11 See FRUS, Japan 1931–1941, II, 325ff.
12 *Ike*, 133ff., 208ff.
13 DGFP, XII, Nos. 78, 218, 266; XIII, Nos. 89, 127, 316, 458, 512, 551.
14 *Ike*, 209–10.
15 Boyle, *China and Japan at War*, 297ff.
16 WP (40) 302, CAB 66/10.

17 See WP (40) 209, CAB 668/; COS report, 25 June 1940, WP (40) 222, CAB 66/9·
18 A. Calder, *The People's War, 1939–1945* (London, 1969), 19; see P. Gore-Booth, *With Great Truth And Respect* (London, 1974), 81.
19 WP (40) 102, CAB 66/6.
20 DC (Ops.), 9 April 1941, CAB 69/2.
21 FEC, 4 July 1941, CAB 96/2; see WP (41) 154, CAB 65/17.
22 WP (41) 230, CAB 66/19; P. Lowe, *Great Britain and the Origins of the Pacific War* (Oxford, 1977).
23 WP (40) 308, CAB 66/10.
24 FEC, 28 Nov. 1940, CAB 96/5.
25 D. Dilkes (ed.), *The Diaries of Sir Alexander Cadogan* (London, 1971; hereafter, *Cadogan Diaries*), entry for 22 Feb. 1941.
26 See J. M. A. Gwyer, *Grand Strategy*, vol. III, part I (London, 1964), 283.
27 See P. Lowe, 'Great Britain and the Coming of the Pacific War', *Transactions of the Royal Historical Society*, 5th series, vol. 24, 1974; AWC, 14 Feb. 1941, A2673, vol. 4.
28 Roskill, *Naval Policy*, II, 477.
29 Eggleston Papers, series 9/40410, 40416; Latham to Curtin, 16 Dec. 1941, Latham Papers, 100a/65/638.
30 Chennault Papers, box 4; Brown, C., *Suez to Singapore* (New York, 1943).
31 Cooper to WSC, 18 Dec. 1941, PREM 3, 161/1. The Shenton Thomas/Duff Cooper files in the Colonial Office records are closed for 50 years.
32 AAWC, 16 Oct. 1941, A2682, vol. III; See *Kirby*, I, 79.
33 FO 371, F4000G and 4535/1193/10.
34 Colonial Office register, CO 967/69.
35 See e.g. WSC directive of 28 April 1941, J. R. M. Butler, *Grand Strategy*, II, appendix IV; J. Kennedy, *The Business Of War* (London, 1957), 193; W. S. Churchill, *The Second World War*, vol. III (London, 1950; hereafter, *Churchill*, III, etc.), 522.
36 WP (39) 125, CAB 66/3; *Churchill* IV, 43.
37 Cab, 8 August 1940, CAB 65/14; DC (Ops.), 29 April 1941, CAB 69/2.
38 Cab, 21 July 1941, CAB 65/23; WP (41) 212, CAB 66/18.
39 DC (Ops.), 21 Oct. 1941, CAB 69/8; Cab, 27 Oct. 1941, CAB 65/23.
40 Cab, 12 Nov. 1941, CAB 65/24; FO 371, F12322/12/23.
41 Butler, *Grand Strategy*, I, 555.
42 E.g. *Kirby*, I; *Roskill*, I; Butler, *Grand Strategy*, II, and Gwyer, *Grand Strategy*, III part I.
43 See WP (40) 95, CAB 66/6.
44 Brooke-Popham to Ismay, 5 Dec. 1940, Brooke-Popham Papers, V/1/3; J. W. Kirby, *Singapore: The Chain of Disaster* (London, 1971), 56.
45 *Kirby*, II, 9.
46 WP (41) 286, CAB 66/20.
47 Perham, *Colonial Sequence*, 189.
48 See e.g. V. Purcell, *The Memoirs of a Malayan Official* (London, 1965), 286ff.
49 See e.g. Purcell, *The Chinese in South East Asia*, passim.
50 Purcell, *Memoirs*, 300.
51 Purcell, *The Chinese in South East Asia*, 311. For an eyewitness account of the role played by the Chinese in Singapore once the war had begun, see Morrison, *Malayan Postscript*, 164ff.
52 See PREM 4, 50/1.
53 Agent in Burma to Laithwaite, 18 April 1941, Linlithgow Papers, vol. 115.
54 See Ba Maw, *Breakthrough In Burma*, cap. 3.
55 Thakin Nu, *Burma Under The Japanese*, 3.
56 Dorman-Smith to Linlithgow, 31 March 1942, Linlithgow Papers, vol. 115.
57 Interview with Sir Reginald Dorman-Smith, and letter from Dorman-Smith to the author, 16 July 1976.
58 PREM 4, 50/1.
59 See e.g. B. N. Pandey, *The Break Up of British India* (London, 1969), 49ff.

60 Bevin to Amery, 24 Sept. 1941, Bevin Papers, box 13.
61 Amery to Linlithgow, 18 Dec. 1941, Linlithgow Papers, vol. 10.
62 WP (42) 59, CAB 66/21; see B. I. Gupta, *Imperialism and the British Labour Movement, 1914–1964* (London, 1975), 254ff.
63 Correspondence in PREM 4, 43A/3, 45/6 and 50/3.
64 Amery to Linlithgow, 18–20 August 1941, Linlithgow Papers, vol. 10.
65 Hansard H.C. Deb. 374, col. 67ff.
66 Amery to Linlithgow, 25 Nov. 1941, Linlithgow Papers, vol. 10.
67 Cabs., 25 Oct. 1939 (CAB 65/1), 2 Feb. 1940 (CAB 65/5), 12 April 1940 (CAB 65/6), 25 July 1940 (CAB 65/8).
68 Linlithgow to Amery, 15 May 1941, Linlithgow Papers, vol. 10, and Viceroy to Secretary of State, 21 Jan. 1942, ibid., vol. 22.
69 Grigg to Grigg, 23 July 1939 and 15 August 1941, Grigg Papers, box 9/6; papers on Indian affairs, ibid, box 2.
70 On the background to this see e.g. Thornton, *The Imperial Idea And Its Enemies*, 195ff.
71 W. H. Hancock, *Smuts, The Fields of Force, 1919–1950* (Cambridge, 1968), 323ff.
72 See e.g. Mackenzie King to WSC, 10 May 1940, PREM 4, 43A/11.
73 See Butler, *Grand Strategy*, II, 558.
74 King to Fedden, 2 August 1941, PREM 4, 43A/13; see Cab, 28 August 1941, CAB 65/19.
75 Freyburg to Fraser, 14 Oct. 1942, DNZ, II.
76 Cab, 9 June 1941, CAB 65/18.
77 See e.g. the strong Australian business connections of Oliver Lyttelton. Lord Chandos, *Memoirs* (London, 1962).
78 *Cadogan Diaries*, 13 Sept. 1939, 26 Feb. 1941.
79 See e.g. PREM 4, 43A/16.
80 J. van der Poel, *Smuts Papers*, IV, WSC to Smuts, 7 Sept. 1939.
81 AAWC, 28 May 1941, A2682, vol. II.
82 AAWC, 11 Nov. 1941, ibid, vol. III. See Edwards, *Bruce of Melbourne* (Melbourne, 1965); *Hasluck*, I, 344ff.; R. G. Menzies, *Afternoon Light* (London, 1967), 31ff., 92.
83 E.g. AAWC, 23 April 41, A2682, vol. II.
84 WP (41) 208 and 217, CAB 66/18.
85 Earle Page Papers, 259/618 and 619.
86 E.g. Cab, 12 Nov. 1941, CAB 65/20; AWC, 15 May 1941, A2673, vol. 7, and 15 Oct. 1941, ibid, vol. 8; AAWC, 5 Feb. 1941, A2682, vol. I, 14 August and 12 Sept. 1941, ibid, vol. III.
87 ADEA, A981/New Caledonia; Evatt Papers, Netherlands Indies file.
88 E.g. AWC, 26 Nov. 1940, A2673, vol. 3, and 7 Nov. 1941, ibid, vol. 9; AAWC, 28 Nov. 1941, A2682, vol. III.
89 E.g. FO 371, file 27615; R. and N. Lapwood, *Through The Chinese Revolution* (London, 1954); Bertram, *The Shadow of a War*. For Chinese Communist fears that Britain and perhaps the U.S.A. might be preparing for a 'Far Eastern Munich', see J. Gittings, *China and the World, 1922–1972* (London, 1974), 78ff.
90 FO 371, F2406 and 6438/60/10.
91 Ibid, F8136/280/10.
92 Clark Kerr to Foreign Secretary, 3 Feb. 1942, FO 800/300.
93 FO 371, F13942/60/10.
94 Ibid, F9211/7183/10.
95 E.g. ibid, F11825/145/10.
96 On British policy towards China from here onwards, see L. Woodward, *British Foreign Policy During the Second World War*, vol. IV (London, 1975; hereafter *Woodward*, IV etc.).
97 *Manchester Guardian*, 27 Sept. 1941.
98 FO 371, F8229/760/10.
99 Ibid, F 3572/60/10.
100 Cab, 26 Sept. 1939, CAB 65/1.

101 WP (40) 400, CAB 66/12.
102 PREM 4, 28/9.
103 E.g. Cabs, 4 Sept. 1938 (CAB 65/1), 23 Jan. 1940 (CAB 65/5), 1 July 1940 (CAB 65/8).
104 E.g. AWC, 1 Dec. 1941, A2673, vol. 9; AAWC, 29 Oct. 1940, A2682, vol. I, and 6 August 1941, ibid, vol. III.
105 WP (40) 302, CAB 66/10.
106 Cab, 25 Oct. 1940, CAB 65/9. See Cab, 13 March 1940, CAB 65/6.
107 Cab, 13 Nov. 1940, CAB 65/10.
108 PREM 4, 42/8.
109 Cab, 25 Sept. 1939, CAB 65/1.
110 E.g. WP (39) 56 (CAB 66/2); WP (39) 152 (CAB 66/4); FO 371, F3572/60/10; F11662/145/10; Clark Kerr to Foreign Secretary, 3 Feb. 1942, FO 800/300.
111 FO 371, F5879/849/10; see F110/110/10.
112 Eggleston Papers, 423/9/1372.
113 Notes on China, n.d., Clark Kerr Papers, FO 800. For a portrait of Clark Kerr, see Hayter, *A Double Life*, 51.
114 See e.g. Harvey, *Diplomatic Diaries of Oliver Harvey*, 23 April 1940.
115 E.g. FO 371, file 27721.
116 WP (41) 131, CAB 65/17.
117 Cabs, 1, 5, 10 July 1940, CAB 65/8; WP (40) 119 and 263, CAB 66/9; *Cadogan Diaries*, 5 July 1940.
118 WP (41) 230, CAB 66/19.
119 E.g. WP (41), 203, CAB 66/18.
120 CAB 96/1, 2, 4, 7, 10.
121 FEC, 13 Feb. 1941, CAB 96/2.
122 Maxwell Hamilton Papers, box 1.
123 FEC, 16 Jan. 1941, CAB 96/2; Cab, 13 Nov. 1940, CAB 65/10; WP (40) 436, CAB 66/13.
124 WP (40) 481, CAB 66/14; WP (41) 13, CAB 66/14; Cabs, 19 Dec. 1940, (CAB 65/10), 29 Jan. 1941 (CAB 65/17), 18 Aug. 1941 (CAB 65/19); Dorman-Smith, 'Report on Burma Campaign, 1941–1942', Dorman-Smith Papers, 215/218; C. L. Chennault, *Way of a Fighter* (New York, 1949), 106; material in Chennault Papers, box 4.
125 FO 371, F565/503/61.
126 FEC, 1 May 1941, CAB 96/2; I. Adamson, *The Forgotten Men* (London, 1965).
127 PREM 3, 90/1; Cab, 11 Nov. 1941, CAB 65/20; FO 371, F11714, 11941/145/10, and F12262, 27655/145/10; Chennault Papers, box 1.
128 Cab, 24 Nov. 1941, CAB 65/20; Feis, *The Road To Pearl Harbor*, 312ff.
129 PREM 3, 156/5.
130 See WP (41) 24, 101, 168 and 254 in CAB 66/14, 16, 17 and 19 respectively; Cab, 29 July 1940, CAB 65/8.
131 WP (40) 289, CAB 66/10.
132 Cabs, 21 July 1941, CAB 65/23, and 3 Nov. 1941, CAB 65/20.
133 DC (Ops.), 8 Aug. 1941, CAB 96/2.
134 FO 371, files 28134, 28151, 28156, 28164.
135 Cab, 26 Sept. 1939, CAB 65/1; WP (40) 263, CAB 66/9; *Woodward*, II, 155.
136 WP (40) 168, CAB 66/7; WP (40) 203, CAB 66/8.
137 E.g. AWC, 24 Sept. 1940, A2673, vol. 4.
138 AAWC, 25 Nov. 1940, A2682, vol. I; ADEA, A981/USA/79.
139 WP (41) 202, CAB 66/18; *Woodward*, II, 130.
140 DC (Ops.), 17 Dec. 1940, CAB 69/1.
141 FO 371, F10625/7762/61.
142 Cabs, 27 Nov. 1939, CAB 65/2, and 10 Feb. 1940, CAB 65/5; WP (40) 265, CAB 66/9; WP (40) 436, CAB 66/13; WP (41) 172, CAB 66/17.
143 FEC, 27 Jan., 24 and 31 July 1941, CAB 96/2.
144 Cabs, 21, 24, 28 July 1941, CAB 65/19.
145 Cab 20 Oct. 1941, CAB 65/23.

146 Sir D. Scott memo., 15 April 1941, FO 371, A3823/118/45.
147 E.g. Cabs, 9 June 1940, CAB 65/7; 27 July 1940, CAB 65/9; DC (Ops.), 19 May 1941, CAB 69/2; Cabs, 19–25 and 28 Aug. 1941, CAB 65/19; WP (41) 282, CAB 66/20.
148 Cab, 16 Oct. 1941, CAB 65/23.
149 Halifax Diary, 26 Nov. 1941.
150 WSC to Eden, 23 Nov. 1941, PREM 3, 156/6.
151 Cab, 19 Aug. 1941, CAB 65/23; WP (41) 203, CAB 66/18; Lowe. 'Great Britain and the Coming of the Pacific War', loc. cit.; FO 371, file 27893.
152 FO 371, file 35957. See R. Craigie, *Behind The Japanese Mask* (London, 1946) for hints of his actual views, and, on differences within the Tokyo Embassy, K. Sansom, *Sir George Sansom and Japan: A Memoir* (Tallahassee, Fa., 1972), 116; Gore-Booth, *With Great Truth and Respect*, 79.
153 See J. C. Grew, *Turbulent Era*, vol. 2 (London, 1953), 1264ff.
154 See e.g. *Woodward*, II, 158.
155 *Churchill*, III, 539.
156 See *Woodward*, II, 92ff.
157 E.g. Cab, 17 July 1940, CAB 65/8; FEC, 18 Oct. 1940, CAB 96/1.
158 FE (40) 110, CAB 96/1; FE (41) 52, CAB 96/2; FEC, 11 Sept. 1941, CAB 96/2.
159 FRUS, 1941, IV, 881.
160 E.g. Lord Avon, *The Reckoning* (London, 1965; hereafter, *Avon*), 308.
161 WP (41) 202 and 220, CAB 66/18.
162 Cab, 22 June 1940, CAB 65/7.
163 Directive of 28 April 1941, PREM 3, 156/6.
164 W. Stevenson, *A Man Called Intrepid* (New York, 1976; hereafter, *Stevenson*), 299; *Churchill*, III, 532.
165 Cab, 1 Dec. 1941, CAB 65/20; Staff conference, 1 Dec. 1941, CAB 79/86.
166 WP (41) 296, CAB 66/20; Cab, 4 Dec. 1941, CAB 65/20; DC (Ops.), 3 Dec. 1941, CAB 69/2; Halifax Diary, 2 Dec. 1941. On the role of the British Minister to Siam in this period, see Allen, *Singapore*, 77ff.
167 Cab, 8 May 1941, CAB 65/22; DC (Ops.), 30 April 1941 and 10 June 1941, CAB 69/2.
168 *Borg and Okamoto*, 222; *Matloff and Snell*, 32ff.
169 *Matloff and Snell*, 65 and 75ff.; *Woodward*, II, 173ff.
170 *Matloff and Snell*, 32ff.; Butler, *Grand Strategy*, II, cap. XVIII; L. Morton, *Strategy and Command: The First Two Years* (Washington D.C., 1962), 87ff.; Morison, *Two-Ocean War*, 34; F. C. Pogue, *George C. Marshall: Ordeal and Hope, 1939–1942* (New York, 1966; hereafter, *Pogue*, I), 126–7.
171 Quoted in *Matloff and Snell*, 74.
172 Quoted in Greenfield, *Command Decisions*, 32.
173 Bullitt to FDR, 5 Dec, 1941, Roosevelt Papers, PPF Bullitt; Stimson Diary, 6 Oct. 1941; E. Roosevelt, *F.D.R.: His Personal Letters, 1928–1945*, vol. 2 (New York, 1950; hereafter, *Roosevelt Letters*), letter of 11 July 1941.
174 *Borg and Okamoto*, 448.
175 Ibid, 442.
176 See *Roosevelt Letters*, 13 Nov. 1940; Feis, *The Road to Pearl Harbor*, 206, 236.
177 J. M. Burns, *Roosevelt, The Soldier of Freedom, 1940–1945* (London, 1971; hereafter, *Burns*), 107.
178 *Roosevelt Letters*, 31 Dec. 1940; Grew, *Turbulent Era*, vol. 2, 1259.
179 Grew to Lindley, 12 March 1941, Grew Papers, vol. III; see Feis, *Road to Pearl Harbor*, 102.
180 J. Leutze (ed.), *The London Observer: The Journal of General Raymond E. Lee* (London, 1972), 4.
181 FRUS, Japan, 1931–1941, II, 516.
182 *Matloff and Snell*, 25; H. Ickes, *The Secret Diary of Harold L. Ickes*, vol. III (London, 1955), 630.
183 B. Berle and T. Jacobs (eds.), *Navigating The Rapids: From The Papers of Adolf A. Berle* (New York, 1973; hereafter, *Berle*), entry for 26 Dec. 1941; F. L. Israel (ed.),

The War Diary of Breckenridge Long (Lincoln, Nebraska, 1966; hereafter *Long*), entry for 14 Sept. 1940.

184 O. Lattimore, *Solution In Asia* (London, 1945, hereafter, *Lattimore*), 5; see Iriye, *Across The Pacific*, passim.

185 Lattimore to Martin, 3 June 1940, IPR, box 373. Lattimore believed at the time that, once she had allies, China would resume an active part in the war. Interview with Professor Lattimore.

186 *Matloff and Snell*, 10. Cf. Lake, *The Legacy of Vietnam*, 228.

187 Stimson Diary, 28 Nov. 1941.

188 Morton, *Strategy and Command*, 125; see Stimson Diary, 28 Nov. 1941, and Morison, *Two-Ocean War*, 45.

189 C. Romanus and R. Sutherland, *Stilwell's Mission To China* (Washington D.C., 1953; hereafter, *Romanus and Sutherland*, I), 13.

190 See below, 170–172.

191 *Romanus and Sutherland*, I, 43, 45.

192 E.g. *Roosevelt Letters*, 15 May 1941.

193 E.g. Morgenthau notes, 24 April 1941, Morgenthau Papers, Presidential Diaries, vol. 4.

194 E.g., Feis, *Road to Pearl Harbor*, 122; Steele, *American People and China*, 22; H. R. Isaacs, *Scratches On Our Minds* (New York, 1963), 37; J. N. Thomas, *The Institute of Pacific Relations* (Seattle, 1974); IPR files, passim.

195 China Defense Supplies, Inc., was set up to channel this aid at the U.S. end.

196 See Young, *China and the Helping Hand*, cap. X.

197 E.g. Fox to Currie, 12 Nov. 1941, H. D. White Papers, box 6; Clark Kerr to Foreign Secretary, 3 Feb. 1942, FO 800/300.

198 Lattimore to Currie, 25 Jan. 1941; FDR to Hull, 21 Nov. 1941, Roosevelt Papers, PSF box 37.

199 *Burns*, 145.

200 *Borg and Okamoto*, 320.

201 E.g. Feis, *Road To Pearl Harbor*, 302, 323.

202 White memos., 3 June 1941 and 17 Nov. 1941, White Papers, box 6.

203 E.g. *Borg and Okamoto*, 105.

204 Ibid, 49.

205 E.g. Stimson Diary, 27 Nov. 1941.

206 DGFP, XII, No. 418.

207 Henry-Haye to Welles, 5 March 1942, NFM, D2 EI18.

208 R. Wohlstetter, *Pearl Harbor: Warning and Decision* (Stanford, 1962), 69.

209 Ibid, 73. Dr. Wohlstetter's book helps confirm that Roosevelt did not deliberately allow the Pearl Harbour disaster to take place in order to get America into the war. There was, rather, a lack of imagination as to what Japan might do if pressed, and an inability to sift out from the mass of information obtained those pieces which pointed to a forthcoming attack on the Hawaiian base.

210 Feis, *Road to Pearl Harbor*, 141.

CHAPTER THREE

THE ANGLO-AMERICAN RELATIONSHIP
ON THE EVE OF PEARL HARBOUR

IT IS a commonplace that the historian's shorthand use of words like 'Britain' and 'Germany' can involve the danger of his writing of the policies and reactions of states as if they emerged from monolithic units, each with a single interpretation of the national interest and a single voice with which to proclaim and pursue it. Nevertheless, the Second World War as a subject may give rise to particular temptations in this respect. Stalin, Hitler, Roosevelt, Churchill: were not these decisive figures, so that what they willed or did may conveniently be taken to represent the totality of their respective state's international behaviour? Perhaps, thirty-five years after Pearl Harbour, a caution against such an oversimplification is unnecessary. It is as well, however, to recall at the outset that a study of Anglo-American relations during the war involves two pluralities, and that this is so even if one is concerned only with the two governments and official machineries.

Not everyone involved was fully aware of such realities at the time. In London, for example, there were those in high places who continued to think of American politics in essentially British terms; whose expectations of what Roosevelt or his opponents could or could not do failed to allow for the fact that, in the words of one historian, 'both major American political parties were heterogeneous alliances of dissimilar groups with diverse views that were drawn together for the purpose of getting into public office and controlling the government.'[1] In effect, Roosevelt was presiding over a 'coalition' government, as was Churchill in a formal sense. Indeed, there were times when Roosevelt's Democratic Administration looked a good deal more fissile than did Churchill's National Government, in which Attlee could later 'remember no case where differences arose between Conservatives, Labour and Liberal along party lines. Certainly not in the War Cabinet. Certainly not in the big things. We applied ourselves to winning the war.'[2] Even leaving aside the two Republicans, Stimson and Knox, who had been brought in by Roosevelt, there was a huge span between, say, Cordell Hull as a key representative of the 'old South', and Henry Wallace (Vice President from 1941 to 1945) as a spokesman for progressive midwestern agrarian interests, who became for Hull one of the 'radical boys' who had to be resisted and removed altogether if possible, because of what the Secretary of State deemed to be their pursuit of 'world-wide social revolution even at the danger of producing revolution in the United States.'[3] Personality clashes—Ickes versus Hopkins and many others—and bureaucratic rivalries and distrust—Hull versus Morgenthau; Ickes versus a State Department which he saw as being 'shot through with Fascism'[4]—added to the confusion.

Not that London was altogether lacking in such attractions. Behind those neat, rational Cabinet Conclusions penned by the Secretary, Sir Eric Bridges, there lay at times scenes of acrimony and turmoil, with four or five Ministers shouting at each other at once.[5] 'I think that we just don't deserve to win the war', Hugh Dalton, President of the Board of Trade, was to write in his diary in February 1942. 'We are all fighting each other instead of the enemy, and with such zest.' Dalton himself was no mean Whitehall warrior, to whom Cripps was 'crazy Cripps' and Beaverbrook 'the asthmatic ape';[6] Beaverbrook in particular attracted hostile feelings, not least from Bevin.[7] Moreover, despite Attlee's subsequent recollections, there were those on the right of the Government who were looking apprehensively at what Bevin and others might achieve during the war that would be of consequence for the ordering of society thereafter. Beaverbrook, for example, saw Bevin as 'working hard for the war and a little harder for socialism';[8] P. J. Grigg was likewise 'very worried over Winston's complete indifference to the way Bevin and his friends are committing us to a syndicalist state';[9] Churchill himself, not, it seems, as indifferent as Grigg believed, snapped at Bevin in Cabinet, when the latter was inveighing against pre-war social 'chaos': 'You are trying once more to prejudice the settlement of our post-war problems. What you call chaos others might call freedom.'[10] Meanwhile to Linlithgow, as Viceroy of India, the Foreign Office was 'spineless' and 'old womanish to a degree',[11] whilst in return some of the most savage comments to be found among Foreign Office minutes were reserved for the Government in New Delhi. Certain Colonial Office officials, for their part, were often scornful in private, especially in 1942, of what they saw as the Foreign Office's 'defeatism' and its 'appeasement' of the United States over colonial issues.[12]

More serious, however, was the threat to the very unity of Churchill's Government which was being posed at the time of Pearl Harbour by a possible split within the ranks of the Conservatives, over the American drive to extract in return for Lend Lease a British commitment to work for a multilateral system of world trade after the war.[13] As Keynes conducted in Washington negotiations which were to result in the Mutual Aid Agreement of February 1942 (the draft article 7 of which pledged both Governments to work for the 'elimination' of discriminatory practices and the 'reduction' of tariffs), Amery, Beaverbrook and the Minister of Agriculture, R. S. Hudson, were vigorously defending imperial preference and the protection of British farming interests against those like Lord Cherwell, Churchill's special adviser, who were arguing for collaboration with the United States. Others, too, were involved in this issue, with Bevin fearing that multilateralism could mean 'the adjustment of a proper equilibrium by the old free-trade process of starvation.'[14] But the major threat lay within the ranks of the Conservative Party, where Churchill himself had no solid base and only a wary acceptance as leader.[15]

Beyond this question of the interplay of forces within Washington and London, other, comparative features of the Anglo-American setting need to be borne in mind. At the widest political extent, for example, there were the differences, as well as similarities, between the political cultures of the two countries, involving in 1941, for instance, the greater number, variety and role of pressure groups on the United States side, as well as what has been described as 'a more complex and less stable . . . political division of labour' there.[16] Interwoven with such contrasts in the area of political culture were the respective political systems and actual political situations existing at the time, the resulting patterns being of a kind that might seem surprising to the uninitiated. Thus Churchill, removable at any time by a vote of Parliament, was in some ways in a stronger position than Roosevelt, reelected in 1940 for another four-year term. Yet even here, no simple contrast is possible. For example, Churchill, for all his apparent indispensability—and between July 1940 and May 1945, never less than 78 per cent of those questioned in opinion polls approved of his leadership[17]—was to face considerable pressure within Parliament for a short period in 1942, whilst Roosevelt, on distant terms with a large portion of Congress,[18] was in 1941 beginning to take executive actions which faced the legislature with a series of faits accomplis in a manner which, in the view of one authority, 'must in the end have produced a serious constitutional crisis had not the Japanese obligingly come to the rescue.'[19] Moreover, the onset of war, besides allowing the President to emphasize his role as Commander in Chief, was to complete a process by which the powerful influence exercised upon foreign policy by Congress in an isolationist direction since 1919 came widely to be held—and held in Congress itself—to have had a deleterious effect on the nation's ultimate safety.[20]

It can be argued, in fact, that there were times when Roosevelt was more cautious in the field of war-time foreign policy than he need have been in terms of possible domestic repercussions. In 1941, however, there still seemed every reason for him to step carefully. During his 1940 election campaign against Wendell Willkie, both candidates had felt obliged to pander to isolationist sentiments, Roosevelt himself pledging: 'I shall say it again and again and again: your boys are not going to be sent into any foreign wars.' The American public were ready to see pressure put on Japan; they were ready (in the ratio of two to one by the summer of 1941) to see aid extended to Britain; at the same time they even believed by a substantial majority that the United States would eventually be drawn into the European conflict. But they remained what they had been in 1939, heavily against entering that conflict voluntarily (79 per cent in a Gallup Poll of May 1941). Even when American destroyers were sunk by German U-Boats in the Atlantic, with heavy loss of life, the underlying mood of passivity did not change, whilst in August 1941 the renewal of the Selective Service Act, without which the drafting of men into the Army would come to an end, passed the House of Representatives by only a single vote.[21]

If caution, even self-effacement, seemed at times to be an American characteristic in 1941, this was scarcely to be the case once battle had been joined. Writing of 1942–43, a British official historian has noted, for example, the confident, expansive approach which American strategic planners were by then bringing to Allied discussions, in contrast to their opposite numbers in London:

'The melancholy experience not only of three war years but of the years preceding them had taught the British the hard lesson that resources of every kind would always be limited and usually quite inadequate; that the demands of one theatre could be met only at the expense of another; that no operation could be considered out of the context of the war as a whole. The Americans, on the other hand, were conscious rather of the enormous potential, in manpower, weapons and equipment, which lay at their disposal. For them shortages were not a problem, as for the British, to be lived with indefinitely, but a passing embarrassment which need not affect long-term strategy.'[22]

This contrast, as Michael Howard indicates, went beyond the war-time situation itself. This is not to say that one cannot find periods of American history when the predominant mood would seem to have been one of a lack of confidence.[23] Nor must it be forgotten that a deeply-ingrained confidence in themselves (perhaps in some ways a relic of the mid-nineteenth century years when the pound sterling and the Royal Navy had indeed been supreme) had stood the British people in good stead in 1940—even finding expression, in some quarters, in a sense of relief when France dropped out of the war since, in King George VI's words, there were now 'no allies to be polite to and to pamper.'[24] Yet Britain was, indeed, in a beleaguered state and was not in a position adequately to defend her empire—facts which could not be dismissed altogether by mere defiance against invasion. Moreover, many of the British people, it seems, were fighting the war to the accompaniment of a belief that their own society was in need of fundamental reorganization and development, a feature which boded ill for the Conservative Party and for Churchill in the long run.[25]

Americans, too, during the period of the New Deal, had disagreed violently among themselves about the organization of their society, but without impairing their fundamental belief in their history as being 'a success story'. There remained 'the quiet conviction that the ends of action are not in doubt: they are prescribed by American principles, or by the "facts of life" ', together with the assumption—more common on the British side a hundred years earlier—'that the values that arise from their [American] experience are of universal application.'[26] Economic abundance (enjoyed in fact by only a portion of the population, but in legend there for all to take on a basis of equal opportunity); years of security from foreign attack; the extension and taming of the territory of the Republic: these and other features of America's history would help colour the approach of her people to the war itself, to foes and to allies. A morally simplistic view of international politics would facilitate the division of the world into tyrants on the one hand and 'freedom-loving nations' (including the one led by Stalin) on the other. 'Implicitly', writes an American historian,

'we understood, of course, that we were the most devoted of all [to freedom] and that, while other countries might prove fickle in their affection, we could pride ourselves upon a record of constant fidelity. It was as if all the world had been presented with a choice between a right principle of government and a wrong one, and we, more than any others, had been unequivocal in choosing the right.'[27]

As Stanley Hornbeck of the State Department was to put it in December 1943, 'In the U.S. we place a much higher valuation upon the concept of political freedom and independence than do the British . . . We assume to a far greater extent that various and sundry now-dependent or quasi-dependent national groups have capacity for self-government.'[28]

Such an assumption was often to grate upon allies, who might cast a glance at, say, Puerto Rico, and who did not always appreciate the immense vigour, optimism, and often generosity which it engendered and which were to contribute so much to the winning of the war. To Europeans, in Sir Isaiah Berlin's words, the 'simpler and grander view of the powers and tasks of modern man . . . the large vista possible only for those who live on mountain heights or vast level plains offering an unbroken view, seems curiously flat, without subtlety or colour, at times appearing to lack the dimension of depth, certainly without that immediate reaction to fine distinctions with which perhaps only those who live in valleys are endowed.'[29] In their turn, many Americans were to find in the pragmatic, shaded, qualified, more pedestrian approach of the British, evidence of a tired people who lacked idealism and had had their day. In this sense, Britain, for all her special features, could come to be lumped together with other European states. And in Europe, the men who had been shaping American policy during the New Deal had seen

'at worst, a ghastly mess that threatened to divert America's "giddy minds" into "foreign quarrels", at best, a battlefield between repellent totalitarian regimes and bloodless, divided democracies that were unable to get over the depression, produce real leadership, or defend their interests. Again [as during the Woodrow Wilson years], there was a legacy of impatience, distaste and reprobation . . . with new overtones of dismay and some contempt—overtones that are not difficult to detect in F.D.R.'s own wartime attitudes.'[30]

In 1941 there were also, of course, special factors by virtue of which Britain did stand apart from the remainder of Europe in American eyes. The United States and Britain had deep ties with one another, and 'certain ways of looking at the world which have a good deal in common.'[31] Furthermore, relations between the two countries, centred upon the Churchill-Roosevelt connection, had developed to a remarkable extent since 1939,* in contrast to the strains which had occurred during the First World War before 1917. By their defiance of Hitler in 1940, reported from the spot by Ed Murrow of C.B.S., and others, Churchill and the people he led had won enormous admiration, not all of which had evaporated by the time of Pearl Harbour. If the British survived the war, the American Military Attaché in London had written, 'they will be bankrupt but entitled to almost unlimited respect.'[32] Wendell Willkie, as much as Harry Hopkins, left Britain in this period impressed by the spirit he had found, and determined, in his own words, that 'anything I can do in America to help Britain in her fight for freedom I shall certainly do.' 'Whither thou goest, I will go', quoted Hopkins privately, ' . . . even to the end.'[33] Others in the American Administration, notably Stimson, had a deeply-rooted sense of Anglo-American kinship, and despite policy differences found it easy to mingle with men from Westminster and Whitehall. (Even Attlee, not altogether Stimson's type, one might have thought, struck the latter when he met him in 1941 as being an 'outstanding labor leader now who is furnishing backbone to the war . . . I was rather impressed by him, as a very serious, thoroughly responsible English leader.')[34]

For the longer term, Roosevelt in this period envisaged the Royal Navy— over whose possible fate there had been much American anxiety during Hitler's early successes—joining the U.S. Navy to police the world, Russia and China not yet having been added to the ranks of global peacekeepers. 'Despite his frequent hostility towards Britain', writes a student of the President's views on a new world order, 'he had a clear understanding of the Anglo-American community of interest, and he never doubted that Britain's continued independence was vital to the security of the United States.'[35] Perhaps, after all, as part of that new order of things, there might come about a fundamental change in Britain which would win the approval of the New Dealers in the United States? One senior member of the State Department, at least, thought that Roosevelt had this in mind when sending to London as Ambassador, early in 1941, John G. Winant, who had been Director of the International Labour Organization:

'The Country Gentleman type, the landed and industrial aristocracy of England', wrote the State Department official, 'are being jolted out of position. If Churchill should fall, a new Government would be drafted from a new type—not the MacDonald type, but more wholly composed of

* The Churchill-Roosevelt relationship during this crucial period has been described by J. P. Lash in his *Roosevelt and Churchill, 1939–1941* (London, 1977) especially chapters 11 and 15. From the examination of that relationship offered below, it will be seen that the present writer shares Mr. Lash's view of its vital nature, and agrees with some of the contrasts he draws between the two leaders. On the other hand, there will also emerge a marked difference of emphasis in over-all terms. In part this arises from the inclusion in the present study of the post-1941 phases of the relationship; in addition, however, the two works diverge in their assessments of Roosevelt especially.

popular interests and definitely labor groups, among whom would be persons now considered radical and with Bevin as the possible head of the Government . . . Roosevelt sees this possibility and is establishing contacts with what may be the Government in the future . . .'[36]

Whether Roosevelt did, in fact, envisage such an outcome is not clear. Certainly, however, Harold Laski, who had been corresponding with the President for some time, was trying to get the latter to put some reforming zeal into Churchill himself:

'Winston is a very great Commander in Chief', wrote Laski in October 1940; '[but] he has yet, in my view, to prove himself a great Prime Minister. He will only do that when he sees that the condition of a real victory is a New Deal for the British, and that he must begin the New Deal as part of the actual strategy of the war . . . That [new] England and F.D.R.'s America in conjunction can take over the leadership of the masses throughout the world. There is the best revolution by consent in world history in this approach. Please use your authority to make him start. He has the imagination and the courage; what he needs is the understanding.'[37]

For all the hopes and heroism to be found in Britain before the United States entered the war, however, there remained on both sides of the Atlantic much fertile soil in which mutual criticism and distrust could spring up thereafter. Perhaps the very existence of a common language contributed to this state of affairs at a fairly superficial level, by making it all the easier to assume unconsciously that nationals of the other country should behave and think as one did oneself. An Englishman might expect an Italian to act in what to him appears an outlandish fashion: the latter is, after all, manifestly a 'foreigner'; but a white American can be regarded as a wayward Anglo-Saxon, mangling the English language into what Keynes contemptuously and openly referred to as 'Cherokee', as well as behaving in altogether too bouncy a manner.[38] Conversely, General Stilwell, for example, even before he plunged into the Burma campaign, was enjoying caricaturing in his diary the 'bored and supercilious limies': 'Monocoled ass at lunch: "One does enjoy a cawk-tail doesn't one? It's so seldom one gets a chawnce. In my own case I hardly have time for a glahss of bee-ah!" '[39]

'The United States', Professor Denis Brogan soon felt it necessary to warn his readers in the *Spectator*, 'is a foreign country and the Americans . . . in short are non-English—a state of affairs to which they are wholly reconciled.'[40] Certainly, there was a tendency on the British side to regard Americans de haut en bas:

'They strike me as very crude and semi-educated', wrote Britain's new Ambassador, Lord Halifax, in his diary early in 1941, 'and have not begun to appreciate . . . that the essential element of education is not to know things but to know how little you know. And I think also that national life has been pretty easy for them and they shrink from things that are

hard. The consequence is that they are tempted . . . to think that everything can be resolved on the emotional level by soft words and fine
thoughts, that are not always reflected in action. Another consequence is
that they are dangerously afraid of public opinion, and when they profess
dislike of our aristocratic system, I am tempted to reply (but hold my
tongue) that at least it gives us a capacity to disregard uninformed public
opinion that has little claim to be regarded.'[41]

Again, the very similarities between the two countries helped foster an
exchange of criticisms concerning standards, a process which each could find
particularly wounding. In Professor Nicholas's words: 'Precisely because we
persist in being each other's keepers to a degree that we would think im-
proper or pointless elsewhere, we often exacerbate our relations. We expect
much more of each other than we expect of third parties, and are proportionately chagrined when we fail to find it. One consequence of this has been
a disposition to overlook the element of power which inevitably enters into
our mutual relations.'[42] In addition, there existed in 1941 a considerable
degree of ignorance and misperception between the two peoples. The First
World War had not led to a sense of shared suffering, or to widespread
understanding; in the inter-war years, contrasting developments in domestic
politics and various diplomatic clashes had taken place against a background
of mutual images which scarcely rose above the level of the Hollywood ones
of America which were projected on to British cinema screens.[43]

Thus, Felix Frankfurter—eminent American jurist and friend of Roosevelt—was probably correct when he identified as 'a central difficulty . . . a
lack of continuing consciousness of comradeship between the two peoples',
a deficiency which meant, for example, that many Americans, convinced that
Britain was no more than an imperialistic, Tory squirearchy, were unaware
of what Frankfurter called 'the actual makeup of the English people, the
reality of their democracy', and did not realize that 'the aims of the British
people in waging this war are substantially our aims.'[44] Halifax for one was,
indeed, marked down at first by many Americans as 'a hopeless Tory', in
Harry Hopkins' phrase ('I would not like to see him have much to say about
a later peace', noted Hopkins, '[and] I should like to have Eden say less'),
although subsequently he became a more popular figure.[45]

Halifax also possessed another handicap in American eyes: his association
with 'appeasement' in 1938, which 'stuck in the craw' of Harold Ickes, for
example.[46] Events such as this from the past—post-war debts; disarmament
quarrels; the Stimson–Simon episode—have already been mentioned as contributing to subsequent tension. It was also common in America to find in the
past proof that Britain was the most subtle, devious and self-seeking of
players of the international game. 'It is always the same with the British',
Roosevelt apparently warned Willkie in this pre-Pearl Harbour period, 'they
are always foxy and you have to be the same with them.'[47] In the eyes of
Breckenridge Long, a wealthy conservative supporter of F.D.R. and an
Assistant Secretary of State, 'the British just do not know how to play

cricket' [sic], and in January 1942 he would speedily conclude that their policy was

'to suck the United States dry. When peace comes ally with Russia. Let Russia have Poland, Eastern Germany, Baltic States, Finland. Hold the Mediterranean; Turkey hold the Dardanelles. Hold Iraq and Iran and India (if the Japs don't get it)—and let the U.S. alone politically and strangle it commercially . . . If they would take the British businessmen and put them in charge of their Army and Navy they would win some battles. They are smart boys . . .'[48]

The private papers of many Americans in official circles are scattered with such assumptions regarding British selfishness, cunning and lack of idealism. Henry Wallace, for example, was to describe the British as 'trying to play their customary role of getting more than they are entitled to.'[49] In June 1941, Adolf Berle of the State Department wrote to Roosevelt suggesting that the Department should try its hand at drafting an outline of the kind of post-war world which the United States desired to see, adding that 'on the record of the past twenty years and of the present conflict, it hardly seems that the British can make any statement of program; and their highly opportunist policy leaves her with little moral authority, outside her own territories.'[50]

In contrast to American innocence ('[our] inexperience in dealing with allies', ran the later 'Master Narrative' of the American Army's China–Burma–India Command, 'became apparent from the hotel lobbies in Washington to the committee rooms in Delhi and Chungking. We lack the international point of view.')[51], it was assumed that British officials, military and civil, would always be skilful at playing 'power politics', seeking to perpetuate to their own advantage that evil system, the 'balance of power', through that equally odious device, 'spheres of influence'. The warning to the American members of the 1941 Anglo-American staff talks has already been quoted to this effect, while among the Army's planners Major-General Stanley D. Embick was quick to suspect British manoeuvring. Even General Marshall himself, usually friendly and as upright as can be imagined in his dealings with Britain, 'never completely rid himself', in his biographer's words, 'of a certain wariness in dealing with strategy that he believed to be motivated by purely British political interests.'[52] Embick's son-in-law, General (as he later became) Albert C. Wedemeyer, who was to play a major part in Southeast Asia Command and the China Theatre, was also highly suspicious. 'To the British', he was to write after the war, 'the true friend might be the man who could be manipulated or enticed to see things as the British themselves saw them. There was no give and take between British and American planners. It was all "take" on their part . . .'[53]

The thorough preparations made by British staff officers before Allied wartime conferences was merely to prove the point as far as Wedemeyer and many of his colleagues were concerned: the British, he wrote, 'always knew in advance what they wanted'; the Americans 'had no clear-cut conception of our own national interest.'[54] It was a picture which, while not devoid of all accuracy, was greatly exaggerated, as we shall see later in our Far Eastern context, and as Dalton was to note ruefully in his diary after talking to Averell Harriman in March 1943:

'He says that most Americans believe that we are so damned clever that we have already got all our post-war plans worked out to the last dot, and intend to inveigle the Americans into accepting them to their own great disadvantage. In view of our chronic indecisions, this is really frightfully funny; but I only tell Harriman that decisions come even more slowly in a Coalition than in a one-Party Government.'[55]

Britain was clever in the extreme. As such, she might seek, so some American officials thought even before Pearl Harbour, to make the Anglo-American partnership too exclusive an affair. 'Increasingly', noted Adolf Berle in his diary, 'there is tension in the Administration between the people who take the English view, i.e. that there are only two civilized peoples in the world—English and American— . . . [and those who believe that] we need every nucleus of continental help we can get.'[56] Hornbeck was to try to put this into wider perspective in May 1943, when noting how easy it was for the British Government to decree that there should be close cooperation with the U.S.A.:

'It is not, however, in reverse, so simple a matter for [us]', he wrote. 'This country has not adopted an attitude or policy paralleling in reverse this British attitude and policy. I would doubt the advisability of trying [to do so]. British foreign policy in modern times has always included among its fundamental principles that of making alliances and relying upon [the] balance of power . . . American policy has avoided alliances, shyed away from special friendships and proffered ententes . . .'[57]

Moreover, quite apart from such contrasts, Britain was seen by many Americans as a major—often the major—trade rival. That was how Roosevelt himself recalled the history of his ancestors of the Delano family in their commercial ventures in China; no doubt this sense of rivalry helped sharpen the President's pleasure when he scooped Canton and Enderbury islands in the late 1930s, despite the counter-claims of the British.[58] This idea of rivalry could also colour other issues arising between the two countries. Henry Wallace, for example, was to comment on this after listening to a friend of both Roosevelt and Churchill, Bernard Baruch, 'hold forth at some length about the bitter-mouthed Englishmen all the time advancing hypocritical arguments, so that they could get in position to exploit subject peoples. In his argument', continued Wallace, 'I was never quite sure whether Baruch was more concerned in getting rid of British competition so American businessmen could make more money, or more interested in the subject peoples.'[59]*

* It is unlikely that many Americans realized that Britain's dependent Empire provided only 1 per cent of her income on the eve of the Second World War. See Gupta, *Imperialism*

Suspicion that Britain would steal an unfair advantage—for example in South American export markets—also lay behind some of the troubles which were to arise over the supply of Lend Lease materials, and over the level of gold and dollar reserves which Britain would be permitted to accumulate while receiving Lend Lease aid.[60] In addition, a feeling of rivalry, together with bitter memories of how slender United States reserves of tin and rubber had become as war approached, sharpened American views on access to and the regulation of the supply of raw materials. In this context we shall see below the effect of wartime American opposition to the international regulation of tin production by Britain and others, and, even more, to the 1938 International Rubber Regulation agreement and the Committee which carried it out. (Jesse Jones, for example, whom Roosevelt made overseer of the American synthetic-rubber programme, charged that the I.R.R.C. were responsible for the shortage in the U.S.A. at the outbreak of war.)[61]

The question of markets had already arisen during the preparation of the Atlantic Charter. On that occasion, the American draft of clause four— 'They will endeavour to further enjoyment by all peoples of access, without discrimination and on equal terms, to the markets and to the raw materials of the world which are needed for their economic prosperity'—was changed at Churchill's insistence, and despite State Department opposition, to: 'They will endeavour, with due respect for their existing obligations, to further the enjoyment of all states . . . of access, on equal terms, to the trade and to the raw materials which are needed for their economic prosperity.' Churchill had in mind, of course, Britain's imperial preferences under the Ottawa agreements, and also the potential splits, noted above, within the Conservative party over this issue, even though he was not personally wedded to the Ottawa structure. ('My own view', he wrote to Eden at the end of August 1941, 'is that there can be no great future for the world without a vast breaking down of tariffs and other barriers. The United States, which will be more than ever the world's creditor, although hitherto the worst offender in tariff matters, seems now disposed to promote a policy of reduction. If this mood were implemented it would be natural that the measures which we have been forced to take should also be thrown into the common pot.') Hull, however, was bitterly disappointed at this Atlantic Charter setback to his crusade for a new world order based on multilateral trade—an order which would include, for example, an open door for the U.S.A. into the economies of Eastern Europe.[62] Future disagreements were facilitated by the self-consoling way in which the American side chose to interpret the Prime Minister's reservation, as referring, in the words of Sumner Welles the Under Secretary of State, merely to 'temporary impediments.'[63]

This matter of post-war trade patterns continued to give rise to friction when it appeared in article 7 of the Mutual Aid Agreement, mentioned earlier. Although Keynes, who did most of the negotiating for Britain, was beginning to change his own views in a multilateralist direction, there was

and the British Labour Movement, 245, and in general on the burden, rather than asset, of the Empire to Britain, C. Barnett, *The Collapse of British Power* (London, 1972).

considerable alarm within the State Department over what was seen as the likely adoption by Britain after the war of a deliberate policy of 'bilateral commercial and economic arrangements with foreign countries.'[64] Churchill's own reluctance to see the matter brought to a head exasperated officials in Washington: 'The qualities which produce the dogged, unbeatable courage of the British', wrote one of them later, 'personified at the time in Winston Churchill, can appear in other settings as stubbornness bordering on stupidity.'[65]* On the British side, Amery, noted above as leading the opposition to article 7, regarded Hull as 'a complete crank and a fanatic on the subject of the most-favoured-nation clause . . . He will try to do everything to get us to abandon inter-imperial preference as well as to prevent Europe coming together as an economic commonwealth. In that way he is a real danger, not only to the cohesion and economic development of our own Commonwealth, but to the prospects of world recovery.'[66] It is hardly surprising to find that when the Agreement, including article 7, was eventually signed in February 1942, there were to be considerable differences of interpretation between London and Washington regarding the degree to which Britain was now committed to abandon imperial preference.[67]

The third point of the Atlantic Charter, in which Britain and the United States declared their respect for 'the right of all peoples to choose the form of government under which they will live', has already been mentioned as causing difficulties within British official circles. (Indeed, in 1945 Richard Law, by then Minister of State at the Foreign Office, was to observe in exasperation that 'the Atlantic Charter has got us into difficulties mainly, I think, because as far as I can make out, nobody at any time believed in it. On our side, and, I think, probably on the American, it was mainly a dodge to get the U.S. a little bit further into the war . . .')[68] Like point four, point three of the Charter also provided a focus for differing approaches and assumptions between the two countries themselves. Churchill, as already indicated, chose to interpret this pledge mainly in terms of 'the nations of Europe now under the Nazi yoke', and to separate from it 'the progressive evolution of self-governing institutions in the regions and peoples which owe allegiance to the British Crown.'[69] It is clear that Roosevelt, on the other hand, as he later asserted publicly, always thought of the pledge and the Charter as a whole as having universal application. The President was by now, in contrast to the paternalist and Mahanite attitude he had adopted during his early days in politics, a confirmed opponent of imperialism, certainly of the European variety. (Harold Macmillan, for one, believed that Roosevelt was 'hostile—perhaps even jealous—' where the British Empire

* Caught between pressure from Washington on the one hand and the danger of a serious Cabinet split on the other, Churchill felt obliged at times to suggest to his colleagues that the President was less concerned over the issue than might appear to be the case. It was not the only time that he 'interpreted' and tempered American forcefulness in this way during the war. This was no doubt valuable in terms of maintaining as smooth a partnership as possible in the face of the enemy. It may, however, have helped to obscure important and lasting realities about Anglo-American relations that the Prime Minister himself preferred not to see.

was concerned.)[70] 'There never has been, there isn't now and there never will be', he had asserted to correspondents in March 1941, 'any race of people on earth fit to serve as masters of their fellow men ... We believe that any nationality, no matter how small, has the inherent right to its own nationhood.'[71] To a friend in 1942 who feared that the United States was assisting the cause of European imperialists, he was to remark, turning over his palm as he did so, 'Why, Pat, I can change all that at the proper time, as easily as this ...'[72] (This was by no means the only occasion when a hint of megalomania hovered around the President.)

Like many Americans, Roosevelt thought of his own country's handling of the Philippines and the pledged date of independence for those islands as 'a model' for other states to follow.* More basically, the abiding lesson of 1776 was sufficient to create in most Americans an instinctive hostility towards imperialism, and to suggest in their minds that in this respect Britain was the chief villain. At an individual level, the reactionary and lofty attitude of expatriate British living in imperial outposts sometimes reinforced this attitude, as it had for both General Stilwell and General Marshall, for example.[73] As for specific issues involving the British Empire, there were already those within the State Department who wished to see pressure put on Britain to grant India full Dominion status. For the moment these officials were not heeded, but not long after Pearl Harbour this question would threaten to bring about a serious breach between Roosevelt and Churchill themselves.

On the British side before December 1941 it was of course Churchill above all, half-American as he was, who sustained the idea of an intimate transatlantic partnership, with the President in the role of Britain's vital friend, and who entertained, in Sir Ian Jacob's later words, 'a vision of the ultimate conjunction of the English-speaking peoples, whose history he had nearly finished writing.'[74] Lord Lothian, too, as Ambassador in Washington before Halifax, had done much to further the cause of Anglo-American collaboration, being aware from the outbreak of war that the United States was crucial for both the defence of the British Empire in the East and the supply of armaments for use against Germany.[75] There were also others who shared Churchill's concern to see a full American involvement in international affairs. Amery, for example, for all his hostility to Hull's commercial designs, was envisaging a special bond between the two states whereby a limited period of residence would qualify Americans and British for full civic rights in each other's countries.[76] Attlee, too, wrote on his return from a visit to the U.S.A. in November 1941:

'In talking with Ministers especially interested such as the Vice President,

---

* One must add, however, that it was perfectly possible for an American to be strongly opposed to granting independence to the Philippines in the foreseeable future, and yet at the same time be a fierce opponent of all European imperialism. Patrick Hurley, a former Secretary of War who had also been a Brigadier General during the 1917–18 war, and who was to become Ambassador to China in 1944, was a case in point. See R. Buhite, *Patrick Hurley and American Foreign Policy* (Ithica, N.Y., 1973), 69, 81.

the Secretary of State and Mr. Welles, I did not find it difficult to agree with them in their general approach to post-war problems, such as social security and nutrition . . . It is, I think, most desirable that the American people should get accustomed to thinking of themselves as bound, through the facts of the situation, to take a big share of responsibility for the post-war settlement and as jointly concerned with us to maintain the democratic way of life. The more they envisaged the end the more must they provide the means.'[77]

Indeed, there were those in Whitehall and Westminster who, during the darkest moments of the war against Hitler, had foreseen the need for Britain to accept a completely subordinate role in relation to the might of the U.S.A. Thus Stafford Cripps—who by 1942 would be giving vent to resentment at American high-handedness—was in June 1940 envisaging a post-war world consisting of four main groups: an Asiatic one under Japan or Japan and China; a Euro-Asiatic one under the Soviet Union; a European group under 'one major European power' (can he have meant Germany?), and an American one under the United States. As possibly 'the only practical and permanent method of saving Anglo-Saxon civilisation', thought Cripps, Britain would go in with the United States. 'No doubt', he added, 'the centre of gravity of political life of the two countries would shift to the American continent, and Great Britain would become merely the European outpost of an Anglo-Saxon group largely controlled in the West.'[78] Moreover, even if so dramatic a solution as that contemplated by the joyless Cripps proved to be unnecessary, it was already becoming apparent to many in London that in any diplomatic confrontation between themselves and Washington, the latter would hold most of the major cards. For Cherwell, for example, advising Churchill over the article 7 dispute, this was the final and decisive argument:

'America is well aware of our balance of trade difficulties', he wrote in September 1941, 'and well appreciates that if we are to cooperate [in establishing world trade on a multilateral basis] we must be helped through the difficult [post-war] period, by some credit or Lease-Lend arrangement. To annoy her and perhaps sacrifice her cooperation, merely in order to retain a free hand to extend these undesirable [bilateral] practices, would surely be disastrous pusillanimity . . . It seems that the time has come for us to abandon our suspicions and decide to play in with the Americans. It is in our interest to do so: for with their vast gold holdings and lending power they will easily win in the long run if both countries compete to capture trade on a narrow bilateral basis.'[79]

Yet the 'suspicions' of which Cherwell wrote remained. Could one, for example, trust a future President or future Congress to hold down American tariffs once Britain had pledged herself to abandon imperial preference? There were also moments of tension and resentment over the extent of the facilities in the West Indies which were sought by the United States in exchange for giving Britain fifty old destroyers in 1940.[80] In a similar vein, this time concerning American demands for the maximum possible financial payments by Britain, including the shipment of gold from South Africa, in return for vital supplies, Beaverbrook wrote to Churchill in December 1940: 'They have conceded nothing. They have exacted payment to the uttermost for all they have done for us. They have taken our bases without valuable compensation. They have taken our gold. They have been given our secrets and offered us a thoroughly inadequate service in return.'[81] Even Churchill himself, although generally far more ready than Beaverbrook to believe that, in A. J. P. Taylor's words, 'the Americans were sentimentally attached to Great Britain as he himself felt towards France',[82] was prepared to bristle over this particular matter. 'Remember', he wrote to Halifax in March 1941, 'their lives are in this business too. We cannot always be playing up to minor political exigencies of Congress politics . . . God knows we are doing our bit.' To the Chancellor of the Exchequer he wrote: 'I am sure we will have to come to a showdown . . . As far as I can make out we are not only to be skinned but flayed to the bone . . .'[83]*

On the Prime Minister's part, such exasperation was never allowed to descend into pettiness or to obscure the bigger picture. (On this occasion, he could also entertain the consoling thought that, when it came to 'getting [the Americans] hooked a little firmer', 'the power of the debtor [was] in the ascendant', especially when he was doing the fighting.) But in some quarters, the resentment went deeper. R. A. Butler, for example, as Parliamentary Under Secretary of State at the Foreign Office, recalled what he described as America's 'betrayal over the League of Nations', and raised the possibility that she might again 'rat on us.' 'At present', he observed, 'it appears that the Anglo-Saxon (Rhodes) ideal is the finest before us. I feel this deeply, yet I intend to approach the ideal realising that my country is, for the second time, doing America's fighting for her, and that my country has more right than wrong on her side.'[84] 'We will never do any good with the United States propaganda', Sir Herbert Williams, M.P., was to write in 1942, 'until we stand up to the Americans. They suffer from a permanent inferiority complex, and the reason they dislike us is because they realise their inferiority. The more we suck up to them the more they dislike us.'[85] Talking to Dalton in July 1942, Sir Arthur Salter, recently returned from working in the U.S.A. on supply matters, was to put such sentiments as Butler's into broader perspective. 'I say', noted Dalton afterwards, 'that I sense in certain circles, both at the F[oreign] O[ffice] and the Treasury, an anti-American prejudice. He says that this is very real. It is the jealousy of the old British governing class at the "passing of power." '[86]

Jealous or not, few British officials in this pre-Pearl Harbour period could remain wholly unaware of the growing significance for the fortunes of their

* See the later recollections of Churchill's aide, Desmond Morton: 'The U.S.A. had bled us white, charging wholly exorbitant prices for the very stuff of life, taking over British firms and capital in the U.S.A. at a tenth or even a hundredth of their true value, etc . . .' (Thompson, *Churchill and Morton*, 32.)

own country of American public opinion. To Lothian on the spot in Washington, it appeared, indeed, to be a vital factor. 'In this country', he wrote to Halifax in February 1940, 'owing to the constitutional equality of status of the Executive and the Legislature, it is public opinion itself which is continually decisive.'[87] Within the Foreign Office, that opinion, together with the pressure groups that tried to influence and use it,[88] were coming to be scanned and analysed with much care and anxiety, not merely for their immediate importance for the war ('the threatening attitude of Japan', ran one minute, 'has been of real help in awakening American opinion')[89], but also for their likely impact on the post-war situation.

'I have little doubt', wrote Professor T. Whitehead, who had pursued a university career in the United States and in consequence had been brought into the Foreign Office to advise on American opinion, 'but that America is likely to be fully in the war before very long, and that our two countries will pull together adequately for the duration; whether they will remain together at the armistice is another and very important question. This, as I see it, depends more on public opinion in the two countries than on formal relations between the Foreign Office and the State Department. Since our need for collaboration will be more apparently obvious than that of the Americans, probably the most vital single factor in our post-war collaboration will be the attitude which public opinion in America adopts towards us. I have already indicated that this attitude at the moment leaves much to be desired. It is, however, not beyond our powers to improve this substantially before the end of the war, and this is one of the most important tasks in front of us.'[90]

We have already observed how, in the Cabinet as well as in the Foreign Office, the state of American opinion was viewed with concern, particularly in the late summer and early autumn of 1941.[91] Professor Whitehead, for his part, reported in November that 'during all the years I have known America, I have never known her so actively suspicious and distrustful of our country.' There were those in London, indeed, who gloomily believed that this element of American suspicion could never be dispelled entirely. 'I doubt whether the British will ever be popular in the United States', concluded one Foreign Office official. 'We may be admired, possibly at times envied, and individuals very frequently accepted and liked, but as a people we are suspected.'[92] One difficulty, as the Foreign Office saw it, was that American moods were 'essentially unstable.' 'The Americans, more than any other people', wrote the Head of the North American Department, 'are prone to emotionalism and exaggeration.' 'They really are the most mercurial people', noted Halifax, 'up and down all the time.'[93] They were also seen as reluctant to accept their responsibilities:

'In practice', wrote Whitehead, 'isolationism for Americans has always meant two things: first an intense dislike of political entanglements in any continent (particularly Europe) outside the Western Hemisphere. In the second place isolationism has signified a disinclination to acknowledge those international responsibilities which result from a given geographical and material position. These two tendencies are different facets of a persistent failure to recognise the inevitable connexion between . . . privilege and responsibility . . . It would be over-optimistic to suppose that so deep and widespread an attitude . . . will disappear overnight and be replaced by the steady exercise of collaboration . . .'[94]

Of course there were those Americans who, on their side of the Atlantic, were seeking to awaken their fellow countrymen to their responsibilities, as Whitehead called them. Henry Luce, for example, publisher of the magazine, *Life*, sought to do this in his article early in 1941 on 'The American Century', in which he lambasted the failure of the New Deal and challenged the United States to prove instead that free economic enterprise and 'American democracy' could create 'a vital, international economy and . . . an international moral order.' 'In any sort of partnership with the British Empire', wrote Luce, 'Great Britain is perfectly willing that the U.S.A. should assume the role of senior partner . . . With due regard for the varying problems of the members of the British Commonwealth, what we want will be okay with them.'[95]

Such an attitude, however, for all its welcome interventionist spirit, engendered additional anxieties in the minds of some British observers. Sir Ronald Campbell, for example, Minister in the Washington Embassy, posed in August 1941 the question of how Britain could achieve a partnership with the United States without at the same time being politically and economically swamped, especially since 'the British Commonwealth will be much exhausted by the war and deeply indebted to the United States, who are likely to be at the height of their mobilised strength.' Campbell discerned, among the various strands of American opinion, 'a continuing, though vague, desire (or assumption of a destiny) to inherit the influence and power of Great Britain and the Commonwealth'; although he 'did not believe that either Government or people at present wish to reduce the British Commonwealth to a subordinate position', he warned nevertheless that 'our vigilance must be unceasing to forestall the emergence of any such desire. In my judgment', he added with reference to the article 7 issue, 'the desire might well emerge if we failed to make any effort to respond to the United States Government in respect of economic matters so near to the heart of the Administration and the people of America.'[96]

Even aside from economic issues, some officials in London felt that Americans wanted a clearer statement of Britain's war aims. 'We have failed to tell them', wrote Whitehead, 'that we are engaged in doing something more than saving what they regard as our conservative skins; they do not know that we also have had some kind of moral rebirth and that, like them, we are facing the future in an idealistic mood.'[97] There were difficulties in the way of attempting something in this direction, however. One was the sheer pressure of events. ('Under present circumstances', observed one of Whitehead's colleagues, 'when we are hanging on by the skin of our teeth, all we can do is to deal with day-to-day problems.') There was also the great danger of appearing to be prompting Americans to undertake some kind of action, in which connection Lothian had uttered a firm warning: 'The one fatal thing for us', he had written in 1940, 'is to offer the United States advice as to what she ought to do . . . Anything which looks like British propaganda designed to influence American policy creates a cold fury in the American mind.'[98] Attlee repeated the warning in November 1941, asserting that 'our own friends in America are our best propagandists', and that it was 'a mistake to send out large numbers of persons to make generalised speeches to public meetings.'[99]

Nevertheless, the British publicity services in the United States came under greater scrutiny as concern increased over the standing of Britain in American eyes, and as suggestions were heard that all was far from well with the organizations in question. (Joseph Alsop, the American columnist, privately described the British Library of Information in New York in 1941 as 'a sort of hive of epicene and depressing young men whose energies are strained to the limit by the composition of pro-British news releases which no one reads and which are not one-tenth as effective as the weekly German news-letter.')[100] The outcome, in May 1941, was the appointment of Sir Gerald Campbell as Director General of a reorganized publicity machine. In the event, this move did not put an end to friction in the area, for example between the Foreign Office and Ministry of Information;[101] nor did it of itself remedy the accompanying problem, which had been commented upon by Geoffrey Crowther of the *Economist* among others, that 'far too many—probably a majority—of the servants of His Majesty's Government do not make themselves liked in the United States . . . [where] reserve can easily be seen as superior disdain.'[102] Campbell's appointment did, however, mark the beginning of a new effort to build a partnership that would rest on as wide a basis as possible within the United States. As Nevile Butler put it in a Foreign Office minute: 'We must keep the conception of an "American front" before us.'[103] In the months and years ahead, no issues on that front would present more difficulties than those involving the war in the Far East. And in that connection, as we shall see, it was a 'front' where, by August 1945, most of the Foreign Office officials involved would deem their efforts over the previous four years to have been in vain.

Meanwhile, aside from the Far East, there was already, by the end of 1941, some foreshadowing of difficulties to come in respect of the relations of the two English speaking states with third parties. In February 1942, indeed, Cordell Hull would be regarding the British as being 'in a very bad way and very stupid' over not only Asian affairs, but also where the Soviet Union and Vichy France were concerned.[104] The Vichy issue, and Britain's espousal of de Gaulle, had in fact been a matter for obsessive irritation and anger on the part of the Secretary of State since 1940, and brought him to the point of 'almost resigning' in January 1942 when Roosevelt declined to put pressure on London over the matter.[105] From Vichy itself, the stolid Admiral William

Leahy, as American Ambassador, soon to be Chief of Staff to the President in the latter's capacity as Commander in Chief, developed not only anti-Gaullist views and an expectation of chaos in post-war France, but also scorn for British 'stupidity.'[106] On the other side, despite Churchill's frequent exasperation with de Gaulle, the Foreign Office maintained the view that the General represented the best hope of bringing about the revived and friendly France which Britain badly needed, and London had officially recognized him in June 1940 as 'the leader of all free Frenchmen wherever they may be.'[107] The brief episode at the end of 1941, when Gaullist forces, to the fury of Hull but not of Britain, seized the Vichy-held islands of St. Pierre and Miquelon off the coast of Newfoundland,[108] brought out the underlying difference of approach between London and Washington. We shall see later that, in the Far East, the question of the future status of Indochina was to do the same, if less dramatically, during the war against Japan.

When Hull and others looked at British policies towards France, they branded them, not only as misguided in themselves, but as a symptom of the deeper malaise mentioned earlier, namely a persistent inclination to play what was termed 'power politics', to seek to 'balance' power in Britain's interest by forming blocs or at least special understandings and 'spheres of interest.' Thus, it was with this in mind that Washington carefully and anxiously watched Eden's visit to Moscow in December 1941, the fear on this occasion being that London might agree to Soviet territorial demands which would infringe the Atlantic Charter.[109] Later, there was to be even more concern lest Britain should eventually bring about a conflict with the Soviet Union through the formation of rival blocs in Europe. The relevant factor for our study of the Far East is the same in each case: that is, the underlying American belief that Britain was inclined to play the international game according to a different, dangerous and corrupt set of rules from those observed by a disinterested and enlightened United States. It was an issue which was to become entangled with that of the strategic and military conduct of the war against the Axis. In Southeast Asia, for example, as in the Mediterranean, British strategy would frequently be dismissed or opposed by Washington for this underlying reason.

Nevertheless, the strains and potential difficulties which existed between Britain and the United States on the eve of the war with Japan were problems between two countries who were already, in Robert Sherwood's well-known phrase, 'common-law allies': that is, allies by reason of their conduct rather than as a result of official signatures to that effect.[110] In other words, the foundations had already been laid for what has rightly been described as 'an integration of effort of truly astonishing proportions between two completely independent countries' (accepting, for the moment, that war-time Britain can be described as 'completely independent').[111] The greatest symbol of this partnership was undoubtedly the Lend Lease Act of March 1941, the culminating response of the United States, and above all of President Roosevelt, to the mounting British appeals for assistance after the fall of France in the summer of 1940.[112]

There are, it is true, certain riders which should be added when this 1941 Lend Lease measure is mentioned. For example, the volume of such aid before Pearl Harbour, both absolutely and proportionately, was as yet not great. In 1940, Britain had produced 83 per cent of all munitions used by the Commonwealth and Empire, and in 1941 the figure actually rose to 84 per cent. (Even for the war as a whole, it was to be as high as 69·5 per cent.) Similarly, the actual dollar value of aid to the Empire during the period March to December 1941 was barely one-thirtieth of the total that was to be achieved by the end of the war.[113] Nor was the transaction an entirely disinterested one. It was, indeed, 'an Act to promote the defense of the United States', and played an invaluable part in gearing-up American industry to meet its own country's war-time requirements.[114] Moreover, although the American Administration was coming to Britain's aid in remarkable fashion, 'Roosevelt and his Cabinet', in the words of a historian of Lend Lease, 'were determined not to fight the war for British goals', and in addition, as we have seen, drove a hard bargain over the price that Britain must pay in terms of her assets in the United States.[115]

Yet despite these features of Lend Lease, and despite also the reciprocal aid given by the British Commonwealth and Empire to the U.S.A. (as a proportion of national incomes, in fact, total American Lend Lease and U.K. reciprocal aid figures were almost identical)*, what stood out already by the end of 1941 was the degree of Britain's dependence on the United States. Without the industrial and financial might of America behind her, Britain would be faced with a task—defeating Germany and Italy—that would be quite beyond her.† As early as May 1940, the Chiefs of Staff had bluntly informed the Cabinet in London of this fact.[116] From that date, too, financial caution had been cast aside in order to obtain vital supplies from North America, with the result that, by the end of 1940, gold and dollar reserves had fallen drastically. During 1941, likewise, disinvestment and borrowing abroad amounted to £820 million, whilst capital equipment and stocks in the U.K. fell by over £350 million.[117] From September 1939 to June 1945, indeed, Britain's external disinvestment (including the rise in her external debt and the decline in her gold and dollar reserves) was to amount to £4,198 million, her total loss of national wealth being about £30,000 million, or a quarter of the pre-war figure.[118] Moreover, the very terms of the original Lend Lease Act, by asserting U.S. property rights in the articles and services that were transferred, and by looking ahead to some form of repayment, helped to fix in many American minds the notion of being owed

---

* The U.K. alone received $27,625 million of Lend Lease aid during the war; it contributed £1·896 million in reciprocal aid, of which £1,201·2 million went to the U.S.A. (i.e. about $5·667 million). W. Hancock and M. Gowing, *British War Economy* (London, 1949), 377.

† At the end of 1940, for example, German-occupied areas had a steel-producing capacity of 212 million ingot tons; the capacity of the British Commonwealth was 18·5 million, and of the U.S.A. 50 million. H. D. Hall, *North American Supply* (London, 1955), 206.

something—a notion that echoed the discordant history of First World War debts and that was to hang over the Anglo-American relationship throughout this new conflict. (75 per cent of the Americans polled in February 1942 believed that Britain should eventually repay the U.S.A. for Lend Lease war material, and this figure was to increase over the following three years.)[119] In the words of one student of the subject, 'from 1942 to the end of the war, Lend Lease kept alive an obsolete theory of inequality which was incompatible with the principles of full partnership and equality of sacrifice that inspired the common war.'[120]

If Roosevelt thus failed in his stated intention to 'eliminate the dollar sign', it had been equally fictitious of Churchill to promise the United States that if they 'gave Britain the tools' she would 'finish the job.' Not only did Britain need American aid to defend herself against Germany; she had no prospect of actually defeating Hitler without a full American entry into the war. Privately, British officials and politicians were admitting as much. Bombing and blockade would not be sufficient. Nor was it enough that Roosevelt had taken over the defence of Greenland and Iceland, exchanged old destroyers for long-leases on British bases in the Western Hemisphere, and extended American patrol zones far out into the Atlantic. As a section of the British Joint Planning Staff wrote in June 1941, 'The active belligerency of the United States has become essential for the successful prosecution and conclusion of the war.'[121] Hence Churchill's subsequent judgment that Japan's attack on Pearl Harbour had been 'a blessing' for Britain, and had ensured ultimate victory.

It would be quite insufficient to describe the complex network of Anglo-American relations at any time in terms of official machineries alone. A full investigation of the relationship as it stood in December 1941 would have to embrace, for example, contacts long established in the worlds of scholarship and of business; it would make use of not only Foreign Office and State Department despatches, but the letters exchanged between, say, Beaverbrook and Roy Howard of the Scripps Howard press group in the United States, or between Felix Frankfurter and Harold Laski. It would include within its compass institutions like the Council on Foreign Relations in New York and the Royal Institute of International Affairs ('Chatham House'); it would observe a small factor such as the respect accorded by American specialists to Sir George Sansom, the British scholar-diplomat, as a result of his studies of Japanese culture and society; in wider circles, it would have to attempt to assess the effects of, say, the Anglophobia of a newspaper like the *Chicago Tribune*.

Here, however, no more will be done than simply to offer this brief reminder of the existence of such relations in non-official spheres. And even where the official side of things is concerned, students would do well to refer to more detailed works on such bodies as the British Supply Council in North America, under the vital leadership of Arthur Purvis; to explore the collaboration achieved in the field of economic planning, where, 'within the limits of "all aid short of war", the United States Administration [had] intermeshed its policies with British policies with a comprehensiveness which has seldom been surpassed by full military allies'; or to examine the work of Harry Hopkins as adviser to the President on Lend Lease.[122] In the military sphere, local collaboration such as that between Chennault and the British authorities in Burma and Singapore, and staff talks of the kind held in Washington early in 1941, have already been mentioned.

Secrets of various kinds were also being exchanged across the Atlantic well before Pearl Harbour. When Hopkins was in London early in 1941, for example, an F.B.I. member of his party had talks with British Secret Service authorities, and there exists in Hopkins' papers to this day complete lay-outs of both Britain's intelligence organizations as a whole and, in detail, including names, of M.I.5. (the security service for Britain itself).[123] In the field of foreign intelligence, William Stephenson, Head of British Security Coordination (B.S.C.) in the U.S.A., was making available to Hoover's F.B.I., despite friction between B.S.C. and that body, information gathered by Britain's Secret Intelligence Service (M.I.6.). Stephenson was also cooperating closely with William Donovan, the President's Coordinator of Information,[124] and according to his latest biographer was sharing with Roosevelt and Donovan the fruits of Britain's 'Ultra' capability of breaking major German military codes.[125] British researchers were also cooperating with the American team who were working on their 'Magic' elucidation of Japan's main codes,[126] while overall B.S.C. were later able to record that 'as much as six months before Pearl Harbour we had secured full American participation and collaboration in secret activities directed against the enemy throughout the world.'[127]

As a reminder that such trust and collaboration was not absolute, however, it can also be revealed that Britain in the pre-Pearl Harbour period had succeeded in breaking at least one of the codes used by the State Department itself. For in a letter to Roosevelt of 25 February 1942 (which he vainly requested the President to burn after reading), Churchill was to admit as much:

'Some time ago', he wrote, '. . . our experts claimed to have discovered the system and constructed some tables used by your Diplomatic Corps. From the moment when we became allies [i.e., presumably, in December 1941], I gave instructions that this work should cease. However, danger of our enemies having achieved a measure of success cannot, I am advised, be dismissed.'[128]

Likewise, some, but not all, vital secrets of a military nature were being exchanged.[129] On atomic energy, for example, Roosevelt shared with Stephenson and Churchill the knowledge of how dangerous German achievements in this field could be; yet American feelers for 'very close collaboration' over nuclear research were treated 'somewhat coolly' in London and were not taken up[130]—a policy that by 1943, when the United States effort in this sphere had caught up and surpassed that of Britain, would appear to have been over-confident and insouciant. This is, indeed, but one example of a changing awareness of the relative strengths and bargaining positions of the two countries, which will form an important contextual element of our Far Eastern analysis.

Within that same analysis, some of the material will, of course, concern the diplomatic machineries of Britain and the United States. It is important at the outset, therefore, to make it clear that the position of the professional diplomat was not the same within the war-time administrations of the two countries, and that cooperation and coordination between the two was handicapped as a result. Once the United States became a belligerent, Hull called upon the State Department to cooperate fully with the American War and Navy Departments, in a way which helped to ensure that his own organization would play a relatively ineffectual role. 'The war had come', he observed to a colleague, '[and] it was now a military and naval responsibility.'[131] More important still was Roosevelt's own lack of sympathy for the Foreign Service (he observed privately that Hull had failed to 'clean up the State Department').[132] The President could not afford an open break with his Secretary of State, given the latter's powerful standing with Congress and his reputation as a man of integrity, but he frequently ignored him in his top-level war-time policy-making, and even when he had to deal with the State Department, often did so, until 1943, through the Under Secretary, Sumner Welles, thus exacerbating the friction that existed between Welles and Hull.[133] Hull himself was left to trail along, a somewhat sad figure, eager, like Coleridge's Ancient Mariner, to pour out to a listener his tale of how the failure of the 1941 Japanese-American negotiations had been none of his doing, or to reiterate his passionate faith in multilateral and low-tariff trade as the key to a better world.

Roosevelt meanwhile treated many of his official Ambassadors with something between contempt and indifference, preferring to develop other channels of communication. Thus, as regards China in 1941, he was employing T. V. Soong and the ambitious Laughlin Currie (one of his own administrative assistants) to maintain contact with Chiang Kai-shek;[134] similarly in London, Winant as Ambassador, inarticulate, but a shrewd observer of the British scene, was reduced to asking Hopkins plaintively to help him to be made some use of and to be kept in the picture, the President preferring to use Hopkins himself and, on a longer-term basis, Averell Harriman, as his main contacts with Churchill.[135] The bulk of the Roosevelt-Churchill messages, in fact, went through the Map Room which the President had established within the White House, and were not known even to Hull.[136] Moreover, the Secretary of State was later to be refused access to the papers arising from a major inter-Allied conference like the one held at Casablanca, while the State Department were to receive no copy of, for example, the 1944 Churchill-Roosevelt agreement on atomic-weapons development, or of the Yalta agreement on the Far East.[137] 'The President runs foreign affairs', observed Hull sourly to Morgenthau in 1943. 'I don't know what's going on. I have to find out from Halifax what's going on between the President and

Churchill.'[138] Small wonder that, by October 1944, Hull would be determined to resign, 'tired of intrigue . . . tired of being by-passed . . . tired of being relied upon in public and ignored in private.'[139]

Thus, the State Department drifted on, in Dean Acheson's later words,

'without direction, composed of a lot of busy people working hard and usefully but as a whole not functioning as a Foreign Office. It did not chart a course to be furthered by the success of our arms, or to aid or guide our arms. Rather it seemed to have been adrift, carried hither and yon by the currents of war or pushed about by collisions with more purposeful craft.'[140]*

In Washington, the Far Eastern Division did not in any case possess the indefinable prestige of the European Division, and there were to be clashes between the two where their spheres of competence overlapped in the area of European colonial territories in Asia. In the field, American diplomats, even those of the standing of Harriman, were often left in ignorance of relevant events or policies.

'I find the British Foreign Office', wrote Harriman to Roosevelt from London, 'has a well-developed method of keeping its ambassadors informed of developments of policy the world over, whereas it seems to me that our State Department informs each ambassador on matters relating only directly to his particular country. As far as I personally am concerned, I have had . . . cables only in direct answer to specific questions. Aside from this my source of information is entirely from the British Ministries.'[141]

This lack of professional efficiency within the American diplomatic machine was not new. It was, however, only a part of a generally chaotic situation in Washington, where Halifax in lordly fashion likened trying to deal with Government departments to 'a disorderly day's rabbit shooting.'[142] Roosevelt, 'a great spiritual figure' in the eyes of Hopkins and many others,[143] was nevertheless a poor administrator, ends, not means, being what concerned him.† It was also part of his method of working to see to it that none of those around him possessed a complete picture of what was going on. As one historian has put it, 'he always thrived on disarray.'[144] This made it all the easier for him to play off one subordinate against another; doubtless it also appealed to his 'relish for power and command', as Dean Acheson has called it.[145] The situation was not improved by the strong element of sycophancy that existed in the circles closest to the President (Adolf Berle, for

* 'More purposeful craft' included the War Department's planning staff, where the distrust of Britain among Major General Embick and his colleagues has been noted above (see *Pogue*, I, 132–3), and the senior officers of the U.S. Navy in Washington, led by Admiral King, whose fundamentally anti-British stance will be encountered frequently in what follows.

† 'I seek an end', Roosevelt had observed in 1925, 'and do not care a rap about the methods of procedure.' Range, *Roosevelt's World Order*, 29.

example, was in the habit of writing to him as 'dear Caesar'),* nor by the patronizing joviality, sometimes amounting to flippancy, with which Roosevelt for his part often conducted business.[146]

In observing this characteristic of the President, one should not overlook the remarkable fortitude which he had long displayed in the face of infantile paralysis,[147] nor the need for someone in his position to make light of burdens and problems if he were to survive. ('Strictly between ourselves', he wrote to Frankfurter, 'I have little sympathy with Copernicus. He looked through the right end of the telescope, thus greatly magnifying his problems. I use the wrong end of the telescope and it makes things much easier to bear.')[148] Likewise, the vast extent of those burdens of Roosevelt's needs to be borne in mind when one finds Judge Rosenman, a close personal aide, despairing in 1942 of what he termed the President's 'complacency.' Roosevelt, he was to tell Morgenthau then, 'doesn't devote more than two days a week to the war. I have tried one month to get him to look at this Executive Order, and you heard him [procrastinating] this morning. I have been up at Shangri-la [Roosevelt's weekend retreat] three times, and he sits there playing with his stamps . . .'[149]

Yet whatever allowances are made, the result of the President's methods was what Stimson privately called 'the topsy-turvy, upside-down system of poor administration [by] which Mr. Roosevelt runs the Government.'[150] Stimson himself, as Secretary of War, met regularly with Knox of the Navy and Hull, but their consultations had little connection with ultimate, Presidential decisions. As for Cabinet meetings, they were neither minuted nor treated as decision-making occasions, and were frequently reduced to a rambling monologue by Roosevelt. Indeed, the wonder is that business ever got done at all.[151]

The resulting nature of the American Administration often created frustration among British negotiators in Washington, where they would find their opposite numbers initially confused and divided among themselves, and never able to commit their Government without a Presidential directive.[152] As Keynes inimitably expressed it in a warning to the British Cabinet:

'Remember that, in a negotiation lasting weeks, the situation is entirely fluid up to the last minute. Everything you are told, even with the greatest appearance of authority and decision, is provisional, without commitment . . . There is no orderly progression towards the final conclusion . . . I liken them to bees who for weeks will fly around in all directions with no ascertainable destination, providing both the menace of stings and the hope of honey; and at last, perhaps because the queen in the White Hive has emitted some faint, indistinguishable odour, suddenly swarm to a single spot in a compact, inpenetrable bunch.'[153]

* Lord Coleraine, who, as Richard Law, Minister of State at the Foreign Office, encountered Roosevelt on several occasions (the latter spoke admiringly of Law to others), has recalled in conversation with the author that what struck him most about the President's face was that it suggested a man who was 'corrupted by power.'

By contrast, the British machinery of war-time administration was already, by the end of 1941, operating in a far more efficient fashion, controlled and stimulated by the driving energy of Churchill, who, in Ronald Lewin's phrase, 'unashamedly enjoyed power—and war.'[154] The Prime Minister's own position at this time was still a towering one: the man who had saved the country in 1940, whose genius shone out across the free and would-be-free world, and whose scope for initiative had not yet been circumscribed by the full impact of Soviet and American power. Many well-placed observers, indeed, believed that only Churchill counted for something in the Government of Britain. 'He is the directing force behind the strategy and the conduct of the war in all its essentials', cabled Hopkins to Roosevelt,[155] while Harriman, as another Presidential emissary, did not find much to impress him at this time among the Prime Minister's colleagues. 'As you well know', he was to write to Hopkins in March 1942, 'Atlee [sic] is a man of small capabilities. He does not lead the Labour Party. It leads him.'[156] Harriman, who was busy developing his own, intimate connections in London, was also to inform the President in the same month that

'There is no other man in sight to give the British the leadership that Churchill does. Cripps wears the hair shirt and wants everyone else to do the same. [The] British are prepared to make any sacrifice to get on with the war, but are not interested in sacrifice for its own sake . . . Eden you know all about. Anderson is an uninspired, competent technician. Bevin has never really risen above labor union politics. And then we have Max [Beaverbrook]! There is no one else on the horizon.'[157]

One visitor to London whom Harriman had earlier, in the summer of 1941, found valuable in this context was Menzies, then Prime Minister of Australia. 'He was one of the few men' reported Harriman, 'who talked up to the Prime Minister.'[158] Menzies himself, as we have seen, had, on his return to Canberra, described Churchill's colleagues in somewhat scornful terms.[159] Like the Australian High Commissioner in London, Stanley Bruce, he also spoke strongly in the same vein to Sir Maurice Hankey, one member of the British Government who agreed that the Prime Minister had become over-mighty.[160] 'The sheep baa'ed in chorus', noted Cadogan after attending a Cabinet meeting at which Churchill had again insisted on having his own way,[161] and indeed there exist ample records of the time to bear out Lord Normanbrook's subsequent observation, that the Prime Minister 'was not much interested to hear what others had to say.'[162] Despite the existence of the Cabinet's Defence Committee, Churchill's colleagues were apparently increasingly content to leave the running of the war to him and the Chiefs of Staff, among whom Sir John Dill, as C.I.G.S., confessed himself to Hankey to be 'profoundly disturbed' about the Prime Minister.[163] 'This is in essence a one-man government, so far as the conduct of the war is concerned', wrote Amery privately, 'subject to a certain amount of conversation in Cabinet.'[164]

Yet for all Churchill's manifest egocentricity and relish for power,* it has

* See Major Desmond Morton's recollection of Churchill's inability to enter into the

rightly been observed that no one was ever dismissed simply for standing up to Churchill, whose burden of responsibility surpassed the imagination, let alone the capacity, of most men,[165] and with whom the Chiefs of Staff, led by Dill's successor, General Sir Alan Brooke, were able, by dint of perpetual watchfulness, to establish and maintain an acceptable, if strained, working relationship.[166] And as we shall see, Harriman, amongst other observers, was soon to be highly concerned over the temporary impairment of the Prime Minister's position which arose from the military disasters of early 1942.

As for the Foreign Office, although Churchill had little love for it, and treated it—as he treated the military planners—with suspicion,[167] it was at least able to contribute more directly than did the State Department to the shaping and execution of war-time policies. After difficulties which lasted until 1942, means were to be found of harmonizing the Prime Minister's direct communications with the President with the more regular procedures of diplomacy,[168] while Eden, as Foreign Secretary, played a far more significant role in the conduct of inter-Allied relations than did Hull. In general, the exchange of information and formulation of advice proceeded as efficiently as during the pre-war years, and in less oppressive circumstances than those that had brought about the eclipse of the Foreign Office when Chamberlain was Prime Minister.

Yet there remained limits, set above all by Churchill's own predilections or inactivity, beyond which the Foreign Office could not influence current British policies. We shall observe this in respect of the Far East, in which the Prime Minister had little sustained interest. ('I must admit', he was to write to Eden in October 1942, 'that my thoughts rest primarily in Europe—the revival of the glory of Europe, the parent continent of the modern nations and of civilization', while at one point he was to refer to the Far East as 'those wild lands.')[169] Moreover, quite apart from divergencies between the Prime Minister and the Foreign Office over specific issues like the role and future of de Gaulle, there was a strong disposition on Churchill's part to concentrate on immediate, war-winning matters, and to look with impatience upon long-term and post-war subjects.* Thus, a lengthy memorandum on a

---

minds of others, and that 'his junior staff, with few, if any, exceptions, disliked him to the point of detestation. He treated them like "flunkeys", without apparent interest in them or humanity.' Morton, who was very close to the Prime Minister at the time, also suggested later that, not only did he have 'an overwhelming desire to dominate', but that he was capable, as in his dismissal of Wavell from command in the Middle East, of sinking to 'depths of selfish brutality' when dealing with more senior figures. Morton believed that Churchill 'heartily disliked any person whose personal character was such that he could not avoid, most unwillingly, feeling respect for that person.' (Thompson, *Churchill and Morton*, 71, 174.)

* Morton's recollection in this respect was that Churchill 'refused to think of the ensuing peace, of Communism, of world economics or anything else. He never even gave thought to international (or national) politics save in their immediate connection of winning the war.' This appears exaggerated in the light of documentary evidence but conveys the essence of the situation. (Thompson, *Churchill and Morton*, 123.)

'Four Power Plan' for a post-war international order, left at Chequers by Eden in October 1942, was to be subject to the Prime Ministerial comment: 'I hope that these speculative studies will be entrusted to those on whose hands time hangs heavy, and that we shall not overlook Mrs. Glass's Cookery Book recipe for Jugged Hare—"First catch your hare." ' As Eden, 'most disappointed' at this reply, pointed out, this was hardly the way to construct a sound foreign policy to carry Britain into the peace,[170] and by forming a Reconstruction Department under Gladwyn Jebb, the Foreign Office went on endeavouring to prepare for the future. It must be added, however, that even within the Office itself there remained a strong tendency to concentrate upon immediate issues. Cadogan, as Permanent Under Secretary, was, in his own words, highly averse to 'planning'—'it is to me as incomprehensible as futile'—[171], even though, by his own admission, the failure to undertake contingency planning after Munich had meant that the Foreign Office in the first part of 1939 had given 'the impression of a number of amateurs fumbling about with insoluble problems.'[172] We shall observe later that, for all its greater professionalism, the Foreign Office, partly as a result of Cadogan's discouraging attitude and partly due to the role played by Sir Maurice Peterson as the Assistant Under Secretary responsible for the area, had fallen far behind the State Department by the later stages of the war, when it came to formulating ideas about the future of various territories in the Far East.

The Foreign Office had also been criticized by Ernest Bevin in 1940 for being 'out of touch with the growing forces of Labour, Trade Unionism, and the socialist organisations of the world', a dissatisfaction that was in part to be reflected in the 1943 White Paper on the Foreign Service.[173] Others, too, were to find fault with the Foreign Office before reforms were initiated after the war.[174] Even so, the outbreak of hostilities in 1939 had resulted in various outsiders being brought in to assist in the work of the Office. These appointments, it is true, were not always a success—R. H. Tawney's unhappy attachment to the Washington Embassy in connection with labour and industrial affairs, for example—but we shall see other newcomers making a significant contribution: Professor Whitehead in the field of American affairs, for instance; and, where Far Eastern matters were concerned, G. F. Hudson of Oxford University, who, via the Foreign Office Research and Press Service (later to become the Foreign Office Research Department), set up by Chatham House and run by Arnold Toynbee, came to play an important part in internal debates.* In addition, Isaiah Berlin was to write a celebrated series of weekly political reports from the Embassy in Washington, where Halifax, successfully living down some early gaffes and his image as an

---

* The Far Eastern Department of the Foreign Office, however, like its counterpart in the State Department, did not have the prestige of, say, the one dealing with Western Europe, and contained within its ranks several 'country specialists' who, for all their expertise, belonged to the Consular Service, and were thus technically junior to all regular Foreign Service colleagues.

effete appeaser, presided in somewhat aloof and lazy fashion over a huge and complex outpost. (At one time during the war there were 9,000 British officials in Washington.)[175]

Halifax established good relations with leading members of the Roosevelt Administration, although Hull's moralizing outbursts could annoy him greatly, and despite the fact that, as we have seen, he was scornful of those American leaders who, in his opinion, were 'almost as afraid of [public opinion] as they are of the Germans.'[176] Meanwhile, within the Foreign Office itself, American affairs were of particular concern to Richard Law as Parliamentary Under Secretary of State and later Minister of State. Law (a son of Bonar Law) had worked in the United States for some years between the wars, and supplied in the upper levels of the Office an element of stability which was lacking in Eden's more testy and temperamental approach. Although the Foreign Secretary was admired by those who served him for his skill as a negotiator, there is evidence in both published and unpublished papers to suggest that he was far from universally popular among officials, and his minutes often have a petulant tone.[177] In addition, Eden made no pretence, in his own words, 'to understand Far Eastern affairs',[178] a factor which, together with the abrupt and unconstructive approach of Sir Maurice Peterson as the Assistant Under Secretary concerned, did not make it any easier for the Far Eastern Department to win greater interest and sustained attention for their problems and recommendations within Whitehall as a whole.

The vital link between Britain and the United States, however, was the one developed by the President and the Prime Minister themselves, with the help of Hopkins, Harriman and to a lesser extent Beaverbrook.[179] Isaiah Berlin has already drawn, in matchless fashion, a portrait of the two leaders in 1940:[180] Roosevelt, with 'his astonishing capacity for life and his apparently complete freedom from fear of the future'; Churchill, whose 'strongest sense is the sense of the past'; the former, a child of the twentieth-century New World, the latter of nineteenth-century Europe, 'not the herald of the bright and cloudless civilisation of the future.' 'Each appeared to the other', writes Sir Isaiah, 'in a romantic light high above the battles of allies or subordinates.' Certainly, that is substantially true of Churchill in 1940 and afterwards. 'My whole system', he was to write to Eden in 1942, 'is based upon partnership with Roosevelt',[181] and however exasperating the latter could be at times (as over Indian affairs), there must never be a word said against him in the Prime Minister's hearing, never a phrase unsuited to not only a great political leader and vital ally, but also a Head of State.[182]

Roosevelt, too, had in the early part of the war a great admiration and liking for Churchill. 'On the way back [from seeing the Prime Minister off from Washington in January 1942]', noted Hopkins, 'the President made it perfectly clear that he was very pleased with the meetings. There was no question but that he genuinely grew to like Churchill.'[183] When Roosevelt later cabled to the Prime Minister: 'It is fun to be in the same decade with you',[184] it reflected something of the nature of the partnership which Sir

Isaiah has sought to describe.* Yet that partnership was not approached in entirely the same fashion on both sides. Roosevelt, as we shall see, was before long ready to belittle Churchill behind his back, to Stalin, to Chiang Kai-shek and to American newsmen. He was ready to imitate him before advisers, in a way in which the edge of criticism was more noticeable than was affection.[185] 'Towards the end of the war', writes Lord Chandos, who, as Oliver Lyttelton, saw a good deal of the President, '. . . he became intensely jealous of Winston', while Morton, too, thought him 'jealous of . . . Winston's ebullience', and believed that he 'never trusted W[inston] a yard.'[186]

Certainly, senior British officials in contact with him were wary of Roosevelt. Halifax, for example, noticed his readiness to lie if it suited his purpose,[187] and described him to Dalton as untrustworthy, capable 'at any time [of playing] politics to our detriment.'[188] Halifax's Minister, Sir Ronald Campbell, likewise warned London that 'in the course of my general experience here [in Washington], I have seen not a few instances in which, even when this was not essential for the exigencies of the war, he has given a small impulsion to the wheel of fortune in such a way as to modify the position in America's favour but to our detriment.' Britain must not, added Campbell, expect 'generosity out of friendship for this country.' Richard Law, for his part, thought that Campbell was right, but, for fear of explosions, it was agreed not to print the despatch for circulation, or to send it to the Prime Minister.[189]

It was not that these officials would have thought of denying the immense amount which Britain owed to Roosevelt. Whether in a long-lasting matter such as Lend Lease, or a single episode like his providing new armour after the fall of Tobruk in 1942,[190] or in his general conviction of the need to support Britain against Hitler, the President was a great and well-nigh indispensable friend. There were, nevertheless, two features of the Anglo-American relationship which need adding to the familiar portrait of hands-across-the-sea, and which will become more pronounced as we move on towards the end of the war. One was the personal factor alluded to above. To Churchill, his friendship with and loyalty to the President were sacred, however much they may have been based upon hard political calculation.[191]† For the President, however, this was certainly not so to the same degree, and it may have been due in part to his awareness that, in an important respect, he was the lesser man of the two. For Churchill, although in one sense his entire life consisted of the playing out of a dramatic role, sustained by his

---

* William Hayter, as a First Secretary in the Washington Embassy, was wont to ask Isaiah Berlin on what evidence his reports were based, and whether a certain one was true. ' "It is true", the reply would come, "at a deeper level." ' Hayter, *A Double Life*, 69. Sir Isaiah has confirmed to the present writer that his interpretation of the Churchill-Roosevelt relationship could not be based upon detailed, first-hand evidence. He never met Roosevelt himself.

† Lord Coleraine, who saw Churchill in private shortly after the latter had received the news of Roosevelt's death, has recalled, in conversation with the author, that the Prime Minister seemed 'remarkably unmoved.'

imagination and dreams,* nevertheless possessed the strength of genuineness. Like him or not, approve of his policies or not, what those who met him encountered was the man himself with all his blazing, egocentric impact. As someone once remarked, 'he is an extraordinarily transparent creature', temperamentally unsuited to intrigue.[192] In Roosevelt's case, on the other hand, for all his political toughness, there was far more of a façade, a willingness to appear and to speak as his listener might be thought to wish it ('Eager to dominate yet reluctant to offend', as one historian has kindly put it), and this coupled with a facile bonhomie that Acheson among others found 'patronising and humiliating.'[193] Roosevelt was a great political animal, and in many ways he possessed more vision than Churchill. But in being less genuine and less loyal to his transatlantic partner, he was the smaller man. One feels that he knew it, and that he was not always comfortable with that knowledge.†

There was more to the matter, however, than personalities alone. To Stalin, Chiang Kai-shek and others, Roosevelt criticized not only Churchill but also Britain as a whole. In conferences with his Chiefs of Staff, for example, he echoed the kind of snide remarks (about, for instance, Britain's alleged profiteering from Lend Lease goods) which were the routine product of Anglophobes in the United States.[194] Furthermore, as we shall see, by the time the war was entering its later stages the Anglo-American partnership was not to have the same degree of priority in the President's mind that it had commanded at the outset. Moreover, in several important respects Roosevelt saw Churchill and his policies as major obstacles to some of the fundamental reforms—in the colonial field, for one—which he hoped to see achieved in the future. 'We will have more trouble with Great Britain after the war than we are having with Germany now', he observed to an adviser at the end of 1942.[195]

For Churchill, on the other hand, however much he might burst out at times against what he considered to be unreasonable American behaviour, the solidarity of 'the English-speaking peoples' was the keystone of all his hopes for the years ahead. In this cause, therefore, minor irritations had to be tolerated, and the Prime Minister continued to see the American people as a whole, as he had first done in 1895, as 'a great lusty youth who treads on all your sensibilities . . . but who moves about his affairs with a good-hearted freshness which may well be the envy of other nations of the earth.' To such a people, the British for their part could offer their solidity, thus producing a combination of 'complementary virtues and resources.'[196] Though not all his war-time colleagues agreed with him,‡ he deeply believed that the interests of the two countries 'could not clash.'[197]

* 'He was a consummate actor, whether he knew it or not', recalled Major Morton. (Thompson, *Churchill and Morton*, 79; but see also 156.)

† Note, for example, how Roosevelt, having witnessed Churchill's anger at Tehran over Stalin's suggestion that several thousand German officers should be shot, privately egged Stalin on at Yalta to repeat the proposal. (*Churchill*, V, 330; FRUS, Malta and Yalta, 570.)

‡ 'Cripps is anti-American', noted Dalton in his diary in May 1942. ' . . . They are

Here lay one of Churchill's greatest strengths during the war—and also one of his less happy legacies. He saw how dependent Britain had become on the support of the United States, and therefore subordinated other considerations to the overriding necessity of maintaining this partnership. 'I never had any doubt', he wrote later, 'that a complete understanding between Britain and the United States outweighed all else.'[198] At the same time, however, despite his extensive knowledge of American history and literature, one may question how realistic was Churchill's grasp of American politics. (Note, for example, his 'astonishment' in December 1945 over the entirely-predictable charging of interest by the United States on the loan then granted to Britain.)[199] Too often, it seems, he projected into a lengthy future the temporary circumstances of the war-time comradeship in arms and the special relationship between himself and Roosevelt which he had done so much to foster. Even before his death, the unrealistic nature of his expectations in this respect were to become apparent; so, too, was the false notion of Britain's standing in the world which his war-time greatness had helped to engender and preserve in his fellow countrymen.

Meanwhile, if one wished to discover an area, even during the war, over which a good many Americans, especially, did believe that their own interests and those of the British could, indeed, clash, then one had only to turn to the Far East. There, more than anywhere else, the element of unrealism in Churchill's image of the transatlantic partnership was to be amply demonstrated.

treating us like a poor dependency. Lyttelton has gone to Washington because F.D.R. summoned him. He is now sending for Leathers and Bevin. It is as though we were all his servants. The P.M. has always gone in for appeasing the Americans, letting them have whatever they like. S[tafford] C[ripps] thinks that he ought to go over to Washington and say, "This must stop." ' (Dalton Diary, 30 May 1942.)

Notes to Chapter Three

1 Cole, in *Borg and Okamoto*, 304.
2 F. W. Williams (ed.), *A Prime Minister Remembers* (London, 1961), 37; see C. R. Attlee, *As It Happened* (London, 1954), 118.
3 E.g. *Burns*, 23ff.; *Long*, 16 Feb. and 9 Sept. 1943; J. M. Blum, *The Price of Vision: The Diary of Henry A. Wallace, 1942–1946* (Boston, 1973; hereafter, *Wallace*), entry for 16 Feb. 1943.
4 Ickes, *Secret Diary*, III, 216.
5 Dalton Diary, 23 Feb. 1942; 4 Aug. 1944.
6 Ibid, 27 Oct. 1942; 9 Sept. 1943.
7 E.g. Christiansen to Beaverbrook, 28 Oct. 1942, Beaverbrook Papers, C/38.
8 Beaverbrook to Hoare, 27 June 1940, Beaverbrook Papers, C/308.
9 Grigg to Grigg, 23 Feb. 1941, Grigg Papers, 9/6.
10 Dalton Diary, 9 July 1942.
11 Linlithgow to Amery, 2 July and 8 Sept. 1941, Linlithgow Papers, vol. 10.
12 W. R. Louis, *Imperialism at Bay* (forthcoming; hereafter, *Louis*).
13 On the background to this, see L. C. Gardner, *Economic Aspects of New Deal Diplomacy* (Boston, 1971), 24ff., and R. N. Gardner, *Sterling-Dollar Diplomacy* (Oxford,

1956), 13ff. The author has also benefited a great deal from discussions on this topic with Lord Coleraine.

14 Bevin to Eden, 24 April 1942, Bevin Papers, box 23.
15 See e.g. R. R. James, *Churchill, A Study In Failure* (Harmondsworth, 1973), 32, 348.
16 H. V. Wiseman, *Political Systems: Some Sociological Approaches* (London, 1966), 23.
17 Calder, *The People's War*, 97.
18 See A. Vandenberg (ed.), *The Private Papers of Senator Arthur Vandenberg* (London, 1953; hereafter, *Vandenberg*), entry for 13 Jan. 1941.
19 Quoted in A. M. Schlesinger, *The Imperial Presidency* (London, 1974), 113.
20 Ibid, 99; but cf. R. Dallek, 'Franklin Roosevelt As World Leader', *American Historical Review*, vol. 76, No. 5, 1971; W. Kimball (ed.), *Franklin D. Roosevelt and the World Crisis, 1937–1945* (Lexington, Mass., 1973), passim.
21 See e.g., R. E. Sherwood, *Roosevelt and Hopkins: An Intimate History* (New York, 1948; hereafter *Sherwood*), 367, 382.
22 M. Howard, *Grand Strategy*, IV (London, 1972), 249.
23 See G. Almond, *The American People and Foreign Policy* (New York, 1965), 65.
24 J. W. Wheeler-Bennett, *King George VI* (London, 1958), 460.
25 See A. Marwick, *Britain In The Century of Total War* (Harmondsworth, 1970), 259ff.; Calder, *The People's War*, 525ff.
26 See e.g. S. Hoffmann, *Gulliver's Troubles* (New York, 1968), 108, 144.
27 D. M. Potter, *The People of Plenty* (Chicago, 1968), 111.
28 Hornbeck memo., 3 Dec. 1943, Hornbeck Papers, box 181.
29 I. Berlin, *Mr Churchill in 1940* (London, 1950), 35.
30 Hoffmann, *Gulliver's Troubles*, 96.
31 H. G. Nicholas, *The United States and Britain* (Chicago, 1975), 2. For a lengthy, if romantic, survey of Anglo-American relations, see H. C. Allen, *Great Britain and the United States* (London, 1954); see also S. Spender, *Love-Hate Relations* (London, 1974).
32 Leutze, *London Observer*, 25.
33 E. Barnard, *Wendell Willkie: Fighter For Freedom* (Marquette, Michigan, 1966) 277–84; *Sherwood*, 235ff.
34 Stimson Diary, 10 Nov. 1941.
35 W. Range, *Franklin D. Roosevelt's World Order* (Athens, Georgia, 1959), 18. See also R. A. Divine, *Second Chance: The Triumph Of Internationalism In America During World War Two* (New York, 1967), 45; *Sherwood*, 359; *Woodward*, I, 379.
36 *Long*, 15 Feb. 1941.
37 Laski to Roosevelt, 20 Oct. 1940, Roosevelt Papers, PSF box 51.
38 See J. W. Wheeler-Bennett, *Special Relationships* (London, 1975), 16.
39 Stilwell Diary, 23 and 26 Feb. 1942.
40 *Spectator*, 3 July 1942.
41 Halifax Diary, 7 March 1941.
42 Nicholas, *The United States and Britain*, 4.
43 E.g. ibid, caps. 7 and 8.
44 Frankfurter to Cripps, 9 July 1942, M. Freedman (ed.), *Roosevelt and Frankfurter* (London, 1967); hereafter, *Freedman*), 664.
45 *Sherwood*, 237; Lord Birkenhead, *Halifax* (London, 1965), 507ff.
46 Ickes, *Secret Diary*, III, 428.
47 Halifax Diary, 17 Feb. 1941.
48 *Long*, 22 Aug. 1941, 29 Jan. 1942, see *Sherwood*, 130–1.
49 *Wallace*, 21 Dec. 1942.
50 Berle to FDR, 21 June 1941, Roosevelt Papers, PSF box 80.
51 CBI 'Master Narrative', 281, Stilwell Papers, box 1.
52 *Pogue*, I, 132–3, 264. See *Vandenberg*, 16 Feb. 1942.
53 A. C. Wedemeyer, *Wedemeyer Reports!* (New York, 1958), 188.
54 Ibid, 106, 179. See e.g. H. H. Arnold, *Global Mission* (London, 1951), 155; G. Smith, *American Diplomacy During The Second World War* (New York, 1965), 14.

55 Dalton Diary, 3 March 1943.
56 *Berle*, 17 March 1941.
57 Hornbeck memo., 7 May 1943, Hornbeck Papers, box 181.
58 *Berle*, 18 Feb. 1941; *Roosevelt Letters*, 12 April 1938 and 11 Jan. 1941. On Berle's own Anglophobia, see Stevenson, *A Man Called Intrepid*, 364.
59 *Wallace*, 17 Dec. 1943.
60 E.g. *Sherwood*, 313; D. Acheson, *Present At The Creation* (London, 1970), 38; Hull, *Memoirs*, II, 923; J. M. Blum, *Roosevelt and Morgenthau* (Boston, 1970), 346; Leutze, *London Observer*, 222; Gardner, *Economic Aspects of New Deal Diplomacy*, 107, 173.
61 E.g. FO 371, U173/173/53 and file 31490; H. Feis, *Seen From E.A.* (New York, 1947), 3ff.
62 See G. Kolko, *The Politics of War* (London, 1969; hereafter, *Kolko*), 167.
63 WSC to Eden, 27 Aug. 1941, PREM 4, 71/1; *Woodward*, II, 200ff.; *Churchill*, III, cap. XXIV; S. Welles, *A Time For Decision* (London, 1944), 140; Hull, *Memoirs*, II, 975; Gardner, *Sterling-Dollar Diplomacy*, 42ff.; Roosevelt, *As He Saw It*, 36ff. (This last book is of very doubtful accuracy.)
64 Hawkins to Hull, 4 Aug. 1941, Roosevelt Papers, PSF box 80; in general see R. F. Harrod, *The Life of John Maynard Keynes* (London, 1951), 512ff.
65 Acheson, *Present At The Creation*, 33.
66 Amery to Smuts, 26 June 1941, in van der Poel, *Selections From The Smuts Papers*, VI. See Amery to Linlithgow, 5 Jan. 1942, Linlithgow Papers, vol. 11.
67 Gardner, *Sterling-Dollar Diplomacy*, 64ff.
68 FO 371, U242/5/70.
69 *Woodward*, II, 207.
70 H. Macmillan, *The Blast of War, 1939–1945* (London, 1967), 159.
71 E.g. *Wallace*, 29 Oct. 1942; E. R. Drachman, *United States Policy Toward Vietnam, 1940–1945* (Rutherford, N.J., 1970), 41–2; Range, *FDR's World Order*, 105, 109; Roosevelt, *As He Saw It*, 25; G. R. Hess, *America Encounters India* (Baltimore, 1971), 29; *Louis* (forthcoming).
72 Gardner, *Economic Aspects*, 177; W. A. Harriman and E. Abel, *Special Envoy To Churchill and Stalin, 1941–1946* (London, 1976), 191.
73 See B. Tuchman, *Sand Against The Wind: Stilwell and the American Experience of China, 1911–1945* (London, 1971; hereafter, *Tuchman*), 38; *Pogue*, I, 121.
74 J. W. Wheeler-Bennett, *Action This Day: Working With Churchill* (London, 1968), 205; see H. Pelling, *Winston Churchill* (London, 1974), 46.
75 E.g. Lothian to Halifax, 15 Sept. 1939, FO 800/324. See Wheeler-Bennett, *Special Relationships*, 115.
76 Amery to Smuts, 3 April 1941, van der Poel, *Smuts Papers*, VI.
77 WP (41) 282, CAB 66/20.
78 WP (40) 310, CAB 66/10.
79 Cherwell to WSC, 26 Sept. 1941, Cherwell Papers, Off. 1.1.
80 E.g. Cab, 29 July 1940, CAB 65/14; Wheeler-Bennett, *King George VI*, 513–14. The idea of obtaining West Indian bases etc. in return for British indebtedness was not new in American circles. See *Thorne*, 293, note.
81 Beaverbrook minute, 26 Dec. 1940, PREM 4, 17/1.
82 A. J. P. Taylor, *Beaverbrook* (London, 1972), 439.
83 WSC to Halifax, 15 March 1941; WSC to Wood, 20 March 1941, PREM 4, 17/2.
84 Butler minute, 3 April 1941, FO 371, A1874/18/45.
85 PREM 4, 25/7.
86 Dalton Diary, 8 July 1942.
87 Lothian to Halifax, 1 Feb. 1940, FO 800/324.
88 See e.g. FO 371, A6398/44/45.
89 Ibid, A1171/3/45.
90 Ibid, A9268/118/45.
91 See also material in PREM 4, 25/2, and PREM 3, 469.

92 FO 371, A9214/44/45; and minutes in A7946/3/45.
93 Ibid, A3266/3/45; A3131/44/45; Halifax Diary, 6 March 1941.
94 FO 371, A1874/18/45.
95 See ibid, A3060/44/45.
96 Campbell to Foreign Office, 15 Aug. 1941, ibid, A7415/18/45.
97 Ibid, A9214/44/45; see A1407/44/45.
98 Lothian to Halifax, 1 Feb. 1940, FO 800/324.
99 WP (41) 282, CAB 66/20.
100 Alsop to Forbes, 28 May 1941, Alsop Papers, box 2.
101 See FO 371, files 26184–26188, and Wheeler-Bennett, *Special Relationships*, 76 and 122.
102 FO 371, A9704/44/45.
103 Ibid, A7415/18/45.
104 *Long*, 7 Feb. 1941.
105 Hull to FDR, 31 Dec. 1941, Hopkins Papers, box 308; Hull, *Memoirs*, II, 1132ff.; W. Langer, *Our Vichy Gamble* (New York, 1947), 186–7; Smith, *American Diplomacy*, 36; M. Viorst, *Hostile Allies: FDR and Charles de Gaulle* (New York, 1975).
106 Leahy Diary, e.g. 24 Feb. 1941, 28 July 1941. See W. D. Leahy, *I Was There* (London, 1950; hereafter, *Leahy*), 30.
107 See *Woodward*, I, xlixff., 330.
108 E.g. *Woodward*, II, 82–4.
109 E.g. ibid, 220ff.; *Sherwood*, 401.
110 *Sherwood*, 270; see in general Harriman and Abel, *Special Envoy*, cap. 1.
111 Gore-Booth, *With Great Truth and Respect*, 121.
112 E.g. *Woodward*, II, 352, 388; *Sherwood*, 224ff.; W. Kimball, *The Most Unsordid Thing* (Baltimore, 1969).
113 Hall, *North American Supply*, 39; Hancock and Gowing, *British War Economy*, 236.
114 Hall, 255; *Burns*, 20.
115 Kimball, *The Most Unsordid Thing*, 235–8.
116 WP (40) 168, CAB 66/7.
117 Hall, 243ff. Britain's cash purchases from the U.S.A. during the war amounted to $7,000 million.
118 Ibid, 174; Gardner, *Sterling-Dollar Diplomacy*, 178.
119 H. Cantril and M. Strunk, *Public Opinion, 1935–1946* (Princeton, 1951; hereafter *Cantril and Strunk*), 411ff.
120 Hall, 298; Hancock and Gowing, *British War Economy*, 377.
121 Butler, *Grand Strategy*, II, 547ff.; Gwyer, *Grand Strategy*, III, part I, 26; van der Poel, *Smuts Papers*, VI, Smuts to Gillett, 6 Jan. 1941; *Cadogan Diaries*, 20 Sept. 1941.
122 E.g. Hall, *North American Supply*, 100, 190ff.; Hancock and Gowing, *British War Economy*, 379; *Woodward*, I, xxv; *Sherwood*, 267; Gore-Booth, *With Great Truth and Respect*, 122.
123 See Leutze, *The London Observer*, 220.
124 See H. M. Hyde, *The Quiet Canadian* (London, 1962), 27ff., and *Stevenson*, passim.
125 See F. W. Winterbotham, *The Ultra Secret* (London, 1974), and *Stevenson*. Peter Calvocoressi, however, who was involved in the Ultra project, has doubts as to whether Stevenson is accurate on this point.
126 *Stevenson*, 143ff.
127 Ibid, 152, 254.
128 WSC to FDR, 25 Feb. 1942, Roosevelt Papers, MR box 7A. I have not discovered examples of this success being utilized in the exercise of British diplomacy at the time, however.
129 See Leutze, *The London Observer*, 314, and *Stevenson*, 143ff.
130 M. Gowing, *Britain And Atomic Energy, 1939–1945* (London, 1964), 123.
131 Hull, *Memoirs*, II, 1109; *Long*, 20 April 1942.
132 *Wallace*, 15 June 1942; C. E. Bohlen, *Witness To History* (London, 1973), 122.
133 E.g. *Long*, 3 Aug. 1941; *Sherwood*, 135.

134 Morgenthau, Presidential Diary, 10 July 1941.
135 E.g. Harriman to Hopkins, 19 Dec. 1942, Hopkins Papers, box 328; Winant to Hopkins, 16 Oct. 1943 and 19 Dec. 1944, Roosevelt Papers, MR box 13; Leutze, *London Observer*, 241; Butler, *The Art of The Possible*, 87.
136 E.g. *Woodward*, I, xxxix; W. F. Kimball, 'Churchill and Roosevelt: The Personal Equation', in *Prologue*, Fall, 1974.
137 Murray to Hull, 2 July 1943, DS, Matthews files, box 14; Hornbeck to Hull, 5 May 1944, Hornbeck Papers, box 43.
138 Morgenthau Diary, 9 July 1943.
139 *Long*, 18 Oct. 1944.
140 Acheson, *Present At The Creation*, 38.
141 Harriman to FDR, 10 April 1941, Roosevelt Papers, PPF. See *Thorne*, 88.
142 Dalton Diary, 29 Aug. 1941; see Halifax to WSC, 13 March 1941, PREM 4, 27/9.
143 *Sherwood*, 266.
144 *Burns*, 105; S. I. Rosenman, *Working With Roosevelt* (London, 1952), 427; R. Tugwell, *In Search of Roosevelt* (Cambridge, Mass., 1972), 253; *Wallace*, 18.
145 Acheson, *Present At The Creation*, 740. For a different emphasis, see Schlesinger, *Imperial Presidency*, 109.
146 See Roosevelt Papers, PSF box 92; Acheson, *Present At The Creation*, 740; Smith, *American Diplomacy*, 8ff.
147 See F. Freidel, *Franklin D. Roosevelt: The Ordeal* (Boston, 1954), 105.
148 FDR to Frankfurter, 11 March 1943, Frankfurter Papers, box 98.
149 Morgenthau, Presidential Diary, 25 Aug. 1942.
150 Stimson Diary, 12 Nov. 1941; see ibid, 1 Dec. 1941 and H. Stimson and M. Bundy, *On Active Service In Peace And War* (New York, 1948; hereafter, *Stimson*), 561–3.
151 Stimson Diary, 1 May 1942.
152 E.g. Gore-Booth, *With Great Truth And Respect*, 124.
153 WP (45) 24, CAB 66/60.
154 R. Lewin, *Churchill As Warlord* (London, 1973), 264. See P. Cosgrave, *Churchill At War*, vol. I (London, 1974), 23, 65ff.
155 *Sherwood*, 257.
156 Harriman to Hopkins, 7 March 1942, Hopkins Papers, box 308.
157 Harriman to FDR, 7 March 1942, Roosevelt Papers, PSF box 50.
158 Harriman to FDR, 7 May 1941, ibid.
159 See above, 63–4.
160 Hankey Diary, 28 and 30 April 1940; 1 May and 9 June 1941.
161 *Cadogan Diaries*, 9 July 1941.
162 Wheeler-Bennett, *Action This Day*, 26.
163 Ibid, 193; Hankey Diary, 13 May 1941.
164 Amery to Linlithgow, 13 Jan. 1942, Linlithgow Papers, vol. 11.
165 Wheeler-Bennett, *Action This Day*, 235; Thompson, *Churchill and Morton*, 100.
166 See Butler, *Grand Strategy*, II, 561ff., and A. Bryant, *The Turn of the Tide* (London, 1957) and *Triumph In The West* (London, 1959), hereafter *Bryant*, I and II respectively.
167 E.g. Wheeler-Bennett, *Action This Day*, 77.
168 *Woodward*, I, 333, note; material in PREM 4, 27/3.
169 WSC to Eden, 21 Oct. 1942, PREM 4, 100/7.
170 Material in PREM 4, 100/7; Dalton Diary, 23 June 1943; *Woodward*, I, liiff.
171 *Cadogan Diaries*, 19 June 1945.
172 Ibid, p. 166.
173 Bevin to Halifax, n.d., 1940, Bevin Papers, box 21; WP (42) 538, CAB 66/31.
174 Thus, Sir George Sansom in 1945 found it 'in need of the most drastic overhaul, physically and morally . . .; the whole machine is slow, cumbrous and obsolete, and there is still too much of the anointment with holy oil . . .' Sansom, *Sir George Sansom*, 141.
175 Wilkinson Journal, 8 Feb. 1944; e.g. *Sherwood*, 247; Birkenhead, *Halifax*, 507; interview with Sir John Wheeler-Bennett, 19 Nov. 1974.

176 Halifax Diary, 24 May 1941; Halifax to Eden, 4 Feb. 1941, Hickleton Papers, A4 410 4.
177 E.g. Dalton Diary, 4 Feb., 8 Aug. 1941; 12 Feb. 1942; Sansom, *Sir George Sansom*, 141.
178 FO 371, F3941/23/40.
179 E.g. *Sherwood*, 269, 276.
180 Berlin, *Mr. Churchill In 1940*.
181 WSC to Eden, 5 Nov. 1942, PREM 4, 27/1.
182 E.g. *Sherwood*, 351, 363.
183 Hopkins memo., 15 Jan. 1942, Hopkins Papers, box 308.
184 *Churchill*, IV, 62.
185 Taussig memo., 13 July 1944, Taussig Papers, box 47.
186 Lord Chandos, *Memoirs* (London, 1962), 310; Thompson, *Churchill and Morton*, 54.
187 Halifax Diary, 20 Feb. 1943.
188 Dalton Diary, 13 July 1944.
189 FO 371, A9963/144/45.
190 See *Churchill*, IV, 344.
191 See *Churchill*, III, 588 et seq.
192 Pelling, *Churchill*, 174.
193 *Wallace*, 36; Acheson, *Present At The Creation*, 740.
194 JCS, 21 Feb. 1944, RG 218.
195 Taussig memo., 30 Nov. 1942, Taussig Papers, box 46. Professor Lloyd Gardner has reminded me that during the First World War, Colonel House had likewise warned Wilson that the U.S.A. would have great trouble with Britain afterwards.
196 Pelling, *Churchill*, 46, 401.
197 Commonwealth Prime Ministers' Conference, 9 May 1944, PREM 4, 42/5.
198 *Churchill*, III, 555.
199 Gardner, *Sterling-Dollar Diplomacy*, 225ff. An interesting comment on Anglo–U.S. relations in 1942 was to be made in a secret O.S.S. Research and Analysis report (No. 315) on 'English Attitudes Toward the United States Since Pearl Harbor', which concluded: 'In comparison with the violent anti-British attitude not only of many influential American newspapers but also of many prominent politicians, the attitudes of both press and politicians in England toward America have been models of friendly cooperation.' See also Harriman's comment below, 145, in a similar sense.

PART TWO

Pearl Harbour to Casablanca
December 1941 to January 1943

CHAPTER FOUR

THE SETTING

PEARL HARBOUR transformed the Second World War into a conflict of global dimensions.[1] On 11 December 1941, four days after the Japanese had launched their attack, Hitler and Mussolini also declared war on the United States, thus relieving the embarrassment of an American Administration which until then still lacked the overwhelming reasons it believed it required for public consumption, as to why the Republic should once more embroil itself in European quarrels. Even then, as we shall see, it was the war against Japan, and not the one against the European dictators, which for many Americans was to remain their country's own, particular fight.

For Germany, too, by the end of 1941, the main conflict now lay outside Western Europe, in the expanses of the Soviet Union. Hitler's offensive into that country had had to be called off with Moscow still untaken; Sebastopol (until July 1942) and Leningrad also remained defiant. In the summer of 1942, however, Nazi forces did make progress towards the Caucasus, thus heightening Allied fears of a three-way link-up between the Germans, descending on the Middle East through Iran and from the North African desert, and the triumphant Japanese advancing from the east. But the tenacity and strength of the Russians, which were eventually to destroy the invader, were demonstrated to the full at Stalingrad between September 1942 and February 1943, and it is worth recalling, for purposes of scale, that in this one battle the Russians lost more men than the United States was to do in all its campaigns of the war.

Russia's great burden in fighting the German Army almost single-handed led to loud cries in the West during 1942 for the opening of a second front in Europe. In London that summer, the Soviet Foreign Minister, Molotov, was assured that this was, indeed, the intention, but was warned at the same time that no promises could be given; in Washington, however, following Molotov's talks there, Roosevelt permitted a communiqué to be issued which stated that in the course of those discussions 'full understanding [had been] reached with regard to the urgent task of creating a Second Front in Europe in 1942.' To his Secretary of the Treasury the President observed: 'The whole question of whether we win or lose the war depends upon the Russians. If the Russians can hold on this summer and keep three and a half million Germans engaged in war, we can definitely win . . . Once we lick the Germans, with the help of England's Fleet we can defeat the Japanese in six weeks.'[2]

It was left to Churchill, however, to explain to Stalin in person in August that there would not, after all, be any major landings in Europe that year. (The Prime Minister's reasoning was reinforced by the costly failure of the Dieppe raid, shortly beforehand.)[3] Instead, there would be the 'Torch' landings in French North Africa. 'The P.M. was at his best', reported Harriman to Roosevelt, 'and could not have handled the discussion with greater brilliance.'[4] Meanwhile Churchill himself had accepted from the outset of the war with Japan that the Soviet Union could not herself be asked to set up a second front in that, eastern part of the world 'in view of the enormous service which [she] was giving to us by hammering the German Army on her Western front.'[5] Nevertheless, the idea of obtaining an eventual Soviet contribution in the Far East, and of bombing Japan from Soviet Pacific bases, was already a part of Allied thinking.[6] Stalin himself, in December 1941, encouragingly told Eden that he would reconsider this matter in the following spring, by which time he hoped to have restored the strength of his Far Eastern armies.[7]

The vital need to sustain the Soviet contribution to the war, to prevent any possibility of a revived Nazi-Soviet understanding, and to ensure Moscow's collaboration after Germany and Japan had been defeated, made Britain in this period more ready than was the United States to recognise the western frontiers which Stalin had acquired before Hitler's attack in 1941. Soviet intransigence over certain conditions that were involved, however, prevented such an agreement with London being formalised, and to Washington's relief the most that was achieved was an Anglo-Soviet twenty-year Mutual Assistance Pact, signed in May 1942.[8] Admiration and hope regarding the Soviet Union were high in Britain at the time. In the United States, although something of the same thing existed, there also remained suspicion of the home of Communism, notably in Republican circles,[9] while for the Administration, too, the partnership with Britain remained the central one. Yet already, in December 1942, Roosevelt was musing in a way which anticipated developments which were to take place within the ranks of the Allies later in the war. Asking Vice President Henry Wallace if, at a conference of the Institute of Pacific Relations, 'the Britishers took their typical [imperialist] slant', the President added 'that when there were four people sitting in at a poker game and three of them were against the fourth, it is a little hard on the fourth.' 'This I took to mean', noted Wallace afterwards, 'that he, Stalin and Chiang Kai-shek would be playing the game together.'[10]

Meanwhile the fourth member had experienced many severe setbacks before at last achieving a major victory (although it was a victory which Churchill, for international and domestic political reasons, made seem even more significant than was actually the case) in the second battle of Alamein. The first part of 1942 had been a dismal time for Britain in this North African theatre, with the loss of Benghazi in January and Rommel's successes of May and June, including the capture of Tobruk. ('What a shock', wrote the First Lord of the Admiralty, A. V. Alexander, in his diary on that last occasion. 'Bevin very shaken. Thinks we should immediately change the High Command. Doubts whether Govt. can survive.')[11] There were, of course, some events to set on the other side of the account: Malta survived its blockade; the Royal Navy, despite the disabling of the battle-ships *Queen Elizabeth* and *Valiant* (an event which was significant for the Far Eastern war), hung on in the Mediterranean; Rommel had already been checked in July before being forced back from Alamein in October; the Allied landings in Northwest Africa were successfully undertaken in November, and were to lead to the eventual clearing of the enemy from the southern Mediterranean shore in May 1943.

Nevertheless, it is important to remember how low the reputation of the British Army had sunk before Alamein, a process that was furthered by defeats at the hands of the Japanese. 'Our generals are no use, and do our men fight?' asked Cadogan in his diary,[12] while Dalton, in his, observed that one reason for avoiding war in the future was 'that we are less good at it than some other people.'[13] Churchill's doctor, for his part, concluded that British fighting morale was lower than it had been during the First World War,[14] and General Wavell was likewise of the opinion that 'for the time being we have lost a good deal of our hardness and fighting spirit.'[15] 'We were undoubtedly softer, as a nation, than any of our enemies, except the Italians', the Director of Military Operations, Lt. General Kennedy, was to write later.[16] 'Too many old men and "nice chaps"' were what Air Marshal Tedder found in the Middle East at the time.[17]

If opinions such as these were fairly widespread on the British side, it is hardly surprising that, by the summer of 1942, in the words of a senior official of the State Department, there was 'definitely a growing feeling in Washington that the British are absolutely incapable of exercising command or using equipment.'[18]* Some drew a conclusion that pointed towards the 'true' American war, in the Far East: 'Why not just tell the British', asked Hornbeck, now Political Adviser in the State Department, 'that in the Libyan theater and the Near Eastern theater they will have to "paddle their own canoe" with what they have and what we have given them—and thereby put an end to their tendency to cave in and look to us to save the situation in those theaters; we, meanwhile, concentrating on first holding Japan and as soon as possible knocking out Japan.'[19]

A similar tendency to swerve in exasperation towards the East was to

---

* Circulating in Washington at the time, for example, were verses mocking the British military effort in the Far East. A small, mild specimen ran as follows:

'To lunch they go at half past one—
Blast me, old chap, the day's half done.
They lunch and talk and fight the Jap,
And now it's time to take a nap.
The staff study starts at three fifteen;
Such progress here you've never seen.
They're working now, as you can see,
But blast me down, it's time for tea . . .'

(Hornbeck Papers, box 180.)

manifest itself during the year among those responsible for the direction of American strategy. At first, however, this was not so. Despite warnings against the dangers which would result from too-exclusive an Anglo-American partnership;[20] despite the lasting fears among American officials over what they saw as Churchill's undue influence upon Roosevelt in strategic matters;[21] despite the absence of a formal Anglo-American alliance (in London, indeed, there was for a time much agonising over whether to dare risk offending the susceptibilities of Congress by publicly calling the United States an 'ally'),[22] what stood out at the beginning of 1942 was the remarkable degree of harmony that was achieved at the highest level of Anglo-American relations. Indeed, these relations were to remain, in the words of one British official historian, 'a close association that was unparalleled',[23] and even the sharp exchanges which took place over Mediterranean strategy later in 1942 have been described as 'a model of how Allies should discuss and resolve their differences.'[24] Many hard words and much disillusionment must figure in our account of the relationship in the Far East especially. But if this side of things has tended to be played down in the past, it would be equally wrong now to overlook the genuineness with which Stimson, for example, could observe that, at a dinner for British and American Service chiefs in Washington in December 1941, 'a spirit of harmony and endeavor pervaded everybody', while he himself fondly recalled the comradeship in arms of 1917.[25] Or again, it was of real significance when Roosevelt wrote to his Chief of Naval Operations, Admiral King, in August 1942: 'The British are our partners, hence we must have the fullest and frankest collaboration with them',[26] just as it was when he and Marshall promptly reacted to the news of the fall of Tobruk by promising Churchill and Brooke new supplies of armour.[27]

Collaboration had also been achieved at the 'Arcadia' Conference held in Washington in December 1941 and January 1942. Building on foundations that had been laid before Pearl Harbour, an inter-Allied structure was then established—the Combined Chiefs of Staff, the Munitions Assignment Board, the Shipping Adjustment and Raw Materials Boards, and (in June) the Production and Resources Board[28]—which, in the later words of General Marshall, led to 'the most complete unification of military effort ever achieved by two Allied nations.'[29] Here, with these two states, lay the vital powers for allocating the economic resources of the United Nations alliance, and others had to fit themselves around such a scheme of things. Strategically, too, the crucial decisions were taken in this Anglo-American context. In these early conferences like 'Arcadia', it was Churchill, in fact, who made the running—on this occasion with his lengthy memoranda which surveyed the war in broad perspective and in which he also developed the idea of landing in North Africa.[30] Above all, and despite the shock of Pearl Harbour, it was agreed in the document W.W.1 to reaffirm the 1941 staff conclusion that the war against Germany, not Japan, should be given priority. 'Her defeat is the key to victory', ran W.W.1. 'Once Germany is defeated the collapse of Italy and the defeat of Japan must follow . . . Only the minimum of force necessary for the safeguarding of vital interests in other theatres should be diverted from operations against Germany.'[31]

The American side still had to organise itself for high level inter-Allied meetings of this kind, and again in June, when Churchill revisited Washington, the diary of the British Chiefs of Staff noted 'the extraordinary lack of coordination in the direction of the U.S. Services.'[32] Nevertheless, on this occasion, too, a further step was taken in the direction of Anglo-American primacy among the allies, when Roosevelt agreed to the sharing of findings in the development of the atomic bomb. Such a sharing would increasingly be of benefit to Britain, whose pioneering work in the field was, in the words of John Anderson, the Minister overseeing the project, 'a dwindling asset', and who could not house a full-scale production plant. Even so, there were shocks ahead, as when Anderson, in January 1943, found the U.S. Army laying down the 'quite intolerable' ruling that information must be withheld from Britain on the grounds that she could not take advantage of it during the current war. The sequel to this belongs to a later section, but the affair was one indication of the shifting balance of power within the alliance.[33]

Meanwhile, at Roosevelt's suggestion, it had been agreed in March 1942 that the world should be divided into three broad areas of strategic responsibility: the Pacific, to be the concern of the United States; the area from the Mediterranean to Singapore, to be overseen by Britain, and the Atlantic and Western European continent to be shared between the two.[34] This issue will be reverted to in the next chapter, but it should be noted here that these arrangements reinforced a situation which Churchill had accepted earlier, wherein Australia and New Zealand lay within the American sphere, and that links with China (where Chiang Kai-shek was recognised to be still in command) were also a matter for the Americans. 'I presume you will take China under your wing at Washington', the Prime Minister had written to Roosevelt in February, and on the telephone to Hopkins he repeated 'that the President would have the primary responsibility for dealing with China in all cases.'[35] Likewise, in the global division of responsibility for clandestine operations, arrived at between Britain's Special Operations Executive and the American Office of Strategic Services in June 1942, China was declared to be 'an American sphere of influence', Burma, Siam, Indochina, Malaya and Sumatra being 'a no-man's land' which could be worked by both parties as proved convenient.[36]

These agreements did not mean, however, that there now existed an entirely settled strategy between the two partners. Indeed, the summer of 1942 witnessed the growth of considerable mutual exasperation and even distrust in this respect. One reason for this was that in April, when Marshall and Hopkins visited London to put their proposals for a full-scale invasion of the European continent in 1943, with possibly a foothold being obtained beforehand, Churchill chose not to express forcefully the strong doubts which he entertained on the matter.[37] Similarly, in Washington in June, the British Chiefs of Staff agreed with their American colleagues that, whilst only in an emergency would a European operation be undertaken in 1942, landings in North Africa should not take place, the main effort being directed instead towards a build-up for a cross-Channel invasion.[38] Hence, when Churchill carried Roosevelt with him in pushing ahead with the idea of landing in North Africa in 1942 (operation 'Torch')—despite the warnings of the Combined Chiefs of Staff that this must seriously delay cross-Channel preparations—much bad feeling was engendered. To the American Joint Chiefs, London appeared to be throwing over the April agreement, and in their frustration not only Admiral King but also Generals Marshall and Arnold (Commander of the U.S. Army Air Force), together with Admiral Leahy, recommended to the President that if Britain refused to cooperate in a speedy, direct attack on the Germans, 'the U.S. should turn to the Pacific for decisive action against Japan.' If for Marshall this was a tactic by which to force Britain into a cross-Channel attack and away from the Mediterranean, for King and the U.S. Navy it represented a persistent desire.[39] And as Marshall observed, such a move to the Pacific 'would tend to concentrate rather than to scatter U.S. forces; it would be highly popular throughout the U.S., particularly on the West Coast; the Pacific War Council, the Chinese and the personnel of the Pacific Fleet would all be in hearty accord, and, second only to [the cross-Channel attack], it would be the operation which would have the greatest effect towards relieving the pressure on Russia.'[40]

Roosevelt rejected this J.C.S. proposal. 'Defeat of Germany', he declared in significant fashion, 'means the defeat of Japan, probably without firing a shot or losing a life.'[41] Nevertheless, out of the ensuing confusion there emerged in July a further Combined Chiefs of Staff document, C.C.S. 94, which reflected the American view that, with progress in Europe being delayed, certain ground and air units should be transferred 'for the purpose of furthering offensive operations in the Pacific.'[42] In Washington, Admiral Cunningham, head of the British naval mission, described C.C.S. 94 as 'a most poisonous document', and the First Sea Lord in London agreed. 'None of us liked [it] very much', wrote the latter, 'but we felt that, having got the American Chiefs of Staff to our way of thinking as regards [the North African landings], it was a pity to be too critical of the precise wording in which they gave their assent.'[43] This understandable laxity was nevertheless unfortunate, since, while London regarded W.W.1. as remaining fully in force, Marshall and his colleagues, especially King, could now look upon it as having been superseded, or at least significantly amended, by C.C.S. 94 in the matter of the demands of the war against Japan. It was a divergence of views and interests that even the inestimable friendship in Washington between Marshall and Sir John Dill, now head of the British Joint Services Mission there, could not remove. As for Churchill, he observed sourly to Halifax that 'just because the Americans can't have a massacre in France this year, they want to sulk and bathe in the Pacific.'[44]

Tension between the two partners was also engendered during 1942 by the question of future tariff policies. The Mutual Aid Agreement, it is true, including its controversial article 7, was signed in February, and on both sides there were hopes thereafter that discussions could lead to a more substantial accord.[45] But opposition within the British Government to signing the Agreement had remained strong up to the last minute, notably from Amery. 'The abandonment by us of Imperial Preference', he wrote early in 1942, 'will not prevent any temporary lowering of the American tariff being promptly reversed by the next Republican majority.' A year later, he was still repeating the warning: 'There are plenty of straws to show that the wind in America is going to blow away from the New Deal and all its works', he wrote then, 'towards something not so very far removed from the isolationism which followed on the last war.'[46] Churchill himself, despite his own inclination towards free trade, was content to let the Cabinet procrastinate over the matter, and had avoided discussing it when in Washington for 'Arcadia'.[47] The result was continued bad feeling on the American side (Hull, obsessed as ever with the issue, referred to Churchill as 'selfish, vindictive, vicious' in this connection),[48] with Amery being seen as something of a menace.[49]* To get the Agreement signed in February required from Roosevelt a combination of reassurances over advanced pledges and veiled threats over the attitude Congress were likely to take towards a renewal of Lend Lease legislation.[50] Even so, there remained a difference of interpretation between the two capitals, especially, as already noted, as to how far article 7 committed Britain to abandon imperial preference after the war.[51] The entire episode also helped to create in Amery's mind the idea —which, as we have seen, Cripps shared—that Britain was tending to be unduly subservient to the United States, a fault which both he and the Viceroy of India, Linlithgow, blamed above all on the Foreign Office. Eden, wrote Amery, 'lives in terror of anything that could conceivably offend a single American.'[52] Such suspicion of the United States were also fostered by Washington's attempt, from the end of this period onwards, to hold down Britain's gold and dollar reserves to a level of no more than $1 billion.[53]

What was already occurring, in fact, was the beginning of a substantial shift in the balance within the alliance. Although in terms of scale per head of population the British war effort remained as great and in many respects greater than the American one,† in absolute terms the huge latent power of

---

* It is interesting to note, however, that, secretly, both Hull and Stimson shared some of Amery's fears. In November 1942, for example, Hull was talking of the 'young Communists' in Roosevelt's entourage, who, he thought, might well provoke a conservative reaction so that 'even at the present day chances would be against us in any effort to set up a liberal regime of low tariffs, etc.' (Stimson Diary, 17 Nov. 1942.)

† U.S. munitions output, scaled to U.K. population, December 1941–June 1944:

	U.K.	U.S.A. scaled		Armed forces as % of total labour force		
				1942	1943	1944
Planes	66,300	62,400	U.K.	20	23	24
A.F.Vs.	77,500	56,300	U.S.A.	7	15	18
Wheeled vehicles	511,000	74,700				
Artillery over 20m.	49,300	27,600				
Small-arms	5,700,000	4,700,000				

(Source: Hall, *North American Supply*, 419, 473.)

the United States was already starting to make itself felt.[54] By the end of 1942, for example, her output of munitions and aircraft was twice that of Britain, of merchant shipping six times as much. Looking ahead, special pleas for the provision of additional shipping resources had to be made by London in November in order to prevent the exhaustion of Britain's food and raw materials in the summer of 1943. By the end of October, Britain was dependent on the U.S.A. for 77 per cent of her supplies of escort vessels, 88 per cent of her aircraft escort vessels, 99 per cent of her landing-force ships, 88 per cent of her landing craft, 68 per cent of her light bombers, nearly 100 per cent of her transport aircraft, 60 per cent of her tanks, nearly 100 per cent of her self-propelled artillery, 100 per cent of her heavy tank-transporters and 10-ton trucks, 50 per cent of her magnesium, refined tungsten and refined molybdenum. Meanwhile, during the course of 1942 U.S. ground forces grew from 37 to 73 active divisions, and air combat units from 67 to 167.[55]

Contrasts such as these greatly affected the approaches of the two partners to strategic issues, as Michael Howard's summary has already emphasized. Moreover, from the very outset of the alliance sections of the American press had been in no doubt that the United States was, in the words of the *New York Times*, 'the natural leader of the democratic forces.'[56] 'If there is to be a partnership between the United States and Britain', declared a belligerent *Chicago Tribune*, 'we are, by every right, the controlling partner. We can get along without them. They can't get along without us.'[57] Similar notions were expressed by Morgenthau to his senior staff at the Treasury. The power of the dollar, he assured them, would mean 'that the United States, when the war is over, is going to settle . . . what kind of Europe it is going to be . . . Who is going to pay for it? We are going to pay for it. The English are going to be busted . . . I think it had better be Franklin Roosevelt, without Winston, [who] . . . writes the peace treaty.'[58] Even the Anglophile Stimson saw British opposition to an early cross-Channel invasion as evidence that 'a fatigued, defeatist government which [had] lost its initiative [was] blocking the help of a young and vigorous nation . . . This war, if it is to be won', he wrote, 'must be won on the morale and the psychology and courage of the American forces and leaders.'[59] There exists a conviction, reported Richard Law to his Government colleagues in London after visiting Washington and New York in the late summer of 1942,

'that the United States stands for something in the world—something of which the world has need, something which the world is going to like, something, in the final analysis, which the world is going to take whether it likes it or not . . . All this is interesting and exhilarating. It is also rather alarming. There is, of course, very great over-simplification. Washington sees world problems through a telescope where we look at them through a microscope. Washington is thinking in terms of centuries and continents when we are thinking of question-time next Wednesday and the Free Austrian Movement. These people are not men of the world. They are children, playing with bricks and "making the world over" . . . [The real danger is that] through lack of guidance they will run their heads against so many and so hard brick walls that there will be utter disillusionment . . . The [senior] position must go to the United States by virtue of their resources and their population. We, for our part, can hope to redress the balance—and more—by virtue of our experience and our greater political sagacity.'[60]

It is important to note that for Law and the majority of his colleagues, even a clumsily interventionist United States was infinitely preferable to an isolationist one. 'Some British observers', wrote Oliver Lyttelton, 'contrive to be alarmed at one and the same time by American imperialism and by fears of her cutting herself adrift from the rest of the world. Both cannot be dangers at once. But of the two . . . the second, in my view, looms much the larger.'[61] Similarly, Isaiah Berlin, in one of his weekly surveys, found it 'natural that this new-found [international] interest should frequently manifest itself in imperial day-dreams and facile schemes to put the world to rights . . . [but] it may be doubted if they will be lasting. They are rather first signs of beginnings of a grasp of world affairs.'[62] There was also the comforting and quite widespread notion that a wise Britain could in any case guide the young giant. Harold Macmillan, for example, was soon talking of the Greeks running the later Roman Empire without the latter realizing it.[63]

Even so, the zeal and confidence of the United States in these early stages of her war effort were accompanied in some quarters by a brashness that caused unease in British minds. Campbell, for example, as Minister in Washington, warned in May 1942 that there were two kinds of American interventionists,

'those of the type of Hull, Acheson and others among the more friendly and more internationally minded; and those of a more imperialistic turn of mind who may lurk anywhere among the interventionists, whether friendly or unfriendly. There are already signs that thoughts and even assumptions of succession to our Empire are beginning to rise above the surface of the subconscious . . . Conversely, . . . there are among the isolationists a type of people who I can easily imagine proceeding from their isolationist reasoning to a stage where they will satisfy themselves that in order to isolate themselves properly the United States must rule the roost.'[64]

'The Willkie–Welles–Luce group', warned Halifax in a despatch of May 1942, 'see the world as a vast market for the American producer, industrialist and trader. They are believers in the American century, energetic technicians and businessmen filled with a romantic, equally self-confident, economic imperialism, eager to convert the world to the American pattern.'[65] Wendell Willkie's best-selling book, *One World*, based on his visit to the Middle East, Russia and China, was to be summarized in a similar way for the

Prime Minister by one of his aides. 'The book', wrote this official, 'aims at founding an American policy against all Empires, and is therefore subtly anti-British. At the same time it points out equally subtly the great opportunities offered to the U.S.A. to exploit the Middle East, Africa, China and Russia, to the commercial advantage of the U.S.A.'[66]

Others were being led to such conclusions by their observation of American practices, rather than precepts. Air Marshal Tedder, for example, noted their blatant commercial manoeuvrings over trans-African and other air routes. (Pan Am, recorded Vice President Wallace, aims at 'a monopolistic position over large areas of the earth . . . Herbert Feis [Economic Adviser in the State Department] proclaimed that he saw a new American imperialism forming.')[67] In a similar vein, the War Office in London summarised for the Cabinet in the autumn of 1942 reports from officers serving in Washington. In their view, there existed within the American War Department an expansionist attitude which

'takes various forms, ranging from the establishment of a "Pax Americana" [as] substitute for the "Pax Britannica" (now regarded by many Americans as having finished its useful life), to a definite American Imperialistic policy which aims at the building up of American power and prestige in various parts of the world. It is difficult to ignore the fact that, under the guise of war effort, this is already being attempted or achieved at Britain's expense, in the Argentine, New Zealand, Persia, Africa, India, Egypt and Turkey, to mention only a few places.'[68]

Oliver Stanley, as Secretary of State for the Colonies, likewise sounded a warning in a Cabinet memorandum of December 1942 over the interest being displayed by American firms like Pan Am and Socony Vacuum in British West Africa,[69] while Attlee, as Dominions Secretary, had reported to the Prime Minister in the preceding June that

'the High Commissioners [representing the Dominions in London] are considerably exercised in their minds as to the habit of prominent Americans, including members of the administration, of talking as if the British Empire was in the process of dissolution . . . [They] are also disturbed by the economic imperialism of American business interests which is quite active under the cloak of a benevolent and avuncular internationalism. In particular, the activities of Pan American Airways and of the radio interests in staking out claims for the post-war period are viewed with considerable apprehension.'[70]

Churchill himself does not appear to have been unduly worried by such reports. Nor was he yet much concerned over how a powerful United States could be brought together with other countries to work within some formal post-war structure of international relations. His own broad vision of the future, as he had expressed it to Congress at the end of 1941, of 'the British and American peoples . . . for their own safety and for the good of all walking side by side in majesty, in justice, and in peace',[71] weighed far more with him than did tentative Foreign Office schemes for an international organization centred upon four major powers (China being included in that category, along with the U.S.A., the Soviet Union and the British Commonwealth, in deference to the views of the Americans). The Prime Minister did not share Bevin's concern to find 'an economic basis for collective security', nor the belief of Cripps that Britain must speedily devise an international scheme to put forward in order to forestall 'the American-century propaganda and all the subtle imperialism of the Republicans.'[72]

The evidence reaching Britain concerning the American political scene was, after all, ambiguous. Certainly, to the unease of Cripps and others, 1942 was a year of Republican Party advances, culminating in autumn elections which gave them forty-two new seats in the House and nine in the Senate, together with control of half the nation's governorships. In Congress, the thirty-seven Republican Senators could now block any motion requiring two-thirds approval, while in the House the Democrats barely had a majority. When account was taken of Southern Democrats who were closer to the Republicans than they were to a man like Henry Wallace, then it was clear that the New Deal was on the defensive. It was a development which gave rise to concern within the Foreign Office in London. The record of the Republicans, the Office reported to the Cabinet, was 'anything but reassuring', and it urged the Government to push ahead with any agreements it wished to make with the U.S.A. during the two years of life that were left to the existing Roosevelt Administration, whose members were 'in a remarkable degree receptive and anxious to co-operate with us.'[73] Meanwhile, some precautionary action had already been taken to cultivate leading Republican figures like Senator Vandenberg[74] and the 1940 Presidential candidate (unloved though he was by his Party machine), Wendell Willkie. Much tact was obviously required in the conducting of such manoeuvres, however. 'More care must be used with the President now', wrote Churchill to Eden in November 1942. 'We must not seem to be in too great a hurry to hail the rising sun.'[75]

The greatest British fear, expressed within the Foreign Office even before the Republicans' election successes, was that disenchantment and the new burdens that would come America's way could lead to 'a really serious outbreak of isolationism in its most virulent form.'[76] Inside the State Department, too, there were those who were urging that a scheme for establishing a new international organization should be 'sold' to the American public before a reactionary mood set in.[77] And yet at the same time there were also clear signs that even the Republicans were in fact now moving in an internationalist direction, encouraged by Willkie and by the publication of a book by ex-President Hoover and Hugh Gibson, *The Problems of Lasting Peace*. In the country as a whole, a poll conducted in July 1942 showed 59 per cent as being in favour of the U.S.A. joining a league of nations after the war, a figure which rose to 72 per cent in January 1943.[78] Advocates of various forms of American involvement in world affairs were increasingly making themselves heard: Willkie, with his 'One

World' theme; Wallace, with his vision of 'the century of the common man' and of something like a global extension of the New Deal; Luce and other aggressive proponents of 'the American century'; and, as always, the Cobdenite, free-trade internationalism of Cordell Hull.

Some Americans also felt that Roosevelt himself should be giving a stronger lead in this debate on the future of the United States in a world setting. 'The people are being spiritually starved for the lack of the right word from the White House', wrote Walter Lippmann privately, 'and indeed the routine publicity that emanates from the President's White House conferences is positively harmful because the tone of it is in general destructive of the mood of high seriousness.'[79] Stimson, too, was, as before, finding Roosevelt far too casual and confused in his leadership within Government circles, listening in dismay as the President talked to Churchill of sombre matters 'with the frivolity and lack of responsibility of a child.'[80] Meanwhile, bitter struggles among sections of the Administration continued to be a feature of the Washington scene, with Hull warning Roosevelt that 'the representation of this country abroad is showing signs of disintegration through a multiplicity of agencies speaking for the Government.'[81] It was also in this period that Hull declared to Elmer Davis, head of the Office of War Information, that he (Davis) and Milo Perkins (assistant to Wallace for Economic Warfare) were more interested in creating 'world-wide social revolution' than in winning the war, 'even at the danger of producing revolution in the United States.'[82]*

Certainly on one, major domestic issue which is of particular relevance to this study, Roosevelt was being careful not to give a lead or to expose himself unduly. The issue was that of race relations—an area in which, as briefly indicated already, some of the President's own ideas were a trifle bizarre. To British observers in 1942, the anxiety which was being created by the question of relations between blacks and whites in America was apparent. 'The Administration', wrote Halifax, 'is seriously worried about feeling among the coloured population, which according to every survey is apathetic to the war, which it considers a white man's conflict.'[83] Such, indeed, was the sense of the reports that were reaching the President, whose response, though essentially cautious, included the setting up of a Fair Employment Practices Commission. 'The fundamental patriotism of the Negroes', warned the O.W.I.'s Bureau of Intelligence, '. . . should not be allowed to obscure the frustration, pessimism, cynicism and insecurity which appear to characterize their attitudes toward the war.' And again: 'Large numbers of [white] people in all regions showed what must be regarded as an illiberal attitude toward Negroes. On such issues, indeed, it appears that rights which have long since been granted to them are still opposed by large numbers of white people.'[84] (The observations of Gunner Myrdal concern-

* One joke then current in Washington listed in order of importance the wars that were being fought. First—easily—there came the war against Roosevelt; then the war against Britain; third, there was the war against Japan; fourth to sixth, various internal battles; and seventh the war against Germany. (Hayter, *A Double Life*, 68.)

ing black attitudes to the Pacific War have already been illustrated, as has the fact that in 1942–3, small pro-Japanese Negro cults were unearthed in a few American cities.)[85]

Many Americans in high places saw no solution to the problems of the country's blacks. 'The social intermixture of the two races is basically impossible', wrote Stimson in his diary, and while the U.S. Navy was still restricted to whites only, the Army kept its blacks segregated in units of their own, mainly of a labouring, rather than of a combat, nature.[86] 'The more I hear', noted Halifax, 'the more I resent their criticism of us in India. We may have been a bit slow politically, but socially and administratively we are miles ahead of them.'[87]

Britain herself in this context was causing special concern to Stimson and others (including John Foster Dulles, the future Republican Secretary of State, and Arthur Sulzberger of the *New York Times*) because of the non-discriminatory treatment which, in the main, was being accorded to black G.I.s when they arrived there as part of the American Army's build-up in the European theatre. Stimson, in fact, was sufficiently disturbed to raise the matter with Roosevelt, friend of the world's oppressed races:

'I told him', Stimson noted subsequently, 'of the current dangerous situation in the U.S.A. and the difficulties that we [i.e. the Army] are having, and then I told him that Mrs. Roosevelt notified me of her coming trip to the U.K. and asked him if he would not caution her on the subject of making any comments as to the different treatment which Negroes received in the U.K. from what they received in the U.S. He was very much interested in this whole subject and very sympathetic to our whole attitude, and told me he would pass the word on to Mrs. Roosevelt.'[88]

As the present writer has indicated at greater length elsewhere,[89] this issue of the Negroes in Britain also caused a flurry in Whitehall, with the Cabinet being divided over whether British forces, male and female, should be 'educated' to accept the American line over segregation. (A report of January 1943 by the Home Intelligence Unit of the M.O.I. described, as one feature of fairly widespread anti-American feeling, 'consistent criticism' of the colour-discrimination policy of the U.S. Army. For Roosevelt, the report somewhat surprisingly added, there existed admiration but not enthusiasm.)[90] Again, this was not an issue which greatly troubled the Prime Minister at this time. When Cranborne, for example, indignantly cited the case of one of his own, coloured officials at the Colonial Office who was now barred from his usual lunch-time restaurant because it was patronized by white American officers, Churchill apparently rejoined: 'That's all right; if he takes his banjo with him they'll think he's one of the band.'[91]

1942 was a year in which the Prime Minister had troubles enough on his hands. His leadership continued to inspire—and to exasperate—those around him.* 'At times you could kiss his feet', observed Admiral Pound,

---

* Churchill was also an inspiring figure to many Americans. The *New York Times* of

the First Sea Lord; 'at others you feel you could kill him.'[92] Meanwhile military disasters in the Far East and North Africa gave rise to considerable unrest in political circles and beyond, unrest which Churchill had to confront in the House of Commons in January and again at the beginning of July.[93] Demands for 'new blood' also led to Cabinet changes, with Cripps for a while appearing to be a figure of great political consequence.[94] Beaverbrook, for his part, continued to intrigue in all directions. ('I might be the best man to run the war', he confessed to Halifax. 'It wants a ruthless, unscrupulous, harsh man, and I believe I could do it.')[95] Certainly, American observers were disturbed by these crises. 'On my return', wrote Harriman to Roosevelt in February, 'I found the position more serious than I had expected',[96] and in March he reported himself to be

'worried about the Prime Minister—both his political status and his own spirits. He did not take well to the criticism he found on his return from Washington . . . Although the British are keeping a stiff upper lip, the surrender of their troops at Singapore has shattered confidence to the core—even in themselves, but more particularly in their leaders . . . Unfortunately Singapore shook the Prime Minister himself to such an extent that he has not been able to stand up in this adversity with his old vigor . . .'[97]

Roosevelt also received highly-spiced reports on the situation from Beaverbrook, who noted what he believed to be a sharp decline in the fortunes of the Tory party during the year,[98] and from Laski (whom Churchill and the President between them had secretly prevented from being invited to visit the U.S.A.), who continued to urge Roosevelt to lead the Prime Minister towards enlightened policies that would bring about a social revolution:

'You have only to hear the troops discussing the Beveridge Report', wrote Laski, '. . . to know that the masses are on the move . . . Above all, I am quite sure that the clue to peace lies in the ability of our rulers to understand that only those appear capable of wisdom in an hour of crisis who can combine magnanimity with audacity. That is why, above all, I hope you will teach our Prime Minister that it is the hope of the future and not the achievement of the past from which he must draw his inspiration.'[99]

In the event, Churchill, while in no way conforming to Laski's wishes, and despite being menaced for the long term by a major leftward shift of public opinion that was taking place,[100] survived the attacks of his domestic critics. Where Anglo-American relations were concerned, however, it was in general a difficult year. (Even in the invaluable B.S.C.–O.S.S. partnership that Stephenson and Donovan had built up, serious strains were beginning to develop—and to be fostered, it seems, by Soviet agents like Kim Philby.)[101] The mutual distrust and criticism that existed was probably more pronounced on the American side. 'There are a lot of things on [our] end which

19 June 1942, for example, described him as being 'so deeply loved in this country and so long since adopted as our own.'

are hard for the British to understand', reported Harriman. 'On the other hand, having been in the war for two and a half years they are not inclined to be as critical of us as we seem to be of them.'[102] Admiral Stark, formerly C.N.O. and now head of the American Naval delegation in London, was able to tell his Secretary of the Navy that 'good will seems to shine forth from everybody's eyes over here',[103] while the London press was loud in its welcome for the arriving American troops—170,000 of them by the end of 1942:

'If the Americans and Englishmen', wrote *The Times*, 'can seize this opportunity to sit down together round the same hearth, and the Americans can be enabled to see how life is lived in England, and the Englishman to hear how it is lived in America, the foundations of the future will be well and truly laid.'[104]

Yet even on the British side, there were also signs of coolness. A Gallup Poll taken in June, for example, revealed that 62 per cent of those questioned believed that the Russians were more popular with the British than were the Americans.[105] Further evidence that the climate of opinion could readily breed disagreement and resentment was to come to light early in the following summer, when Gallup Polls conducted in the two countries asked which of the United Nations had up to then made the greatest single contribution towards winning the war, the British sample answering the Soviet Union (50 per cent), Britain (42 per cent), China (5 per cent) and the U.S.A. (3 per cent), as against the American response which placed the United States first (55 per cent), followed by the Soviet Union (32 per cent), Britain (9 per cent) and, last of all, China (4 per cent).[106]

Nor was it any more difficult than it had been before Pearl Harbour to find in British official circles critical attitudes towards the United States and towards Americans—mercurial, unstable and unduly sentimental creatures, as opinion in the Foreign Office tended to have it, with Halifax in Washington loftily finding fresh evidence in the off-duty behaviour of high-ranking Americans with which to sustain his view 'of how immature these people are; it is really', he added, 'the reproduction of an undergraduate atmosphere.'[107] Distrust of American political behaviour was likewise being reflected in the diary kept by Sir Alexander Cadogan,[108] while the Head of the Foreign Office's North American Department was moved to observe in June 1942 that, at a meeting held in the Secretary of State's room on the previous day, 'we discussed America almost as an enemy.'[109] (Sir Arthur Salter's comments on the jealousy of some officials over 'the passing of power' have already been noted in this connection.)[110]

To one official in the Foreign Office, indeed, there was an interesting degree of similarity in the suspicions that were running back and forth between the two countries:

'The Americans', he wrote, 'when viewing our Empire, accuse us of economic imperialism; we . . . see considerable evidence that the Americans regard Latin America as their preserve, reserved to American exploitation. They think the disorderly inter-war world [was] the result of British failure to accept proper responsibility for its ordering; we are quite sure that it was largely due to American refusal to take a hand in its regulation. They think British selfishness will spoil the next peace; we nurse the suspicion that America won't cooperate fairly in the work of reconstruction. They fear that we want to use the Empire as a means of balancing growing American importance; we fear they want to attract its members into their orbit in order to lessen our world-influence.'[111]

Such comments, of course, involved, then as now, huge generalizations. When observing the American scene, for example, one can find both sustained hostility towards Britain during this period, in, say, the pages of the *Chicago Tribune*, and sustained sympathy in the *New York Times*.[112] The notorious 'Open Letter to the People of Britain' that was published in October in Henry Luce's *Life* and criticized Britain's lack of unselfish war aims and her imperial repression, brought forth pro-British rejoinders from the *New York Herald Tribune*, the *Chicago Daily News*, the *Christian Science Monitor* and others. A speech by Willkie on an anti-imperial theme did the same.[113] Likewise, against General Stilwell's finding that all the Americans he spoke to in the Middle East were 'unanimous about limies. Bored and supercilious attitude everywhere',[114] or against Willkie's scorn for those Royal Navy officers in Alexandria who, according to him, spoke to him in terms of 'Rudyard Kipling untainted even by the liberalism of Cecil Rhodes',[115] one could set off the degree of harmony achieved by Eisenhower throughout his Anglo-American staff who were preparing in London for the North African landings. Willkie himself described the British people in June as being 'brave, heroic and self-sustaining.'[116] 'This thing of calling the English a decadent race is just bunk', Henry Morgenthau assured his staff on his return from London.[117]

Nevertheless, it was generally agreed among observers in the United States that Britain's stock fell to an exceptionally low level during 1942, and especially at the time of the defeats in the Far East and North Africa. One survey by the O.W.I., entitled 'Attitudes Towards Our Allies', showed anti-British sentiments among Americans to be greater than anti-Russian or anti-Chinese feeling, 40 per cent of the sample taken in cities and 48 per cent of the rural mid-West being recorded as falling within the first of these categories. 'About 40 per cent of Americans', concluded the survey, 'think that the British got us into the war, and a slighly smaller percentage believe that the British will try to get us to do most of the fighting.' Another such report in December 1942 described 'approximately one quarter of the American public' as being 'more or less anti-British.'[118] Criticism of Britain was 'substantial', according to Halifax in March, and in May he was again reporting: 'Anti-British feeling is still strong.' In the following month Denis Brogan wrote on his return from the U.S.A. that 'the American people think of England as being both Conservative and Radical, conservative of absurd anomalies and dangerously radical in many important departments of life . . . [And] it would not be much of an exaggeration to say that the American thinks of this war as having been fought by Australians, Canadians, etc., armed with American weapons.'[119]

In July, members of the Embassy in Washington felt it necessary to draw up a list of 'Things Which Americans Hold Against The British': their imperialism; their class system; their tendency now to 'go Red'; their bunglers in high places; their large army which remained in the British Isles, not engaged in any fighting; their defeats and retreats; their acceptance of Lend Lease while still owing money borrowed during the First World War; their conservative role in Europe (this opinion coming mainly from Europeans who had emigrated to the U.S.A.); the fact that 'anti-British sentiment is part of the central patriotic American tradition'; the superior airs of Britons in the U.S.A.; their lack of forthrightness and their accent; the snobbish, inward-looking Embassy itself 'which has a quite fantastically low reputation'; a lack of appreciation of the British war effort; repercussions from the lack of understanding encountered by Americans in Britain, and from the unpopularity of American Anglophiles, who were often seen as wealthy snobs; embarrassment arising from the lack of American suffering in the war up till then; the stonewalling tactics adopted by British officials in the face of aggrieved foreigners; the class-consciousness of some British books and films; a romantic sympathy for the Chinese and Indians, who painted a dark picture of the British in Asia; hatred for Roosevelt, which tended to carry with it a dislike of the British, whom the President was thought to like; and the assumptions made about British guile in international affairs.[120]

This last idea did, indeed, remain widespread throughout the period, helped, in the country at large, by Churchill's admission in a speech in February that he had 'dreamed of, aimed at, and worked for' American entry into the war.[121] Suspicions were as deep as ever in official quarters, as well. United States Service chiefs, for example, frequently expressed in private the belief that Britain was managing to get far more than her rightful share of American arms production.[122] Welles, for his part, assured a sub-committee of the State Department's Advisory Committee on Post-War Foreign Policy that 'Britain definitely desires to assume jurisdiction in one form or other over certain French possessions, particularly Jibuti and Tunisia.'[123] The British Foreign Office, Roosevelt told his Joint Chiefs of Staff, was not to be trusted in its manoeuvrings over French issues (further complicated as they had been by the landings in North Africa and the Darlan–de Gaulle–Weygand troubles); Admiral Leahy, too, was confiding similar convictions to his diary.[124] It was also in this period that the President began conveying to Churchill the belief that he, Roosevelt, would be better able to handle Stalin than would the Prime Minister.[125] Long accustomed to maintaining the balance of power and playing the 'honest broker', wrote a senior official of the State Department's European Division,

Britain would naturally now seek to act in such a fashion between the United States and the Soviet Union—though he acknowledged that it was understandable that the British should find it difficult to adjust to their reduced status at a time when 'perhaps the most important single factor in Anglo-American relations today is the passing of world leadership from the British to ourselves.'[126] Other, more biting comments by American officials in this period have already been cited, as have the observations of Hornbeck on the fundamental aversion of the United States, in contrast to Britain, to forming a lasting alliance with fellow Anglo-Saxons or anyone else.[127]

If Hornbeck was right in this—and though his history needed amending, he was close to an important, underlying contrast as regards the World War Two relationship—then no amount of effort on the part of British officials was likely to bring about the exclusive and unrestrained partnership which Churchill, for one, desired. Meanwhile as others saw it, the very inequalities that existed between the two countries were also bound to create severe strains. Arnold Toynbee, for example, with the aid of historical analogues, suggested this to an audience at Chatham House after his return from a visit to the United States between August and October 1942:

'The great difficulty in our relations with America', he argued, '. . . is the fact that [she] still has, and will have, compared to us, a margin, while we have no margin now; a margin of security, a margin of wealth, a margin of time and leisure to give to things other than the war . . . Again and again when I was in America I said to myself: Now I know how the French have felt, and how very good it is for me to know that. Now I understand what they could never make me and my fellow-countrymen understand until it was too late . . . Now [also] I know how the poor Austrians felt in the nineteenth century when Gladstone denounced their vile rule in Lombardy . . . They felt: We Austrians . . . have an empire round our necks. We did not invent the thing just to be nasty. It is a traditional thing, a historic thing . . . It is a very complicated, difficult thing to run, but there it is and we have got to do what we can about it, and after all we are rather proud of it . . . And now here come these Anglo-Saxons and say: "We have no time to learn about this thing, but it is a scandal and we denounce it." . . . And our denunciations gave a certain push to the Austrian Empire and the Turkish Empire which helped to topple them over, and after they had toppled over we saw that there had been some point in them . . . The situation between us and the Americans is very like that.'[128]

Here and there, there were also those in 1942 who were anxious to see time given, on both sides of the Atlantic, to obtaining a new perspective and understanding of the changing state of Anglo-American relations. 'The real trouble', wrote Walter Lippmann to Keynes in letters he sent in April,

'is that since the death of [Lord] Lothian [British Ambassador in Washington in the early days of the war] there has been no one here who has had any philosophy and doctrine about the changing relationships between the United States, the British Commonwealth, and the British Empire. There is almost a complete intellectual vacuum on the subject . . . The whole approach of your people here is ad hoc on details of this and that arising from the conduct of the war itself. There is no general conception among them which they propose to our people which provides any political philosophy into which all of the mighty changes now going on in the world might fit.' 'Americans believe', he wrote in a second letter, 'that their war aims are profoundly different from those of Great Britain . . . There is a strong feeling that Britain east of Suez is quite different from Britain at home, that the war in Europe is a war of liberation and the war in Asia is for the defence of archaic privilege . . . The Asiatic war has revived the profound anti-imperialism of the American tradition [which] is . . . a controlling cause of the anti-British sentiment which . . . developed after the fall of Singapore.'

To this, Keynes himself added that there was also a need for people to re-think their ideas about the relationship in terms of those matters which were his particular concern:

'The present position financially', he responded, 'is one of the by-products of the total failure to revise Anglo-American relations, political, financial and economic—in fact in any field outside the military and supply fields . . . It is lamentable and in the long run may be disastrous.'[129]

As for Roosevelt's close friend, the Anglophile Felix Frankfurter, what he felt was lacking, as we have seen, was 'a continuing consciousness of comradeship between the two peoples', and he regretted that Britain's case and the idealistic element in her war aims were not being put across in the United States as they had been during the First World War, he recalled, by H. G. Wells, Norman Angell and others.[130] At least, however, Frankfurter could derive comfort from the clear instructions given by General Marshall at this time to senior officers of the U.S. Army, that steps must be taken to counteract the enemy propaganda which Marshall believed to be responsible in many instances for 'a marked hostility or contempt for the British' among American soldiers.[131] (Marshall thought, as did Stimson, that 'the best cure for Anglophobia was close contact with each other between the American and British troops.')[132]

In London, meanwhile, the Foreign Office for its part was studying how to improve further British publicity in the U.S.A., making use of larger, and more appealing themes, such as the magnitude of Britain's war effort and the similarity of the two countries' war aims.[133] (It was in this context that one official, as noted earlier, observed that the British Government had become as responsive to American as they were to British public opinion.)[134] In proposing action of this kind, officials believed that they could act with complete sincerity. Many of them genuinely thought that 'a new Britain' was emerging from the war, and that it was this development above all that had to be conveyed to an American public that appeared all too eager to seize upon the self-critical portraits of the British produced by the cartoonist Low and others.[135] As Richard Law minuted in connection with an article in the *Economist* in December on 'America and Britain': 'I believe the British people are experiencing a spiritual regeneration . . . Why *can't* we get it across?'[136]

In addition, there was a belief in Whitehall that a special effort had to be made over one of the major issues that had arisen between the two countries, an issue on which Toynbee, Lippmann and a good many others were placing particular emphasis: that of the existence and future of the British Empire. But as Lippmann also observed, this question was inextricably bound up with another, concerning the entire conduct of the war against Japan. It meant Hongkong, Burma and Malaya, India. The Anglo-American relationship following Pearl Harbour was, as we have seen, remarkably close and yet particularly strained. And it was the Asian, more than the European, setting for the alliance which was helping to create the second of these two, contrasting features. It is therefore to this Far Eastern war in its many aspects that we must now turn.

Notes to Chapter Four

1 For a study of the war as a whole, see P. Calvocoressi and G. Wint, *Total War* (London, 1972; hereafter *Calvocoressi*).
2 Morgenthau, Presidential Diary, 16 June 1942.
3 *Stevenson*, 381, offers a dramatic version of the thinking behind the Dieppe raid, though it must be regarded as unproven as yet.
4 Harriman to FDR, 14 Aug. 1942, Roosevelt Papers, MR box 12.
5 Cab, 10 Dec. 1941, CAB 65/24.
6 E.g. *Matloff and Snell*, 121.
7 *Churchill*, III, 560.
8 See *Woodward*, II, cap. XXVI, and *Sherwood*, 401–2.
9 See in general H. B. Westerfield, *Foreign Policy and Party Politics* (New Haven, 1955).
10 *Wallace*, 16 Dec. 1942. Hopkins, too, was already stressing the need for Soviet help against Japan. *Sherwood*, 641.
11 Alexander Papers, AVAR 6/1.
12 *Cadogan Diaries*, 9 Feb. 1941.
13 Dalton Diary, 11 Sept. 1942. For an interesting exploration of the background to Britain's 'softness', see Barnett, *The Collapse of British Power*.
14 *Moran*, 27.
15 Butler, *Grand Strategy*, III, part II, 419.
16 J. Kennedy, *The Business of War* (London, 1957), 198.
17 Lord Tedder, *With Prejudice* (London, 1966), 313.
18 *Long*, 25 June 1942.
19 Hornbeck memo., 30 July 1942, Hornbeck Papers, box 425.
20 See e.g. FO 371, A10445/31/45.
21 E.g. Stimson Diary, 8 Jan., 23 Sept. 1942; 21 Jan. 1943.
22 FO 371, A1207/60/45.

23 J. Ehrman, *Grand Strategy*, vol. V (London, 1956), xvi.
24 Howard, *Grand Strategy*, IV, 128.
25 Stimson Diary, 23 Dec. 1941.
26 FDR to King, 24 Aug. 1942, King Papers, series I, box 2.
27 *Churchill*, IV, 344; *Bryant*, I, 408.
28 See *Hancock and Gowing*, 388ff.
29 Hall, *North American Supply*, 353. At an individual level, one could cite, for example, the good relations established in North Africa in this period between Macmillan and the President's representative, Robert Murphy (even though the latter was greatly distrusted in the Foreign Office). Macmillan, *The Blast of War*, 237.
30 E.g. *Churchill*, IV, 572ff.
31 'Arcadia' papers, CAB 99/17.
32 'Argonaut' papers, CAB 99/20.
33 'Tube Alloy' papers, PREM 3, 139/8A.
34 E.g. JCS, 9 March 1942, RG 218.
35 Hopkins Papers, box 136.
36 Goodfellow Papers, box 4.
37 DC (Ops.), 14 April 1942, CAB 69/4; CCS, 21 April and 20 June 1942, CAB 88/1.
38 CCS memo., 20 June 1942, CAB 99/20.
39 See Howard, *Grand Strategy*, IV, introduction; *Matloff and Snell*, 268ff.; Marshall to FDR, 6 May 1942, Hopkins Papers, box 133; Stimson Diary, 23 and 27 July 1942.
40 JCS, 10 July 1942, RG 218.
41 JCS, 25 Aug. 1942, Roosevelt Papers, MR box 7A. See material in CAB 99/19.
42 CAB 99/21.
43 Cunningham to Pound, 31 July 1942; Pound to Cunningham, 24 Aug. 1942, Cunningham Papers, BM Add. 52561.
44 Halifax Diary, 15 July 1942.
45 E.g. Pasvolsky to Hull, 20 Jan. 1943, DS, Pasvolsky files, box 4; WP (42) 159, CAB 66/23.
46 WP (42) 23, 25, CAB 66/21; Amery to Linlithgow, 5 Jan. 1942 and 5 Jan. 1943, Linlithgow Papers, vols. 11 and 12 respectively.
47 Cabs, 2 and 6 Feb. 1942, CAB 65/25; WP (42) 62, CAB 66/21; material in PREM 4, 47/1; Halifax to Eden, 17 Feb. 1942, Hickleton Papers, A4. 410.4.
48 Long, 13 Jan. 1942; see Acheson, *Present At The Creation*, 33.
49 Winant to Frankfurter, 29 Dec. 1941, Frankfurter Papers, box 112; DS, Notter files, box 80; FRUS, 1942, I, 191.
50 WP (42) 58 and 66, CAB 66/21; Cab, 12 Feb. 1942, CAB 65/25.
51 Gardner, *Sterling-Dollar Diplomacy*, 64ff.
52 Amery to Linlithgow, 23 Dec. 1942; Linlithgow to Amery, 21 Sept. 1942, Linlithgow Papers, vol. 11.
53 Blum, *Morgenthau and Roosevelt*, 484.
54 See Butler, *Grand Strategy*, III, part II, 665.
55 WP (42) 486, CAB 66/30; Howard, *Grand Strategy*, IV, cap. 1. *Matloff and Snell*, cap. XVI.
56 *New York Times*, 12 Dec. 1941.
57 *Chicago Tribune*, 10 Jan. 1942.
58 Blum, *Morgenthau and Roosevelt*, 490.
59 Stimson Diary, 23 and 27 July 1942.
60 WP (42) 492, CAB 66/30. The substance of Law's Cabinet paper got back to Hull and others in Washington. Taussig Papers, box 46.
61 WP (42) 591, CAB 66/32, and e.g. FO 371, A4741/31/45, A5722/399/45.
62 FO 371, A7567/31/45.
63 Dalton Diary, 1 Jan. 1944.
64 Campbell to Butler, 8 May 1942, FO 371, A4747/399/45.
65 FO 371, A4741/31/45.
66 PREM 4, 26/6.

67 Tedder, *With Prejudice*, 156, 219ff.; *Wallace*, 26 Feb. 1943.
68 WP (42) 515, CAB 66/30.
69 WP (42) 601, CAB 66/32.
70 PREM 4, 42/9.
71 *Churchill*, III, 596.
72 WP (42) 532, CAB 66/31; Bevin to Eden, 8 Dec. 1942, Bevin Papers, box 23; see also WP (42) 516, CAB 66/30; Cabs, 23 and 27 Nov. 1942, CAB 65/28; WP (43) 31 and 39, CAB 66/33; material in PREM 4, 100/7.
73 WP (42) 586, CAB 66/32.
74 E.g. *Vandenberg*, 13 Dec. 1941.
75 PREM 4, 27/1.
76 FO 371, A2206/31/45; see various minutes in files 30653–4.
77 E.g. memos, by Division of Special Research, DS, Pasvolsky files, box 4.
78 Divine, *Second Chance*, 68ff.
79 Lippmann to Frankfurter, 13 July 1942, Frankfurter Papers, box 78.
80 Stimson Diary, 27 March, 22 June and 10 Aug. 1942.
81 Hull to FDR, 15 April 1942, Hull Papers, vol. 50
82 *Wallace*, 16 Feb. 1943.
83 FO 371, A5948/31/45; see A2742/31/45.
84 Reports of 16 March and 5 Aug. 1942, Roosevelt Papers, PSF boxes 170, 171.
85 See above, 9.
86 Stimson Diary, 13, 17, 24 Jan. 1942; 12 May 1942.
87 Halifax Diary, 8 March 1942.
88 Stimson Diary, 24 Sept. and 2 Oct. 1942; Dulles report, IPR, box 374.
89 C. Thorne, 'Britain and the Black G.Is.', *New Community*, vol. III No. 3, 1974.
90 FO 371, A670/32/45.
91 *Cadogan Diaries*, 483.
92 Alexander Diary, 10 June 1942, AVAR 6/1.
93 See *Churchill*, IV, 53ff., 351ff.; Taylor, *Beaverbrook*, 506ff.
94 See e.g. P. Addison, *The Road to 1945* (London, 1975; hereafter, *Addison*), 190ff.
95 Halifax Diary, 25 March 1942; see Dalton Diary, 19 Feb. and 24 Aug. 1942, and Donovan to FDR, 2 March 1942, Roosevelt Papers, PSF box 162.
96 Harriman to FDR, 7 Feb 1942, Roosevelt Papers, MR box 12; see Harriman and Abel, *Special Envoy*, cap. VI.
97 Harriman to FDR, 7 March 1942, Roosevelt Papers, PSF box 50; see Hopkins memo., 11 March 1942, Hopkins Papers, box 154.
98 Beaverbrook to FDR, 15 Sept. 1942, Roosevelt Papers, PSF box 37.
99 Laski to FDR, 27 Dec. 1942, Frankfurter Papers, box 75; FDR to Hopkins, 30 July 1942, Hopkins Papers, box 314; Churchill to Hopkins, 14 Aug. 1942, Roosevelt Papers, MR box 13. Laski also wrote to the President: 'The common people have faith in you. So long as you keep their devotion, nothing else really matters.' Laski to FDR, 11 Oct. 1942, Frankfurter Papers, box 75.
100 *Addison*, 15 and 127ff.
101 *Stevenson*, 411.
102 Harriman to Hopkins, 7 March 1942, Hopkins Papers, box 308.
103 Stark to Knox, 2 May 1942, Knox Papers, box 1.
104 *Times*, 29 July 1942. See ibid, 3, 6, 11, 15 July 1942, 26 Nov. 1942, 22 Dec. 1942; *News of the World*, 2 April 1942; *Daily Express*, 4 July 1942, 13 and 19 Aug. 1942, 21 Oct. 1942.
105 Pelling, *Churchill*, 561; *Daily Express*, 13 Aug. 1942.
106 Gallup Poll archives, London; *Cantril and Strunk*, 275.
107 Halifax Diary, 20 Nov. 1942; see e.g. FO 371, A1286/31/45; A4574/60/45.
108 E.g. *Cadogan Diaries*, 17 Nov. and 17 Dec. 1942.
109 FO 371, A8566/G.
110 See above, 105.
111 Evans minute, 12 May 1942, FO 371, A4410/60/45.

112 E.g. *New York Times*, 19 and 23 Dec. 1941, 22 June and 18 July 1942; *Chicago Tribune*, 6 June, 12 Oct. and 3 Dec. 1942.

113 See PREM 4, 26/8 and *New York Herald Tribune*, 13 Oct. 1942; *Chicago Daily News*, 13 Oct. and 12 Nov. 1942; *Christian Science Monitor*, 12 Dec. 1942; *Saturday Evening Post*, 21 Nov. 1942.

114 Stilwell Diary, 23 Feb. 1942.

115 Barnard, *Willkie*, 351.

116 Ibid, 345.

117 Blum, *Morgenthau and Roosevelt*, 482.

118 FO 371, A3480/3/45; A852/32/45.

119 Ibid, A2206, 4741 and 6223/31/45.

120 Ibid, A6681/60/45. See Rostow to Martin, 11 Jan. 1943, Kingsley Martin Papers, box 1.

121 See Halifax to Eden, 24 Feb. 1942, PREM 4, 27/9, and *Vandenberg*, 16 Feb. 1942.

122 E.g. JCS, 7 March 1942, RG 218; Stilwell Diary, 11 Jan. 1942; King to Stark, 21 May 1942, King Papers, series I, box 2.

123 Committee on Political Problems, 12 Dec. 1942, DS, Notter files, box 55.

124 JCS, 7 Jan. 1943; Leahy Diary, 9 and 24 Dec. 1942.

125 *Churchill*, IV, 177.

126 Hickerson, 'Notes on British Policy', n.d., 1943, DS, Hickerson-Matthews files, box 2; see FO 371, A995/399/45.

127 See above, 100.

128 Address of 7 Dec. 1942, Toynbee file, RIIA.

129 Keynes–Lippmann correspondence, FO 371, A4574 and 8566/60/45.

130 Frankfurter to Cripps, 9 July 1942, and memo., n.d., Frankfurter Papers, box 126.

131 Marshall to Frankfurter, 19 Dec. 1942, ibid, box 126.

132 Stimson Diary, 18 Dec. 1942.

133 Material in FO 371, file 30670; see e.g. editor of *New Republic* to Martin, 2 June 1941 Kingsley Martin Papers, box 30; Luce letter, 'to some of my friends in Britain' 11 Nov. 1942, Beaverbrook Papers, C/227; WP (42) 208, CAB 66/24.

134 FO 371, A1070/3/45.

135 E.g. Aubrey Morgan report, ibid, A995/399/45.

136 Ibid, A126/32/45. One reason why some American observers remained unconvinced that Britain was undergoing a social transformation was bound up with the defeats of her Army, discussed above. Thus, a secret O.S.S. report of March 1942 on 'Morale in the British Armed Forces', while praising the spirit to be found in the R.N. and R.A.F., concluded that 'In the Army, the problems of officer-men relationships have become immensely complicated, resolving at times into a class struggle which threatens the whole organization with disunity, . . . [and with] a new generation of subalterns, with the approval or by the orders of Commanding Officers, . . . [creating] a renewed emphasis on privilege and social precedence.' R and A, 617.

CHAPTER FIVE

THE WAR AGAINST JAPAN

IN THE six months following Pearl Harbour, the Japanese achieved against the Western powers a remarkable series of military triumphs, the political effects of which no subsequent counter-victories could entirely erase. The Asian scene would never be the same again. Within days, the *Prince of Wales* and the *Repulse*, those intended deterrents from a passing era of British naval supremacy, were at the bottom of the sea; within weeks, Hongkong, symbol of Britain's world-wide commercial interests, was in Japanese hands. Worse was to follow, for the fall of Hongkong, already surrounded by Japanese forces, had clearly been inevitable. By the end of January 1942 the British and Australian defenders had been swept from the Malay peninsula into Singapore, the very heart of the Empire's defensive system in the East. Then, on 15 February, to the astonishment of the world, Singapore itself surrendered. Nor did a hastily-erected inter-Allied defence structure fare any better. On 15 January General Wavell took up his command of the A.B.D.A. (American, British, Dutch, Australian) area, centred upon the Netherlands East Indies; by 25 February, his Command dissolved, he was flying back to India, with resistance in the East Indies coming to an end early in April. Meanwhile the Japanese were also advancing into Burma, where Rangoon fell to them on 7 March. The Burma Road to China had been cut by the end of April, and by mid-May nearly all of Burma was under Japanese control; only a trickle of supplies continued to reach China by the 'Hump' air-transport route over the Himalayas from India. Even India itself already appeared to be seriously threatened. Early in April a Japanese striking force of aircraft carriers and battleships had moved into the Indian Ocean and raided Ceylon, forcing the main units of the British Eastern Fleet to withdraw towards East Africa.[1] For a time—and in the event the Japanese raiders chose to pull back—the Northeast of India appeared to be wide open to attack.

For the Americans, too, as for the Europeans, it was a time of defeat. In the Philippines, for all the earlier confidence displayed by General MacArthur, the main body of defenders were forced to surrender on the Bataan peninsula on 9 April; further resistance came to an end on 6 May with the fall of the island fortress of Corregidor—although MacArthur himself, on the orders of the President, had by then made his way out to

Australia, where he took command of the newly-created South West Pacific Area. It was the Americans, however, who delivered the first check to the triumphant Japanese. In the naval–air battle of the Coral Sea, early in May, and despite the severely depleted number of units at Admiral King's disposal after Pearl Harbour, the enemy's aircraft carriers failed to gain a clear victory over a rival U.S. Navy force. A month later, at the battle of Midway, they were decisively defeated, four of their large carriers being sunk to the Americans' one. It was, in fact, one of the turning points of the war, for never again was Japan's Navy to hold the initiative in the Pacific.

Yet even so, the Japanese remained a formidable foe, as became apparent during the bitter American struggle for the island of Guadalcanal in the British Solomon Islands Protectorate, which lasted from August 1942 to early February 1943. The same lesson was made plain during the Australian–American campaign to check and drive back the Japanese in eastern New Guinea, which lasted from July until January 1943. Only when victory had been gained in these two fights, on Guadalcanal and in New Guinea, were the Allies in a position to begin the task of advancing back up the line of Japanese conquests in the Southwest Pacific. Nor had any significant impression yet been made on the other, Southeast Asian, arm of those conquests, on the borders of Burma and India. By February 1943, Japanese expansion had been brought to a halt, but had still to be rolled back.

These developments in the Far East obviously had a considerable impact in Britain, as demonstrated, for example, by the serious Parliamentary situation, already referred to, which faced Churchill on his return from the 'Arcadia' Conference. The Japanese had inflicted not simply defeat but humiliation on the Empire, and in a poll taken early in 1943 only 6 per cent of those asked disapproved of the intention to fight on until Japan was beaten, even if Germany were defeated beforehand.[2] Churchill himself had publicly made such a pledge to the United States at the end of 1942, thus helping, so the Embassy in Washington reported, 'to meet the undercurrent of suspicion which has been increasingly felt [here] that once the European phase of the war is over, the United States will be left to deal with Japan alone, or with only token British aid.' The Prime Minister also, at Casablanca, offered to enter into a formal treaty in order to allay further suspicions of this kind.[3]

Yet it remained the case that for the bulk of the British public the war was being fought above all against Hitler's Germany, whence had come the bombs and the threat of invasion itself. 'The Japanese war', writes a student of the home front, 'impinged remarkably little on the consciousness of the British people, except of course in those families who had members serving in the Far East. Save at the time of the fall of Singapore, its advances and reverses meant little in Britain. Only thirty thousand British servicemen died in the war against Japan, as compared to two hundred and thirty-five thousand in the war against Germany . . . , first and always the real enemy.'[4] Kingsley Martin for one, as editor of the *New Statesman*, believed that there was a 'really important job of work' to be done in awakening the British to

Far Eastern affairs, and vainly sought an additional allowance of paper on which to print a special monthly supplement devoted to this purpose.[5]

The contrast with the United States was considerable. There, opinion might be confused as to the ends for which the war was being fought (or so the O.W.I. reported to the President),[6] but the need to be revenged upon the Japanese stood out clearly enough. Pearl Harbour was an insult to the entire nation, and the barbaric treatment meted out to American prisoners taken in the Philippines (notably during the notorious Bataan death-march) had to be punished with all speed. 'We're going back to Bataan!' proclaimed the daily masthead of the *Chicago Tribune*. Indeed, such had been the hysteria following Japan's first attacks, that thousands of Japanese-Americans living on the West Coast had been interned in camps inland.[7] On this West Coast, too, as well as in former isolationist circles, the idea was prevalent that the United States should focus her efforts upon Japan as being, in the words of the *Chicago Tribune*, 'the principal and proximate enemy.'[8] 'Public opinion at the present', reported the O.W.I. to Roosevelt in April 1942, 'is that our strength should be concentrated first on defeating Japan', while by February 1943 public opinion polls were still showing that 53 per cent regarded Japan as the major foe.[9] Japan is 'enemy number one', declared the *San Francisco Examiner*. 'For Uncle Sam . . . the Pacific Ocean is HIS show, [the aim being to prevent] the extermination of 75 per cent of the English-speaking peoples and substitution of Japanese-speaking peoples.'[10] Such sentiments were eagerly voiced by enemies of Roosevelt, with his European-oriented priorities, and they had their own hero to hand in the person of Douglas MacArthur, who was depicted as being hampered in his fight by Washington and America's allies alike.[11] Even those who accepted the President's lead were stirred by the struggle in the Far East. The *New York Times*, for example, which endorsed a strategy of 'Germany first', nevertheless saw 'the siege of Asia' as being crucial: 'If Asia holds out', the paper declared, 'the United Nations can win a clear-cut and conclusive victory . . . But if Asia falls to the Axis war will simply become chronic, the chief occupation of mankind for horrible, endless years.'[12] Some went further still. In a speech in February 1942, the celebrated novelist and Sinophile, Pearl Buck, proclaimed that

'The American stake in the Far East is far greater than it is in Europe. If the American way of life is to prevail in the world, it must prevail in Asia, whether it prevails in Europe or not . . . In Europe our influence has been of little importance. In Asia it has long been the chief influence. We have so far the ideological leadership in Asia, and Japan knows it . . .'[13]*

Evangelical zeal of this kind was quite absent from British approaches to the war against Japan, something which is not surprising in the light of those features of international politics in the Far East that we have observed in the years before 1939. There was, however, an apprehensive awareness in

---

* Note Thomas Mann's statement in Dec. 1942, that 'the Americanization of the world, in a certain fundamental moral sense, would be a piece of good fortune for mankind.'

official quarters that a widespread and emotional pull away from a policy of 'Germany first' existed in the United States. Hopkins underlined this by warning the Cabinet's Defence Committee in London in April that 'if public opinion in America had its way, the weight of American effort would be directed against Japan', and it was a danger which clearly dwelt in Churchill's mind at the time.[14] Moreover, there continued to be an awareness on the part of some British officials and commentators of one of the developments towards which Pearl Buck and others in the United States were pointing: that a new era was opening in relations between East and West. When the *New York Times* meditated on the import of Chiang Kai-shek's talks with Nehru and others in India, for example ('India and China', it suggested, 'are no longer suppliants at the white man's door. Not all the faded trappings of imperialism, not all the pomp of viceroys, not all the arrogance of the "old China hands" has much meaning for them now'),[15] the theme was echoed by the *Manchester Guardian*.[16] Even the Secretary of State for India, Amery, observed uneasily to Smuts: 'It looks as if we were on the eve of very great changes in the relation of Asia to Europe. Indeed the whole question arises whether in the future empires like our Asiatic empire, based on a very low degree of militarization and interference with the life of the people, can subsist.'[17] In a memorandum to his Cabinet colleagues, part of which has already been quoted, Attlee declared:

'India has been profoundly affected by the changed relationship between Europeans and Asiatics which began with the defeat of Russia by Japan at the beginning of the century . . . The reverses which we and the Americans are sustaining from the Japanese at the present time will continue the process. The gallant resistance of the Chinese for more than four years against the same enemy makes the same way. The fact that we are now accepting Chinese aid in our war against the Axis Powers and are necessarily driven to a belated recognition of China as an equal and of Chinese as fellow fighters for civilisation against barbarism makes the Indian ask why he, too, cannot be master in his own house.'[18]

'Nationalism and social factors', Chiang Kai-shek informed Roosevelt, could well be increasingly important elements in the war in Southeast Asia; in a similar vein, American military intelligence reported that in the areas they had occupied the Japanese were stimulating native nationalisms to such an extent that 'the idea of Asia for the Asiatics will not vanish on the day of Japan's complete military defeat.'[19] Indeed, in both London and Washington, but more especially in the American capital, the fear was already growing that Tokyo might succeed in turning the war into a racial crusade. Admiral Leahy, for example, from his place at Roosevelt's side, agreed with Pat Hurley, later Ambassador to China, that 'unless we administer a defeat to Japan in the near future, that nation will succeed in combining most of the Asiatic people against the whites.'[20] Hence, as we shall see in more detail in the next chapter, the belief that it was vitally important to keep China and India in the fight on the Allied side. 'The whole position in Asia might change very rapidly', ran the minutes of a Cabinet discussion in London, 'and we should not exclude the possibility of a Pan-Asiatic movement.'[21] (With this in mind, the Government of India, like the State Department, was averse to giving publicity to the humiliations inflicted upon white prisoners by the Japanese.)[22]

Post-war as well as war-time implications were involved. For example, the Australian Minister in Chungking, Sir Frederick Eggleston, warned Canberra that, after the current conflict was over,

'the Asiatic peoples might band together to forward their mutual interests; in fact, a Pan-Asiatic movement. India might be able to come to an arrangement with Japan; China might then join in and with her millions she would be a tremendous asset to the combination . . . The idea has an attraction to the Asiatic mind and I feel it must be watched.'[23]

In the gulf between whites and coloureds, likewise believed a senior member of the Institute of Pacific Relations, lay 'the greatest threat to the future peace of the Pacific area in particular and the world in general', and Hornbeck among others was anxiously discussing the same subject.[24]

Another person who was taking an interest in future inter-racial developments in general, and not merely in the need to keep China's millions as friends of the West, was Roosevelt. The President's natural inclination was to look ahead in a broad way. He was also being encouraged, now that America was in the war, to see himself as the supreme arbiter of the eventual peace. (Colonel Donovan, for example, as head of the O.S.S., told him after touring the Middle East that the small nations 'look upon Churchill as the great defender, but they look upon you as the great liberator.')[25] It has already been suggested, however, that Roosevelt's ideas about race, and in particular about inter-racial developments in the Far East, appear to have been of a somewhat cloudy kind. To the Pacific War Council, for example, he observed that, since 'human beings, given equal opportunities, mix successfully', then, in the post-war world, 'racial prejudices, as we know them in the past, will . . . probably be subordinated, and the countries of the world will more or less become melting pots.' ('If we accept the President's thought in this matter', dryly observed the Australian representative on the Council, 'it would seem to be of little importance who wins the war.')[26]

More specifically, Roosevelt had earlier suggested, during a private conversation at his Hyde Park home with the British Minister in Washington, 'that [Britain] and the United States should try to think of some arrangement by which India found its place in the . . . Western orbit rather than in the Asiatic . . .' 'The President said', reported the Minister afterwards, 'that, after all, racially the mass of Indians were really the cousins of us Westerners (Aryans, Iranians!).'[27] Moreover, as was indicated briefly in an earlier chapter, Roosevelt also talked on this occasion of the possibility of effecting a racial crossing in order to improve conditions in the Far East, where the evil-doing of the Japanese might be due to the less-developed skulls of their basic stock. He had a professor at the Smithsonian Institution working on the matter. Meanwhile, 'As far as I could make out', noted the Minister, Sir Ronald Campbell (who was a careful reporter), 'the line of the President's thought is that an Indo-Asian or Eurasian or (better) Euroindoasian race could be developed which would be good and produce a good civilization and Far East "order", to the exclusion of the Japanese, languishing in Coventry in their original islands.'[28]*

Subjects to do with breeding and race seem, indeed, to have held a certain fascination for the President—a topic which 'psycho-historians' will no doubt deal with in time, but some of the evidence for which a writer of more limited compass may note in passing. Thus, for example, Roosevelt felt it in order to talk, jokingly, of dealing with Puerto Rico's excessive birth rate by employing, in his own words, 'the methods which Hitler used effectively.' He said to Charles Taussig and William Hassett, as the former recorded it, 'that it is all very simple and painless—you have people pass through a narrow passage and then there is a brrrrr of an electrical apparatus. They stay there for twenty seconds and from then on they are sterile.'[29] In more serious vein, it seems, the President told Morgenthau that 'you either have to castrate the German people or you have got to treat them in such a manner so they can't just go on reproducing people who want to continue the way they have in the past.'[30] In addition, Roosevelt was ready to make sweeping generalizations about the characteristics of specific nationalities. Thus the Vietnamese, he was to inform Stalin at Yalta, were 'people of small stature . . . and not warlike', while we have already seen his scornful dismissal of the Burmese as dislikable.[31] †

Such facile and somewhat ugly ramblings apart, one also encounters again in this period various American ideas about the Far East which have been observed in earlier, pre-war years. Thus Stimson, for example, was still thinking, as Secretary of War, of the special destiny of the United States in that part of the world and of her special relationship with China in particular, just as he had done as Secretary of State during the 1931–33 crisis. The supplying of American war-time aid to China, he now wrote in his diary in February 1942, was 'a unique opportunity to play for the highest stakes in the Far East.'[32] Some officials were also encouraged to think in similar terms by their belief that no other country besides the United States was likely to be involved in the act of rescue. Numerous

---

* The bulk of the document is given in the notes to this chapter. The scientist in question was Dr. Ales Hrdlicka, Curator of the Division of Phsyical Anthropology at the Smithsonian Institution until his retirement in 1942. He died in 1943. For a summary of his career, see *American Anthropologist*, vol. 46, no. 1, 1944.

† In his *Price of Revolution* (London, 1951), Denis Brogan was to remind his readers of an important general point in this field. 'It would be highly unrealistic', he wrote, 'not to note the fact that in the years between the wars, the United States was only outdistanced by Germany as a market for race theories, some of them crude enough to have suited Hitler.' Also relevant are the racial attitudes among American whites which surrounded the eviction of Japanese-Americans from the West coast in 1942. See A. Girdner and A. Loftis, *The Great Betrayal* (Toronto, 1969).

pieces of evidence of Britain's weariness, wrote Hornbeck, 'tend to confirm
. . . that the saving of the situation in eastern Asia and the Indian Ocean . . .
is going to depend upon the efficiency and efficacy of American efforts, plus
whatever can be made of Chiang Kai-shek's political genius, Chiang's will
to fight, Chiang's command over three or four million soldiers, and the
terrain of China as a base for air operations against Japan.'[33]

It followed that American strength, employed on its own, could help to
ensure not only a better future for Asia, but a more prosperous one for the
United States herself. 'After we have won the war in the Pacific', declared
the former Consul-General in Batavia, '*and we must win it alone*, . . . we shall
be in a position to insist on the "open door" in matters of imports, exports,
industries, the development of resources and the improvement of the condition of the native.'[34] (More senior men will be found speaking and writing
in this vein in subsequent periods of the war.) There were those, indeed, who
were thinking of the Japanese war rather in terms of a crusade. Therefore
American policy in Asia must be based on the highest principles, and must
conform to the Atlantic Charter, which was of universal relevance—
although some in the U.S.A., as well as Evatt for Australia, thought that
perhaps a companion, 'Pacific Charter' was needed. In this connection one
could proudly hold up the case of American policy in the Philippines as
being, in Hull's words, 'a perfect example of how a nation should treat a
colony or dependency in cooperating with it . . . in making all necessary
preparations for freedom.'[35]

Ideas such as these were frequently accompanied by the belief, in American
minds, that Britain was unfortunately less enlightened in these matters.
The myth of having been 'let down' by Britain in 1932, for example, retained
a wide currency.[36] Hornbeck, who had figured prominently in that earlier
episode, was for his part still capable of bursting out when face to face with
British officials (he did so to Ashley Clarke, Head of the Foreign Office's
Far Eastern Department, when the latter visited Washington) about London's
unawareness of vital trends in the Far East, especially those concerning the
greatness of China.[37] The conviction was also widespread that Britain,
like others, was fighting in Asia and elsewhere a 'political' war, in a
way that the United States was not. 'We have not bled enough for the liking
of the Russians, the British or the Chinese', General Stilwell's diplomatic
adviser was to write early in 1943. 'With political considerations looming so
large in their calculations, they are each fighting not only the common
enemies but also, in a negative fashion, their allies.'[38]

These American suspicions and beliefs were, in part at least, known to
British Ministers and officials. The response from Churchill himself was at
times an adamant one, as we shall see in the case of India and of the British
Empire in general. Before the anniversary of the signing of the Atlantic
Charter, for example, the Prime Minister made it clear to Roosevelt that he
was opposed to any interpretation of that document in universal terms:

'I should not be able', he wrote, 'without mature consideration, to give it a wider interpretation than was agreed between us at the time. Its proposed application to Asia and Africa requires much thought. Grave embarrassment would be caused to the defence of India at the present time by such a statement as the Office of War Information has been forecasting . . .'[39]

'We also have our traditions', he insisted to an American official over lunch at 10 Downing Street, 'and as long as I am here we will hold on to them and the Empire.'[40] In public, too, he made his celebrated declaration that he had 'not become His Majesty's First Minister in order to preside over the liquidation of the British Empire.'

Elsewhere in Westminster and Whitehall there were also outbursts of exasperation, for example within the Foreign Office over what was described as 'a noticeable tendency [on the part of the Americans] to play down or even ignore the part played by the United Kingdom in the Pacific war.'[41] In general, however, officials were anxious to do something to diminish American criticisms concerning the Far East, a list of which—including a reference to the Simon–Stimson episode of 1932—was drawn up by the Ministry of Information. (In response to this document, and in apparent ignorance of what the Prime Minister had told Roosevelt, the Foreign Office asserted that the British Government 'have never contested the universal application of the Atlantic Charter and are equally determined to see the Four Freedoms* established in their Far Eastern and Pacific territories and elsewhere.')[42]

Britain's Far Eastern policies were seen in the Foreign Office, in fact, as being vital for the preservation of good relations with Washington. 'In our attitude towards the Far Eastern struggle', ran one memorandum by Sir John Brenan, a former Consul General in Shanghai, 'we have at all times to keep in line with the United States';[43] 'Anglo-Chinese relations', minuted another official, 'are . . . in themselves and at present of no great importance. There is little either side can or will do more than it is doing to help or harm the other. Where our relations with China are important is in their very great potentiality to affect, for better or worse, our relations with America. The Americans are pathological about China, and keenly suspicious of any possible unfriendliness towards her on the part of others.'[44] The same conclusion was drawn when it came to looking ahead to later years. 'We should now seriously begin to clear our minds on the problems of a post-war settlement in the Far East', urged the Head of the Far Eastern Department after visiting Washington, 'and . . . while United States views are still in the formative stage, devise some means of joint consideration of such problems with the United States authorities.' 'The readiness of the United States to cooperate with us in the Far East', he added, 'both now and after the war, will, I am convinced, depend on the degree to which we make it plain that

---

* In January 1941, Roosevelt had enunciated 'Four Freedoms' on which the world of the future should be built: freedom of speech and expression; freedom of worship; freedom from want; freedom from fear.

we also want to help China for her own sake.'[45] In this connection, both the Far Eastern and North American Departments saw an American involvement in post-war peace-keeping in the Far East as being vital for the security of Britain's own interests; both Departments believed, in the words of Brenan, 'that our best hope for peace and stability after the war lies in close collaboration with the United States in all matters concerning post-war reconstruction.' 'Therefore', Brenan added, 'our plans for the future of the Far Eastern countries should fit in with this general picture.' When consideration was given to a specific issue that might give rise to trouble in the future, such as the possibility of a Sino-French clash over Indochina, the answer was the same: Anglo-American cooperation was essential.[46]

It is true, as we shall see below, notably where India was concerned, that not every British official dealing with Asian matters in 1942 was as anxious as the Foreign Office to cater to American susceptibilities. Nevertheless, a predominant pattern was already forming in connection with Far Eastern affairs—one that was to last throughout the war: on the American side, suspicions of the British and an assumption of conflicting interests; on the part of the British, a belief in mutual, long-term Anglo-American interests and hopes for close collaboration. Already, too, associated difficulties and strains were becoming apparent, for example in the field of political warfare. In this connection, an inter-departmental Committee on Political Warfare Against Japan was set up in London in March 1942, while the Office of War Information (together with the O.S.S.) was beginning to operate in this field from the United States. Liaison arrangements between the two were established, and few difficulties were encountered over such matters as the devising of propaganda aimed at weakening Japanese morale.[47] Among the British departments involved, however, a major problem did arise when the Ministry of Information proposed to make use of propaganda in free China 'to turn our Far Eastern disasters to good account by showing . . . that the fall of Singapore symbolized the passing of a whole phase of Britain's relations with the peoples of the East, and that there is arising in Britain a new attitude towards them based no longer on the idea of exploitation and racial superiority but on equality, mutual respect and friendship in a common struggle.' The difficulty was that, as the M.O.I. recognized, a prior requirement was for the Government itself to make 'a major declaration of policy and some statement further interpreting the Atlantic Charter.' And with Churchill in command, no such declaration or statement was likely to be forthcoming.[48]

At the same time as the British were attempting to build a structure of political warfare without the firm foundations of a positive, long-term political policy, tension was also developing between the two Western Allies, especially where the question of propaganda directed at supposedly loyal Asian peoples was concerned. 'The United States attitude towards Britain in that part of the world was not altogether friendly', observed the Political Warfare Against Japan Committee uneasily.[49] And when, for example, by some means or other, a secret O.S.S. Psychological Warfare

Division paper on 'British Malaya' found its way to Whitehall, it was discovered that the document advised American propagandists not to identify the United States with Britain, and not to refer to 'British' Malaya 'since many inhabitants of Malaya do not wish to see [the country] revert to its old status.' This and other pieces of evidence suggested to one Foreign Office official 'that unscrupulous elements in the American organisation intend, perhaps without the direct consent of their superiors, to direct some of their political warfare activities against us as well as against the enemy.'[50] We shall see later that such a reading of the situation was to figure more prominently still in London by 1944 and 1945.

Meanwhile, there existed a more immediate cause for anxiety among British officials, in the shape of an American tendency to direct a greater military effort against Japan than a strict policy of 'Germany first' would allow. Admiral King, in particular, sought to push ahead in this direction, while at his new Australian headquarters MacArthur was doing likewise. Others, too, like Leahy and Hornbeck, were thinking in a similar manner: 'America's war effort should now be concentrated on Japan', noted the former in September 1942.[51] In the event, no official change of policy was forthcoming since Roosevelt, for all his fears at one time of the degree of damage the Japanese could inflict if they attacked in force in the Indian Ocean,[52] stood by the agreement reached at the 'Arcadia' Conference. Even so, the July document drawn up by the Combined Chiefs of Staff, C.C.S. 94, did, as we have seen, complicate the situation. Moreover, by the end of 1942 the American military effort in the Pacific was already considerably exceeding the level which had been originally intended. (346,000 American troops were then serving in the area, a figure roughly equal to that for the U.K. and North Africa combined, and 150,000 more than the one originally projected.) 'The Army planners', write two American official historians, 'continued to work on the principle—which was never stated in so many words—that further "diversions" to operations in the Mediterranean, as required to maintain the momentum of "diversionary" operations initiated there in 1942, justified parallel "diversions" to operations in the Pacific, as required for the same reasons.'[53]

This tendency greatly perturbed the British Chiefs of Staff.[54] It was not that they were completely indifferent to the Far Eastern theatre: quite apart from obvious British interests such as the defence of Australia and New Zealand, the raw materials of the area alone were sufficient to compel anxiety in London over the enemy's advance. Churchill himself, in the strategic surveys mentioned earlier,[55] made it clear that he was as eager as Admiral King to do something to regain the initiative against Japan. He was also ready in 1942 to agree that the reopening of land communications with China was 'an immediate and essential need.'[56] Nevertheless, a major attack against the Japanese, as the Prime Minister saw it, would have to wait until 1943, although preparations could be made 'all along the Californian shore' in the meantime.[57] And nothing must be allowed to interfere with the 'primary object' of defeating Germany. ('Disasters in Far East cloud the nearer scene', wrote Cadogan in his diary, 'but on a longer view all that matters is defeat of Germany.')[58]

Meanwhile some comfort could be derived from the thought, expressed by Smuts in the Pacific War Council in London, that 'one or two good blows at the heart of the Japanese resistance would cause a surprising collapse.'[59] This idea, of an eventual fierce assault upon 'the heart', rather than a prolonged war of attrition on the periphery, of the Japanese-held area, was what attracted the Prime Minister, also. Thus, in June 1942, he summarized his thoughts for the benefit of his liaison officer with MacArthur, in the form of a nursery rhyme: for the outlying Japanese forces, once their homeland was under severe bombardment, it would be a case of '"Lady bird, Lady bird, fly away home, your house is aburning, your children are gone."'[60] One could also hope—although senior Foreign Office officials doubted that the moment was near at hand—that the Soviet Union, too, would lend her weight to the fight against Japan, as Stalin had already indicated he wished to do.[61]

For the moment, however, the extent of Britain's military weakness in the Far East reinforced the inclination to think only in modest terms of what could be achieved in that area in the immediate future. This same military weakness also helped to bring about another development: that of the Americans becoming closely involved in the British sphere of Far Eastern operations. We have seen how the regions from Singapore westwards were made a British responsibility in the global allocation drawn up in the spring of 1942.[62] Yet, as the Chiefs of Staff warned the Cabinet in London, 'once Japan has effectively breached the Malayan Barrier, she has a clear run into the Indian Ocean, where we are dangerously weak in all respects.'[63] And when the Japanese threat in that Ocean did, indeed, come to pass, Churchill was speedily forced to confess to Roosevelt that 'we have more than we can bear', and to appeal for American naval and air reinforcements.[64] Thus, the growing material predominance of the United States which was noted earlier, together with Washington's concern for reestablishing links with China through Burma, ensured that strategy and campaigns in Southeast Asia were to be very much an inter-Allied affair—this, despite the main responsibility carried by the C.O.S. in London and despite a sometimes unreasonable tendency on the part of that body to bridle at what they saw as American interference.[65]

Similar factors also ensured that there would be an American war-time predominance in China itself, a development which completely reversed the pre-war relative positions of Britain and the United States. For the supplying of military equipment, China was officially placed within America's area of responsibility;[66] in general strategic matters, Churchill himself acknowledged to Roosevelt that 'Chiang Kai-shek is primarily your concern', and suggested 'that you will weave her in with the Combined Chiefs of Staff in Washington, while keeping us constantly informed, and will bring everything to a final solution there.'[67] At the same time, Britain's weakness and America's swelling power helped to ensure that, on the other side of the

Malay Barrier from Southeast Asia—on the other side, that is, of Japan's extensive circle of conquests that effectively split the Allied efforts being made from east and west on its periphery—a very different situation obtained from the one within Britain's area of responsibility. Despite London's obvious concern for the fate of Australia and New Zealand, it was the United States that was now their protector, both in fact and under the worldwide division of responsibilities. Whilst the Americans became increasingly involved in Southeast Asia, where the South West Pacific Area was concerned the British Chiefs of Staff found themselves reduced to 'largely conjecture' as to what was happening there.[68] Likewise, at the Casablanca Conference in January 1943, the British planners discovered, in the words of the official historian, 'that while their American colleagues were quite prepared to expound their plans for the Pacific theatre, they resolutely refused to discuss them. They were settled and not open to debate: the British had no *locus standi* in the matter.'[69]

Thus the strategic and military components of World War Two politics in the Far East had already taken shape: Britain labouring under the legacy of a series of defeats which seemed to demonstrate to the world that her Asian Empire had been little more than an anachronism and a façade, dependent on American assistance even in Southeast Asia, and retaining only slender links with Australia and New Zealand; the United States, despite its share in the initial defeats, gathering up its power to strike back, solely in charge of the main, Pacific operations against Japan, and pre-eminent in the Southwest Pacific and China. Given the strains inherent in this situation, together with the divergencies between London and Washington over global strategy, as outlined in the preceding chapter, what is remarkable is not that, at the Casablanca Conference, there was conflict, but that a formula for agreement was achieved at all. (Apart from other reasons for this success, such as the adherence of Roosevelt and, fundamentally, Marshall, to a policy of 'Germany first', together with the admirable role played by Sir John Dill in Washington, it may well have helped that the State Department, at Roosevelt's insistence, was not represented at Casablanca. The element of disarray on the American side, and the clashes over command and strategic issues in the Pacific that were taking place between the U.S. Army and Navy, also made things easier for the British delegation.)[70]

Even so, the disagreements that emerged at Casablanca were significant for the future. Before the Conference assembled, Admiral King had been urging his colleagues on the Joint Chiefs of Staff in Washington that 'the United States, [which] now has the principal power, therefore . . . should take the lead' at such inter-Allied meetings. (He also expressed considerable scorn for Britain's relative quiescence against Japan, even attributing the Royal Navy's loan of the aircraft carrier *Victorious* for Pacific operations to 'their apparent desire to keep their [Eastern] Fleet immobilised.')[71] At the Conference itself he proposed that the proportion of Allied resources devoted to the Japanese war should be increased from 15 to 30 per cent in order to prevent the enemy from making himself impregnable; the manpower of China, too, he asserted, must be brought into play at the earliest opportunity.[72] Marshall for his part warned that unless a major advance into Burma (operation 'Anakim') were undertaken by land and sea, aimed at retaking Rangoon, reopening the Burma Road, and easing the pressure in the Southwest Pacific, then 'a situation might arise in the Pacific at any time that would necessitate the United States withdrawing from the commitments in the European theatre . . . He insisted that the United States could not stand for another Bataan.' Roosevelt, too, stressed his desire to see more done to increase air supplies into and air operations within China. In all, the pressure upon the British representatives to agree that greater emphasis should be placed upon the Far Eastern war was considerable.[73]

In the event, however, an agreed basis for detailed planning was found. Although the chances of mounting a cross-Channel invasion during 1943 were clearly dwindling, the hope of defeating Germany in that year was reiterated, with approval also being given for operations in the Mediterranean aimed at the capture of Sicily. Meanwhile 'adequate forces' would be committed against Japan in order to retain the initiative and prepare for a full-scale offensive after Germany had fallen. Planning for 'Anakim' would go ahead, with a final decision on that operation to be taken in July 1943. In the Southwest Pacific, Rabaul and the Bismarck Islands barrier should be the target, and in the Central Pacific a line of advance towards the Marshall and Caroline Islands should be developed if resources permitted. In addition, it was also declared publicly that the war would be prosecuted until the 'unconditional surrender' of the enemies of the United Nations had been achieved. This celebrated pronouncement, it is now known, was not the unpremeditated act, either on the American or on the British side, that Roosevelt chose to make it appear at the time, although its implictions had not been thoroughly explored.[74]* For Britain, adherence to the idea of unconditional surrender was in part a response to the accusations being levelled against her by certain Pacific-first circles in the United States, and to Admiral King's sour question at the Conference itself: 'On whom would fall the principal burden of beating Japan once Germany had been knocked out?' Churchill had already pledged in private that 'all of the British resources and effort' would eventually be turned against Japan, but the unconditional-surrender formula was a means of offering further, public reassurance.

Nevertheless, the question of whether to demand unconditional surrender was not settled for ever at Casablanca, as we shall see. Nor had the strategic compromise reached at the Conference done anything to resolve the political tensions that existed between Britain and the United States in the Far East, tensions which were in some ways being exacerbated by the military situation. Over various long-term issues, as well as over immediate military ones in Southeast Asia, the Allies were still not in step. In order to see how this

---

* Desmond Morton, however, subsequently maintained that Churchill had in fact been completely surprised by Roosevelt's statement at Casablanca, which he much disliked. (Thompson, *Churchill and Morton*, 87.)

was so, we must return from Casablanca to the year that preceded it, and examine developments in each of the main areas involved in the war against Japan.

Notes to Chapter Five

1 See e.g. *Churchill*, IV, 161.
2 Poll findings in Hornbeck Papers, box 117.
3 FO 371, A11498/31/45, and *Churchill*, IV, 613.
4 Calder, *The People's War*, 488.
5 Martin to Bracken, 11 May and 4 June 1942, Martin Papers, box 30.
6 'Americans and the War', 13 May 1942, Roosevelt Papers, PSF box 170.
7 See A. Girdner and A. Loftus, *The Great Betrayal: The Evacuation of the Japanese-Americans During World War Two* (Toronto, 19_9), and the essay by S. Conn in K. R. Greenfield (ed.), *Command Decisions* (London, 1960).
8 *Chicago Tribune*, 14 Jan. 1942.
9 Report of 29 April 1942, Roosevelt Papers, PSF box 170; material in DS, Pasvolsky files, box 6.
10 *San Francisco Examiner*, 2 and 7 Jan. 1942, 13 Jan. 1943.
11 E.g. *Chicago Tribune*, 15 April 1942; *San Francisco Examiner*, 5 May 1942.
12 *New York Times*, 19 July 1942.
13 Material in Hornbeck Papers, box 40.
14 DC (Ops), 14 April and 16 Nov. 1942, CAB 69/4; *Moran*, 35; FO 371, A6124/31/45.
15 *New York Times*, 19 Feb. 1942.
16 *Manchester Guardian*, 18 Feb. 1942.
17 Amery to Smuts, 13 Feb. 1942, van der Poel (ed.), *Smuts Papers*, VI.
18 WP (42) 59, 2 Feb. 1942, CAB 66/21.
19 Chiang Kai-shek to FDR, 7 Jan. 1942, Roosevelt Papers, PSF box 36; Military Intelligence memo., 26 Feb. 1943, DS 740.0011 P.W./3132½.
20 Leahy Diary, 2 Oct. 1942.
21 Cab, 5 Feb. 1942, CAB 65/25.
22 FO 371, F2044/1193/10; F565/560/61; F5986/5329/61.
23 Eggleston, 'The Outlines of a Constructive Peace in the Pacific', 2 Feb. 1943, ADEA, A989/44/655/25.
24 Tarr to Carter, 23 Sept. 1942, IPR Papers, box 36; Hornbeck to Buck, 13 July 1942, Hornbeck Papers, box 40.
25 Donovan to FDR, 25 April 1942, Roosevelt Papers, PSF box 163.
26 PWC (W), 28 Oct. 1942, Roosevelt Papers, MR box 168.
27 Campbell to Cadogan, 5 Aug. 1942, FO 371, F5902/2428/10.
On the Aryans in India, see Mason, *Patterns of Dominance* (London, 1971).
28 Campbell to Cadogan, 6 Aug. 1942, PREM 4, 42/9. The main part of Campbell's letter ran as follows: '[The President said that] he had set one Professor Hrdlicka of the Smithsonian Institute to work on a private study of the effect of racial crossing. A preliminary report had been given him, with all of which he by no means agreed. But it seemed to him that if we got the Japanese driven back within their islands, racial crossings might have interesting effects, particularly in the Far East. For instance, Dutch–Javanese crossings were good, and Javanese–Chinese. Chinese–Malayan was a bad mixture. Hrdlicka said that the Japanese–European cross was bad, and the Chinese–European equally so. It was here he disagreed with the Professor. Experience, the President said, had shown that unlike the Japanese–European mixture, which was, he agreed, thoroughly bad, Chinese–European was not at all bad.

The President had asked the Professor why the Japanese were as bad as they were, and had followed up by asking about the Hairy Ainus. The Professor had said the skulls of these people were some 2,000 years less developed than ours (This sounds very little, doesn't it?). The President asked whether this might account for the nefariousness of the Japanese, and had been told that it might, as they might well be the basic stock of the Japanese.' [Campbell then summarized the President's ideas, as indicated in the text of this chapter.] I am most grateful to Dr. T. Dale Stewart, a former Director of the Museum of Natural History, Smithsonian Institution, and a colleague of Dr. Hrdlicka's, for discussing this document with me. Dr. Stewart finds Campbell's report 'entirely plausible', adding that Hrdlicka's ideas in the field of racial characteristics were 'idiosyncratic' and that they 'have not stood the test of time.' The probable accuracy and validity of Campbell's report has been further confirmed for me by Hrdlicka's own correspondence with Roosevelt, which Dr. Stewart arranged for me to see. From the first time that he wrote to the President, in 1933, Hrdlicka urged the latter to realise that the leaders of Japan were 'utterly egotistic, tricky and ruthless, . . . working steadily towards the exclusion of all, and particularly the white man, from the Pacific . . . and eastern Asia.' The apparent civilization of these men, he wrote in 1933, was only 'a veneer, covering primitive fanaticism and ruthlessness'. Applauding Roosevelt's 'quarantine' speech in 1937, Hrdlicka again declared that the Japanese were no more than 'insular pirates, who have but a veneer of civilization and whose late history is full of perfidy, usurpation and brutality.' They respected in Americans, he added, 'but one factor, . . . which is that of greater than theirs *intellectual* and material *power*.' (Italics added.) In the summer of 1941, Hrdlicka was writing frequently to Roosevelt to urge him to 'Rouse our people. Rouse the women, the young, the very children, regardless of obstruction', and to take up arms forthwith against Japan. 'What an eternal shame and source of weakness if we stayed out.' It is against this background that, in part, the subsequent Roosevelt–Hrdlicka 'scientific' exchanges concerning the Japanese need to be seen.

For details of studies on migration and settlement that were prepared for F.D.R. during the war by another scientist, Henry Field, see the latter's book, '*M*' *Project for F.D.R.* (Ann Arbor, Michigan, 1962), especially, as regards the Far East after the war, 147, 187, 218, 220, 251, 257, 327.

29 Annex to memo. of 15 March 1945, Taussig Papers, box 52.
30 Morgenthau Presidential Diary, 19 Aug. 1944.
31 FRUS, Malta and Yalta, 766; and see above, 6.
32 Stimson Diary, 29 Jan. and 3 Feb. 1942.
33 Hornbeck memo., 7 May 1942, DS 740.0011 P.W./2414.
34 'The Future of the Netherlands Indies', 21 June 1942, Hull Papers, box 50.
35 Hull to FDR, 11 Aug. 1942, Hull Papers, box 62; Hornbeck to Hull, 6 May 1942, Hornbeck Papers, box 48; PWC (W), 21 April 1942, FO 371, F3053/1417/61; Hull to Phillips, 18 Nov. 1942, Hull Papers, box 50.
36 E.g. FO 371, A4410/60/45.
37 Interview with Sir Ashley Clarke; and see e.g. Johnson to Drumright, 22 July 1942, Johnson Papers, box 40.
38 Davies to Gauss, 9 March 1943, Roosevelt Papers, PSF box 36.
39 WSC to FDR, 9 Aug. 1942, PREM 3, 470.
40 Taussig memo., 17 Dec. 1942, Taussig Papers, box 46.
41 FO 371, A1169/60/45.
42 Ibid, F8172/628/61.
43 'British and American policy Towards China', 28 Dec. 1942, ibid, F8539/54/10.
44 Young minute, 9 Dec. 1942, ibid, F8170/4072/10.
45 Clarke report, 11 June 1942, ibid, F4320/4320/10.
46 E.g. ibid, A1684 and 5545/1684/45; F4320/4320/61; F7542/623/61.
47 E.g. ibid, files 31759–61; 31779; 31786–96.
48 Ibid, F2660 and 5781/2000/61.
49 Ibid, F7178/2000/61.
50 Ibid, F6404/2000/61.
51 Leahy Diary, 20 Sept. and 1 Oct. 1942, and e .g. JCS, 4 May1942; King to Marshall

3 Sept. 1942, King Papers, series 1, box 3; Hornbeck memo., 3 Oct. 1942, Hornbeck Papers, box 180; FRUS, 1942, China, 84.

52 FDR to Hopkins, 26 Feb. 1942, Hopkins Papers, box 308; but contrast a draft, unsent message of FDR to WSC, 18 March 1942, Roosevelt Papers, MR box 2.

53 *Matloff and Snell*, cap. XVI and 367.

54 E.g. COS, 13 and 14 Aug. 1942 (CAB 79/22) and 29 Oct. 1942 (CAB 79/23); CCS, 6 Aug. 1942, CAB 88/1; *Bryant*, I, 545, 555.

55 And see *Churchill*, III, 578ff.

56 PWC (L), 21 Oct. 1942, CAB 99/26.

57 WSC to FDR, 5 March 1942, CAB 69/4.

58 *Cadogan Diaries*, 31 Dec. 1941.

59 PWC (L), 21 Oct. 1942, CAB 99/26.

60 Wilkinson Journal, 30 March 1943.

61 See FO 371, files 31827, 31834, 31835, 31847.

62 See *Churchill*, IV, 174, and above, 155.

63 WP (42) 94, 21 Feb. 1942, CAB 66/22.

64 See in general *Roskill*, II, 25ff.; also *Sherwood*, 525.

65 E.g. COS, 23 Sept. 1942 (CAB 79/23) and 8 Dec. 1942 (CAB 79/24).

66 See FRUS, Washington and Casablanca, 349.

67 WSC to FDR, 3 Feb. 1942, PREM 3, 470.

68 COS, 26 Oct. 1942, CAB 79/23.

69 Howard, *Grand Strategy*, IV, 243.

70 See FRUS, Washington and Casablanca, 496; JCS, 6 April 1943, RG 218; *Matloff and Snell*, 368ff.; Lord Ismay, *Memoirs* (London, 1960), 286; Morison, *Two-Ocean War*, 264.

71 JCS, 14 Jan. 1943, loc. cit.

72 For the CCS discussions at Casablanca, see CAB 88/2 and 99/4. Major documents from the Conference are printed as appendices to Howard, *Grand Strategy*, IV.

73 See Tedder, *With Prejudice*, 389.

74 See Howard, *Grand Strategy*, IV, 282; FRUS, Washington and Casablanca, 506; Harriman and Abel, *Special Envoy*, 187ff.

CHAPTER SIX

THE UNITED STATES, BRITAIN AND CHINA

The American approach

SHORTLY BEFORE the Casablanca Conference convened, the Australian Minister to China, Sir Frederick Eggleston, drew up a paper on 'Anglo-American Relations in the Far East', briefly referred to in an earlier chapter. During his time in Chungking, and later as Minister in Washington, Eggleston, a physically handicapped and ponderous individual, but a shrewd and thoughtful one, looked on both leading Western powers with a fairly detached eye, critical alike of British failure to 'kindle to the new idea' and of American 'arrogance and aggression . . . based on intellectual clichés.' At the same time, he applauded the strong qualities that each possessed, and deplored what he saw as their bad relations with each other in the Far East. 'Why should two nations of such outstanding achievements', he was to write in his diary in April 1943, 'stand and glare at each other like this when a very slight increase of warm human feeling, a small movement towards one another, might do so much good to the world?'[1]

It was thus Eggleston's belief, and it is also a theme of the present work, that, fundamentally, there existed in China more common ground between the British and Americans than some protagonists of the time—above all on the American side—realized or would admit. Nevertheless, Eggleston was able to see reasons why trouble and suspicions had occurred over such matters as military collaboration and supply, as well as in the field of economics and finance, where 'indications . . . suggest', he wrote, 'that the United States intend to pursue a policy of economic development in the Far East after the war in competition with all comers.' The Chinese themselves, he believed, had exacerbated matters by seeking to profit from the 'mutual suspicion' of the Americans and British. At the same time, he perceptively suggested other causes of trouble:

'There are, indeed, several reasons why disagreement should be more likely here than nearer the centre', he wrote. 'Although Britain had large interests in China, they have received little attention for some years . . . British representatives, both military and diplomatic, come here without any Eastern point of view, and inhibited by the British attitude of world

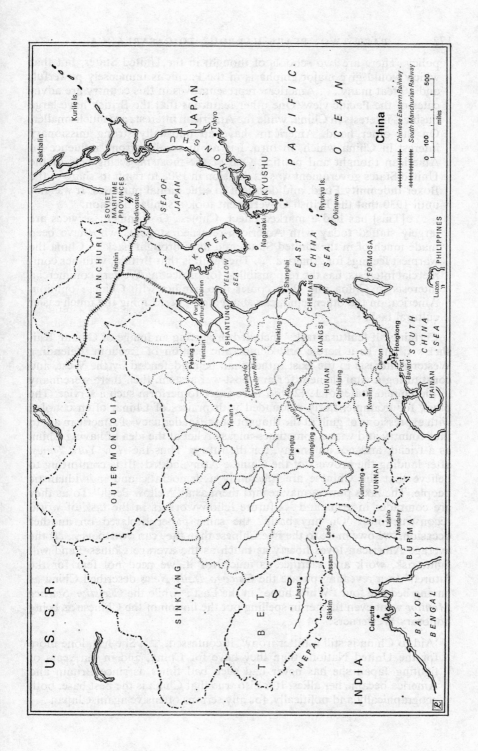

China

Chinese Eastern Railway · · · · · · ·
South Manchurian Railway ┼┼┼┼┼┼┼┼

0   100   500
└─┴─┴─┴─┴─────────┘
        miles

U.S.S.R.

SOVIET MARITIME PROVINCES

MANCHURIA

Sakhalin

Kurile Is.

JAPAN

HONSHU

Tokyo

PACIFIC

OCEAN

KYUSHU

SEA OF JAPAN

Vladivostok

Harbin

KOREA

Nagasaki

Ryukyu Is.

Okinawa

Port Arthur Dairen

SHANTUNG

YELLOW SEA

Tientsin

Peking

Hwang-Ho (Yellow River)

Nanking

Shanghai

CHEKIANG

EAST CHINA SEA

FORMOSA

KIANGSI

Yenan

Yangtze Kiang

HUNAN

Chihkiang

Kweilin

Canton

Port Bayard

Hongkong

SOUTH CHINA SEA

HAINAN

PHILIPPINES

Luzon

OUTER MONGOLIA

Chengtu

Chungking

YUNNAN

Kunming

Lashio

Mandalay

BURMA

Ledo

SINKIANG

TIBET

Lhasa

Assam

Sikkim

NEPAL

INDIA

Calcutta

BAY OF BENGAL

policy. There are two schools of thought in the United States, but that which would give major emphasis in the Pacific is immensely powerful, and a great many . . . American representatives in this country are advocates of the Pacific view. One other feature is that the British have large business interests in China, while the American interests are much smaller. On the other hand, Americans have an unusually strong missionary interest in China which, in turn, has an unusually strong influence on American thought and politics. One of the most far-seeing acts of the United States government was its decision in 1908 to remit its share of the Boxer Indemnity Fund, and devote it to educational purposes. It was not until 1930 that the British Government took a similar decision.

. . . [This] has had a marked effect. Chinese Government services are largely staffed today with American-returned students who have been made much of in the United States and have brought back to China the warmest feelings for America . . . The result is that Britain, with her commercial interests, has the responsibility for protecting Western commercial interests in China and thus comes into conflict with Chinese opinion. America, on the other hand, can stand aloof, performing the much easier cultural task.'2

Certainly, if 'cultural tasks' included projecting an image of Chiang Kai-shek's China as a heroic and democratic bastion of freedom, defending Western interests in the East rather than being defended by the West, and constituting a vital element for any post-war system, then there were many in the United States of 1942 who were eager to perform such a service. The press, for example, fairly resounded with praises of China, often coupled with expressions of guilt at the thought of the inadequacy of American aid to that country and with a sometimes-uneasy relief at the idea of having China as a friend, and not an enemy, for the future. Thus the *New York Times*, after lauding the prowess of the Chinese Army, added: 'It is comforting to believe that the Chinese are inherently a democratic and individualistic people. The Axis powers may regard them as a "Yellow Peril." To us they are comrades in arms and . . . future fellow-workers in the task of world reconstruction.'3 'On any basis', the same paper declared on another occasion, 'we owe more to the free Chinese than they can owe to us . . . If the average American loves liberty as much as the average Chinese, and will fight, risk, work and sacrifice as much for it, we need not fear for the future.'4 In a revealing phrase the *Chicago Daily News* described China as having become 'our "White hope" in the East',5 while the *Christian Science Monitor* went even further in spelling out the notion of the Chinese as being honorary Westerners:

'Aid to China is still a bitter irony', it confessed. '. . . She has done more for the United Nations than they have for China, and in ten years of fighting Japan she has never had such bad times as since Britain and America became her allies. It is also true that China is the best base, both geographically and politically, for any serious offensive against Japan . . .

Politically, China is the main bridge between western and eastern cultures. So long as 400,000,000 people of the yellow race belong to the United Nations, Tokyo cannot split the world on the basis of race hatreds, colored against white . . . How many have considered what a different balance the world might have today were not the Generalissimo a Christian and his wife American-educated?'[6]

Prominent American visitors to or students of China underlined this message of hope. After the war, declared Owen Lattimore, China would emerge as one of the world's great democracies and would, make the next hundred years 'a Chinese century.'[7] (In private, Lattimore had already described Chiang Kai-shek's China in 1940 as 'a genuinely democratic democracy'.)[8] Wendell Willkie, visiting China in the autumn of 1942 likewise manifested his enthusiasm for his hosts, who had, he assured them, a special role to play now that 'mankind was on the march' and 'the old colonial times were past.'[9] It mattered little that the American public at large remained hugely ignorant of the real China (it will be recalled that, four months after Pearl Harbour, 60 per cent of a sample poll could not locate China or India on an outline of the world).[10] Enthusiasm reached new heights, spurred on by a visit by Madame Chiang Kai-shek to the United States from November 1942 to the spring of 1943.[11] Congress was dazzled and ready to vote money for the sister republic—perhaps all the more generous, one writer has suggested, 'because no one envisaged China as a post-war rival for power or commerce.'[12] The public, too, contributed directly through United China Relief Inc., which disbursed over $3 million between December 1941 and the end of September 1942, and over $7 million between then and September 1943. (Directors of the fund included Willkie and Pearl Buck.)[13] T. V. Soong, banker and businessman, brother of Madame Chiang Kai-shek, and China's Foreign Minister, was skilfully cultivating his connections in Washington—especially Hopkins, through whom he could reach the President—'attentively served', in John Davies' words, 'by a variety of American sinophiles and retainers with broad contacts in the American Government.'[14] One of those who was flattered for the time being by Chinese attention was Laughlin Currie, a Canadian-born American serving as an administrative assistant to the President. Currie ordained himself a China-expert, assuring Roosevelt after a visit to that country that 'we do not need to lay down any conditions or tie any strings to our support', and openly expressing to his master his ambition to become Ambassador in Chungking in place of the professional encumbent, Clarence Gauss.[15]

The time was to come when Currie and others of those in official positions in Washington who now, in 1942, were joining in the chorus of acclaim and concern for China, would realize how wide was the gulf between reality and the idealized portraits of Chiang Kai-shek and his country which they had helped to display in America. And yet, despite their new awareness, they would in a sense be prisoners of the very public enthusiasm which they had done much to encourage. Even now, as will be seen below, there were those who were endeavouring to bring about a more realistic attitude, related to the true state of affairs in China. But in 1942, in official circles as well as among the public at large, the admirers of China were still in the ascendant, depicting her as being, in the words of an O.S.S. survey, 'one of the world's staunchest strongholds of democracy.'[16] Even as late as March 1943, Roosevelt himself, as was briefly mentioned in the opening chapter, his China policy ill-conceived, inefficient and irresponsible, would solemnly be describing Chiang and his country to General Marshall in terms of sheer fantasy:

> 'All of us must remember', the President was to warn his Chief of Staff privately, 'that the Generalissimo came up the hard way to become the undisputed leader of four hundred million people—an enormously difficult job to attain any kind of unity from a diverse group of all kinds of leaders—military men, educators, scientists, public health people, engineers, all of them struggling for power and mastery, local or national, to create in a very short time throughout China what it took us a couple of centuries to attain . . . One cannot speak sternly to a man like that or exact commitments from him the way we might do from the Sultan of Morocco.'[17]

Alas for the Sultan of Morocco. What is more—and this anticipated a similar process during the Vietnam war[18]—those who dared to doubt or to criticize could find themselves being subjected to pressure. The only views and information wanted, in other words, were those which reinforced the 'party line'. Thus Hornbeck suggested in March 1942 that Army officers on the spot who were being critical of Chinese efforts should be made to bring their utterances 'into harmony with the officially adopted policy of the Government.'[19] (He even proposed that Dutch criticisms of the Chinese should also be 'flattened out.')[20] 'The less our recruits know about China the better', wrote the head of the newly-formed American Navy Intelligence unit in that country, 'for if they are willing to learn we can indoctrinate them so they will meet with Chinese approval.'[21] Meanwhile Stimson, as Secretary of War, was pursuing a similar course:

> 'I called in General Strong', he recorded in April, 'and told him that I was tired of the kind of statements that came to me from the J[oint] I[ntelligence] C[ommittee] communiqués knocking the Chinese and warning us against trusting their military ability . . . I told General Strong that such statements were likely to make a great deal of trouble . . . [He] agreed with me perfectly . . . He came back and told me he traced it to a member of the Navy and I told him to see that it didn't happen again. He said he would.'[22]

In this connection, a common version of the situation was that, while the Chinese did, of course, have a special affection for the United States, if great care were not taken to avoid critizing them and to prevent the U.S.A. from being associated in their eyes with Britain, then anti-foreign tendencies could spread out to embrace Americans as well as Europeans.[23] Therefore, in the opinion of true believers, a man like Gauss, the dour Ambassador in

Chungking, who had few illusions about the nature of the regime to which he was accredited, should be removed from his post—a campaign which was joined by Roosevelt himself, although he failed to get his way for the time being.[24]*

Thus, despite the critical reports about Nationalist China that were available to the President, Stimson, and other senior men in Washington, that country and Chiang Kai-shek alike were seen as being vital to the Allied cause. 'If the Generalissimo's regime should fall', warned the head of the American military mission in Chungking, 'all Asiatics, including the Chinese, will be attracted to the enemy.'[25] The result of such an eventuality, in Hornbeck's words, would be 'China no longer in the war; China's soil no longer available to the United Nations for operations against Japan; China's natural resources and manpower available to Japan . . .'[26] In an informal memorandum that was passed on to the Foreign Office in London, the Chief of the State Department's Far Eastern Division spelt out in greater detail the assets which China possessed and which now stood at risk: not merely three million troops in the field, but 'the most important defense which the United Nations have at this time against Japanese efforts to promote race warfare.' If she collapsed,

> 'psychologically Japan might well obtain such a secure place as the leader of the Asiatic races, if not the colored races of the world, that Japan's defeat by the United Nations might not be definitive . . . There might develop in the Far East such a feeling of solidarity that it would be impossible to create in that area groups of peoples or nations friendlily disposed to the democratic principles motivating the United Nations. This development would seriously hamper the implementation of long-range high policy of the United States in its foreign relations.'[27]

Stimson likewise told Morgenthau that the Chinese must be kept going at any price,[28] while Leahy envisaged a possible American defeat in the Pacific if this were not done.[29] Even someone like John Davies, political adviser to Stilwell, who realistically pointed to Chungking's desire to fight as little as possible and to husband its resources in order to ensure its domestic supremacy, could nevertheless proclaim that 'probably nowhere in this war can we do so much with so little as in the China–Burma–India theater.'[30]

Moreover, the prize was seen in terms far wider than simply those of the war itself. After the enemy had been beaten, China must become one of the four 'big policemen' of the world, as Roosevelt put it to Chiang Kai-shek at the end of 1942 under the guise of a letter from Lattimore, Chiang's former political adviser.[31] China would help America to maintain order in the Western Pacific; China could play a special role in a scheme of 'trusteeships' which should come into force 'in certain colonial areas of the Southern Pacific and Southeast Asia.' For those whose minds ran in commercial directions, there was also the prospect of a greatly expanded post-war trade

* Gauss' approach to China and the Chinese may well have been influenced by his consular, rather than diplomatic, background. He had been Consul General in Shanghai,

with China's market of 450 millions, and of a special place for the United States in the economic and industrial development of that country.[32]

The Chinese themselves strove to keep American anxieties alive by hinting that, unless a great deal more help were forthcoming, morale would collapse and elements come to the fore that would insist on coming to terms with Japan.[33] In much of the American press and in Far Eastern circles within the State Department the cry was the same: send more aid to China.[34] Chiang Kai-shek himself kept up the pressure in this direction. Surely Roosevelt, he declared, 'the one great friend of China', would disprove the prediction which Gandhi had made to him, the Generalissimo, that ' "they will never voluntarily treat us . . . as equals; why, they do not even admit your country to their staff talks." '[35] Therefore, in order to demonstrate the falsity of this charge, China should be given a place on the Combined Allied Boards for the allocation of supplies, and her own share of those supplies should be much increased.

Neither Chungking nor China's fervent supporters in the United States were satisfied with the extent of the American Government's response to these appeals, but in several respects there were at least some moves in the required direction. Lend Lease goods continued to be supplied, although with all land communications cut from May onwards, deliveries fell well below the 7,500 tons a month which the Chinese were then seeking.[36] Apart from increasing the amount of supplies sent by air and planning to open a new road through northern Burma, the possibilities were also explored of sending goods through Persia and the Soviet Union, or via Tibet; meanwhile technical experts of various kinds were sent out to assist the Chinese on the spot.[37] As for the military sphere, since nothing came of the proposal to organize an international guerilla force in China, the Americans did not share the disillusion which the British, as we shall see, experienced as a result of their own efforts in that field.[38] Instead, the volatile but experienced General Joe Stilwell was sent out with orders 'to increase the effectiveness of United States assistance to the Chinese Government for the prosecution of the war and to assist in improving the combat efficiency of the Chinese Army.'[39]

By June 1942, Stilwell's mission had expanded to include command of American forces in the new China–Burma–India theatre, where the aim was above all to reopen a land route to China. In the words of General Marshall, who firmly supported Stilwell against his critics, 'the British cannot do this alone; the Chinese certainly can't manage it; neither side would admit of leadership by the other. So our only hope is to secure guidance by an American.'[40] At the end of 1942, therefore, Stilwell took over responsibility from the British for driving a new road from Ledo, through northern Burma, to link up with the old Burma Road, the way forward being cleared, as he planned it, by a converging attack by Chinese forces from Yunnan and American, British and Chinese forces from India.[41] Stilwell also set about the thankless task of advising Chiang Kai-shek on urgent military reforms. From the outset, however, he was faced with a rival American military group in China, with its own strategic arguments and its own demands upon supplies coming over the 'Hump'. General Chennault's A.V.G. had been absorbed into the U.S. Army Air Force, and its leader now claimed, in a letter to Roosevelt in October 1942, that his units could bring about the collapse of Japan if supplied with a mere 105 fighters, 30 medium bombers and 12 heavy bombers.[42] For the moment, it was Stilwell and his land strategy that held the field, thanks to Marshall above all; Chennault's supporters, however, included Madame Chiang Kai-shek, and, led by the pre-war columnist Joe Alsop, who was on Chennault's staff, they lost no opportunity of putting the claims of their champion before Hopkins and others in Washington, denigrating Stilwell at the same time.[43]*

Chiang Kai-shek, meanwhile, wanted more than military advice and supplies. He wanted money. The argument was that the financial and economic crisis facing China in 1942 was as great as the threat from the Japanese. Price levels early in the year had risen to such a height that money had less than five per cent of its 1937 purchasing power; by the end of the year it had fallen further still, to about one sixty-sixth of the 1937 level, and in such a situation, the efforts of the Anglo-American–Chinese Stabilization Board had become virtually irrelevant.[44] Meanwhile, on 30 December 1941, Gauss had reported that the Generalissimo was asking for a loan of $1 billion, half from Britain and half from the United States, the intention being not only to help steady the economy but to 'silence the doubters, the dissenters and the ignorant.'[45]

In Washington, the Hornbecks and the Stimsons were enthusiastic over this project, so much in keeping, in the latter's words, with his 'conception of the whole relation of the United States to China.' 'Now is the time', urged Hornbeck, 'to tie China into our war (which is still her war) as tight as possible.'[46] Thus, while Hull originally thought of offering $300 million only, $500 million was eventually accepted as the sum which the United States should find. Although Morgenthau at the Treasury tried to devise a scheme (and succeeded in interesting Roosevelt and Churchill in it) whereby the money would be used to finance the Chinese Army in some direct fashion, Chiang Kai-shek's opposition to the idea was allowed to kill it; although Morgenthau, and even Hornbeck, wanted to attach conditions to the loan regarding its use, here, too, Chinese resentment carried the day, and Washington rested content with an assurance that the Secretary of the Treasury would be kept informed by Chungking. Roosevelt recommended the loan to Congress in glowing terms, and it was passed forthwith. The detailed agreement between the two States was signed on 21 March, and

---

* Stilwell greatly admired the ordinary Chinese soldier, but in general held a low opinion of Chinese officers. His idea of putting white American officers in to command Chinese troops was from the outset likely to be rejected in China, however, and burdened all his efforts. Chiang Kai-shek's Minister of War and Chief of Staff, General Ho Ying-chin, for example, conceived his own main task to be, in Barbara Tuchman's words, 'keeping the army loyal through the manipulation of cliques and control of supplies and funds.'

before long $200 million of the total had been paid over as backing for an issue of securities within China.[47]*

There was one further action that the United States and other western countries could take to give the Chinese comfort of a less material kind: the abolition of those extraterritorial rights and privileges in various parts of China which originated in the nineteenth century, and negotiations over which had been cut short by the Japanese seizure of Manchuria in 1931. China's Western allies were already on record as looking towards the ending of such rights after the war, and during the spring and early summer of 1942 this was considered by the State Department to be sufficient a gesture for the time being, London signifying its agreement with this judgment. During August and September, however, the strong trend of American public opinion towards treating China as a complete equal, coupled with a somewhat improved military situation and 'a more activist attitude' on the part of the Chinese Government, prompted a change of mind in Washington. (Privately, Hull was also thinking that immediate renunciation of extraterritorial rights might help to ease Britain out of her favourable position in Shanghai and Hongkong.)[48]

It was therefore suggested to London, which agreed, that the time had come to take the initiative and to propose to China treaties abolishing extraterritoriality altogether. A draft document to this effect was forwarded for the Foreign Office's comments at the beginning of October, and the Chinese themselves were informed shortly afterwards of what was intended.[49] There followed negotiations in which Chungking pressed for an early agreement, and in which Washington, by giving way on almost every point of difference (despite the fears being expressed by some American commercial interests),[50] in turn put pressure on London to make concessions to speed up the parallel set of Anglo-Chinese exchanges. Separate American-Chinese and Anglo-Chinese treaties abandoning extraterritoriality were eventually signed on 11 January 1943, to the accompaniment of loud rejoicings in the American press. It was, declared the *New York Times*, 'the dawn of a new epoch in the Far East.'[51]

The Anglo-American differences which arose during these extraterritoriality negotiations will be considered below, in the context of British policy. The tactics Washington had employed, however, were sufficiently exasperating to officials in London for Eden to feel called upon to protest. 'Several times', he wrote, '. . . the United States Government have, with the object of saving time, conceded to the Chinese points of great importance to His Majesty's Government, before our Ambassador in Chungking could be in a position to discuss them with the Chinese Government . . . We are dealing with questions of the greatest importance to our commercial, financial and

---

* Between 1943 and the end of the war, $220 million more went to enable the Chinese to purchase gold, $55 million was used for the purchase by them of banknotes, while the remainder, in 1945 and 1946, went on the purchase of textiles and raw cotton. Department of State, *United States Relations With China* (Washington, 1949; hereafter, *U.S. and China*), 471.

shipping interests in the Far East, and the decisions which we reach now will have an inevitable effect on the negotiations for the comprehensive modern [commercial] treaty to be concluded subsequently.'[52] Nor did the State Department comply with the Foreign Office's wish that the former should support the stand that London was taking—eventually successfully—against the Chinese desire to have the Kowloon Leased Territory, adjoining Hong-kong, included in the retrocession. (Hornbeck was inclined towards the British case on this occasion, but the Far Eastern Division in Washington believed that 'the sympathy of the American public would lie almost entirely with China and would be strongly critical of this Government.')[53]

Clearly, the factor emphasized by the Australian Minister, Eggleston, was at work on this occasion: that is, that the relative smallness of her existing commercial stake in China made it easier for the United States to negotiate over a matter like the surrender of extraterritoriality. There was an additional reason, however, briefly referred to above, for not aligning Washington's position too closely with that of London. Chinese officials, from Chiang Kai-shek and his wife downwards, were losing no opportunity in 1942 of making known to Americans their hostility towards the British.[54] (On behalf of the Chinese Communists, Chou En-lai likewise claimed that the British 'discriminated against and treated as inferiors the Chinese who fought with the British at Hong Kong and in Malaya.')[55] The accompanying suggestion, that in so far as the United States worked with Britain she risked incurring some of this odium, was expressed to Roosevelt by Willkie on the latter's return from Chungking:

> 'The British position in India,' he wrote, 'diversion of American planes to British fronts, the complete absence of British aid to China [sic], the deep-rooted suspicion that America has given at least acquiescence to British plans for restoration of its earlier imperial position in Asia—all are factors tending to deplete the reservoir of good-will we started with in China.'[56]

Moreover, American officials themselves tended to regard the British in Asia, and particularly those concerned with Chinese affairs, as indifferent, clumsy and anachronistic in their attitude. 'They give little evidence of being interested in China', reported Gauss,[57] and while Davies depicted British policy in Asia as being both selfish and supine, Stilwell commented that if Britain would only 'take a small cut in her enormous allocations [of supplies] for the year', China could be 'kept in line.'[58] Various incidents were seized upon to reinforce such interpretations. At the end of December 1941, for example, General Wavell, as C. in C. India, accepted at first only a portion of the two Chinese Army corps that were offered to him by Chiang Kai-shek to help in the defence of Burma. Or again, in Burma itself, there was the action of the Governor (taken with the agreement of an American official, but not with that of the Chinese) in removing for local defence purposes some American Lend Lease supplies, destined for China, that were threatened with destruction by Japanese air raids. (Both of these incidents will be examined more fully in the section below dealing with British policy.) In the

State Department it was assumed that Wavell's hesitation over the offer of Chinese troops was due to a reluctance 'to accept assistance from Orientals as derogatory to British prestige in Asia.' 'The Chinese are in no way comparable to or to be thought of as something like India and the Hindus', urged Hornbeck to the American Ambassador in London, while Roosevelt later expressed himself strongly to Stimson 'as to Wavell's lack of tact and his inability to get along with the Chinese.'[59]

Even where the Chinese themselves were only indirectly involved, many American comments from the region during this period were based upon a latent or overt sense of rivalry with the British, rather than a feeling of comradeship. Manuel Fox, for example, the American member of the international Stabilization Board in China during the early part of 1942, saw himself as battling with the British, and particularly with Sir Otto Niemeyer who, as we have seen, was seeking to assist the Chinese Government over financial matters.[60] Chennault, too, bitterly but vainly trying to prevent the induction into the American Army Air Force of his Volunteer Group which had been fighting in Burma, blamed the British for the proposal (he was wrong in this), which he saw as being their way of getting the A.V.G. completely under Wavell's control. 'Not satisfied with the support which we have furnished them by permission of the Generalissimo', wrote Chennault to his 'princess', Madame Chiang Kai-shek, 'they desire to consume the entire group in an area where they made no proper preparations for air defense.'[61]

In a similar spirit, and in the field of clandestine warefare, the representative in China of the O.S.S. reported to General Donovan in Washington, concerning his success in winning the confidence of the Chinese authorities: 'I have the jump on the British in many ways.' (This was before the O.S.S./ S.O.E. agreement that China should be 'an American sphere of influence' in such matters.)[62] Captain (later Rear-Admiral) Milton ('Mary') Miles, also involved in clandestine operations in China as head of the U.S. Naval Group there, saw the British as being 'mad' at his achievement in working with Tai Li, head of the Chinese Secret police. 'They'd do anything to wreck me', he warned Washington, sneering meanwhile that the British Army was on the run in Asia to such an extent that it would not stop until it got to 'the middle of Kansas.' His hostility was increased when he learned through an Australian friend who was employed on censorship duties that the British in India were 'steaming open all the mail they can lay their hands on, including U.S. Army and U.S. Navy and U.S. State Department mail . . .'[63]* When Anglo-Chinese relations showed signs of improving at the end of 1942, one of Miles' staff wrote that such a development was 'bad for our postwar future', and later, in 1945, we shall find the Admiral himself haranguing his officers on the overriding importance of the coming trade war with Britain for the markets of the Orient.[64]

Thus, in 1942 there existed in both public and official circles in the United

---

* Although Miles was a highly unreliable witness where the British were concerned, his sources on this occasion were such that it is quite possible that there was some truth in his accusation.

States a concern and admiration for China which tended to be accompanied by the assumption—repeated subsequently by American historians of widely differing persuasions[65]—that Britain was relatively unsympathetic in that regard, and sometimes by a sense of rivalry with the British over the destiny of the heroic Chinese people. And yet, even if such a crude picture of the British position were accurate—and we shall see that in fact it was a simplification which amounted to a considerable distortion—there was at the same time another side to the United States' own attitudes and judgments: a side which was to become more prominent in the following years, but which was already creating a certain ambivalence towards China in some quarters of Washington; a side which, indeed, was to spread and grow until it had created a state of disillusionment and even bitterness towards Chiang Kai-shek's China which exceeded anything known in Britain.

From the outset of the American entry into the Pacific War, there were, as already indicated by Stimson's hostile reaction to them, military and naval observers on the spot in Chungking who were reporting the realities of the situation: that the Chinese Army was scarcely employed at all in fighting the Japanese and that the tales of its marvellous achievements were, in General Magruder's words, 'entirely without foundation'; that military resources in China were valued above all for their usefulness in 'fighting against fellow-countrymen for economic and political supremacy', and that in any case by the time supplies in decisive quantities were able to reach China, 'we will be well on our way toward defeating Japan.'[66] As Stilwell himself rapidly became disillusioned with 'the Chinese cesspool. A gang of thugs with the one idea of perpetuating themselves and their machine',[67] and as the chances of getting the Chinese to develop an offensive into northern Burma dwindled,[68] he, too, came to believe that the only way to get any action from the General-issimo—'Peanut', as Stilwell began referring to him in his diary—would be 'pressure and bargaining.'[69] This attitude on the part of Stilwell and those working with him became all the more pronounced as Chinese importuning increased, with Chiang demanding at the end of June three American divisions to join in the fighting from India, 500 planes to be delivered by August, and 5,000 tons of supplies per month to arrive by air over the 'Hump.'[70] 'If he threatens to make peace with Japan', wrote one of Stilwell's staff, 'tell him to go ahead. In all probability the Japanese would laugh at him now.'[71]

Ambassador Gauss, although not on particularly good terms with Stilwell, was reporting in a similar strain. China, he wrote, was 'not prepared physically or psychologically to participate on a major scale in this war'; Chiang Kai-shek himself, however, was 'irrevocably committed to the policy of continued resistance to Japan', and all talk of making other arrangements if his demands were not met was simply a bluff, which should be called. 'China is only a minor asset to us', Gauss warned, '[but] she might ... become a major liability ... If [the Generalissimo] persists in demanding more and threatens peace with Japan ... he should be told ... that when he undertakes to negotiate a peace with Japan the American military and diplomatic missions will immediately be withdrawn ... and that finishes all

American assistance to China—now and for the future.'[72] Aeroplanes and supplies sent in from outside would be useful, wrote another diplomat in China, John Carter Vincent, later Chief of the Far Eastern Division in Washington, but 'the continuation of resistance does not depend upon the reception of allied aid.'[73]

Moreover, both Vincent and Gauss dismissed the notion that the ruling Kuomintang were interested in bringing about a democratic China or in finding a radical solution to her many ills. 'The end of the party', advised the Ambassador, 'is to remain in power . . . It seeks to remedy defects in its own organization for control rather than to correct the basic defects in the social and economic structures.' 'The Kuomintang', wrote Vincent, 'is a congerie of conservative political cliques whose only common denominator and common objective is desire to maintain the Kuomintang in control of the Government.'[74] There were also individuals within the State Department itself who were ready to write of the 'alarming . . . growing strength of ultra-conservative or reactionary officials in the Chungking Government', while the Far Eastern Division as a whole submitted that 'our concept of government with the consent of the governed is not native to China.'[75]

The idea was also gaining ground in some quarters that the Chinese Government were secretly deriding the Americans for being such easy targets for extortion. Chou En-lai, representing the Yenan Communists in Chungking, warned O.S.S. officers of this tendency. 'American generosity', he observed, 'excites contempt and gives them reason for pride in the effectiveness of their finesse.'[76] Foreign diplomats in Chungking thought likewise.[77] Even Harry Hopkins, greatly naïve where that country was concerned, was by the end of the year describing the Chinese and Chiang Kai-shek as experts in 'sucking folks in and deceiving them.'[78] The episode of the $500 million loan helped to foster such feelings. In Gauss' eyes, the sum was 'out of all proportion to the needs of the situation viewed from the political-psychological or the financial-economic standpoint—or both.'[79] Morgenthau at the Treasury was inclined to agree, as well as suspecting, rightly, that much of the money would find its way into the pockets of China's ruling clique. His abortive scheme for paying Chinese troops directly was designed to bring about a situation whereby 'if they don't fight, no money', and when that idea had been rejected, then 'my heart wasn't in it.' It was, he agreed with the Soviet Ambassador, blackmail, and that 'at a time when we have our back to the wall in the Pacific.'[80] Matters were made worse by the absurdly inflated exchange rate which the Chinese insisted on for the fapi—a rate which put the Chinese currency early in 1942 at about 18 per cent of its 1937 value instead of the true 5 per cent, and which led not only to a black market in dollars, but almost certainly to huge profits being made by some in privileged positions.[81]

The United States put up with these things. It is important to note, however, that, despite the loan and other gestures, there were limits in practice to what was done for China in various important respects. For example, Chiang Kai-shek's proposal, made immediately after Pearl Harbour, for an

American–British–Chinese–Dutch military staff to be set up to coordinate the war against Japan from Chungking was quietly ignored. So, too, was the Chinese desire to obtain a place on the key Anglo-American combined boards and committees. Moreover, when the military situation in the Middle East became serious, Washington was prepared to divert to that theatre planes originally destined for China; also, although more planes were promised for the Hump in response to Chiang's three demands of June 1942, no sizeable commitment of American troops to the C.B.I. theatre was contemplated.[82] Nor, despite the ending of extraterritoriality, was anything yet done to remove the ban on the immigration of Chinese into the United States. They were loved, but at a suitable distance, and when the Chinese Ambassador in Washington raised the matter, he obtained from Hull nothing more in return than clouds of the old man's rhetoric.[83]

In short, although the U.S.A. was now doing more for China than at any time since the latter's struggles with Japan began in 1931 and 1937, there remained a considerable gap between American protestations of affection and the means which the United States was ready to adopt, the price she would pay, in order to realize the dream of a modern, democratic China, acting as her special protégé and friend in the Far East. For many Americans, there also continued to exist a similar gap between image and reality where Chiang Kai-shek's regime and its war effort were concerned; so great a gap, indeed, that the way was being prepared for a strong, disillusioned reaction later on.

Meanwhile, although information was scanty and direct contact maintained only through Chou En-lai in Chungking, there were some Americans who were beginning to suspect that, away in the north-west, where they were blockaded by Chiang's armies, the considerable force of Chinese Communists might be more wholehearted than Chungking in their opposition to the Japanese, as well as being ready for some form of genuine collaboration with the Kuomintang to that end, if only the latter would agree to it.[84] Moreover, it seemed also, as Captain Evans Carlson had already suggested to Roosevelt,[85] that Mao Tse-tung and his colleagues might not be extremists politically. One report from a Frenchman who had been in Yenan, for example, indicated that for those in control there Communism was only a very long-term goal, to be preceded by a democratic phase based on the principles of Sun Yat-sen.[86] Owen Lattimore likewise told two O.S.S. officers that 'he believed Chu Teh [Commander of the Chinese Communist armies] was running a Democratic rather than a Communist regime in North China.'[87] Might not Mao, Chu, Chou En-lai and others also constitute, as Carlson had claimed in 1938, 'a group of Chinese whose attitude towards the problems of life, and whose conduct, more nearly approach our own than do those of any other large Chinese group'?

Americans, it seemed, needed someone to admire and rely upon in wartime China. For the moment, Chiang Kai-shek held that position. But if Chiang should prove to be a broken reed—or worse, a rotten one—might not his enemies fit the bill?

The British approach

The British as a whole, or at least British officials, were not looking for heroes in China in 1942. And certainly there was no inclination to search for them in Yenan. Clark Kerr, the Ambassador in Chungking until early in the year, was interested in Mao Tse-tung's regime, which he saw as being determined to fight the Japanese to the end and which, as we have seen, he described to Eden as 'the mild Radicalism which in China is called communism', and to his Australian colleague as one of 'agrarian reformers', whom he admired.[88] On the other hand, an official of the Government of India, in very different vein, was already forecasting civil war in China after the defeat of Japan, with the Communists, 'an indigenous growth, not an offshoot of Russia', hanging like 'a sword of Damocles' above the heads of the Kuomintang.[89]

Whatever one's views, however, all thought of becoming involved with the Yenan movement or of intervening in its relations with the central Chinese Government was ruled out. Clark Kerr himself was firm on this point when, after he had left Chungking to become Ambassador to the Soviet Union, he was approached by S.O.E. with a scheme to set up a British agent in Chinese Communist territory in order to organize sabotage attacks on major industrial targets in North China, Manchukuo and Korea. 'Probably the Chinese Communists would be as apt at such work as any other Chinese, but certainly no apter', wrote Clark Kerr, 'and I see no point in making use of them when, by doing so, we risk giving offence to the Chinese Government with whom we are in close and friendly relations.'[90] There was, in addition, a particular reason for adopting such a stance. To become involved in any way would remove a strong argument which was being employed by London when trying to get Chungking to desist from commenting publicly on matters concerning India. 'I think the best rule for Allies to follow', Churchill cabled to Chiang Kai-shek, 'is not to interfere in each other's internal affairs. We are resolved in everything to respect the sovereign rights of China, and we have abstained from even the slightest comment when Communist–Kuomintang differences were most acute.'[91]

When it came to judging China in private, however, British officials were nearer to the Gauss school of realists than to the American worshippers of all things Chinese, whose 'unbounded . . . innocence of the real China' forcibly struck Ashley Clarke, Head of the Foreign Office's Far Eastern Department, when he visited the United States.[92] As for Churchill, he for one saw China as likely to be subservient to the U.S.A. after the war, 'a faggot vote* on the side of the United States', as he put it, 'in any attempt to liquidate the British Overseas Empire.'[93] Nor did China's internal regime command great respect in London. Sir Otto Niemeyer, for example, described it on his return from Chungking as 'a Fascist head surrounded by a corrupt oligarchy and supported by exceedingly skilful use, both in and

---

* That is, the vote of someone essentially unqualified to possess it, likely to be cast at the direction of another.

outside China, of publicity.'[94] 'China as a democracy is a legend', wrote an
official of the Government of India, and he, too, described the Kuomintang
regime as 'Fascist, in a new and special, oriental sense.'[95] Even Clark Kerr,
who, as we have seen earlier, greatly admired Chiang Kai-shek and urged
that Britain should support him to the fullest extent, admitted that the
Generalissimo was 'a dictator'—though one who possessed, he believed,
'the unquestioning faith and affection of the millions he rules.'[96]

Clark Kerr's successor as Ambassador, Sir Horace Seymour, observed for
his part that China's forces were doing scarcely anything in the way of
attacking the Japanese along their 4,000-mile front. (Stalin had put the same
point to Eden when the latter visited Moscow.)[97] 'The world has been told',
the Foreign Office duly reported to the Cabinet, 'of Chinese victories,
desperate resistance, brilliant exploits, massacres of Japanese and so on,
most of which are grossly exaggerated and some entirely untrue.'[98] This
verdict was reinforced by the experiences of two military groups which
Britain sent to China with the intention of assisting in the fight. The first
consisted of 150 soldiers specializing in guerilla warfare, who, as 204
Military Mission, entered China from Burma in January 1942 in order to
train and work with battalions of Chinese 'surprise' troops. The Chinese,
however, showed no inclination to let the resulting mixed, Anglo-Chinese
units see action, whereupon morale among the British declined; most of
them were therefore withdrawn to India in October.[99]

The second and similar episode involved an S.O.E. group of Danes, who
were recruited before Pearl Harbour and sent out to China ostensibly in the
employ of a Danish arms manufacturer, their real purpose being to establish
training schools and carry out commando raids. John Keswick, the peace-
time head of the large British commercial firm in China, Jardine Matheson,
was overseeing the project on attachment to the British Embassy, but again
the Chinese showed no desire to have the tranquillity of their front with the
Japanese disturbed. General Chow Wei-lung put various obstructions in the
way of the group, and in March 1942 Chiang Kai-shek himself suddenly
ordered the Danes to be withdrawn, on the grounds that they had been
meddling in domestic politics. Those involved blamed not only the Chinese
desire for a quiet life but also their wish to hide the fact that their budding
commando troops were 'being built up as a political army on the lines of
the Gestapo and not as a fighting unit on the front.'[100] No doubt it did not
greatly help, either, that Tai Li, the secret-police friend of America's
Captain Miles, had been imprisoned for a time by the British in Hongkong
in 1941. A few other British soldiers stayed on in China, like the peace-time
North China manager for the Asiatic Petroleum Company, who trained
Chinese guerillas in sabotage. Other groups, as we shall see later, were also
to be involved in rescuing Allied flyers from behind the Japanese lines.
Essentially, however, the idea of a small but specialized and valuable British
military effort alongside the Chinese had come to an end. 'They are just
sitting back waiting for us to win the war for them elsewhere', wrote the
Military Attaché in Chungking, '. . . [intending] to build up now as strong

an army as they can with the object of coming to the peace table and confronting the powers with as formidable a force as they can muster.'[101]

Even if the Chinese were not fighting, however, the predominant belief in London, as opposed to Washington, was that they were unlikely to collapse or to make peace with the Japanese, and that they were, in the words of Sir John Brenan, 'not in the least sentimental in their international relations, but . . . astute diplomatists and propagandists.' 'We do not see any reason at present to expect the Chinese resistance to collapse in the next twelve months', reported Seymour in September, 'if (a) Japanese confine themselves to activities on present scale, (b) no major disaster to the Allies occurs, especially in the Middle East or India, (c) crops are sufficient to ensure food supplies.'[102] But even supposing that the Japanese were to advance again and virtually to knock the Chungking regime out of the war, it was still not thought in London that Tokyo's forces would thereby gain great freedom of action:

> 'The immediate result in China', the Cabinet were advised in June, 'might well be a renewal of civil war. The Communists would probably oppose a compromise peace settlement, and there might be a revival of provincial autonomy and misrule. It is doubtful whether the Japanese would be enabled to withdraw many of their troops; they would have to stay and keep order if they wished to exploit the occupied territories.'[103]

Although the Joint Intelligence Committee reported in rather less sanguine terms to the Chiefs of Staff in the same month, they, too, believed that 'the communists, who constitute a considerable part of the forces opposed to Japan, are doubtless as determined as ever to continue the fight',[104] while at the end of August the Chiefs of Staff themselves approved a planners' report which concluded: 'We consider that the Chinese cannot be equipped to take the offensive . . . If they cease to fight as a United Nation, it is unlikely to result in the release of any appreciable Japanese forces.'[105] China could continue in the war, asserted the J.I.C. at the end of September, although without overland reinforcement she would become weaker. Again, at the end of the year, the Committee reported that as yet 'no marked general deterioration in the economic situation of China' was discernible, while the Military Attaché in Chungking had already written that he saw 'not the slightest danger at the moment' of China's seeking a separate peace.[106]

All this did not mean, as we shall see, that a desire to assist China or an awareness of her significance were entirely lacking. It was easy, however, to feel a sense of helplessness when it came to actually doing something to improve relations, as the memoirs of Eden and others indicate.[107] China had been allocated to the United States for both strategic liaison and supplies. In any case, Britain's resources were inadequate for her own needs (together with her supplying of the Soviet Union), let alone for those of China as well. Even small gestures, like the commando schemes mentioned above, tended to go awry or, as happened to a proposal to send out a fighter squadron, to prove impracticable.[108] Collaboration with the Chinese at a strategic-planning level also ran into the serious problem that their cyphers were thought to be far from secure, quite apart from the tendency for information to leak out from Chungking across the Japanese lines.[109] In addition, General Wavell, never the most expansive of men, shied away from taking Chiang Kai-shek into his confidence when it came to planning operations for the recapture of Burma in the summer and autumn of 1942.

Specific incidents helped to worsen relations. As briefly noted earlier, Chungking took offence when Wavell, on being offered the Chinese 5th and 6th Armies* on 23 December 1941 to assist in the fight to save Burma, accepted only two divisions for immediate use (although both Armies later fought in Burma under Stilwell). Wavell had logistical reasons for his decision—communications in North Burma were very poor—and he doubted the wisdom of leaving Yunnan uncovered, which the proposed move would entail. But despite his subsequent claim not to have made a diplomatic mistake ('I make any number of military blunders, but I've never made a political blunder in my life'),[110] it is apparent that he had, indeed, been motivated partly by political reasons. 'It was obviously better to defend Burma with Imperial troops than with Chinese', he explained to Churchill, 'and the Governor particularly asked me not to accept more Chinese for Burma than was absolutely necessary.'[111] The Governor's own correspondence confirms this, and enlarges upon his alarm at Chinese political ambitions over at least parts of his territory.[112] The Foreign Office, for its part, certainly believed that Wavell had committed an error—Ashley Clarke even feared that another Stimson–Simon type of legend might have been created —and so, too, did Churchill.[113] The Prime Minister also reacted critically when the Governor of Burma, although he had secured local American approval, caused an outcry by ordering the unloading of the ship *Tulsa* at Rangoon and the temporary use of some of its cargo of Lend Lease supplies bound for China. This time, however, there had been no ulterior motive; simply a common-sense decision in a critical military situation and at a time when enemy air-raids were imminent.[114]

Over the surrender of extraterritorial rights, too, as has already been indicated, there existed more difficulties on the British than on the American side. Ironically, one of the delicate issues involved—the notion that some special status might be retained for Shanghai after the war in order to encourage the development there of foreign business activity—had been raised in the first place by a Chinese official and adopted by the Foreign Office (who speedily dropped it once it was opposed) only in the mistaken belief that the Chinese themselves would be glad to see this come about.[115] Three other issues, however, were emphasized by the British themselves as being of considerable importance for the future: the right of British citizens to be treated on the same basis as Chinese nationals for commercial purposes; their right to acquire real property; and their right to participate in

---

* A Chinese army was about the size of a British division.

coastal trade and inland navigation.[116] On all these points, largely as a result of indirect American pressure ('really', noted Cadogan, 'their behaviour is most cavalier!'),[117] London eventually gave way. With the backing of the Cabinet, however, no surrender was made over the Chinese demand that the Kowloon Leased Territory at Hongkong should be included in the rendition, and on this, at the eleventh hour, it was the Chinese who gave way and thus enabled the agreement as a whole to be signed.[118] This did not mean, of course, that all British businessmen with interests in China were satisfied over what had occurred, any more than were their American counterparts. The British American Tobacco Company, for example, remained apprehensive over the possibility of Chinese Government monopolies being established which could affect their particular commodity, whilst over-all, the hopes of those like Messrs. Butterfield and Swire that one could 'retain the substance [of extraterritoriality] and give away only the shadow' had certainly not been realized.[119]

Further difficulties arose over the question of a possible British loan to China. Chiang Kai-shek had originally sought £100 million to accompany the sum being provided by Washington, but this figure was regarded in London as absurd. After a first thought of £30 million instead, £50 million was offered when it was learned that the Americans were coming up with their $500 million loan. In the British case, however, unlike the American, certain conditions were insisted upon: the money (apart from £10 million to be used to guarantee an internal loan if so desired) must be spent in the sterling area and on war needs only, and although Eden privately had some doubts as to the wisdom of attaching such strings to the transaction,[120] the Treasury remained adamant. 'After the war', the Cabinet were warned, 'we shall have to face the very difficult task of paying out of our current exports for our imports . . . and we cannot afford to give China a first call on those exports . . . It would be impossible to defend having let China "in on the ground floor" to this extent, in priority to our own Dominions and Colonies.' As the Chinese nevertheless persisted in making proposals that would in effect enable them to use the credit after the war, no agreement was reached during this period.

It was a failure which provided ready ammunition for those in China and the United States who wished to contrast British unhelpfulness with American generosity, even though the financial considerations involved were appreciated within the State Department.[121] Meanwhile the distorted Chinese exchange rate disturbed British as much as it did American officials. Keynes, for example, who was Treasurer of the United Aid to China Fund, estimated at the end of 1942 that sterling was fetching only about one-ninth of what it was worth. 'Thus', he wrote, 'for every £100,000 sent to China by the . . . Fund, only about £10,000 went directly to the purpose for which it was intended and the remaining £90,000 went into somebody's pocket.'[122]

The deadlock over the loan, like the differences between the two countries over Indian affairs, which will be related in a later chapter, only increased angry and contemptuous sentiments towards Britain among Chinese officials. Little attempt was made to disguise these feelings, especially since they made good listening for quite a number of Americans. Madame Chiang Kai-shek, for example, decried to the Governor of Burma Britain's 'selfish policy of over-concentration on defence of her own island', and in an April number of the *New York Times* magazine, made derisive references to the swift fall of Hongkong and Singapore.[123] 'Our prestige has never been so low', wrote the Military Attaché in Chungking, while he described the Chinese as having 'now reached a pitch of arrogance and conceit that is unbelievable.'[124]

Not the least reason for London's concern at such a state of affairs was the harm that it might do to Britain's standing in the United States. Walter Lippmann specifically warned Halifax that, in the latter's words, 'a good deal of the criticism of ourselves by [American] intellectuals flowed from the sympathy of the said intellectuals with China, whom they persisted in thinking we had never been anxious to treat on fully-equal terms . . .'[125] It was a situation which disturbed Churchill sufficiently for him to invite, during his June visit to Washington, the ever-fruitful Laughlin Currie to put forward his own suggestions for improving Sino-British relations. When Currie's list duly appeared, it proposed, amongst other things, that London should allow its loan to China to go through, should consult more with Chiang Kai-shek over plans to recapture Burma, and should offer China a pact on the lines of the Anglo-Soviet one.[126]

This last idea, of signing some kind of treaty with China, had in fact already been considered within the Foreign Office, partly in response to the Generalissimo's proposal, made immediately after Pearl Harbour, for an alliance among the Allies. Eden himself was at one time interested in the possibility of drawing up even a bilateral, Sino-British agreement, as a form of encouragement to the Chinese, a way of preparing for post-war collaboration, and 'a counterpoise to any agreement with Russia.' In the end, however, the arguments against such a treaty were adjudged decisive. China was expected to be too weak after the war to make any mutual guarantee at all equal in its benefits and obligations; the position of the Soviet Union over Manchuria and Korea was an unknown factor which could complicate matters at some future date; above all, there was no likelihood—and Harry Hopkins confirmed as much—of the United States, whose position would in many ways be decisive, participating in anything in the nature of a formal alliance. ('Much as the Americans may like the Chinese', commented Brenan correctly, 'they emphatically do not accept China as an equal partner in the planning and prosecution of the war.')[127]

For some officials and politicians in London, and even more, in New Delhi, there was an additional reason for moving warily where China was concerned. In brief, it was the fear that a newly-assertive and nationalistically arrogant China might after the war make an attempt either to secure or to control territories at present belonging to Britain or of direct concern to her. Tibet, for example, was one case which was to the fore in this connection in 1942, the de facto independence of that country being a matter of importance to the Government of India, as well as anxiously being asserted by the Tibetans themselves in the context of proposals from London and Chungking for a supply route to China running through their land.[128] Some British officials, meanwhile, were even suggesting that China might try to establish wider claims still, based on those of the Manchu Empire in the past. 'There is a great potential danger of Chinese imperialism', noted Dalton in his diary after hearing a talk by Sir Muhammed Zaffrullah Khan, who had recently been representing the Government of India in Chungking.[129] Zaffrullah Khan likewise suggested to a Far Eastern study group at Chatham House that China would want to lay her hands on parts of French Indochina and Tibet, was already emphasizing her former suzerainty over Upper Burma, and might even claim a share in the administration of Malaya on the grounds of the substantial numbers of Chinese living there.[130]

Others, Sir George Sansom among them,[131] were talking in a similar vein. Duff Cooper, for example, thought that post-war China 'would be more difficult and perhaps more dangerous than Japan',[132] a comparison that was also made by Amery for Eden's benefit.[133] 'It is evident that these Chinese tendencies threaten to raise questions of the first magnitude in Asia after our common victory', observed Seymour, and John Keswick approvingly forwarded to the Foreign Office an anonymous memorandum which suggested that 'the Chinese plan to obtain control of most of the Far East, the immediate objects being Hongkong, Indochina, Burma and Tibet.'[134] Mongolia, too, was thought by some to be a target for repossession,[135] whilst Brenan expected to see Chinese 'immigration, commercial penetration and political intrigue' threaten the Netherlands East Indies as well as Burma and Malaya.[136] Dr. H. J. van Mook, the Dutch Minister for Colonies, agreed: taking a long view, he put it to Lord Cranborne, the United States and China between them could constitute a greater threat than Japan.[137]

The outline given thus far of Britain's relations with China in 1942 would more or less have fitted into the picture as it was seen by many Americans at the time: severely limited cooperation on London's part, tinged with suspicion and a certain distaste. And yet the outline is seriously incomplete. There was, in fact, another side to British thinking, and one which put the over-all position of London distinctly closer to that of Washington, even though the peculiarly American euphoria over China was largely absent. This other aspect of British approaches can immediately be illustrated with reference to the subjects of Tibet and possible Chinese imperialism which have just been raised. Thus Eden, for one, did not go along with the Government of India over Tibet. 'I do not find it possible', he minuted, 'to accept the argument that Tibet must be maintained as a buffer state against an ally, China.'[138] And in the margin of Amery's letter which contained the comment that China after the war might well prove 'even more dangerous than Japan', the Foreign Secretary put a large exclamation mark, describing the document as 'a very depressing effusion.'[139] More typical, in fact, than

Amery's emphasis was the one embodied in a Foreign Office summary of the position vis-à-vis the Chinese that was put before the Cabinet:

'So long as they continue to function and to pay at least lip service to the common cause, the only policy for the Allies is to remember their many admirable qualities, to overlook their less pleasant tendencies, and to go on giving them all the help and encouragement that may be possible.'[140]

Moreover Churchill himself, for all his subsequent scorn for the idea of China being a great power, was ready in 1942 to talk of her in 'American' terms. 'When we remember', he cabled to Wavell in January over the aid-to-Burma affair, 'how long the Chinese have stood up alone and ill-armed against the Japanese, and when we see what a very rough time we are having at Japanese hands, I cannot understand why we do not welcome their aid.' There was also, he reminded Wavell, the American factor to consider in this: 'China bulks as large in the minds of many [Americans] as Great Britain . . . And never forget that behind all looms the shadow of Asiatic solidarity, which the numerous disasters and defeats through which we have to plough our way make more menacing. If I can epitomise in one word the lesson I learned in the U.S.A., it was China.'[141]

As for the situation on the spot in China, the observations of Eggleston are of some interest:

'British prestige', he wrote to Canberra in April, 'was never lower in China than it is today . . . [But] there is nothing in the attitude of British officials and soldiers in Chungking today to justify this feeling. I do not know anyone among them who is not genuinely friendly to China and anxious to keep on the best of terms . . . So far as my observation goes, there is far greater personal hostility to the Chinese, and criticism of their inefficiency, among American diplomats and military officials and journalists than among the British. There is, however, an ineradicable preference for the Americans among the Chinese.'[142]

Nor, in London, was it simply a matter of caring about China for the sake of Anglo-American relations alone, even though, as already indicated, this was an aspect of great importance.[143] There was in addition a genuine concern, especially during the early part of 1942, to keep China going. Churchill, speaking in both Washington and London on the subject, fully recognized the need to keep the Burma Road open for supplies to Chiang Kai-shek's Government.[144] 'Taking the widest view', he informed the Cabinet's Defence Committee on 21 January, 'Burma was more important than Singapore. It was the terminus of our communications to China which it was essential to keep open.'[145] The C.I.G.S. and the Director of Military Operations agreed with this judgment,[146] and the Chiefs of Staff had already recorded their opinion that 'we shall require Chinese help for the final defeat of Japan. Cooperation with Chiang Kai-shek', they added, 'must therefore remain a cardinal point in Allied policy.'[147] During the defence of Burma, the C.O.S. continued to be as anxious as Clark Kerr that the Generalissimo should be kept 'more fully in the picture', and both they and the Prime Minister endorsed a proposal—which proved abortive—that retreating British/Indian forces should withdraw into China rather than towards India.[148]

Even after the initial crisis of December 1941 to the spring of 1942 had passed, pro-Chinese sentiments continued to be expressed in official British circles. Supplies to China were still a matter of concern to Churchill later in the year. 'All our difficulties will be aggravated', he wrote in June, 'if China is forced out of the war. The danger of the collapse of Chiang Kai-shek is one of the greatest we have to face at the present time.'[149] Projects for reopening overland routes to China received the support of the Cabinet, the Chiefs of Staff and the Foreign Office, the last-named devoting much time to trying to obtain agreement from the countries concerned in order to open up a route through Tibet and another from India via East Persia, the Soviet Union and Sinkiang. Even the Burma Office, which might have been expected to fear the possible political repercussions involved, urged that a road from Ledo to Myitkyina—what was to become, in fact, the famous Ledo Road, built by the Americans to link up with the old Burma Road—should be constructed 'with all possible speed.'[150]

The Cabinet, too, like the Military Attaché in Chungking and the Foreign Office, were keen to see an R.A.F. squadron operating in China if possible, since it would have 'a political effect out of all proportion to the sacrifice involved',[151] but this project was killed, not only by a shortage of suitable planes, but by Stilwell's opposition to it.[152] Eden for one, however, went on making the over-all case:

'The Chinese war effort', he informed his Cabinet colleagues in August, 'is largely maintained by the vitalising leadership of Chiang Kai-shek and by his success in keeping up the morale of the people . . . But his ability to maintain morale . . . depends very much on the help which he receives from ourselves and the United States, and on the evidence which we provide of our continued close interest in, and support of, the Chinese war effort.'[153]

At the same time, the Joint Planners and Joint Intelligence Committee agreed that, were China to leave the ranks of the Allies, there would be 'grave political drawbacks.' 'The morale [sic; 'moral' ?] and political value of China as a member of the United Nations', advised the latter in January 1943, 'is out of all proportion to her material contribution. Her resistance adversely affects Japan's prestige and morale and vitiates Japan's propaganda claim to be freeing Asia for the Asiatics.' Keeping China in the fight ranked second only to weakening the enemy's war machine in the aims that were drawn up for carrying out political warfare against Japan, while Chinese assistance in developing anti-Japanese propaganda in Burma was welcomed.[154]

In public, too, moreover, there was much enthusiasm for the cause of China, stimulated in part by prominent individuals who had had dealings of various kinds with that country. Where the press was concerned, indeed, the degree of praise bestowed upon China was not much less than that to be found in the United States. The warmth displayed by the *Manchester Guardian* in this respect might have been expected, it is true:

'The Chinese Revolution is a constructive achievement not less remarkable than the Russian', it declared. '. . . A people ready to suffer for its ideals is led by a man who does not fear to ask for sacrifices from his nation because he knows that his countrymen are confident that in his hands they will not be wasted . . . The British people are proud to be associated with the great enterprises and the great ideals to which the Chinese people have shown such heroic devotion.'[155]

Yet the *Daily Express* was equally forceful in urging an increase in aid to China,[156] while the *Daily Telegraph* described 'the deliverance of China' as being 'the keystone to the security of the free nations in the Far East and the Pacific.'[157] 'If China goes', asserted the *News Chronicle*, 'all goes, so far as the war in the Far East is concerned. Remember, too, that no nation has a greater contribution to make to the world's future.'[158] As for *The Times*, it was downright apologetic about the unequal status that had been accorded China in the past—'full redress will have to be made to her national self-respect'[159]—and enthusiastic about her role in the years ahead:

'It is sufficient proof of the part which China is playing in the alliance of the United Nations', it proclaimed in January 1942, 'that the only decisive victory over Japanese forces since December 7 has been won by the Chinese forces at Changsha, and that China is the only member of the alliance with an unlimited reserve of manpower available in a place where it can be immediately brought to action. To this it may be added that the Chinese, alone of the allies, have behind them an experience of nearly five years of active campaigning against the enemy . . . Equally impressive . . . are the growth and strength of the Chinese national spirit . . . The failure of the Japanese to make any serious breach in the national front is the best possible proof of the solidarity of the new China . . . These facts make it impossible to doubt that China is destined to play an increasingly important, and eventually a dominant, part in the struggle between the United Nations and Japan . . . To establish the full independence and authority of China at the earliest possible moment is one of the principal aims of the allies in the Far East, and nothing must be left undone to complete the machinery of a partnership that will not end with victory.'[160]

Sentiments similar to these were also being expressed in speeches by Stafford Cripps in particular, who, it will be recalled, had visited China early in the European war. Cripps, who had found Chiang Kai-shek 'impressive in his modesty and sincerity' and Madame Chiang Kai-shek 'extraordinarily intelligent', managed to combine enthusiasm for left-inclined social experiments in China, such as the Industrial Cooperatives Movement (in fact, disliked intensely by the ruling clique), with a fantasy picture of the Kuomintang leading China into a democratic and peaceful future. ('Through the operation of that party', declared Cripps, 'thousands of ordinary Chinese citizens have been brought into contact with democratic ideas.')[161] Propaganda for the Kuomintang was also in effect promulgated in Britain by Lady Cripps' United Aid to China Fund, which took much of its information for pamphlets and speeches on China from official Chinese sources.* Those few people in Britain who were aware of and supported the left in Chinese politics—notably the members of the China Campaign Committee led by Dorothy Woodman—were hardly in a position yet to attack the Chiang Kai-shek regime.[162]

As for the handful of Britons who were actually living in Communist-held areas—notably Michael Lindsay, son of the Master of Balliol—their enthusiastic reports had scarcely begun to filter down to Chungking and London. Endorsement of the existing Government of China, meanwhile, was also forthcoming from a Parliamentary good-will mission which visited that country during the autumn and winter of 1942. In confidential memoranda sent to the Prime Minister on their return, the mission, although they commented upon the weakness of the Chinese Army and on the regime's aim to conserve as much strength as possible for use against the Communists, nevertheless approved, in somewhat patronizing terms, of the autocratic nature of Chiang Kai-shek's rule:

'Among a people who are as deficient in these virtues of self-sacrifice and loyalty . . . as the Chinese have always been', the mission concluded, 'discipline must come before freedom if any improvement in the condition of the country is to be made . . . [But] the defeat and disarmament of Japan will probably leave China with a government and a people who will possess both the will and the means to rise from the depths of anarchy to the heights of industrial and military strength.'

'It is clear', declared one member of the mission at a reception in the House of Commons, 'that the Chinese should be the great power in the East.'[163]

Against such a background, there existed in at least some parts of Whitehall more than simply the desire to help China to pin down large portions of the Japanese Army. When Richard Law, for example, talked in the Commons of the need to work with China 'on terms of absolute equality in the world that is to come', it was not a case of his concealing private Foreign Office cynicism behind a suitable public façade.[164] One finds Sir John Brenan, for instance, who, as the result of his service in Shanghai, was quite often a stern critic of the Chinese,[165] writing in an Office minute in April:

'I agree that the superior attitude which many of the British have been inclined to show towards the Chinese in the past is unjustified and

* In its first year of operation, 1942–3, the Fund raised £703,000. Humanitarian aid for China was also provided by various other bodies. (See Cripps Papers, file 676, and FO 371, file 31646.)

dangerous, and that from now on we shall have to accept the idea of complete equality and reciprocity in our political relations with China. A useful step in that direction would be to give up our extraterritorial jurisdiction while it is still possible to do so voluntarily and as a friendly gesture. Its exercise is becoming increasingly embarrassing from our own point of view and it has long been regarded by the Chinese as an intolerable affront to their nationhood.'[166]

Possible means of improving the state of Sino-British relations were also discussed several times in Cabinet, and were the subject of a lengthy talk between Churchill and the Chinese Ambassador, Wellington Koo. Encouraging messages were sent to Chungking by the Prime Minister, and Cripps broadcast to China; other measures that were considered included inviting Madame Chiang Kai-shek to visit Britain, and bestowing honours of various kinds on her husband.[167] Some steps were meanwhile being taken to develop cultural and scientific relations between the two countries. Professor E. R. Dodds of Oxford visited China in this connection, while, more importantly, Dr. Joseph Needham, the future historian of Chinese science and technology, left for that country in the autumn of 1942 to work with universities there and with the Academia Sinica.[168]

As for the extraterritoriality issue which Brenan had raised within the Foreign Office, Eden himself was keen to surrender these privileges, writing in March: 'I should like to do it in such a manner that [the] Chinese know that the initiative is ours and not American.'[169] Both Seymour in Chungking and the Far Eastern Department in London supported him (unlike the position in Australia, there was no British policy of immigration restriction to complicate matters).[170] Only reluctantly, in April, did the Foreign Secretary accept the unfortunate advice of Cadogan (a diplomat whom contemporaries and historians may have somewhat overrated) and Sir Maurice Peterson that it would be better to wait until Britain's military position in the Far East had been improved in order to make the gesture look less like one born of weakness. The result was that, when extraterritoriality was abolished shortly afterwards, very little credit accrued to Britain, the assumption in Chungking being that Washington had pressed a reluctant London to agree to rendition. Many Americans, too (and perhaps even those numerous American historians who have subsequently and unthinkingly based their descriptions of Britain's China policies on their own country's mythology), would have been surprised to learn of the degree of willingness over the surrender of extraterritoriality that existed in London. There was even in some quarters—including, remarkably enough, the Colonial Office, as well as the Head of the Foreign Office's Far Eastern Department—a preparedness to discuss with China after the war a possible ending of British sovereignty over Hongkong itself, within the context of a United Nations security system for the Far East as a whole.[171]

The Prime Minister, of course, would almost certainly never have endorsed this last proposal, and the Cabinet agreed that even the matter of the Kowloon lease must not be discussed until a peace conference met.[172] Nevertheless, the question demonstrated that some officials, including highly-placed ones, were indeed ready to think in new terms. Moreover, within the China Association, which represented Far Eastern commercial interests in London, despite the desire of some businessmen to try to secure new safeguards for their non-extraterritorial future, there were those who had for some time been arguing that an entirely fresh and equal basis needed to be found for relations with the Chinese.[173] The press, for its part, right across the political spectrum, hailed the ending of extraterritoriality when it came in January 1943. 'China', declared *The Times*, 'is now offered the guarantee that with victory she will take her part, as a Great Power, . . . in shaping and sustaining the coming new order in Asia. A resplendent destiny is opening for her.'[174]

One reason for Whitehall's positive approach to this whole question had been the belief that, even without extraterritoriality, there would continue to be considerable commercial opportunities for Britain in China after the war. 'Participation must be in the spirit of cooperation and not exploitation', ran a report by the Department of Overseas Trade. 'British nationals should be impressed with the necessity for recognising and conforming with the changed spirit of China.'[175] Difficulties were foreseen, however, Niemeyer being one who was less sanguine about the outcome. Would credits be available, for example, with which to prime the market in China? Above all, it was agreed that there must be no attempt to embark upon a course of rivalry with the United States in this field. Americans and British must 'act in unison', urged the Treasury's representative at an inter-departmental meeting on the subject,[176] while the Ministry of Supply declared itself to be 'most perturbed about the present state of Anglo-American collaboration in China, particularly so far as industrial supplies are concerned.' Similarly, when the Chinese themselves made known their readiness to discuss business with a British firm, the Far Eastern Development Company, care was taken to ensure that there were no American objections to this before official approval was given.[177]

Such British hopes of future cooperation with the United States in China were based on a genuine belief that the interests of the two countries were broadly similar and could best be served in this way. In addition, however, hopes of this kind arose naturally from the rapidly weakening position in China in which Britain found herself, her pre-war dominance among the Western powers there swept away by the exigencies of global conflict and by the resources and special position possessed by the United States in current, war-time circumstances. The simultaneous ending of extraterritoriality by London and Washington had, indeed, marked a certain degree of collaboration. Already, however, there existed differences of approach, as well as of strength, between the two countries, deriving from developments and beliefs which, as has been suggested in the first part of this book, went back a long way before the Second World War. There was a strong tendency on the part of the United States to see herself as possessing a monopoly of virtue among the foreign powers dealing with China, and to attribute to Britain, sometimes correctly, sometimes not, insensitivity if not outright selfishness.

Among Americans, too (and we shall see this emerging more clearly still in later periods of the war), there was an inclination to look to the future in China and the Far East in terms, less of collaboration than of rivalry with Britain: rivalry over trade; rivalry over the kind of world that was to emerge from the fight against the Axis. This was also evident as regards the area of war adjoining China, in Southeast Asia.

Notes to Chapter Six

1 Eggleston Papers, MS 423/9/1148.
2 Eggleston despatch, 4 Jan, 1943, ADEA, A989/43/315/1/2.
3 *New York Times*, 23 Jan. 1942.
4 Ibid, 7 July 1942. And e.g. 9 and 30 Dec. 1941; 29 Feb. 1942.
5 *Chicago Daily News*, 15 Jan. 1943.
6 *Christian Science Monitor*, 25 July 1942.
7 *New York Times*, 24 Oct. 1942.
8 Lattimore to Yarnell, 18 June 1940, and to Martin, 3 June 1940, IPR Papers, box 373; and see Lattimore speech of 2 May 1942, Hornbeck Papers, box 274. In describing China as 'a democracy', Lattimore, who had not at the time met any of the Kuomintang leaders, was influenced by the spirit he had found among bourgeois-liberal-academic circles in Tientsin. Interview with Professor Lattimore.
9 Barnard, *Willkie*, 365ff., and J. P. Davies, *Dragon By The Tail* (New York, 1972; hereafter, *Davies*), 255.
10 H. R. Isaacs, *Scratches On Our Minds* (New York, 1963), 37.
11 E.g. ibid, 174; *Tuchman*, 349ff.
12 J. M. Blum, *From The Morgenthau Diaries: Years of War* (Boston, 1967), 124.
13 United China Relief Papers, boxes 76 and 77.
14 *Davies*, 244.
15 *Romanus and Sutherland*, I, 186; FRUS, 1942, China, 62; Currie to FDR, 13 Nov. 1942, Roosevelt Papers, PSF box 145.
16 OSS, R and A, 341.
17 FDR to Marshall, 8 March 1943, OPD, Exec. file 10, item 70. On FDR's fondness for recalling his family's involvement in the China trade, see F. Freidel, *Franklin D. Roosevelt: The Apprenticeship* (Boston, 1952), 9.
18 See Halberstam, *The Best and the Brightest*, cap. 18; Lake, *The Legacy of Vietnam*, 161.
19 Hornbeck memo., 4 March 1942, Hornbeck Papers, box 52.
20 Hornbeck to Welles, 11 Feb. 1942, ibid, box 440.
21 Miles letter, Sept. 1942, USNOA, Naval Group China files.
22 Stimson Diary, 16 April 1942; see FRUS, 1942, China, 153.
23 E.g. DS 740.0011 P.W./2387, 2454; OSS, R and A, Psychology Division, 'Short Guide To South China', 27 June 1942, Goodfellow Papers, box 3.
24 E.g. DS 740.0011 P.W./2476½; FDR to Hull, 19 Nov. 1942, Hull Papers, box 50; FDR to Hull, 21 Nov. 1941, Roosevelt Papers, PSF box 37. Hornbeck, to his credit, defended Gauss. See material in Hornbeck Papers, box 175.
25 FRUS, 1941, IV, 769.
26 FRUS, 1942, China, 49.
27 Ibid, 71. Walter Lippmann likewise assured Foreign Office officials that without China 'you would get a set-up of East against West.' FO 371, F6518/54/10.
28 *Morgenthau Diary, China*, vol I (Washington, 1965), 632.

29 JCS, 11 Aug. 1942, loc. cit.
30 FRUS, 1942, China, 126.
31 Ibid, 185.
32 E.g. ibid, 733, and Gardner, *Economic Aspects*, 248.
33 E.g. FRUS, 1942, China, 8, 55.
34 E.g. ibid, 18, 20, 135; *New York Times*, 4 and 13 June 1942; *San Francisco Examiner*, 11 Jan. 1943.
35 FRUS, 1942, China, 33; see Mme. Chiang Kai-shek to Currie, 18 May 1942, Roosevelt Papers, PSF box 145.
36 FRUS, 1942, China, 566ff.; *Romanus and Sutherland*, I, 159ff.
37 See FRUS, 1942, China, 591ff., 624ff., 697ff.
38 See *Romanus and Sutherland*, I, 91; Magruder to Stimson, 7 Jan. 1942, Hornbeck Papers, box 150.
39 Stilwell's briefings are in OPD, Exec. file 10, item 17.
40 FRUS, 1942, China, 159.
41 *Romanus and Sutherland*, I. 181, 306ff.
42 Ibid, 250ff.; Chennault, *Way Of A Fighter*, 212.
43 Material in Hopkins Papers, box 331. Alsop got on well with Britons in China.
44 FRUS, 1942, China, 495ff., *Young*, 189, 257.
45 *U.S. and China*, 471.
46 Stimson Diary, 29 Jan. 1942; FRUS, 1942, China, 433, 442.
47 FRUS, 1942, China, 419ff.; *Morgenthau Diary, China*, I, 587ff.
48 Gardner, *Economic Aspects*, 243.
49 See FRUS, 1942, China, 268ff.
50 Hiss memo., 8 Jan. 1943, Hornbeck Papers, box 350.
51 FRUS, 1942, China, 309ff.; 'Narrative of Negotiations for Extraterritoriality Relinquishment', DS 793.003/4–1443; e.g. *New York Times*, 13 Jan. 1943, *Christian Science Monitor*, 12 Jan. 1943, *Chicago Daily News*, 12 Jan. 1943.
52 FRUS, 1942, China, 390.
53 Atcheson to Hornbeck, 29 Dec. 1942, DS 793.003/12-2942.
54 E.g. Currie to FDR, 16 Sept. 1942, Roosevelt Papers, PSF box 36; FRUS, 1942, China, 35; *Morgenthau Diary, China*, vol. II, 862.
55 *Morgenthau Diary, China*, II, 862ff.
56 Barnard, *Willkie*, 376.
57 FRUS, 1942, China, 119.
58 Ibid, 126; Stilwell to War Dpt., 8 Dec. 1942, OPD, Exec. file 10, item 22.
59 See Magruder to War Dpt., 25 Dec. 1941, and Beaverbrook to Hopkins, 31 Dec. 1941, Hopkins Papers, box 135; FRUS, 1942, China, 2, 6; FRUS, Washington and Casablanca, 152, 271; Hornbeck to Winant, 9 Jan. 1942, Hornbeck Papers, box 445; Stimson Diary, 29 March 1942.
60 *Morgenthau Diary, China*, I, 585.
61 Chennault to Mme. Chiang, 26 Jan. 1942, Chennault Papers, box 1.
62 Lusey to Donovan, 23 May 1942, Goodfellow Papers, box 3.
63 Miles to Lee, 1 and 20 May 1942; Miles to 'Abie', 23 Aug. 1942, USNOA, Naval Group China files. See M. E. Miles, *A Different Kind Of War* (New York, 1967).
64 Naval Group China letter, 18 Nov. 1942, Naval Group China files; see below, 536.
65 See e.g. Kolko, *The Politics of War*, 221; *Tuchman*, 237.
66 E.g. FRUS, 1942, China, 13, 31; *Romanus and Sutherland*, I, 43.
67 Stilwell Diary, 19 Jan. 1943.
68 E.g. *Romanus and Sutherland*, I, 250ff.
69 Stilwell to JCS, 30 July 1942, Stilwell Papers, box 5.
70 *Romanus and Sutherland*, I, 172.
71 Ibid, 182–3. On contacts that did take place between China and Japan during the war, see L. Allen, *The End of the War in Asia* (London, 1976), 219ff.
72 FRUS, 1942, China, 24, 27, 91, 109.
73 Ibid, 104.

74 Ibid, 193, 211, 260.
75 Ibid, 191, 258.
76 *Morgenthau Diary, China*, II, 862ff.
77 E.g. Dixon record of talk with Bos, 4 Jan. 1943, ADEA, A989/43/735/319.
78 *Wallace*, 18 Dec. 1942.
79 FRUS, 1942, China, 505, 585.
80 *Morgenthau Diary, China*, I, 576, 635.
81 *Young*, 234ff.; FRUS, 1942, China, 534, 559, 562.
82 FRUS, 1942, China, 89; *Romanus and Sutherland*, I, 224; *Sherwood*, 598.
83 FRUS, 1942, China, 344.
84 E.g. ibid, 206, 228, 246.
85 See above, 42.
86 Currie to FDR, 13 Nov. 1942, Roosevelt Papers, PSF box 145.
87 Tolstoi and Dolan memo., 6 Oct. 1942, Goodfellow Papers, box 3.
88 See above, 68.
89 Weightman memo., 'China, Fact and Fiction', 1942, n.d., FO 371, A9511/122/4
90 Two memos., n.d., ? 1942, FO 800/300.
91 WSC to Chiang, 26 Aug. 1942, FO 371, F6122/54/10; see F5797/2428/10.
92 Ibid, F4320/4320/61.
93 WSC to Eden, 21 Oct. 1942, PREM 4, 100/7.
94 FO 371, F2950/7/10.
95 Ibid, A9511/122/45. A rather different picture of China, in which he forecast the
   retention of power after the war by the Kuomintang and dismissed the Communists
   as 'not doing anything', was given to the Far Eastern Group of Chatham House on
   28 Oct. 1942 by Colin McDonald, former *Times* correspondent in Chungking. Far
   Eastern Group files, RIIA.
96 Clark Kerr to Eden, 3 Feb. 1942, FO 800/300.
97 E.g. FO 371, F2918/4/10; F1448 and 2543/54/10.
98 WP(42)236, CAB 66/25.
99 See FO 371, F6402/54/10, F3650/74/10; I. Adamson, *The Forgotten Men* (London,
   1965).
100 Reports on China Commando Scheme, in Goodfellow Papers, box 3, and Naval
   Group China files, USNOA.
101 Grimsdale to Ismay, 15 Aug. 1942, Ismay Papers, IV/Gri/3.
102 E.g. FO 371, F2543 and 7756/54/10; F6316/1689/10.
103 WP(42)236, CAB 66/25.
104 JIC(42)213(0), PREM 3, 143/1.
105 COS, 28 and 31 Aug. 1942, CAB 79/22.
106 COS, 25 Sept. 1942 (CAB 79/23) and 4 Jan. 1943) CAB 79/25); Grimsdale to Ismay,
   15 Aug. 1942, loc. cit.
107 E.g. *Avon*, 366; M. Peterson, *Both Sides Of The Curtain* (London, 1950), 239.
108 COS, 3 Sept. 1942, CAB 79/23.
109 E.g. COS, 3 Jan. 1942 (CAB 79/18) and 15 April 1942 (CAB 79/20); Wavell to WSC,
   14 Sept. 1942, PREM 3, 143/9.
110 Sansom, *Sir George Sansom*, 139.
111 Wavell to WSC, 26 Jan. 1942, PREM 3, 154/1.
112 Dorman-Smith to Linlithgow, 5 Feb. 1942, Linlithgow Papers, vol. 115.
113 FO 371, F4285 and 4597/18/10; F1369/4/23; WSC to Wavell, 22 Jan. 1942, PREM 3,
   154/1.
114 FO 371, F76 and 286/76/10; material in PREM 3, 90/2, and in Dorman-Smith
   Papers, E 215/44; COS 7 Jan. 1942, CAB 79/17.
115 FO 371, F6364 and 6482/828/10.
116 E.g. ibid, F8081 and 8450/828/10.
117 *Cadogan Diaries*, 20 Oct. 1942.
118 FO 371, F3782, 8408, 8482 and 8566/828/10; *Cadogan Diaries*, 28 Dec. 1942.
119 FO 371, F13942/60/10; F1104 and 2619/456/10. A further sign of changing times was

the ending of the tenure of Sir Frederick Maze of the traditionally British-held post of Inspector General of Chinese Maritime Customs. FO 371, file 31625.

120 Ibid, F3688/4/10.
121 See ibid, files 31618–20; WP(42)370, CAB 66/27; Cab, 2 Feb. 1942, CAB 65/25; FRUS, 1942, China, 519, 521.
122 FO 371, F8311/7/10.
123 Ibid, F4089/1689/10; Dorman-Smith to Linlithgow, 7 April 1942, Linlithgow Papers, vol. 115; *Sherwood*, 660.
124 Grimsdale to Ismay, 8 March and 15 Aug. 1942, Ismay Papers, IV/Gri/1 and 3.
125 Halifax to WSC, 22 Oct. 1942, PREM 4, 27/1; FO 371, F3343/3187/10.
126 Currie to WSC, 25 June 1942, PREM 3, 90/5.
127 See FO 371, F13469/13469/10; F4839 and 5716/54/10; F2031/74/10.
128 See ibid, files 31635, 31637–41, 31700.
129 Dalton Diary, 21 Jan. 1943.
130 Far Eastern Group, 3 Feb. 1943, RIIA.
131 Sansom, *Sir George Sansom*, 137.
132 Dalton Diary, 22 Dec. 1942.
133 Amery to Eden, 13 Aug. 1942, FO 371, F5964/74/10.
134 Ibid, F3751 and 8438/1689/10.
135 E.g. i bid, file 31702.
136 Ibid, F4297/3187/10.
137 Ibid, F4533/90/61.
138 Ibid, F78/78/10.
139 Ibid, F5964/74/10.
140 WP(42)236, CAB 66/25.
141 PREM 3, 154/1. See *Churchill*, IV, 119, and on his failure to meet Mme. Chiang in the U.S.A., ibid, 712.
142 Eggleston despatch, 6 April 1942, ADOD, A816/19/306/139.
143 See above, 161.
144 E.g. FRUS, Washington and Casablanca, 74, 220.
145 CAB 69/4.
146 Kennedy, *The Business of War*, 187.
147 DC(Ops.), 20 Dec. 1941, CAB 69/3.
148 E.g. COS, 13 and 17 Dec. 1941 (CAB 79/16), 3 and 26 Jan. 1942 (CAB 79/17), 21 Feb. 1942 (CAB 79/18), 30 March 1942 (CAB 79/19); material in FO 800/300; Wavell to COS, 22 March 1942 and WSC to COS, 25 March 1942, PREM 3, 152/3. General Slim for one, however, was greatly opposed to the idea of sending British forces into China. R. Lewin, *Slim: The Standardbearer* (London, 1976), 97.
149 WSC to COS, 7 June 1942, PREM 4, 28/9; see ibid, 8 April 1942, PREM 3, 142/2; 16 June 1942, PREM 3, 143/1; WSC to First Lord of Admiralty, 1 June 1942, PREM 3, 163/8.
150 See Cabs, 9 March 1942, CAB 65/25, and FO 371, files 31635–43.
151 Cabs, 11 June 1942 (CAB 65/26) and 31 Aug. 1942 (CAB 65/27); Military Mission and Attaché to War Office, 24 Feb. 1942 and 12 Aug. 1942, PREM 3, 90/5; FO 371, F4219, 5995 and 6978/24/10.
152 FO 371, F5987/24/10; Wavell to Stilwell, 28 June 1942 and Stilwell to Wavell, 7 July 1942, Stilwell Papers, box 6.
153 WP(42)375, CAB 66/28.
154 COS, 7 June 1942 (CAB 79/21) and 4 Jan. 1943 (CAB 79/25); J.P. Sub. Cttee. 20 April 1942, CAB 84/4; Amery to WSC, 30 April 1942, PREM 3, 152/3.
155 *Manchester Guardian*, 26 Sept. 1942.
156 *Daily Express*, 11 Sept. 1942.
157 *Daily Telegraph*, 21 July 1942.
158 *News Chronicle*, 30 July 1942.
159 *Times*, 6 June 1942.
160 Ibid, 31 Jan. 1942.

161 Cripps speeches, 3 and 10 Oct. 1942, Cripps Papers, files 1158 and 1159; C. Cooke, *Stafford Cripps* (London, 1957), 258.

162 See Martin Papers, box 50, and Cripps Papers, box 527. For the experiences of Britons in contact with the Chinese Communists at this time, see R. and N. Lapwood, *Through The Chinese Revolution* (London, 1954); C. and W. Band, *Dragon Fangs* (London, 1947); M. Lindsay, *The Unknown War: North China, 1937–45* (London, 1975).

163 See FO 371, F8510/1689/10 and files 31693–5; PREM 4, 28/5. The delegation consisted of Lord Ailwyn and Capt. Scrymgeour-Wedderburn (Cons.), John Lawson (Lab.) and Lord Teviot (Lib.).

164 Hansard, HC Deb. 385, col. 155.

165 See e.g. *Thorne*, 228–9.

166 FO 371, F3133/54/10.

167 Cabs., 1 June 1942 (CAB 65/26), 3 and 31 Aug. 1942 (CAB 65/27); WSC-Koo talk, 3 June 1942, PREM 4, 45/4; Cripps broadcast, 14 July 1942, Cripps Papers, box 81; material in PREM 4, 28/7 and 8, and in FO 371, file 31654.

168 FO 371, F7252/1689/10.

169 Ibid, F2031/74/10.

170 On the problems caused by the 'White-Australia' policy, see ADEA, A989/43/735/313 and A989/44/655/37.

171 See FO 371, F5965/74/10 and F37822/828/10. In general, see Chan Lau Kit-Ching, 'The Hong Kong Question During The Pacific War', *Journal of Imperial and Commonwealth History*, vol. II no. 1.

172 See Cabs, 30 Nov. 1942 and 21 and 28 Dec. 1942, CAB 65/28, and on the negotiations generally FO 371, files 31657–60, 31663–65, 31679–80, 31683–4, 31715.

173 General Cmttee. minutes, 25 Nov. 1941, 30 Oct. 1942, Ch.A.; FO 371, F7845 and 8109/828/10.

174 *Times, Daily Telegraph, Manchester Guardian, News Chronicle*, 12 Jan. 1943.

175 FO 371, F5853/4350/10, and in general, files 31713–14; for Niemeyer's views, see F2950/7/10.

176 Ibid, F7193/4356/10.

177 Ibid, F5668 and 7125/4356/10.

CHAPTER SEVEN

SOUTHEAST ASIA AND THE FUTURE OF EMPIRES

Defeat

THE MILITARY reasons for the rapidity of the British defeat in Hongkong, Malaya, Singapore and Burma have been analysed in detail elsewhere.[1] Many of those reasons, of course, as was suggested earlier, stretched well back into the 1930s and beyond, and were not to be laid at the door of the commanders, troops or civilian officials involved in the débâcle itself. This was not what the world stopped to see, however. All that stood out at the time was the astonishing ease with which British rule had been pushed aside. In the Malayan campaign alone, for example, out of total British Empire and Commonwealth losses of 138,700 and against Japanese battle casualties of only 9,824, 130,000 men were marched off as prisoners of war. Between the opening of the fight and 8 March, the loss of manpower in all reached 166,500, as against Japanese casualties of around 15,000.[2] 'It was clear now', the Cabinet in London were belatedly informed, 'that Japan was a most formidable and dangerous antagonist . . . Our military performance in Malaya had left much to be desired.'[3] To Roosevelt, Churchill bluntly described the fall of Singapore as 'the greatest disaster in our history.'[4]

The manner of this defeat gave rise to many questions and criticisms on the British and Commonwealth side, as well as among foreign observers. Acts of heroism and defiance, examples of devotion to duty amid the most difficult circumstances,[5] could easily appear less significant than evident shortcomings on the part of individuals or of British rule as a whole. Over Hongkong, for example, the Commanding Officer of the colony's Field Ambulance Unit, who had escaped from Japanese confinement into unoccupied China, where he was subsequently to lead the British Army Aid Group, wrote of 'apathy, inertia and self complacency' on the part of a Hongkong Government that was 'rotten to the core, its people [having] no confidence whatever in their leaders', and of a garrison that had been 'psychologically defeated' well before the actual surrender.[6] Another memorandum, on the subject of poverty and racial discrimination in Hongkong, together with the haughty manner in which the local Chinese had been treated, brought from the experienced Brenan in the Foreign Office the comment: 'I am afraid that there is some justification for many of [these] criticisms.'[7]

As for the case of Singapore, we have already seen the concern expressed by Duff Cooper at what he found there when sent out from London to investigate late in 1941. Of the Governor, Sir Shenton Thomas, Cooper wrote in extremely severe terms, as being unable to adjust his mind to war conditions and having 'lost his grip on the situation.' Senior members of the Governor's staff came in for even stronger criticism, while the Malayan Civil Service as a whole had, in the Minister's opinion, 'failed lamentably in making adequate preparations for war.' As for the military Commander, Lt. General Percival, Cooper found him, as we have seen, 'not a leader.'[8] The local Australian Commander, Major General Gordon Bennett, also subsequently criticized before the War Cabinet in Canberra the poor leadership that had been given to British troops, 'due', he claimed, 'to the "old school tie" method of selection', while he described the quality of the Indian forces involved in the campaign as inferior.[9] (Not that Bennett's own performance had been particularly glorious. As the end came at Singapore, and having urged on Percival the need to surrender, he abandoned his troops and, without Percival's knowledge and without appointing anyone in his place, slipped away to safety.)[10] Two of the last men in responsible positions, a doctor and a civil engineer, who managed to evade the Japanese at Singapore, also gave a statement to the authorities in Bombay which included the charge that 'every department of the Civil Administration [in Malaya] was rotten with graft and corruption';[11] another report from a different quarter, submitted to the Colonial Office in London, castigated 'the faulty policies and methods of the Malayan Government and [the] Colonial Office', above all for 'concentrating on developing a separatist Malayan nationalism; a selfish nationalism which demanded a privileged position for Malays within the states, and more particularly power and wealth for Malays of the aristocracy, whether they deserved it or not.'[12]

In retrospect, the official British military historian of the area has written in his own, private study of the Singapore disaster, of the Governor as being 'far too easily swayed by the last person with whom he had been in contact', of those responsible for the land campaign against the Japanese as committing 'every conceivable blunder', and of Churchill as giving instructions which 'bore no relation to the facts.' In addition, much harm was done at the time by the preference accorded to whites over Asians during some of the evacuations in the peninsula.[13] Over Burma, too, some of the widespread criticisms of the time were to be echoed by the subsequent judgment of Field Marshal Sir William Slim, that many senior members of the administration of that country were unable to produce the vigour and flexibility that the emergency demanded.[14]

It is not being argued here that every one of these and similar accusations is absolutely proven. Through other eyes one can come up with a very different emphasis—on, for example, the constructive work performed by the Governor and his civil service in Malaya,[15] or on the endeavours of some members of the administration in Burma to cope with a problem like the sudden exodus of Indians from Rangoon and other parts of the country

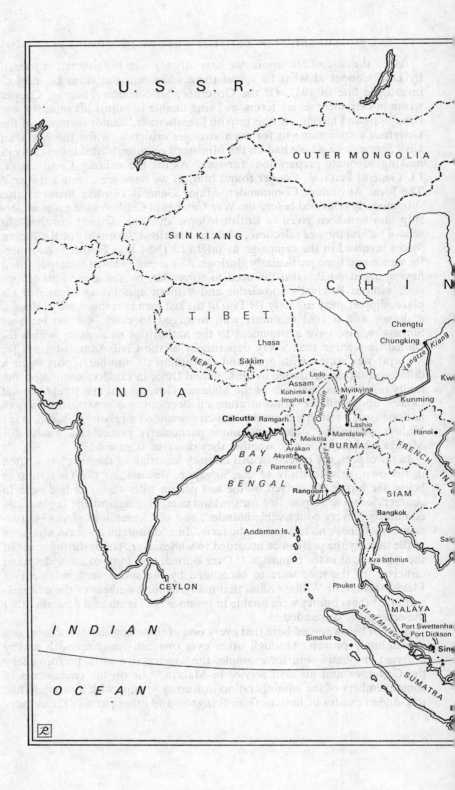

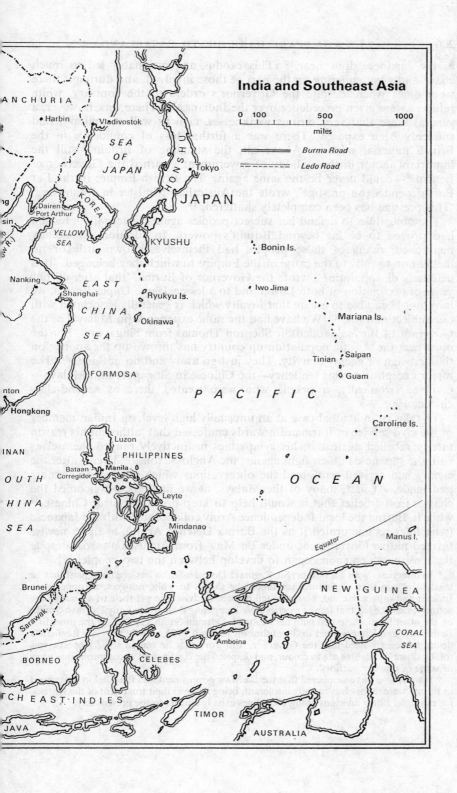

India and Southeast Asia

0   100   500   1000
                 miles

————————— Burma Road
- - - - - - Ledo Road

MANCHURIA

Harbin

Vladivostok

SEA
OF
JAPAN

HONSHU

Tokyo

JAPAN

KOREA

Dairen
Port Arthur

YELLOW
SEA

KYUSHU

Bonin Is.

Nanking

EAST
CHINA
SEA

Shanghai

Ryukyu Is.

Iwo Jima

Okinawa

Mariana Is.

Saipan
Tinian
Guam

FORMOSA

PACIFIC

Hongkong

Caroline Is.

Luzon

PHILIPPINES

Bataan
Corregidor

Manila

OCEAN

Leyte

Mindanao

Manus I.

Equator

Brunei

NEW   GUINEA

Sarawak

CORAL
SEA

Amboina

BORNEO

CELEBES

DUTCH EAST INDIES

TIMOR

JAVA

AUSTRALIA

as the Japanese drew near.[16] (This exodus unquestionably led to much chaos and great suffering on the part of those involved, and during it there were times when, despite the Governor's orders to the contrary, white refugees were given precedence over the Indians.)[17]* There was, however, a general sense that very serious weaknesses, civil as well as military, had suddenly been exposed. There was a further loss of confidence in the British imperial mission. Above all, the standing of Britain—'still the important factor in the stability of government', warned the Governor of Bengal[18]—could never be the same again. 'The British Empire in the Far East depended on prestige', wrote the Australian Minister in Chungking. 'This prestige has been completely shattered.'[19]

The obligation to defend her subject peoples against external aggression had proved to be far beyond Britain's powers. In addition, as already mentioned, many of those peoples had themselves shown little or no inclination to rally to the cause of the Empire to which they belonged. 'It is definitely disappointing', wrote the Governor of Burma, 'that after all our years of occupation of both Lower and to a lesser degree Upper Burma, we have not been able to create that loyalty which is generally associated with our subject nations.'[20] 'We have had the same experience [in Malaya] as the Governor of Burma', added Sir Shenton Thomas from Singapore. 'For the most part the Asiatic population up country has thrown up the sponge on the first sign of enemy activity. They just go away and do nothing.'[21] (The major exception to this tendency—the Chinese in Singapore and Malaya—involved, ironically, a people who were treated there as second-class citizens.)[22]

To take an individual case at an unusually high level, an Indian member of the civil service in Burma afterwards confessed that 'although his reason utterly rebelled against it, his sympathies instinctively ranged themselves with the Japanese in their fight against the Anglo-Saxons.'[23] Events after the enemy had arrived reinforced the observations which the two Governors had made. At first, many of the Malays, as we have seen, welcomed the change in the belief that it would help to keep down the local Chinese,[24] while in Burma the local Independence Army collaborated with the Japanese (who later reinaugurated it as the Burma Defence Army), as did a newly-formed native Government under Ba Maw from August onwards, despite the tension which soon began to develop between the two peoples.[25]†

* In interviews with the author, Sir Reginald Dorman-Smith has been adamant that he tried to ensure that no favouritism should be shown to white refugees, as opposed to Indians and others. He did, however, tell his white advisers to get their wives out of the country, since he felt that family worries were hampering their work. Lady Dorman-Smith, on the other hand, stayed on with her husband. Dorman-Smith's A.D.C. at the time, Eric Battersbee, in a letter written to the author on 12 April 1977, shortly after Sir Reginald's death, has emphasized that the Governor, 'old Tory that he was in some respects, was totally liberal in his attitude to colour, and despised the rigidity and uncompromising ways of some of our compatriots'.

† It must also be remembered that the Ba Maw government and the Thakin movement in Burma were themselves racially intolerant, being fierce in their treatment of the Karens, for example. Bitter divisions along these lines exist in Burma to the present day.

The manner and consequences of these defeats were to burden British Far Eastern diplomacy and Anglo-American relations for the remainder of the war. Empires per se were deplorable enough in many American eyes; yet here was something even worse: an Empire that could not even protect its peoples, win their active allegiance, or put up a stern resistance to the common foe. Only a swift and successful military response, for which Britain lacked the necessary resources—and perhaps the spirit, might have done something to erase the impression that had been created. As it was, Allied observers were sometimes moved to scorn by what they saw. Some American press correspondents in Singapore, for example, fell foul of the authorities over what they wished to reveal, and Cecil Brown of C.B.S. had his facilities withdrawn in what he termed 'the City of Blimps.'[26] Roosevelt passed on to Churchill a similarly scathing denunciation of the state of affairs in Burma, written, according to the President, by 'one of our best newspapermen',[27] while Chiang Kai-shek, after visiting the country early in 1942, wired to the Prime Minister: 'In all my life of long military experience, I have seen nothing to compare with the deplorable unprepared state, confusion and degradation in the war area of Burma.'[28]

Critical reports of this kind were also circulating privately in American official circles, reinforcing impressions there which were all the stronger as a result of the shock occasioned by the swift surrender of Singapore. (The need to hold Singapore had been felt as keenly in some American quarters as in London. Stimson, for example, had warned Roosevelt that its fall would be 'an almost vital blow to the British Empire as well as to our own future commercial interests in the Pacific.'[29] Likewise, the Chief of the State Department's Far Eastern Division had described the base as 'a symbol of the power, the determination and the ability of the United Nations to win this war', the fall of which would 'lower immeasurably . . . the prestige of the white race and particularly of the British Empire and the United States in the eyes of the natives of the Netherlands East Indies, of the Philippines, of Burma and of India.')[30]

In some cases, it is true, American military observers on the spot in Southeast Asia did appreciate the difficulties which Britain had encountered, even though her forces were described as 'beaten and groggy, slow to adapt to new conditions of warfare.'[31] Where civilian expatriates and administrations were concerned, however, few saving graces appear to have been found. In Singapore, the British were a 'tight little social group, until recently . . . antagonistic toward Americans.'[32] On Hongkong, the former U.S. Consul there wrote in a report that was circulated within the State Department after his repatriation:

'The British were the ruling caste and to justify their primacy which they took to be their natural right they developed a conceit and a complacency that were amazing . . . The local British were also predisposed to regard the war, not as the resistance of a united community . . . but rather as a struggle between two ruling groups for the control of a subject populace

... Hongkong was not really home for its defenders: why should they die for it?... Hongkong had become a little never-never land living in the rhythm of Rudyard Kipling, far away from wars or any possible challenge to the white man's rule. Real preparation for war was thus psychologically impossible ... The essential set-up of the Hongkong British had also made them an easy prey to defeatism ... [Their] doubt was the product and the precipitant of all that other weakness: when its spirit had reached up to the Governor and down to the ranker, resistance ceased.'[33]

Likewise, Stilwell's political adviser reported after the fall of Burma:

'One of the outstanding phenomena of the Burma campaign was the refusal of the Government of Burma to recognise impending catastrophe and to take effective action to cope with the situation ... The American military officers felt that the civil government in Burma was representative of the worst type of colonial bureaucracy. The administration was cumbersome and inefficient ... Unless the same decadent and unintelligent course in India is corrected, India may be expected to collapse under attack as Burma did. The British have shown no volition to correct this situation. The only remedy would seem to be pressure from Washington on London.'[34]

Reports reaching Washington also stressed the disaffection of native populations. 'The ordinary affairs of life', ran one such document, 'have been generally conducted in Burma in such a way as to uphold British prestige and to put the Burmese in their place ... The Burmese deeply resent the contemptuous treatment the British have given them.'[35] At the same time, surveys also tended to suggest that there existed a natural affinity between these Southeast Asian peoples and Americans: 'The Burman is the kind of person we Americans like and can get along with'; 'the Malayan Chinese hold the United States in very high esteem ... and wholeheartedly support enterprises conducted by Americans in Malaya.'[36] The Chinese of the region were seen in one summary as being especially important for the future, thus reinforcing the significance already attached by United States officials to China itself: 'Not unreasonably, the Chinese feel that their losses in Southeast Asia entitle them to a voice in its affairs ... Sooner or later the Chinese of this area must be used in the struggle against Japan, and they can be used effectively only through the Nationalist Government at Chungking.'[37]

The course of the war thus increased American interest in Southeast Asia, its peoples and future. (Up till then, the American diplomatic presence in the area had been very limited.)[38] Besides military considerations, there were other factors involved, such as the supply of raw materials from the region. American officials were tending to say in private what we have already seen papers like the *Chicago Tribune* bellowing in public:[39] that the European imperialists in Southeast Asia had, by their selfish policies, helped to make the United States herself unprepared for war. Herbert Feis, for example, the

State Department's Economic Adviser, declared 'with great vehemence' to the Dutch Minister for Foreign Affairs, 'that never again would the great American nation allow the British and Dutch to dictate the prices at which it could buy its tin and its rubber.'[40] The Under Secretary of State, Sumner Welles, likewise observed to the State Department's Advisory Committee on Postwar Foreign Policy that 'he could not see the United States fighting to maintain British rubber or tin monopolies.'[41]

There was thus all the more reason to be concerned over the postwar fate of what a memorandum by the State Department's Division of Special Research described as 'a vast wealth of raw materials and of large populations ... which constitute actual or potential markets of great value.'[42] This also involved, however, the larger question of the entire future of colonial empires in general and, in terms of Anglo-American relations in 1942, of the British Empire in particular.

The British Empire: the public debate

In an earlier section, concerned with Anglo-American relations as a whole, it was briefly mentioned that the future of the British Empire was one issue which, in 1941–42, was complicating and in some ways worsening those relations.[43] It is again important to bear in mind, however, a consideration that has also been suggested in another context: that, on each side of the Atlantic, one is dealing with national opinions that were far from homogeneous.

It is true that, where the American scene was concerned, the most noticeable feature in this respect was the extensive criticism, direct or implied, of the British Empire as a selfish and dangerous anachronism. *Life*, for example, in its open letter to the people of Britain already referred to, urged them to 'stop fighting for the British Empire and fight for victory', warning that 'if you cling to the Empire at the expense of a United Nations victory you will lose the war because you will lose us.'[44] Similarly, Wendell Willkie, in proclaiming his theme of 'One World', chose India as the symbol of Asia's doubts, when he demanded on its behalf: 'Is freedom supposed to be priceless for the white man ... but of no account to us in the East?' Likewise it was Hongkong that he selected to illustrate the foreign privileges that were barring the way to China's true independence.[45] Whether it was the articles of a left-wing magazine like *Amerasia*[46] or a public speech by a prominent member of the Administration like Sumner Welles,[47] the message was fundamentally the same: the age of imperialism was past and must speedily be recognized as such. In a poll conducted in June 1942, 56 per cent of those Americans questioned agreed that the British could be described as oppressors 'because of the unfair advantage ... they have taken of their colonial possessions.'[48]

Even so, there were other voices to be heard speaking in the United States in very different terms. 'How much of the British Empire can Americans afford to see liquidated', asked the *Christian Science Monitor*, 'before a better system of collective defense has been developed?'[49] Americans were not fighting in order to destroy that Empire, declared the *Chicago Daily News*, adding that 'Mr. Churchill's remark [that "we mean to hold our own"] should be taken to heart by some of our overzealous brethren . . . and it is too bad that he even had to say it.'[50] As the *New York Herald Tribune* saw it, 'It is quite true that the American people are not fighting to preserve the less lovely aspects of a British imperialism already dead. But neither are the vast majority of the British.'[51]

This last point was also conceded by Willkie himself. 'British public opinion on these matters', he wrote in *One World*, 'is even ahead of opinion in the United States. The British have no doubt—and, so far as I can see, little regret—that the old imperialism must pass.'[52]* This was probably an accurate summary of the situation. True, American attacks like the one in *Life* did bring forth, even in the *Daily Herald*, indignant and sometimes sweeping denials that British imperial policies were 'unprincipled.'[53] The Labour Party, like the Conservatives, tended to view overseas possessions, like the Commonwealth, 'as actually or potentially an immense power for good in the world', with even Harold Laski emphasizing around this time that the system, for all its oppressive faults, gave people like the Indians an opportunity to advance towards their freedom.[54] When studying the deliberations and papers of a body like the Labour Party's Advisory Committee on Imperial Questions, for example, one is struck by their moderation, when emphasizing the extreme unreadiness for independence of some colonies (in Africa, for instance), or when rejecting some form of international government (as distinct from general international supervision) for dependent areas.[55] The paternalist tradition, indeed, survived within the Labour ranks. 'The fact of Empire', as one student of the subject has observed, 'was still the plainest of challenges to all men of goodwill. Socialism, like Benthamite utilitarianism before it, might find there a fertile field wherein to apply itself. Socialists, missionaries in their own kind, recognised the nature of their mission . . . They believed, with Kipling, that a white man's burden existed, and that it had to be borne.'[56]

Nevertheless, what stands out in retrospect is the extent to which opinion in Britain by 1942 did recognize (when it considered the subject, that is) the need for new developments in the colonial sphere. In part, such a recognition involved having to adopt a suspicious attitude—and rightly so—towards Churchill himself, who in so many other respects was proudly taken to be speaking for the people he led. 'Mr. Churchill was an active Tory', warned the *Daily Herald*. 'He may again, after the war, become an active Tory . . . We think he has not found time to study and grasp the vital bearing of political issues upon the outcome and aftermath of the war.'[57] In a *Times* leader, Margery Perham expressed similar sentiments, albeit in slightly more veiled terms: 'The pride and achievement of the modern British Empire',

* The important but elusive link between domestic social and political developments on the one hand and imperial attitudes on the other is explored by Mason in *Prospero's Magic*, especially 26ff.

she wrote, 'are that it has become in a certain sense a self-liquidating concern . . . Its aims can be defined in terms not of "have and hold" but of the Atlantic Charter and the "four freedoms".'[58]

Likewise, in contrast to Churchill's angry response to Willkie's anti-imperialist speeches (most notably the Prime Minister's declaration in November 1942 about having no intention of 'presiding over the liquidation of the British Empire'), the American's advice was received with appreciation in much of the British press. 'When Mr. Wendell Willkie argues that the whole of civilized mankind has an interest in the advancement of dependent peoples', acknowledged *The Times*, 'he can encounter no dissent here . . . Moreover, some understanding upon colonial objectives belongs naturally to the common effort to break the Japanese hold upon Malaya and other Eastern territory which they have seized.'[59] Willkie's *One World* itself was to receive a good press when it was published in 1943.[60] Meanwhile the case for collaboration with the Americans in this field was developed at greater length by Margery Perham in two articles in *The Times* on 20 and 21 November:

'The Americans are forward-looking people', she wrote, 'and we must do more than explain that, as empires go, ours is doing meritorious work . . . They want us to convince them that we are liquidating this idea [of "colonial possessions"] from above by a readiness for international cooperation and from below by strenuous education in self-government. It is not enough for those of us who move in government or colonial circles to convince ourselves in our own undertones that this is exactly what we are doing. Clarity and urgency are needed . . . Is it too much to hope that a voice might be heard from this country with a ring of leadership, proclaiming a clear plan of advance that would catch the imagination of the common man in Britain and in the colonies and give them the sense of working together to achieve it?'

In the House of Commons, too, there were those who were trying to prod the Government into adopting more progressive measures (such as increasing the niggardly amount allocated under the 1940 Colonial Development and Welfare Act), developing a new approach to colonial issues generally and to the specific question of India, or recognizing publicly the universal validity of the Atlantic Charter.[61] Others elsewhere were expressing the belief that an imperial era was coming to an end. 'The British Empire of the past, with its mixture of paternalism and repression, has plainly had its day', asserted the *Manchester Guardian*.[62] Privately, Laski wrote to Frankfurter: 'The weakness of our method is that we keep our war effort, so far as the Four Freedoms go, mainly on the plane of rhetoric instead of beginning to make them operate on the plane of action. The collapse of British power in Burma and Malaya, its exhibited weakness in India, derive from this.'[63] 'Asia is at last coming into her own', observed R. H. Tawney to a friend. 'The British imperial game is up. The British governing class has been tried and in spite of exceptions found wanting.'[64] Even Smuts, in an interview published in *Life* in December 1942, outlined possible future developments within the Empire in a way which emphasized the eventual independence and freedom of its constituent units.

One particular forum that was involved in this Anglo-American ventilating of ideas and accusations over colonial matters was the Institute of Pacific Relations. It was an organization which had its headquarters in the United States and affiliated branches—the British one being based on the Royal Institute of International Affairs at Chatham House—around the world.[65] After the war, as already mentioned, the size and significance of the Institute, and in particular of its American branch, were to be greatly exaggerated by those who included it among the targets for their attempts to rout out so-called 'traitors' who had helped the United States to 'lose' China.[66] Nevertheless, the I.P.R. had, in peace-time, made an important contribution to the study of Asian issues, with its regular publications, *Pacific Affairs* and *Far Eastern Survey*; after Pearl Harbour moreover, with a much larger audience to hand, it took on wider educational work. Above all, its international conferences, of which there were two during the war, the first being held at Mont Tremblant, Quebec, in December 1942, gave the I.P.R. a status well beyond its actual size.

An entire study could be devoted to these war-time I.P.R. conferences and their ramifications. (A report drawn up at the time on the 1942 meeting can be read in book form under the title of *War and Peace in the Pacific*, published in 1943.) Here, one must be content simply to mention three particularly interesting aspects that relate to the present work. The first is that, through its conferences especially, the I.P.R. embraced both the official and the non-official worlds. In the United States, for example, a leading member of the Institute like Owen Lattimore (he had been editor of *Pacific Affairs* from 1933 to 1941) had been drawn into the ranks of America's officials, first, as we have seen, as an adviser to Chiang Kai-shek, and then as Director of Pacific Operations for the O.W.I.; at the same time, a prominent Washington official like the State Department's Stanley Hornbeck was in attendance when the Institute met at Mont Tremblant. In Britain, the Foreign Office and other Government departments likewise took a considerable interest in that conference.[67] There already existed a direct connection between the I.P.R.'s London branch, Chatham House, and the Foreign Office, in that the former, as noted earlier, was providing for the Government as a war-time measure the Foreign Research and Press Service. Additionally, an F.R.P.S. member like G. F. Hudson, Head of its Far Eastern Section, was quite often included in the circulation of Foreign Office papers, to the minuting of which he could, and did, make a significant contribution.

Official involvement in the 1942 I.P.R. conference itself was increased when Chatham House was obliged to seek Government funds in order to send its delegation to Canada, the Foreign Office in return asking to be consulted on the composition of that delegation, as well as briefing certain members of it on relevant aspects of British policy. In the event, Britain's representatives were led by Lord Hailey, who himself spanned the worlds of

Whitehall and of the scholarly study of colonial affairs and who, like Harold Macmillan as Parliamentary Under Secretary at the Colonial Office, was engaged in developing the idea of 'partnership' between Britain and her dependent territories, as distinct from schemes for some form of international supervision for all colonies.[68] The delegation also included Sir John Pratt, now retired but formerly a prominent member of the Foreign Office's Far Eastern Department, and Sir George Sansom, currently serving in the Embassy in Washington. Likewise, reports of the proceedings at Mont Tremblant were to be fed into the official machinery of both the Australian and Netherlands Governments.[69]

The extent to which some delegations had received official approval gave rise to comment at the time. Among American I.P.R. officials, for example, it was caustically observed that the party from India—chosen by the Indian Institute of International Affairs—would be 'more British than the British', and that the latter were themselves noticeably lacking in representatives of 'the lower classes.'[70] Nevertheless, the very presence of officials and members of influential non-official circles contributed to the second noteworthy feature of these conferences: that they acted as arenas where blunt criticisms could be exchanged between such people in a way which was normally precluded by the basic courtesies of international diplomacy or the requirements of preserving good-feeling between war-time allies.

In the case of the Mont Tremblant gathering, the main feature in this respect was the considerable degree of suspicion and criticism of British imperial policies in Asia that was expressed by various other delegations, led by that of the United States. It had already been appreciated in London that such views were prevalent among the international secretariat of the I.P.R. itself, and if confirmation of this had been needed it was forthcoming in an article in the December issue of *Pacific Affairs*, written by W. L. Holland, the Institute's Research Secretary, which gave rise to much resentment in Chatham House. Now, at the conference itself, there developed, in the words of the Secretary to the R.I.I.A. delegation, 'sustained criticisms of British policy . . . at practically all of the Round Tables, particularly during the early part of the meeting. British policy in India, her colonial policy and the British defeats in Southeast Asia . . . had all come under heavy fire of criticism from members of the United States, Chinese, Canadian, Australian and Indian groups. Doubts had also been expressed as to the sincerity of Britain's intentions in carrying out the terms of the Atlantic Charter.' In Washington after the conference, Hornbeck similarly reported to Hull that for the most part it had been 'Britain against the field.'[71] In return, the British delegation—even someone like Arthur Creech-Jones (who was to be Colonial Secretary in the post-war Labour Government), who, in a domestic setting, was wont to prod and criticize the Government over colonial matters—quickly became exasperated with what they saw as uninformed and high-flown American ideas in this field.[72*]

* Of the other delegations, that of the Netherlands, as its report shows, came closest to sharing the British views.

The proceedings at Mont Tremblant were not entirely destructive, however, and the third interesting aspect of this and the succeeding conference is the extent to which they helped to focus attention on major themes and problems, such as political and social developments within Japan, which would have to be faced in the Far East when the war was over, if not before.[73] Again, the ideas put forward in December 1942 cannot be given in detail here. As an illustration, however, mention can be made of Lord Hailey's proposal for a Pacific Zone Council, to act after the defeat of Japan as the local agency for the United Nations in matters of safeguarding the peace, and as a consultative body for the promotion of international cooperation in the area of common social and economic problems. ('It was intended in the first place', wrote Hailey later, 'to provide an answer to those who demanded some recognition of the principle of accountability in Colonial administration. But we felt that it also had merits of its own.') In addition, the preparation of papers before the conferences, or local discussions afterwards, enabled officials and delegates to air views which did not accord entirely with their own country's current policy. In London, for example, H. V. Hodson put forward a paper on security in the Indian Ocean area in which he urged the enlistment of China to help administer the post-war system, while Pratt argued vehemently in a Chatham House study group— as he could not do, out of loyalty, at Mont Tremblant itself—that 'to retain Hongkong would not further British interests in the slightest degree; on the contrary to retain it would mean that British interests could never revive in China.'

Thus, the future of the British and other colonial empires was being debated in various public or semi-public quarters during 1942, against the background of the Japanese triumph in Southeast Asia and the Pacific. At the same time, the issue was also receiving a great deal of attention in private, within more strictly official circles.

Colonial issues: the policy debates

As was the case among American newspapers, views on colonial issues held by politicians and officials in Washington were far from unanimous. Stimson, for example, had a great deal of sympathy for the aims and existence of the British Empire, while Hull saw Welles' public denunciations of imperialism as being harmful to the Allied cause.[74] In general, however, it is clear that the climate of opinion regarding existing colonial structures was a hostile one, with the accompanying belief, as we have seen, that America's handling of the Philippines, due to receive their independence in 1946,* was a model for the less enlightened European imperial powers to copy.

* Roosevelt thought that the date of 1946 should be adhered to for Philippines independence, even if the war ended well beforehand, his argument being that a period of 'repair and readjustment' would probably be required. (FRUS, 1942, I, 906.) This was not so very different from the way in which the Governor of Burma, for example, was approaching the question of that country's post-war prospects.

Roosevelt himself set the tone for this at the top. A paternalist and imperialist in the past, notably during his days as Assistant Secretary of the Navy,[75] the President still had a keen eye for the possible acquisition by the United States of bases that would enhance her strength at sea or in the development of new air routes.[76] We shall encounter one or two episodes later on which suggest that the old Adam of the Assistant Secretary was not entirely dead in him. In other respects, however, as indicated already in relation to article three of the Atlantic Charter, Roosevelt had by now become a confirmed anti-imperialist. (The memoirs of his son, Elliott, though highly unreliable over details, probably catch the spirit of the President's observations on the subject.) Episodes such as his visit to Gambia when en route to Casablanca served to confirm his feeling of scorn for the small amount which had been achieved in their overseas territories by some of the European Colonial powers. As for the future, his idea of United Nations 'trusteeships' was already taking shape,[77] while over-all he remained convinced, as he emphasized to the press, that the Atlantic Charter was applicable 'to all humanity.'[78]

Similar opinions were to be found at the other end of the official structure, where it overlapped with individuals who, while not holding an official position, were of importance in the influencing of American elite opinion. For example, in the sub-committees on Political Problems and on Territorial Problems of the State Department's Advisory Committee on Post-War Foreign Policy, officials like Welles, Berle and Hornbeck sat with distinguished outsiders like Isaiah Bowman (President of Johns Hopkins University), H. F. Armstrong (editor of *Foreign Affairs*), and Norman H. Davies (President of the American Red Cross). Here, too, of course, opinions concerning colonial affairs varied.[79] John V. A. MacMurray, for example, a former American Minister to China, warned that 'it would be a mistake on our part to force the hand of the present sovereign powers', while Hornbeck and Berle raised the question of the embarrassment which might arise over America's own external possessions. (Might not Hawaii 'make trouble on the issue of self-determination'? And what of the Panama Canal zone?) Welles for his part, however, brushed aside such irritating objections, blatantly applying a double standard where the United States was concerned. Trusteeship principles, he declared, need not be thought of in connection with the Western Hemisphere;[80] as for the question of Panama, 'that would be answered by saying that we had acquired certain bases and that was all we needed'—a suggestion that he had no difficulty in reconciling with his proposal that Singapore, among other strategic centres, should be placed under international control. There was always, after all, the Philippines example to fall back upon—so long as one did not acknowledge the extent to which its history had made it atypical. 'Without it', admitted James Shotwell, a prominent figure from the inter-war peace movement, 'our position would be almost impossible.'

The predominant opinion in these committees in 1942, however, was again strongly reformist—an emphasis which we shall later see beginning to be modified even in 1943. On 8 August, for example, the sub-committee on Political Problems declared itself to be

'in agreement that as a general principle the United States should work toward the liberation of the peoples of the Far East; and that some form of international trusteeship should be established in giving effect to this principle so as to accomplish two objectives: (a) to assist the peoples of the territories to attain political maturity, and (b) to control the raw materials of the area in the interest of all peoples.

It was felt that the United States must take a stand on its principles at the end of the war, since the imperial powers might desire to return to the status quo ante. However, it was considered that the former sovereigns should be associated with the process of liberation . . . It was suggested that the solution of the problem lay primarily in persuading the British to cooperate, perhaps by placing Burma under trusteeship. The other countries would then more readily fall in line. It was thought that opposition from Great Britain would be inspired mainly by the City, together with the Treasury and Board of Trade . . . It was not felt that France had any claim to regain Indochina.'

Possible patterns for the future that were under discussion included a federation of various territories in Southeast Asia. In broader terms, officials began to draw up drafts of an international trusteeship system, although in this regard Hull made the important and limiting suggestion that a distinction should be made between colonial territories on the one hand and existing mandates or territories to be taken from the enemy on the other.[81] The Secretary of State had also stated in a radio broadcast in July the carefully qualified belief that 'all peoples, without distinction of race, color, or religion, who are prepared to accept the responsibilities of liberty, are entitled to its enjoyment.' In addition, as we shall see below, he proposed in passing to Halifax that perhaps some declaration of colonial principles could be devised, to which both Britain and the United States could subscribe.

When it came to considering the future of individual territories, however, certain developments were already taking place on the American side which were likely to lead to differences with Britain, rather than to a common stand. The idea, for example, that countries belonging to Britain's own Empire, such as Burma and Malaya, should be removed from her sovereignty was obviously a case in point, but other areas were also involved. One of these, Siam, was not, in fact a colonial possession but an independent state. Even so, the question of its post-war status did become a matter for debate, and by 1945 would be creating considerable tension between Washington and London. For the moment, during this first phase of the Pacific war, two significant developments occurred where Siam was concerned. One was that that country, like Indochina, was not included in the British area of strategic responsibility, but was placed instead within the command zone of Chiang Kai-shek. This decision, endorsed at the time of the setting up of the

A.B.D.A. command, came to have an anti-colonial significance—especially where Indochina was concerned. Initially, however, it was taken above all in order to bolster up the prestige of Chiang Kai-shek. 'If we relegate [him] to China alone', noted Stimson in his diary, 'he won't feel he is regarded very highly among us and he may not be as helpful as he would be otherwise.'[82] The second development involving Siam was that when, under Japanese impulsion, she declared war on Britain and the United States (but not on China) on 25 January 1942, Washington, unlike London, chose not to respond, but to treat Siam simply as an enemy-occupied territory. At the same time American officials were sympathetically inclined towards a proposal of Chiang Kai-shek's—one that was eventually carried out by him in February 1943—that he should publicly reassure the Siamese that they were still regarded as friends, and that the Allies had no designs on their territory.[83]

Meanwhile, where conditions inside Indochina were concerned, reliable information had been hard to come by since the Japanese occupation. Even so, the State Department and the O.S.S. gleaned material which suggested that the politically-conscious natives were both anti-Japanese and anti-French, an O.S.S. survey also concluding that 'the Annamites have proven themselves capable of self-government.'[84] Nor did the State Department see any reason to comply with French wishes by trying to prevent operations into Indochina from being conducted by China, where the voices of exiles were already being raised on behalf of at least Vietnamese independence after the war.[85] Nevertheless, the over-all American policy position as regards Indochina was still unclear. This was due in large measure to the chaotic system presided over by Roosevelt and described in some detail earlier; matters were not improved, either, by the sharing of responsibility for such European colonial areas in Southeast Asia between the Far Eastern and European Divisions of the State Department.[86]

Moreover, uncertainty remained even though United States representatives had, on several occasions, formally recognized, in the words used by Welles to the Vichy Ambassador in April 1942, 'the sovereign jurisdiction of the people of France over the territory of France and over French possessions overseas.'[87] In fact, the current was flowing strongly in the opposite direction. The advisory sub-committee on Political Problems, as seen above, was emphatic on the matter: 'the title of France to Indochina', it declared, 'was clouded by the failure of the Vichy Government to resist Japanese aggression.' Welles described it as 'a great moral question', which exemplified the general situation of 'exploitation by European powers with very little if any advantage to the peoples concerned.'[88]

Above all, Roosevelt himself was already dwelling more upon the case of Indochina than on that of any other colony. Moreover, he was airing his views on the subject in a way which showed that he would be quite content if the French themselves came to hear of them. To the Allied representatives on the Washington Pacific War Council, for example, he 'casually observed' on 20 May, in the words of Halifax, who was present, 'that he did not feel at all sure that it would be a good plan after the war to return all French Pacific islands to France. Nor was he at all sure about Indochina. French administration had left a good deal to be desired, and he hinted at the possibility of Indochina being placed under an international trusteeship.'[89] The President spoke again to the Council in December, brazenly and falsely affirming in response to a question that 'no firm commitment had been made' to the French regarding the sovereignty of their empire.[90] Roosevelt was in fact well aware of the various pledges referred to above, but told his Chiefs of Staff in January 1943 that Robert Murphy, for example, had 'exceeded his authority' when he, among others, had assured French leaders that their empire would be restored.[91]

The President's own reading of the situation, loftily conveyed to an irate de Gaulle at Casablanca, was that since 1940 the French people had not been in a position to assert their sovereignty, so that France was 'in the position of a little child unable to look out and fend for itself, and that in such a case a court would appoint a trustee to do the necessary'—including, it would seem, removing some of the child's possessions.[92] (The United States, wrote de Gaulle himself later, 'delighting in her resources, feeling that she no longer had within herself sufficient scope for her energies, wishing to help those who were in bondage anywhere, yielded in her turn to that taste for intervention which concealed the instinct for domination.'[93] As it was, the Gaullists were already seeking to preserve their interests from friend and foe alike by developing their own contacts with the Vichy army in Indochina through a military mission in China.)[94]

The European power to come best out of these American deliberations was in fact the Netherlands, to whose colonial administration in the East Indies warm tributes were paid by the State Department's Advisory Committee,[95] and whose promises of future reform, underlined by Queen Wilhelmina in a broadcast of December 1942, were noted approvingly.[96] Roosevelt himself, who liked to talk of his Dutch ancestry and also enjoyed the snobbery of his relationships with visiting royalty such as Wilhelmina,[97] assured both the Queen and Dutch officials that the East Indies would be returned to them.[98] Typically, while he also criticized British imperial policy to the Netherlands Foreign Minister, to Sir Ronald Campbell, on the contrary, he described it as being unlikely that the Dutch, 'the poor dears', could have the East Indies back as they liked to imagine.[99]

The European colonial powers, for their part, were sufficiently aware of these trends in American thinking to be greatly concerned over the future. The Vichy Government, for example, took up through its Ambassador in Washington a slighting reference made by Roosevelt in a broadcast to the surrender of Indochina to the Japanese, and, as mentioned earlier, listed at great length the occasions in 1940 and 1941 when France had vainly sought the assistance of the United States in order to resist Japanese pressure.[100] The Gaullists, too, got wind of the President's pronouncements about Indochina.[101] As for the Netherlands Government in exile, the Colonial

Minister, van Mook, privately expressed his concern over American intentions, and suggested to a Chatham House audience that international supervision of the East Indies could in fact retard the development of that territory's autonomy.[102] His Prime Minister, Dr. Gerbrandy, was, amazingly, still hoping well into 1942 that 'the main centre of gravity of control' of the Pacific war would not shift from London to Washington,[103] while Queen Wilhelmina's speech of December 1942, in which she promised autonomy and 'complete partnership' for the units of the Netherlands Kingdom after the war, was carefully designed with the need to quieten American opinion in mind.[104]

Meanwhile within the Foreign Office in London there existed a desire to see Britain and the Netherlands stay close to each other over these matters. 'They are an important Far Eastern ally', wrote the Head of the Far Eastern Department, 'whose cooperation later on will be indispensable.'[105] As for the case of Indochina, there was scepticism as to whether the Free French would be able to supply much help from that territory; in addition, however, apprehension was expressed over the possibility of future clashes concerning its fate between France on the one hand and China and the United States on the other. Moreover, although Britain herself, unlike the United States, had not pledged to restore the French Empire in its entirety, Roosevelt's musings over the fate of Indochina aroused the fear in London that similar proposals might be forthcoming for putting British possessions, too, under some form of international control.[106]

The seeds of possible difficulties with Washington were also being sown by the British themselves where Siam was concerned. In response to the latter's declaration of war, Churchill's Government had felt bound to reply in kind, especially in the light of the measure of assistance that the Siamese had given to the Japanese during the attack on Malaya. And although there were some officials, including the former Minister in Bangkok, Sir Josiah Crosby, who argued that, even so, the Siamese should be treated as 'victims of circumstances', as the Americans were doing, others like the essentially negative Sir Maurice Peterson were more aggressively critical, foreshadowing in this an insensitivity that was to mark Whitehall's handling of the issue during the later stages of the war.[107] More specifically, the Prime Minister himself was already burdening British policy towards Siam with an element which was later to make it extremely difficult to arrive at an agreement with the United States over that country. In connection with the Chinese proposal to assure the Siamese that the Allies had no designs on their territory, one of Churchill's secretaries wrote to the Foreign Office in May to say that the Prime Minister 'has asked me to draw your attention to the fact that it might be found necessary after the war to consider some sort of Protectorate over the Kra Peninsula area . . . in the interests of the future security of Singapore.' Clearly, difficulties in reconciling this idea with the assurances contained in the Atlantic Charter, difficulties which the Foreign Office at once foresaw, did not trouble Churchill.[108]

The insensitivity and conservatism of the Prime Minister over major issues that were beginning to arise in regard to Southeast Asia and colonies generally were already a serious handicap to the development of constructive British policies. His own assumptions and approach were apparent in the bland allusions to the future which he made during a broadcast in December to the Japanese-occupied territories in the Far East—'rather an extraordinary performance', Cadogan termed it[109]—and in the conclusion which, as we have seen earlier, he drew from a report presented to the Pacific War Council on the situation in the Netherlands East Indies: that 'the natives were looking to Europeans for their future and were not making common cause with their fellow Asiatics. This augured well.'[110]

Among Foreign Office officials, however, there was considerable concern over the warnings being received from the Embassy in Washington that, in Campbell's words, 'official [American] opinion is tending towards the conclusion that as part of the post-war settlement the existing Colonial Empires ought to be liquidated, or at all events greatly modified.'[111] As we have seen earlier, there was also in some quarters an accompanying fear that a form of American economic imperialism might seek to replace those colonial empires. One reaction, not surprisingly, was resentment. 'The American attitude to the Pacific', minuted Eden, 'if it is correctly reported by Russians, is to give away other people's property . . . to an international committee on which America will be one of three or more.'[112] Others like Grigg, Secretary of State for War, were more indignant still over what they saw as an American 'assumption of proprietary rights in more and more of the British Empire.'[113] It made him, confessed the Governor of Burma, 'all Colonel Blimpish. By Gad, Sir, why should these foreigners poke their noses into the British Empire?'[114] In more detailed terms, papers were drawn up by officials to demonstrate that three centuries of Spanish rule had made the Philippines atypical among Southeast Asian colonies, thus rendering meaningless the never-ending use of that example by Americans when upbraiding others.[115]

Nevertheless, it was widely agreed, by the Cabinet as well as within departments, that a positive response was called for, including a bid, in Campbell's words, 'to educate [American] opinion on the real facts of our stewardship and the nature of our Empire and our Commonwealth.'[116] Furthermore, some revision of British colonial policy itself might, it was thought, be called for. Cranborne, who for the time being was Colonial Secretary, suggested to his Cabinet colleagues that more effective action was needed, 'especially in respect of economic development and social welfare',[117] while the Foreign Office wanted Cranborne's officials 'to do their utmost to ensure that no substantial accusation lies against H[is] M[ajesty's] G[overnment] of a failure to put their colonial house in order.'[118] In the opinion of the Head of the Office's North American Department, 'it would be a great step towards war-time comradeship and the continuing of it into the peace if we could evolve a Colonial policy revised in the light of war and on lines that command American respect.'[119]

The major difficulty was that, as Margery Perham had suggested in *The*

Times, a forthright and forward-looking statement of policy from the highest Government level was still lacking. 'Neither we nor the C[olonial] O[ffice]', wrote a senior Foreign Office official, 'appear to have any clear idea of what is likely to be a workable post-war policy governing our relations with the non-white inhabitants of our 1939 Empire.' 'We have no colonial policy', added Law.[120]*

It was not that all individual departments or officials were lacking in ideas. Within the Colonial Office, for example, although there was, as mentioned earlier, some scorn for the Foreign Office's 'appeasement' of the Americans, the notion was being developed of setting up regional bodies to facilitate international cooperation over colonial affairs.[121] Or again, where Burma was concerned, the Governor, Sir Reginald Dorman-Smith, who was convinced that the promulgation of the Atlantic Charter had to mean 'the end of the British Empire', wanted a programme set out for a period of direct rule after the war whilst reconstruction took place, with a time limit being set for this stage and with measures to be taken thereafter that would lead to 'full self-government.' He also wished to see the Government of Burma participate in the running of big firms so that the Burmese people would know that limits were being set on the amount of profits that foreigners were taking out of the country. Within the Burma Office in London, too, officials recognized the need 'to provide for a fundamentally *nationalist* sentiment', and argued that policies established on the resumption of British rule would have to lead 'incontestibly and immediately . . . to freedom for Burma.'[122] Amery himself (Secretary of State for Burma as well as for India) was inclined to back Dorman-Smith. The two of them could make no headway, however—and we shall see that a direct confrontation was to occur in the following year—against the one great obstacle to progress: the Prime Minister, encouraged in his reactionary stance by individuals like Grigg in the Cabinet and Lord Linlithgow in India.

Beneath this disastrous blockage at the top, those officials who were concerned at the American outcry over the British Empire were left to do the best they could. One major stimulus was provided by Wendell Willkie, on whom considerable thought and care was already being focussed by Whitehall, as a prominent Republican who had supported the cause of Lend Lease for Britain and who, it was hoped, could help prevent his Party from adopting an isolationist attitude after the war.[123] During his world tour in the autumn of 1942, Willkie called on the British Ambassador in Moscow, Clark Kerr, and expressed his alarm at the prevalence of anti-British sentiments that he had encountered among Americans on his way out, through the Middle East. He added a warning which the Ambassador was quick to pass on to London: 'If he were confident that our future [colonial] policy would be liberal and progressive, he would use all his influence to swing American opinion into the fullest appreciation of it. If, however, he were not

---

* In April 1943, a senior Colonial Office official would likewise be admitting that it had not been worked out how colonies would achieve Dominion status. (G. E. Gent minute, 19 April 1943, CO, 967/23.)

convinced, he must tell me frankly that he would be obliged to come out against us.' (The Washington Embassy, too, was warning that Willkie might seek to rally support for himself within the Republican party 'by an anti-imperialism campaign which would very easily become anti-British.')[124]

This message from Clark Kerr was taken with great seriousness within the Foreign Office. Cadogan, for example, wrote: 'Until we can recapture a sense of the need of a moral aim—"tear the guts out of Hitler", but what then?—and until someone can translate this feeling into speech and action, we shall not be respected by Americans.' 'The trouble is', argued Sir George Gater, Permanent Under Secretary at the Colonial Office, 'that we have given the appearance of stagnation and lack of effort in the colonies and of being on the defensive.'[125] (Both men, of course, were in effect pointing to one of the Prime Minister's most serious failings, in the field of the development of forward-looking policies.) A high-level inter-departmental committee was therefore set up in December 1942, consisting of senior officials from the Foreign Office, Dominions Office, Colonial Office, India Office and Ministry of Information, and chaired by Richard Law. Its aims, as redrafted, were '(a) to study the state of American feeling about the British Empire with a view to ascertaining the measure and extent of favourable and hostile reactions; (b) to study and make recommendations concerning the best methods of stimulating favourable and moderating hostile feeling with a view to securing a general sentiment sympathetic to the maintenance of the British imperial system and to recognition of the Empire as a suitable partner with the U.S.A. in world affairs.' An informal committee, to correspond to this one of Law's, was also set up within the Washington Embassy.[126]

The establishing of committees was, of course, far from solving the problem. One particular area where many difficulties clearly lay ahead was that involving raw materials produced in colonial territories. Here, as noted earlier, American hostility was, for example, making uncertain the future of the International Rubber Regulating Committee; also, American displeasure was further aroused at this time by the signing, in September 1942, of an agreement between Britain, Belgium, the Netherlands and Bolivia on the control of the production and export of tin.[127]

One development did take place, however, which for a time at least was to foster the hope that a closer understanding over colonial matters could be reached with the United States. This was the introduction of the idea, first raised by Hull with Halifax in August 1942, that the two countries, in the latter's words, might make 'some general statement in which we might . . . assert broad purposes, making plain that attainment of freedom involved mutual responsibility of what he called parent states and of those who aspired to it.' There followed a complicated and protracted series of discussions in London—the process had not been completed by the end of this period—which went up to Cabinet level, and the aim of which was to devise a draft declaration of colonial principles, with special, practical application to the Southeast Asian region, that could be submitted to the Americans.[128]

The details of succeeding drafts and counter-drafts need not be followed here ('Very soon', observed Cranborne, now Lord Privy Seal, 'Colonial Policy will become, like House of Lords reform, an inextricable tangle of conflicting theories').[129] The issues involved included the degree of supervisory and coordinating powers to be accorded to international regional organizations; the extent to which the creation of regional defence organizations should be stressed; and the degree of emphasis to be placed upon the eventual independence of colonial territories. (We all know in our heart of hearts', wrote Cranborne to Eden, 'that most of the Colonies, especially in Africa, will probably not be fit for complete independence for centuries.') Individuals had their own, particular causes which they wanted to see adopted. Bevin, for example, was anxious to see India given a position on any post-war regional body overseeing colonial affairs in Southeast Asia; Amery, supported by Oliver Stanley, the new Colonial Secretary, wanted to seize the opportunity to abolish the old League of Nations mandates system, which cast doubts, he believed, on the authority of the administering state.[130] In general, the most radical position was that adopted by Attlee, with Amery and Stanley tending towards the other extreme and Cranborne and the Foreign Office (in particular, the Economic and Reconstruction Department under Gladwyn Jebb) somewhere in between.

So fierce did the disagreements become, that Jebb saw 'a real danger that our foreign policy may be paralysed on the one hand by the attitude of Mr. Amery, whose tendency is to restore the status quo everywhere, and on the other by Mr. Attlee, who seems to wish to internationalise the whole of our colonial Empire.'[131] The Dominions, too, had to be consulted, with Australia emphasizing the need to give an international body real authority in colonial matters, and questioning whether all pre-war sovereignties in Southeast Asia and the Southwest Pacific should be restored. As for the Prime Minister, while ready to try to encourage the Americans to adopt a responsible attitude over these issues, he remained at bottom opposed to change. When Halifax cabled to ask for a strong public statement of the principles of British colonial rule, he declined to respond;[132] when the Ambassador reported that Roosevelt had not been consulted before Hull made his original proposal for a joint declaration, Churchill wrote to Eden: 'Please note how very informal and insecure is the foundation on which the "Parent States" policy is being elaborated';[133] when the Viceroy, Linlithgow, cabled from India to warn against taking too meek an attitude and accepting American interference, the Prime Minister was 'inspired', as Amery reported to Linlithgow, 'to a most fervid harangue [in Cabinet] against giving away the Empire.'[134]

Eventually, in January 1943, an agreed draft was forthcoming. It represented the highest common factor obtainable in Whitehall and Westminster at the time, and did go some way towards meeting the kind of demands that were emanating from the United States. There were references to the Atlantic Charter and the Four Freedoms. 'Parent states', besides being called upon to enter into 'general defence schemes', were accorded 'the duty . . . to guide and develop the social, economic and political institutions of the colonial peoples until they are able, without danger to themselves and others, to discharge the responsibilities of government.' The natural resources of colonial territories were to be 'organised and marketed not for the promotion merely of commercial ends, but rather for the service of the people concerned and the world as a whole.' And regional commissions should be set up, consisting of, in addition to parent states, others having 'a major strategic or economic interest' in the area concerned.

It was something, but it might not be enough. The British draft did not propose that the administrative responsibilities of parent states should be diminished; regional commissions were not to supervise, but merely to promote consultation and collaboration; there was no suggestion of firm dates being set for the granting of independence. Nor did London's proposals relate to India, whose future, as we shall see, constituted a major issue in American minds, and one which they seldom distinguished from questions concerning colonial empires in general. Meanwhile, away from the context of future policy and within that of immediate action against the enemy in Southeast Asia, there, too, the divergencies between the Allies remained considerable.

Campaign issues in Southeast Asia

In the previous chapter, the point was made that not only the Americans, but Churchill, too, was concerned during 1942 to sustain China as a combatant. Even without this consideration, however, the Prime Minister was eager to see the fight carried back to the Japanese in Burma after the Allies had been so humiliatingly driven out in the spring; his natural aggression, together with the urgent need to do something towards restoring the prestige of British arms, provided impulsion enough. Thus, from April to the end of the year, he was urging General Wavell, first to attempt to retake Rangoon by mounting an amphibious operation before the end of September, and then, when the impossibility of this had been reluctantly accepted, to launch alternative attacks with all speed.[135] In addition, the Prime Minister was alert to the need to maintain harmonious relations with General Stilwell, once the latter had become the American commander in the area, who would also control, under Wavell's over-all direction, any Chinese forces fighting in Burma.[136] As for the entire American interest in what was a British sphere of responsibility, Field Marshal Dill in Washington did his best to explain to the somewhat prickly Chiefs of Staff in London that Burma's crucial position in regard to assisting China made this reasonable.[137] Dill also endeavoured, with Marshall, to smooth over difficulties which arose between Wavell and Stilwell,[138] and even Wavell reported privately to the Prime Minister that his American colleague, for all his sharpness, was likeable, 'cooperative and genuine.'[139]

In the event, however, as was to be the case so often in the following years, the outcome in this theatre was one of disappointing military achievements and strained Anglo-American relations. The details of the various plans and setbacks involved can be read elsewhere,[140] but the result was that no impression had been made upon the Japanese position in Burma by the end of this period. Contrary to the belief of some Americans, it was not that Wavell himself was averse to taking the offensive; even Churchill, despite the great difficulty he had in communicating with the taciturn Wavell,[141] continued to believe in the latter's ability, and, against Grigg's strong opposition, accepted the case which the General himself unblushingly made out that he should be promoted to Field Marshal as soon as possible.[142]*

However, in the face of not only a formidable enemy but also of problems of terrain, communications, the monsoon season and inadequate base facilities in India, the resources of men and matériel at Wavell's disposal were not sufficient to carry out the kind of dramatic advance that Churchill and the Americans so eagerly awaited. Stilwell himself, it should be noted, was at times ready to acknowledge the limitations that were involved. In January 1943, for example, he privately expressed relief that a planned attack had been postponed, with the comment that 'We'd have been hung.'[143] Earlier, at a staff meeting with Wavell, he produced, according to one who was present,† the following blunt responses:

Wavell: 'Are you satisfied that this operation is not feasible?'
Stilwell: 'Yes I am.'
Wavell: 'Are you satisfied on purely military grounds?'
Stilwell: 'Yes I am.'
Wavell: 'What will you say to Chiang Kai-shek?'
Stilwell: 'I shall tell him the bloody British won't fight.'
Stunned silence.[144]

It must also be said, however, that the need for close liaison with the Americans and Chinese appears to have been appreciated far more in London than in New Delhi, and that Wavell himself was slow to act in this respect. It was the middle of October before he let Stilwell know of his major plans, while he was more cautious still where the Chinese were concerned.[145] Relations with Chiang Kai-shek were also complicated by Churchill, who, in the spring of 1942, sketched for the former what in retrospect were unduly sanguine plans for establishing before long a naval

---

* Grigg refused to believe that Wavell had great ability, or 'fire in his belly', or 'enough iron in his body.' As for Wavell, having been told by Churchill that his request would be granted in the New Year's Honours List, he responded: 'I hoped and still hope that you could announce it forthwith. After all, I feel that it was in 1941 that I earned it, not in 1942, and that it will look rather like an old-age-pension in the New Year list. Life is uncertain and my military career is beginning to draw to an end. I confess I should like to enjoy prestige as long as possible. Also it might help in dealing with Americans and Chinese in forthcoming negotiations on Burma. Gingerbread is always gingerbread, but may I have it with gilt on please.'

† There is no documentary evidence with which to substantiate this piece of verbal testimony. On the other hand, the witness concerned is himself a professional historian of great note.

force that could command the Indian Ocean. The Generalissimo seized upon this, together with the achievement of Allied air superiority over Burma, as preconditions to be fulfilled before he would launch Chinese troops into an attack upon Burma from Yunnan, in the north. Thus, when developments in the Mediterranean prevented the planned build-up of the Eastern Fleet (just as operation 'Torch' prevented Wavell from assembling sufficient landing craft), Chiang claimed that promises had been broken, and declined to move his Yunnan forces.[146]

Other Chinese troops earmarked for a Burma campaign, their nucleus being made up of units which had retreated into India when the Japanese overran Burma earlier in the year, were being trained by Stilwell at Ramgarh. Here, too, there existed a significant difference of approach between on the one hand the authorities in New Delhi, together with those responsible for Indian affairs in London, and on the other the Foreign Office and Chiefs of Staff. When Stilwell announced his desire to fly in to India for training at Ramgarh more Chinese troops, making 23,000 there in all, the Viceroy was all for refusing permission. 'Chinese are expert poker players', cabled his Private Secretary to London. 'Their side interest in this business is the future of China . . . If they get a good footing of this nature in India, we can with some confidence anticipate that internally in India and externally in relation to the future of Burma and Malaya it will be expensive.'[147] Amery, too, was uneasy, as was the Secretary of State for War, Grigg, who, it will be recalled, had once been a prominent Indian Civil Servant.[148] Eden, for his part, was angered when Roosevelt corresponded directly with Chiang Kai-shek on the matter, without consulting London. 'I regard this', wrote the Foreign Secretary, 'as almost intolerably impertinent . . . We might as well not exist.' Yet the Foreign Office line in general was that the need for good relations with China and the United States made agreement over the Ramgarh increase advisable, and as Wavell, like the Chiefs of Staff, was not unduly perturbed, the Cabinet eventually decided that the proposal should be 'warmly accepted.'[149]

There existed, however, a more fundamental strain underlying Anglo-American relations in Southeast Asia, and involving future operations into Burma. In short, the British tended to look south-east, towards Lower Burma, Rangoon and beyond; the Americans, in contrast, looked only north-east, across Upper Burma to China. On the British side this did not mean, as we have seen, that no concern existed over the supplying and sustaining of Chiang Kai-shek's forces. There was, however, a growing scepticism as to whether the best way to achieve this was to push a road through the harsh terrain of North Burma from Ledo. Even if such a road could be built, suggested the Vice Chief of the Imperial General Staff in London, it would not be capable of being used to deliver much to China, since a great deal of its capacity would have to be taken up with maintenance work.[150] A better way to help, it seemed, would be to recapture the major port of Rangoon, and from there open up again the old Burma Road, meanwhile keeping up the flow of supplies over the Hump.

In adopting this approach—and as we shall see, the basic difference of opinion persisted throughout the following years—the British were eventually proved to be both wrong and right. They were wrong in that they underestimated the capacity of American drive and technological resources to get the Ledo Road built; indeed, in no theatre were there better exemplified the contrasting British and American approaches inculcated by paucity of resources on the one side and immense reserves on the other.[151] The British were nevertheless to be proved correct in their belief that, by the time the task had been completed, the prospect would have opened up of getting supplies through to China in far larger quantities by other means, including the old Burma Road, and above all the possibility of being able to use a port on China's coast.

In addition to their lack of faith in the Ledo Road project, two other, and stronger, factors directed the British gaze away from Upper Burma. One was Churchill's marked preference for amphibious operations over a renewed and desperate battle with the Japanese amid the jungles of Burma, which seemed to suit their fighting abilities so well.[152] The other was the desire to recover British territories, meaning not so much the remote and rugged areas of Northern Burma as the richer and more populous lower regions of the country, and, beyond them, Malaya. Thus, despite the fact that Washington, too, wanted to see Rangoon retaken (the reason being its potential role as the main port for supplying China), there was built into the military situation in Southeast Asia a difference of approach, partly political, partly technical, that was to bedevil Anglo-American relations there. More serious still, this situation helped to reinforce two American assumptions which have been examined above and which, although they were by no means fully justified, were sufficiently strong and widespread to impair the entire Anglo-American partnership: the belief that Britain had no concern for China and saw her still through 'treaty-port' eyes; and the conviction that Britain was bent upon restoring the status quo ante in her imperial domain, having no intention of developing colonial policies that would be in accord with the broader aims for which the war was being fought.

Nor did this last assumption, that the British interest in the war in Southeast Asia stemmed solely from a desire to snatch back her lost territories, preclude an American belief that Churchill and his generals were reluctant to set about even this task if it meant making a major military effort. In Washington, the need to advance into Burma and open up a route to China was seen as urgent, doubly so in that Chiang Kai-shek was making it clear that action on his own part depended on a vigorous attack being launched against the Japanese from India.[153] This impatience helped to foster the suspicion that when Wavell and others enumerated various practical difficulties that were preventing immediate action on a large scale, they were in fact simply revealing a basic lack of interest in fighting the Japanese.[154] 'The British appear to have no intention of attempting to retake Burma in the foreseeable future', wrote Davies, Stilwell's political adviser, in July. 'The reason would seem to be the conviction that no Asiatic possession is worth any appreciable diversion of strength from the British Isles; that the war will be won in Europe; and that lost possessions will at the Peace Conference revert with clear title to the British if those colonies remain up to the termination of hostilities under enemy occupation, whereas if those possessions are reoccupied with Chinese and American assistance, British title may be compromised.'[155]

It is true that good relations between the two Allies were, even so, sometimes achieved locally. Major General Lewis Brereton, for example, commander of the U.S. Air Force in India, wrote to Washington to say how well he got on with Wavell and Air Marshal Peirse of the R.A.F.;[156] likewise, an O.S.S. unit, Detachment 101 under Major Carl Eifler, was soon on good terms with the local British authorities and civilians when it arrived in Assam in order to begin operations behind the Japanese lines in Upper Burma.[157] Stilwell for his part, however, was setting for those serving under him an example that entailed exasperation, suspicion and even contempt where the British were concerned, the General's tone being reflected subsequently in a book like *Wrath in Burma*, written by a former member of his staff, Fred Eldridge.[158] In Stilwell's view, Wavell (or 'Weevil', as he referred to him in private) was a pleasant but 'tired old man';[159] the 'cock-eyed limies' were 'poor fools' and 'bastards' who were out to sabotage his vital scheme for building up fully-trained Chinese units at Ramgarh, and whose procrastinations gave Chiang Kai-shek just the excuse he was looking for in order to do nothing in the way of fighting the Japanese.[160] Likewise, Americans working on the Ledo Road soon became convinced that the local British were not only cool towards the project, but were engaging in 'passive resistance' to it.[161]

Military difficulties and disappointments in Southeast Asia in 1942 were thus contributing towards a general lack of sympathy and understanding between the Allies in that part of the world. In this they were joined by political differences that were focussed upon the base from which operations would have to be launched against the Japanese: India itself.

Notes to Chapter Seven

1 E.g. *Kirby*, I, 454ff.; II, 218ff.; Slim, *Defeat Into Victory*, 15, 89; Kirby, *Singapore: The Chain of Disaster*; Lewin, *Slim*.
2 *Kirby*, I, 473.
3 Cab, 16 Feb. 1942, CAB 65/25.
4 DC(Ops.), DO(42)21, CAB 69/4.
5 See e.g. *Churchill*, III, 563; Morrison, *Malayan Postscript*, 188–9.
6 FO 371, F4000/1193/10; see F6407/1193/10.
7 Ibid, F5219/1095/10.
8 Material in PREM 3, 161/1 and FO 371, F348/182/23. See B. Bond (ed.), *Chief of Staff: The Diaries of Lt. General Sir Henry Pownall*, vol. II (London, 1974; hereafter, *Pownall*), entry for 8 Jan. 1942; WP(42)92 (CAB 66/22) and WP(42)145 (CAB 66/23).
9 AWC, 2 March 1942, A 2673, vol XI.

10 Kirby, *Singapore*, 223, 246; Allen, *Singapore*, 178.
11 FO 371, F4138/182/23.
12 Luckham memo., 'Some of the Causes of the Loss of Malaya', 30 March 1942, CO 865/1.
13 Kirby, *Singapore*, 151, 195, 213; Allen, *Singapore*, 247ff.; Morrison, *Malayan Postscript*, 69.
14 Slim, *Defeat Into Victory*, 31; see Dorman-Smith to Amery, 2 April 1942, PREM 3, 152/3, and Linlithgow to Amery, 15 April 1942, ibid.
15 Purcell, *Memoirs of a Malayan Official*, e.g. 316, 318, 321.
16 M. Collis, *First and Last in Burma* (London, 1956), 125ff.; Dorman-Smith, 'Report on the Burma Campaign, 1941–1942', appendix V, Dorman-Smith Papers, E215/28.
17 H. Tinker, 'A Forgotten Long March: The Indian Exodus From Burma, 1942', *Journal of Southeast Asian Studies*, March 1975.
18 N. Mansergh (ed.), *The Transfer of Power, 1942–7*, vol. I (London, 1970; hereafter, *Transfer of Power*) no. 615.
19 Eggleston to Evatt, 4 May 1942, Evatt Papers, Ext. Affs., Misc. Corr. See F. Spencer Chapman, *The Jungle Is Neutral* (London, 1949).
20 FO 371, F2274/4/23.
21 Ibid, F182/182/23.
22 E.g. ibid, F182 and 348/182/23; material in PREM 4, 43A/10; Allen, *The End of the War in Asia*, cap. 1.
23 Elsbree, *Japan's Role in the Southeast Asian Nationalist Movements*, 163.
24 See above, 59.
25 See Ba Maw, *Breakthrough In Burma*, 38ff., 261ff., and Elsbree, op. cit., 62.
26 FO 371, F566 and 783/289/61. See OSS R and A, 24, on Singapore, 12 Dec. 1941.
27 PREM 3, 152/1.
28 PREM 3, 152/3.
29 FRUS, Washington and Casablanca, 44.
30 DS 740.0011 P.W./1891.
31 Reports by Lt. Col. Clear and Col. Brink, 20 April 1942, Roosevelt Papers, PSF box 163; see Stimson Diary, 8 April 1942.
32 OSS R and A, 34.
33 DS 740.0011 P.W./2795.
34 Ibid, 2869.
35 Ibid, 1675. See ibid, 1959 and e.g. Clear report, cited above.
36 OSS, Psychology Division, 'Short Guide to Burma', 26 June 1942, Goodfellow Papers, box 3; OSS R and A, 750, 'British Malaya: A Social–Political–Economic Survey', 20 June 1942.
37 OSS R and A, 840, 'Our Chinese Allies in Southeast Asia', 25 May 1942.
38 In December 1941 the U.S. had only a Legation in Bangkok, Consulates General in Batavia, Singapore and Rangoon, and Consulates in Saigon, Penang, Medan and Surabaja. R. H. Fifield, *Southeast Asia in United States Policy* (New York, 1963), 34.
39 E.g. *Chicago Tribune*, 9 April and 7 June 1942.
40 FO 371, A2492/60/45.
41 Sub-committee on Political Problems, 8 Aug. 1942, DS, Notter files, box 55.
42 'Statement of Major Postwar Problems in the Pacific Area', 20 Feb. 1942, DS, Pasvolsky files, box 2.
43 See above, 102–3.
44 *Life*, 9 Oct. 1942.
45 Barnard, *Willkie*, 378; W. Willkie, *One World* (New York, 1943), 109.
46 *Amerasia*'s critical line against Britain was such as to cause dissension among its editorial board. Material in IPR Papers, box 358.
47 E.g. Halifax despatch, 11 June 1942 and Campbell despatch, 14 July 1942, PREM 4 42/9.
48 *Cantril and Strunk*, 274.
49 *Christian Science Monitor*, 12 Dec. 1942.

50 *Chicago Daily News*, 12 Nov. 1942.
51 *New York Herald Tribune*, 13 Oct. 1942. See *New York Times*, 20 Jan. 1942.
52 Willkie, *One World*, 174.
53 *Daily Herald*, 10 Oct. 1942. See ibid, 13 Aug. 1942, for a T.U.C.-Labour Party state-ment on the necessity for arresting extreme nationalists in India.
54 Calder, *The People's War*, 99; Laski, Labour Party pamphlet, 1940, 'Is This An Imperialist War?'
55 Leonard Woolf Papers, boxes 35, 36, 40. Woolf was secretary to the Committee.
56 Gupta, *Imperialism and the British Labour Movement*, 260; Thornton, *The Imperial Idea and its Enemies*, 278.
57 *Daily Herald*, 18 Nov. 1942.
58 *Times*, 21 Nov. 1942, and Perham, *Colonial Sequence*.
59 *Times*, 16 Oct. 1942.
60 E.g. *Daily Telegraph*, 14 May 1943; *News Chronicle*, 9 April 1943.
61 E.g. Hansard HC Deb 376, cols. 177, 515, 546; ibid, 377, cols. 111–13; ibid, 378, cols. 231, 271; ibid, 380, cols. 2043ff., 2110.
62 *Manchester Guardian*, 6 Oct. 1942; see C. H. Rolph, *Kingsley* (London, 1973), cap. 10.
63 Laski to Frankfurter, 16 Sept. 1942, Frankfurter Papers, box 75. Laski went on to add absurdity to sense: 'Had Winston understood this, we should have won in 1942.'
64 FO 371, A4406/399/45.
65 See J. N. Thomas, *The Institute of Pacific Relations* (Seattle, 1974), and C. Thorne, 'Chatham House, Whitehall and Far Eastern Issues, 1941–1945', in *International Affairs*, January 1978.
66 E.g. material in IPR Papers, box 360. Interviews with Dr. Dorothy Borg and Professor Owen Lattimore.
67 All the following material on the Foreign Office and Chatham House aspects of the IPR in 1942 comes from FO 371, files 31801–3, and RIIA archives.
68 See Macmillan, *The Blast of War*, 161ff.
69 ADEA, A989/43/735/34; NFM, Washington archive, P.1.8/41.9.
70 Carter to Jessup, 17 Nov. 1942, and Holland to Carter, 21 Aug. 1942, IPR Papers, boxes 379 and 62 respectively.
71 Hornbeck to Hull, 31 Dec. 1942, Hornbeck Papers, box 218.
72 Louis, *Imperialism At Bay*.
73 Such issues were also raised at an informal gathering at Princeton earlier in 1942. IPR Papers, box 376.
74 Stimson Diary, 2 June 1942.
75 Freidel, *Franklin Roosevelt: The Apprenticeship*, 270ff.
76 E.g. memo. to Hull, 11 Jan. 1941, *Roosevelt Letters*, and see Clipperton Island affair, below, 666–7.
77 E.g. letter to Smuts, 24 Nov. 1942, *Roosevelt Letters*.
78 See e.g. Range, *Franklin Roosevelt's World Order*; F. Dulles and G. Ridinger, 'The Anti-Colonial Policies of Franklin D. Roosevelt', *Political Science Quarterly*, March 1955; *Wallace*, 29 Oct. 1942; E. R. Drachman, *United States Policy Toward Vietnam, 1940–1945* (Rutherford, N.J., 1970), 42; Roosevelt, *As He Saw It*.
79 The following summaries and quotations are taken from the 1942 minutes of the sub-committees, DS, Notter files, boxes 55 and 59.
80 This position was, in fact, adopted by Welles at a subsequent meeting on 10 April 1943.
81 On this, and the work of various advisory and preparatory bodies in general, see H. A. Notter, *Postwar Foreign Policy Preparation* (Washington D.C., 1949; hereafter, *Notter*).
82 Stimson Diary, 29 Dec. 1941. See FRUS, Washington and Casablanca, 134, 141, 283.
83 FRUS, 1942, China, 32; FRUS, 1942, I, 913ff.; FRUS, 1943, China, 13; OSS R and A, 301, 19 June 1942.
84 DS 851 G.00/75 and 76; OSS R and A, 719, 'Strategic Survey of Indochina', 4 March 1942. For an overall survey, with some documents, see PP, vol. I, 1ff.; also C. Thorne,

'The Indochina Issue Between Britain and the United States, 1942–1945', *Pacific Historical Review*, Feb. 1976.
85 FRUS, 1942, China, 730, 749ff.
86 See Hornbeck memo., 6 May 1942, Hornbeck Papers, box 173.
87 E.g. material in ibid, box 172, and summary in PP, vol. I, 9.
88 Sub-committee minutes, 1 and 8 Aug. 1942, DS, Notter files, box 55.
89 FO 371, F3825/1417/61.
90 PWC(W), 9 Dec. 1942, Roosevelt Papers, MR box 168.
91 FRUS, Washington and Casablanca, 506.
92 Ibid, 694.
93 C. de Gaulle, *War Memoirs: Unity, 1942–1944* (London, 1960), 83. See P. Devilliers, *Histoire du Viêt Nam, 1940–1952* (Paris, 1952), 116.
94 G. Sabbatier, *Le Destin de l'Indochine* (Paris, 1952), 68; J. Sainteny, *Histoire D'Une Paix Manquée* (Paris, 1953), 17; D. Lancaster, *The Emancipation of French Indochina* (London, 1961), 102.
95 Sub-committee on Political Problems, 15 Aug. 1942, 10 April 1943, DS, Notter files, box 55.
96 E.g. OSS R and A, 209, 8 Jan. 1943.
97 Hassett, *Off The Record With F.D.R.*, 64; Freidel, *Roosevelt: The Apprenticeship*, 6.
98 Loudon despatch, 8 Jan. 1943, NFM Londens Archief G.A., D 2 D 31a; FDR to Wilhelmina, 6 April 1942, *Roosevelt Letters*.
99 Campbell to Cadogan, 6 Aug. 1942, PREM 4, 42/9.
100 See above, 84.
101 Interview with M. René Massigli.
102 FO 371, F4533/90/61; Far East Group, 15 July 1942, RIIA; see Soejono memo., 5 Oct. 1942, NCol.M, XI.11.D.
103 PWC(L), 13 March 1942, CAB 99/26.
104 Loudon to van Kleffens, 5 June 1942; van Mook to Council of Ministers, 21 Oct. 1942, NCol.M, XIA.B11.
105 FO 371, F7267/828/10; see F4533/90/61 and F495/107/61.
106 Ibid, F3825/1417/61; F5855/5855/61; F614/582/61.
107 Ibid, files 28164, 31856, 31860–2, 31869.
108 Ibid, files 31866–7. Amery was also in favour of such a move over the Kra peninsula. Amery to Smuts, 7 Jan. 1943, van der Poel, *Smuts Papers*, VI.
109 FO 371, F8184/243/61.
110 PWC(L), 21 Oct. 1942, CAB 99/26. For Churchill's attitude to Britain's colonial record, see *Churchill*, IV, 824.
111 FO 371, A8329/1684/45; see A4741/31/45.
112 Ibid, F4608/74/10.
113 Grigg to WSC, 6 May 1942, PREM 3, 152/1.
114 Dorman-Smith to Amery, 1 Dec. 1942, Dorman-Smith Papers, E215/53.
115 E.g. FO 371, F5874/3806/61. It is significant that in private, some U.S. officials were ready to describe the Filipinos as being used only to government 'imposed from above', as having been socially segregated from Americans, as not to be 'trusted with Government funds or official positions as far as an Occidental', and as unlikely to stand up for 'justice and right.' OSS R and A, 760, July 1942.
116 FO 371, A7003/31/45; Cab, 18 Nov. 1942, CAB 65/28.
117 WP(42)249, CAB 66/25.
118 FO 371, A9030/60/45.
119 Ibid, A7436/65/45.
120 Ibid, A5545/1684/45.
121 *Louis*.
122 See WP(42)346, CAB 66/27; Cab, 12 Aug. 1942, CAB 65/27; Dorman-Smith to Amery, 23 Feb. 1943, Dorman-Smith Papers, E215/53; memos. in IO, Private Office Papers, L/PO/236. Also, interviews and correspondence between the author and Sir Reginald Dorman-Smith.

123 E.g. material in PREM 4, 26/6 and 27/1; FO 371, files 30715, 31723, 34162.
124 Clark Kerr to Eden, 28 Sept. 1942, FO 371, A9030/60/45; A10395/31/45.
125 Ibid, A1502/3/45.
126 See ibid, files 34086ff.
127 Ibid, files 31490, 31493.
128 Material in ibid, files 30707, 31521, 31526–7; in PREM 4, 26/8 and 42/9; in WP(42)575
    and 606 (CAB 66/32), WP(43)6, 7, 8, 9, 33 (CAB 66/33); Cabs, 9 Dec. 1942 (CAB
    65/28) and 7 and 20 Jan. 1943 (CAB 65/33). See J. Williams, 'The Joint Declaration
    on the Colonies', British Journal of International Studies, 2, 1976.
129 Cranborne to Halifax, 29 Dec. 1942, Hickleton Papers, A4.410.4.
130 Amery to Stanley, 8 Jan. 1943, and Stanley to Amery, 9 Jan. 1943, IO, Private Office
    Papers, L/PO/261.
131 FO 371, U828/828/70.
132 WSC to Eden, 2 Nov. 1942, PREM 4, 26/8.
133 WSC to Eden and Stanley, 7 Jan. 1943, PREM 4, 42/9.
134 Amery to Linlithgow, 5 Jan. 1943, and Linlithgow to Amery, 2 Jan. 1943, Linlithgow
    Papers, vols. 12 and 24 respectively.
135 E.g. WSC to Wavell, 12 June 1942, and WSC to COS, 4 and 8 April 1942, PREM 3,
    143/9; WSC to Wavell, 6 July 1942, PREM 3, 142/6; COS, 19 Nov. 1942, CAB 79/24.
136 COS, 30 March 1942, CAB 79/19.
137 E.g. Dill to COS, 12 Dec. 1942, PREM 3, 143/10.
138 E.g. Dill to Marshall, 7 Oct. 1942, 19 Dec. 1942, OPD, Exec. file 10, item 65.
139 Wavell to WSC, 31 Oct. 1942, PREM 3, 143/9.
140 On the British side, see especially Howard, Grand Strategy, IV, caps. 5 and 6, and
    Kirby, II.
141 See J. Connell, Wavell: Scholar and Soldier (London, 1964), 254.
142 Material in PREM 4, 83/2, 84/3.
143 Romanus and Sutherland, I, 262.
144 Interview with Philip Mason.
145 Wavell to WSC, 14 Sept. and 19 Oct. 1942, PREM 3, 143/9.
146 E.g. FDR to WSC, 8 Jan. 1943, PREM 3, 143/6; WSC to COS, 18 May 1942, PREM
    3, 143/9; Wavell to COS, 15 Nov. 1942, PREM 3, 143/10.
147 Laithwaite to Monteath, 2 Oct. 1942, Linlithgow Papers, vol. 23.
148 Amery to Linlithgow, 10 Oct. 1942, ibid, vol. 23; Brooke to Grigg, 8 Oct. 1942,
    Grigg Papers, box 9.
149 FO 371, F6781 and 6821/2428/10; F7347/4/23; WP(42)449, CAB 66/29; Cab, 8 Oct.
    1942, CAB 65/28.
150 COS, 19 Dec. 1942, CAB 79/24.
151 See e.g. the contrasting emphases of plans dealt with in CCS, 18 Sept. and 2 Oct.
    1942, CAB 88/1.
152 E.g. Churchill, IV, 702.
153 E.g. JCS, 13 Oct. 1942, RG 218; Marshall to King, 5 Jan. 1943, Roosevelt Papers,
    MR box 3; Chiang Kai-shek memo., 6 Aug. 1942, ibid, PSF box 36.
154 E.g. JCS, 7 March 1942, loc. cit.; FRUS, Washington and Casablanca, 558, 594.
155 FRUS, 1942, China, 126. See CBI 'Master Narrative', 276, Stilwell Papers, box 1.
156 Brereton to Arnold, 6 March 1942, Stilwell Papers, box 6.
157 See W. Peers and D. Brelis, Behind The Burma Road (London, 1964); R. H. Smith,
    O.S.S. (Berkeley, 1972; hereafter, OSS), 243; N. Barrett, Chinghpaw (New York,
    1962); Dorman-Smith to Amery, 25 March 1943, Dorman-Smith Papers, E215/43;
    interview with Sir R. Dorman-Smith.
158 F. Eldridge, Wrath In Burma (New York, 1946), e.g. 134, 156. For the American side
    in general, see Romanus and Sutherland, I, passim.
159 J. P. Stilwell, The Stilwell Papers (New York, 1948; hereafter, Stilwell Papers), entry
    for 30 Aug. 1942.
160 Stilwell Diary, 29 and 30 Sept. and 9 Oct. 1942.
161 L. Anders, The Ledo Road (Norman, Oklahoma, 1965), 24, 80.

CHAPTER EIGHT

BRITAIN, THE UNITED STATES
AND INDIA

INDIA DOES not lie within the Far East. Nor was India, as Burma and Malaya were, the scene of fighting between the Allies and Japan. In 1942, however, it was closely involved with developments taking place further east in three important ways: as the base for launching attacks into Burma and from which American supplies continued to be sent into China; as the outstanding case at issue when Americans and others held forth on the subject of the British Empire; and, related to that, as a major factor in discussions on the danger that Japan might succeed in leading a pan-Asiatic movement, and on the likely pattern of relations between Asia and the West after the war.

India's declaration of war in 1939, decided upon by the Viceroy alone; the promulgation of the Atlantic Charter in 1941 and Churchill's interpretation of it; the general feeling that the European conflict that was taking place called in question more than ever the entire existing order of things: all these elements had helped to unsettle further the Indian scene, even before the Japanese arrived at the country's borders in 1942. Congress Party ministries in the provinces had resigned, an individual civil-disobedience movement had arisen, and nationalists had not been placated by a British declaration in 1940 which described the Government's goal as being the attainment of Dominion status by India 'with the least possible delay' after the war, to be reached via the setting up of a representative body charged with the devising of a constitution. At the same time, Congress and Jinnah's Muslim League stood wide apart from each other, the latter having already proclaimed a plan for independent Muslim states, Pakistan.

The approach of the Japanese aroused some hopes, as well as fears, within India, for there were those who believed that liberation from British rule might be at hand. Subhas Chandra Bose, who was to lead an Indian National Army in support of Japan and to proclaim a Government of Free India in Singapore in 1943, was already assuring his fellow-countrymen by radio from Germany that Japan was their 'ally' and 'helper'.[1] Meanwhile, for those responsible for the administration and protection of the country, an even more disturbing factor was the frailty of India's defences. 'If the Japanese adopt a bold policy', warned the Joint Planners in London in March 1942, 'we are in real danger of losing our Indian Empire—with incalculable consequences to the future conduct of the war.'[2] Yet for Churchill and his colleagues, this threat had to be weighed against others, notably in the Middle East; it was thus easy for those in New Delhi to feel that their needs were not fully appreciated by the men responsible for controlling Britain's war effort. Wavell, for example, once more C. in C. India after the A.B.D.A. failure, cabled to the C.I.G.S. in April to protest against the diversion of promised reinforcements and 'the casual way in which [the] Indian defence problem has been treated.' He added: 'War Cabinet must really make up their minds whether or not they propose to defend India and Ceylon seriously.'[3] Wavell's charge was probably overstated—certainly the Chiefs of Staff were alert to the dangers hanging over Ceylon above all.[4] But the fact that this criticism could be formulated by the C. in C. on the spot makes it all the less surprising when one encounters various American observers who also doubted whether Britain was really concerned to defend India at this time.

Meanwhile, the Far Eastern war in 1942 was rapidly affecting the Indian situation in other ways. For example, under arrangements made in 1940, Britain's financial obligations incurred in the defence of India were now beginning to rise steeply, to an extent that had been entirely unforeseen. Indeed, it appeared that India's sterling balances would be as high as £400 to £450 million by April 1943, a state of affairs which greatly perturbed the Chancellor of the Exchequer when he looked ahead to the financial difficulties which Britain would face after the war. (What, for instance, if India wished to convert such balances into gold and dollars?) The situation also aroused indignation on the part of the Prime Minister, who was determined to prevent a development whereby it would be a case of 'Britain to defend India against the Japanese . . . ; Britain, if successful, to be turned out of India if India wishes; and Britain thereafter to owe India an immense financial debt.' Amery and the Viceroy, however, strenuously warned of the disastrous effects on Indian and world opinion that would be created by any disclaimer of financial liability on the part of London, and they managed to prevent any formal move of that kind being made for the time being. Amery still despaired, however, of getting Churchill to see that India, a poor country, 'does pay for British forces now defending India . . . [and] that most of this debt is incurred in respect of goods supplied for other theatres of war or for India's fighting in these theatres.' The Prime Minister, unmoved, still wished to prepare for eventually making a counter-claim, 'in which such items as the naval, air and military defence of India by British forces will play their part.'[5]

This determination that India, despite its desire to see the British gone, should pay for being defended by the Imperial power coexisted in Churchill's mind with an extreme reluctance to yield anything to Indian demands for constitutional advancement. This had been his attitude from the outset of the war, as well as during the preceding years, and the fact that the enemy was now at India's gates served only to reinforce his stubbornness. His entire inclination was to seek to prolong Britain's sovereignty over the sub-continent. Thus, in February 1940, as we have noted earlier, he had privately declared his satisfaction at the continued existence of the Hindu–Muslim feud, 'the bulwark of British rule in India.'[6] Now, at the beginning of 1942, he was joined by Amery and the Viceroy in believing that 'there is no immediate further interim constitutional advance that we can make' beyond the announcement issued in 1940.[7] Linlithgow's position, in fact, was, as we have seen, unambiguously that of a conqueror ruling unwilling subjects who were 'alien by race, history and religion' and had no 'natural affection' for the Empire.[8]

Nevertheless, as the Japanese threat drew closer, the pressure increased for Britain to make some new political gesture. To the alarm of Muslim leaders,[9] appeals were sent from India to London for 'a transformation of the entire spirit and outlook of the administration of India', including the creation of a 'truly National Government.'[10] Within the British Cabinet itself, meanwhile, Attlee put it to Churchill that the latter's 'strong views on India . . . [were] not widely shared', and fiercely rejected the 'crude imperialism of the Viceroy, not only because I think it is wrong, but because I think it is fatally short-sighted and suicidal . . . Now is the time', Attlee added, 'for an act of statesmanship. To mark time is to lose India.'[11] Even Amery was coming to see possible benefits accruing from such an innovation as a popularly-elected defence council,[12] while the Prime Minister himself, who in January had written confidently to Attlee, 'I do not think you will have any trouble with American opinion [over India]',[13] now, in the weeks that followed, began to feel the need to respond to the pressures that were building up—not least, as will be seen below, from the direction of the United States. As Amery put it in a private letter to Linlithgow in March: 'There is a certain sense of humour in that Winston, after making infinite difficulties for both of us . . . , has now, as is his wont, seen the red light (especially the American red light) overnight.' 'The pressure outside upon Winston from Roosevelt', he added, 'and upon Attlee and Co. from their own party, *plus* the admission of Cripps to the War Cabinet, suddenly opened the sluice gates.'[14] Churchill himself cabled to Linlithgow that 'it would be impossible, owing to unfortunate rumours and publicity, and the general American outlook, to stand on a purely negative attitude.'[15]

The outcome—and these developments have been documented in detail elsewhere[16]—was the Cripps mission to India in late March and early April, 1942, involving proposals that had been hammered out by a Cabinet Committee in London.[17] Britain was ready to declare that she would set up an elected, constitution-making body for India immediately after the war, with the aim of bringing about full Dominion status—although any province wishing to stand aside and frame its own constitution could do so; meanwhile representatives of the principal parties would be invited to join the Government of India as counsellors to the Viceroy.

The negotiations that ensued were surrounded by confusion. Linlithgow, inimical to the whole project, quickly became offended by Cripps' behaviour:

'You may safely presume', he minuted on a message from Amery, 'that Sir S.C. consulted me about nothing at any time.'[18] The Government in London also found themselves in the dark on occasions, but Churchill and Amery soon realized that, in his discussions with Indian leaders, Cripps had gone further than authorized in the direction of complete Indianization of the Executive (apart from the Viceroy and C. in C.), and of something approaching a national government.[19] Cripps himself, with the encouragement of Roosevelt's personal representative on the spot, Louis Johnson, tried to straddle the gap between the caution of his colleagues at home and the impatience of his Indian interlocutors. But while London sharply reminded him of the limits which had been set to his offer, Congress, for its part, rejected both the long-term aspect of those proposals (including, as they did, a Pakistan option), and, eventually, the short-term ones as well, on the grounds that full responsibility for defence matters should be handed over to an Indian within a freely-functioning national government.[20]

In Churchill's opinion, everything possible had now been done in the way of putting forward new proposals, and the matter could be put on one side whilst the more urgent and important task of winning the war was attended to. 'The effect throughout Britain and in the United States has been wholly beneficial', he cabled to Cripps,[21] while to Amery's astonishment he decided, in the latter's words, that 'there was no particular point in [Cripps'] telling the Cabinet anything about his experiences and conclusions, and in fact the Cabinet has not discussed the matter at all since his return!'[22] (Cripps did eventually present to the Cabinet a written report, in which he blamed the failure to achieve a settlement on Gandhi above all, together with other factors such as 'the decline in confidence in our prospects of victory due to the Japanese successes in the Far East.')[23]

The conclusion seemed to be, as Amery put it to Smuts, that an impasse had been reached, especially when, in August, Congress began a campaign of civil disobedience in the face of Britain's refusal to surrender power in India immediately.[24] The decision that was then taken in London to imprison Gandhi and other Congress leaders was backed by the Labour members of the Government. 'The Cabinet are all perfectly sound', noted Amery, 'none sounder than Bevin, who hitherto, next to Cripps, has been most inclined to favour Congress.' Once more Churchill assured his colleagues that Congress 'did not represent the masses of the Indian people', and worked to avoid a Parliamentary debate on the issues involved.[25] Thereafter, he did become enthusiastic for a while over the possibility of 'sidetracking the whole political crisis by a vigorous policy of social reform'[26] (a policy which Cripps and Bevin also vainly hoped would enable an appeal to be made to the Indian masses over the heads of the nationalist élite).[27] That apart, however, the Prime Minister's public pronouncements on the Indian situation tended to be coldly dismissive, to the dismay of Amery and others. 'I really begin to think', wrote Halifax in his diary in this connection, 'that whatever his merits as a war leader, on many things Winston is little short of a disaster.'[28] The Ambassador himself, of course, had, at times, been 'little short of a disaster' as Foreign Secretary, and, if given the responsibility, might well have led Britain in 1940 to what amounted to defeat. That in no way invalidates his observation on this occasion, however.

Meanwhile, although it appeared that the British Government had weathered this latest storm in India, the war was already bringing into contact with the affairs and condition of the sub-continent far more outsiders than usual. The impressions and reactions that followed, moreover, were often directed against the existing state of things. Thus, for example, a British war-time soldier, never having been in India before, wrote with bitterness of the way in which he and his kind were treated as 'filth beneath the feet of the white civilians', of rampant snobbery and 'a rigid caste system [which] is in every way opposed to the principles for which we are supposed to be fighting.'[29] Likewise, Andrew (later Sir Andrew) Gilchrist, a Foreign Office official on war-time attachment to S.O.E. in Southeast Asia, was greatly shocked when he arrived in Calcutta by the misery and apathy that he encountered there, asking himself whose responsibility it was.[30] Or again, looking ahead to early 1944, Irene Ward M.P. was to return from a visit to Calcutta during a famine there, and to report that British troops were saying: '"If this is what India is like and the Indians do not want us, what are we here for and why do we bother to fight?"'[31]

More noticeable still in 1942 was the involvement in Indian affairs of China, in the shape of a visit by Chiang Kai-shek and his wife in February. This project, which was to be followed by an exchange of representatives between Chungking and New Delhi,[32] had been eagerly sponsored by Clark Kerr during his last weeks as Ambassador to China, when he declared his 'completest confidence in [the Generalissimo's] decency and discretion' as regards the latter's proposed talks with Indian leaders.[33] The Foreign Office were also keen on the idea, with a view to improving Anglo-Chinese relations, even if it meant seeing Chiang in private conference with Gandhi. 'We cannot afford at this very critical juncture to strain our relations with Chiang Kai-shek', wrote the Head of the Far Eastern Department. 'We have swallowed a good deal in the interests of relations with Russia. I suggest that we must be prepared to swallow a good deal also in the interests of the alliance with China.'[34] Even the Viceroy, usually so resentful of outside interference, welcomed the proposal, found the Generalissimo 'a thoroughly sound person', and was soon pronouncing the visit 'a decided success.'[35]

This self-congratulation was a little premature, however. True, Chiang Kai-shek did allow himself to be dissuaded, at the Prime Minister's insistence, from making a special journey to visit Gandhi. (He could not be allowed to travel across India, wrote Churchill, 'to parley with Gandhi about whether the British Empire in India should come to an end or not.')[36] True, he also fulfilled the main British hope by publicly—and, it seems, privately— urging the Indians to fight wholeheartedly against the savage Japanese aggressor.[37] At the same time, however, Chiang emphasized his sympathy for Indian aspirations, and in his farewell message to the country called upon Britain to give India 'real political power' with all speed.[38] He adopted a similar position in private during the August civil-disobedience crisis, proposing that the United States should be invited to mediate between the British Government and Congress, and sending messages for the imprisoned Congress leaders, which the Viceroy declined to transmit.[39] It was on this occasion that Churchill, as noted earlier, felt obliged to remind the Generalissimo of Britain's careful non-interference in China's domestic affairs, with particular reference to the Kuomintang–Communist conflict.[40]

Behind the backs of the British, in fact, the Chinese, whatever they may have been thinking, were certainly speaking in terms even further removed from the loyalty and understanding in which Clark Kerr had naïvely believed. 'The Limeys thought they were impressing their guests', noted Stilwell after talking to Madame Chiang Kai-shek, 'but the Chinese were laughing most of the time.'[41] The Generalissimo for his part warned Roosevelt: 'If the British Government does not fundamentally change their [sic] policy toward India, it would be like presenting India to the enemy and inviting them to occupy India.'[42] As the situation reached a new climax in July and August, culminating in the arrests of Congress leaders, Chiang again appealed to the President to put pressure on Britain to give India her freedom. 'The outcome of this question', he averred, 'may in very great part determine the outcome of the war in the Far East.'[43] For him, the Congress Party represented 'the desire of the Indian people'—a contrast to the view of the Chinese Communists, who, it was reported, saw Congress and Muslim League alike as 'reactionary on virtually every issue save that of independence.'[44] In turn, Gandhi publicly assured the Generalissimo that, if Britain would quit India, the Allies could nevertheless continue to maintain forces there for the purpose of fighting the Japanese.[45]

Despite this pledge of Gandhi's, however, the belief that his policy of non-violence would amount to surrendering India to the Japanese was widespread in the United States as well as in Britain, and Nehru did his best to counteract it by insisting to Roosevelt that a free India could fling herself into the common struggle against the Axis in a way which was impossible under British rule.[46] Gandhi may not have helped matters, either, when he added to his own appeal to the President a sting in the tail, by referring, as mentioned earlier, to the 'Negro problem' in America in conjunction with Britain's repressive imperial policies.[47]

The main Indian criticism of the United States, however, was not that her Negroes were badly treated but that she was not forcing Britain to change those same imperial policies. Even some of those Indians who were in America on official, war-time business, pleaded for action on the part of their hosts, one of those who did so being K. C. Mahindra of the Indian Supply Mission there.[48] Sir Girja Shankar Bajpai, too, the Government of India's Agent General attached to the British Embassy in Washington, tended to employ a different emphasis when talking to American officials from when he was reporting to London and New Delhi. Thus, Bajpai privately encouraged the idea of intervention by Roosevelt in Anglo-Indian affairs, deploring the obstinacy of Churchill and Amery as well as of

Congress, and suggesting that a firm date should be fixed for Indian independence.[49]

Out in the open, meanwhile, Indian nationalists and the British Government alike strove by means of propaganda to win the support of the American public on the issue, the nationalist cause being championed also by such diverse figures as Pearl Buck and Clare Booth Luce, as well as many others in the United States.[50] (Writing to Mrs. Roosevelt, Pearl Buck warned that the Indians were 'so filled with bitterness against the English that we must look for revengeful massacres against all white people . . .')[51] Although Americans in general were greatly ignorant of India,[52] the ready response of many of them to anti-imperialist cries was clearly reflected in opinion polls in this, as in other cases. At the end of March 1942, for example, 41 per cent of those questioned felt that India should be granted Dominion status immediately, as against 24 per cent who believed that a better time for this would be the end of the war; again, in July, of the 43 per cent who favoured complete Indian independence, 55 per cent advocated its immediate inauguration.[53] 'The rooted feeling of America', wrote Frankfurter to Halifax in June, 'is that India is Britain's victim . . . The American people look to Mr. Churchill to act greatly . . . As in the case of the Philippines, a definite date should be fixed for the self-rule of India . . . and . . . must be guaranteed internationally. The effect upon America of some such step and such a declaration will lift Anglo-American relations to a new plane and will be of incalculable benefit for the new international order.'[54] Promptings of this kind could be uttered all the more easily when Britain's own public, as distinct from her Government, were seen as being ready for such a move. Thus, an intelligence report presented to Roosevelt in March, for example, depicted the British people as being more critical of their Government than ever before over this matter: 'There is genuine sympathy for Indian aspirations and demands for generous action.'[55]

Scorn for the status quo was also aroused in a good many American troops who arrived in or passed through India—about 250,000 of them during the entire war. Although there was a tendency on the part of these men to regard the natives slightingly as 'wogs',[56] they, too, were frequently dismayed at the poverty they encountered, and often contrasted unfavourably the Indian atmosphere with the one they found in China. Stilwell himself wrote that 'every trip from India to China I get a shock. In India the natives are depressed, dejected, hopelessly poor, ragged, underfed, skinny, sick, unsmiling, apathetic. In China they have their heads up, are bright, cheerful, laughing and joking, well fed, relatively clean, independent, going about their business, appear to have an object in life. India is hopeless.'[57]

Even so, when the Cripps offer was announced by Britain, the response of the American press was overwhelmingly favourable, and in several cases included strong criticism of what the New York Times described as 'a dismaying flood of opposition' to the offer on the part of Indian leaders. In July, over the 'quit-India' demand of the Congress Party, the same newspaper observed: 'The effect of what Gandhi is now saying may be to defeat everything for which he stands . . . The All-India Congress does not represent all India . . . The British are not blameless . . . [but] if they were to do precisely what Gandhi now demands they would create more wrongs than they would end.'[58] Thereafter, as Indian political activity and the Japanese threat both declined, so, too, did American interest, and by April 1943 a clear majority of those who responded to a poll by supporting the idea of Indian independence indicated that they thought the time for this to come about was after the war, and not immediately.[59]

Even before the Indian crisis of 1942 came to a head, various American officials had been concerned over the affairs of that country. During 1941, for example, Adolf Berle and Wallace Murray within the State Department had urged in vain that pressure should be put upon Britain to get her to grant India full Dominion status, and thus full partnership in the war effort.[60] Roosevelt himself, at the end of that year, had talked to the journalist and author, Edgar Snow, of the possibility that India could become 'our problem', and of the need to persuade Britain to give her her independence in order to enlist her sympathies fully on the Allied side.[61]

As the situation worsened in 1942, however, there also remained officials who advocated extreme caution in approaching this issue. Davies, for example, as adviser to Stilwell, reminded the General that 'India is not a nation but a sub-continent containing a conglomeration of political units with varying relations to the ruling or paramount British authority. Cutting across and complicating these political differences', he continued, 'are the more fundamental racial, linguistic, religious, social and economic differences . . . It would seem to be both much too late and much too early for any orderly solution to the problem of India, if such a solution is possible.'[62] Few Americans perceived the problem so acutely, but Stimson did privately regard it as 'foolish' for Roosevelt to attempt to intervene in such matters,[63] while even Henry Wallace acknowledged that the United States would be just as resentful if Britain were to 'butt in on Puerto Rico.'[64] As for Hull, while he reiterated that the Atlantic Charter was universally applicable, he also emphasized publicly, with India in mind, that those who aspired to independence had obligations of their own to live up to; in addition, the Secretary of State discussed with Halifax ways in which American opinion could be calmed over the Indian issue.[65]

Despite such reservations, however, the predominant reaction in American official circles during the first part of 1942 was one of alarm over the apparent dangers inherent in the Indian question. 'It seems to me', wrote Berle in February, 'that the State Department must immediately get to work on the changed situation in the Far East arising out of the fall of Singapore. The first item on the list ought to be to tackle the Indian problem in a big way.'[66] In his diary, Berle likewise asked: 'Why should India defend a freedom she hasn't got?'[67] As the Japanese advanced further into Southeast Asia, reports reaching Washington warned that the great mass of Indians, intensively disliking the British, were likely to be apathetic in the event of a threat of invasion.[68] This theme was echoed throughout the summer that followed. 'I found a situation', cabled a senior diplomat in May, 'which promises no real or substantial resistance to Japanese invasion if attempted.'[69] An O.S.S. survey likewise concluded that 'most Indians feel that Britain is their first and most immediate enemy',[70] while an Assistant Secretary of State, Breckenridge Long, noted in April: 'India is about to fall. The uncomprehending philosophy of England is meeting its reward. Blind, self-centred and tenacious of the phantoms of the past . . .'[71] 'A desperately serious situation is going to break out in India', Welles warned Roosevelt in July. '. . . This is a question of vital concern to our own military and naval interests in the Far East.'[72]

Moreover, the danger was viewed as being more than simply a military one. Disastrous consequences for America's prestige and influence were foreseen should she become identified with Britain in the minds of the Indians themselves. As Laughlin Currie put it to Wallace, the United States must 'maintain her own position with regard to races like the Indians and Chinese and not get sucked into taking the British position.'[73] 'There are disturbing evidences', he warned Roosevelt in August, 'of a tendency on the part of Congress supporters to identify American forces and attitudes in India with the British.'[74] An O.S.S. survey regarding propaganda in the region emphasized: 'Do not identify our cause with British policies in India',[75] and an official statement was issued to the effect that American troops were in that country solely for the purpose of aiding China, and that they would not become involved in suppressing local disorders, unless they themselves were attacked.[76]

If the United States thus had good reason to make her views known on Indian affairs, she also, in the opinion of many in Washington, had the right to do so. Not only were the lives of 'American boys' at stake, but, as the Senate Foreign Relations Committee forcibly expressed it in February (reflecting in this the changing balance of power within the alliance, observed in our contextual chapter above), the extent of the aid being given to Britain justified an accompanying demand for 'autonomy' to be granted to India, thus permitting a full mobilization of the resources of the British Empire for the fight against Japan.[77] 'India', observed H. F. Armstrong, editor of *Foreign Affairs*, 'had become a touchstone.'[78] The right of the United States to act in the matter was also reinforced, it was felt, by the fact that India herself, already in receipt of Lend Lease supplies, was evidently in urgent need of further American assistance, both military (Wavell at one point appealed directly to Washington for planes with which to stave off an invasion)[79] and industrial.[80] A move towards meeting the latter requirement had, in fact, already been made by the despatch to India in the spring of 1942 of an economic and production mission under Henry Grady, a former Assistant Secretary of State, although his ensuing recommendations were shelved by the Joint Chiefs of Staff, who feared losing valuable American material during a full-scale Indian revolt.[81] Meanwhile, it also occurred to some of those in Washington that, especially if Britain were forced to allow

New Delhi to keep its own dollar earnings, India could become an important market for American goods.[82]

In the public eye, the United States came closest to intervening in the Indian crisis of 1942 in the person of Colonel Louis Johnson, a prosperous West Virginian lawyer and former Assistant Secretary of War—'a man', in the later words of an American diplomat on the spot, 'uniquely unsuited to deal with the British and the Indians. Coarse, bombastic, and essentially ignorant regarding matters into which he was muscling.'[83] Johnson was specially chosen by Roosevelt to go out to India as his personal representative at the time of the Cripps mission. Thereafter, he vainly endeavoured, with Cripps, to find a formula concerning the allocation of defence responsibilities to which Congress could agree. More important than the details of these attempts, however, is the picture which Johnson sent back to Washington of the prestige of the United States ('The magic name over here is Roosevelt; the land the people would follow and love [sic], America'); of British incompetence ('Wavell is worn out and defeated; the hour has come when we should consider a replotting of our policy in this section of the world'); and of the wrecking tactics which, he believed, were being employed by Churchill's Government ('Cripps and Nehru could solve it in five minutes if Cripps had any freedom or authority... London wanted a Congress refusal').[84]*

Behind Johnson, however clumsy he might be, there stood Roosevelt himself, far more formidable a problem for London to face. Towards the end of February, the President had begun to move closer to the Indian issue by sounding out Winant and Harriman on the way Churchill was thinking on that matter.[85] At the same time he had drafted a message to the Prime Minister—it was not sent—in which he set out the context of his current concern:

'I have been for many years', he wrote, 'interested in the problem of the relations between Europeans and Americans on the one side with the many varieties of races in eastern and southern Asia and the Indians on the other side... There is no question in my mind that the old relationship ceased to exist ten or twenty years ago, and that no substitute has yet been worked out except the American policy of eventual freedom for the Philippines... In somewhat similar circumstances the older policy of master and servant has not been altered by the Dutch... nor by you... and this rather recent surge under the generic name of "Asia for the Asiatics" has in a sense come rather suddenly upon the Dutch and the British, for the very good reason that you... have not had time to work out a different plan for the future...

I feel that there is real danger in India now that there is too much suspicion and dissatisfaction in too many places, and that resistance to

---

* One comment in the State Department, however, on the charge that London had sabotaged Cripps, was that it had 'not been proved.'

Japan would therefore not be nearly as sincere and wholehearted as it should be . . .'[86]

The specific suggestions which followed in this draft did survive in the message that Roosevelt eventually sent to Churchill on 10 March.[87] Using the example of the thirteen American colonies, together with their Articles of Confederation and Constitutional Convention, the President proposed that a 'temporary government' should be set up in India, headed by 'a small, representative group covering different castes, occupations, religions and geographies—this group to be recognized as a temporary Dominion government'; in turn, the body would establish an assembly to draft a more permanent constitution. It was a scheme that Roosevelt raised again on 11 April, this time after the Prime Minister had reported the breakdown of the talks between Cripps and Indian leaders.[88] On this occasion, however, the President, urging that the negotiations should be reopened, added a sharper warning on the state of American opinion, as he chose to interpret it. 'The feeling is held almost universally', he claimed, 'that the deadlock has been due to the British Government's unwillingness to concede the right of self-government to the Indians, notwithstanding the willingness of the Indians to entrust to the competent British authorities technical, military and naval defense control.'

This last message marked the height of Roosevelt's efforts to force Churchill's hand over India. Perhaps he was relying in part upon the re-forming temper of the British public over this matter, which had been reported to him. But his implied threat relating to American public opinion was clearly an exaggerated one: the tendency of the press in the United States, as we have seen, was to blame the Indians rather than the British for the failure of the Cripps mission, and the public at large was not greatly aroused over the issue. Important though the question was in Washington, London, if pressed, and despite being the weaker partner, would place upon it a higher value still. In the event, rebuffed by the Prime Minister, as we shall see below, the President adopted thereafter a more cautious approach. Thus in May, when Johnson cabled from India to suggest that the United States should press for the formation of a national government there, Roosevelt replied that the situation had to be judged in military terms above all, and that 'the risks involved [in Johnson's proposal] outweighed the advantage that might be obtained.'[89] Similarly, when Chiang Kai-shek suggested in July that the U.S.A. should intervene in order to resolve the dispute between London and the Congress party, Roosevelt asked for Churchill's comments before composing a reply, which was to the effect that America and China should refrain from interfering.

The President repeated this conclusion in August, when the Generalissimo expressed his concern over the arrest of Congress leaders: Washington and Chungking, he wrote, should step in only 'if we are called in by both sides', and he added that it was to be regretted that Gandhi did not see the need for providing vigorous assistance in waging war against the Axis.[90] 'Frankly', he told the Pacific War Council, 'he did not think India was ready today for complete independence. He did not feel that China and the United States . . . could tell the British Empire what it must or must not do . . .'[91] To Senator George W. Norris, who suggested in September that American and Chinese good-offices should be used to change Britain's attitude, Roosevelt likewise deplored the adoption by Congress of a civil-disobedience campaign at a time of danger from Japan, and emphasized that, although the Indian situation was grave, 'this country must not get into a serious dispute with Great Britain . . .'[92]

The same approach to the question was expressed in the State Department's Advisory Sub-Committee on Post-War Problems, where, as the result of a meeting at the end of 1942, a statement on the desirability of Indian independence was followed by the rider: 'But in its own interests the United States should refrain from intervening in the Indian situation during the war.'[93] The complexity and intractibility of the issue, as well as the easing of the Japanese threat, had thus helped to diminish earlier American confidence and bold concern. So, too, of course, had British resistance.

In London, the limits within which American interference over India would be accepted were marked out by Churchill above all, urged on throughout by Linlithgow from New Delhi. For a while, the Viceroy was quite impressed by Louis Johnson, whom Cripps also described to the Prime Minister as an 'invaluable intermediary.'[94] Linlithgow soon came to feel, however, that the President's representative had in fact been less than helpful, whilst the Cabinet in London became alarmed lest Johnson's intervention should be construed as representing official action on the part of the United States Government.[95] That this was not the case was made clear to Churchill by Hopkins, who happened to be in London at the time; the Prime Minister promptly cabled this important information to New Delhi, and it probably helped to ensure that Cripps would not be granted additional room for manoeuvre. Thereafter, in May, Churchill let Hopkins know that Johnson's views and his presence in India were not regarded as helpful by the British Government.[96]

Nor did the Prime Minister give any encouragement to the ideas formulated by the President, rightly regarding the latter's analogue with the thirteen American colonies in the late eighteenth century as facile, emphasizing what he later termed 'the Moslem side of the picture' and the danger of totally disrupting the Indian Army by giving in to the demands of the Congress party.[97] Thus, in his comments on Chiang Kai-shek's July appeal to Roosevelt, Churchill assured the latter: 'The Congress party in no way represents India . . . [but] represents mainly the intelligentsia of non-fighting Hindu elements, and they can neither defend India nor raise a revolt. The military classes on whom everything depends are thoroughly loyal . . . Their loyalty would be gravely impaired by handing over the Government of India to Congress control.'[98] Responding more fiercely still to a subsequent appeal sent to Washington by the Generalissimo ('I take it amiss', wrote the Prime

Minister, 'that Chiang should seek to make difficulties between us'), he added: 'You could remind Chiang that Gandhi was prepared to negotiate with Japan on the basis of a free passage for Japanese troops through India in the hopes of their joining hands with Hitler. Personally, I have no doubt that in addition there would have been an understanding that the Congress would have the use of sufficient Japanese troops to keep down the composite minority of 90 million Moslems, 40 million untouchables and 90 million in the Princes' States.'[99]

As for the President's brandishing of the picture of a highly critical American public opinion, Churchill was ready to respond with a larger and successful threat of his own, in addition to intimating that 'anything like a serious difference between you and me would break my heart and would surely deeply injure both of our countries.' Quite simply, the threat was that he would resign if coerced over the question of India. 'I do not feel I could take responsibility for the defence of India if everything had again to be thrown into the melting pot at this critical juncture', he cabled on 12 April. For this reason, he added (thus giving Roosevelt the chance to back down), he had not yet brought the President's message before the Cabinet. Indeed, in his original draft of this response, the Prime Minister had set out to be more forceful still, utilizing the likely reactions of his own legislature and public:

'I cannot feel', he had sketched, 'that the common cause would benefit by emphasising the serious differences which would emerge between our two countries if it were known that against our own convictions we were conforming to United States public opinion in a matter which concerns the British Empire and is vital to our successful conduct of the war in the East.

I should personally make no objection at all to retiring into private life, and I have explained this to Harry [Hopkins] just now, but I have no doubt whatever that Cabinet and Parliament would be strongly averse from reopening the Indian constitutional issue at this juncture.'[100]

Churchill himself, just as the President had been when making his own threat, was obviously bluffing in part, being no more likely to surrender power amid the excitement of war—least of all in a manner which would jeopardize his dream of an everlasting Anglo-American partnership—than would a fish climb out of the sea. Nevertheless, Roosevelt's suggestions over India received short shrift in London. (On a report, in March, concerning one of the President's verbal rambles around the subject, Eden commented: 'It is a terrifying commentary on the likely Roosevelt contribution to the peace, a meandering amateurishness lit by discursive flashes.')[101]

At the same time, however, there was a great deal of concern to improve Britain's standing over the matter in American eyes. A member of Cripps' staff who visited the United States after the failure of his master's mission reported that 'the trend of American opinion on British relations with India is towards sympathy for the more extreme and usually Congress Party points of view', and that at times of tension the Indian issue could become 'of first significance' in Anglo-American relations. As it was, he suggested (and the North American Department of the Foreign Office agreed),[102] there was important work to be done in trying to remove the many misconceptions entertained by Americans on the subject.[103] Meanwhile Cripps himself made a broadcast to the U.S.A. in order to assert that 'to have agreed to the Congress Party's or Mr. Gandhi's demands would have meant inevitable chaos and disorder',[104] while Attlee, in Churchill's absence abroad, sought to justify in advance to Roosevelt the arrest of the Congress leadership in August.[105] Also, as far as non-political American involvement in India was concerned, the Cabinet welcomed the idea, set out in the report of Grady's technical mission, of the United States assisting in increasing the sub-continent's war-time industrial capacity.[106]

Over this question of how far Britain should go in taking account of American susceptibilities concerning India, there was a marked difference of emphasis between London and New Delhi. The Viceroy did claim to be fully aware of the problem, citing the extent to which he himself entertained visiting Americans and his appointment (it was not considered by others to have been a very happy one) of Sir Evelyn Wrench, long associated with the English Speaking Union, as American Relations Officer, with instructions to ease those relations as much as possible from the social point of view.[107] At the same time, however, Linlithgow greatly resented the way in which passing Americans like Laughlin Currie and Louis Johnson interfered in Indian affairs. 'I cannot resist the conclusion', he cabled to Amery, 'that the Americans are not running entirely straight with us over India. Every one of them of any political eminence who comes through here flirts with Congress.' And by letter he added: 'I do not feel any doubt . . . that we shall have to stand firm over the general Indian business as against the U.S.A. unless we are prepared to contemplate throwing our hands in altogether.'[108]

The Viceroy's appeal to be shielded from yet more American visitors, such as Wendell Willkie and Sherwood Eddy,[109] won more sympathy from Churchill than from the Foreign Office. The latter believed that it would be better to welcome and seek to influence a man like Willkie, and tended to view the outlook of New Delhi as being far too narrow. Eden's own summary of the Government of India's reactions to the American interest in India was that they were 'unimaginative, even foolish', while he found the India Office in London 'slow and sluggish.'[110] As for ways of improving Anglo-American relations in this context, a suggestion by Halifax, that the United States should be invited to send out to India a three-man fact-finding mission, did not find favour.[111] The Foreign Office, to the dismay of Linlithgow, did, however, come up with the idea of getting Washington to install in New Delhi, where he could be taken into the Viceroy's confidence, 'a really high-calibre American in whom we have confidence and who would equally have the confidence of the President and be a sufficiently well-known figure to command the confidence of the American people too.'[112] Even Amery approved of the proposal as being 'our best hope of keeping the United States Government straight regarding India.' When the United States Administration agreed in turn to the idea and selected William Phillips for the job (the other likely candidate having been Joe Grew), there was general satisfaction in London and in the Washington Embassy. Phillips, cabled Halifax to the Viceroy, was 'an extremely good man. You are lucky to get him.'[113]

An old friend of Roosevelt's and a man with a distinguished career in diplomacy behind him, very much a member of the East-coast élite, and indeed in some ways, as recalled by those who met him, seemingly more British than the British, Phillips did indeed appear to be someone likely to sympathize with Britain's imperial problems during war-time. He was already serving in London when, early in November 1942, he was formally offered the post of the President's Personal Representative in India, with the rank of Ambassador. There was no question of American intervention, instructed Hull, and he must avoid 'objectionable pressure upon either side [which] would probably result . . . in the case of the British in a possible disturbance of the unity of command and of cooperation both during and following the war.' On the other hand, Hull continued, Phillips could talk in a friendly but blunt way to British officials, and remind them that the Philippines provided 'a perfect example of how a nation should treat a colony or dependency in cooperating with it in all essential respects calculated to assist it in making all necessary preparation for freedom.'[114]

Armed with this much-used and largely irrelevant model of the Philippines, Phillips had numerous discussions in London before his departure for New Delhi. With a reservation concerning Churchill, who was 'less liberal-minded than the general feeling here in official and unofficial circles', the new Ambassador was able to report to Roosevelt in December that he had found that there was 'a complete readiness to give effect to the principles of self-determination in India, a duty however which cannot be fulfilled merely by walking out and leaving the India the British have created, including the millions of minority groups, to muddle through to a solution.'[115] Amery urged Phillips to try to persuade the Indians themselves 'to pull together', though he believed that the Muslims would require separate states in the North-West and North-East; Brendan Bracken produced the remarkably ignorant assertion that 'trade unionism and the raising of wages throughout India . . . was the basis of all the present problems'; Cripps 'was outspoken in his criticism of the present Viceroy, who he said was impossible.'[116] In general, Phillips found it all to be in marked contrast to the climate of opinion that he encountered in India itself, when he arrived in January 1943. There, he reported to the President, the British he met 'could not really envisage a free India fit to govern itself.'[117]

Contrary to London's expectations, in fact, Phillips was to prove a severe critic of British policies in India, and to figure in an incident which added to the strains in Anglo-American relations. This will be related in due course, as will the repercussions on those relations caused by famine in Bengal and

of a growing American interest in post-war commercial links with India.*
Even so, by 1943 the crisis which the affairs of the sub-continent had brought
about between London and Washington had passed its peak. The Japanese
advance had come to a halt; India as a base from which to move back to the
aid of China remained intact; even apart from British intransigence, it seemed
that perhaps the simple cry of anti-imperialism and the majestic example of
1776 might not, after all, provide a sufficient and ready solution.[118]

Over an issue like article 7 of the Mutual Aid Agreement, Roosevelt had
been able in 1942 to use American (and more specifically, Congressional)
opinion, combined with his country's superior resources, to extract an
important concession from the British Government. Over India, however,
despite Britain's increasing material inferiority, the factors and values
involved had not permitted the President a similar success. The basic American dislike of Britain's imperial position remained, but would not again be
pressed upon London as it had been during the spring and early summer of
1942.

* During the war years, American exports to India increased from 1 per cent to 5 per
cent of the U.S. total, and the American share of India's total imports increased from 6 to
17 per cent. Hess, *America Encounters India*, 158.

Notes to Chapter Eight

1 On Bose's activities in Germany in 1941, see DGFP, XIII, Nos. 120, 213, 521. In
   general, see Allen, *The End of the War in Asia*, cap. 5.
2 COS, 1 April 1942, CAB 79/20. See Kennedy, *The Business of War*, 219.
3 WP(42)184, CAB 66/24.
4 See COS, 13 March 1942 (CAB 79/19) and 9 April 1942 (CAB 79/20).
5 WP(42)325, 328 (CAB 66/27); WP(42)421, 422, 447 (CAB 66/29); Amery to Linlithgow, 26 Sept. 1942, Linlithgow Papers, vol. 11; WSC to Linlithgow, 24 Sept. 1942,
   IO, Private Office Papers, L/PO/325.
6 See above, 62.
7 WP(42)42, CAB 66/21.
8 See above, 62.
9 See WP(42)110, CAB 66/22.
10 Sapru et al. to WSC, 2 Jan. 1942, WP(42)53, CAB 66/21.
11 Cabs, 12 Jan. and 5 Feb. 1942, CAB 65/25; WP(42)59, CAB 66/21.
12 WP(42)87, CAB 66/22.
13 *Churchill*, III, 615.
14 Amery to Linlithgow, 2 and 10 March 1942, Linlithgow Papers, vol. 11.
15 *Transfer of Power*, no. 294.
16 Ibid, passim.
17 See WP(42)105, 109, 115 (CAB 66/22); Cab, 9 March 1942 (CAB 65/25); material in
   CAB 91/1; Cooke, *Cripps*, 283ff.; *Churchill*, IV, cap XII.
18 Amery to Linlithgow, 31 March 1942, Linlithgow Papers, vol. 11; *Transfer of Power*,
   no. 582.
19 Amery to Linlithgow, 11 and 29 April 1942, Linlithgow Papers, vol. 11; Gopal,
   Nehru, I, 281.
20 *Transfer of Power*, no. 587; see Gopal, *Nehru*, I, 280.

21 *Transfer of Power*, no. 597.
22 Amery to Linlithgow, 6 May 1942, Linlithgow Papers, vol. 11.
23 WP(42)283, CAB 66/26. See Gopal, *Nehru*, I, 287.
24 Amery to Smuts, 12 Sept. 1942, van der Poel, *Smuts Papers*, VI.
25 Amery to Linlithgow, 8 Aug. and 1 Sept. 1942, Linlithgow Papers, vol. 11. See Dalton Diary, 9 April 1942; Cabs, 13 and 24 July, 31 Aug. 1942, CAB 65/27; WP(42)255, CAB 66/25; Gopal, *Nehru*, I, 295.
26 Amery to Linlithgow, 30 Oct. 1942, Linlithgow Papers, vol. 11.
27 Gupta, *Imperialism and the British Labour Movement*, 272.
28 Amery to Linlithgow, 5 Oct. 1942, Linlithgow Papers, vol. 11; Halifax Diary, 11 Oct. 1942.
29 Amery to Linlithgow, 22 Jan. 1943, Linlithgow Papers, vol. 12; and see Cripps to Amery, 3 Nov. 1942, IO, Private Office papers, L/PO/81. For Wavell's rejection of such complaints, see Wavell to Linlithgow, 9 March 1943, Linlithgow Papers, vol. 125.
30 A. Gilchrist, *Bangkok Top Secret* (London, 1970), 143.
31 Far Eastern Group meeting, 6 April 1944, RIIA.
32 See FO 371, F1319 and 2199/1273/10; *Transfer of Power*, no. 383.
33 *Transfer of Power*, no. 69.
34 FO 371, F1523/74/10.
35 Linlithgow to Amery, 9 and 16 Feb. 1942, Linlithgow Papers, vol. 11. See Clark Kerr to Cripps, 26 April 1942, Clark Kerr Papers, FO 800/300.
36 WSC to Eden, 13 Feb. 1942, FO 371, F1533/74/10.
37 Gopal, *Nehru*, I, 277.
38 *Transfer of Power*, no. 173.
39 FO 371, F5756 and 5797/2428/10.
40 See above, 184.
41 *Stilwell Papers*, 9 March 1942.
42 FRUS, 1942, I, 604; see FRUS, 1942, China, 140, and DS 740.0011 P.W./2101.
43 FRUS, 1942, I, 695; see ibid, 714.
44 FRUS, 1942, China, 98.
45 FRUS, 1942, I, 674.
46 Ibid, 635.
47 See above, 9.
48 FRUS, 1942, I, 723, and Mahindra to Waring, 19 Aug. 1942, Hopkins Papers, box 313.
49 E.g. Donovan to FDR, 10 Feb. 1942, Roosevelt Papers, PSF box 162; FRUS, 1942, I, 639, 679, 735, 740; *Long*, 13 May 1942.
50 See G. Hess, *America Encounters India* (Baltimore, 1971), 91, 113ff.
51 Buck to Mrs. Roosevelt, 7 March 1942, Roosevelt Papers, PSF box 53.
52 See Isaacs, *Scratches On Our Minds*, 239ff.
53 Cantril and Strunk, 327.
54 Frankfurter to Halifax, 30 June 1942, Frankfurter Papers, box 62.
55 British Home Intelligence report, 16 March 1942, Roosevelt Papers, PSF box 162.
56 Isaacs, *Scratches On Our Minds*, 317.
57 *Stilwell Papers*, 4 Jan. 1943. See Peers and Brelis, *Behind The Burma Road*, 40.
58 *New York Times*, 31 March, 2, 3, 11 and 12 April, 16 July 1942.
59 See Hess, *America Encounters India*, 127ff.
60 See M. S. Venkataramani and B. K. Shrivastava, 'The United States and the Cripps Mission', *India Quarterly*, vol. xix, no. 3, 1963.
61 E. Snow, *Journey To The Beginning* (London, 1959), 254.
62 Davies memo., 20 May 1942, Stilwell Papers, box 7.
63 Stimson Diary, 20 April 1942.
64 *Wallace*, 21 Oct. 1942.
65 E.g. FRUS, 1942, I, 733; Hull, *Memoirs*, II, 1205, 1482ff.
66 FRUS, 1942, I, 602.

67 *Berle*, 28 Feb. 1942.
68 E.g. DS 740.0011 P.W./2060. See CBI 'Master Narrative', 276, Stilwell Papers, box 1.
69 FRUS, 1942, China, 38.
70 OSS R and A, 283, 14 May 1942.
71 *Long*, 7 April 1942.
72 Welles to FDR, 29 July 1942, Roosevelt Papers, MR box 2.
73 *Wallace*, 27 Aug. 1942.
74 FRUS, 1942, I, 712.
75 OSS R and A, 740, 27 May 1942.
76 War Dept. to Stilwell, 6 Aug. 1942, OPD, Exec. file 10, item 21; FRUS, 1942, I, 715.
77 FRUS, 1942, I, 606; DS 740.0011 P.W./2298.
78 Sub-committee on Political Problems, 12 Dec. 1942, DS, Notter files, box 55.
79 DS 841.248/1199.
80 See e.g. FRUS, 1942, I, 593.
81 Ibid, 735, and, on Lend Lease and reverse aid, ibid, 555; *Romanus and Sutherland*, I, 207–9.
82 See Gardner, *Economic Aspects*, 185.
83 *Davies*, 236.
84 FRUS, 1942, I, 630–2, 657–62.
85 FDR to Winant, 25 Feb. 1942, Roosevelt Papers, PSF box 3.
86 Draft of 25 Feb. 1942, ibid, MR box 2.
87 FRUS, 1942, I, 613; WP(42)118, CAB 66/22.
88 FRUS, 1942, I, 633.
89 FDR to Johnson, 7 May 1942, Roosevelt Papers, PSF box 91.
90 FRUS, 1942, I, 695, 700, 705, 714–7.
91 PWC(W), 12 Aug. 1942, FO 371, F5705/2428/10.
92 FDR to Norris, 23 Sept. 1942, Roosevelt Papers, PSF box 11.
93 Sub-committee on Political Problems, 12 Dec. 1942, DS, Notter files, box 55.
94 Linlithgow to Amery, 7 April 1942, Linlithgow Papers, vol. 11; *Transfer of Power*, no. 574.
95 Linlithgow to Amery, 18 May 1942, Linlithgow Papers, vol 11; *Transfer of Power*, no. 567.
96 FRUS, 1942, I, 629; Hopkins memo., 9 April 1942, Hopkins Papers, box 308; WSC to Hopkins, 28 and 31 May 1942, ibid, box 136; *Sherwood*, 530–1.
97 See *Churchill*, IV, 186ff.
98 WP(42)334, CAB 66/27.
99 WSC to FDR, 13 Aug. 1942, PREM 4, 45/4.
100 Draft of 12 April 1942, PREM 4, 48/9. See *Churchill*, IV, 195.
101 FO 371, A2421/122/45.
102 E.g. ibid, A7709/122/45, A9872/399/45.
103 WP(42)318, CAB 66/26.
104 Cripps Papers, file 1143.
105 FRUS, 1942, I, 703.
106 WP(42)461, CAB 66/29; Cab, 19 Oct. 1942, CAB 65/28.
107 Linlithgow to Amery, 30 June 1942, Linlithgow Papers, vol. 11; Wrench to Amery, 10 Oct. 1943, IO, Private Office papers, L/PO/81.
108 Linlithgow to Amery, 13 Aug. 1942, Linlithgow Papers, vol. 23; ditto, 21 Sept. 1942, ibid, vol. 11.
109 FO 371, A8241/122/45; IO, Private Office papers, L/PO/446.
110 FO 371, A9008 and 10250/122/45; see A8627 and 9625/122/45.
111 Halifax Diary, 14 Aug. 1942.
112 FO 371, A7869/122/45; ibid, A7567/31/45; Amery to Linlithgow, 7 Oct. 1942 and Linlithgow to Amery, 18 Sept. 1942, Linlithgow Papers, vol. 23.
113 FO 371, A11302/122/45.
114 Hull to Phillips, 18 Nov. 1942, Hull Papers, box 50; FRUS, 1942, I, 744ff.; W. Phillips, *Ventures In Diplomacy* (London, 1955), cap. 22.

115 Phillips to FDR, 17 Dec. 1942, Roosevelt Papers, PSF box 51.
116 Phillips' Indian Diary, Nov. and Dec. 1942, Phillips Papers, vol. 32.
117 Phillips to FDR, Phillips Papers, vol. 33.
118 See Hess, *America Encounters India*, 127.

CHAPTER NINE

AUSTRALASIA AND THE SOUTHWEST PACIFIC

NOWHERE DID the first, swift triumphs of the Japanese create more shock and alarm than in Australia and New Zealand. We have seen how, for many years, these Dominions had been given assurances by Britain as to the means available for their protection, and how, even in 1941, Churchill and others had tended to belittle the idea that Japan posed a serious and immediate threat to their safety.[1] Now, as the *Prince of Wales* and *Repulse* were swept aside and Singapore was so easily taken, there arose both fear and a measure of bitterness towards Britain.[2] The American Consul in Adelaide wrote that, on the day following the sinking of the two capital ships, 'the general public [here] . . . were the closest to actual panic that I have ever seen. Staid businessmen who only the day before were complacent about the menace of "the yellow dwarf" were now reduced almost to wringing their hands.'[3] 'Everywhere', reported the American Minister in Canberra to Roosevelt later, 'one got the feeling that Australia was ready to give up without a struggle; that if it had been possible to leave the country the people would have gone.'[4] The former Prime Minister, Robert Menzies, talking to a British official towards the end of 1942, spoke of 'a real ugly fear over the prospect of invasion among many of the Australian Government leaders around February/March . . . —men turning [a] "nasty colour" etc.'[5] Reports from New Zealand were less dramatic, but there, too, the sense of shock was evident.[6]

In retrospect, the alarm which spread throughout Australia at the end of 1941 and during the early months of 1942 is readily understandable, fuelled as it was by such local incidents as the bombing of Darwin and a submarine attack on Sydney harbour. It was easy to believe that there were scarcely any limits to the aims and capabilities of the triumphant Japanese—and, indeed, we have seen that the eventual conquest of Australia and New Zealand did figure in long-term Japanese plans. Throughout the spring and early summer of 1942, therefore, the Prime Minister of the Labour Government in Canberra, John Curtin, continued to proclaim that his country was in danger of invasion. Even after the major victory of the U.S. Navy at Midway, he still declared, in a broadcast in June, that Australia 'could be lost.'[7]

From London, however, this threat had to be seen and weighed alongside many others, and these differing viewpoints helped to bring about a period of severely strained relations between Britain and Australia. At times, indeed, the language employed was remarkably sharp ('The evacuation of Singapore', Curtin warned Churchill towards the end of January, 'would be regarded as an inexcusable betrayal').[8] Moreover, Canberra's disillusionment was made plain for the world to see, with Curtin stating at a press interview towards the end of December 1941 that he wished to 'make it quite clear . . . , without inhibitions of any kind', that 'Australia [looked] to America, free of any pangs as to [her] traditional links or kinship with the United Kingdom.'[9] In the eyes of Curtin and his colleagues, London was not giving due consideration to the extent to which Australia's own land and air forces were away serving in other theatres—48,000 of them still in September 1942; likewise, Australian strategic proposals—for example, that a single, powerful Anglo-American fleet should be formed to wrest the initiative from the Japanese at once[10]—appeared to go unheeded. When Wavell's new A.B.D.A. Command was set up during the Churchill–Roosevelt talks in Washington at the turn of the year (albeit with misgivings on the British side, especially over saddling one of their generals with almost certain defeat, and on the part of Roosevelt and Marshall with the idea in mind of replacing Wavell with an American commander later on),[11] keen resentment was felt by the Australians, as it was by the Dutch, over the lack of consultation involved.[12]

There followed, moreover, various other, well-known disputes, such as the one when Canberra refused, against the strongly-expressed desire of Churchill, to allow the 7th Australian Division, on its way back from the Middle East to Australia, to be diverted to Rangoon.[13] Curtin's Government also insisted that their 9th Division should likewise come back from the Middle East, and although Roosevelt succeeded in getting the move delayed for a while, it was to be carried out at the end of 1942.[14] Sharp exchanges again took place between Churchill and Curtin—and were made public— over the former's appointment, against Curtin's wishes, of R. G. Casey, the Australian Minister in Washington, as British Minister in the Middle East, with a seat in the War Cabinet.[15] Less dramatic, but foreshadowing major disagreements later in the war, were the indications that already existed that Curtin's Government was far more keen than its British counterpart to see the trusteeship principle applied to colonial possessions at the end of the war, especially where Australia's part of the world was concerned.[16]

Above all, the Australian Government—New Zealand's was also anxious, but less vociferous[17]—pressed vigorously throughout this period for more land, sea and air reinforcements to be sent out to their theatre of operations, aiming, amongst other things, at a target of 73 squadrons for the Royal Australian Air Force. Dr. Herbert Evatt, for example, the country's ambitious, talented and overbearing Minister for External Affairs, came in person to London to hammer the message home.[18] ('You've stated Australia's case in no uncertain terms', wrote his more tactful companion, the prominent Australian businessman, W. S. Robinson, a man with many high-level connections in London. 'The manner in which you have stated it eliminates

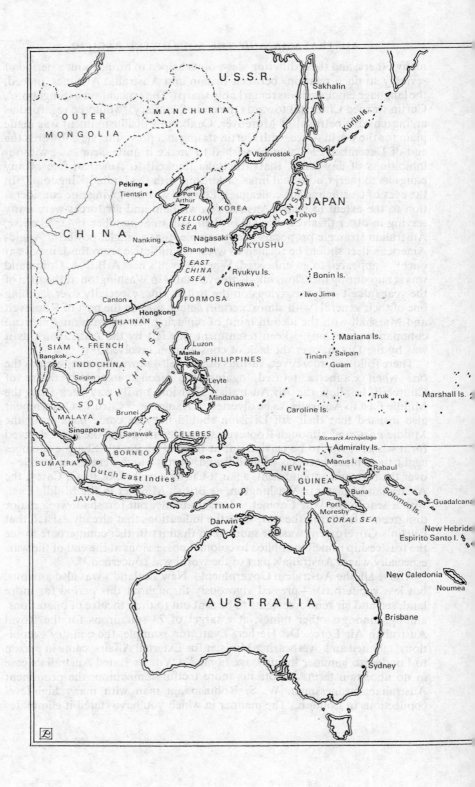

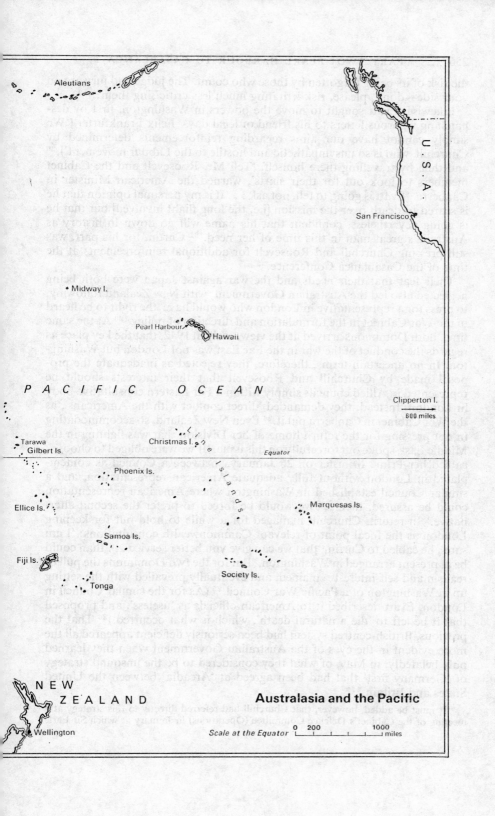

Aleutians

U.S.A.

San Francisco

• Midway I.

Pearl Harbour
Hawaii

P A C I F I C   O C E A N

Clipperton I.

600 miles

Tarawa
Gilbert Is.

Christmas I.

Equator

Phoenix Is.

Line Islands

Ellice Is.

Marquesas Is.

Samoa Is.

Fiji Is.

Society Is.

Tonga

N E W
Z E A L A N D

Australasia and the Pacific

Wellington

Scale at the Equator 0   200   1000
                                                    miles

the risk of its being forgotten by those who count. The judge and jury are on your side—don't, please, risk irritating much less criticising them!')[19]

Likewise, Evatt sought to move the powers in Washington, first by despatching vigorous letters to his friend of legal days, Felix Frankfurter ('We simply cannot have our aims regarding reinforcements determined by Churchill, who is so unsympathetic and hostile to the Labour movement'),[20] and then by travelling there himself. 'Tell Mr. Roosevelt and the Cabinet members to look out for their shirts', warned the American Minister in Canberra. 'Evatt is going to tell, not ask . . . It is my personal opinion that he is scared to death over the mission [i.e. the long flight involved] but that he is going nevertheless, confident that his name will go down in history as Australia's great man in this time of her need.'[21] Curtin, for his part, was still pressing Churchill and Roosevelt for additional reinforcements at the time of the Casablanca Conference.[22]

Their fear that their needs and the war against Japan were both being neglected also led the Australian Government, with New Zealand following, to press for a representative in London who would have 'the right to be heard in the War Cabinet in the formulation and direction of policy.'[23] At the same time, both Dominions arrived at the view, early in 1942, that the key place as regards the conduct of the war in the Far East was not London but Washington. In no uncertain terms, therefore, they rejected as inadequate the proposal made by Churchill and Roosevelt that their interests should be represented in Allied councils simply within a Far Eastern consultative body in London. Instead, they demanded 'direct contact with the Americans', as the War Cabinet in Canberra put it.[24] Even New Zealand, so accommodating in not pressing for the return home of her Division that was fighting in the Middle East, spoke out forcefully on this issue. 'If we were obliged to choose', cabled her Prime Minister on 26 January, 'between a Council as contemplated in London without fully adequate American representation, and a similar Council established in Washington where American representation could be assured, then . . . we would be forced to prefer the second alternative.' In return, Churchill managed for a while to hold out for keeping London as the focal point of relevant Commonwealth consultations: 'I am sure', he cabled to Curtin, 'that we can give you better service . . . than could be at present arranged in Washington.' But for the two Dominions the pull of realism and self-interest remained, and eventually prevailed with the setting up in Washington of a Pacific War Council.[25] (As for the similar Council in London, Evatt described it to American officials as 'useless', and proposed that it be left to 'die a natural death', which is what occurred.)[26] That the previous, British-centred system had been seriously deficient appeared all the more evident in the eyes of the Australian Government when they learned only belatedly, in May, of what they considered to be the unsound strategy of 'Germany first' that had been agreed at 'Arcadia' between the United States and Britain.[27]*

---

* It must be added, however, that Churchill had referred directly to this strategy at a meeting of the Cabinet's Defence Committee (Operations) in January at which Sir Earle

In London, the seriousness of this rapid decline in relations with Australia made a deep impression in at least some quarters. Indeed, at a Cabinet meeting towards the end of January, one of those present went so far as to scribble on a piece of paper: 'Australia is the most dangerous obstacle in the path of this Government.'[28] More thoughtfully, Lord Cranborne, who was Dominions Secretary at the time, put the matter within the wider, Commonwealth perspective that was outlined in an earlier chapter, warning his colleagues that it could be 'disastrous' to underrate the strength of Australian feeling, and that with 'centrifugal tendencies' already present in South Africa and elsewhere, 'a rot which started in Australia might easily spread to other Dominions.'[29] The King, too, conveyed to Churchill his 'genuine alarm at the feeling which appears to be growing in Australia', while from Australia itself, a former Prime Minister, Billy Hughes, sent a private message to Churchill to warn that, under pressure from more extreme colleagues, Curtin might 'plump for America as against Britain.'[30] The British High Commissioner in Canberra, Sir Ronald Cross, likewise suggested that Evatt, the strongest influence in the Australian Cabinet, was channelling his desire for personal advancement into 'nationalistic or possibly secessionist' directions.[31]

To a limited extent, London did take steps, therefore, to try to assuage Australian fears and to improve relations. Churchill, for example, assured Curtin and Evatt that even when Australia came within the area of American strategic responsibility, the British Government regarded itself as still bound by the pledge that, 'if you are actually invaded in force . . . we shall do our utmost to divert British troops and British ships . . . to your succour, albeit at the expense of India and the Middle East.'[32] In addition, Australia kept her 'accredited representative' in the War Cabinet in London, Evatt himself briefly filling that role during his visit, and being succeeded by the High Commissioner and former Australian Prime Minister, Stanley Bruce. Churchill also went out of his way to soothe Evatt, promising to send some squadrons of Spitfire fighter planes to Australia,* and exploring the possibility of despatching even an aircraft carrier there in order to help 'our permanent relations . . . [and] the future of the Empire.' The Prime Minister also, early in 1943, invited Curtin to visit Britain, although without success.[33]

In general, however, Australia did not win for herself a great deal of sympathy or stimulate action on her behalf in London. In private, Churchill reacted bitterly to Curtin's statement at the end of 1941 about Australia looking to the United States, and at the end of January he suspended special, premier-to-premier telegrams to Canberra 'in view of Mr. Curtin's tone.'[34]

Page of Australia was present. Nothing on this matter appears to exist in the Earle Page Papers. (DC(Ops.), 21 Jan. 1942, CAB 69/4; *Hasluck* II, 165. And see DS, 740.0011 P.W./2528.)

* The Middle East crisis in June 1942 forced Churchill to delay sending the bulk of the promised Spitfires to Australia, thus prompting Evatt to register with Brendan Bracken his 'utter disgust.' At the end of 1943, moreover, MacArthur was to complain to a party of British press executives that, even when they had eventually arrived, the Spitfires had been antiquated, their pilots raw and their achievements poor. The British Chief of the Air Staff was able to demonstrate the falsity of these charges. (Material in PREM 3, 159/2.)

Cadogan at the Foreign Office, for his part, was still employing scornful terms when writing in his diary about Australians,[35] while from Canberra, Cross (a poor choice for the post, and not highly regarded either by his hosts or by British visitors)[36] proposed that, in the face of a virulent anti-British campaign that was being 'inspired and conducted by Ministers', London should refuse to meet Australian desires over economic and financial questions. 'The time has come', he cabled, 'to collect all our weapons and to fight for British prestige in Australia'—though his particular selection from the armoury was sensibly rejected by Cranborne as being certain to make matters a great deal worse.[37]

Meanwhile on the military side of things, the British Chief of Staff in A.B.D.A., Lt. General Pownall, found the Australians 'the most egotistical, conceited people imaginable';[38] the Chiefs of Staff in London (who, rightly as we now know, refused to believe that a major Japanese offensive against Australia was imminent) subsequently made it clear to Churchill that, for their part, they were opposed to staff officers from Australia being 'let into all our secrets', and that in their view Dominion prime ministers should receive only the same kind of periodic summary of the war situation which Churchill was in the habit of sending to Stalin.[39]

As for the Prime Minister himself, he continued to blend firmness with sympathy in his communications with Curtin.[40] Yet there was never any likelihood that he would accord the Australians the kind of respectful attention which he continued to bestow upon Smuts.[41] Bruce—who was not in Evatt's confidence either—soon found his role in the War Cabinet in London a hollow one. 'I am given so little information and consulted so little', he protested to Churchill in September 1942. And indeed, as Cranborne was to point out to the Prime Minister a year later, the High Commissioner was not even being allowed to attend all those Cabinet meetings at which questions affecting Australia were discussed, contrary to the assumption made by his Government in Canberra. Churchill was persuaded by the Dominions Office to tone down most of his written responses to Bruce to an adequately courteous level, but he was nettled by the latter's suggestion that he, Churchill, was treating the War Cabinet as a whole with indifference. Early in 1943, the Prime Minister was writing to Attlee that the High Commissioner 'should be brought up with a round turn', reasoning in a manner which casts some light on his own, over-all view of the Japanese war, and on his limited sympathy for Australia. 'The position of Mr. Bruce is highly anomalous', he wrote. 'The Australians have now moved their last troops away from the general war zone [i.e. the Middle East] to their own affairs. Why should Australia be represented on the War Cabinet when Canada, which has five Divisions, and New Zealand and South Africa, which each have one, are not similarly represented?'[42]*

It was Evatt, rather than Curtin, who was looked upon askance in London.

* The insistence of Mackenzie King, Prime Minister of Canada, his eye upon the United States, that existing Commonwealth consultative arrangements were entirely adequate, was one of the handicaps Australia had to face throughout the war.

Attlee, among others, thought that the Minister for External Affairs was conducting his aggressive diplomacy in part with a view to supplanting Curtin at the head of the Australian Government.[43] From Cross and the British political-warfare representative in Australia there also came reports that Evatt was 'entertaining grandiose ideas about Australia's future position in the South West Pacific and South East Asia', ideas which would involve, it seemed, Australia's becoming senior partner in a condominium to manage the Netherlands East Indies, obtaining a preponderant influence in Malaya, and securing a privileged economic position throughout the region. Within the Foreign Office, these 'wild ideas' were thought to be 'potentially dangerous', cutting across, as they did, the Office's inclination to work alongside the Netherlands in that part of the world.[44] (Rumours of such Australian ambitions also came to the ears of the Dutch themselves.)[45]* Moreover, Evatt trod on various toes, as was his wont, during his visit to London.[46]

Personalities apart, however, the Japanese threat in 1942 was only bringing into sharper focus developments and problems that had been in the making since even before the First World War, involving for Australia and New Zealand (although their attitudes were by no means identical in this context) a trend which was to reach its logical conclusion with the signing of the ANZUS Pact in 1951. During a crisis of world-wide proportions, it was to the United States, rather than to Britain, that these Dominions had to look for their security. And as the Pacific War Council in London passed, inevitably, from inconsequence into silence (the only meeting after 2 October 1942 was one on 4 August 1943),[47] the crisis in Anglo-Australian relations became interwoven with developments involving Australia and the United States.

In their moment of gravest danger, Australia and New Zealand obtained vital support from the Americans. They were, after all, as Admiral King put it in a note already quoted, 'white men's countries', which the United States must therefore defend against Japan in order to prevent adverse repercussions spreading 'among the non-white races of the world.'[48] In Washington, as Canberra and Wellington had desired, a Pacific War Council was set up in April 1942, where the two Dominions, together with other Allies, could meet with the Americans under the chairmanship of Roosevelt himself.

In the war zone, meanwhile, where the Pacific as a whole was now recognized as being a United States responsibility, Australia, together with the Philippines, most of the Netherlands East Indies, New Guinea and other islands, was allocated to the new Southwest Pacific Area, under the command of General MacArthur, who arrived in Melbourne in March to a hero's welcome. (New Zealand, to its disappointment, was placed within a separate, South Pacific Area, a sub-division of the Pacific Ocean Area under Admiral Nimitz, where the United States Navy took over responsibility for the defence of Fiji and Tonga, for example.)[49] As Australian diplomats keenly surveyed

* However ambiguous Evatt's position was vis-à-vis the Netherlands East Indies, he was nevertheless firm in his support for the idea that French possessions in the Far East and Pacific should revert to that country. (E.g. ADEA, A981 War/France/13.)

developments within the United States itself, watching, in particular, the standing of their country there,[50] so there arrived in the S.W.P.A., ready to fight alongside the Australians in New Guinea and elsewhere, a growing number of American servicemen: 89,000 by June 1942; 178,000 a year later; 511,000 by June 1944; 863,000 by June 1945.[51]*

There can be little doubt that these developments were accompanied by a widespread Australian desire for closer relations generally with the U.S.A. The Australian–American Cooperation Movement, for example, led by the press magnate Sir Keith Murdoch among others, embodied this attitude, while in 1943 Murdoch was to argue publicly that a United States interest in the area after the war—leading, he hoped, to an alliance with Australia— could be stimulated by granting Australian citizenship to American soldiers who fought there.[52] Meanwhile, in the combat areas (things were often rather different back in Australia itself) relations between men of the two countries were in many cases extremely good. As for the situation at the highest political level, MacArthur himself told his British liaison officer in October 1942

'that when he had reached Australia in March, Curtin had indicated to him that Australia was ready to shift over to the U.S. away from the British Empire, but that he (MacA.) had refused to listen to any such talk . . . His quotation of Curtin's remark is probably extravagant, but he —MacA.—has previously told me that Curtin and Co. more or less offered him the country on a platter when he arrived from the Philippines.'[53]

Certainly, relations between MacArthur and Curtin were soon established on a basis of mutual confidence and respect[54] (the Dutch in Australia were also impressed by MacArthur),[55] with the General joining his powerful voice to that of the Government in Canberra in urging that greatly increased reinforcements should be sent to his Command.[56] To the Australian Advisory War Council, he declared that, although 'a considerable body of opinion in the United States and the United Kingdom regarded the European theatre as the predominant one, to others, including himself, the Pacific was the real centre.'[57] In turn, moreover, the presence in Australia of someone of MacArthur's stature and temperament was itself enough to complicate further the already difficult relations between Canberra and London. Churchill found to his disquiet, for example, that the General was supplying Curtin with the estimates of military requirements which figured in the demands that the Australian Prime Minister sent to the British Government.[58] As Henry Stimson noted in his diary in Washington, '[MacArthur] is . . . really egging the Australians on to try to make the Australian theater the main theater of the war, and to postpone what we are trying to do in regard to fighting Hitler first . . . He has been doing it in a very disloyal way.'[59]

In addition, MacArthur was at one with members of the Government in

* New Zealand also contributed land, sea and air units to the Pacific war, but its main effort was made in the Mediterranean and, later, European theatres. (For a summary, see e.g. Lussington, *New Zealand and the United States*, 66ff.)

Canberra in being highly suspicious of any attempts on the part of London to establish links with his Command. Thus, as the present writer has set out at length elsewhere,[60] although the General got on extremely well with Lt. Colonel Gerald Wilkinson, the British liaison officer who had been with him since the campaign in the Philippines ('I hold him', cabled MacArthur to Marshall, 'in the highest personal and professional regard')[61]*, he came to regard Wilkinson's channel of communications with Churchill through the British Secret Intelligence Service (M.I.6.) as a barrier to his serving on the S.W.P.A. staff. Likewise, MacArthur and Curtin were both hostile to the presence of a small British Army and Air Force Liaison Staff which eventually arrived in Australia early in 1943 under the command of Major General R. H. Dewing.[62] (In the Pacific theatre, too, matters at this time were little better in the way of inter-Allied liaison.)[63]†

And yet, despite the rapidly growing ties between Australia and the United States in 1942, there were difficulties and limitations involved, some of which make it less surprising when one finds later that, by 1944, the Australians were tending to move back in a British direction. (This development was more to be expected where New Zealand was concerned, for, despite welcoming American protection, she had continued, in the words of one student of the subject, 'to view the United States with some reserve', with 'the Commonwealth association always looming larger than the American link.')[64] Essentially, the United States military presence in Australia was part of an independently-conceived strategy—first in connection with a supply route to the Philippines, then as a fall-back position and base for an eventual advance. MacArthur himself, not surprisingly, was pursuing a vision that was centred upon the interests of the United States as he saw them, having long been convinced, as noted earlier, that America's future and 'very existence' were 'irrevocably entwined with Asia and its island outposts . . ., Western civilization's last earth frontier.'[65] Now, as sensitive about his personal position as he was able, imaginative and given to self-dramatizing, he was bent upon redeeming the shame of defeat in the Philippines.

Indeed, there was more than simply defeat for MacArthur to wipe out. A belief in the staunch loyalty to the United States of the Filipinos was a

* So much for the statement put out by an official of the MacArthur Library (made, it seems, in response to a request from the State Department, which apparently was concerned at the possible effects on American–Australian relations of the present writer's articles indicating MacArthur's strong reservations about the quality of his Australian troops) that Wilkinson was virtually unknown and counted for nothing so far as MacArthur was concerned.

† Although Churchill offered a British aircraft carrier to work with the U.S. Navy in the Pacific—*Victorious* eventually went out—attempts to coordinate the activities of the American Fleet there and those of the British Eastern Fleet operating in the Indian Ocean scarcely got anywhere. Each side privately blamed the other. Admiral Sir James Somerville, commanding the Eastern Fleet, wrote to Admiral Sir Andrew Cunningham in Washington to emphasize his anxiety to help the Americans, but also his ignorance of their plans. Cunningham himself found Admiral King, at the head of the U.S. Navy, 'a determined non-collaborator.' King, meanwhile, privately deplored the inactivity of Somerville's Eastern Fleet and belittled the loan of the *Victorious*.

cardinal element in the American vision of the country's place, achievements and destiny in the Far East, as well as in the use of the Philippines case as a model for the European powers to follow. Yet early in 1942 it had been feared within the State Department that President Manuel Quezon of the Philippines might seek to come to an arrangement with the advancing Japanese.[66] Moreover, as the enemy's attack closed in, Quezon, bitter at the American failure to protect his people, had indeed gone so far as to propose to Roosevelt that the Philippines should be given immediate independence and allowed to make terms with the invader. Worse still, in the eyes of a horrified Stimson in Washington, MacArthur himself had gone 'more than half way towards supporting Quezon's position.' Thereupon, a draft reply which, it seems, had been drawn up within the President's entourage and which envisaged granting Quezon the right to surrender, had been hastily scrapped, and Stimson had helped Roosevelt to produce instead a message which, in the Secretary of War's own words, 'put our attitude to the Philippines upon a correct and elevated basis.' There would be no sudden independence, no separate surrender. The necessary myth was preserved: the Filipinos were loyal, steadfast and loving to the end. Now, however, with the colony lost to the enemy, it was all the more urgent for the United States, and for MacArthur personally, to redeem their position in Filipino eyes before independence actually came about.[67]

Not only was the United States eager to recover her own territory in the Pacific. Already there were those in Washington who were looking ahead to the need to secure new island bases after the war was over, bases that would ensure America's military supremacy and security, as well as facilitating the development of new commercial air routes. 'I think we should grab as many as possible', wrote William Bullitt to Roosevelt,[68] while the U.S. Navy were even now making plans for the military government of islands taken from the Japanese.[69] The President himself was keenly interested in the future of a strategically-placed territory like Clipperton Island, which was within range of the Panama Canal and which for the moment happened to belong to France. And while Roosevelt's own ideas at this time appear to have inclined towards giving sovereignty over various islands to the United Nations, there were others who were thinking in more strictly national terms.[70] For the moment, Australia was only too glad to see a growing American presence in the area, and at the end of the war she would still be anxious to have a United States screen across the Pacific between her and Japan. The time would come, however, when America's desire for bases and tendency to regard the future of Pacific territories as being hers to dispose of were to arouse disquiet and even opposition in Australian circles.

Meanwhile, in embracing MacArthur so closely the Australian Government was indirectly becoming involved in the complicated cross-currents of internal American political and military affairs. As a focus for those 'Pacific-first' sentiments which were especially strong among some sections of Roosevelt's opponents, MacArthur was already a potential force in American politics, and the idea of running him as a Republican candidate was being aired in some quarters during 1942. (This was one reason why some British officials thought it important to maintain close and friendly relations with the General.)[71] At the same time, in more strictly military and strategic terms, MacArthur's was only one of the contending factions that existed within American Army and Navy circles, and could thus by no means guarantee the success of Australian pleading in Washington.

Nor did the new comradeship in arms between Australia and the U.S.A. entirely enhance the former's standing in American eyes—just as there were instances of bad feeling in the reverse direction. During the bitter campaign to halt and force back the Japanese in New Guinea (a campaign in which the majority of Allied casualties were Australian), MacArthur sweepingly observed to his British liaison officer: 'Gerry, I tell you, these Australians won't fight.'[72] He likewise told one of his American commanders, Major General Eichelberger, 'They won't fight.'[73] Whether the General was referring to Australian troops or to their leaders in the field is not clear; a generally poor impression, however, filtered back to Government circles in Washington. Frank Knox, for example, Secretary of the Navy, noted privately that 'the Australians were not doing too well in New Guinea', and that they lacked initiative.[74] Stimson, for his part, wrote in his diary of 'the rather feeble efforts of the Australian divisions', and recorded General Arnold, Commander of the U.S. Army Air Force, and just back from a visit to MacArthur, as reporting: 'One of the most striking things in Port Moresby was that the Australians would not fight. As MacArthur put it, they were not good in the field, they were not good in the jungle, and they came from the slums of the cities in Australia and they had no fighting spirit.' Stimson also wrote that Roosevelt himself told his Cabinet in confidence that MacArthur had 'concealed that the work [in New Guinea] was really rescued by the Americans and let the credit go to the Australians so as to bolster up their morale.'[75]* (It is worth noting here that in 1943 British observers were to describe the American soldiers in the S.W.P.A. as 'very poor indeed', as compared to Australian 'first-class fighting men.' The view of General Dewing, head of the British liaison mission in Australia, was that MacArthur was 'working steadily to exclude the Australians from any effective hand in the control of land or air operations or credit in them, except as a minor element in a U.S. show.')[76]

In addition, there were Americans on the spot, in both official and non-official capacities, who, like some of their British counterparts,[77] thought that the Australian war effort left much to be desired. Such views were encouraged by, for example, the fierce industrial disputes, involving strikes, that continued to be a feature of the Australian scene, and by the fact that,

* One of the lighter moments that occurred during the minor storm created in Australia by the present writer's articles, which first revealed these private opinions of MacArthur and senior members of the Government in Washington, was supplied by a senior official of the U.S. Embassy in Canberra, who sought to rebut the above entries from private diaries, letters, etc. by citing MacArthur's *public* tributes to his Australian forces. (The *Australian*, 26 June 1974.)

unlike the volunteer Australian Imperial Force, the conscripts of the Australian Military Force could not be required to serve overseas. Thus, *Colliers Magazine* wished to publish an article in the United States—it was prevented from doing so by the intervention of General Marshall—which painted a savage portrait of poor Australian morale, of an army that lacked discipline, of hostility to American troops, and of crippling industrial anarchy among dockside workers in Sydney and elsewhere.[78]

More important still were the opinions formed by the American Minister to Australia, Nelson T. Johnson, which reached Washington through a series of letters that he wrote to Hornbeck in the State Department. Although he admired Curtin, Johnson was at times scathing about Evatt and other members of the Government, suggesting on occasions motives for their behaviour that even now were best not published. Above all, the Minister tended to be scornful of the average Australian, used to living 'like a parasite on the body of the Empire', having refused to spend adequate sums on defence preparations and yet now 'seeming to expect us to do everything for him, fight for him and work for him'; a creature incapable of seeing 'beyond his surfing beaches', isolationist and unable to face facts.[79] As for the experiences of American soldiers who found themselves in Australia, they, too, were not always conducive to improved relations between the two countries. 'It was regrettable but true', observed Sumner Welles to the State Department sub-committee on Political Problems, 'that the friendly sentiments of the United States people toward Australia have diminished since our troops arrived there. Personal friction has developed and it has hurt good feelings.'[80]

Meanwhile, the results of Australian appeals to Washington, and the outcome of Canberra's hopes of exerting influence there, were scarcely any more satisfactory on the whole than what had been achieved vis-à-vis London. The blustering Evatt tended to overplay his hand both before and during his visit to the United States, exasperating even his friend Frankfurter and encountering firm resistance in the persons of Stimson and Marshall.[81] 'You know how sensitive poor relations are', Frankfurter wrote to Roosevelt, 'and the Australians feel like poor relations. What is needed is to satisfy them psychologically.'[82] The President did his best in this direction, and obtained Churchill's blessing for him to issue an invitation to Curtin to visit Washington. But supplies of war materials to Australia were another matter, and had to be fitted into the global situation in that respect. Thus, Roosevelt rejected Canberra's requests for 100,000 American troops and 1,000 planes to be stationed in its country, which was to be regarded, Stimson and the War Department agreed, as 'a secondary theater.'[83]

At the same time, American officials recognized that, in political terms, United States relations with Australia were a delicate matter. (Johnson, for example, was to write in 1943 of the Dominion 'being pulled in two directions', between the British Empire, with which it had strong economic ties, and the U.S.A., whose protection it could not do without.)[84] In the main, moreover, Washington's response to this situation was to seek to avoid creating trouble with Britain where Australia was concerned, rather than to look for advantages in it for the United States. Thus, when Australia and New Zealand were first included within an American sphere of strategic and military responsibility, the ever-upright Marshall warned that 'care should be exercised vis-à-vis Great Britain in this regard', while the Advisory Committee on Post War Foreign Policy, when discussing the same subject, agreed that the preservation of the British Commonwealth and its internal ties was in the American interest.[85]

Although in the United States generally, as Halifax reported to the Foreign Office, public clashes between London and Canberra were taken as being further evidence that the Commonwealth and Empire (many Americans thought of these two different associations simply as one 'Empire') were falling apart,[86] Roosevelt himself was embarrassed by these episodes, urging that they should be cleared up and preferring to deal with London as agent for the Commonwealth as a whole, rather than with separate Dominions.[87] The President was likewise quick to try to prevent MacArthur from supplying Curtin with ammunition to use against Churchill over the question of military reinforcements.[88] In addition, the Washington Pacific War Council, so keenly sought after by Canberra and Wellington alike, soon turned out to be, in Halifax's phrase, 'merely a façade.' Its meetings were not attended by the American Chiefs of Staff, had no bearing on decision-making, and were taken up by Roosevelt, in his own words, 'telling stories and doing most of the talking.' The President, reported the Australian Minister in Washington to his Cabinet, 'always avoided critical issues.' Long before the end of the war, the Council's meetings were regarded by most of those taking part as a waste of time.[89]

Thus, Evatt's early hopes of achieving something approaching an over-riding American–Australia–New Zealand partnership, based on Washington, came to nothing.[90] At times, it is true, as over the issue of whether the 9th Australian Division should be moved from the Middle East, Canberra was able to feel that Roosevelt was more sympathetic in his approach than was Churchill. Essentially, however, Allied grand strategy continued to be made by the United States and Britain alone, with the 'Germany-first' decision remaining unaltered, despite its modification in practice, as we have seen, by the switching of large numbers of additional American forces to the fight against Japan, especially on Guadalcanal.

Australia's growing assertiveness and sense of independence had been demonstrated, and with them, the need to develop a new basis for relations between Canberra and London. It is difficult to feel, however, that, amid the pressures of war, many British politicians or officials appreciated this to any great extent. Cranborne was one exception. For Churchill, on the other hand, the clashes of 1942 seem to have been merely an unpleasant episode to be put behind him, rather than a lesson for the future. As we have seen, he remained unsympathetic to Australia's desire to have Cabinet-level representation in London, while he could rest easy in the knowledge that the United States herself was restricting any tendency on Canberra's part to stray in that direction. Lunching with Colonel Wilkinson in March 1943,

'Churchill chuckled rather grimly', as the latter recorded, 'at my reference to Australian political wanderings last year, and asked me if I knew what Washington's reply had been. I said I did, to which the P.M. replied, "Yes, they told them they would not have them."'[91]

By the time this conversation occurred, the threat to Australia was in any case well past its peak, the battles of Midway, Guadalcanal and Buna (in New Guinea) having been won. Even so, political difficulties between London and Canberra were to reappear. So, too, were problems arising from the presence in a Commonwealth area of an American figure of the size and complexity of MacArthur (described by Wilkinson to Churchill as 'ruthless, vain, unscrupulous and self-conscious ... but ... a man of real calibre, with a vivid imagination, a capacity to learn rapidly from the past, a leader of men ... [with] a considerable understanding of personalities and political development'). In addition, there were the strains created by the growing imbalance between the American and the British and Commonwealth shares of the war effort against Japan. Regardless of whose sovereignty had been exercised before the war over the territories involved,* it was the United States, led in the field by MacArthur and, to the north, Admiral Chester Nimitz, which was assuming by far the greater part of the burden.

In some ways, this last feature of the situation was welcome to a man like Admiral King at the head of the U.S. Navy, who wanted to get on with the job of avenging Pearl Harbour without being encumbered with inter-Allied command and consultation problems. It also fitted in with the fairly widespread American view that it was this struggle against Japan that was the country's 'real' war—'Ernie King's war', as it was sometimes called. Yet the possibilities of resentment, misunderstanding and friction were also present in this state of affairs. There were already those in the United States, for example, who were demanding to know why so much of their countrymen's blood should be shed on, say, Guadalcanal, when it was a British possession.† There were even stories circulating—they were without foundation—that

---

* A brief mention should be made of Portugal's involvement in the area, in the shape of Portuguese Timor. This territory had been occupied by Australian and Netherlands forces at the end of 1941 in order to forestall the Japanese there. Portuguese protests duly followed. (See Cabs, 19 Dec. 1941, CAB 65/20, and 5 Jan. 1942, CAB 65/25; FO 371, file 31734; *Hasluck*, II, 100–102.)

† Where New Caledonia was concerned (which was French, but vital for U.S. war-production as a result of its nickel deposits), a survey was drawn up by the U.S. Navy following difficulties that involved the local American Commander as well as rival French factions. This report, while justifying (and reasonably so) American activities on the island, added the following interesting observations: 'Many members of the American Armed Forces [there] have two ideas which lead them to conclude that the United States should take over New Caledonia. The first is that the Americans do things right while other people fumble along in an inefficient, haphazard manner—therefore everyone should want to be closely associated with the United States in order to be assured of a happy existence ... The second idea is that the Americans came over to the Pacific to fight someone else's war ... and that the people who have been saved owe everything to the United States.' ('Report on Franco-American Relations In New Caledonia', Admin.

Britain was charging the U.S.A. for every one of the palm trees destroyed during the battles for such islands. It was not difficult, therefore, for those who were in any case not particularly well-disposed towards Britain to assume that she was deliberately letting the United States take on the dirty work against Japan, while waiting to have her property handed back to her on a plate. Nor was it difficult to come to the conclusion that the American Government and people, having been left the task of beating Japan throughout the Pacific, should also, when the time came, dictate the peace in that part of the world.

True, Churchill was doing his best to make it clear that Britain would undertake her full share of the fight against the Japanese once Germany had been overcome. There remained those Americans, however, whom no amount of speeches could convert on this subject. Nor could Churchill defy the weight of circumstances, which ensured that, as it entered its post-Casablanca phase, the Far Eastern partnership between the two Western allies would remain an unbalanced one, and full of difficulties.

Hist., appendix 34 (10) (C), S.W. Pacific Area and Forces, USNOA. See also C. de Gaulle, *Mémoires de Guerre: L'Appel* (Paris, 1954), 189–91, and JCS, 16 March 1942, RG 218.)

Notes to Chapter Nine

1 See above, 4, 56.
2 See P. Hasluck, *The Government and the People*, vol. II (Canberra, 1972; hereafter, Hasluck, II), 71.
3 Hutchinson to State Dept., 12 Jan. 1942, Hornbeck Papers, box 22.
4 Johnson to FDR, 12 Oct. 1942, ibid, box 262.
5 Wilkinson Journal, 29 Oct. 1942.
6 E.g. WP(42)67, CAB 66/21.
7 See, in general, Butler, *Grand Strategy*, III, Part II, 429ff.
8 WP(42)34, CAB 66/21; see *Churchill*, IV, cap. 1 and 136ff.
9 *Hasluck*, II, 39.
10 DC(Ops.), 31 Dec. 1941, CAB 69/2.
11 Cab, 29 Dec. 1941, CAB 65/20; WP(41)307, CAB 66/20; COS, 'Arcadia', 26 and 27 Dec. 1941, CAB 99/17; FRUS, Washington and Casablanca, 109.
12 E.g. FRUS, Washington and Casablanca, 306, 321; van Kleffens to Loudon, 4 Jan. 1942, NFM, Londens archief, DZ, D31a, E.1. 18 (13).
13 E.g. Cab, 23 Feb. 1942, CAB 65/25; *Hasluck*, II, 73ff.
14 E.g. WP(42)119, CAB 66/22; *Hasluck*, II, 169ff.
15 E.g. Cab, 23 March 1942, CAB 65/25; ADEA, A981/War/Casey; Lord Casey, *Personal Experience, 1939–46* (London, 1962), 93ff.
16 E.g. Australian Govt. to Sec. of State, Dominions Affairs, 2 Jan. 1943, ADEA, A989/43/735/221; material in ibid, A989/43/735/1021.
17 See DNZ, III, passim; material in PREM 3, 151/3; and, on New Zealand's continuing sense of loyalty to Britain and the Commonwealth, M.P. Lussington, *New Zealand and the United States, 1840–1944* (Wellington, 1972), 23, 49, 97.
18 Cabs, 4 and 21 May 1942, CAB 65/26; PREM 3, 163/6; *Hasluck*, II, 175ff.
19 Robinson to Evatt, 18 May 1942, Evatt Papers, Robinson file.
20 Evatt to Frankfurter, 22 Feb. 1942, Frankfurter Papers, box 53.
21 Johnson to Hornbeck, 11 March 1942, Hornbeck Papers, box 262. On Evatt, see A. Watt, *Australian Diplomat* (Sydney, 1972), 49.

22 PREM 3, 142/7; Roosevelt Papers, MR box 12.
23 Cab, 22 Jan. 1942, CAB 65/20; DNZ, III, 150; AAWC, 30 Jan. 1942. A2682, vol. IV.
24 AWC, 21 Jan. 1942, A2673, vol. X.
25 DNZ, II, 142ff.; ibid, III, 141ff.; material in PREM 3, 145/4 and 5.
26 DS, 740.0011 P.W./2715.
27 Australia's Pacific-first inclinations did not prevent Evatt and others from being highly critical of China. E.g. Johnson to Hornbeck, 9 Nov. 1942, Hornbeck Papers, box 262.
28 Alexander Papers, box 5/6.
29 WP(42)29, CAB 66/21. See Cab, 20 Dec. 1941, CAB 65/20.
30 Hardinge to WSC, 22 Jan. 1942, PREM 3, 167/1; Hughes to WSC, 30 May 1942, PREM 4, 50/6.
31 Cross to Dominions Office, 27 March 1942, PREM 4, 50/6.
32 WSC to Curtin, 20 March 1942, PREM 3, 165.
33 Material in PREM 3, 151/2 and 4, 150/7; PREM 4, 50/8; Cabs, 4 and 21 May 1942, CAB 65/26.
34 Cab, 29 Dec. 1941, CAB 65/20; Moran, 21; WSC minute, 30 Jan. 1942, PREM 4, 50/7.
35 Cadogan Diaries, 19 Jan. 1942.
36 C. Thorne, 'MacArthur, Australia and the British', Australian Outlook, April 1975.
37 Material in PREM 4, 50/6 and 7; WP(42)33, CAB 66/21.
38 Pownall, 25 Feb. 1942.
39 COS, 27 Jan. 1942 (CAB 79/17); 17 March 1942 (CAB 79/19); 1 April 1942 (CAB 79/20); Ismay to WSC, 9 May 1943, PREM 4, 50/8.
40 Material in PREM 3, 150/3, 5; 151/1; and in CAB 69/4.
41 See Edwards, Bruce of Melbourne, 337ff.
42 Bruce–WSC and Attlee–Cranborne–WSC correspondence, PREM 4, 50/1; Bruce to Evatt, 27 May 1942, Evatt Papers, War/Cab/Aust. Participation.
43 Attlee to WSC, 25 June 1942, PREM 3, 150/7.
44 FO 371, U1909/828/70; F7601 and 8361/2000/61; F4533/90/61; C. Thorne, 'Engeland, Australië en Nederlands Indië, 1941–1945', Internationale Spectator (The Hague), August 1975.
45 Van der Plas report, 29 Dec. 1942, NFM, van Kleffens Papers, VI/23. See unpublished Ph.D. thesis (A.N.U.) of M. George, 'Australian Attitudes and Policies Towards the Netherlands East Indies and Indonesian Independence, 1942–1949'; hereafter 'George Ph.D.'.
46 Wilkinson Journal, 15 April 1943.
47 Minutes in CAB 99/26; Material in PREM 3, 165 and 167/3; Cadogan Diaries, 21 Oct. 1942.
48 King to FDR, 5 March 1942, King Papers, series I, box 2, USNOA.
49 E.g. DNZ, III, 191, 318ff.
50 E.g. material in Watt Papers, MS 3788.
51 Hasluck, II, 218ff.; also Kirby, II, and R. L. Eichelberger, Our Jungle Road To Tokyo (New York, 1950).
52 WP(43)170, CAB 66/36.
53 Wilkinson Journal, 19 Oct. 1942.
54 Hasluck, II, 114; correspondence in MacArthur Papers, RG 4; MacArthur to Marshall, 31 March 1942, Roosevelt Papers, PSF box 4.
55 See FO 371, F3212/415/61.
56 E.g. MacArthur to Curtin, 12 May 1942, and MacArthur to Marshall, 8 May 1942, MacArthur Papers, RG 4.
57 AAWC, 26 March 1942, A2682, vol. IV.
58 Material in PREM 3, 151/1.
59 Stimson Diary, 13 May 1942.
60 C. Thorne, 'MacArthur, Australia and the British, 1942–1943', Australian Outlook, April and August, 1975.
61 MacArthur to Marshall, 24 Aug. 1942, MacArthur Papers, RG 4.

62 Thorne, 'MacArthur, Australia and the British', loc. cit., and MacArthur to JCS, 2 Oct. 1942, MacArthur Papers, RG 4.
63 Somerville to Cunningham, 9 Oct. 1942, Cunningham Papers, BM, Add. 52563; Cunningham to Pound, 12 Aug. 1942, ibid, Add. 52561; WSC–FDR correspondence, Dec. 1942, PREM 3, 470; Halifax Diary, 25 Aug. 1942; King to Marshall, 7 April 1943, King Papers, series I, box 2, USNOA; JCS, 14 Jan. 1943, RG 218. In general, see Roskill, *The War At Sea* (hereafter, *Roskill*), vol. II, 229ff. WSC also believed the Eastern Fleet to have been unnecessarily inactive, but the official historian finds Somerville's behaviour justified. Iibd, 237.
64 Lussington, *New Zealand and the United States*, 37, 97.
65 See above, 12.
66 FRUS, 1942, I, 883.
67 Ibid, 888–900; Stimson Diary, 9 Feb. 1942; draft reply to Quezon in Roosevelt Papers, PSF box 4.
68 Bullitt to FDR, 17 Dec. 1942, Roosevelt Papers, PSF box 12.
69 D. E. Richard, *United States Naval Administration of the Trust Territories of the Pacific Islands* (Washington D.C., 1957), vol. I, cap. III.
70 Material in Roosevelt Papers, MR box 162; Dixon reports of PWC(W), 8 Jan. 1943 and 2 April 1943, ADEA, A989/43/735/251; Taussig memo., 26 Oct. 1942, DS, Hickerson files, box 2.
71 *Pogue*, I, 374; Hassett, *Off The Record With F.D.R.*, 88; Thorne, 'MacArthur, Australia and the British', loc. cit.
72 Wilkinson Journal, 19 Oct. 1942.
73 J. Luvaas (ed.), *Dear Miss Em.* (Westport, Conn., 1972), 31.
74 Knox to Mrs. Knox, 9 Sept. 1942, Knox Papers, box 3.
75 Stimson Diary, 22 Sept., 3 and 29 Oct. 1942.
76 Somerville Diary, 31 Dec. 1943; Dewing to Wilkinson, 10 Feb. 1943, Wilkinson Papers. See Luvaas, *Dear Miss Em.*, 33.
77 Thorne, 'MacArthur, Australia and the British', loc. cit.
78 Marshall to Hopkins, 5 Oct. 1942, Hopkins Papers, box 133. For a fuller description, see C. Thorne, 'Evatt, Curtin and the United States', Melbourne *Age*, 31 May and 1 June 1974. On Australian dockside strikes, see *Roskill*, II, 421. And see King and Whitehill, *Fleet Admiral King*, 161.
79 Johnson–Hornbeck letters, passim, Hornbeck Papers, box 262. For a fuller account, see C. Thorne, 'Australia and the Americans: Letters From The Minister', Melbourne *Age*, 8 and 9 Jan. 1975.
80 Sub-committee on Political Problems, 12 Dec. 1942, DS, Notter files, box 55.
81 Stimson Diary, 17 and 23 March 1942; *Pogue*, I, 372; Frankfurter to Hopkins, 9 March 1942, Frankfurter Papers, box 53.
82 Frankfurter to FDR, 30 March 1942, Frankfurter Papers, box 98.
83 FDR to WSC, 28 May 1942, PREM 3, 470; Stimson Diary, 6 March 1942; *Matloff and Snell*, 217–21.
84 Johnson to Hornbeck, 27 Nov. 1943, Hornbeck Papers, box 262.
85 JCS, 9 March 1942, RG 218; sub-committee on Political Problems, 12 Dec. 1942, DS, Notter files, box 55.
86 E.g. FO 371, A2963/31/45.
87 FDR to WSC, 23 March 1942, PREM 3, 470; see FRUS, Washington and Casablanca, 287.
88 FDR to MacArthur, 6 May 1942, MacArthur Papers, RG 4.
89 FO 371, A6050G; Roosevelt Letters, 17 June 1942; Halifax to Eden, 23 April 1942, Hickleton Papers, A4.410.4; AWC, 12 May 1942, A2673, vol. XIII; AAWC, 13 May 1943, A2682, vol. VI; *Hasluck*, II, 228.
90 Evatt to Hopkins, 31 March 1942, Hopkins Papers, box 308.
91 Wilkinson Journal, 15 March 1943.

PART THREE

Casablanca to Cairo
January 1943 to December 1943

CHAPTER TEN

THE SETTING

It was now the turn of the Allies to move over to the offensive against Germany and Italy. In battles such as those of the Kursk salient in July 1943, retaking Kharkov, Kiev and in all 140,000 square miles during the year, the Soviet forces dealt the Germans heavy blows. Meanwhile the Western Allies, although they failed to establish a new front in North-west Europe, were subjecting Germany itself to round-the-clock bombing, and —vitally—were beginning at last to overcome the U-boat menace in the Atlantic. In May, victory was completed in Tunis—a reminder, in Marshall's words to Churchill, of the severe injury which was being done to the Axis cause by 'the ability of our two nations . . . to work and fight as a team.'[1] ('It is as well to remember', writes one of the British official historians, 'that the area of [Anglo-American] consent remained larger than the area of dispute, and that even when the partners differed they remained close partners.')[2] Sicily fell in July. In the same month, Mussolini was deposed, and in September, when the Allies began to fight their way up from the toe of Italy, that country surrendered.

This gathering pace of success and the development of new, offensive strategic plans did not put an end to the divisions that existed between, for example, the U.S. Army and Navy.[3] Nor did the achievement of inter-Allied teamwork preclude serious strains arising between the British and the Americans, strains which were apparent during the major conferences of the period, in Washington in May, in Quebec in August, and in Cairo, then Tehran, then Cairo again at the end of November and early December. On the American side, the belief remained widespread that Britain was fighting a 'political' war, and was seeking to manoeuvre the United States within that context. 'Most American military men', wrote Stilwell's political adviser, 'think of the war as a soldier's job to be done . . . as soon as possible with a minimum of fuss over international political and economic issues . . . To our allies, the conduct of the war is a function of overall political and economic policy. Military logic is therefore always subordinated to and sometimes violated in favour of political and economic considerations.'[4] '[The British] swarmed down upon us like locusts', observed one of the United States planners after Casablanca, '. . . to insure that they not only accomplished their purpose but did so in stride and with fair promise of continuing in their role of directing strategically the course of the war.'[5]

Meanwhile, from the West coast of the U.S.A., Isaiah Berlin was reporting to London the existence there of 'very widespread suspicion of our post-war intentions . . . [where] it is thought we must have many an ace up our sleeve.'[6]

As was to be expected, a newspaper like the *Chicago Tribune* was also trumpeting such views.[7] In addition, however, Senator Vandenberg and other members of a sub-committee of the Senate Foreign Relations Committee, men who were certainly less Anglophobe than the *Tribune*, were anxiously probing Marshall in order to find out just how far Britain was, indeed, making America's decisions for her.[8] Moreover, Roosevelt himself expounded to the Joint Chiefs of Staff his belief that political motives lay behind Britain's desire to see France become a major power once more, behind her proposals concerning zones of occupation in Germany, her strategy in Southeast Asia, her manoeuvring to secure control of Abyssinia, and her schemes, devised by the Foreign Office, involving the future of the Balkans. In the same vein, the President warned against allowing Britain to 'get [the United States] roped into accepting any European spheres of influence.'[9]

Mediterranean affairs, especially, provided a focal point for these American suspicions. 'Some of our officers', noted Admiral Leahy in his diary, 'have a fear that Great Britain is desirous of confining allied military effort in Europe to the Mediterranean area in order that England may exercise control thereof, regardless of what the terms of peace may be', and subsequently the President's Chief of Staff took such an interpretation to be proven.[10] From the Balkans and North Africa, reports came in to Roosevelt and to Hopkins of fears of British imperialist ambitions on the part of local peoples, in contrast to the high, unsullied reputation of the United States.[11] The British, wrote the Anglophile Stimson privately, were 'straining every nerve to lay a foundation throughout the Mediterranean area for their own empire after the war is over.'[12]

In actual fact, Churchill's main concern at this time was, in the words of the official strategic historian, centred upon 'the desirability of continuing to provide employment and glory for British arms', a cause for which the Mediterranean provided more ample opportunities than did, say, the Bay of Bengal or North-west Europe.[13] And although in London Amery, for one, was indeed hankering after 'a Monroe doctrine [for Britain] covering the Middle East and the countries round the Indian Ocean',[14] the Chiefs of Staff, for their part, were 'coldly professional' in their approach to the question of where the Mediterranean should stand in Allied strategy. Nevertheless, the outcome, apparent both at and in between the conferences named above, was a considerable degree of tension between the C.O.S. and the J.C.S., with Marshall in particular, of the Joint Chiefs, fearing that Mediterranean operations would become a 'suction pump', drawing off resources from the build-up for a cross-Channel invasion (scheduled, after Quebec, for the beginning of May 1944).[15] As arguments swirled around such topics as the allocation of scarce landing-craft and schemes like that

of Churchill's for an assault on Rhodes, Roosevelt observed in exasperation
to the Joint Chiefs: 'The British look upon the Mediterranean as an area
under British domination.'[16]

Other senior men in Washington emphasized what they saw as a British
war-weariness and reluctance to face a major operation such as the cross-
Channel one. 'The shadow of Passchendael and Dunkerque still hangs too
heavily over the imagination of [their] leaders', wrote Stimson to the
President after visiting London.[17] All the more reason, then, for insisting
upon American leadership, and doubly so in that such a development would
assuage the fear of the American public that the U.S.A. was being manipulated by subtle Europeans. Thus, Stimson urged upon Roosevelt that 'our
only hope of carrying the United States into a post-war organization such
as we all hope for will be by having the people realize that this whole war has
been run from Washington.'[18]

This shift in emphasis, away from the idea of equal partnership and
towards that of United States pre-eminence, begins to be discernible in a
number of American quarters during this period—nothwithstanding the
recognition by Stimson among others that Churchill was still in some ways
the foremost public spokesman for the alliance,[19] and notwithstanding the
chaos which continued to surround Roosevelt's politico-strategic direction
of affairs, by comparison with the machinery which was operating in
Whitehall.[20] Thus, for example, at Cairo Harry Hopkins talked privately of
the U.S. as now being 'the senior partner.'[21] 'In the autumn of 1943', writes
Ronald Lewin, 'the course of events was transforming Churchill's role . . .
The days when [he] could initiate and impose his private strategic concepts
had ended. American predominance and Russia's increasing self-confidence
remained prime factors until the end of the war.'[22] Moreover, as Ian Jacob
(then Military Assistant Secretary to the British War Cabinet) was to put it
later, the evident determination of Roosevelt not to be tied by the British
when it came to negotiating with the Russians 'went clean against
[Churchill's] concept of the English-speaking peoples as a combined force
for good in the future world.'[23]

Hence the Prime Minister's alarm when the President proposed that he,
Roosevelt, should meet Stalin à deux, and, when that idea had been aban-
doned, that nothing should be done which Stalin could interpret as a sign
that the British and Americans were 'ganging up on him.'[24] Whereas
Churchill—although there were waverings to come—was beginning to
foresee 'grave troubles' with the Soviet Union,[25] the hopes at this time of
Roosevelt and those around him were epitomized by the outlook of Averell
Harriman, later a leading cold-warrior, who proclaimed himself to the
President 'a confirmed optimist in our relations with Russia because of my
conviction that Stalin wants, if obtainable, a firm understanding with you
and America more than anything else.'[26] And although Roosevelt himself
did at times express concern about possible Soviet post-war attitudes, he
also, if William Bullitt is to be believed, assured the latter privately that
'if I give [Stalin] everything I possibly can and ask nothing from him in

return, noblesse oblige, he won't try to annex anything and will work with me for a world of democracy and peace.'[27] Cordell Hull came away from the Moscow Conference of Foreign Ministers in October 1943 with a similar optimism, privately belittling the part which Eden had played in the talks.[28]

Thus, at Tehran, Churchill (who had earlier been concerned at the prospect of Roosevelt and Beaverbrook working together for the speedy opening of a Second Front) had to watch the President put Stalin in the position of arbiter between differing British and American strategies; likewise, the President made a point of siding with the Soviet ruler against the Prime Minister in the banter which surrounded the business of the Conference.[29] 'I thank the Lord that Stalin was there', wrote Stimson in his diary back in Washington. '. . . He brushed aside the diversionary attempts of the Prime Minister with a vigor which rejoiced my soul.'[30] Soon afterwards, Henry Morgenthau, too, was at work on his diary, in order to record that

'The Roosevelt–Stalin axis is gaining strength and the Roosevelt–Churchill axis is losing strength in about equal ratio. That is the opinion of Leo Crowley [the administrator of Lend Lease] and it is based on what the President said at the Cabinet meeting right after his return [from Tehran and Cairo] . . . "If I were going to write a story I'd certainly say that Roosevelt had to play the role of peacemaker both at Cairo and Tehran", Crowley said, "and that he thoroughly relished the role. There could be no mistaking that, the way he talked at the Cabinet meeting . . . Of course Roosevelt was in a commanding position at both conferences because back of him he had our enormous industrial output, which our allies think of in terms of lend lease . . . But it was perfectly obvious that the President is very much impressed with Stalin and not quite so much impressed as he has been with Churchill . . ."'

Morgenthau later showed this entry to Roosevelt. The latter did not contradict what Crowley had said.[31]

The shifting balance and consequent strains in the Anglo-American partnership will be examined further below. Before leaving the question of relations with third parties, however, we should note that there were implications in terms of the Far East in the Soviet Union's growing stature, especially in the light of Stalin's assurance, given to an excited Hull during the Moscow Conference, that he would join in the war against Japan once Germany had been defeated.[32] Likewise, there were Far Eastern implications involved in the question of the future status of France. Here, at least, Churchill and Roosevelt continued to find common ground in their strong reactions to the behaviour of de Gaulle.[33] And yet, as the President observed to his Chiefs of Staff (his own estimate was that France 'would certainly not again become a first-class power for at least twenty years'),[34] the British were far more committed than were the Americans to restoring the position of that country in the world, 'a sacred duty', as Churchill described it in the House of Commons.[35] And whilst the Foreign Office continued to take a more Francophile and pro-Gaullist line than the Prime Minister,[36] American officials still distrusted what London was up to—'The British Government seems determined to exploit de Gaulle at our expense', wrote Leahy—and blamed the Foreign Office in particular for refusing to keep in step with the United States.[37] The contrast in tone between the British and American official statements, issued in August, regarding the position of the French Committee of National Liberation—the British one sympathetic and positive, the American grudging and restricted[38]—underlined a general difference of approach which we shall see repeated in the particular case of Indochina and the question of the French title to that territory.

Various possible consequences for the Far East—involving, for example, the post-war positions there of China and the U.S.S.R., and the future of dependent territories—also arose out of ideas which were being developed during 1943 as regards the world order that was expected or desired to emerge from the existing conflict. In this respect, the Four Power declaration, issued from Moscow in the name of the Soviet Union, the United States, Britain, and, significantly, China, marked a major step forward, envisaging, as it did, 'a general international organisation . . . for the maintenance of international peace and security.'[39] A great deal of public debate was also taking place on such matters in the United States, where even the Republican Party was moving towards an endorsement of the idea of America's involvement in an international body of this kind.[40] Within American official circles, however, there remained disagreement and uncertainty. For example, State Department drafts involving a central, world-wide body did not square with Roosevelt's emphasis at the time upon the 'four policemen', who would operate on an essentially regional basis.[41] In London, too, the ideas being developed by Jebb and others in the Foreign Office ran up against Churchill's notion of separate, regional councils and his emphasis upon the overriding role of the Anglo-American special relationship.[42]

The need for a continuing and close Anglo-American partnership, a 'fraternal association', as he called it, lay indeed at the heart of the Prime Minister's thinking. He revealed as much to his American listeners in a speech at Harvard in September,[43] and developed the idea over lunch at the White House, extolling 'Anglo-Saxon superiority' as he did so.[44] Some of those in the United States who heard him were inclined in a similar direction. Stimson, for one, believed that it was essential 'to continue after the war the same controls as have saved us during the war, namely close association between the English-speaking countries.'[45] A study produced by the Yale Institute of International Studies likewise argued that only the most intimate Anglo-American relations could provide the basis for an international security system, while Walter Lippmann among others was prepared to contemplate even an Anglo-American alliance as a major feature of the post-war scene.[46] Needless to say, however, there were others in the United States who reacted with suspicion and hostility to any such ideas. 'We are not going backwards into the British Empire as inferiors', warned the

Chicago Tribune after Churchill's Harvard speech, and the *Washington Times* and others agreed.

Fears of this kind, involving the idea that Britain might seek somehow to take over the United States, are all the more remarkable in retrospect when seen against the background of a British power that was in sharp decline relative to that of the U.S.A.—a state of affairs that again was a factor of major significance where the Far Eastern war was concerned. It is true that the British Empire in 1943 still had more divisions in fighting contact with the enemy than did the United States;[47] true, also, that Britain's effort, if measured in war expenditure as a percentage of national income, was ahead of that of its more powerful ally.[48] Nor must it be forgotten that the Americans, too, were having their problems in the area of manpower, for example.[49] Moreover, Britain's difficulties at this stage were not so overwhelming, or at least were not seen as such, to rule out optimism over the future. 'I am not at all sure', wrote Gladwyn Jebb in the Foreign Office in April 1943, 'that I accept the thesis that our relative power [his interpretation of the term 'power' was somewhat superficial] will have declined at the end of the war . . . For instance, our greatest enemy—Germany—will we hope have been defeated, and Japan and Italy as well should be out of action for a long time to come. In addition, the Soviet Union will have been seriously weakened economically, if not militarily.'[50]

Nevertheless, in 1943 Britain was reaching the boundary of her manpower resources, with mobilization coming to its peak in September. 'The limits of population', writes an official historian, 'both determined and reflected the limits of the war effort, and affected strategic thought.'[51] The decision was taken, therefore, to make a maximum effort in 1944; thereafter, however—and this was obviously decisive where the Far East was concerned—the country would be increasingly dependent upon the Americans:

> 'Our manpower is now fully mobilised for the war effort', Cherwell wrote to Churchill in October. 'We cannot add to the total; on the contrary it is already dwindling. All we can do is to make within that total such changes as the strategy of the war demands . . . If the war with Germany continues after the end of 1944 we shall have to rely increasingly on U.S. resources to make up for the declining scale of our own war effort.'[52]

Britain's shipping resources and stocks of raw materials were also seriously inadequate. In the spring, the U.K. stockpile of food, raw materials and petroleum reached its lowest level throughout the entire war. Earlier still in 1943, sailings to the Indian Ocean for the Far and Middle Eastern theatres had had to be cut by half, thus gravely affecting not only the economies but also the political stability of some of the major territories concerned.[53] Meanwhile, in purely military terms, the vast resources of the United States were already beginning to overshadow those of Britain, for example in the matter of shipbuilding. By 1944 the U.S. Navy would be roughly three times the size of the Royal Navy, with nearly one hundred American aircraft carriers of various sizes ranging the Pacific by August of that year.

Where the ultimate weapon of the war was concerned, also, the junior status of Britain was by now apparent. 'The truth was', writes the historian of the atomic-bomb project, 'that the British [by mid-1943] were increasingly conscious that, in the absence of American cooperation, Tube Alloys [the code name for the bomb] could not be pursued as a war-time British project, for the war in Europe was sure to finish before an independent plant was working.'[54] Moreover, Roosevelt had to be pushed by Churchill and Hopkins before he signed an agreement at Quebec for full collaboration between the two countries in this field, and even then there remained those in important positions on the American side who were not in favour of a total exchange of information with the British. (Suspicion still existed that the latter's interest lay mainly in the commercial development of nuclear energy after the war. In fact, the concern of those in London who were a party to the secret was, in Sir John Anderson's words, that 'we cannot afford after the war to face the future without this weapon and rely entirely on America, should Russia or some other power develop it.')[55]

Above all, it was by now evident—although Churchill was angered when Oliver Lyttelton dared to use the term[56]—that Britain after the war would be a debtor state. Yet even so, the full extent of the crisis that the country would have to face was not yet known, and there was disconcerting evidence to suggest that in Washington, particularly, there existed a tendency to overlook the magnitude of the problems that were gathering. For example, after some internal wrangling the United States Administration argued that a ceiling of $1 billion should be placed upon Britain's gold and dollar reserves, given the Lend Lease aid that was being sent across the Atlantic. What it amounted to, as Kolko has pointed out, was that the United States wished 'to keep [Britain] neither too weak nor too strong at the same time as it invaded prewar British markets and made direct efforts to break into the colonies.'[57] In vain did Churchill remonstrate that, while gold and dollar reserves in London were, indeed, increasing at the rate of $600 million per annum, the net position, taking into account liabilities (the largest of which was the mounting debt to India), was a decrease of $3 billion per annum.[58]

Even more alarming to the British Government was the growing talk in the United States—talk that Roosevelt did not attempt to oppose openly— of the need for Britain to repay eventually at least some of the Lend Lease aid she was receiving.[59] 72 per cent of those Americans questioned in April 1943 believed that this restitution should be made, and papers like the *Chicago Tribune* were loud in the same cause.[60] Five members of the Senate added to such demands by reporting, after a tour of various war zones, that Britain was misusing Lend Lease goods,[61] whilst in private Patrick Hurley, on a mission to the Middle East for Roosevelt, declared that the British were 'using American lend lease and American troops not for the purpose of creating a brave new world based on the Atlantic Charter and the four freedoms, but for British conquest, British imperial rule and British trade monopoly.'[62] To his Cabinet colleagues in London, Richard Law emphasized: 'There is unfortunately little doubt that the Administration is being forced . . . to put Lend Lease back on to [a repayment] kind of basis. In short, the War Debts issue is being revived, and unless steps are taken to kill it, [it] will poison all our relations with the United States as it poisoned them in the period between the two wars.'[63] It was largely for this reason that the Government published a White Paper showing how extensive was the reciprocal aid being furnished by Britain to the U.S.A.[64] Meanwhile, on the related subject of article 7 of the Mutual Aid Agreement and post-war trade policies, informal and preliminary talks were held with the Americans;[65] but continuing splits over this issue within the British Government—involving, as before, Amery and Beaverbrook among others—ensured that there remained little prospect of an early agreement being reached.[66]

Whatever the question arising between London and Washington, however, Britain's inferior position over-all was increasingly preventing her from being able to adopt an intransigent attitude in the long run. ('Our lack of bargaining power at any time', Churchill's assistant, Major Desmond Morton, was to recall after the war, 'was . . . because we were broke.') This situation was reflected, for example, over the matter of the regulation of the sale of rubber, on which American dislike of the existing International Rubber Agreement—a dislike now backed by the possession of a formidable synthetic industry—deterred the British Government from renewing that Agreement as had at first been intended.[67] The same was true over Middle East oil, over which some eager eyes in Washington were being cast, and where American intentions seemed to point towards a demand for 'Open Door' principles to be recognized—until the U.S.A. herself was securely installed in, say, Saudi Arabia, whereupon the door would be shut.[68] The most that Britain felt able to do in this connection was to delay replying to Washington's suggestion that informal talks should be held on the subject.[69] Or again, over the future of civil aviation, despite the readiness of some British officials for a showdown as regards what Cherwell called 'Pan American infiltration in the immediate post-war period',[70] and despite a tendency even within the State Department to see Britain's position as being a strong one,[71] the general conclusion in London was the one expressed by the Secretary of State for Air, Sir Archibald Sinclair: that some form of arrangement was desirable since 'in the immediate post-war period our bargaining power vis-à-vis the U.S.A. would be small.'[72]

In these circumstances, there continued, not surprisingly, to be grudging talk in some British quarters of American economic imperialism and general high-handedness. One civil servant, for example—it was Douglas Jay, who was to be a post-war President of the Board of Trade—prophesied that Britain would find herself after the war driven 'to line up with Western Europe in a combination against American Imperialism.'[73]* 'The Yanks', wrote Grigg to his father from the War Office, '. . . are busily engaged in laying the foundations for post-war commercial penetration.'[74] Likewise, Sir John Pratt suggested to a Far East Group at Chatham House that in the

* There is, of course, some irony in the remark in the light of Jay's subsequent fierce opposition to Britain's membership of the E.E.C.

United States 'the old die-hard isolationists will come back into power towards the end of the war . . . as a new style of American imperialism, economic imperialism.'[75] 'American big business—American imperialism as it is now beginning to be called', remarked another speaker at Chatham House, '. . . constitutes perhaps the greatest threat of all to Anglo-American relations in the post-war era.'[76] Guy Wint, a civil servant who specialized in Indian affairs, speculated for his part that 'in an organisation such as Pan-American Airways, there may possibly be reborn the ideas and methods of the East India Company and the chartered corporations of Africa. Their aims will be economic, their ambitions to enjoy commercial power without administrative responsibility.'[77] As for the Embassy in Washington, it reported that during the first quarter of 1943 'a fairly clear imperialist line' had emerged in the United States in the shape of public demands for post-war bases and commercial advantages. Later in the year, the Embassy added that 'an imperialism which demands economic privilege without political responsibility is a common ground on which Isolationists . . . and realistic Nationalists . . . can meet, mobilise and manoeuvre.'[78]

Resentment against the United States also found expression in Parliament during this period. 'We are not fighting . . . against the tyranny of the industrial rings of Central Europe', one M.P. declared, 'in order to submit after the war to any thraldom by Pan American Airways . . .'[79] Among the public, too, there existed a certain coolness towards the U.S.A. (only one-third of those questioned by Mass Observation gave a favourable opinion of Americans),[80] even though Roosevelt received warm tributes in the press.[81] Sour feelings were again to be heard within the Cabinet itself. 'Hostility, jealousy, and general touchiness against the Americans are painfully evident among my colleagues', wrote Law, and he added on another occasion that the Chancellor of the Exchequer was one of those who argued that since the Democrats would not retain power after the Presidential election of 1944, 'it is hardly worth while doing anything to attract the old Administration because it won't be there when we need it.' Law also observed that he had 'heard some very strange people [in Government circles] denouncing "appeasement" of the Americans—people certainly who ought to be good judges of appeasement since they practised it so faithfully in days gone by.'[82] As for Eden, who visited the United States in the spring in order to try to establish closer relations between the Foreign Office and the State Department, Law found him to be 'in a constant state of irritation with the Americans', though he did agree on 'the overwhelming importance of Anglo-American relations.'[83] After his talks with Roosevelt, Hull and others in Washington, the Foreign Secretary told the Heads of British and Commonwealth Missions there that while 'the Administration seemed anxious to cooperate with Great Britain . . . he could not help entertaining some doubts about the cooperation being realised, having regard to the difficulties existing in the United States.'[84]

One person who, at the end of 1943, expressed to Churchill his anxieties about the state of transatlantic relations was Richard Casey, formerly

Australian Minister in Washington and now, it will be recalled, Britain's Minister of State in the Middle East. 'I do not believe', he wrote, 'that Anglo-American relations are "good" now', and he continued:

> I believe that a vast number of the American people (probably enough to control the American electorate in normal times) has wholly wrong ideas about "the British", i.e. they believe, for a variety of reasons, that the people of the United Kingdom are old-fashioned, class-conscious, super-cilious, patronising and imperialistic, and look down their noses at honest-to-God Americans . . .
>
> I do not believe in the sentimental approach . . . The British and Americans are *different* people and we do not naturally understand one another. I believe that the real basis of collaboration must be our political common interests . . . Until a generation ago we ran the world. Now the job is too big for us alone. We want their cooperation. But we cannot have our cake and eat it too . . . We must admit the American right to share the guidance and advancement, the privileges and responsibilities of the world with us. And we must do it with a good grace. The world is big enough for both of us . . .
>
> So far as I know, we have nothing whatever to hide from the Americans in this area. I cannot think offhand of a single file of papers on any Middle East subject that could not be read by the Americans without damage to our interests. And yet, for some reason or other, we are nothing like as close to them on Middle East matters as we should be . . . We dissipate our potential combined strength by working in almost watertight British and American compartments. I would expect this to be so in other parts of the world too.'[85]

Felix Frankfurter in Washington agreed with what Casey had to say, deploring 'the growing manifestation of separation in feeling and thought between the British and ourselves', and being particularly concerned over the false picture of the British Empire entertained by most of his fellow-Americans.[86] There were those in London, too, in addition to Law, who shared these anxieties. Cripps was one, despite his resentment during 1942 at American high-handedness, and in a letter to Frankfurter he regretted the tendency of the two peoples to 'concentrate on each other's imperfections.'[87] Cranborne was another, being fearful as to what would happen 'if the American people are allowed to feel that they alone have won the war.'[88] Likewise, in the North American Department of the Foreign Office, a troubled watch was still being kept on the images that Americans held of the British, with much critical comment being directed against the British Information Services in the United States. Attention was also paid, as before, to maintaining good relations with key figures such as Willkie—still possibly the man to lead the Republicans away from isolationism in 1944— and with prominent Congressmen like Vandenberg, although the use of any 'tricks' to win over the Republican old guard, such as playing up 'the Bolshevist menace', was firmly ruled out in the Foreign Office.[89]

One piece of propaganda for Britain that did make a considerable impact upon the United States was the Beveridge Report, published at the end of 1942 and something of a shock for those Americans who regarded both Churchill's Government and British society at large as being reactionary and undemocratic.[90] In fact, a wide programme of social and economic reconstruction was being set on foot in London, a process which did not engage the sympathies of Churchill as it did those of some of his colleagues, and which carried with it significant political implications for the future where he was concerned, even though his position at this time remained entirely secure. A Gallup Poll conducted in the spring of 1943, which recorded that 93 per cent of those questioned approved of the Prime Minister, also gave Labour a lead of more than 10 per cent over the Conservatives.[91] 'Reconstruction', writes a student of the domestic war-time scene, '. . . could not come about through Churchill. But gradually it flowed around and past him, like a tide cutting off an island from the shore.'[92]

By contrast, there were signs that the United States, in the words of the well-known broadcaster, Eric Sevareid, was 'going rightist again', with the eclipse of 'Dr. New Deal's' role in caring for the country's health.[93] In Washington, this development helped ensure that bitter in-fighting continued, coming as it did on top of jurisdictional disputes like the one between Henry Wallace at the Board of Economic Warfare and Jesse Jones of the Reconstruction Finance Corporation.[94] 'We are getting some of those radical boys out of the way and more will go', remarked James Byrnes, Director of Economic Stabilization and a key figure in the managing of American domestic affairs, while Wallace, prominent among those 'radical boys', noted in his diary that 'an inner-circle conflict' was shaping up.[95] Meanwhile, confusion continued to be a feature of Roosevelt's system of Government as a whole ('The President', confided Stimson to his diary in March, 'is the poorest administrator I have ever worked under in respect to the orderly procedure and routine of his performance'),[96] with the State Department remaining largely on the sidelines—Admiral Leahy, for example, refused even to let Hull have the record of the proceedings at Casablanca.[97] Links between the Department and the White House became particularly tenuous after the resignation from the post of Under Secretary of Sumner Welles, Hull's bête-noir, about whom William Bullitt had spread rumours concerning his homosexuality.[98] (In the Foreign Office, the State Department as a whole was seen as being much impaired by internal disunity. As for Bullitt, Eden fittingly described him as 'poisonous'.)[99] Congressional leaders, for their part, were bemoaning what Vandenberg called 'a complete and total lack of authentic liaison between the White House and Congress in respect of war responsibilities', and indeed the Executive under Roosevelt was extending its control of affairs in a way which was significant for the future powers of the Presidency generally.[100]

One feature of the American scene in 1943 which the Administration, however, for all its power, could not remove was acute racial tension. This burst out in, for example, riots in Detroit in June (25 blacks and 9 whites were killed), and further disturbances in Harlem in August.[101] 'This trouble in Detroit', noted Stimson apprehensively after reading a military report on the situation, 'is merely an omen of what may come anywhere.'[102] Some American commentators at the time also related these events to a world-wide problem involving white and coloured peoples[103]—a connection that, as we have seen, was being made by blacks themselves.*

Such racial currents were again of general significance, as will be shown below, when it came to the war in the Far East. Meanwhile, within the United States, bitter opposition to Roosevelt continued to be linked in a good many cases with Anglophobia. The *Chicago Tribune*, as before, provided a pathological example of this. Sneering at the President's wife, for example, for saying that there was no anti-American prejudice in Britain, the paper, in a passage which throws some light on the part played in both the domestic politics and external relations of the U.S.A. by a sense of inferiority, declared:

'In decrying Americans and exalting the British, Mrs Roosevelt voices the attitude of the seaboard social set into which she was born. The members of that set are determined to return this nation to the status of Colonialism, so that from the bottom rung of the British social ladder they may look down on their fellow-Americans whom they hold in contempt.'[104]

Some British observers believed that remarks such as these represented more than simply the thinking of a lunatic fringe. Sir Ronald Campbell, for instance, Minister at the Embassy in Washington, wrote that he now 'felt sure that Americans congenitally hate us',[105] which was almost certainly a considerable overstatement. There was also, however, another feature of the anti-Roosevelt movement in the United States which, like the racial issue there, was relevant to the Far Eastern conflict in 1943. For, as in the preceding period, many of those who attacked the President and his notional subservience to the British were continuing to call at the same time for the highest priority in terms of America's military effort to be given to the war against Japan. And it is to that war that we must now turn again.

---

* In Britain, sympathy continued to be displayed by the public for black American troops against hostile white Americans. The Secretary of State for War, still anxious to adapt to the U.S. Army's segregation policies, lamented to Churchill: 'Though in the Army we have managed to foster a reasonably sane attitude, the outlook of the public at large is much less understanding.' (PREM 4, 26/9.)

Notes to Chapter Ten

1 Marshall to WSC, 8 June 1943, PREM 4, 72/3.
2 J. Ehrman, *Grand Strategy*, vol. V (London, 1956), xvi.

3 E.g. F. C. Pogue, *George C. Marshall: Organizer of Victory, 1943–1945* (New York, 1973; hereafter, *Pogue*, II), 206.
4 M. Matloff, *Strategic Planning For Coalition Warfare, 1943–1944* (Washington, D.C., 1959; hereafter, *Matloff*), 287.
5 Ibid, 107.
6 FO 371, A10611/34/45.
7 E.g. *Chicago Tribune*, 2 and 3 Aug., 4 and 8 Oct. 1943.
8 *Vandenberg*, 10 May 1943.
9 JCS, 6 April, 10 Aug., 15 and 19 Nov. 1943, Roosevelt Papers, MR box 29.
10 Leahy Diary, 2 and 7 May, 7 Oct. 1943.
11 E.g. Hurley to FDR, 5 May 1943, Roosevelt Papers, MR box 12; Earle to Hopkins, 2 April 1943, ibid, box 13; Murphy to FDR, 6 July 1943, Hopkins Papers, box 330.
12 Stimson Diary, 1 June 1943.
13 Howard, *Grand Strategy*, IV, 500; see WP(44)9, CAB 66/45, and *Churchill*, V, cap. XII.
14 Amery to Dorman-Smith, 7 July 1943, Dorman-Smith Papers, E215/37.
15 E.g. Howard, *Grand Strategy*, IV, 420, 561; Ehrman, *Grand Strategy*, V, 75.
16 FRUS, 1943, Cairo and Tehran, 476.
17 FRUS, 1943, Washington and Quebec, 496; see JCS, 10 Aug. 1943, RG 218.
18 Stimson Diary, 29 Oct. 1943.
19 Ibid, 22 Sept. 1943. See the comments of an Australian observer, Watt to Hodgson, 24 May 1943, Watt Papers.
20 E.g. *Matloff*, 41; *Pogue*, II, 5.
21 E. Roosevelt, *As He Saw It*, 151.
22 Lewin, *Churchill As Warlord*, 218.
23 Wheeler-Bennett, *Action This Day*, 209.
24 See FRUS, Cairo and Tehran, 3, 10, 11, 79.
25 E.g. FRUS, Washington and Quebec, 966; *Moran*, 140.
26 FRUS, 1943, III, 581.
27 J. L. Gaddis, *The United States And The Origins of the Cold War* (New York, 1972), 64.
28 *Long*, 18 Nov. 1943. On the Conference, see *Woodward*, II, 581.
29 Taylor, *Beaverbrook*, 543; e.g. C. Bohlen, *Witness To History* (London, 1973), 146; *Woodward*, II, 600, 603; R. Beitzell, *The Uneasy Alliance: America, Britain and Russia, 1941–1943* (New York, 1972), 264; *Churchill*, V, 330.
30 Stimson Diary, 5 Dec. 1943.
31 Morgenthau Presidential Diary, January 1944 and 7 April 1944.
32 FRUS, Cairo and Tehran, 147.
33 E.g. FRUS, Washington and Quebec, 320; FRUS, Cairo and Tehran, 189.
34 FRUS, Cairo and Tehran, 194.
35 Hansard, HC Deb 392, col. 101.
36 E.g. Avon, *The Reckoning*, 397.
37 Leahy Diary, 6 April 1943; and e.g. Matthews to Atherton, 25 June 1943, DS, Matthews files, box 9; FRUS, 1943, III, 9.
38 FRUS, Washington and Quebec, 1169; *Woodward*, II, cap. XXXI.
39 *Woodward*, II, 588.
40 See Divine, *Second Chance*, 85ff.; *Vandenberg*, 4 Aug. 1943.
41 E.g. Hull, *Memoirs*, II, 1625ff.; *Notter*, 169ff.; FRUS, Cairo and Tehran, 529; *Burns*, 359.
42 E.g. FO 371, files 35363ff.; Gladwyn, *Memoirs*, 131; WP(43)31 and 39 (CAB 66/33) and 447 (CAB 66/41); Woodward, *British Foreign Policy in the Second World War*, vol. *V* (London, 1976; hereafter, *Woodward*, V), passim.
43 WP(43)398, CAB 66/40. See PREM 4, 30/3; WSC to Attlee, 14 Sept. 1943, PREM 4, 30/1; *Churchill*, V, 110.
44 *Wallace*, 22 May 1943.
45 Stimson Diary, 11 May 1943; see entries for 22 May, 7 and 8 Sept. and 28 Oct. 1943.
46 FO 371, A6188/57/45; see A7147/57/45.

47 *Hancock and Gowing*, 367.
48 Ibid, 369.
49 E.g. *Matloff*, 112ff.
50 FO 371, U1970/1970/70.
51 Ehrman, *Grand Strategy*, V, 41.
52 Cherwell to WSC, 22 Oct. 1943, Cherwell Papers, Off. 13A. 1. See WP(43)539, CAB 66/43.
53 Howard, *Grand Strategy*, IV, 292.
54 Gowing, *Britain and Atomic Energy*, 165.
55 Ibid, 171; FRUS, Washington and Quebec, 631, 633, 639; material in PREM 3, 139/8A.
56 Lyttelton to WSC, 9 April 1943, Cherwell Papers, Off. 39. 1.
57 *Kolko*, 284.
58 FRUS, 1943, III, 48, 81, 98, 101, 104; FRUS, Cairo and Tehran, 822; Blum, *Roosevelt and Morgenthau*, 484ff.; WP(43)331, CAB 66/39.
59 Cab, 13 Sept. 1943, CAB 65/35.
60 *Cantril and Strunk*, 411; *Chicago Tribune*, 5 Feb. and 1 Oct. 1943.
61 See Campbell to Foreign Office, 18 Oct. 1943, PREM 4, 73/1.
62 Hurley to FDR, 7 Nov. 1943, Roosevelt Papers, PSF box 151.
63 WP(43)478, CAB 66/42.
64 Cabs, 27 July 1943 (CAB 65/35), 27 Oct. and 1 Nov. 1943 (CAB 65/36).
65 WP(43)559, CAB 66/44.
66 E.g. WP(43)136 (CAB 66/35), 168 (CAB 66/36), 388 (CAB 66/40), 576 (CAB 66/44); Cabs, 8 April 1943 (CAB 65/34) and 27 July 1943 (CAB 65/35); Dalton Diary, 8 April and 23 July 1943.
67 Cab, 6 Aug. 1943, CAB 65/35; and see below, 458, and Thomson, *Churchill and Morton*, 58.
68 See *Kolko*, 302.
69 WP(44)119, CAB 66/47; Stimson Diary, 4, 11 and 28 June 1943; Feis, *Seen From E.A.*, 93ff.
70 Cherwell to WSC, 18 June 1943, Cherwell Papers, Off. 1. 1.
71 FRUS, Washington and Quebec, 679, 1320.
72 Committee minutes, 17 Sept. 1943, Beaverbrook Papers, Civil Aviation file. See Cranborne to Amery, 14 Sept. 1943, IO, Private Office Papers, L/PO/218.
73 Dalton Diary, 24 Aug. 1943.
74 Grigg to Grigg, 9 Sept. 1943, Grigg Papers, box 9/6.
75 Far East Group, 17 March 1943, R.I.I.A.
76 War Strategy Group, 8 April 1943, R.I.I.A.
77 FO 371, A8894/3/45.
78 Ibid, A8229/34/45; see A10220/34/45.
79 See Hansard, HC Deb 386, col. 777; and ibid, HC Deb 387, col. 1103.
80 Calder, *The People's War* 309; see FO 371, A670/32/45.
81 E.g. *Manchester Guardian*, 6 July 1943.
82 FO 371, A10579/32/45; A1005/34/45; A8485/32/45.
83 Ibid, A7757/32/45.
84 Dixon to Evatt, 28 March 1943, ADEA, A989/43/735/1021.
85 Casey to WSC, 29 Dec. 1943, Evatt Papers, Casey file. Casey sent Evatt a copy of this letter in 1956, as being 'still true in essence.'
86 Frankfurter to Casey, 8 Jan. 1943, Frankfurter Papers, box 126; Frankfurter to Halifax, 14 May 1943, ibid, box 62.
87 Cripps to Frankfurter, 26 May 1943, ibid, box 50.
88 FO 371, A8485/32/45.
89 Ibid, A5950G, A9823/144/45 and A72/32/45; Halifax to WSC, 2 Nov. 1943, PREM 4, 27/9.
90 See WP(43)59, CAB 66/34.
91 Pelling, *Churchill*, 504.

92 *Addison*, 14, 126. See e.g. the contrast between WP(43)18 (CAB 66/33) and WP(43)255 (CAB 66/38); also Dalton Diary, 29 Oct. 1943.

93 Sevareid notes, 22 Dec. 1943, Sevareid Papers, box D3; Tugwell, *In Search of Roosevelt*, 264.

94 *Burns*, 331ff.

95 *Long*, 9 Sept. 1943; *Wallace*, 18 Dec. 1943.

96 Stimson Diary, 28 March 1943.

97 Ibid, 4 May 1943; see ibid, 16 Feb. 1943.

98 E.g. *Long*, 29 Aug. 1943.

99 FO 371, A7563 and 8103/144/45.

100 *Vandenberg*, 16 Feb. 1943; *Burns*, 343.

101 See R. L. Lingeman, *Don't You Know There's A War On?* (New York, 1970), cap. IX; *Burns*, 388.

102 Stimson Diary, 24 June 1943.

103 E.g. *Christian Science Monitor*, 20 Nov. 1943.

104 *Chicago Tribune*, 14 Feb. 1943.

105 FO 371, A33/6/45.

CHAPTER ELEVEN

THE WAR AGAINST JAPAN

In 1943, as in the preceding year, there were individuals and groups at work in the United States, seeking to increase the proportion of American, if not Allied, effort devoted to the war against Japan: people who caused a great deal of concern to those responsible for British policy. As Gallup Polls in February confirmed, a majority of Americans continued to regard the Japanese as the 'chief enemy' of their country.[1] Newspapers such as the *San Francisco Examiner* and *Chicago Tribune* went on demanding that the struggle in the Pacific should be given priority,[2] while in Congress, the same theme was propounded by Senators Chandler, Wheeler and Tydings (Democrats), Shipstead and Bridges (Republicans) and others, probably egged on by individuals within the press, the Navy and the Army's Services of Supply under General Brehon Somervell.[3] Such 'Pacific-first' manifestations were noted with anxiety by British officials, as were the loud repercussions after Churchill, in a major survey of the war, had failed to pay the warm tribute to China that American sentiment demanded.[4] Henry Stimson, on a visit to Britain, added his own warning to the Prime Minister, reminding him that 'the enemy whom the American people really hated . . . was Japan, which had dealt them a foul blow.'[5] Harry Hopkins, too, sent a message through Law to say that anti-British outbursts in the U.S.A. could be traced back to discontent over the degree of collaboration that was being achieved by the two Western partners against Japan.[6]

At the same time, the Far Eastern war continued to contribute to the difficulties that were arising between British and American senior officers in the field of Allied grand strategy. Within the Combined Chiefs of Staff, there was disagreement, for example, over how the decisions of the Casablanca Conference should be interpreted as regards the distribution of forces between the European and Far Eastern theatres, with the British representatives objecting to what they saw as unwarranted assumptions on the part of the Americans, while Admiral King, for the J.C.S., talked of 'a difference of opinion that would always remain . . . on the adequacy of forces in the Pacific.'[7] During the Washington Conference in May, Sir John Dill privately warned his colleagues who had arrived from London that 'the nearer the Presidential Election approached, the more the political pull would be to the Pacific.' Brooke, for his part, had already noted in his diary: 'Their hearts are really in the Pacific', adding later: 'It is all so maddening, as it is not in this case difficult to see that, unless our united efforts are directed to defeat Germany and hold Japan, the war may go on indefinitely.'[8]

During the ensuing sessions of the Combined Chiefs of Staff, in which Brooke spoke out against what he feared would be the suction effect that would be created by operations against Japan, Leahy from the other side of the table insisted that 'should the situation in the Pacific become dangerous to United States interests . . . it would be necessary to supplement United States forces in this theatre, even at the expense of the early defeat of Germany.'[9] Likewise, during the run-up to the Cairo Conference, the Joint Chiefs declared that an endeavour 'to maintain and extend unremitting pressure against Japan' should be made 'simultaneously' with efforts directed against Germany. If the British reneged on the cross-Channel operation in the interests of their Mediterranean schemes, Marshall advised Roosevelt, then the United States should 'pull out [of Europe] and go into the Pacific with all our forces.'[10] And at Cairo itself, the very concentration on Far Eastern and, more specifically, Chinese affairs, promoted by the presence of Chiang Kai-shek, was a matter of great irritation to Churchill.

Meanwhile Washington was, indeed, committing additional forces in order to maintain the momentum of the war against Japan, so that by the end of 1943 1,878,152 men were employed in that task as against 1,810,367 who were engaged in the fight against Germany. The figures for U.S. aeroplanes were 7,857 deployed against Japan and 8,807 against Germany; for combat ships, 713 and 515 respectively.[11] Such an allocation of American resources not only threatened the strategy of 'Germany first'; it also constituted a very great contrast with the meagre amount of men and matériel which the British, for their part, could conceivably commit to the Far Eastern war, and hence underlined the predominant role which the United States could and would play in the shaping of Allied strategy in that conflict.[12]

Churchill was well aware of what he called 'the natural urge which existed in America to devote resources to the war against Japan.' 'Public opinion in the United States was much more concerned about [that] war . . . ,' he reported to the Cabinet after the Washington Conference. 'It was almost true to say', he added, 'that the American public would be more disturbed if China fell out of the war than if Russia did so. Though this was not the view of the President and leaders of the administration, they could not fail to be influenced to some extent by public opinion.'[13] For his part, he again sought, in speeches on both sides of the Atlantic, to reassure that public that Britain would bear her full share of the fight against Japan, going so far as to declare in a press conference in Washington that 'if the war continues on both fronts [it] will be waged with equal force as our reserves grow. Instead of being consecutive our efforts will be concurrent.'[14] At the same time, the Prime Minister tried to promote the idea of 'showing the Americans that we take a real interest in their operations in the Pacific' by sending a powerful British battle squadron, via the Panama Canal, to work with the U.S. Navy before passing on to operate in the Indian Ocean.

Needless to say, however, Admiral King's response to this proposal was decidedly cool.[15]

The great majority of the British public—88 per cent, according to one poll—approved of Churchill's pledge that the country would fight on against Japan after Germany had been defeated.[16] Officials dealing with Far Eastern affairs, however, continued to be concerned over what was seen as the public's lack of interest in those aspects of the war. (One report spoke of 'events in the Far East, of which the public knows little and cares less.')[17] In this respect, special problems were foreseen as regards the period after Germany had capitulated. 'It is very desirable', insisted the Foreign Office during a Whitehall discussion on whether to reveal how the Japanese had ill-treated their prisoners-of-war, 'to bring home to everyone in this country the terrible nature of the Japanese enemy . . . and to rouse our people to a fuller determination to defeat Japan.'[18] Likewise, Churchill and other members of the Government were raising during the year the question of whether special inducements would need to be provided for British forces in the Far East after the European war was over. 'We cannot fight with raw, lightly-trained youths', the Prime Minister asserted. 'The war against Japan may well take several years and will require a large proportion of our best troops. The heart-burnings which will arise about all this will be fierce.'[19] Moreover, it was also felt by those dealing with the Far East that even in Whitehall itself there were still very few who took an interest in such matters, which one Foreign Office official sourly described as 'largely ignored or forgotten except by the depressed classes whose business it is to deal with that region.' 'No section of H[is] M[ajesty's] G[overnment]', wrote Sir Maurice Peterson in May, 'is at present very much interested in, or very much linked up with, operations [against Japan].'[20]*

That officials and public alike should take a greater interest in the Far Eastern conflict was held to be all the more important in that Britain's contribution in that sphere might considerably affect American attitudes towards her, both during and after the war. 'The war in the Pacific', wrote Sir Ronald Campbell from Washington, 'will afford a [great] opportunity for engraving deep in the American consciousness the feeling that we are the right partner in a dangerous enterprise . . . In the conduct of the war in the Pacific may well lie the determining (though by no means the sole) factor in the attitude towards us of the American people for as far ahead as I can see.'[21] Other officials echoed these views. 'The greatest danger and the greatest opportunities will arise when the offensive is mounted against Japan', wrote one. 'Britain will then be not the aided but the ally of America.' And to another, the Far Eastern war would be 'a great opportunity of getting Anglo-American relations onto a new and healthier level.' It was, declared a third, 'a very great chance to work an important change in Anglo-American relations.'[22]

---

* During this period, the suggestion made earlier by Duff Cooper, that a separate Far Eastern civil service should be established (see above, p. 58), was turned down. (WP(43)29, CAB 66/33.)

Hopes such as these, however, accompanied as they were by Churchill's public assurances as to Britain's full commitment against Japan, were by no means matched on the United States side when American officials came to think about the role the British could or should play in the Far Eastern war. Their greatest anxiety concerned, not the relationship between the two white Allies in that context, but, as before, the danger of a racial or colour conflict developing. Thus, one member of the State Department wrote about the major problem of how to direct 'the nationalism of colored peoples' into 'healthy channels', while in general, China's continuing presence as an active partner on the side of the Allies was still seen as being 'the best insurance that the present war does not become a race war.'[23] Stanley Hornbeck, who was one of those emphasizing the benefits which China contributed as 'a good friend of and a willing co-worker with the Anglo-Saxon countries', also forecast 'serious trouble in this country arising out of "color" and the characteristics etc. that go therewith . . ., [together with] a great deal of trouble throughout the Far East for the "white" race.'[24] A watch must be kept, the State Department's Committee on Colonial Problems were told, on certain organizations in Harlem 'which seek primarily to unite all colored peoples into a common cause',[25] while Representative Charles A. Eaton warned the Advisory Committee on Political Problems in dramatic terms that 'the desire is for the Oriental peoples to have independent and civilized nations and eventually the United States might be pushed off the map too . . .; there might be racial war between the yellow man and the white man in the future—we may be liquidated.'[26] Even beloved China might contribute to such a terrifying prospect, and with this in mind, Senator Elbert D. Thomas added his alarmed voice to that of Eaton: 'Genghis Khan', he recalled, 'got into Europe, and we can loose in Asia forces so great that the world will be deluged and there will be no way to prevent it.'[27]

One possible reaction to such disturbing notions, of course, was to decide that the United States should stick close to Britain and the Commonwealth in a white, Anglo-Saxon partnership. This was, indeed, the policy that Representative Eaton advocated to his committee, and J. V. A. MacMurray, a former American Minister to China, agreed with him. 'It is more valuable for the peace of the world', insisted MacMurray, 'that we should maintain our relations with the British than that we should jeopardise them . . . by participating in the breaking up of the British Empire.'[28] Likewise, Nelson T. Johnson wrote from his Legation in Canberra to suggest that the Australians, for all their shortcomings, were 'our natural racial allies in dealing with the problems of the Pacific.'[29] Meanwhile a portion of the American press, and, it would seem, a majority of public opinion, did accept Churchill's assurances about Britain's determination to see the war against Japan through to a conclusion—a pledge doubly welcome to those who, like the Secretary of the Navy, Frank Knox, secretly entertained sacrilegious doubts as to whether the American people on their own would 'have the guts to stay with it to the finish.'[30]

And yet, more common among American officials and members of the Administration was the feeling that, in a situation fraught with the danger of a racial or colour conflict, Britain was, to say the least, something of a liability as a partner. Her aims in the war against Japan, Roosevelt assured the Joint Chiefs of Staff, were essentially selfish.[31] She was primarily interested in the Far Eastern campaigns, reported Hornbeck after visiting London, 'in order to win back parts of the Empire which [she] had lost, rather than to defeat Japan.'[32] Likewise, Davies, as Stilwell's political adviser, warned that Churchill possessed 'the power and influence to force through . . . a policy of nineteenth-century imperialism and power politics',[33] while in another paper he set out what he saw as being the consequent peril for the U.S.A.: 'In the minds of most Americans', he wrote in October 1943, 'a better world is identified with the abolition of imperialism, and there is a very real danger that the United States may again become isolationist after the war as a result of a feeling by the American people that they have been made dupes of British imperialism.'[34] The fact had to be faced, insisted the Chief of the State Department's Far Eastern Division, that, over India, Burma and China, major differences existed between Washington and London,[35] and Hornbeck added his own summary of the situation in that regard: 'The British Government', he wrote, 'never had understood the fundamental facts which underlie the so-called Far Eastern problem . . . They were not really interested in it. They were not really aware of it.'[36] Britain and the United States 'are miles apart in Asia', declared Adolf Berle to Roosevelt in October, 'notably on the Chinese question, race question, attitude towards Indian aspirations and a lot of things.'[37] On the basis of this fixed assumption, the American mission in Delhi were warned

'to keep firmly in mind that American and British interests in the field of psychological warfare in Asia are by no means identical. The United States is fighting without imperialist design, solely for the defeat of Japan. The British in Asia can, on the other hand, be assumed to be fighting primarily for the retention, if not expansion, of their Empire . . . The Department [of State] has been constantly opposed to any integration of American and British psychological warfare programs in the India–Burma area, lest we identify ourselves in the eyes of the Asiatic peoples concerned with British imperialism.'[38]

Despite such ritual disclaimers of selfish aims as far as the U.S.A. was concerned (Theodore Roosevelt's earlier pronouncements in this respect will be recalled),[39] there did also exist other lines of thought on the American side which reinforced the belief in the need to stay apart from Britain in the East, but in this case out of a sense of rivalry with her over the commercial opportunities which would open up in that part of the world once the war was over. Thus Phillip C. Ferguson, for example, a former Congressman who in 1943 was serving with the Marines against the Japanese, expressed something of this mood in a letter which he wrote to Vice President Wallace, and which the latter passed on approvingly to Hull.

'We must have absolute control of all necessary bases in the Pacific', declared Ferguson. 'We must have free trade in the Pacific..., with Australia, New Zealand and the Orient. That will do more to secure our position than all the treaties in the world. We will have the ships and the manufacturing capacity... No country will be unknown to us. Every community will have some returned member of the armed forces to give first-hand information. The American public must know what over a million potential customers out here can do toward keeping our tremendous shop open for business... The whole Pacific is not too big for us, not right now.'[40]

An even more significant letter, in view of the treatment that it received, was written in March by William Howard Gardiner, a former President of the Navy League, to Joseph Grew in the State Department. In this, Gardiner listed at length the selfish and untrustworthy acts committed by Britain in the Far East, but went on to point out that, even if little help in the current conflict could be expected from that quarter, that was not something to be greatly regretted:

'It would be of very, very great post-war importance to the United States', he suggested, 'both politically and commercially, if the war to crush Japan could be carried on, in the main, by the United States, with merely such secondary help from Australasia, China and Russia rather than, so to speak a "United Nations" undertaking. Let the recovery of the Netherlands East Indies, the Philippines and all other islands in the Pacific, as well as the removal of the Japanese from Singapore and all of Southeast Asia, follow as the manifest results of American naval and aerial operations... For such a procedure would improve immeasurably the peace settlements we would be able to make in the regions of the Pacific, and our future political standing and commercial opportunities in Asia and in Australasia.'[41]

We shall later encounter MacArthur, amongst others, talking in exactly the same vein. Meanwhile Hornbeck, who read Gardiner's letter, regarded it as being of great importance, and urged Grew to ensure that it was seen by the President.[42] Grew himself warmly thanked Gardiner for his 'admirable exposition', and promised to 'keep the picture as you present it very much in mind.' Later, he did discuss the letter with Roosevelt, and although there appears to be no record of the latter's reaction to it, we do have that of his Chief of Staff, Leahy, who, reported Grew to Gardiner,

'has written me that he has read your letter... with much interest and with much advantage to his efforts to visualize a correct attitude for America to take at the present time, and in future negotiations with both our present enemies and our present friends.'[43]

Thus, largely as a consequence of American assumptions, but also, in part, as a result of the fact that it was Winston Churchill who appeared to speak for Britain in the matter of imperial and Far Eastern affairs, the two Allies remained on uneasy terms where the war and the future in Asia were concerned. They were alike, however, in that neither, in this period, had formulated a clear and decisive plan for the defeat of Japan. In over-all terms, both Churchill, with his talk of attacking the octopus at its centre rather than at the tentacles, and Roosevelt, whose own analogue was that of the centre, as opposed to the corners, of a pie, were anxious to strike at Japan proper.[44] In the meantime, however, neither leader imposed a dominant strategy on the Far Eastern war. The President, for his part, tended to shift his ground, for example over whether to back Stilwell or Chennault in China, and over the general significance of that country in the war effort. The Prime Minister, too, varied his position. For instance, he declared to the Cabinet in April that 'it could not be said that the conquest of Burma was an essential step in the defeat of Japan. Nor would the occupation of North Burma mean immediate traffic on the Burma Road ... Everything pointed to an alternative line of action.'[45] Yet in August, by contrast, he was telling the Chiefs of Staff that 'we ought to make a strong new feature of the offensive from Assam into Upper Burma ... to help reopen the Burma Road and form a permanent overland contact with the Chinese forces in Yunnan and elsewhere.'[46] And even then, the Prime Minister's favourite scheme for an amphibious assault upon Sumatra tended to overshadow his other, shifting ideas concerning Southeast Asia.[47] It is thus hardly surprising to find Cadogan in the Foreign Office describing British planning for the war against Japan as reminding him of 'a blind man searching for a black cat in a dark room.'[48] Churchill did not improve matters at the Quebec Conference when, in response to a submission by the Chiefs of Staff that a choice must be made between a Burma–China axis of attack and a Malaya–South China-port one, he refused to contemplate any decision whereby, as he short-sightedly put it, 'the dead hand of a long-term plan paralysed action in the near future.'[49]

The American Joint Chiefs, too, approached the Cairo Conference at the end of this period still with no agreed, long-term plan of their own for the Far Eastern war.[50] And when that Conference assembled, a number of important questions had yet to be answered. For example, how long after the defeat of Germany was it likely to take the Allies to achieve victory over Japan? (American planners were thinking in terms of twelve months; their British counterparts inclined towards a longer period.)[51] What role could China be expected to play in the fight? Would an actual invasion of the Japanese home islands be necessary?[52] Meanwhile, planning staffs put forward outlines of possible stages during which Japan would be approached from the Pacific, Southeast Asia and China—with alternatives which bore very differing implications for the part that Britain in general and the Royal Navy in particular might play in the final, decisive thrusts.[53]

Eventually, however, the Combined Chiefs of Staff did agree at Cairo on an over-all plan which placed the main emphasis on the Pacific theatre, where there was to be a two-pronged attack: one through Japan's mandated islands in the Central Pacific, the other along the New Guinea–Netherlands Indies–Philippines axis.[54] As for the British naval contribution, this would be made mainly in the Pacific, rather than in the Bay of Bengal; British operations in Southeast Asia would thus be reduced to what Leahy described as 'a diversionary effort.' Despite this last feature of the plan, Churchill, together with Roosevelt, initialled the report in which it was contained. We shall see later, however, that, in the following period, the Prime Minister was to have very pronounced second thoughts on the subject, and in doing so was to throw the planning process in London into great confusion.

Such is the barest outline of the strategic-planning aspect for the Far East during the months between Casablanca and Cairo. Some of the specific issues involved, however, together with the progress that was being made at this time in the actual fighting, need to be sketched in before we turn again to the various areas of American and British endeavour. As regards the Pacific, for example (where, to the north, the Japanese were cleared from the Aleutians between May and August), the eventual decision to develop a two-pronged attack was reached only after considerable strife had arisen between the U.S. Navy, with its commitment to a central axis of advance, and MacArthur in the South-West.[55] MacArthur himself, meanwhile, operating under a new directive issued in March, was in overall command of two separate thrusts in his own area: one moving up the Solomons from Guadalcanal, the other advancing along the north-east coast of New Guinea, and aimed at outflanking the Japanese stronghold of Rabaul in the New Britain islands. These campaigns in the Southwest Pacific involved the battle of the Bismarck Sea in March, in which a large Japanese convoy of reinforcements for New Guinea was destroyed; they also witnessed the seizure by Admiral 'Bull' Halsey's amphibious forces of Emirau island, and landings in the Admiralty Islands as MacArthur developed his 'leapfrogging' tactics.[56] Meanwhile, the decision had been taken in Washington to launch a major attack along the Central Pacific chain of islands, again involving the by-passing of forward Japanese defences with the aid of fast aircraft-carrier units, and avoiding the need to 'hop' from one island to the next.[57] In November 1943, the execution of this plan led to landings in the Gilbert Islands, with U.S. Marines becoming involved in extremely bloody fighting on the small, British-owned island of Tarawa.[58] This step in turn brought the Americans close to the Marshalls, with the Carolines and Marianas beckoning beyond. In short, they were already beginning to hammer at the perimeter of the Japanese Empire itself.

These advances in the Pacific also had implications of an inter-Allied kind. Both MacArthur and the U.S. Navy, for example, were contributing greatly to that pull towards the Pacific theatre which has been noted above in terms of grand strategy and of public opinion. Admiral King, for one, was acting on the principle of getting his forces involved on the spot to such an extent that no second thoughts of a strategic nature would be possible. 'We must be so committed in the Central Pacific', he urged his commanders, 'that the British cannot hedge on the recall of ships from the Atlantic.'[59] (In his diary, Stimson commented: 'The Navy has been dead anxious to fight in the Pacific . . . And they have been barely loyal in regard to following out the plans.')[60] In addition, and despite the contribution made to MacArthur's advance by Australian forces, this major, Pacific scene of activity against Japan continued to be directed exclusively by Washington. As the American planners put it when listing the advantages of making this the main sphere of Allied effort in the Far Eastern war, 'In effect, it gives the Joint Chiefs of Staff almost complete liberty of action in the Pacific without reference to the British Chiefs of Staff.'[61] Pacific projects, a leading U.S. representative informed the British members of the Combined Staff Planners, 'were exclusively United States', though he did add that he would be glad to let his colleagues from across the water have a look at them.[62] During the major inter-Allied conferences, the British Chiefs of Staff encountered—and in the main accepted—the same attitude.[63]

Despite their acquiescence over this matter, however, senior British officers were beginning to have serious doubts as to whether their American partners would ever welcome a contribution in the Pacific on the part of the Royal Navy. Even when the surrender of Italy appeared to make such a project much more feasible, the situation remained uncertain.[64] And there were, indeed, good grounds for such doubts, for although Roosevelt, personally, warmed to the idea (mentioned above) of a British battle squadron operating in the Pacific whilst en route to the Bay of Bengal, King remained hostile to all proposals of this kind. 'We have all the naval force that we can properly manage deployed in that area', he informed his colleagues on the Joint Chiefs of Staff, while to the senior American naval officer in London he wrote scornfully: 'The seeming "helplessness" of our cousins strikes me as amusing when it is not annoying. I am sure that what they wish in their hearts is that we would haul down the Stars and Stripes and hoist the White Ensign in all of our ships.'[65]

Meanwhile, by comparison with the striking developments that were taking place in the Pacific, little or no progress was being made on the ground during this period, either in China or Southeast Asia. As we shall see in the following chapter, China's potential role continued to be stressed by United States officials, which in turn led to strong differences of opinion with the British over the degree of emphasis to be placed on the need to reopen a land route from Burma into Yunnan. The Chinese themselves did what they could to keep eyes turned in their direction by inventing major military successes for use by their propaganda machine, as when they claimed to have 'halted' a Japanese offensive in the Yangtze region in March. Her participation in the Four Power Moscow declaration and in the policy statement issued at the Cairo Conference (in which she was promised the restoration of all her territories lost to Japan) also appeared to enhance China's status. Yet strategically, the development of the Central and Southwest axes of attack in the Pacific foreshadowed a decline in even the potential military significance of Chiang Kai-shek's forces and land-space in American, as well as in British, eyes. So, too, did the intimation received towards the end of the period that the Soviet Union would eventually enter the war against Japan—a development which Churchill (who later, for the purposes of argument, claimed to have been surprised by it) had been forecasting earlier in July.[66] As an American staff planner put it at Cairo: 'With the possibility of Russia coming into the war and with the chances of successful action in the Pacific, the value of the Burma Road was now less.'[67] 'The promise of China', writes the American official historian, 'was now to be replaced by the promise of the Soviet Union as the valuable ally in the Far East.'[68]

By the same token, the British contribution in Southeast Asia could well come to be overshadowed by the work of the Red Army in pinning down the Japanese forces—thought to be powerful still—that were stationed in Manchuria and North China. Even as it was, Britain's campaign achievements were sufficiently small to bring forth yet more American scorn, and to foster the conviction that the United States was defeating the Japanese virtually single-handed. An offensive in Arakan between September 1942 and February 1943 failed to achieve decisive results, and by May a Japanese counter-attack had pushed the British and Indian forces back to where they had started.[69] True, some help for sagging morale was furnished by the first Chindit operation which was carried out behind the Japanese lines between February and April—an exercise that encouraged the Japanese themselves to believe that they, in turn, could attack across the Assam–Burma frontier, a campaign which, when attempted later, was to bring them to disaster.[70] Meanwhile the leader of the Chindits, Brigadier Orde Wingate, was seized upon by Churchill as a figure who could help refurbish Britain's tarnished martial image in Southeast Asia. Accordingly, Wingate was taken by the Prime Minister to the Quebec Conference, where American military leaders did, indeed, find him 'a breath of fresh air' and, in Marshall's words, 'a best bet.'[71]

The promise held out by one unusual and assertive figure such as Wingate was not enough, however. What was required, it was increasingly felt in higher circles on both sides of the Atlantic, was a fundamental reorganization of Britain's military effort against the Japanese. The outcome was the setting up in this period of the new Southeast Asia Command. The disagreements and disappointments that lay behind this development will be examined in more detail in the chapter dealing with Southeast Asia. As an important modification to the inter-Allied framework within which the war against Japan was conducted, however, the main outline of the creation of S.E.A.C. will be given here.

The need to make changes in the system of command which would ensure that hard-hitting operations would be conducted against the enemy in Southeast Asia was set forth to the Cabinet by Churchill in June 1943. 'We must fight the Japanese with vigour at all points where they could be engaged', he declared. 'We must devise at once all possible means for increasing the power of our offensive on this front.'[72] To the Chiefs of Staff

in the following month the Prime Minister went on to complain angrily of
the way in which 'all the [existing] Commanders on the spot seem to be
competing with one another to magnify their demands and the obstacles
they have to overcome.' Therefore, while Wingate, 'a man of genius and
audacity', should be given the task of controlling the land campaign (this
thought being a good example of Churchill's capacity for impetuous folly in
the field of military direction), an over-all commander was also needed, and
General Sir Claude Auchinleck (now C. in C. India in succession to Wavell,
who had become Viceroy) would not do for the job. ('The kind of paper [it
was a cautious strategic appreciation] that we have just received from
General Auchinleck', Churchill observed, 'would rightly excite the deepest
suspicion in the United States that we are only playing and dawdling with
the war in this theatre.')[73] Already, in May, the Secretary of State for
India, Amery, had suggested the appointment of a Supreme Commander for
Southeast Asia, independent of the Government of India and its Commander
in Chief. It was also Amery who suggested Lord Louis Mountbatten for the
job, although the Prime Minister at first brushed aside the idea as impossible—perhaps on the grounds of Mountbatten's youth.[74]

The first thing that had to be done, however, was to reach agreement over
the matter with the Americans, among whom Stilwell in particular had
already been lobbying behind the scenes for a change of British commander.[75]
One of the issues involved, which was argued back and forth between June
and the meeting at Quebec, was what type of command should be set up.[76]
Should it, as the British wanted, be based on the model established by
MacArthur in the South West Pacific area, whereby the separate Chiefs of
Staff concerned—in MacArthur's case the Americans; in that of the new
command in Southeast Asia, the British—had effective control of strategy?
Or should it, as the Americans wished, be based instead on Eisenhower's
North African model, with over-all instructions being issued by the Combined Chiefs of Staff, and transmitted by the Chiefs of Staff in London?
Churchill, Brooke, Portal and Pound were strongly committed to their
preference, arriving at Quebec agreed that 'the MacArthur model should be
insisted on', and that they 'should not hesitate to threaten to proceed on the
basis of a purely British command if the Americans did not fall in with our
wishes.'[77] Yet the Americans were equally insistent that control should be
vested in the Combined Chiefs. Such an outcome, Marshall told his colleagues of the J.C.S., was essential in view of the vital nature of United
States relations with China and of the importance of Burma in this connection.[78] Roosevelt himself added the argument that S.E.A.C. operations
would need to be coordinated with those in the Pacific, foreseeing that
'centralization in Washington will eventually be required.'[79]

In the event, and not surprisingly, it was the American side that appeared
to obtain the greater success over this matter of the command structure. The
Combined Chiefs, it was agreed at Quebec, would exercise 'a general
jurisdiction over strategy' in Southeast Asia, and would also be responsible
for allocating resources between that theatre and the Chinese one. The

British Chiefs of Staff, for their part, as well as being the channel for communications between the Combined Chiefs and the new Supreme Commander, were to oversee 'all matters pertaining to operations.'[80]* Over-all, some kind of compromise was clearly intended by these arrangements, but even so they were to give rise to friction from time to time. Before 1943 was out, for example, Brooke was finding it necessary to insist that the Joint Chiefs in Washington did not have the right to be consulted over specific S.E.A.C. operations, as distinct from general strategy.[81]

Concurrent with this debate was the one over who should be nominated to command the new theatre. Churchill's first proposal to Roosevelt was that it should be Air Marshal Sir Sholto Douglas, but this was rejected by the Americans as a result of the unfavourable reactions of some of their officers who knew Douglas.[82]† The President in turn proposed either Air Marshal Sir Arthur Tedder or Admiral Sir Andrew Cunningham, both serving in the Mediterranean theatre; the Prime Minister replied that neither could be spared, and urged instead that the Americans should accept Mountbatten, who had risen to more-than-naval prominence as the youthful head of Combined Operations, with the acting rank of Vice Admiral.[83]

Mountbatten was accordingly appointed, but there were also other staffing difficulties to be faced, not least the position of General Stilwell. Churchill suggested that Stilwell should be made answerable to both the new Supreme Commander of S.E.A.C. and Chiang Kai-shek, thereby providing an important link between Southeast Asia and the China theatre. On Roosevelt's initiative, however (and doubtless Marshall was hoping by this to ensure that the new Command adopted an aggressive outlook), Stilwell, in addition to retaining operational control over American and Chinese forces in the field in Burma, was also named Mountbatten's Deputy Supreme Commander. Given that Stilwell's American C.B.I. Command was not co-terminous with S.E.A.C., and that he remained Chief of Staff to Chiang Kai-shek as well, the complexity of the situation was thus considerable. Even a more flexible man than 'Vinegar Joe' would almost certainly have found the satisfactory fulfilment of all the roles involved to be beyond him.[84]

Further problems still were entailed in the creation of S.E.A.C. In theory, Stilwell would have to work in part under a British Land Commander in Chief (in practice, he was to take strongly against General Giffard, who

---

* As an additional quid pro quo, Churchill was also authorized to send a senior officer to MacArthur's headquarters as his liaison man in the S.W.P.A. Meanwhile, an attempt was made to facilitate cooperation and good relations in the S.E.A.C./India area by establishing a Combined Liaison Committee in New Delhi to deal with quasi-military activities. American agencies wishing to carry out such operations had first to obtain permission from the Viceroy, or the C. in C. India, or the new Supreme Allied Commander of S.E.A.C.

† Churchill's subsequent account of the appointment of Mountbatten and the agreement over S.E.A.C. command arrangements is less than satisfactory. (*Churchill*, V, 70, 77.) Brooke, for his part, was to imply that Mountbatten's appointment was accepted by the President as something of an 'exchange' for Churchill's agreement to an American Supreme Commander for the cross-Channel attack. (*Bryant*, I, 707.)

first filled that position),[85] while all three British Commanders in Chief would in turn need to establish a smooth working relationship with a Supreme Commander who, in the normal course of events, would have been considerably junior to them. We shall see later that, where the naval C. in C., Admiral Sir James Somerville, was concerned, such a relationship was not achieved. Meanwhile, as his Chief of Staff Mountbatten was given the experienced Lt. General Sir Henry Pownall, whose task, as he noted it in his diary, was to 'keep [the former] on the rails.' (When visiting Whitehall, the Governor of Burma was told the same thing: that 'though Dickie [Mountbatten] would be the supremo . . . Pownall would be the really important man as he would be the steadying influence.')[86] As Deputy Chief of Staff, Major General A.C., 'Al' Wedemeyer went out ⟨to⟩ S E.A.C. from Washington, where he had been a member of the Army's planning staff. Wedemeyer, greatly ambitious and given to self-importance, was later to claim that he had been 'eased out' into his new job because he was too ready to stand up to the British in planning matters; at the time, however, he appeared to find the appointment to his liking.[87] Another American, Lt. General R. A. Wheeler, became at the same time S.E.A.C.'s much-liked Principal Administrative Officer, while Major General Stratemeyer commanded the U.S. Army Air Force in the theatre—Mountbatten eventually obtaining agreement that these units should be combined with those of the R.A.F. into a single force.[88]

Yet another problem concerned the boundaries of the new Command. In his initial proposal, Churchill had referred to it as an 'East Asian' one, but he was able to assure Roosevelt at once that he had not intended to suggest that the China theatre, under Chiang Kai-shek, should form a part of it. It was to make this clear that the name was changed to 'Southeast Asia'.[89] A more difficult question, however, arose over the territories of Indochina and Siam, since both at the time fell within the Generalissimo's sphere of jurisdiction, yet both might well become the scene of military thrusts or at least clandestine operations initiated by Mountbatten. (Many of the supplies for the Japanese forces in Burma came through these countries.) The Prime Minister's answer was to include them within the proposed S.E.A.C., together with Burma, Malaya and Sumatra.[90] And interestingly enough, in the light of later developments, an early American draft, too, prepared for Roosevelt possibly by Marshall, included Indochina and Siam in the new Command, so that the President cabled Churchill at the end of June 1943 accepting the boundaries that the latter had submitted.[91] Second thoughts then arose in Washington, however—not, it would seem, because of any long-term political calculations (although some historians have leaped to this tidy conclusion), but because the proposed arrangements would, in Leahy's words, be 'unsatisfactory to Chiang Kai-shek', who might easily feel that he had lost face if so large an area were removed from his Command.[92] At Quebec, therefore, Leahy proposed a compromise: that Indochina, where operations were far distant, should remain in the Generalissimo's theatre, whereas Siam should, as originally intended, go to S.E.A.C.

It was on this basis that the boundaries of the new Command were officially drawn up in Washington and London.[93]

Despite this apparent agreement, however, considerable confusion was still to surround the subject for some time to come.[94] In part, this was a result of what took place soon after the Quebec meeting. In October, Mountbatten, together with Lt. General Brehon Somervell of the U.S. Army, paid a visit to Chiang Kai-shek, who confirmed American assumptions by imaginatively declaring that 'under existing circumstances . . . the inclusion of Thailand* and Indochina in the Southeast Asian Theatre would not be practicable . . . [because of] the effect which a change of boundary would have on the Chinese people, on the people of Thailand and Indochina, and on the Japanese.' In other words, Siam, as well as Indochina, must remain in the China theatre. Nevertheless, Mountbatten did manage to reach an understanding with the Generalissimo that 'as the war develops, the scope of operations of . . . the Southeast Asia Theatre . . . may involve Thailand and Indochina . . . [when] the boundaries between the two theatres are to be decided at the time in accordance with the progress the respective forces make.'

This agreement, while never formalized, was accepted by the British and American Chiefs of Staff, although Churchill and the Foreign Office ruled out Chiang Kai-shek's accompanying suggestion, that political issues arising in the area should be dealt with by a Chinese–British–American committee sitting in Chungking. Meanwhile Mountbatten also raised with the Generalissimo the question of his being able to initiate clandestine (or 'quasi-military') operations in Siam and Indochina—a matter that was to create much trouble between Mountbatten and Wedemeyer after the latter had been elevated from his S.E.A.C. post to command the American forces in the China theatre. It is important to note, therefore, that Chiang Kai-shek's agreement on this point, although it was not forthcoming until November, when he was on a visit to the Chinese military training camp at Ramgarh in India, was known at the time, both to the War Department in Washington and to Wedemeyer himself. Mountbatten signalled to Wedemeyer at the end of November: 'I asked [the Generalissimo] to confirm that he did not mind my sending agents into Siam and Indochina from now onwards. He confirmed this but asked me to keep him generally informed of my activities. I replied, "I will of course do the same as you do."'[95] In the light of this message, Wedemeyer's subsequent assertions and behaviour in 1945 appear surprising, to say the least.

Difficulties over these boundary questions lay in the future, however. For the moment, despite a certain sourness in some American quarters (elements of the press, encouraged by MacArthur and his staff, suggested that S.E.A.C. had been established at the expense of the Southwest Pacific Area),[96] there was widespread hope that the new Command would supply fresh vigour for the war that was being conducted against the Japanese from

* On the use of either 'Thailand' or 'Siam', see the introductory note on p. xxii, above.

bases in India. How S.E.A.C. did in fact fare during its early days will be examined in the chapter on Southeast Asia. Before that, however, we must take up again the closely related subject of developments in China—developments which, in 1943, appeared to most Western observers to be both confused and disheartening.

Notes to Chapter Eleven

1 Polls of 29 March 1943, DS, Pasvolsky files, box 6.
2 E.g. *San Francisco Examiner*, 4 May, 13 Oct. 1943; *Chicago Tribune*, 10 Aug., 2, 8 and 9 Oct. 1943.
3 E.g. FO 371, A4853/144/45; A5569 and 5958/361/45.
4 Ibid, A3055/144/45.
5 FRUS, Washington and Quebec, 444.
6 Campbell to Foreign Office, 8 Oct. 1943, PREM 3, 158/7.
7 CCS, 23 and 30 April 1943, CAB 88/2.
8 *Bryant*, I. 601, 610, 619.
9 COS, 12 May 1943, CAB 99/22; CCS, 14 and 24 May 1943, CAB 88/2. And see CSP, 15 May 1943, CAB 88/51.
10 FRUS, Cairo and Tehran, 157, 257.
11 *Matloff*, 397–9.
12 See Ehrman, *Grand Strategy*, V, 133–5.
13 Cabs, 29 April and 5 June 1943, CAB 65/34.
14 See Hansard, HC Deb 386, col. 1476; FO 371, file 34118 on WSC speech to Congress, 19 May 1943; press conference of 25 May 1943 in PREM 4, 72/2.
15 CCS, 9 Sept. 1943, CAB 88/3; DC(Ops.), 28 Sept. 1943, CAB 69/5; COS, 5 Aug. 1943, CAB 79/27; King–Nimitz conference, 26 Sept. 1943, USNOA, series III; *Churchill*, V, 119.
16 British Institute of Public Opinion poll, Hornbeck Papers, box 117.
17 E.g. FO 371, A4955/3/45; A3856/361/45.
18 WP(43)484, CAB 66/42.
19 WP(43)327, CAB 66/39. See WP(43)232, 238, 239, 241 (CAB 66/37), and WP(43)259 and 294 (CAB 66/38).
20 FO 371, F2446/25/10; F2637/11/10.
21 Ibid, A10220/34/45.
22 Ibid, A7129/3/45; A7355/32/45; A5904/3/45. See also A10634/144/45.
23 FRUS, 1943, China, 14 and 322.
24 Hornbeck memo., 6 July 1943, Hornbeck Papers, box 119.
25 Committee on Colonial Problems, 15 Oct. 1943, DS, Notter files, box 120.
26 Committee on Political Problems, 13 March 1943, ibid, box 55.
27 Ibid.
28 Ibid.
29 Johnson to Howard, 12 May 1943, Johnson Papers, box 42.
30 E.g. *New York Times*, 20 May 1943; FO 371, A5721/32/45; Knox to Pratt, 23 Dec. 1943, Knox Papers, box 1.
31 JCS, 6 April 1943, RG 218.
32 Hornbeck memo., 28 Oct. 1943, DS, Notter files, box 79.
33 Davies memo., 17 Sept. 1943, Stilwell Papers, box 15.
34 FRUS, 1943, China, 878.
35 Ibid, 14.
36 Hornbeck memo., 10 Nov. 1943, Hornbeck Papers, box 181.
37 DS 740.0011 P.W./3499a. See *Sherwood*, 712.

38 DS 740.0011 P.W./3471.
39 See above, 21–2.
40 Wallace to Hull, 20 May 1943, Wallace Papers, box 52.
41 Gardiner to Grew, 12 March 1943, Roosevelt Papers, PSF box 80.
42 Hornbeck to Grew, 7 April 1943, Hornbeck Papers, box 189.
43 Grew to Gardiner, 23 March and 3 May 1943, Grew Papers, vol. 115.
44 JCS, 6 April 1943, RG 218.
45 Cab, 29 April 1943, CAB 65/34.
46 WSC to COS, 7 Aug. 1943, PREM 3, 147/3.
47 *Bryant*, I, 712.
48 FO 371, A10965/361/45.
49 COS, 19 Aug. 1943, CAB 99/23.
50 *Matloff*, 312, 338.
51 E.g. COS, 20 Aug. 1943, CAB 99/23; CSP, 1943, passim, CAB 88/51; planners' appreciation, 18 Aug. 1943, PREM 3, 147/1.
52 E.g. CCS, 17 Aug. 1943, CAB 88/3.
53 E.g. JPS 67/5, 26 May 1943, CAB 99/22; Ehrman, *Grand Strategy*, V, 159–61.
54 FRUS, Cairo and Tehran, 681, 810.
55 See JCS, 8 June 1943, RG 218; MacArthur, *Reminiscences*, 183. In June 1943, the U.S. planners favoured the Central over the Southwest Pacific. *Pogue*, II, 253.
56 See Morison, *The Two-Ocean War*, 284.
57 JCS, 6 July 1943, RG 218; *Matloff*, 193; *Kirby*, II, 83ff.
58 Morison, *Two-Ocean War*, 299ff.
59 King–Nimitz conference, 30 July–1 Aug. 1943, USNOA, series III.
60 Stimson Diary, 18 June 1943.
61 Handy to Marshall, 3 Dec. 1943, OPD, Exec. file 5, item 15.
62 CSP, 14 Aug. 1943, CAB 88/51.
63 See Howard, *Grand Strategy*, IV, 447.
64 *Roskill*, III, part 1, 240; material in PREM 3, 163/7.
65 JCS, 9 Sept. 1943, RG 218; King to Stark, 5 Nov. 1943, King Papers, box 3, USNOA.
66 WSC to MacArthur, 20 July 1943, PREM 3, 158/5.
67 CSP, 5 Dec. 1943, CAB 88/51.
68 *Matloff*, 373.
69 *Kirby*, II, 253ff., 331.
70 Ibid, 309ff.
71 JCS, 18 Aug. 1943, RG 218; *Churchill*, V, 62.
72 Cabs, 5 and 15 June 1943, CAB 65/34 and 65/38 respectively.
73 WSC to COS, 24 and 26 July 1943, PREM 3, 143/8.
74 Amery to Linlithgow, 25 May and 8 Sept. 1943, Linlithgow Papers, vol. 12.
75 Stilwell Diary, 31 May 1943.
76 E.g. *Romanus and Sutherland*, I, 355ff.
77 WSC–COS meeting, 7 Aug. 1943, PREM 3, 147/2; WSC to FDR, 3 July 1943, PREM 3, 471.
78 JCS, 16 Aug. 1943, RG 218.
79 FDR to WSC, 9 July 1943, PREM 3, 471.
80 Material in PREM 3, 147/4 and WP(43)414, CAB 66/41.
81 E.g. COS, 22 Nov. 1943, CAB 99/25; COS to JSM, 5 Nov. 1943, PREM 3, 148/1.
82 WSC to FDR, 19 June 1943; FDR to WSC, 9 July 1943, PREM 3, 471.
83 FDR to WSC, 30 June 1943, ibid.
84 WSC to FDR, 28 June 1943; FDR to WSC, 30 June 1943, ibid.
85 Stilwell Diary, 18 Nov. 1943.
86 *Pownall*, 14 Sept. 1943; Dorman-Smith Papers, E215/19; *Bryant*, I, 693.
87 *Pogue*, II, 259; Wedemeyer, *Wedemeyer Reports!*, 248.
88 Material in PREM 3, 142/4.
89 WSC to FDR, 19 and 28 June 1943; FDR to WSC, 25 June 1943, PREM 3, 471.
90 WSC to FDR, 28 June 1943, ibid.

91 Draft, 'Problems of South East Asia/China', 22 June 1943, and FDR to WSC, 30 June 1943, Roosevelt Papers, MR box 3.
92 Leahy Diary, 16 July 1943; JCS, 23 Aug. 1943, RG 218.
93 FRUS, Washington and Quebec, 941; War Dpt. to State Dpt., map of command areas, 1 Nov. 1943, DS 740.0011 P.W./3575; Mountbatten directive from WSC, 21 Oct. 1943, PREM 3, 147/4.
94 See e.g. FO 371, F5154/4022/23.
95 Somervell to Dill, 3 Nov. 1943, OPD, Exec. file 1, item 23; Mountbatten to WSC, 26 Nov. 1943, ibid, file 5, item 15; Dill to COS, 6 Nov. 1943, FO 371, F5914/4022/23; Mountbatten to COS, 9 Nov. 1943, ibid, F5915/4022/23; Mountbatten memo., 25 Nov. 1943, COS (Sextant) 1, CAB 99/25; Mountbatten to Wedemeyer, 30 Nov. 1943, PREM 3, 147/7; Earl Mountbatten, *Report to the Combined Chiefs of Staff by the Supreme Commander, Southeast Asia, 1943–1945* (London, 1951; hereafter, *Mountbatten*), 6–7.
96 *Pogue*, II, 281.

CHAPTER TWELVE

THE UNITED STATES, BRITAIN AND CHINA

China as an issue in Anglo-American relations

WE HAVE already seen that, when tension arose between Americans and British over military issues in Southeast Asia, one of the basic causes was to be found in their apparently differing evaluations of the strategic significance and potential of China. And although, as we have also seen, by no means all the American assumptions regarding British views of China were warranted; despite the fact, as well, that American ideas about China were themselves soon to be modified, it is clear that there did, indeed, exist at this time a marked difference of opinion over this question. Among the Combined Staff Planners, for example, it was the American members who exerted pressure on China's behalf, in June being 'unanimous in emphasising that, until the defeat of Japan, they could envisage no situation in which they did not consider it essential to assist China and keep her in the war . . . The United States', they added, 'anticipated a long war against Japan . . . but if China should collapse it would be prolonged indefinitely.'[1]

Similarly, at the Washington Conference it was Leahy, Stilwell and others on the American side who urged that it was 'essential to do something for China . . ., [whose] geographical position and manpower were vital to the defeat of Japan.'[2] (Roosevelt, interestingly enough, put it somewhat differently: 'It was imperative', he observed, 'that the United Nations [should] not be put in a position of being responsible in any way for the collapse of China.')[3] And again, at Quebec, it was Marshall who argued that China was vital for the air bases that she could provide, from which the Allies could strike at Japan proper.[4] Thus, from premises such as these, it followed for the Americans that a campaign in North Burma to reestablish overland contact with China remained essential, both to sustain her morale and to furnish her with a greater volume of supplies.[5]

By comparison, the British approach to the question of China's military and strategic value was cool—cooler, indeed, than it had been during the crisis of 1941–42. Churchill himself epitomized this attitude when he remarked during the Washington Conference that he was 'not prepared to undertake something foolish purely in order to placate the Chinese.'[6] Brooke, too, in the words of his biographer, 'did not believe that any advantage could come from pouring resources into that bottomless pit of Oriental inefficiency and corruption, Chiang Kai-shek's China.'[7] The British planners reported that, for their part, they were less optimistic than their American counterparts over the potential of the Chinese Army; that they could envisage alternatives—Formosa, for example—to China as bases for bombers; that they were less sanguine than the Americans about the volume of supplies that could be carried into China, and less pessimistic over the possibility of China's dropping out of the war altogether.[8] Moreover, even if it were a matter of importance to provide China with large quantities of supplies, the opening up of a port on her south-eastern seaboard would be a far more effective way of doing it than would struggling to push a road through North Burma.

Meanwhile, a low view was held in London, both by the Foreign Office and by the Services, of China's current military effort. Sir Maurice Peterson, for example, wrote on one report: 'Our impression that the Chinese don't mean to fight in *this* war is confirmed.'[9] At the same time, however, it was considered unlikely that China would make peace with Japan, and even if such an eventuality came about, the Communist forces in the north were expected to fight on, thereby continuing to pin down a substantial number of Japanese troops.[10] In a paper specially prepared for the military planners in the light of their disagreements with their American colleagues, the Foreign Office summed up in July the underlying British position, using, interestingly enough, the same major criterion as did Washington, that is, the necessity of defeating Japan as soon as possible:

'We do not want China to drop out of the war', they insisted, 'and we should like to prevent it, but not at the expense of prolonging the war against Japan . . . Assistance to China should only be a primary consideration if it is in the interests of strategy; otherwise it should be a secondary, though not a negligible consideration. In the worst eventuality it is better that the Chungking Government should collapse than that the allied military effort against Japan should be dissipated in an effort to keep it alive.'[11]

In 1943, the American response to this paper would of course have been that the survival of Chiang Kai-shek's Government was, indeed, essential, in both military and political terms, to the successful prosecution of the Far Eastern war. Even had they not believed this, however, it would have been extremely difficult for politicians, officials and staff officers in the United States to emulate the detached nature of the Foreign Office's appraisal. Although for some Americans disillusionment was now not far away, there remained in 1943 a strong inclination on the part of many to indulge in adulation where China was concerned, a country that was 'standing as an unchallenged equal beside us in the war', as the *New York Times* put it.[12] Further public appearances in the United States by Madame Chiang Kai-shek helped to sustain this climate of opinion. 'No figure on the world stage', declared the *New York Times*, 'stirs the American imagination more than hers', while in private Harry Hopkins had the satisfaction of hearing her say that 'we could be sure China would line up with us at the peace table.'[13] Her brother, T. V. Soong, likewise continued to exercise his persuasive powers on the Senate Foreign Relations Committee and others in Washington.[14]

China was still widely seen by Americans, high and low, as a fellow-democracy, looking to the United States not only for aid but for leadership and inspiration. Thus, an itinerant Presidential envoy, Patrick Hurley, was able to reassure Roosevelt after visiting Chungking before the Cairo Conference took place that 'the Generalissimo and the Chinese people favor the principles of democracy and liberty . . . [and] are opposed to the principles of imperialism and communism . . . [Chiang Kai-shek] has implicit confidence in your motives . . . [and] will therefore follow your leadership on the diplomatic and political questions that will be considered in the impending conference.'[15] In return, the President assured this admirably humble protégé that he would continue to press for China to be acknowledged as a complete equal of the other Allied powers.[16] Nor was Roosevelt, in saying this, simply speaking for the record, for it was during this period, in March 1943, that he conveyed privately to Marshall his view of China and of Chiang Kai-shek that was quoted earlier, describing the Generalissimo as having created in a very short time throughout his country 'what it took us in a couple of centuries to attain.'[17]

If this personal belief were not sufficient incentive in itself, Roosevelt also had to reckon with public demands for more aid to be sent to China, some of them, though not all, coming from his political enemies.[18] Chiang Kai-shek himself went on loudly asking for more help during 1943, seeking in particular an independent air force for Chennault to command in China, supplies to the tune of 10,000 tons a month to be flown over the Hump, and 500 planes, to be delivered by November. Chungking's statements of such requirements were accompanied, as before, by hints that, if her demands were not met, China might seek to reach a compromise peace with Japan,[19] and there were still those in Washington who were indeed ready to believe that, in Leahy's words, Chiang 'might drop out of the war.'[20] Even if the Generalissimo's forces were not beaten in the field, his regime, so many American officials thought, could easily suffer an economic collapse. (The purchasing power of the Chinese currency, one sixty-sixth of the 1937 level at the end of 1942, was one two-hundred-and-twenty-eighth a year later.)[21] Therefore China must be supplied with increased aid and be accorded an enhanced status within the councils and war-administration of the Allies;[22] also, criticism of her in the American press must if possible be prevented.[23] Similarly, Roosevelt, when en route to Cairo, announced his desire to see Chiang Kai-shek on his own and before any meeting with the British delegation.[24] It all amounted to an immediate concern and esteem for China which was not matched by Churchill and his colleagues.

Anglo-American differences also continued to exist over China's future status. Throughout 1943, the President was again stressing that she must be regarded as one of the four great powers who, from a position at the heart of a new international organization, would 'police the world' after the war. There was a selfish, as well as a benevolent aspect to this idea. Roosevelt, noted Hopkins after one of the talks held with Eden in Washington in March, 'feels that China, in any serious policy conflict with Russia, would undoubtedly line up on our side', and although the British Foreign Secretary's own reaction was somewhat sceptical, he saw to it that the message was duly received in London.[25] The President also ensured that Mountbatten, in Southeast Asia, understood his point of view. 'I really feel', he wrote to the new Supreme Commander, 'that it is a triumph to have got four hundred and twenty-five million Chinese on the Allied side. They will be useful twenty-five or fifty years hence . . .'[26] He brought the subject up again at Tehran, this time with Stalin—who, like Eden, tended to be sceptical.[27] And at Cairo the President rambled on on the same theme to Stilwell and Davies, totally failing, as he did so, to meet the General's request for precise instructions and a definition of American policy as regards China.[28] ('God-awful is no word for it', wrote Stilwell in his diary afterwards. '. . . The man is a flighty fool. Christ, but he's terrible. We came out puking. Sat around, but nothing happened.')[29]

Meanwhile, in marked contrast to Roosevelt, Churchill, though willing to humour the former to some extent over China's place in a proposed international organization, remained scornful of the entire notion that she had a leading role to play. 'It is affectation', the Prime Minister wrote to Eden, 'to pretend that China is a power in any way comparable to the other three. It is quite possible that with the removal of the Japanese menace, and above all if anything should happen to Chiang Kai-shek, China might fall again into a state of great confusion and possibly civil war.' Thus, in a speech he delivered in Washington in September, Churchill included a reference to China alongside the other great powers only at the urging of his advisers and 'with much blasphemy' during the drafting process.[30*]

Other factors also helped prevent the development of a close and harmonious Anglo-American approach to questions involving China. One was the strong dislike of the British that, so American officials reported, continued to be entertained by the Chinese themselves. 'The blunt fact is', wrote Berle in Washington, 'that Chinese–British relations are deteriorating to a point where they are in conflict in a number of very important details; and conflict is developing along certain very fundamental lines.'[31] (As if to emphasize the point, anti-British articles written by Chinese were appearing in the American press.)[32†] The danger for America that was seen to arise

---

* Churchill subsequently described the Chinese aspect of the Cairo talks as having been 'lengthy, complicated and minor.' (*Churchill*, V, 289.) Brooke, too, was convinced by what he heard at Cairo that 'there was little to be hoped for from Chiang's China.' (*Bryant*, II, 76, 81.)

† One issue not much remarked upon by Americans at the time—in part, perhaps, because they, too, were open to awkward questions in this field—concerned Australian–Chinese negotiations over the ending of extraterritoriality. In 1943 no agreement was reached between the two countries, as a result of difficulties which arose from 'white-

from this situation was, in the words of the Chief of the State Department's Far Eastern Division, that 'Chinese resentment toward the British (which is severe) tends to turn, at least indirectly, toward the United States because the United States and Great Britain are so closely allied in the formulation of global strategy.'[33] In addition, the British for their part were seen in some American quarters as being, not merely cool towards China (Eden appeared to confirm this by telling Roosevelt that he 'did not much like the idea of the Chinese running up and down the Pacific' after the war),[34] but anxious to see China remain weak and divided. It was an assumption that was to flourish in Washington during the final stages of the war, and that has tended to be repeated subsequently by American historians, their national heritage seemingly outweighing their knowledge and powers of investigation.[35]

It followed that many Americans continued to hold the belief that the United States was far more enlightened in its approach to China than was Great Britain. For example, even after having a series of amicable talks in London, in which scarcely any difficulties had seemed to arise, Hornbeck went on uttering his usual refrain: 'The British', he reported, 'tend to look at China and the Chinese in the light of their experience in India, and hence are less inclined [than we are] to consider China as a sovereign state.'[36] Earlier, in a memorandum which he had given unofficially to Halifax, he had demanded: 'Would it not be to the greatest advantage of the greatest number were the British Government . . . and the people of Great Britain and the governments and peoples of the British Dominions to adopt toward China the attitude and policy which, generally speaking, are those of the Government and people of the United States . . . ?'[37] Such an approach was encouraged by the Chinese themselves, who were wont to comment warmly on the greater degree of friendship they received from Americans.[38] In return, Stilwell for one was glad to list for Chiang Kai-shek's benefit belittling remarks about the Chinese Army that he had heard made by British officers.[39]

Not that there is any reason to think that these quotations of Stilwell's were invented. As in the previous period, there was at least some foundation for the view which Hornbeck and others took of British attitudes towards China, just as there was some justification for the reciprocal belief which was held in the Foreign Office that Americans had a distorting 'obsession' with that country and that a revision of Washington's opinions on the subject—'the dawn of intelligence', one London official called it—was long overdue.[40] On the British side there remained, for example, those who saw China as constituting something of a menace for the future, and on one occasion rumours of Chinese territorial ambitions were openly referred to in Parliament.[41] To members of the Foreign Office, the existence of such ambitions appeared the more likely in the light of various pieces of evidence that came to hand during 1943—Chinese maps showing Burma as part of that country,

Australia' immigration policies. (See e.g. ADEA, A989/43/150/5/1/2; Eckersley memo., June 1943, ibid, A989/43/735/301; Eggleston despatch, 15 March 1943, ibid, A989/44/655/37.)

for example; statements made in Chungking about expatriate Chinese living in Southeast Asia; Chiang Kai-shek's own book, *China's Destiny*, which blamed foreigners for China's misfortunes over the preceding century, and the translation of which into English was held up by the Generalissimo; a private warning from President Quezon of the Philippines, speaking when none of his American mentors was around, that the Chinese were 'the greatest potential danger in Asia, far greater than Japan.'[42]

Parallels between the Kuomintang's rule in China and Fascism in Europe were again being drawn in London, Peterson in the Foreign Office, for example, commenting that 'large parts of [*China's Destiny*] might have been written by Hitler or at least by Franco.'[43] As before, however, it was the Government of India that was outstanding for the extent to which it expressed apprehension where China was concerned. Sir Mahommed Zafrullah Khan, for instance, continued to prophesy that 'China after the war was going to be a very formidable problem indeed', stating that the Chinese 'had very much the same kind of ideas as the Japanese.'[44] Likewise, Sir Olaf Caroe, the head of New Delhi's External Affairs Department, argued to the Chatham House Far Eastern Group that 'history had proved that there was such a thing as Chinese imperialism.' (Sir John Pratt, who was one of those present, retorted that 'there was no danger to India from China . . . Indeed', he added, 'we had called Chinese imperialism into existence by our own follies . . . [and] the real danger was from Japan.' A small incident, it nevertheless serves to illustrate how crude was the lumping together by American observers of all Britain's Caroes and Pratts, Linlithgows and Dorman-Smiths, where attitudes to Asia and Asian countries were concerned.)[45]

Various local issues heightened New Delhi's disquiet and, at times, ire. There was the discourtesy of Madame Chiang Kai-shek when she passed through India en route from the United States without notifying the authorities in advance.[46] Worse still, there were her remarks to the American press in support of freedom for India.[47] Questions also continued to arise over the training of Chinese troops by Stilwell at Ramgarh, with the Viceroy and Secretary of State for India alike displaying much alarm when the aggressive American proposed to increase the numbers involved from 42,000 to 100,000.

'The presence in India of Chinese troops', Amery emphasized to the Defence Committee in London, 'may cause the Chinese Government to raise a claim in certain eventualities to meddle in Indian politics. They have already shown an embarrassing tendency in that direction . . . There might even be a danger of Chinese troops assisting the Congress Party . . . in the event of really serious civil disorders breaking out in India . . . [And] the greater the part which Chinese troops play in the reconquest or the subsequent garrisoning of Burma, the greater the voice China will expect to have in the settlement of Burma's future.'[48]

Tibet, too, was again a subject for concern. In this period, there were growing rumours to the effect that China was concentrating troops with the intention of invading and enforcing its claim to sovereignty over that territory, and the Government of India was loudest among those in British official circles who expressed their disquiet accordingly.[49] Fear of Chinese designs on Tibet was also the main reason why New Delhi, to the apprehension of the Foreign Office in London, decided to start pushing its area of effective administration in northern Assam up to the McMahon line of 1914, thus countering Tibetan encroachments in those regions.[50] Meanwhile the over-all policy of the Government in London was to seek to prevent Chinese–Tibetan issues coming to a head, although at the same time insisting that Britain's recognition of Chinese suzerainty was dependent on China's own acceptance of Tibetan autonomy.[51] For its part, Chungking continued to proclaim China's sovereign rights over that country, while denying that any act of military coercion was being planned.[52]

As far as London was concerned, however, Tibet was a secondary matter. Far greater difficulties seemed likely to arise over Hongkong, in which case the Chinese Government might receive the support of the United States. The signing in January 1943 of the agreement to end extraterritoriality had not prevented the Chinese from reserving the right to raise at a later date the question of the future of the Kowloon Leased Territory, their aim being, it seemed clear, to secure eventually the rendition of Hongkong in its entirety.[53] In response to this situation, the China Association in London, strongly opposed by Sir John Pratt but supported by John Keswick of Jardine Matheson (now, as we have seen, in Government service), urged that Britain should leave no doubt that she intended to retain the colony. As for the Foreign Office, while there remained those officials who were ready to issue a statement to the effect that the question of Hongkong's future could be discussed after the war, the general feeling was that it would be best to preserve such a bargaining counter for possible use later. Indeed, attitudes in Whitehall as a whole appear to have been hardening at this time, as compared to the more flexible approach which had been adopted by even the Colonial Office in 1942, when the pressures upon Britain had been greater. Churchill himself, needless to say, remained adamant on the subject, and specifically mentioned Hongkong when stating to Roosevelt and Stalin at Tehran that 'nothing would be taken away from [Britain] without a war.'[54] Thus, Roosevelt's own hope, that Britain would give up Hongkong 'as a gesture of goodwill' (another idea circulating among American officials was that the port might become 'a great international depot'), seemed unlikely to be realized.[55] Nor was there forthcoming during this period an alternative gesture on London's part in the shape of a loan for China, negotiations over the proposed £50 million grant of 1942 remaining deadlocked, largely as a result of the insistence of the Treasury that no use must be made of such funds by China for post-war commercial purposes.[56]

British apprehension over China's intentions regarding the future in East and Southeast Asia, and also over the role that the United States might choose to play in that respect, were not lessened by the affair of the Cairo communiqué. What occurred on that occasion was that the Americans showed their draft of this public declaration first to the Chinese, and only afterwards to the British delegation, with the result that Cadogan and his colleagues had great difficulty in obtaining what they held to be important amendments. Indeed, two of the original features of the document to which they objected were still there in the final version: that is, the naming of Manchuria and other territories as having been stolen from China by Japan, and therefore due for restoration to the former (the Foreign Office view was that the Soviet Union would insist on being consulted where Manchuria was concerned); and the failure to name at the same time territories which should be restored to Britain, the Netherlands and other Western powers with interests in the area. Cadogan did manage to have inserted in the communiqué the pledge that none of the signatories (the United States, China and Britain) coveted anything for itself or had thoughts of territorial expansion.[57] Even so, the experience could only reinforce the feeling in London that the United States was developing a tendency to act independently of Britain where the Far East, and particularly China, was concerned.

The retirement in 1943 of Sir Frederick Maze as Inspector General of Chinese Customs, and his replacement by the first American to hold the post, appeared to symbolize a new era.[58] It was in this year, also, that Sir Eric Teichman, Britain's most experienced adviser on Chinese affairs, drew up his report, quoted in the first chapter above, on the striking contrast with the scene of ten years earlier, arising from the way in which China now 'depended on America and [accepted her] leadership', and from Britain's enforced 'abdication from the position of leadership which we have occupied in China for the past hundred years.'[59]

Being clearly overshadowed in this way appears in retrospect to have helped inhibit British officials from undertaking anything very much in the nature of planning for the future in the Far East—this, of course, in addition to Cadogan's unfortunate lack of sympathy for any such exercise. The Military Attaché in Chungking did suggest in forceful fashion that some long-term thinking was urgently required, but his submission was rejected in the Foreign Office on the grounds that it was too early to discern adequately either the problems that would be encountered or the resources that would be available for meeting them.[60] It was a regrettable contrast to the more constructive line that the Head of the Far Eastern Department had himself been taking in 1942.[61] Eggleston, from his vantage point in the Australian Legation in Chungking, noticed at the time that 'the British are fond of emphasising the imponderables.' In a diary entry that has been briefly referred to earlier, he also observed of the British in China:

'There is [in them] no kindling to the new idea or to opportunities of cooperation . . . I doubt whether many of the British staff have read the Beveridge Plan. Those who read, read 18th century literature . . . On the other hand the Americans are arrogant and aggressive, quite rude in their condemnation of things which they do not understand and quite resentful

when their criticism provokes a hostile reaction or causes the Englishman
to go into reserve. The worst of it is that their criticism is based on
intellectual clichés by which modern facts are interpreted . . . [But] I have
great faith in the Americans—they are constructive. You can get into
discussion with them on all the big problems of the day, and you can't
with the products of Oxford and Cambridge . . .'[62]

Meanwhile, viewed from London, it was the Americans who appeared to
be lukewarm as regards opportunities for cooperation over Chinese affairs.
The Sino–American–British Currency Stabilization Board, for example,
which the Foreign Office saw as being a potential basis for later collaboration over China's post-war reconstruction, was brought to an end during
this period at Washington's insistence and as a concession to Chinese dislike
of foreign interference.[63] British proposals for a three-power screening
board to be set up in China to deal with supplies needed by that country
also met with a negative response in Washington. The American attitude in
this case is scarcely surprising, given their well-nigh exclusive role when it
came to providing the supplies in question, but it was frustrating for London
to remain in virtual ignorance of what was being done.[64] It also came as
something of a shock to British officials when they learned that, despite
previous assurances exchanged between the State Department and the
Foreign Office about consulting and keeping each other fully informed on
such matters, Washington had gone ahead and agreed to explore with the
Chinese the chance of concluding a comprehensive Sino-American commercial treaty.[65]

Indeed, the possibility that commercial rivalry might arise between the
United States and Britain in China after the war was already beginning to
cast its shadow, even at this comparatively early stage of the Far Eastern
conflict. In Washington, Chinese plans for post-war industrialization were
being carefully watched, together with indications concerning, for example,
the likely extent of Chinese Government monopolies and control over
business generally.[66] In October 1943, as a service organization for American firms who wished to deal with China, the China–America Council was
established, its founder-members including the U.S. Rubber Company, the
International Harvester Company, Coca-Cola, International General
Electric, Remington Rand, Time Inc., the Chase Manhattan Bank, and
Standard Vacuum Oil. As for the prospectus of the Council, it contained a
clear call to American firms to meet and overcome the rivalry of Great
Britain:

'Unless American industry is fully prepared for immediate action', it
declared, 'considerable competitive advantages will fall to other nations
who have already realized the necessity of cementing and expanding their
trade position in China in anticipation of a very prosperous post-war
era . . . The British have always profited by a successful organization of
their foreign commercial interests . . . If this advantage is to be neutralized,

similar steps must be taken by American business toward that end without delay.'[67]

Meanwhile, on the spot in Chungking, an American like Captain 'Mary' Miles was still conducting his affairs on the basis of assumed Anglo-American rivalry (between them, for example, U.S. intelligence officers and Tai Li, head of Chiang Kai-shek's secret police, with whom they were working, appear to have suppressed some of the reports that the British academic, Michael Lindsay, was trying to send to Chungking from the Communist-held areas in the north).[68] Amongst other things, Miles had the previous commercial connections of British officials and officers serving in China carefully noted,[69] while he was only one of the U.S. representatives who suspected that some ulterior motive must lie behind continuing British attempts to open up a supply route into China via Iran, the Soviet Union and Sinkiang.[70]

Yet to the British themselves, what stood out at the time were not the opportunities that were available to them in China, but the difficulties that stood in the way of becoming involved in the affairs of that country to even a limited extent, let alone being able to lay firm foundations for subsequent commercial expansion on a large scale. One example of the frustrations that were involved arose as a result of the interest displayed by the Chinese Government in obtaining transport planes from Britain for use on various internal routes, an interest that was coupled with a proposal that Britain should also participate in a joint corporation for developing an air route from India to Sinkiang. Despite their obvious attractions in terms of post-war civil aviation, however, the projects quickly foundered when Washington's dislike of the transport-aircraft deal was made clear, London rightly feeling that they could scarcely provoke American hostility over the matter when Britain herself was dependent on the United States for the supply of such aeroplanes.[71] A separate scheme, involving the possibility that Jardine Matheson (who had the advantage of John Keswick's frequent presence in China) might participate in a Sino-British air-transport company, was running up against similar difficulties.[72] Meanwhile, American displeasure had been apparent when, at the request of Chiang Kai-shek, Air Vice Marshal Pattinson and six other R.A.F. officers arrived in Chungking to run the Chinese Air Staff College. Stilwell had tried to have the appointment cancelled; in addition, he continued to oppose the despatch of British fighter squadrons to China and, according to General Carton de Wiart, was 'very much against' the latter's appointment to Chungking as the military representative there of Churchill and of Mountbatten.[73]

In short, whether one looks at the broad question of China's post-war role in the world or at the detailed conduct of the war as it involved China, one could again easily conclude that Britain and the United States were far apart where that country was concerned. And yet during this period, as in the previous one, there did exist other elements in the reactions and policies of each Western Ally which suggest in retrospect that a close accommodation might possibly have been arrived at, especially had there existed on the part of the Americans a greater will to such an end, unencumbered by the emotion and rhetoric with which many of them continued to surround the subject of China.

Britain and China

Whatever might be thought of the American preoccupation with China, it continued to be accepted within the Foreign Office that Britain's own relations with that country could have a significant bearing on the state of the transatlantic partnership. As a member of the Far Eastern Department put it, 'the essential fact about Anglo-Chinese relations . . . is that they are relatively unimportant in themselves, but very important—and potentially very dangerous—as an aspect of Anglo-American relations.'[74] It was thus thought to be all the more necessary for it to be emphasized, as it was by Eden, for instance, at an Albert Hall 'Salute to China' rally, that Britain wanted 'a strong and united China',[75] and that the latter could be sure that, as Churchill expressed it at a meeting of the Pacific War Council, 'the entire forces of the British Commonwealth would, at the earliest possible moment, be hurled into the battle against Japan.'[76]

It also followed that the American 'obsession for China' must be treated with great delicacy. 'It is useless for us to try to debunk [that] obsession as such', wrote the Head of the North American Department,

'though we can tell the truth in season and in private on concrete issues such as China's war effort, and it is dangerous for us to seem to slight China by not admitting her as a Great Power, for such apparent slights would make it easier for her to range U.S. opinion against us at the peace settlement . . . Moreover, if we let ourselves appear as unsympathetic or even unimaginative towards China, the moral effect on the ingrained evangelical side of the United States character, combined with the condemnation that Russian policy is almost certain to incur, might conceivably reverse the present current towards interventionism . . . and might give an advantage to U.S. commercial competition against our own.'[77]

British officials, from whatever department, who were visiting the U.S.A. were therefore warned in a confidential set of notes that,

'For various reasons, some historical, the Chinese enjoy in America today a prestige second to none. Admiration for the Chinese may sometimes lead to their being credited with a degree of virtue which few Chinese would seriously claim. Unless you have first-hand knowledge of the Far East [however], do not attempt to correct American opinion; and if you do have such knowledge, stick to your personal experience.'[78]

Meanwhile, in the military field, British attitudes did extend beyond mere coolness and doubt. Chennault's programme for the use of air power within

China, for example, continued—in contrast to the schemes of Stilwell—to command British support.[79] Plans for increasing the flow of supplies over the Hump also had the approval of the Chiefs of Staff in London.[80] Nor were the objections put forward by the Government of India to an increase in the number of Chinese troops training at Ramgarh allowed to win the day, even though Eden, personally, had some sympathy with the Viceroy over the matter. The decisive argument within the Foreign Office—many Americans would have been astonished to read it—was that 'our main objective must be to defeat the Japanese with any help we can get', and the issue was finally argued out in military rather than political terms, agreement being given to Stilwell's revised increase of 15,000 (rather than the 58,000 addition that he had originally proposed).[81]

In both the diplomatic and commercial spheres, also, the overriding desire continued to be to work as closely as possible with Washington. Over the Tibetan question, for example, London vainly hoped to see the United States become involved, and welcomed as an encouraging sign the decision to send O.S.S. representatives to that country. (Even more pleasing was the sympathy expressed by those O.S.S. officers for Tibet's demand for freedom from Chinese interference.) Again, of course, this desire for cooperation sprang partly from Britain's own helplessness. 'If China administers a rebuff to us', wrote Sir John Brenan, 'and follows it up with a military demonstration against Tibet, there is not much that we can do about it, especially if the U.S. Government proves unsympathetic towards our side of the dispute.'[82] Where propaganda efforts that involved China were concerned, meanwhile, the need to develop a harmonious Anglo-American approach in this field was again emphasized in London.[83]

As for commercial matters, the Foreign Office had reason to believe that American 'advisers' in China, together with others connected with bodies like the Universal Trading Corporation (a Sino-American company handling Chinese cash-purchases in the U.S.A.) were engaged in seeking post-war orders as well as in carrying out their official, war-time duties; hence there was a feeling that British firms should not be discouraged from exploring the potential market in China for themselves, if they were able to do so. Even so, it was strongly believed that, in the words of the Ambassador in Chungking, 'we should . . . take every precaution not to expose ourselves to any appearance of undermining existing United States trade interests [in China].' Again, given Britain's weak position, Anglo-American cooperation in this field was bound to remain the hope for the future. There was also, however, a belief in it for its own sake. It was in this spirit, for example, that a Foreign Office official proposed that 'even if, as it appears, . . . the Americans are pulling fast ones over us . . . we ought to stick to the rules on our side.'[84]

In the same cause of cooperation, an attempt was also made to maintain close contact with the State Department over Far Eastern affairs, notably by means of an exchange of letters between Ashley Clarke, Head of the Far Eastern Department in London, and Stanley Hornbeck. Sometimes this link did prove useful, as when Clarke was able to set out the reasons why Britain was not ashamed to be seeking to 're-take Burma', any more than the Americans were ashamed of wanting to liberate the Philippines; fundamentally, both countries, submitted Clarke, were in any case 'fighting for their lives.'[85] In general, however, Hornbeck's usefulness as a contact was lessened in that, in contrast to what he had to say within his own, Washington, circles, he tended in his letters to London to play down Anglo-American differences. 'It is a matter of constant gratification to me', he wrote in January 1943 in one of his less-mangled prose efforts, 'to find that you [in the Foreign Office] feel regarding various aspects of current problems and probable future policies very much as we here feel.'[86] The same thing happened when Hornbeck, at the invitation of the Foreign Office, visited London in person towards the end of the year. (The conferment on him of an honorary Oxford degree was contemplated, in the knowledge that it would add great pleasure to his stay in Britain; it was eventually concluded, however, that even the cause of Anglo-American partnership could not warrant so great a lowering of the University's standards.)[87] Hornbeck did urge on this occasion that China should be treated as an equal; but in the series of talks that followed, issues were seldom brought to a head, and the members of the Foreign Office who were involved would almost certainly have been surprised to see Hornbeck's own summary of what had transpired, prepared for consumption in Washington, in which, as we have seen, he duly returned to the standard American theme of how far apart the two countries were in the Far East.[88]

To British officials, indeed, Hornbeck, for all his prickliness, appeared to be a friend. Even before he set off for London, for example, he had indicated to Halifax 'off the record' that he did not agree with those of his colleagues who believed that Britain should give Hongkong back to China, although he hoped to see that port become a 'key point in the [post-war] United Nations defence strategy.'[89] As for his own views on the future within China, in conversation with Clarke and others he dismissed the idea that after the war 'there would be a period of chaos [and] civil war between the Kuomintang and Communists.' Chiang Kai-shek's Government, he assured his British listeners, was 'by far the strongest power among the Chinese', and by the end of the war its resources would be 'overwhelming.' What was more, argued Hornbeck, 'this Government had the great majority of the people behind it. What could the Communists do', he asked, 'against such a show of power?'[90] His predictive ability was again, as so often, shown to be limited when he cast doubt on the suggestion, made by his Foreign Office hosts, that the Soviet Union might well want to control the major railways in Manchuria; access to a warm-water port, he thought, would be enough to satisfy Moscow.[91]

Meanwhile Hornbeck's main concern and message was, in the words of a British official, 'that we should back Chiang Kai-shek right through.' And yet, not long after he had impressed this line upon London, he himself was to be eased out of the State Department, with his ideas being superseded there in some measure by an increasing exasperation with Chiang and a more flexible approach towards the question of who should govern China. As it was, the Foreign Office for their part were quite ready to accept what Hornbeck had had to say. 'We should have no difficulty', wrote Ashley Clarke, 'in going most of the way with him on the various matters which we have discussed.'[92]

It was all the easier for Clarke and his colleagues to come to such a conclusion in that the assurances which they had given their visitor, to the effect that Britain did desire to see a strong and stable China, were not simply designed for American consumption but, as we have seen in the preceding period, were genuine. As Clarke now put it in an internal minute: 'The more united and orderly and the more confident in her own strength China was, the more likely it was that we could maintain reasonable political and economic relations with her.'[93] The China Association, too, for all its 'treaty-port' past, was making a similar point in private, hoping for 'a strong and stable government in China without which there cannot be a steady flow of trade for the benefit of China and the outside world alike.'[94] Even the supplanting of British by American leadership among the foreigners in China was accepted philosophically in some quarters, so that Teichman, in his paper already quoted, received an appreciative hearing in the Foreign Office when he wrote: 'There is something instinctively purposeful, if slow and clumsy, about the development of United States policy in China; and it is in accordance with modern political and geographical circumstances, and perhaps in the long run in the interests of ourselves as well, that China and America should draw together and the former accept the latter's leadership in the Far Eastern world.' (Again, this is a line of thinking that has almost entirely escaped American historians of war-time Chinese affairs.) Even in Government of India circles, not all was hostility towards China. For example, many members of an unofficial 'brains trust' in New Delhi, comprised of Sir Olaf Caroe and other leading officials, found 'the vision of a Sino-British entente . . . attractive.'[95]

The idea of a 'new' China and of the need for a qualitative change in relations between her and the rest of the world was also by now even more widely accepted in London than it had been in 1942. 'We have got to deal with an entirely new China, politically at any rate', Ernest Bevin wrote to Eden,[96] while one of the latter's own officials observed that 'modern China has come to stay and we must like it or lump it.'[97] Another member of the Foreign Office likewise bluntly informed a representative of the China Association 'that [his] committee should get their minds clear on one point, namely that there was going to be a clean cut between the past and the future, and that henceforth H.M.G. would treat China as a sovereign independent state.'[98] In turn, members of the Association, having been assured by T. V. Soong during one of his visits to London that an expansion of commercial relations 'on a basis of full equality' would be welcomed, set about trying to find ways of adapting to the changed circumstances, such as setting up new businesses under nominal Chinese control, or tying up with T. V. Soong's own commercial interests.[99]

It was during this period, also, that the Parliamentary delegation, whose visit to China has been described already,[100] returned to Britain with its glowing accounts of China's 'sense of unity and achievement', her 'new sense of nationhood that . . . is going to have a profound effect upon the world's future.' In return, Chinese military and 'goodwill' missions arrived in London during the year,[101] while Madame Chiang Kai-shek (whose influence within China still tended to be overrated) was told that she, too, would be made welcome if she could come.[102] As for the Generalissimo himself (elected President of the Republic of China in September), when Carton de Wiart wrote from Chungking to ask if Churchill agreed that 'to treat a man who has achieved a position like his present one as a coolie is ridiculous', the Prime Minister minuted: 'I do indeed.'[103] Moreover, as well as being flattered by Roosevelt, Chiang Kai-shek at Cairo managed to make his mark with the British party at the Conference. 'Winston fell for Madame Chiang Kai-shek', recorded Cadogan, '. . . [and] Chiang Kai-shek himself made an impression . . .', while Eden told Ministers on his return that 'the P.M. . . . likes both her and her husband much better than he did before, never having met either of them.'[104]

In their small ways, British attempts to aid China in practical fashion were also continued during 1943. The slender possibility of opening up new supply routes, through either the Soviet Union or Tibet, went on receiving attention,[105] while at Hornbeck's instigation (though in the event nothing came of it) Washington was informed that Britain would not object to China's being granted representation on Allied supply boards.[106] In China itself, a handful of British officers were still training special 'surprise' (i.e. commando) battalions of local troops, though handicapped by the inadequate amount of supplies which reached them through the American-controlled system.[107] Meanwhile the United Aid to China Fund was again remitting substantial sums to Chungking (£703,000 was collected between July 1942 and July 1943; £507,000 in the year after that),[108] with aid also being supplied by the British Red Cross and Friends ambulance unit.[109] In the field of scientific, technological and cultural relations, too, valuable work was being performed in China by Dr. Joseph Needham, who had been asked by the British Council in 1942 'to do everything in my power to renew and extend the cultural bonds between the British and Chinese peoples, which had been disrupted since the outbreak of the Sino-Japanese conflict.'[110]* At the same time a Universities China Committee in Britain dealt with such matters as the development of Chinese studies and the placing of visiting Chinese students.[111]

These endeavours are cited, not because they rivalled the American

* In marked contrast to the situation in almost every other field of Anglo-American relations in China, Dr. Needham encountered in his work no sign of hostility on the part of the Americans, while Dr. Fairbank, who was involved in related, though not overlapping, activities on behalf of the U.S.A., recalls the situation in similar terms. Indeed, various U.S. Government agencies were ready at times to work through Dr. Needham. In retrospect, Dr. Needham attributes this state of affairs partly to the existence of an international fraternity of scientists and scholars. (Interviews with Dr. Needham and Professor Fairbank.)

presence in and dealings with China, but in order to demonstrate that, for all Britain's reduced ability to play some kind of role there, concern and good-will did remain—something that was often, probably usually, overlooked in the United States. This is not to claim, of course, that the British approach was essentially the same as the American one. The underlying differences which have been traced back into the pre-war years still existed. The good-will that was exhibited within official circles in London, for example, was allied to a more pragmatic attitude than was generally to be found in Wash-ington, less inclined towards acute anxiety and other strong emotions when the Chinese scene was being surveyed. An illustration of this is provided in connection with the closely-linked questions of Chinese Communism and of possible Soviet influence in China in the future.

Although, as we have seen, some British individuals like Michael Lindsay and Claire and William Band (Band had been Professor of Physics at Yenching University before Pearl Harbour) were living with the Communists in northern China, and were enthusiastic over what they saw,[112] no British diplomatic contact with Yenan existed, and information as to what was happening in the Communist areas was scarce. Nevertheless, from such pieces of evidence that he could put together, the Ambassador in Chungking, Seymour, felt able to report in July that 'there seems little doubt that the agrarian policy of the Communists has proved superior to that of the Kuomintang in the economic security and social well-being it has brought to the masses of the population.' He also believed that, despite the existence of 'a Communist oligarchy [with] semi-dictatorial powers', some basis of popular representation had been established, 'an achievement which as yet cannot be claimed for Kuomintang China.'[113]

As for the question of whether the Yenan regime was a genuinely Com-munist one, Seymour's judgment was essentially correct. 'It is clear', he wrote, 'that the Chinese Communists have no intention of abandoning Marx-Leninism as their guiding principle, but aim rather to adapt it to present and future Chinese conditions.' G. F. Hudson of the Foreign Office Research Department likewise took issue with Ashley Clarke's suggestion (which echoed the opinion of Teichman) that the Chinese Communists were 'more interested in an agrarian new deal in China than in world revolution.' Mao Tse-tung's 1940 pamphlet, *The New Democracy*, argued Hudson, made it entirely clear 'that Mao at any rate regards Chinese Communism as part of a world proletarian revolution, and that its aim is to establish in China the same economic and political system which exists in the U.S.S.R., though owing to the backwardness of China there must be a transitional period in which the Communists would be ready to cooperate with the Kuomintang, provided they were given a share in the Government, until such time as they are ready to push out the Kuomintang and suppress them.'[114]

The idea that the Communists in China were not genuine Marxists was nevertheless to prove a difficult one to erase altogether, as we shall see in later periods. Meanwhile, what were the prospects for the future? Some—for example Hudson himself and F. C. Jones, a fellow-academic serving in the

Foreign Office Research Department—foresaw a Kuomintang victory in the event of a civil war in China, unless the Soviet Union intervened on the side of the Communists.[115] Yet G. P. Young of the Far Eastern Department— a diplomat with a conventional background (Westminster School and Oxford), but a markedly independent mind*—declared in a highly prescient minute in May 1943:

'It is impossible not to gain the impression that the Chinese in [the Communist] areas are as far ahead of the Kuomintang Chinese as Dr. Sun Yat-sen's original party were ahead of the Manchus. They have what the Kuomintang conspicuously lacks—an alive ideology . . . [If, as was likely, Kuomintang repression were to continue,] there is every possibility that the first thing that will happen on the defeat of Japan—though it may well happen before—will be an open clash between these new "communist" Young Chinese and the Kuomintang. Even if Russia does not throw her weight into the scales on the side of the former, the odds are, in my opinion, that the Young Chinese will produce a revolutionary army which will achieve successes as remarkable as those of the early armies of the French Revolution . . . I suppose there is little if anything we can or should do. To urge on Chiang Kai-shek the necessity for a reconciliation with the Chinese Reds would, I think, be wholly profitless.'[116]

Young's final sentences underline what has been said about the cool and pragmatic nature of most British reactions. A flexible approach was also displayed in a propaganda plan that was drawn up for the guidance of those sending material into China, the document emphasizing that 'we should not tie ourselves . . . to the Kuomintang Party or to the existing set-up of the Chinese Government.'[117] Even so, the predominant view in the Foreign Office was that the authority and status of Chiang Kai-shek's Government must continue to be respected, and a group of M.P.s who called on Eden to ask why some of the funds collected in Britain for China could not be sent direct to the Communist areas were told that any such interference in China's internal politics would be strongly resented in Chungking.[118] This belief in the need to deal with whatever government happens formally to hold power in another country, regardless of one's private opinions of that regime, tends to be a feature of British foreign policy, of course. On this occasion, there was also another consideration, one which has appeared already, in the section covering the events of 1942. Thus, a brief on the Communist/ Kuomintang split prepared for Eden before he saw T. V. Soong concluded that 'the matter is obviously an internal one', and went on to remind the Foreign Secretary that 'in addition, [British interference would] invite intervention in what we rightly regard as the internal affairs of India.'[119] Should the time ever come when British influence could usefully be brought to bear, then it should be exerted in favour of a compromise whereby the Communists

* After health problems had jeopardized his career, Young went on to become Minister in the Paris Embassy, but he died at a comparatively early age.

would disband their separate armies but would be guaranteed political rights
as a party throughout China. 'The Communists', commented Clarke, 'might
[then] leaven the fascist tendencies of the K.M.T. lump.'[120]

What of the Soviet factor in Chinese affairs? Again, the approach to the
question was a cool one. It was not believed in London that Moscow was
sending aid to Yenan at that time.[121] Should the Soviet Union enter the war
against Japan, however, she would probably obtain 'a considerable voice in
re-drawing the map of east Asia.' Manchuria, Outer Mongolia and Sinkiang
were all seen as being areas where friction could easily arise between her and
China, while she might also, it was thought, want to have a say in the future
of Korea. It behoved Britain to walk carefully where those regions were concerned, therefore, but no great alarm bells were sounded about the destiny
of China or the East as a whole. There was little Britain could do except
watch and take note.[122] As an attitude on which to build one's policies it may
have lacked satisfying and dramatic overtones, but not realism.

The United States and China

If the British in 1943, for all their doubts about China, possessed more
good-will towards her than most Americans, officials and otherwise,
allowed, then Americans themselves, or a good many of them who were in a
position to know what was going on, were privately experiencing a growing
degree of disappointment and disillusionment over their Asian protégé.

True, there remained the hope, as we have seen in the chapter on the war
as a whole against Japan, of keeping China going militarily, so that she could
come to play a vital role against the enemy. The Cairo Conference in a way
symbolized this hope, as had, to a lesser extent, the visit to Chungking paid
by General Arnold, together with Sir John Dill, after the Casablanca meeting
earlier in the year.[123] There were even occasional moments when it seemed
as if fulfilment was at hand, as when Chiang Kai-shek agreed in writing in
July that, in conjunction with advances from the Indian side of Burma,
Chinese forces would attack southwards from Yunnan. ('The little bastard is
hooked, after 14 months of struggle', wrote an excited Stilwell in his diary.
'Well, by Jesus, that much is accomplished, in spite of hell and high water.
And what a headache it has been! Insult, delay, obstruction, intrigue, double-
cross, ignorance, hate, jealousy, corruption and general cussedness. Nobody
will ever know what it has meant.')[124]

Yet there remained a fundamental element of uncertainty over American
strategic plans involving China. Was the main effort—and restricted supplies
meant that a choice had to be made—to be put into renovating the Chinese
Army, as Stilwell proposed; or into the campaign in Burma; or into Chennault's schemes for increasing his air attacks on the Japanese from bases in
China? In Washington there was no agreement on the issue. 'As July drew to
a close', writes the official historian, 'the divergent trends in U.S. policy were
in the open. Reform of the Chinese Army, an augmented air effort and the
recapture of Burma conflicted logistically . . . Stilwell's Commander in Chief

[i.e. Roosevelt] indicated little interest in his mission, but it remained unchanged.'[125] In fact, over the struggle between Stilwell and Chennault—each wanting a major share of the tonnage being flown over the Hump—the President was inclining towards the latter. He had already encouraged Chennault to correspond with him direct, while Joseph Alsop, still serving on Chennault's staff, wrote often and at length to Hopkins to condemn Stilwell and his schemes.[126] Nevertheless, Presidential favour could not prevent Chennault from having to call out for Army protection for his new air bases, as Stilwell and Marshall had foretold, when the Japanese began to advance in their direction.[127] Nor was the conflict over resources resolved. By the end of this period Roosevelt was still ready to grasp at some new, cheap way of helping to win the war through China, this time by staging at Chinese airfields B 29 bombers on their way from their home base near Calcutta to smash Japan's steel-making capacity. (For this operation 'Matterhorn', Churchill also promised his support.)[128]

As for Stilwell, although he was still proposing before Cairo that Chiang Kai-shek should ask the United States to train and equip as many as ninety Chinese divisions,[129] his illusory schemes for transforming the Chinese Army were being ground away by the harsh realities of the local scene. Formally, his orders remained unchanged, but, in the words of the historians of his Command, 'the days of the Stilwell mission, the days in which [he] personally sought to prepare the Chinese Army for the ordeals ahead of it, were ended.'[130] 'Chiang Kai-shek sits in the local Berchtesgaden and writes books', the embittered General informed Washington in March. 'No unpleasant reports reach him except through me and he finds it hard to believe a foreign devil in preference to his own people. As a result he is confirmed in his belief that all China needs to run the Japs out is a lot of airplanes. His ideas on training, organization and tactics are childish . . . The constant fulsome praise of him and his troops in the American press confirms him in his warped ideas . . .'[131] 'His usual, affable, pleasant self, the little bastard', Stilwell noted of 'Peanut' in June on his own return from a visit to Washington and London. '"What did we *git*?" . . . The gratitude of the bastard is overwhelming.'[132] In return, the Generalissimo, with the encouragement of T. V. Soong, sought to have Stilwell removed from his post,[133] and only the intervention on the General's behalf of Soong's sisters, Madame Chiang and Madame Kung, plus the help of Somervell and Mountbatten when they arrived in Chungking in October, succeeded in smoothing things over for the time being. (Soong, himself, was about to suffer eclipse.)[134]

Stilwell was by no means alone among Americans in portraying Chiang Kai-shek's regime as inactive yet grasping. 'The Chinese', wrote a senior member of the Embassy in Chungking, 'continue to wait for the Allies (chiefly the United States) to defeat Japan.'[135] General Donovan of the O.S.S. was likewise of the opinion that the ruling clique were setting aside arms which they were being given, 'for future use in internal affairs.' Visiting China in December, Donovan went so far as to sack the egregiously and uncritically pro-Kuomintang Captain Miles from his post of Chief of the

O.S.S. in the Far East, though he could not prevent Miles continuing to work with General Tai Li in the intelligence-gathering Sino-American Cooperative Organization.[136]

Meanwhile, many American observers in China, from the Ambassador downwards, were assuring Washington that Chiang Kai-shek would not be so foolish, at a time when an Allied victory was beginning to look increasingly certain, as to seek peace with Japan.[137] It followed, therefore, that the United States was in a better position than she appeared to realize to do what Stilwell had always advocated, and demand solid returns for U.S. aid. 'We have a stronger bargaining position with Chiang Kai-shek than we seem to be willing to acknowledge', wrote John Davies. 'He cannot desert us without disastrous results to himself and most of his principal supporters. We can, on the other hand, accomplish our immediate objective in Asia—the defeat of Japan—without his aid. We may have to in any case.'[138] Laughlin Currie, his passion for China now cooled, and his advice consequently swinging round 180 degrees since 1942, likewise urged Roosevelt that 'we are dealing with a large group of men who have definite interests with which they fear we may interfere, who have no particular affection for us, and who are determined to secure as much from us as possible, while parting with as little as possible . . . The Chinese have in every way sought to create the impression that our bargaining position is weak . . . Actually the Chinese Government's bargaining position is quite weak and ours is strong.'[139]

To the disgust of Stilwell in particular, however, the President continued what the former called his 'softy-stuff' approach, in effect declining to put strong pressure on Chiang. (Roosevelt's usual masking of disagreement with an unctuous bonhomie failed to have much effect on this occasion. 'F.D.R.', wrote Stilwell after seeing him, 'calls me "Joe". The double-xxing bastard.')[140] Yet already in some quarters of Washington strategic evaluations of China's place in the war were beginning to change, away from the optimism of old and towards something very like the view that predominated in London. Thus, in November the War Department's Strategy Section concluded that any land effort that could be made in China would come too late to be of assistance in the attack on Japan proper, recommending, therefore, that only thirty Chinese divisions should be trained by the U.S. Army and that only a limited bomber offensive should be mounted within China, with Burma to be by-passed.[141] And although Marshall and the Joint Chiefs of Staff as a whole chose for their part to go on emphasizing China's potential, the development of the main, Central Pacific offensive, as we have seen, together with the long-term promise of Soviet help against Japan, were beginning to overshadow anything that China appeared likely to provide. Moreover, the decision that Roosevelt took during the second phase of the Cairo Conference, to fall in with British wishes and postpone a planned amphibious operation across the Bay of Bengal (operation 'Buccaneer', whose fate will be examined more fully in the next chapter) that had been intended to facilitate a major land attack into Burma, marked a significant down-grading of the attempt to get through to China via the new road from Ledo. In the words of the American official historian, it was in fact 'a turning point for China and its importance to the Allies in the War.'[142]

The rambling remarks that Roosevelt made at Cairo to Stilwell and Davies on the subject of America's policy towards China[143] reflected this change, in that they seemed to indicate that she should be kept in the war simply as a flank position that needed protecting. What is more, the President (who remained entirely cynical in his attitude towards his official diplomatic representatives in China)* also appeared on this occasion to be less than totally committed to Chiang Kai-shek's regime: if the Nationalist Government began to crumble, he observed to Stilwell, then the United States would 'look for some other man or group of men to carry on'—though whether he had in mind a dissident war-lord or even the Communists, Roosevelt did not say.[144]

In the United States at large, of course, China was still, in high-sounding phrases, being proclaimed a major friend both then and for the future. Yet even such a devotee of this cause as the Research Secretary of the Institute of Pacific Relations was having to admit privately that China was not yet fitted to be one of the world's leading guardians of security.[145] (Others, as noted earlier, were even coming to regard her as a possible menace to the very existence of the white man.)[146] Also, in strictly practical terms, the fact remained that, of the Lend Lease aid that was flowing out of the U.S.A., China received only 0·4 per cent in 1943,[147] while it was only after much difficulty that Congress, at the end of the year, was persuaded to repeal the laws preventing Chinese immigration into America, their place being taken by legislation which established, instead, a princely annual quota of 105.[148]

Meanwhile, quite apart from the complaints already cited regarding China's military inactivity, criticisms of the Chungking regime were growing. Reports reaching Washington indicated 'increasing unrest and dissatisfaction with the Central Government', and that that body 'had no real solution to the problem of peasant revolts save that of force.'[149] As in London, Chiang Kai-shek's *China's Destiny* also received unfavourable attention, with Gauss among others referring to 'the Chinese brand of Fascism which masquerades under Sun Yat-sen's San Min Chu I.'[150] Conversely, much resentment was aroused in Chinese ruling circles when reports in the I.P.R.'s *Far Eastern Survey* and elsewhere in the American press began to suggest that China might not, after all, be the democracy which popular acclaim had made her out to be.[151] Madame Chiang Kai-shek, for example, despite her triumphs in the United States, was said to have returned home with 'something of an anti-American bias.' Perhaps she realized that she herself had outworn her welcome in Presidential and other official circles. (Stimson, for one, had changed his judgment of her from 'a most attractive and beguiling little lady' to 'that little devil.')[152]

* At the request of a Democratic Party intermediary, for example, Roosevelt proposed that one of the Party's faithful should be given the post of Ambassador in Chungking. (Hooker to FDR, 15 Oct. 1943, and FDR to Stettinius, 22 Oct. 1943, Roosevelt Papers, PSF box 80.)

Unease about the Chinese scene was spreading to such an extent, that the *New York Times* felt obliged to insist: 'It is not true that China is a dictatorship. It is not true that the ruling element in China have fascist inclinations.'[153] The same newspaper also expressed concern over the rift between the Kuomintang and the Communists,[154] a concern that was increasingly shared in official circles, even though Hornbeck, as we have seen, tended to play down the problem.[155] It was the serious nature of the conflict that others were now emphasizing, with Gauss, for example, warning that the evidence pointed towards a civil war breaking out 'at some undetermined future date.'[156] As in London, opinions among American officials were divided over the question of how genuine or deep was the Communism of the Yenan regime. John Davies, for instance, reported that, although Mao Tse-tung and his colleagues appeared to follow the Comintern line,* foreign observers described them as being 'far removed from orthodox Communism' and as better termed 'agrarian democrats.' The Chief of the Far Eastern Division, too, was referring in this period to 'the so-called "Communists".'[157] One fairly junior American diplomat in China, however, John S. Service, thought that a Communist government 'would probably not be democratic in the American sense', and he joined Davies in warning that such a regime would be likely to look towards Moscow rather than to the U.S.A. for help and guidance. (It was noted during the year that the Soviet press was beginning to champion the cause of Yenan.)[158] All the more reason, therefore, for the United States to try to avert a final rift between the two centres of power in China, quite apart from the consideration that the Communists might be able to render considerable assistance in the fight against Japan. (Davies put the 8th Route Army at 60–100,000; the American Military Attaché thought that, altogether, the Communists could muster something like 600,000 troops, though they would be lacking in equipment.)[159] Hence, both Davies and Service made the suggestion during 1943 that the United States should improve its position by establishing contact with Yenan.[160]

The greatest fear, outlined for example by Davies, was of America being drawn into a Great Power struggle with the Soviet Union over China, a fear which again led to the conclusion that 'we cannot afford to incur the risk of our present hands-off policy toward China.'[161] But what were the intentions of the Soviet Union herself as regards the Far East? The question appeared to be all the more urgent when it became known—and Stalin reaffirmed it at Tehran—that she would enter the war against Japan once Germany was defeated.[162] Stalin's comment that 'the Chinese must be made to fight, which they had not so far done' suggested that he had few illusions in that direction.[163] But were the Chinese, for their part, correct in distrusting and fearing Russia's own motives?[164] One State Department estimate was that Moscow would seek to obtain a warm-water port, with transit facilities to it and to Vladivostok across Manchuria, and would try 'to gain control of or create Sovietized governments among the peoples of Inner Mongolia, Manchuria, Korea, and possibly other areas in the Western Pacific.'[165]

* As a gesture towards his Western allies, Stalin dissolved the Comintern itself in 1943.

Stalin himself, at Tehran, was content merely to ask what could be done for the Soviet Union in the Far East, and appeared to give his approval when Roosevelt brought up the idea of Dairen becoming a free port under international guarantee. (Churchill agreed that the Soviet Union deserved to obtain access to a warm-water port, and suggested that the matter could be settled 'as between friends.')[166] Roosevelt also claimed later, at a meeting of the Pacific War Council, that Stalin wanted the Kuriles and Sakhalin, but that he recognized that the Manchurian railways were the property of China. There is no record, however, of the Soviet leader having raised these points at Tehran.[167]

Whatever the detailed desiderata which were put forward, the United States was obviously going to be closely concerned; already, moreover, the possibility could be seen that she might find herself in a most embarrassing position, between the desires of the Soviet Union on the one hand and the claims of China on the other. At the same time, as noted above, the need was increasingly felt to become involved in the internal strife between Chungking and the Communists. Add to all this the contrast, more acknowledged in official circles now, between the image of China that had been fostered among the American public and the dismaying realities of the situation in that country, and it will be seen that the leading role which the United States had assumed in China was proving to be by no means an unmixed blessing. Nobody at the time envied the British, now pushed on to the sidelines. In retrospect, however, the situation was such that there was something to be said for being comparatively helpless, and recognizing as much.

Notes to Chapter Twelve

1 CSP, 16 May 1943, CAB 88/51.
2 CCS, 14 May 1943, CAB 88/2. See JCS, 16 Jan. and 15 May 1943, RG 218.
3 Plenary meeting, 12 May 1943, CAB 99/22.
4 CCS, 14 Aug. 1943, CAB 88/3.
5 E.g. FRUS, 1943, China, 57, 111, 154. Some Chinese officials, however, were cool towards the idea of reopening the Burma Road. E.g. ibid, 118.
6 Plenary meeting, 14 May 1943, CAB 99/22.
7 *Bryant*, I, 654.
8 Joint Staff report, 11 Aug. 1943, CAB 99/23. See JCS, 10 Aug. 1943, RG 218.
9 FO 371, F894/16/10. See Ismay to WSC, 23 July 1943, PREM 3, 90/5.
10 E.g. FO 371, F3275/351/23; F3885/387/23.
11 Ibid, F3885/387/23.
12 *New York Times*, 11 July 1943.
13 Ibid, 19 Feb. 1943; *Sherwood*, 706. See e.g. *Tuchman*, 349ff. and Carter memo., 5 March 1943, IPR, box 363.
14 *Vandenberg*, 16 June 1943.
15 FRUS, Cairo and Tehran, 263.
16 Ibid, 47.
17 See above, 371.

18 E.g. *New York Times*, 14 Nov. 1943; *Chicago Tribune*, 10 Feb. 1943; see *Leahy*, 185–6.
19 E.g. *Romanus and Sutherland*, I, 275, 326–7.
20 *Leahy*, 251–2. See *Berle*, 26 May 1943.
21 *Young*, 257. See FRUS, 1943, China, 57.
22 E.g. FRUS, 1943, China, 4, 9, 17.
23 Ibid, 102, 126.
24 FRUS, Cairo and Tehran, 194.
25 FRUS, 1943, III, 34, 36, 38; Eden to WSC, 17 March 1943, PREM 4, 28/9; Eden to WSC 29 March 1943, PREM 4, 30/3; Cab, 13 April 1943, CAB 65/34.
26 FDR to Mountbatten, 8 Nov. 1943, *Roosevelt Letters*.
27 FRUS, Cairo and Tehran, 529.
28 *Davies*, 280–1.
29 Stilwell Diary, 6 Dec. 1943.
30 WSC to Eden, on WP(43)130, PREM 4, 30/3; WSC to Eden, 8 Oct. 1943, PREM 4, 30/5; WSC to Eden, 22 March 1943, FO 371, F1686/25/10; *Cadogan Diaries*, 6 Sept. 1943. See e.g. WP(43)31 and 39, CAB 66/33.
31 FRUS, 1943, China, 40; see ibid, 47, 55, 233.
32 See FO 371, F3563 and 4118/10/10.
33 FRUS, 1943, China, 4.
34 FRUS, 1943, III, 34.
35 See e.g. *Davies*, 273, 279; *Tuchman*, 370.
36 Hornbeck memo., 28 Oct. 1943, DS, Notter files, box 79. See Hornbeck memo., 29 Nov. 1943, Hornbeck Papers, box 400.
37 Hornbeck memo., 9 July 1943, Hornbeck Papers, box 197.
38 E.g. FRUS, 1943, China, 11, 65.
39 Stilwell to Chiang, n.d., 1943, Stilwell Papers, box 14.
40 E.g. FO 371, F1878 and 2156/25/10; F3108/1591/10.
41 Hansard, HC Deb, 394, col. 1604.
42 E.g. FO 371, F1878/25/10; F4780/3546/10; F6332/6332/10; Wyatt-Smith report, 18 May 1943, PREM 3, 158/7; S. R. Chow, IPR Conference paper, 'A Permanent Order for the Pacific' (in FO 371, file 35906); Tuang-sheng Chien article, *Foreign Affairs*, July 1943.
43 FO 371, F2351/682/10. See ibid, F4480/10/10; F2377/13/10; Grimsdale to Ismay, 15 Feb. and 1 July 1943, Ismay Papers, IV/Gri/6 and IV/Gri/7/2; Chiang Kai-shek, *China's Destiny* and *Chinese Economic Theory* (ed., P. Jaffe; New York, 1947).
44 FO 371, F282/120/10.
45 Far Eastern Group, 17 Nov. 1943, RIIA.
46 FO 371, F3586/73/10.
47 Ibid, F2078/120/10.
48 DO(43)13, CAB 69/5; Viceroy to Secretary of State, 25 Feb. 1943, Linlithgow Papers, vol. 24.
49 Material in FO 371, files 35755, 35758; WP(43)225, CAB 66/37.
50 FO 371, F1737/40/10. On the background to this, see A. Lamb, *The McMahon Line* (London, 1966) and *The China–India Border* (London, 1964).
51 WP(43)267, CAB 66/38; Cab, 7 July 1943, CAB 65/35.
52 E.g. FO 371, F3864/182/10; F2641/58/61; FRUS, Washington and Quebec, 134.
53 FO 371, F285/1/10.
54 See ibid, F3095/682/10; material in file 35824; F1409/25/10; General Cmttee, 25 May 1943, Ch.A.; FRUS, Cairo and Tehran, 552.
55 Hopkins memo., 29 March 1943, Hopkins Papers, box 329; sub-cmttee of Advisory Cmttee on Post War Foreign Policy, 13 March 1943, DS, Notter files, box 55.
56 FO 371, F238, 5722 and 6670/39/10.
57 Material in PREM 4, 74/2; Cabs, 29 Nov. and 13 Dec. 1943, CAB 65/36; FRUS, Cairo and Tehran, 401–2, 404, 448.
58 See FRUS, 1943, China, 687.
59 See above, 13.

60 FO 371, F3805/102/10; Grimsdale to Ismay, 1 July 1943, Ismay Papers, IV/Gri/7/1.
61 See above, 161.
62 Eggleston Diary, April and May 1943, Eggleston Papers, 423/9/1148ff.
63 FO 371, F3047, 4065, 4273 and 6277/39/40; file 35752; FRUS, 1943, China, 457ff.
64 FO 371, F2711, 3329 and 3524/11/10; F6751/1/10; FRUS, 1943, China, 503ff.
65 FO 371, F2996/1/10; F2387/525/10; FRUS, 1943, China, 710ff.
66 E.g. FRUS, 1943, China, 865ff.
67 FO 371, F689/16/10. See below, 583, note 94.
68 Lindsay, *The Forgotten War* (no page numbers; a disgrace).
69 E.g. Miles to Wright, 6 March 1943, and memo. for Embassy, 29 May 1943, Naval Group China files, USNOA.
70 FRUS, 1943, China, 590ff. and 609.
71 FO 371, F329/11/10, and material in files 35691, 35694–6, 35699.
72 Ibid, material in file 35842.
73 FRUS, 1943, China, 10, 33, 40; COS, 25 Feb. 1943, CAB 79/25; FO 371, file 35831; SEAC War Diary, minutes of Chungking conference, 16 Oct. 1943; Carton de Wiart to Ismay, 30 Oct. 1943, PREM 3, 158/7.
74 FO 371, F1317/1317/61.
75 FRUS, 1943, China, 84.
76 PWC (L), 4 Aug. 1943, CAB 99/26.
77 FO 371, F1878/25/10; see F5682/25/10.
78 Ibid, A2750/3/45; see A3225/144/45.
79 E.g. Grimsdale to Ismay, 8 Jan. 1943, Ismay Papers, IV/Gri/5; Ismay to WSC, 21 May 1943, PREM 3, 90/5.
80 E.g. Howard, *Grand Strategy*, IV, 405.
81 FO 371, F3071/25/10; DO(43)14, CAB 69/5; material in PREM 3, 154/1.
82 FO 371, files 35755 and 35759; WP(43)343, CAB 66/39; FRUS, China, 1943, 620ff.
83 FO 371, F3506/72/10.
84 Ibid, material in files 35739, 35785–7, 35790, 35802, 35817–9. As before, however, exchanges with the Chinese were restricted in the light of London's knowledge that the Japanese had broken major Chinese ciphers. *Bryant*, I, 718.
85 FO 371, F5765/25/10; letters in Hornbeck Papers, box 118.
86 FO 371, F1472/1/10.
87 Ibid, F4386/25/10.
88 See above, 309.
89 FO 371, F3561/25/10.
90 Ibid, F5468/74/10.
91 Ibid, F5466/3801/10.
92 Ibid, F5460/5251/10.
93 Ibid, F5468/74/10.
94 Ibid, F2913/964/10.
95 Ibid, F2890/1953/10.
96 Bevin to Eden, 1 Feb. 1943, Bevin Papers, box 12.
97 FO 371, F3895/254/10.
98 Ibid, F4593/4593/10.
99 Executive Cttee, 6 Aug. and 8 Dec. 1943, Ch.A.; material in FO 371, files 35681 and 35725–6.
100 See above, 194.
101 FO 371, files 35766–7 and 35849–50.
102 Ibid, files 35737–8, 35775. But see WSC and Eden minutes in PREM 4, 28/7.
103 Carton de Wiart to Ismay, 20 Dec. 1943, PREM 3, 159/14.
104 *Cadogan Diaries*, 586; Dalton Diary, 21 Dec. 1943.
105 FO 371, files 35692, 35697–8, 35704–5, 35707–8, 35710, 35909.
106 Ibid, F5461, 5679 and 6745/25/10.
107 Ibid, F2706, 2839, 3133/11/10.
108 Ibid, file 35714; Cripps Papers, file 676.

109 FO 371, files 35715-6, 35719-23.
110 Ibid, files 35784, 35788, 35790 and 35799; Cripps Papers, file 624; J. Needham, *Science in China* (London, 1945), and *Science Outpost* (London, 1948).
111 FO 371, file 35791.
112 E.g. Band, *Dragon Fangs*, 238; Lindsay, *The Forgotten War*, passim.
113 FO 371, F3895/254/10; see F644/74/10.
114 Ibid, F1893 and 2315/1893/10.
115 Ibid, F2273/74/10. F2431/254/10.
116 Ibid, F2431/254/10. See F894/16/10.
117 Ibid, F1213/72/10.
118 Ibid, F4233/11/10.
119 Ibid, F4265/74/10. See F3637/254/10.
120 Ibid, F4852/74/10.
121 Ibid, F6732/11/10.
122 Ibid, material in files 35737, 35768, 35770, 35860, 35917.
123 For conferences in New Delhi en route to Chungking, see PREM 3, 143/1.
124 Stilwell Diary, 12 July 1943.
125 *Romanus and Sutherland*, I, 341, 328-9.
126 Material in Hopkins Papers, box 331; *Romanus and Sutherland*, I, 277ff., 320ff.; *Sherwood*, 739.
127 See Stilwell Diary, 28 July 1943.
128 C. Romanus and R. Sutherland, *Stilwell's Command Problems* (Washington, D.C., 1956; hereafter, *Romanus and Sutherland*, II), 15ff.; FRUS, Cairo and Tehran, 172, 188.
129 *Romanus and Sutherland*, II, 56-8.
130 Ibid, I, 385.
131 Stilwell to War Dpt., 7 March 1943, OPD, Exec. file 10, item 22.
132 Stilwell Diary, 17 June 1943.
133 See FRUS, 1943, China, 133.
134 Ibid, 387.
135 Ibid, 111.
136 Somerville Diary, 12 Dec. 1943; *O.S.S.*, 258; Miles, *A Different Kind Of War*, 159ff.
137 E.g. FRUS, 1943, China, 25, 37, 168, 257.
138 Ibid, 257. See Gauss to Hornbeck, 4 Sept. 1943, Hornbeck Papers, box 175.
139 Currie to FDR, 18 May 1943, Roosevelt Papers, PSF box 145.
140 Stilwell Diary, 29 June and 22 Nov. 1943.
141 *Matloff*, 326.
142 Ibid, 373.
143 See above,
144 *Romanus and Sutherland*, II, 73.
145 Far Eastern Group, 3 Nov. 1943, RIIA.
146 See above, 291.
147 *Young*, 350.
148 FRUS, 1943, China, 769ff.; material in Long Papers, box 89.
149 FRUS, 1943, China, 238, 344.
150 E.g. ibid, 76, 244, 351. An OSS survey (R and A 951) of 15 July 1943 observed that if *China's Destiny* were to be published in an English translation, 'in America it would explode the China myth', and that 'the strictures against liberalism and inter-nationalism', like 'the ardent nationalism and totalitarian position of the Kuomin-tang', would make especially bad reading.
151 Ibid, 80; Thomas, *I.P.R.*, 24; *Shewmaker*, 144ff.
152 FRUS, 1943, China, 80; Hassett, *Off The Record With F.D.R.*, 182; Stimson Diary 23 Feb. and 18 Oct. 1943.
153 *New York Times*, 15 Sept. 1943.
154 Ibid, 12 Aug. 1943.
155 See FRUS, 1943, China, 201, and above, 317.

156 Ibid, 351.
157 Ibid, 257, 322.
158 Ibid, 193, 285, 316.
159 Ibid, 382.
160 For Mao Tse-tung's own long-established theme of the need to work temporarily with other, imperialist, powers against Japan, see Gittings, *China and the World*, cap. 3.
161 FRUS, 1943, China, 257.
162 FRUS, Cairo and Tehran, 487.
163 Ibid, 565.
164 See FRUS, 1943, China, 62.
165 FRUS, Washington and Quebec, 627; see FRUS, 1943, China, 317.
166 FRUS, Cairo and Tehran, 565.
167 Ibid, 868.

CHAPTER THIRTEEN

SOUTHEAST ASIA AND THE FUTURE OF EMPIRES

Campaign issues in Southeast Asia

AS WE have seen in the strategic outline of the period, the question of China's potential role in the war continued in 1943 to create considerable strain between the British and the Americans over Southeast Asia. Marshall and Stilwell were clear in their minds that priority should be given to a campaign which would enable the new road from Ledo (construction of which had been taken over from the British in December 1942) to be pushed through, via Mytkyina, to link up with the old Burma Road, and thence into Yunnan. Hence, British schemes which pointed in a different direction were regarded as well-nigh subversive, while what was described in an official report as British 'passive resistance' to the actual building of the Ledo Road was a betrayal of all that the United States was striving to achieve.[1]

The British planners, however, were convinced for their part that any realistic completion date for the road would lie too far ahead to be of help to China in her hour of crisis; in addition, they believed that 'practically the entire capacity of the Ledo–Mytkyina route, even when developed into a two-way all-weather road, would be taken up in supplying the forces protecting it. Only token quantities of urgently-needed supplies might be passed through to China . . .'[2] As for the British Chiefs of Staff, the position they adopted at the Washington Conference, when they were confronted by Stilwell himself, was that it had not been shown that the reconquest of Burma, 'however desirable the political effect, especially on China and India', was 'indispensable from the military point of view.'[3] Churchill, too, despite waverings, was continually reverting to the idea that the Allies should 'by-pass Burma and its swamps and jungles and strike out eastward across the sea' by means of an 'Asiatic "Torch"' operation.[4]

Matters were further complicated by the fact that, in order for Burma to be retaken, the assistance of the Chinese themselves appeared highly desirable, in the form of a coordinated drive south from Yunnan. Yet British commanders placed little reliance upon such an attack,[5] doubly so in that Chiang Kai-shek, citing what he held to have been a promise of Churchill's 1924 in about the augmentation of the Eastern Fleet to 8 battleships and 3 aircraft carriers was, indicating that, before his own troops could move, a major operation must be launched across the Bay of Bengal.[6] Nor was the position greatly improved by the formation of the new South East Asia Command, even though the orders given to Mountbatten added to his 'prime duty' of engaging and wearing down the Japanese (thus forcing them to divert strength from the Pacific) the 'second [task], but of equal consequence,' of maintaining links with China by air and of establishing direct contact via North Burma.[7] True, Mountbatten, like Churchill himself at times, did his best to keep Chiang Kai-shek happy.[8] But there was not a great deal of faith in the Chinese at S.E.A.C. headquarters: the Chief of Staff, for example, wrote in his diary that to plan on the assumption that the Chinese would move south from Yunnan was to build 'on a foundation of sand', while the Commander of the Eastern Fleet, Admiral Somerville, regarded the Generalissimo himself as being 'a pretty slippery customer [who] can never really be relied upon.'[9] Mountbatten, also, found the Chinese staff officers who attended the Cairo Conference 'very difficult and rather truculent.' 'The Chinese', he wrote, 'really can be very maddening . . . Chiang Kai-shek made several . . . illogical suggestions and I cannot help wondering how much he knows about soldiering.' He added that he was glad that the Prime Minister and President were 'at last being given first-hand experience of how impossible the Chinese are to deal with.'[10]

The situation was made worse by the continued decline, rather than enlargement, of the Eastern Fleet, with Chiang Kai-shek nevertheless still insisting on his Bay of Bengal precondition.[11] Perhaps unwisely, Churchill attempted to rescue matters by promising the Generalissimo, in a letter of October:

'There is to be a considerable amphibious operation in the Bay of Bengal or Indian Ocean. For this purpose I shall concentrate during February [1944] a powerful fleet based on Ceylon and comprising some of the finest and most modern units in the Royal Navy. This Eastern Fleet will in our judgment be strong enough to fight a general engagement with any detachment of the Japanese Navy which the enemy may dare to make from the Pacific.'[12]

By the time the Cairo Conference convened, the Prime Minister was having to talk of 'late spring or early summer' as the date when the new units of the Eastern Fleet would assemble. Even so, he still gave the Chinese—and the Americans—reason to believe that a powerful collection of British warships ('no less than' 5 modern capital ships, 4 heavily-armoured aircraft carriers and up to 12 auxiliary carriers) would be made available. By emphasizing this (for reasons that are entirely understandable), he was storing up future trouble, as we shall see.[13]

To these problems of the Chinese contribution and that of the Royal Navy, there must again be added the difficult features which had surrounded the Southeast Asian Theatre in the preceding period: a limited campaigning season, between November and May; the shortcomings of India as a base for major operations;[14] bottlenecks involving the Assam line of communications and the shortage of engineering resources;[15] inadequate shipping and supplies of landing craft;[16] the need to train a far larger number of troops in jungle warfare; and the need for more forces and equipment generally. In this last connection, the Chiefs of Staff in London thought of asking Washington for increased assistance, but Churchill, revealingly, was opposed to bringing in American troops. Marshall, for his part, was also against any move that would entail putting U.S. soldiers under British command in Southeast Asia, even though Roosevelt toyed with the idea of sending in two divisions. As it was, the only American ground force in Burma, apart from the engineers constructing the Ledo Road, was the 'Galahad' commando unit, whose development had been inspired by Wingate's example, and which was serving under Stilwell.[17]

The first major casualty brought about by these various difficulties was operation 'Anakim', which had aimed at the reconquest of Burma, including Rangoon. Stilwell and the American planners fought to save this project. By April 1943, however, neither the Commanders in Chief on the spot nor the Chiefs of Staff in London believed that such an operation would have much chance of success during the 1943–44 season, while Churchill himself was comparing it to 'a man attacking a hedgehog by pulling out its bristles one by one.'[18] These British opinions did nothing to diminish the widespread American conviction that the entire approach of their Allies was one of great feebleness. 'Somehow or other', wrote General Arnold later, in connection with his post-Casablanca visit to India, 'I could not get the impression out of my head that the British had been using India as a place to which to send officers who had more or less outlived their usefulness in other theaters.'[19] Admiral King was likewise scornful of the limited efforts of the Royal Navy's Eastern Fleet,[20] while at the Washington Conference, General Wavell, whom Stilwell was already seeking to have removed, made a very poor impression on the American representatives when he emphasized the difficulties that were facing him.[21]

Marshall and his colleagues were not alone in their impatience, however. On the spot in Burma, for example, a middle-ranking British officer's view of the performance of his country's generals in Arakan was that it was to be equated 'with New Orleans, Passchendaele and the blockheaded stupidities of the Boer War.' Meanwhile, on a higher plane, the Prime Minister, as we have seen, was greatly perturbed at the delay in mounting a major and successful operation, despite his general aversion to Burma as a place in which to fight the Japanese. 'A poor tale!', 'this lamentable tale', 'this lamentable scene', were some of his minuted comments, and he was keenly aware, as he told the Defence Committee, of the likelihood of provoking American criticism of 'our lack of enterprise and drive.'[22] During the Washington Conference, indeed, he made no secret of his displeasure when talking to Stilwell. 'He asked', recorded the latter, 'if I thought the British had been dilatory and lacked energy. I said "yes." He thought so too.' He was 'thoroughly dissatisfied with the way his commanders [in India and

Burma] had acted', he told Stimson.[23] Hence, as noted above, his eagerness to seize upon the audacity and the success, such as it was, of Wingate,[24] together with his desire for the kind of fundamental reorganization that eventually emerged with the setting up of S.E.A.C. Hence, also, his increasing emphasis upon the need to carry out, in the spring of 1944, operation 'Culverin', a landing in Sumatra designed to outflank the Japanese, despite the fact that the Chiefs of Staff remained doubtful as to what could be achieved in such a direction without substantial American assistance.[25]

Even the establishment of S.E.A.C. did little to lessen the Prime Minister's impatience, and he was soon fiercely questioning, for example, the ratio of British (meaning, throughout, 'British and Indian') to enemy forces that the Command deemed necessary to achieve before launching an operation.[26] Meanwhile, S.E.A.C.'s plans for the 1943–44 dry season hinged upon a landing in the Andaman Islands (operation 'Buccaneer'), together with land advances (operation 'Tarzan') along the Burmese coast, in central Burma, and in the north along the line of the Ledo Road, with the Chinese 'Y' force striking down from Yunnan and Wingate's Long Range Penetration Force operating in the Japanese rear.[27] At Cairo, however, the British Chiefs of Staff, to the dismay of their American colleagues, made clear their doubts and opposition as regards both the land and the amphibious aspects of such plans. 'Tarzan', Brooke argued, could develop into major operations that would require more forces to be sent out to Burma, while 'Buccaneer', even if desirable, would tie up landing craft that would be needed for more important operations in Europe.[28] The outcome of the disagreement was that Roosevelt, to the great disquiet of the J.C.S., eventually agreed to the cancellation of 'Buccaneer', offering Chiang Kai-shek the alternatives of either carrying on with 'Tarzan' without its Bay of Bengal complement, or delaying matters until the next campaigning season. Meanwhile, even an alternative operation, 'Pigstick', which envisaged a landing on the Arakan coast behind the Japanese lines, found little favour on the British side.[29] It seemed, indeed, that the Cairo decision on grand strategy—to put the weight of the Allied attack against Japan into the two Pacific spearheads—meant that S.E.A.C. as a whole was to be relegated to a secondary role, and that, in the words of its Supreme Commander on his return from the Conference, 'a completely new orientation of plans must be faced.'[30]

Disappointments of this kind did nothing to lessen the strains which already, in the first few months of its existence, were beginning to bedevil S.E.A.C. It must be emphasized that such strains were not entirely of an Anglo-American nature. There soon arose, for example, differences of opinion between Mountbatten and his land commander, General Giffard, and tension between the former and his naval C. in C., Somerville. One close observer believed that the trouble in this second instance lay in the fact that Somerville, far senior to his Supreme Commander in the ordinary course of events, had expected to be able to dominate the younger man.[31] Aside from this factor, two specific issues were involved. One was Mountbatten's desire to establish his own war-planning staff, as distinct from the planners who were working with each C. in C. Somerville opposed this idea as entailing too complex an arrangement, and it is true that, although Mountbatten did eventually get his way, he later abandoned the new system.[32] The second issue concerned Somerville's responsibility to the Admiralty, and not to the Supreme Commander, for offensive action and the security of shipping, both within and outside the S.E.A.C. area. Originally, Mountbatten accepted this situation: 'I fully understand your direct responsibility to the Admiralty for sea communications', he wrote to Somerville in September. At Cairo, however, according to the First Sea Lord, Admiral of the Fleet Sir Andrew Cunningham, the Supreme Commander 'asked to have the whole Eastern Fleet area placed under him.' Cunningham refused and there the matter rested, but Somerville continued to feel, as he wrote to Cunningham, that Mountbatten wanted 'a finger in every pie', and, as he complained to Ismay, 'that he's got swung right off his feet and is determined to be the central figure of a S.E.A.C. which is going to MAKE HISTORY . . . He is out MacArthuring MacArthur . . .'[33]

It must be noted that by no means all the established British commanders and officials in the area resented the arrival of the youthful Mountbatten— Wavell, for example, welcomed his appointment.[34] More central to the present study, however, is the fact that the new Supreme Commander clearly went out of his way to try to achieve Anglo-American harmony in his theatre, and was acknowledged by American officers to be acting most laudably in this respect.[35] 'All in all', wrote General Somervell to Marshall in October 1943, 'personal relationships are decidedly favorable', and he thought that Mountbatten had exhibited a most heartening offensive spirit.[36] Wedemeyer, for his part, reported to the Joint Chiefs in Washington that he was 'greatly impressed with the ability, energy and sincerity of Admiral Mountbatten', while even Stilwell felt able to write to Marshall early in November that 'relations with Mountbatten and his staff are excellent.' 'Louis', he wrote privately, 'is a good egg.'[37] Conversely, Generals Wheeler and Wedemeyer made a very good impression on their British colleagues.[38] Moreover, where dislikes did arise, they were sometimes of an inter-American variety, for example between Stilwell and his C.B.I. staff on the one hand and Wedemeyer on the other. 'This guy Wedemeyer', wrote Stilwell scornfully, 'thinks Wedemeyer is a hell of an important guy.' At the same time, relations between the Allies were often good at the actual fighting level. 'The closer you got to the front', one British officer recalled later, 'the more that you found that the Americans, whether or not they saluted with great punctilio, meant business, and the closer become the ties between them and the rest of us.'[39]

Yet despite all this, there can be no doubt as to the strains that developed on an Anglo-American basis within S.E.A.C. and neighbouring India. One American staff officer, for example, has recalled 'endless confused, petty bickerings over trivial issues', while regarding the triangular situation of S.E.A.C., C.B.I. and Britain's India Command, he writes: 'The two Delhis, the American and the British, hated each other not the less that they hated

Mountbatten the more.' He goes on to describe the eventual pattern as being one in which 'all the Americans aligned themselves in one camp—even if they continued to quarrel among themselves within it—and the British from England formed an unhappy but united imperial front with the colonial sahibs and tuans.'[40] The Governor of Burma likewise noted 'constant criticisms' of Mountbatten on the part of Americans in Delhi, and that, even at S.E.A.C. headquarters, 'it was impossible even for a visitor not to sense a measure of unhappiness in the relationship between the British and the Americans.'[41] 'We are having quite a lot of bother with the Americans', recorded Mountbatten's Chief of Staff, Pownall, who went on to observe that those U.S. officers on the staff who were not involved in this friction were often accused by their compatriots of being 'pro-British.'[42]

The main immediate source of the trouble on the American side was Stilwell and his C.B.I. Command, whose complex and awkward relationship with S.E.A.C. in practical terms has been noted earlier. Stilwell's fierce anti-British sentiments were not known at the time by all British officers on the spot, but his staff quickly became greatly disliked. Meanwhile, for all his early good impressions of Mountbatten, Stilwell soon came to believe that the latter was simply 'playing the "Empah" game', and was writing of him by January 1944: 'The Glamour Boy is just that. He doesn't wear well and I begin to wonder if he knows his stuff. Enormous staff, endless walla-walla, but damn little fighting.'[43] Moreover, Stilwell was informed by Marshall that 'the limies' were trying to have him removed from his post,[44] and although he continued to like and respect General William Slim, he soon set a sour anti-British example for C.B.I. generally to emulate. Thus 'S.E.A.C.' became 'Save England's Asiatic Colonies', while songs were sung of the variety: 'The Limeys make policy, Yank fights the Jap, And one gets its Empire and one takes the rap.'[45] In return, Stilwell quickly came to be much disliked by some of his British colleagues. General Pownall wrote in this sense; so, too, did Admiral Somerville, who described Stilwell as 'this bone-headed, obstinate old man.'[46]

As for Mountbatten himself, he claimed that, although Stilwell was difficult to work with, he was glad that he and others had persuaded Chiang Kai-shek not to sack the American from his post as the Generalissimo's Chief of Staff and as Commander of Chinese troops in Burma.[47] The diary of Admiral Somerville, however, conveys a somewhat different impression:

'10 October 1943. The three Commanders in Chief held a meeting and afterwards proceeded to the Supreme Commander's quarters . . . On our arrival the Supreme Commander informed us that General Stilwell was to be given his congée by the Generalissimo . . . No regrets were expressed at the news . . .'
'23 October 1943 [after Mountbatten's return from Chungking]. From what the Supreme Commander said, it appeared he felt so positive that General Stilwell would go he felt no harm would result if he softened the blow of it by suggesting to the Generalissimo he should be grateful for all

that General Stilwell had done in the past . . . It appears that the Supreme Commander overplayed his hand, since late that evening the Generalissimo sent for General Stilwell, kissed him either physically or metaphorically on both cheeks, and said he was his friend for life. So Joe is still with us and it is not clear how he can be got rid of.'

Meanwhile, arrangements that were made for S.E.A.C. on the civilian side also had their unfortunate aspects. Stilwell, as we have seen, had his own political adviser in the person of John Paton Davies, seconded from the Embassy in Chungking, a diplomat who at this time tended to take a suspicious view of British motives and to emphasize the gulf between American and British interests in Southeast Asia. (The Foreign Office made enquiries about Davies as the importance of his position came to be recognized; the impressions of him that were gathered were favourable.)[48] Mountbatten himself had a political adviser from the Foreign Office, Esler (later Sir Esler) Dening, an appointment that took the place of the one which the Foreign Office, in pre-S.E.A.C. days, had been hoping to secure, whereby someone from the Office would have gone out to India as adviser to the Viceroy. The Supreme Commander also had an adviser on Chinese affairs, John Keswick being nominated for this task despite uneasiness on the part of the Foreign Office as to how the Chinese would react to his pre-war connections with Jardine Matheson and his war-time work in China on behalf of S.O.E.[49] One other appointment, however, which Mountbatten, Dening and the Foreign Office all favoured, of an American political adviser to the Supreme Commander, to be of equal standing with Dening, was not taken up by Washington. An opportunity of reducing mutual misunderstanding and suspicion was thus missed.[50]

Difficulties at the command level were again reflected in troubles in the fields of political warfare and quasi-military activities—this, despite Anglo-American cooperation in the United States over Far Eastern intelligence matters,[51] and despite occasional instances of good relations on the ground, as in the case already mentioned, involving Carl Eifler's O.S.S. team in Burma and the Governor, Dorman-Smith.[52] Before S.E.A.C. was set up, there were several examples of rivalry in such matters.[53] And although Mountbatten established a 'P' Division, under Captain G. A. Garnon-Williams, R.N., to coordinate S.O.E., S.I.S., O.S.S. and political warfare work, Anglo-American suspicion and the mounting of separate, nationally-based enterprises soon became common within the new Command.[54] The O.S.S. and Office of War Information, wrote Mountbatten at the end of November, were still 'carrying on independent operational activities in South East Asia Command without being coordinated', and we have already seen how, on the American side, local agencies were being warned by Washington of the great differences that existed between British and United States aims in their part of the world.[55] For this same reason Washington also declined to appoint an American representative to a New Delhi Emergency Co-ordinating Committee for Political Warfare which it had been intended to set up alongside similar bodies in London and Washington. 'O.S.S. and O.W.I. seem likely to adopt a neutral attitude', wrote Dening, 'and expect us to show appreciation if they refrain from being hostile.'[56]

Clearly, S.E.A.C. was already feeling the effects of those underlying Anglo-American political differences regarding the future of imperial territories which have been explored for the previous period, and to which we must now turn again.

The future of empires; British territories in Southeast Asia

'Asia', observed Elmer Davis, the head of O.W.I., to the Joint Chiefs of Staff, 'had proved especially difficult in the way of propaganda ... The British particularly did not like the playing up of China, although this constituted the best talking point from the standpoint of the Orient. The difficulty had been increased', he continued, 'by the effects of the theoretical independence granted by Japan to former portions of the English and Dutch empires ...'[57] (In fact, the Philippines, as well as Burma, were given their 'independence' during this period, which also witnessed the Great East Asia Conference in Tokyo, referred to earlier.)[58] At Stilwell's elbow, John Davies developed the same theme. 'Britain can be a first-class power', he wrote, 'only as it has the empire to exploit. Imperial rule and interests means association with other peoples on a basis of subjugation, exploitation, privilege and force ... It means a turning by the colonial peoples to any nation or group of nations which can promise them a change, nations to whom the colonial peoples would not turn if it were not for their servitude.'[59] Much of the British public and many officials, added Davies, might not want such a policy of exploitation, but Churchill's philosophy was one of '19th century imperialism and power politics, and Mr. Churchill has the power and influence to force through such a policy.'[60] The consequence, he believed, was to place the United States in a dilemma:

'Our policy is apparently based on the conviction that we need Britain as a first-class power; Britain cannot be a first-class power without its empire; we are accordingly committed to the support of the British empire ... [Yet] in the minds of most Americans a better world is identified with the abolition of imperialism, and there is a very real danger that the United States may again become isolationist after the war as a result of a feeling by the American people that they have been made dupes of British imperialism.'[61]

This direct and perceptive statement by Davies of the difficulty facing the United States—it involved only one of several fundamental war-time questions over which Roosevelt failed to supply a clear lead—was an uncomfortable one for some of his colleagues. 'I think', wrote Berle, '[that] Mr. Davies is getting into pretty deep water.' Yet Berle, too, recognized the need to face squarely the problem 'of whether, in the Far East, we are reestablishing the

Western colonial empires, or whether we are letting the East liberate itself if it can do so.'[62] Only the President, it was felt in the State Department, could provide an answer; however, perhaps not surprisingly in view of the difficulties involved, none was forthcoming that was sufficiently clear and unequivocal to form a basis for a consistent policy.

To say that is not to overlook Roosevelt's frequent anti-colonial utterances regarding the specific case of Indochina, which will be examined below. It is also evident that his general inclinations still lay in the same direction, as his son, for all the errors of detail in his account, has recorded in the context of the Cairo and Tehran Conferences.[63] To Charles Taussig, Roosevelt observed, in the former's words, 'that we are getting nowhere with the British on colonial post-war planning. He said they were impossible.'[64] Nor, interestingly enough, was the President particularly impressed when Taussig, on another occasion, informed him that the British were at least proposing to offer a new constitution to Jamaica. His first thought, rather, was not to let himself or the United States be upstaged in any way; he therefore told Taussig that he would make a public statement himself, giving Puerto Rico the right to elect its own governor, and that he would do it 'before the British offer came out.'[65] In retrospect, such a combination of halo-polishing and hard politics is not without its amusing side.

Roosevelt's anti-imperialism was in harmony with the continuing views of very many of his fellow-Americans and much of their press.[66] The *New York Times*, for example, was again emphasizing the importance of the Atlantic Charter as 'the covenant of the new world', and calling for a clarification of the Allies' political aims in the Pacific War.[67] 'We propose', proclaimed *Fortune* magazine, 'that the Western powers surrender all their exclusive rights or preferential positions in Asia after this war . . . [when] the function of British imperialism in the Orient will have been fulfilled.'[68] A member of the I.P.R.'s staff in New York similarly urged a colleague that there now existed 'a special opportunity of cashing in on public interest as the carpet of Japanese occupation is rolled back . . . Here', he declared, 'is an opportunity for creative work: let the American public, at the time Burma is freed or Indochina occupied, get a sense of what countries they are, what the problems for international decision are, and how the Atlantic Charter, if taken seriously, will affect their future . . . We cannot fight imperialism in the Pacific by tripping behind and challenging every imperialist proposal; we ought to be there first with our democratic proposals.'[69]

Other, related aspects of the question were also of direct interest to the United States: for example, the raw materials of colonial areas. In this connection, it was stated with alarm in the State Department's Advisory Committee on Post-War Foreign Policy that 'the rapid rate at which we are depleting vital resources means that our position in the future will be perilous . . . Because of the post-war scramble for raw materials it will be necessary to the United States to see that the resources of the world do not slip away under controls and methods hostile to American interests.'[70] As for the need for markets, the remarks made by Bernard Baruch at this time, implying that it was essential for the U.S.A. to get into a position to sell in British colonies, have already been noted.[71]

In private, some constructive Anglo-American dialogues on the colonial issue were taking place, it is true. For example, papers on aspects of the Far East after the war were beginning to be exchanged between a Chatham House group under Sir Frederick Whyte and a number of interested individuals in the United States, brought together by Professor William C. Johnstone of Washington.[72] (The Foreign Office kept in touch with Chatham House over these developments, and over the repercussions of the somewhat stormy I.P.R. Conference that was mentioned in the preceding period.)[73] There also existed some American officials and advisers who felt that the gap between the two countries over colonial questions was now less wide than it had been. Leo Pasvolsky, for instance, who was a leading State Department adviser of Hull's on post-war matters, commented that 'the British were going pretty far in their colonial policy. Their recognition of the idea of trusteeship was equivalent to a recognition of their responsibility to the public opinion of the world.' Similarly, the Advisory Committee on Colonial Problems was 'disposed to believe that the British pledges to colonial peoples did not depart widely from the Atlantic Charter.'[74]

At the same time, some modifications were being made within these circles to the more extreme American hopes of 1942. On the Advisory Committee for Post-War Foreign Policy, for example, doubts were now expressed as to whether members of the United Nations should be required to place their own colonies under trusteeship, the conclusion being that 'perhaps the most that can be hoped for is that the administration of such colonies will be kept in harmony with the principles of trusteeship by the pressure of international public opinion.' It was also urged that, at a time when the trend was towards a demand for 'Asia for the Asiatics', the United States should not appear to be in any way responsible for the elimination of the British Empire in the Far East, which might be involved. In addition, a certain embarrassment continued to be felt over the question which, this time, Representative Eaton brought up, of 'whether it was intended that the Virgin Islands, Puerto Rico and Hawaii should be placed under the trusteeship principle.'[75]*

Even so, the American response to the British draft declaration of colonial principles (which we noted in the previous period, and which was left with Hull at the beginning of February)[76] still spoke of colonial powers 'fixing, at the earliest possible moment, dates upon which the colonial peoples shall be accorded the status of full independence within a system of general security . . .'[77] This 'Draft Declaration on National Independence', as the

---

* In addition to the notion of international trusteeships, ideas being explored in Washington during 1943 included the setting up of regional councils and, more specifically, the establishing of some form of association between Malaya, the Netherlands East Indies, Borneo and the Philippines. (E.g. Committee on Colonial Problems, 26 Nov. 1943, DS, Notter files, box 120.)

State Department called it, was handed to Eden during his visit to Washington in the spring, and then again during the Moscow Conference of Foreign Ministers. In Australian eyes, at least, it was a satisfactory piece of work, for the idea of establishing trusteeships and regional commissions for colonies was playing an important part in Canberra's internal deliberations; the Americans were informed, therefore, not only that their draft was perfectly acceptable, but that Australia would go further than Britain probably would over this whole question.[78]

In making this last suggestion, Canberra was correct, for Hull's document was encountering an extremely cool reception in London. At a meeting between Eden, Cranborne, Stanley and (be it noted) Attlee, it was agreed that the draft was objectionable on several grounds: its emphasis on colonies obtaining 'independence', rather than on their moving towards 'self-government'; its demand for a timetable—quite unacceptable in view of the widely differing degrees of development among Britain's colonial territories and the need in many cases to settle religious and racial differences before the granting of independence could be contemplated; and its suggestions for what appeared to be an elaborate machinery to oversee the whole process.[79] Churchill himself renewed his strictures against 'the vague American aspirations which cost them nothing to make and exposed our whole Empire to great embarrassment', while Eden agreed that the State Department's document 'must be radically transformed, not merely amended.'[80] As for Oliver Stanley at the Colonial Office, one of his officials reported that he was 'rather bored and irritated by the whole business', and the general feeling was that, especially since the intense pressures of 1942 had now been reduced, a joint declaration with the Americans had become less urgent a matter, besides looking very difficult to achieve.[81]

Meanwhile, further forthright defences of the British Empire were being made in public. 'Let us not overlook the fact', declared Attlee, 'that faith in our rule and in British justice has been exemplified by many gallant actions by our fellow-subjects of many different races.'[82] Warnings were also issued to the effect that Britain firmly intended to continue controlling the administration of her own colonies after the war,[83] and at a scholarly level Professor W. K. Hancock published his *Argument of Empire*, which upheld the same idea, as against proposals for international control. In private, an eye was being kept at the same time on signs of American interest in the economic resources of the colonies, one example—it took the form of a detailed questionnaire on Burma—leading the Governor of that territory to warn Amery that 'the Yanks are out for all the information which they can get about our ordinary peace-time trade.' (The American Consul-General in Calcutta also asked the Governor 'how Burma would react to coming under international control.')[84] In addition, an uneasy watch was kept on American political-warfare activities involving Southeast Asia. It was noted, for example, that the O.W.I.'s directive for Burma emphasized 'the building up of Roosevelt as a symbol' and did not suggest the likelihood of a return to British rule. The Pacific Bureau of the O.W.I., operating from California, was deemed to be particularly hostile to British interests, directed as it now was by Owen Lattimore, 'who', it was reported, 'is such a Sinophile that he inevitably is also Anglophobe [and] is opposed to the return of Colonial Government after the war.' There was thus all the more reason, it was felt, to increase the effectiveness of the Ministry of Information's own Far Eastern Bureau as a counter to such American activities.[85]

Yet in Britain, as well as in the United States, calls were still being made in 1943 for fresh thinking on the subject of the country's colonies. In Parliament, Stanley had to face further questions on, for example, the significance of the Atlantic Charter in this respect and the possible role of regional advisory councils.[86] The Labour Party's Advisory Committee on Imperial Questions was recommending, for its part, that all colonial powers should be made accountable to an international authority for their stewardship,[87] while even the War Office did nothing to prevent the distribution to troops of educational material containing ideas that were far closer to Washington's than to Churchill's, or, indeed, to those of Grigg, the Secretary of State for War. Thus, in a *British Way and Purpose* pamphlet issued in January 1943 by the Directorate of Army Education, soldiers were told that

'We no longer regard the Colonial Empire as a "possession", but as a trust or responsibility. "Imperialism" in the less reputable sense of that term is dead: there is obviously no room for it in the British Commonwealth of equal nations, and it has been superseded by the principle of trusteeship for Colonial peoples . . . The conception of trusteeship is already passing into the more active one of partnership . . . Self government is better than good government . . . We must see if that can become a common Colonial policy accepted by all Colonial irresponsible powers and concurred in by other nations. Of the cooperation of the United States we may be assured.'[88]

One would like to have heard the Prime Minister's reactions had he read this. 'Self government is better than good government'? Nevertheless, within other official quarters, including the Colonial Office and the Foreign Office Research Department, attempts were being made to envisage the changed circumstances in which the country's Colonial Empire would find itself after the war.[89] The inter-departmental Committee on American opinion and the British Empire, chaired by Law, also continued to function, as did the parallel group within the Washington Embassy.[90] Here, too, the thinking was far from purely defensive and conservative. The general feeling in the Committee was reflected in a paper by its Secretary, a document which, in part, unwittingly echoed one of the reports which we have seen despatched to the State Department by John Davies, and which looked ahead to the vital need for Anglo-American cooperation after the war:

'American public opinion in regard to such cooperation is decisive, as compared to American Government opinion. It is much more likely that American disillusion in regard to the Empire will influence Americans in the direction of withdrawal from political responsibility than it will result in American imperialism of a kind which is likely to replace British administrative control ... The problem in general is therefore to keep America "in" politically rather than to keep her "out."'

'I am convinced', minuted Gladwyn Jebb in the Foreign Office, 'that we must somehow or other both more closely associate America with the British Empire and adopt measures which will be pleasing to America, not only in the Far East but also in the Caribbean and Africa.'[91]

Could one, therefore, as Denis Brogan suggested, appeal for understanding to United States businessmen on the grounds that the Empire 'performed ... great service for American capitalist enterprise by creating and maintaining a system of law and order in which American business can function easily'?[92] Could one, as Law proposed, 'encourage American participation in development work'?[93] Could some form of cooperation be created over colonial raw materials like rubber and tin?[94] 'There can be no doubt', wrote a Colonial Office official, 'that it is of the first importance for the successful operation of any post-war Rubber Regulation scheme that the United States should be full parties to it in view of the predominant position they will have, ... both as consumers and producers.' Similarly, it was with American objections in mind that the Cabinet itself decided that the existing International Rubber Regulating Committee, with its accompanying restrictive agreements, should be brought to an end, its place to be taken by an International Rubber Committee with a 'consultative and advisory capacity' only.[95]*

The belief that action of some kind was required in respect of colonial policies made itself felt throughout the Law Committee's proceedings. Apart from anything else, domestic opinion, it was argued, needed to be awakened to imperial issues. 'People in England', observed the Permanent Under Secretary at the Colonial Office, 'have no very convinced belief that the Empire is a good thing, and this affects America.'[96] A more direct move, however, was required if an impact was to be made on the American public, and the Permanent Under Secretary at the India Office wondered whether 'something ... dramatic' might not be possible where Burma was concerned.[97] Yet despite the airing of such ideas and despite the very existence of the Committee, the coordination of Whitehall's efforts in the field remained very imperfect. Thus, when Stanley made a major speech in the

---

* The Colonial Office nevertheless rejected American allegations concerning the injurious effects of the old I.R.R.C. before the war. 'Put briefly', Stanley wrote to Eden, 'the essential facts are that in the two years immediately prior to the attack on Pearl Harbour, far more rubber was produced than in any previous two years in the history of the industry; that every demand actually made by those responsible for building up the Government stockpile in the United States was met ... that for all practical purposes restrictions had been completely inoperative since the early stages of the war; and that the major reason why the United States Government's stockpile was not higher still was that those responsible in America had completely failed to control private consumption and the accumulation of private stocks by American manufacturers.' From December 1939 to November 1941, 1,880,000 tons of rubber were exported to the U.S.A., compared to 925,000 tons during the preceding two years.

Commons on colonial policy, when a Colonial Development Report was published, and when a new constitution was offered to Jamaica, in none of these instances had advance notice been given that would have enabled publicity in the United States to be properly organized.[98]

The major obstacle to progress, however—of greater consequence than the caution of the India and Colonial Offices, which at times irked the Foreign Office[99]—remained the conservatism of the Prime Minister, as displayed, for example, over the question of Burma. During this period, both the Governor, Dorman-Smith, and the Secretary of State, Amery, were urging that the Cabinet should be given the opportunity to endorse a major statement of British policy as regards that territory, a statement which should look towards 'the establishment of full self-government as soon as possible', and lay down a maximum period (the Governor proposed the figure of seven years)[100] in which interim British post-war rule would be exercised. Dorman-Smith also continued to entertain some fairly radical ideas, glanced at in passing in an earlier chapter, whereby the Government of Burma 'should to some degree participate in the running of big firms' so that the Burmese people could have a check on the amount of profits being taken out of their country. 'If necessary', he wrote to Amery, 'we must be very tough with the business boys, in spite of their blooming shareholders.'[101]

Churchill's approach, however, remained very different. Thus, when the Governor, in a press interview, looked ahead to the eventual self-government of Burma, the Prime Minister wrote angrily to Amery: 'He [Dorman-Smith] seems to have been talking a lot of nonsense about our handing over Burma, etc. Let me see a full report of his speech.' And when Amery replied to the effect that the Governor's words had been entirely in keeping with British policy, Churchill reiterated that it was 'a most ill-timed utterance.'[102] His face-to-face response to Dorman-Smith, as we have seen, was more un-constructively blunt still—even brutal, his general attitude leading the latter to draw up a letter of resignation in November 1943, though Amery dis-suaded him from sending it.[103]

Similarly, when the question of Burma's future and a possible announce-ment of Britain's policy came up in Cabinet, Churchill again displayed what Amery described as 'his most impossible mood', and it was with reference to this occasion that the Secretary of State made the observation, quoted earlier, about the Prime Minister's 'hatred of self-government in any shape or form.'[104] Grigg, however, as Secretary of State for War, gave Churchill encouragement, writing that he had 'always believed that the future welfare of Burma, as of India, depends on the British retaining quite unashamedly the ultimate authority there.'[105] Even the Cabinet as a whole allowed itself in April to be guided by the Prime Minister, failing to heed Amery's warning that both political warfare and reconstruction planning required a major policy decision to be made.[106]* The Secretary of State was thus reduced to

* It is interesting to note that Dorman-Smith, as Governor of Burma, found Cripps, like Amery, always most helpful in London, but Attlee 'entirely unsympathetic.' (Interviews with Sir Reginald Dorman-Smith.)

telling the Commons that self-government within the Commonwealth would be introduced for Burma 'as soon as circumstances permitted',[107] a state of affairs which failed to satisfy Mountbatten on the spot in Southeast Asia when, later in the year, he sought to win the support of the Burmese people for his campaigns.[108] Amery therefore raised the matter once again with Churchill, but he got no change. 'There is no need for haste', wrote the latter, missing the point, perhaps deliberately. 'Burma is not yet in our control.'[109]

Yet whatever the Prime Minister's short-sightedness, immediate, practical issues in Southeast Asia were already foreshadowing the arrival of wider and more difficult ones. Around the end of this period, men of S.O.E.'s Force 136, operating behind the Japanese lines in Burma, made contact with native elements that were anti-Japanese but also strongly nationalist. Similarly, unknown to London, British agents in occupied Malaya reached an agreement in December 1943 with the Communist-controlled Malayan Peoples' Anti-Japanese Army whereby the latter would follow the instructions of the Allied Commander in Chief in return for being supplied with arms and ammunition.[110] In both Malaya and Burma, however, the further question was bound to arise of what political line Britain should take regarding such potentially difficult allies, and of what promises for the future could or should be made in order to win and retain their support against the Japanese. As we shall see in the following periods, issues such as these were to force their way to the front before the war was over. Whatever views might be held within 10 Downing Street, in other words, there could be no comfortable return to the status quo for Britain in Southeast Asia. And many in London, as well as in the United States, recognized as much.

Other territories in Southeast Asia

Of the Southeast Asian territories outside the British Empire, the Netherlands East Indies, it will be recalled, fell for the most part within MacArthur's South West Pacific Area and will therefore be dealt with in that context, in a later chapter. The British were involved, however, to the extent that Sumatra lay within the new South East Asia Command. The Foreign Office also continued to regard the Dutch as 'our natural allies' in the region, and looked forward to 'close contact on all planning for the future of our colonial territories', as well as to an arrangement whereby the Dutch would resume control in their own lands as soon as they were reoccupied.[111] Mountbatten likewise asked for a Dutch official to supervise political warfare directed against Sumatra,[112] while there existed an added common factor in the fact that the Dutch, like the British, continued to cast an anxious eye at American opinion concerning the future administration of colonies.[113]

Siam posed more difficult questions, quite apart from the blurred one that has been noted already, of whether it lay within S.E.A.C. and whether that Command could conduct pre-operational activities there.[114] Siam, as we have seen, was technically at war with both Britain and the United States, a challenge which Washington had ignored but to which London had responded in kind. For the British, too, there arose an additional issue in 1943 when Siam accepted as a gift from the Japanese four Confederate Malay States and the two Shan States.[115] In return, Churchill, as noted earlier, already had his eye on Siam's Kra Isthmus for post-war defence purposes, and the Vice Chiefs of Staff went on record in a similar, if broader, sense during 1943.[116] The Colonial Office likewise suggested that there would be advantages in obtaining the Siamese 'appendix' that lay between Burma and Malaya.[117] Within the Foreign Office, opinions were divided, with Sir Maurice Peterson continuing to take a harsh and dismissive view of the nascent Free Siamese Movement, while others, in the Far Eastern Department, saw that resistance Movement as 'commanding a measure of support in the country such as to make its recognition worth while.'[118] Sir Josiah Crosby, the former British Minister in Bangkok, suggested for his part that some sort of protectorate for Siam might be needed in the future, but that such a role should be played by the United States, rather than Britain. (There was some irony in this, in that a subsequent article of Crosby's was to be taken by American observers as 'proof' that Britain was bent upon absorbing Siam in some fashion.)[119]

The British position over Siam was made more awkward in February 1943, when Chiang Kai-shek broadcast the assurance that 'China and her allies have no territorial designs on Thailand and no intention to violate Thailand's sovereignty'—a pledge that was publicly endorsed by Roosevelt in the following month, with the State Department strongly hinting that London should come out in a similar sense.[120] The Foreign Office were indeed in favour of Britain's making some declaration of this kind, as were Mountbatten and Dening later in the year from their S.E.A.C. vantage-point. 'A common front with the United States [regarding Siam] is in our opinion essential', wrote Dening then, and he urged that action should be taken without waiting for the leaders of the Siamese resistance to make some overt move.[121] Yet there remained the Prime Minister's declared intention to retain a free hand over the Kra Isthmus, and therefore the best that could be done, at the end of this period, was for a draft statement to be prepared for Cabinet approval, carefully omitting any reference to Siam's territorial integrity.[122] Herein lay the seeds of future trouble between London and Washington, for American officials were already suspicious that Britain was up to something shady as regards the future of Siam.[123] The State Department was looking more positively at signs of a resistance movement in that country,[124] and Hornbeck's view, that post-war strategic requirements might make it advisable not to guarantee her territorial integrity, put him, as he privately admitted to Sir George Sansom of the British Embassy, in a minority of one among his colleagues.[125]

Trouble over Siam lay in the future. Already, however, there was ample evidence to indicate the existence in 1943 of difficulties in respect of another territory: French Indochina. In this connection, the different attitudes adopted by the United States and Britain respectively regarding the future of France as a power—attitudes that have been outlined in an earlier chapter— were obviously relevant. So, too, were the various ideas about Indochina that had been formed in 1942. Yet in some American official quarters, modifications were made during 1943 to opinions that had been expressed in the previous year, a development which has already been noted as regards colonial issues generally. Isaiah Bowman, for example, as a member of the State Department's Advisory Committee on Post-War Foreign Policy, was now advocating that France should, after all, get back Indochina, though subject to international agreement on the character of her administration there.[126] Even Sumner Welles was beginning to talk in similar terms,[127] although the Far Eastern Division of the State Department were emphasizing the rider 'that the Annamites are fundamentally capable of self-government', and that any post-war administration should speedily 'train [them] to resume [those] responsibilities . . .'[128]

Roosevelt, however, whatever second thoughts some of his officials might be having, continued to push in a more wholeheartedly anti-French direction. Thus, to the Pacific War Council in Washington, to a group of foreign ambassadors, and to Eden during the Foreign Secretary's visit to the U.S.A., the President again made clear his view that 'the French should not be allowed to return to Indochina . . . To permit France to return', he continued, 'would make bad feeling throughout the Far East. The French had done nothing for the population but had misgoverned and exploited it.' Therefore, he reiterated, the territory should become a United Nations trusteeship,[129] while to his Chiefs of Staff, en route to Cairo and Tehran, he added that France should not get back New Caledonia, the Marquesa Islands or Dakar either.[130]

In the inter-Allied talks that followed, Roosevelt drew a blank when airing these ideas to Eden and Churchill. According to the President himself later, the Prime Minister dismissed as 'nonsense' the suggestion, amongst others, that China had no wish to impose her own control on Indochina, whereupon, as he recalled it, Roosevelt bluntly retorted:

'"Winston, this is something which you are just not able to understand. You have 400 years of acquisitive instinct in your blood and you just don't understand how a country might not want to acquire land somewhere if they can get it. A new period has opened in the world's history, and you will have to adjust to it."'[131]*

Chiang Kai-shek himself assured Roosevelt that China had no designs on Indochina, and that he accepted his proposals for the territory, while Stalin, too, reacted favourably to what the President had to say, agreeing that 'France would certainly not again become a first-class power for at least 25 years.'[132] Despite this encouragement, however, Roosevelt still failed to issue a clear-cut directive which the whole of Washington could follow over Indochina, and when the French themselves expressed their fear of a possible Chinese armed incursion into that territory, he merely informed the State

* Likewise, and with little regard to history, John Carter Vincent in the State Department argued that, far from the Annamites and Chinese being enemies, 'the Annamites by and large have for the Chinese a feeling of friendliness and cultural affinity.'

Department that it was 'essentially a military problem.'[133] Ample room was thus left for confusion on the American side in the future.

The French, for their part, were not only strenuously suggesting that there would be serious adverse consequences if the Chinese were allowed to undertake military action in Indochina, but were active in other ways.[134] Thus, when China belatedly broke with Vichy, the Free French sent to Chungking in the autumn of 1943 both a military mission and a diplomatic representative, General Ziaovi Pechkoff. The Gaullists also succeeded in bringing under their control clandestine operations being launched from China into Indochina, which had been initiated by a party loyal to General Giraud, a rival of de Gaulle's.[135] Meanwhile in London the French were pressing for permission to send out to Southeast Asia a military mission under General R. C. Blaizot, together with a body of specially trained French troops, the Corps Léger d'Intervention, and for France to be given some say in Allied military planning as it affected Indochina.[136]

These proposals were received with caution by the British authorities. In the Foreign Office, for example, the belief that de Gaulle himself had advanced, that almost all the French troops in Indochina were loyal to him and at his bidding would rise and massacre the Japanese, was regarded as 'nonsense'. 'All our information goes to show', Dening had written in April, 'that the French in Indochina are putting up a very poor show of resistance', while in October the request for Blaizot to be allowed to join Mountbatten was turned down on the grounds that there was no immediate prospect of the French Army operating in the Far East.[137]

At the same time, however, British thinking in general continued to lean in a pro-French direction rather than towards the radical policies of Roosevelt. For political reasons, the Foreign Office would have liked to see Indochina placed within S.E.A.C. instead of remaining under Chiang Kaishek, and it was Chinese machinations that were thought to lie behind manifestations of Annamite nationalist sentiment.[138] It was believed to be very likely that China intended by such means to dominate Indochina after the war; in contrast, British political warfare in the region 'carefully refrained', in Dening's words, 'from taking a line with the native population which would undermine French sovereignty.'[139]

As for Roosevelt's ideas on Indochina, they continued to get a somewhat scornful reception in the Foreign Office, even though the Head of the North American Department wrongly believed that the President was not being very serious, needing, merely, 'to make a noise like a liberal leader' and to 'dress the post-war settlement in the Pacific in some kind of Atlantic Charter costume.'[140] William Strang, also, failed to emphasize Roosevelt's fundamental anti-colonialism, speculating that the latter might be concerned with what seemed to be a potential weak spot as regards a post-war security system, or with the possibility that France might at some future date collaborate with a newly-revived Germany.[141] On the other hand, to the official responsible for liaison between the Office and the Services, V. Cavendish-Bentinck, the President's statements on Indochina suggested 'that [he] is suffering from the same form of megalomania which characterised the late President Wilson and Mr. Lloyd George (the latter to a lesser extent) at the end of the last war . . . I trust', he added, 'that we shall not allow ourselves to quarrel with the French without being on very strong grounds, for the benefit of a United States President who in a year's time may be merely a historical figure.'[142] The one Foreign Office official who showed some sympathy for Roosevelt's conclusions, if not his premises, was Sir Maurice Peterson, who felt that France would have difficulty enough reestablishing herself as a European and Mediterranean power without adding to her burdens by struggling on in the Far East, where Vichy's collaboration with Japan had already discredited her.[143]

A British policy over Indochina had not yet been worked out to the extent of receiving Cabinet endorsement. (This, as we shall see, was to be done in the following period.) But in the Foreign Office a draft was prepared that anticipated some of the broad ideas that were to be involved: the firm belief, for example, that it was not in Britain's interest to see France weakened or to sour relations with her; the extension of this to the conclusion that she should receive back her Far Eastern empire on condition that she accepted any measures of an international kind that Britain applied to her own colonies; and the conviction that international control of Indochina would only open the door to Chinese, and perhaps later, Japanese intrigues there, although it was also recognized that there were limits beyond which Britain would find it difficult to go if it came to opposing American designs in this respect.[144] In conformity with this generally pro-French approach to the whole issue, the Foreign Office suggested at the end of the year that the question of whether to allow a mission under Blaizot to proceed out to S.E.A.C. should be reopened.

Already, however, the Office found that it was running into an obstruction in the person of the Prime Minister. Churchill had no sympathy with Roosevelt's ideas over Indochina; yet at the same time, he was himself exasperated with de Gaulle, and above all was not prepared at this stage to focus attention on a disagreement between the President and himself over what appeared to be a comparatively minor issue. Thus, when the question arose of whether France should be provided with a seat on the Pacific War Council, he wanted to 'leave it quiet'; similarly, when Cadogan suggested that, 'in view of the well-known American attitude towards the restoration of colonies generally, there is much to be said for the Colonial Powers sticking together in the Far East', the Prime Minister merely minuted in November: 'This can certainly wait.'[145]

Thus, on the British side, as well as on the American, and above all when it came to an interchange on the subject between the two, there existed a lack of clarity where Indochina was concerned. In some respects the same was true, as we have seen, regarding Southeast Asian affairs generally. Churchill's fierce conservatism did at least appear to provide one certain element in the situation, but by the same token the Prime Minister was setting a severe limit to the articulation of constructive and forward-looking British policies for the region. As for the Americans, a solution was still awaited to the dilemma outlined by Davies: how to reconcile a general dislike of colonial empires with support for an ally who possessed just such an empire?

At least each side had formulated proposals for a joint declaration on colonial policy, and in retrospect it can be suggested that, taking into account all the domestic differences that lay behind their respective documents, the possibility of an eventual agreement being reached was not negligible. As we have seen, there were those in Washington who privately accepted that they and the British were not, after all, so very far apart, whilst Lord Halifax, for one, thought that the American draft was not too bad from Britain's point of view.[146] Nevertheless, the continuing need for the Americans to express their deeply-seated anti-colonialist sentiments, together with an undue readiness on the part of British Cabinet Ministers to be discouraged from continuing the search for common ground, had virtually put an end to the project. Given the mutual misunderstandings and suspicions that existed, this was unfortunate. Meanwhile, further difficulties also continued to arise across the border from Burma and Southeast Asia, in India.

Notes to Chapter Thirteen

1 See Anders, *The Ledo Road*, 80.
2 COS, 23 Jan. 1943, CAB 79/25.
3 Aide memoire, 8 May 1943, CAB 99/22. See CCS, 20 May 1943, CAB 88/2.
4 COS, 9 May 1943, and White House meeting, 12 May 1943, CAB 99/22; material in PREM 3, 147/3 and 143/10.
5 JP(43)277, PREM 3, 143/10.
6 FDR to WSC, 8 Jan. 1943; WSC to FDR, 10 Jan. 1943, PREM 3, 143/6.
7 WSC to Mountbatten, 21 Oct. 1943, PREM 3, 147/4.
8 E.g. Mountbatten–Chiang Kai-shek talks, 19 Oct. 1943, SEAC War Diary; Mountbatten to WSC, 5 Oct. 1943, PREM 3, 90/5; WSC to Chiang Kai-shek, 11 Aug. 1943, PREM 3, 143/10.
9 *Pownall*, 6 Dec. 1943; Somerville to Cunningham, 4 Dec. 1943, Somerville Papers, box 8/2.
10 SEAC War Diary, 24 and 27 Nov. 1943.
11 *Roskill*, II, 425; Carton de Wiart to WSC, 17 Dec. 1943, PREM 3, 147/6.
12 WSC to Chiang Kai-shek, 2 Oct. 1943, PREM 3, 147/10.
13 FRUS, Cairo and Tehran, 311, 335.
14 E.g. Vice Chief of Imperial General Staff to CIGS, 15 Aug. 1943, PREM 3, 147/9.
15 E.g. Mountbatten to WSC, 23 Oct. 1943, PREM 3, 90/3; Howard, *Grand Strategy*, IV, cap. XXI; *Romanus and Sutherland*, I, 334.
16 See *Roskill*, III, part I, 344.
17 Material in PREM 3, 148/1; JCS, 20 May and 26 July 1943, RG 218. On force levels over-all, see Ehrman, *Grand Strategy*, V, 146–7.
18 COS, 28 April 1943, PREM 3, 143/7, and 19 April 1943, CAB 79/88; Cab, 29 April 1943, CAB 65/38. See Howard, *Grand Strategy*, IV, cap. XXI.
19 Arnold, *Global Mission*, 208.
20 King to Marshall, 7 April 1943, King Papers, USNOA.
21 Stilwell Diary, 31 May 1943; *Leahy*, 205.
22 J. Masters, *The Road Past Mandalay* (London, 1961), 128; material in PREM 3, 143/10; DC(Ops.), 28 July 1943, CAB 69/5.

23 FRUS, Washington and Quebec, 165, 172.
24 For varying views on Wingate, see e.g. C. Sykes, *Orde Wingate* (London, 1959); Slim, *Defeat Into Victory*; Lewin, *Slim*, 143; Howard, *Grand Strategy*, IV, 548–9; Masters, *The Road Past Mandalay*, 155ff.
25 WSC to COS, 27 Sept. 1943 (PREM 3, 147/10) and 23 Oct. 1943 (PREM 3, 148/1); DC(Ops.), 28 Sept. 1943, CAB 69/5; *Bryant*, I, 602.
26 WSC to Mountbatten, 6 Dec. 1943, and COS to WSC, 7 Dec. 1943, PREM 3, 147/7.
27 See Ehrman, *Grand Strategy*, V, 153.
28 E.g. COS, 4 and 5 Dec. 1943, CAB 99/25; FRUS, Cairo and Tehran, 675, 681, 699; JCS, 17 Nov. and 5 Dec. 1943, RG 218.
29 FRUS, Cairo and Tehran, 719, 725, 815; COS to WSC, 24 Dec. 1943, and WSC to COS, 28 Dec. 1943, PREM 3, 147/6. See *Churchill*, V, 363ff.
30 Meeting of 9 Dec. 1943, SEAC War Diary.
31 *Pownall*, 14 Dec. 1943. On Giffard, see Lewin, *Slim*, 124, 203.
32 Somerville Diary, 12 Dec. 1943; *Mountbatten*, 12; *Kirby*, III, 49; *Roskill*, III, part I, 218.
33 Mountbatten to Somerville, 2 Sept. 1943, Somerville Papers, box 8/3; Cunningham to Somerville, 19 Dec. 1943, and Somerville to Cunningham, 4 Dec. 1943, ibid, box 8/2; Somerville Diary, 2 Dec. 1943; Somerville to Ismay, 3 Dec. 1943, Ismay Papers, IV/Som/2; *Roskill*, III, part I, 214.
34 P. Moon (ed.), *Wavell: The Viceroy's Journal* (London, 1973; hereafter, *Wavell*), entry for 26 Aug. 1943.
35 E.g. Mountbatten minute, 7 Dec. 1943, SEAC War Diary.
36 Somervell to Marshall, 25 Oct. 1943, OPD, Exec. file I, item 23.
37 JCS, 22 Nov. 1943, RG 218; Stilwell to Marshall, 8 Nov. 1943, Roosevelt Papers, MR box 165; *Stilwell Papers*, 7 Oct. 1943. See Leahy Diary, 22 Nov. 1943.
38 E.g. Somerville to Cunningham, 27 Oct. 1943, Somerville Papers, box 8/2.
39 Masters, *The Road Past Mandalay*, 162; Stilwell Diary, 25 Nov. 1943. See Eldridge, *Wrath In Burma*, 198.
40 E. Taylor, *Richer By Asia* (London, 1948), 31, 34, 42.
41 Dorman-Smith Papers, E215/44.
42 *Pownall*, 14 Dec. 1943.
43 Masters, *The Road Past Mandalay*, 154–5; *Stilwell Papers*, 10 Nov. 1943 and 12 Jan. 1944.
44 Stilwell Diary, 4 Dec. 1943.
45 Eldridge, *Wrath in Burma*, 263.
46 *Pownall*, 28 Oct. 1943; Somerville to Ismay, 9 Dec. 1943, Ismay Papers, IV/Som/3.
47 E.g. Mountbatten to WSC, 23 Oct. 1943, PREM 3, 90/3; interview with Earl Mountbatten.
48 FO 371, A6422, 7339 and 8280/93/45.
49 Material in FO 371, file 35967.
50 Ibid, F6413/4022/23; Dening to COS, 23 Oct. 1943, SEAC War Diary.
51 See Wilkinson Journal for 1943 and 1944.
52 E.g. Dorman-Smith to Amery, 25 March 1943, Dorman-Smith Papers, E215/43.
53 E.g. COS, 7 and 12 Aug. 1943, CAB 79/27; B. Sweet-Escott, *Baker Street Irregular* (London, 1965), 139.
54 Garnon-Williams directive, 4 Oct. 1943, SEAC War Diary; A. Gilchrist, *Bangkok Top Secret* (London, 1970), 188ff.; *O.S.S.* cap. 9. See Dening to COS, 21 Oct. 1943, SEAC War Diary.
55 COS, 27 Nov. 1943, CAB 99/25; see above, 292.
56 Material in FO 371, files 35895–6, 35899–900.
57 JCS, 26 Oct. 1943, RG 218. O.W.I. policy was to concentrate on attacking Japanese imperialism, but also to avoid suggesting that there would be a return to the colonial status quo in Asia. Interview with Professor Owen Lattimore.
58 See above, 10; Friend, *Between Two Empires*, 241, and Ba Maw, *Breakthrough in Burma*, 325 and 336.

59 *Davies*, 275.
60 Davies memo., 17 Sept. 1943, Stilwell Papers, box 15.
61 FRUS, 1943, China, 878.
62 Ibid, 883.
63 Roosevelt, *As He Saw It*, 155, 180.
64 Taussig memo., 24 June 1943, Taussig Papers, box 47.
65 Taussig memo., 18 Feb. 1943, ibid, box 47.
66 E.g. *Chicago Tribune*, 5 April 1943.
67 *New York Times*, 12 April, 17 Oct. 1943.
68 FO 371, file 34140.
69 Lasker to Farley, 14 March 1943, IPR Papers, box 392.
70 Sub-committee on Political Problems, 1 May 1943, DS, Notter files, box 55.
71 See above, 59.
72 Council minutes, vol. 23, RIIA; Whyte to Johnstone, 4 May 1943, RIIA.
73 FO 371, F4767 and 5163/1953/61; F3430/186/61; file 35905.
74 Sub-committee on Territorial Problems, 5 March 1943, DS, Notter files, box 59; Committee on Colonial Problems, 30 Nov. 1943, ibid, box 120.
75 Sub-committee on Political Problems, 13 March, 3 and 10 April 1943, ibid, box 55. Already, indeed, an OSS survey (R and A 797, 1942) was suggesting that American 'promises to the nationalist movements in [the Far East] must be such as to be consonant with the type of economic and military security we hope to see develop there. This implies', it added, 'a moderate definition of the term "independence" and a process of achievement of independence which does not involve a sudden political or economic break with Britain, the Netherlands, or the United States.'
76 WP(43)33, CAB 66/33.
77 See FRUS, 1943, I, 747; 1943, III, 28; Washington and Quebec, 717; *Notter*, appendix 12.
78 E.g. papers on proposed South-Seas Commission, ADEA, A989/44/735/321/5; memo., 15 April 1943, 'Departmental View on Australian Interests in the Colonial Question', and Dixon to Canberra, 25 March 1943, ibid, A989/43/735/1021.
79 FO 371, U2039/14/70. See Cab, 13 April 1943, CAB 65/34.
80 WSC to Eden, 15 Sept. 1943, and Eden to WSC, 16 Sept. 1943, PREM 4, 30/4.
81 FO 371, U4018 and 5376/14/70.
82 Attlee speech at Carmarthen, 3 Sept. 1943, Attlee Papers (University College), box 14. See also BWP, 3 (Jan. 1943).
83 E.g. Hansard, HC Deb, 387, col. 1181, and ibid, 391, col. 47ff.
84 Dorman-Smith to Amery, 6 May 1943, Dorman-Smith Papers, E215/57.
85 Material in FO 371, files 35879, 35881, 35883, 35890.
86 E.g. Hansard, HC Deb, 390, cols. 1152, 1167.
87 Material in Bevin Papers, box 17.
88 BWP, 3 (Jan. 1943).
89 E.g. FO 371, F4830/1953/61.
90 Ibid, A3480/3/45.
91 Ibid, A1070/3/45; A444/32/45.
92 Ibid, A1143/3/45.
93 Ibid, A1103/3/45.
94 Ibid, A6188/57/45.
95 Ibid, files 35253–5; Cab, 6 Aug. 1943, CAB 65/35.
96 FO 371, A78/3/45.
97 Ibid.
98 Ibid, A8483/3/45; A2760/32/45.
99 E.g. ibid, A9506/361/45.
100 WP(43)131, CAB 66/35; Amery to WSC, 2 April 1943, PREM 4, 50/3.
101 Dorman-Smith to Amery, 23 Feb. and April (n.d.) 1943, Dorman-Smith Papers, E215/53.
102 Material in PREM 4, 50/3.

103 See above, 60, and draft letter to WSC, 8 Nov. 1943, Dorman-Smith Papers, E251/3.
104 See above, 16.
105 Grigg to WSC, 7 April 1943, PREM 4, 50/3.
106 Cab, 14 April 1943, CAB 65/34.
107 Hansard, HC Deb, 388, col. 1807.
108 FO 371, F5434/783/61.
109 WSC to Amery, 5 Nov. 1943, PREM 4, 50/3.
110 See F. S. Donnison, *British Military Administration In The Far East, 1943–46* (London, 1956; hereafter, *Donnison*), caps. XIX and XX.
111 FO 371, F6673/260/61. See my article, 'Engeland, Australië en Nederlands Indië, 1941–1945', *Internationale Spectator* (The Hague), August 1975.
112 FO 371, F6016 and 6141/71/61.
113 E.g. Loudon to van Kleffens, 22 Nov. 1943, NFM, van Kleffens Papers, file III/I; NCM, 9 July 1943.
114 See above, 301, and COS, 6 Aug. 1943, CAB 79/27.
115 FO 371, file 35949.
116 Ibid, F6444/169/10.
117 Ibid, F3088/222/40.
118 Ibid, material in file 35977.
119 Ibid, F606/169/40 and F696/222/40. On the internal situation in Siam, see Allen, *The End of the War in Asia*, cap. 2.
120 Lawford to Martin, 19 March 1943, PREM 3, 158/7; material in FO 371, file 35983. See FRUS, Cairo and Tehran, 323.
121 FO 371, F5829/169/40.
122 Ibid, F6089/169/40; F6582/6582/61.
123 See ibid, F6362/71/61.
124 FRUS, 1943, III, 1118.
125 FO 371, F6717/69/40.
126 Bowman memo., 29 Oct. 1943, DS, Notter files, box 70. See my article 'The Indochina Issue Between Britain and the U.S.A.', *Pacific Historical Review*, Feb. 1976.
127 Sub-committee on Political Problems, 13 March 1943, DS, Notter files, box 55; FO 371, F1851/877/61.
128 FRUS, 1943, China, 885. A French request for a seat on the Pacific War Council was evaded in Washington. DS 740.0011 P.W./3648.
129 FO 371, F3812/58/61; F6656/1422/61; FRUS, 1943, III, 36, 38.
130 *Matloff*, 339.
131 T. M. Campbell and G. C. Herring (eds.), *The Diaries of Edward R. Stettinius Jr., 1943–1946* (New York, 1975; hereafter *Stettinius*), entries for 17 Jan. and 17 March 1943.
132 FRUS, Cairo and Tehran, 322, 482; Cab, 13 Dec. 1943, CAB 65/40; WSC to Attlee, 1 Dec. 1943, PREM 4, 74/2.
133 FRUS, 1943, China, 886.
134 Ibid, 882.
135 See FO 371, F5070/4249/10; Miles, *A Different Kind of War*, 183ff.; Sainteny, *Histoire D'Une Paix Manquée*, 17; Sabattier, *Le Destin de l'Indochine*, 69.
136 FO 371, F4870, 4871 and 6059/1422/61.
137 Ibid, F1726/779/61; F1422 and 5242/1422/61; COS, 4 Oct. 1943, CAB 79/27.
138 FO 371, F6582/6582/61; F1784/779/61; F6441/4023/61.
139 Ibid, F242/71/61.
140 Ibid, F4646/1422/61.
141 Ibid, Z4105/77/17.
142 Ibid, F6656/1422/61.
143 Ibid, F6441/4023/61.
144 Ibid, F4646/1422/61.
145 Ibid, F5379 and 5608/1422/61.
146 Ibid, U2026/14/20.

CHAPTER FOURTEEN

BRITAIN, THE UNITED STATES
AND INDIA

IN SOME respects, Indian affairs in 1943 presented less of a problem to the British Government than had been the case during the year before. Political activity in the country was at a much lower level, partly as a result of fiercely repressive measures taken by the authorities,[1] and a fast by Gandhi, which at one time threatened to cause trouble, was brought to an end by him in March. The military danger from the Japanese also seemed less acute, although under their auspices an Azad Hind 'Government of Free-India' was set up in Singapore in October.[2]

Even so, the supply problem as regards India remained acute, and in the autumn famine in Bengal brought over a million deaths. (The 1942–3 rice crop was a poor one, while the Japanese were of course preventing the normal arrival of such food from Burma.)[3] The Indian economy as a whole, Amery reported to his colleagues in July, was 'strained almost to breaking point', and in September the Chiefs of Staff declared that 'unless the necessary steps are taken to rectify this situation, the efficient prosecution of the war against Japan by forces based in India will be gravely jeopardised and may well prove impossible.'[4] Thus, quite apart from the continuing problem represented by the separate existence of the Congress party and the Muslim League, serious difficulties faced Wavell, whose appointment as the new Viceroy in place of Linlithgow was announced in June, after Churchill had played with the idea of sending out Eden instead.[5] (The Prime Minister also, in October, sounded out Halifax as a possible replacement for Amery at the India Office, but the Ambassador responded, as he recorded afterwards, that 'our feeling about India was too different to make the kind of partnership he suggested very fruitful.')[6]

Following the tumult of 1942, Britain adopted an essentially negative approach to the Indian constitutional and political question in this period. Over the specific case of Gandhi, for example, the Cabinet accepted the Viceroy's advice that no weakness must be shown in the face of the former's fast,[7] while on broader issues Linlithgow remained unhopefully conservative to the end:

'I am inclined to be pessimistic', he wrote to Amery, 'about the prospect of any solution coming out of the post-war constitutional discussions . . . I am quite certain that any conclusions that did emerge can be implemented and any scheme held together only by the continued and effective presence of Great Britain ... Here, as in the colonial field (and the same is even more true of Burma), I think we are entitled to bear in mind that it is we who have created and developed these great territories, given them peace and good order and held them together, and there are limits to the sacrifices that we can reasonably be expected to make.'

Apart from 'a small coterie of ambitious politicians', he informed Amery in August, there was 'precious little interest [in India] in any radical change in the system of government.'[8]

Amery himself inclined towards gloom over the prospects that lay ahead, and was thinking of means of avoiding eventual chaos which echoed the bizarre ideas of Roosevelt[9] (and, indeed, to some extent, of Alfred Rosenberg) about inherent racial characteristics and the possibilities of interbreeding. 'If India is to be really capable of holding its own in the future', he wrote, 'without direct British control from outside, I am not sure that it will not need an increasing infusion of stronger Nordic blood, whether by settlement or intermarriage or otherwise.'[10] The saviour of the East, it seems, was to be neither a Gandhi nor a Curzon, but Siegfried with a sitar. Meanwhile, the Secretary of State was also concerned that the drastic expansion of the Indian Army from around 180,000 in 1939 to nearly 2 million might have increased the chances of its allegiance being undermined, especially since 'the Indian soldier's belief in the power of Britain has been shaken.'[11] (In the event, the Army, which was to comprise about 2,500,000 men in 1945, was remarkable for its loyalty to the Raj.)[12]

The Prime Minister, for his part, was at times even more apprehensive than Amery over this last possible danger. 'Winston at the moment', wrote the latter to Linlithgow in June, 'has got one of his fits of panic and talks about a drastic reduction of any army that might shoot us in the back.'[13] 'He has got a curious complex about India', noted Wavell when Churchill made the same point to him, 'and is always loth to hear good of it and is apt to believe the worst. He has still, at heart, his cavalry subaltern's idea of India.'[14] Despite Amery's efforts to demonstrate the magnitude of the Indian war effort, the Prime Minister also continued to become indignant about that country's growing sterling balances, and he again insisted 'that we ought to reserve the right to put in a counter-claim in respect of all that we had done to defend India from conquest by Japan.'[15] It was during this period, too, that Churchill gave vent to his feelings, already quoted, about the 'gross, dirty and corrupt ... baboos' of India, warning at the same time that Britain would be bound 'by the Americans if by nobody else' to the promises which she had given, and that the area as a whole would 'prove extremely distracting to British statesmen' in the future.[16]

Churchill was not opposed with any vigour in Cabinet over Indian questions, despite the presence of Cripps and Bevin, for example, whose concern for the people of the sub-continent was proven. Nor did Linlithgow and

Amery evoke a very sympathetic response in London when they pressed hard for an increase in the grain supplies being despatched to India. 'We should be very chary of sending ships with grain for the civil population [there]', Cherwell wrote to Churchill, and in general his advice was followed. Cherwell's repugnance against coloured people has been noted earlier;[17] now Amery wrote despairingly that he was regarded by the Prime Minister 'as an authority on everything, and especially on India.'[18] Some Ministers, it is true, did have ideas for change in the future, notably Bevin, who wished to see a new basis created on which to build a post-war defence partnership between Britain and an industrialized India, a drive undertaken to increase the latter's living standards, and a major role secured for her on the Asian scene after the defeat of Japan.[19] But Bevin in 1943 also wanted 'to turn the minds of the people of India [away] from political agitation', and it was left to Wavell to press for a new initiative to be taken on that front, proposing that leaders of Indian parties should be invited to join the Viceroy's Executive Council.[20]

Despite obtaining some support from the Cabinet's India Committee, however, the new Viceroy did not find Ministers in general very responsive. 'I have discovered', he wrote in his journal, 'that the Cabinet is not honest in its expressed desire to make progress in India', and he saw around him in London only 'spinelessness, lack of interest, opportunism.'[21] Consequently, Churchill had little difficulty in killing the idea of undertaking a major constitutional initiative. With a new military offensive being planned for 1944, 'there could hardly be a less suitable time', he declared, 'for raising again the political agitation on its old and well-known lines . . . The fact that a new Viceroy is going out to India', he added, 'affords no reason for running such risks.'[22] Thus, Wavell's directive from the Government reminded him that his first duty was 'the defence of India from the Japanese menace and invasion'; the 'material and cultural conditions of the many peoples of India' also received a mention, but he must 'beware above all things lest the achievement of victory and the ending of the miseries of war should be retarded by undue concentration on political issues while the enemy is at the gate.'[23]

Aside from such major questions of policy, the Government of India continued in this period to be the subject of considerable hostile comment from within the Foreign Office. The main complaint was that it had little grasp of the political aspects of the Far Eastern conflict, and was thus entirely unsuited to the task of directing the propaganda and psychological warfare activities that were carried on in India. 'Officials who return from New Delhi', noted the Head of the Far Eastern Department, 'tell a story of cumbrous machinery, parochialism and lack of reality', while Sir Maurice Peterson, sour as usual, wrote of 'the myopic vision of the Government of India [which], while it may reach as far as Burma, certainly does not extend as far as Japan.' A Foreign Office memorandum on the subject concluded that 'there is nothing in the present position of the Government of India . . . to encourage the idea that the Indian administration are in a position to give confident and vigorous direction to the war against Japan . . . Their self-complacency is . . . in part inspired by the absence of any real consciousness that the enemy is the Japanese and that such questions as the danger of an extension of Chinese influence over Burma and Eastern India itself, as well as the Quisling India forces being recruited by the Japanese . . ., are wholly subsidiary ones.'[24]

It cannot be said that the Foreign Office itself, for all that its views in this respect had evident substance, was always constructive over the issue. For example, it cold-shouldered Sir Olaf Caroe, who was responsible for foreign affairs in New Delhi, when he was back in Britain for a while.[25] Meanwhile related questions, the complex details of which need not be explored here, embraced both principles and personalities involved in the direction of the Ministry of Information's Far Eastern Bureau and the links between India and bodies in London like the inter-departmental Political Warfare Against Japan Committee. Suffice it to say that the Director General of the Far Eastern Bureau resigned in October, but that the Foreign Office failed in its efforts to have the Viceroy required to correspond directly with itself on such matters. The Office failed also to get a senior official of its own appointed to the Viceroy's staff, Dening's posting to S.E.A.C. being the most that could be secured.[26]

Meanwhile, India continued to be a subject for concern in the United States, though at a lower level than in 1942. (A poll taken in April 1943 indicated that 62 per cent were in favour of Indian independence, but that only 19 per cent of that number thought it advisable to bring it about immediately, 40 per cent of them advocating that it should await the end of the war.)[27] Appeals by Indian nationalists were still being directed at the American public over such matters as Gandhi's imprisonment and the famine in Bengal; American troops and correspondents went on seeing for themselves the unhappiness of the sub-continent, and continued to be struck by the differences between India and China. 'The contrast', broadcast Eric Sevareid of C.B.S., 'is strong and vivid. Down on the plains of India, you saw proud buildings and sad faces; in China you see sad buildings and proud faces. With the people of India you felt instant pity; with the people of China, instant liking.'[28] Also, the fear was still expressed that the United States might become identified with Britain in Indian eyes.[29] At the same time, Pearl Buck and others went on urging that the problem of India was one in which the U.S.A. had to become involved,[30] while leading members of the Senate Foreign Relations Committee emphasized their belief that, given the prominent American war-time role in that part of the world (financial and economic, as well as military: in this period Washington agreed, for example, to lend the Government of India 20 million ounces of silver to help stabilize the latter's economy),[31] the President should 'turn the heat' on Churchill and make him settle the Indian constitutional question.[32]

Calls for American action of some kind were also being made by William Phillips, now installed in New Delhi, where he remained for the early part of

1943. Phillips, as we have seen, had been sent out there with wholehearted British approval, the feeling in the Washington Embassy and Foreign Office being that he would help to bring about a more stable, understanding and responsible American approach to Indian affairs. Instead, what happened was that the new Presidential Representative, for all his old-school-diplomatic and East-coast-élite backgrounds, soon came to conclusions which, in Roosevelt's words, were 'amazingly radical for a man like Bill.'[33]

It will be recalled that, with the exception of Churchill, the men Phillips had talked to in London had given him the clear impression that 'the English people were ready and even eager to grant dominion status to India if only the Indians would agree among themselves with regard to the form of their government.' In India itself, however, he found that, led by Linlithgow, 'the British whom I have met seem unaware of the changing attitude in England and cannot really envisage a free India fit to govern itself.' Unable to keep out of the public eye, besieged by Indian requests to help over Gandhi's imprisonment and fast, Phillips came to believe that only a cast-iron pledge by Britain to grant independence on a certain date after the war, with an immediate transfer of substantial powers to an interim, coalition government meanwhile, could save the situation. In addition, he argued, the United States must make its own position on these matters clear beyond doubt, and should possibly intervene, if London agreed, by getting an American to preside over a meeting of Indian leaders, and by giving what would amount to a guarantee by Washington of Britain's promises.

'The Indians', Phillips wrote in one of his frequent letters to Roosevelt, 'are caught in the new idea which is sweeping over the world, of freedom for oppressed peoples.' The British, on the other hand, were, he believed, merely keeping the lid on an explosive situation by holding 20,000 Congress leaders in jail without trial, while on neither side, British or Indian, was there any zeal for prosecuting the war against the external foe. (The Indian Army, he asserted, was 'purely mercenary.')*

'It is hard to discover any pronounced war spirit against Japan, even on the part of the British', he wrote in April. 'Rather, it seems to me, the British feel that their responsibility lies on this side of the Burma–Assam frontier . . . As I see it, unless the present atmosphere is changed for the better, we Americans will have to bear the burden of the coming campaign in this part of the world, and cannot count on more than token assistance from the British in British India.

As time goes on, Indians are coming more and more to disbelieve in the American gospel of freedom of oppressed peoples . . . India, China and Burma have a common meeting ground in their desire for freedom from foreign domination . . . Chinese apathy and lack of leadership and, moreover, Chinese dislike of the British, meet a wholly responsive chord in India . . . Color consciousness is also appearing more and more and under

* The 'mercenary' Indian Army was to win 20 out of the 27 Victoria Crosses awarded during the fighting for Burma. (Mason, *A Matter of Honour*, 507.)

present conditions is bound to develop. We have, therefore, a vast bloc of
Oriental peoples who have many things in common, including a growing
dislike and distrust of the Occidental.

I see only one remedy to this disturbing situation, and that is to try with
every means in our power to make Indians feel that America is with them
and in a position to go beyond mere public assurances of friendship.'[34]

While Phillips was writing reports such as this to the President, the O.W.I.
in India were already emphasizing publicly the difference between the American and British positions, pointing out in advertisements the United States
policy of granting freedom to the Philippines at a stated time, and declaring
that 'the Expeditionary Forces of the United States of America are in India
today to defend the future of Asia . . .'[35]* The President's Representative
himself, however, did not stay long enough to try to bring about the new
initiative in which he believed. At the end of April he left India for the United
States, and spent most of the summer of 1943 on leave in Washington, after
first making a direct attempt to get Roosevelt to see the urgency of the
situation. In September, it was announced that, although he would retain his
Presidential appointment to New Delhi, Phillips was going to undertake War
Department work—it was with the Headquarters of the Allied Expeditionary
Force for Europe—in London.

This restricted use made of Phillips in India reflected the restrained nature
of the American official responses to the situation there in 1943, responses
that contrasted with Roosevelt's attempts to influence Churchill—coerce
him, even—in the preceding year.† Hull in particular was anxious to 'make
every effort to prevent this question from becoming a matter of serious contention and general discussion here', and to 'keep down in this country any
sentiments against Great Britain.' 'We cannot have a serious breach, personal or political, with [Churchill] now', he noted, 'even if we were disposed
to do so.'[36] Only within these limitations, therefore, was some effort made to
influence events. Roosevelt's view that Gandhi should not be allowed to die
in prison was made known to London through Halifax,[37] and American
concern over the Bengal famine was also indicated (although on the Combined Food Board in Washington the British representatives took the line
that their country alone was responsible for the supply of foodstuffs to
India).[38] Where intelligence and political warfare activities based in India
were concerned, care was taken, as in S.E.A.C., to see that the American

---

* Phillips himself, however, had serious reservations about the O.W.I. set-up in India.
'The personnel', he wrote to Welles, '. . . is far from what it should be. There is a cheapness
about it which does us . . . considerable harm.' He also took note of Indian fears of
American 'dollar diplomacy' and 'economic imperialism.' (Phillips to Welles, 17 Feb. 1943,
Phillips Papers, vol. 33; memo. for Phillips, 20 April 1943, ibid, vol. 34.)

† It should also be noted that there was a marked limit to what the United States would
do to put itself out in a practical way on India's behalf. Thus, although officially requested
to do so, the Administration would make no effort to get Indian immigration into the
U.S.A. permitted, along with the new trickle of Chinese being allowed in. (FO 371,
A10200/144/25.) See below, 644, note 19.

position remained well apart from the British one.[39] Meanwhile, one gleam of hope was discerned as regards the future, in that both Phillips and the Ambassador in London, Winant, were impressed by the new Viceroy, Wavell, and welcomed his appointment.[40]

Roosevelt, however, was apparently thinking along lines more drastic than anything that the most well-meaning representative of the British Throne could achieve. 'At some future date', the President remarked to Stalin at Tehran, 'he would like to talk with Marshal Stalin on the question of India; . . . he felt that the best solution would be reform from the bottom, somewhat on the Soviet line.' To this ingratiating observation, Stalin merely replied that the matter was a complex one, and that 'reform from the bottom would mean revolution.'[41] Ironically, his own general view, as summarized by 'Chip' Bohlen who was present at the Tehran meetings, was, by contrast, that 'because of the British military contribution, the Soviet Government considers that there should be no reduction in the British Empire, but on the contrary it should if necessary be increased by turning over to Great Britain on the basis of trusteeship certain bases and strong-points throughout the world.'[42]

Roosevelt's remarks on this occasion were not known to the British, or no doubt the Prime Minister would have had a few words to say. As it was, Linlithgow in New Delhi had, earlier in the year, soon become disillusioned with Phillips, whose arrival he had greeted with relief—'He has admirable manners, is most friendly, and seems to me better really than anything we could reasonably have hoped for.' The President's Representative became in the Viceroy's eyes 'a centre for discontented [Indian] politicians', and the latter rejected Phillips' request to be allowed to visit Gandhi. Yet another American, Linlithgow now believed, had turned out after all to be sentimental in his approach and unable to grasp the complexities of Indian politics.[43] It made no difference that the Foreign Office, from its more sheltered vantage-point in London, looked on Phillips' activities sympathetically, nor was the Viceroy convinced by Law's opinion, conveyed by Amery, that India was indeed now the United States' business as well as Britain's.[44] Linlithgow continued to be highly suspicious of American intentions generally, and was certain that 'the Wendell Willkie–Luce group' and others had their eye on trade possibilities in India; even the increasing number of U.S. diplomats being posted to India were part of a scheme, he believed, 'to dig in in this country with a view to the post-war period.' In consequence, he foresaw a major struggle over such matters as air routes and oil resources taking place between Britain and the United States, and denounced as 'profoundly unwise . . . and [potentially] very expensive for us' what he described as the Foreign Office line of 'treating the United States as if they were children and could not bear to hear anything unpleasant.' 'American uneasiness lest we should move over into the Russian camp,' he added, 'is a factor that ought not to be overlooked when we are considering what we hold in our hand'—a bizarre touch, this, in the light of history, coming from a Viceroy of India.[45]

The Foreign Office, on its side, winced at some of Linlithgow's opinions, believing that New Delhi failed to appreciate the complexities and significance of the American scene, just as it failed to place the struggle against Japan in its correct perspective.[46] In his resentment over American interference, however, and in his essentially pessimistic view of India's future, the Viceroy continued to the end of his time in office to have Churchill behind him. The Prime Minister met Phillips in Washington in May, and took the occasion to warn the latter in the strongest terms against what he believed to be his recipe for solving India's problems. As Phillips recorded it later: '"Mark my words", he concluded, shaking a finger at me, "I prophesied the present war and I prophesy the blood bath." I was helpless to argue. Never had I mentioned the sudden withdrawal of British power, and yet he insisted upon thinking that that was my proposal. It was only too clear that he has a complex on India from which he will not and cannot be shaken.'

Phillips reported all this afterwards to Roosevelt. The President was 'rather amused.'[47] He clearly did not, in 1943, share Churchill's vision of the future, any more than he had done in the year before.* During this period, however, he was not prepared to challenge him either. Phillips' recommendations were not taken up. Nevertheless, his analysis of the Indian situation, as we shall see, was to create trouble in the coming year.

* Insofar as Churchill's expectation of 'a blood bath' referred to strife between Hindus and Muslims were British rule to be removed, he was proved correct, of course, although many Indians would lay the blame for this at Britain's own door.

Notes to Chapter Fourteen

1 See Gopal, Nehru, I, 300–1.
2 See Holland, Asian Nationalism and the West, 295.
3 Howard, Grand Strategy, IV, 292ff.; Casey, Personal Experience, 190ff.
4 WP(43)349 (CAB 66/39); WP(43)467 (CAB 66/41).
5 Avon, The Reckoning, 382–5; Wavell, 27ff.
6 Halifax Diary, 18 Oct. 1943.
7 Cab, 12 Jan. 1943, CAB 65/33.
8 Linlithgow to Amery, 26 Jan. and 2 Aug. 1943, Linlithgow Papers, vol. 12.
9 See above, 167–8.
10 Amery to Linlithgow, 1 Oct. 1943, Linlithgow Papers, vol. 12.
11 WP(43)197, CAB 66/36.
12 P. Mason, A Matter of Honour (London, 1974), 472, 513.
13 Amery to Linlithgow, 21 June 1943, Linlithgow Papers, vol. 12.
14 Wavell, 24 June 1943.
15 Cab, 27 July 1943, CAB 65/35. See also Cabinet Committee on Indian Financial Questions, CAB 91/5. Dalton, for one, accepted the picture of Indian war profiteering. Dalton Diary, 16 Aug. 1943.
16 See above, 5.
17 See above, 6.
18 Cherwell to WSC, 20 Jan. and 4 March 1943, Cherwell Papers, Off. 1.1; WP(43)504, CAB 66/43; Amery to Linlithgow, 5 and 17 Aug. 1943, Linlithgow Papers, vol. 12.
19 Cab, 15 June 1943, CAB 65/34; draft paper, 21 June 1943, Bevin Papers, box 12. See WP(43)300, CAB 66/38.
20 Cab, 7 Oct. 1943, CAB 65/36.

21 *Wavell*, 7, 8 and 12 Oct. 1943.
22 WP(43)445, CAB 66/41. See WP(43)435, 436 and 442, CAB 66/41.
23 WP(43)450, CAB 66/41.
24 FO 371, F4797/25/10; F3375/71/61.
25 Interview with Sir Olaf Caroe.
26 E.g. FO 371, F1145, 3489, 3598 and 5007/71/61; material in files 35893, 35894 and 35931; Cab, 11 Aug. 1943, CAB 65/43.
27 Hess, *America Encounters India*, 128.
28 Broadcast of 11 Sept. 1943, Sevareid Papers, box D3.
29 E.g. *New York Herald Tribune*, 27 Nov. 1943.
30 E.g. *Daily Express*, 20 April 1943.
31 See FRUS, 1943, IV, 273.
32 *Vandenberg*, 1 July 1943.
33 FDR to Hopkins, 19 March 1943, Roosevelt Papers, PSF box 53.
34 Phillips to FDR, 19 April 1943, FRUS, 1943, IV, 217. The preceding summary of Phillips' views is based on other letters to be found in FRUS, 1943, IV, 178ff. See also Phillips, *Ventures In Diplomacy*, 227ff.
35 FO 371, A4735/3/45; A1058 and 2789/93/45.
36 FRUS, 1943, III, 28, 40. See Amery to Linlithgow, 20 April 1943, Linlithgow Papers, vol. 24.
37 FRUS, 1943, IV, 199.
38 Ibid, 296ff.
39 Ibid, 239–40.
40 Ibid, 227–8.
41 FRUS, Cairo and Tehran, 482.
42 Ibid, 845.
43 Linlithgow to Amery, 11 Jan., 16 March and 2 May 1943, Linlithgow Papers, vol. 12; Linlithgow to Amery, 28 Jan. and 11 Feb. 1943, ibid, vol. 24.
44 FO 371, A2732/93/4. See ibid, A1864 and 3779/93/45; Amery to Linlithgow, 19 March 1943, Linlithgow Papers, vol. 24.
45 Linlithgow to Amery, 30 Jan., 2 March, 10 May and 20 Aug. 1943, Linlithgow Papers, vol. 12; Amery to Law, 31 March 1943, FO 371, A3155/93/45. On the Viceroy's hostility towards the International Secretariat of the I.P.R., see his telegrams to Amery of 6 June and 4 Aug. 1943, Linlithgow Papers, vol. 25.
46 E.g. FO 371, A5095/93/45. London also took a wider view than New Delhi of the question of reciprocal Lend Lease to the U.S.A. from India. Material in PREM 4, 46/4A. See FRUS, 1943, IV, 246ff.
47 Diary of 22 May 1943, Phillips Papers, vol. 34.

CHAPTER FIFTEEN

AUSTRALASIA AND THE
SOUTHWEST PACIFIC

ALTHOUGH THE Allies were now turning back the enemy's advance in the Far East, in the spring of 1943 there still remained in Australian Government circles the fear that Japan might yet succeed in invading their country.[1] MacArthur himself, who continued to be on very good terms with Curtin and other leading Australian politicians,[2] was again privately supplying the Prime Minister and Minister for External Affairs in Canberra with material to use when they presented their case for further reinforcements, for example to bring the R.A.A.F. up to 72 squadrons.[3] Curtin in turn pressed his requirements upon Churchill and Roosevelt by cable,[4] while in April Evatt left once more for Washington and London, where he could put Australia's arguments in person. (Curtin, no doubt aware of the resentment that Evatt's aggressive tactics had already aroused, advised him 'to fish for a request . . . for Australian demands . . . rather than to waken disfavour by forcible intrusion.')[5]

Nevertheless, the improvement in the general military situation was not without effect, and in June Curtin did at last abandon his thesis that the country stood in danger of invasion. He also interpreted Churchill's remarks to the press after the Washington Conference as meaning that the war against Japan would now rank equal with that against Germany—this being more than the British Prime Minister had intended.[6] In addition, Curtin strengthened his domestic base by winning a general election during this period, and even before that had managed to get through a bill whereby conscripted, as distinct from volunteer, Australian forces (the militia or A.M.F.) could be called upon to serve outside Australian territory, within what was called a 'Southwest Pacific Zone', which covered much of MacArthur's Command.[7] This move was clearly made in part with United States opinion in mind, and what Americans thought about Australia continued to be a matter of concern to a body like the Advisory War Council in Canberra.[8] Reassuringly, the country's representatives in the United States tended to feel that, in the words of one of them, 'the epidemic of adverse publicity concerning Australia which was so troubling in the last months of 1942 seems to have spent its force.'[9]

Even so, some strains were still apparent where Australian–American relations were concerned. For example, there arose the question of the overall allocation of the Australian war effort, in which connection, as was also the case in New Zealand, serious manpower difficulties were now having to be faced.[10] When, however, as a result of a major review of the problem, Curtin informed MacArthur that some diminution in the provision of supplies and labour for his forces might be necessary, the General bluntly retorted that such a move 'could not fail to endanger the basic cooperation between our two countries.' Curtin in turn warned MacArthur that the latter's own suggestion, that exports of food from Australia to Britain should be diverted in order to make up any deficiencies in the supplies reaching American forces in the Southwest Pacific, could be contemplated only if the amounts involved were made up to Britain by the United States. For two men who had been so much at one, it was a notably chilly exchange.[11]

Meanwhile, the presence of American troops in Australia was leading at times to friction, with the publicity barrage and cult surrounding MacArthur coming in for sidelong glances on the Australian side.[12] What appeared to be ambitious American ideas about the future of the region as a whole also aroused attention. Thus, a telegram drafted in the Department of External Affairs in Canberra for possible despatch to London (in the event, it was apparently not sent) spoke of

'considerable American interest in the Southwest Pacific Area. Investigations have been carried out', it continued, 'on behalf of the U.S. Board of Economic Warfare into the supply position in Pacific Islands and mineral resources in New Caledonia and Australia. Air and naval works have been constructed in the New Hebrides and the Solomons which have the appearance of permanent rather than merely wartime bases. We have evidence that local American officers have sometimes been inclined to disregard British and French sovereign rights in the New Hebrides . . . The training of large numbers of military administrators in the United States suggests that recaptured and conquered territories in the Pacific, including Japan, will be subjected to direct American influence in the important formative stage immediately following the cessation of hostilities. British, Dutch, French and Australian interests would be closely affected . . . In regard to civil aviation, the control and operation of the current trans-Pacific service is in American hands and . . . is shortly to be expanded.'[13]

In similar vein, a Department of External Affairs memorandum on the colonial question foresaw that 'a security system in the Pacific might lead to Australia being dominated by the strongest partner in the system', and suggested that she 'might later need some European counter-weight to Asiatic or American influence . . .'[14] Roosevelt's pronouncements on the future of Indochina were likewise noted with some unease, while the American idea of establishing China as a post-war colonial trustee was rejected by Evatt in conversation with Hull.[15] To Sir Walter Layton, a prominent member of the British press establishment who visited Canberra in October, Curtin himself urged that Britain should keep her flag flying in the Pacific war and thus counter American commercial ambitions in the region.[16]

A major reason for this Australian disquiet was the feeling—to be reinforced strongly by the Cairo Conference, over which Canberra was not consulted and of which it learned the details only belatedly—that the country was still not being accorded its rightful status in the major decision-making circles of the Allies. Where the future of the South and Southwest Pacific was concerned, however, concern was all the greater as a result of Australia's own ambitions. Evatt, for example, spoke to Eden about obtaining Timor from the Portuguese (the same idea occurred to Roosevelt),[17] while memoranda written in the Department of External Affairs stressed the desirability of Australia's securing bases at Rabaul and Port Moresby and in the Solomons, with her influence being 'extended over a wide area of the South Pacific [by becoming] more closely associated with the administration of British dependencies.'[18] Evatt also hoped to secure a long lease for Australia of Dutch Timor and Dutch New Guinea, above all for defence purposes, and told his High Commissioner in London, Bruce, to sound out the Netherlands Government in exile on the matter.[19] At the same time he wished to keep the situation fluid where even the Netherlands East Indies were concerned, and instructed Bruce to try to prevent the planned departure from London for Australia of Dr. H. J. van Mook, who had been appointed Lieutenant Governor of that Colony.[20] Evatt failed in this, and van Mook was to arrive in Australia early in 1944; in retrospect, however, the episode helps to justify the unease which some Dutch officials felt over Australia's intentions, an unease that was manifested in a démarche after Evatt had made a speech in New York in which he talked ambiguously of Australia and the Netherlands becoming 'partners' in the future development of the Indonesian people.[21]

British officials, too, were aware that Evatt's restless mind was dwelling upon the East Indies among other areas. Indeed, in a conversation with Cross, the British High Commissioner in Canberra, the Minister for External Affairs was quite open on the subject. He observed, as Cross reported it, 'that he was anxious that we should not tie our hands much at this stage and in particular he had in mind the relinquishment of sovereignty . . . He said that for one thing he had the Netherlands East Indies in mind. He agreed to my suggestion that he was thinking of an economic and political participation in these territories . . . He was seeking time, feeling that something more favourable for Australia might be obtained later on.'[22]

Evatt's visit to Britain in May went more smoothly than his stay in 1942.[23] Reports reaching London, however, including one which repeated comments made in private by the Australian Minister in Washington, continued to suggest that Curtin was by far the more reliable and sound of the two Australian leaders.[24] This was a matter of some importance, since the Commonwealth factor as a whole was beginning to receive more attention. As Britain's relative position as a great power declined and as her Empire again came under attack, there was a growing desire in London to hear Dominions like Canada and Australia speak out, especially to the people of the United States, on the merits of the Commonwealth.[25] There was also an increasing belief that, without a closely-knit Commonwealth operating as a unit in international affairs after the war, Britain, in Attlee's words, would not be able to continue 'to exist as a world power.'[26] How to achieve this state of affairs, and yet at the same time to 'satisfy the legitimate claim of each of the Dominions to rank in the world as an independent nation', was recognized as presenting a considerable problem, not least as regards the question of representation in a new world organization.[27] For this reason among others, invitations were sent out to Commonwealth Prime Ministers to assemble in London in November. Curtin, however, felt unable to leave Australia at such a time, and the earliest date that could be arranged for the meeting was found to be May 1944.[28]

Meanwhile from his post in Canberra, Cross was pressing for Britain to increase in the region her own military showing, as distinct from that of the United States, for the sake of 'the future development of Anglo-Australian relations and . . . our popular influence in this country.'[29] It seemed that such an increase in the British presence would, indeed, be in accord with Australia's own wishes,[30] while in reports put before the Cabinet it was suggested that both Australia and New Zealand were 'cooling' in their attitude towards the U.S.A.[31] 'There has been a noticeable swing in Australian feelings from anti- to pro-British', ran one message reaching the Foreign Office.[32] In another private report, written by the News Chronicle representative in New Zealand and endorsed by the Chief of the New Zealand Air Staff, reference was likewise made to the growing awareness in both South Pacific Dominions of American post-war commercial ambitions. The writer had been told by the Australian Minister of Supply, Beasley, for example, 'that he had found that opposition by American supply officers to the development of an Australian aluminium industry emanated from officers who in private life represented American aluminium interests.'[33]

As for Britain's links with the leading American in the area, MacArthur, these were disrupted for a while when the General declined to have Colonel Wilkinson back as liaison officer, despite what he termed 'my real affection for him', on the grounds that Washington forbade the use of such a direct channel of communication to Churchill.[34] General Marshall, however, was prepared to admit privately that Britain had not been kept sufficiently in touch with military developments in the Southwest Pacific Area, and as something of a quid pro quo for his conceding that the Combined Chiefs of Staff, and not the British C.O.S. alone, should oversee the affairs of S.E.A.C., Churchill was permitted to send to MacArthur's headquarters a senior staff officer, Lt. General Sir Herbert Lumsden.[35] Even so, Curtin for his part found the new appointment 'somewhat abnormal and unconstitutional', and while MacArthur himself welcomed Lumsden gracefully enough, he retained his extraordinary suspicions, and was to refer in private to Lumsden's successor as 'Churchill's spy.'[36] Meanwhile, he decided nevertheless to give London the benefit of some of his strategic thoughts, including the proposal that Britain and the United States should 'throw in all their reserves' on the Russian front. ('The General's ideas', noted Churchill, '. . . are singularly untroubled by considerations of transport and distance.')[37] In turn, London kept a careful eye on MacArthur's political prospects. Members of the General's staff were, indeed, secretly in touch with Senator Vandenberg and others over the possibility that their master might run for the Republicans against Roosevelt in 1944, while a Gallup Poll taken in September on the subject of just such a hypothetical contest gave MacArthur as much as 42 per cent of the vote against the President's 58 per cent.[38] The North American Department of the Foreign Office conferred with Colonel Wilkinson on such matters, concluding that MacArthur was 'not without certain dangerous possibilities', and that British military planners should take care not to offend him—though there is no indication that this ever became part of Service policy.[39]

In addition to being of potential political significance, MacArthur in his American context also embodied his country's responsibility for the future of the Philippines. Concern over those islands was heightened in the United States during this period by Japan's own promise of early independence for their people, and by the establishment of a puppet government which worked closely with the invader. In response to this situation, Roosevelt somewhat casually approved a Congressional resolution by which the United States would itself have granted immediate independence to the Philippines. Stimson among others managed, however, to prevent so precipitate a move (which could have been taken as tantamount to recognition of the puppet government of the colony), and in the event the legislation was amended so that it referred only to independence being given 'as soon as feasible.'[40] Meanwhile President Quezon waited in the United States, his term of office, due to expire before the end of 1943, eventually being extended by special act of Congress. According to an anti-Roosevelt report reaching MacArthur, Quezon's position was far from a happy one, 'a prisoner of the White House ... [who] will not make any public statements or manifestations which are against the "party line" of F.D.R. Two things keep him in line: operations of the Philippines Government are financed by an authority of the [U.S.] Treasury ... [which] can be rescinded at any time ... The other is the question of succession upon expiry of [his] term of office in November 1943— he wants to continue in power and if he gets out of hand Roosevelt can over- look him and let [Vice President] Osmena take the Presidency.'[41]*

Besides his connection with the Philippines, MacArthur also remained the major link tying the United States to Australia. Nelson Johnson, too, con- tinued in his post as the American Minister in Canberra, even though, in what was widely seen as a crude political move, Roosevelt early in 1943 had nominated a Democratic Party functionary, Ed Flynn, for Johnson's job. (The President hastily withdrew the proposal when a storm of disapproval

* The Foreign Office in London also saw Quezon's position as less than a heroic one, the belief being that Jorge Vargas in the Philippines was collaborating with the Japanese with Quezon's full approval. Quezon's aim, it was thought, was to secure all the benefits of collaboration while on the surface preserving 'a spotless reputation for loyal resistance in contrast to the alleged apathy or 5th columnism of Malaya and Burma.' (FO 371, F3539/ 71/61 and F272/272/61.)

arose.)[42] Johnson, as briefly noted earlier, now saw Australia as 'being pulled in two directions. The primary and greater pull', he wrote to a colleague, 'is towards the British Empire ... But the Japanese bid for control of the Pacific has increased the pull in the opposite direction, namely toward demand of more independent national status, with freedom of relations with the United States, because of its dominant position in the Pacific and Australia's dependence on the United States for protection here ...'[43] Despite their tendency to turn in an American direction, however, the Australian people continued to exasperate Johnson, who saw them as being 'unwilling to pay for the planes and guns and munitions which are needed to defend Australia', and who was outraged by the 'scandalous' behaviour of the Sydney longshoremen in striking and 'malingering' during the war emergency.[44] The Minister also remained cynical about Evatt, who evidently wished to make use of his visit to the United States in order to gain prestige for himself in the context of domestic politics. (Evatt secretly asked the American Legation to pass the word to Washington—although not as if in response to a request by him—that decisions regarding increased aid for the Southwest Pacific should be deferred until he arrived.)[45]*

The United States Government, for its part, was still ready to make helpful gestures in Australia's direction, even though the Japanese menace had passed its height. Roosevelt, for example, promised Evatt that he would hand over to her six squadrons of obsolescent U.S. Army and Navy planes during the remainder of 1943.[46] But Australia continued to be left outside the inner circle where Allied strategy was being directed, giving rise to resentment in Canberra. In addition, moreover, there were already signs that trouble might occur between Australia and the United States over the shaping of the post-war order in the Pacific, especially where bases and territories in the vicinity of the former were concerned. For although victory was still clearly a long way off, more people on the Allied side were beginning to turn their minds towards that post-war scene, and even to make their voices heard as to some of the features it should contain.

* Johnson also found Evatt's senior permanent official, Colonel Hodgson, 'didactic and opinionated ... staunchly pro-Empire and pro-Melbourne Tory. His tory bias', added the Minister, 'makes him anti-American ... He never misses an opportunity to belittle American effort.' (Johnson to Hornbeck, 1 March 1943, Hornbeck Papers, box 262.)

Notes to Chapter Fifteen

1 See *Hasluck*, II, 207ff.
2 Correspondence in MacArthur Papers, RG 10.
3 MacArthur to Shedden, 31 March 1943, ibid, RG 4.
4 Curtin to WSC and FDR, 18 March 1943, and to WSC, 30 March 1943, PREM 3, 142/7.
5 Curtin to Evatt, 13 May 1943, ADEA, AA1971/360. See material in Evatt Papers, 1943 Overseas Trip file.
6 Curtin to WSC, 3 June 1943, PREM 3, 158/7; *Hasluck*, II, 216.

7 *Hasluck*, II, 326ff.
8 AAWC, 2 Feb. 1943, A2682, vol. VI.
9 Heymanson to Evatt, 16 Feb. 1943, Evatt Papers, U.S.A. file.
10 *Hasluck*, II, 283ff.; Lussington, *New Zealand and The United States*, 64, 72.
11 MacArthur to Curtin, 6 Nov. 1943, and Curtin to MacArthur, 13 Nov. 1943, APMD, file CP 290/16.
12 E.g. memo., by war-correspondent 'A', 16 Oct. 1943, Evatt Papers, War/U.S.A. file.
13 Draft telegram, 24 Aug. 1943, ADEA, A989/43/735/321.
14 Memo., 15 April 1943, ADEA, A989/43/735/1021.
15 Hull memo., 15 April 1943, DS 740.0011 P.W./3208.
16 Layton notes, 3 Feb. 1944, PREM 3, 159/2.
17 Cab, 15 June 1943, CAB 65/34; FDR to WSC, 22 June 1943, PREM 3, 471.
18 Forsyth memo., 12 July 1943, ADEA, A989/43/735/310/2; research report, March–April 1943, ibid, A989/43/735/321/3.
19 Evatt to Bruce, 20 Nov. 1943, ADEA, A989/44/600/5/1/5.
20 Evatt to Bruce, 9 and 13 Dec. 1943, ibid.
21 Correspondence between Australian and Netherlands Governments, ADEA, A989/43/600/5/1/2; in general, 'George Ph.D.'
22 Cross to Dominions Office, 16 Jan. 1943, IO, Private Office papers, L/PO/261.
23 E.g. Evatt to WSC, 6 May 1943, PREM 4, 50/8.
24 E.g., Campbell minute, 1 Sept. 1943, PREM 4, 73/1; Dewing report, 29 June 1943, PREM 3, 158/5.
25 E.g. FO 371, A7707/3/45.
26 WP(43)44, CAB 66/33; see WP(43)115, CAB 66/35.
27 WP(43)244; CAB 66/37.
28 Material in PREM 4, 42/2.
29 Cross to WSC, 11 Aug. 1943, PREM 3, 151/4. See *Churchill*, V, 572.
30 WP(43)417, CAB 66/41.
31 WP(43)123, CAB 66/35; WP(43)225, CAB 66/37.
32 FO 371, A3970 and 4359/3/45. See Somerville Diary, 23 Dec. 1943.
33 FO 371, F3575/387/23.
34 Marshall to WSC, 12 April 1943, PREM 3, 158/5.
35 Material in PREM 3, 158/5; JCS, 16 Aug. 1943, RG 218.
36 Lumsden to WSC, 19 Nov. 1943, PREM 3, 158/7; Luvaas, *Dear Miss Em.*, 280. See anti-British material contained in memo. to MacArthur by Colonel McMicking, 11 July 1943, MacArthur Papers, RG 3.
37 Material in PREM 3, 158/5.
38 *Vandenberg*, cap. 5; *Pogue*, II, 282.
39 FO 371, A1052/144/45; Wilkinson memo., 15 Oct. 1943, Wilkinson Papers. Wilkinson wrote: 'MacArthur is shrewd, selfish, proud, remote, highly strung and vastly vain. He has imagination, self-confidence, physical courage and charm, but no humour about himself, no regard for truth, and is unaware of these defects. He mistakes his emotions and ambitions for principles.'
40 FRUS, 1943, III, 1097ff.; Stimson Diary, 27 Sept. 1943; Friend, *Between Two Empires*, 237.
41 McMicking memo., 11 July 1943, MacArthur Papers, RG 3.
42 Johnson to Hornbeck, 12 Jan. 1943, Hornbeck Papers, box 262; Watt to Heydon, 22 Jan. 1943, Watt Papers; *New York Times*, 12 Jan. 1943.
43 Johnson to Hornbeck, 27 Nov. 1943, Hornbeck Papers, box 262. Australia in this period finally granted the U.S.A. most-favoured-nation treatment commercially. Negotiations for an Australian–American trade agreement failed, however. FRUS, 1943, III, 115ff.
44 Johnson to Hornbeck, 2 April and 20 May 1943, Hornbeck Papers, box 262.
45 Stewart Memo., 13 April 1943, Hornbeck Papers, box 157.
46 *Matloff*, 99.

CHAPTER SIXTEEN

JAPAN AND THE POST-WAR ORDER
IN THE FAR EAST

DURING 1943, demands were already being made in public in the United States concerning the country's requirements in the Pacific after the war. 'Permanent safety', argued the *Chicago Tribune*, for example, would require American possession of New Caledonia, Fiji and the Solomons (all belonging at the time to fellow-Allies), as well as of the Japanese mandated islands—the Carolines, Marshalls and Marianas.[1] Of those questioned in an O.W.I. survey, 61 per cent believed that the United States should keep 'Guadalcanal and other territories in the Pacific that we have conquered',[2] while a programme put before the Republican Party's Mackinac conference bluntly declared that 'the Pacific Ocean must become an American lake.'[3]

Meanwhile in official circles, too, post-war desiderata were being formulated. In the first instance, wrote Admiral King to one of his staff, a study of the country's requirements in terms of bases should be undertaken without reference to 'considerations of sovereignty', the sole factors to be taken into account being 'geographical-strategic' ones.[4] During the year the Navy's General Board for its part produced several surveys of the kind King wanted, listing as territories needed by the U.S.A. for bases Canton Island, New Caledonia, the Solomons, Samoa, the Marquesas, Tonga and the Society Islands among many others, with 'all French possessions in the South Pacific except the interest in the New Hebrides [to] pass to the control of the United States', and with Britain and the Dominions being required to transfer to American sovereignty Samoa, the British Line Islands, Ellice Island, the Phoenix Islands and the Gilberts. In addition, the United States must have possession of the Japanese mandates, together with a permanent base in the Philippines.[5]

Others in Washington had ideas of their own, not always so stridently nationalistic or ambitious as those of the Navy, but generally pointing in the direction of a re-ordering of the Pacific scene at the behest of the United States. Thus, Harry Hopkins, for example, mentioned the need for bases in Formosa when talking to Molotov and Eden at Tehran,[6] while in the State Department it was thought that various islands which had been in dispute before the war between the U.S.A. on the one hand and Britain and New Zealand on the other—islands that could be of considerable significance in terms of the development of air routes—should be handed over to inter-national trusteeship.[7] As for the President, his ideas, too, tended to involve international, rather than national, ownership of various key territories like the Japanese mandated islands and New Caledonia (which, like Dakar, should be taken from France and handed over to the United Nations). Similarly, Roosevelt declined to endorse the full list of suggested annexations by the United States that the Navy Board put forward.[8]

This emphasis of the President's upon the future role of the United Nations (though not his anti-French leanings) was in accord with official thinking in London, where a Cabinet memorandum submitted by Eden envisaged all suitable military bases in the Western Pacific and East Asia being put at the disposal of the international organization's notional Pacific Council of Defence.[9] There was no intention, of course, of handing over British possessions to the United States, but the latter's increased involve-ment in all matters pertaining to security in the Far East was thought to be highly desirable. 'It was a major British interest', Churchill told the Cabinet, 'that the United States should secure full mobility of their sea and air power throughout the Pacific. It should be the basis of our policy that we would not object to any American proposals to acquire further bases in this area.'[10] Within the Foreign Office the emphasis was the same: on how to ensure American post-war involvement. 'What we really want', wrote Jebb, 'is an Anglo-Soviet-American *alliance*. If we had that there is little to suppose that we should not have a long period of peace. Unfortunately everybody knows that we are unlikely to get it with America, and this being so the more we can, so to speak, entangle her by means of proposals for pooling bases, or what-ever it may be, the better.'[11]

The need for some form of defence arrangement in the Far East was obviously tied up with the question of what was to happen to Japan. On this, the views of Churchill at this stage appear to have been of a limited and somewhat crude variety, though no doubt he had the predilections of his American audience in mind when he spoke to Congress in May of 'the process, so necessary and desirable, of laying the cities and other munitions centres of Japan in ashes, for in ashes they must surely lie before peace comes back to the world.' (The Political Warfare Against Japan Committee thought that this statement was likely to harden the resolution of the Japanese, rather than to terrify them.)[12]

Others had time to think in more detailed terms. Should Japan, for example, be totally and lengthily occupied by the Allies? The tendency within the Foreign Office was to believe that this would be a burdensome and un-necessary business, since, in contrast to Germany, a Japan stripped of her overseas possessions could be denied armaments by means of economic controls, provided that adequate naval and air power were kept in reserve by the victors.[13] As for the general treatment to be accorded to the Japanese, members of the Foreign Office were appalled when their former colleague, Sir John Pratt, who was visiting the United States after attending the I.P.R. Conference, argued that the Japanese should not be humiliated and should speedily be brought back within the community of nations.[14] Nevertheless, there existed opinions within official circles, too, that inclined towards a 'soft' rather than a harsh peace in the Far East. Esler Dening, for instance, agreed with a fellow Japan-specialist in the Far Eastern Department that 'the Japanese would find it by no means difficult, in the event for example of total defeat, to cast all [their] beliefs and theories upon the rubbish heap and adopt some entirely different basis for a new structure.'[15] Moreover Sir George Sansom, supreme among the Office's students of Japanese affairs, was himself thinking in terms not far removed from those of Pratt. 'Japan's record is certainly a discreditable one in many important respects', he wrote, 'but there is a better chance of her good behaviour if she can be invited to join the club and observe the rules instead of being blackballed.' He also agreed with Hornbeck that the Japanese should be left to evolve for them-selves the form of government that suited them best.

As for the question of what should become of the Emperor and the Throne, Sansom was scornful of what he saw as an undue preoccupation with this on the part of the Americans, but his own ideas, as revealed in unofficial correspondence, by implication allowed for the preservation of the institu-tion, if not the man. Speaking to Hornbeck, indeed, he went even further, suggesting that it would be 'extremely inadvisable to depose the Emperor.'[16] This was plainly a dangerous and delicate issue, however, and Eden, for his part, chose to sidestep it when, in conversation with the Chinese Ambassador in London, he observed that Britain would 'regard the Chinese Government as being the experts' on the subject.[17]

There was another question that was disturbing some officials, however. Might not a 'hands-off' policy towards Japan's internal affairs after the war lead to severe disorders in that country, and might not 'something like a communist government' emerge there in consequence? Ashley Clarke, Head of the Far Eastern Department in London, was one who feared as much, and although Hornbeck, when talking to the former, declared that he himself did not find the prospect of a period of chaos in Japan a disquieting one, he was not in this respect typical of those in American official circles who were thinking about the future of their Far Eastern enemy.[18]

The State Department, indeed, largely thanks to its network of advisory committees, was considerably further advanced than the Foreign Office when it came to setting out ideas about various aspects of the post-war scene in the East. And where Japan herself was concerned, what most of those involved in Washington envisaged was a country stripped of her overseas territories, but also encouraged in a very direct way to develop liberal political institu-tions and creeds, and allowed 'to share in the development of a world economy on a non-discriminatory basis, looking toward a progressively higher standard of living.' As a major element in this line of thought, the belief existed in the minds of State Department specialists like Hugh Borton that there would be found in Japan a body of liberals who, emerging from the ruins of the country's militarism, could form a progressive government and become the nucleus of a new, stable and moderate system.[19]

These ideas implied that Japan would come to form part of that low-tariff post-war trading world that was so important in Hull's mind. They were also accompanied by two notions which, as we have seen, were simultaneously developing in the minds of British officials. First, there was the belief that the Japanese as a whole would prove malleable. 'My own guess is', wrote Joseph Grew, 'that after the military machine has been wholly beaten, the futility of aggressive militarism will be recognized and there will be an automatic turnover among the Japanese people, who will be ready to cooperate in any reasonable program which will offer them some hope of building up their shattered national structure.'[20] Second—although this was strongly opposed by some officials like Alger Hiss, and was far removed from the vengeful mood of America at large[21]—there was a growing feeling that the institution of the Throne in Japan should not be destroyed, but, in Grew's words, 'should be preserved . . . as a symbol [which] can be made to serve as a cornerstone for healthy and peaceful internal growth . . .'[22]

This question of the future of the Japanese Throne was raised by Roosevelt at Cairo with Chiang Kai-shek. And although on this occasion the Generalissimo merely commented that it should be left to the people of Japan to decide,[23] it seemed to American officials that, in the shaping of any post-war system in the Far East, the desires and role of their Chinese allies would be of immense significance. The hopes of Roosevelt and the doubts of Churchill in this regard have already been indicated. In addition, there were more specific questions that were now beginning to push their way into the minutes and memoranda of those concerned with Far Eastern policies. What, for example, should be done with Manchuria? The Chinese were insisting that it should return to them, and the leaders of Britain and the United States were agreed that this should be done.[24] In the Foreign Office, too (contrary to rumours which arose at the I.P.R. Conference about a British desire to internationalize that territory, or hand it over to the Soviet Union), it was accepted that Chungking's aim was a legitimate one.[25] The future of Korea appeared to pose greater difficulties—a self-styled Provisional Government in exile in Chungking was asking for, but not receiving, official recognition by the Allies—although in both London and Washington the tendency was to think in terms of some form of international trusteeship.[26]

The future of Manchuria and Korea alike, however, involved another and far larger question, one that was raised in an earlier chapter. What would be the role and the demands of the Soviet Union in the Far East, especially if and when she had joined in the fight against Japan?[27] Here was a major unknown element for officials in London and Washington to ponder over as 1943 drew towards a close and the war in the Far East entered its post-Cairo phase.

Notes to Chapter Sixteen

1 *Chicago Tribune*, 1 Feb. 1943.
2 FO 371, A5721/32/45.
3 *New York Times*, 26 Aug. 1943.
4 King to Hepburn, 21 Oct. 1943, King Papers, box 4, USNOA.
5 General Board Studies, no. 450 (20 and 27 March and 6 April 1943), USNOA.
6 FRUS, Cairo and Tehran, 568.
7 Ibid, 167.
8 Ibid, 509; FRUS, 1943, III, 36; Louis, *Imperialism at Bay*.
9 WP(43)300, CAB 66/38.
10 Cab, 13 April 1943, CAB 65/38.
11 FO 371, A3360/34/45.
12 Ibid, F2618/71/61.
13 E.g. ibid, F4976/4905/61; WP(43)300, CAB 66/38.
14 FO 371, F233/186/61.
15 Ibid, F1651/403/23.
16 Ibid, F186/186/61; F4976/4905/61; Hornbeck memo., 28 July 1943, Hornbeck Papers, box 370.
17 FO 371, F4020/25/10.
18 Ibid, F5470/4905/61.
19 A. Iriye, 'Japan and the Cold War in Asia', in Y. Nagai and A. Iriye (eds.), *The Origins of the Cold War in Asia* (Tokyo, 1977). For a broad outline of State Department ideas, based on published sources only, see F. S. Dunn, *Peace-Making and the Settlement With Japan* (Princeton, 1963).
20 Grew to Fearey, 30 Nov. 1943, Grew Papers, vol. 115.
21 E.g. Hiss to Hornbeck, 30 Dec. 1942, Hornbeck Papers, box 237.
22 Grew to Hornbeck, 30 Sept. 1943, Grew Papers, vol. 116. And e.g. Dickover to Hornbeck, 11 Nov. 1943, Hornbeck Papers, box 237.
23 FRUS, Cairo and Tehran, 322.
24 Ibid, 329, 387.
25 See FRUS, 1943, China, 844; FO 371, material in file 35793; F4260/3004/10.
26 FRUS, 1943, III, 1090ff.; FO 371, file 35956.
27 See e.g. FO 371, F5138/294/61.

PART FOUR

Cairo to the Second Quebec Conference
December 1943 to September 1944

CHAPTER SEVENTEEN

THE SETTING

1944 SAW the Allies closing in on Germany on all fronts. The Russians, having relieved Leningrad earlier in the year, commenced new attacks into Poland in June from White Russia and the Ukraine; in Southeast Europe, their spearheads entered Rumania, Hungary and Bulgaria. It was increasingly apparent that the might of the Red Army would constitute a major factor in the post-war international situation. Meanwhile in Italy the Western Allies (together with Poles, New Zealanders, Indians and others) had overcome the disappointing outcome of the Anzio landing, moving on to take Rome in June and Florence in August. These successes, however, were overshadowed by the invasion of Normandy in June, with secondary landings taking place in the South of France in August (operation 'Anvil'). Paris was liberated in August, Brussels and Antwerp in September, as Eisenhower's armies advanced towards the Rhine, although in the middle of that month there came the setback at Arnhem.

This opening of a new front in Northwest Europe, so long desired by Washington as well as Moscow, eased some of the tension over grand strategy between Britain and the United States. Even so, activities in the Mediterranean theatre continued to form the subject of disputes, for example over the degree of priority to be accorded to the campaign in Italy and the desirability or otherwise of undertaking operation 'Anvil', as opposed to, say, an advance into the Balkans.[1] Over this last issue, indeed, the American Ambassador in London, Winant, thought it important to let Roosevelt know 'how deeply the Prime Minister has felt the differences', adding that he had 'never seen him as badly shaken.'[2] In Washington, too, Stimson recorded in his diary the anger to which he and Marshall, on their side, had been moved in the same dispute.[3]

Moreover, these Mediterranean issues again had links with the Far Eastern scene, through, for example, the question of how best to utilize scarce landing craft, or of whether or not to transfer from Italy the additional forces that had to be found if an operation were to be launched for the seizure of Rangoon.[4] Developments in the West and in the East were likewise associated when it came to judging when the war against Germany might be won—a subject which again involved Anglo-American differences in the shape of well-known disagreements between Eisenhower and Montgomery, but on which the answer, by the end of September, was clearly not going to be 'in 1944', as had at one time been hoped. For Britain this was a development which was bound to have very serious consequences since, as we have seen, she had staked everything on making a maximum effort in that year, and would find herself in increasing difficulties and more than ever dependent on American aid the longer the war went on thereafter.[5]

Meanwhile there took place in September 1944 the second Anglo-American Quebec Conference, convened because, as Churchill saw it, the affairs of the Allies were 'getting into a most tangled condition.' The Conference superseded the idea of a meeting à trois with Stalin, and was once more held on the Western side of the Atlantic because, in American eyes, that would look less like leaving the Soviet Union 'out in the cold' than would a gathering in Europe.[6] To the press at the end of these Quebec proceedings, Churchill spoke of 'a blaze of friendship' between Britain and the United States, the only difficulty he referred to being the desire of some Americans to keep to themselves too much of the war against Japan.[7] Yet this was to be the last of the major Anglo-American meetings, and again, for Britain, this was a matter of some consequence. It reflected the fact that the bilateral relationship of the Anglo-Saxons was no longer supreme, that the Soviet Union was increasingly making its presence felt, and that Britain's position relative to those of the other two great powers was a declining one.

Where the swift rise of the Soviet Union was concerned, the picture of Western reactions which is sometimes displayed—a picture featuring, above all, unrelieved Churchillian fears and naïve Rooseveltian optimism—requires some refinement. It is true, of course, that the Prime Minister was considerably troubled by the Soviet question in this period. His doctor recorded in August, for example, that he was 'always harping on the dangers of Communism', and that 'he dreams of the Red Army spreading like a cancer from one country to another. It has become an obsession . . .'[8] In strategic terms, this led Churchill to a belief in 'the extreme importance . . . of our having a stake in Central and Southern Europe and not allowing everything to pass into Soviet hands . . .'[9] It meant also that an issue like that of the future of Poland, which in this period was already coming to the fore, took on an added significance.[10] Brooke, too, reflecting a belief that was to become increasingly pronounced among senior officers, was concluding that 'Russia . . . cannot fail to become the main threat in fifteen years from now.'[11]

And yet London was ready to accept, for instance, that the Soviet Union should keep the Baltic States.[12] More significantly, Churchill himself told the Commonwealth Prime Ministers in private when they assembled in May that 'he refused to consider the possibility of a confrontation between Russia and the English-speaking peoples.'[13]* In the Foreign Office, as well, when various draft plans concerning post-war security had revealed that, as Jebb put it, there existed 'an undoubted tendency in the Service Departments

* Major Desmond Morton later asserted that Churchill failed 'to grasp the truth about Stalinism and about its inventor' until after the war. (Thompson, *Churchill and Morton*, 102.)

to regard the Soviet Union as a *potential enemy*', what was emphasized was that 'the policy of His Majesty's Government', in Sir Orme Sargent's words, 'is not based upon the assumption that in the foreseeable future we may have to deter the Soviet Union by force of arms from advancing their own interests at our expense.'[14]

Meanwhile, Roosevelt, for his part, did indeed still believe that he could successfully handle Stalin and the Soviet Union. The general tendency in Washington, moreover, was to assume that Britain, in the words of a State Department briefing paper prepared for the President in September, was 'seek[ing] to maintain a balance between the United States and the Soviet Union and to play the role of "honest broker" between them.'* In the opinion of the State Department, however, matters stood very differently. As one memorandum put it, 'the absence of any conflict of vital interest between the United States and the U.S.S.R. . . . and the number of points at which the British and Soviet interests impinge make it appear probable that we, whether we choose it or not, may be forced to play such a [mediating] role.'[15] Similarly, the Joint Chiefs of Staff had declared in May that 'so long as Britain and Russia cooperate and collaborate in the interests of peace, there can be no great war in the foreseeable future.'[16]

Yet despite these sanguine views—so striking in the light of what was to follow in 1945—concern over the Soviet Union's intentions was even now growing in some American minds. The new Secretary of the Navy, James V. Forrestal, for example (his predecessor, Knox, had died in April), was one of those who already feared Soviet expansionism, while William Bullitt continued to utter his warnings along similar lines.[17] Even the State Department concluded, in a briefing paper submitted to the President in September, that 'a greater degree of firmness in our attitude and policy toward the Soviet Union would avoid more serious difficulties in the future', while a few days later Harriman, as Ambassador in Moscow, alerted Washington to the fact that, in his opinion, the Soviet Government was 'showing signs of indifference' to American requests and that a 'startling' deterioration in relations was taking place.[18]

It is also worth noting that Roosevelt himself (who, in private, was ready to direct remarks against Communism)[19] accepted in this period Churchill's line about what to do about the Soviet Union in connection with the West's development of the atomic bomb. The Prime Minister had set his face against sharing the secrets of the new weapon with Stalin, and had snubbed Sir John Anderson, who was overseeing the British end of the project, when the latter, partly at the prompting of the eminent Danish physicist, Niels Bohr, pressed for a study to be made of means whereby international

---

* Some British leaders did indeed see matters in such a light. Cranborne, for example, urged that Britain must remain a great power lest 'the three-power system . . . [become] a two-power system, with the rival giants, Russia and the United States, which represent the conflicting political philosophies of Capitalism and Communism, facing each other across the world.' 'I can imagine', he concluded, 'nothing more calculated to lead to another and greater world war.' (Cranborne to Halifax, 9 Feb. 1944, Hickleton Papers, A4 410 4.)

control and collaboration with the Russians could be achieved.[20] In the United States, on the other hand, Bohr, having enlisted the help of Felix Frankfurter, was led to believe, as did the latter, that he had won the sympathy of the President for his fears and proposals.[21] Yet at Hyde Park in September, following the Quebec Conference, Roosevelt joined Churchill in deciding, not only that full Anglo-American collaboration on the bomb should continue, but that 'the suggestion that the world should be informed . . . with a view to an international agreement regarding its control and use is not accepted.' 'Enquiries should be made', the resulting aide-mémoire went on, 'regarding the activities of Professor Bohr, and steps taken to ensure that he is responsible for no leakage of information, particularly to the Russians.'[22] Typically, the President chose not to inform his senior advisers about this agreement; nor can it be said with any certainty whether or to what extent he envisaged an Anglo-American nuclear monopoly which would overshadow his 'four-policemen' concept when it came to the ruling of the post-war world. What is clear, however, is that for the war in the Far East and for the making of the peace there, both the creation of the atomic bomb and the continuing rise of Soviet power were to be of great significance.

Between Cairo and Quebec there were also implications for the Far East, and more particularly for the fate of Indochina, that arose from the resurgence of France in this period. Not that all was now well between de Gaulle and his Western allies. In fact, as is well known, bitter disputes continued, involving, for example, the question of civil-affairs arrangements in France after D-Day, while over-all there also remained a great deal of anti-Gaullist sentiment in Washington. According to one firmly-based report reaching London, for instance, the ponderous Admiral Leahy was still advising the President early in 1944 that when Allied troops entered France 'the most reliable person to whom we could look for help in rallying the French was . . . Pétain.'[23] Leahy also continued to prophesy that there would be revolution in France after the liberation.[24] As for Cordell Hull, Stimson noted in June that he 'hates de Gaulle with such fierce feeling that he rambles into almost incoherence whenever we talk about him.'[25] By extension, American officials also tended to resent British, and above all Foreign Office, support for de Gaulle, and on one occasion even the usually calm Marshall burst out angrily to Eden on the subject.[26]

Roosevelt's line, meanwhile, was that he could not recognize any government of France until the people of that country had had the opportunity to make a free choice.[27] In turn, the Prime Minister sent a message via Harriman to the effect that he would follow the President's lead on these matters, and to this end he resisted Foreign Office proposals for the official recognition of the French National Committee as the Provisional Government of France.[28] To de Gaulle himself, Churchill apparently bluntly observed: 'There is something you ought to know: each time we have to choose between Europe and the open sea, we shall always choose the open sea. Each time I have to choose between you and Roosevelt, I shall always choose Roosevelt.'[29]

Nevertheless, the Prime Minister did remain convinced of the need for France to 'rise again in greatness and power',[30] and he was ready to point out to Roosevelt that 'in practice, I think it would be found that de Gaulle and the French National Committee represent most of the elements who want to help us.'[31] Moreover, even Washington now felt obliged to begin the process of admitting that France was one of the Western powers, a development symbolized by the visit of de Gaulle to the American capital in July 1944, when he took advantage of the occasion to reiterate that Indochina, despite changes in her administration, would remain French.[32]* And although Roosevelt, at the time of the Quebec Conference, continued his refusal to recognize de Gaulle's Committee as a Provisional Government, the State Department had by then come to believe that such a move would be advisable. When Churchill, in October, proposed recognition, therefore, the President at last gave way, and it was formally announced on the 23rd.[33] This event falls just outside our period, but it is recorded here as the logical conclusion to a process of French resurgence which had become evident during the preceding months, and which cast further doubt over Roosevelt's plans for Indochina, which will be set out in the chapter on Southeast Asia.

The role that France was to play, and even more the basis of future relations between the West and the Soviet Union, were both important elements in the continuing debate over the nature of the post-war international order. In the United States, especially, this subject was attracting increasing attention, and by July 1944 polls were indicating that over 70 per cent were in favour of joining some kind of 'world league.'[34] Books such as Walter Lippmann's *United States War Aims* (in which he advocated the establishment of spheres of influence and attacked the Wilsonian approach to world peace) helped to sustain discussion; on the Republican side, John Foster Dulles, the future Secretary of State, was one of those who was closely involved, although it was agreed privately to keep the issue out of the political arena.[35] Roosevelt's own idea of control by the 'Big Four' was not boldly stated, however, much to the frustration of some observers, but was 'leaked' in the shape of articles by a journalist friend of the President's.[36] Like so many people of the time, Roosevelt was thinking essentially in terms of preventing a 1939-type conflict from breaking out again. 'Wilson's "This is the war to end all wars" went too far', he wrote to a friend. 'We are not omniscient, but we ought to set up machinery that has a reasonable chance to prevent a similar war [to this one] happening for a good long time—say a couple of generations.'[37] Also, with the memory of 1919–20 very much in mind, great care was being taken to involve Congress in the debate, a bipartisan committee led by Senator Tom Connally being set up shortly after the end of this period 'to advise and consult with the Secretary of State' on plans for an international organization.[38]

* Not that the General was above fishing for American sympathy. To Forrestal, for example, he emphasized, as the latter recorded it, that France and the United States were 'the only two major powers with no imperialistic ambitions', and stressed Anglo-French differences. (Forrestal Diary, 18 Aug. 1944.)

On the British side, Churchill continued to place more emphasis on the regional structure that such an organization could be given than did either the Foreign Office or the Commonwealth Prime Ministers, with whom he discussed the subject in May.[39] The Chiefs of Staff, for their part, were seen by the Foreign Office as 'not accepting the Four Power thesis.' 'They argued', reported Jebb, 'that what in practice was likely to happen was that the Combined Chiefs of Staff would continue in being; that the Russians would have a very large sphere of their own in which they would have their own "security" organisation; and that China was anyway rather a joke.'[40] Nevertheless, the Foreign Office's own plans continued to make progress, aiming as they did at the creation of 'a centre where the policies of the principal states of the world can be harmonised', but again tending to look backwards, with their emphasis that 'the object, in the first instance, of any world security organisation should be the prevention of renewed aggression by Germany and Japan.'[41] Internationally, too, a major step forward was taken during this period with the Conference at Dumbarton Oaks in August and September, at which broad principles for the future organization were agreed upon, even though such major issues as voting rights remained outstanding. (The proposals of the Conference were to be published in October.)[42]

There remained no doubt in Churchill's mind that, whatever the structure that was created for an international body, the British Empire and Commonwealth, the 'Union of our World-Wide Brotherhood' as he called it, would have a special role to play in the post-war world.[43] So, too, of course, would his beloved 'fraternal association' between Britain and the United States, two countries, he assured the Commonwealth Prime Ministers, 'whose interests could not clash.'[44] 'It is my deepest conviction', he wrote to Law (reprimanding him for publicly rejecting the idea of 'an Anglo-American governess' for the world), 'that unless Britain and the United States are joined together in a special relationship, including the Combined Staff organisation and a wide measure of reciprocity in the use of bases—all within the ambit of a world organisation—another destructive war will come to pass.'[45]

And yet, even more than during the preceding period, it was becoming increasingly apparent in 1944 that in any future Anglo-American relationship, however 'special', Britain's role would be a junior one. True, the British war effort, as before, remained at least the equal of that of the United States in terms of a proportion of the resources available to each country. During 1944, for example, 24 per cent of the total British labour force were in the armed services, as compared to the American figure of 18 per cent.[46] War expenditure as a proportion of national income also continued to be higher than was the case in the U.S.A., while even in absolute terms it was only in the middle of the year that the number of American divisions in fighting contact with the enemy overtook that of British Empire divisions so employed.[47]

Nevertheless, Britain's problems in meeting the requirements of total war were becoming increasingly severe. The manpower question, for instance, which had begun to come to the fore during 1943, now occupied much of the Government's time as it looked ahead to 1945. The working population, it was estimated, would decline by 1,630,000 in that year; hence, a cut of about 1,100,000 in the armed forces and munitions workers had to be contemplated. If, moreover, following the defeat of Germany, the country was, at one and the same time, to make a significant contribution to the downfall of Japan, to take part in the occupation of Europe, to increase her exports, and to rebuild her cities and raise somewhat her living standards, then there would be a gap of 1,750,000 between estimated manpower supplies and requirements.[48]

As mentioned above, the date when Germany would be defeated and the length of the war against Japan thereafter assumed great significance in this context.[49] And in all, what it amounted to was that, as Churchill admitted at Quebec, 'the British Empire effort had now reached its peak, whereas that of their [American] ally was ever-increasing.'[50] By the middle of 1944, in fact, the United States had nearly twice the British number of civilians employed on war work.[51] Or to take a specific, Far Eastern example, at a time when the Royal Navy was still having to spread its resources with care, the U.S. Navy was able to assemble for a single operation such as the assault on the Marianas a vast array of warships: 14 battleships, 15 large and medium aircraft carriers, 10 escort carriers, 24 cruisers, 140 destroyers and escorts, together with over 50 transports.[52] Meanwhile in the field of nuclear development Britain's secondary role was now evident, while the Americans involved in the project were showing increasing confidence in their ability to carry it through to a successful conclusion.[53] As for the future, a survey written within the U.S. War Department during this period was already forecasting that 'the British Empire will emerge from the war having lost ground both economically and militarily.'[54]

Remarkably enough, there were those in high circles in Britain who, even now, did not accept that the economic and financial outlook for the country was a bleak one, and who were far from convinced of the need to work closely with the United States in order to erect an entirely new structure for the post-war world in those respects. True, agreement was reached between the two countries at the Bretton Woods Conference on the desirability of establishing an International Monetary Fund and Bank, but London was not to ratify this until forced to do so after the war was over.[55] As for the related question of tariffs and article 7 of the Mutual Aid Agreement, the Anglo-American talks held at the end of 1943 were not resumed during the remainder of this period, while in Westminster and Whitehall the resistance of Amery, Beaverbrook and others was carried on as fiercely as ever. Far from fearing for Britain's position, Amery, for example, was convinced that her monetary system was faced with exciting prospects. 'I don't believe', he wrote to Beaverbrook, 'that even you realise what we have made out of the sterling area during this war. At this moment the reserve banks in the sterling area countries hold about two thousand millions of sterling paper. Before the war is over it will be three thousand, or even four thousand millions . . . In other words, thanks to the credit we have established in the world, our paper is treated as being as good as gold, and we have an almost unlimited gold mine in our printing presses here at home . . .' More aggressively still, he declared that 'the present Dick Law policy . . . would certainly bust the Conservative Party if the Government were once definitely committed to it and the facts became known . . . I should go all out on the war-path against the Government', he added, 'and I imagine a great many other Conservatives would follow suit.'[56]

Given the continued existence of such brontosaurian beliefs, it is not surprising that battles within the Cabinet over this aspect of Britain's external relations were at times extremely fierce, as Law and others responded to Amery that the Government had signed the Mutual Aid Agreement in the belief 'that the policies indicated in Article VII offered the most hopeful prospect of a solution of the very serious problems with which we ourselves will be faced after the war.' 'The whole thing develops into the worst pandemonium I have ever seen in the Cabinet', recorded Dalton after one particularly lively session. 'Towards the end, four or five Ministers are often shouting at once.'[57] Beaverbrook, in particular, was now devoting much of his attention not only to this one issue but to what he saw as a fight to preserve Britain's independence as a whole vis-à-vis the United States.[58] In addition, there were also the varying views of the Dominions to be considered. Small wonder, then, that Churchill continued to hold back from arriving at a committed policy position, maintaining merely 'that we should not agree to depart from [Imperial Preference] unless in return for some such offer by the United States as full free trade or the reduction of United States tariffs, at an international conference, to a negligible level.'[59] If he went further than that, he told Law, there would be 'grave difficulties in the Conservative Party.'[60]

But for all the success of Amery and his allies in holding Britain back from committing herself to Hull's vision of a world of minimal tariffs, the harsh fact that the country was going to be dependent on American aid after the war was being presented to Ministers with mounting emphasis in this period. 'It would be impossible to maintain sterling', Anderson, as Chancellor, warned the Cabinet in April, 'without some assistance from the United States . . . [and] if we antagonised the United States, the generous assistance we needed from that country would not be made available.'[61] Cherwell likewise told Churchill that 'without either lend lease or a loan from the U.S.A. immediately after the war, we shall be completely at the mercy of our overseas suppliers and our economic position and standard of life will be affected for a generation.'[62] As a senior economic adviser in the Foreign Office saw it, 'We face appalling risks and difficulties unless the U.S.A. can be induced to help us in Stage II and III [the war against Japan alone, and the early post-war period] in a manner, and to a degree, unparalleled in international relations.'[63]

At the beginning of July, Anderson made use of a memorandum that had been prepared for him by Keynes to put the matter to his colleagues in the bluntest terms.[64] The country's overseas liabilities, he pointed out, now amounted to £2,000 million, and were increasing at a rate of over £600 million a year. In addition, a deficit of about £1,000 million was foreseen for the early post-war years, between what could be earned by the export of goods and services and what would be needed to cover the import of food and raw materials. Exports, Keynes had written, 'a luxury to the United States, are a matter of life and death to us'; yet even if they could be increased substantially, Britain would still need to obtain from the U.S.A., ideally, $1 or $2 billion in goods on lend-lease terms, and another $1 or $2 billion as an interest-free cash loan. If terms such as these were unforthcoming, then the country would simply have to 'borrow all we can from the United States on any terms available, and in due course shuffle out.'

The Chancellor felt obliged to return to the subject in yet another paper, insisting once again, for the benefit of the Amery brigade, that 'from being the world's largest creditor, we shall have become at the end of the war the world's largest debtor.'[65] In the Foreign Office, too, the position was now viewed with extreme seriousness, and a major review was put in hand of the consequences for British diplomacy. It 'might well involve a change in our diplomatic methods', forecast Sir Orme Sargent. 'We could no longer rely on the weapons of the rich man, such as credits, loans and subsidies . . . [And] whereas *we* would not be able to provide credits, the U.S.A. would. That might result in a considerable extension of United States influence compared to our own, and might even lead us into conflict.' Yet could Britain dare allow such a conflict to arise? The Head of the North American Department, for one, drew the conclusion that she could not:

'Our conduct of our foreign policy during the period for which we need U.S. financial support', he wrote in forthright fashion, 'must be such as to commend itself to the U.S. In particular we shall need to show that we are a reliable and potentially strong partner, and one whose policies are on lines broadly acceptable to American public opinion . . . The American Administration, Congress and public opinion will need to be persuaded that "We mean to hold our own" is not the be-all and end-all of British policy.'[66]

This implied rejection by a British official of Churchillian attitudes ('We mean to hold our own') as being inadequate, accompanied the existence of an obvious external threat to the Prime Minister's policies, a threat which was embodied in the perceived extent of the country's future dependence on the U.S.A., and which was likely to manifest itself in the Far East as much as anywhere else. Churchill himself was evidently aware of the situation, though without a solution to it. 'We should bear in mind', he warned the Cabinet, 'the risk that (e.g. in regard to India) if we accepted the financial help of the United States we might also be parting with political authority and control. Finance was interwoven with the power and sovereignty of the state.'[67]

Meanwhile, if there were those on the British side who were taking time to appreciate the gravity of the country's position, Roosevelt, too, behaved on occasions as if he were not fully aware of what lay ahead. Thus, although Stettinius for one advised him that, when set against her liabilities, Britain's reserves did not look unduly high, the President went ahead and asked Churchill to try to cut down those reserves to $1 billion.[68] The Administration also bowed to pressures in both official and non-official quarters by reducing certain non-military Lend Lease supplies to Britain, while a senior Washington spokesman denied publicly that Lend Lease of any kind would continue once the war was over.[69] When Morgenthau returned in August from a visit to London and reported to Roosevelt: 'England really is broke', the latter responded that he had had 'no idea' that this was the case. Jokingly, he added that he would 'go over there and make a couple of talks and take over the British Empire.'[70]

The extent to which, even before peace came, Britain would be dependent on the United States during Stage II (when Japan alone would be the enemy) was spelled out during the Quebec Conference. The Cabinet in London had concluded before Churchill and his advisers set out that, in the first year of fighting following the defeat of Germany, the country would need from the U.S.A. $4 billion worth of munitions and $3 billion of other supplies, with $1·2 billion and $1 billion respectively to come, it was hoped, from Canada.[71] Morgenthau and Hopkins were both sympathetic in their responses, though the latter's influence in White House circles had by now declined.[72] At one stage during his Quebec talks with Roosevelt and Morgenthau, however, the Prime Minister was reduced to bursting out with the resentful question: 'What do you want me to do? Get on my hind legs and beg like Fala [the President's dog]?'[73]* Moreover, although at Quebec agreement was reached in principle on figures of $3½ billion for munitions and $3 billion for non-munitions during Stage II, with detailed talks on the subject to follow, this was not a decision that, on the American side, was regarded as binding one. Thus, while the Cabinet in London were informed that the outcome of the Quebec talks on Lend Lease had been eminently satisfactory,[74] it was not to be long—in November, in fact— before Morgenthau was recording in his diary that Roosevelt was insisting that 'he had never promised them anything at Quebec', that he was querying items which appeared in the draft detailed agreements ('"And what is this ship for, and what's that plane for?"'), and that 'he wanted to be able to tell the newspapers that there was no agreement, and simply that there was a recommendation from us [Morgenthau and his colleagues] to him and he can take it into consideration.'[75] Thus far was the President to be trusted.

* It is difficult to accept later testimonies to the effect that Churchill did not realize that Britain had fallen to 'second place' until after the Yalta Conference. (See Thompson, *Churchill and Morton*, 84.)

Even the fragile agreement that had been reached at Quebec had involved the granting of something of a concealed quid pro quo on Churchill's part, for Harry Dexter White was surely correct in claiming later that the Prime Minister's acceptance of Morgenthau's plan for the de-industrialization of the Ruhr and the Saar—Churchill and Roosevelt agreed that Germany should be converted 'into a country primarily agricultural and pastoral in character'[76]—was linked to the assurances he had received about aid during Stage II. Morgenthau's own record of the sequence of events which led up to the Prime Minister dictating a minute on the subject of Germany, despite Eden's objections, is instructive in this connection. Churchill, he noted, had 'tears in his eyes' when accord was reached over the Lend Lease issue. 'When the thing was finally signed he told the President how grateful he was, thanked him most effusively, and said this was something they were doing for both countries. Then Churchill, turning to Lord Cherwell and myself, said: "Where are the minutes on this matter of the Ruhr?"'[77] Moreover, Morgenthau's later denials that the two matters had been connected with one another look weak in the light of the record in his diary of an exchange between himself and White in October:

White: 'The important thing in your mind is that in their [British] mind this thing [Stage II] was tied upon that [Germany]. Now whether they will deliver on this other thing remains to be seen, so we shouldn't deliver on this wholly without any chance to—'

Morgenthau: 'Dear Harry, the old man [i.e. Morgenthau] was doing a little bargaining last night when he brought this German Directive to their attention and said, "I should be pleased to see it." And I am going to keep doing this thing while this is before me. What do you think I was doing last night?'

White: 'Yes, that is all right.'

Morgenthau: 'We are together, all right.'[78]

Hopkins also told Cherwell later that, in the latter's words, 'He had no doubt I had supported Morgenthau [over Germany] because I was anxious to get Stage 2 through . . .'[79]

Morgenthau's plans for the de-industrialization of Germany were, in fact, to come to nothing, owing to the opposition to them that was mounted by the War and State Departments. Nevertheless, the idea of using Britain's Lend Lease needs as a lever with which to move her in directions pleasing to the United States was present in other minds in Washington in this period. Hull, for one, bemoaned the fact that Roosevelt had not seized the opportunity at Quebec to insist that 'the soundness of the economic policy adopted by Great Britain' would be a criterion by which the granting of further aid would be judged, while one of his senior officials listed all the other things, besides the implementation of Article 7, which could be demanded of London in return for supplies, including the recognition of America's title to various islands in the Pacific whose ownership was in dispute between the two countries.[80] Earlier, Hornbeck for his part had written to Hull: 'We are in a position to get from the British agreement to and cooperation in any reasonable course of action upon which we may choose to insist. This is especially the case in the circumstances which now prevail, wherein they are to a great degree dependent upon us for their preservation.'[81]

More harshly and specifically, General Brehon Somervell, head of the U.S. Army's Services of Supply, wrote a memorandum at the time of the Quebec Conference in which he argued that after the defeat of Germany Lend Lease should be severely restricted to materials needed for actually fighting Japan. Other Lend Lease items then in Britain's possession, he submitted, should be handed back on demand, while 'in partial compensation' for the remaining balance against Britain resulting from all Lend Lease transactions, the U.S. should obtain the following: 'any extension that may be needed' of the rights she had acquired in 1941 to bases in the West Indies and Newfoundland; 'rights of a similar kind in any part of the world under British control'; 'assurance of full commercial rights for the U.S. and its nationals throughout the British Empire'; assurance of no discrimination against American purchases of raw materials 'such as petroleum, metals and rubber' which had been produced under 'British control or auspices'; and (can he have thought that the list so far was unduly modest?) cash or long-term credit reimbursement of any substantial Lend Lease balance remaining in the United States' favour after taking into consideration benefits received under the foregoing items.[82] Similar agreements, argued the General, should then be concluded with other states which had benefited from American Lend Lease.

Somervell's vision of a world dominated by a new ring of American bases, its markets and resources available to the United States on an 'Open Door' footing, reflected an awareness of the country's increasing might which we have already noted as being present in the minds of some of the General's compatriots, not least in relation to the future of the Far East. A common accompanying belief, that American and British commercial and economic interests were and would be in conflict, was seen by British observers in the United States to be growing in this period,[83] fostered by developments over such particular issues as oil resources and civil aviation routes.

Where oil was concerned, the fluctuating tension created by the American interest in acquiring new rights in the Middle East cannot be followed here in any detail. (It involved, for instance, talks between the two countries and the signing in August of a draft interim agreement; Roosevelt's assurance to Churchill that the United States was not 'making sheeps eyes' at Britain's oilfields in Iraq or Iran; and the Prime Minister's warning that Britain would 'not be deprived of anything which belongs to her . . ., at least so long as your humble servant is entrusted with the conduct of her affairs.')[84] What does need to be noted, however, besides the expansionist tendencies of the United States, is the considerable degree of resentment that the issue engendered on the British side of the relationship. Dalton, for example, recorded in his diary that in Cabinet circles there was 'some anti-American feeling in the air', and that Churchill himself had declared: '"We may be only poor, god-fearing men, serving the Lord Jesus Christ in humbleness of heart, but there is no reason why we should allow ourselves to be knocked about.'[85]

And yet, although Beaverbrook in particular urged defiance over the oil issue,[86] there was a significant awareness on the part of Eden and others that Britain simply could not afford to clash with the United States over such a matter. 'I cannot share your views that we should benefit by a "free for all"', the Foreign Secretary wrote to Beaverbrook in June. 'On the contrary, I believe that we have every reason, commercial as well as political, for wishing to avoid unrestricted commercial competition with the Americans at the present time . . . Once we embark on an "oil war" we shall in present conditions stand to lose heavily.'[87] Likewise, over the question of post-war civil aviation (where Britain's proposal for the establishment of an international authority with executive powers did not meet with American approval), there was a belief in London that a United States company like Pan American Airways was in a highly advantageous position.[88]* Nor did British Ministers and officials feel themselves to be able to resist American pressure, even when the country's existing interests seemed likely to be endangered as a result. Thus, when Washington withdrew its Ambassador from the Argentine (without consulting London), the Cabinet reluctantly decided that it had to follow suit, while later in 1944 Churchill felt obliged to agree to an American request that Britain should not sign a long-term meat contract with the Argentinians, despite the threat that such a move might pose to British food supplies.[89]

Meanwhile, in official and Congressional circles in Washington there continued to exist a strong suspicion that Britain, perhaps all the more so because of her material weaknesses, was up to her old game of playing 'power politics' to her own advantage. Admiral Leahy, for example, still situated at Roosevelt's right hand, found room in his diary for a good many entries to this effect,[90] while both Stettinius and Hull warned the President that Britain was intending to set up, in agreement with the Soviet Union, separate spheres of interest in the Balkans.[91] Others remained convinced that Britain's deep imperialist and acquisitive instincts were far from dead. 'British imperialism seems to have acquired a new lease of life', Pat Hurley wrote to Roosevelt, attributing the fact to '. . . the infusion, into its emaciated form, of the blood of productivity and liberty from a free nation through lend lease.'[92]

A memorandum on 'Britain's imperialistic policy' in the Middle East was likewise sent to Hopkins by the State Department,[93] while Roosevelt himself drew up a policy statement which declared that 'in the Middle East,

* In Washington, the President of Pan. Am., Juan Trippe, was lobbying in official circles as zealously as ever. (E.g. Leahy Diary, 30 March 1944; Stimson Diary, 1 Aug. 1944.)

as elsewhere, the objective of the United States is to make certain that all nations are accorded equality of opportunity. Special privileges . . . have little place in the type of world for which this war is being fought.' (He did have the grace to add that 'the realization of such aims will naturally further the broad interests of the United States in that it will assure equality of treatment being afforded to this country.')[94] To advisers, the President commented that 'the British would take land anywhere in the world, even if it were only a rock or sand-bar', and that 'we are still going to have a tough time with the British on this issue.'[95] Meanwhile both the British and American senior civilian representatives in the Mediterranean area observed in this period that relations between Washington and London were not as close as they once had been.[96]

British imperialist instincts remained associated in American minds with what Morgenthau privately called 'the ruling class of England of which Mr. Churchill is one and of which Mr. [sic] Halifax is another.' 'At the top', he concluded, 'they evidently haven't learned anything.'[97] Rather than vigorous villains, however, these were tired old dogs up to their usual tricks, for the image of the heroic, embattled Britain of 1940 now lay well in the past. 'I have come to the conclusion', wrote the Anglophile Stimson in April, 'that if this war is to be won, it's got to be won by the full strength of the virile, energetic, initiative-loving, inventive Americans, and that the British really are showing decadence—a magnificent people, but they have lost their initiative.'[98] Roosevelt, too, according to Hopkins when he lunched with Law in Washington in August, 'did not expect us [the British] to play the role that we had played in the past . . . [although] it would be necessary to bolster us up and pretend that we were still a great power.' (Law found this 'the most sinister part of a somewhat sinister conversation.')[99]

In many, probably most, American eyes, the United States, by contrast, was not only far stronger than Britain but more enlightened. 'I am thrilled', Roosevelt wrote to Hurley, 'with the idea of using our efforts in Iran [for the distribution of Lend Lease supplies there, rather than allowing the British to do it] as an example of what can be done by an unselfish American policy.'[100]* Meanwhile, it could be proclaimed in Anglophobe quarters like the *Chicago Tribune* that 'we Americans are winning this war. We are doing virtually all of the fighting in the Pacific and have made virtually all the advances in France . . . This is an American-made victory and the peace must be an American peace.'[101] Beliefs of this kind were far more disturbing to British officials than were short-lived Anglo-American difficulties, over, for example, Oliver Lyttelton's clumsy public assertion that the United States had manoeuvred Japan into starting the Far Eastern war,[102] or complaints by Roosevelt's opponents that Britain was seeking to meddle in the Presidential election.[103]

Thus, Eden in January uneasily observed that 'Americans have a much

* Leahy suggested to Roosevelt in April that he should put up a plaque at Bernard Baruch's country home, indicating that he had come there, not simply for a rest, but 'to escape from the British.' (Leahy Diary, 23 April 1944.)

exaggerated conception of the military contribution they are making in this war. They lie freely about this ... The result ... is that the Americans advocate the claims of Washington as capital of the country making the major fighting effort, which it certainly is not.' Halifax agreed. 'Amazing and deplorable ignorance prevails among even friendly and usually well-informed Americans', he reported after D-Day, 'about the extent of British participation in the present operations', while in August Beaverbrook, visiting the United States, found there that British prestige had sharply declined.[104] As usual, the subject gave rise to questions about the effectiveness of Britain's publicity machine in the U.S.A., some of them being asked in the House of Commons.[105]

Again, moreover, expressions of resentment against the United States were to be heard in Parliament as well as within official circles in London. Emmanuel Shinwell, for example, a belligerent Labour Party patriot, asked for it to be made clear that 'as far as Europe is concerned, we cannot allow our foreign policy to be dictated by the United States', while Arthur Greenwood, a former member of the Government, likewise declared from the Labour benches: 'We cannot become the vassal of the United States and I think we are entitled to say so.'[106] As for those in official positions, the Secretary of State for War, Grigg, revealed his usual suspicion of Americans when, in what a Foreign Office report wincingly described as 'one hour and forty minutes of unalleviated hectoring and admonishment', he addressed an Anglo-American dining club, thumping his fist on the table and announcing to the Americans in the audience: '"I tell you, gentlemen, whether you like it or not, imperial preference is here to stay."'[107] And although the Foreign Office regarded this particular incident with despair ('A silly speech', minuted Eden. 'The man is not wise. I suppose this is the kind of thing the Tory Party wants when it complains that I am not tough enough!'), they, too, including the Foreign Secretary, were moved to exasperation and scorn by some American behaviour and claims that United States policies were based entirely on the highest principles.[108] A scheme was also discussed in the Office whereby ill-founded American criticisms would be 'answered back' by British officials in the U.S.A.[109]

At this point, however, it must be emphasized once again that, for all the growing imbalance and areas of tension between the two partners, it would be quite wrong to see their relationship as being an entirely sour one in this period, any more than it had been before. The extent of the cooperation that was being achieved remained remarkable, and a visit which Stettinius and a number of American officials paid to London in April demonstrated the degree of good-will and readiness for accommodation that still existed. (To Halifax, Stettinius on his return to Washington expressed 'his deep conviction that we should stick together as a permanent partners', and his belief that it was in America's interest for the Commonwealth to be 'strong and prosperous.')[110] Similarly, numerous personal relationships, like the one between the civilian heads of the two navies, for example, remained excellent.[111]

Moreover, however great exasperation with Americans became in London, far stronger was the anxiety there to see the United States remain closely involved in international affairs after the war was over. In this connection, much attention was paid in the Foreign Office to the state of American opinion and politics as it stood in 1944, compared to what it had been in 1918–19. In other words, the vital question being asked was whether the eventual repudiation of President Wilson and the League of Nations might be repeated. Some disturbing similarities with those earlier years were noted, but in general the analyses that were made were hopeful. From the Washington Embassy, for example, Isaiah Berlin described 'the incomparably greater skill shown by the Roosevelt Administration' in rallying the majority of public opinion and opinion-forming groups behind its foreign policy. Likewise, the Foreign Office Research Department concluded that there was now 'a much fuller realisation [than in 1918] that the United States is a world Power and cannot escape the responsibilities which that involves.'[112]

Naturally there was also much British speculation about the outcome of the forthcoming Presidential election. Churchill himself was sure that Roosevelt would be returned. 'I do not believe', he wrote with unconscious irony, 'that a great people will desert the pilot who weathered the storm.'[113] Nevertheless, might not a hostile Congress prevent the President from carrying out his chosen policies?[114] Would the old-guard Republicans (and this period saw the eclipse of their main foe within the Party, Willkie, who was to die in October) prove to be anti-British at heart, or were they, as some insisted, essentially friendly?[115]

While waiting for the answers to such questions, efforts were made to improve the outlook generally by making arrangements for visits to Britain by a growing number of U.S. Congressmen.[116] As for the future shape of the hoped-for partnership with the American giant, some in senior positions were consoling themselves with the thought that the quality of her diplomatic skills could make up for Britain's material inferiority. 'What really matters', wrote Halifax, 'is surely that by every means we should seek to make an enduring reality of our present partnership in arms with the United States. And I have enough confidence in our experience and inherited wisdom to feel pretty sure that, if we play our cards right in this kind of fashion, we need not be too apprehensive of the final outcome.'[117] 'Instead of trying to use the Commonwealth as an instrument which will give us the power to out-face the United States', ran a Foreign Office memorandum, 'we must use the power of the United States to preserve the Commonwealth and the Empire, and, if possible, to support the pacification of Europe.'[118]

Such were some of the main British hopes for the future. Where this period was concerned, however, it is evident in retrospect that the Anglo-American partnership, which had grown so strong in the earlier part of the war, was in something of a decline—a factor of considerable significance for the war in the Far East, which, at the same time, was increasing in importance. The machinery of combined planning, for example, including the Combined Chiefs of Staff, tended to play a less active part after D. Day.[119] Nor did the Churchill–Roosevelt link (to which, as we have seen, the President had accorded a somewhat lower priority during 1943 than he had earlier) recover the strength it had possessed in 1941–42. For the Prime Minister, of course, this relationship remained of paramount importance; but the weight that he could bring to bear through it was reduced, and his behaviour at times suggests that he was well aware of this. 'We do wish he would *reason* with Pres.', wrote Cadogan despairingly. 'He won't.'[120] As for Roosevelt, Lewis Douglas, a prominent American Anglophile, observed to Halifax that 'he thought he noticed a tendency in that quarter to ride rather more roughshod and to be less painstaking about reaching agreements by honest give and take', while it was in this period that the Ambassador himself made the remark noted earlier, that the President was quite capable at any time 'of playing politics to [Britain's] detriment.'[121]

Halifax also recorded in his diary various pieces of information which came to him suggesting that Roosevelt's grip on the running of affairs was now less than sure.[122] We know today, of course, that the President was a dying man from at least April 1944 onwards—not that his liking for power seems to have been impaired[123]—which explains why British representatives at the Quebec Conference noted a striking deterioration in his appearance.[124] The functioning of the Joint Chiefs of Staff was not greatly affected by what was happening to their Commander in Chief—his relationship with them had never been as close or as active as Churchill's with the British Chiefs of Staff.[125] But the continuing administrative chaos in Washington, which a despairing Hopkins vividly illustrated for the benefit of a visitor,[126] meant that there was no adequate machinery to ensure that decision-making and execution flowed on, despite the President's decline. The State Department, like most ambassadors in the field, was still left on the sidelines, with Roosevelt dismissing the idea that it should be represented at Quebec on the grounds that the Conference was to be of a military nature. (There was thus much consternation on the part of Hull and his colleagues when they learned that Eden and Cadogan were in attendance on the Prime Minister nonetheless.)[127]

Roosevelt remained, of course, a huge and vital figure on the American scene when it came to bringing the country to accept that involvement in post-war international affairs which London was so anxious to see. Nevertheless, as his grip slackened during the last year of his life, and as major problems concerning the post-war world built up—problems for which he often had no answer beyond a belief in his personal ability to win agreement among men of good-will—the President became in some ways a liability in terms of the effective conduct of United States and Allied business. Domestically too, his refusal to face the facts concerning his own state of health, coupled with his decision to run again for the Presidency, suggest, not so much heroism, as is usually argued, but irresponsibility and an undue belief in his indispensability, if not a love of power.

What of Churchill, within his British setting? Although the Cabinet agreed in September 1944 to extend the life of Parliament for another year,[128] this was a period of increasing strain as regards British domestic politics, both between the two major parties of the coalition and within the Labour Party.[129] Thus, Labour's National Executive agreed that they would fight the first election after the defeat of Germany on an independent basis, while even so staunch a supporter of the coalition as Ernest Bevin (much criticized by militants like Aneurin Bevan) was 'tending', in Dalton's words, 'to think more and more in Party political terms.'[130]

Meanwhile, as post-war social and economic issues became increasingly prominent,[131] not only was Conservatism in eclipse, but Churchill himself was left further out of touch with the times. 'I have a very strong feeling that my work is done', he admitted on the way back from Quebec. 'I have no message. I had a message. Now I only say, "Fight the damned socialists." I do not believe in this brave new world.'[132] To some observers, the Prime Minister's grasp of affairs also appeared to decline around this time, with Cabinet business not being transacted efficiently, and with what seemed to be an increasing reliance on his part on the opinions of Beaverbrook and Cherwell. 'It's terrible', wrote Cadogan privately, 'that we have a P.M. who simply *can't conduct business*.'[133] Others, the C.I.G.S. and Secretary of State for War among them, were coming to feel that, in the latter's words, 'Winston is a very old man and . . . his two illnesses have taken away a good deal of his power of decision.'[134]

In the event, Churchill was far from finished, and his powers of recuperation proved to be extraordinary. He remained a gigantic figure, symbolizing Britain's determination to see the war through to the end, and by his very presence bridging part of the gap between the country's status as a great power and her limited resources when compared to the might of the United States and the Soviet Union. Yet we shall see in the next chapter that not only Cabinet business but vital strategic decisions were to be handled poorly by the Prime Minister in 1944. Moreover, as well as being increasingly out of touch with domestic opinion where the future—political, social and economic—was concerned, he was likewise, in the international setting, far removed from a sympathetic understanding of the new Asia of strong and impatient nationalisms that was emerging from the war. Nor was he the man to help bring Britain to a realization and constructive acceptance of her new and much diminished place in world politics.

As in the case of Roosevelt, it is difficult to imagine the scene without Churchill's leadership, even at this stage of the war. But again as with Roosevelt—and in contrast to the context of Britain in 1940–41—the Prime Minister cannot in retrospect be described as an unqualified asset to his country in 1944. In certain respects, indeed, he was already a liability.

Notes to Chapter Seventeen

1 See Ehrman, *Grand Strategy*, V, caps. VI and VII, and e.g. *Bryant*, II, 51, 180.
2 Winant to FDR, 3 July 1944, Roosevelt Papers, MR box 11.
3 Stimson Diary, 28 June 1944.
4 E.g. COS to WSC, 9 Sept. 1944, PREM 3, 149/8; COS, 8 Sept. 1944, CAB 99/29.
5 WSC to FDR, 29 Sept. 1944, PREM 3, 472; Ehrman, *Grand Strategy*, V, 377ff., 506.
6 WSC to Hopkins, 19 July 1944, Roosevelt Papers, MR box 13; FRUS, The Conference At Quebec, 2. See Ehrman, *Grand Strategy*, V, cap. XIII.
7 Press conference, 16 Sept. 1944, PREM 4, 75/2.
8 *Moran*, 173. See Hancock, *Smuts*, 414.
9 WSC to COS, 9 Sept. 1944, PREM 3, 149/8.
10 *Woodward*, III, 115, 154ff.
11 *Bryant*, II, 242.
12 *Woodward*, III, 112ff.
13 Meeting of 5 May 1944, PREM 4, 42/5.
14 FO 371, U6253/748/G. See various drafts in ibid, files 40740 and 40741A.
15 FRUS, Quebec, 190.
16 FRUS, The Conferences at Malta and Yalta, 103.
17 W. Millis (ed.) *The Forrestal Diaries* (London, 1952; hereafter, *Forrestal*), entry for 2 Sept. 1944; *Leahy*, 280.
18 FRUS, Quebec, 192, 198.
19 On one occasion in September, the President defended the Pope against an attack made by Mrs. Roosevelt, saying that 'he [the Pope] had always been for private property and was against communism.' Morgenthau, Presidential Diary, 2 Sept. 1944.
20 Anderson to WSC, 21 March 1944, PREM 3, 139/2; Wheeler-Bennett, *Anderson*, 297.
21 See M. J. Sherwin, 'The Atomic Bomb And The Origins of the Cold War', American Historical Review, Oct. 1973 (hereafter, 'Sherwin, *Am. Hist. Rev.*') and his subsequent book, *A World Destroyed: The Atomic Bomb and the Grand Alliance* (New York, 1975); *Freedman*, 728.
22 Agreement dated 19 Sept. 1944, PREM 3, 139/8A.
23 FO 371, Z1146/275/17.
24 Stimson Diary, 8 June and 14 Sept. 1944.
25 Ibid, 14 June 1944.
26 Ibid, 22 June 1944; and e.g. Matthews to Hull, 9 May 1944, DS, Matthews files, box 9.
27 E.g. FDR to WSC, 13 May 1944, PREM 3, 472. See *Woodward*, III, 22, 38.
28 Harriman to FDR, 29 May 1944, Roosevelt Papers, MR box 11; *Woodward*, III, 73ff.; P. Dixon (ed.), *Double Diploma* (London, 1968), 87ff.
29 de Gaulle, *War Memoirs: Unity, 1942–1944*, 227.
30 Hansard, HC Deb, 403, col. 493.
31 WSC to FDR, 20 June 1944, PREM 3, 472.
32 Drachman, *U.S. Policy Toward Vietnam*, 53; Viorst, *Hostile Allies*, 208; FRUS, 1944, III, 724.
33 FRUS, 1944, III, 735, 737, 739, 741.
34 *News Chronicle*, 3 July 1944; Divine, *Second Chance*, 183.
35 E.g. Dulles to Lippmann, 5 July 1944 and other material in Dulles Papers, boxes 2 and 3; Divine, *Second Chance*, 219.
36 Divine, *Second Chance*, 199.
37 FDR to Burlingham, 29 May 1944, Frankfurter Papers, box 98. See E. May, '*Lessons' of the Past* (London, 1975).
38 Material in Connally Papers, box 103.
39 Material in PREM 4, 30/7; e.g. FRUS, 1944, III, 1; *Woodward*, V.
40 FO 371, U1751/748/G; see Dalton Diary, 17 Jan. 1944; Hankey Diary, 2 June 1944.
41 Foreign Office memo., 16 April 1944, APW, CAB 87/67; APW minutes, 22 April 1944, CAB 87/66.
42 See Divine, *Second Chance*, 221; *Cadogan Diaries*, 654ff.; *Stettinius*, 103ff.

43 WSC note, 8 May 1944, PREM 4, 30/7.
44 Minutes of 9 May 1944, PREM 4, 42/5; Hansard, HC Deb., 399, cols. 577ff.
45 WSC to Law, 16 Feb. 1944, PREM 4, 27/10.
46 Hall, *North American Supply*, 473.
47 *Hancock and Gowing*, 369, 367.
48 WP(44)173 (CAB 66/48); WP(44)316 (CAB 66/51); WP(44)379, 380, 381 (CAB 66/52); WP(44)431 (CAB 66/53); Cab, 8 Aug. 1944 (CAB 65/43).
49 See *Hancock and Gowing*, 515ff.
50 *Matloff*, 518. See *Bryant*, II, 225.
51 *Hancock and Gowing*, 368; *Churchill*, VI, 62.
52 *Roskill*, III, part II, 191.
53 Gowing, *Britain and Atomic Energy*, 233ff., 340.
54 *Matloff*, 523.
55 See Gardner, *Sterling-Dollar Diplomacy*, cap. VII.
56 Amery to Beaverbrook, 11 and 22 Feb. 1944, Beaverbrook Papers, C/7.
57 Dalton Diary, 23 Feb. 1944.
58 Taylor, *Beaverbrook*, 555ff.
59 Meeting of 8 May 1944, PREM 4, 42/5.
60 FO 371, U3795/238/50. On the issue in general, see Cabs, 11 Feb. (CAB 65/45), 23 Feb. (CAB 65/41), 14 April (CAB 65/46), and 18 July 1944 (CAB 65/43); WP(43)559 and 576 (CAB 66/44); WP(44)41 (CAB 66/45); WP(44)64, 75, 81, 95 (CAB 66/46); WP(44)121, 129, 138, 145, 148 (CAB 66/47); WP(44)176 (CAB 66/48); Dalton Diary, 11 and 14 Feb. 1944, 8 May 1944.
61 Cab, 14 April 1944, CAB 65/40.
62 Cherwell to WSC, 17 March 1944, Cherwell Papers, Off. 1.1.
63 FO 371, AN3460/6/45.
64 WP(44)360, CAB 66/52. See Hall, *North American Supply*, 445, and on Keynes' efforts, Harrod, *Keynes*, 525ff. and 586ff.
65 WP(44)419, CAB 66/53.
66 FO 371, UE615/169/53.
67 Cab, 18 July 1944, CAB 65/43.
68 Stettinius to FDR, 22 Feb. 1944, Roosevelt Papers, MR box 7A; FDR to WSC, 22 Feb. 1944, ibid, MR box 5; FRUS, 1944, III, 45.
69 Blum, *Roosevelt and Morgenthau*, 133ff.; e.g. JCS, 29 Aug. 1944, RG 218; material on the Truman Committee in FO 371, file 38539; *New York Herald Tribune*, 8 Aug. 1944; Leahy Diary, 16 and 27 March 1944.
70 Morgenthau, Presidential Diary, 19 Aug. 1944.
71 WP(44)419 and 448, CAB 66/53; Cab, 4 Aug. 1944, CAB 65/43; FRUS, Quebec, 159.
72 Blum, *Roosevelt and Morgenthau*, 310; Cherwell–Hopkins talk, 3 Oct. 1944, Cherwell Papers, Off. 23.2.; Halifax to WSC, 20 Aug. 1944, PREM 4, 75/2; Lubin to Hopkins, 4 Aug. 1944, Hopkins Papers, box 335.
73 FRUS, Quebec, 348.
74 Ibid, 344, 468; Cab, 18 Sept. 1944, CAB 65/47.
75 Morgenthau Diary, 16 and 21 Nov. 1944.
76 FRUS, Quebec, 466.
77 Ibid, 360.
78 Morgenthau Diary, 18 Oct. 1944.
79 Cherwell–Hopkins talk, 3 Oct. 1944, Cherwell Papers, Off. 23.2.
80 Hull to FDR, 30 Sept. 1944, Roosevelt Papers, PSF box 92; Matthews to Stettinius, n.d., 1944, DS, Matthews files, box 12.
81 Hornbeck to Hull, 3 Jan. 1944, Hornbeck Papers, box 181.
82 Somervell memo., 7 Sept. 1944, Hopkins Papers, box 335.
83 E.g. FO 371, AN1690/20/45.
84 FDR to WSC, 3 March 1944; WSC to FDR, 4 March 1944, PREM 3, 472. See also FRUS, 1944, III, 94ff.; Cabs, 6 March (CAB 65/41), 5 April, 31 May and 16 June (CAB 65/42) and 3 and 4 Aug. 1944 (CAB 65/43); WP(44)313, 324 (CAB 66/51);

WP(44)454 (CAB 66/54). On the Middle East background, see Gardner, *Economic Aspects*, cap. 11.
85 Dalton Diary, 23 Feb. 1944.
86 Material in Beaverbrook Papers, unclassified 'Oil' file; WP(44)102, 109 (CAB 66/47); WP(44)281 (CAB 66/50).
87 Eden to Beaverbrook, 12 June 1944, Beaverbrook Papers, 'Oil' file.
88 Cabs, 1 and 25 Sept. 1944, CAB 65/43; WP(44)472, 473, CAB 66/54; Beaverbrook Papers, 'Civil Aviation' file; Gardner, *Economic Aspects*, 270ff.
89 Cabs, 14 and 17 Jan. 1944 (CAB 65/41) and 3 July 1944 (CAB 65/43); WSC to FDR, 1 July and 13 Oct. 1944; FDR to WSC, 11 Oct. 1944, PREM 3, 472. Gardner, *Economic Aspects*, 201ff.
90 Leahy Diary, 12 and 23 May, 15 and 29 June 1944.
91 Stettinius to FDR, 10 June 1944, Hull to FDR, 17 June 1944, Roosevelt Papers, MR box 6.
92 Hurley to FDR, 21 Dec. 1943, Roosevelt Papers, MR box 7A. See Hurley to FDR, 3 Feb. 1944, ibid, MR box 12, and WSC to FDR, 21 May 1944, ibid, PSF box 50.
93 State Dpt. memo., 29 Aug. 1944, Hopkins Papers, box 332.
94 FRUS, 1944, V, 1.
95 *Stettinius*, 17 March 1944, and see ibid, 33.
96 Macmillan, *The Blast of War*, 521.
97 *Morgenthau Diary, China*, II, 1116.
98 Stimson Diary, 10 April 1944.
99 FO 371, AN3333/20/45.
100 FDR to Hurley, 25 March 1944, *Roosevelt Letters*.
101 *Chicago Tribune*, 2 Aug. 1944.
102 FO 371, AN2478/20/45; AN2381/34/45; WSC to FDR, 23 June 1944, PREM 3, 472.
103 E.g. *Chicago Tribune*, 2 and 5 April 1944, 12 Aug. 1944; *San Francisco Examiner*, 3 May 1944.
104 Eden to Halifax, 28 Jan. 1944; Halifax to Eden, 11 Feb. 1944; Halifax to Bracken, 8 June 1944, PREM 4, 27/9; Beaverbrook to Halifax, 29 Aug. 1944, Hickleton Papers, A4 410 4.
105 Hansard, HC Deb, 401, cols. 826ff.
106 Ibid, 398, col. 1412; ibid, 399, cols. 390ff.
107 FO 371, AN2951/6/45.
108 E.g. ibid, AN1327/34/45.
109 The scheme was not fully implemented. See ibid, AN91/20/45; AN1037 and 2575/34/45.
110 Ibid, AN2071/78/45. See also FRUS, 1944, III, 1ff.; DS, 740.001, 'Stett. Mission' files.
111 E.g. Knox to Alexander, 3 Jan. 1944, Alexander Papers, box 5/9.
112 FO 371, AN2678/34/45; AN3332/325/45.
113 WSC to Beaverbrook, 5 Aug. 1944, PREM 4, 27/10.
114 See Halifax to Eden, 14 Feb. 1944, PREM 4, 27/9.
115 Berlin report, 13 March 1944, PREM 4, 27/1; Bracken to Halifax, 3 Feb. 1944, Hickleton Papers, A4 410 4; material in FO 371, files 38542-3.
116 FO 371, AN3743/78/45.
117 FO 371, AN447/6/45.
118 Ibid, AN1064/16/45.
119 Hall, *North American Supply*, 437.
120 *Cadogan Diaries*, 18 May 1944.
121 Halifax Diary, 28 Feb. 1944; Dalton Diary, 13 July 1944.
122 E.g. Halifax Diary, 31 March, 21 May, 5 Oct. 1944.
123 See e.g. Morgenthau Diary, 2 and 7 Sept. 1944.
124 See J. Bishop, *F.D.R.'s Last Year* (New York, 1974), passim, and e.g. Ismay, *Memoirs*, 373. Interview with Lord Coleraine.
125 See e.g. JCS, 21 Feb. 1944: 'The President greeted the Chiefs of Staff and asked what they were concerned about.' RG 218.

126 Davies memo., 4 Sept. 1944, Stilwell Papers, box 15.
127 See FRUS, Quebec, 36, 44, 46. The State Department also came in for considerable public criticism in this period. See e.g. FO 371, AN1176/325/45.
128 Cab, 27 Sept. 1944, CAB 65/43.
129 E.g. Bullock, *Bevin*, II, 315ff.; Chandos, *Memoirs*, 322.
130 Dalton Diary, 1 Sept. 1944.
131 *Addison*, 229ff.
132 *Moran*, 183.
133 Wheeler-Bennett, *Action This Day*, 52; Dalton Diary, 23 March, 15 June and 13 July 1944; *Cadogan Diaries*, 30 May and 3 Aug. 1944.
134 Grigg to Grigg, 10 April 1944, Grigg Papers, box 9/6; Montgomery to Grigg, 8 Aug. 1944, ibid, box 9; *Pownall*, 10 June 1944; *Bryant*, II, 22–3, 185.

CHAPTER EIGHTEEN

THE WAR AGAINST JAPAN

IN 1944, the racial aspects and possible racial consequences of the Far Eastern war continued to be a matter of concern to some in the West. Not that it was widely appreciated that the position of the white man in Asia was undergoing a fundamental change: even an Indian—though a very 'establishment' one, Sir Firoz Khan Noon—could tell the Commonwealth Prime Ministers when they met in London that the point of encouraging the French, Dutch and Portuguese to follow Britain's lead in granting increased political responsibility to Asian subject peoples was to enable the latter 'to take their rightful place as friends and supporters of their European rulers.' No one contradicted him.[1]

To some, however, the outlook was a far less comfortable one. 'The white race has lost considerable prestige', the Australian Minister to China warned the Advisory War Council in Canberra, adding that '. . . it would be an error to suppose that we would be welcomed by the native populations when we return.'[2] In the United States, too, the whole subject of racial prejudice and conflict was receiving increased and anxious attention in 1944,[3] while even Churchill talked of the need to make use of a Council of Asia after the war 'to prevent trouble arising with the yellow races.'[4]

Yet for the Prime Minister, it was Europe—'the storm centre; the place where the weather comes from'—that remained the focus of his attention. Nor did a common 'whiteness', as against 'the yellow races', prevent the British and the Americans from continuing to experience considerable trouble in their dealings with one another East of Suez. 'We have been finding Far Eastern affairs chronically difficult as an element in Anglo-American relations', wrote a senior member of the British Embassy in Washington, and Halifax himself noted 'a very general popular attitude of distrust' on the subject in the United States, where the State Department appeared to regard it as axiomatic that the aims of the two countries were fundamentally divergent.

'The disturbing fact remains', cabled the Ambassador in May 1944, 'that when, for reasons of domestic politics or for the promotion of some private interest or doctrine, it appears expedient to belabour the British, attacks on our conduct of affairs in the Far East can be sure not only of popular acceptance but also of approval by a great number of individuals in the armed services and in Government departments. For in both spheres there are many who are highly conscious of the rapid growth of American power and . . . have no doubt that America must dominate the Pacific scene. This is a prospect which gives pleasure not only to American imperialist and American commercial and financial leaders, but also to missionaries and educators and to almost every kind of league and association seeking to regenerate Asia by the spread of the principles which they uphold.'

The Far Eastern Department of the Foreign Office summarized matters by writing of 'a steady deterioration in Anglo-United States collaboration as regards that part of the globe, which is itself adversely affecting the prosecution of the war.'[5]

Assumptions about American predominance, present and future, in Far Eastern affairs were indeed by now widespread in the United States. Even the cry of 'Pacific first', though still to be heard in, for example, the columns of the *San Francisco Examiner*, was now being sounded less often as the growing might of the country's presence in that ocean made it seem superfluous.[6] Meanwhile the interests of the United States in the region were seen as being paramount. She had, the State Department's Office of Far Eastern Affairs pointed out, 'longer coastlines on the Pacific than has any other power. [She has] more trade in and across the Pacific than has any other power. [She has] more wide-flung cultural interests in the Pacific than has any other power.'[7] Some also continued to advocate that Washington should not merely take the lead in the making of the peace in that part of the world, but should dictate it. Having beaten the Japanese single-handed, argued the *Washington Times Herald*, 'we can restore such of those pieces of empire as we decide upon to the British, Dutch, French and Portuguese on our own terms, and they will have them henceforth by grace of our sufferance and generosity, and the world will know it.'[8]

At the same time there was a growing emphasis upon the vital economic role that the Far East could play in the post-war life of the United States.

'Good relations with China', argued Congressman Walter H. Judd, 'are also of importance from the standpoint of our future economic interests in the Pacific. In order to furnish food and supplies for ourselves, . . . our Allies and hungry millions being liberated from Axis tyranny, we are being compelled to build up American production far in excess of what we at home can buy and pay for . . . A free Orient will become a huge market.'[9]

Owen Lattimore, writing in 1944, made the same point: 'Americans must realize that Asiatic problems are not academic. They work out to a plus or minus in American exports, imports, jobs—or breadlines, because unless we do our share in developing markets in Asia for what we produce, . . . we shall not be able to employ all the men who should do the producing.'[10] In a similar spirit, the magazine *Amerasia*—a decidedly left-wing journal in

American terms, be it noted—described India as 'the "new economic frontier" for the American economy',[11] while Vice President Wallace, after visiting China, talked of America entering 'the era of the Pacific', which would bring with it vast possibilities for trade and development. (He had already outlined this theme in a pamphlet, *Our Job in the Pacific*, which was drafted with the help of Lattimore's wife and published by the American Council of the I.P.R.)[12] In other words, it was by no means solely the right-wing, capitalist element in American life that looked forward to a successful commercial assault in Asia.

Such an endeavour would, of course, require that equality of opportunity for the U.S.A. that Roosevelt had demanded as regards the Middle East. As one American staff officer, then serving in S.E.A.C., was to comment subsequently,

'In Southeast Asia, as in China, United States policy, it seemed, was to dissociate ourselves as often as possible from the imperialist aims of our colonialist allies, while vigorously asserting on occasion our claim to enjoy equally with them the commercial—and implicitly the strategic—rewards of colonialism, in the measure that the institution survived our disapproval.'[13]

This summarizes well what had been, from the nineteenth century, a basic ambiguity about America's attitude towards colonial territories. It also underlines what we have already noted in the context of Western policies towards China from the signing of the 'unequal treaties' onwards: an element in the American approach which, perhaps best described as self-deception on a large scale, looked to other white imperialists like downright hypocrisy.

Thus, closely allied to the very understandable American image of itself in 1944 as being the predominant power in the Far East, there continued to exist those critical views of Britain's effort and motives in the area that Halifax had so deplored. There were still, it is true, a few appreciative voices to be heard, of which the *New York Times* was one.[14] Nor should the open and extreme contempt of the *Chicago Tribune* for Britain's contribution against Japan be taken as typical.[15] In addition, one or two Americans in prominent positions were becoming concerned over the possible effect on future Anglo-American relations if Britain were not permitted by Washington to take as full a part as possible in the Far Eastern war. If she were kept out, wrote James Byrnes to Roosevelt, 'the feeling engendered would make difficult the settlement of peace problems.'[16] Similarly, Winant submitted from London that if the United States insisted on keeping the war to herself, there would spring up in America 'a hatred for Great Britain that will make for schisms in the post-war years that will defeat everything that men have died for in this war.'[17] Hull himself warned the President that the avoidance of commercial friction, the settlement of the Lend Lease issue, and the building up of 'collaboration to face the problems of the post-war world' would all be jeopardized unless the British were 'brought . . . into the war operations in the Far East to the greatest possible extent.'[18]

Yet there remained, as British officials ruefully noted, a marked duality about American attitudes in general: on the one hand, a quickness to criticize Britain for not doing more against Japan; on the other—and we shall see this to be particularly marked in U.S. Navy circles—a jealous belief that that war was a United States preserve.[19] There continued to exist, also, a tendency to adopt a low estimate of Britain's motives in the same context. To Morgenthau at Quebec, for example, Roosevelt observed 'that he knew why the British wanted to join in the war in the Pacific. All they want is Singapore back.'[20] Similarly, the assumption that the two countries were far apart in their aims was made outside as well as within the State Department. Henry Luce, for instance, head of the *Time-Life* group, asserted to a number of British acquaintances that 'we lacked in the East the common ideals which animated us in the West', while the remarks of John Davies and others on the subject led an official in London to conclude that 'all Americans seem to have it firmly in their minds that it is impossible for Britain and America to see eye to eye on anything east of Suez.'[21] Political warfare questions thus continued to give rise to friction, and the head of the relevant British mission to the United States reported that Elmer Davis and others below him in the O.W.I. 'made no secret of the fact that they wanted to see us thrown out of our Far Eastern colonies for good and all.'[22]

This strong American criticism, bordering at times on hostility, aroused disquiet and resentment on the fringes of, as well as within, official circles in London. Thus, a special meeting of the Council of the Royal Institute of International Affairs was convened at the instigation of Lord Hailey in order to discuss whether or not Chatham House should remain affiliated to the I.P.R., which 'had developed into an organisation which was perpetually critical of Great Britain and her policy.'[23] At the same time attempts were made to analyse what it was that lay behind the United States' own sense of destiny in the Far East, with G. F. Hudson of the Foreign Office Research Department writing of 'the American geopolitical wind which now fills [Roosevelt's] sails', and of 'a special form of national romanticism inspired by traditions . . . of Frontier pioneering', which 'in Wallace's ideology is consciously anti-imperialist . . . yet can easily become bellicose if it meets with obstruction.'[24]

Nevertheless, whatever America's motives and however exasperating her criticisms, the overriding need, in British eyes, remained that of keeping in touch and as far as possible in step with Washington over Far Eastern affairs, and of trying once again to make out Britain's case. This was the conclusion, for example, which was arrived at by the special Council meeting at Chatham House, mentioned above, and it also continued to be the prevailing line within the Foreign Office. Indeed, the Office impatiently wanted more public statements to be made regarding the country's determination and existing contribution in terms of the fight against Japan. Britain's entire standing in the United States, it was again asserted, was likely to depend 'upon the part played by [her] arms in the Pacific war.'[25]

Even so, those in Whitehall and Southeast Asia who were directly concerned with Far Eastern affairs still believed that in several respects Britain herself was making the problem greater than it need be. They continued to feel, for example, that far too little attention was being paid to the subjects in question in London, where Mountbatten's Chief of Staff in S.E.A.C., who arrived for a short visit, found that '"they" ... were absorbed ... in European affairs to the almost total exclusion of Far Eastern problems.'[26] 'We still feel as unloved, unhonoured and unsung East of Suez as ever we did', wrote Dening from S.E.A.C. headquarters.[27] Coupled with this was the failure to take major decisions at a high level as to what Britain's long-term policies should be regarding various aspects of the Far Eastern scene. Again, Dening wrote to urge that this should be remedied, while the Head of the North American Department in London admitted that 'our apparent lack of frankness [with the Americans] is often accounted for by the fact that we have not yet got agreement in the War Cabinet on a policy.' In order to make clear what Britain's policy was, concluded the Far Eastern Department, 'we must [first] formulate it ourselves. This is a formidable task and it may be argued that it is impossible to tackle such long-term issues now. But they must be tackled some day, and the longer we put it off the more will American aversion increase.'[28]

Once again, in other words, British pragmatism and American millennial attitudes were making for an uneasy partnership. In more specific terms, the obstructive role of Churchill over the case of Burma, which has been illustrated for earlier periods, will again become apparent below. Siam, too, will figure as an example of British procrastination over policy in 1944, while an even greater failure, this time involving the whole of war-time strategy and politics in the region, will be dealt with later in this chapter.

Meanwhile, concern also continued to be expressed about the degree of enthusiasm which could be expected from the British public and armed forces for the war against Japan alone. Thus, a Foreign Office memorandum suggested that Whitehall 'still [had] to tackle the job of stirring up or reviving anti-Japanese feeling among our own people as an incentive to our contribution in the final onslaught against Japan.'[29] An M.P. who visited India supplied supporting evidence for the fears of some officials when she reported that British troops there 'were anxious to defeat the Germans whom they consider to be their enemies, but they could not see that the Far East mattered to them';[30] the Prime Minister himself believed that 'financial inducements' should be offered to those who would find themselves still fighting after the war in Europe had come to an end.[31] Considerations such as these were, indeed, now coming more to the fore, as great strides were taken towards defeating Germany, and as the Far Eastern conflict itself entered a phase of increasing Allied success.

Anglo-American difficulties east of Suez were now occurring against a background far removed from the one of defeat, confusion and peril in 1942. The decline in Japan's fortunes that was taking place was symbolized by the resignation of General Tojo as Prime Minister in July, his successor being General Koiso Kuniaki. Only from the Chinese theatre was there still no Allied success to report, with the Japanese themselves mounting a vigorous spring offensive there in the direction of the Hankow–Canton railway and the bases of the American 14th Air Force, while the long-awaited Chinese attack southwards from Yunnan into Burma came to nothing when eventually attempted.[32]

In South East Asia Command, in contrast, the fortunes of the Allies at last changed decisively during the period. In the north of Burma, where the road and pipeline from Ledo were slowly being pushed ahead, Stilwell surprised not only the Japanese but also the British[33] by seizing the airfield at Myitkyina in May—the town itself was not secured until August—thus taking a large step towards linking up with the Chinese by land, and providing an important staging post on the air route to Kunming. At the other, southern extremity of the front, in Arakan, gains had been made and Japanese attacks repulsed during the winter months as a prelude to further successes in the spring and summer.[34]

In between the two wings, the second Chindit operation took place in March, during the course of which Wingate himself was killed; thereafter the Chindits moved northwards to come under Stilwell's command during April and May.[35] Above all, however, beginning in March, there were fought the ferocious battles of Imphal and Kohima, as the Japanese strove to break through into India, were held, and, in June, decisively broken, with Slim's Fourteenth Army, campaigning now in the monsoon season, taking up the pursuit.[36] These last successes represented the vindication of British and Indian arms against the Japanese, following the humiliations of 1941–42. Even so, they tended to be overshadowed by the dramatic events in Europe following 6 June; nor could they undo all the consequences of those earlier defeats in terms of British prestige and the future of British rule in Southeast Asia.

Meanwhile, a reinforced British Eastern Fleet, though checked for a while by reports of a strong Japanese naval concentration at Singapore, carried out raids across the Indian Ocean and Bay of Bengal.[37] In terms of seapower, however, the Pacific remained the decisive theatre, where the submarines of the U.S. Navy were beginning to demonstrate to the full Japan's economic vulnerability by strangling her shipping movements to an extent which promised to limit severely Tokyo's ability to continue the war. American (and in MacArthur's case, Australian) advances in land–sea–air operations were likewise more spectacular than the successes being won, mile by mile, as it were, in Burma. In the South West Pacific Area, landings were carried out in the Admiralty Islands in February, and in March on the northern coast of New Guinea, the campaign in that territory being brought to a triumphant conclusion by the end of July.[38] The way was now open for MacArthur to move on towards his main target, the Philippines. Shortly after the end of our period, in October 1944, after first covering his flank by landing in the Palau group, the General achieved the goal of his planning since he had been driven from Corregidor, when he launched his forces against Leyte. As he had dramatically promised, he had returned.

The most direct threat of all to Japan's empire, however, was being mounted by Admiral Nimitz in the Central Pacific. There, the Marshall Islands were assaulted in January 1944, and in the following month the Japanese base on Truk, in the Carolines, was destroyed. In June, a massive air victory was won above Guam in the Mariana islands, in the Philippine Sea, while in June and July a series of amphibious attacks were carried out on the same Marianas—on Saipan, Tinian and Guam itself, islands that were to provide vital bases from which B 29 bombers could strike at Japan's home islands.[39]

In all, these military developments underlined the predominant part being played by the United States in the Allied war effort against Japan. Despite the size of the Japanese forces remaining in China—and their offensive in the east of the country was the largest land operation that they mounted during the war, involving 620,000 troops[40]—the American successes in the Pacific also diminished the perceived value and likely role of Chiang Kai-shek's army and territory, with the alternative bomber bases in the Marianas becoming available at a time when, as we shall see in the following chapter, Washington's impatience over the Chinese contribution to the struggle was greatly increasing.[41] In contrast, the expectation of an eventual Soviet intervention against Japan continued to figure prominently in the thinking of the Western Allies.[42] Such a development promised to over-shadow the role of not only China, but quite possibly Britain as well, and again it was the Americans, not the British, who were to conduct the detailed military negotiations that were involved and which Stalin indicated could begin soon after the Quebec Conference.[43]

It was also within the American ranks that there took place the major debate on Pacific strategy in this period, a debate which exacerbated existing Army–Navy tensions and which centred on the question of whether to by-pass the Philippines in order to strike at Formosa, as King and Nimitz advocated, or, as MacArthur insisted, to include an invasion of the Philippines as an essential element in the plan of campaign. The President himself was drawn into the argument, meeting Nimitz and MacArthur at Pearl Harbour in July. On the General's side, a strong political element was involved, as indicated in his declaration that 'the failure of the United States to liberate its people would be a blot upon its honor.' (He would personally land with the first of his troops, he told Stimson, whereupon 'the whole Philippines people will arise, with their faith in the United States restored.') The outcome was a victory for MacArthur, despite the fact that, earlier in the year, the Joint Chiefs of Staff, who, in purely strategic terms may well have been correct in their judgment, had inclined very much in favour of the Central Pacific thrust.[44]

Other major strategic questions likewise awaited American, rather than

British, answers and decisions. How much time after the defeat of Germany, for example, should it be assumed that it would take to bring Japan to her knees? The British estimate was two years; American planning was based originally on one year; the figure presented in the final report of the Combined Chiefs of Staff at Quebec was that favoured by the U.S. Joint Chiefs: eighteen months.[45] Or again, was Japan to be invaded, or could she be blockaded and bombed into surrender? Against a background of much debate in Washington, Marshall gave the Combined Chiefs of Staff the answer that an invasion would be necessary.[46] Should nuclear weapons, if successfully developed, be employed in the Far East? Following the Quebec meeting, Roosevelt and Churchill agreed at Hyde Park that, were a bomb to become available, 'it might perhaps, after mature consideration, be used against the Japanese, who should be warned that this bombardment will be repeated until they surrender.'[47]

Over all such issues, Britain's position was a secondary one, and Churchill recognized as much. 'We must regard ourselves as junior partners in the war against Japan', he told the Commonwealth Prime Ministers in May.[48] One might disapprove of certain features of that war—Churchill, for example, thought that the Americans were 'using steam-hammer methods to crack nuts in the Pacific'[49]—but there was little to be done about it. Essentially it was a matter of resources, and the growing imbalance between the two partners which was noted above in over-all terms was especially marked in the Far East. As the official historian of Britain's military campaigns against Japan has put it, 'by the end of 1943, America was in a position to launch her [Pacific] counter-offensive, its speed accelerating month by month in almost geometrical progression. In a short period of eighteen months it had advanced some 4,000 nautical miles from the Gilbert and Solomon Islands to Iwojima and Okinawa . . . The Southeast Asia theatre was a complete contrast. The Pacific, Middle East and European theatres needed practically all the assault shipping and landing craft that the United States and Britain could produce. As a result, all major operations in Southeast Asia until 1945 had to be on land, aided by such small-scale amphibious assaults as could be undertaken. In these circumstances the only contribution the Allied forces there could make initially towards the defeat of Japan was to secure India as a firm base, to contain as much of the Japanese strength as possible in Burma and Malaya, and to gain contact with China by both air and land if possible . . .'[50]

As Churchill acknowledged at Quebec, Britain's effort had reached its peak, while that of the United States was still increasing. This meant among other things that, at the same time as pressing for Britain to be allowed her 'fair share' of the main operations against Japan, as the Prime Minister did at the same Conference in the name of 'the future good relations of the two countries', one had also to ask to be provided with some of the essential means (such as tank-landing craft) to make such a British contribution practicable in the first place.[51] The question was even raised at Quebec, though it came to nothing, of possibly obtaining one or two

American divisions from Europe to help in operations in Southeast Asia aimed at recapturing Rangoon.[52]

Within this Southeast Asian theatre, meanwhile, the underlying divergence between the American pull in the direction of China and that of Britain towards Singapore continued as before. It was epitomized by the affair of the 'Axiom' and Stilwell missions, which, in anticipation of the chapter dealing in detail with Southeast Asia, will be outlined here since it concerned strategic planning of the broadest kind. The matter came to a head in January 1944, when Mountbatten, supported by his Commanders in Chief, produced a new plan, 'Axiom', for S.E.A.C. operations, a plan which he claimed was in accordance with his over-all directive to maintain and improve links with China. Nevertheless, this 'Axiom' scheme did not have a place within it for Stilwell's intended drive overland to China via Myitkyina, the reason given for the omission being Chiang Kai-shek's refusal to play his full part by attacking from Yunnan regardless of the absence of major amphibious operations in the Bay of Bengal. 'In view of this refusal', Mountbatten submitted, 'it is not possible to establish overland communications with China within any reasonable period.' Instead, the aim should be to open up a port in the China Sea via operations against Sumatra and Malaya, S.E.A.C.'s boundaries being extended accordingly to include not only the port selected but also Hongkong.

Stilwell, for his part, vigorously opposed this 'Axiom' proposal in a memorandum which Mountbatten duly forwarded to London and Washington. An attack by way of Sumatra, the Deputy Supreme Commander argued, would be a frontal one and would require the construction of new air bases; to proceed via Burma and Yunnan, on the other hand, would be a flanking movement, with air bases already available in India, would raise instead of prolong the blockade of China with its own valuable airfields, and would not depend for its execution on the early defeat of Germany and the arrival in S.E.A.C. of extensive new resources. As John Davies, still advising Stilwell on political affairs, put it in a supporting memorandum to Hopkins:

'S.E.A.C.'s plans for the future heavily discount the importance of China as an ally and the Chinese position on Japan's flank . . . [They] reinforce the argument that Lord Louis' command is primarily concerned with the reoccupation, under British leadership, of colonial Southeast Asia. The main American concern is, of course, to strike the Japanese where it hurts them most. This is not in Sumatra and Malaya. It is in East China, Formosa, Manchuria and Japan itself. The quickest and most direct approach to this vital area is straight across Burma and Southeast China.'[53]*

In order to argue the 'Axiom' case, Mountbatten despatched to London

* Looking back thirty years later, John Davies believes that Stilwell's campaign across northern Burma to reach China, which he himself supported so emphatically at the time, was a futile enterprise. (Conversations with the author.)

and Washington a mission led by Wedemeyer. Stilwell also, without consulting his Supreme Commander, sent Davies and two staff officers ahead of the Wedemeyer party in order 'to combat S.E.A.C.' in Washington.[54] The outcome, not surprisingly, was that the Americans supported Stilwell, even though his fellow-countryman, Chennault, was still fiercely critical of his ideas. Hopkins endorsed Davies' memorandum on the situation when passing it on to the President; the Joint Chiefs insisted that the campaign in upper Burma must go ahead; Roosevelt, too, joined in the rejection of Mountbatten's proposal, emphasizing the importance of obtaining air bases in China as the American Pacific advance approached the China–Luzon–Formosa triangles.[55] 'The British have never been whole-hearted in regard to Burma', wrote Stimson in his diary, 'and this would seem to confirm all the suspicion that their critics have said of them.'[56]

Churchill's support for the 'Axiom' plan was thus not enough to secure its adoption,[57] and Stilwell's surprise seizure of Myitkyina airfield in May helped to ensure that the North Burma cause would be sustained. When Mountbatten's new directive eventually arrived from the Combined Chiefs of Staff early in June—and Anglo-American differences had helped delay it by six months—the development of land communications with China remained one of its features, as part of a maximum ground and air effort that was to be made during the current monsoon season.[58] Even then, however, the affairs of S.E.A.C. could not be taken as settled, since the resounding defeat of the enemy in the Imphal–Kohima area proceeded to open up a new range of possibilities. Mountbatten had thus to ask in July for further instructions, with his Commanders in Chief and Stilwell, together for once, all anxious to pursue the retreating Japanese overland, whereas the Chiefs of Staff in London were inclined to wait until the resources were available for an amphibious assault on Rangoon.[59]

The Combined Chiefs therefore produced a new directive at Quebec. Once more, the desirability of opening a road into China was included in the document at the insistence of Marshall and his colleagues. Mountbatten's task was now set forth as being to clear Burma of the enemy at the earliest possible moment, with an advance across the Chindwin River (operation 'Capital') taking place as required to protect the air and land routes to Yunnan, and preparations being made for an air- and sea-borne attack on Rangoon (operation 'Dracula') in March 1945.[60] The need to accommodate both American and British desires in the region was thus again apparent.

The delays during 1944 in producing new directives for S.E.A.C. were not, however, simply a matter of Anglo-American divergencies. They sprang also from a major difference of opinion and a prolonged struggle within British official circles over the country's contribution to the Far Eastern war—an issue which had significant political as well as purely strategic aspects. A detailed narrative of the debate in question can be read elsewhere,[61] but its main features need to be illustrated here. It originated with the Prime Minister's belated rejection of the final report that the Combined Chiefs of Staff had presented to him and the President at Cairo, a report which set forth in broad terms the strategy that the Allies should pursue against Japan, and which had been initialled by the President and Prime Minister as being approved in principle as a basis for further investigations.

What the report had envisaged, it will be recalled, was a concentration of effort in the Pacific, where a British naval contribution might begin to be built up in the summer of 1944; operations in Southeast Asia would mean-while be restricted to land and minor amphibious movements in Burma. Now, however, at a meeting of the Defence Committee on 19 January, Churchill declared that 'it was the first he had heard of these proposals', and that the promised intervention against Japan by the Soviet Union (a pledge which had, of course, been known when the C.C.S. document was approved at Cairo) entirely altered the circumstances involved, fore-shadowing as it did the use of bases in the Soviet Maritime Provinces. Nor was the Prime Minister at all content when he read—or re-read—of the limited role that was envisaged for S.E.A.C. 'He was dismayed at the thought that a large British army and air force would stand inactive in India during the whole of 1944.' Above all, he argued, operation 'Culverin', his long-sought landing in Sumatra, should not be discarded.[62]

There thus began what the official historian has called 'perhaps the most serious disagreement of the war' between the Prime Minister and the Chiefs of Staff, a disagreement that was to continue in various forms until the eve of the Quebec Conference, and that Field Marshal Brooke (as he had become) believed, in March, might well 'lead to the resignation of the Chiefs of Staff Committee ... [since] Winston ... overrides our opinions and our advice.'[63] Brooke and his two Service colleagues based their arguments, both on what they saw as being best for the Allies as a whole, and on what they believed to be in Britain's separate interest. In each case, the matter of timing was of the greatest importance. Thus, from the Allied point of view, the Chiefs of Staff held that to concentrate on a single main attack from the east would bring them to the Philippines six months earlier than would converging advances from both east and west.[64] As for the purely British effort, the earliest that 'Culverin' could be mounted would be the spring of 1945, with a move on to Singapore perhaps becoming possible by January 1946; by then, however, the Americans would be far advanced with their Pacific drive, and might even have reached Formosa.[65] In short, 'whatever strategy we follow, the major credit for the defeat of Japan is likely to go to the Americans. Their resources and their geographical position', the C.O.S. continued, 'make them the predominant partner in Japan's defeat. The first mortal thrust will be the Pacific thrust, upon which the Americans have already embarked. We should not be excluded from our part in this thrust.'[66]

In advancing such arguments, the Chiefs of Staff did not ignore political considerations, concerned as they were for Britain's prestige and citing as they did in support of their case Australian and New Zealand calls for an increased British presence in the Pacific area of operations. (Curtin, for example, emphasized in London in May that 'he desired to see the British flag flying in the Far East as dominantly and as early as possible.')[67] These Commonwealth wishes, it was suggested, could be met, not only by a Royal Navy presence, but by building up a British and Commonwealth land and air force which could operate in the Southwest Pacific, with Australia as its base; this could lead after the defeat of Germany, the C.O.S. thought, to a British command in the area, although the Central Pacific and supreme command would remain in American hands.[68]

Not surprisingly, however, political arguments figured more prominently still as part of the opposing case developed by the Prime Minister. In this, he summarized British aims in the Far Eastern war as being 'to engage Japanese forces with the maximum intensity, and the same time to regain British territory.'[69] The first of these objects was for him to be attained, not by a land advance in Burma—'he was determined that the minimum of effort should be employed in this disease-ridden country'—nor by 'dragging our lines of communication all round the south of Australia.'[70] The place to utilise the British military strength that was based on India, he asserted, was across the Bay of Bengal, in an amphibious attack directed against Sumatra, for preference, or as a second best, Rangoon.[71] Beyond them, moreover, there beckoned Singapore, which he was describing by September as 'the supreme British objective in the whole of the Indian and Far Eastern theatres . . ., the only prize that will restore British prestige in this region.'[72]

Here, in other words, the Prime Minister was concerned with the second of his two objectives, the recovery of Britain's territories, and in this context he saw the long-term threat as likely to come, not from Japan, but from Britain's ally, the United States:

'If the Japanese should withdraw from our Malayan possessions', he wrote, 'or make peace as a result of the main American thrust, the United States Government would after the victory feel greatly strengthened in its view that all possessions in the East Indian Archipelago should be placed under some international body upon which the United States would exercise a decisive control. They would feel with conviction: "We have won this victory and liberated these places, and we must have the dominating say in their future and derive full profit from their produce, especially oil."'[73]

So much for Churchill's own assertion that British and American interests 'could not clash.' Meanwhile, for the more strictly military side of his case, the Prime Minister sought assistance from Roosevelt, and obtained it, despite the latter's dislike of a Malaya–Sumatra strategy: questioned by cable in March, the President replied that American operations in the Pacific would not require the presence there of the Royal Navy during 1944, and probably not before the summer of 1945.[74] For support in political terms, on the other hand, Churchill turned to his own Cabinet colleagues, and again he was rewarded, at least in the early stages of the debate. Oliver Lyttelton, for example, warned the Chiefs of Staff that 'if our operations formed merely a part of the great American advance, we should be swamped.

It was essential', he suggested, 'that we should be able to say to our own possessions in the Far East that we had liberated them by our own efforts.' Attlee agreed. 'The effect in India, and, indeed, in England, of strong operations against Malaya to recapture Singapore', he argued, 'would be very much greater than the effect of operations through New Guinea towards the Philippines, in which far the greater share would be borne by the Americans. It was in Malaya, Borneo and the Netherlands East Indies that our reputation has suffered, and it was there that the world would expect to see it rehabilitated.'[75]

Eden, too, weighed in in February on behalf of the Foreign Office, writing to Churchill: 'If we are merely dragged along at the tail of the Americans in the Pacific, we shall get no credit whatever for our share in the joint operations.' He attached to his note a paper by Dening, 'Political Implications of Far Eastern Strategy', in which Mountbatten's political adviser attacked the existing strategy in that part of the world as being 'an American one in which the British role is merely contributory and in which there is no place for an essentially British effort.' Operations carried out against Pacific islands, continued Dening, would make little impact on the minds of Asian peoples, including the Japanese, whereas the Sumatra–Malaya approach being proposed by S.E.A.C. would have 'immediate psychological and political effects.' If the Pacific strategy were to be accepted, he concluded, 'and if there is no major British role in the Far Eastern war, then it is no exaggeration to say that the solidarity of the British Commonwealth and its influence in the maintenance of peace in the Far East will be irretrievably damaged.'[76]

Before the major issue, thus defined by each side, could be decided, there were also various practical questions to be answered. One involved the base facilities that would be available for the rival strategies. Could India, with its grave economic and social difficulties, sustain an enlarged campaign from the west?[77] The Chiefs of Staff were extremely doubtful. On the other hand, could the necessary bases for an attack from the east be built up in Australia, bearing in mind that country's own problems in the field of manpower and its economy generally—problems which Curtin spelled out when he came to London for the Commonwealth meeting in May? With some reluctance, the Australian Government agreed to a British mission going out to investigate the matter, but the resulting report was not available until the end of the summer.[78]

Meanwhile there emerged a compromise proposal that envisaged a line of attack in between the extremes of the Bay of Bengal and the Philippines. This so-called 'middle strategy', as put forward by the Chiefs of Staff and welcomed by Canberra and Wellington, would entail British and Commonwealth forces, based on Australia, operating in the Southwest Pacific on the left of MacArthur. In the original version, the axis of advance was to be Timor–Celebes–Borneo–Saigon; then, as revised, it became Amboina–Borneo, with the possibility of moving thereafter either northwards towards China or westwards towards Malaya.[79] As the difficulties that lay in the way of mounting operation 'Culverin' became more apparent, Government Ministers were attracted by this 'middle-strategy' compromise. The Foreign Office, too, shifted its ground, accepting 'the relegation of S.E.A.C. to a secondary role for the time being' and declaring that the new proposal would meet the wide-ranging desiderata of reestablishing British prestige, stimulating the Chinese and the peoples of British territories occupied by the Japanese, supporting the Dominions, and making possible collaboration with the Americans in the final assault on Japan.[80]

Even the 'middle strategy' gave rise to another question, however. What would be the relationship between such a British and Commonwealth force and General MacArthur? This extremely delicate matter, which involved the wishes of the Australian Government and Army, as well as the rivalries within the American armed Services, will be considered in more detail in the chapter dealing with the Southwest Pacific. For the moment, it is sufficient to say that, at the London end of things, Churchill's first idea, as expressed in June, was that a force operating on MacArthur's left would be so distinct operationally that it could come under Mountbatten and within an extended S.E.A.C. area.[81] The Chiefs of Staff, however, envisaged that the force would function under MacArthur's supreme command, he in turn becoming responsible to the Combined Chiefs, instead of to the Joint Chiefs alone.[82] This last possibility was discussed in an informal way, with generally encouraging results, when Marshall and King visited Britain in June, although the outcome, as we shall see, was the arousing of much suspicion and turbulence in some American circles, with Churchill having to reassure MacArthur that Britain had no intention of trying to undermine his position.[83] As for the Joint Chiefs of Staff in Washington, the most that they would do before the Quebec Conference was to accept the idea of 'a British Empire task force' operating under MacArthur, while giving no undertakings as to the General's becoming responsible to the C.C.S.

Quite apart from this problem, however, the 'middle strategy' began to decline in favour. Criticisms of it made by the U.S. Joint Chiefs, together with S.E.A.C.'s successes at Imphal and Kohima, prompted Churchill to a further outburst against the idea of relegating Mountbatten's forces to a minor role, and to return to his schemes for landings on the island of Simalur, followed by ones in Sumatra and at Singapore.[84] (These 'Culverin' operations, of course, like an attack on Rangoon, which was increasingly favoured in London,[85] would absorb the troops who might otherwise go to Australia.) The idea of sending a British and Commonwealth force to the Southwest Pacific did nevertheless go forward to the Quebec meeting, along with other, alternative British proposals, but was there withdrawn in the light of the American acceptance of a Royal Navy task force for Pacific operations, and of the new opportunities for S.E.A.C. that were opening up in the direction of Rangoon.[86]

By this time, however, the length of the internal debate on these politico-strategic issues had seriously delayed Britain's preparations for the Far Eastern war. It had also strained matters greatly between the Chiefs of Staff and Prime Minister, the former adhering firmly to their position even when Churchill attempted to get his way by communicating with them individually rather than collectively, and by beginning to work directly with the planning staff on 'Culverin'. For all those involved, it was a wearying and exasperating business. 'Really ghastly', was how Eden described one of the many meetings that were entailed, while Attlee summarized another as having been 'two hours of wishful thinking.'[87] Within the Foreign Office, the official responsible for liaison with the Services lamented the delay in coming to a decision because it was preventing 'a frank discussion with the Americans.' Rightly, he went on to place the blame for this state of affairs upon the Prime Minister's repeated postponing of a final choice rather than accept the demise of 'Culverin'. 'I do not think', he added, 'that when the history of the discussions on our Far Eastern strategy which have taken place comes to be written it will be found very edifying.'[88]

Leading military figures shared these sentiments.[89] 'From first to last', wrote Mountbatten's Chief of Staff, 'there has been muddle and mismanagement',[90] and from his position at Churchill's right hand, General Ismay agreed. 'When history comes to be written', he confided to a friend in May, 'I believe that the waffling that there has been for nearly nine months over the basic question of our strategy in the Far East will be one of the black spots in the record of British Higher Direction of War . . .'[91] As for Brooke, he summed up the position as he saw it in a despairing diary entry in May:

'Curtin and MacArthur are determined to stand together, support each other, and allow no outside interference. Winston is determined Mountbatten must be given an operation to carry out; Andrew Cunningham [now First Sea Lord] is equally determined that Mountbatten should not control the Eastern Fleet; Americans wish to gather all laurels connected with the Pacific fighting, and Winston is equally determined that we should not be tied to the apron strings of the Americans! How on earth are we to steer a straight course between all these snags and difficulties?'[92]

Despite the Prime Minister's chief share of the responsibility for this situation, however, he did in the end loyally and vigorously put forward to the Americans at Quebec a proposition that he had earlier opposed: that a major British naval contribution should be made to the main operations in the Pacific. (This was necessary, he had come to recognize, on political grounds if no other, and whatever the outcome. 'A refusal of our offer by the Americans', he wrote in August, 'would be of enormous value as a bulwark against any accusation that we had not backed them up in the war against Japan.')[93] It was not a project which commended itself to Admiral King on behalf of the U.S. Navy. In the meetings of the Combined Chiefs of Staff he continued to raise difficulties, and to protest that 'it would be entirely unacceptable for the British main fleet to be employed for political reasons in the Pacific and thus necessitate the withdrawal of some of the United

States fleet.' To Nimitz in private he observed sourly 'that the British should be told what they can get, not [asked] what they want.'[94]

Roosevelt, however, during one of the main sessions at Quebec, had already decided otherwise: 'The British Fleet', he declared, 'was no sooner offered than accepted.' The final report of the Combined Chiefs of Staff therefore recorded as much, with the proviso that the Royal Navy's units must be 'balanced and self-supporting'—a major problem, this, in the light of Pacific distances—and that their specific employment would be decided 'from time to time in accordance with the prevailing circumstances.'[95] Thus, the naval question received a clearer answer than did the accompanying British proposal that the R.A.F. should participate in the very-long-range bombing of Japan. This last matter was likely to involve considerable difficulties where the provision of bases was concerned, and at Quebec was left open for more detailed consideration.

At the end of this period, then, the broad shape of Britain's contribution to the later stages of the war against Japan was at last decided. She would have at least some part in the main thrust; meanwhile, in Southeast Asia, she would press on in the direction of Rangoon and of Singapore, where, Churchill frankly informed his American listeners at Quebec, 'a grievous and shameful blow to British prestige must be avenged in battle.' Nevertheless, the contribution of not only Britain but of the Commonwealth as a whole to the defeat of Japan, however useful, was clearly going to remain a fairly small one when compared to that of the United States. Nor did the achievement of an agreement over strategy mean that the two Allies were about to enter the final phases of the war at one politically, where the East was concerned. Even where the gap between their respective expectations had in practice been narrowed, long-standing assumptions and suspicions, particularly on the American side, continued to hamper the development of anything in the nature of a joint approach. The case of China showed as much.

Notes to Chapter Eighteen

1 Minutes of 5 May 1944, PREM 4, 42/5.
2 AAWC, 5 April 1944, A2682, vol. VII.
3 See e.g. *New York Times*, 4, 14 and 18 April, 6 June 1944; *New York Herald Tribune*, 6 March 1944; *Christian Science Monitor*, 28 Sept. 1944.
4 Minutes of 9 May 1944, PREM 4, 42/5.
5 FO 371, F2300, 2469 and 3896/993/61.
6 See comments in ibid, AN830/34/45.
7 FRUS, 1944, V, 1232.
8 *Times Herald*, 16 Sept. 1944, in PREM 3, 159/14.
9 *Pioneering for A Civilized World*, in FO 371, file 38542.
10 *Lattimore*, 16.
11 *Amerasia*, 8 Sept. 1944, in FO 371, AN3679/34/45.
12 *New York Herald Tribune*, 10 July 1944; Wallace, *Our Job In The Pacific* (New York, 1944).
13 Taylor, *Awakening From History*, 280.

14 E.g. *New York Times*, 14 and 18 Sept. 1944.
15 E.g. *Chicago Tribune*, 5 April 1944.
16 Byrnes to FDR, 8 March 1944, Roosevelt Papers, PSF box 79.
17 Winant to Hopkins, 1 Sept. 1944, Hopkins Papers, box 332.
18 FRUS, 1944, III, 53.
19 FO 371, W7599/1534/G and F2300/993/61.
20 Morgenthau Presidential Diary, 15 Sept. 1944.
21 FO 371, AN3558/78/45; F2151/100/23; F4314/1/61.
22 Ibid, F1671/1/61. See e.g. F1160/1/61. On the other hand, Lattimore, of the O.W.I., was found to be less unfriendly in this period. Material in ibid, files 41702–3.
23 Council minutes, 15 March 1944, RIIA.
24 FO 371, F3861/3755/61 and F3464/1776/10.
25 Ibid, AN830/34/45; AN3519/16/45. WSC draft, 2 Sept. 1944, PREM 3, 149/11.
26 FO 371, F3457/34/10.
27 Ibid, F3169/100/23.
28 Ibid, F2151 and 2200/100/23; F2469/993/61.
29 Ibid, F3624/94/23.
30 Irene Ward, M.P., lecture to Far Eastern Group, 6 April 1944, RIIA.
31 COS, 9 Aug. 1944, PREM 3, 149/7. See Ismay to Auchinleck, 27 July 1944, Ismay Papers, IV/Con/1/1F; Somerville Diary, 27 Jan. 1944.
32 *Kirby*, III, 390ff.
33 Stilwell had, however, told Slim his plans in secrecy. Slim, *Defeat Into Victory*, 207; see *Bryant*, II, 248.
34 *Kirby*, III, 113ff., 265ff.
35 Ibid, 169ff., 205ff., 279ff.
36 Ibid, 187ff., 355ff.; Slim, *Defeat Into Victory*.
37 *Roskill*, III, part I, 347ff.
38 *Kirby*, III, 417ff.
39 Morison, *Two-Ocean War*, 318ff.
40 *Kirby*, V, 430.
41 See *Matloff*, 445.
42 E.g. JCS, 5 Sept. 1944, RG 218; WSC to Mountbatten, 1 June 1944, PREM 3, 148/8. For WSC's unease over Soviet delay and motives, see *Churchill*, V, 621.
43 Harriman to FDR, 24 Sept. 1944, Roosevelt Papers, MR box 11; J. R. Deane, *The Strange Alliance* (London, 1947), cap. XV.
44 MacArthur to Leahy, 7 Aug. 1944, Leahy files, JCS correspondence, USNOA; Stimson Diary, 21 Jan. 1944; see also JCS, 29 Aug. and 1 Sept. 1944, RG 218; *Leahy*, 269, 294; Morison, *Two-Ocean War*, 421ff.; Greenfield, *Command Decisions*, 'Luzon versus Formosa'. On Army–Navy tensions in general, see e.g. MacArthur to Marshall, 27 Feb. 1944, MacArthur Papers, RG 4; Marshall to King, 10 Feb. 1944, OPD, Exec. file 1, item 68.
45 JCS, 14 Sept. 1944, RG 218; COS, 13 Sept. 1944, CAB 99/29; Ehrman, *Grand Strategy*, V, 520ff.
46 CCS, 14 July 1944, CAB 88/4. See *Matloff*, 487ff.
47 FRUS, Quebec, 492.
48 Minutes of 3 May 1944, PREM 4, 42/5.
49 COS, 25 Feb. 1944, CAB 79/89.
50 *Kirby*, V, 427.
51 E.g. WSC to FDR, 4 April 1944, PREM 3, 472.
52 Minutes of 16 Sept. 1944, CAB 99/29.
53 Mountbatten to COS, 4 Feb. 1944, and Stilwell memo., 31 Jan. 1944, OPD, Exec. file 1, item 23a, and Leahy files, 'Pacific Strategy', USNOA; Davies to Hopkins, 16 Jan. 1944, Roosevelt Papers, MR box 10.
54 Stilwell Diary, 16 Jan. 1944; *Mountbatten*, 31, 55.
55 FDR to WSC, 25 Feb. 1944, PREM 3, 472; CCS, 24 March 1944, CAB 88/4. See *Tuchman*, 430.

56 Stimson Diary, 17 Feb. 1944.
57 WSC to Mountbatten, 2 March 1944, PREM 3, 147/10. From Quebec onwards, WSC had continued to hanker after a Sumatra operation. See *Bryant*, II, 44.
58 CCS, 2 June 1944, CAB 88/4; Ehrman, *Grand Strategy*, V, 490; *Kirby*, III, 255, 441.
59 Ehrman, *Grand Strategy*, V, 492; *Kirby*, III, 428.
60 Ehrman, *Grand Strategy*, V, 506ff.
61 Ibid, caps. XI and XII.
62 DC(Ops.), 19 Jan. 1944, CAB 69/6.
63 *Bryant*, II, 161, 166, and in general 152ff.
64 COS, 25 Feb. 1944, CAB 79/89.
65 COS, 13 March 1944, ibid.
66 COS memo., 8 March 1944, PREM 3, 160/7.
67 Minutes of 3 May 1944, PREM 4, 42/5.
68 Material in PREM 3, 160/7.
69 COS, 8 Sept. 1944, CAB 99/29. See *Churchill*, V, 511ff.
70 COS, 15 Sept. 1944, CAB 99/29; WSC to MacArthur, 12 March 1944, PREM 3, 159/14.
71 E.g. WSC to COS, 24 July 1944, PREM 3, 148/9.
72 WSC to COS, 12 Sept. 1944, PREM 3, 160/6; see WSC to Ismay, 24 June 1944, PREM 3, 160/5.
73 WSC memo., 29 Feb. 1944, PREM 3, 160/7.
74 WSC to FDR, 10 March 1944, PREM 3, 160/8; FDR to WSC, 13 March 1944, PREM 3, 164/6.
75 COS, 13 March 1944, CAB 79/84.
76 Eden to WSC, 21 Feb. 1944, PREM 3, 160/7; FO 371, F1040/100/23. See ibid, F3699/100/23.
77 Ehrman, *Grand Strategy*, V, 462ff.
78 Material in PREM 3, 160/1 and 2; Ehrman, *Grand Strategy*, V, 470ff.
79 E.g. COS (44) 449(0), PREM 3, 160/4; COS, 20 April 1944, CAB 79/89; Ehrman, *Grand Strategy*, V, 459–61.
80 Foreign Office memo., 4 May 1944; Eden to WSC, 12 June 1944, PREM 3, 160/4.
81 WSC to Ismay, 24 June 1944, PREM 3, 160/5; *Pownall*, 19 June 1944.
82 COS (44) 553(0), PREM 3, 160/5.
83 Hollis to WSC, 30 June 1944, ibid; CCS, 11 and 14 June 1944, CAB 88/4; Thorne, 'MacArthur, Australia and the British', *Australian Outlook*, April and August, 1975; FRUS, Quebec, 244, 257.
84 COS, 6 July 1944, PREM 3, 160/5.
85 See August COS meetings, PREM 3, 149/7.
86 COS, 12 Sept. 1944, CAB 99/29; CCS, 14 Sept. 1944, CAB 88/4.
87 *Avon*, 461–2.
88 FO 371, F3699/100/23.
89 E.g. Kennedy, *The Business of War*, 323.
90 *Pownall*, 29 June and 29 Aug. 1944.
91 Ismay to Pownall, 27 May 1944, Ismay Papers, IV/Pow/4/2.
92 *Bryant*, II, 192. And see ibid, 250, 266, 270, 272.
93 COS, 9 Aug. 1944, PREM 3, 149/7. See COS, 13 March 1944, CAB 79/89 and Cunningham, *A Sailor's Odyssey*, 598.
94 CCS, 14 Sept. 1944, CAB 88/4; King–Nimitz meeting, 29 Sept. to 1 Oct. 1944, King Papers, series III, USNOA.
95 Quebec minutes, 13 Sept. 1944, CAB 99/29; FRUS, Quebec, 469.

CHAPTER NINETEEN

THE UNITED STATES, BRITAIN AND CHINA

China as an issue in Anglo-American relations

AMERICAN OPINIONS concerning China and its Government were becoming troubled and divided in this period, as we shall see below. Nevertheless, whether one still looked to Chiang Kai-shek as the guardian of his country's future greatness or emphasized the role that might be played by the Communists from Yenan, it continued to be commonly assumed that the British attitude towards China was one of unappreciative selfishness, a facet of that same unregenerate 'imperialism' against which Americans were bracing themselves in the Mediterranean as well. As Hornbeck put it in July 1944 in his prolix way, 'the British not only have a conception of China and of China's potentialities very different from the conception which prevails among the people and within the Government of the United States, but the British are actively engaged in propagating in this country points of view and expressions of misgivings calculated to undermine and alter the American concept and attitude.[1]*

In some quarters, suspicion and accusations regarding British policies were more specific still. Patrick Hurley, for example, felt able to report to the President that British and other European officials were together working to secure the appointment of Mountbatten as commander of all United Nations forces in China, which would constitute, he warned, 'an overwhelming victory for the hegemony of the imperialist nations.'[2] In China itself, Rear Admiral Miles (as he had become) likewise voiced an assumption that was to be echoed by Hurley and others, that Britain would in all likelihood 'go so far as to work for the downfall of the central government in China in order to bring about a measure of provincial autonomy, and thereby create a situation where a reinforcement of foreign authority in China would again become necessary.'[3]

This belief that Britain and the United States remained far apart where China was concerned was also shared by Roosevelt himself. Over the case of

* Hornbeck's assurances to Foreign Office officials should still be borne in mind: 'It is a matter of constant gratification to me to find that you feel regarding various aspects of current problems and probable future problems [in the Far East] very much as we feel here [in Washington].' (See above, 317.)

Hongkong, the President continued to be sure that he would have 'no difficulty in getting the Chinese to make [it] a free port', if only the stubborn British would surrender it to Chiang Kai-shek in the first place.[4] In wider terms, his comments on the situation were conveyed to the Generalissimo by Vice President Wallace when the latter visited Chungking in June 1944: 'That the British did not consider China to be a great power; that President Roosevelt wanted China to be a great power in fact as well as in theory; that at Cairo the British were opposed to giving any reality to China's position as one of the "Big Four" . . . Mr Wallace', the record runs, 'then quoted to President Chiang the following statement made by President Roosevelt: "Churchill is old. A new British Government will give Hong Kong to China and next day China will make it a free port."'[5]

Wallace's own pamphlet, *Our Job In The Pacific*, which has been mentioned earlier, emphasized that a very new order of things was coming about in the East.[6] Similarly, when in Chungking, he issued with Chiang Kai-shek a joint statement proclaiming 'the right of self-government for Asiatic peoples now dependent', having beforehand pointedly refrained from paying a courtesy visit to the British Ambassador and having made deprecating remarks about Britain in public.[7] In other ways, too, the Americans appeared as determined as ever to keep apart from Britain on matters relating to China. For example, further suggestions from London for the setting up of joint machinery for screening Chinese requests for supplies were again rejected,[8] while in the military field Stilwell once more made clear his opposition to having R.A.F. units operating from within China.[9] In the diplomatic sphere, Washington avoided becoming involved with Britain over the tense situation that was developing between China and Tibet,[10] and where financial matters such as exchange rates were concerned the American Treasury dealt directly with Chungking with little or no reference to London.[11]

As before, such American behaviour and the assumptions that lay behind it were often found extremely trying by British officials. Wallace's actions and words, for example, aroused resentment, as Halifax later made plain to him.[12] (Cordell Hull sympathized over this. 'I would like you to tell Eden', he growled to Halifax, 'that nothing would please me better than to see him step right out in the House of Commons and kick the hell out of [Wallace].')[13] Likewise, there was a degree of exasperation within the Foreign Office when it was learned that Hornbeck believed that Britain, together with the other Allies, should adopt a healthier attitude towards China and provide more assistance for Chiang Kai-shek. 'It is a travesty of the truth to say we are playing China down to justify our own inactivity', wrote one official. 'The Americans played China up so hysterically that there was bound to be a reaction; our "inactivity" is due to material causes of which Dr. Hornbeck is well aware and which need no justification.'[14]

Above all, Churchill—correct in the short but not the long term—continued to find absurd the American insistence that China must be thought of and treated as a great power. It was, he wrote to Eden, 'an absolute farce. I have told the President I would be reasonably polite about this American obsession, but I cannot agree that we should take a positive attitude on the matter. The latest information from inside China points to the rise already of a rival government to supplant Chiang Kai-shek, and now there is always a Communist civil war impending there. While not opposing the President's wish I should object very much if we adopted other than a perfectly negative line, leaving him to do the needful with the Russians.'[15]

The Prime Minister made the same point to his Commonwealth colleagues when they assembled in London, pointing out (though Fraser of New Zealand registered his disagreement) the absurdity of giving China a say in the affairs of Europe.[16] Nor did he trouble to conceal his views from the State Department's Stettinius when the latter visited London, scornfully referring to the Chinese as 'pigtails' and questioning both their ability to unite and their potential as guardians of world peace.[17] Eden, too, while warning that for the sake of American opinion it was necessary to accept China as one of the 'Big Four', felt confident that 'in practice . . ., for a long time China would be so dependent on the other Great Powers that she would not be likely to pursue any very independent policy . . . in matters affecting international peace and security.'[18] Rooseveltian rhetoric on the subject, produced when announcing Wallace's forthcoming visit to China, was likewise greeted with scorn in the Foreign Office, where it was suggested that the President was 'intoxicated with the exuberance of his own verbosity.'[19]

It was, of course, still recognized in London that the American presence in China had come to far outweigh that of Britain. Moreover, the Embassy in Washington reported that there existed 'increasing evidence that the United States regards China as, in a special sense, an American "sphere of influence."'[20] From China itself, information also came in which suggested that American business interests, such as the United States Steel Products Corporation, were already seeking to lay the foundations of a major post-war presence in that country.[21] One case, on which a considerable amount of material accumulated in the Foreign Office, involved a firm of consulting engineers, H. A. Brassert and Co., which had both American and British branches, and on whose behalf a British representative went out to China in order to discuss the condition of the iron and steel industry there. According to the Chinese Minister of Economic Affairs, Dr. Wong Wen-hao, American pressure was then exerted to prevent his Government signing an agreement with this representative of the firm, and to direct further business towards its United States branch instead. Dr. Wong expressed his anger at what had occurred, bitterly remarking in private that 'China was not yet an American colony.'* For his part, the frustrated British engineer wrote

* Of course, Dr. Wong may have been playing off the British and Americans against each other. It is quite likely, however, that his resentment against the U.S.A. was genuine. See the footnote below, 729.

home: 'From what Mr [Donald] Nelson and other Americans [in China] told me and tell me, there is a strong tendency to declare China a "no-trespassers-admitted" territory; this policy seems to be backed by the American Greater-Navy bloc who appear to lay claim to "essential bases in China, such as Formosa, in preparation for the coming war against Russia."'[22]

Dr. Wong was not the only member of the Chinese Government in this period to suggest that a British commercial and financial presence would be welcomed back after the war.[23] Even so, the Foreign Office remained anxious to avoid misunderstandings with the United States over any transactions of this kind that might be undertaken while hostilities with Japan continued, and still looked forward to Anglo-American collaboration, rather than rivalry, in the China market of the future.[24] The China Association, too, while seeking 'to establish a united British front on all matters affecting trade with China', were thinking in terms of setting up some form of cooperation with the Americans, and, with Foreign Office encouragement, wrote to the United States National Foreign Trade Council to this end.[25] Speaking at Chatham House, a former Financial Counsellor of the British Embassy in Chungking likewise welcomed the prospect of a major American commercial involvement in China, where he felt sure there was 'room for both of us.'[26]

Meanwhile in the political, as well as in the commercial field, the Foreign Office continued to hope for Anglo-American collaboration. (In this context, the Far Eastern Office of the State Department—'Divisions' were turned into 'Offices' there early in 1944—was seen as being essentially friendly towards Britain, though constrained by American public opinion; even Hornbeck, for all his prickliness, was accepted as being well-meaning as well as tedious, and Joseph Grew, who replaced him as Director of the Far Eastern Office in the summer, was respected in British circles.)[27] It was thus emphasized within the Foreign Office that no attempt should be made to capitalize on Sino-American differences when these began to be more apparent during this period.[28] The intention to work for partnership with Washington remained paramount.

There was, however, a certain wry satisfaction among British officials as it became clear that, in Halifax's words, there now existed 'a slump in general Chinese stock' in the U.S.A.

'Those sections of the public who think about it all', wrote a member of the Washington Embassy in July, 'are now rather bewildered. They are beginning to doubt whether China will be a friendly democracy protecting American interests in the Pacific and whether the China market will be so lucrative after all. And many thoughtful people are asking themselves whether the United States would really wish to get involved in Sino-Russian disputes about Manchuria, Korea, Mongolia, etc.'[29]

The general British reaction to this was that a greater measure of realism on the part of Americans towards China was long overdue. When Halifax wrote that the claims of China to be a first-class power now tended to be treated with 'an ironical attitude', Churchill noted in the margin: 'Good. They are becoming sane on this point.'[30]

Similarly, although no attempt was made to score off the Americans, there was a certain dry pleasure in London when it was observed that, as Sino-American strains increased, the Chinese, in Eden's words, 'now turn almost embarrassingly towards us!'[31] In April, Carton de Wiart reported that Madame Chiang Kai-shek was 'swinging pro-British hard', and that 'American shares [were] slumping'; likewise, the Generalissimo's wife declared to a member of the British Embassy, Berkeley Gage, that 'she believed in Anglo-Chinese friendship because Britain and the Empire were one of the most important stabilising forces in the world—which was good for China.'[32] This emphasis on a common interest in conservatism, although far removed from the hostility that had been displayed towards the British Empire by Madame Chiang Kai-shek and other Chinese in 1942, was in fact well-suited to the nature of the Kuomintang regime. It was also evoked in part by the greater circumspection with which the British, as opposed to the Americans, approached the Communist issue in China.

The Generalissimo himself now joined his wife in displaying warmer sentiments than hitherto. Britain's attitude towards China, he told Seymour in July, was 'very fair', and he hoped, the Ambassador reported, that 'once the war was over we would help China in her industries.' According to the Vice Minister of Foreign Affairs in Chungking, Chiang had instructed 'that relations between Britain and China were to be made as friendly as possible, [and he] was determined that the present alliance should be continued after the war.'[33] To American officials in China, also, it was intimated that the Generalissimo 'now feels that the British way is more to his liking than the American as "the British do not indulge in undignified criticism of their leaders, in contrast to the criticism of President Roosevelt by Congress and the American press."'[34]

The response in London to these new Chinese overtures was cool: one must wait to see if Chungking would back up its pleasant words with practical measures reflecting good-will. Moreover, even if there had not existed the overriding desire to work for cooperation with the United States, Britain was in no position to take advantage of the latter's difficulties in China by seeking to supplant her there. Chiang Kai-shek, in other words, would not find adequate compensation in that direction for his worsening relations with Washington.

As for the Anglo-American side of the triangle, we have seen how deep-seated American suspicions and treaty-port image of Britain, together with a continuing belief in the special role of the United States where China's future was concerned, helped prevent any close accord coming about. This was so, even though in general terms Washington, faced with the growing dangers and intractable problems inherent in the Chinese situation, was beginning to place increased emphasis upon the need, in the words of a State Department memorandum, for 'collaboration among the four principal powers in the Far East—the Soviet Union, the British Commonwealth, China and ourselves.'[35]

It was one thing to state the desirability of such collaboration; it was another to wipe away the past and work on equal terms and on a basis of trust with the possessors of Hongkong. Moreover, the continued failure to achieve a close Anglo-American working relationship over China in 1944 is all the more striking in that the opinions of American officials were now shifting considerably closer to those of their British counterparts concerning the military contribution that China might make during the war and the extent to which she was ready to play a leading political role on the world stage.

The United States and China

The emotive language surrounding American hopes over China had become too pervasive to disappear entirely when there appeared grounds for increasing disillusionment. Instead, it coexisted uneasily with the growing expression of doubt in public, and with an exasperated writing-down of Chinese prospects within official circles. To some degree, the American Administration found itself a prisoner of the exaggerated beliefs about China which it had itself helped to develop in the earlier part of the war. In the light of what one official described as 'the unique position . . . that China and Chiang Kai-shek have come to hold in wide sections of public opinion throughout the world . . . as the leaders in Asia of the war against the Axis',[36] there was considerable reluctance to undertake in public that drastic revision of past expectations which the evidence now suggested was required.

Yet quite apart from what the American people had been led to believe, the Administration itself had too much invested in the hope of seeing China become a grateful and cooperative major power to make such revision at all easy. This in turn, as the crisis in China deepened, brought out the continuing discrepancy between the high aspiration of seeing China come into her own—her door open to American commerce and political influence—and the limited means which the United States was ready to adopt to bring this about. In this respect, the mounting problems of 1944 showed up the ambiguities and uncertainties surrounding American policy in much the same way as had the Japanese demands upon China during the First World War and the attacks upon her in 1931 and 1937.

At the same time, the tensions that were involved on the American side continued to contrast with the less emotional and more pragmatic way in which British policy-makers reacted to what was happening in China. Having in the first place expected more from Chiang Kai-shek than had the British, Americans tended to respond in sharper fashion as the shortcomings of his regime became increasingly apparent. And in continuing to hope for more from China and the Chinese, some American officials and newsmen now turned away from the corruption of Chungking to hail the new society of Mao Tse-tung's Yenan with an enthusiasm whose quality was scarcely to be found in British circles. (There was also, of course, the more prosaic reason for this last contrast, that British officials in 1944 did not have the contacts with Yenan which became available to the Americans. In addition, the difference in official styles does not mean that individual Britons who saw something of the Communist areas could not themselves be enthusiastic, as we shall observe below.) Moreover, by being more involved on the ground in China and in a position to exert greater influence there than could the British, American policy-makers had to face questions which in London were rendered less urgent by comparative impotence.

The United States sponsorship of China as a great power was reflected in this period by China's presence at Dumbarton Oaks, the proposals of that conference assigning her a permanent seat on the Security Council of the new world organization. The continuation of American rhetoric on the subject of China was meanwhile amply illustrated during the Wallace visit to Chungking, which occasioned what John Davies has since described as an outbreak of 'political flatulence.'[37] (Wallace himself was clearly out of his depth when it came to both Soviet and Chinese politics, and Owen Lattimore, who accompanied him to those two countries, has confirmed this to the author.) In public, the cause of increasing aid to China went on being supported in papers such as the *New York Times* (which described that country as 'the hope of future peace in the Pacific')[38] and by individuals like Representative Walter Judd, whom we have heard before, and who was a former medical missionary in China:

'We have never had a major conflict between ourselves and the Chinese', Judd declared. 'The two peoples are nearer alike, we are nearer to the Chinese in our basic beliefs, our basic emphasis on the rights of the individual, and in our basic personal habits of democracy, than we are to most of the countries of Europe ... We have nothing to fear from an independent China; it is enormously to our interests, first because it is necessary in order to save American lives and money from war ... Secondly from our economy, because China is a natural complement.'[39]

In official circles, Stanley Hornbeck, although increasingly at odds with State Department colleagues and eventually, to their relief, removed to the post of Ambassador to the Netherlands, also went on pleading China's cause, deploring the increasing criticism of the Chungking regime and the inadequacy of American aid.[40] (Lend Lease to China in 1944 was still only 0·4 per cent of the total given by the U.S.A. in that year.)[41] Within China, too, various American agencies still sought to promote closer ties between the two countries, although the Ambassador, Gauss, felt that 'the law of diminishing returns had long since come into play' as far as the extensive O.W.I. organization there was concerned. (Gauss also reported to Washington his regret that John K. Fairbank, who was working on a cultural relations programme, had a 'strong and unconcealed prejudice against the Kuomintang and all its ways and works.')[42]

In the economic field, Roosevelt himself, in despatching Donald Nelson, former head of the War Production Board,* on a mission to China, emphasized the possibility of American war-time aid leading to a close post-war relationship. Such expectations were also encouraged by various Chinese officials, who held out the prospect of extensive American participation in areas like the development of the steel industry. Meanwhile the State Department continued to work on the draft of a commercial treaty between the two countries which would ensure the best possible opportunities for United States businessmen in that long-standing source of American dreams, the China market.[43]

But were the prospects in and for China so very good after all? A visiting representative of an American steel corporation, for one, feared, in the words of a local U.S. diplomat, 'that post-war China will be so poor that it will be impracticable for his organization to operate here, either now or in the immediate post-war period, on a conventional basis of selling its products to consumers, either government or private.'[44] Moreover, commercial doubts of this kind were only one facet of a growing American tendency to question and criticize where China was concerned. In the press, for example, the conclusion was increasingly being drawn that, as the *New York Times* at last admitted, 'democracy does not yet exist in China.' Reports of corruption and totalitarianism on the part of Chiang Kai-shek's regime were underlined when it became known that Chungking's agents were attempting to enforce political 'thought control' on Chinese students living in the United States. Nor could the disillusionment that now existed in various official quarters be concealed. 'The tales told parents and friends by American soldiers who have served in China are beginning to spread', observed the *Christian Science Monitor*. 'And the sentiments on China held by the State Department and War Department in Washington are strong enough to be heard above the scratch of the censor's black pencil.'[45]

Reports which discredited China—for example of the extent of the Soong family's corruption—were indeed circulating among officials.[46] More serious, however, was the growing prospect of China falling apart as its military, economic and political situation worsened. In addition to the unresolved problem of Chungking's relations with the Communist regime in

* It is important to note that Nelson, like Wallace, was in 1944 on the way down, not up, the Washington greasy pole. Indeed, it became a common jest that, if Roosevelt wanted to speed someone on his way out of the higher circles of the Administration, he would send him on a mission to China. This might possibly have been the case when Pat Hurley was sent to Chungking in 1944. Some officials believed that the President did not know at the time what to do next with his peripatetic, all-American representative. A story went round that, after seeing Hurley before the latter's departure, Roosevelt quipped: 'Well, the next thing we'll hear from Pat will be his memoirs. The title will be: "Alone In China."' (Interview with Owen Lattimore.)

As for Nelson, Stimson thought him 'weak, dishonest and inefficient.' Hopkins, for his part, suggested that Nelson would be entirely happy in China if his hosts 'provided him with four or five girls—that would keep him quiet.' (Stimson Diary, 24 Aug. 1944; Davies memo., 4 Sept. 1944, Stilwell Papers, box 15.)

Yenan, which will be considered below, there was also the mounting threat of a separatist movement being led by Marshal Li Chi-shen in Kwangsi province, from whom Chiang Kai-shek withheld reinforcements in the face of a Japanese attack.[47] Increasing dissatisfaction with the Kuomintang regime was also manifesting itself in Yunnan and among groups of younger army officers.[48] 'The problem of the United States', observed John Carter Vincent of the State Department in January 1944, 'far from being that of building up China to become [a] stabilizing power, will be to keep China from disintegrating.'[49]* 'Chinese morale is low', reported Wallace in June, 'and demoralization is a possibility with [a] resultant disintegration of [the] central authority . . . The political situation is unstable and tense, with [a] rising lack of confidence in the Generalissimo and his reactionary entourage.'[50]

By July, Cordell Hull had come to feel that China had 'only a fifty-fifty chance to reestablish [sic] herself as a great power.' In September, even Harry Hopkins revealed to John Davies his declining optimism over China, where the likelihood of internal conflict 'did not seem to give much scope for the rosy plans which were being drawn up for expansive post-war economic development . . . by the United States.' Roosevelt himself had admitted to his Cabinet in May that 'he was apprehensive for the first time as to China holding together for the duration of the war.'[51]

Declining hopes in the political stability of China were accompanied by impatience and a reduced valuation regarding her likely contribution in the military sphere. Rather than providing fresh opportunities for closing in on Japan, danger and frustration seemed to be the China Theatre's main donation to the Allied cause during this period. By their successful summer advance against the airfields in East China, the Japanese demonstrated the continuing weakness of the Chinese land forces, amply bearing out Stilwell's warnings that the activities of Chennault's 14th Air Force, on whose behalf Roosevelt had altered the allocation of Hump supplies in 1943, could well provoke a response from the enemy that the Army was not yet strong enough to meet. (The Japanese drove into Hunan in May; in August they opened a new offensive in Chekiang, and on 12 November captured the air base at Kweilin.) Chennault himself, whose rivalry with Stilwell for the ear of Washington continued, and who had beguiled both Chiang Kai-shek and Roosevelt with his promises of great gains from a small investment, was now reduced to crying out that 'we are . . . faced with the possible loss of China as an allied base unless drastic counter-measures are promptly taken.'[52] 'What I am trying to find out', declared the President for his part, 'is where is the Chinese Army and why aren't they fighting, because the Japanese seem to be able to push them in any direction they want to.'[53] Even the bombing of industrial targets in Japan by B 29s using the Chengtu base

* Vincent added that 'consideration of American policy in the Far East is "second drawer" and is the concern . . . of relatively few people in the American Government.' This has a ring about it that is interestingly similar to the complaints being made by Far Eastern officials in London.

in China—a scheme in which Washington invested almost blind faith and a high proportion of the material reaching Yunnan, and which, like Chennault's earlier proposals, appeared to offer a tempting short-cut to victory—was in fact achieving only a minute proportion of the results expected of it.[54]

Increasingly, indeed, it was only such short-cuts towards success as the B 29 programme which interested Washington where China was concerned, an attitude which was in keeping with the long-standing American reluctance to become heavily involved on the ground in East Asia, however much it might be out of step with the proclaimed political intention of building up China as a major power. As early as January 1944, U.S. Army planners were coming to the conclusion that by the time the Chinese Army was adequately trained and equipped it would be too late to be of any assistance in the fight against Japan. There could be no pulling out of China altogether, but the aim should now be no more than to develop air bases there and to keep the Japanese forces in that country from moving elsewhere. 'Henceforth', comments the American official historian, 'planning could be conducted on a more realistic basis. China's role would be considered less and less important.'[55]

What this meant for Stilwell was spelled out to him in May by the Joint Chiefs of Staff and, in particular, Marshall. His former primary task of increasing the efficiency of the Chinese Army was now down-graded, and the main intention must instead become that of supporting operations in the Pacific: 'Japan should be defeated without undertaking a major campaign against her on the mainland of Asia if her defeat can be accomplished in this manner.'[56] By the end of the period, with Nimitz's advance gathering pace in spectacular fashion, and with the decision being taken in Washington that even a landing on the coast of China would not now be necessary, 'there was no longer a military reason for a major U.S. effort in the China Theater', involvement there being reduced to 'a sort of insurance policy to be drawn on if anything went wrong with the central Pacific offensive.'[57]

This new evaluation, so far removed from those eager ideas for utilizing the manpower of China which had flourished in the early stages of the Pacific war, and so much closer to the view long held in London, meant that America's political aspirations and her military actions were now more than ever out of alignment with each other. In terms of the political struggles within China, it also meant that Chiang Kai-shek would not, after all, have at his command the sixty modernized divisions that Stilwell's programme had envisaged—Roosevelt at Cairo had casually agreed, even, to increase the final number to ninety—though it must be added that Chiang himself, whose position rested upon the placing of personal loyalties above the demands of efficiency or the national good, had given Stilwell little assistance in that direction. At the same time the scaling down of American expectations was not accompanied by a reduction in friction between Washington and Chungking. On the contrary, it was during this period, when China's performance appeared more lamentable than ever and the Soviet alternative could be taken as certain, that Roosevelt came much closer to following the line that Stilwell had always advocated, of demanding action from the Chinese in return for continued aid.

The relevant exchanges between the President and the Generalissimo need not be recounted here in detail.[58] On his side, Roosevelt sought two things in purely military terms (the financial matters at issue between the two countries will be dealt with below): first, that the Chinese 'Y' force in Yunnan should aid the operations of S.E.A.C. in Burma by attacking southwards across the river Salween—even though this demand involved overlooking the choice which the President had offered Chiang and the latter had accepted when operation 'Buccaneer' had been cancelled at Cairo, of postponing his Salween offensive until the autumn of 1944. As the patience of both Roosevelt and Marshall dwindled (inactivity on the part of 'Y' force was 'inconceivable', the former signalled to Chiang in April), the Generalissimo once more tried to insist that major operations in the south of Burma should take place as a prerequisite, and to argue that his units were too weak for the task envisaged for them. Eventually, in April, Chungking was given to understand that unless 'Y' force moved, Lend Lease supplies for it would come to an end. An attack across the Salween was duly opened in May.

The second of Roosevelt's military demands, which followed on from American suggestions that a war council should be formed in China in order to coordinate the activities of the country's armies, including those of Yenan, was that Stilwell should be placed in command of all Chinese forces, Communist as well as Kuomintang. This proposal was first put forward in July, at the instigation of the Joint Chiefs of Staff, who reported that 'the Chinese ground forces, in their present state of discipline, training and equipment, and under their present leadership, are impotent. The Japanese forces can, in effect, move virtually unopposed except by geographical-logistical difficulties.'[59] As the Salween offensive ran into trouble and the military crisis in East China deepened—and although the Japanese did not in fact have plans to do so, the fear was that they would sever the Chinese end of the Hump air route by seizing Kunming and perhaps then drive on to Chungking itself—so Washington became more pressing. Chiang Kai-shek, however, whose entire system of maintaining power through a network of personal loyalties was threatened by the proposal, would agree only 'in principle' that Stilwell should take command. For his part, he now insisted that the relationship between the General and himself must be clearly defined, that the Communist forces must be excluded from the new arrangement until they agreed to accept the orders of the Chinese Government, and that Lend Lease supplies to China should be removed from Stilwell's control. In addition, the Generalissimo asked the President to send out a special representative 'to adjust the relations between me and General Stilwell.'

Stilwell himself, meanwhile, was coming to the conclusion, as he expressed it to Marshall in September, that 'the United States will not get any real cooperation from China while Chiang Kai-shek is in power. I believe', he went on, 'that [Chiang] will only continue his policy of delay, while grabbing for loans and post-war aid, for the purpose of maintaining his present position, based on one-party government, a reactionary policy, and the suppression of democratic ideas . . .'[60] Matters came to a head at the time of the Quebec Conference, when Stilwell reported that Chiang was proposing to withdraw his forces back across the Salween unless he, Stilwell, promptly launched an attack from Myitkyina, on the other side of the Japanese position in North Burma. Thereupon Roosevelt, following a draft prepared by Marshall, delivered his strongest rebuke to the Generalissimo, holding the latter personally responsible for the outcome if the necessary steps on his part were not taken. 'I have urged time and again in recent months', he cabled, 'that you take drastic action to resist the disaster which has been moving closer to China and to you. Now, when you have not yet placed General Stilwell in command of all forces in China, we are faced with a loss of a critical area in east China with possible catastrophic consequences.'[61]

This fierce message of Roosevelt's gave joy to Stilwell,[62] who, as Chiang Kai-shek read it, watched 'the harpoon hit the little bugger in the solar-plexus and [go] right through him.' But victory went to the Generalissimo, and will be recorded here even though it falls just outside the period ending at Quebec. Roosevelt had begun to give the appearance of getting tough, but a thoroughgoing policy of such a kind was made difficult for the United States by her own failure to fulfil all her past promises of material help to China. Furthermore, despite the strong support he received throughout from Marshall, Stilwell was far from having a solid American backing for the stand he had long wanted to make. Already, in June, his recall had been recommended by Wallace after the latter's visit to China, when the Vice President's ear had been gained by Chennault's staff and, above all, Alsop. Hopkins, too, remained essentially a supporter of Chennault, while Admiral Leahy believed that Stilwell had 'failed completely to adjust himself to the authority of Chiang as Generalissimo and President of China.'[63] Nor was Roosevelt himself the man to see matters through to a showdown with his Asian protégé.

Thus, various concessions were now made in the face of Chiang's stubbornness. Stilwell, in an endeavour to get things moving, dropped the proposal that Communist forces should be included within his command. Then the President, advised by a thoroughly disillusioned Marshall, withdrew even the suggestion that an American should take control of China's armies; he also proposed that Stilwell should be relieved as the Generalissimo's Chief of Staff, remaining only as commander of the Chinese forces in Burma and Yunnan. Even this, however, was not enough for Chiang Kai-shek, whose 'face' was now at stake. Quite possibly encouraged by a report from H. H. Kung to the effect that Hopkins had indicated that Roosevelt would make a new military appointment to China if this was insisted upon, the Generalissimo simply repeated his complete lack of confidence in Stilwell, and demanded his recall. The process was completed by Patrick Hurley, who was sent to China by the President as his special representative. Stilwell, wired back Hurley, was 'the only issue' that now stood between the two heads of state, while Chiang Kai-shek remained the man whom the United States should support in China.[64] Marshall, meanwhile, had reached the conclusion that Stilwell's 'loss of prestige and his influence with the Chinese will make fruitless further dealings with the British, who have never been in accord with his aggressive policy.'[65] On 18 October, Roosevelt issued the order for Stilwell's recall. The policy of standing up to Chiang would not be seen through to the end, and the Generalissimo could draw the conclusion that over other matters, too, such as the effecting of basic political reforms, he could defy the United States and get away with it.

Even before this, Stilwell had learned from a staff officer that, as a result of the strategic decisions taken at Quebec and in Washington, 'this theater', as he put it, 'is written off, and nothing expected from us.' His own fall, he was convinced, was more than a matter of personalities:

'Real issue', he jotted down in note form, 'China make effort or not . . . Given a mission and no means. Hamstrung by "no bargaining." Three years of struggle . . . Bucked by the Br[itish]. Bucked by the Ch[inese] . . . Asked for *policy* at Cairo. All I was told was "we want to keep China."'[66]

Yet for all his justifiable complaints, Stilwell himself had shared in the widespread American illusions as to the nature and capabilities of China and what the United States in particular could achieve there. His fall symbolized a frustration of American hopes that was inevitable.[67] The entanglement in China was to continue, but even Roosevelt now appeared to lose much of his interest in her cause. His exchanges with Chiang became infrequent and more distant, and at Yalta, as we shall see, he would be ready to infringe China's interests without consulting Chungking. These very swings in his China policy both derived from and illustrate its essentially facile and irresponsible nature.

So long as Washington believed that it was vital to sustain China, and so long as Chiang Kai-shek was accepted as being the only man who could hold that country together against the Japanese, the Generalissimo was in a position to capitalize on his weakness, and to exercise considerable leverage against his infinitely more powerful ally. (This tactic, of course, was to be successfully employed by South Vietnamese regimes during a later war.) Quite apart from her long-standing, if largely inactive, sympathy for China, the United States, by her policy of bringing Japan to surrender unconditionally and of removing the latter as an influential unit on the international scene, made it appear essential to go on propping up China as the state that would fill the ensuing power vacuum in the Far East, whatever disappointments she now provided. And although Stilwell among others thought that he could see possible alternatives to Chiang as the leader of that country, the Generalissimo's position as one of the outstanding Allied statesmen had too long been lauded and accepted to make it easy for Washington to think of transferring its support from him to another. We have already seen the exalted terms in which Roosevelt himself, in private, had thought of Chiang and his role in 1943. Now, in 1944, even when severely criticizing the policies of the Chungking regime, Wallace for his part concluded after his visit that 'there seems to be no alternative to support of Chiang.'[68] Owen Lattimore, too, was still publicly praising the latter's qualifications as the symbol of a new phase in China's history and 'a coalition statesman of genius.'[69]*

Nevertheless, in 1944, even more than during the preceding period, various Americans in official positions were expressing opinions which tallied with the Stilwell thesis that Chiang could and should be coerced by the United States. Gauss, for example, argued from Chungking that there was no likelihood of the Generalissimo's seeking a compromise peace with Japan, as had been threatened, and that he depended on the support of the Allied powers for the very existence of his regime.[70] Gauss' Second Secretary, John S. Service, put it more forcefully still, depicting Chiang as being

'completely dependent on the United States—in foreign relations, militarily and economically. Even his internal position', insisted Service, 'would be endangered if American support were withdrawn . . . [Therefore the United States should] make up its mind what it wants from him and then get hard-boiled about it.'[71]

The Secretary of the Treasury, Morgenthau, was by now taking a similar line. 'We have everything they want and the Chinese haven't got a penny!' he observed. 'And so what? We are in a perfectly good position . . . I think it comes to a point where you have to tell these people to fish or cut bait . . .'[72]

Meanwhile, in addition to the matter of the employment of the Chinese Army, two other issues were bound up with this question of the extent to which the United States should acquiesce in the position taken up by Chiang Kai-shek. One was the political situation within China, with particular reference to the relationship between the Kuomintang regime and the Communists; the other concerned the demands that Chiang was making for further financial assistance.

It was immediately after he had attended the Cairo Conference, when he was informed that there would not take place, after all, a major amphibious operation in the Bay of Bengal, that the Generalissimo requested, as a vital means of keeping China in the war, a new loan of $1 billion in gold.[73] Within the State Department (where, typically, the matter was learned of in

* Lattimore believed that Chiang Kai-shek had not only held together the various factions of the Kuomintang, but that he had played a vital part in sustaining some sort of common front with the Communists against the Japanese invasion after 1937. In the light of Chiang's attitude and policies towards the Communists from about 1940–41 onwards, however, to describe him in 1944 as 'a coalition statesman of genius' would seem highly questionable. Similarly, in view of the fundamental conservatism made clear by the Generalissimo in his book, *China's Destiny*, quite apart from his failure to support basic social, political or economic reforms, he would appear in retrospect to have been a less-than-ideal symbol of China's new age. (Interview with Professor Lattimore.)

haphazard fashion) the belief was that, in the interests of long-term Sino-American relations, the request should be handled sympathetically. Hornbeck, for example, warned against the risk of letting China become 'aligned in a nascent and potentially powerful grouping of the colored races banding and banded together in and for a struggle against the domination or fancied domination of the earth by the white races.'[74] A memorandum put forward in the name of the Department as a whole went further still, revealing the hopes which, even now, were entertained in Washington of securing a patron–client relationship with a grateful China after the war.

'That China be a well-disposed member of the "Big Four" combination is desirable', the document began. 'But that, when there come stresses and strains in the relations of the United States with, on the one hand Great Britain and with, on the other hand, the Soviet Union, China will be well disposed toward the United States is, from the point of view of United States interests and concerns, even more imperatively desirable . . . It is important that nothing be allowed to develop from which it might result that China withdraw from confidence in and reliance upon the United States and move into a position of reliance upon the Soviet Union or an acceptance of the Japanese thesis that oriental peoples must combine in opposition to the influence of occidental peoples.'[75]

Others, however, reacted very differently to this latest Chinese demand. Gauss reported that the Embassy in Chungking saw 'no sound basis, political or economic, for supporting any such loan proposals at this time.'[76] In Washington, stronger objections still were voiced. General Somervell, for example, declared that the Army

'had decided that they were going to be tough with the Chinese Government. They were very dissatisfied with the cooperation they were getting in China and with the small amount of actual combat fighting which the Chinese armies were carrying on. The Army were willing to go to the limit if necessary. They were even prepared to stop building airports in China and were ready to approach Japan from another direction . . . They could break Chiang Kai-shek by withdrawing American support or if they wanted to with an expenditure of $100 million by "buying" one of his competitors . . . There were lots of candidates.'[77]

Stimson, as Secretary of War, was indeed in the mood indicated by Somervell. 'I have been feeling that China has been riding us pretty hard with the aid of Madame Chiang Kai-shek's influence over the President', he wrote in his diary, 'and that it was time to stop.'[78] Morgenthau at the Treasury felt the same, describing the Chinese as 'a bunch of crooks'. The blunt rejection of the request for a loan which he drafted, and which Roosevelt at first approved, was, however, toned down by Hull.[79] Eventually, State, War and Treasury agreed to propose that, in place of a loan, an American commission should visit China to explore ways of helping her through her economic crisis, and that the costs incurred by the U.S. Army in China, estimated at about $25 million a month, might be borne by Washington.[80]

There followed the arrival of unacceptable Chinese counterproposals, and lengthy negotiations then took place, involving the amount which should be paid on behalf of the U.S. Army (the Chinese were pressing for large sums in return for work such as the construction of the B 29 air base at Chengtu) and the rate of exchange to be adopted (the Chinese originally proposed 20–1 in yuan to dollars, and the U.S. Treasury 100–1; the final settlement worked out at about 74–1, although the free-market rate at the time was about 200–1).[81] Eventually, beyond this period, at the end of 1944, it was agreed that the United States would pay $210 million to cover Army expenditure up to the end of September.[82] The particular sum involved, however, mattered less than did the greatly increased resentment and suspicion that was felt towards the Chinese by officials in Washington as a result of the way in which the former had approached the whole affair. Within the Treasury, particularly, the Chungking regime had few friends by now, and Harry Dexter White and other officials were deliberately delaying shipments of gold to China which had been promised back in 1943.[83]

More threatening still to Chiang Kai-shek was the growing American interest in the Communist regime in Yenan, and in the notion of somehow transforming the Chinese political scene. Whatever the arguments for not intervening in China's domestic affairs—and we shall see that they carried greater weight in London—the growing military and political crisis in that country made it appear urgent to make contact with Chiang's main opponents, whose dissatisfaction and independent position threatened to prevent a unified China arriving on the world scene after the war. Moreover, the Communists had at their disposal men and above all territory that could prove valuable in the struggle against Japan. Such considerations, put forward by John Davies in January 1944, were accepted by Roosevelt, for whom there was the added desire to ensure that a Kuomintang–Communist clash would not embroil the Soviet Union and the United States on opposite sides, and thus endanger the basis of the entire post-war international system. The President had expressed such a fear to Sumner Welles in 1943.[84] Now, in 1944, the dangers seemed greater still, as Chungking sounded the alarm over clashes between Chinese and Soviet forces in Sinkiang, and as John Service warned from his position on the spot that Chiang Kai-shek's short-sightedness was likely to bring about even greater trouble with Moscow.[85] Any issue that could lead to a Sino-Soviet conflict must be settled, Wallace urged Chiang, who in turn indicated that he would welcome American assistance in improving his relations in that direction.[86]

Rather than act as intermediary between Chungking and Moscow, however, Washington, encouraged by Stalin's agreement that the Generalissimo was the best man available in China (even though, Stalin added, he needed to be dealt with firmly),[87] saw its chance of avoiding trouble as lying in ending the split within China itself. 'Peaceful unification', as Professor

Tang Tsou writes, 'was the keystone of the whole structure of American policies.' In the words of a State Department paper, 'unity in China, based on democratic tolerance, is vital to the prosecution of the war.'[88] Thus, after receiving Davies' advice in January, Roosevelt sought Chiang Kai-shek's agreement to an American observer mission proceeding to North China. Receiving approval from the Generalissimo only as regards those areas that acknowledged the authority of the Nationalist Government,[89] the President returned to the charge during the Wallace visit to China, which, with an optimism that in retrospect appears extraordinary, was designed to try to bring to an end that country's political divisions.[90] Roosevelt, Wallace informed Chiang, suggested that the Kuomintang and Communists might 'call in a friend'—that is, himself—to help settle their differences. The President's entire approach, indeed, seems to have been based on an assumption that the Yenan–Chungking conflict could be handled in the same way that he dealt with difficulties within American politics. 'Nothing', he now observed, 'should be final between friends.'[91]

Chiang Kai-shek gave way to the extent of informing Wallace that an American party could proceed to Yenan. The outcome of this was the so-called 'Dixie' mission, led by Colonel David Barrett and including, along with its military personnel, Foreign Service officers.[92] The sending of this mission to Yenan marked a considerable increase in America's involvement in the Communist–Kuomintang struggle, an involvement that had hitherto been restricted to what Roosevelt himself described as 'doing my best to keep some of the Chinese leaders from taking more positive action against the Eighth Route Army leaders.'[93]

Moreover, following Wallace's visit and as the military crisis in East China worsened, Washington's line was advanced further still, from one of advocating the need for reconciliation between Chungking and Yenan to one of suggesting the setting up of a unified military command (under Stilwell, as outlined above), the enactment of reforms by Chiang Kai-shek's regime, and even the establishment of some form of coalition government. As Grew, now in charge of the State Department's Office of Far Eastern Affairs, wrote to Gauss in August,

'We are endeavouring to keep our eyes open for any and every possibility to bring about improvement along lines which we consider urgently needed . . . There is urgent need for broadening the base of support of the Chinese Government, and anything that we can do to hasten such a reform will be all to the good.'[94]

Even Chennault, later so vehement in his denunciation of Americans who, in his eyes, had sold out Chiang Kai-shek to the Communists, was writing to Roosevelt in September to urge that the only way to avoid a Russian-backed victory for Mao Tse-tung's forces was 'for us to sponsor thorough political reconstruction at Chungking, followed by true unification between Chungking and Yenan. Only in this way', he concluded, 'can we insure a strong, united, and above all independent China.'[95] Earlier still, Hull, through Gauss, had passed on to Chiang Kai-shek the suggestion, agreed between himself and the President, that some form of coalition council could help to bring about a much-needed spirit of tolerance and unity.[96]

The more urgent the Americans believed the need for political reconstruction in China to be, the more impatient they became over the Generalissimo's rigid stance. Gauss, for example, declared that Chiang failed to see that time was on the side of the Communists, and believed that 'he does not have any realistic conception of either the character or uses of democracy.'[97] The conclusion could be drawn—and in defiance of the Hornbeck approach, officials within the State Department were beginning to do so—that the United States should take care not to commit itself too firmly to Chiang. Already, at the end of 1943, Davies had given a warning to this effect, advising that 'we should be ready during or after the war to adjust ourselves to possible realignments in China. We should wish, for example, to avoid finding ourselves at the close of the war backing a coalition of Chiang's Kuomintang and the degenerate puppets [of the Japanese] against a democratic coalition commanding Russian sympathy.'[98] And again, in August 1944, in a memorandum that Hopkins passed on to the President, Davies argued that

'We must recognise that the isolation or overthrow of Chiang does not necessarily mean the collapse of China. A coalition which may overshadow or overthrow Chiang may well (1) play a more active and cooperative role in the war against Japan, and (2) serve to unify and strengthen China to a degree which Chiang has not recently been able to do.'[99]

We shall see later that this proposed policy of flexibility, even when it had been approved by the State Department itself, was to be negated by Patrick Hurley who, at the suggestion of Stimson and Marshall, was appointed in August to be Roosevelt's special representative in China, with the prime task, as noted above, of composing the differences between Chiang Kai-shek and Stilwell, and who was soon to become, as he wished, Ambassador in succession to Gauss.[100]* As for the American hopes of bringing the Communists and Kuomintang together, in retrospect they appear to have been predestined to frustration. The very nature of the Kuomintang regime precluded any such accommodation; for the Communists, too, whose fortunes had been reviving since 1942 and whose forces numbered about 474,000 regulars and 2 million militia by October 1944,[101] the ultimate intention (as the Embassy in Chungking, though not every field officer,

---

* Hurley's subsequent line of policy scarcely chimed with the disillusioned attitude of Stimson and Marshall—but then, Eden, as British Foreign Secretary before the war, had nominated Sir Nevile Henderson to be Ambassador in Berlin, where he was a disaster. In the light of Hurley's subsequent clash with John Davies, it is also ironic to find the latter, in conversation with Hopkins in September 1944, welcoming Hurley's appointment as 'a verbally expansive emissary.' (Davies memo., 4 Sept. 1944, Stilwell Papers, box 15.)

recognized) remained the seizure of power, whatever the tactics of delay and restraint needed in the meantime.[102]

It was not the ruthlessness, however, but the vigour and popularity of the Communist regime that struck American observers in this period when they were at last allowed to travel to Yenan. This was the case with newsmen, as well as officials, although the findings of the former, eventually contained in articles and in books such as Harrison Forman's *Report From Red China*, usually had to await publication until the censor in Chungking could be circumvented.[103] John Service, too, who arrived with the Dixie Mission in July, was much impressed by what he found, reporting that the Communist leaders were 'modern' and Western in their outlook, in contrast to the obscurantism of Chungking, and that their control was genuinely democratic. 'As for the ideas that China is "different"', he wrote, 'that the fundamental economic laws do not apply here, or that "foreigners cannot understand China"—they laugh at them.'[104]

Were Mao and his colleagues, then, Communists or not? Service himself had, earlier in 1944, summarized Mao's *New Democracy*, which emphasized that, whatever the need in China for an interim, bourgeois-democratic phase, 'Communist principles' must not be abandoned, and that China's ultimate revolution would be 'part of a great world movement.'[105] (One of the American press representatives, Theodore H. White, was likewise struck by the pride taken by Yenan's leaders in their Communist principles, though he was also impressed by their nationalism.)[106] Yet once he was in Yenan, Service came to stress the moderation of his hosts and their democratic aims, quoting remarks that Mao Tse-tung had made to the correspondent, Gunther Stein, that 'what China needs most is democracy, not socialism', that there should be 'proper treatment of capital, both Chinese and foreign, after the war', and that 'the Comintern has no place in the Far East.'[107]

Stalin, too, encouraged American thoughts and hopes in a similar direction, describing Mao and his colleagues to Harriman in June as 'margarine communists', while Molotov reiterated to Nelson in August that they had 'no relation whatever to communism.'[108] This scornful Soviet attitude, together with Stalin's agreement that Chiang Kai-shek was the man to back in China, played a major part in fostering the American belief that the U.S.A. could, indeed, bring the Kuomintang and the Yenan regime together. Hurley, for example, was quick to relay such Soviet assurances to the Generalissimo who, while renewing his promise that he would seek to solve the Communist problem only by political means, nevertheless remained convinced that the American estimate of that question was naïve and wrong.[109]

Roosevelt himself, meanwhile, having long been encouraged to think in such terms by Major Evans Carlson, as we have seen, cited Hurley's conclusions when declaring to Stettinius in September that the Chinese Communists 'were agrarians.' Wallace had received a similar answer when, in March, he had asked Laughlin Currie, John Davies and John K. Fairbank 'what the Chinese Communists were like' and was told 'that they were agrarian reformers.'[110]* Several American broadcasters and correspondents were disseminating conclusions of the same kind, even when, as in the case of Edgar Snow, this involved placing on the subject an emphasis that was very different from the one put forward in earlier writings, such as his *Red Star Over China*. As they did so, they were also encouraging that comfortable and self-flattering belief, which we have seen expounded by Congressman Walter Judd, that the Chinese were in many essential ways like Americans. 'The Chinese Communists are no more Communistic than we Americans are', wrote Harrison Forman.[111]

Previous historians have already commented on this tendency of American officials and press representatives in 1944–45 to underestimate the role of Marxist-Leninist ideology within the Chinese Communist movement, to focus upon what, to Mao Tse-tung, was only the intermediate goal of 'democratic revolution' as distinct from the ultimate one of 'socialist revolution',[112]† and to project on to the Chinese scene assumptions, involving the use of terms like 'democracy', 'agrarians' and 'opposition', that were derived from the American political tradition and political culture.[113] Such tendencies, together with the strong preference for the Yenan regime over the corrupt and backward-looking Kuomintang dictatorship which their own egalitarian, humanitarian and democratic principles gave to American observers, are of infinitely greater significance than the original Communist sympathies of a few of those who were commenting on China in this period. The charges made after the war by Senator McCarthy and in the hearings on the Institute of Pacific Relations, of a centrally-directed Communist conspiracy to deceive the American people where China was concerned, remain totally unproven and in many cases grotesque.[114]

---

* Two of Wallace's interlocutors on this occasion, John Davies and Professor Fairbank, have been somewhat surprised when presented with this evidence by the author. It is quite possible, of course, that Wallace's record of what was said was distorted or over-simplified when he entered it in his diary. On the other hand, the 'agrarian' image of the Communists was undoubtedly a pervasive one at the time.

† See, e.g., Mao Tse-tung, *The Chinese Revolution and the Chinese Communist Party* (? 1940): 'The character of the Chinese revolution at the present stage is not proletarian-socialist but bourgeois-democratic. However . . . this new-democratic revolution is part of the world proletarian-socialist revolution: it resolutely opposes imperialism, i.e. international capitalism. Politically, it means the joint revolutionary-democratic dictatorship of several revolutionary classes . . . Economically, it means nationalisation of all big capital and big enterprises of the imperialists and reactionary traitors, distribution of large landed property among the peasants and at the same time assistance to private middle and small enterprises without the elimination of the rich-peasant economy. Hence, while clearing the way for capitalism, this democratic revolution of a new type creates the precondition for socialism. The present stage of the Chinese revolution is a transitional stage between putting an end to the colonial, semi-colonial and semi-feudal society and establishing a socialist society—a new revolutionary process, that of the new-democratic revolution . . . China must go through this revolution before she can go forward to a socialist revolution . . .' (S. Schram, *The Political Thought of Mao Tse-tung* (Harmondsworth, 1969), 230. On Mao's theory of semi-colonialism in particular, see Gittings, *China and the World, 1922–1972*, 37ff.)

The Dixie mission to Yenan reinforced the belief that Mao Tse-tung and his colleagues not only represented a vital, yet reasonable force within Chinese politics, but that they were especially anxious to work with the United States. Mao himself, for example, asked Service soon after the latter's arrival if a U.S. Consulate could be established in Yenan, while Chu Teh, as commander of the Communist armies, urged that American troops should be landed on the coast of China. At the end of September, Mao went further still, pressing for United States help to bring about a coalition government (even though he described Chiang Kai-shek as 'fundamentally . . . a gangster'); he also reiterated that China needed free enterprise and foreign capital in order to industrialize, and declared that the Communists 'must and will cooperate with the United States.' Every American soldier in China, Mao continued, 'should be a walking and talking advertisement for democracy. After all, we Chinese consider you Americans the ideal of democracy.'[115]

The tactical advantages to be gained by the Communist leadership by speaking in this manner are obvious, and it is highly likely that, whatever the American response had been, Mao would have gone on 'leaning to one side' in the direction of the Soviet Union rather than the West.[116] Even so, it also seems likely that the admiration for American revolutionary traditions to which Mao referred was a genuine one,[117] and it is quite possible that here, in Yenan towards the end of 1944, there was an opportunity to improve the quality of long-term Sino-American relations—an opportunity that Roosevelt was to squander by his acceptance of Hurley's adherence to Chiang Kai-shek and his failure, as during the Stilwell crisis, to follow a strong but flexible policy through to its conclusion.

Meanwhile Service, for his part, in calling for American assistance to be given to Yenan even if Chungking were to oppose such a policy, was pursuing a belief that he had set forth earlier, in April: that a new, unified China in which the Communists would play an important part 'would naturally gravitate towards the United States, and that the United States, by virtue of a sympathy, position and economic resources, would enjoy a greater influence in China than any other foreign power.'[118] Thus, even as belief in Chiang Kai-shek crumbled away, new foundations were being laid by some officials and observers on which they could continue to build the long-standing American expectation that their country had a special role to play and a privileged position to occupy in an 'awakening' China. In this sense, a Hornbeck and a Service, far apart though they were on the issue of how to deal with the China of 1944, had something in common in their broad approach. And from Roosevelt downwards, as we have seen, this approach, together with America's very much greater involvement on the ground in China, continued to help prevent the development of a full partnership with Britain in East Asia.

Britain and China

There was no British equivalent of America's Dixie mission to Yenan.

Instead, the Embassy in Chungking had to rely upon reports made by various Europeans who came south after staying in the Communist areas. Such reports were strongly favourable towards Mao Tse-tung's regime, as Sir Horace Seymour noted when forwarding to London the observations of the British academic, William Band, who with his wife, Michael Lindsay and the latter's wife, had fled into guerrilla territory at the time of Pearl Harbour.[119]

'Mr Band', wrote Seymour in March 1944, 'confirms the favourable view which all previous foreign observers have expressed regarding the Chinese Communists and their administration. He agrees with the general opinion regarding the success of the Communist policy in regard to such matters, in particular, as the enlistment of the support of the peasants for the 8th Route Army; the reduction of taxes and abolition of illegal levies; the limitation of rentals; the elimination of corruption; freedom of speech and belief; promotion of universal education; an effective system of democratic government. He emphasises as others have done that the very success of this policy has won for the Communist leaders the enthusiastic support of all classes of people. One cannot but be impressed by the unanimity of these observers . . . and it is worthy of note that the majority of them have been people of long experience of China.'[120]

In Britain itself, similar views were now reaching the public through the activities of the China Campaign Committee, which reissued as a pamphlet two articles, originally published in *Amerasia* in the spring of 1944, by Michael Lindsay, who was also inserting occasional pieces in *The Times* via his father, the Master of Balliol. In his preface to the pamphlet, which was to be reprinted again in 1945, this time by no less than the Government Stationery Office, Lord Listowel, a junior Minister, summarized the contents as revealing 'a new political and social consciousness among the peoples of North China . . . a sudden leap forward in social organisation which is moving rapidly towards democratic government, public education, equality between the sexes, honest administration, and an agrarian reform that will sweep away feudal practices and privileges, by giving the peasant his place in the sun.'[121] Favourable views of Yenan were also being formed by Gunther Stein of the *Manchester Guardian*, who was one of the correspondents allowed to go there in the summer of 1944. (In Stein's case, the unproven charge, which he denied, was later made that he had been a Soviet agent. Whatever the truth of the matter, however, his enthusiasm for Mao Tse-tung's administration and disillusion with Chungking were in no way unusual.)[122] In Parliament, too, the subject of the Kuomintang's blockade of Yenan was raised by a Communist M.P., while questions were also asked about the share being received by the Communist areas, and in particular by the International Peace Hospitals there, of United Aid to China funds being sent to China from Britain.[123]

As during the preceding period and as in American official and press circles, the ideological complexion of the Yenan regime continued to be the subject of widely differing views. Band's opinion, conveyed by Seymour, was that the theories of Mao and his colleagues were 'Marxist Leninist in origin and essence, but have been modified and adapted to meet native conditions and requirements. They have fashioned their own brand of Communism, which is ideologically connected with the Soviet variety, but owes nothing to Soviet leadership or control.' Stein likewise judged that his hosts 'are and intend to remain Communists', but 'found Chinese national-ism a more characteristic trait of Yenan's ideology than Marxism',[124] while Lindsay, in a private letter, emphasized that Yenan's leaders were genuinely anxious to see China unified and 'would make a lot of concessions [to the Kuomintang] . . . if only they could get their fundamental demands about democracy realised . . .'[125]

Within official circles, Clark Kerr kept up from Moscow his pressing but erroneous argument that the Yenan regime was 'in no sense Communist', citing Molotov's view to that effect.[126] However, the Foreign Office Research Department, and in particular G. P. Hudson, strongly disagreed. Hudson was scornful of the use (by Band among others) of the word 'democracy' in a Western sense to describe such an administration, arguing that, even if it were not controlled by Moscow (as, indeed, seemed to be the case), 'Com-munists are devoted to the interests of the U.S.S.R. because it is an essential part of their political faith.' 'The Communists do not', he wrote, 'any more than the Kuomintang, think of "democracy" as a system which gives a chance to opposition parties. What is really meant by the "democracy" of the Communists is that they are strongly supported by the poorer peasantry who are the "masses" in rural China.' Members of the Far Eastern Depart-ment agreed. 'The "Communist" administration', minuted G. P. Young, 'should be given credit for their real achievement, which is agrarian and social reform, and not for their resemblance to a democracy.'[127] Although no complete comparison is possible, since British officials did not have the experience of seeing Yenan at first hand, it may be suggested that in general they tended to arrive at a more realistic evaluation of the Chinese Com-munist movement than did their American counterparts, and were less prone to project on to the Chinese scene images and assumptions derived from domestic, Western political cultures and experience.

In addition, and again in contrast to a good many American officials and politicians, most British officials were agreed in taking a pessimistic view of attempts to find a *modus vivendi* between the Communists and Chungking, and in believing that anything more than a 'papering of the cracks' was improbable.[128] As for the outcome of the expected conflict, opinions con-tinued to differ. Hudson, for example, still thought it unlikely that the Communists could win control of the whole of China and that any Soviet assistance they received would probably be balanced by American aid to the Kuomintang. Young, on the other hand, was, as before, impressed by the vigour of the Yenan regime, and believed that 'the Chiang Kai-shek dynasty has had its day and is as far removed from the set-up which will emerge from post-war China as the Manchus were from the China which was to emerge in 1911.'[129]

Meanwhile, when it came to the possibility or advisability of outside intervention, there was again a marked contrast with the optimism and urgency that were being expressed on the American side. This was so, even though the Foreign Office shared the United States view that increased trouble between China and the Soviet Union was all too likely. (Smuts, also, raised this possibility at the Commonwealth Prime Ministers' meeting, speculating that 'China might . . . in the end find herself much under Russian influence.')[130] Seymour's advice from Chungking was that 'pressure from the Western powers . . . might be resented by the Communists and the Central Government alike', and the Foreign Office accepted that it would be best to keep out of the matter. Only at the very end of this period, in September, did a new Head of the Far Eastern Department, J. C. Sterndale Bennett, raise the possibility of seeking permission from Chungking for an official observer to go up to Yenan, and even then he was persuaded to drop the issue for the time being.[131]

Reluctance to intervene in the Kuomintang–Communist struggle was not due to any great admiration on the part of British officials for Chiang Kai-shek's rule. On the contrary, it was observed that the Generalissimo was becoming, in Seymour's words, 'more and more autocratic', the intention of the Kuomintang being, as Hudson saw it, 'to exalt [him] to the position of Emperor in everything but name.' Again the term 'fascist' was used in the Foreign Office to describe the Kuomintang regime, as it also was by a director of I.C.I. (China) in a talk he gave at Chatham House.[132]* (In Canberra, too, Sir Frederick Eggleston was depicting China as 'a Fascist state.')[133] Episodes like the one involving the 'thought control' of Chinese students abroad—deplored in London, as in Washington—helped to reinforce the conclusion that was reached in a Ministry of Information survey, that 'the most marked feature of Chinese political life today is the combination of an increased tendency towards one-party, authoritarian rule by the Kuomintang with protestations of devotion to constitutional and democratic practices . . . , [resulting in] the temporary decline in political importance of those sections of the population most likely to be friendly to Great Britain.'[134]

The possibility of expansionist tendencies on the part of the Chinese Government also continued to engage the attention of British officials. Chinese maps that claimed parts of Burma and Malaya were noted, while the Indian Agent General in Chungking saw 'sinister possibilities' in the existence in India of Chinese who could serve as a fifth-column for the Kuomintang.[135] In New Delhi in particular, as during earlier periods, much

---

* The same I.C.I. official described the Chinese Communists as 'not as Communistic as one would imagine. In fact', he went on, 'they are very open-minded. If you could get rid of this ultra-nationalistic clique in the saddle at present in Chungking, and many Government officials are extremely broad-minded, I think that the way would be open for a compromise with the Communists.'

concern was also being expressed over Chungking's apparent intention to reabsorb Tibet, the long-term precaution being taken, as noted earlier, of carrying on pushing British administration up to the McMahon line in northern Assam. Yet apart from sending Sir Basil Gould, the Political Officer in Sikkim, on a visit to Lhasa, and reiterating Britain's readiness to see an agreement whereby a Tibetan recognition of Chinese suzerainty would be exchanged for a Chinese acceptance of Tibetan autonomy, it seemed that there was little that could be done over the matter. Certainly, no promise of military assistance could be given to the anxious Tibetans.[136]

Meanwhile there also remained the question of the future of Hongkong, on which there was still no agreed long-term policy in London beyond the Prime Minister's refusal to contemplate the surrender of any part of the British Empire. The view was again being expressed within the Foreign Office that the colony would eventually have to be ceded to China, but that this should be done 'not [as] a futile gesture of appeasement . . . but [as] a contribution to arrangements for international security.' Others, Amery among them, went on arguing the case for Hongkong's retention on the grounds of prestige, commercial opportunity, and 'the uncertainty of China's future.'[137]

Not that British reactions to China in this period were all criticism and suspicion, any more than had been the case before 1944. During the early part of the year, especially, glowing tributes to her continued to appear in the press, with *The Times*, for example, declaring that 'sympathy for the Chinese cause is universal in this country', referring to 'admiration for unflinching valour . . . struggling to rebuild a liberal and progressive China', and to Britain's desire 'for the most cordial relations with that great country.'[138] Lord Teviot, who had been a member of the Parliamentary mission to China, wrote to *The Times* in praise of 'the grand leadership of the Generalissimo, who is looked up to and respected by all', while Churchill himself described Chiang Kai-shek in the Commons as 'a world figure and the main hope and champion of China.'[139] As if to lend substance to such expressions of good-will (though in fact it was the Chinese who in the end had to give way over the terms involved), agreement was at least reached over the £50 million British loan, on which, it will be recalled, negotiations had been deadlocked since 1942.[140]*

Other tokens of British friendship and cooperation were also still being given in this period, such as the work of the Friends Ambulance Unit in China, which was supported by a Government grant.[141] Dr. Joseph Needham, his activities looked upon askance in some quarters of Whitehall but supported by the Embassy in Chungking, went on developing wide cultural and scientific contacts in that country on behalf of the British Council.[142]

---

* Signed on 2 May 1944, the agreement provided for £10 million in the first instance to secure an internal loan, £10 million for printing banknotes in the sterling area during the war, £20 million for the purchase of goods in the sterling area for war purposes, and the remaining £10 million to be used for the purposes of the agreement as might be proved necessary. A Lend Lease agreement was signed at the same time.

Donations also continued to be sent out by the United Aid to China Fund, although, as noted above, there was increasing disquiet in some quarters, notably on the part of Dorothy Woodman, Victor Gollancz and other members of the China Campaign Committee, over the way in which the Fund was being distributed. In this connection, the integrity of Madame Chiang Kai-shek was questioned, and a case was made out for more money to be sent to the International Peace Hospitals in Communist areas. There was also a good deal of resentment in London (the Chancellor of the Exchequer withheld his own subscription from the U.A.C.F. on these grounds) over the absurd exchange rate—more than ten times less than the open-market one—which the Chinese authorities at first insisted on maintaining for these U.A.C.F. payments.[143]*

At the same time, hopes were still being entertained and plans developed by the China Association as regards the commercial opportunities which it was believed would exist in China after the war. Individual firms who were thinking in similar terms included British American Tobacco,[144] the Peking Syndicate (which had established an important position in war-time trade with the Chinese Government), I.C.I. (which had plans for establishing a joint company with the Chinese on a 50–50 basis), and the British China Corporation (which, in conjunction with John Keswick of Jardine Matheson, was still exploring the possibility of setting up a Sino-British corporation in the field of civil aviation.)[145] Whitehall, like Washington, was also now slowly preparing a draft commercial treaty with China. A strong difference of opinion was already emerging, however, and was to become more marked still in the final period of the war, between those who, like the Far Eastern Department of the Foreign Office, argued forcefully for the granting of post-war credits to China as a means of reestablishing British commerce there, and hence of restoring British prestige and influence ('We cannot abdicate in the Far East', wrote Sterndale Bennett in this connection), and those who, on the other hand, believed that in the straitened circumstances in which Britain would find herself after the war, it would be foolish to risk putting money into a country as unstable, politically and economically, as China.[146]

Moreover, whatever the hopes that might be entertained regarding the future, there was no disguising the continuing slenderness of the current British presence in and collaboration with China. The two British military organizations that remained there, although valued in London as 'to some extent replacing, in the areas in which they operate, the influence formerly exercised by our consuls and the leaders of our trading communities', were small and, as before, handicapped by the difficulty of getting adequate

---

* Of instalments which generally amounted to about £140,000, £10,000 was usually earmarked for the International Peace Hospitals. The official exchange rate was 80 Chinese $ to the pound, while the open-market rate was about $1,000 to the £. The Chinese authorities at first supplemented U.A.C.F. payments to make an effective rate of $160; later, agreement was reached on a rate of $700 for such instalments.

'Hump' supplies allocated to them.[147]* The amount of British Lend Lease aid to China was still extremely limited (even in India, about one-third of the value of supplies given to the Chinese Army units there came from U.S. sources), and hopes of opening a new route to China through Sinkiang were abandoned in this period.[148] Suspicions concerning Chinese motives and security also helped to prevent collaboration in the intelligence field, while Chiang Kai-shek was not given full details of British military plans in Southeast Asia.[149]

Nor was there by the summer of 1944 any disguising the chaotic and perilous stituation in which China found herself, and which cast uncertainty over both the political and the commercial future. As the Japanese attack progressed, previous low estimates of the military value of the Chinese forces appeared to be amply confirmed. (The Foreign Office also found 'illuminating' a report from Needham, in which he described the appalling medical conditions existing amongst Kuomintang units, contrasting these with information he had received on the excellent state of affairs in 'the so-called Communist areas', with their Eighth Route and New Fourth Armies.)[150] In the press, as well as in official circles, reports were circulating of corruption and confusion in China—a 'debunking' process which the Foreign Office thought useful if not carried too far.[151]†

Overall, the picture as seen in London by the middle and later parts of this period was one of increasing disintegration in China, and what one Foreign Office official described as 'alarming possibilities' there—although he added, 'there's nothing we can do.'[152] In May, the Commonwealth Prime Ministers were told by Eden of worsening Kuomintang–Communist relations, and of runaway inflation. (Smuts, who was listening, confessed that 'he had not [till then] appreciated the inherent weakness of the Chinese state.')[153] By August, Chiang Kai-shek's domestic authority was seen as having been considerably diminished. G. P. Young in the Foreign Office, as we have seen, believed that the Generalissimo's regime was finished, though Eden observed that 'it is not in our interest that China should relapse into chaos, which will, I fear, occur if he can't win through.'[154]‡

---

* The organizations were (1) the British Army Aid Group under Colonel Ride (the officer who had written a scathing report on the Hongkong Administration as it was at the end of 1941; see above, 202), which operated an escape network, had a small S.O.E. wing, and supplied intelligence to G.H.Q. India and to the Colonial Office, where plans were being prepared for an emergency administration to be set up in Hongkong should Chinese forces get there before major British units; and (2) officers of 204 Military Mission, who were still training special Chinese 'surprise' battalions.

† Interestingly enough, such 'debunking' of China in the British press threatened to disturb an arrangement that had been arrived at in 1943 between the authorities in Chungking and New Delhi, each bent on preserving the status quo and now finding a common, conservative ground that contrasted with their tense relations in 1942. Under this arrangement, reports on each other's internal situation were cleared before publication with officials of the country concerned. The Indian Administration was therefore not pleased when the press in Britain was allowed freedom to publish more or less what it wanted about the Chungking regime.

‡ The Australian Chargé d'Affaires in Chungking also thought that Chiang Kai-shek

Whether China would, eventually, become a major power was still arguable—there were those in the Foreign Office and its Research Department who held that within ten or twenty years she would have solved her internal problems, developed the capacity to resist any invader, and begun to exert 'very formidable' influence, especially in Southeast Asia.[155] For the moment, however, the evidence appeared to support Churchill when he scornfully dismissed American claims that China should be treated as a great power. At the same time, such evidence also reinforced British scepticism over the value of the effort which the Americans, for all their own re-thinking over strategy, were insisting should be put into attempts to reopen land communications with China by South East Asia Command.

was the one strong man in China, the running of which had best be left to him without outside interference. (Officer to McDougall, 18 July 1944, Officer Papers, MS 2629/1/966.)

Notes to Chapter Nineteen

1 Hornbeck memo., 13 July 1944, Hornbeck Papers, box 181.
2 Hurley to FDR, 21 May 1944, OPD, Exec. file 10, item 61.
3 Miles memo., 19 Sept. 1944, Naval Group China files, USNOA.
4 Taussig memo., 14 Feb. 1944, Taussig Papers, box 47. In conversation with an official of the I.P.R., Vincent of the State Department expressed the opinion that the British 'were in all probability through in Hong Kong.' Dennett memo., 18 Jan. 1944, IPR Papers, box 358.
5 FRUS, 1944, China, 231. For further material on the Wallace–Chiang talks, see *U.S. and China*, 549ff.
6 Memo. of 10 April 1944, Wallace Papers, box 61; *Wallace*, 9 May 1944.
7 FO 371, F3045/1776/10; Eden memo., 4 Aug. 1944, PREM 4, 27/10.
8 FRUS, 1944, China, 952, 964; material in FO 371, files 41539–40.
9 Material in PREM 3, 142/7.
10 See FRUS, 1944, China, 969.
11 See *Morgenthau Diary, China*, II, passim.
12 FO 371, AN4068/20/45; *Wallace*, 3 Oct. 1944.
13 Halifax to Eden, 30 Aug. 1944, Hickleton Papers, A4 410 4.
14 FO 371, F3503/28/10.
15 WSC to Eden, 23 Aug. 1944, PREM 4, 30/11.
16 Minutes of 4 May 1944, PREM 4, 42/5.
17 *Stettinius*, 15 April 1944. It was during this period that the Prime Minister, when receiving a Chinese delegation, apparently chose to discuss the subject of ma-jongh. FO 371, F2248/34/10.
18 Eden to Halifax, 12 Aug. 1944, PREM 4, 30/11; APW, 20 July 1944, CAB 87/66.
19 FO 371, F2480/1776/10.
20 Ibid, AN3199/34/45.
21 Ibid, F1866/16/10.
22 Material in ibid, files 41617–8.
23 See e.g. ibid, F689/16/10.
24 E.g. ibid, F1175/16/10 and the case of the floating power stations, in files 41569 and 41572.
25 China Association Exec. Cttee., 14 July 1944 and General Cttee., 18 July 1944; minutes of meeting at Foreign Office, 12 April 1944, Ch.A.
26 Far Eastern Group, 30 Aug. 1944, RIIA
27 FO 371, AN1241/20/45; Hornbeck to Clarke, 28 March 1944, Hornbeck Papers, box 118.

28 FO 371, F2017/28/10.
29 Ibid, F3467 and 3976/357/10; see F3598/14/10, AN3268 and 3658/20/45.
30 Halifax despatch, 20 Aug. 1944, PREM 4, 27/10.
31 Ibid.
32 Carton de Wiart to Ismay, 24 April 1944, PREM 3, 159/14, and 25 April 1944, PREM 4, 28/7; FO 371, F2397/127/10.
33 Seymour despatch, 12 July 1944, PREM 3, 159/14; FO 371, F2970/34/10; F3308/127/10.
34 FRUS, 1944, China, 385.
35 FRUS, 1944, V, 1232; see FRUS, 1944, China, 784.
36 FRUS, 1944, China, 877.
37 *Davies*, 305. Wallace declared that the end of the war would mark 'the beginning of the century of the common man.'
38 *New York Times*, 13 Feb. 1944.
39 Judd press conference, 24 Aug. 1944, Dulles Papers, box 2.
40 Hornbeck to Hull, 6 July and 2 Aug. 1944, Hornbeck Papers, box 380; Hornbeck to Hull, 17 July 1944, Hull papers, vol. 63.
41 *Young*, 350. United China Relief also disbursed about $8½ million between Sept. 1943 and Sept. 1944. Most of the money came from the National War Fund. UCR Papers, boxes 48 and 77.
42 FRUS, 1944, China, 16; Gauss to Hornbeck, 8 Jan. 1944, Hornbeck Papers, box 175.
43 FRUS, 1944, China, 249, 1018, 1045, 1062.
44 Ibid, 1049. American firms were also anxious about the requirements the Chinese Government sought to lay down for their registration, though the deadline set for this, 30 July 1944, was shifted, first to the end of the year and then to the end of June 1945. Ibid, 983.
45 *New York Times*, 5 May and 19 Aug. 1944; Nathaniel Peffer article, *New York Times Magazine*, 7 Nov. 1943; *Christian Science Monitor*, 11 April 1944.
46 E.g. *Wallace*, 20 June 1944. On FDR's exasperation with the Soongs, see Stimson Diary, 23 June 1944.
47 See Boyle, *China and Japan At War*, 319.
48 FRUS, 1944, China, 319, 457, 470, 492, 581.
49 Dennett memo., 18 Jan. 1944, IPR Papers, box 358.
50 FRUS, 1944, China, 234.
51 Davies memo., 4 Sept. 1944, Stilwell Papers, box 15; FRUS, 1944, China, 230; Hull, *Memoirs*, II, 1586.
52 Chennault to FDR, 26 May 1944, Roosevelt Papers, PSF box 103; material in Hopkins Papers, box 334; Stimson Diary, 1 June and 2 Aug. 1944; *Romanus and Sutherland*, II, cap. XI.
53 Blum, *Roosevelt and Morgenthau*, 537.
54 *Romanus and Sutherland*, II, 370.
55 *Matloff*, 436–7.
56 Ibid, 440; *Romanus and Sutherland*, II, 363.
57 *Romanus and Sutherland*, II, 457, 463.
58 See ibid, 80, 304ff.
59 JCS memo., 4 July 1944, OPD, Exec. file 10, item 68; subsequent material in ibid, item 60 and Roosevelt Papers, MR box 10. See FRUS, 1944, China, 120ff.
60 Stilwell to Marshall, 26 Sept. 1944, OPD, Exec. file 10, item 60; see *Stilwell Papers*, 317.
61 JCS, 16 Sept. 1944, RG 218; FRUS, 1944, China, 157.
62 E.g. Stilwell Diary, 19 Sept. 1944.
63 Leahy Diary, 16 Oct. 1944.
64 FRUS, 1944, China, 166; *Romanus and Sutherland*, II, 459ff.
65 Marshall draft memo., 4 Oct. 1944, OPD, Exec. file 10, item 60.
66 Stilwell notes, n.d., Stilwell Papers, box 21; Stilwell Diary, 4 Oct. 1944.
67 See *Davies*, 338.

68 FRUS, 1944, China, 240; Cf. Lake, *The Legacy of Vietnam*, 329, 362.
69 *Lattimore*, 52–4.
70 FRUS, 1944, China, 100, 149.
71 Ibid, 37.
72 *Morgenthau Diary, China*, II, 1211.
73 FRUS, 1943, China, 180.
74 FRUS, 1944, China, 843, 847.
75 FRUS, 1943, China, 484.
76 Ibid, 476.
77 *Morgenthau Diary, China*, II, 1027.
78 Stimson Diary, 19 Jan. 1944.
79 *Morgenthau Diary, China*, II, 1022; Blum, *Roosevelt and Morgenthau*, 473; FRUS, 1943, China, 479.
80 FRUS, 1944, China ,847, 855.
81 *U.S. and China*, 492; *Morgenthau Diary, China*, II, passim; *Young*, 286ff.
82 FRUS, 1944, China, 948; *Morgenthau Diary, China*, II, 1352.
83 Blum, *Morgenthau Diaries: Years of War*, 285ff.; *Young*, cap. XVIII. China also made claims in this period for extensive aid from U.N.R.R.A. *Young*, cap. XIX.
84 Welles, *Seven Decisions That Shaped History* (New York, 1950), 152.
85 FRUS, 1944, China, 41, 761, 777.
86 *U.S. and China*, 549, 555.
87 FRUS, 1944, China, 97.
88 Tang Tsou, *America's Failure In China, 1941–50* (Chicago, 1962; hereafter, *Tang Tsou*), 156; FRUS, 1944, China, 484.
89 FRUS, 1944, China, 102, 307, 329, 348, 355; *Davies*, 300.
90 FDR to Wallace, 21 June 1944, Roosevelt Papers, MR box 12; *U.S. and China*, 549ff.
91 *Wallace*, 18 May 1944.
92 See D. Barrett, *The Dixie Mission: The United States Army Observer Group in Yenan, 1944* (Berkeley, 1970); *Romanus and Sutherland*, II, 375.
93 FDR to Carlson, 2 March 1944, Roosevelt Papers, PSF box 36.
94 Grew to Gauss, 17 Aug. 1944, Grew Papers, vol. 118.
95 FRUS, 1944, China, 158.
96 Ibid, 567; *U.S. and China*, 560, 563.
97 FRUS, 1944, China, 69, 544, 573.
98 FRUS, 1943, China, 397.
99 Davies memo., 30 Aug. 1944, Roosevelt Papers, MR box 165.
100 Stimson Diary, 3 Aug. 1944; FDR directive to Hurley, 18 Aug. 1944, Roosevelt Papers, PSF box 151; FRUS, 1944, China, 247.
101 At the end of 1943, the Communist-controlled base areas covered 155,000 square miles and contained 54 million people. By 1945, the Communists controlled 225,000 square miles and about 65 million people. *Tang Tsou*, 51; Donovan to FDR, 28 Sept. 1944, Roosevelt Papers, PSF box 167.
102 FRUS, 1944, China, 559; see e.g. *Tang Tsou*, 136.
103 *Shewmaker*, 162ff., 173ff., 199ff.
104 FRUS, 1944, China, 517, 551, 623.
105 Ibid, 420.
106 White and Jacoby, *Thunder Out Of China*, 220; *Shewmaker*, 247.
107 FRUS, 1944, China, 536, 559, 585.
108 Ibid, 97, 253.
109 Ibid, 154.
110 *Stettinius*, 8 Sept. 1944; *Wallace*, 9 March 1944.
111 See *Shewmaker*, 239ff.; *Tang Tsou*, 224ff.
112 For example, on the ignorance of Vincent, Chief of the Division of Chinese Affairs, in the field of Marxist ideology, see *Tang Tsou*, 221.
113 See *Tang Tsou*, 219ff., and *Shewmaker*, 297ff.
114 The position is well summarized in *Shewmaker*, 269ff.

115 FRUS, 1944, China, 522, 589, 599.
116 See *Tang Tsou*, 208ff.; cf. Gittings, *China and the World*, 92. See e.g. Mao's address, 'Stalin Is Our Commander', in Schram, *The Political Thought of Mao Tse-tung*, 426.
117 See S. Schram, *Mao Tse-tung* (Harmondsworth, 1967), 226, and, Gittings, *China and the World*, 98.
118 FRUS, 1944, China, 615, 777.
119 C. and W. Band, *Dragon Fangs* (London, 1947).
120 FO 371, F1546/159/10.
121 Lindsay, *North China Front*, in Cripps Papers, file 676; in general, see *Shewmaker*, 134ff., and Lindsay, *The Unknown War*.
122 G. Stein, *The Challenge of Red China* (London, 1945); *Shewmaker*, 283, 295.
123 Hansard, HC Deb, 399, col. 1326; FO 371, F2755/5/10.
124 Stein, *Challenge of Red China*, 81ff., 113.
125 FO 371, F4519/159/10.
126 Ibid, F4114/3913/10.
127 Ibid, F2375, 1546 and 975/195/10.
128 E.g. ibid, F2375/159/159/10; F4356/34/10.
129 Ibid, F4519/159/10; F3503/28/10.
130 Material in ibid, file 41637; minutes of 5 May 1944, PREM 4, 42/5.
131 FO 371, F1546 and 4023/159/10.
132 Ibid, F1003/34/10; F1441/159/10; F399/34/10; Far Eastern Group, 9 Aug. 1944, RIIA.
133 AAWC, 5 April 1944, A2682, vol. VII.
134 FO 371, F2000/1031/10; F2017/28/10.
135 Ibid, F400 and 2821/34/10; see Officer Diary, 20 Feb. 1944, MS 2629/2/19.
136 WP(44)271 (CAB 66/50); WP(44)352 (CAB 66/52); WP(44)538 (CAB 66/55); material in FO 371, files 41585–8; *Wavell*, 25 March 1944.
137 FO 371, F2172 and 3681/1505/10; W2166/1534/G.
138 *Times*, 18 Jan. 1944; see also e.g. *Evening Standard*, 11 Jan. 1944.
139 *Times*, 19 April 1944; Hansard, HC Deb, 397, col. 696.
140 FO 371, files 41546–7.
141 Ibid, F467/5/10.
142 Ibid, material in files 41567, 41570–1, 41579.
143 Ibid, material in files 41548–61.
144 On British American Tobacco's record in China, see Gittings, *China and the World*, cap. 1.
145 FO 371, F3571/4/10; F3617/16/10; F437/120/10; file 41626 passim; China Association-Dpt. of Overseas Trade meeting, 9 May 1944, China Association Exec. Cttee., Ch.A; Far Eastern Group, 9 Aug. 1944, RIIA; Hansard, HC Deb, 402, col. 168.
146 FO 371, files 41601 and 40952.
147 See ibid, F5347/20/10; F1194/2/10; file 41623, passim.
148 By June 1944, about £3 million worth of supplies had been sent from Australia, £6 million had been provided in supplies and services for Chinese troops in India and Burma, and £50,000 of supplies had been sent from Britain. FO 371, F2855/2/10 and files 41536 and 41591; *Romanus and Sutherland*, II, 279.
149 Carton de Wiart to WSC, 15 Sept. 1944, PREM 3, 159/14; FO 371, file 41676B. On separate British intelligence activities in China, organized from the U.S.A., see Wilkinson Journal, vol. 3.
150 FO 371, F2235/5/10; Carton de Wiart to Ismay, 18 Sept. 1944, PREM 3, 159/14.
151 E.g. Dalton Diary, 7 June 1944; *Observer*, 4 June 1944; FO 371, F2611/28/10; F2243/159/10; material in files 41612–14.
152 FO 371, F2880/34/10.
153 Minutes of 4 and 5 May 1944, PREM 4, 42/5; FO 371, W7599/1534/G.
154 FO 371, F3659/3659/10; F4046/34/10. For a report by Needham on the various factions within the Kuomintang, see F436/159/10.
155 Ibid, F399/34/10.

CHAPTER TWENTY

SOUTHEAST ASIA AND THE FUTURE OF EMPIRES

Campaign issues in Southeast Asia

DESPITE THE fact that considerable military success was eventually achieved during this period against the Japanese in Southeast Asia, many of those serving in that theatre continued to experience a sense of frustration. Notwithstanding the efforts of a Supreme Commander who was very publicity-conscious, the feeling remained that this was 'a forgotten war.' (Remarks to this effect by Dening and Pownall, for example, have already been quoted.)[1] Worse still, there were the delays, described above, in obtaining revised strategic directives from London and the Combined Chiefs of Staff, as Churchill conducted his tussle with his military advisers and as planners in Washington began to question the entire American presence in Southeast Asia.[2] For the British involved in S.E.A.C.'s affairs, there also existed the usual difficulty of inadequate resources, a deficiency that enabled the Americans, to Churchill's anger,[3] to impose material constraints upon any strategy which they did not themselves support.

> 'The hard fact is', wrote Mountbatten's Chief of Staff in April 1944, 'that the Americans have got us by the short hairs . . . We can't do anything in this theatre, amphibious or otherwise, without material assistance from them . . . So if they don't approve they don't provide, and that brings the whole project automatically to an end. They will provide stuff for north Burma operations . . . but they won't for anything else . . . Who pays the piper calls the tune.'[4]

The outcome for Mountbatten and his staff was a period of great uncertainty, as various operations emerged as possibilities only to become surrounded with questions. Could the necessary landing craft be retained in order to carry out an attack behind the Japanese lines, along the Arakan coast (operation 'Pigstick'), as the Americans wished?[5] Would the Prime Minister's private campaign for an operation against Sumatra ('Culverin') prove successful? Could one hope to obtain sufficient resources to carry out a seaborne attack on Rangoon ('Vanguard') before the defeat of Germany?[6] In addition, there again was Churchill's impatience to contend with, directed as it was against such matters as the degree of numerical superiority over the enemy deemed necessary by S.E.A.C.'s planners, and, in particular, against 'the disgrace', as he saw it, of the small number of fighting divisions in Burma produced by the huge Indian Army, described by the Prime Minister as 'a gigantic system of outdoor relief.'[7]

Problems also continued to surround the role of India as a base and the supply line connecting it with the fronts in Burma, though in the latter case improvements were achieved when Americans took over responsibility for the Bengal–Assam railway.[8] Meanwhile, uncertainty still hung over the degree of cooperation that could be expected from the Chinese forces in Yunnan, Mountbatten quickly becoming exasperated by Chiang Kai-shek's renewed attempts to lay down preconditions for their employment, and passing on to London the speculation that the Generalissimo was 'keeping these troops, which are said to be the best in China, in case he needs to use them against his political opponents.'[9] Chiang Kai-shek, wrote Admiral Somerville, was 'a stupid old man.'[10] Somerville's own presence, and his belief that Mountbatten should 'act more as a Chairman of a Committee [of his Commanders in Chief] than as a Supreme Commander' also continued to present problems up to his relief by Admiral Sir Bruce Fraser in August.[11] So, too, until his death in March, did the demanding zeal of Wingate: in Churchill's eyes 'a man of genius who might have been a man of destiny'; to some in the higher echelons of S.E.A.C., on the other hand, someone whose end came as a relief: 'This may shock you', observed Air Marshal Sir Philip Joubert to an American staff officer, 'but I was delighted at Wingate's death because I felt that these [Chindit] forces then would be pulled out of central Burma and put to some use elsewhere.'[12]*

The major trouble bedevilling S.E.A.C., however, continued to be that of the contending British and American pulls towards Singapore and Yunnan respectively.[13] This involved in 1944, as we have seen within the context of grand strategy, the affair of the 'Axiom' and Stilwell missions to the West, and the arguments of the S.E.A.C. staff—including at first, it should be noted, American officers such as Wedemeyer—against Stilwell's Ledo Road project. ('The acceleration of the U.S. programme in the Pacific', wrote Mountbatten in April, 'has made the construction of a road and pipeline to China through Northern Burma more than ever out of step with global strategy.')[14] An even greater degree of polarization, in fact, took place in the summer, as Wedemeyer and other American staff officers shifted away from Mountbatten's and towards Stilwell's position, so that Dening, reporting to London in July, could talk of 'our different [national] attitudes about aid to China.'[15]

In general, London and Washington went on backing the rival views of their respective commanders on the spot. The British Chiefs of Staff disliked the North Burma campaign; so, too, did Churchill, although he vacillated over whether or not it was worth trying to take Myitkyina, and was ready to reassure the Americans that Britain would not try to undermine Stilwell's

* Note also the later comment of Major Desmond Morton: 'The death of Orde Wingate must have been an act of divine providence.' (Thompson, *Churchill and Morton*, 181.)

efforts.[16] In Washington, meanwhile, Marshall remained solidly behind Stilwell. And although, as we have seen, the U.S. Army's planners had begun to place a reduced valuation on the latter's operations in a way which made agreement with London far more feasible (even Roosevelt, when talking to Wedemeyer in March, 'did not appear', the latter reported, 'to attach importance to [the Ledo Road], at least not as much as he had on previous occasions'),[17] Stilwell's dramatic seizure of Myitkyina airfield in May, using as his spearhead the American troops of 'Merrill's Marauders', gave new life to the North Burma campaign. ('Will this burn up the Limies!' wrote a jubilant Stilwell in his diary.)[18] Thereafter, as already noted, the push towards China had to remain a feature of S.E.A.C.'s task as laid down by the Combined Chiefs of Staff. Wedemeyer himself not only swung round to adopt the standard American view, but began sending back to Washington messages that probably helped increase the suspicion and impatience that already existed there. The British, he commented, were 'primarily interested in restoring their prestige throughout Southeast Asia' and only secondarily in defeating the Japanese.[19] (Churchill's private definition of Britain's aims in a different sense will be recalled.)[20] Now secretly arguing against his Supreme Commander, Wedemeyer likewise wrote to Marshall in August to urge 'that the U.S. Chiefs of Staff insist once more that S.E.A.C. conduct operations without delay to secure the overland route to China.'[21]

Against this background of discord over basic strategy, Anglo-American relations within S.E.A.C. continued to be uneasy and if anything, as the case of Wedemeyer illustrates, to worsen. Mountbatten himself, whatever shortcomings he may have displayed in collecting an over-large staff or in what Ismay called 'the undue amount of ego in his Cosmos',[22] worked hard to bring about inter-allied harmony. And as before, of course, there were instances where this was achieved, as when the U.S.S. *Saratoga* worked with the Eastern Fleet.[23] On both sides, however, observers recorded the strains which remained. 'In conversation with American and British officers connected with S.E.A.C.', wrote a United States diplomat, '. . . I have noted a regrettable lack of any spirit of camaraderie between British and American sections, or any real evidence of mutual frankness and trust.'[24] 'I am very much afraid', remarked a compatriot, 'that the majority of American officers in this theater, outside all those who have the privilege of serving on the Staff of the Supreme Commander, are pessimistic about the chance of any real Allied cooperation being achieved here, suspicious of British intentions, bitter over many real or fancied grievances, and convinced of the essential bad will and hopeless inefficiency of the Indian administration, both civil and military.'[25] Memoirs already referred to, such as Eldridge's *Wrath In Burma*, Davies' *Dragon By The Tail*, and Taylor's *Richer By Asia*, tell a similar story for this period.

One particular area of difficulty involved various command arrangements within the theatre: the question, for example, of whether Mountbatten could divert American planes from the Hump during an operational emergency; of what was to be done about Stilwell's refusal to serve under General

Giffard; of whether there should be an over-all Allied land C. in C. (General Oliver Leese was appointed to this position in September, although his career in S.E.A.C. was not to be an entirely happy one).[26] The sending of instructions by Washington direct to Stilwell and Sultan (who took over from Stilwell as U.S. Commander in Burma and India) also aroused British resentment,[27] while Mountbatten and the Chiefs of Staff in London, on their side, proposed that Stilwell's several posts should be separated, and that he should be moved from S.E.A.C. in order to concentrate on the job of Chief of Staff to Chiang Kai-shek.[28]

A particularly bitter episode occurred when the Chindits, now commanded by Major General Lentaigne, came under Stilwell's operational control for a while in the summer of 1944, the British holding that Stilwell proceeded to demand the impossible of them, Stilwell that his orders were being disobeyed. So fierce did feelings run that, for example, one British officer involved has recalled that a member of Stilwell's staff, whom the General was wont to send on missions 'solely to tell Chindits they were yellow', was later hunted by another British officer intent on killing him.[29]

Stilwell's opinion of the British in general, which tended to be accepted in the State and War Departments in Washington, remained that 'they simply do not want to fight in Burma or reopen communications with China.'[30] In his diary, he also gave vent to an increasing scorn for Mountbatten personally—'the Glamour Boy', 'an amateur', 'a fatuous ass', 'childish Louis, publicity crazy', 'pisspot'—and to a bitterness against all things British: 'The more I see of the Limies, the worse I hate them'; 'the bastardly hypocrites do their best to cut our throats on all occasions. The pig-fuckers.'[31] In return, many senior British officers were by now more angered than ever by Stilwell's attitude and behaviour (though Slim got on with him well enough), with Dening conveying to London as early as February the conviction 'that General Stilwell has been disloyal to [Admiral Mountbatten] throughout', and that 'the showdown . . . must come some day.' 'We cannot have an American general', concluded Dening, 'fighting against us in our own territory.'[32]

Matters were made worse still by the appearance in the American press of reports of the rival strategies proposed by Mountbatten and Stilwell.[33] American correspondents were being briefed by members of the latter's staff, and duly wrote about the disinclination of the British to fight. Much bad feeling was also engendered where the publicity and credit given for specific operations were concerned, Americans believing, for example, that too much was made in public of the Chindits, that the British tried to steal some of the applause following the seizure of Myitkyina, and that the role of the U.S. Air Force in supporting Wingate was played down.[34] Trouble also arose over films of the campaign. To the British, the American picture about the fighting in Southeast Asia, 'The March of Time', was a slight upon their country's arms, Henry Luce, responsible for its making, being bluntly informed by press correspondents and officials in London that it was Stilwell who was being uncooperative and the British who were doing the greater part of the fighting, rather than vice versa.[35] For their part, Stilwell's staff, supported by the State Department, opposed Mountbatten's wish for a joint, Anglo-American film to be made about S.E.A.C., lest such a project should be taken as implying an American acceptance of the British claim to be making a genuine effort in that part of the world.[36]

What the American deputy-director of S.E.A.C.'s 'P' Division (for coordinating clandestine activities) later called 'pathological suspicion' of each other had also come to infect relations between the S.O.E. and O.S.S. in the Command, although the head of S.O.E. there again blamed the trouble on Stilwell rather than on the O.S.S. itself.[37] In the field of political and psychological warfare, the American desire to avoid a contaminating partnership with the British in no way lessened, and led to the demise of the Combined New Delhi Emergency Committee on such matters.[38] Likewise, the O.W.I. personnel working within S.E.A.C. still refused to come under the direction of the Supreme Commander, and although a Combined Liaison Committee, placed within Air Marshal Joubert's Information and Civil Affairs area of responsibilities, was eventually set up in June, John Davies promptly warned his fellow members of that Committee that 'American political warfare will avoid identifying itself with British political warfare to the peoples of Southeast Asia . . . [and] will keep its American identity.'[39] The State Department similarly refused to agree to Mountbatten's suggestion that American civil-affairs officers should be attached to his Command, on the grounds that such appointments 'would further increase the widespread belief in India and in the Far East that our policy and British imperialism are the same, or that we are dupes of the British.'[40]

Yet another potential source of Anglo-American friction was provided by the question of S.E.A.C.'s boundaries, which Mountbatten in January hoped to see 'extended further eastwards to cover part of the South China Sea and if possible parts of the China coast . . . [including] Hong Kong'— this as a necessary step towards obtaining a role for the Command 'in the final thrust against Japan.' The issue of who should control operations in Indochina and Siam ('more important to S.E.A.C. than to any other theatre', in Dening's words, 'because through them lies the enemy land and air reinforcement route to Burma and Malaya') also remained in the inconclusive state created by the 1943 Mountbatten–Chiang Kai-shek interim agreement.[41]

In short, by the end of this period Anglo-American differences over strategic and command questions in Southeast Asia had become thoroughly entangled with political considerations. For the British, for example, Mountbatten himself was to bring the two aspects together early in October, when registering his acute disappointment at the news that he would not after all receive the resources needed to mount an air–sea attack on Rangoon:

'Failure to give us these resources', he wrote to Churchill, 'may permanently injure our position in the Far East. Although I find the view widely held out here that our prestige in the Far East is unlikely to recover from the blow of having the British Empire handed back to us, possibly with strings attached, by a peace treaty imposed as a result of a predominantly American victory, I realise that this is a political aspect that does not concern me. My concern is a military one, and I feel deep disquiet at the inevitable effect on the morale in this theatre if it should later become apparent that, although the Americans have speeded up their attack on the Philippines, . . . we are in grave danger of postponing our first airborne and amphibious assault by 9 or 10 months after the previous postponement of 12 months.'[42]

For the Americans, Davies had already summarized the political considerations arising as he saw them at the end of 1943:

'In so far as we participate in S.E.A.C. operations', he had argued, 'we become involved in the politically explosive colonial problems of the British, Dutch and possibly French. In doing so we compromise ourselves not only with the colonial peoples of Asia but also the free peoples of Asia, including the Chinese. Domestically, our Government lays itself open to public criticism—"Why should American boys die to recreate the colonial empires of the British and their Dutch and French satellites?" Finally, more Anglo-American misunderstanding and friction is likely to arise out of our participation in S.E.A.C. than out of any other theater . . .'[43]

The future of empires; British territories in Southeast Asia

In the opinion of many Americans, the British Empire was now in rapid and inevitable decline. In Asia, judged Davies correctly, it could not survive 'because the people of the United Kingdom, Mr. Churchill notwithstanding, have lost their will to empire, and because the historical dynamics of nationalism throughout Asia will sooner or later bring about the downfall of colonial imperialism.'[44] Some also continued to believe that it was necessary to hasten the end of such an iniquitous system, as attacks by press correspondents like Drew Pearson and Louis Fischer and papers such as the *Chicago Tribune* demonstrated. Even a friendly source like the *New York Times* felt obliged to point out that it would be a tragedy for relations between East and West 'if the old abuses of imperialism were restored', while, as a minor but faintly amusing episode, one finds the Duchess of Windsor, speaking as a fellow-American to a State Department official, urging that 'the Empire must be cut down, particularly in the Far East.'[45]

Roosevelt, too, continued to deplore British imperial policies in private, mimicking Churchill on the subject in none-too-kindly a fashion, and declaring the Prime Minister to be 'warped on the idea of sovereignty.'[46] Early in September, the President was warned by Hull that Britain appeared bent upon using S.E.A.C. to restore its 'highly unpopular . . . political and economic ascendancy in Southeast Asia', including a 'predominant influence over the post-war Government of Thailand.' As a riposte, Hull suggested that the United States should press the European colonial powers to make 'early, dramatic and concerted announcements' concerning the steps towards and timing of independence for the territories of Southeast Asia, together with a pledge of equality of economic treatment there for other states.[47]

Yet as we saw even at the outset of the war, there were those Americans who approached the colonial issue in notably moderate fashion, and this remained the case in 1944. Thus, for example, a pamphlet published by the Foreign Policy Association dealt sympathetically with the economic problems which a change in policy would create for the colonial powers.[48] Even Davies now recognized that 'temporarily, the British imperial system may be regarded as a stabilizing influence in Asia', while an article in *Fortune* magazine went so far as to hail the evolutionary process of Empire into Commonwealth as 'one of the very few constructive ideals by which an orderly evolution can be achieved toward freedom under law rather than revolution outside the law.'[49]

Moreover, despite the President's general attitude, no clear and co-ordinated anti-colonial policy existed in Washington, where military planners still lacked all guidance on the matter, where the Far Eastern and European sections of the State Department continued to approach the subject of Southeast Asian colonies in very differing fashions, and where the President himself was said by Hopkins in conversation with Davies in September to be 'more interested at this stage in European problems.'[50] The tone in which the question was discussed in Washington also tended to be far less strident now than it had been in 1942, and when Isaiah Bowman (the President of Johns Hopkins University and, it will be recalled, an adviser to the State Department on such matters) returned from discussing it in London as a member of the Stettinius mission, he could report that the two sides had been 'much closer in our thinking . . . than we could have hoped.'[51] One reason for this was that Bowman himself had told British officials that

'the United States Administration had now definitely discarded all idea of approaching this problem from the aspect of political independence. They recognised', he had continued, 'that the disparity in the matter of political competence between the overseas dependencies in question was too marked: far too many of them were obviously unripe for independence: the goal of actual independence was too remote: the gradual attainment of "self government" was the only political object at which we could usefully aim now. The political status of these territories, moreover, was relatively very much less important than their economic prosperity.'[52]

Bowman, in saying this, had gone farther than a good many of his colleagues would have done, and to this extent his reassuring words had given the Colonial Office in London something of a false sense of security where American intentions were concerned. Even so, moderation was also to be found elsewhere in Washington. From the State Department's

Committee on Colonial and Trusteeship Problems and its inter-Divisional Area Committee on the Far East, for example, the modest idea was emerging of setting up regional international commissions for colonial affairs (including one for Southeast Asia and one for the South Seas) that would have 'advisory, cooperative and collaborative' rather than executive functions. The opinion was also to be heard that 'many of the peoples in Southeast Asia were too backward to govern themselves', and the Colonial Committee were unanimous that, as Bowman had suggested when in London, any declaration on colonial principles should stress 'self-government' rather than 'independence', and should not encourage the peoples concerned 'to take matters into their own hands.' It was also reported that Hull and Eden had reached an understanding whereby dependent territories other than mandates/trusteeships should remain under the sovereign administration of the parent state, and not be placed under the direct jurisdiction of a world organization.[53] Even the limited plan drawn up by the State Department for a United Nations trusteeship system which would assume responsibility for League of Nations mandates and 'certain territories' to be taken from the U.N.'s current enemies had to be withheld from the Dumbarton Oaks Conference, owing to opposition to it on the part of the War and Navy Departments, which wished to see American sovereignty established over Japan's mandated islands.[54]

Meanwhile Britain in this period, as during earlier ones, did not lack defenders of her Empire. Those who spoke out in 1944 included not only Lord Hailey in his book, *The Future of Colonial Peoples*, but Bertrand Russell and, from the Labour benches in the Commons once more, a belligerent Emmanuel Shinwell, who declared himself to be 'in hearty accord with the view [the Prime Minister] expressed some time ago on the suggested liquidation of the Empire', and who warned that 'we have no intention . . . of throwing the British Commonwealth of Nations overboard in order to satisfy a section of the American press . . .'[55] For the benefit of British troops, the Directorate of Army Education also published a defence of the country's colonial and Indian policies (using terms such as 'the ladder of self-government'), together with an explanation of why international administration of colonial territories would prove unsatisfactory.[56] In Whitehall, senior Colonial Office officials were at the same time undertaking a major review of policy, reaching conclusions which again emphasized the need for Britain to retain control of her own territories and not to place them within a scheme of international trusteeship.[57]

American opinion on the subject still could not be ignored, however, and Richard Law's inter-Departmental Committee, maintaining its study of this aspect of Imperial affairs, received from one of its officials, Graham Spry, a lengthy report which concluded that 'American nationalism is the first obstacle to healthy Anglo-American relations and the root attitude in the mind of the American people as a whole towards Britain and the British.' Further disturbing evidence was supplied by Hopkins, who, over lunch in Washington with Law and Sir Ronald Campbell, talked of Roosevelt's anti-colonial ideas. 'From this', wrote Campbell afterwards, 'it looks as if we must expect what I have always feared, that in the name of benefiting the backward populations and improving standards of life, we will get here a combination of Wallace up-lift and National Association of Manufacturers export drive, much to the detriment of the nations who will be forced to run before they can walk. It also seems to bear out anticipations that the President means to be tough.'[58] (The Netherlands Embassy in Washington was also expressing such fears at the time.)[59]

In consequence, the attitude adopted by Whitehall towards the United States over colonial issues continued to be in part a prickly and defensive one. Now that the storm of 1942 was well passed, for example, the Ministers concerned agreed to abandon the pursuit of a joint declaration with Washington on colonial policy, America's own approach being scornfully described by Stanley, the Colonial Secretary, as one of seeking to 'enable the United States to get away with the retention of the Marshalls and Carolines . . . although wrapped up in a rather diaphanous cover of the usual idealism.'[60] Stanley also carried his colleagues with him in hoping to do away with the mandate system—in other words that existing mandated territories such as Tanganyika should revert to the status of ordinary colonies—a notion which was in direct conflict with American plans for an extension of the trusteeship principle.[61] As for Britain's own colonies, the Cabinet, like the Colonial Office, remained firmly opposed to any suggestion that the administration of them should in some way be overseen by an international body.[62]

Nevertheless, just as there existed moderate and sympathetic attitudes on the American side, so positive responses and hopes continued to be expressed in Britain. In public, for example, Margery Perham wrote that 'America's armed partnership with Britain throughout the Empire carries with it a right to criticise', while in private the Colonial Office endorsed her suggestion that officials from the State Department should be invited to London 'to get an inside view of recent developments in British colonial policy and administrative machinery.'[63] The Colonial Office also judged that there was no need to fear American economic competition in the colonies, while in this connection the hope expressed in the Spry report to the Law Committee, that a new relationship as 'partners' could be established with the U.S.A., was reflected over the specific issue of rubber, where, as foreshadowed in the preceding period, the old International Rubber Regulating Committee was now entirely wound up in deference to American hostility, and plans were made, with United States representatives participating, for the setting up of a new international study group which would include Americans among its members.[64]

There was also a degree of convergence between British and American ideas concerning the establishment of international regional commissions to facilitate cooperation on colonial matters—always provided that it was not intended to give such commissions any executive powers.[65] (In this respect, however, as we have seen already and as was to become more apparent still in the final phase of the war, Australia and New Zealand, apprehensive of the dangers to themselves that could arise from 'weak parent states', as one memorandum called them, returning unconditionally to their Asian and Pacific possessions, were closer to the more radical section of Washington opinion than to British officials in wanting to see some form of international supervision of colonial areas.)[66]

Meanwhile ideas were being developed in London regarding individual British territories in Southeast Asia. For Malaya, the Cabinet approved a scheme whereby a Malayan Union—excluding Singapore—would come under a single authority, the jurisdiction of the various Sultans being ceded to Britain and the basis of the country's political institutions being broadened to take in non-Malays. (At S.E.A.C. Headquarters it was felt that these plans did not go far enough towards ending the special position of the Malays, and, in company with the Foreign Office, that more publicity should in any case be given to the proposed reforms.) In Borneo, too, the British Government was to extend its control by taking over powers from the North Borneo Chartered Company, the Sultan of Brunei, and the Rajah of Sarawak, this area, like Malaya, to come under the over-all authority of a Governor General for the region, residing in Singapore.[67]

In the case of Burma, the Governor, Dorman-Smith, continued in this period to press for 'a big and generous' reconstruction programme, a recognition that the country was capable of governing itself, and the setting of a time limit for the granting of an independence that would include the right to secede from the Commonwealth.[68] (At this stage, it is worth noting, Dorman-Smith and Mountbatten, who were later to fall out over Burmese politics, were at one in their reforming approach to the country's status and problems, Mountbatten writing in his diary in October that the Governor had 'first-class ideas on the future of Burma' and that 'we see eye to eye on all Burma questions.')[69]* A group of Conservative back-bench M.P.s were also studying Burma's future with concern, although their proposals were linked to a form of self-government which would leave defence matters and external affairs in British hands;[70] Amery, too, as Secretary of State, favoured the announcement of a date for the establishment of self-government. It is scarcely necessary to say that the Prime Minister, on the other hand, continued to stand in the way of any programme of constitutional reform, and it was as a means of by-passing his hostility that Amery and Dorman-Smith agreed at the end of this period to ask for a Cabinet Committee to be set up in order to make policy recommendations.[71]

These constitutional issues apart, other questions were arising over British territories in Southeast Asia. How would the Chinese behave in North Burma, for example, where their forces were now operating? (Some reassurance was provided in this respect by an agreement in principle that

* There is all the more irony in this in that, while Dorman-Smith—unfairly in the author's opinion—was later adjudged, not least by Mountbatten, to have been a failure and was cast aside, Mountbatten himself was to ride on to glory as the man who wound up British rule in India.

British civil-affairs officers could accompany them.)[72] What would be the attitude of China concerning the Chinese who lived in Malaya?[73] How should Britain deal with the Malayan Peoples' Anti-Japanese Association which, though Communist-controlled, had 'attracted the best of the Chinese youth irrespective of their political convictions'? Or with the Burmese all-party Anti-Fascist Peoples' Freedom League, set up by Aung San in August 1944 in order to resist the Japanese?[74] At least, in facing such an uncertain future, there existed by now, both within S.E.A.C. and in Whitehall, a growing awareness that nationalism in Asia was a rapidly-growing force and that, Churchill notwithstanding, there could be no return to the pre-war status quo as Britain re-entered her Southeast Asian territories.

Other territories in Southeast Asia

The Netherlands East Indies, for which a Provisional Government was set up in this period under the former Colonial Minister, Dr. H. J. van Mook, will again be dealt with in the context of MacArthur's South West Pacific Area. Britain still retained her operational responsibility where Sumatra was concerned, however. Moreover, in view of strong post-war Dutch suspicions over the attitude of the British Government towards the colony as a whole,* it is important to make clear that neither in London nor in S.E.A.C. was there any deviation from the firm intention to hand over recaptured Netherlands territory to a Dutch civil administration 'as rapidly as practicable.'[75] Both the Colonial and Foreign Offices were anxious to cooperate with the Dutch regarding future developments in Southeast Asia (Dutch fears over the possible role of the Chinese living in the region had not abated in this period), while Churchill himself assured the Netherlands Prime Minister, Gerbrandy, 'that he was going to stand up for the Dutch Empire after the war.'[76] 'Of all our allies in this war', declared Mountbatten's Chief of Staff, 'the Dutch are the most cooperative and reliable', to which a Foreign Office official added: 'Hear, hear!'[77] At the same time it was being assumed in Washington, too, that recaptured Dutch territory would be handed back to its owners, although it was intended to preserve 'the rightful interests of others' in the arrangements made for such colonies.[78] We shall also see in the following period how quick American officials were to suspect that the Dutch were banding together with the British and French in order to restore the status quo in Southeast Asia, and how attempts were thereupon made to forestall any such move.

Even now, indeed, tension was growing between Washington and London over the future of Siam, a situation which, it will be recalled, had been created in part by the reservations placed upon British policy by Churchill in 1942. Now, in March 1944, the State Department drew up a summary of

* I am particularly grateful to those friends in or formerly of the Netherlands Foreign Ministry and Service, who are mentioned in the Preface, for instructing me in the post-war Dutch scene in this respect. The officials and other participants at a meeting of the Nederlandsch Genootschap Voor Internationale Zaken were also most helpful.

United States policy towards Siam, which was approved by Roosevelt: she should be regarded as an enemy-occupied and not as an enemy state; her existing government would not be recognized, while, although no commitment would be undertaken in respect of any particular group, sympathy would be shown towards the Free Siamese Movement; and above all, Siam should be reestablished as an independent state.[79] (The State Department's Inter-Divisional Area Committee on the Far East did feel, however, that there might have to be an interim post-war period before an independent Siamese government could be set up, and hoped to see the administration of civil affairs during such a phase come 'predominantly under American control, with Allied participation.' They also recognized that the territories taken from Malaya and Indochina and given to Siam by the Japanese would have to be returned, although adding that this should be done without prejudicing subsequent claims and negotiations.)[80]

At the same time the suspicion was by now firmly implanted in a good many minds in Washington that Britain, who had not followed the lead of Chiang Kai-shek and Roosevelt in publicly endorsing Siamese independence, was developing sinister designs of her own upon that country. The O.S.S., for example, who shared an uneasy relationship with the S.O.E. as regards operations into Siam, informed the State Department that British work in that field 'appeared to be more political than military in intent.'[81] More specifically, they claimed that some British officials were thinking in terms of a federation of Burma, Malaya, Indochina and Siam that would come under Britain's aegis, a story that was repeated, with some variations, by the Siamese diplomat, Mani Sanasen.[82]

American disquiet was increased by the appearance in the July 1944 issue of *International Affairs* of an article by Sir Josiah Crosby, the retired British Minister to Siam, in which he wrote of the need for 'some form of political tutelage [being] required for a period throughout Southeast Asia after the war', and suggested that Siam herself would benefit from 'a system of foreign advisers.'[83] (Ironically, as we have seen, Crosby's private thought was that the United States should oversee such a stage in Siam's affairs.)[84] Worse still, there was London's failure to produce an acceptable declaration concerning Siam's future and her territorial integrity and independence. In this respect, the drafts which the Foreign Office proffered were rejected by Washington during a lengthy series of exchanges which culminated in September 1944 in the admission by Eden that, in Britain's opinion, 'some special strategic arrangements may be necessary in the Kra Isthmus within the framework of an international security system.'[85]

In the Foreign Office, the hardening attitude of the State Department over Siam was noted with regret and some exasperation, Hornbeck having earlier indicated privately that he disliked the activities in the area of the O.S.S. 'gumshoe boys', as he called them, and that he hoped Anglo-American friction could be avoided.[86] Nevertheless, there were also those British officials who were themselves anxious to see the country's policy as regards Siam clarified. Mountbatten and Dening both argued in this sense, as did the S.O.E., who felt that London and S.E.A.C. Headquarters alike were being dilatory over the matter and feared lest an unsympathetic British policy should 'drive [the Free Siamese Movement] into the O.S.S./Chinese camp.'[87] Some Foreign Office officials, too, were prepared to assert that 'we want a strong and independent Siam',[88] while from the sidelines Crosby also believed that the country's Regent, Luang Pradit, who was secretly cooperating with the F.S.M., was 'working in his own way for ultimate collaboration with us and . . . [was] the natural leader of the future Siam.'[89]

Even so, as the Americans realized, Britain was far from disinterested where Siam was concerned. In addition to her pre-war commercial investments in that country—in tin and teak production, for example—there was now a growing interest in securing Siam's surplus rice supplies in order to feed Malaya, Hongkong and other territories in the area after the war.[90] On top of this, Amery suggested during this period that Britain should seek to obtain those Malay states under Siamese suzerainty which separated Malaya from Burma. More generally, it was believed in London that if Siam did not throw over her alliance with Japan before the ending of hostilities, some form of Allied military government should be imposed upon her when she surrendered. Nor was there much expectation that the Siamese would act in such an outright anti-Japanese fashion.[91] Dening, for example, described them as 'a child-like people, incapable of any worthwhile military effort', while Sir Maurice Peterson, whom we have encountered before as the Assistant Under Secretary of State in the Foreign Office who was responsible for the area, continued to be particularly scornful of the F.S.M.[92]

Eden himself was at his shrill worst over Siamese affairs, describing attempts to draft a declaration of Britain's policy as 'a silly business [and] an increasing bore', and still assuming that Luang Pradit, as Regent, was 'a supporter of the Japs' and 'a creature who collaborates with the Japs . . .'[93] Nor would the Minister responsible for the S.O.E., Lord Selborne, do battle in London on behalf of his units working in the field on Siamese operations. Moreover, the Cabinet as a whole were, if anything, more insensitive still on the subject, being determined that Siam should be regarded as an enemy until she had 'worked her passage home' by turning against the Japanese, not prepared to enter into any commitments as regards her future boundaries, and indifferent to the need to allay American and Asian suspicions of Britain's intentions.

Small wonder, then, that, with Churchill's reservation about the future of the Kra Isthmus also remaining in force, a succession of Foreign Office attempts (submitted without enthusiasm by Eden) to draft a declaration of policy that would satisfy both the Cabinet and the Americans came to nothing in these months. The most that Mountbatten could obtain, meanwhile, was Cabinet approval at the end of the period for S.O.E. operations to be undertaken in Siam, provided that no political obligations were entailed.[94]

As Britain and the United States drifted further apart over Siam, they came no nearer to achieving an understanding where French Indochina was concerned. Again, this was due in part to the confusion and uncertainty that existed within both Washington and London. On the American side, for example, a senior State Department official was driven to compose a memorandum to the President, asking for guidance over Indochina, but got no reply.[95] Hull himself admitted to Halifax in January 1944 that he was in the dark over Roosevelt's alleged remarks on the subject, and sent over to the White House a reminder of past United States pledges that France should have her Empire restored to her.[96] The President, meanwhile, had in fact spoken out on 16 December 1943 to diplomatic representatives of China, Turkey, Egypt, Persia, the U.S.S.R. and Britain, declaring that 'he had been working hard to prevent Indochina being restored to France who, during the past hundred years, had done nothing for the Indochinese people under their care', and advocating a U.N. trusteeship to prepare the territory for independence.[97]

In January, Roosevelt was forthright enough to Hull, for a change, as well as to Halifax. Those past pledges that Hull had brought up were not of importance, and Robert Murphy in North Africa had gone further than he should have done in that respect. Indochina, he reiterated, which the French had 'milked for a hundred years', should become a trusteeship, and since Stalin and Chiang Kai-shek agreed about this, there were 'three votes to [Churchill's] one' on the matter. To the Pacific War Council Roosevelt went on to add that New Caledonia, where the French administration was 'a disgrace', should also be taken away, and given to Australia either outright or for her to rule on behalf of the United Nations. 'He would say to the French in other places that as they could not manage this sort of possession they could not have them back. The French would protest, so what?'[98] The President repeated these ideas to Stettinius and others as the year went on, asserting at various times that 'no French troops whatever should be used in operations in Indochina', that 'we are still going to have a tough time with the British on this issue', and that China should play a leading part in the new scheme of things.[99]

Yet already difficulties were arising which could thwart Roosevelt's intentions. China was looking less and less prepared to take on a stabilizing role in East and Southeast Asia after the war, while conversely, as we have seen, the Gaullists, despite American hostility, were establishing themselves at the head of a reviving and assertive France. (Even the President, it seems, made soothing noises to de Gaulle about Indochina when the latter visited the U.S.A. in July.) Such difficulties also helped to promote disagreements over Indochina at lower levels in Washington. The State Department's Inter-Divisional Area Committee on the Far East, for example, although agreed on the ultimate goal of independence, was split evenly between those who favoured an interim international trusteeship and those who, like Hull, preferred a return to French administration under some form of international accountability.[100]

Some American officials shared Roosevelt's critical view of the French record in the territory, and it became known that Vietnamese nationalists were looking to the United States for support for their cause.[101] There were also direct American interests to be borne in mind. For example, the Consul General in Kunming, William R. Langdon, in a despatch which received much praise in the State Department, suggested that it was important to 'secure American enterprise against a continuation of French commercial monopoly of that rich country.'[102] Both commercial and security considerations were also put forward by two senior State Department officials, Joseph Grew and James Dunn, in a memorandum they drew up for the President early in September:

'These areas [of Southeast Asia]', they wrote, 'are sources of products essential to both our wartime and peacetime economy. They are potentially important markets for American exports. They lie athwart the southwestern approaches to the Pacific Ocean and have an important bearing on our security and the security of the Philippines. Their economy and political stability will be an important factor in the maintenance of peace in Asia.'[103]

However, American diplomats in China were not impressed meanwhile by the Annamite independence groups which had taken refuge in that country; they were also more suspicious than was Roosevelt of Chinese intentions, which might well be, they thought, to make use of such groups 'to establish and increase Chinese influence and control in Indochina to as great a degree as circumstances render practicable.'[104] Even Consul General Langdon, who castigated French rule as having been 'unconscionable exploitation of the Annamite people', asserted that

'the Annamites are not yet materially or politically prepared for independence or capable of resisting aggression from neighbours. Nor would they be able alone to hold back the peaceful but nonetheless racially annihilating, smothering penetration of Chinese immigration . . . [Therefore] a further period of dependence and protection seems to be the only logical proposition for Indochina, and the question resolves itself as to which power should exercise this temporary dominion. Obviously the power must be France for practical reasons . . .'[105]

In a similar strain, Isaiah Bowman, when visiting London, confided that the American approach to the question would now be 'entirely realistic', with the French to be asked merely to accept 'certain standards of colonial administration';[106] even in the long term, argued Grew and Dunn in their memorandum cited above, 'close voluntary association with western powers' would help make Southeast Asian territories like Indochina more stable. According to the French Ambassador in Chungking, who had passed through Washington, General Marshall and John J. McCloy, Assistant Secretary of War, went further still when talking to him in private, and 'expressed sympathy for France and the restoration of the empire.'[107]

Amidst these American differences and uncertainties, one common assumption to be found from the President downwards, an assumption reinforced by reports from U.S. representatives in the S.E.A.C. area, was that the British were working closely with the French in order to obtain an outcome regarding Indochina that would be favourable to the continuation of colonial rule in Southeast Asia as a whole.[108] As we shall see, this was an overstatement and oversimplification of the case, especially where Churchill was concerned. It was true, nonetheless, that British officials were becoming increasingly uneasy as a result of continuing reports of American revisionist intentions over the case of Indochina, partly because such reports appeared to fit into a general pattern whereby the activities of S.E.A.C. were to be restricted and Britain's own role in the Far Eastern war was to be reduced to a minor one.[109] Thus, Roosevelt's repeated pronouncements on the subject, though dismissed by Churchill as idiosyncratic and 'chance remarks' that he had always refused to endorse, were greeted by many officials with a mixture of apprehension and scorn. Might the President not take it into his head to extend his proposal for international trusteeships to cover British and Dutch territories? However preposterous his ramblings to the Pacific War Council ('One of the President's most half-baked and unfortunate obiter dicta', minuted Cadogan on one occasion), should not a caveat be entered there and then?[110]

In direct contrast to Roosevelt's views, a paper was drawn up for the Prime Minister by the Foreign Office and F.O.R.D. in which they emphasized, not only the importance of Indochina to France, but the economic and social improvements which had been brought about there under French rule, together with the looser forms of political association with metropolitan France that were being contemplated. Similarly, an aide-mémoire prepared for the Prime Minister to take to the Quebec Conference concluded:

'It cannot legitimately be said that France has misruled Indochina. Whatever criticisms may be levelled against the French administration . . ., French rule has preserved Indochina from tyranny and other evils and has given peace and political cohesion to a territory which has no geographical or ethnographical unity . . . Any attempt to interfere with French sovereignty in Indochina . . . would put in question the future of all other Far Eastern colonial possessions which have been overrun by Japan.'[111]

The expectation in the Foreign Office (and Air Marshal Joubert of S.E.A.C. agreed) was that a resurgent France would be able to reclaim Indochina despite Roosevelt. Almost everyone concerned on the British side, in fact (Major General S. W. Kirby in the War Office was an exception), failed entirely to appreciate that native nationalism was going to present a major problem. Insofar as difficulties were anticipated, they concerned Chinese ambitions in the area and the possibility of Sino-American collaboration against France.[112] The nationalist factor thus failed to figure in the guidelines for British policy which were drafted by the Foreign Office and Post Hostilities Planning Committee, and were approved by the Cabinet in February 1944, a Ministerial committee also endorsing a summary of that policy before the meeting of Commonwealth Prime Ministers in May.[113]

Two overriding desiderata figured in these statements. First, there was the need to remain on good terms with and to sustain France:

'The menace of a rearmed Germany being greater than the menace of a rearmed Japan, a friendly and prosperous France is a strategic necessity to the Commonwealth and Empire as a whole . . . To deprive France of her economic stake in Indochina would weaken her severely. Any such deprivation would be passionately resented, with the result that the possibilities of friendly collaboration with France in post-war Europe would be jeopardised, and France would be encouraged to form a *bloc*, possibly with the Russians, opposed to an Anglo-American *bloc*.'

Moreover, international control of Indochina would not work, and would merely 'open the door to Chinese intrigue and provide possibilities for Japanese exploitation.' Neither Britain, the Netherlands or the Soviet Union would want to be responsible for Indochina on their own; Chinese rule would be even worse than an international regime; American control, which might be popular in Australia and New Zealand and would make it harder for the United States 'to point their fingers at our colonies', was likely to be ruled out by the American anti-colonial tradition. Again, therefore, everything suggested that France should return to Indochina, as to her various possessions in the Pacific.[114]

There remained, however, the second of the main desiderata: the need to ensure that Indochina would be strongly defended in the future.

'France', noted the Post Hostilities Planning Committee in this connection, 'is unlikely for some time at least, to be strong enough to defend Indochina by herself, and it is therefore important to the future security of India, Burma and Malaya, and of the British Commonwealth and Empire in the Southern Pacific, that the United States should be directly involved in the event of an attack on Indochina . . . This might best be achieved by the establishment of some system of United Nations bases in Indochina . . .'

In short, as the Cabinet concluded, France should return to her Far Eastern and Pacific possessions, subject to her acceptance of an international security scheme which would embrace those territories.

It was one thing, however, to state such a policy in general terms; another altogether to arrive at decisions on immediate, practical issues at a time when the Prime Minister retained his aversion to de Gaulle and, more important still, his determination not to jeopardize his relations with Roosevelt over what still appeared to be a secondary matter. The Indochina question could not be ignored, even so. The French National Committee themselves, their colonial policies having been given a new, reforming look at the Brazzaville Conference early in 1944,[115] were pressing for greater participation in the Far Eastern war. By the spring, the battleship *Richelieu* was already operating successfully with the Royal Navy's Eastern Fleet, and in the second half of the year French agents, to the dislike of the O.S.S., were working with S.O.E.'s Force 136 in order to foster resistance to the Japanese in Indochina.[116] In addition, the French were continuing to seek representation on the Pacific War Councils, the acceptance of a military mission under General Blaizot at S.E.A.C. Headquarters, the despatch to S.E.A.C. of the Corps Léger d'Intervention (about 500 men), and agreement to the eventual sending out of a full-scale expeditionary force.[117] Mountbatten's view of all this was that Indochina was of great military importance as a Japanese supply route, and that 'French help was essential' for its reconquest; by the end of the summer he was also anxious to commence the pre-operational activities that had been allowed for in his 'gentleman's agreement' of 1943 with Chiang Kai-shek.[118]

Even before this, in April, the Supreme Commander had been joined by the Chiefs of Staff, Lord Selborne for S.O.E., and the Foreign Office, in recommending that France should have her requests granted, save that she should not become involved in the preparation of plans against Japan until the stage was reached of launching military operations into Indochina.[119] When the Head of the Foreign Office's North American Department entered a reservation to the effect that, in the interest of good relations with the Americans, direct collaboration with the French should be avoided, Eden disagreed. 'I really cannot accept this', he minuted. 'We must have some freedom in our foreign policy.'

The predominant attitude within the Office, in fact, was one of exasperation at the delays in meeting French wishes. 'I cannot follow the purpose of a policy of estranging, and often to our disadvantage, the only French authority that at present exists', wrote Cadogan. 'I don't understand it—I don't know what is at the back of it.'[120] Mountbatten, in a letter he sent to Eden in August, added a further fear, though it was in fact not a well-founded one at the time:

'I have felt all along', he wrote, 'that it was vital that the French should liberate French Indochina in collaboration with us, and that they should be properly grateful to us for doing it for and with them. As I understand it, however, the President's attitude to the future of French Indochina after the war made the whole matter too tricky for us to take a firm line about.

Now, however, his line towards de Gaulle has changed, and I have heard rumours that the Americans are about to start making up for lost time, and are embarking on a kind of competition with us in trying to secure the good graces of the French for after the war ... [and] I feel apprehensive lest they should try cutting us out with the French in the Far East ... It may well suit the Americans in their new mood to see that the [French Military] Mission goes to China, and to offer the French the liberation of French Indochina without our collaboration, and under purely American auspices.'[121]

The cause of the impatience in London and in Kandy (Ceylon) was, as before, the Prime Minister. As already emphasized, he dismissed the very idea that the United States could take away Indochina against the wishes of a properly constituted French Government.[122] He also suggested, in January, that the Foreign Office should 'develop a very strong movement on this issue . . . through the State Department.'[123] By March, however, he was arguing that it would be 'a great mistake to raise this matter before the Presidential election. 'I cannot conceive it is urgent', he added. '. . . Nothing is going to happen about this for quite a long time.'[124] In keeping with this view, he had instructed that 'a negative and dilatory attitude' should be adopted in response to French requests for an increased presence in the Far East.[125] And when Eden pressed him again on the matter in May, the Prime Minister reiterated both the American and the French considerations that weighed with him:

'It is hard enough to get along in S.E.A.C. when we virtually have only the Americans to deal with', he expostulated. 'The more the French can get their finger into the pie, the more trouble they will make in order to show that they are not humiliated in any way by the events through which they have passed. You will have de Gaullist intrigues there just as you now have in Syria and the Lebanon.
    Before we could bring the French officially into the Indochina area, we should have to settle with President Roosevelt. He has been more outspoken to me on that subject than on any other colonial matter, and I imagine it is one of his principal war aims to liberate Indochina from France . . . Do you really want to go and stir all this up at such a time as this ?'[126]*

Eventually, however, Churchill gave way to the continuing pressure from S.E.A.C., the Foreign Office and Chiefs of Staff, being influenced, perhaps, by reports that the French inside Indochina might be ready to turn against the Japanese. Early in August, therefore, he approved a suggestion to despatch the Corps Léger to India and to allow the Blaizot Mission to join Mountbatten.[127] Yet no sooner had matters been advanced to this extent in London than they ran into an obstruction in Washington. When the Joint Chiefs of Staff there were asked by their British colleagues to endorse the Blaizot and Corps Léger proposals, they were ready to agree, subject only to the condition that French participation in planning and political warfare must be confined to the S.E.A.C. area, and with the reminder that Indochina still fell within the China Theatre. Roosevelt, however, vetoed this approval by the J.C.S., saying that the entire question should await discussion between himself and the Prime Minister at Quebec.[128]

* I.e., on the eve of D-Day.

Yet, in the event, no such discussion took place, either during the Conference itself or while the two leaders were alone together at Hyde Park.[129] Each no doubt hoped that time and circumstances would help to solve things in the direction he wished. As it was, developments in China and France were such that the autumn of 1944 was not a good time for Roosevelt, for his part, to press his case, even had his officials been wholeheartedly behind him, which we have seen they were not. For Churchill, on his side, when so many delicate and important issues had arisen between London and Washington—for instance over Lend Lease—there must have seemed every reason not to allow a secondary matter like Indochina to dampen the 'blaze of friendship.'

The only blunt speaking between Allies over the future of the French Far Eastern Empire came in fact from Canberra—surprisingly so in view of the greater desire of Australia, as distinct from Britain, to see reforms made in the field of colonial administration.[130] Evatt defended the French record, and advised Curtin that it would 'probably be found in the end that the status quo ante in Indochina will be the safest post-war policy.' Taking up Roosevelt's remarks on the subject to the Pacific War Council, and ignoring the President's blandishments over New Caledonia, Evatt also warned Hull 'that Australia is under a deep obligation to fighting France. It is publicly pledged', he continued, 'to do its utmost to maintain the sovereignty of France in its present South Pacific possessions. Similar pledges', he added pointedly, 'have been given by other governments.'[131]

We have seen that there were those in London who would have liked Britain to be as forthright as this, not only as regards Indochina but over the colonial issue in Southeast Asia as a whole. Thanks to Churchill above all, however, undertainty still surrounded her own strategic and political plans for that part of the world; this in turn helped to increase American suspicions as to what the ever-wily British were up to. The differences between the two major Allies were indeed real and extensive enough, but they could at least have been clarified and faced more squarely. As it was, Southeast Asia remained an area where Anglo-American relations, so successful in many ways, were extremely poor.

Notes to Chapter Twenty

1 See above, 405 and R. Arnold, *A Very Quiet War* (London, 1962).
2 See e.g. Mountbatten to COS, 3 May 1944, PREM 3, 148/9; Somerville Diary, 15 Jan. 1944; *Pownall*, 10 Sept. 1944. On the Washington scene, see e.g. *Matloff*, 478, 496.
3 WSC to COS, 5 May 1944, PREM 3, 148/9.
4 *Pownall*, 29 April 1944.
5 Material in PREM 3, 147/6.
6 Material in PREM 3, 149/7.
7 Material in PREM 3, 147/7; WSC to COS, 7 May 1944, PREM 3, 148/9; Cherwell memo., 14 July 1944, Cherwell Papers, Off. 1.1; Dalton Diary, 4 Aug. 1944.

8 Material in PREM 3, 90/3; *Young*, 339.
9 Mountbatten to COS, 24 Dec. 1943 and 16 Jan. 1944, PREM 3, 147/6 and 148/6 respectively.
10 Somerville to Ismay, 19 Jan. 1944, Ismay Papers, IV/Som/5/1.
11 Somerville Diary, 4 Feb. 1944 and e.g. Pownall to Ismay, 28 April 1944, Ismay Papers, IV/Pow/3.
12 On Wingate's death see *Pownall*, 1 April 1944 and Eldridge to Stilwell, 24 Aug. 1944, Stilwell Papers, box 6. For the views of WSC and Mountbatten, see material in PREM 3, 147/10.
13 See the summary in *Pownall*, 13 July 1944.
14 Material in PREM 3, 147/8, 148/4, 5, 9; SEAC War Diary, 1 and 3 Feb. 1944.
15 FO 371, F3699/100/23.
16 COS memo., 23 Feb. 1944, PREM 3, 148/2; WSC to COS, 24 July 1944, PREM 3, 148/9; WSC to Dill, 20 March 1944, PREM 3, 148/10; WSC to CIGS, 2 April 1944, and to COS, 15 May 1944, PREM 3, 148/11.
17 Wedemeyer to WSC, 21 March 1944, PREM 3, 148/12; *Romanus and Sutherland*, II, 228.
18 Stilwell Diary, 17 May 1944.
19 DS 740.0011P.W./7–2944.
20 See above, 412.
21 Wedemeyer to Marshall, 17 Aug. 1944, OPD, Exec. file 1, item 23b.
22 Ismay to Auchinleck, 2 Feb. 1944; Auchinleck to Ismay, 26 Jan. 1944, Ismay Papers, IV/Con/1/1E and F.
23 Somerville Diary, 1 May 1944.
24 DS 740.0011P.W./7–2944; see ibid, 9–544.
25 FO 371, F2983/1/61.
26 See Ehrman, *Grand Strategy*, V, 407ff. and *Grand Strategy*, VI, 173; *Kirby*, III, 439ff.; *Pownall*, 14 May 1944; Lewin, *Slim*, 206, 245.
27 Mountbatten to COS, 13 May 1944 and COS to Dill, 18 May 1944, PREM 3, 148/12; Pownall to Ismay, 26 April 1944, Ismay Papers, IV/Pow/2/2; *Pownall*, 20 April 1944; *Mountbatten*, 57; *Kirby*, III, 257.
28 *Kirby*, III, 260; *Pownall*, 10 and 17 June 1944; *Bryant*, II, 218.
29 *Kirby*, III, 403ff.; *Romanus and Sutherland*, II, 220ff.; *Pownall*, 20 July 1944; Stilwell Diary, 25 May and 4 July 1944; Masters, *The Road Past Mandalay*, 289, 267.
30 *Romanus and Sutherland*, II, 362; Stettinius memo., 23 Feb. 1944, DS 740.0011P.W./3792; Stilwell Diary, 18 May 1944; Stilwell to Marshall, 3 July 1944, Double Zero file 31, USNOA; Eldridge, *Wrath In Burma*, 212.
31 Stilwell Diary, e.g. 1 and 24 Jan., 3 and 17 April, 19 May, 8, 24 and 25 Aug. 1944.
32 FO 371, F993/993/61. See Somerville Diary, 31 Jan. 1944. For Slim's views, see Lewin, *Slim*, 91, 141.
33 *Pownall*, 25 Feb., 11 March and 10 Oct. 1944; *Romanus and Sutherland*, II, 170; Stimson Diary, 4 March 1944.
34 See Eldridge to Stilwell, 24 Aug. 1944, Stilwell Papers, box 6; Stilwell Diary, 19 May 1944; *Davies*, 302; Sykes, *Wingate*, 524; Eldridge, *Wrath In Burma*, 238, 245, 266; *Life*, May 1944; FO 371, AN3575/20/45.
35 FO 371, AN3558/78/45; AN3463/118/85.
36 DS 740.0011P.W./9–1944.
37 Taylor, *Richer By Asia*, 77, and *Awakening From History*, 279; *O.S.S.*, cap. 9; Sweet-Escott, *Baker Street Irregular*, 227 ff.; FO 371, F3770/100/23.
38 FO 371, F758 and 1004/1/61.
39 Ibid, F1024, 1160, 1301, 1671, 2532, 3146 and 3605/1/61; SEAC War Diary, 22 Feb. 1944; DS 740.0011P.W./3685. Difficulties were also caused by the proliferation of British agencies in the political-warfare field, involving the Far Eastern Bureau of the M.O.I., the Government of India and GHQ India, with S.O.E., S.I.S. and the Ministry of Economic Warfare also being involved in an indirect way. See FO 371, F1118/1/61.
40 DS 740.0011P.W./3751, 3745½; FRUS, 1944, V, 1195.

41 SEAC War Diary, 4 Jan. and 9 Sept. 1944; COS, 6 Sept. 1944, CAB 99/29.
42 Mountbatten to WSC, 11 Oct. 1944, PREM 3, 149/8. See *Pownall*, 29 Aug. 1944. In weighing political considerations, Mountbatten was broadly in agreement with his political adviser. Observers noted, however, that Dening's standing with the Supreme Commander was not high. Eggleston Diary, 9 Jan. 1944; interview with Lord Mountbatten.
43 FRUS, 1943, China, 188.
44 Davies memo., 18 Feb. 1944, Stilwell Papers, box 15.
45 E.g. material in PREM 4, 27/10; *Chicago Tribune*, 5 June 1944; *New York Times*, 11 March 1944; Taussig memo., 26 Jan. 1944, Taussig Papers, box 47.
46 Taussig memo., 13 July 1944, Taussig Papers, box 47.
47 Hull to FDR, 8 Sept. 1944, Roosevelt Papers, MR box 166; Hull, *Memoirs*, II, 1600. For a report to the State Dpt. on the unpopularity of the British in Burma, see DS 740.0011P.W./2-2744.
48 L. K. Rossiter, 'Independence For Colonial Asia—The Cost To The Western World', *Foreign Policy Reports*, vol. XIX, no. 22.
49 Davies memo., 18 Feb. 1944, Stilwell Papers, box 15; *Fortune*, Jan. 1944.
50 *Matloff*, 513; Hornbeck to Hull, 3 Feb. 1944, Hornbeck Papers, box 151; Davies memo., 4 Sept. 1944, Stilwell Papers, box 15.
51 Stettinius to FDR, 22 May 1944, Roosevelt Papers, PSF box 93; Bowman to Winant, 28 April 1944, DS, Notter files, box 79; Dependent Areas Cttee., 16 May 1944, ibid, box 120; Woodward, *British Foreign Policy in The Second World War*, 440ff.
52 FO 371, U3427/910/70.
53 Cttee. on Colonial and Trusteeship Problems, 8 and 23 Feb., 7 March 1944, DS, Notter files, boxes 119 and 120; Inter-Divisional Area Cttee. on Far East, 29 and 30 May 1944, ibid, box 118. It is also worth noting that an OSS survey of March 1944 (R and A 1253) took a line over certain Burmese nationalists that was 'harder' in some ways than the one eventually followed by Britain. 'The dictatorial Ba Maw clique, the Thakins, and known Japanese agents', it ran, 'must of course be removed.'
54 *Notter*, 387ff. and Appendix 39; Taussig memo., 1 Sept. 1944, Taussig Papers, box 47; Hull, *Memoirs*, II, 1599. The U.S.A. also returned a cool response when the Chinese Government sought to discuss colonial issues. FRUS, 1944, China, 1165–7; FRUS, 1944, VI, 46.
55 Hailey, *The Future of Colonial Peoples* (Princeton, 1944); Russell, 'Can Americans and Britons Be Friends?', *Saturday Evening Post*, 3 June 1944; Hansard, HC Deb, 399, cols. 390ff.
56 BWP, 16 (March 1944) and 17 (April 1944).
57 Louis, *Imperialism at Bay*.
58 FO 371, material in files 38522–4; AN2108 and 3199/34/45; AN3333/20/45.
59 Washington Embassy to van Kleffens, 21 Sept. 1944, N Col. M, Londen bundel Amerika, and material in Afdeling X.
60 FO 371, U3625 and 3408/910/70.
61 Material in ibid, file 42678. On Stanley's approach to the domestic discussion of colonial matters, see PREM 4, 42/9.
62 Cab, 4 Aug. 1944, CAB 65/43.
63 Perham, *Colonial Sequence*, 250ff.; FO 371, AN3118/78/45.
64 FO 371, AN102 and 1577/16/45; files 40461–2, 40943–5.
65 Stanley memo., 18 April 1944, PREM 4, 31/4; minutes of 9 May 1944, PREM 4, 42/5; Hansard, HC Deb, 400, cols. 1223ff.
66 E.g. minutes of 9 May 1944, PREM 4, 42/5; Fraser-Bowman talk, 6 July 1944, Long Papers, box 192; memo., 27 March 1944 and Curtin to Forde, 16 May 1944, ADEA, A989/44/735/321/5.
67 Cab. Cttee on Malaya and Borneo, minutes and papers, CAB 98/41; WP(44)3, CAB 66/45; WP(44)258, CAB 66/50; Cab, 31 May 1944, CAB 65/42; SEAC War Diary, 24 Dec. 1943, 13 June and 24 July 1944; FO 371, file 41625.
68 Dorman-Smith to Amery, 18 Aug. 1944, IO, Private Office, L/PO/238. For an example

of American unawareness of the existence of such ideas among British officials, see Ludden memo., 28 Jan. 1944, Stilwell Papers, box 15. But see also Hull to FDR, 8 Sept. 1944, Roosevelt Papers, MR box 166.

69 Dorman-Smith to Munster, May 1944, Dorman-Smith Papers, E215/21; SEAC War Diary, 25 Oct. 1944; *Donnison*, cap. IV.

70 Amery memo., 28 Sept. 1944, IO, Private Office, L/PO/238; *Blueprint For Burma* (London, 1944).

71 Amery to Dorman-Smith, 7 Sept. 1944, IO, Private Office, L/PO/237; Dorman-Smith to Amery, 13 Sept. 1944, ibid, L/PO/238.

72 Dorman-Smith to Mountbatten, 4 May 1944, Dorman-Smith Papers, E215/17; material in FO 371, files 41594, 41642, 41675; *Donnison*, cap. V.

73 FO 371, F1436/295/10.

74 See Purcell, *Memoirs*, 349; Thakin Nu, *Burma Under The Japanese*, 98ff.

75 FO 371, U3386, 4968 and 5210/3386/74; *Donnison*, cap. XXII.

76 FO 371, files 41726 and 41627; WSC note, 11 Feb. 1944, PREM 3, 326.

77 FO 371, F2741/100/23.

78 FRUS, 1944, V, 1195.

79 DS 892.01/50.

80 Inter-Divisional Area Cttee. responses, 21 and 22 March 1944, DS, Notter files, box 119.

81 DS 892.01/46; see Gilchrist, *Bangkok Top Secret*, 188ff.; *O.S.S.*, 295ff.

82 DS 740.0011P.W./7–2944; DS 892.01/7–2744. Ironically, Sanasen was suspected by both British and Americans of working against their respective interests. DS 892.01/6–1244; FO 371, F3881/23/40.

83 See *O.S.S.*, 303.

84 See above, 347.

85 DS 892.01/53; FRUS, 1944, V, 1312ff.; WP(45)102, CAB 66/62.

86 FO 371, F331 and 1399/23/40.

87 Ibid, F3770/100/23; F242, 3849 and 3941/23/40; Gilchrist, *Bangkok Top Secret*, 86ff. There was still confusion in London as to whether Siam was within S.E.A.C. or not FO 371, file 41076.

88 FO 371, U5426/3386/74.

89 Ibid, F2196/168/61; F3836/23/40.

90 Ibid, files 41076, 41853, 41851.

91 Ibid, W2166/1534/G; U3386/3386/74; SEAC War Diary, 14 April 1944.

92 FO 371, F3849/23/40; F3770/100/23.

93 Ibid, F881, 2156 and 3941/23/40.

94 See WP(43)574 (CAB 66/46); WP(44)72 (CAB 66/46); WP(44)208 and 233 (CAB 66/49); WP(44)365 (CAB 66/52); WP(44)514 (CAB 66/55); Cabs, 3 Jan. 1944 (CAB 65/41), 10 July 1944 (CAB 65/43), 25 Sept. 1944 (CAB 65/43).

95 Stewart to Hornbeck, 3 April 1944, Hornbeck Papers, box 262.

96 FO 371, F66/66/61; FRUS, 1944, III, 768; Hull, *Memoirs*, II, 1579.

97 Eden to WSC, 20 Dec. 1943, PREM 3, 178/2.

98 FO 371, F360/66/61; F285/285/61; FRUS, 1944, III, 773.

99 FRUS, 1944, V, 1205; Stettinius, *Roosevelt and the Russians*, 211; *Tuchman*, 430.

100 Far East Area Cttee., 23 Feb. 1944, DS, Notter files, box 118; Hull, *Memoirs*, II, 1598.

101 E.g. Hornbeck to Hull, 3 April 1944, Hornbeck Papers, box 173; DS 851G.00/8–2444.

102 DS 851G/8–344.

103 DS 851G.01/9–844.

104 DS 851G.00/96, 8–2444, 9–944, 9–3044.

105 DS 851G.00/8–344.

106 FO 371, U3386/3386/74.

107 Ibid, F1450/100/23.

108 E.g. DS 740.0011P.W./3625, 7–644 and 7–2944; Hull to FDR, 8 Sept. 1944, Roosevelt Papers, MR box 166.

109 FO 371, F4348/9/61.
110 WSC to Eden, 11 March 1944, PREM 3, 178/2; FO 371, F360 and 478/66/61; F285 and 301/285/61; Z605/605/17.
111 FO 371, F478/66/61; Dixon to Martin, 24 Jan. 1944, PREM 3, 178/2; Martin note, 20 Sept. 1944, PREM 3, 180/7.
112 FO 371, U3386/3386/74; F791/295/10; F4261/9/61; F3713/66/61; SEAC War Diary, 19 April 1944.
113 WP(44)111, CAB 66/47; Cab, 24 Feb. 1944, CAB 65/41; FO 371, AN 1560/6/45; U3524/G; W5270 and 5449/1534/G.
114 The Post Hostilities Planning Sub-Cttee. did suggest in April that the New Hebrides islands should, for defence reasons, be partitioned, with Britain or Australia obtaining Espiritu Santo. As for Indochina, if the scheme for U.N. bases failed, Britain herself should obtain bases there through an alliance with France. FO 371, U3524/G.
115 See Marshall, *The French Colonial Myth*, 102ff.
116 Somerville Diary, 29 March 1944; Somerville to First Sea Lord, 21 April 1944, Somerville Papers, box 8/5; Sweet-Escott, *Baker Street Irregular*, 238ff.; *Donnison*, cap. XXI; *O.S.S.*, cap. 10.
117 FO 371, F1475/1/61; F9 and 2702/9/61.
118 Mountbatten to COS, 14 Sept. 1944, PREM 3, 178/3; SEAC War Diary, 3 Feb. 1944. The matter of military jurisdiction in Indochina was still not clear to all at S.E.A.C. H.Q. Joubert, for example, wrongly believed that Chiang Kai-shek had agreed to leave to S.E.A.C. 'the conduct of operations with Indochina.' SEAC War Diary, 20 April 1944.
119 Material in PREM 3, 180/7; FO 371, files 41719, 41723–4, 41797; WP(44)444, CAB 66/53; Cab 14 Aug. 1944, CAB 65/43.
120 FO 371, F3788 and 2223/66/61; *Cadogan Diaries*, 12 May 1944.
121 FO 371, F3948/9/61.
122 WSC to Eden, 21 Dec. 1943, PREM 3, 178/2.
123 FO 371, F118/66/61.
124 Ibid, F1176/66/61.
125 WSC minutes, 17 Dec. 1943 and 4 May 1944, PREM 3, 180/7.
126 WSC to Eden, 21 May 1944, PREM 3, 180/7.
127 SOE memo., 28 July 1944 and COS to WSC, 2 Aug. 1944, ibid.
128 FO 371, F4018/9/61; FRUS, Quebec, 247, 251, 252; JCS, 29 Aug. 1944, RG 218.
129 Martin note, 20 Sept. 1944, PREM 3, 180/7.
130 The New Zealand Prime Minister also recalled in public pledges by U.N. countries to restore the French Empire.
131 Evatt speech, 19 July 1944, and Fraser speech, 29 March 1944, ADEA, A989/43/735/ 310/3; Evatt to Curtin, 5 May 1944, ibid, A989/43/735/310/2; 1944 memo., 'Australian Interests in the Future of Indochina', ibid, A989/43/735/302; Evatt to Hull, 24 Feb. 1944, PREM 4, 50/12.

CHAPTER TWENTY-ONE

BRITAIN, THE UNITED STATES AND INDIA

JUST AS some British officials were attempting to plan for the development of Burma and the colonial territories of Southeast Asia after the war, so there were those who, as in 1943, continued to give some thought to the role that India might play in the future. For example, Ernest Bevin, G. F. Hudson of the Foreign Office Research Department and various officials in the India Office all had ideas which would involve India's becoming a vital element in a regionally-based defence scheme for the Commonwealth and Empire.[1] In wider terms, Wavell, as Viceroy, believed that Britain's 'prestige and prospects in Burma, Malaya, China and the Far East generally are entirely subject to . . . [her securing] India as a friendly partner in the British Commonwealth.'[2]

As matters stood in 1944, however, the situation was far from encouraging, even though political dissent continued to be damped down. The Governor of Bengal (now Richard Casey) reported, for instance, that there still existed no enthusiasm for the war there, and that 'it would be a brave man who would say that the majority of Indians want to remain within the British Commonwealth.'[3] Inflation remained a major problem, with New Delhi and the India Office in London both warning in February that 'an economic collapse' was on the cards.[4] Moreover, following on the Bengal famine, a new food crisis now developed, made worse by an explosion in the docks at Bombay, when about 40,000 tons of food were lost and 500 people killed.[5] With Amery's help, Wavell strove in vain to bring home the urgency of the situation to the Cabinet in London, where Cherwell and others were able to point to inadequate shipping facilities and see to it that only a limited response was forthcoming. Mountbatten reported that Churchill, for his part, 'seemed to regard sending food to India as an "appeasement" of Congress', while Amery was driven to describe the Prime Minister's attitude over the question as 'Hitler-like.'[6] In other words, in addition to strategic and logistic considerations, there appears to have been present as a contributory factor an especially ugly aspect of Churchill's racism, and possibly that of Cherwell as well. Meanwhile, in private, Wavell recorded that the approach of the Cabinet as a whole to Indian affairs had been 'negligent, hostile and contemptuous to a degree I had not anticipated.'

From London's viewpoint, India's mounting sterling balances continued to present a major problem. A Cabinet Committee was set up to examine it, but could offer only the hope that, in more propitious circumstances, especially when British prestige had been restored by the defeat of Japan, 'Indian opinion will be ready to accept a settlement which is in fact reasonable.'[7] This was a topic that was still guaranteed to arouse indignation on the part of the Prime Minister, who also remained totally opposed to dealings with Gandhi, Britain's 'bitter enemy', as he described him, over constitutional matters.[8]

In all, indeed, such were Britain's difficulties as regards India in this period that she could not avoid having to seek some assistance there from the United States, however regrettable this might appear in the light of Washington's impatience over the Indian constitutional issue. Thus, having resolved in March not to do so (and not wishing to bring India within U.N.R.R.A.'s sphere of competence), the Cabinet were driven at the end of April to appeal to Roosevelt for ships to help carry grain from Australia to India, a request which the President, on the advice of the Joint Chiefs of Staff, turned down with regret at the beginning of June. (The Chiefs of Staff in London thereupon released additional British shipping for the task, but this was not sufficient to prevent 'semi-famine' conditions from obtaining in parts of India.)[9] Extra railway waggons for India also had to be sought from the United States, while it was during this period that the provision of 100 million ounces of silver under Lend Lease was negotiated with Washington in order to help stem inflation in the sub-continent.[10]

American help thus proved essential, but any kind of United States involvement in India's affairs continued to give rise to very mixed reactions on the British side. Within the Foreign Office, it was still accepted that 'a real settlement in India is of valid strategic and economic concern to the Americans', a fact that the India Office and New Delhi were both thought to be slow to recognize. The Government of India did, however, send Sir Frederick Puckle to the U.S.A. to report on the interest in India which existed there (he found it 'intermittent and emotional') and to discuss the subject with Pearl Buck and other writers.[11] Over-all, it seemed that the attention paid in the United States to Indian matters was declining, reviving only temporarily at the time of the Japanese attack at Imphal. Nevertheless, the sour attitude of American troops in India itself continued to give rise to concern among British officials, who were too readily inclined simply to blame Stilwell for this state of affairs.[12]

In some quarters, the response to American contacts with and interest in India was again grudging and defensive. Even Wavell became annoyed over what he saw as 'a constant criticism and denigration of the British effort', agreeing with General Giffard that 'we were a very great nation, greater than the Americans, and would remain so.'[13] Churchill gave vent to a similar impatience at Quebec, in a tirade directed at Morgenthau and others. 'I will give the United States half of India to administer', he declared, 'and we will take the other half, and we will see who does better with each other's half [sic].'[14] The Cabinet as a whole also opposed a proposal put forward by

Halifax, Wavell, Amery and, more diffidently, Eden, that the Indian Agency General in Washington should be separated from the British Embassy there and made a Legation under a Minister, the fear being that the United States would in turn press for more substantial representation for itself in India, 'with results that might be very embarrassing.'[15]

In fact, far from encouraging an American presence in India, the British Government sought to minimize it. This attitude was reinforced by delayed repercussions from William Phillips' stay in India in 1943 as Roosevelt's personal representative. In the *Washington Post* in July 1944, Drew Pearson published part of the text of Phillips' final report to the President in which, it will be recalled, he had deplored Britain's unwillingness to institute constitutional reforms, had described the Indian Army as 'mercenary', and had forecast that only 'token assistance' could be expected from Britain and India in the war against Japan. Churchill himself was not troubled by this new incident—Pearson, he noted, was known as a 'champion professional liar', and there was no point in dragging the President into so minor an affair when he had been understanding and restrained about India generally.[16] The Foreign Office and Government of India, however, were greatly concerned at the unwillingness of the American Administration to repudiate publicly Phillips' views, the State Department merely regretting that the leak had occurred (Roosevelt and Hull suspected Welles over this).

Matters were made worse in August, when Pearson revealed that he had access to secret British cables, in one of which it was declared that Phillips would not be welcome to return to India. Although the State Department denied that any such representation had been received from the British Government, sharp questions were asked in Congress by Senator A. B. Chandler, and some of the old anti-British feeling over India was revived. When Phillips was recalled from his duties in London with the Supreme Headquarters of the Allied Expeditionary Force—in fact for family reasons —some Americans concluded that this was yet another case of Britain interfering in their domestic affairs.[17]*

By his own silence over this latest Phillips affair, Roosevelt appeared to be dissociating himself publicly from the British in India, even though in private he deplored the leaks that had occurred. Already, in February, he had issued a statement stressing that American troops were in India solely in order to defeat Japan, his intention in this being 'to clear up a good deal of anti-American feeling' in that country, and to put an end to any suggestion that the United States was bolstering British rule there.[18] Hull, too, wished to keep silent about the Phillips business, telling the President that the State Department 'shared in general the views expressed in the Ambassador's

---

* What Pearson had seen, thanks to the connivance of an Indian officer serving on the staff of the Agent General in Washington, Bajpai, was a cable to London from Sir Olaf Caroe for the Government of India, declaring Phillips to be persona non grata. The issue had not been raised officially by London with Washington, however. The officer who had leaked the cable was quietly transferred to a fighting front. He is named in the Foreign Office documents on the affair and the subsequent enquiry.

letter.'[19] In the opinion of Vincent, Chief of the Chinese Division, India might still emerge as 'the point of major disagreement between the U.S. and the U.K.', while prominent American liberals like Pearl Buck and Reinhold Niebuhr, encouraged by the Indian League of America, went on calling for a more enlightened British policy and the release of Nehru and other detainees.[20] At the same time, as noted earlier, the magazine *Amerasia* was proposing that the United States should create a new world economic system in which Britain would no longer have to exploit India; enlightenment and self-interest would thus go hand in hand for the U.S.A., with India becoming her 'new economic frontier.'[21]

There were still those on the left of British politics, of course, who also retained a vision of a new, free India. But when Americans thought of Britain and India they thought in terms of Churchill rather than of Laski. And with Churchill dictating the limits of British policy, the United States and the United Kingdom entered upon the final stages of the war with their differences over India muted but far from resolved.

Notes to Chapter Twenty-One

1 FO 371, U4136/1970/10; Bevin to Cranborne, 1 Feb. 1944, Bevin Papers, box 13; material in IO, Private Office, L/PO/296.
2 *Wavell*, 24 Oct. 1944. A group of Wavell's officials made a comparison between India and China as future powers. Their conclusion was 'that there was not much in it but that China was tougher . . .' Ibid, 18 Sept. 1944.
3 WP(44)326, CAB 66/51.
4 WP(44)96, CAB 66/46.
5 *Wavell*, 14 and 15 April 1944.
6 Ibid, 10 March, 15 Aug., 7 and 21 Sept., 20 Oct. 1944; Dalton Diary, 3 Aug. 1944; Wavell to Ismay, 8 Feb. 1944, Ismay Papers, IV/Con/2/3; WP(44)63 and 99 (CAB 66/46); WP(44)103 and 118 (CAB 66/47); WP(44)165 (CAB 66/48); WP(44)216 (CAB 66/49); WP(44)351 (CAB 66/52); Cabs, 14 and 21 Feb., 20 March 1944 (CAB 65/41), 24 April 1944 (CAB 65/42).
7 WP(44)398, CAB 66/52; Cab, 4 Aug. 1944, CAB 65/43; material in CAB 91/5.
8 Cab, 3 Aug. 1944, CAB 65/43. For Brendan Bracken's facile comments on the Indian political situation, see memo. of 13 Aug. 1944, Harry Dexter White Papers, box 7.
9 WSC to FDR, 29 April 1944, PREM 3, 472; Cttee. on Indian Food Grain Requirements, CAB 91/6; FO 371, AN2726/6/45; FRUS, 1944, V, 271; Ehrman, *Grand Strategy*, V, 469.
10 Cttee. on Indian Financial Questions, 17 May 1944, CAB 91/5; FRUS, 1944, V, 248ff.
11 FO 371, AN2804/181/45; AN1254/181/45.
12 Ibid, AN278, 1049 and 3072/20/45; AN333 and 532/181/45.
13 *Wavell*, 24 June 1944.
14 Morgenthau Diary, 13 Sept. 1944.
15 WP(44)221, CAB 66/49; Cab, 9 June 1944, CAB 65/42; FO 371, AN482 and 2264/181/45.
16 WSC to Halifax, 15 Sept. 1944, PREM 4, 27/10.
17 FO 371, material in files 38611–13.
18 DS 740.0011 P.W./3680; Hull, *Memoirs*, II, 1494.
19 FDR to Phillips, 30 Aug. 1944; Hull to FDR, 15 Aug. 1944, Roosevelt Papers, PSF

box 92; FRUS, 1944, V, 239ff.; Hess, *America Encounters India*, 146; Phillips, *Ventures In Diplomacy*, 269.

20 Dennett memo., 18 Jan. 1944, IPR Papers, box 358; FO 371, AN3159/181/45; AN3812/34/45.

21 FO 371, AN3679/34/45; *Amerasia*, 8 Sept. 1944. Professor Lloyd Gardner has informed me that speeches on the same subject were made at conventions of the National Foreign Trade Council.

CHAPTER TWENTY-TWO

AUSTRALASIA AND THE SOUTHWEST PACIFIC

BY 1944, both Australia and New Zealand were facing more serious problems still regarding their manpower and war effort. Decisions as to the future size of the armed forces of the two Dominions were taken during the Commonwealth Prime Ministers Conference in London in May,[1] for Australia the question being bound up with another one, referred to already, concerning the extent to which she was to provide base facilities for an increased British naval and military presence in the region.

Practical difficulties of this kind apart, Curtin was emphatic that such a British contribution would be most welcome, his tone contrasting markedly with the one he had adopted in 1942, even though he still believed that Australia had at that time pursued a correct policy.

> 'He made no apology', he told his Commonwealth colleagues, 'for asking for American assistance in the days when Australia was seriously threatened. . . . [But] the acceptance of American help had in no way affected the Australians' deep sense of oneness with the United Kingdom. He desired to see the British flag flying in the Far East as dominantly and as early as possible. He was eager to see the prestige of the British Empire reestablished . . . in the Far East and to see a practical demonstration of the British as a civilising agent.'[2]

Curtin put the same point again to Churchill in August, this time with a warning attached:

> 'There is developing in America', he wrote, 'a hope that they will be able to say they won the Pacific war by themselves . . . I am deeply concerned at the position that would arise in our Far Eastern Empire if any considerable American opinion were to hold that America fought a war on principle in the Far East and won it relatively unaided, while the other Allies including ourselves did very little towards recovering our lost property.'[3]

The Australian Prime Minister also put forward suggestions for increased Commonwealth cooperation in the fields of defence and foreign policy, entailing regular meetings between the British Prime Minister and the High Commissioners in London, and the possible establishment of a permanent

Commonwealth secretariat.[4] Here, however, Canberra once more ran into the reluctance of Canada—her eye very much on the United States—to participate in anything that could look like a Commonwealth 'bloc', while Churchill himself, much to Curtin's private irritation, did not display much enthusiasm or even interest in what was being proposed.[5]

This renewed emphasis on their Commonwealth loyalties did not mean that the Australian Government wished to see MacArthur displaced from his position as defender of the Southwest Pacific. On the contrary, Curtin went out of his way to make clear his country's gratitude for the General's presence and performance.[6] There now existed, nevertheless, a certain disquiet among Australians over the use that was being made—or, it seemed at times, not made—of their forces in the Far East.[7] More important still, the Australian and New Zealand Governments continued to feel that, despite all their efforts, the United States, like Britain, still paid too little attention to their views. The casual and belated way in which they were appraised of the decisions taken at the Cairo Conference appeared to prove as much. Uneasiness was also created by Roosevelt's arbitrary statements to the Pacific War Council regarding the future of various Pacific and Far Eastern territories, and by unofficial American statements about the need for the United States to retain her war-time Pacific bases.

The outcome of this resentment, inspired by an ever-assertive and ambitious Evatt, was an Australian–New Zealand Conference and published Agreement in January 1944.[8] Here, the two countries let it be known that they desired amongst other things to be represented at the highest level on all bodies dealing with the conclusion of the war against Japan, to see a regional defence zone established, and to help create an international commission for the South Seas that would harmonize the development towards self-government of dependent territories in that part of the world. In addition, they asserted that the construction and use of war-time bases provided no grounds for post-war claims regarding the possession of the areas concerned, and that enemy territories in the Pacific should be disposed of only as part of an over-all settlement for that ocean in which Canberra and Wellington should participate.

This Agreement on the part of Australia and New Zealand was clearly directed in the main against United States high-handedness, and although New Zealand leaders had managed to tone down some of its more aggressive passages as originally drafted, its publication was followed by a testy exchange between Evatt and Hull over the former's wish that an international conference on the future of the Southwest Pacific should be held in Australia as soon as possible.[9] Evatt's strong desire to secure an enhanced role for his country was also made clear once more in a cable that he had sent to the Dominions Secretary in London, in which he called for Australia to be given after the war 'full responsibility for the policing of Portuguese Timor, Australian New Guinea and the Solomon Islands Protectorate, and . . . a share in the responsibility for the policing of the Netherlands Indies, particularly Java, Dutch New Guinea and also the New Hebrides.'[10]

As he had emphasized to the Dutch Minister in Canberra, Evatt was especially keen to secure 'close cooperation . . . in regard to the future security and welfare of the peoples of the [East Indies] region.' Within the Australian Department of External Affairs, indeed, the hope was that fear of isolation and of American interference would make the Dutch in the Indies amenable to Canberra's influence, which could then be asserted in such a way as not to 'offend Indonesian aspirations or compromise our long-term aims' in the area.[11]

On the Dutch side, this Australian eagerness was viewed with some apprehension by a number of senior officials.* The new Lieutenant Governor of the East Indies, van Mook, wrote in June to warn his Prime Minister, Gerbrandy, that

'in Australia there undoubtedly exists an annexationist group. Australia feels under-valued in this war, and some officials strive to increase their popularity by . . . getting from participation in this war tangible gains . . . The British have no designs upon Netherlands Indies territory . . . but I question how far London is opposing such [Australian] designs; the Government in London might be appeasing the Australians by letting them go ahead with such unwise annexationist designs in order to maintain imperial harmony.'[12]

These fears were increased by MacArthur, who in private warned a Dutch official that the C. in C. of the Australian Army, General Blamey, together with 'a powerful group', sought to split the Netherlands Indies from his South West Pacific Area as a step towards annexing them. Appealing for Dutch support to prevent the boundaries of his Command from being reduced, MacArthur proclaimed himself to be 'the guardian of unimpaired Dutch sovereignty in this area', and warned against not only Australian intentions but a readiness on the part of Britain to build up 'an economic and political predominance' in the Indies.[13]

Even before this, van Mook, supported by his Foreign Minister, van Kleffens, was in any case arguing that Dutch interests would best be served if the East Indies were to remain within MacArthur's South West Pacific Area rather than being transferred to Mountbatten and S.E.A.C. S.E.A.C., he pointed out, would take far longer to liberate the area from the Japanese, while it was desirable to counteract the impression that existed in some American circles 'that in our military contribution and colonial policy we are merely playing second fiddle to London.'[14] Not all Dutch Ministers and officials accepted this kind of emphasis: the Prime Minister himself, for example, tended, as we have seen in an earlier period, to look towards the British Government for help in resisting American pressure against the colonial powers, while in the war zone Admiral Helfrich of the Royal Dutch Navy made little secret of his resentment at the way in which Admiral King

---

* The qualification is necessary since interviews have made it apparent that the fears of van Mook were not shared at the time by all his senior officials in Australia, and that some of them, indeed, were unaware of the extent of his apprehension.

and the U.S. Navy were laying down the law.[15] In general, however, the Dutch remained satisfied with MacArthur, while at the same time seeking to guard their interests in more direct fashion by obtaining Australian agreement 'in principle' to the arrival and training in Australia of 30,000 Netherlands troops, who would thus, they hoped, be ready to move quickly into the East Indies when the moment came.

Meanwhile the Australian–New Zealand Agreement had caused some surprise in British official circles. It was only by chance that the High Commissioner in Canberra, Cross, had learned that the conference between the two Dominions was to take place, and Curtin failed to carry out his promise that he would announce it as being a preliminary step only, to be followed by consultations in London. The ensuing Agreement was attributed by Cross to Evatt's desire 'to burst upon the world with what he regards as a development in British-Empire relations, and to appear as the author of a foreign policy which was obviously free from overseas influence.' In the Dominions Office the document was pompously dismissed as 'a deplorable monument to egregious amateurism in international affairs', while the Colonial Office, not surprisingly, singled out for attack Evatt's separate wish to secure Australian control over the Solomons. Nevertheless, there was also some satisfaction in the Foreign Office and elsewhere at what was seen to be a rap over the knuckles for the Americans, and the Cabinet, guided by Cranborne, welcomed the concern that the two Dominions were displaying over future defence arrangements in the Pacific. Furthermore, Evatt himself privately described the Agreement to a British official as having been prompted above all by apprehension over American expansionist tendencies in the South Pacific, Australia and New Zealand, while the New Zealand Prime Minister, Fraser, also hastened to make it known that the Agreement had in no way been intended to embarrass Britain.[16]

Indeed, Commonwealth relations, and especially those between Britain and Australia, appeared to be much improved during this period when compared to the tempestuous days of 1941–42. At the meetings of Prime Ministers in London in May, the visitors, as Eden noted in his diary, 'were whole-hearted in approval of [Britain's] foreign policy'; in return, they received a renewed pledge from Churchill that Britain would mount a full-scale effort against Japan once Germany had been defeated, and that the importance of the Commonwealth for the post-war world was fully appreciated in London.[17]* In addition, reports were continuing to reach British officials and officers that, especially away from the front line, there existed 'quite an amount of apparent ill-feeling [among Australians] towards the Americans.'[18] General Blamey in particular was said to have returned home

---

* There remained tension, however, over the British desire that the Commonwealth should speak in the United Nations of the future with a single voice, as compared to the Dominions' wish for separate representation. There was also a marked difference between Churchill's scheme for regional councils of the U.N. and the emphasis that the Dominions, like the Foreign Office, placed on the need for a single international political body. (Cab, 27 April 1944, CAB 65/42; WP(44)370, CAB 66/52; *Cadogan Diaries,* 9 and 19 May, 1944.)

from a visit to London 'full of admiration and loyalty towards all things British', being 'not now on as good terms as formerly with General Mac-Arthur', and 'appearing to favour the operation of Imperial forces under an independent command and on an axis separate from that of the American forces.'[19]

In general, the feeling was being encouraged in London that, as one official put it, although Australia would 'naturally as a Pacific nation have close relations with the United States, her closest relations will, unless we play our cards extremely badly, be with the United Kingdom and the other nations of the Commonwealth.'[20] The Foreign Office, too, in a circular sent out in December 1943, expressed its hopes for the future vitality of the Commonwealth, sustained by British leadership and by her status as a world power. At the same time, it was argued in this paper, 'we must in future regard the Dominions not so much as offspring of the Mother Country as fellow makers of the United Nations'; moreover, it continued, 'we must accept with good grace, though with no apologies for the past, and indeed some insistence on our rights, the fact that the United States is now in an undefined way associated with the Commonwealth.' (It was even acknowledged by the Foreign Office that 'in their habits and ways of living, people of the Dominions, with the exception of French Canadians and possibly South Africans, are in many respects more akin to Americans than to ourselves.')[21]

As for the immediate problem of the prosecution of the war against Japan, we have seen that the Chiefs of Staff in particular were arguing throughout much of 1944 for a British effort to be based on Australia and to include operations on MacArthur's left flank.[22] In the debates that surrounded this question, Churchill, for his part, did at one time put forward the idea that S.E.A.C. might be extended to take in such a new operational area, while the Chiefs of Staff also thought in terms of an eventual British commander for the region as a whole when the time came for American units to shift northwards. For the moment, however, the proposal that held the field was for a Commonwealth force to operate under MacArthur's direction, and when the General let it be known that he suspected London of working against him, the Prime Minister hastened to tell him, with at least an approximation to the truth, that 'I never had the slightest idea of diminishing your command.' Churchill similarly sought to reassure Curtin—who, unlike Blamey, insisted on remaining close to MacArthur—that there was no intention of interfering with the Australian Government's direct relations with the General.[23]

Even before he received these assurances, MacArthur on his side was declaring to British officers and officials on a number of occasions that he supported their Imperial cause. 'It always had been and was his firm wish to see a strong British Empire', he told General Lumsden, 'and to see the best of relations between the peoples of America and the British Empire.' He advised, moreover, 'that it was obviously very much in the interests of the British Empire that, as soon as any territory [in the Pacific] had been reconquered, it should be garrisoned and held by troops of the British Empire. Possession', he observed, 'is nine-tenths of the law.' To Cross he also emphasized how keen he was to have units of the Royal Navy working in his Area, going so far as to remark that it would be 'a great thing that an American general should sail into Manila under the British flag.' For good measure he endorsed the British view of Stilwell's overland drive through Burma towards China, a campaign which he described as 'nonsense', and supported Churchill's idea of launching an attack on Singapore via Sumatra. [24]

These protestations of friendship on MacArthur's part were accepted as genuine by the British officers and officials to whom he was talking at the time. Nor did Cross carry Churchill with him when describing the General as being 'absorbed with the business of being a great man.' Nevertheless, as we have seen in the case of his dealings with the Dutch, MacArthur was very ready to cast suspicion on the motives of the British behind the latter's backs, once he believed that they were threatening to take away some of his South West Pacific Area. And this belief did become implanted in his mind, despite the fact that he was correctly told by Marshall after the Chief of Staff had visited London in the summer of 1944 that what the British Chiefs of Staff were thinking of was a Commonwealth task force operating under his, MacArthur's, command. [25]

Aside from the part played in all this by the General's vain, sensitive and suspicious nature, the trouble was exacerbated by the manoeuvrings of Admiral King, who had accompanied Marshall to London, but who chose to warn MacArthur that Britain 'might' propose to absorb most of the Netherlands East Indies within S.E.A.C. (One can only surmise that King may have been seeking to build up a common American front against a British presence in the Pacific. Certainly, he admitted in private to Nimitz that what he had told MacArthur was no more than speculation on his part.) [26] MacArthur's suspicions were deepened further still by Curtin, who, with more justification than King had had, repeated to him the idea which he had heard raised in London in May, that a Commonwealth force might eventually, when the Americans had moved north, take over responsibility for military operations in the Australia–Borneo–East Indies area. [27]

MacArthur reacted fiercely to what he suspected and had been told, despite the fact that his attention was by now focussed above all upon the prospect of liberating the Philippines.* In private, he castigated General

---

* For all the emotional capital invested in the freeing of the Philippines, the American Administration displayed at this time little interest in planning the rehabilitation of those islands. (Friend, *Between Two Empires*, 252.) In London meanwhile, the American colonial record in the Philippines was regarded as being far from the model one that Washington held it up to be. There also continued to be a certain wry satisfaction in British official circles over the collaboration that was taking place between native officials in the Philippines and the Japanese. Comparisons were drawn, in addition, between American and Filipino attacks on 'British imperialism' and the likelihood that the U.S.A. would demand post-independence bases in the Philippines. (FO 371, AN2993/34/45; material in files 41814 and 41818.) See above, 231, note 115.

Blamey in particular, who, he believed (rightly, it seems), favoured an independent Commonwealth military zone.[28] To Washington, where Admiral Leahy agreed with him, he uttered the warning that if the British once got into the Netherlands East Indies it would be 'difficult to prise them loose.' Above all, he spelt out (and accompanied with a veiled threat) what he saw as being at stake for the United States in terms of influence and hard cash:

'Entirely aside from any consideration of equity', he wrote to Marshall, 'the division of the area and the assignment of the major portion thereof to a British commander would be completely destructive of American prestige in the Far East and would have the most serious repercussions. It is my belief that such a line of action would not receive the approval of the American people . . . [and] that any form of appeasement will be followed in due course by deterioration not only of British–American relationships but of American prestige and commercial prospects throughout the Far East.'[29]

Moreover, MacArthur had little difficulty in convincing Roosevelt himself that the British had sinister expansionist designs, when he conferred with the President in Hawaii in July. (Perhaps mutual disgust for a third party helped to ease the underlying tension that must have existed between the two men when they met face to face, following the uncovering of Mac-Arthur's continuing condemnation of the New Deal and his flirtation with the Republicans as a possible Presidential candidate. In any case, *les absents ont toujours tort*.)[30] The President, Leahy recorded later, 'did obtain information [at this meeting] on what the British are planning to do in the Western Pacific', while Roosevelt himself subsequently told an official that Mac-Arthur had revealed 'that [the British] have made plans for exerting a maximum influence in the Dutch East Indies', going on to deplore such unregenerate imperialist tendencies and Britain's 'disgraceful' rule in an area like West Africa, which he had seen for himself.[31]

That there were some grounds for MacArthur's belief that an eventual take-over of part of his Command was contemplated in London, despite the intention to work under him in the first place, has been demonstrated above. There was no substance, however, in the idea that Britain had designs upon the Netherlands East Indies. That Roosevelt and others in Washington should so readily accept such a notion is merely further proof of how pervasive and lasting were the suspicions and misunderstandings that surrounded Anglo-American relations over colonial and, in particular, Far Eastern matters.

Meanwhile American–Australian relations, too, had been strained, in this case as a consequence of the evident anti-American aspects of the Australian–New Zealand Agreement in January—a document that the United States Minister in Canberra, Johnson, described as 'the Anzac Monroe Doctrine.' The situation was made worse by Hull's subsequent refusal to agree to Evatt's wish to convene as soon as possible a conference on the future of the Southwest Pacific.[32] Nevertheless, Curtin, like Fraser of New Zealand, was clearly anxious that the United States should not be antagonized, and when he visited that country in April he hastened to put things right with the President, at the expense of his colleague, Evatt:

'In the course of the conversation', recorded Rear Admiral Wilson Brown, who was present, '... Curtin expressed concern lest the accounts published about the agreement between Australia and New Zealand ... might be misunderstood and possibly resented in the United States and United Kingdom ... President Roosevelt said that he thought he had already figured out what had occurred. His guess was that Prime Minister Curtin had had very little to do with the drafting, but that Evatt had done most of it and the others had merely agreed. Curtin said that was exactly right: that a group had discussed the future of the white man in the Pacific and that they had all disapproved of the [British] Government's India policy and feared that unless properly handled China might turn against all white men.* While pursuing this theme the proposal for an agreement between Australia and New Zealand was made and carried in what may well prove to be an excess of enthusiasm.

President Roosevelt directs that the record show that his present opinion is that it will be best to forget the whole incident.'[33]†

Even Evatt himself, however much his 'rudeness and crudeness', as Roosevelt called it,[34] caused offence in Washington, appeared to be conscious still of the need for Australia and the United States to work closely together, suggesting to American officials in September 1944 that the two countries should settle the affairs of the South Pacific area between them.[35] The perils of 1942 had shown up, after all, a degree of Australian dependence on the U.S.A. for its safety that could not be forgotten simply because the Japanese had now been pushed back.

Yet the episode of the January Agreement between Canberra and Wellington had indicated that the perceived interests of Australia and the United States respectively were not necessarily always in harmony. Moreover, this was to emerge in even clearer fashion during the final stages of the war against Japan and the early months of the peace, when it became

* It seems unlikely, although documentary evidence on the point has not been found, that Curtin's account of the genesis of the 'Anzac' Agreement was correct. In the first place, written and oral testimony points overwhelmingly to resentment at not having been consulted over the Cairo Conference's dealings regarding the Far East as having provided the main impetus. Secondly, Evatt's own attitude towards China, as indicated elsewhere in the present volume, was one of unconcealed suspicion and a certain loftiness. Curtin's emphasis on racial dangers and his employment of British imperial policies as a scapegoat seem, rather, to have been a transparent attempt to placate Roosevelt.

† Leahy privately described Curtin and his wife as 'speaking with a strong accent of the uncultured inhabitants of [Australia].' (Leahy Diary, 25 April 1944.) That a Leahy should think in this manner underlines the extent to which there now existed a pervasive sense of American superiority.

evident that the United States intended to dictate the shape of the new order in the Far East.

Notes to Chapter Twenty-Two

1 Minutes of 3 May 1944, PREM 4, 42/5; *Hasluck*, II, 550ff.; Ehrman, *Grand Strategy*, V, 473ff. The May decision was for Australia to maintain its existing naval strength and to have 6 divisions and 53 squadrons by the end of 1944. New Zealand was to maintain its naval strength, and to provide 20 squadrons and 1 division for the Pacific war in 1945.
2 Minutes of 3 May 1944, PREM 4, 42/5.
3 DO(44)13, CAB 69/6. See AAWC, 7 Sept. 1944, A2682, vol. VIII.
4 WP(44)210, CAB 66/49; FO 371, material in file 42678; minutes of 15 May 1944, PREM 4, 42/5.
5 Cab, 27 April 1944, CAB 65/42; Ismay to Casey, 13 June 1944, Ismay Papers, IV/Cas/4; Dalton Diary, 25 May 1944; Hankey Diary, 7 and 25 May 1944.
6 Minutes of 3 May 1944, PREM 4, 42/5; AAWC, 7 Sept. 1944, A2682, vol. VIII.
7 *Hasluck*, II, 569ff.
8 See ibid, 436 and 480ff.; Reese, *Australia, New Zealand and the United States*, 32ff.; Lussington, *New Zealand and the United States*, 82.
9 FRUS, 1944, III, 168ff. Hull was privately supported in his refusal by Fraser of New Zealand.
10 Australian Government to Dominions Secretary, 25 Jan. 1944, ADEA, A989/43/735/324.
11 Evatt to van Aersson, 24 April 1944, ADEA, A989/43/735/435; Hood memo., 22 Sept. 1944, ibid, A989/44/600/5/1/7; Evatt to van Aersson, 5 April 1944, and Departmental memo., 6 March 1944, ibid, A989/44/600/5/1/5.
12 van Mook to Gerbrandy, 29 June 1944, NFM, Londens archief, Brandkast Ia 13. See Hillgarth report, 28 March 1944, PREM 3, 159/10, and 'George Ph.D.'
13 van der Plas reports, 14 and 19 Aug. 1944, NFM, Londens archief, Brandkast Ia 13.
14 van Mook to Gerbrandy, 29 June 1944, loc. cit., and 11 Sept. 1944, ibid.
15 Somerville Diary, 4 July 1944.
16 Material in PREM 4, 50/12; WP(44)108, CAB 66/47; Cabs, 9 and 11 Feb., CAB 65/41; FO 371, W8408/1534/G and F1555/153/61; DO, DO 35/1214, WR 227/11. Officials in London sought to refute Australian suggestions that she was inadequately informed. FO 371, W7087/1534/4.
17 *Avon*, 442; minutes of 2 and 11 May 1944, PREM 4, 42/5.
18 Layton to WSC, 3 Feb. 1944, PREM 3, 159/2; Somerville to Ismay, 19 Jan. 1944, and Ismay to Somerville, 12 Feb. 1944, Ismay Papers, IV/Som/5/1 and 7. The New Zealand Premier, Fraser, was also concerned over a remark of Admiral King's, that 'there were political reasons against the employment of New Zealanders in the Central Pacific.' DO(44)12, CAB 69/6. On the American side, the Minister in Canberra disliked the activities of the O.W.I. in that country. Johnson to Hornbeck, 6 Jan. 1944, Hornbeck Papers, box 262.
19 Lumsden to Ismay, 15 July 1944, PREM 3, 159/4; Hollis to WSC, 30 June 1944, PREM 3, 160/5.
20 DO, DO 35/1118/G579/19.
21 FO 371, W12262/5467/68. A senior officer in Australia nevertheless expressed concern at the 'economic stranglehold of the whole area' that he thought the Americans were seeking through their war-time predominance. Somerville Diary, 11 March 1944.
22 See above, 413, and material in PREM 3, 160/1–8.
23 Material in PREM 3, 159/4, and WSC to Curtin, 15 Sept. 1944, PREM 4, 75/2.
24 Cross to WSC, 30 Aug. 1944, and Ismay to WSC, 21 Sept. 1944, PREM 3, 159/4;

Hillgarth report, PREM 3, 159/10; Lumsden to Ismay, 24 April 1944, PREM 3, 159/14; MacArthur to Marshall, 2 Feb. 1944, MacArthur Papers, RG 4.

25 Marshall to MacArthur, 21 Aug. 1944, MacArthur Papers, RG 10. See *Pogue*, II, 452.
26 King to MacArthur, 21 July 1944, King Papers, box 4, USNOA; King–Nimitz minutes, 13–22 July 1944, ibid, series III.
27 Shedden to MacArthur, 26 June 1944, and MacArthur to Marshall, 27 Aug. 1944. MacArthur Papers, RG 4.
28 Lumsden to Ismay, 15 July 1944, PREM 3, 159/4.
29 MacArthur to Marshall, 27 Aug. 1944, MacArthur Papers, RG 4; *Leahy*, 299; Luvaas, *Dear Miss Em.*, 155.
30 See *Vandenberg*, cap. V.
31 Leahy Diary, 16 Aug. 1944; Taussig memo., 13 Nov. 1944, Taussig Papers, box 47.
32 FRUS, 1944, III, 175; Johnson to Hornbeck, 26 Jan. 1944, Hornbeck Papers, box 262; Watt to Hood, 4 April 1944, Watt Papers.
33 FRUS, 1944, III, 180, 192; Brown memo., 25 April 1944, Roosevelt Papers, MR box 168. See also FDR to WSC, 5 April 1944, PREM 4, 27/3, and FDR to Curtin, 3 Jan. 1944, *Roosevelt Letters*.
34 Taussig memo., 16 Jan. 1945, Taussig Papers, box 48.
35 DS 740.0011P.W./9–244. An OSS survey of April 1944 (R and A, 1971) suggested: 'It is possible that future historians will regard World War II as a landmark in the coming of age of Australia and New Zealand. Present trends suggest that this war will introduce a rather profound change in the Anzac position in the Pacific [and] in their relationship to the British Commonwealth of Nations.'

CHAPTER TWENTY-THREE

JAPAN AND THE POST-WAR ORDER
IN THE FAR EAST

IN AUSTRALIAN and New Zealand eyes, the main threat to be guarded against in the future was that of a revived Japan.[1] Among British officials, too, the warning was to be heard that 'it would be most unwise to assume that the problem of Japan will be solved by the mere fact of defeat.' 'We presume', wrote the Head of the Foreign Office's Far Eastern Department, 'that the major objective of a post-war settlement in the Far East is to prevent a recurrence of aggression by Japan.' More forcefully still, the Post Hostilities Planning Sub-Committee predicted that the Japanese, 'a progressive and ambitious people', would be likely 'to seize any opportunity to avenge their defeat in the present war.'[2] Yet at the same time, there existed within the Service Departments in Whitehall, as noted in an earlier chapter, what Gladwyn Jebb described as 'an undoubted tendency to regard the Soviet Union as a potential enemy'—a view that was generally deplored by the Foreign Office.

When it came to drafting ideas about Britain's post-war security needs, and trying to reconcile military and diplomatic opinions in this respect, the Foreign Office was handicapped by Cadogan's unreasonable objection to not only the Services but also his own officials occupying themselves with what he liked to dismiss as 'crystal gazing.' A full study of possible post-war international political developments which could affect defence policies in various ways was thus lacking, although Jebb did his best. Cadogan should not have been surprised or indignant, therefore, when the Service Departments, which had sought the Foreign Office's advice in the first place, went ahead largely on the basis of their own assumptions.

Concern over a possible threat from the Soviet Union thus made its appearance in a series of drafts prepared by the Post Hostilities Planners on the subject of 'security in Southeast Asia and the Southwest Pacific.' What was required, these documents suggested, was a chain of bases along the line Marshalls–Carolines–Philippines–Formosa–China coast, bases which, happily, would serve as a defence against both Japan and the U.S.S.R. As for China, the danger would lie not so much in aggression on her own part, but in her possible subordination by one of the two aforesaid states. Therefore Britain should 'build up and foster the friendliest relations with a strong China and encourage her to maintain a complete independence from the

U.S.S.R. and Japan.' In addition, it was argued in these drafts, the best way to provide further cover against an attack via China would be 'to secure the northern frontier of Indochina and the China–Burma border.' 'Control of land communications in Siam' would also be a valuable asset.[3]

Apart from their own, inter-departmental difficulties in drawing up tentative post-war plans of this kind for the Far East and Pacific, British officials had to work largely in the dark where the intentions of the United States were concerned, although the Embassy in Washington did its best to piece together various scraps of evidence that came its way.[4]* On one point, at least, Churchill continued to be clear: if the United States wished to hoist its flag over the Japanese mandated islands, that would be entirely acceptable to the United Kingdom.[5] And this was, indeed, what a considerable body of American opinion, both within and outside official circles, by now intended should be done. Congressmen like Senator Chandler and newspapers like the *Chicago Daily News* and *Chicago Tribune* were speaking out loudly to this effect, and a poll suggested that nearly 70 per cent of the American people were with them.[6] On behalf of the Joint Chiefs of Staff, likewise, Leahy informed Hull that 'the Japanese Mandated Islands should be placed under the sole sovereignty of the United States. Their conquest is being effected by the forces of the United States', he continued, 'and there appears to be no valid reason why their future should be the subject of discussion with any other nation.'[7]

Even within the State Department, there were senior officials like Adolf Berle and Breckenridge Long who wanted to see the U.S.A. 'simply go out and take' the Carolines, Marshalls and Marianas, if necessary placing them under American sovereignty. Stettinius, too, who was to wobble around in a somewhat weak manner over the issue, was ready in July to agree with the more forceful Forrestal 'that there should be nothing equivocal about our position as to these islands being under United States sovereignty in the future.'[8] More extensive plans still were meanwhile being drawn up by a senior official of the Bureau of the Budget, Wayne Coy, sourly described by Stimson as 'one of the "angels around [Roosevelt's] throne."'[9] Coy's proposals, which he submitted to Hopkins, would require Britain, France, the Netherlands, Australia and New Zealand all to bow to American wishes. His assumption was that the United States

'will hold by possession, mandate, lease, purchase or agreement general control over Polynesia and Micronesia, adequate participation in Melanasia, and a strong position in Indonesia . . .† The United States will

---

* The State Department did agree to an unofficial exchange of papers, but little came of this. (Note of 29 Jan. 1944, DS, Notter files, box 79.) It was not known in London, for example, what American intentions were regarding the twenty-three Pacific islands that had been in dispute between the two countries before the war. Concern was also aroused by reports that in some British Pacific islands that were currently occupied by U.S. forces, natives had petitioned for a change of allegiance to the United States. (FO 371, file 38570.)

† Polynesia was defined as 'the mid-Pacific triangle located by the Hawaiian Islands, Easter Island and the North Cape of New Zealand'; Micronesia as 'the northern island

exercise civil authority in its Pacific possessions and mandates; and it will acquire special representation in civil affairs in all other islands groups in which it will maintain bases . . . [In the Philippines, following independence, the United States] will establish a special form of civil representation appropriate to a protectorate . . .'[9]

However, within the State Department some officials were becoming uneasy over talk and schemes of this kind that would involve American possessions being extended to take in the Japanese mandates and other territories. Concern was aroused, for example, by a report prepared at the President's request and submitted to him in June by Rear Admiral Richard E. Byrd, dealing with Pacific islands in relation to national defence needs. In his report, Byrd argued 'that the Pacific will be our sphere for the keeping of world peace', and that to this end 'we must know how, without antagonising our allies, to get control of whatever islands we need and to neutralize or get participating rights in what we may fail to get control of.' Byrd's entire approach, submitted Grew, was out of step with the declared policy of the President and Secretary of State, which was to work for a post-war system of security within the framework of an international organization.[10] Roosevelt himself reminded the Joint Chiefs in July 'that we have agreed that we are seeking no additional territory as the result of this war.' His own idea, he continued, was 'that the United Nations will ask the United States to act as Trustee for the Japanese Mandated Islands. With this will go the civil authority to handle the economic and educational affairs of their many inhabitants, and also', he added reassuringly, 'the military authority to protect them, i.e. fortifications etc. It does not necessarily involve a decision on permanent sovereignty.'[11]

While Washington was thus engaged in a sometimes fierce internal debate over the fate of strategically placed Pacific islands, on a few other aspects of the post-war order in the Far East rather more interest was displayed in what London had to say. It was agreed, for example, that the State Department and Foreign Office would exchange ideas about the means by which Korea should be brought to independence, as promised at Cairo, and that the Chinese, too, should be invited to contribute to this discussion. The State Department's own view continued to be that some form of interim international administration would be required, probably involving the U.S.A., Britain, China and the Soviet Union.[12] Korea, however, was a peripheral matter, as well as being complicated by uncertainty as to what actions and policies would be forthcoming in that area from Moscow. Far more central and more widely controversial was the question of what should be done with Japan after she had been defeated. And here, although there

bridge between Polynesia and Indonesia with a spur north to Japan including the Ellice, Gilbert, Marshall, Caroline, Mariana and Bonin Islands'; Melanesia as 'the southern bridge between Polynesia and Indonesia, including the Fiji, New Hebrides, New Caledonia and Solomon Islands, the Bismarck Archipelago, New Guinea and adjacent islands.' Coy's memorandum included in its list of problems to be faced in these areas 'the preservation of racial homogeneity.'

were informal exchanges between American and British officials, involving in particular individuals like Hugh Borton on the one side and Sir George Sansom on the other, everything pointed towards the issue being preserved by the United States as one for its own, separate decision.

In public in the U.S.A., to a far greater extent than in Britain, concern was being expressed more loudly in 1944 than a year earlier that there should be no 'appeasement' of or 'soft' peace for Japan.[13] One reason for this, obviously, was that victory and the moment of decision were now clearly closer at hand; another, no doubt, was the impact of the fresh revelations that were made in this period concerning Japanese war-time atrocities.[14] At the same time, even over this matter of the future of the enemy, there existed in some American quarters suspicions of what the British might be up to. Vice President Wallace, for one, apparently believed that the British Government wanted to see Japan remain strong after the war.[15]

Such a supposition, as we have seen in the preceding period, was not justified. For instance, over the question of whether or not to retain the Throne in Japan, British officials were divided, Sansom continuing to advocate its preservation but others, like Ashley Clarke and G. F. Hudson, having serious doubts as to the desirability of this. (British political warfare did avoid attacking the existing Emperor, but this was done partly because it was believed that the opposite course would prove counter-productive.)[16] In general, British officials with a knowledge of Japan, in contrast to some of the more enthusiastic evangelicals in Washington, remained cautious as to how far a fundamental change of spirit and character could be brought about throughout that society. Some hopes were placed on what Sansom described as the 'considerable number of liberals' who might emerge from the ruins of Japan's defeat; on the other hand a member of the Far Eastern Department rightly recalled that many so-called Japanese 'liberals' were better described as 'the level-headed, worldly-wise element', and that they had in many cases disagreed with 'the military fanatics' over the means of the country's policy, rather than over the end of making her the dominant power in East Asia. Defeat, he suggested, was likely to bring about among Japanese ruling circles 'not a change of heart but an accession of worldly wisdom.'[17]

It was in the United States, however, that the question of what should be done with the Emperor and Throne in Japan was attracting most attention. Grew had contributed to this process at the end of 1943, when he had made a speech that revealed something of his belief that the Throne should be utilized by the Allies when they came to construct a new Japan. 'The institution', he again argued privately to Hull, '. . . is a cornerstone and sheet anchor', although he also emphasized that the myth of divinity must be removed from around it.[18] The Far Eastern Sub-Committee of the State Department's Postwar Programs Committee likewise came to the conclusion, although against the advice of some of its members, that it would be 'indispensable' to retain the Emperor 'as an instrument of the will of the Supreme [Allied] Commander', the belief being that the roots of Japanese militarism lay in an attitude of mind rather than in the existence of the Throne. Hornbeck, on the other hand, was thinking in terms of setting the Emperor aside temporarily, during the period of Allied occupation, while in the public debate Owen Lattimore, more in tune with popular sentiment, called for 'a revolution' in Japan to solve the entire question.[19]

In general, American officials were indeed proceeding against the current of public opinion. Thus, the State Department's Inter-Divisional Committee on the Far East advised, as Sansom was doing on the British side, that, while militarism in Japan must be rooted out, she must at the same time be given the prospect of a better future and 'a share in the world economy on a reasonable basis.' In approaching this eventual condition, three phases were envisaged: first, 'the stern discipline of occupation', followed by a period of 'close surveillance', and finally the arrival of a Japan 'discharging its responsibilities in the family of peaceful nations.' During the initial stage, as the State Department saw it, key political, economic and strategic centres would be occupied, although the Allies would reserve the right to install themselves throughout the country if that proved necessary. Above all, there would be a single, centralized administration, and not separate zones, each for a different Ally, as was planned for Germany.[20]

In London, meanwhile, there was a keen awareness of the desirability of the two leading Western Allies keeping in step with one another over this question of the treatment of Japan. This was also the case where the politics of the Japanese surrender were concerned, as demonstrated in September 1944, when news of a peace feeler from within the enemy's ranks was received from Stockholm, and was immediately passed on to the State Department.[21]* Nevertheless, British thinking about post-war Japan was far less organized and advanced than was the case on the other side of the Atlantic. This alone would have made a coordinated approach to the subject difficult, even had the desire for such a procedure been strongly present in Washington. As it was, State Department officials kept in touch with Sansom only in a general and informal way. And while, in their own planning, they allowed for a share in the occupation of Japan by all the other Allies who had fought against her, they were entirely clear that the predominant role must and would be played by the United States.[22]

The same was true as regards the longer-term shaping of Japan's future and the construction of a new order in the Pacific and Far East generally. In the State Department, and even more in the War and Navy Departments, the assumption was that what had been largely an American war would be followed by an essentially American peace. As a part of that peace, an influential body of United States officials envisaged the creation of a liberalized, democratic, free-trading Japan. An Americanized Japan, in fact. Perhaps here, after all, rather than from amidst the perpetual chaos of

* This news from Stockholm was regarded in London as being worthy of serious attention, even though the significance of the resignation of General Tojo and his replacement by a Koiso-Yonai Cabinet in July had been somewhat underrated. In fact, however, the Stockholm move was only a peripheral affair.

China, there would arise the protégé so long sought in East Asia: not only a peaceful and grateful friend, but regenerate proof of the universal validity of American values.

As the war entered its final eleven months, the Far Eastern triumphs of United States arms, together with the country's growing economic might, were helping to ensure that, despite all disappointments and complexities, many still felt as Pearl Buck had done in 1942, that 'if the American way of life was to prevail in the world, it had to prevail in Asia.'

Notes to Chapter Twenty-Three

1 E.g. Murdoch speech reported in *New York Times*, 24 June 1944.
2 FO 371, F3240/94/23; W7599/1534/G; U4150/748/G.
3 Ibid, material in files 40740 and 40741A.
4 Ibid, W3776 and 4536/1534/G; APW(44)2, CAB 87/67.
5 Minutes of 9 May 1944, PREM 4, 42/5.
6 E.g. *Chicago Tribune*, 8 Feb. 1944; *Chicago Daily News*, 2 and 28 Feb. 1944; *New York Times*, 17–23 Jan. and 24 May 1944; *Times*, 16 Aug. 1944.
7 FRUS, 1944, V, 1201; JCS, 18 Jan. 1944, RG 218.
8 *Berle*, 22 June 1944; Forrestal Diary, 7 July 1944. Vincent thought that American policies on these matters would be set by the Navy. Dennett memo., 18 Jan. 1944, IPR Papers, box 358.
9 Coy to Hopkins, 10 Jan. 1944, Hopkins Papers, box 334.
10 DS 740.00119/7–1244; Grew to Hull, 11 July 1944, Grew Papers, vol. 120; see also Cttee. on Colonial and Trusteeship Problems, 23 Feb. and 21 April 1944, DS, Notter files, box 120.
11 FDR to JCS, 10 July 1944, Roosevelt Papers, MR box 167.
12 FO 371, files 40798 and 41801; FRUS, 1944, V, 1224, 1290ff.
13 E.g. *Chicago Daily News*, 17 March 1944.
14 See e.g. Cab, 24 Jan. 1944, CAB 65/41; WP(44)51, CAB 66/46; FO 371, AN427/20/45. On difficulties arising between the U.S., Britain, Australia and Japan over the exchange of civilian internees and prisoners of war, see Cabs, 6 March 1944, CAB 65/41, and 28 July 1944, CAB 65/43; WP(44)127, CAB 66/47.
15 FO 371, AN3582/20/41. In March 1943, Hornbeck had written to Hull: 'There are some indications of a British desire to avoid as far as possible any intensification of Japanese hostility to Great Britain, with a view, presumably, to a resumption of at least a quasi-friendly relationship with Japan in the post-war period.' Hornbeck Papers, box 27.
16 FO 371, F1629, 3324, 4139/1/61; F94 and 459/94/23; F2061/208/23; FRUS, 1944, China, 1112; memo., 5 Jan. 1944, DS, Notter files, box 79.
17 FO 371, F4015/1/61.
18 Material in Grew Papers, vols. 118–20. For Foreign Office relief that an American and not a British official was raising the issue, see FO 371, AN20/20/45.
19 Ballantine Diary, cap XI; Hornbeck to Hull, 29 April 1944, Hornbeck Papers, box 237; Hornbeck to Hull, 25 April 1944, ibid, box 380; *Lattimore*, 31. See FRUS, 1944, V, 1250, and *Long*, 23 April 1944.
20 FRUS, 1944, V, 1235, 1257; Inter-Divisional Cttee. on Far East, minutes, passim, DS, Notter files, box 119.
21 FO 371, F4370/208/23 and F3514/241/23; R. J. Butow, *Japan's Decision to Surrender* (Stanford, 1954; hereafter, *Butow*), 29, 40ff.
22 Inter-Divisional Area Cttee. on Far East, 13 March 1944, DS, Notter files, box 119.

PART FIVE

The Second Quebec Conference to the Japanese Surrender

September 1944 to August 1945

CHAPTER TWENTY-FOUR

THE SETTING

THE SURRENDER of Germany early in May 1945 left Japan alone and facing inevitable defeat. Even in its final phases, however, the war in the West had continued to affect developments in the Far East. For Britain in particular, the additional months beyond the end of 1944 which it took to bring about Germany's surrender meant increasing strain, and made the burden all the heavier when the time came to contribute an extra effort against Japan. The setback at Arnhem in September 1944 and the German offensive in the Ardennes in the following December and January, for example, held up the transfer of forces to Mountbatten's South East Asia Command in a period when the extent and speed of the American advances in the Pacific were already overshadowing the British part in the Far Eastern conflict.[1] Meanwhile the formidable military power displayed by the Soviet Union as her forces moved in across the Vistula to crush Hitler and dominate Eastern and Central Europe underlined the impact which it could have on the East Asian scene if and when Moscow chose to turn it in that direction.

Despite the approach of victory, strategic disagreements continued to arise during these final stages of the war in Europe between the British and the Americans—disagreements which, while tending to centre upon individual figures like Montgomery and Eisenhower,[2] involved such wide issues as the speed with which Germany could be defeated and, even more, the politics of the peace. Should there be a single, main thrust into the Ruhr? Should an offensive be launched into the Balkans towards Vienna? Should everything be subordinated to a drive to capture Berlin? Linked with questions of this kind, moreover, was the greater one still, brought into prominence at the Conferences of Yalta (4–11 February 1945) and Potsdam (17 July–2 August), of what was to be expected in regard to future relations with the Soviet Union. Here, too, as we shall see, significant implications were involved where the Far East was concerned. These were bound up with such issues as how desirable it was for the West, and more especially the United States, to obtain the promise of a Soviet military offensive against the Japanese Kwantung Army in Manchuria; of what benefits could be derived from using the atomic bomb against Japan; and of what policy the U.S.A. should adopt as regards the Asian colonial empires of its West European allies.

Following on from what was said about Western attitudes to the Soviet Union during the previous period, it must again be emphasized that concern and alarm in Washington and London over Moscow's behaviour did not, in late 1944 and the first half of 1945, increase in a steady, unrelieved or uniform manner. For example, whilst, before Yalta, Soviet insistence on recognizing the Lublin Committee as the Provisional Government of Poland gave rise to much disquiet, Churchill, during a visit to Moscow in October, had not found it difficult to arrive at an understanding with Stalin over the rough proportions of influence that their respective countries should exercise in the Balkans and Eastern Europe. (This understanding, it should be noted, did not cover the case of Poland, although the future of that country was mentioned during the talks.)[3] Moreover, the Yalta Conference itself, where agreement appeared to be reached over even the Polish issue,[4] was hailed by Western officials, as well as by their publics, as a major step towards the achievement of lasting friendship with the U.S.S.R. In Hopkins' words, it seemed to be 'the dawn of the new day we had all been praying for.'[5] Even Churchill, whose own recollections were to exaggerate the consistency and perspicacity of his concern over the Soviet menace,* assured his Cabinet colleagues on his return from the Crimea that Stalin 'meant well to the world and Poland.' 'Poor Neville Chamberlain believed he could trust Hitler', he went on. 'He was wrong. But I don't think I'm wrong about Stalin.'

During the months that followed Yalta, of course,[6] the Prime Minister rapidly became alarmed at what he now saw as an 'enormous . . . Russian peril', doubly so as he contemplated American plans to switch their forces from Europe to the Far East once Germany had been defeated, and to be gone altogether, according to Roosevelt, 'as rapidly as transportation problems permitted', and at the most within two years. Truman, too, after succeeding Roosevelt, declined to hold up the transfer of American units to the war against Japan.[7] In London, Attlee, as well as Churchill, increasingly distrusted Soviet intentions.[8] But although growing concern also existed in Washington, there was far from being a complete Anglo-American alignment against the U.S.S.R. Roosevelt—cool over Churchill's visit to Moscow in October and, as noted in an earlier chapter, ready at Yalta to egg Stalin on over a matter (the possible shooting of German officers en masse) which he knew distressed the Prime Minister[9]—remained convinced that he could handle the Soviet leader. Truman, for his part, proposed, to Churchill's dismay, that he should meet Stalin alone before the Potsdam Conference.[10]

* In his war memoirs, Churchill misleadingly emphasized only his *public* declaration of faith in Stalin after Yalta, explaining that he had felt the need to make such a statement in order to encourage Soviet good behaviour. (*Churchill*, VI, 351; and see above, 380, footnote.) On the other hand, the Prime Minister's remarks to his colleagues (not only recorded at the time by Dalton, but recalled by Lord Coleraine in conversation with the author as having been striking and even somewhat puzzling) help to show the degree of exaggeration present in some 'revisionist' historical writings. (See, e.g., *Kolko*, 25, where the assertion is made that the Prime Minister's letters to Stalin were 'full of feigned warmth and solicitude, [revealing] the extent of his duplicity.')

Meanwhile, American officials continued to suspect Britain of seeking 'to play off the United States and the U.S.S.R. against each other', Joseph E. Davies, a former U.S. Ambassador in Moscow, declaring after a visit to London in May 1945 that Churchill was 'more concerned over preserving England's position in Europe than in preserving peace.' Hopkins, too, so staunch a friend of Britain's in many ways, remained as late as May 'skeptical about Churchill' as regards the Soviet Union, and 'thought it of vital importance that we not be maneuvered into a position where Great Britain has us lined up with them as a bloc against Russia to implement England's European policy.'[11] Instead, the role which Washington still tended to envisage for itself—to the disquiet of the Foreign Office—was that of a mediator between Britain and the Soviet Union, the visit of Hopkins to Moscow in May being designed partly with this in mind.[12]

Nevertheless, American attitudes towards the Soviet Union were hardening.[13] Roosevelt himself, increasingly unable to reconcile the public expectations that he had aroused over the future of Eastern Europe with the limits of United States power there which he recognized in private, joined Churchill in protesting to Stalin over developments in Poland. And although it is difficult to be precise about the degree to which the President's ideas were changing, given the likelihood that he played little part in drafting a good many of the messages that went out in his name at this time, he does appear to have been reflecting, shortly before his death in April, that the West would soon be in a position to take a 'tougher' line than hitherto on these matters, while he had already held up proposals for granting a $10 billion loan to the U.S.S.R. until her intentions became clearer.[14]

At the same time senior members of the Administration like Forrestal and Stettinius were calling for what the latter termed 'serious determination in our relations with Russia', whilst Harriman from Moscow declared that only the greatest firmness would suffice in the face of a Soviet desire, as he interpreted it, 'to see [their] concepts extend to as large an area of the world as possible.'[15] A similarly disillusioned and hard approach was to be found among the U.S. delegation to the United Nations San Francisco Conference in April and May. 'The basic problem', proclaimed Representative Eaton in private, 'was who was going to be masters of the world . . .', while Isaiah Bowman envisaged a time 'when perhaps the inevitable struggle [would take place] between Russia and ourselves.'[16]*

As for Truman, it did not take him long to arrive at a decision to take the 'tougher' line that Roosevelt had spoken of, despite the fact that, at the crucial meeting with his senior advisers on 23 April, Stimson and Marshall advocated caution ('he was evidently disappointed by my . . . advice', recorded Stimson), and even Leahy ('not a very acute person', as the same diarist had written earlier) confessed that he had always regarded the

---

* Note, for example, the typically brave public comment of I. F. Stone on 4 May 1945. 'The tendency, which is very strong, if not dominant, in the American delegation, is to regard the United Nations Conference . . . as a conference for the organization of an anti-Soviet bloc.' (I. F. Stone, *The Truman Era* (New York, 1973), 11.

Yalta agreement on Poland as being open to differing interpretations, including the one that Moscow was putting upon it.[17] For the benefit of the outside world, there were still some suggestions of continuing Allied harmony to come: the West's recognition of the new Provisional Polish Government, for example, and the agreement at Potsdam on Poland's western frontier. In private, however, both American and British officials went on anxiously debating the question, as summarized by Pierson Dixon, Eden's Principal Private Secretary, of 'whether Russia is peaceful and wants to join the Western Club but is suspicious of us, or whether she is out to dominate the world and is hoodwinking us.'[18] Moreover, the Potsdam exchanges—and in particular, curiously enough, those concerning international waterways—were enough to convince Truman, for one, that he now knew the answer. It was, as he later put it, that 'the Russians were planning world conquest.'[19]

In terms of the Far East, this conviction of Truman's clashed with the concept of a Soviet-American understanding which, as described below, had formed the basic element of the framework that Roosevelt had sought to erect for that part of the globe at Yalta. Meanwhile, these developments involving relations between Washington and Moscow also had their effect upon American attitudes towards the creation of the atomic bomb, a subject too extensive to be explored here, but one on which widely differing interpretations have been put forward. Suffice it to say that, as early as April, the Secretary of State elect, James F. Byrnes, was telling Truman that the bomb 'might well put us in a position to dictate our own terms at the end of the war', a view which Churchill appeared to share when, at Potsdam, he heard of the successful test explosion in New Mexico ('Now we could say, "If you insist on doing this or that, well . . . And then where are the Russians!"');[20] that Truman, advised by Stimson, followed Roosevelt in agreeing with the Prime Minister that no details of the bomb should be imparted to Stalin;[21] and that the use of the weapon against Japan was connected, in the minds of some American officials, with the future pattern of relations with the Soviet Union.

By this last point it is not intended to deny that for many of those involved, probably the majority, the overriding consideration in the decision to use the bomb was to save American lives and hasten the defeat of Japan. Simply to take a single source, however, one finds recorded in the diary of Henry Stimson, who had a special responsibility in the matter, not only the belief that the successful development of the weapon would provide a 'master card' when it came to settling issues between the U.S.A. and the Soviet Union, but also the wish to see this new power displayed for all—including Moscow, of course—to see. On 6 June, for example, Stimson told Truman that he was 'a little fearful that before we could get ready the Air Force might have Japan so thoroughly bombed out that the new weapon would not have a fair background to show its strength.' The President, recorded Stimson, 'laughed and said he understood.'[22]

By comparison with the Soviet Union, France meanwhile presented fewer and less vital problems for Britain and the United States in this final period of the war. Here, too, however, the state of relations among the three countries continued to have its repercussions in the Far East, notably in regard to the question of Indochina. In this context, matters developed in two opposing directions. On the one hand, Washington's lack of sympathy for the French imperial cause was reinforced by the onset of yet more difficulties with de Gaulle. The General was not invited to Yalta, for example, and in return refused to meet Roosevelt on the latter's journey back from the Crimea to the United States. In June, moreover, when de Gaulle belligerently declined to withdraw his troops from the Val d'Aosta, as London and Washington were both insisting, affairs even reached a point where Stimson could record that 'we thus suddenly and unexpectedly seemed to be on the brink of war with France.'[23] Churchill, too, was greatly incensed by both this Val d'Aosta confrontation and French behaviour and hostility towards Britain in the Levant during the spring of 1945. We shall see that these developments, which helped prevent the conclusion of an Anglo-French treaty at the time, also made the Prime Minister disinclined to champion the French cause in Indochina against the wishes of Washington.[24]

Yet on the other hand, the Foreign Office in London continued to argue that Britain should help build up a strong France and work closely with her.[25] Even in the State Department, moreover, the recovery of France was now recognized and generally welcomed, marked as it was during this period by the promise of a zone of occupation in Germany and the allocation of a permanent seat on the Security Council of the United Nations. Thus, briefing papers prepared for Yalta and Potsdam acknowledged France's 'great strides towards . . . resuming her former position of influence in world councils', and recommended that 'her usefulness to us and her contribution to the construction of a peaceful future world will be increased by her full participation in world affairs on a basis of parity with the Great Powers.' Hopkins, too, went out of his way to improve Franco-American relations when he visited Paris in January, while Truman, encouraged by senior State Department officials, did the same when Georges Bidault, de Gaulle's Foreign Minister, came to the United States in the spring.[26] All of this helped to make the imposition of a radical, anti-French solution in Indochina increasingly unlikely.

The new world organization in which France was to have an important place was brought nearer during this period by agreements reached at Yalta and at the San Francisco Conference a few months later, this despite major problems being encountered on the way over such issues as the veto and the number of seats to be allocated to the U.S.S.R.[27] Much of the credit for what was achieved belonged to Roosevelt, who had fostered an American public opinion favourable to such an organization; who, to the end, sought to guard against a Republican repudiation of it (Republicans such as Senator Connally, John Foster Dulles and Harold Stassen were included in the San Francisco delegation); and who was careful nevertheless to warn against 'perfectionism [which], no less than isolationism or imperialism or power politics, may obstruct the paths to international peace.'

In London, an eager welcome was given to any sign that there was to be no repetition of America's retreat from international responsibilities after 1918. In this respect, encouraging pieces of evidence included Senator Vandenberg's speech in January on the need for the United States to play her full part in the world community, and poll findings in April which indicated that over 80 per cent of the Senator's fellow-countrymen were in favour of joining an international organization possessing policing powers. (The proportion answering in favour of a post-war military alliance between the U.S.A. and Britain was significantly less, though still as high as 52 per cent.)[28] Even so, the Embassy in Washington warned the Foreign Office that there was far less awareness on the part of the American public of the need for economic, as distinct from purely political, cooperation among nations, while the Minister of State, Law, still foresaw the possibility of 'a swing back to . . . an expansionist isolationism of a highly inconvenient character.'[29]

As it was—and in the light of American distrust of Britain's addiction to 'power politics' it was ironical—occasions were already arising when manoeuvring by the United States in order to extend and protect her interests disconcerted British observers. For example, the tortuous efforts of the American delegation at San Francisco to prevent any United Nations interference with their country's regional arrangements in Latin America (Dulles among others coolly wished at the same time to veto all other regional agreements) brought from Eden the warning that they could undermine 'the whole concept of World Organisation.'[30] We shall also encounter another instance, shortly after the end of the war, when, viewed from London, the determination of the United States to secure strategic predominance over a wide area began to take on some of the less endearing characteristics of a runaway rhinoceros.

However enlightened or otherwise the policies and actions of the United States might be, it was more apparent than ever during this final stage of the war that her position vis-à-vis Great Britain was already that of senior partner. This situation will be evident when we turn to the Far Eastern war and to such questions as whether or not to use the atomic bomb against Japan. In over-all terms, Churchill himself was to recall later: 'Up to July 1944 England had a considerable say in things; after that I was conscious that it was America who made the big decisions.'[31] To Forrestal in April 1945, Eden suggested 'that there was an analogy between the position of England and Austria after 1815 and the position of England and the United States now: the United States has taken the place of England [as] England [had] taken the place of Austria.'[32]

Naturally, it was a state of affairs that was scarcely welcome within the Foreign Office in London, which was uneasily aware that Washington was indeed increasingly thinking of Britain in terms of a second-rate power, and of Soviet-American relations as being those which held the main key to the future. 'The United States', reported Halifax in August 1945, 'is now groping towards a new order of things in which Great Britain, whilst occupying a highly important position as the bastion of Western European security and as the focal point of a far-flung oceanic system, will nevertheless be expected to take her place as junior partner in an orbit of power predominantly under American aegis.'[33]

Such notions were to be heard both in public and in private, official circles in the United States. 'Every American', declared the *New York Herald Tribune*, 'faces himself and his countrymen with a new confidence, a new sense of power . . . We cannot if we would shut our eyes to the fact that ours is the supreme position. The Great Republic has come into its own; it stands first among the peoples of the earth.'[34] The *Chicago Tribune*, needless to say, was not to be outdone over such sentiments. 'The good fortune of the world', it concluded, 'is that power and unquestionable intentions go together.'[35] Meanwhile in private, Bernard Baruch, financier friend of both Churchill and Roosevelt, urged the latter that he now possessed all the material power necessary to dominate entirely the shaping of the peace.[36] Similarly, Wallace emphasized to Truman that the world was hungry for leadership, and that he, not Churchill, was the man who could supply it; according to a member of the White House staff, it was with such a belief firmly implanted in his mind, 'feeling that the U.S. is by far the strongest country in the world', that the new President approached the Potsdam Conference.[37] As for relations with Britain, Harry Dexter White in the Treasury was among those who judged that these 'mattered little . . . if the problems between the United States and Russia can be solved.'[38]

This growing sense of power among American politicians and officials had a financial and economic, as well as a military basis, as has been indicated in the context of earlier periods.* Morgenthau, for example, was able to tell Truman proudly, soon after the latter had entered the White House, that the financial centre of the world was now located, not in London, but at his desk in the Treasury in Washington.[39] Meanwhile in the Foreign Office, it was recognized even more clearly than before that Britain's growing financial difficulties would seriously handicap the country's post-war diplomacy, with 'a shift in influence' being bound to take place in Washington's favour, and a significant degree of British dependence upon the U.S.A. becoming inescapable. (The acknowledgement that 'in order to preserve the good relations required we may well find ourselves forced to follow the United States in a line of policy with which we do not fundamentally agree' was removed from the final version of the Office's survey of

---

* 'The U.S.A.,' writes Professor Milward, 'emerged in 1945 into a world of exhausted nations with its enormously expanded industries working at full capacity and at higher levels of efficiency than ever before, and with its population enjoying a higher standard of living.' He concludes that the increase in American productive capacity was possibly 'the most influential consequence of the Second World War for the post-war world.' Milward, *War, Economy and Society*, 63ff., and 94.

the subject, not because its sense was rejected, but because of the poor impression that it would create if the document fell into the wrong hands.)[40]

As it was, Britain ended the war, it will be recalled, having lost a quarter of her national wealth since 1939, and needing to increase exports by between 50 and 75 per cent over pre-war levels in order to compensate for what had occurred.[41] At the end of June 1945 the country's external liabilities had reached £3,355 million (£2,723 million of it owed to states within the sterling area), while liquid assets amounted to only £453 million; external disinvestment since 1939 totalled £4,000 million.[42] The forecast made by Keynes in a vital paper written in April and put before the Cabinet in the following month was that, at the end of the war, 'we shall be running an overseas deficit . . . at a rate of about £1,400 millions per annum.' He went on to warn backward-looking spirits like Amery that it was far from being 'a well-chosen moment for a declaration of our financial independence of North America', and to estimate that a minimum of $5 billion would be needed in aid from the United States 'with up to (say) $8 billion possibly required to give us real liberty of action . . .'[43]

Meanwhile, Britain's war-production capacity had become severely strained; there was also a serious shortage of workers available for the tasks of raising the standard of living of the population, restoring capital equipment and reviving exports. Demobilization plans were being affected by the situation; demobilization in its turn, especially where it involved the repatriation of men who had had a long spell overseas, threatened to produce serious consequences for the operations of South East Asia Command.[44] At the same time, Britain's war effort in the Far East was also running into difficulties over inadequate shipping, while Washington's own proposals for saving shipping space by cutting back supplies of food and raw materials to Britain were themselves causing great concern in London.[45]

There was indeed a tendency among American officials to overrate the size of British stockpiles in 1945 and to conclude that they were more than adequate.[46] As for the United Kingdom's dependence upon American supplies in an area like that of S.E.A.C., this was seen within the State Department as providing a means whereby control could be exercised over British behaviour towards Siam, for example. Looking further ahead, the Department's Economic Adviser, Herbert Feis, echoing the approach we have seen adopted by General Somervell earlier,[47] proposed that, in return for American aid, Britain should give the U.S. 'free rights with her citizens in exploring and exploiting the portions of her empire that were not self-governing . . .'[48]

Some of those concerned in Washington did recognize that Britain would need help in overcoming her financial problems after the war and in making the transition to a low-tariff trading basis.[49] Here, too, however, there was a tendency to underestimate the seriousness of the situation and to expect the British economy to make a quick recovery.[50] Bernard Baruch, who was sent to London by Roosevelt in the spring of 1945, was prominent among those who argued that the British should learn to stand on their own feet and that care should be taken not to supply them with aid unnecessarily.[51] Moreover, as Keynes was to discover when he arrived in the U.S.A. in September 1945 to seek desperately-needed American money, arguments about 'equality of sacrifice' in regard to the war now carried far less weight. Britain, in short, was going to have to bow to the United States' grand design for the post-war economic order, in which Washington's position would be predominant, if she was to obtain the assistance she so urgently required. As Feis had observed at the time of the Bretton Woods Conference, 'capital is a form of power.'[52]

Not surprisingly, therefore, the question of Lend Lease continued to be one which not only reflected the imbalance between the two countries—the United States was to end the war a net creditor to the U.K. by over $20 billion—but created strains between them.[53] It also formed a most significant part of the framework within which Britain had to approach the Far Eastern war during this final period. As noted earlier, a broad agreement had been reached between Churchill and Roosevelt at Quebec, in September 1944, on the matter of Lend Lease during Stage II, the first year of the war with Japan alone. During the detailed negotiations that followed (Britain sought just over $3 billion in military aid and $2¾ billion in non-munitions),[54] sympathy was shown on the American side by Hopkins and Morgenthau in particular, whilst even the hatchet-men of Leo Crowley's Foreign Economic Administration suggested that a campaign should be launched to publicize British military efforts in the Far East in order to help make Congress more ready to loosen the purse strings. Roosevelt, too, was reported by Hopkins in November to 'believe that there is going to be another war' and to have 'made up his mind that in that war there will be a strong Britain on the side of the United States.' 'He wants you to be strong', Hopkins assured a member of the British Embassy, 'and will help you to be so.'[55] Moreover the outcome of the talks—the United Kingdom was to receive $2.8 billion in military aid and $2.6 billion in non-munitions—was regarded as highly satisfactory by British Ministers and officials, Keynes echoing Hopkins by attributing the settlement to 'the ever-increasing and ever-deepening conviction in the minds of all responsible Americans that a strong Britain after the war is . . . an indispensable requirement of American policy.'[56]

And yet in private, as already illustrated,[57] Roosevelt was being extremely sour and unenthusiastic about the new Lend Lease proposals, denying that he had promised anything at Quebec and being advised by Leahy, at his elbow, that 'the American people [would] react with violent disfavor' to any fresh commitment, which should be avoided at all cost.[58] Therefore, the programme of aid that emerged was regarded on the American side as being in no way binding, but 'subject to the changing demands of strategy as well as to supply considerations.' Or, as Roosevelt bluntly expressed it to Stettinius, 'They must rely on our good will.'[59] The President maintained this attitude up to his death, and his successor, highly sensitive to Congressional opinion, proved to be if anything less forthcoming still. Thus, in May,

Truman authorized a cut-back in the volume of Lend Lease deliveries, while in July, again with Leahy doing some prompting, he directed that munitions supplies should be strictly limited to those needed for the fighting against Japan.[60]*

In London meanwhile, insufficient attention was paid to some of the warning signs about Lend Lease that were there to be seen—for example, the action of Congress in April in amending the Lend Lease Act in such a way as to prevent aid being given for post-war rehabilitation purposes, or the information passed on to British colleagues by American officials in May, that they did not expect Lend Lease to be continued for more than 'perhaps a month or so after V-J day.'[61] From May onwards, however, Halifax and the British Service delegations in Washington were reporting a 'serious deterioration' in the attitude of American Government departments concerned with Stage II supplies, with the needs of U.S. forces in the Far East being given priority and 'the whole allocation and assignment machinery [being] virtually at a standstill' by July, when Truman's 'Japan-only' ruling on military deliveries became known.[62] Churchill had already raised the whole issue with Truman in May, but did not obtain a response until the Potsdam Conference, when the President further alarmed British officials by calling for payment to be made in dollars for certain items being sent to Britain. Worse still, Truman displayed in the process an unawareness of the extent to which Britain's gold and dollar reserves, although higher than had been expected, were dwarfed by the country's overseas liabilities.

Truman did also reveal a basically sympathetic attitude at Potsdam, it is true, declaring to the Prime Minister that Britain's staunchness in 1940 'justified the United States in regarding matters as above the purely financial plane.' In addition, he went on to agree that the United Kingdom's military Lend Lease needs should be met after all, with the exception only of matériel involved in the occupation of Axis territories. Nevertheless, the final shock for London was still to come, following the surrender of Japan. On 20 August the news was received that Lend Lease supplies were to be terminated immediately, with even goods already in the pipeline having to be paid for in cash. At an emergency meeting called by Ernest Bevin, now Foreign Secretary, Washington's behaviour was denounced as 'shabby'. No amount of resentment, however, could alter the situation that was being demonstrated: that Britain was now dependent on the United States to a very great extent for the preservation of her economy and the well-being of her people.[63] Indeed, as the Foreign Office's draft review of the circumstances had tacitly admitted,[64] although she was emerging from the war victorious, in an important sense Britain had already become much less of a truly 'sovereign, independent' state than had been the case in 1939. A statesman of vision and of true greatness in peace-time as well as war-time terms might have conceived it to be a vital task to educate his countrymen

* An unpublished poll taken at the time revealed that 76 per cent of those Americans questioned believed that Britain should pay back the Lend Lease she had received for the war against Germany.

to this reality and all that it implied. Churchill was ill-qualified to do so.

Alongside and in some ways reflecting this growing imbalance in power, there also remained clear indications that the Anglo-American partnership, although still a remarkable achievement and a major contribution to the winning of the war, was playing a less prominent part within the Allied cause than it had before D. Day.* (One personal factor in this decline was the death, in the autumn of 1944, of Sir John Dill, who, as the Washington representative of the British Chiefs of Staff, had won both trust and affection from Marshall and Stimson.)[65] Thus, before Yalta Roosevelt agreed only with reluctance to a preliminary meeting of the British and American Chiefs of Staff at Malta, while the Joint Chiefs declined a British suggestion that they should visit London for talks before the Potsdam Conference.[66] As for the proposal that the Combined Chiefs of Staff organization should be continued after the war, a project so close to Churchill's heart and put forward by the British at Yalta and again at Potsdam, the American response was to stall, Truman remarking privately to the Joint Chiefs at Potsdam that 'our relations with our allies were not sufficiently stabilized to warrant consideration of a permanent military relationship between the military commands.'[67] Also highly indicative of the declining partnership was the American request, a month after Roosevelt's death, that Stephenson's British Security Coordination organization, the most vital secret link between the two countries, should leave the United States.[68]

Meanwhile the Churchill–Roosevelt relationship, as already suggested for the preceding period, had lost something of the brightness that had surrounded it during the earlier part of the war. The Prime Minister, of course, still placed his highest hopes upon it, telling the President in November 1944 of his 'indescribable relief' at the latter's re-election, and in the following March depicting their friendship as 'the rock on which I build for the future of the world.'[69] His description of Roosevelt, after the latter's death, as 'the greatest American friend we have ever known' was patently sincere (and was echoed throughout the British press),[70] even if, as indicated earlier, it is possible that he was less deeply involved with the President on a personal level than Sir Isaiah Berlin and many others have tended to believe.[71]

On Roosevelt's part, however, certain reservations had by now become more marked. Perhaps, as Halifax, Lyttelton and Morton believed, he had come to be jealous of Churchill in various respects.[72] Certainly, over colonial issues, as we shall see once more below, he regarded the Prime Minister as being wholly out of touch with the times and an obstacle to peace and progress. Moreover, he also found him now to be 'excitable and dangerous' where the Soviet Union was concerned,[73] and declared in private to Mackenzie King, the Prime Minister of Canada, that his relations with Churchill were less good than those with Stalin.[74] The decline of Hopkins through worsening health and a loss of Presidential favour also meant the

* One significant indicator of the changing state of affairs was the growing number of British cables marked 'Guard'—i.e. for British eyes only, and not to be shown to Americans.

weakening of what had previously been a vital link between Washington and London. The ailing man himself noted in August 1945: 'To hear some people talk about the British, you would think the British were our potential enemies.'[75]

Roosevelt, too, was in any case in markedly failing health by the end of 1944, despite his electoral triumph in November, and despite a continuing, immense stature which was to be emphasized by the reactions of the majority of the American people at the time of his death and by the view they retained of him thereafter.[76] To many who encountered him, the President's advancing sickness was increasingly apparent. (Richard Law, for example, when lunching with him at Quebec, observed that his hand was trembling so much that he had difficulty in finding his mouth with his fork; at Yalta, Cadogan's opinion was that 'most of the time he hardly knew what it was all about.')[77] As the confusion and delay surrounding American decision-making increased, some of the messages that went out in Roosevelt's name had not been absorbed, let alone drafted, by him. His assistant, Samuel Rosenman, told Morgenthau in April that 'recently anybody could get the President to sign anything, and . . . often the President didn't know the contents of the document he signed.'[78] (To what extent this was the case where communications to Churchill were concerned is a matter upon which American scholars working on the subject are not entirely agreed;[79] certainly, Leahy, who, as we have seen, was suspicious and often resentful towards the British, seems to have played a significant part at least in the drafting that was done.)

At the same time, the international difficulties facing the dying man were rapidly growing, in some instances exacerbated by his own facile approach to them in the past. To Harold Laski, who was urging him on towards a revolutionary peace, he wearily wrote in January: 'Our goal is, as you say, identical for the long-range objectives, but there are so many new problems arising that I still must remember that the war is yet to be won.'[80] In some ways, it was probably fortunate for Roosevelt's reputation that he died when he did.

As the President declined, so there remained little likelihood that the State Department could provide the necessary coordination of American foreign policies. Hull himself resigned at the end of November 1944, bitter at his long neglect by Roosevelt and furious at the way in which the latter had ignored the State Department during the Quebec Conference. ('In Christ's name', Hull burst out to Stettinius, 'what has happened to the man!')[81] In selecting the same Stettinius to be the new Secretary of State, the President made quite clear his intention to run foreign affairs himself.[82] An amiable man, the incoming Secretary was certainly publicity-conscious.* However, he had little knowledge of international politics, and possessed a mind the mediocrity of which, and its predilection for trivia, are reflected in

---

* At one important moment during a discussion among the U.S. delegation to the San Francisco U.N. Conference, when the Secretary of State, as leader of the delegation, had yet to appear, the minutes appropriately read: 'Mr. Stettinius arrived at this point, accompanied by a photographer.'

contemporary records and recalled as an embarrassment by men who worked with him. (Behind his back, senior State Department officials were wont to refer to him as 'Junior.')[83]

Stettinius did reorganize his Department in December (critics found the new appointments disquietingly conservative over-all), with Grew becoming Under Secretary and James Dunn the Assistant Secretary with responsibility for Europe and the Far East among other areas; in addition, 'Chip' Bohlen was sent across to improve liaison with the White House.[84] Nothwithstanding such changes, however, and despite the fact that, at last, the State Department was represented at the major Allied Conferences of Yalta and Potsdam, the situation remained fundamentally unchanged. Roosevelt (as a senior official who accompanied him has recalled for the author's benefit) did not trouble to study the detailed briefing papers which had been prepared by the Department before Yalta. Records of that Conference were not made available to the Department's leading members, and only one or two of them knew of the agreement that the President had reached with Stalin there over Far Eastern affairs; nor was State aware of the understanding that he had concluded earlier with Churchill on the development of nuclear weapons.[85] The only significant step taken towards improving what Stimson called 'the present chaotic situation' in Washington was the institution, in December, of regular meetings between the Secretaries of State, War and Navy, and of a State–War–Navy Coordinating Committee (S.W.N.C.C.) at the level of senior officials and officers.[86]

In London, Stettinius was regarded as a friend of Britain's, although it was realized that he was essentially a glorified messenger-boy for the President. The Foreign Office were also particularly glad to see Grew appointed as Under Secretary, his knowledge of foreign affairs being much respected and a 'warmer and more cooperative tone' on Washington's part being subsequently attributed largely to him.[87] James Byrnes, on the other hand, who succeeded Stettinius as Secretary of State after the San Francisco Conference, was judged in London to be 'of provincial outlook and somewhat unsure of himself.'[88]

As for the change in the Presidency, some apprehension was at first expressed by British diplomats lest the Joint Chiefs of Staff should obtain and misuse a greater freedom of action under the new regime, and lest 'foreign policy by Congress' should now prove to be the rule.[89] Truman's 'slick and snappy manner' was also felt by Cadogan, writing after Potsdam, to militate against a proper consideration on his part of British views and interests.[90] Nevertheless, Truman quickly won the approval of most British observers. He should not be underestimated, wrote Halifax, and the Ambassador concluded that 'his attitude on international questions is, from our point of view, impeccable.' He was also described as being 'warmly pro-British.' Eden, who met Truman in April, echoed these opinions, while Churchill for his part was delighted with the President's performance at Potsdam, coming to regret later that he had not responded to the latter's wish for the two of them to meet immediately following Roosevelt's death.[91]

To some Americans who saw him in action, Churchill himself appeared to be in decline in this period. Stettinius, for example, told Forrestal after returning from Yalta that 'the Prime Minister seems to be going through some sort of menopause; he talked with great eloquence in meetings but did not follow up in subsequent sessions ... with the same vigor.'[92] This question of Churchill's condition at the time was to become a controversial one, especially after the publication of Lord Moran's memoirs. As has been suggested in a chapter dealing with the preceding period, however, it does seem that, as was only to be expected, the huge burden that the Prime Minister had been carrying was beginning to tell. Sir William Hayter was noting at Potsdam, for example, that Churchill 'was tired and below his form, [and] suffered from the belief that he knew everything and need not read briefs.' Lord Bridges, too, has recalled that the Prime Minister now appeared to need longer to make up his mind, while Bevin, in the summer of 1945, was bluntly describing him in private as 'going completely Ga-Ga.'[93]

In more measured terms, Attlee had earlier, in January, written privately to Churchill to complain of the way in which he was conducting Cabinet business, and of the 'very scant respect' he displayed for the views of his colleagues in the Government, other than Beaverbrook and Bracken:

'When [the reports of Cabinet committees] do come before the Cabinet', Attlee continued, 'it is very exceptional for you to have read them. More and more often you have not read even the note prepared for your guidance. Often half an hour is wasted in explaining what could have been grasped by two or three minutes reading of the document. Not infrequently a phrase catches your eye which gives rise to a disquisition on an interesting point only slightly connected with the subject matter ...'

These views, Attlee stated, were shared by 'many colleagues in the Government, whether Conservative, Labour, Liberal or independent.' Churchill's response was brief. 'You may be sure', he wrote, 'I shall always endeavour to profit by your counsels.'[94]*

Attlee's comments on this occasion have to be seen against a background of increasing restlessness within the Labour Party, and the foreshadowing of a resumption of inter-party battles. 'He's all right as a National leader', Bevin commented on Churchill in April, 'but when he turns into the leader of the Tory Party, you can't trust him an inch. He just becomes a crook.'[95] In May, the Prime Minister first proposed to the Labour leaders that a general election should await the defeat of Japan, and then offered a choice between such a delay or an immediate contest. Although both Attlee and Bevin were in favour of continuing the coalition until the end of the war, the National Executive of the Labour Party thereupon voted to set a deadline of October for the holding of an election. Churchill therefore resigned on

---

* Attlee did not fail to observe the usefulness of the abrupt and evasive qualities of Churchill's reply. Soon after the end of the war he used the same style when responding to Laski, who, at great length, was instructing him by letter on how to bring about the socialist millennium within the near future.

23 May and formed a caretaker administration. The election followed on 5 July, with Labour's massive victory being announced on the 25th. The shift of political opinion in the country which had been under way since at least 1942 had now been given full expression; Conservatism, already in eclipse as the reconstruction measures of 1943–45 took shape, had been decisively rejected.[96]

Foreign policy, however, had not been an election issue, and the impression of continuity in this field had already been enhanced by Attlee's agreement, notwithstanding a flurry involving Laski in his capacity as Chairman of the Labour Party Executive, to accompany Churchill to the Potsdam Conference before the election result was announced.[97] Nor did the Foreign Office itself find it at all difficult to adjust to the arrival of Bevin in place of Eden, whose other political commitments had in any case been creating an unsatisfactory situation within the Office, and who, as suggested in an earlier chapter, was by no means popular with many of his officials.[98]

Meanwhile in the United States the result of the British election and above all the rejection of Churchill had come as a considerable shock—further evidence of the degree of ignorance and unawareness that continued to exist between the two countries. 'The news', wrote Hopkins to Beaverbrook, '. . . is almost unbelievable.' (Beaverbrook himself had been confidently predicting a Conservative victory to his American friends.)[99] There was, indeed, concern at what had occurred. Even Leahy, so often sour about Britain, wrote in his diary: 'I do not know how the Allies can succeed without the spark of genius in [Churchill's] qualities of leadership.'[100] (If the Admiral meant by 'succeed', win the war, then his comment, although interesting, does not increase one's respect for his powers of judgment.) Others, like Forrestal and Vandenberg, were disturbed at such a swing to the left, in what the former naïvely called a 'Communistic' direction. The *San Francisco Examiner*, for example, likewise described the new British Government as having 'the relentless and frank purpose of turning England ultimately to Communism.'[101]

Thus, for some in the United States, Britain changed almost overnight from being an imperialist, reactionary threat to world peace to representing a disruptive force for social and economic revolution. Nevertheless, there was pleasure on the left of American politics over Labour's victory, with messages arriving at the Embassy in Washington 'welcoming us back into the progressive fold.' Bevin, for his part, was already beginning to provide some reassurance for Forrestal and his kind, telling the latter at Potsdam that he was 'quite familiar with the tactics of the Communists because he had had to deal with them in his own labor unions in England.'[102]

What American opinion thought of Britain had continued to be seen in London throughout this period as a matter of great importance. Some of the signs had been encouraging: Eden, for example, when passing through Washington in April 1945, found Congressional leaders far more friendly than had been the case in 1943 ('Eden', wrote Vandenberg, 'is a great guy'); in addition, an increasing number of Congressmen were paying visits to

Britain.[103] On the other hand, the Foreign Secretary, the Foreign Office and the Embassy in Washington were greatly perturbed over the small amount of attention that was being paid in the American press to Britain's military effort, an issue which Sir Ronald Campbell described as being

> 'of really vast importance for the future. Our utter failure hitherto', he added, 'to counteract the false legend that has been growing up in American opinion may cost us dear. Opinion in the U.S.A. is assuming . . . that they alone saved us. On this myth they will build a sentimental and political attitude and . . . will consider that we must concede any demands they make on us as of right. Administrations will base their policy on public opinion—and there you are.'

Within the Foreign Office, indeed, there were now some who, in contrast to the hopes that had been entertained earlier in the war, despaired of ever being able to influence American public opinion to any appreciable extent. Others blamed the Services in particular for not 'doing their stuff' in terms of publicity in the U.S.A., whilst in return there was scorn in some Service quarters for the efforts there of the Ministry of Information and the British Information Service.[104]

The subject of publicity was becoming especially important in connection with the British contribution to the war against Japan, as we shall see in a subsequent chapter. Meanwhile the setting within which the Anglo-American relationship was conducted in the Far East was also affected by the continuing existence of various issues, and the arrival of new ones, between the two countries. Over the matter of oil, for example, Congress was holding up the ratification of the Anglo-American agreement of 1944 in which, as Ickes, the Petroleum Administrator, acknowledged, it was 'the British, not the American side, that is making the concessions.'[105] The interests of London and Washington again came into conflict over the subject of civil aviation, a sphere in which Britain still sought a major degree of international control and where only a limited measure of agreement was reached at a conference in Chicago at the end of 1944. In this context, Churchill and some of his colleagues expressed a fear of what the Prime Minister called 'American pressure to run us off the air'; Roosevelt in return adopted a tough line over the matter, brandishing the prospect that Congress might well reject proposals for new Lend Lease aid for Britain if London did not give way at Chicago.[106]

A similarly forceful approach was adopted by Washington towards the end of 1944 over the question of Britain's purchases of meat from the Argentine. As part of a campaign against the pro-Axis regime in Buenos Aires, Roosevelt and the State Department sought to prevent the United Kingdom from signing a new, long-term meat contract with that country, as she had intended. At one moment, indeed, it even appeared in this context that the State Department was threatening to withhold certain Lend Lease supplies if compliance was not forthcoming, though this was denied in Washington, probably correctly. In any event, the decisive factor in London was the obvious need to maintain the best possible relations with the United States during the negotiations over Stage II assistance, and the Government therefore agreed reluctantly to deal with the Argentine on a month-to-month basis only.[107]

At the same time American pressure continued to be exerted, although in this case with less success, over Britain's future commercial policy as a whole and article 7 of the Mutual Aid Agreement. Discussions on this topic between American and British officials were resumed at the end of 1944; thereafter, however, whereas Roosevelt on his side pressed for the talks to be raised to Ministerial level, Churchill, aware that the divisions within the Cabinet and Conservative Party in this sphere were as deep as ever, continued to stall, and to Truman at Potsdam emphasized again that Britain was under no obligation to put an end to imperial preference. Agreement between the two Governments was in fact not reached on this issue, nor did Britain ratify the Bretton Woods proposals, until the end of 1945, amid economic and financial conditions which had by then weakened even further London's bargaining position.[108]

More acute and public still, though not so long-lasting, were the disputes between Britain and the United States over Greek and Italian affairs, these episodes bursting into the open at the end of 1944 and confirming many Americans in their existing suspicions of British motives in the field of international politics. As Churchill saw it—and he was supported by his Cabinet colleagues—the uprising of the Communist-led E.A.M. and E.L.A.S. in Athens in December was a threat to orderly government and to the interests of the West as a whole; therefore, 'painful and thankless' though the task might be, it must be suppressed by British troops who were on the spot.[109] In the United States, on the contrary, Britain's behaviour was widely seen as reflecting her desire to establish a sphere of influence for herself in Greece and to support an outdated, monarchical form of government against a popular movement. Much resentment was aroused on the British side when Stettinius, on 5 December, therefore issued a statement declaring that the administrations in liberated United Nations territories should 'work out their problems of government on domestic lines without interference from outside.' ('It must be remembered', recorded the Washington Embassy sourly, 'that despite peculiar vagaries of their own foreign policy, Americans think of themselves as inflexibly dedicated to the principles of liberty and equality everywhere.') It was also learned in London that Admiral King had taken it upon himself to order that American ships must not carry British supplies to Greece.

Meanwhile in the United States, even stronger anti-British feelings were aroused when Drew Pearson obtained and published a secret cable in which Churchill had instructed his Army commander in Athens to act 'as if you were in a conquered city where a local rebellion is in progress.' So sensitive was American opinion by now, Roosevelt warned Churchill, that an alignment of the two countries over the troubles in Greece was out of the question.[110] This was all the more the case in that the crisis in Athens was coinciding with Anglo-American tension over Italian affairs, centring upon London's objection to a place in the Rome Government being given to Count Sforza, whom they regarded as 'a clever rascal.' From Washington, this again looked like a pro-monarchical, sphere-of-influence policy, and to Churchill's intense resentment Stettinius publicly proclaimed that the Italians, too, should be left to work out their domestic political problems without outside interference.[111]

Thus, as in previous periods, the American suspicions of British motives and hostility towards her imperialism which we shall again see displayed in a Far Eastern context were only a part of a wider distrust. Moreover, this distrust was to be found among both reactionary, would-be isolationists (who were attacking Roosevelt for being a dupe of Stalin as well as of Churchill),[112] and liberals who hoped to see the United States take its place in a world raised above the selfish, dangerous level of mere 'power politics.'

'We seem to have little visible support in any camp', reported the British Embassy in Washington in February 1945. '. . . It seems clear that the new isolationist and to some extent liberal line . . . will be the thesis that with the Atlantic Charter dead, whatever does not fall to Britain's share will fall to Russia's, and that in this division of spoils neither side is entitled to America's material help.'[113]

We have observed already how pervasive was the belief in Washington that Britain was seeking to manoeuvre the United States against the Soviet Union. Similarly, London's ideas for fostering closer ties with the states of Western Europe were denounced in the State Department before Yalta as 'smacking of power politics.'[114] And although Anglo-American relations generally did improve during the spring of 1945 after the troubles of December and January ('everything has been going beautifully', Stettinius told Truman in April), Dean Acheson, as an Assistant Secretary of State, remained concerned in July at what he saw as 'an increasing number of incidents indicating that the Department is building up a hostile attitude toward Great Britain.'[115]

Within Britain itself, meanwhile, Churchill had been far from alone in being roused by American criticisms concerning Greece and other matters. Indeed, more resentment was expressed publicly than at any time since the beginning of the war. (Stettinius, in a note to Roosevelt, put it down to 'the emotional difficulty which anyone, especially any Englishman, has in adjusting himself to a secondary role after having always accepted a leading one as his natural right.')[116] Thus, for the *Economist* among others it was time that the United States stopped preaching at Britain in an aloof fashion and instead took on their proper share of the maintenance of international stability. 'How can the ordinary Englishman', it asked, 'be expected to listen without mockery to all the lofty generalities that are proclaimed in America when he hears them against such a background [of economic imperialism]?'[117]

In official circles, and less constructively, Grigg, the Secretary of State for War, imparted to Montgomery his 'growing conviction that the Americans and the Russians intend that we shall emerge from this war a third-rate power.'[118] As for the Prime Minister, he refused to be disturbed by 'every trashy press article in America'. Yet even he, the foremost champion of Anglo-American partnership, was moved by Stettinius' platitudes on the subject of 'power politics' to an outburst which encompassed more than simply the immediate incident or even the never-ending doses of American self-deception-cum-hypocrisy. Here, in addition, was surely a cry in private against the fates that were robbing Britain of her international standing and Churchill himself of much of his influence, at the very moment of victory:

'Would you ask [Stettinius]', he dictated as a draft cable to Halifax, 'to give me a definition of "power politics"? . . . Is having a Navy twice as strong as any other "power politics"? Is having an overwhelming Air Force, with bases all over the world, "power politics"? Is having all the gold in the world buried in a cavern "power politics"? If not, what is "power politics"? Is it giving all the bases in the West Indies which are necessary to American safety to the United States—is that "power politics"? Was bleeding ourselves white financially, while the Americans were preparing and arming, "power politics"? Is holding the ring in Greece to enable the people to have a fair election "power politics"? . . . I could continue at length . . .'[119]

Of this final period of the war, it can once more be said that the degree of collaboration achieved between Britain and the U.S.A. continued to be a remarkable one. Nevertheless, the strains were there, and if some had lessened, others were now greater than before. The partnership, in fact, had passed its peak.

Moreover, many of the difficulties that existed between the two countries were of particular significance in terms of the war in the Far East. For it was there that relations remained most tenuous; there that suspicion and misunderstanding, differences and even rivalries, came most frequently to the fore. It was also there that the rapidly growing imbalance between the power of Britain and that of the United States was being demonstrated in its most dramatic fashion as events moved towards the defeat of Japan.

Notes to Chapter Twenty-Four

1 See e.g. *Bryant*, II, 288.
2 E.g. ibid, 370, 395.
3 *Woodward*, III, 146ff.; *Churchill*, VI, 198.
4 *Woodward*, III, 252ff.
5 *Sherwood*, 870; see e.g. L. Snyder, *The War: A Concise History, 1939–1945* (London, 1962), 419.
6 Dalton Diary, 23 Feb. 1945; Cabs, 12 Feb. 1945, CAB 65/49; Ismay to Mountbatten,

17 Feb. 1945, Ismay Papers, IV/Mou/2B; *Cadogan Diaries*, 717; *Woodward*, V, Caps. LXVIII and LXIX.

7 *Churchill*, VI, 485–7, 498.

8 WSC to Eden, 10 May 1945, PREM 4, 31/7; FDR to WSC, 19 Nov. 1944, PREM 3, 472; WSC to HST, 12 May 1945, PREM 3, 473; Dalton Diary, 16 May 1945; CP(45)30, CAB 66/66; *Moran*, 19 and 23 July 1945; Attlee, *As It Happened*, 146; Williams, *A Prime Minister Remembers*, 78; Stettinius, *Roosevelt and the Russians*, 121. For the feeling among some British officials that the time was right for standing up to the Soviet Union, see e.g. FO 371, U5471/5471/G and COS, 23 May 1945, CAB 79/33.

9 See above, 121, note.

10 FRUS, Conference of Berlin, I, 64; *Woodward*, III, 581ff.; *Churchill*, VI, 502.

11 FRUS, Conference of Berlin, I, 64; Cox memo., 4 May 1945, Hopkins Papers, box 337; Forrestal Diary, 20 May 1945; *Leahy*, 443.

12 E.g. FRUS, Berlin, I, 256; FO 371, AN1722 and 2156/4/45; *Woodward*, III, 580ff.

13 For press examples, see *Chicago Tribune*, 3 April 1945; *San Francisco Examiner*, 3 and 7 May, 6 July 1945.

14 FDR to WSC, 11 March and 6 April 1945, Roosevelt Papers, MR box 7; *Woodward*, III, 515. See also Harriman and Abel, *Special Envoy*, 444.

15 Forrestal Diary, 2 and 20 April 1945; DS, Secretary's Staff Cttee., 20 April 1945, box 88H.

16 FRUS, 1945, I, 790ff.

17 Stimson Diary, 14 Sept. 1944, 2 and 23 April 1945; Leahy Diary, 10 Feb. 1945; Forrestal Diary, 23 April 1945; Truman, *Year of Decisions*, 80.

18 Dixon, *Double Diploma*, 165.

19 Truman, *Year of Decisions*, 342.

20 Ibid, 87; *Bryant*, II, 478.

21 The best brief survey of American policies is Sherwin, op. cit., *American Historical Review*. Material on British policies is contained in PREM 3, 139/9 and 11A. Notes on an HST–WSC talk on the subject are in PREM 3, 430/8.

22 Stimson Diary, 10, 13, 15 May, 6 June, 21, 22, 30 July 1945; see Gardner, *Economic Aspects*, 320ff.

23 Stimson Diary, 5 June 1945; Leahy Diary, 7 June 1945.

24 *Woodward*, III, 95ff.; *Churchill*, VI, 489ff.

25 E.g. Eden to WSC, 29 Nov. 1944, PREM 4, 30/8; *Cadogan Diaries*, 20 and 22 Oct. 1944, 18 and 26 June 1945; *Avon*, 496.

26 FRUS, Malta and Yalta, 300; FRUS, Berlin, I, 251; Caffery to State Dpt., 28 and 30 Jan. 1945, Hopkins Papers, box 337; Stettinius Diary, 19 April 1945, DS, Notter files, box 29; Grew–HST conversation, 19 May 1945, Grew Papers, vol. 7.

27 *Cadogan Diaries* provide a valuable record, as does *Woodward*, V; on the U.S. side see *Notter*, and FRUS, 1945, I.

28 Material in FO 371, files 44535–7; *Vandenberg*, cap. 8.

29 FO 371, AN763/763/45; U242/5/70. This was the time when Law made his disillusioned observations about the Atlantic Charter. See above, 102.

30 FRUS, 1945, I, passim, esp. 663, 674, 691.

31 *Moran*, 5 July 1954.

32 Forrestal Diary, 21 April 1945.

33 FO 371, AN2560/22/45. See e.g. AN649/4/45 and U5471/5471/G.

34 *New York Herald Tribune*, 15 Aug. 1945.

35 *Chicago Tribune*, 8 Dec. 1944.

36 Baruch to FDR, 18 March 1945, Roosevelt Papers, PSF box 115.

37 *Wallace*, 29 May 1945; OPD memo., 16 June 1945, OPD, Exec. file 10, item 71.

38 White memo., 30 Nov. 1945, White Papers, box 7.

39 Blum, *From The Morgenthau Diaries: Years of War*, 422.

40 FO 371, UE813/813/53.

41 Gardner, *Sterling-Dollar Diplomacy*, 178–9.

42 Hall, *North American Supply*, 474–5.

43 WP(45)301, CAB 66/65. See Cab, 25 July 1945, CAB 65/57, and *Cadogan Diaries*, 16 Aug. 1945.
44 Ehrman, *Grand Strategy*, VI, 20ff., 238ff.; *Mountbatten*, 167.
45 E.g. FO 371, UE2010/32/71; Cabs, 7 Feb. and 21 March 1945, CAB 65/49; material in PREM 4, 78/1.
46 E.g. DS, Secretary's Staff Cttee., 22 Feb. 1945, box 88G.
47 See above, 390.
48 Inter-Divisional Area Cttee. on Far East, 16 Jan. 1945, DS, Notter files, box 118; Stimson Diary, 22 Nov. 1944.
49 E.g. FRUS, 1945, VI, 54.
50 E.g. FRUS, Berlin, I, 810.
51 Baruch memo., 1 Dec. 1944, Baruch Papers, box 37; DS, Secretary's Staff Cttee., 3 Jan. 1945, box 88G; B. Baruch, *The Public Years* (London, 1961), 319. See Isaiah Berlin's comments on Baruch, FO 371, AN1170/7/45.
52 Gardner, *Sterling-Dollar Diplomacy*, 191; *Kolko*, 258; see Williams, *A Prime Minister Remembers*, 134.
53 The U.S.A. supplied the U.K. with about $27 billion; British reciprocal aid amounted to about $6 billion. If adjusted for size of population and relative industrial power, however, the British figure was equivalent to about $20 billion. Hall, *North American Supply*, 481.
54 WP(44)586, CAB 66/56; *Hancock and Gowing*, 524ff.
55 Cherwell note, 3 Oct. 1944, Cherwell Papers, Off. 23.2; Morgenthau Diary, 6 Oct. and 13, 22, 27 Nov. 1944; FO 371, UE2019/32/71; AN4451/20/45.
56 WP(45)24, CAB 66/60; WP(45)77, CAB 66/61; Dalton Diary, 14 Dec. 1944.
57 See above, 388.
58 Leahy Diary, 18, 21 Nov. 1944; Morgenthau Diary, 16, 18, 21 Nov. 1944.
59 Morgenthau memo., 13 Dec. 1944, Roosevelt Papers, PSF box 20; *Stettinius*, 21 Nov. 1944.
60 Blum, *Roosevelt and Morgenthau*, 635; Leahy Diary, 2 and 5 July 1945; FO 371, AN2241/4/45.
61 Gardner, *Sterling-Dollar Diplomacy*, 176; FO 371, UE2081/32/7.
62 FO 371, material in files 45851–2; COS, 21 June 1945, CAB 79/35.
63 WSC to HST, 28 May 1945, PREM 3, 473; WSC note, 18 July 1945, PREM 3, 430/8; material in PREM 4, 80/1 and CAB 99/39; FO 371, files 45852–3. See FRUS, Berlin, II, 1180ff.; Gardner, *Sterling-Dollar Diplomacy*, 185; Williams, *A Prime Minister Remembers*, 129.
64 See above, 503–4.
65 Stimson Diary, 4 Nov. 1944; *Pogue*, II, 483.
66 FRUS, Malta and Yalta, 29–32; FRUS, Berlin, I, 99.
67 Minutes of 9 Feb. 1945, CAB 99/31; minutes of 19 July 1945, CAB 88/4; JCS, 18 July 1945, RG 218.
68 *Stevenson*, 465.
69 WSC to FDR, 8 Nov. 1944, PREM 3, 472; WSC to FDR, 18 March 1945, PREM 3, 473.
70 Cab, 13 April 1945, CAB 65/50: Hansard, HC Deb, 410, cols. 73ff.; WSC to Hopkins, 13 April 1945, Roosevelt Papers, MR box 13; Dalton Diary, 13 April 1945; British press files for 13 and 14 April 1945; *Christian Science Monitor*, 13 April 1945.
71 See above, 120, note.
72 See above, 120, and e.g. *Moran*, 3 July 1958.
73 Bishop, *F.D.R.'s Last Year*, 239.
74 *Times*, 3 Jan. 1976.
75 *Sherwood*, 804ff., 832ff., 921.
76 See Lingeman, *Don't You Know There's A War On?*, 351; J. E. Mueller, *War, Presidents and Public Opinion* (New York, 1973), 191.
77 E.g. Bishop, *F.D.R.*, passim; *Burns*, 448; *Moran*, 4 Feb. 1945; Cadogan to Halifax, 20 Feb. 1945, Hickleton Papers, A4 410 4; interview with Lord Coleraine.

78 Morgenthau Presidential Diary, 16 April 1945; *Burns*, 453.
79 Discussions with Professor Robert Dallek, who is preparing a large-scale work on Roosevelt, foreign policy and American opinion, and Professor Warren Kimball, who is editing a definitive series of volumes covering the Churchill–Roosevelt correspondence.
80 FDR to Laski, 16 Jan. 1945, Frankfurter Papers, box 75.
81 Halifax Diary, 5 Oct. 1944; Hull–FDR letters, 21 and 23 Nov. 1944, Hull Papers, box 54.
82 E.g. *Berle*, 23 Dec. 1944.
83 See e.g. Stettinius Diary, 18 March–17 April 1945, DS, Notter files, box 29; Watt, *Australian Diplomat*, 69; interview with H. Freeman Matthews.
84 Bohlen, *Witness To History*, 166.
85 J. F. Byrnes, *Speaking Frankly* (London, 1948), 23; interview with H. Freeman Matthews; Stettinius Diary, 11–17 March 1945, DS, Notter files, box 29.
86 See Stimson Diary, 19 and 27 Dec. 1944; *Notter*, 370–2.
87 FO 371, AN4551 and 4584/20/45; AN1737/4/45; Halifax to Foreign Office, 27 Nov. 1944, PREM 4, 27/10.
88 FO 371, AN2156/4/45, AN2003, 2479/6/45.
89 E.g. ibid, AN1198/4/45; UE3133/32/G.
90 Ibid, AN2438/35/45.
91 Halifax to Foreign Office, 14 April 1945, PREM 4, 27/9; Eden to WSC, 16 April 1945 and WSC to Eden, 24 April 1945, PREM 4, 27/10; Rowan memo., 17 July 1945, PREM 4, 79/2; *Cadogan Diaries*, 13 April and 16 July 1945; Stettinius Diary, 8–14 April 1945, DS, Notter files, box 29.
92 Forrestal Diary, 13 March 1945.
93 Wheeler-Bennett, *Action This Day*, 231; Bevin to 'Ivy', 5 June (? July) 1945, Bevin Papers, box 19.
94 Attlee to WSC, n.d. and WSC to Attlee, 22 Jan. 1945, Attlee Papers (Churchill College), box 2/2.
95 Dalton Diary, 19 April 1945.
96 Attlee–WSC correspondence, Attlee Papers (Churchill College), box 2/2; Dalton Diary, 19 May 1945; Bullock, *Bevin*, II, 374; Williams, *A Prime Minister Remembers*, 64; *Addison*, 252ff.
97 Attlee to WSC, 8 June 1945, Attlee Papers (Churchill College), box 2/2; Cab, 20 June 1945, CAB 65/54.
98 Sansom, *Sir George Sansom*, 141; *Cadogan Diaries*, 3 and 6 Oct. 1944, 8 Jan. and 31 July 1945; Hayter, *A Double Life*, 77. Interviews with Sir William Hayter, Lord Gladwyn, Sir Ronald Campbell, Lord Coleraine, Sir John Wheeler-Bennett.
99 Beaverbrook–Hopkins correspondence, July 1945, Beaverbrook Papers, C/175.
100 Leahy Diary, 26 July 1945.
101 *Forrestal*, 85; *Vandenberg*, 218; *San Francisco Examiner*, 21 July 1945.
102 FO 371, AN2306/4/45; Forrestal Diary, 29 July 1945.
103 *Avon*, 531; *Vandenberg*, 13 May 1945; FO 371, file 44547.
104 Material in FO 371, file 44575; on B.I.S. expenditure, see ibid, AN2065/6/45; Somerville Diary, 12 Dec. 1944, 15 Jan., 15 Feb. and 5 March 1945. On anti-British sentiments among American officers in Europe, see *Bryant*, II, 323.
105 DS, Secretary's Staff Cttee., 12 March 1945, box 88F.
106 Cabs, 26 Oct. 1944 (CAB 65/44), 22 and 30 Nov. and 4 Dec. 1944 (CAB 65/48), 19 Feb. 1945 (CAB 65/51); WP(44)680 (CAB 66/58); WSC–FDR correspondence, Nov. 1944, PREM 3, 472; FDR to WSC, 16 March 1945, PREM 3, 473. See *Berle*, Nov.–Dec., passim; *Leahy*, 329; Gore-Booth, *With Great Truth And Respect*, 130–2.
107 Material in DS, Matthews files, box 12; Winant to FDR, 26 Nov. 1944, Roosevelt Papers, MR box 11; Cabs, 4 and 30 Oct. and 24 Nov. 1944, CAB 65/44; Cherwell to WSC, 9 and 14 Nov. 1944, Cherwell Papers, Off. 1. 1; FDR–WSC correspondence, Oct.–Nov. 1944, PREM 3, 472; Hopkins to WSC, 16 Dec. 1944, Roosevelt Papers, MR box 13.

108 WP(45)96, CAB 66/62; WP(45)152, CAB 66/63; FRUS, Malta and Yalta, 962; FRUS, Berlin, II, 21, 54; WSC–HST talk; 18 July 1945, PREM 3, 430/8; Gardner, *Sterling-Dollar Diplomacy*, cap. VIII.

109 *Churchill*, VI, cap. XVIII. The left-wing of the Labour Party, the *Times*, the *Manchester Guardian* and others in Britain were critical of the Government's Greek policy. See ibid, 255.

110 See *Woodward*, III, 410ff.; Stettinius Diary, Dec. 1944, DS, Notter files, box 29; *Stettinius*, 6 and 12 Dec. 1944; FO 371, material in files 38551 and 44635; FDR to WSC, 13 Dec. 1944, Roosevelt Papers, MR box 7; Somerville Diary, 10 Dec. 1944.

111 *Woodward*, III, 440ff.; FRUS, Malta and Yalta, 266ff.; FO 371, AN4618/20/45.

112 E.g. *Chicago Tribune*, 1 and 13 Oct., 11 Dec. 1944.

113 FO 371, AN4730/20/45.

114 Yalta briefing papers in Roosevelt Papers, MR box 165; and see Leahy Diary, 15 Dec. 1944.

115 Stettinius Diary, 16 April 1945, DS, Notter files, box 29; DS, Secretary's Staff Cttee., 17 July 1945, box 88H.

116 Stettinius to FDR, 3 Jan. 1945, Roosevelt Papers, PSF box 93.

117 *Economist*, 30 Dec. 1944.

118 Grigg to Montgomery, 6 Dec. 1944, Grigg Papers, box 9. See e.g. Hansard, HC Deb, 407, col. 519; Watt to Hood, 3 Jan. 1945, Watt Papers.

119 WSC to Eden, 3 Jan. 1945, PREM 4, 27/9; WSC to Halifax, 8 Jan. 1945, PREM 4 27/10.

CHAPTER TWENTY-FIVE

THE WAR AGAINST JAPAN

THIS PERIOD from September 1944 onwards witnessed a series of major triumphs for the American forces in the Far East, nothwithstanding the continuation of what Marshall and Stimson saw as a ruinous 'hatred' between MacArthur and prominent officers of the U.S. Navy.[1] United States submarines were rapidly reducing Japan's capacity to wage the war: her merchant-shipping tonnage, for example, 6 million in 1941, was only 1·8 million by August 1945; oil stocks, which had amounted to 43 million barrels in December 1941, were less than 4 million barrels by the middle of March 1945; steel production, likewise, was down to about 1 million tons a year.[2] The bombing of Japan by B 29s based in the Marianas added to the process of enfeeblement from November 1944 onwards. Meanwhile, despite the suicide, kamikaze attacks by Japanese planes which commenced in October, the American amphibious advance continued. On 21 October, MacArthur's men went ashore on Leyte in the Philippines; during the following days, in the immense naval–air battle of Leyte Gulf, the Japanese failed to take the opportunities that were presented to them, and finally retreated with the loss of 4 aircraft carriers, 3 battleships and 10 cruisers. American landings then took place in Luzon in January and in Mindanao in March, the whole Philippines campaign being brought to a successful conclusion early in July.

Further north, the United States forces under Nimitz were closing in on Japan itself. The island of Iwo Jima, only 750 miles from Tokyo, fell to them after a bitter struggle in February and March. In April—although success was not fully achieved until June—an even greater blow was struck when landings were made on the island of Okinawa in the Ryukyus (remnants of the Japanese Navy, seeking to intervene, were destroyed in the battle of the East China Sea), thus severing the last of Japan's communications to the south and providing a base for the final assault on her home islands. The plan to proceed with such an invasion of Japan, operation 'Olympic', aimed at the island of Kyushu and to be commanded by MacArthur, was endorsed by Truman at a meeting with the Joint Chiefs of Staff on 18 June. King, it should be noted, agreed with his colleagues and the President at the time, though subsequently he was to argue, like Leahy, that an invasion would have been unnecessary.[3]

Just as these operations were essentially American affairs—although Australians were still fighting under MacArthur and units of the Royal Navy saw action off the Ryukyus—so the direction of the Pacific campaigns remained firmly in the hands of Washington. The Chiefs of Staff in London were sometimes informed only belatedly of what was taking place, for example in the matter of command changes, while by the middle of June they themselves had still not given any detailed thought to possible operations against the Japanese homeland.[4] At Potsdam, Brooke and his colleagues sought to change matters by proposing that the entire war against Japan should now come under the 'general jurisdiction' of the Combined Chiefs of Staff. Neither the British Joint Planners nor the Foreign Office thought that Britain had adequate grounds for urging such a case, however, and the American Joint Chiefs rejected it outright. They would be glad to consult with their British opposite numbers, but, in Leahy's words, 'the war with Japan was pretty much of an American show', and where the Pacific theatres were concerned, they would carry on exercising full control.[5]

Within S.E.A.C., of course, the British Empire continued to provide the major contribution. Indeed, the original, Anglo-American nature of the Command was rapidly diminished as the Americans concentrated their efforts elsewhere. In January, at Malta, the Joint Chiefs of Staff again emphasized that 'United States resources are deployed in India–Burma to provide direct or indirect support for China'; moreover, although it was accepted that any transfers out of S.E.A.C. which the British thought would jeopardize operations would be discussed by the Combined Chiefs of Staff, Marshall made it clear that Mountbatten must not count on being able to employ U.S. forces outside Burma.[6] A reduction of American effort in the area was now all the more likely in that the Ledo Road had at last been completed early in January 1945, the first convoy to take that route arriving in China in the following month. (As indicated earlier, the feat had been accomplished far quicker than Mountbatten and the British had expected; on the other hand, as they had prophesied, it came too late to have any significant effect upon the course of the war, and the volume of supplies which began to be sent along the Road was far less than the 45,000 tons a month that were now being flown over the Hump.)

Washington now looked towards a complete American withdrawal from S.E.A.C., with Marshall being prepared by the time the Potsdam Conference took place to hand over entire control of the Command to the British as a quid pro quo for the retention of sole American direction in the Pacific.[7] For Mountbatten, as we shall see in more detail later, all this meant that his operations had to be dovetailed with a timetable for the removal to China of General Sultan's American brigade and U.S. Air Force units. In addition, Chinese divisions were being withdrawn from S.E.A.C., in the first place, at the end of 1944, in order to help meet the crisis created by a Japanese advance in China,* and then, in the early summer of 1945, to

---

* After offensives in Hunan and Chekiang provinces in the summer of 1944, the Japanese, taking the Kweilin air base in November, appeared to have an almost clear road to Kunming and even Chungking if they wished to take it.

contribute to an offensive which was being launched by Chiang Kai-shek's forces towards the East China coast.[8] Meanwhile, in matters such as shipping, the Joint Chiefs insisted that priority must be given to preparations for the invasion of Japan, even if this meant holding up British operations directed towards Singapore.[9]

Yet despite these considerable complications, to which was added the delay in transferring British troops and aircraft from the European theatres, a growing momentum was achieved along the line of advance long favoured for S.E.A.C. by Mountbatten and London. From Malta, the Combined Chiefs of Staff sent the Supreme Commander a new directive, to replace the one that had been issued from Quebec and that had been upset by the setback at Arnhem and other European considerations.[10] This time, operations to the south did not have to be balanced by instructions about the drive towards China: thus, S.E.A.C.'s first task was set out as being to liberate Burma with the forces already at its disposal, while thereafter it was to free Malaya and open the Straits of Malacca.[11] In the event, the speed with which this programme began to be carried out surprised and delighted the Chiefs of Staff in London, to whom an attack on Singapore at the end of 1945 now began to seem a possibility.[12] In the south, an offensive in Arakan, opened in December, resulted in the capture of Akyab in January. Further north, Slim's remarkable Fourteenth Army crossed the Irrawaddy in February and, taking Meiktila en route, had reached Mandalay before the end of March, while in Upper Burma Chinese forces linked up to enable the old Burma Road to be reopened. Rangoon itself was abandoned by the Japanese at the start of May, British forces landing there from the sea and joining up with the Fourteenth Army as it advanced overland, through the monsoon.[13] Planning then went ahead for an assault on the Port Swettenham–Port Dickson area of the coast of Malaya, with an operation against Singapore to follow by the end of the year.

When the time came for Mountbatten to receive his final directive from the Combined Chiefs on 2 August, however, he found his responsibilities greatly enlarged, encompassing a huge area of the outer zone of Japanese conquests and involving projected operations into the Netherlands East Indies and Siam as well as against Singapore.[14] In the light of the suspicions of the British entertained by MacArthur and others in 1944, it must be emphasized that this new development in the summer of 1945 came about as the result of an American, not a British, initiative, despite the fact that it was not to MacArthur's liking. On 13 April, the Joint Chiefs of Staff proposed that, as MacArthur moved northwards to prepare for the assault upon Japan, all of his South West Pacific Area, with the exception of the Philippines and Hainan, should be taken over by S.E.A.C., or by a separate British command.[15] After much deliberation, in which political as well as military and logistical considerations were weighed, the British Chiefs of Staff decided that the suggestion should be accepted, Brooke and Portal concluding, against Cunningham's objections, that the best way to effect it would be to extend S.E.A.C., while the easternmost parts of the S.W.P.A.

should go to an Australian command under the direction of London.

It was also decided, for reasons that will be indicated in the chapter on Southeast Asia, to ask for Indochina as well to be transferred to S.E.A.C., in this case from Chiang Kai-shek's China Theatre.[16] At Potsdam, the Joint Chiefs of Staff responded with a proposal to include Indochina south of 15° latitude in Mountbatten's Command; finally, it was agreed that the line should be drawn at 16°, with the recognition that it might later become necessary for S.E.A.C. to take over the entire territory. Mountbatten's responsibility for Siam was confirmed at the same time. The British and United States Governments were to seek Chiang Kai-shek's approval for the change which, together with the transfer of the bulk of the S.W.P.A., was to be made 'as soon as possible.' Then, when the Japanese surrender suddenly became imminent, the handing-over date was specified as being 'as soon as possible after 15 August', and finally, despite the fears of the British Chiefs of Staff that all was not ready, as 15 August itself.[17]

By the end of the war, the campaign in Southeast Asia had justified itself from London's point of view by the fact that at least some of Britain's lost territory—though not Malaya or Singapore—had been recovered by her own force of arms. For Washington, the overland route to China had also been opened, though too late to be of much consequence. In addition, the campaign had resulted in the deaths of 128,000 Japanese—over 10 per cent of those killed in all theatres—and had kept the enemy engaged at the end of a long and increasingly tenuous line of communications.[18]

Nevertheless, the Pacific remained the focal point of the Far Eastern war, and Britain was still anxious to make a significant contribution in that area. To this end, units of the Royal Navy's Pacific Fleet arrived in Australia in December 1944 under Admiral Sir Bruce Fraser, plans being made for reinforcements to follow that would bring the total up to 4 battleships, 10 aircraft carriers and 16 cruisers by June 1945. Some major difficulties remained, however.[19] One was the need for a base much nearer than Australia to the main scene of operations. Neither of the American proposals in this regard—Manus, in the Admiralty islands, or Brunei Bay in North Borneo (not to be captured until June, in any case)—were acceptable to the Admiralty, and London continued to press for facilities to be made available to the Royal Navy in the Philippines. At the same time, problems were encountered over providing a sufficiently large train of auxiliary ships, which would enable the Fleet to stay at sea for lengthy periods.[20] More serious still, the U.S. Navy continued to appear reluctant to give Fraser's units a permanent place in the main operations, preferring, rather, to keep them as a strategic reserve to be used here and there as the need arose. Relations between British and American commanders on the spot were excellent ('Nimitz, Halsey and Spruance', wrote Fraser later, 'are our greatest friends'), but British representatives in Washington remained convinced that Admiral King was determined to keep the Royal Navy out of the forefront of the battle.[21]

Difficulties were also encountered over the British proposal—accepted in principle by the Joint Chiefs of Staff in October 1944—to contribute to the long-range bombing of Japan, the aim being to employ eventually three groups, one of them Canadian, each consisting of 12 squadrons of heavy bombers and 6 squadrons of long-range fighters. A suitable site for a base was again the problem, together with the need to ship out large numbers of construction workers from Britain and, it was hoped, Canada, in order to make it ready. In the spring of 1945 the Americans offered an area in Northern Luzon, one which presented serious obstacles but which Portal, the Chief of the Air Staff, thought would have to be accepted since the whole endeavour was 'more of a political than a military question.' On the American side, there were those who saw and resented these British political considerations, and General Arnold already had all the planes he needed for the attack on Japan. Even so, the Joint Chiefs made a more attractive offer at the end of May, of a site for bases on Okinawa, to take 10 squadrons in the first place. This proposal was quickly accepted by London, but in the event the end of the war came before the airfields were even constructed.[22]

In addition to these naval and long-range-bombing issues, there was the question of what could and should be the British and Commonwealth contribution to the main invasion of Japan (operation 'Coronet'). Once more, this was a matter of political importance on the British side:

'The effect of our non-participation', wrote Halifax, 'would be in the highest degree unfortunate for us. Apparent justification would be given to those who are already out to maintain that Britain will only participate in the Pacific war to the extent necessary to regain British colonial possessions ... [and] there would be a general feeling ... that the British had quit when the boar was at bay, whereas the United States had seen it through in Europe.'[23]

Again, moreover, there were those on the American side who were less than eager to see their Allies come in on the act, even though Marshall among others did appreciate the need for Britain's wishes in this respect to be met. Thus, in a somewhat exaggerated reference to such a jealously exclusive approach, Morgenthau was telling his Treasury staff in October 1944 that 'he didn't think the Army really wanted the English in the Pacific ... and if they could have them come there with a tin sword and a lead helmet and as ineffective as possible, that would please the Army very much.'[24]

The details of what Britain and the Commonwealth could offer for 'Coronet' were under examination in London from May 1945 onwards. Among the main questions that arose were those of the size and composition of the force (the planners originally suggested either $3\frac{2}{3}$ or $5\frac{2}{3}$ divisions; Churchill subsequently hoped to employ 2 British, 1 Anglo-Indian, 1 Australian and 1 from New Zealand); of whether a Canadian element would be merged with American forces or form part of a Commonwealth unit; of whether Australian troops could be spared in time, given their existing tasks in the Southwest Pacific; of how the necessary shipping could be found and whether the Americans would provide the assault lift and post-assault supplies. In the end, however, it was the Joint Chiefs of Staff, and even more the commander of the operation, MacArthur, who, in July, laid down the limits and conditions regarding what Britain and the Common-wealth could do in this context. Three divisions only could be accepted: one British, one Australian and one Canadian, Indian troops being ruled out on political and administrative grounds. These divisions were to be made available without having to await the completion of engagements elsewhere, and were to be trained in American methods and equipped by the United States; they would not be allotted a separate sector in the assault, but would function as a corps within an American army, and as part of the reserve at that. These conditions were accepted in London with only a few qualifica-tions. One had to be grateful, after all, to be let in at all upon what was clearly a United States enterprise. Even then, the Joint Chiefs of Staff were raising new difficulties and doubts when the surrender of Japan brought the whole project to an end.[25]

In any event, the military contribution that Britain could make to the final stages of the attack upon Japan—described by Marshall to Truman as something of 'an embarrassment'[26]—had for some time been of far less significance in the minds of many of the Americans concerned than had the potential role of the Soviet Union. Here, too, it was United States rather than British opinions which counted, just as it was American officers, officials and members of the Administration who conducted both the political and the technical negotiations that were involved.[27] The matter as a whole was bound up with Washington's hopes and fears over the internal divisions and future international role of China, a subject that will be covered in a later chapter, leaving the direct, strategic and political questions surrounding the Soviet involvement in the war to be dealt with here.

It will be recalled that Stalin had already, in 1943, promised to join in the fight against Japan once Germany had been defeated. In September 1944, he enquired of the British and American Ambassadors whether this assistance was still required, and in the following month renewed his pledge to Churchill and Harriman during the former's visit to Moscow, talking of employing 60 divisions against the Japanese about three months after Germany had surrendered. (He also made it clear at this time that he envisaged operations by the Red Army in North China, and not simply inside Manchuria.) Churchill was delighted. 'When we are vexed with other matters', he cabled to Roosevelt, 'we must remember the supreme value of this [offer] in shortening the whole struggle.'[28]

It was now, however, first in October and then again in the middle of December, that Stalin began to spell out to Harriman the price that he expected to be paid for his assistance, a subject on which he had been studiedly vague and moderate at Tehran. The Kuriles and South Sakhalin, he told the Ambassador, should be returned to the Soviet Union; and although he insisted that he had no intention of interfering with China's sovereign rights in Manchuria, he revealed that the U.S.S.R. wished to obtain a lease of the railway lines linking Dairen to Harbin and thence running east towards Vladivostok and north-west to Manchuli, together with a lease of Port Arthur, Dairen 'and the surrounding area.' (Harriman interjected that he thought the President had in mind an international free port there; Stalin responded that this could be discussed.) Stalin also laid it down that the independence of Outer Mongolia—a territory which in fact had been under Soviet domination since 1921—must be maintained.[29]

Roosevelt for his part was, not untypically, tending to minimize the difficulties which might be involved, telling the Pacific War Council that Stalin 'looked with favour upon making Dairen a free port for all the world' and 'agreed that the Manchurian Railway should become the property of the Chinese Government.'[30] The President must have realized in any case that Stalin could obtain by force a great deal more than he was then asking for if he were so minded; also, and in addition to the growing need to obtain Soviet good-will and forbearance over China's internal affairs, there was the high value that Washington, like Churchill for one in London, placed upon the employment of Soviet arms against Japan. In part this arose from the continuation of what we have seen had long been a self-imposed limitation upon United States activities and policies in the Far East: the desire not to become involved militarily to any large degree on the mainland of Asia. Roosevelt himself made it clear to Stimson in October 1944 that he shared this aversion, 'and implied that for fighting on the mainland of China we must leave it to the Russians.' Stimson agreed, telling Marshall that he 'did not think the country would stand for' the sending of a large number of U.S. troops to China.[31] Arguments such as these were reinforced by the manpower difficulties that the Army was beginning to experience;[32] they were clinched by a serious overestimation in Washington of the strength of the Japanese Kwantung Army in Manchuria, which was thought to contain the cream of the enemy's troops. (This overestimation was shared by Field Marshal Brooke in London, who, as late as July 1945, was judging that Army to be capable of 'serious delaying actions' in the face of a Soviet attack.)[33]*

Hence, the Joint Chiefs of Staff informed the President in January that Soviet military assistance in Manchuria should be obtained as early as possible, and although Leahy had his doubts on the matter, MacArthur gave strong and continuing support to the majority view.[34] Above all, Marshall remained clear in his own mind, at least until July, that the aid of the Red Army was needed, and Truman, like Roosevelt before him, duly accepted the Chief of Staff's advice. Even when, at Potsdam, Marshall

---

* On paper, the Kwantung Army in 1945 had 24 divisions, 9 independent mixed brigades, 2 tank brigades, 1 independent infantry brigade and 1 tank training unit. But 8 of the divisions and 7 of the mixed brigades were new and almost untrained, while apart from 3 divisions brought from China proper, all the rest were newly-raised formations. Morale was poor; there were no anti-tank guns and less than half the authorised number of medium and light machine guns; there was a shortage of artillery and ammunition, and nearly all the infantry's guns were obsolete. The Japanese themselves estimated that the average efficiency of each division was not more than three-tenths that of a pre-war front-line one. (*Kirby*, V, 196; and see Allen, *The End of the War in Asia*, 193ff.)

appeared to change his position and to agree with Stimson that the successful testing of the atomic bomb had altered the situation, he went on to point out that there was still nothing to prevent the Russians from entering Manchuria and taking whatever they wanted.[35]

Long before this conversation took place, Roosevelt had in any case agreed in essence at Yalta that Stalin's price should be paid, his action in doing so behind the back of Chiang Kai-shek emphasizing his much-diminished regard and concern for China, and revealing once more that, for all the verbiage surrounding America's China policies, it was the perceived interests of the United States herself in that context which took first place. It is true that, in the light of Stalin's ability to obtain more or less whatever he desired in North China and Manchuria, the Yalta terms, had they been more carefully phrased and more strictly observed by him, would have placed a significant degree of restraint upon his actions. It is also true that, in the exchanges which took place at Yalta, Roosevelt did secure some modifications to the Soviet proposals concerning the Manchurian railways and the status of Dairen. On the other hand, the President accepted the use of phrases which gave Stalin plenty of room to obtain the essence of what he had sought in the first place; and while the need to obtain Chiang Kai-shek's concurrence over Manchurian and Outer Mongolian matters was recognized, the Generalissimo was to be informed of what had been decided only when Stalin thought the time suitable—for the valid reason that the secrecy of Soviet military intentions had to be preserved from the Japanese. Moreover, the Yalta agreement included the pledge that Moscow's terms would be 'unquestionably fulfilled', the clear understanding being that Roosevelt would ensure that Chiang Kai-shek fell into line.[36]

The Soviet Union, then, would enter the war against the Japanese within two or three months of Germany's defeat. In return, she would obtain from Japan the Kuriles, South Sakhalin and adjacent islands, and from China a lease of Port Arthur as a naval base. Whilst Dairen was to be internationalized, the 'preeminent interests' of the U.S.S.R. there were to be safeguarded; the same applied to Soviet interests in the South Manchurian and Chinese Eastern Railways, even though the management of those lines was to be a joint, Sino-Soviet affair, while in Outer Mongolia the status quo—that is, Soviet domination—was to be preserved. Reassuringly, Moscow at the same time pledged its recognition of full Chinese sovereignty in Manchuria (although this was scarcely in harmony with the port and railway arrangements), and indicated its readiness to conclude with Chiang Kai-shek's Government a pact of friendship and alliance for the purpose of 'liberating China from the Japanese yoke.'* Such was the Yalta agreement on the Far East.[37] It marked the end of an age when Britain and, increasingly, Japan had been the predominant powers in that part of the world, and sought to put in its place an arrangement based upon Soviet–American understanding.

* This did not amount to a promise to support Chiang Kai-shek against the Yenan Communists, which was made later.

Whether such an understanding would last, and what roles would be played by China and the colonial areas of Southeast Asia were still to be seen.[38]

There remained the need to obtain Chiang Kai-shek's endorsement (which Stalin made a prior condition for Soviet military action) of those parts of the agreement which concerned China; the military details of the promised collaboration also had to be arranged, and here the Soviet negotiators in Moscow were soon causing disquiet among their American opposite numbers by declaring that U.S. forces could not, after all, make use of bases in the U.S.S.R.'s Maritime Provinces.[39] Two other outstanding questions required an answer. One was the actual timing of the Russian entry into the war, a vital matter in American eyes in that what was required was for the Kwantung Army in Manchuria to be fully engaged before the landings in Japan itself took place. In May, Stalin said that he would be ready to move by 8 August; at Potsdam, this was changed to the second half of August, but in the event, spurred on by the dropping of the atomic bomb on Hiroshima, Moscow declared war on the 8th of that month, even though no agreement with Chungking had then been signed.[40]

The other question concerned the inconvenient fact that the Soviet–Japanese Neutrality Pact of 1941 remained in existence. On 5 April 1945, Moscow informed Tokyo of its intention to terminate this agreement, but even then it still had a year to run before it ceased to be binding on the two signatories. However, any embarrassment that Stalin and his colleagues might possibly have felt on this account was avoided with the help of Washington when Molotov, at the end of July, sought from the Soviet Union's allies a formal request for her to enter the Far Eastern conflict. Obligingly, Byrnes drafted a letter which Truman then sent, a document which in effect justified the U.S.S.R.'s breaking of the Soviet–Japanese Pact on the somewhat extraordinary and flimsy grounds of the Four Power Moscow declaration of October 1943 (in which the signatories had agreed to consult 'with a view to joint action on behalf of the community of nations'), and of articles 103 and 106 of the proposed—but not yet ratified—United Nations Charter, which reiterated the Moscow pledge and also stated that obligations incurred under the Charter should take precedence over any other international agreements (that is, the 1941 Neutrality Pact) with which they were in conflict. London was informed of this ingenious communication of Truman's, but was not consulted or asked to follow suit.[41] The Foreign Office's lawyers were thus spared what could have been a difficult and embarrassing task.

As it was, and despite the fact that the United States Government thus remained eager to the end over Soviet entry into the war, there were already those on both sides of the Atlantic who were not happy about what was being done. In London, for example, Eden had warned Churchill before the Yalta Conference that Manchuria and Korea were likely to become disputed territories and that it was therefore advisable 'to go warily and to avoid anything like commitments or encouragement to Russia.' Likewise at Malta the Foreign Secretary suggested to Stettinius that, since the Russians would enter the Far Eastern war because it suited their own interests to do so, 'there was . . . no need for us to offer a high price for their participation, and if we were prepared to agree to their territorial demands in the Far East we should see to it that we obtained a good return in respect of the points on which we required concessions from them.'

Moreover, at the Yalta meeting itself Eden, supported by Cadogan, urged Churchill not to endorse the secret agreement which Roosevelt— without the Prime Minister's participation—had made with Stalin.[42] Churchill did so nevertheless, reasoning that this was necessary in order to preserve an active role for Britain in Far Eastern affairs (although he later wrote that, as far as the U.K. was concerned, the issue had been 'remote and secondary').[43] He also assured Stalin that Britain 'would welcome the appearance of Russian ships in the Pacific', going on to repeat this at Potsdam, where he added a reference to 'access to the warm waters of the Pacific.' In private, the Prime Minister continued to emphasize the value of Soviet action against Japan 'at the earliest moment.' By May, however, as relations with Moscow over European affairs deteriorated, he, too, was qualifying this belief: the Russians, he now wrote, 'having regard to their own great interests in the Far East . . ., will not need to be begged, nor should their entry be purchased at the cost of concessions prejudicing a reign of freedom and justice in Central Europe and the Balkans.'[44]

Others, in Washington, were having even more pronounced second thoughts on the matter, again in the context of increasing tension over European issues and also of continuing disintegration in China. It was not, it must be emphasized, simply a question of whether Stalin was himself, by his actions over Poland, nullifying all the Yalta agreements. What Grew, Forrestal, McCloy and Harriman were discussing when they met together on 12 May was, in Grew's words, 'whether we were going to support what had been done at Yalta'—in other words, whether the United States should, on its own initiative, go back on the terms Roosevelt had settled with the Soviet leader as regards the Far East.[45] How great was the need for Soviet military intervention, Grew asked the War and Navy Departments. Was it so vital that one could not demand, as the State Department now thought advisable, that before the Yalta price was paid Moscow should promise to influence the Chinese Communists in the direction of a unified China, and to respect the Cairo Declaration concerning the independence of Korea and the return of Manchuria to China?[46] In a reply of 21 May, Stimson, supported by Forrestal for the Navy, repeated that Soviet armed assistance would 'almost certainly . . . materially shorten the war and thus save American lives'; he also pointed out that Soviet forces, which would intervene regardless of American inducements, could in any case occupy Manchuria, Korea, North China and South Sakhalin before the United States could do anything to prevent it.[47]

Yet by the end of July, Stimson, too, as we have seen, had come round to the opinion that the U.S.A. could do without the aid of the Red Army, his change of mind being brought about by the final achievements in the development of the atomic bomb. James Byrnes, the new Secretary of State, was also 'most anxious to get the Japanese affair over with before the Russians got in, with particular reference to Dairen and Port Arthur. Once in there he felt it would not be easy to get them out.'[48]

The speed with which victory could be achieved, together with the price which would have to be paid en route, whether in lives or political concessions, was bound up with the question of how rigidly the Allies should hold to their demand, announced at Casablanca, that Japan should surrender unconditionally. Should some gloss now be placed upon this proclaimed intention, in order to encourage the Japanese to give in? And how should the West respond to peace-feelers on the part of the enemy? In London, the overriding consideration regarding the various peace initiatives that came to light was the need to keep in step with the United States. At the same time, the Government's attitude was to refuse to make any reply to indirect approaches of this kind, however serious they might appear; and since this was in fact the only variety which emerged, none of the Japanese who attempted to make contact with the West received any encouragement from Britain. Moreover, a direct approach by Tokyo was thought to be highly unlikely. Even when the Koiso Government fell early in April 1945, following the shock of the Okinawa landings, the succeeding Administration of Admiral Suzuki Kantaro (described in the Foreign Office as 'a man of high character and level-headed views') was not expected by British officials to negotiate once it realized that a defeated Japan would have to undergo occupation. Similarly, the advice of the Joint Intelligence Committee in the first part of July was still that Japan would almost certainly fight on to the end. (A decision to do exactly this had in fact been taken in Tokyo early in June.)[49] The Japanese attempt to get the Soviet Union to mediate, however, which was revealed to Churchill by Stalin at Potsdam, had been anticipated by some officials in London.[50]

On the American side, even before Potsdam, their ability to break Japanese codes had made them aware that the Tokyo Government was seeking, in the words of its Foreign Minister, 'to obtain the good offices of the Soviet Union in ending the war short of unconditional surrender.' It has already been pointed out by scholars that Washington failed to react to the knowledge at its disposal in a positive and imaginative fashion. As for earlier approaches which had been made in an American direction, for example through the O.S.S. in Switzerland, they were regarded, in Grew's words, as having 'come from sources which have given no satisfactory evidence that they speak with authority', and as being 'purely fishing expeditions on the part of individuals.'[51]

And yet in both Washington and London, there were those in official circles who were concerned to see something done which would make it easier for Japan to surrender. Opinion on the British side, indeed, was remarkably solid in this sense, but again it was accepted that it was for the Americans, as the Chiefs of Staff put it after Hiroshima, 'to take the lead in any matters regarding the framing of armistice and surrender terms.'[52] Within the Chiefs of Staff Committee, Brooke's opinion was that 'unconditional surrender was an objective which we did not require and which, if achieved, might even impede the liberation of territory now occupied by the Japanese, as it appeared likely that the Japanese forces in those territories would only capitulate if instructed to do so by the Emperor.'[53] Officials of the Foreign Office's Far Eastern Department, together with Dening in S.E.A.C. and Sansom in Washington, were also in favour—if the Americans would take the lead and with the proviso that China should be consulted*—of an interpretive statement being made about unconditional surrender. Such a statement, it was believed, should be to the effect that no particular form of government would be imposed upon Japan by the Allies, that the Emperor would not necessarily have to go, and that a reasonable standard of living would be granted to the Japanese people. 'Unconditional surrender est magnifique', wrote Sir Orme Sargent, 'mais ce n'est pas la paix.'[54]

Already, at Yalta, Churchill himself had observed to Roosevelt that 'some mitigation [of unconditional surrender] would be worthwhile if it led to the saving of a year or a year and a half of war', though he was careful to add that 'Great Britain would not press for mitigation but would be content to abide by the judgment of the United States.'[55] The Prime Minister subsequently raised the same point with Truman at Potsdam, suggesting that a way could be found to obtain all the essentials for a stable peace while yet allowing the Japanese 'some show of saving their military honour and some assurances of their national existence.' When the President countered that the Japanese possessed no military honour after Pearl Harbour, Churchill commented 'that at any rate they had something for which they were ready to face certain death in very large numbers.' He took away from the meeting the impression that the Americans were 'searching their hearts' on the subject, and that they did not need to be pressed any further.[56]

Heart-searching had indeed been going on in Washington for some time. Grew, as Under Secretary of State, had argued to Truman in May that a statement should be made indicating that surrender would not entail the destruction of Japan or the abolition of the Throne; when he returned to this idea in June the President appeared to respond favourably, but said that he would wait until he could discuss the issue with Churchill and Stalin. Meanwhile Stimson, Forrestal and Marshall had all agreed that a statement such as Grew had in mind would be useful, although they thought that, for military reasons, the end of May was too early for its promulgation.[57] Stimson in particular was becoming greatly concerned over the matter, in

---

* That it was mainly British, rather than American officials who, throughout these final stages of the war, bore in mind the desirability of involving China in major decisions regarding Japan serves as yet another, ironic comment upon the myths woven around the subject of U.S.–British–Chinese relations by Americans at the time and American historians subsequently.

June drafting a message to Japan which he got the Navy and State Departments to approve, and pressing the President on the subject early in July and again shortly before the Potsdam Conference. The Japanese, he felt, should be assured that a constitutional monarchy for their country was not ruled out, that they would have 'access to trade and raw materials,' and that there was no intention to destroy them as a race. Despite the fact that the Secretary of War also believed that Japan would probably need to be 'sufficiently pounded, possibly with S-1' (that is, atomic bombs) before she would listen to reason, he was still pressing Byrnes on 9 August 'that he should make it as easy as possible' for the enemy to give in.[58]

Grew and Stimson could at least derive some satisfaction from a public statement issued by Truman on 8 May, that unconditional surrender did not mean 'the extermination or enslavement of the Japanese people', but they knew that more than this was required. It was not forthcoming. Before he left for Potsdam, Byrnes consulted Hull on the question, and found him firmly opposed to Stimson's idea of giving an assurance about the future of the Japanese Throne, the old man's grounds for this being that such an action would be tantamount to 'appeasement' of the enemy. Byrnes, apparently impressed by this argument and doubtless with an eye upon American public opinion, duly saw to it that no reference to the Emperor or the Throne figured in the declaration concerning Japan that was issued at Potsdam on 26 July, with the result that the peace party* in Tokyo were seriously handicapped in their endeavours.[59]

During the discussions on the subject that took place at Potsdam, British delegates did submit and manage to carry amendments to the American draft declaration which resulted in its being addressed to the Japanese Government rather than, over that Government's head, to the Japanese people, and in reference being made to the occupation by the Allies of 'points in Japanese territory', thus avoiding a commitment to take over the entire country. Eden did not, however, press for mention to be made of the preservation of the Throne, his reason being, as one of his senior officials put it, that 'the Americans would no doubt like to get such advice from us and then say they had reluctantly concurred with us.' As it was, the declaration did promise Japan access to raw materials, participation in world trade, and its continuation as a nation. It also called, as before, however, for 'unconditional surrender', promising, as the alternative, 'prompt and utter destruction.'

In arriving at this ultimatum, no thought was given by either the British or the American officials concerned to consulting Australia and New Zealand. As for China, Truman at first argued that it would take too long to obtain her views and concurrence—an attitude that suited Churchill, who wanted the statement to go out in the names of himself and the President alone. Without conferring further with their British colleagues, however, the

---

* This term is not meant to suggest that those in favour of seeking peace were entirely of one mind or highly organized.

United States delegation then decided that Chiang Kai-shek should be brought in as a signatory after all, and this was done.[60]

The Japanese Government's reaction to this Potsdam ultimatum was to declare that they would 'take no notice' (*mokusatsu*) of it, apparently a careless use of phrasing which failed to reflect the 'wait-and-see' policy that the Foreign Minister, Togo Shigenori, and others were advocating.[61] There followed the dropping of atomic bombs (a weapon successfully tested in New Mexico in the middle of July) on Hiroshima on 6 August, and on Nagasaki three days later.

Once more, this was essentially an American decision. At the end of 1944, General Groves, in charge of the project in the U.S.A., had informed Marshall that a bomb would be ready around the beginning of August, and in April he was able to confirm to Truman that the date would be no later than the end of August. Meanwhile in the discussions that were being conducted in Washington on the subject, with Stimson playing a key role, the dominant question was not whether or not to use the weapon against Japan, but how best to do so. The general assumption was that the bomb should be employed in order to shorten the war and thereby save American lives.[62] London, for its part, was informed in April of the intention of the United States authorities to resort to the new weapon 'some time in August.' More detailed plans followed at the end of June, accompanied by a request for Britain's approval of what was intended. That approval was duly given on 4 July with 'never a moment's hesitation', as Churchill later put it, and without any knowledge of the various arguments which had been taking place among Americans involved in the project. In the words of an official historian, the British Government 'had found that they were most successful when they acknowledged the limits of their contribution, and the manner in which they now gave their consent to the use of the weapon was designed to respect that fact. The balance of power, both in the atomic project and in the Pacific, lay too heavily with the United States for the British to be able, or to wish, to participate in this decision.'

This accommodating attitude was sustained by Churchill at Potsdam, when he again assured Truman that he believed the bomb should be used with all speed. Attlee, too, never doubted that it was right to go ahead.[63] American radicals, then and since, might have been surprised to learn, however, that the Far Eastern Department of the Foreign Office, which had had no previous knowledge of the new weapon's existence, drew up a strong protest when the news arrived that nuclear weapons had been dropped on the Japanese:

'The present tactics in the employment of the bomb', wrote the Head of the Department on behalf of all its members, 'seem likely to do the maximum damage to our own cause . . . A more intelligent way of proceeding would surely have been to have given publicity to the discovery and its possible effects, to have given an ultimatum with a time limit to the Japanese before using it, and to have declared the intention of the Allies to drop a bomb on a given city after a given date by way of demonstration, the date being fixed so as to give time for the evacuation of the city.'

The Department, together with their colleagues in Political Intelligence, were also greatly concerned lest it should emerge that the bomb had been ready for use against Germany but had been reserved to inflict upon 'Asiatics.' This was not, in fact, the case, as we have seen. It is certain, however, that there were those in the West who, if asked, would have agreed with the Prime Minister of Canada, Mackenzie King, who privately expressed his relief that the weapon had been employed against an Asiatic people and not against the 'white races of Europe.'[64]

On 10 August, the Japanese Government accepted the terms of the Potsdam Declaration, 'with the understanding that the said declaration does not comprise any demand which prejudices the prerogatives of His Majesty as a Sovereign Ruler.' Leahy for one was all for accepting this response; the Cabinet in London also concluded that 'it would be inexpedient to insist on terms of surrender involving the abdication of the Emperor of Japan if it seemed likely that this would have the result of delaying substantially the end of hostilities in the Far East.' Again, however, it was a decision for the United States Government above all, and Byrnes persuaded Truman that there was no need to go so far as to make a direct pledge about the Emperor's position. (Stimson noted that Hopkins, Acheson and Archibald MacLeish, an Assistant Secretary of State, also remained 'strong anti-Emperor men.') Tokyo was therefore informed merely that 'from the moment of surrender the authority of the Emperor and the Japanese Government to rule the state shall be subject to the Supreme Commander of the Allied powers . . .' The Emperor himself decided on 14 August that this must be accepted as a sufficient assurance.

Thus, on the same day, 14 August, Japan's surrender was announced. To the disquiet of Foreign Office officials in London over the possible long-term consequences, however, the Imperial Rescript which was delivered to the Japanese people in order to explain the disaster glibly proclaimed that the country's aim in fighting the war in the first place had been, not to 'infringe upon the sovereignty of other nations', but merely 'to ensure Japan's self-preservation and the stabilization of East Asia.' Nevertheless, the Allies let this pass, and although some Japanese officers protested to the last, the capitulation went ahead. On 2 September, the surrender documents were signed on board the battleship *Missouri* in Tokyo Bay.[65]

As the Allied advance towards victory was reaching these final stages, it was not fully appreciated in London just how far Roosevelt was inclining towards what would be an essentially Soviet-American settlement in the Far East, a settlement that would contain little room within it for influence to be exercised by the European colonial powers. (Over Korea, for example, to take a specific case, the President told Stalin at Yalta that he saw no reason why Britain should share in the international trusteeship that was envisaged for that country.)[66] It was realized, however, that, as the Embassy in Washington put it, 'most Americans still view the war against Japan as their own concern, to be concluded on their own terms.'[67] True, some kindly opinions were even now being voiced within the U.S.A., for example by the *New York Times*, welcoming Britain's contribution and partnership in the Far East.[68] At the same time, however, others were expressing the sour thought that, as the *Chicago Tribune* put it in February 1945, 'we have done all the fighting in the Pacific so far [and] we expect our allies to do some fighting from now on.' (In addition, high-ranking U.S. officers were among those who were still talking at the end of 1944 of the need for their country to pull out of what they regarded as Britain's European war in order to concentrate on its own, true contest, the one against Japan.)[69] Over-all, Stettinius, in Washington, was hearing 'from Americans in responsible positions in the Pacific' so much talk of Britain's selfishness—and of her indifference towards China—that he felt bound to warn Halifax of what was happening. Similar information was passed on from the British Embassy in Chungking.[70]

To British officials, it seemed that American reactions of one kind and another had the effect of placing them in a cleft stick.

'We must naturally be prepared for criticism from some quarters whatever we do', concluded the Washington Embassy in May. 'If we prosecute the Far Eastern war with might and main, we shall be told by some people [in the United States] that we are really fighting for our colonial possessions the better to exploit them ... while if we are judged not to have gone all out, that is because we are letting America fight her own war with little aid after having let her pull our chestnuts out of the European fire. There are probably elements throughout the Navy Department likely to be prey to both these lines of simultaneous thought ...'[71]

Officials also remained concerned over the lack of recognition in the United States of the effort Britain was already making against Japan. Eden, for example, reported from San Francisco in April that he was seriously perturbed about the likely consequences of this state of affairs. The Chiefs of Staff also turned their attention to the question on several occasions, while in May the Head of the Foreign Office's Far Eastern Department recalled with exasperation that months of trying to improve matters had come to nothing. 'Many times', he wrote, 'we have put up suggestions for a speech by the Prime Minister on these subjects. But a kind of paralysis seems to descend on all our efforts.'* One reason for this was that Churchill himself

* To complicate matters further, the Washington Embassy now suggested that no credit would accrue to Britain as a result of her Far Eastern efforts unless her standing was already high in the U.S.A. As Law minuted: 'We began to get excited about the Far Eastern war in part because we felt that, if we were not recognised to be doing our bit in the Far East, our stock would go down elsewhere. Now the position is reversed—if our stock is not already high elsewhere we shall not be recognised to be doing our bit in the Far East. Means and ends seem to have got a little confused!' (FO 371, AN564/4/45.)

did not share the general concern. 'I do not fear these particular dangers', he minuted in May; and again: 'Don't worry.'[72] He did, however, assure both Roosevelt and Truman once more that Britain would see the war against Japan through to its end. Attlee, too, after his election as Prime Minister, repeated as much both publicly and in private at Potsdam, thus doing something to counteract suggestions being made in the United States that a Labour Government might not wish to strive for the recovery of Britain's imperial possessions.[73]

American attitudes and behaviour towards Britain in the Asian and Pacific context in 1944–45 aroused in London, as before, not only a measure of despair but also resentment. Thus, the Head of the Far Eastern Department, Sterndale Bennett, wrote in April, and again in May, that the evidence showed that 'the Americans are virtually conducting political warfare against us in the Far East and are seeking not only to belittle the efforts which we have hitherto made in that theatre of war, but also to keep us in a humiliating and subsidiary role for the future.'[74] The Embassy in Washington also foresaw that the United States would create more trouble for Britain in the Far East than anywhere else in the world.[75] In addition, fears of American imperialism—economic, but even territorial as well—which we have encountered in earlier periods, continued to weigh upon a number of British and Commonwealth figures in prominent positions. The Prime Minister of New Zealand, Fraser, for example, reported at Commonwealth discussions in London in April 1945 that members of the United States armed forces in the Pacific were talking in 'imperialist' terms; similarly, the Australian Minister to the United States, as he now was, Eggleston, drew up a list of prominent American businessmen who were, he thought, fostering their peace-time interests in the Far East while serving there in some war-time capacity, concluding that such men were 'busy coining new "freedoms" to cover some attempt to use their superior capitalistic position to secure a monopoly.'[76]

Nor were such fears of an all-out American economic drive after the war devoid of substance, as we have already observed in preceding periods. Truman's personal representative in Chungking for economic affairs, for example, was looking forward to 'a China with close economic, political and psychological . . . ties with the U.S.'[77] Admiral Miles, still working on intelligence matters in China in conjunction with the head of Chiang Kai-shek's secret police, put it in more aggressive and anti-British terms in an address which he delivered to his staff in May:

'From an economic standpoint', he declared, 'China cannot be ignored because they have the biggest post-war market. We have to look for foreign markets because we can feed those markets, utilizing our war-time converted factories and facilities to do this. We don't want to permit England or any other country to run us off the commercial map again. We Americans here in this group are the most outstanding group ashore in any foreign country . . . [and] it is our job now to look at the commercial

field we will have to protect . . . . Our biggest competitor will be England—
she is starting it now.'[78]

MacArthur, too, although he ritually denied any 'imperialistic' intentions
on the part of the United States, was privately defining her interests in the
Pacific as being 'the development of markets and the extension of the
principles of American democracy . . ., the lifting of people by the billions
from a mere subsistence level to an economic system which will represent
the greatest purchasing power in world history.'[79] In other words, here,
once again, was that combination of seeking to make money and desiring to
spread the American way of life that Stimson had outlined as the goal of the
United States during the Far Eastern crisis of 1931–33.[80] In tune with this,
officials in Washington who were setting themselves the target of ensuring
employment for 56 million Americans, together with outlets for an annual
gross national product of $150 billion after the war, regarded the markets of
the Far East as vital.[81]

British officials did not know, of course, what men like Miles and
MacArthur were saying in private to their fellow-countrymen. Nevertheless,
the signs of Anglo-American strain were clear enough, so that when an
inter-departmental Far Eastern Committee was reconstituted in Whitehall
in November 1944 the representative of the Foreign Office asserted at its
first meeting that 'the overriding problem throughout the Far East was our
relations with the United States.' The Foreign Office, he continued, 'were
much concerned at the misconceptions in the United States of our aims and
objects. These were due partly to wilful misunderstanding and partly to
ignorance. But we had to take the fact of their existence into account.' At
the same time, however, there could be no question of responding here, any
more than in those other areas of Anglo-American disagreement that have
been mentioned earlier, by pursuing a futile and foolish rivalry with the
U.S.A. The perceived need for American understanding and assistance in
the post-war world was far too great for that. Thus, a central point of
reference for the Far Eastern Committee was, in the words of its chairman,
'the vital necessity to bring about the greatest possible degree of cooperation
with the United States.'[82]

In pursuit of this objective, the Foreign Office informed the American
Embassy in London, in January and again in the spring of 1945 that they
were keen to have informal talks with the State Department on Far Eastern
matters. Washington's response, however, was almost entirely negative. In
the first place it was suggested—and reasonably so—that a prior need was
for London to bring its own studies of the questions involved up to as
advanced a stage as those that had been produced within the State Department. Yet this was followed, at the San Francisco Conference, by a senior
official of the Department's Office of Far Eastern Affairs arguing in an
opposite sense, that insufficient preliminary work had been done on the
American side to enable the proposed talks to take place. The same official
also put forward as an additional inhibiting factor the change of President

that had recently occurred. The Foreign Office therefore waited until July, and then tried again, suggesting that John Carter Vincent and Eugene Dooman, members of the Office of Far Eastern Affairs who were attending the Potsdam Conference, should come to London for informal discussions. The answer was returned that Secretary Byrnes thought this 'inadvisable', and again, on 4 August, that 'Mr. Byrnes . . . had not yet formulated his policy.' As a British diplomat observed with admirable restraint, 'One cannot help being a little disappointed by the way the State Department say in one breath that we are so far behind that it is hardly worth talking, and in the next that they really have no policy and are therefore not ready to talk.'[83]*

In short, it is clear that the main responsibility for the failure of Britain and the United States to cooperate over Far Eastern affairs and planning during this final stage of the war lay with Washington. This was in keeping with the exclusive American approach which has been observed during previous periods. Even so, there were also limiting factors on the British side. In terms of the wider setting, for example, there still existed far less interest in the Far Eastern war among the British public than was the case in the United States, as a survey by the Ministry of Information emphasized.[84] Again, within Whitehall itself, officials who were dealing with Far Eastern matters continued to have to work against a background of relative indifference. Sir Orme Sargent, in a major survey of British policies which he wrote in July, acknowledged as much. 'In spite of our participation in the Far Eastern war', he concluded, 'and occasional statements about our interest in the Far East and in China in particular, we tend to be apathetic on the subject and to underestimate the importance of the Far East in our future policy.'[85]

Moreover, studies in the Office of possible developments in that part of the world and of the best course for Britain in that context were far fewer and less advanced than were equivalent exercises being carried out in the State Department. We have already seen that Cadogan's insistence on a pragmatic approach (planning being to him, it will be recalled, 'as incomprehensible as it is futile') was partly responsible for this state of affairs.[86] Meanwhile, to officials in the field, like Dening, as to American liberal commentators, far too many questions still hung over Britain's political intentions east of Suez.[87] Yet so long as Churchill remained at the head of the country's affairs, preoccupied as he was with the tasks of winning the war and keeping a relatively declining Britain in the front rank of the Allies,

* In fact, the apparent contradiction involved can be explained, and indeed lies at the very heart of American Far Eastern policies, dilemmas and failures. As during earlier periods, studies or knowledge of a particular, restricted area or problem were often available. What was lacking, however, both in 1945 and in the late-nineteenth and twentieth centuries as a whole, was a coherent, over-all view and a reconciliation of aspirations, goals and means. One is reminded of Hippolyte Taine's description of the contents of the Englishman's head as he found them in the 1860s: 'Beaucoup de faits . . . quantité de renseignements utiles et précis . . . nulle vue d'ensemble . . .' (H. Taine, *Notes sur l'Angleterre* [Paris, dix-septième édition], 325.) Cf. Lake, *The Legacy of Vietnam*, 380.

uninterested in the Far East and reactionary as regards the future of the Empire, there was little likelihood that this state of uncertainty would be drastically changed.

Among the broader questions that were still engaging the attention of people on both sides of the Atlantic was that of the likely consequences of the Far Eastern war from a racial point of view. As before, the subject of racial problems in general retained a special significance within the United States— not only in terms of black and white, but of minorities like the Japanese Americans.[88] The issue was also brought out into the open during the San Francisco Conference, where Nehru's sister, Mrs. V. L. Pandit, launched on behalf of India a strong attack on the racial policies of Smuts and his South African Government.[89] The possible repercussions of Britain's attitude towards India's own political problems was another aspect of the question which continued to concern American officials. William Phillips, for example, was still urging in the spring of 1945 that Washington should provide support for Wavell in his struggle against Churchill, Phillips' hope being that there might follow constitutional reforms that would in turn help to sustain 'the prestige of the white race in Asia.' In May, Grew spoke to Eden in this sense, observing 'that we must always reckon with the future development of an "Asia for the Asiatics" movement', and that 'progressive steps in India would tend to offset the strengthening of such a movement.'[90] Similarly, Roosevelt had emphasized to Stettinius in January 'the import- ance of turning the Chinese away from anti-white race attitudes which could easily develop.'[91]

On the British side, meanwhile, a more unusual consideration was put forward by Dening in January from his post in S.E.A.C.—although once more the context was that of a possible pan-Asiatic movement. What Dening suggested was that, were the victorious white nations to inflict upon Japan a destructively harsh peace, then other Asian countries might react unfavourably.

'If we impose a peace which at heart is not acceptable to the East', he wrote, 'the Japanese will make every kind of mischief for us ... Pan- Asianism has ... received a stimulus from the circumstances of war rather than from the propaganda of the Japanese ... Some comfort might be derived from the fact that we and America are on the same side in this ... But I think that in this instance it is cold comfort because the last thing that either of us wants to do is to create a colour cleavage ...'[92]

Instead of such a cleavage, a new and constructive partnership, it was hoped, might come about between East and West. For, as Sir Josiah Crosby reminded a study group at Chatham House, the war had destroyed for ever the prestige and ruling position of the white man in the Far East. Therefore he must endeavour to win 'a new and higher prestige' there by returning 'as friend and mentor bent upon showing [the Asiatics] the road to progress and to government by themselves within the shortest possible space of time.'[93]

Even these well-meant proposals, however, would prove to be too gradualist in temper, as we shall observe in a later chapter. For many Asians, even 'friendly mentors' were by now a distrusted and distasteful anachronism.

The racial issue was one of the subjects which were prominent at the conference of the Institute of Pacific Relations that was held in Hot Springs, Virginia, in January 1945, and an outline of which was to be published under the title, *Security in the Pacific*. Mrs. Pandit of India, for example, asserted that, in essence, the Far Eastern conflict was a race war, while— bearing out what Dening was suggesting at the time—'Asiatic members of the conference', as one report described it, 'repeatedly warned against too harsh a treatment of Japan because this might lead to an anti-Western feeling in the whole of the Far East.'[94] Even more than had been the case at the I.P.R.'s Mont Tremblant conference in 1942, this Hot Springs gathering provided a setting where officials could join in the fray in an ostensibly private capacity. Thus, Chatham House received Foreign Office assistance in selecting—and Treasury money for sending—the British delegation, half of whom were Government servants at the time. (On the 'private' side, there were, for example, Sir Andrew McFadyean, the leader of the delegation and a director of the British North Borneo Company, Sir Frederick Whyte, Arthur Creech Jones, M.P., the future Labour Colonial Secretary, and representatives of three Far Eastern business concerns; among officials were Sir George Sansom, G. F. Hudson, John Keswick and Sir Paul Butler.)[95] Likewise, one quarter of the American delegation were Government officials, including Owen Lattimore, Harry Dexter White and John Carter Vincent.[96]*

Some of the private discussions that took place within the American delegation to Hot Springs remain of considerable interest, and will be referred to in subsequent chapters dealing with specific aspects of Far Eastern affairs. As for the relations between various delegations that developed at this conference, there was respect among the Americans for the calibre of the British team, while McFadyean felt able to report to London at first that the atmosphere was better than it had been at Mont Tremblant, with 'less disposition to twist British tails just for the fun of seeing how the animal reacts.'[97] Nevertheless, the proceedings of the meeting once again developed into an Anglo-American confrontation, with the hostility that was displayed by American members of the I.P.R. Secretariat causing especial resentment in the British ranks. ('It has been catch-as-catch-can', declared McFadyean in his closing speech, 'with no holds barred and occasionally, when the referee was not looking, I think there was some biting.')[98]

* It must again be emphasized that, as was the case in 1942, at the time of the previous conference, the American branch of the I.P.R. as such did not have any direct influence on U.S. Government policies regarding the Far East. Still less did Chatham House have any say in what came out of the Foreign Office in London. But war-time circumstances had brought members of each institution into the ranks of officialdom, while the international exchanges carried on under the aegis of the I.P.R. as a whole provided a significant supplement to the generally more restrained transactions of formal diplomacy.

Colonial issues again formed a major area of controversy during the sessions of the conference, even though McFadyean assured those present that Britain's policies in that respect had been considerably reorientated since Mont Tremblant, and despite the fact that, as an Australian diplomat who was present noted, the British representatives tended to be more advanced than was their own Government in their acceptance of the need for some form of international accountability for colonial powers to be instituted after the war. United States delegates continued to deplore Britain's 'complacency' and her failure to adopt 'a progressive policy', reiterating that Americans were not fighting in order to reconstitute and maintain the British Empire. In return, the British, followed by the Dutch and the French, defended their country's colonial record, and warned, as McFadyean put it, that 'we shall not permit ourselves to be hustled out of evolution into revolution.' 'Every desire for the enlargement of freedom in the British Empire', he added, 'is the direct result of British teaching and British traditions.' The obvious suggestion, that the United States might do well to look to her own Negro problem, was also heard.[99]

At the same time, another focus for disagreement was provided by a Chatham House paper on 'Japan In Defeat', prepared before the conference met by a group headed by Sir Paul Butler. This emphasized the need to preserve stability in Japan after the war, warning against undue interference by the Allies with the economic structure of that country and suggesting that the retention of the Throne could help to prevent chaos. To American delegates this was all too far removed from the fundamental changes which they desired to see enforced in Japan (an approach which, to Butler, Hudson, and others among the British delegation, appeared to ignore practical problems). Drew Pearson also got wind of the arguments that were taking place at Hot Springs on this subject, and publicly charged Britain with wanting a 'soft' peace with the savage enemy.[100*]

When the conference had dispersed, the reactions in Chatham House to what had taken place were similar to the attitude of the Foreign Office towards the State Department: that the Anglo-American differences which had been made so apparent must be faced, and, if possible, overcome. To this end, it was decided to invite the American Council of the I.P.R. to send over a group of representatives for further discussions with members of Chatham House.[101] On the American side, meanwhile (where the I.P.R. was already beginning to be subject to accusations that it was Communist-controlled), Edward C. Carter, the Institute's Secretary General, summarized those same Anglo-American differences and fears—of continuing imperialism as a threat to world peace and of anti-colonialism as a recipe for chaos; of imperial tariff preferences as a barrier to world trade and of America's economic might as a potential bludgeon—ending with the warning that in

* For an example of warnings in the American press against certain Washington officials who were also believed to desire a 'soft' peace with Japan, an accommodation with leading Japanese industrialists (the zaibatsu), and an alignment with post-war Japan against the Soviet Union, see Stone, *The Truman Era*, 15.

the Far East, more than anywhere else, there lay a grave threat to understanding between the two countries.[102]

Others, as we have seen, including a good many British diplomats, had been coming to very much the same conclusion.[103] And among the areas of tension to which they could point in evidence during this final phase of the war, China once again provided an excellent example.

Notes to Chapter Twenty-Five

1 Stimson Diary, 22 Nov. 1944.
2 Morison, *Two-Ocean War*, 511; *Kirby*, V, 95ff.; *Roskill*, III, part II, 233; Milward, *War, Economy and Society*, 82–3.
3 FRUS, Berlin, I, 903; King and Whitehill, *Fleet Admiral King*, 396; *Leahy*, 449.
4 COS, 25 Jan. 1945 (CAB 79/29), 7 and 12 April 1945 (CAB 79/31), 28 May 1945 (CAB 79/34), 14 June 1945 (CAB 79/35); CCS, 1 Feb. 1945 (CAB 88/4).
5 COS, 17 July 1945, CAB 99/39; CCS, 18 July 1945, CAB 88/4; FO 371, F4055/69/23; FRUS, Berlin, I, 921, and ibid, II, 1313; *Leahy*, 478.
6 CCS 452/36, CAB 99/31; Ehrman, *Grand Strategy*, VI, 186.
7 FRUS, Berlin, II, 39; C. Romanus and R. Sutherland, *Time Runs Out in C.B.I.* (Washington, 1959; hereafter, *Romanus and Sutherland*, III), 321ff.
8 CCS, 16 March 1945, CAB 88/4; FRUS, Malta and Yalta, 494; Ehrman, *Grand Strategy*, VI, 180ff.
9 COS, 12 April 1945, CAB 79/31, and 31 May 1945, CAB 79/34.
10 See Ehrman, *Grand Strategy*, V, 531ff.
11 CCS 776/3, CAB 99/31.
12 COS, 4 July 1945, CAB 79/36.
13 See *Kirby*, IV, 253ff., 381ff.; Slim, *Defeat Into Victory*, books V and VI.
14 Ehrman, *Grand Strategy*, VI, 253.
15 Wilson to COS, 13 April 1945, PREM 3, 159/7.
16 COS, 13 April 1945 (CAB 79/31), 26 April and 1 May 1945 (CAB 79/32), 26 June 1945 (CAB 79/35); Ehrman, *Grand Strategy*, VI, 228–31.
17 Potsdam material in CAB 99/39; COS, 8 and 14 Aug. 1945, CAB 79/37.
18 See Ehrman, *Grand Strategy*, VI, 256–7.
19 See ibid, 221ff.; *Roskill*, III, part II, 321ff.; Cunningham, *A Sailor's Odyssey*, 614ff.
20 See WP(45)323, CAB 66/65, and material in PREM 3, 164/5.
21 Fraser to Alexander, 5 Sept. 1945, Alexander Papers, 5/10; Somerville Diary, 10 Jan., 20 Feb. and 19 April 1945; Halifax to Eden, 5 Dec. 1944, Hickleton Papers, A4 410 4. Problems of morale among British personnel, which had been anticipated, did not arise in the event. See WP(44)670, 671 (CAB 66/58), WP(44)722 (CAB 66/59), WP(45)10 (CAB 66/60).
22 COS, 7 April 1945 (CAB 79/31), 19 April and 1 May 1945 (CAB 79/32), 4 and 12 June 1945 (CAB 79/34); CP(45)76 (CAB 66/67); material in PREM 3, 142/5 and 7; JCS, 17 July 1945, RG 218; memo. of 29 May 1945, Leahy files, JCS correspondence, USNOA; Ehrman, *Grand Strategy*, VI, 233, 263.
23 FO 371, F4057/69/23.
24 Morgenthau Diary, 20 Oct. 1944.
25 COS, 11 and 17 May 1945 (CAB 79/33), 24 May 1945 (CAB 79/34), 21 and 29 June 1945 (CAB 79/35), 4 July 1945 (CAB 79/36), 27 and 31 July 1945 (CAB 79/37); CCS, 17 July 1945 (CAB 88/4); Chifley to WSC, 20 July 1945, PREM 4, 80/1; FRUS, Berlin, II, 1334–6; Ehrman, *Grand Strategy*, VI, 264ff. Other issues included the use to be made of Commonwealth tactical air force units. An OSS survey (R and A 2424) of 1944, noting likely sources of Anglo-American friction in the Far East after

the war, concluded, however, that 'Britain has lost her initiative in the area and will have to assume a more or less defensive role, following America's lead.'

26 JCS, 18 June 1945, RG 218.
27 On technical talks in Moscow, see FRUS, Malta and Yalta, 361ff.; material in Roosevelt Papers, MR box 34; J. R. Deane, *The Strange Alliance* (London, 1947).
28 Harriman to FDR, 24 Sept. 1944, Roosevelt Papers, MR box 11; WSC to FDR, 17 Oct. 1944, PREM 3, 472.
29 FRUS, Malta and Yalta, 378.
30 PWC(W), 1 Dec. 1944, Roosevelt Papers, MR box 168.
31 Stimson Diary, 13 Oct. 1944, 27 Feb. 1945.
32 See *Pogue*, II, 490, 512.
33 COS, 11 July 1945, CAB 79/36.
34 FRUS, Malta and Yalta, 396; King and Whitehill, *Fleet Admiral King*, 382; *Leahy*, 344; *Forrestal*, 28 Feb. 1945.
35 FRUS, Berlin, I, 903, 929; Stimson Diary, 23 and 24 July 1945; *Pogue*, II, 527ff. The War Department, however, ceased to regard the use of Siberian air bases as important.
36 See in general Harriman and Abel, *Special Envoy*, 399.
37 FRUS, Malta and Yalta, 766, 894, 984.
38 See A. Iriye, *The Cold War In Asia* (Englewood Cliffs, N.J., 1974), 96.
39 Deane, *The Strange Alliance*, 259.
40 FRUS, Berlin, I, 41; ibid, II, 345; FRUS, 1945, VII, 887.
41 See *Butow*, 155–7; FO 371, F5737/1057/23.
42 FO 371, F710/185/61; FRUS, Malta and Yalta, 498; *Avon*, 511–13; *Cadogan Diaries*, 715.
43 *Churchill*, VI, 342.
44 Yalta minutes, 10 Feb. 1945, CAB 99/31; Potsdam minutes, 18 July 1945, PREM 3, 430/6; FO 371, F185/185/61 and F2872/1057/23; minutes of 6 April 1945 in PREM 4, 31/6.
45 Grew–Stettinius phone record, 12 May 1945, Grew Papers, vol. 7; *Forrestal*, 12 May 1945.
46 FRUS, 1945, VII, 869.
47 Ibid, 876–8.
48 Stimson Diary, 23 July 1945; Forrestal Diary, 28 July 1945; Byrnes, *Speaking Frankly*, 208.
49 *Butow*, 92ff.
50 Cab, 25 Sept. 1944, CAB 65/43; WP(45)254, CAB 66/65; COS, 3 May 1945 (CAB 79/33), 10 and 11 July 1945 (CAB 79/36); FO 371, F4370/208/23, and material in file 46453; minutes of 17 July 1945, PREM 3, 430/7, and of 28 July 1945, PREM 3, 430/9; *Woodward*, V, cap. LXX.
51 FRUS, Berlin, I, 873ff.; FRUS, 1945, VI, 475ff.; Grew–Halifax conversation, 10 July 1945, Grew Papers, vol. 121; *Butow*, 103ff., 130–1.
52 COS, 10 Aug. 1945, CAB 79/37.
53 COS, 11 July 1945, CAB 79/36.
54 FO 371, F4058/584/61; F3620/364/23.
55 Yalta minutes, 9 Feb. 1945, CAB 99/31.
56 Potsdam record, 18 July 1945, PREM 4, 79/2.
57 Material in Grew Papers, vol. 7; Grew, *Turbulent Era*, vol. 2, 1428ff.
58 Forrestal Diary, 26 June 1945; FRUS, Berlin, I, 888; ibid, II, 1265; Stimson Diary, 26 June, 2 July, 9 Aug. 1945.
59 Forrestal Diary, 6 Feb. 1945; Stimson Diary, 17 and 24 July 1945; Hull, *Memoirs*, II, 1593; *Butow*, 140.
60 FRUS, Berlin, II, 1277, 1288; CP(45)88, CAB 66/67; FO 371, F4785/584/61; F4605, 4606, 4767, 4783 and 4789/364/23.
61 FRUS, Berlin, II, 1293; *Butow*, 142ff.
62 FRUS, Malta and Yalta, 383; see H. Feis, *Japan Subdued* (Princeton, 1961), passim; *Stimson*, and Sherwin, *A World Destroyed*.

63 Material in PREM 3, 139/8A and 11A; Gowing, *Britain and Atomic Energy*, 371ff.; *Churchill*, VI, 553; Ehrman, *Grand Strategy*, VI, cap. IX; Truman, *Year Of Decisions*, 350; Williams, *A Prime Minister Remembers*, 73.

64 FO 371, F4953 and 4954/16/61; *Times*, 3 Jan. 1976.

65 *Butow*, 190ff.; FO 371, F4974 and 5160/630/23; Stimson Diary, 10 Aug. 1945; *Bryant*, II, 484.

66 FRUS, Malta and Yalta, 766. Stalin for his part told Truman at Potsdam that the British had little interest in the Far Eastern war. FRUS, Berlin, II, 1582. See D. Clemens, *Yalta* (New York, 1970), 248.

67 FO 371, AN2253 and 791/4/45. For Australia, Eggleston deplored what he saw as 'an almost complete acquiescence in this position' by British officials. Washington notes, 11 Nov. 1944, Eggleston Papers.

68 E.g. *New York Times*, 17 Dec. 1944, 21 Feb., 11 March, 11 June 1945.

69 *Chicago Tribune*, 1 Feb. 1945; *San Francisco Examiner*, 19 July 1945; *Stettinius*, 18 Dec. 1944.

70 Halifax to Eden, 3 Jan. 1945, PREM 4, 27/10; FO 371, F214/127/61.

71 FO 371, AN1513/4/45.

72 E.g. ibid, F5788 and 5848/208/23; AN2192/4/45; AN1409/36/45; Eden to WSC, 28 April 1945, WSC to Law, 11 May 1945, WSC minute, 28 May 1945, PREM 4, 27/10; COS, 4 May 1945 (CAB 79/33), 13 July 1945 (CAB 79/36), 30 July 1945 (CAB 79/37).

73 FO 371, AN2306/4/45; Potsdam minutes, 28 July 1945, PREM 3, 430/9.

74 FO 371, F1955 and 2873/69/23.

75 Ibid, AN4614/34/45.

76 Minutes of 4 April 1945, CAB 99/30; Washington notes, 12 Dec. 1944, Eggleston Papers; Eggleston to Evatt, 5 Dec. 1944, Evatt Papers, Washington file.

77 *Kolko*, 616.

78 Staff conference, 29 May 1945, Naval Group China files, USNOA.

79 Forrestal Diary, 22 Nov. 1944.

80 *Thorne*, 55, 124.

81 Gardner, *Economic Aspects*, 263, 283; *Kolko*, 253ff.

82 FEC, 15 Nov. 1944, CAB 96/5.

83 FO 371, F2342/186/10; F2792/91/61; F626, 1274 and 2061/127/61; F4664 and 4797/4644/61; F4866/186/10; F2774/364/23.

84 Ibid, F851/69/23.

85 Ibid, U5471/5471/G.

86 See above, 118.

87 E.g. FO 371, F5802/993/61; AN3812/34/45.

88 An opinion poll early in 1945 asked if Japanese living in the U.S.A. should have 'as good a chance as white people to get any kind of job.' 61 per cent answered that the policy should be one of whites first. FO 371, file 44605.

89 See Hancock, Smuts: *The Fields of Force*, 469.

90 FRUS, 1945, VI, 249, 251.

91 *Stettinius*, 11 Jan. 1945.

92 FO 371, F514/327/23.

93 War Strategy and Reconstruction Group, 21 June 1945, RIIA.

94 Dennett Hot Springs survey, IPR Papers, box 326; report of Netherlands IPR delegation, 31 March 1945, NFM, DZ/D12.

95 Council minutes, 13 Dec. 1944, RIIA; FO 371, file 41769.

96 Dennett survey, IPR Papers, box 362; delegation minutes, 28 Oct. 1944, ibid, box 358.

97 Material in ibid, box 363; McFadyean to MacAdam, 9 Jan. 1945, Pacific Council Papers, RIIA.

98 Dennett survey, loc. cit.; Washington notes, 22 Jan. 1945, Eggleston Papers; IPR Cttee., 5 Feb. 1945, RIIA; McFadyean speeches, Council Papers, vol. 25, RIIA.

99 Dennett survey, loc. cit.; Watt to Hood, 23 Jan. 1945, Watt Papers; Eggleston Diary, 423/10/1669; Netherlands IPR delegation report, loc. cit.

100 FO 371, F714 and 831/327/23; Dennett survey, loc. cit.; Eggleston Diary, 4 Jan. 1945; Far East Group, 23 May 1945, RIIA.

101 Council minutes, 11 April and 11 June 1945, and report of IPR Cttee., 5 June 1945, RIIA.

102 Thomas, *The Institute Of Pacific Relations*, 36ff.; 'India and the Test in the Pacific', in IPR Cttee. papers, RIIA.

103 Among other symptoms, the persistent anti-British attitude of the journal *Amerasia* was noted in London. FO 371, file 41749.

CHAPTER TWENTY-SIX

THE UNITED STATES, BRITAIN
AND CHINA

China as an issue in Anglo-American relations

EARLY IN 1943, it will be recalled, a lengthy commentary on the unsatisfactory nature of Anglo-American relations over China had been composed by the Australian Minister in Chungking at the time, Sir Frederick Eggleston.[1] Now, as the war approached its end, another Australian diplomat, Keith Officer, who, as Chargé d'Affaires, had succeeded Eggleston, was finding that matters had changed very little.

'From my first arrival here', he wrote to Canberra in February 1945, 'I was struck by the absence of the close relations I had been accustomed to in Moscow, and earlier in Tokyo, between the United States and the various British missions, and disturbed by the extent to which the U.S. Army kept aloof from their British colleagues. In recent months the departure of General Stilwell . . . has wrought a very considerable improvement. But the situation is still not what it should be between close allies, and recent developments in Indochina threaten to raise the difficulties to a dangerous temperature.

The difficulties have their origin in the special situation which exists here. It is a United States theatre of operations, not an allied theatre . . . This, and the amount of aid they have been giving the Chinese has conferred on the U.S. representatives a very predominant position which inclines them to be sensitive to anything which appears to threaten that position. Then some Americans no doubt have great plans for the future development of China, and to them the Chinese market with its "four hundred million customers" seems to offer great possibilities to U.S. industry, and certain U.S. officials and businessmen may intend to obtain the monopoly of that market. Finally there is the difference between British and U.S. views as to future policy in Southeast Asia.

From the above causes a mutual suspicion is likely to arise and threaten Anglo-American relations in this area and react on them elsewhere.'[2]

One American official whom Officer noted as being amiable to the British he encountered was Patrick Hurley, who had arrived in Chungking in September 1944 as Roosevelt's personal representative with Chiang

Kai-shek, and was then nominated to be Ambassador there at the end of November. In private, American circles, however, Hurley, too, was fiercely critical of Britain. It did not take him long after his arrival, being strongly predisposed in this direction, to reach the conviction—as firm as it was false—that British policy aimed at maintaining China in a state of weakness. London's Ambassador, Seymour, he claimed, tried to impress upon him 'the desirability of China remaining divided', a cause for which, Hurley imaginatively insisted, not only British but French, Dutch, Australian and Canadian agencies in that country were working zealously and in collaboration. As angry as ever at what he held to be the abuse of Lend Lease aid by the allies of the United States, he demanded of Truman in May 1945: 'Will we now permit British, French and Dutch imperialists to use the resources of American democracy to reestablish imperialism in Asia?'[3]

Not every American official in China accepted Hurley's version of events. His level-headed Counsellor of Embassy, for example, George Atcheson, later wrote that he had seen 'no evidence of any actions on the part of the British, French or Dutch diplomatic representatives seeking any derogation of the authority of the Chinese National Government or of any desire that China should emerge from the war anything but a stable, unified nation.' Britain's own commercial interests, he pointed out to Hurley, were sufficient to make her wish to see a peaceful, organized China.[4] John Davies, too, was later to pour scorn in his memoirs on the way in which Hurley had sought to explain away the failure of his mission to China by 'imagined foul play by the weary Europeans.'[5]

Yet Davies himself, before his final clash with Hurley and his consequent departure from China, had joined in the anti-British chorus. The Communists in Yenan, he reported in November 1944, believed that Britain was up to her old imperial game of divide and rule,* and, agreeing with this assessment, he warned Hopkins that 'the British oppose the unification of China by either Chiang or the Communists . . . and will be satisfied if they can have Chiang as a quasi-puppet in the area between the Yangtze valley and the Indochina border.' 'The British', he added later, 'do not deceive Chiang . . . The Chinese have not forgotten a hundred years of experience in dealing with [them].' And again, in January 1945, he declared: 'The British . . . want a disunited China.'[6]† Davies' view was echoed by the

---

* Apparently the Communist leaders told Colonel Barrett that they had had an offer from Britain of Lend Lease aid, regardless of the views of Chungking. Even Hurley found their report 'incredible.' The present writer has found no evidence in British records to suggest that there was any truth in it. (FRUS, 1944, China, 732.)

† In conversations with the author, John Davies has confirmed that he had no tangible evidence to support these views at the time. That so perceptive a diplomat should have reported with such conviction on the basis of a stereotyped image of the British in the Far East underlines, more than do any assertions by the erratic Hurley, the strength of American misperceptions in this regard. (For his later views, see Davies, 340, 426.) In the same connection, an outstanding American historian of Far Eastern affairs, Dr. Dorothy Borg, has recalled in discussions with the author how, at the 1942 I.P.R. Conference (where she was a member of the secretariat), she was convinced that Sir John Pratt, whom

representative in Chungking of the U.S. Treasury, Sol Adler, although the latter, like Davies, thought Hurley himself 'a major fiasco.'[7] General Wedemeyer, appointed to be U.S. Commander in China following the recall of Stilwell, was another who subscribed to these convictions about Britain's policies.

Originally so cooperative a member of Mountbatten's S.E.A.C. team, then swinging towards the Stilwell line, as we have seen, Wedemeyer was now regarded by some—though not all—British officials as being decidedly hostile, especially when he assured Dening that after the war the British Empire would no longer exist.[8] Meanwhile he was indeed informing both Chiang Kai-shek and Washington that British activities in China were opposed to the American aim of making that country a great power, his Chief of Staff at the same time voicing contempt for Britain as being dependent on American aid in China and yet seeking to gain all the credit for herself in that part of the world.[9] Admiral Miles, likewise, was again warning his staff in this period against British intrigues aimed at restoring the era of foreign privileges in China.[10]

In arriving at such conclusions, Americans in China were able to seize upon, and sometimes distort, odd scraps of evidence which seemed to reveal an indifference on Britain's part to the fate of her Far Eastern ally. John Keswick, for example, now attached to the Chungking Embassy as Mountbatten's political adviser in China,* advanced to U.S. officials there the view that outside powers could do little to put an end to the divisions within the country, and that although 'a strong, unified China would be ideal', what was more likely to emerge from the war was some kind of loose federation, with the writ of the central government not running very far.[11] Or again, there was Churchill's somewhat slighting reference to China in a House of Commons speech, in which he described her military performance as disappointing, and especially so in the light of the 'lavish aid' provided by the United States.[12] But hard and fast evidence of sinister British designs and activities was not really needed in any case. The stereotyped picture which Americans, especially those concerned with their country's destiny in the East, had of the British in Asia—as before, a pleasing contrast to their self-image as China's special friends, guides and protectors—supplied conviction enough.

she knew quite well, firmly believed that Hongkong should remain in British hands. We have seen above that Pratt, within British circles, was in fact emphatic that Hongkong must be returned to China as swiftly as possible. As a recently retired official, however, he obviously felt constrained not to oppose Government policy in public, so that, unlike the case of John Davies in China, the misperception was on this occasion actually encouraged. (See above, 547.)

* Numerous interviews with those concerned, together with documentary evidence, have made it clear that Mountbatten relied far more on Keswick's advice than he did on that of his chief political adviser, Dening. It is equally apparent, however, that Keswick's approach to questions involving China was a 'harder' one than that of the Foreign Office itself, that the Office was not entirely comfortable over Keswick's position in the light of his Jardine Matheson connections, and that its senior Far Eastern officials had a high regard for the abilities and reporting of Dening.

In turn, the version of Britain's aims that was put forward by American officials and officers in China was widely accepted in Washington. Leahy, for one, believed what Hurley was reporting.[13] Likewise Representative Mike Mansfield, yet another agent sent on a brief visit to China by Roosevelt, relayed to the President the opinion that the British 'want a weak China where the United States want a strong China', and that they were not pulling their weight in the Far Eastern war.[14] A State Department briefing paper prepared for the Yalta Conference summed up the situation by describing Britain's approach to China as 'less optimistic and more cynical' than that of the U.S.A.—though, amusingly, it hastened to add that American policy was 'not based on sentiment . . . [but] on enlightened self-interest.'[15] Hopkins, for his part, informed Stalin in May 1945 that British and American attitudes towards China 'had been quite different',[16] while as for Roosevelt himself, he had told Stettinius in the preceding January that the information being supplied by Hurley, Wedemeyer and others

'seemed to indicate that the British and the French, but more particularly the British, were working to undermine our whole policy in regard to China. He said', recorded Stettinius afterwards, 'that apparently the British did not desire to see a strong China after the war, and still clung to the idea of white supremacy in Asia. He said this was entirely contrary to his idea and the policy of the United States Government. Our policy was based on the belief that despite the temporary weakness of China and the possibility of revolutions and civil war, 450 million Chinese would some day become united and would be the most important factor in the whole Far East.'[17]

As one step towards his goal, Roosevelt continued to hope that he could persuade the British Government to surrender Hongkong to the Chinese, who would then, he believed, turn it into an international free port. According to Hurley later, the President was also concerned lest the Soviet Union should make use of Britain's presence in Hongkong as an argument for obtaining a port of their own in China. In Hurley's version (and we shall see below how unreliable and devious a witness he could be), Roosevelt declared in March that he intended to insist on a change in London's policy over this issue, if necessary going over Churchill's head and appealing to the British people. Certainly, the President used Baruch as a messenger in the spring of 1945 to press the Prime Minister again on the matter.[18] Moreover, in pursuing this policy, Roosevelt, according to a State Department paper that was laid before the State–War–Navy Coordinating Committee, had behind him informed opinion throughout the United States, which, it was stated, regarded Hongkong as 'typifying British colonial imperialism in China', and which wished to ensure that an American victory in the Far East would not be followed by 'the restoration of British domination there.'[19] To Hurley's disappointment, however, Truman took a more cautious line on the matter than had his predecessor, hoping merely that a solution could be found that would satisfy both China and Britain, and failing in August to resist London's determination (and Whitehall's stance was by now a more unyielding one than it had been in 1942) that British, and not Chinese, forces should receive the surrender of the Japanese who were holding Hongkong.[20]

Meanwhile, where other aspects of relations with China were concerned, British officials and officers continued to receive little cooperation from their American colleagues. Thus, for example, Wedemeyer and his staff opposed Britain's attempts to increase her military aid to China, while at the same time emphasizing to Chiang Kai-shek how reluctant the British were to release Chinese divisions from operations within S.E.A.C.[21] ('Unconcealed hostility . . . to European interests in the Far East' was how one British member of S.O.E. in China later described the American attitude he had encountered there.)[22] In Washington, too, officials again showed no inclination to allow the British to participate in the allocating of supplies to China, while the State Department, despite promises to the contrary, presented its draft commercial treaty to the Chungking Government in April without first consulting with London, and even then refused to allow British diplomats to see the document in question. 'When it comes to deeds', wrote a member of the Foreign Office, 'there is very little sign of cooperation.' (Inter-departmental wrangles prevented Whitehall's own draft commercial treaty from being ready until November 1945.)[23] In addition, as we have seen in the previous chapter, the State Department failed almost entirely to respond to the Foreign Office's desire for informal talks on all aspects of Far Eastern affairs, including China. Likewise, in the non-official sphere, the National Foreign Trade Council of the U.S.A. had declined a suggestion from the China Association in London that they should discuss plans for the development of the trade of the two countries with China.[24]

British and American approaches to the Kuomintang–Communist issue within China were also regarded in Washington as being very different, a State Department review in June 1945 concluding that 'the British Government . . . supports the Chinese National Government and opposes the Chinese Communists more unreservedly than does the United States.'[25] (The irony of this view, given previous American rebukes to the effect that Britain was not providing sufficient support for Chiang Kai-shek, is evident.) Yet in this context, as noted in regard to the preceding period, the feeling was growing in Washington that the United States was going to need the cooperation of not only the Soviet Union but even that of Britain as well to help prevent China's international divisions from giving rise to great-power conflict in the Far East after the war. The State Department advanced this view before Yalta, again when Truman came into office, and once more before Potsdam. 'Britain and Russia', wrote an official of the Division of Chinese Affairs, 'are vitally concerned with developments in China.'[26] And at Malta, in January 1945, Stettinius put it directly to Eden that any help that Britain could give in reconciling the Communists and the Kuomintang would be welcomed.[27]

By now, however, the idea that the United States might actually wish to see some activity in China on the part of the United Kingdom was quite difficult for British officials to accept, especially those on the spot. 'I think you will find', wrote Seymour, 'that the Americans . . . will want to keep everything under their own control and will not welcome British participation.'[28] True, the new Head of the Far Eastern Department in London, Sterndale Bennett, expressed the opinion in December 1944 that 'we ought to be on the lookout for opportunities of supporting the Americans in getting the [Kuomintang–Communist] differences . . . composed.'[29] As we shall see in more detail below, however, Seymour in Chungking continued to believe that Britain's involvement in that issue would not affect the outcome, and that in any case no lasting solution was in sight. Sterndale Bennett himself accepted in February that 'the situation is much too complicated for us to start making suggestions at present.'[30]

London did, nevertheless, pin considerable hopes on the idea of talking over the question with Hurley, who was thought (wrongly) by Seymour to be 'genuinely friendly'—although the Ambassador felt obliged to add that 'we certainly do not spend our time trying to slip one over on [the Americans] in the various odd ways they suspect.' Hurley, however, was thoroughly two-faced, as Halifax for one suspected him to be. In contrast to his outbursts in American circles, he told Halifax that 'he thought the United States Government and His Majesty's Government were working for substantially the same thing in China', and even deprecated Roosevelt's policy over Indochina—which in fact he passionately supported to the President's face. Hurley also sought to ingratiate himself by warning another British official that John Davies was 'venemously anti-British'—thereby prompting the Foreign Office to have a special watch kept on Davies' activities in Moscow, when he was transferred there from China.

As for the visit which Hurley paid to London in April, for which the Foreign Office needlessly, if sensibly, prepared copious briefing papers ('He can be told quite categorically', the Prime Minister was informed, 'that we are not engaged in anything nefarious behind the backs of the United States Government'), the Ambassador's performance was a huge anti-climax. Invited to address the Chiefs of Staff, he produced a few generalizations, including the 'fact' that the Chinese Communists were not Communist, and blandly concluded that there were 'no conflicts between British and U.S. aims in China.' Thereafter he saw Churchill, and, in the latter's words, 'seemed to wish to confine the conversation to civil banalities.' 'I took him up with violence about Hongkong', added the Prime Minister with a hint of satisfaction, 'and said that never would we yield an inch of territory that was under the British flag . . . The General-Ambassador accepted this without further demur.' Hurley then completed his performance by writing a long report for Stettinius and Truman in which he vividly described how he had traded blow for blow with Churchill over Hongkong and other subjects, and how he had told the Prime Minister in no uncertain terms 'that President Roosevelt had given him the British Empire which . . . was lost up until the time we entered the war.'³¹* Further comment would appear superfluous.

As it was, Churchill's attitudes towards questions concerning China were still, quite clearly, far removed from those of Roosevelt, and in talks with Commonwealth representatives he again referred to the American 'illusion' that China was a great power. (Attlee, too, thought such a notion 'a piece of folly' on the part of the United States.)³² Within the Foreign Office, as well, long-suffering references continued to be made to China as 'an object of [American] devotion.' 'The difference between American and British aid to China in the "spiritual and moral" sphere', wrote one official, 'is that the Americans hitch their Chinese waggon to a star, while we believe in keeping its wheels firmly on the ground. It experiences less of a jolt if the hitching comes loose.'³³ At the same time, London could observe that such a 'jolt' was, indeed, now occurring, as China's shortcomings became still more apparent in some American eyes. Similarly, though in private, bitter Chinese complaints against the United States were to be heard.³⁴

Yet however detached the British official attitude might appear to be in comparison with the American one, this did not mean, as has already been indicated, that the suspicions of Hurley and his fellows were correct. Even Churchill, although it cannot be said that he was especially zealous over the matter, talked in private of 'owing China nothing but goodwill in her long struggle', and of the need 'to help her in any way possible.'³⁵ Nor was Eden being insincere when, at Malta, he assured Stettinius that Britain wished to see a united China.³⁶ Memoranda and briefing papers prepared in the Foreign Office emphasized on several occasions that 'a weak and divided China would be a menace to world peace', and that it was therefore in Britain's interest to help her to be 'strong, united and prosperous . . . [and] an essential element in future security in the Far East.' Seymour, who had almost certainly been maligned by Hurley, was also anxious to see this policy spelt out in public, and accordingly Cranborne sought to do this in a speech in the House of Lords in January.³⁷ Finally, it must again be emphasized that the Foreign Office continued to accept completely that 'the old regime' of extraterritoriality in China had gone for ever, and to resist any suggestions—for example, from the China Association—which appeared to involve an attempt to put back the clock in some way or other.³⁸

Thus, British and American aims and interests were seen in London as being basically similar. As the end of the war drew nearer, however, there was also concern at the extent to which the United States had established a dominant position in China. 'The plain fact is', reported the Foreign Office, 'that the primary strategic responsibility for China which America has assumed is working out in such a way that China has become for the time being an exclusively American field of political, military and economic influence. This bids fair to have far-reaching effects not confined to the prosecution of the war.'³⁹ The commercial aspect of this situation was particularly troubling to some people and was even raised in Parliament,

* Hurley had also told British officials in the autumn of 1944 that he had no wish to become Ambassador to China. In fact he had already asked to be given that post.

with an accompanying description of how extensive the China market was likely to prove after the war.[40] In this respect, officials in London, Washington and Chungking watched with some apprehension as evidence continued to accumulate of American business representatives, some in the role of wartime 'advisers' to the Chinese, striving to secure post-war contracts; even more disturbing was what Sansom described as 'a widespread conviction . . . in both official and private circles . . . that China must be an almost exclusive field for American investment and enterprise.' The visit of Donald Nelson to China (referred to briefly in the previous chapter and described in more detail below) and the setting up of a Sino-American War Production Board aroused particular interest, while it was even suspected that American 'big business' might be behind the decision, encouraged by Wedemeyer for military purposes, to change China's rule of the road from left- to right-hand drive. The predominance of the United States in U.N.R.R.A.'s activities in China, together with her exclusive attitude in that context, also cause eyebrows to be raised, as did China's own large claims upon the funds of that organization.[41]

In all of this, more than simply commercial profit was seen by British officials as being involved. What was at stake, declared Sterndale Bennett, was 'the extent to which this country could sustain its authority in the Far East and influence the future political development of China.' Even so, the response to tension with the United States over China was again the one that has already been observed for this period in terms of the Far East as a whole: that is, a desire, not for competition but for cooperation. One reason for adopting this attitude was, of course, supplied by Britain's dependence on the U.S.A. for her very future. 'To appear to compete with the Americans in either the political or economic fields in China', wrote Edmund Hall-Patch, whose career spanned the Foreign Office and the Treasury, 'would be . . . disastrous until the Stage III negotiations [over post-war American financial aid to Britain] are well out of the way . . . If we attempt to do anything [in China] . . . it should only be done in complete agreement with the Americans.'[42]

Quite apart from this consideration, however, the Foreign Office continued to see American and British interests in China as running side by side, and consultation and collaboration between the two countries as being in itself the most desirable way in which to proceed—even though it was recognized that 'the United States are necessarily playing the hand there at present.'[43] It was in this spirit, therefore, that the Economic Sub-Committee of the Far Eastern Committee argued for 'the closest harmony with the Americans' over commercial developments in China, envisaging the possibility of joint enterprises being established and, at the very least, a full exchange of information in order to eliminate misunderstanding and wasteful competition. Lord Strathallan of the Ministry of Production, the Board of Trade and members of the Chungking Embassy were similarly inclined, even though the mood of Americans in China was proving to be far from encouraging.[44]

Here, then, was the framework of Anglo-American relations as they concerned China during this final phase of the Far Eastern war. Once more, what stands out is the suspicion and sense of rivalry that predominate among the Americans involved, while for the British there are the familiar feelings of being dwarfed, misunderstood and overlooked, but also, notwithstanding this, a continuing desire for collaboration. For both sides, however, the situation in China was itself creating much perplexity and uncertainty, as we can now turn to observe in rather more detail.

Britain and China

Despite the obvious strength of the American position in China, a measure of optimism continued to be expressed in 1944–45 by various British officials and businessmen about their country's commercial prospects there. Seymour, for example, from his vantage point in Chungking, believed that the long experience of British bankers, shippers, insurers and the like would reap its reward, even though he acknowledged that among Chinese politicians there existed 'a dislike . . . for some at least of the old-established firms which have operated in China.' Above all, and supported over this by the Far Eastern Department of the Foreign Office, he urged that Britain should foster trade relations by granting China some form of commercial credits, suggesting that the unused portion of the 1944 war-time loan should be used for this purpose after the defeat of Japan.[45] The Board of Trade, too, adopted a similar if somewhat more cautious line, while in February the Far Eastern Committee as a whole decided that, even if not justified on purely economic grounds, credits for China could be seen as a political necessity, since 'the part we play in China is of such great importance to our whole position in the Far East.' At the same time it was judged that, provided due regard was paid to the need to keep closely in touch with the Americans and that goods received from the U.S.A. on Lend Lease were not involved, there was no obligation to that country which prevented Britain from beginning to 'generally foster the market' in China while the war was still in progress.[46]

Hopes of revived opportunities were also being expressed within the China Association, where there existed a division of opinion between those who wished to make strong representations against any new Chinese regulations which were 'repugnant to English law', and those who believed it essential to acknowledge the ending of all forms of foreign privileges and to show regard for China's new status 'as one of the four Great Powers.'[47] Neither businessmen nor the Far Eastern Committee, however, received any encouragement from the Treasury, already grappling with the financial crisis that was going to face Britain once the fighting had come to an end.

In a series of interventions which culminated in a memorandum by the Chancellor of the Exchequer himself early in April, three things were made abundantly clear: first, that the purchases China could make with the £50 million granted in 1944 would continue to be severely restricted to goods required for the prosecution of the war (an order for floating power stations, for example, was excluded from the loan arrangement on these grounds); second, that unspent portions of that 1944 loan could not be used for post-war commercial purposes; and third, that after the war there would be no granting of credits to the Chinese or to anyone else unless the transaction in question could be justified on strictly economic grounds. Exports, in other words, would have to go to those countries that could pay for them on the spot, and China was not expected to fall into this category.[48] These restrictions imposed by the Treasury, coupled with a continuing desire not to create friction with the Americans, led the Foreign Office to postpone taking action on a proposal by the China Association, supported by the Chungking Embassy, that a British commercial mission should be sent to China. Indeed, the project was still frozen when the war came to an end.[49]

The Treasury was not alone, in fact, in looking coolly at the prospects of trade with China. Dalton, for example, as President of the Board of Trade, heard the view expressed that, by leaving that country's commercial field wide open to the United States, Britain would be helping to ensure that the Americans were 'definitely anchored on the other side of the Pacific', thus in turn guaranteeing the defence of Australia and New Zealand.[50] Dalton himself agreed with this opinion, finding both political and financial reasons for keeping out of China:

'If . . . we and the Russians and the Americans can't maintain a triangular friendship', he noted at the end of March 1945, 'it were best for us that the failure, if there must be failure, should be in the maintenance of Russian–American friendship. With this thought at the back of my mind I am inclined to let the Americans do practically all the trade and development in China. In any case, I don't see us getting paid for exports to China for a long while, if ever . . . It will also make it easier for the Americans to go slower for their export drive in other parts of the world. No doubt there will be a screech from our Shanghailanders and Hong-konkers, but I have never been much impressed by that crowd. Indeed, I would like to have very few British hostages to Chinese fortune in the coming years.'[51]

In the Foreign Office, Hall-Patch was arguing in similar terms. The Americans, he submitted, were obviously determined to take the lead in China (he quoted Stilwell, Willkie and Laughlin Currie—'it is now our turn to bat in Asia'—to this effect). Very well, let China 'improve her economy at American expense and not ours . . . America', he continued, 'has many lessons still to learn as a creditor nation, and while she is learning we can build up our strength. . . . There is at least a prospect that before America has learned her lessons we shall again be on our feet and be able to compete on equal terms.'[52]

Hall-Patch also found another reason for holding back over trade with

China: that the achievement of both a stable political situation and a convertible currency in that country still seemed to be 'far distant'. The Chinese internal situation did indeed appear grave by this time. Inflation had now reached extraordinary proportions, goods indexed at 100 in 1937 standing in 1945 at 125,000. Politically, separatism and strife continued, despite changes that were made within the Chungking regime at the end of 1944, involving the dismissal of Kung as Minister of Finance and the revival of T. V. Soong's fortunes as he became Acting Vice President and Acting President of the Executive Yuan. These moves were welcomed in the Foreign Office in London as 'a step in the right direction', but strong doubts remained as to whether Chiang Kai-shek himself would learn to become less autocratic. Kuomintang pledges of future democratic reforms, greeted approvingly in the British press, were likewise treated with caution by officials, and in June 1945 Seymour was still reporting that the reactionary and ultra-nationalist elements in the Kuomintang were dominating the Party's affairs.[53]

Was China, in fact, facing a complete collapse? From his position within the Chungking Embassy, Keswick for one thought so at the end of November 1944, describing Chiang Kai-shek's Government as being 'very nearly on its last legs', and dismissing the likelihood of any compromise between it and the Communists 'as long as the Generalissimo and the right wing of the Kuomintang remain in power.'[54] By the following February, Seymour for his part believed that the overall position had greatly improved as the Japanese military threat receded and Chiang Kai-shek's prestige seemed to revive; nevertheless, despite what he now saw as 'a healthy desire to come to terms' with the Communists on the part of the Chungking regime, the Ambassador, like Keswick, still thought a lasting settlement of the dispute unlikely.[55]

Leaving aside the Communist issue for the moment, however, there remained the question of whether there was anything that Britain could do to help improve China's internal condition. Was British policy towards that country, as the *Observer* charged, 'merely drifting'?[56] Certainly, the Far Eastern Department of the Foreign Office were anxious to explore all possibilities, and strongly rejected a wholly pessimistic review of the situation by the Services' Joint Intelligence Committee, which appeared to argue 'that China could be written off and that we can regard even her complete collapse with equanimity.'[57] Yet little enough emerged in the way of practical suggestions. Perhaps Eden could visit China at some suitable time—which meant not then but later; perhaps that old and greatly overrated standby,* an invitation to Madame Chiang Kai-shek to visit Britain, should be

---

* Sir Berkeley Gage, who, as First Secretary of the Embassy in Chungking, was the British diplomat who maintained the closest relations at the time with Madame Chiang Kai-shek, has in conversation with the author agreed with the view that her political significance within China tended to be greatly overrated in London. Professor Owen Lattimore has done the same in terms of Washington and the American body-politic at large.

revived.[58] Meanwhile, one could point to the continuing work being done by Dr. Needham in the scientific and cultural fields, or to the donations of £20,000 per month which were still being sent to China by the United Aid to China Fund. (Even this last contribution was not free of difficulties, however, with renewed problems cropping up over the exchange rate on which the Chinese were insisting, and with further accusations being made by the China Campaign Committee—the charges were not accepted within the Foreign Office or Chungking Embassy—that the Fund was being misused at the Chinese end, to the continuing detriment of the International Peace Hospitals in the Communist areas.)[59]

Likewise in the military sphere, it seemed that very little could be done to assist China. Churchill did raise the possibility, during the Malta talks with the Americans, of British troops moving from Burma into China, but Brooke and Marshall both promptly ruled this out as being 'not a practical proposition.'[60] As for the dangers facing China during the Japanese advance towards Kunming at the end of 1944, these were urgently presented to London by Carton de Wiart, the Prime Minister's personal representative with the Generalissimo; de Wiart also supported Chiang's demand for the return of Chinese divisions from Burma, and highly praised the work of Wedemeyer and Chennault on China's behalf.[61] The Chiefs of Staff, however, took a much more detached view of the situation, judging that the Japanese were unlikely to take Kunming, let alone Chungking, and that even if Chiang Kai-shek's regime were to fall, 'the Communist influence would probably spread southwards and guerilla activities against the Japanese would correspondingly be intensified.'[62]

Meanwhile the work of Britain's 204 Military Mission in China continued for a time, its orders being 'to do all in [its] power to improve the fighting efficiency of the Chinese Army.' The scale of the Mission's operations remained small, however, and the Americans still declined to provide the transport facilities which would enable the Chinese 'surprise battalions' to be properly equipped. Eventually, in May, it was decided to end the Mission's separate existence.[63] The British Army Aid Group for its part went on helping Allied personnel to safety from behind the Japanese lines, but the whole field of clandestine operations, shared by B.A.A.G., S.O.E. and S.I.S., and directed from London, New Delhi and S.E.A.C. Headquarters, was in a somewhat confused state, Carton de Wiart finally being given a coordinating role in an attempt to improve matters.[64] S.O.E. activities in China continued to be very limited in scale, and a scheme to train guerillas in the vicinity of Hongkong, with the 'ulterior aim' of setting up a British administration in the colony immediately the Japanese capitulated, was turned down by the Ambassador, Carton de Wiart and the new G.O.C. China, General Hayes, on the grounds that 'our military position in China is now so difficult and precarious that it is essential that any project of this nature, if it is to have any chance of success, must be previously cleared with both the Chinese and Americans and at the highest level.' The commander of B.A.A.G. added that, if the British were to go ahead with such an operation, they 'would be damned in the eyes of both Chinese and Americans for a long time afterwards.'[65]*

As it was, there were those in Whitehall who remained doubtful as to whether Britain could in any case impose her will over the future of Hongkong. In the Foreign Office, for example, Hall-Patch and Sir Ronald Campbell (now returned from Washington, and an Assistant Under Secretary of State) were agreed that the port 'cannot be used as a commercial entrepot or a defence base if the Chinese do not acquiesce in our so doing.'[66] Within the Chiefs of Staff Committee, too, Brooke described the colony as 'virtually indefensible', and expressed the wish to avoid all military commitments there.[67] Nevertheless, the Colonial Office, urged on by the China Association, argued strongly that British rule should be restored in Hongkong, and laid long-term plans for obtaining China's agreement to maintain the colony's vital services when the lease of the New Territories fell due in 1997; discussions were also held on how the population could be more closely associated with the machinery of government.[68]

Churchill's own continuing determination in this period not to cede Hongkong has already been illustrated, while Attlee lent his name, too, to such a policy by affirming in the House of Commons that the colony was covered by the Prime Minister's earlier pledge that there was to be no 'liquidation' of the British Empire. Even so, it was not until the end of June 1945 that the Chiefs of Staff considered plans for getting British forces into Hongkong, which still fell within Chiang Kai-shek's China Theatre. Finally, the Americans having been informed beforehand, naval units were ordered to the colony immediately after news had been received of the Japanese capitulation. Despite the protests from Chiang Kai-shek that ensued, it was thus a British officer who received the surrender of Hongkong. Washington, now well into the post-Roosevelt era, acquiesced in what had been done.[69]

Like Hongkong, Tibet also continued to be the subject of Anglo-Chinese differences in 1944–45. Of necessity, however, the British approach in this instance remained far more restrained, and there was never any likelihood of action being taken to defend Tibet against a possible Chinese incursion. The situation, in fact, remained deadlocked to the end of the war. Chungking still maintained that Tibet was a part of Chinese territory; Tibet sought, and failed to obtain, a promise of British support if she were to resist an invasion by Chiang Kai-shek's troops; the Government of India, its eye, as before, on the possibility of a future confrontation with China in the area, went on establishing its administration up to the McMahon Line of 1914, thereby arousing Tibetan protests and disquieting the Foreign Office, which wished to keep the entire question as quiet as possible.[70]

As before, indeed, New Delhi was far louder than London in expressing fears that China could well become a menacing, expansionist power. In this

* Some British intelligence operations, however, were carried on in Hongkong, with the knowledge of both Chiang Kai-shek and Wedemeyer. (Wedemeyer–Chiang conversation, 8 Jan. 1945, Wedemeyer Papers, box 7; and Wilkinson Journal for 1944–45, passim; interview with Professor Konrad Hsu.)

connection, for instance, a study group under Sir Olaf Caroe, India's Foreign Secretary, cited both Sun Yat-sen's San Min Chu I and Chiang Kai-shek's *China's Destiny* as evidence of the will which existed in that country to establish an empire in Burma, Malaya, Indochina and elsewhere. The Governor of Burma shared this unease.[71] So, too, as in earlier periods, did Dutch officials, among whom their Ambassador in Chungking foresaw the setting up of a Chinese 'coprosperity sphere', to the exclusion of Westerners. Likewise, the Australian High Commissioner in London, Bruce, believed that 'China could, under certain circumstances, become as great a menace as Japan.'[72]*

In the Foreign Office, however, it was not so much the potential strength of China that was receiving attention as the international dangers that could arise from her current weakness. Given such a situation, the Soviet Union was more than ever seen as being likely to play a significant part in the area, not merely by reasserting herself in Sinkiang, but perhaps by becoming the mentor of a separate regime in northern China. 'I can conceive nothing but difficulties', Hall-Patch wrote, 'if China becomes a bone of contention between Russia on the one hand and the Americans and ourselves on the other.' 'The Polish problem', added Hudson, 'would be child's play compared to this.'[73] And yet, over the vital matter of the Sino-Soviet talks that were held in the summer of 1945 and that led to the signing in August of a treaty of friendship and alliance between them, London was left almost completely in the dark.[74] In the political sphere, as in the military one, it was Washington that continued to deal single-handedly with Moscow over Far Eastern affairs.

There remained, however, the related question which was referred to briefly above, of what attitude and action, if any, Britain should take in connection with the Kuomintang-Communist split in China. Unfortunately, discussions on this issue within the Foreign Office did not now have the benefit of the opinions of G. P. Young, whose prescience regarding the vitality and ultimate victory of Mao Tse-tung's forces has been illustrated in earlier periods. Moreover, despite the efforts of G. F. Hudson to establish the contrary view, there remained a widespread tendency to see the Yenan regime as being not a truly Communist one. Keswick, for example, described it as 'nothing more than a provincial government by a group whose policy sprang from an agrarian revolt.' 'It is unlikely', he added, 'that they would interfere with private ownership of property or would move away from Dr. Sun Yat-sen's San Min Chu I.'[75]† Sterndale Bennett, at the Head of the Far Eastern Department, accepted this interpretation, writing of 'the so-called Communist area.'[76] Consequently, the Foreign Office briefing paper prepared for Eden and Churchill before Hurley's visit to London asserted

* It also seems apparent, from reading between the lines of certain reports within Whitehall, that British agencies were monitoring communications between the Chinese Embassy in London and Chungking. (See FO 371, F1530/1530/60.)

† Sun Yat-sen's Three Principles of the People: nationalism, democracy and the people's livelihood.

that 'the Communists . . . are not Communist in the usual sense of the word, nor are they a political party in the usual sense. They are an autonomous faction capable of developing into a rival Government of China.' (The survey did add, however, that the policies of Yenan appealed to 'great numbers' of Chinese; it also made the point so often advanced by Hudson, that while both the Kuomintang and Communists invoked concepts of democracy, 'neither can be called democratic; they are in fact rival forms of dictatorship.')[77]

In the British press, meanwhile, it tended to be the moderation of Mao and his colleagues that was emphasized. Gunther Stein, for example, whom we have encountered earlier and who had just spent four months in Yenan, asserted in the *News Chronicle* that the 'virile new democracy' he had been witnessing was 'no more Communistic than is Britain's wartime democracy.' *The Times*, too, moreover, majestically reassured its readers that 'the Yenan system is not Communism; it resembles an agrarian democracy.'[78] Stein for one was by now also fiercely critical of the Chungking regime, and his views in this respect received some attention in the Foreign Office. Officials took note of the opinions of Michael Lindsay, as well, who continued in letters home to deplore the Kuomintang's corruption and tyranny—'in some ways [they] are nearly as bad as the Nazis'—and to blame Chungking for the drift towards civil war.[79] As for the contrasting achievements of Yenan, Seymour, the senior British representative on the spot in China, accepted, as he had done earlier, that the reports of Stein and others before him showed these to be 'positive and important' in both 'practical and moral' spheres, although he was not prepared to forecast what were the military or political prospects of the movement.[80] Carton de Wiart, on the other hand, almost as politically naïve as he was brave, not only detested but dismissed the Communists on principle (having met Mao Tse-tung himself later, he described him as a fanatic, but added: 'I cannot believe he means business'); thus, when invited to address the Cabinet in London in January 1945 on the situation in China, he apparently ignored the Yenan factor altogether and simply declared that there was no one in sight to challenge the rule of Chiang Kai-shek.[81]

Carton de Wiart's superficial reading of Chinese affairs was not shared by the Far Eastern Department of the Foreign Office, where Sterndale Bennett in October again raised the possibility of some form of British initiative to help improve matters, beginning, perhaps, with a visit to Yenan by a member of the Chungking Embassy.

'We do not seem well placed to make any positive contribution', he wrote to Seymour, 'and our intervention would probably be disliked as much by the Americans as by the Chinese. At the same time it is becoming increasingly clear . . . that we have a very great interest in building up a strong, united (and yet democratic) China . . . I am wondering if we could not achieve our purpose without anything in the way of a threat, merely by showing an active interest in the Communists—as the Americans are doing . . . In any case, can we afford to let matters drift without attempting to take a hand? Assuming that the Kuomintang and the Communists do not reach a settlement, will not the Communists tend to drift into the exclusive orbit of Soviet Russia? Supposing that Russia were eventually to decide to enter the war against Japan? What with the special security arrangements which she might subsequently demand in Manchuria and her special relations with the Communists in North-West China, might she not penetrate North China to such a degree as to make Chinese unity more or less permanently unrealisable? . . . Is it not therefore in our interests to cultivate the Chinese Communists and to do what we can to bring about a reconciliation between them and the Kuomintang for the sake of Chinese independence and unity?'[82]

These arguments, so close to those of American diplomats in China like Davies (who, as we have seen, was assuring Washington that British policy aimed at keeping China divided), continued to carry weight in the Foreign Office. Thus, the proposal that Britain should 'be ready to consider lending a hand . . . should the opportunity arise'—possibly bringing Moscow in on the matter as well—was repeated in the briefing paper prepared for Hurley's visit in April. Various inhibiting factors, however, were sufficient to ensure that in the event no British intervention over the Communist question was forthcoming. One of the less important of these was the fact that the United Kingdom lacked the military reasons which the United States had been able to advance for making contact with Yenan. More significant was the slenderness of Britain's presence and her over-all lack of leverage in China, again in contrast to the American position. In addition, despite what Stettinius had said during the Malta talks, London continued to entertain doubts as to whether the U.S.A. would, indeed, welcome an initiative in China on Britain's part.

As for the actual political situation on the spot, the argument that British Governments in the past had often treated on a de facto basis with various regional regimes in China could be countered by emphasizing the need to respect the position and wishes of the one, Chungking Government which had been formally recognized. (Much stress had been placed upon this in the past, it will be recalled, when requesting Chiang Kai-shek to cease interfering in Britain's private affairs in India.) This approach was reinforced by a tendency to see the Generalissimo, for all his faults, as still being the one man who could lead a united China. Finally, there was the considerable weight which—in contrast to Rooseveltian practice—was given to the opinions of the Ambassador concerned.

Seymour, as we have seen, continued to the end of the war to believe, and rightly so, that there was little or no hope of a lasting settlement being achieved between Chungking and Yenan.[83] Moreover, he judged that intervention on the part of the United States had already helped to drive Chiang Kai-shek into the arms of the Kuomintang's extremists, since the Generalissimo was 'the last man to lay himself open to the charge of yielding to foreign advice or pressure in the matter of internal politics'; at the same time, American sympathy for the Communists had made them, too, more intransigent.[84] In addition, the Ambassador could not envisage any plan for the solution of the question that would satisfy both Washington and Moscow, so that the danger would always be present of 'transferring the Kuomintang/Communist dispute into an argument between the major Allies.' 'I do not believe', he concluded, 'that our participation would affect the result.' Hence, Britain would be well advised to stay clear of the issue.[85]

Seymour's line of reasoning was supported in the Foreign Office by Hudson. 'Our experience in the Balkans', he wrote, 'suggests that the attempt to ride two horses at once does not last for long and that in the end we must either support the established Government or eliminate it. In Yugoslavia we backed Tito* and discarded Michailovitch; in Greece we are now fighting E.L.A.S. It may be a matter of controversy which side we and the Americans ought to back in China, but I do not see how we can back both.'[86] Hudson's own preference was dictated by the conviction that Yenan would always gravitate towards Moscow, and that Chungking, for all its failings, did have to its credit years of struggle against Japan, and would incline towards the West. 'If the Americans do not support Chungking' he wrote in June 1945, '. . . they risk losing all their influence in China, for it is extremely unlikely that a Communist China would be any more pro-American than Tito's Yugoslavia is pro-British. The Moderator of the Church of Scotland *might* have more influence over the Catholic Clergy than the Pope, but probably not.'[87]

Unlike G. P. Young earlier, Hudson failed to discern the extent of the underlying weakness of Chiang Kai-shek's regime, and there were others in the Foreign Office who held that, faced with a choice, Britain should put her money on the Generalissimo.[88] Nor was it likely that Churchill, his alarm at the threat of Communism in Europe rapidly mounting, would conclude any differently. 'Chiang Kai-shek', he told Commonwealth representatives in London in April, 'seemed . . . to be the best figure in China that we were likely to see.' Under his leadership, the Prime Minister continued, China would probably line up with the United States in the United Nations Security Council, but at least that would mean that she would not 'join with Russia.'[89]

Thus, during the final phase of the Pacific War, Chungking had good reason to be pleased with the 'correct' and essentially passive attitude of the British Government. This reaction, of course, was far removed from the one China had displayed towards Britain in 1942. The irony of the 1945 situation lies, however, in another contrast: that between London's 'correctness' on the one hand and on the other the ambivalence towards Chiang Kai-shek

---

* A separate essay could be written on the ways in which, in both London and Washington, the notion that Mao Tse-tung was in certain ways the 'Tito' of China, together with comparisons between that country's situation and Yugoslavia's, influenced perceptions of and attitudes towards the Chungking–Yenan problem.

now being displayed by Washington—whence, in the past, reproaches had so often been cast at Britain for her failure to show sufficient regard for the position, interests and wishes of the Generalissimo and his Government.

The United States and China

In the year that followed the Second Quebec Conference, as we observed during the preceding period as well, American admiration for China and for Chiang Kai-shek in particular still proved to be too deep-seated, too independent of the facts of the situation, to disappear entirely.* Prominent individuals who, after the war, were to constitute part of the membership of what was loosely termed 'the China lobby'—Representative Walter Judd, for example; Henry and Clare Booth Luce; William Bullitt—were still as loud as ever on Chungking's behalf.[90] Even where disillusion had begun to set in, the choice in China could nevertheless seem a clear one: thus, the *Chicago Tribune* declared that, for all Chiang Kai-shek's undemocratic tendencies, 'America's interests are infinitely better served by the existing order as long as the war lasts than they would be by the rise of a Communist government.'[91] And was not Chiang, in any case, promising to introduce democratic reforms in the near future?[92] As for China's international position, she took her place at the San Francisco Conference as one of the principal members of the United Nations, while at Potsdam Truman sustained the fiction of her Great Power status by obtaining a seat for her on the proposed Council of Foreign Ministers. (China, it was understood, would participate when 'problems concerning the Far East ... of world-wide significance' were under discussion. In the event, however, the Council had little to do with Far Eastern questions.)

Nor were the hopes of a vast market for American goods in post-war China easily dampened, as the remarks of MacArthur, Miles and others have already indicated. After causing some alarm in the U.S.A. over the possibility that it would introduce nationalistic, high-tariff trade regulations, the Chungking Government itself continued to encourage American anticipation in this respect, announcing that no restriction would be placed on the percentage of foreign capital invested in any Sino-foreign enterprise, and assuring Washington that it would follow the United States in adopting a free-trade policy based upon the Atlantic Charter and article 7 of the Mutual Aid Agreements. Also, the introduction of new and potentially awkward company registration requirements was postponed.[93] Another promising sign, it seemed, was the return to prominence in the Chungking Administration of T. V. Soong, who was not only commercially-minded, but regarded as something of a Westerner who had merely had the misfortune to be born with a yellow skin.[94]

* At least the outline of what follows on U.S. aspects of the subject may well be familiar to American students of war-time history. In the light of the lesser degree of awareness obtaining in Britain, however, the material has not been compressed to the extent that would otherwise have been possible.

The Chinese Government, of course, had expectations of its own—not least that substantial American assistance would be forthcoming for the development of China's industry and economy after the war.[95] Already, technical advisers of various kinds were arriving from the United States, and their involvement in, for example, the study of extensive hydro-electric schemes encouraged the hope that full American partnership would follow in order to carry through a specific project like the one for obtaining electrical power from the waters of the Yangtze Gorges.[96] And indeed, Washington was preparing an over-all plan for the industrialization of China, an outline of it being published in May 1945, with the estimated expenditure required being put at just under $2 billion.[97] American involvement in this whole field was also increased when Donald Nelson, sent to Chungking by Roosevelt, it will be recalled, helped to set up there Chinese War Production and War Transport Boards, each with United States advisers. The benefits which the U.S.A. herself could derive from this wartime partnership were spelled out by Nelson in his report to the President at the end of 1944:

'The success of China's venture in planned war production', he wrote, 'if properly followed up through American government and business channels, will make for close post-war economic relations between China and the United States. China has the capacity and the desire to develop herself industrially with American aid. If that aid is realistically planned and if financial arrangements are put on a sound basis, China should soon after the war begin to replace Japan as the leading industrial nation of the Orient. In that event, a market of enormous size should progressively open up for American export industries. I believe, too, that with American guidance, China's development can be turned into peaceful and democratic channels . . .'[98]

Quite apart from the lure of the market which they seemed able to offer, however, Chinese officials had some reason to believe that they would never have undue difficulty in loosening the purse-strings of the United States Government.[99] The continuation of American financial aid to China in this period is all the more striking in that, as we have already seen in the preceding months, a growing number of U.S. officials were disillusioned and resentful over what was taking place. The Treasury in Washington learned, for example, that the Chinese Government were selling gold in a 'frenzied' and absurd fashion, some of that gold finding its way into the Japanese zone; American proposals for helping to correct matters by setting up a new stabilization fund were rejected by Chungking.[100] It was also known that U.S. goods and munitions that had been sent to China were being hoarded by her Government, while Morgenthau and his senior officials had in their hands a list of those Chinese in high places—the Soong family being prominent among them—who were believed to have benefited personally from the sale of American bonds and savings certificates.[101] Similarly the

Director of the O.S.S., Donovan, submitted a memorandum to the President in May in which he referred to the possibility that T. V. Soong had been making money out of U.S. aid transactions.[102]

Against this background, as was mentioned in passing earlier, Harry Dexter White* and other Treasury officials had for some time been holding up promised shipments of gold to China—a move which suited even Ambassador Hurley, who wished to use Chungking's desire for this gold to extract from them certain concessions.[103] Yet this strong line was abandoned in May 1945 when T. V. Soong reminded a shocked Morgenthau (who had forgotten the matter, and blamed his officials for not having called it to his attention) that in 1943 he, the Secretary, had promised in writing that, as part of the $500 million 1942 loan, China would be sent nearly $200 million in gold, with no strings attached. Morgenthau decided that his pledge would have to be honoured; the money, he observed, would go 'down the rat-hole', but there it was.[104] Shipments were therefore resumed, while in July the greatly-suspected H. H. Kung was even allowed to take back to China in person $10 million of currency. (Kung's argument was that this was a vital move in the fight 'to hold the economic line' in China against inflation. The picture of this gentleman, having won his point, departing from the United States loaded down with dollars in this fashion provides a delightful reductio ad absurdum of Sino-American war-time relations in this field. As for Morgenthau, not, perhaps, the sharpest man in Washington, he persisted during his interview with Kung in calling the latter 'Soong', which did not go down too well. Possibly, all Chinese Ministers and ex-Ministers seemed alike to him.)[105] In addition, and at Truman's insistence, it was agreed to provide China with 45 million yards of cotton textiles which, it was hoped, would do more than Kung's suitcases of dollars to help check the rate of infflation.[106]

One reason for this softer behaviour on Washington's part during the summer of 1945 was that the Chinese were at last achieving something in military terms. This was due in part to the groundwork that Stilwell had done, but also to the efforts and ambitions of Wedemeyer who had succeeded him as Chiang Kai-shek's Chief of Staff† and who managed to tidy things up by bringing under his control all American military and intelligence activities in China, such as those of the O.S.S. and of Miles' Naval Group.[107] Significantly, the exact military and political nature of Wedemeyer's mission was not in fact clear in Washington, such were the disappointments and

---

* After the war, it was strongly argued that White had been a Communist agent for a considerable time. Despite a recent biography by David Rees, the charge still appears to be unproven (for an attempted refutation of it, see Stone, *The Truman Era*, 48). It is important to note that, whatever the truth of the matter, the opinions that White was expressing about the Chungking Government in 1944–45 were essentially those of his Washington colleagues—many of whom were far from being Communists—and of his own Secretary, Morgenthau.

† Wedemeyer did not, however, command the Chinese Army, Washington having retracted its proposal that an American should be given that role. The India–Burma Theatre was also now a separate command, under Lt. General Daniel I. Sultan.

revisions which had occurred since the brave days of Stilwell's appointment.[108] Nevertheless, once the Japanese advance of 1944 had come to a halt, and a final thrust towards Chinkiang in Hunan had been defeated in the spring of the following year, Wedemeyer developed ambitious plans for a drive towards the coast by Chinese divisions, backed by American advisers as well as by the 28,000 other U.S. servicemen in the theatre. The original object was to open up a port in the Hongkong–Canton area early in 1946; these ideas had to be somewhat modified subsequently, but the Japanese themselves then facilitated matters by withdrawing towards the North China plain, with the Chinese following up behind them. The target of Wedemeyer's offensive was therefore switched to Port Bayard, and Chiang Kai-shek's forces were approaching this area of the coast when Japan surrendered.[109]

Yet for all Wedemeyer's efforts and late achievements, the fact remained that Washington had already relegated China to an altogether secondary position in the military effort against Japan. It was now the shortcomings, rather than the potential, of the Chinese Army that were emphasized. Wedemeyer himself, as the Japanese advanced with ease in the summer and autumn of 1944, had described Chiang Kai-shek's divisions as 'not organized, equipped and trained for modern war.' 'Psychologically', he added, the Chungking regime itself was 'not prepared to cope with the situation because of political intrigue, false pride and mistrust of leaders' honesty and motives.'[110] Donovan passed on to Roosevelt a similar O.S.S. report which stated that 'China's strength, which was never as great as generally believed, has seriously declined. We cannot', it concluded, 'expect much of the future.'[111] In turn, the President admitted to Churchill in December 1944: 'We can do very little to prepare China to conduct a worthwhile defence.'[112] The morale of America's own forces stationed in China was also declining, with an increasing number of unpleasant incidents taking place between them and the local population.[113] The whole strategic emphasis now lay elsewhere, in the Pacific; thus, in January, even the B 29s operating through the expensive Chengtu air-base were withdrawn and switched to the Marianas.[114] When the Chinese advance did eventually take place in the summer it was a pleasant surprise, but it came far too late to restore China to the place she had once occupied in American estimates and plans for the Far Eastern war.

As part of the effort to obtain a greater degree of military success in China, the idea was developed towards the end of 1944 by Colonel Barrett, leader of the Dixie mission to Yenan, by O.S.S. representatives and also Wedemeyer's Chief of Staff, Major General Robert B. McClure, of supplying U.S. arms to Communist Chinese forces, and of employing some of those forces under American direction in conjunction with the despatch of United States airborne troops to Communist territory and a possible amphibious landing in Shantung. Stimson in Washington was also hoping that some form of cooperation with Yenan's armies could be established, describing the Communists as 'the only live body of military men there is in China at the present.' Mao Tse-tung, for his part, indicated his readiness to collaborate. Chiang Kai-shek, however, refused outright to allow arms to be sent to Yenan, while Hurley, when he found out what had been going on, erupted into one of his well-known displays of anger, even publicly challenging General McClure to a fist fight, and refusing to speak to Wedemeyer for some days. Wedemeyer in turn promptly fell into line, instructing his officers to avoid all involvement in China's domestic politics and to 'support the Chinese National Government.' There were to be no further military negotiations with the Communists, moreover, unless approved beforehand by the Generalissimo.[115]

This incident highlighted a more fundamental matter, and one that would take more than a display of tantrums by Hurley to settle. The question was, what was the primary purpose of the United States presence in China: to help win the fight against Japan; to create a strong China; or to prop up Chiang Kai-shek? To the very end of the war, confusion was to surround this issue, thus continuing what we have seen to have been a long-standing characteristic of United States Far Eastern policies. That this was the case was scarcely the fault of the State Department, however, which, by 1945, was doing its best to supply a clear answer—an answer that did not bode well for Chiang Kai-shek. At the end of February, for example, the Department produced a policy paper for the guidance of the War Department and its commanders in the field. In this, a distinction was made between the short-term aim of unifying and utilizing China's resources against Japan, and the long-term one of helping to develop 'a united, democratically progressive and cooperative China.' Such a China, it was stated, would not necessarily be ruled by the Generalissimo.[116]

A similar note of reservation about Chiang Kai-shek was sounded in another paper that was prepared in April. Here, it was asserted that after the war 'it would be unwise to commit ourselves in any way to the present National Government', especially in terms of supplying it with arms, unless and until it could bring about unity and stability, achieve the support of the Chinese peoples, and establish an economy that could sustain a modern army and air force.[117] And again, in June, a major State Department survey of Far Eastern affairs described America's diplomatic tactics as being to maintain sufficient flexibility 'to permit cooperation with any other Chinese leadership which may give greater promise of achieving United States policy toward China.'[118] In a similar vein, Wedemeyer was instructed on 10 August that the United States would 'not support the Central Government of China in a fratricidal war', while the General himself had already come to the conclusion that Chiang Kai-shek, as well as the Communists, would have to be coerced in some way if a coalition government was ever to be brought about.[119]

Such a flexible approach as regards the position of the Kuomintang Government was in accordance with the advice that John Davies had continued to submit until Hurley had him removed from China: that the United States 'must not indefinitely underwrite a politically bankrupt regime.'[120] John Service and Raymond P. Ludden, colleagues of Davies, in China, were likewise recalling that support for Chiang Kai-shek was merely a means, not the end, of American policy, and that the Kuomintang and National Government were manifestly in decay.[121] It cannot be emphasized too strongly, however, that officials in Washington too, and not simply those in the field, had for some time been moving towards conclusions of this kind.[122] The Under Secretary of State, Grew, shared them; so did the Division of Chinese Affairs. Moreover, Grew saw to it that Hurley was informed accordingly,[123] while both the State-War-Navy Coordinating Committee and the Joint Chiefs of Staff endorsed the decision not to build up China's armed forces after the war until her Government had fulfilled the basic political and economic requirements that were deemed essential.[124] Roosevelt himself, indeed, who, in conversation with Stalin at Yalta blamed the Kuomintang more than the Communists for the failure to achieve unity in China, was still talking in private in February 1945 of going on working with both Chungking and Yenan. Prompted by Hurley, the President also helped ensure that the Communists were represented on the Chinese delegation to the San Francisco Conference.[125]*

If so many individuals holding senior positions within United States official circles were by this time advocating or at least contemplating a flexible policy towards Chiang Kai-shek's regime, where, then, did the confusion arise? The answer lies with two men above all: with Hurley, and—inevitably, one is tempted to say—with Roosevelt. In order to demonstrate how this was so, one has first to set out the acute differences of opinion that arose in this period among those Americans in Washington and China who were concerned with East Asian affairs. On one point, at least, there was a broad measure of agreement: that is, the intermediate aim of bringing about a reconciliation between Chungking and Yenan. As we have observed in the preceding stage of the war, this had become central to American hopes of improving China's contribution against Japan, building up her post-war position, and avoiding a Great Power confrontation over her internal political situation. Roosevelt, Hurley, Stettinius, Davies and others all believed, unlike Seymour on the British side, that some form of a settlement was still possible—and in this were almost certainly wrong. Roosevelt, for example, repeated this desire to see reconciliation come about to Hurley in November 1944. 'I wish you would tell the Generalissimo from me', he cabled, 'that a working arrangement between [him] and the North China forces will greatly expedite the objectives of throwing the Japanese out of China from my point of view and also that of the Russians . . . You can emphasize the word "Russians" to him.'[126]

Even when the difficulties that were involved for Chiang Kai-shek were

---

* The extent to which Chungking's stock had fallen can also be seen in the remarkable comment made by Admiral Harry E. Yarnell, former Commander of the U.S. Asiatic Fleet, to his fellow American delegates to the I.P.R. Hot Springs conference. 'In the event of a civil war [in China]', declared the unusually thoughtful and flexible Admiral, 'the U.S.S.R. would support the Communist element *as would the United States*.' (Minutes of 28 Oct. 1944, IPR Papers, box 362; emphasis added.)

appreciated, there remained the wish to see a settlement achieved, as Stettinius indicated to the President in January:

'Chiang', he wrote, 'is in a dilemma. A coalition would mean the end of conservative Kuomintang dominance and open the way for the more virile and popular Communists to extend their influence to the point perhaps of controlling the government. Failure to settle with the Communists, who are daily growing stronger, would invite danger of an eventual overthrow of the Kuomintang. Chiang could, it is felt, rise above party selfishness and anti-Communist prejudice to lead a coalition government which might bring new life to the war effort and assure unity after hostilities.'[127]

Already, however, we have entered an area of controversy. Were the Communists truly 'more virile and popular', as the Secretary of State, no less, avowed? Gauss for one, who after much provocation finally resigned as Ambassador in Chungking in the middle of November, thought that the odds did, indeed, lie in favour of Mao Tse-tung and his colleagues.[128] Davies was more emphatic still, being impressed, as was Service, by the popularity the Yenan regime had achieved, and echoing the judgment that had been put forward within the Foreign Office in London by Young in 1943: 'The Communists are in China to stay', wrote Davies in November 1944. 'And China's destiny is not Chiang's but theirs.'[129] Yet Hurley, on the other hand, rated the strength of the Communists far less highly and believed in the ability of Chiang and his Government to survive and even to strengthen their position. This basic difference of opinion helped to ensure that the new Ambassador was far less inclined than were Davies, Service, George Atcheson (Counsellor of Embassy) and others to attempt to coerce the Generalissimo into reaching an agreement with Yenan.[130]

This split within the ranks of American officials was reinforced by another clash of views, this time over the role which the Soviet Union was likely to play in Chinese affairs, Davies, for his part, rightly believed that the Chinese Communist movement was a genuinely domestic product and not a creature of Moscow's. Nevertheless he greatly feared that before long the situation in China could be 'ripe for Russian intervention', and that Soviet troops might well move into and dominate northern China. Therefore, he argued, the need was all the greater for the United States to win for itself the friendship of Mao Tse-tung and those with him, and to press Chiang Kai-shek to revise his own policies before it was too late.[131] From Moscow Harriman likewise warned that, if no accommodation had been reached in China before the Soviet Union entered the war against Japan, it had to be assumed that Stalin would back the Yenan regime; George Kennan, Counsellor of Embassy under Harriman, also emphasized that Soviet policy towards China would remain fluid and would aim at 'the achievement of maximum power with the minimum responsibility on portions of the Asiatic mainland lying beyond the Soviet border.'[132]

Hurley, on the other hand, retained the conviction which we have already seen him acquire during visits to Moscow: that Stalin would continue to support American policies in China and would acknowledge Chiang Kai-shek as the one leader of that country. Stalin helped by repeating his assurances to Hurley in April and to Hopkins when the latter visited Moscow in May. Hence, the Ambassador could again believe that Yenan was not, in fact, in a strong position, and would eventually have to come to terms with Chiang Kai-shek once the latter had concluded an agreement of his own with the Soviet Union.[133]

To both Service and Davies—the latter placing more emphasis than his friend and colleague on reasons of *realpolitik**—it was essential that the United States should respond speedily to the professions of friendship which Mao Tse-tung continued to make. These even included an offer, in January 1945, that he and Chou En-lai would go to Washington if necessary. 'Without the help of American influence', he told Service in March, 'real unity and democracy will have to be won [in China] by a long and bitter struggle.'[134] At least on one, related issue, however, there was some measure of agreement between the two junior diplomats and their Ambassador. For Davies and Service, like Hurley, continued to argue that to call the Yenan regime simply a 'Communist' one was misleading.[135] In a memorandum written in November 1944 and entitled 'How Red Are The Chinese Communists?', Davies described Mao Tse-tung, Chou En-lai and their comrades as realists and nationalists. 'They have now deviated so far to the right', he asserted, 'that they will return to the revolution only if driven to it by overwhelming pressure from domestic and foreign forces of reaction.' This judgment—which, as Davies himself was later to acknowledge, entailed an underestimation of the role played by ideology within the Chinese Communist movement—was repeated in essence after he had been transferred to Moscow, from where he described Yenan's immediate aim as being the achievement of 'agrarian democracy', with 'socialism' lying somewhere in the distance.[136]

On the other hand, Davies was of course correct in emphasizing the nationalist aspect of the movement, as Mao's writings on the Sinification of Marxism, for example, make clear.[137]† Another junior American diplomat who visited Yenan, Raymond Ludden, reported in a similar sense, describing the position of his hosts as being, not only 'liberal-democratic' but also 'soundly nationalistic'; Communism, added Ludden, was 'no more than an idea to be achieved in the distant future.'[138] Meanwhile Hurley, for his part, basing his opinion partly on the economic set-up that he found when he, too, went to Yenan, and again ignoring the fundamental role of ideology,[139] was

---

* Service, like Hudson in London, though in a more favourable sense, suggested a parallel between Mao Tse-tung's Yenan and Tito's position in Yugoslavia. (FRUS, 1944, China, 708.)

† Mao Tse-tung had also used the occasion of the dissolution of the Communist International in 1943 to emphasize the independent achievements of his own Party. (See Schram, *Mao Tse-tung*, 223.)

likewise informing Washington that 'the Communists are not in fact Communists, they are striving for democratic principles.' In April, indeed, he went so far as to endorse a report which described Yenan's aims as being to establish 'democratic capitalism' in the first instance, and a socialist state only in the long-term and by a process of evolution, not revolution.[140] Thus, the Ambassador, like others, failed to place his emphasis on the maximum as opposed to the intermediate, minimum Communist programme, and overlooked Mao's clear and open determination to maintain the ideological purity of his Party. (The contribution made towards this misunderstanding by American political culture has already been indicated.)[141]

In Washington itself, these views of Yenan held by men on the spot continued to be echoed by others in official circles, as well as by the press. Representative Mike Mansfield, for example, on his return from China, reported to the President that the Communists were 'more reformers than revolutionaries.' (He also described the Kuomintang as being 'more hated every day . . . corrupt and dictatorial.')[142] Stilwell, too, when he arrived back in Washington, told Stimson that the Communists were 'really the agricultural liberals of China' (Henry Wallaces, in other words; good Iowa men).[143] When the Military Intelligence Division of the War Department argued, in July 1945, that 'the Chinese Communists *are* Communists' and that they had 'a strong attachment to the Soviet Union', it was a minority view.[144] Roosevelt himself continued to the end to refer to 'the so-called Communists.'[145]

Nevertheless, there remained the wide differences of opinion between Hurley and his subordinates in China over the relative strengths and prospects of the two rival regimes and the position of the Soviet Union in that connection. In addition, there existed a more fundamental reason still for the strong element of confusion that was referred to above. Hurley interpreted his instructions as requiring him to sustain Chiang Kai-shek, come what may. Moreover, he maintained this position in the face of not only the advice of other American diplomats on the spot, but also the clear decision of the State Department itself, illustrated earlier, that there must be no unqualified and binding commitment to support the Generalissimo and the Kuomintang Government.

It was Roosevelt who allowed this dichotomy to continue. More important still, it was Roosevelt who, when finally faced with the necessity for choice, permitted Hurley to continue on his way unchecked, and, as he had done at the end of the Stilwell–Chiang crisis in the autumn of 1944, backed away from bringing to bear upon the Generalissimo the entire weight of American influence. In one sense, perhaps, it may not have mattered very much, in that the entire idea that the United States could decisively shape the course of events in China was an illusion. But to go on upholding Chiang Kai-shek in 1945—not even requiring him to cease taking repressive measures against innocuous, non-Communist parties outside the Kuomintang—was a fittingly weak and futile end to Roosevelt's war-time policies towards China.[146] Thereafter, Truman, too, supported Hurley's interpretation of American interests and lines of action—hardly surprising, given the daunting array of problems which the new President, totally unprepared by his dying predecessor, was called upon to face at short notice.

Just to what extent Roosevelt himself had emphasized to Hurley that Chiang Kai-shek must be supported is not entirely clear. The Ambassador's written instructions were brief, focussing on the tasks of promoting efficient and harmonious relations between the Generalissimo and Stilwell, and of facilitating the latter's command of Chinese forces.[147] But the President did not query Hurley's interpretation of his orders in this sense when the latter wrote back from China in October and December 1944. In fact, in a report prepared for Roosevelt in November by one of his aides, the Ambassador's version was accepted as being the correct one: that 'the President [had] told him, as he was leaving Washington, that his overall aim was to prevent a collapse in China and to keep China in the war. As part of a plan to do this, the President said that he had decided to sustain the leadership of Chiang Kai-shek.' Stettinius passed along to the White House a similar summary of his task that Hurley wrote in December, and again Roosevelt allowed it to stand.[148] Nor did the State Department at this important, early stage choose to resist the Ambassador's version of American policy, despite its own increasing emphasis on the need for flexibility. (The issue, it has been suggested, was not sufficiently developed at the time to encourage the staging of a confrontation, while the State Department may have been anxious to do nothing that would discourage Hurley from reporting to them, for a change, and not simply to the President direct. The weakness of Stettinius might also have been a contributory factor.)[149]

The outcome was a growing unrest on the part of the diplomats serving under Hurley's idiosyncratic leadership in China. Their views on the need to put pressure on Chiang Kai-shek to offer better terms to the Communists, on the desirability of avoiding being tied to him, and on the value of supplying aid to and cooperating over military matters with Yenan were summarized for Washington's benefit in February 1945 by Atcheson, who was acting as Chargé d'Affaires at the time during Hurley's absence, and who, in submitting these opinions, was behaving in an entirely proper fashion. Grew in turn endorsed Atcheson's approach to China's domestic problems when passing on one of the latter's cables to Roosevelt, for the State Department, too, was becoming increasingly alarmed at Hurley's 'intransigent and inflexible attitude', and could make no headway in discussions with him when the Ambassador visited Washington in March.[150] Hurley himself then made the situation worse still by expressing his sense of outrage at what Atcheson had done in his absence; he also voiced his belief that his subordinates were deliberately, as a result of personal political convictions, seeking to undermine his efforts—an accusation that he was to make in public after his resignation later in the year, by which time he had had Service and others, like Davies before them, 'Hurleyed' out of China, as the saying went.

This attitude on the part of the Ambassador was a self-serving and distorted one, and was matched by his readiness to help the Chungking regime in its attempts to stifle American press criticism of the Kuomintang.[151] Even so, he did have reason to believe that he was doing no more than carrying out the President's wishes as regards China's domestic affairs, and he was allowed to continue in this conviction when he called on Roosevelt in March. The latter knew what the State Department's line on the issue was, and he could have enforced it. Apparently he chose not to do so.[152] At the same time, he failed to adopt the alternative course of taking issue with Stettinius, Grew and their officials over the Department's increasing emphasis on the need for flexibility as regards Chiang Kai-shek and the Kuomintang. Hence, American policy remained essentially ambiguous.

If the ultimate responsibility for this state of affairs and for the Ambassador's approach thus lay with Roosevelt (and where its assumptions about the role that the Soviet Union would play were concerned, that approach was, indeed, in accord with what the President had sought to achieve over the Far East at Yalta), so, too, it was he who had in the first place chosen to entrust the complex and delicate negotiations in China that were involved to a man like Hurley. This, again, was a fitting commentary on the President's handling of his relations with that country. It has already been indicated that Hurley was not only insensitive and blustering, but a braggart and a liar, a man who, behind his dashing and vigorous exterior, had a central streak of weakness in him.[153] Nor was he the person to speak with care and precision, or to listen to the views of others. 'The trouble about talking to General Hurley', wrote the Head of the Foreign Office's Far Eastern Department, 'is that he branches off almost imperceptibly from one subject to another without allowing time for interjections.'[154] 'His discourse', observed Colonel Barrett, 'was by no means connected by any readily discernible pattern of thought.'[155]

Moreover, for all his carefully preserved appearance, Hurley was something of an unwitting buffoon, and came to be mocked both by Westerners and the Chinese themselves. (Some Kuomintang officials were in the habit of referring to him as 'The Second Big Wind.') For example, as a legacy of legal work he had once undertaken for that tribe, he was fond of emitting ear-piercing Choctaw warcries, and it was in this fashion, on stepping from his aeroplane, that he greeted the dignified Communist leaders who had hastily assembled to greet the Ambassador on his first visit to Yenan. Even being in more enclosed spaces did not deter the senior representative of the United States. Thus, the Dutch Ambassador in Chungking wrote home to his Foreign Minister:

'Is it part of "modern" trends in diplomacy to say of diplomatic colleagues of other countries that they are "idlers", or to utter Indian war-cries in the most unexpected places and times, especially at official receptions or at dinner in my house?!! Choctaw calls might have sounded well on the plains of Oklahoma in the days of Buffalo Bill. And in diplomatic and

Chinese official circles there is an appreciation of the need for innovation. But Hurley's performance reduces everyone to laughter.'[156]

Hurley with his war-cries and his offer to punch General McClure on the nose; Kung being loaded up with still more of Uncle Sam's ever-ready dollars and Hornbeck earnestly penning yet another tangled, illusion-based memorandum on America's destiny in the East; a stream of ignorant emissaries arriving in Chungking from Washington to add their quota of rhetoric and acquire instant expertise; Roosevelt rambling on to Stilwell and Davies at Cairo, unable or unwilling to give them the policy-guidance they so urgently needed: the Great Republic has known better moments in its foreign relations. What is more, those elements of genuine well-meaning and concern that, alongside hypocrisy, condescension and self-seeking, formed a part of the United States' response to China, deserved something more than this.

Mention of condescension recalls one further and important aspect of Hurley the man that should be set down before we turn back to examine the outcome of his mission in China. Long before the war, he had shown himself to be, in common with many of his contemporaries, a strong believer in the right of the white peoples of the world—or at least those of the United States—to a position of pre-eminence. As a public figure he had proved indifferent and insensitive to the condition and grievances of the blacks in his own country; over the question of the future of the Philippines he had revealed that he shared, in his biographer's words, 'many of the views of the turn-of-the-century imperialists.'[157] And now, when he arrived in China as the senior representative of the power that proclaimed itself to be her champion and admirer, he did so clad in the private conviction that he was one of an inherently superior species. 'Hurley', recalls Professor Lindsay, who met him in Yenan in 1945, 'despised the Chinese [and] asked whether I did not agree that they were hopeless people who must have a strong man on top to keep them in order.'[158]

During the first phase of his mission, beginning in September 1944, Hurley did seek to balance between Chungking and the Communists. This was possible for him because he managed to believe that there was 'very little difference' between the avowed principles of the rival regimes. Further encouragement was forthcoming when he was able, after discussions with Mao Tse-tung, to get the Yenan leaders to agree (with a few amendments) to a five-point basis for reconciliation that he had personally drafted. This document envisaged the unification of China's military forces, the establishment of a coalition government, legal recognition of the Communist Party, and the institution of political freedoms—all those freedoms being couched in American political terminology. Hurley thereupon endorsed what Mao had agreed to, and when Chungking rejected the proposals outright, he blamed Kuomintang extremists for the failure, even describing them privately at one point as 'fascists'. By January, however, the Ambassador had come to see Mao Tse-tung as a trickster, and it was now Chungking's readiness to reach an agreement which he chose to believe in and to emphasize. When the Communists then broke off negotiations, he also blamed their intransigence on the prospect of American military aid which had been held out to them by General McClure and others.

Hurley's own position over such matters was by now very clear, and indeed in April he made it public: no military assistance should be provided to anyone in China unless Chiang Kai-shek agreed to it; nor should there be any Stilwell-like attempt to bring strong pressure to bear upon the Generalissimo. Thereafter, as the deadlock between the two sides continued, the Ambassador increasingly placed the responsibility upon Yenan; his staff, on the other hand, together with the Treasury's representative in Chungking, pointed to Chiang Kai-shek's determination not to surrender any of his power as being at the heart of the trouble—a judgment the correctness of which was demonstrated by Chiang's repressive policies, mentioned above, towards not only the Communists but other, minor parties that possessed no military power with which to threaten the position of the Kuomintang. Meanwhile, Hurley's growing identification with the Chungking Government led in turn to public attacks being made upon him by the Communists from their North-Western stronghold.[159]

The details of each proposal and counter-proposal which passed between Chungking and Yenan in this period need not be recounted here. What Chiang Kai-shek was demanding on his side was the incorporation of Communist forces under his overall command, in return for which some vaguely defined form of constitutional rule would be set up. But that new political structure plainly was not going to alter, so far as the Generalissimo was concerned, the dominant position of the Kuomintang; nor was it intended to include a coalition government. (Even the superficially attractive idea of summoning a People's Congress, which Chiang proposed, was designed in such a way as to maintain Kuomintang supremacy.) The Communists, on the other hand, aware of their growing strength* and the popularity of their programme, would accept nothing less than a genuine coalition government.[160]

By August, American hopes of bringing the two sides together had greatly diminished. Vincent of the State Department, for example, told a British colleague early in that month that the prospect of a compromise agreement 'had now receded almost to vanishing point, and that in the end a showdown was inevitable, the result of which would depend to a great extent on the Russian attitude towards Yenan.'[161] Indeed, what the Soviet Union might do in China was by now causing much disquiet among

---

* Mao, in April 1945, claimed that his army now numbered 910,000 and his militia over 2,200,000. The Communists were also poised to take over some of the key strategic areas of China. Gittings (*China and the World*, 63) gives the following figures for the Communist strength:

	1937	1945
Communist armies:	92,000	880,000
Population of border areas under Communist control:	5 million	80 million.

American officials. The idea that Moscow might have sinister intentions in this regard was also aired in the press, as were fears of a Soviet-American clash over China and hopes that some kind of accord between the two powers could be reached that would prevent such a grim outcome.[162] (Within the American delegation to the I.P.R. Hot Springs Conference, for instance, it was suggested that there was an increasing danger of China's becoming 'the Spain of the Far East.')[163]

Much depended, or so it seemed in Washington, on what would occur between Chungking and Moscow when the Chinese learned of the terms for Russian entry into the Pacific War which Roosevelt and Stalin had agreed upon at Yalta. In this connection it is worth noting that Hurley, who was later to denounce what had been done by the President at that Conference as a betrayal of China, made no objection at the time, when Roosevelt put him in the picture, and accepted the need to delay before informing Chiang Kai-shek of what had occurred.[164] As it was, it was not until early in June that Truman passed on the Yalta terms to T. V. Soong, telling him that he himself stood by what his predecessor had agreed.[165]

In the light of what the Soviet Union could seize if she wished, the news may not have caused too great a shock in Chungking; there is reason to believe, however, that it did arouse consternation in Yenan, where the Communist leaders had earlier assured Davies that 'they were positive that [Soviet intervention against Japan] would not involve Russian demands for concessions or special rights in Manchuria.'[166] Chiang Kai-shek's Government, for its part, received soon afterwards a statement of the terms on which the U.S.S.R. was prepared to conclude with it a treaty of friendship and alliance. There followed, from the end of June until the middle of August, lengthy negotiations in Moscow between T. V. Soong and the Soviet authorities.[167]

Washington, which had already sought to disclaim any desire to act as arbiter between the Chinese and the Russians, now found itself placed in an extremely awkward position. Not unreasonably, Soong wished to know what had been intended by such Yalta phrases as 'preeminent Soviet interests' and 'status quo'. Yet he was told by Grew that no interpretation of the agreement Roosevelt and Stalin had drawn up could be provided; indeed, under the Rooseveltian system of conducting foreign affairs, the State Department did not even possess a copy of the document in question, nor records of the conversations that had led up to its signing, while Truman, of course, had not been involved in any way at the time.[168] The best that Soong could obtain before he left for Moscow was the new President's assurance that Stalin, in conversation with Hopkins and Harriman, had again been emphasizing his respect for China's sovereignty in Manchuria and elsewhere, and that he had promised to support Chiang Kai-shek's leadership and promote the unification of his country.[169]

During July, however, concern in Washington grew as the unhappy Soong, not dealing now with effusively naïve Americans, found himself pressed by Stalin to agree, for example, that an acceptance of 'the status quo' in Outer Mongolia would entail the recognition by China of that country's independence; that the Manchurian railways should be Soviet-owned and -managed (though jointly operated); and that Soviet military control should be established over all of the old Russian Kwantung Peninsula leased area, including Dairen. These last two demands clearly went beyond what Roosevelt had envisaged at Yalta, even though they could nevertheless be fitted within a rendering of such elastic phrases as those referring to 'preeminent interests' and to 'the former rights of Russia' that had been violated by Japan in 1904. Moreover, Harriman, and above all Stimson, the latter treasuring the memory of his celebrated endeavours in 1932, were now urging upon Truman that there must be no endangering of the sacred American right to an Open Door in Manchuria—an emphasis on the interests of the United States, rather than of China, which was wholly consistent with past American policies. 'Again and again', recorded Stimson, '[I warned the President] to be absolutely sure that the Russians did not block off our trade by their control over the Chinese Eastern Railway.'[170]

Truman, therefore, did now take a few steps towards intervening, and at Potsdam, after talking to Stalin about the matter, felt able to assure Stimson that he had managed to safeguard the Open Door in Manchuria. (Stalin had also promised Hopkins in May that he would respect this American interest, a pledge which Washington later requested him to put in writing.) The President, in addition, reminded Chiang Kai-shek on 23 July that the Chinese Government were not required to go beyond the terms that had been agreed at Yalta; finally, on 5 August, he sent a message to Stalin, indicating that he believed that Soong had met those terms by the offers he had already put forward and asking that no arrangements which might affect American interests—for example in Dairen—should be concluded without referring the matter to Washington beforehand.[171]

Further than this, however, the President felt he could not go. Thus, Chiang Kai-shek's suggestion that the United States should itself participate in the use of Port Arthur as a naval base, and in the Sino-Soviet agreement as a whole, was rejected. As for Britain, whom the Generalissimo also wanted to see brought into the agreement to help offset the pressure of the Russians, she was not consulted by the United States over this question, and it was left to Attlee to raise the matter on 6 August, when he asked if London and Washington should coordinate their views on how the Yalta agreement ought to be implemented.

The entire episode, indeed, underlined again the strength of the Soviet position as a genuine East Asian power, together with the limitations—partly self-imposed, and long having been a feature of her involvement in Far Eastern affairs—which faced the United States, despite her current military triumphs in the Pacific. Thus, although Byrnes was anxious to see a Sino-Soviet agreement concluded before the Soviet Union entered the war against Japan, both he and Truman believed, as Leahy recorded it in the middle of July, that the treaty in question 'can only be reached through radical concessions by China, and that Stalin will enter the war whether or not such concessions are made and will thereafter satisfy Soviet demands regardless of what the Chinese attitude may be.'[172] On the mainland of Asia, in other words, no alternative could be seen in Washington to accepting that the Soviet Union would play a major role, the recognition of which had already formed one of the bases of the Yalta agreement.

As it turned out, Chiang Kai-shek had good reason to be satisfied with the terms which Stalin finally agreed to accept on the night of 13–14 August —doubly so in that Soviet forces had already swarmed over the Japanese in Manchuria.[173] Trouble for Chungking arose, not so much from the new treaty—which included pledges by Moscow to withdraw its troops from Manchuria within three months of the ending of hostilities, to avoid interfering in China's internal affairs, and to give its support there solely to the National Government of Chiang Kai-shek—but from subsequent Soviet actions. Indeed, it was again Yenan that had most reason to be concerned at the nature of the Sino-Soviet understanding, in that it appeared to indicate that Stalin was still hedging his bets over Chinese internal political rivalries.[174*]

The treaty between Moscow and Chungking, moreover, was seen in the Western press, as well as by some American officials,[175] as being a triumph for Chiang Kai-shek, 'Russia has clearly disowned the Chinese Communists', declared the *Manchester Guardian*; the Central Government, wrote *The Times*, was now in 'an overwhelmingly strong position', while the *New York Times* assured its readers that the Soviet promises had 'pulled the rug from under the Chinese Communists.' At the same time, the treaty was hailed as what the *New York Times* called 'a victory for peace as great as any scored on the battlefield', with the U.S.S.R. 'becoming a partner in America's traditional policy toward China.'[176]

With the Soviet aspect of the question apparently well on its way to being settled, American expectations of a healthy future for China could revive. Yet nothing could disguise the extent to which those expectations, so extravagant not long before, had been shaken by the time the war approached its end. We have already seen how this was so in the military sphere—one consequence being an increasing discrepancy between Service opinion in Washington and Hurley's frantic efforts to enable China to make a greater contribution against Japan. The same was true of Sino-American political relations. In China itself, there were growing signs of mutual resentment and even bitterness between the two peoples. (One minor but nevertheless significant incident involved Brigadier General Lyle H. Miller of the U.S. Marine Corps, who, at a Sino-American dinner party in Chungking, delivered a speech which included scathing remarks about Chiang Kai-shek

---

* Other points in the Sino-Soviet agreement included: recognition of the independence of Outer Mongolia, following a plebescite there; Chinese chairmen but Soviet managers to be appointed for both the S.M.R. and C.E.R.; Soviet military authority in Dairen to be exercised in time of war only; Port Arthur to be used jointly by the two states, though with a Soviet predominance there; and Chungking's representatives to be allowed into Manchuria while Soviet troops were operating in that territory.

and his wife and references to China as 'a twelfth-rate power', as well as demands for 'sing-song girls' to be produced.) Hurley, too, after an initial honeymoon period with T. V. Soong, revealed something of his low regard for the Chinese in general by referring to the latter as 'a crook'.[177] Strongly critical comments about the Generalissimo's Government also continued to be published in the American press by writers like Harold Isaacs, Brooks Atkinson and Theodore White, and in journals such as the I.P.R.'s *Far Eastern Survey*, now under the editorship of an outspoken former Foreign Service officer, Lawrence Salisbury.[178]

Roosevelt himself, his direct communications with Chiang Kai-shek now far less frequent, tended during his last months to speak of China in somewhat cool, even at times slighting, terms. 'Three generations of education and training would be required before China could become a serious factor', he told Churchill and the Combined Chiefs of Staff at Malta, while during one of the plenary sessions at Yalta he proposed that the discussion should concentrate on the major subject of general peace aims 'rather than [on] Dakar and China.'[179] The significance of the Far Eastern agreement he concluded with Stalin on that occasion, without consulting or informing Chiang Kai-shek, has already been indicated.

Meanwhile others with a special interest in the politics of the post-war world were likewise looking doubtfully at the role that China might play. In this respect, it is interesting, for example, to find John Foster Dulles, the future Republican Secretary of State, who before long was to bow readily before the storm of pro-Chiang Kai-shek fantasies brought on by Senator Joe McCarthy, the 'China lobby' and their like, suggesting privately in March 1945 that some means should be provided whereby permanent members of the U.N. Security Council could be deprived of that status if, as might well be the case with China, he thought, they proved not to be one of the 'great nations' after all.[180] At the other end of the political spectrum from Dulles, a wealthy Communist or crypto-Communist member of the American I.P.R. delegation to Hot Springs, Frederick V. Field, spoke in private to his fellow-delegates in somewhat similar terms, describing the Dumbarton Oaks U.N. scheme as being based on 'a false premise, as China is not in fact a major power. The future security of the United States', he continued, 'depends on a strong and united China as the pivot of any successful security machinery in the Pacific. Yet this pivot does not now exist. This presents us with a very serious dilemma to which I wish someone would suggest an answer.'[181]

Mention of Dulles, Field and the I.P.R. has already served as a reminder, however, that American disappointments over China, both in 1944–45 and in the post-war years, were not to be followed by a cool reappraisal and readjustment of the country's policies, however much the State Department (as indicated, for example, by the publication of the *China White Paper*) might wish it. Various factors—not least the emotional and illusory nature of the attitudes of a good many Americans towards China, together with what Richard Hofstadter has termed 'the paranoid style' in United States politics—would ensure that the shock of the revealingly-termed 'loss' of China to the Communists, of the discovery that the U.S.A. could not impose its will within that country, and of the belated realization that a grateful protégé was not going to be found there after all, would come to be explained for many by that crudest of means: a conspiracy theory.

Already, during the period now under consideration, there were fore-shadowings of this. Alfred Kohlberg, for example, a member of the I.P.R., was publicly accusing that body of following a 'Communist line'. Hurley, for his part, was, as we have seen, beginning to build up in his mind the picture which he was soon to make public, of disloyal American diplomats who were working for the downfall of Chiang Kai-shek and, indirectly if not more, in the interests of Communism in East Asia.[182] In June, following a raid by the O.S.S. in March, charges were brought against Philip Jaffe, editor of *Amerasia* (a journal which Field had helped to found), together with the diplomat John S. Service and others, on the grounds that classified official documents had been passed to the *Amerasia* office.[183]*

Jaffe was to plead guilty. Service, on the other hand, was exonerated in August 1945, and was cleared again in several subsequent investigations, both within and outside the State Department. Like John Davies, however, Service was to be dismissed from the Foreign Service as the McCarthy hysteria reached its height, Dulles being content to sacrifice his officials as the need arose.

Meanwhile, the views of China that were entertained in American official circles as the Pacific war came to an end had in general moved some way towards those which had long been heard in Whitehall. Considerable Anglo-American contrasts remained, of course, including that between the continuing embroilment of the United States in Chinese affairs and Britain's position of relative detachment. Nor, as we have seen, were American suspicions of British attitudes towards China greatly diminished. Moreover, a not dissimilar pattern was emerging in the related field of colonial affairs, only in this case it was Britain which was the more involved of the two Western powers. Here, too, there was a degree of convergence of the policies of London and Whitehall. Here, too, nevertheless, American distrust of Britain retained much of its strength.

* The *Amerasia* case helped to swing Mao Tse-tung towards adopting an openly anti-American stance. Jaffe, for his part had prepared an unexpurgated—and hence revealingly reactionary and anti-Western—translation of Chiang Kai-shek's *China's Destiny*. (See Schram, *Mao Tse-tung*, 231.)

Notes to Chapter Twenty-Six

1 See above, 170.
2 Officer despatch, 24 Feb. 1945, ADEA, A1066/P45/136/2.
3 FRUS, 1944, China, 692, 745; FRUS, 1945, VI, 40, 107; Officer Diary, 29 Dec. 1944; Buhite, *Hurley* (hereafter, *Buhite*), 239ff.

4 FRUS, 1945, VII, 731.
5 *Davies*, 368, 416.
6 FRUS, 1944, China, 667, 695, 724; FRUS, 1945, VII, 155.
7 *Morgenthau Diary, China*, II, 1457.
8 E.g. FO 371, F5800/993/61; Somerville Diary, 23 Jan., 9 and 10 March 1945.
9 Wedemeyer–McClure–Chiang Kai-shek record, 13 Jan. 1945, and Wedemeyer–Chiang comments, 26 Dec. 1944, Wedemeyer Papers, box 7; *Romanus and Sutherland*, III, 158ff.; Wedemeyer, *Wedemeyer Reports!*, 281.
10 Miles staff conference, 20 March 1945, Naval Group China files, USNOA.
11 FRUS, 1944, China, 700; FRUS, 1945, VII, 35.
12 FO 371, AN3859/20/45.
13 *Leahy*, 338.
14 FRUS, 1945, VII, 2.
15 FRUS, Malta and Yalta, 352.
16 FRUS, Berlin, I, 41.
17 *Stettinius*, 2 Jan. 1945.
18 *Leahy*, 368; *Moran*, 11 Feb. 1945; FO 371, F3171/1147/10; *Buhite*, 244; Baruch, *The Public Years*, 319, 321.
19 SWNCC 111, SFE, 111, 14 May 1945.
20 FRUS, 1945, VII, 120; *Buhite*, 246.
21 Material in Wedemeyer Papers, box 7.
22 J. Amery, *Approach March* (London, 1973), 418.
23 FO 371, F621 and 3625/12/10; F1926/57/10; material in files 46220–1, 46223; FRUS, 1945, VII, 1258ff.
24 Executive Cttee., 17 Oct. 1944, Ch.A.
25 FRUS, 1945, VI, 556ff.; see FRUS, 1945, VII, 294.
26 FRUS, Malta and Yalta, 352; FRUS, Berlin, I, 858; FRUS, 1945, VII, 93, 249; JCS, 4 Feb. 1945, RG 218.
27 FO 371, F804/186/10.
28 Ibid, F458/186/10.
29 FEC, 21 Dec. 1944, CAB 96/5.
30 FO 371, F1085, 1156/186/10; see F1331/409/10.
31 Ibid, F234, 1415, 1417 and 1565/127/61; F1113/11/61; material in ibid, file 41685 and in PREM 3, 159/12; COS, 6 April 1945, CAB 79/31; FRUS, 1945, VII, 329.
32 Minutes of 6 April 1945, CAB 99/30; Williams, *A Prime Minister Remembers*, 60.
33 FO 371, F454 and 3063/36/10; F1288/409/10. For a study of the 'China lobby' in Washington, see ibid, AN4360/20/45.
34 E.g. ibid, F4684/16/10; AN3658 and 4213/20/45; F5799/34/10.
35 Minutes of 6 April 1945, CAB 99/30.
36 Minutes of 1 Feb. 1945, CAB 99/31.
37 FO 371, F409 and 1331/409/10; briefing paper, 30 March 1945, PREM 3, 159/12.
38 E.g. FO 371, F1441/19/10.
39 PREM 3, 159/12; FEC, 29 Nov. and 21 Dec. 1944, CAB 96/5. U.S. Lend Lease to China (excluding loans and credits) during the war amounted to $800 million; that of Britain to China was $44 million. *Young*, 403.
40 Hansard, HC Deb, 406, cols. 226ff.
41 FO 371, material in files 41149, 41576, 41605, 41618, 46129, 46136, 46170, 46178–9, 46181, 46184, 46217–8, 46232; Wilkinson to Sansom, 28 Dec. 1944 and 9 March 1945, Wilkinson Papers.
42 FO 371, F1331/409/10.
43 Memo., 30 March 1945, PREM 3, 159/12.
44 FEC 28 Feb. 1945, CAB 96/5; FO 371, F5799/34/10; F4608 and 4921/120/10; F2781/12/10; F4171/186/10.
45 FO 371, F4608/120/10; F1534/13/10; UE615/169/53; UE2189/813/53.
46 FE(E) (45), 2, CAB 96/8; FEC, 21 Dec. 1944, 28 Feb. 1945, CAB 96/5; FO 371, F5643/120/10; F1853 and 2209/12/10.

47 Executive Cttee., 17 Oct. 1944 to 18 Sept. 1945, passim, Ch.A. On problems involving the registration of foreign companies under new regulations in China, see FO 371, file 46178.
48 FO 371, F6046/16/10; F1482/12/10; F4162 and 6278/13/10; APW memo. (45) 51, CAB 87/69.
49 FO 371, files 46182 and 46263; Executive Cttee., 3 May 1945, Ch.A.
50 Dalton Diary, 3 April 1945.
51 Ibid, 27 March 1945.
52 FO 371, UE615/169/53.
53 Ibid, F5737/34/10; F5558 159/10; F5435/3682/10; F3723/186/10; and see e.g. Times, 2 Jan. 1945.
54 FO 371, F6140/34/10.
55 Ibid, and F1181/186/10.
56 Observer, 25 Feb. 1945.
57 FO 371, F387 and 439/186/10; F136/136/10.
58 Ibid, F4757/4757/10; material in file 46266.
59 Ibid, F1761/186/10; material in files 46142, 46152, 46156–8.
60 Minutes of 2 Feb. 1945, CAB 99/31.
61 COS, 3 Jan. 1945, CAB 79/28; de Wiart to Ismay, 21 and 28 Nov., 1 Dec. 1944, PREM 3, 149/2; de Wiart to Ismay, 6 Nov. 1944 and WSC to Chennault, 7 Jan. 1945, PREM 3, 159/14.
62 COS, 16 Jan. 1945, CAB 79/28; FO 371, F387 and 439/186/10. Dening also held that Britain should not rush to the aid of China at the expense of her own interests elsewhere. FO 371, F4794/34/10.
63 FO 371, material in files 46196–7; F5039/5039/10; COS, 25 May 1945, CAB 79/34.
64 FO 371, F5347/120/10; F4950/485/23; material in file 46196; Somerville Diary, 27 Feb. 1945; SEAC War Diary, 29 Jan. 1945; COS, 14 March 1945, CAB 79/30.
65 FO 371, F1954/88/10; F4153 and 4449/1147/10; Amery, Approach March, 425; Sweet-Escott, Baker Street Irregular, 252.
66 FO 371, F2577/127/61.
67 COS, 21 Feb. 1945, CAB 79/29.
68 FEC, Econ. Sub-Cttee. memos., CAB 96/8; Executive Cttee., 17 Oct. 1944, Ch.A.; Donnison, cap. VIII.
69 COS, 21 and 29 June 1945, CAB 79/35; ibid, 10, 13, 14, 15, 17, 20, 21 Aug. 1945, CAB 79/37; Donnison, 150ff. and cap. XI; Allen, The End Of The War In Asia, 251ff.
70 WP(44)697 (CAB 66/58); WP(44)730 (CAB 66/59); CP (45)88 (CAB 66/67); FO 371, material in files 46121–3, 46201.
71 FO 371, F4220/4220/10; Dorman-Smith to Caroe, 22 May 1945, Dorman-Smith Papers, E215/13. For China's continuing interest in Southeast Asia, see FO 371, F3274/186/10.
72 McGuire memo., 3 Dec. 1944, ADEA, A989/44/600/5/1/7; Bruce despatch, 22 Nov. 1944, ibid, A989/43/150/5/1/2; Lovink cable, 18 Nov. 1944, NFM, Political Reports, China, 3b; Lovink to van Kleffens, 6 Feb. 1945, ibid, Political Reports, Chungking, 20.
73 FO 371, F5799/34/10; F4098/1776/10; F1690/35/10; material in files 46187–9.
74 Ibid, F4283 and 4719/186/10; material in file 46227.
75 Ibid, F6140/34/10.
76 Ibid, F5126/159/10.
77 Paper of 30 March 1945, PREM 3, 159/12.
78 News Chronicle, 2 Jan. 1945; Times, 25 Jan. 1945.
79 FO 371, F35 and 102/35/10.
80 Ibid, F5126/159/10.
81 de Wiart to Ismay, 6 Sept. 1945, Attlee Papers (University College), box 5; Cab, 11 Jan. 1945, CAB 65/51; de Wiart, Happy Odyssey, 270.
82 FO 371, F4857/34/10; F4609/159/10.
83 E.g. ibid, F261 and 4479/35/10.
84 Ibid, F5710 and 6119/34/10.

85 Ibid, F1085/186/10.
86 Ibid, F6002/159/10.
87 Ibid, F2251/35/10; F3065/36/10.
88 E.g. ibid, F102/35/10.
89 Minutes of 6 April 1945, CAB 99/30.
90 See Steele, *The American People and China*, 239.
91 *Chicago Tribune*, 14 Dec. 1944.
92 E.g. *New York Times* and *New York Herald Tribune*, 1 Jan. 1945.
93 FRUS, 1944, China, 1086–7; FRUS, 1945, VII, 57, 1206ff., 1332, 1337.
94 See e.g. State Dpt. to Hopkins, 6 Dec. 1944, Roosevelt Papers, PSF box 36. In its Annual Report for 1944–5, 'New Horizons for China Trade', the China-America Council of Commerce and Industry (see above, 313) remained evangelically confident. Declaring that 'it is important to us that the basis of China's industrialization be the free-enterprise system', the report described the Chinese as 'awake to the promises of modern industrial civilization . . . , industrious and kindly.' It also expected vital support for American enterprises in China, springing from 'the minds and hearts of thousands of Chinese who, having been educated in American universities, have gone back to China to become leaders in China's government, industry, arts, sciences and professions. They are', it concluded, 'the builders of tomorrow!'
95 FRUS, 1945, VII, 1351.
96 FRUS, 1944, China, 1154; FRUS, 1945, VII, 1425ff.
97 FO 371, F2513 and 4118/334/10.
98 FRUS, 1944, China, 249, 261, 287.
99 Between Sept. 1944 and Sept. 1945, UCR also sent out $11½ million. UCR Papers, box 78.
100 FRUS, 1945, VII, 1063, 1081–3.
101 *Morgenthau Diary, China*, II, 1425, 1486, 1520, 1541.
102 Donovan to HST, 12 May 1945, Truman Papers, White House central files, OSS.
103 See FRUS, 1945, VII, 1056; Young, cap. XVIII.
104 *Morgenthau Diary, China*, II, 1543ff.
105 Ibid, 1626, 1683; FRUS, 1945, VII, 1091.
106 *Morgenthau Diary, China*, II, 1596; FRUS, 1945, VII, 1095.
107 Donovan to FDR, 12 Dec. 1944, Roosevelt Papers, PSF box 168; Miles, *A Different Kind of War*, 434, 454.
108 FRUS, 1945, VII, 34.
109 JCS, 13 March 1945, RG 218; material in Wedemeyer Papers, box 2; *Romanus and Sutherland*, III, 5ff., 19, 333ff., 386ff.; material in PREM 3, 90/4.
110 Wedemeyer to Marshall, 4 Dec. 1944, OPD, Exec. file 1, item 29; see Wedemeyer to Marshall, 6 Nov. 1944, Wedemeyer Papers, box 1.
111 Donovan to FDR, 17 Nov. 1944, Roosevelt Papers, PSF box 168.
112 FDR to WSC, 10 Dec. 1944, PREM 3, 472.
113 *Romanus and Sutherland*, III, 390.
114 Ibid, 161ff. More tonnage was being flown over the Hump, however. Ibid, 12.
115 Ibid, 72–5, 249ff.; Barrett typescript, 'The Dixie Mission', 86, Barrett Papers; *Davies*, 383, Stimson Diary, 14 Dec. 1944; FRUS, 1945, VII, 172; *Buhite*, 190.
116 *Romanus and Sutherland*, III, 337; FRUS, 1945, VII, 37, 116; and see FRUS, Malta and Yalta, 356.
117 FRUS, 1945, VII, 74; see also San Francisco briefing paper, Roosevelt Papers, PSF box 6.
118 FRUS, 1945, VI, 556ff.
119 *Romanus and Sutherland*, III, 393.
120 FRUS, 1944, China, 695.
121 FRUS, 1945, VII, 217 and e.g. *U.S. and China*, 567ff.
122 E.g. FRUS, 1944, China, 792.
123 FRUS, 1945, VII, 249; Grew to FDR, 2 March 1945, Roosevelt Papers, PSF box 36; J. S. Service, *The Amerasia Papers* (Berkeley, 1971), 119ff.; *Buhite*, 212.

124 SWNCC, 83/13, China.
125 FRUS, Malta and Yalta, 766; FRUS, 1945, VII, 283, 307; Service, *Amerasia Papers*, 125; Snow, *Journey To The Beginning*, 348.
126 FDR to Hurley, 17 Nov. 1944, Roosevelt Papers, MR box 11.
127 Stettinius to FDR, 4 Jan. 1945, ibid, PSF box 36.
128 Morgenthau Diary, 27 Nov. 1944.
129 FRUS, 1944, China, 670.
130 See e.g. FRUS, 1945, VII, 242.
131 Ibid, 155, 333.
132 FRUS, 1944, China, 737; FRUS, 1945, VII, 341–2.
133 FRUS, 1945, VII, 338; *Sherwood*, 902.
134 FRUS, 1945, VII, 272. See FRUS, 1944, China, 615, and B. Tuchman, 'If Mao Had Come To Washington', *Foreign Affairs*, Oct. 1972.
135 For Service's subsequent emphasis to the contrary, see his *Amerasia Papers*, 165.
136 FRUS, 1944, China, 669; FRUS, 1945, VII, 333; *Davies*, 362, 371.
137 See e.g. Schram, *The Political Thought of Mao Tse-tung*, 164, 171.
138 FRUS, 1945, VII, 158.
139 See e.g. *Tang Tsou*, 183ff.
140 FRUS, 1945, VII, 205, 223, 350.
141 See above, 438.
142 FRUS, 1945, VII, 2.
143 Stimson Diary, 13 Dec. 1944.
144 L. van Slyke (ed.), *The Chinese Communist Movement: A Report of the United States War Department* (Stanford, 1968), 1, 221.
145 E.g. FDR to Carlson, 15 Nov. 1944, Roosevelt Papers, PSF box 36; FRUS, Malta and Yalta, 766.
146 See *Davies*, 428.
147 *U.S. and China*, 71.
148 'The President and U.S. Aid to China', Roosevelt Papers, MR box 165; Stettinius to FDR, 26 Dec. 1944, ibid, PSF box 36.
149 FRUS, 1944, China, 215, 745; Service, *Amerasia Papers*, 102.
150 *U.S. and China*, 87, 92; FRUS, 1945, VII, 242, 254, 348; *Morgenthau Diary, China*, II, 1457.
151 See *Shewmaker*, 174ff.; White and Jacoby, *Thunder Out Of China*, 231.
152 FRUS, 1945, VII, 345, 350, 406; Leahy Diary, 16 March 1945; *Burns*, 590. For a full development of the conspiracy theory over China and U.S. diplomats, see A. Kubek, *How The Far East Was Lost* (Chicago, 1963).
153 See above, 551–2.
154 FO 371, F2213/127/61.
155 Barrett, 'The Dixie Mission', 60, Barrett Papers.
156 Lovink to van Kleffens, 2 Feb. 1945, NFM, Political Reports, Chungking, 20. See Morgenthau Diary, 1 March 1945.
157 *Buhite*, 38, 69ff.
158 Lindsay, *The Forgotten War* (no pagination).
159 *U.S. and China*, 74; FRUS, 1944, China, 659–66; Hurley–FDR correspondence, Oct.–Dec. 1944, Roosevelt Papers, MR box 11; *Morgenthau Diary, China*, II, 1379, 1416ff.; FRUS, Malta and Yalta, 346; FRUS, 1945, VII, 154, 172, 223, 242, 300, 406, 426, 433; *Davies*, 364ff.; Schram, *The Political Thought of Mao Tse-tung*, 400.
160 See *U.S. and China*, 74ff.
161 FO 371, F4866/186/10.
162 E.g. *San Francisco Examiner*, 24 July 1945; *New York Herald Tribune*, 26 April and 20 June 1945; *New York Times*, 6 July 1945; *Lattimore*, 133.
163 Minutes of 28 Oct. 1944, IPR Papers, box 362.
164 FRUS, 1945, VII, 338; *Buhite*, 204ff.
165 FRUS, 1945, VII, 896.
166 Ibid, 279.

167 FRUS, Berlin, I, 861; FRUS, 1945, VII, 900, 911ff.
168 FRUS, 1945, VII, 898, 906, 914, 934.
169 Grew, *Turbulent Era*, II, 1466; *Buhite*, 224. See FRUS, 1945, VII, 101; *Sherwood*, 902–3. For Hopkins' optimism see Morgenthau Diary, 20 June 1945.
170 FRUS, 1945, VII, 943–4, 950; Stimson Diary, 15 July 1945.
171 FRUS, 1945, VII, 950, 955.
172 Ibid, 903, 907, 956–7; Leahy Diary, 17 July 1945.
173 *U.S. and China*, 120.
174 FRUS, 1945, VII, 971.
175 Snow, *Journey To The Beginning*, 361.
176 *Times*, 17 Aug. 1945; *Manchester Guardian*, 27 Aug. 1945; *New York Times*, 28 Aug. 1945; *New York Herald Tribune*, 28 Aug. 1945.
177 See e.g. FRUS, 1944, China, 163, 171; Donovan to FDR, 27 Oct. 1944, Roosevelt Papers, PSF box 167; Morgenthau Diary, 8 Dec. 1944.
178 See *Shewmaker*, 158ff.
179 Minutes of 2 Feb. 1945, CAB 99/31; FRUS, Malta and Yalta, 624.
180 Dulles to Vandenberg, 5 March 1945, Dulles Papers, box 3.
181 Minutes of 28 Oct. 1944, IPR Papers, box 362.
182 See *U.S. and China*, 581.
183 See Service, *Amerasia Papers*, 35ff.; *O.S.S.*, 277; Thomas, *I.P.R.*, 36ff., 51; E. J. Kahn, *The China Hands* (New York, 1975).

CHAPTER TWENTY-SEVEN

SOUTHEAST ASIA AND THE FUTURE OF EMPIRES

Campaign issues in Southeast Asia

THE MOUNTING successes achieved within S.E.A.C. in this period have been outlined in an earlier chapter. Even now, however the Theatre was far from obtaining all the resources it required, largely as a result of military developments in Europe. In October 1944, Mountbatten's plans received a severe setback when operation 'Dracula', an amphibious assault on Rangoon, had to be postponed owing to the inability of the Chiefs of Staff in London to free the necessary forces from fronts in the West.[1] It was small comfort only when Eden, at a meeting in Cairo in November that was attended by Churchill as well, told Mountbatten that the Prime Minister was well aware that S.E.A.C. was getting 'a thin diet.'

Nevertheless, the Supreme Commander outlined at this conference a new and ambitious set of proposals, aimed at 'the capture of Singapore at the first possible moment', with the interim stages to be an advance into central Burma across the Chindwin river (operation 'Capital') and 'a bold step to the Southward, probably to the Kra Isthmus', from where an attack could be launched against either Rangoon or Singapore.[2] Churchill himself liked this idea of going for the Kra Isthmus, being impatient for action of a dramatic kind and declaring that Japan's powers of resistance in the Malay peninsula as a whole were 'much over-rated'. At the end of November he was writing to Ismay: 'This Mountbatten business drags on and should not be neglected further. There seems to be stalemate everywhere.' Likewise he was still urging the Chiefs of Staff in April 1945 that 'a tremendous effort should be made to sustain Mountbatten', and that 'we must have Rangoon at all costs by June 1st.'[3]

By the time the Prime Minister was writing this minute in April, important developments had already been taking place within S.E.A.C. itself. In the north, the Americans and Chinese, together with the British 36th Division, had at last, in January, achieved Washington's object of driving the Ledo Road through to China. Churchill, in his message of congratulation on the feat to Mountbatten, chose to place his emphasis on the way in which the British contribution within the Command had helped to make this success possible; also in a grudging spirit, there was a certain amount of petty resentment in the Foreign Office when Chiang Kai-shek, with good cause even if not with absolute tact, given that British territory was involved, later renamed the road into Burma after Stilwell.[4] In return, at the Sino-American ceremony held in Kunming when the first American convoy arrived from Ledo early in February, only passing reference was made to the role played in the Theatre by the British and Indians.[5]

Meanwhile, to the south, Mountbatten had had his plans for an Arakan offensive approved, and had taken Akyab and Ramree island by the middle of February. The proposed attack on the Kra Isthmus had had to be cancelled, however, owing to the demands being made by the China Theatre upon S.E.A.C.'s resources, a subject that will be dealt with separately below.[6] Even so, the Supreme Commander had continued to plan ambitiously, working now within a new directive, despatched to him by the Combined Chiefs of Staff early in February, which, it will be recalled, instructed him to clear Burma and then open the Straits of Malacca.[7] On 23 February the decision was taken to advance overland to Rangoon before the arrival of the monsoon, this move to be followed by landings on Phuket island in June (operation 'Roger'), in the Port Swettenham–Port Dickson area of Malaya in October (operation 'Zipper'), and finally at Singapore itself between December 1945 and March 1946 (operation 'Mailfist').

Once again, serious difficulties were encountered. American and Chinese units within S.E.A.C. continued to withdraw in order to operate in China instead, while there were delays in building up the East Indies Fleet (as the Eastern Fleet had now been renamed, its Commander being Admiral Power from November onwards) after it had been weakened by the creation of the new Pacific Fleet.[8] Despite such obstacles, however, and with Sultan's forces moving south to reach the Lashio–Mandalay road in March, Slim's Fourteenth Army took Mandalay itself on 20 March; an even more striking success was achieved early in May, when Rangoon was taken by troops landing from seawards, who then linked up with Slim's forces driving down from the north. Mountbatten was thus able to revise his plans, bringing operation 'Zipper' forward to the second half of August, without a preliminary attack on Phuket island, the aim now being to reach Singapore by the end of the year. Staff studies of operations designed to liberate Siam also continued to be made, although, as we shall see below, a Cabinet decision as regards policy towards that country was still awaited.

New difficulties were also beginning to arise from two other directions, despite the fact that the war against Germany was now over: preparations for the final Allied assault on Japan's home islands were now receiving priority over S.E.A.C. operations; and demobilization plans—in particular the reduction of the Southeast Asian repatriation qualification from 3 years 8 months to 3 years 4 months—threatened to create major problems for 'Zipper' and 'Mailfist.' Preparations went ahead, nonetheless, until, at Potsdam, Mountbatten was told of the intention to use the atomic bomb and of the need to make plans for an early Japanese surrender. He then received a new directive on 2 August, whereby, as we have seen, S.E.A.C.

was to be greatly extended into the South West Pacific Area controlled until then by MacArthur.[9]

By the time the war came to an end, Anglo-American tension over strategic questions concerning S.E.A.C. had been resolved by what was essentially a parting of the ways. During much of this final period, however, the contrast between the American orientation northwards towards China and the British one southwards towards Singapore—a contrast spelled out once more by senior individuals within the Command as well as by the Joint Chiefs of Staff in Washington[10]—had continued to create difficulties. These centred above all on the desire of Chiang Kai-shek and of Wedemeyer, in the main supported by Washington, to remove Chinese and American units from S.E.A.C. to China, in the first place in order to meet the threat created by the Japanese advance there in 1944,* and then to prepare for the counter-offensive towards the China coast that we have observed Wedemeyer planning. In turn, Mountbatten and the Chiefs of Staff in London—despite the views of Carton de Wiart to the contrary—felt that China's needs in this respect were being exaggerated, and tried to prevent S.E.A.C.'s operations from being jeopardized by the demands being received from Chungking and the U.S.A.; the Chiefs of Staff also strove to retain for themselves some jurisdiction over the entire issue via the Combined Chiefs of Staff Committee.

Matters first came to a head in November 1944, when Chiang Kai-shek sought the return of three Chinese divisions. Wedemeyer persuaded the Generalissimo to reduce this demand to two divisions, which were duly released, with Churchill's approval. Wedemeyer himself, however, also wanted 50 combat-transport aircraft to be transferred (Mountbatten's counter-proposal of 48 bombers was accepted by the Combined Chiefs), and, despite the opposition of the British Chiefs of Staff, was given in addition the right to call upon American air units operating under General Sultan in the U.S. India–Burma Theatre. (Sultan, like Stilwell before him, came under Mountbatten within the area covered by S.E.A.C.) Moreover, the Joint Chiefs in Washington insisted on retaining the right to act independently of the Combined Chiefs of Staff Committee over air allocations should an emergency arise in China. Some of the planes that had been removed from Mountbatten were in fact returned at the end of January, but in late February and early March a new series of demands began to be made upon him. Wedemeyer and Chiang Kai-shek now wished to transfer to China in rapid succession the American brigade ('Mars force') that was serving under Sultan, together with all the Chinese divisions that remained in S.E.A.C. Quite apart from the loss of troops that would be involved (and the Generalissimo was now drawing a line in Burma beyond which Chinese

* It remains one of the more remarkable aspects of Japan's war-time strategy that, with so many of her troops involved there, she allowed the conflict in China to stagnate, in effect, for several years. Political calculations involving China were obviously involved, but in retrospect the decision seems highly questionable. See in general Boyle, *China and Japan at War*.

forces would not be allowed to operate), the diversion of the air transport that would be required for the carrying out of such transfers posed a major threat to Mountbatten's drive towards Rangoon.

There ensued a series of exchanges that need not be followed in detail, but which included a visit by Mountbatten to Chungking early in March, and a personal intervention by Churchill at the end of that month, when he appealed to Marshall's 'sense of what is fair and right between us.'[11] Marshall in return proposed that Mountbatten should keep the American air resources that he needed in order to take Rangoon, the terminal date being either the fall of that town or 1 June, whichever was earlier; even so, the Joint Chiefs still reserved the right to remove the aircraft concerned if Rangoon had not been captured by the time the monsoon set in, and rejected Mountbatten's request to be allowed to keep them for two or three months after Rangoon became his. Eventually, in the middle of April, a timetable for all withdrawals from S.E.A.C. was agreed. The remainder of the U.S. 'Mars' brigade would be gone by the end of that month; in May, one Chinese division and part of the headquarters of the U.S. air forces in India–Burma would depart, to be followed in June by the remainder of that H.Q., two combat-cargo air groups and two more Chinese divisions; remaining units of the American Air Force would then leave in stages between July and September. S.E.A.C. would thus rapidly become an essentially British and Empire affair.[12]

Yet another series of disagreements between Wedemeyer and Mountbatten, this time over Indochina, will be outlined later in this chapter. Meanwhile within S.E.A.C. itself, however, a considerable improvement in Anglo-American relations at senior levels took place once Wedemeyer, as well as Stilwell, had left the Command, and when, on the British side, General Giffard had been replaced by Lt. General Sir Oliver Leese, who became Commander of all Land Forces. Both Lt. General Daniel Sultan as Commander of the U.S. India–Burma Theatre and Lt. General Raymond Wheeler as Mountbatten's Deputy were privately warm in their praise for the Supreme Commander. Mountbatten, Washington was told at the end of 1944, was 'motivated by a sincere desire to promote harmonious and friendly relations with Americans . . . [and] was always sympathetic to American requests and complaints and took prompt action wherever possible.' General Leese was also applauded in the same report.[13]

In March, Wheeler suggested to the War Department that Mountbatten should be 'brought more prominently into the news and played up consistently as Supreme Allied Commander.' 'He deserves credit', Wheeler added, 'for organising a successful Allied offensive with meagre resources.'[14] In a tone far removed from that of Stilwell, Sultan, too, wrote to Marshall in February 1945:

'Our relations with the British in this theater are excellent. Field Marshal Wavell and General Auchinleck have been most friendly and most cooperative in every way . . . My relations with [Admiral Mountbatten] are on a very frank and cordial basis. General Leese . . . is doing a fine job. He is a fighter. There is absolutely no friction of any kind evident at this time. [However], Admiral Mountbatten is much inclined to integra-tion of American forces and agencies with the British. This I have always resisted . . .'[15]

In return, Mountbatten regarded Sultan as being 'a good friend', and was equally pleased with Wheeler (who in June took over Sultan's India–Burma Command, while remaining Deputy Supreme Commander of S.E.A.C.).[16] Wavell and Dening were others who held Wheeler in high esteem.[17]

Unfortunately, however, this new degree of harmony among the Com-mand's senior officers did not prevent a continuation of mutual Anglo-American suspicion and resentment, both in the U.S.A. and in Britain as well as within S.E.A.C. itself. In Washington, for example, Stimson was writing in his diary towards the end of 1944 of British 'incompetence and sluggishness' in Southeast Asia, while Representative Mansfield reported to Roosevelt in January after his visit to the Far East that 'the American military . . . are fed up with the dilatory tactics of the British out there.'[18] Meanwhile, on behalf of those much-criticized British, Dening was writing to London in December:

'Militarily the Americans are taking their eyes off the ball, which is the defeat of Japan. Politically they are damaging our position in the Far East to a degree which it would be unwise to ignore. . . . It is an ugly and sinister situation and I think if we are to fight this war against Japan at all [in S.E.A.C.] we must eventually fight it alone. Otherwise we shall be continually sabotaged.'[19]

Dening also continued to be very critical of the British Chiefs of Staff for not standing up more strongly to the Americans when the latter imposed their own strategic pattern on the war in the Far East, and for overlooking Britain's political requirements in the area.[20] In London, it was justifiably felt by senior officials in the Foreign Office that, in developing this case so strongly, Dening was overlooking the wider problems which the Chiefs of Staff were having to face. Nevertheless, Eden himself had emphasized to Mountbatten 'the need for reconquering the British Empire with mainly British force of arms',[21] while we have already encountered the view, ex-pressed by the Head of the Far Eastern Department and others in the spring and early summer of 1945, that the Americans were 'virtually conducting political warfare' against Britain in the Far East, and were deliberately restricting her military role in that part of the world.[22]

A particular area of activity within S.E.A.C. which troubled Dening was that of public relations, where he felt that too little regard was being paid to possible implications for foreign affairs.[23] Here, too, Anglo-American difficulties continued. Some Americans serving in the Command, for instance, were again inspiring anti-British reports in United States news-papers.[24] ('It is horrifying', Mountbatten wrote in his diary in June, 'to think that the American and Indian press evidently still regard us as merely Imperial monsters, little better than the Fascists or Nazis.')[25] Films, too, went on causing trouble, yet another American one that concentrated entirely on the drive by U.S. and Chinese forces in North Burma being declared unacceptable by the Ministry of Information in London, while questions were asked in Parliament on the same subject.[26]

Less publicly, antagonism also persisted in the field of political warfare. Both Dening and London looked askance at the activities of the O.W.I., which, as before, appeared to be directed against the interests of the European colonial powers in the region, and which were undertaken with little consultation with the British beforehand. On the Combined Liaison Committee in New Delhi, Dening wrote in March, there were 'constant manifestations . . . that the United States reserve the right to take an entirely independent line in psychological warfare addressed to all Asiatics other than the Japanese. It follows that they object when we associate them by the use of the word "Allies" in any of our leaflets.' The British line, on the other hand, was that, just as propaganda directed towards the Philippines had been left to the Americans, so material aimed at Britain's Asiatic subjects should be a matter for London. There was much relief among British officials when the O.W.I. ceased its broadcasts to Burma in May.[27]

It must again be emphasized that some of Britain's troubles in this field were of her own making, arising from a lack of clear and comprehensive policies for Southeast Asia. Thus, Halifax's suggestion in October that high-level talks should be held with the Americans in order to resolve differences over political warfare met with a cool reception from the Foreign Office, Political Warfare Executive and M.O.I., who jointly concluded that 'it was neither practicable nor desirable to draw up a cut and dried statement of British policy in the Far East. Consequently, it would be dangerous to send a delegation to Washington . . . since they would probably be faced with a demand for such a statement.'[28] Squabbles also continued to arise among the various British agencies involved in anti-Japanese political warfare, Joubert for S.E.A.C. clashing with the M.O.I.'s Far Eastern Bureau, for example.[29]

Nevertheless, the Americans, on their side, were indeed approaching the subject in a spirit of suspicion and determined independence, as Dening was suggesting. Thus, Washington instructed its officials on the spot that there should be no identifying the U.S. effort with that of the British over political warfare, and that in the neighbouring field of clandestine operations 'O.S.S. in Burma . . . should not under any circumstances become associated in Burmese minds with S.O.E. or in any British political propaganda organization.'[30] By May, indeed, General Sultan thought the only satisfactory answer would be to go further still, and to pull all Americans, including those of the O.S.S., out of the India–Burma Theatre altogether.[31]

Meanwhile, although Sultan himself had an American political adviser in the person of Consul-General Max Bishop, whose loud warnings against British machinations will be noted below, the desire of Mountbatten and

Dening to have a representative of the State Department on the S.E.A.C. Headquarters' staff was still resisted. 'The assignment of political officers to S.E.A.C.', wrote Bishop, 'could hardly avoid placing the United States in a position of a greater measure of responsibility for and participation in S.E.A.C. political manoeuvres and policies.'[32] Thus, the United States could continue to have it both ways: suspicious of British activities, yet declining to appoint officials who might have helped to increase mutual understanding. As it was, the main reason that Bishop adduced for maintaining an American presence in the Command at all was the need to ensure that, even after U.S. forces had departed, 'whatever American assistance is given to S.E.A.C. . . . is utilized in a manner to promote American national interests . . .'[33]

Tension between the two partners over the affairs of S.E.A.C., then, lasted into the final stages of the war. The withdrawal of United States units, along with those of China, did nevertheless help to ease matters in the summer of 1945. What is more, some degree of Anglo-American convergence was also taking place as regards policies towards colonial territories in general—this despite the substantial differences that remained and the lasting American antipathy towards European empires, in Asia especially.

The future of empires; British territories in Southeast Asia

Denunciations of European imperialism continued to be heard in the United States to the very end of the war. Thus the *Chicago Tribune*, for example, was declaring in February 1945 that American public opinion would not tolerate the reimposition of 'slavery' on the colonial peoples of Southeast Asia.[34] Likewise, the columnist Marquis Childs described attempts to maintain the colonial system as 'a betrayal' and—once more— held up the example of U.S. policy towards the Philippines as a model for others to copy. Colonialism, insisted the National Association for the Advancement of Colored Peoples, was 'a primary and implacable obstacle to the evolvement of world peace.'[35]

Britain in particular remained a special target for much of this criticism. 'The British game never varies', observed the *Chicago Tribune* in April. 'What Britain has she will hold. What other nations obtain Britain will share . . . [Her] colonial administrators, notably at Guadalcanal and Tarawa, landed and took charge as soon as our forces had made possible a safe return . . . [But] the British mandates and colonial territories, where native populations have long been oppressed, must . . . be subject to discussion.'[36] Raymond Gram Swing, a popular broadcaster, similarly assured his listeners that 'we are not going to spend American lives and treasure in freeing imperial possessions from the Japanese and then turn them back to their pre-war owners.' The Embassy in Washington reported that such views were widespread and that Britain was thought to have a poorer record than the Netherlands in colonial matters.[37] To a question posed in an opinion poll early in 1945: 'The English have often been called oppressors because of the unfair advantage some people think they have taken of their colonial possessions. Do you feel that there is any truth in this charge?', 56 per cent answered in the affirmative.[38]

The word 'feel' in this somewhat tendentiously-framed question was appropriate, since hostility towards colonialism in general and the British Empire in particular was essentially an emotional matter. Thus, when the Colonial Secretary, Oliver Stanley, visited the United States early in 1945 and attempted to outline in public Britain's progressive attitude towards colonial affairs, he was accorded very little attention; similarly, the publication in London of a White Paper on policy proposals for Burma went, in the words of the Washington Embassy, 'virtually unnoticed.'[39] What Britain actually did counted for far less than what she was believed to stand for. The only event during this period which did cause some individuals, Sumner Welles among them, to adopt a more hopeful attitude was the election victory in July of the Labour Party, with its record of opposition to at least the worst features of imperialism.[40]

Meanwhile in American official circles, too, there remained a substantial degree of hostility towards European colonialism, especially in Asia. An additional reason for anxiety in this regard was conveyed to Roosevelt by Hull in October 1944, when the Secretary of State drew the President's attention to the recent promise by Japan of independence for the Netherlands East Indies:

'The Japanese move,' wrote Hull, 'is important as indicating adoption of a "scorched earth" political course as they retreat, in order to put the United Nations on the defensive and to lay the foundations for a possible resurgence of Japanese influence in Asia by identifying themselves as the champions of liberation who were thwarted and defeated by the Western imperial powers . . . [This] emphasizes the need for prompt formulation of American policies towards the regions of Southeast Asia and the importance . . . of a concerted, dramatic announcement by the appropriate United Nations regarding the future of these regions.'[41]

Yet reports from Asia itself suggested that the European colonial powers were already seeking to sabotage a policy of the kind Hull was advocating. Thus, Hurley informed Roosevelt from China in November that

'The British, French and Dutch in the Far East are bound together by a vital common interest, namely repossession of their colonial empires . . ., because without their empires [they] would be impoverished and weak. This interest is also binding because it is based on the desire of the British to extend to the Far East the same character of imperial hegemony of the three great imperialistic nations as they have arranged for the control of Western Europe . . . You may therefore expect Britain, France and the Netherlands to disregard the Atlantic Charter and all promises made to other nations by which they obtained support in the earlier stages of the war . . . In the foregoing you have an outline of the reason why the

Council of the three Empires recently formed at Kandy [S.E.A.C.'s Headquarters] has been built up without the consent or approval of the United States.'[42]

Hurley's description of events—not totally devoid of truth, as we shall see below, but greatly exaggerated and inaccurate—was backed up by General Wedemeyer, who cabled to Marshall (from whom the message reached Roosevelt): 'British-French-Dutch are integrating intensified effort to insure recovery of political and economic pre-war position in Far East.'[43] (In a separate comment which arrived in Washington via Gauss, Wedemeyer admitted that he had no first-hand evidence for his charges—the similar cases of John Davies and Admiral King will be recalled[44]—but increased his estimation of European aims from the recovery to the 'expansion' of their interests.)[45] Donovan likewise reported that the O.S.S. representative in S.E.A.C. had 'little doubt' (again, it should be noted, firm proof was lacking) that 'the British and Dutch have arrived at an agreement with regard to the future of Southeast Asia and now it would appear that the French are being brought into the picture . . . It would appear', the O.S.S. survey continued, 'that the strategy of the British, Dutch and French is to win back and control Southeast Asia, making the fullest possible use of American resources, but foreclosing the Americans from any voice in policy matters.'[46]

Roosevelt, for his part, was undoubtedly impressed by these reports, which fitted so readily within the framework of his own assumptions. He asked Hurley, therefore, for further information about 'the activities of British-French-Dutch missions in Southeastern Asia.'[47] Furthermore, on his instructions the American Embassy in London told the Foreign Office that it had been learned that some form of colonial understanding was in the process of being reached by the European states concerned, and that the United States Government expected to be consulted before any arrangements were arrived at, regarding the future of Southeast Asia.[48] As for the President's own ideas for the future in this respect, he continued until his death to hold many of those which have been observed during previous stages of the war: that the colonial era must be brought to an end, and that as a major step towards this goal the principle of trusteeship must be established;[49] that as one, specific case, Hongkong should be returned to China by Britain,[50] while the United States itself should set an example to others by granting independence to the Philippines with all speed.[51] (A bill was also brought into Congress in this period to grant 'independence' to Puerto Rico—though carefully hedged about with provisions that would ensure free access for the U.S. Army and Navy to that territory at all times.)[52]

Moreover, the future of Asia as a whole, and not simply of its imperial regions, continued to concern the President. To an adviser on colonial policy in March 1945 he talked of 'the brown people of the East.' 'He said', recorded the official in question, 'that there are 1,100,000,000 brown people. In many Eastern countries they are ruled by a handful of whites and they resent it. Our goal must be to help them achieve independence—1,100,000,000 potential enemies are dangerous. He said he included 450 million Chinese in that. He then added, Churchill doesn't understand this.'[53] Roosevelt had made similar remarks about the Prime Minister to American correspondents who accompanied him back from Yalta, declaring that 'Dear old Winston will never learn on that point', and that the latter was 'mid-Victorian' over colonial matters.[54] By contrast, he described Queen Wilhelmina of the Netherlands as being enlightened in this respect, and said that she had promised that she would grant dominion status to the East Indies, together with the right to opt for total independence.[55]

Yet if Roosevelt knew what he disliked about colonialism, and had broad ideas about what he wanted to see put in its place, he still lacked, as one historian has put it, 'a carefully conceived strategy to carry out [his ideals], given the global strategic considerations and the checkered and volatile politics of Southeast Asia.'[56] We shall see below how even his thinking in respect of Indochina was beginning to shift shortly before his death. Similarly, he remarked to an official in January: 'As to Burma . . . I don't know yet just how we will handle that situation.'[57] It has been suggested, indeed, and rightly so, that, had he lived longer, the President might well have been obliged to modify considerably his approach to colonial issues, along lines similar to those that in the event were followed by the succeeding Administration.[58]

Meanwhile, among officials and politicians in Washington, there remained those whose ideas on colonial subjects were far from radical. During his visit there in January 1945, for example, Oliver Stanley was not treated at all roughly during the discussions, official and otherwise, that took place. The Colonial Secretary's scheme for abolishing the distinction between mandates (or trust territories) and other colonies was firmly resisted, and he was taken up sharply by Felix Frankfurter when he tried to argue that Britain was 'trustee of its own colonies.' (Frankfurter held that, as a basic legal principle, a trustee could not judge its own acts; when Walter Lippmann, who was present, remarked that this was all quite unimportant and 'merely a matter of semantics', it led to a blunt exchange between the two Americans.) Nevertheless, some of those who talked to Stanley went out of their way to show understanding. Vice President Truman, for example, asked those present at a dinner party at the British Embassy: 'Suppose Great Britain had Puerto Rico as a colony and treated the colony as we do, what would be the United States reaction to Great Britain?' Roosevelt himself went so far as to tell Charles Taussig that he liked Stanley, while Taussig responded that 'although [the Colonial Secretary] was hard-boiled, I felt there was a genuine streak of liberalism in him, and that under his leadership the British would make some substantial changes in their whole colonial policy.'

Both sides in the discussions envisaged a role for international regional commissions as regards dependent territories, although the scope of such commissions' activities, which Stanley wished to restrict, had yet to be decided. In all, Leo Pasvolsky, a senior State Department official concerned with post-war planning, could report that the talks had been 'unexpectedly successful.' 'The British', he added, 'are prepared to go very far to reach agreement.' Stanley's own record shows Pasvolsky, for his part, concurring that the two countries should strive to reach a common policy before the United Nations Conference met in San Francisco, and that 'the one thing that must be avoided was discussion at the conference on a basis of disagreement between the United States and the United Kingdom.'[59]

Stanley's experiences in the U.S.A. apart, there were other indications that Washington might well wish to avoid a confrontation with Britain over colonial issues. It was known in London, for example—the subject had been aired by Lawrence Salisbury in the *Far Eastern Survey*—that in this respect there existed major differences of opinion within the State Department, between the Office of European Affairs and some of those officials who specialized in Far Eastern matters; the Washington Embassy was also able to report that those individuals with whom it dealt in the Department appeared to be 'genuinely anxious to be as cooperative as possible' over colonial problems.[60]

In addition, various direct hints were being dropped to the effect that the United States would pursue a more moderate line than some of Roosevelt's remarks might have led other States to expect. Thus, State Department officials indicated to the Australian Minister, Eggleston, that they did not share the President's views on colonial matters, while Grew laughed incredulously when Eggleston told him that some of the American delegates at the I.P.R. conference had talked of granting immediate independence to such territories or bringing them under international control. Even Owen Lattimore, one of those who spoke out strongly at that conference, surprised Eggleston when later, in March, he delivered a talk on the same subject of the future of colonies in a much more moderate vein.[61]* More important still, Hopkins at Yalta gave Eden a broad hint that Roosevelt himself would not in fact push Britain too hard over the question of her colonial Empire.[62]

The proposal that the United States Government put forward at that Yalta meeting, and, with some modifications, was agreed to by Britain and the Soviet Union in a Protocol of the Conference, was indeed modest enough. Under it, the trusteeship principle was to be applied only to three categories of territories: existing League of Nations mandates; areas detached from current enemy states; and colonies voluntarily placed under trusteeship by the sovereign states concerned. The five permanent members of the U.N. Security Council were to consult on these questions before the forthcoming San Francisco Conference of the organization, but neither in

---

* Even before the Hot Springs Conference, Lattimore, in discussions within the U.S. delegation, had approached the question of the future of colonial territories partly in terms of *realpolitik*. Thus, for example, he observed that 'differences in area must be considered. Large areas that are mistreated are capable of rebellion, but the small areas can do little more than protest, or strike on a small scale.' He also suggested that a distinction could be made 'between annexation of a base and annexation of a dependency. The first is a security problem, the second comes under the dependency question.' (Minutes of 28 Oct. 1944, IPR Papers, box 362.)

these discussions nor at the Conference itself were specific territories to be referred to, this being a matter for subsequent agreement.[63]

Even then, after making so moderate a submission, the United States remained in an uncertain position—so much so that the five-power talks that had been envisaged did not take place before the U.N. delegations assembled at San Francisco. The heart of the trouble lay in the continuing determination of the War and Navy Departments in Washington that nothing should be done which might possibly impede the establishment of full American control over Japan's mandated island groups. We shall return to this subject in more detail in a later chapter dealing with post-war arrangements in the Pacific. Here, it is sufficient to note that, following the Yalta agreement over dependent territories, various drafts that the State Department prepared regarding a U.N. trusteeship scheme ran up against the desire of War and Navy to exempt the Marianas, Carolines and Marshalls from such a system, and to postpone discussion of the entire issue. The State Department in turn tried to bridge the gap by suggesting that, where the Japanese mandates were concerned, the trusteeship principle should be 'applied in form but not in substance.'

Even so, with Stettinius hovering uncertainly between his own officials on the one hand and Stimson and Forrestal on the other, the question could not be resolved without a Presidential decision. Roosevelt, therefore, was about to supply this (and it is clear that he was going to pronounce essentially in favour of the State Department's approach) when he died. Truman thereupon reached agreement over the matter with Stettinius, Stimson and Forrestal, with the final drafts of the U.S. Government's official position being hastily prepared by officials on the train en route to San Francisco, where they were approved by the American delegation. Briefly, the solution which the War and Navy Departments had reluctantly accepted was that certain trusteeship areas could be designated as having special strategic significance; in those cases, the functions of the World Organization would be exercised by the Security Council, rather than by the Assembly.[64]

The Army and Navy might have got less than they wanted, but those in American official or quasi-official circles who, on the contrary, had advocated a radical approach to the colonial issue were by now on the defensive. The atmosphere of the time in this regard can to some extent be recaptured from the records of the discussions that took place in private among the U.S. delegates to the I.P.R. Conference at Hot Springs. For example, one finds the Negro, Ralph Bunche, later to become an outstanding U.N. official, expressing the fear that the United States would not be able to insist upon a new colonial order unless 'our hands are clean.' 'If we free the Philippines on the one hand', he continued, 'and take over the [Japanese mandated] islands on the other hand, it won't prove much and would lead to the development of an American empire in the Pacific.'[65]

That had been in October 1944. Now, on the eve of the San Francisco Conference, Charles Taussig, who was a member of the American delegation, visited Mrs. Roosevelt on the afternoon of 12 April, exactly at the moment when her husband, attended by his mistress among others, lay dying at Warm Springs away to the south. Taussig's purpose was to enlist the help of Mrs. Roosevelt in encouraging the President to resist the War and Navy Departments, together with the more conservative members of the State Department, over the colonial question. The help was readily promised: Mrs. Roosevelt, it was agreed, would relay to her husband any messages that Taussig might send her from San Francisco; she further made her feelings clear by describing one of the senior State Department officials concerned as 'a fascist'.[66] She and her visitor, however, were fighting for a cause that was already lost, and when Taussig saw Mrs. Roosevelt again, in August, it was to describe in bitter terms the conservative, even reactionary approach which his fellow-delegates had adopted at San Francisco, and 'how little influence the memory of F.D.R. had [had] with [them].'[67]

The discussions within the American delegation to San Francisco had indeed gone strongly against Taussig, and this against a background that included a public warning by Walter Lippmann that the principle of accountability in colonial affairs should not be carried too far.[68] Senator Vandenberg, for example, declared to his colleagues that Congressional opinion was 'totally in sympathy with the position of the Secretaries of War and Navy', and was in turn reassured by the State Department's Pasvolsky that, under the proposals the delegation were putting forward, 'it would be entirely possible for the United States to control every territory it might need and want.' General Embick added that the United Nations had in any event less chance of survival than had been the case with the League of Nations, and that therefore the U.S.A. must have 'an entire chain of island bases.' As for the idea of trusteeship, John Foster Dulles described it as merely 'a legal device', and assured his listeners that 'the church groups with which he was associated were satisfied . . . with self-government or autonomy as objectives of the Trusteeship system, and had never insisted on independence.' (Dulles' habit of suggesting some rather special connection between the will of the Lord and the interests of Republican conservatism was not merely a feature of his years as Secretary of State.)

Senator Connally, Chairman of the Senate Foreign Relations Committee, who, it will be recalled, had castigated Britain over India in 1942–3,[69] likewise observed that the word 'independence' should be avoided, otherwise disorder might well follow. Harold Stassen, the able young Republican who was representing the United States on the trusteeship committee of the Conference, agreed: self-government might lead to independence in some cases, but independence itself 'was a provocative word'; therefore the U.S. delegation must resist Soviet attempts to have it included in the U.N. Charter, and aim only for 'self-determination [which] should be established according to the individual circumstances of the territories involved. There were some areas', Stassen added, 'which could never govern themselves and hence could not, for their own welfare, be allowed to determine their own political status.' He continued by suggesting that the United States should not seek in this connection to go beyond a position which could be agreed by all the Great Powers. In particular, he observed, 'we did not wish to find ourselves committed to breaking up the British Empire.' Isaiah Bowman seconded this last comment. 'When perhaps the inevitable struggle came between Russia and ourselves', he declared (it was now the middle of May 1945), 'the question would be, who are our friends . . . Would we have the support of Great Britain if we had undermined her position?'[70]

Thus, while still by no means in agreement on all aspects of the colonial question, the United States and Britain were to be found together at San Francisco, resisting the demands of the Chinese and others that 'independence' rather than 'self-government' should be laid down as the goal for such territories, opposing the Soviet wish to include in the Charter a phrase concerning 'the right of self-determination', and seeing to it that, over the matter of the supplying of information to the U.N., qualifying reference was made to 'security and constitutional considerations.'[71]*

As for the thought expressed by Bowman, in which he related the colonial issue to the rising tension between the United States and the Soviet Union, this was to be echoed in several other American quarters during the final months of the war. Harriman, for example, home from the Embassy in Moscow, remarked to the Secretary of State and others that 'the Russians were going on in a high-minded way about colonies being given their freedom when they were at the same time subjugating Poland.' Likewise, the State Department itself, in a major survey of the Far Eastern situation that was prepared towards the end of June, observed that the 'adoption in [Southeast Asia] of an ideology contrary to our own, or development of a pan-Asiatic movement against Western powers would seriously affect our future security and interests.' Self-government for colonies did remain the American aim, and was one that still required that Britain be prodded forward; nevertheless, the survey continued, 'Soviet ideology will be a rising force throughout the entire Far East', and care must therefore be taken that U.S. policies 'will not undermine the influence of the West.'[72]†

The same point had already been expressed more bluntly still by the O.S.S. (though many of that organization's research staff and officers in the field would have strongly disagreed) in a memorandum written in April which reached the White House. This document foresaw the emergence, after the war, of an immensely powerful Soviet Union, with which the U.S.A. might come into conflict. If such an event occurred, then, 'if at all feasible we

---

* Eventually, the word 'independence' was included in the Charter, but not in the significant position that China had wanted. Article 73 of the Charter sets forth the obligation of colonial powers 'to develop self-government . . . according to the particular circumstances of each territory, and its peoples and their varying stages of advancement.' Article 76 refers to the goal of 'self-government or independence as may be appropriate' for U.N. trusteeships.

† The tension between on the one hand the American belief in the right of all peoples to self-expression and their choice of governments which 'derive their just powers from the consent of the governed', and on the other the conviction that, even where many manifestly support a Communist form of government, such a development must be resisted, is well known. A reminder, and not a full exploration of it, is all that can be provided here.

should fight abroad rather than at home, and with Allies rather than alone.'

'In this connection', the memorandum continued, 'the United States should realize also its interest in the maintenance of the British, French and Dutch colonial empires. We should encourage liberalization of the colonial regimes in order the better to maintain them and to check Soviet influence in the stimulation of colonial revolt. We have at present no interest in weakening or liquidating these empires or in championing schemes of international trusteeship which may provoke unrest and result in colonial disintegration and may at the same time alienate from us the European states whose help we need to balance the Soviet power.'[73]

Already, in other words, judgements were being expressed which were to lead the United States five years later to underwrite financially the French war in Indochina, and to help bring about America's own military involvement, and defeat, in Vietnam.

In London, meanwhile, the eventual mildness of the line taken by Washington over colonies came as a relief. Churchill, especially, had been preparing to encounter and resist something far worse. Thus, in the House of Commons in January, he had reaffirmed his 1941 statement that the Atlantic Charter did not apply directly to the British Empire, and that it was 'a standard of aims and an indication of the direction in which we are proceeding . . ., not a law.'[74] Likewise, at the Yalta Conference, when he had failed to grasp that the American trusteeship proposals would not in fact be binding upon British territories, he had burst out angrily that under no circumstances would he permit other states to pry into the affairs of the Empire.[75] Within the Foreign Office, too, Roosevelt's message about reports of European machinations in Southeast Asia and his demand that Washington must be consulted before any arrangements were made there were found 'singularly irritating', suggesting, as they did, 'that we are engaged in something underhand or reprehensible.'

In fact, contrary to what Hurley, Wedemeyer and others were proclaiming, no agreements had been entered into with either the French or the Dutch, and Seymour, for one, termed the accusations 'ludicrous'.[76] At the same time, British officials also continued to express a measure of scorn for the way in which Americans went on holding up the Philippines to the rest of the world as 'the ideal Asiatic state'. The presence of Communist guerillas in the islands, for example, was noted with a certain *Schadenfreude*, as were the activities of Filipino collaborators and the clear signs that the United States intended to retain a considerable say in the economic affairs of the colony after it had been given its freedom. 'In practice', wrote one official who had served in that territory, 'the "independent" Philippine Republic will be a good deal less independent than our Dominions.'[77]

Moreover, despite the measure of accord that was reached at Yalta over trusteeships, there remained apprehension on the British side. Some Colonial Office officials, for example, were by no means happy when they realized that that agreement, embodied in a formal Protocol, had committed the United Kingdom to accept some degree of involvement by the U.N. where the administration of British mandated territories was concerned. Nor was there yet a firm belief that the United States would continue to adopt a moderate attitude as regards the issue as a whole. Thus, when Halifax reported in March that Washington was said to be going to put forward at San Francisco a fairly advanced declaration of colonial principles, Eden saw this as an additional reason (besides Soviet-Western difficulties) for postponing that Conference, while Churchill minuted his own misgivings.[78] The Foreign Office, meanwhile, thought it as well to seek from the Colonial Office 'a brief with some stunning examples of our progressive beneficence and striking statistics for the American mind, to show our unselfishness, etc. etc.'[79]

Led by the Prime Minister—who, to the consternation of the Foreign Office, was even prepared at one point to throw over unilaterally the commitment contained in the Yalta Protocol to continue the mandate system—the Cabinet, Labour Ministers included, determined that whatever proposals might arise at San Francisco, there would be no surrender of Britain's right to administer and exercise sovereignty over her own colonies, and that there could be no question of voluntarily placing those colonies under trusteeship. (Stanley even for a time persuaded his colleagues on the Cabinet's Armistice and Post-War Committee that they should seek to reject the Yalta Protocol's acceptance of this scheme of voluntary placement, on the grounds that it would lead to constant pressure being put on Britain by the U.S.A. to apply it to parts of the Empire.) '"Hands off the British Empire" is our maxim', Churchill wrote to Eden, while the latter, in terms that would have warmed even the dour hearts of American admirals, expressed the hope that the United States would 'not go in for half-baked international regimes in any ex-enemy colonies they may take over, nor advocate them for others, but . . . accept colonial responsibilities on the same terms as ourselves.' In the event, the American proposal at San Francisco, that certain 'strategic areas' should be placed outside the usual obligations of trusteeship, was regretted in London, in that it would apparently enable Washington to take a less realistic view of that trusteeship system generally; nevertheless, the British delegation, on the instructions of the Prime Minister, supported the plan.[80]

In continuing to adopt an essentially defensive and conservative stance over colonial questions, the British Government had to resist pressure from Australia and New Zealand. That difficulties were going to arise from that quarter became apparent early in November 1944 when, following discussions between the two of them, Canberra and Wellington issued a statement calling for a comprehensive trusteeship system to be established by the U.N., with a body analogous to the League's Permanent Mandates Commission being empowered to inspect all dependent territories.[81] This public proposal aroused no little resentment in London, not only because of its disturbing nature, but because Britain had not been consulted beforehand, and indeed appeared to have been misled by the mild line which Curtin had adopted in this regard during the Prime Ministers' conference in the preceding May. 'We ought to take the strongest exception', wrote Cranborne. 'The time has come when we should speak frankly to the two Governments.' Representations were made accordingly, but although the two Dominions offered some reassurances, they remained essentially unrepentant, and continued to develop their own ideas for the effective international supervision of colonies.[82]*

During discussions that were held in London in April, before the San Francisco Conference, Fraser for New Zealand and Evatt for Australia urged their British Government colleagues to make what Fraser called 'a magnificent gesture [that] would stir the world' by voluntarily placing their colonial territories under trusteeship. Otherwise, Fraser warned, 'the United Kingdom Government would be placed in an isolated position and stigmatised as reactionary.'† Evatt, agreeing, added that 'some colonial people in Asia had been badly treated [and] deserved better. Furthermore', he continued, 'the bad administration of colonial territories in Asia, some of which the Japanese had occupied without resistance, led to a feeling of insecurity in our lands.'[83]

The British Government refused to entertain Fraser's suggestion, however, and it had to be accepted that at San Francisco the Commonwealth would speak with separate and differing voices on the subject. Thus, Evatt in particular vigorously made out a case at the U.N. Conference for an extension of the trusteeship principle. He was thwarted, nevertheless, by the way in which Stassen for the U.S.A. kept fairly close to the British position. Nor did Evatt's abrasive approach make him popular with his fellow-delegates. ('Everyone by now hates Evatt so much', noted Cadogan, 'that his stock has gone down and he matters less.')[84] Cranborne and Eden for Britain did not in the event find the efforts of Australia and New Zealand unduly embarrassing. 'On the whole we are a pretty good Empire party here' the Foreign Secretary reported to Churchill. '. . . Evatt is the most tiresome and Fraser the most woolly. But between them they are making clear to the Americans and all concerned that we do not control their votes.'[85]

As for relations between the British and American delegations at San Francisco, several differences of opinion arose over colonies and trusteeships and were overcome only with difficulty. The problem for Cranborne, representing Britain on the Trusteeship Committee, was that, as Fraser had

---

* The Opposition in Australia, however, advocated a policy over colonies that was much closer to that of Britain, while Curtin's Government itself had no intention of leaving Papua or New Guinea, and indeed wished to secure the right to fortify the latter, which was a mandate territory. (Material in ADEA, files A1066/P45/153/2, pts. 1 and 2.) As for the Australian Government's two-fold concern over Pacific colonies—for their welfare and their potential role in terms of a security system—the emphasis in 1944–45 was tending to shift towards the second of these considerations. W. D. Forsyth, who played a leading role in working on these matters in the Department of External Affairs in Canberra, has confirmed this interpretation in conversation with the author.

† One New Zealand official had even described Stanley's colonial ideas as being 'close to Hitler talk.' (Louis.)

forecast, the United Kingdom found itself in a somewhat isolated position (though usually able to count upon the support of the Netherlands and France, who had themselves been consulting together on how to preserve their colonial interests against American pressures).[86] Hence, she was extremely dependent on United States backing.

'Our difficulty is political', Cranborne wrote back to Stanley. 'We cannot count on carrying any point which may be pressed to a vote in Committee unless the United States supports us. We are therefore in a dilemma, that if we feel so strongly on any point that we cannot meet United States views and must force the issue, the almost certain result will be that we lose altogether . . . I felt I must let you know quite frankly the extremely difficult bargaining position in which the colonial powers are placed.'

Thus, when Stassen joined Cranborne in resisting the use of the word 'independence', it came as a great relief, and formed the basis of a common position in Committee. (Although some officials in the Colonial Office in London still felt strongly that too much had been conceded to the American view,[87] they were being quite unrealistic, politically, in this; indeed, in retrospect it is apparent, as Cranborne indicated, that the U.S. representatives could have exerted far more pressure on their British colleagues than they chose to do.) Cranborne was thus able to report what seemed to be 'a genuine conviction [on the part] of the United States delegation that the unity and strength of colonial empires (not only British) is essential to world security.' It was, he added, 'a very healthy development in United States opinion.'[88]

If the British position remained an essentially conservative one, London had nevertheless, even before San Francisco, been modifying some of its ideas on colonial issues, partly in order to avoid a clash with the United States. Thus, Stanley had returned from his visit to Washington early in 1945 reluctantly convinced that, in the light of what he had heard there, and of the Yalta Protocol and the attitude of Australia and New Zealand, Britain could not after all oppose a continuation of the mandate principle.[89] In addition, an attempt was made to meet at least some of the demands that were emanating from the United States for an international involvement in colonial affairs by putting forward proposals for regional commissions, including ones for Southeast Asia and for the South Pacific. This gesture was a limited one, however, in that London at the same time sought to render such commissions as harmless as possible by indicating that their role should be to foster consultation and collaboration, and not to supervise or interfere in the administration of territories by the individual colonial powers concerned. When it was accepted that mandates/trusteeships would have to continue, moreover, the regional-commission proposal was still further reduced by making it apply to these territories only and not to straightforward colonies; the idea of setting up an international Colonial Centre to receive annual reports from the administering powers—again designed to meet American demands for 'accountability'—was also with-drawn altogether.[90]*

More positively and straightforwardly—although the political aim involved was once more fundamentally conservative—Stanley, after a tussle with the Chancellor of the Exchequer, obtained the agreement of the Cabinet to extend the 1940 Colonial Development and Welfare Act (which had allowed for the paltry sum of up to £5 million a year for ten years to be spent on development and welfare) and to increase its provision to £120 million to be spent over the ten years beginning in 1946. 'The next few years may determine the course of the Colonial empire', argued Stanley. 'The participation of the Colonies in the war and the gratitude felt by this country for their efforts have increased our awareness of past deficiencies in our administration. . . . Here we have an opportunity that may never recur . . . of setting the Colonial Empire on lines of development which will keep it in close and loyal contact with us.'[91]

In the economic sphere, as in the political one, unease continued to be felt in London over the possibility that the rest of the world, led by the United States, might force its way into Britain's colonial territories. Here, too, however, evidence was continuing to accumulate which pointed towards the necessity for arriving at some form of accommodation with Washington in this respect—even if one were to leave aside the overall state of financial and political dependency in which Britain now found herself. The country's uneasy position as regards Southeast Asian economic matters in particular was outlined by Hall-Patch in the Foreign Office in January 1945:

'As producers of rubber and tin', he wrote, 'we have common interests with the Dutch and French which may conflict with the interests of the U.S. as the principal consumer of these commodities. We should do nothing which would prevent us from a free exchange of views with the Dutch and French as to how best to protect our common interests . . . if the United States . . . are not prepared to collaborate. We are offering collaboration with open hands, but it is still uncertain if the Americans will respond.

Malaya is one of our greatest potential sources of dollars in the years immediately after the war, when our balance of payments difficulties will be most acute. We should give due weight to this important factor in discussing Southeast Asia with the Americans. They want cheap rubber and tin. We require reasonable prices for those commodities, firstly, because we want the dollars, and secondly, because unless the producer is given a reasonable price for his product, the Colonial Government is deprived of the fiscal resources necessary for a progressive colonial

* In the event, colonial powers agreed only in general terms 'to cooperate with one another' (U.N. Charter, article 73), while powers exercising trusteeship had to report annually to the General Assembly and accept periodic visits arranged by the Assembly's Trusteeship Council (articles 86–88).

policy. Unless we can pursue such a progressive policy, the Americans will be the first to accuse us of "imperialistic exploitation." They cannot have it both ways, which is what they want.'[92]

Yet however logical this line of reasoning might be, the difficulty remained that the United States, as we have observed in the preceding period, was rapidly developing an extremely strong bargaining position over rubber in particular. As a report reaching the Foreign Office in March made clear, there now existed in that country 'ample capacity for the production of synthetic rubber to supply current and immediately prospective consumption requirements.' (The U.S. Government had in fact invested about $800 million in synthetic plants, and by the end of 1944 America's consumption of natural rubber was only about 16 per cent of the total rubber used. The performance of the synthetic product—for example as tyres—was also being greatly improved.) The total post-war world production capacity of rubber, indeed, looked like being about twice the size of the expected demand, while loud cries were being uttered within the United States for the synthetic programme to be continued on strategic and economic grounds, regardless of what could be the crippling consequences for a natural-rubber producer like Malaya.* Small wonder, then, that Hall-Patch observed in March that Britain 'could not afford to quarrel with America' over this matter.

London therefore dealt warily with Washington over a French request to be given a seat on the rubber committee of the Combined Raw Materials Board, and on the International Rubber Study Group. (France eventually obtained membership of the latter body in November 1945.) There was also a great deal of relief on the British side when talks held in Washington in the spring of 1945 revealed that American officials, and even some sections of the U.S. rubber industry, were ready to seek an agreement that would take account of the need to preserve the natural sources of supply.[93]† Altogether, this single issue concerning the future of Britain's colonial rubber industry in Southeast Asia provided a vivid illustration of the dependence of a weakened United Kingdom on the good-will and cooperation of a United States that was growing mightier by the month.

---

* Estimates prepared by the Technical Sub-Committee of the Rubber Advisory Panel were as follows:

Potential supply (in 1,000 long tons), 1950:

Natural:	1,599
Synthetic:	1,349
Total:	2,948

Potential demand, 1950:

U.S.A.:	827
Others:	700
Total:	1,527

† Problems also hung over the post-war revival of the Malayan tin industry, the U.S.A. having greatly increased its own smelting capacity during the war and having developed ties with Bolivia as an alternative source of supply. (FO 371, files 45686, 45727.)

Meanwhile Malaya, and even more so Burma, were by now beginning to present the British Government with difficulties of another kind, potentially more serious still and involving developments among native movements which we have seen foreshadowed during the earliest days of the war. The significance of these movements was still not fully appreciated in London, although a greater degree of awareness existed on the spot, within S.E.A.C. Nevertheless, by the time Japan surrendered, the activities of some native peoples in Southeast Asia were coming to cast an element of uncertainty over the constitutional plans which Churchill's Government had at last got round to formulating.

Where Malaya was concerned, the Cabinet's proposals were developed from the ones that had been outlined in the summer of 1944,[94] the groups involved in this work being, in addition to the Colonial Office itself, the Far Eastern Committee and a Cabinet Committee on Malaya and Borneo. It was decided at first to tread warily regarding the intention to increase the degree of union between the Malay States and to bring all races within the pale of the constitution; there were, after all, the possible reactions of the Malay Rulers and of the Malays generally to consider. Therefore, although Mountbatten was urging the need to make the Government's intentions known, the most that Stanley would contemplate at the turn of the year was the circulation in 'restricted circles' of a broad statement of the problems involved, while, as a special mark of favour, it seemed, 'restricted circles which could guide and influence thought and discussion' were to be allowed to have a brief summary of the measures Britain was proposing to introduce.

Such a surreptitious—and obviously futile—approach was eventually modified in June as the result of criticism from various quarters; even then, however, the Colonial Office only went as far as to circulate an outline of London's ideas to certain official agencies so that they could 'direct public attention and discussion towards a political and social development of Malaya along lines which the provisional policy envisaged.' It was not thought necessary to consult the United States on these matters, even in the case of North Borneo, which happened to fall within MacArthur's South West Pacific Area, and where the intention remained to substitute direct British Government responsibility for the existing powers of the British North Borneo Company and others.[95]

Force 136 of S.O.E. had meanwhile been extending its activities behind the Japanese lines in Malaya, and in February 1945 learned of the agreement that had already been made between a British officer and the Malayan People's Anti-Japanese Union and Army (or Forces)—an agreement in which Malayan Chinese Communists had played a leading role, they having been the only group to have offered a significant degree of resistance to the Japanese.[96] Some of Malaya's civilian administrators were already fearing that trouble with these Chinese Communists lay ahead.* Mountbatten's

---

* Some administrators, however, emphasized, rather, the division between Malays and Chinese, or the gap between Chinese property-owners and the Chinese Communists. (Observations of Lt. Col. Purcell, recorded in SEAC War Diary, 1 Jan. 1945.)

view, nevertheless, was that the assistance of the M.P.A.J.U. should be welcomed (he reported reassuringly that the majority of its members 'appear to have little or no interest in politics and are constantly asking when the British will return'), and that London should quickly spell out its intention to grant the Chinese equality of status with the Malays after the war. 'Presumably', he wrote to Stanley in May, 'we have not found Colonial subjects rising to fight on our behalf when we were about to occupy their territory,* and the fact that they are doing so today seems to me a wonderful opportunity for propaganda to the world in general, and to the Americans in particular, at a time when we are being accused of reconquering our Colonial peoples in order to re-subjugate them.'[97]

The Supreme Commander did not obtain all that he sought in this connection, however. He was allowed to furnish aid to the resistance movement in Malaya, but the Cabinet was not yet ready to publicize its constitutional proposals. London was also anxious to ensure that any Malays who chose to resist the Japanese should also be assisted, 'in order to avoid creating the impression that we are supporting the Chinese alone.' Matters remained in this state to the end of the war, although early in August Mountbatten was again proclaiming that the M.P.A.J.U. and its army, being 'pro-Malayans', could be won over as supporters of the new order there, whereas the pro-Kuomintang Chinese in Malaya, who had separatist tendencies and looked to Chungking for their instructions, should not receive any aid from Britain.[98]

Mountbatten's forces had not entered Malaya by the time the Japanese surrendered. They had, however, retaken Burma, and the problem involving native movements that was encountered there proved to be more acute still. At least the Government in London had eventually set forth its plans for the future of Burma more clearly than in the case of Malaya. We have seen how, in the preceding period, impatience in this respect had been mounting in several parts of Whitehall and Westminster,[99] and this process continued throughout the winter of 1944–45. Within the Foreign Office, for example, there was a tendency to blame the Burma Office for failing to make up its mind on the subject,[100] while from his post in S.E.A.C. Dening, in a letter written to the Head of the Far Eastern Department in London at the end of 1944, deplored 'the loss of confidence in nearly every quarter resulting from the allegation out here that H.M.G. is always hedging as regards the Far East . . .'

'I think it right to say', Dening continued, 'that what we do in Burma is likely to be the acid test of our good intentions in the Far East. Our future policy in Burma, therefore, . . . becomes a matter of world importance, and of particular importance to the Foreign Office in the light of Anglo-American and Anglo-Chinese relations. I hope that some day in the not too distant future it will be possible to make some pronouncement which is not open to the suspicion that we do not mean what we say . . . [and

* The question that needed an answer, of course, was what was meant by 'on our behalf.'

intend] doing nothing when the time comes, and returning to the status quo. You and I know that this is both unjust and untrue, but the fact remains that it is the way in which we are judged by the world at large.'[101]

Likewise, those who were responsible for conducting political warfare in S.E.A.C. were anxious to be able to assure the Burmese people 'that within a reasonable time Burma will be a Dominion.'[102] The Governor, Dorman-Smith, also continued to argue that Britain should proclaim her intention to grant self-government to Burma following a period of reconstruction (financed by Britain on a large scale) and direct rule, a period strictly limited to seven years. 'We would be deluding ourselves', he wrote to Amery, 'if we thought for one moment that either the Burmese or indeed world opinion would regard the mere restoration of the constitutional status quo as anything but an indication of our determination once more to possess Burma for our own needs, purposes and profit ... Our handling of the Burma problem will be regarded in many quarters as a test case of our sincerity and ability to deal with post-war Asiatic questions.'[103]

One particular anxiety of the Governor's at this time was the fact that many senior Burmese appeared to be much impressed by American war-time efficiency and drive, while their younger compatriots were tending to look admiringly in the other direction, towards the Soviet Union. Hence the need, Dorman-Smith argued, to 'take the trouble to put over "the British way" effectively and sincerely.'[104] The Burma Office, too, for all the strictures directed against it within the Foreign Office, recognized that it was 'very important that our policy in Burma should be clearly stated vis-à-vis the Americans.'[105] Amery, for his part, accepted that the status quo in Burma could not be 'a measure of our requirements', as he put it, while a group of Conservative backbench M.P.s came out with their own, published proposals, entitled *Blueprint For Burma*, which envisaged a six-year limit to direct rule, followed by self-government and Dominion status (though with Britain retaining control of defence and external relations).[106]

As before, the main obstacle to progress was the Prime Minister. In Cabinet he openly abused Amery,[107] and when the Government Chief Whip indicated in December that among Conservatives in the House of Commons there existed a considerable degree of concern over Burma's future, he responded with an angry summary of his own, blindly unconstructive attitude:

'I was much astonished to read the statement ... in your letter', he wrote, '... and I think you might have told me about this and how many Conservative members take this view. Hitherto I have been inclined to think it would be better to re-conquer Burma before giving it away. But I see that the policy which has brought us to the present miserable pass in India is still thriving in some quarters, and that we are being urged to take steps in miniature in Burma which will afterwards bring the destruction of our Indian Empire.'[108]

Churchill did now give way to Amery, however, to the extent of accepting the latter's proposal for the setting up of a Cabinet Committee to consider the subject, the task being given, early in December, to the existing India Committee.[109] This body then proceeded to consider a variety of opinions: for example, on the economic and commercial side of things, Dorman-Smith again emphasized the need to give Burmese 'a fair chance to participate in the management of companies which will exploit Burma's resources', and to make it clear that the country itself was obtaining 'a fair share of the profits derived from exploitation.' R. A. Butler, on the other hand, echoing the Chancellor of the Exchequer's caution over the proposal to supply large sums of Government money for reconstruction purposes, produced the insensitive and unimaginative proposal that private enterprise, in the shape of 'the great commercial corporations interested in Burma', should be used to undertake that task. Likewise in the constitutional sphere, there was a considerable gap between Grigg, the Secretary of State for War, who was ready to contemplate a further lengthy period of British rule, and Cripps, who, like the Governor, stressed the need to meet nationalist opinion by promising an early transfer of power.

Eventually, it was agreed that the Government should provide £84 million for reconstruction purposes, spread over two years. The Committee's constitutional proposals, however (and it should be remembered that an unsympathetic Attlee was in the chair), were cautious. Three years of direct rule were envisaged, during which time the Governor could establish an Executive or Advisory Council in order to broaden the basis of his administration; thereafter, there should be a return to consitutional government under the provisions of the 1935 Act, with preparations being made for full self-government under a new constitution, to be drawn up by the Burmese themselves. No date was set for this translation to self-government, however, and the prior (and to Burmese, obviously disquieting) requirement was laid down that treaties should be signed 'safeguarding the continuing obligations of His Majesty's Government in Burma.' Britain would also continue to administer the Shan States and tribal areas, until their inhabitants signified a desire to join an independent Burma.[110]

On 17 May 1945 a Government White Paper was published, setting out these proposals. In Parliament it was accorded a mixed reception, but a mainly favourable one, while Amery for his part was relieved to have got past the Prime Minister with what he called 'so advanced and flexible a scheme.' (One reason for this success, he thought, was that Churchill had probably not bothered to read the papers involved.)[111] Dorman-Smith, however, was greatly disappointed at what London had produced. 'You probably now know', he wrote to a senior official in the India Office, 'how really badly the cold wording of the White Paper policy statement was received by one and all [here]. It may be that it had to be so worded, but it was a shocker from our point of view and has most unfortunately put us on the defensive again instead of on the offensive.'[112]

The Governor's belief that the Government were not aware of the urgency of the situation as regards nationalist feeling in Burma was shared by Mountbatten. It should again be noted, as it was in the chapter dealing with the preceding period in Southeast Asia, that the Supreme Commander found that he and Dorman-Smith saw eye to eye on the need for an early transfer of power. Mountbatten, as we have seen, was writing privately of the latter's 'first-class ideas', and as late as the middle of June was referring to 'excellent meetings' with him and his staff.[113] By then, however, the source of trouble between the two men had begun to emerge. On 27 March, the Burma National Army under the Thakin, Aung San, who had formerly collaborated with the invader, had risen against the Japanese. Mountbatten's reaction to this development was to submit that the B.N.A.'s assistance should be welcomed, and Aung San provided with supplies;[114] in wider terms, moreover, he was determined that his own forces should advance into Burma as liberators, and that there should be 'no . . . persecution, mass trials or arrests.' Thus, at a meeting in April, he emphasized that 'he wished the problem of Burma to be treated in a sensible manner as we had done in South Africa after the Boer War, and that we should not use a heavy hand which might result in disaster as it had in Ireland. . . . The eyes of the world would be upon us', added the Supreme Commander, 'to see how we handled the first part of the British Empire to be recovered from the enemy.'[115]

Dening, too, agreed on the need for S.E.A.C. to welcome the cooperation of the B.N.A., provided that no political commitments regarding the post-war years was entered into.[116] Further considerations pointing in the same direction had also been put to Dorman-Smith earlier by the Head of Political Warfare Section of S.O.E.'s Force 136:

> 'We should do well', the latter had written to the Governor in November 1944, 'to deal sympathetically with these people, cooperate with them as far as possible and turn a blind eye to many of their past misdemeanours and present failings and exaggerations . . . [The existence of a native resistance movement working with British forces] would be a crushing reply to one of the most prevalent slanders against British rule in the East. In fact one might almost say that if this Burmese resistance movement did not exist it would be justifiable to invent it.'

He added the thought that when self-government was granted to Burma, the 'young, active and politically-minded group' associated with Aung San would inevitably play a large part in the politics of the country. Hence, there was all the more to be said for establishing cooperation with them beforehand.[117]

The Governor, together with the Cabinet's India Committee in London, went along with these arguments a certain way. Thus, with Churchill's authorization, Mountbatten was told that he could work with the B.N.A. in military terms. In addition, however, it was made clear to him that there must be no political discussions with Aung San and his lieutenants, who should be left in no doubt that they had to 'work their passage home.' 'We must at all costs', the India Committee concluded, 'avoid building up a Burmese E.A.M. and E.L.A.S.'[118] Indeed, there was by now some unease in London over S.E.A.C.'s intentions in this regard. A senior official of the Burma Office, who visited Burma in April, reported that 'the Army view had changed altogether. Whereas in the past we were afraid of undue rigour in their attitude to the Burmese, the converse is now the case.' Mountbatten himself, when hearing Aung San described as a dangerous extremist, had replied 'that he could well understand any young Burman who had waited so long and anxiously for freedom under the British accepting unreservedly the promises of independence by the Japanese.'[119] It was this kind of approach that led Eden to write anxiously to Churchill regarding one of Mountbatten's urgent requests to be allowed to support the B.N.A.: 'The tone of this telegram is reminiscent of too much we have had from S.O.E. in the past. Surely we should not boost these people so much. They will give us great trouble hereafter.' 'I cordially agree with you', responded the Prime Minister.[120]

Matters came to a head in the middle of May when Aung San, who proclaimed himself to be the military representative of a Provisional Government of Burma, led by Thakins of the Anti-Fascist Peoples Freedom League, entered the British lines at the invitation of General Slim. Mountbatten now proposed to rename the B.N.A. the 'Burma Guerilla Army', to bring it within the S.E.A.C. structure, and to give individual members of it the chance to transfer to the regular Burma Army. The alternative of declaring the B.N.A. to be illegal was, he argued, out of the question, since it would mean taking on an additional 10,000 enemies and 'would be tantamount to proclaiming to the world that we were prepared to engage in a civil war against forces we had announced were on our side . . .' The Supreme Commander went further still, however, and asked if Slim could inform Aung San that the Governor would consider including members of the self-proclaimed 'Provisional Government' in his Advisory Council once civil rule was restored in Burma. (In his diary, indeed, Mountbatten wrote of Aung San and the B.N.A.: 'I am completely on their side.')

To Dorman-Smith, on the other hand, it was unthinkable that such a degree of recognition should be accorded to Aung San and his colleagues, while Churchill, for once on the Governor's side, minuted: 'I hope Mountbatten is not going to meddle in Burmese politics.' The Chiefs of Staff accordingly instructed the Supreme Commander that no political discussions must be held, that he must correct the pretensions of the 'Provisional Government', and that the aim must be to disarm the B.N.A. after first using it to help mop up the remaining Japanese forces in the country.[121] At this point, a certain sharpness began to enter into Mountbatten's communications with Dorman-Smith. Both men, one can see in retrospect, had a case. For the former it was the need to win over the dynamic elements within Burmese politics; for the latter—who did not rule out working with the Thakins, but declined to promise them official places in advance— there was the desire to uphold the rule of law, to punish anyone who, during the Japanese attack and occupation, had committed an atrocity, and to show no undue favours to those who had helped the invader against the British when other Burmese had risked so much by remaining loyal.

In taking this line, the Governor was backed by Amery in London.[122] Moreover, the situation was further complicated in that some of Mountbatten's own senior staff officers were in favour of arresting Aung San, and in the eyes of their Supreme Commander were behaving in a disloyal manner in this connection.[123] Nevertheless, a way forward was found. At a conference in Delhi at the end of May, Mountbatten and Dorman-Smith agreed that the B.N.A. should be renamed, and that the Governor should meet representatives of all Burmese political groupings—including Aung San and his fellow Thakins—in order to explain Britain's policy. This meeting accordingly took place on board H.M.S. *Cumberland* at Rangoon on 20 June, with Keswick being present to keep an eye on things on Mountbatten's behalf. Both Keswick and Dorman-Smith, in fact, pronounced the event a success, the latter having striven to put the Government's intentions in the best possible light. 'I think—but only think—', he wrote afterwards, 'that we can get these young men [that is, the B.N.A. and its associated A.F.P.F.L.] to play with us if we can show them that we do recognize that they are not without influence in the Burma of today, without in any way seeking to exaggerate that influence at the expense of those who remained utterly loyal to us.'

Mountbatten, too, was relieved, although, like Keswick, he thought that some of the Governor's officials had shown themselves to be 'old blimps' and not up to the task ahead. Aung San, for his part, had already pledged that he would cooperate with the British military authorities, while Dorman-Smith agreed with the Supreme Commander that the B.N.A. leader should be given a commission and a senior position in the Burma Army. The B.N.A. itself was meanwhile renamed the 'Patriotic Burmese Forces', those members of it who were suitable being earmarked for transfer to the Burma Army. In London, the thought of making Aung San a Brigadier was distasteful to some, but Attlee eventually agreed to this early in August.[124]

So matters stood uneasily poised in Burma when the war came to an end. We shall see, briefly, in a concluding chapter, how things then fell apart, with Dorman-Smith—so well-intentioned and in several important respects forward-looking—being saddled with the blame and being abruptly dismissed from his post. As Wavell, too, was to find, it was not the best of times to be the man on the spot, responsible for easing the dying stages of Britain's rule in Asia while Governments in London cast around for solutions and for some escape from the rapidly mounting burdens of Empire.

Other territories in Southeast Asia

In Burma, the British were thus, even before the end of the war, having to face some of the problems created by the upsurge of Asian nationalisms.

Where the Netherlands East Indies were concerned, however, there was an almost total unawareness in the West, as well as among Dutch officials who were waiting in Australia to return to that colony, of the extent of nationalist fervour—this at a time when the Japanese were doing all they could to stimulate that fervour by the use of anti-Western propaganda and promises of forthcoming independence.* One finds, for example, a State Department survey of June 1945 suggesting that 'at the conclusion of the war there will probably be a generally quiescent period in the relations between the Dutch and the native population . . . The great mass of natives will welcome the expulsion of the Japanese and the return of the Dutch to control.'[125]

At the same time—and ironically so, in view of what was to happen after the war—some Americans, including Roosevelt himself, had more sympathy for the Dutch than for the British or the French imperial cause. 'The return of the Dutch to their islands will be welcome to the United Nations', declared the *New York Times*, 'for they were among the most liberal colonial administrators. Their rule therefore was enlightened . . . They have become as necessary to Indonesia as Indonesia is to them.' Likewise, the *New York Herald Tribune* was convinced that 'the return of decent and honest officials will be welcomed in Java and Sumatra as it has in New Guinea.'[126] Even an anti-imperialist like Admiral Leahy looked with sympathy on the increasingly insistent Dutch requests to have their troops shipped out to the Far East, while on the spot in the Southwest Pacific MacArthur readily signed an agreement with van Mook, now Lieutenant Governor-General of the East Indies, whereby civil administration would be handed over to the latter and his officials 'as rapidly as practicable' by the U.S. Army when the time came.[127]

Among those Dutch officials, meanwhile, van Mook himself remained one of those who favoured staying close to the United States as regards the liberation of the East Indies. In private, he complained that 'at Mountbatten's headquarters [the Dutch] were always being put off with the statement that this or that could not be discussed with [them] until it had been discussed with the Americans.' (So much for the Hurley/Wedemeyer thesis of an Anglo-Dutch conspiracy within S.E.A.C.)[128] The Prime Minister, Gerbrandy, however, continued on the other hand to look towards London. 'My Queen and I', he told Major Desmond Morton, 'would prefer to do whatever is to be done in the Far East in partnership with the British rather than . . . with the Americans. I have no doubts about the British attitude towards the Dutch possessions in the Pacific', he added, '[but] I am not happy about the American attitude in that regard.'[129]

* The Japanese announced in March the setting up of a committee of enquiry into preparations for Indonesian independence. Early in July, however, it was decided to change the tempo and to grant that independence as speedily as possible. A committee to prepare for such a move was announced on 7 August. Following Japan's surrender, an Indonesian Republic declared itself independent on 17 August. (Elsbree, *Japan's Role in Southeast Asian Nationalist Movements*, cap. 3; Allen, *The End of the War in Asia*, cap. 3. For the recollections of a prisoner-of-war on the spot, see L. van der Post, *The Night of the New Moon* [London, 1970].)

London was indeed still strongly sympathetic towards the Dutch cause. Both Churchill and the Foreign Office wished to see Netherlands forces participating in the Far Eastern war, and the Prime Minister's first inclination was to respond favourably when Gerbrandy suggested reviving the Pacific War Council in London as a means of keeping his Government in touch with what was going on. 'I will not lend myself to any trickery to deprive the Dutch of their territories', he wrote to Eden.[130] The British Chiefs of Staff, too, were sympathetic towards Dutch requests to have their troops shipped out to the East, welcoming the prospect of their help in liberating and garrisoning the East Indies, and undertaking to provide the necessary equipment.[131] Meanwhile negotiations were preparing the way for the signing of an interim civil-affairs agreement between the Dutch and S.E.A.C. in the latter part of August 1945.[132]

Yet there remained considerable limitations upon what the British, so dependent themselves on the U.S.A., especially in the Far East, could do to further the interests of their fellow-Europeans. Thus, although the Chiefs of Staff tried to obtain a more forthcoming response from their American colleagues, they felt obliged at Potsdam to accept the ruling laid down by the Joint Chiefs of Staff, that no firm commitments over shipping facilities for the transfer of Dutch or French forces to the Far East could be made for 1945.[133] A request by Dutch leaders that they should be given a personal hearing at that same conference was also turned down in London, as well as in Washington.[134] Even when S.E.A.C. was enlarged at the end of the war, taking over the remainder of the East Indies in the process (in addition, that is, to Sumatra), the order of priority decided upon for occupation was first Singapore, then Indochina (Saigon being the centre of the Japanese command for the entire region), then Siam (of strategic importance and with its vital supplies of rice), and only after that Java, and finally Sumatra.[135]

We have noted earlier that, thanks mainly to MacArthur's manoeuvrings behind the scenes, British intentions with regard to the future of the Netherlands East Indies were viewed with unwarranted suspicion in Washington. A far greater degree of Anglo-American tension, however, was by now centering upon the question of Siam. In October 1944, following the removal of Stilwell, this country was placed by Washington within General Sultan's India–Burma Command. It did not fall within the boundaries of S.E.A.C. proper (although the Head of the Foreign Office's Far Eastern Department was still unaware of the fact at the end of 1944), and for operational purposes remained subject to the Mountbatten–Chiang Kai-shek 'Gentleman's Agreement' of 1943. Only at Potsdam, in fact, and against the wishes of both the Generalissimo and Wedemeyer, was it transferred fully to Mountbatten.[136]

Among American officials, Siam, the one Southeast Asian territory that had already become an independent state, was seen as having special significance. It could be of considerable value as regards the security of the region; moreover, in the words of Kenneth Landon, a former missionary in

Siam and now Chief of the State Department's section working on the affairs of that country, 'with our interest in expanding export markets after the war, an independent Thailand may be of particular importance to the United States as the only market in Southeast Asia not complicated by colonial relationships.' Landon added that 'the United States would suffer serious loss of prestige throughout Asia if as an outcome of the war where we are taking a leading role, Thailand . . . should lose pre-war Thai territory or have its sovereignty impaired by the victors.'[137]

The main threat in this last respect was not seen in Washington as coming from the direction of China, although the O.S.S. reported that there existed among the Siamese fears of being swamped by Chinese immigration and cultural penetration, and despite the fact that Chiang Kai-shek himself seemed eager to become involved in Siamese affairs when he proposed that the United Nations should establish and work through a Free Siamese committee in Chungking.[138] The danger to Siam's freedom appeared to U.S. officials, rather, to come from Britain, whose Government, as we have seen, had still not met American wishes by issuing a statement recognizing Siam's independence and territorial integrity.[139] Luang Pradit himself told an O.S.S. officer that he was 'very concerned lest Great Britain establish armed bases within Thailand and refuse to withdraw for a long time.'[140] Likewise, it was believed within the O.S.S. and in some quarters of the State Department that Britain was seeking some form of special privileges in Siam—at the least, a hold on the Kra Isthmus—and perhaps even a protectorate over the entire country.[141] The State-War-Navy Coordinating Committee therefore laid it down that British ideas of obtaining some kind of separate status for the Kra Isthmus were 'without merit', and that the whole of Siam—less those territories taken from Indochina and Malaya early in the war—should recover its independent and sovereign status.[142]

The difficulty for Washington lay in the fact that American military operations were passing Siam by, whereas Britain, through S.E.A.C., was likely to move into that area. The State Department therefore encouraged the O.S.S. units within S.E.A.C. and China to increase their independent activities into Siam, as being the best means available of manifesting United States good-will and securing American influence. For the same reason, British suggestions that joint clandestine operations should be mounted as regards Siam were rejected, with the result that there was an intensification of the existing O.S.S.–S.O.E. rivalry in that part of Southeast Asia. Thus, O.S.S. agents, acting on their own, brought out proposals by Luang Pradit for the setting up of a Provisional Free Thai Government in the U.S.A., an appeal by him for military assistance, and the gift of a gold cigarette-case from the Regent to Roosevelt.[143] In return, Washington looked with favour on the Free Siamese Movement, and recognized the value of establishing at least a committee in exile to represent its interests among the Allies.[144] In only one important respect, indeed, was American policy at this time aligned with that of Britain: both countries warned the Siamese resistance not to rise against the Japanese prematurely. (Some qualification is needed, in other words, to the notion that it was Britain alone who, having demanded that the Siamese should 'work their passage home' by turning against Japan, then deterred them from taking that very action.) Even so, there were still hopes within the State Department that London could be persuaded, perhaps via the Combined Chiefs of Staff, to bring its entire policy over Siam into line with that of the United States.[145]

Meanwhile on the British side there were indeed those officials who were anxious to achieve just such an alignment with the U.S.A. Dening, for example, had for some time been arguing from S.E.A.C. that Britain should 'forget and forgive' where Siam was concerned, and that the American attitude in that respect was 'more realistic' than that of the United Kingdom, being likely to lead to American popularity in Siam at Britain's expense should the contrast between the two approaches be allowed to continue. In order to make things easier, he suggested, Siam should be made a co-belligerent of the Allies, as had been done in the case of Italy; at the same time, London should quickly state its own terms—which should be lenient—for resuming normal relations with Bangkok.[146] The Siam country section of S.O.E. were also striving to persuade higher authority to accept that the Regent, Luang Pradit, was making great efforts 'to turn the Free Siamese Movement into an effective weapon'; and although they found S.E.A.C. Headquarters slow to accept that this was so, by June Mountbatten was proposing to London that the resistance movement should be given arms and training, in order to enable it to take part in coordinated action after the recapture of Singapore.[147]

That the Americans were suspicious of British intentions over Siam was by now well understood in the Foreign Office. Sansom, for example, reported from Washington that 'a general attitude of mistrust' prevailed there, while a State Department official openly described Siamese affairs as being 'a focal point of distrust' towards Britain.[148] A further series of direct exchanges between the Foreign Office and State Department, moreover, left no room for doubt that Washington wished to give official encouragement to the Free Siamese Movement, to recognize a new Siamese Government as soon as the country's subservience to Japan was completely thrown off, and to see Britain place her own aims—political, strategic and economic —above suspicion.[149]

Yet for all the Foreign Office's strong desire to stay close to the United States over Far Eastern affairs, its response in the case of Siam was a grudging one. Thus, when the State Department listed at the end of June 1945 those aspects of Siam's future which needed clarifying, the Head of the Far Eastern Department in London described the document in question as 'smug and provocative.' 'It has a superficial air of reasonableness', he continued, 'and in theory its suggestions are unexceptionable. But it takes no account whatever of realities. The State Department are only too ready to gloss over Siamese faults and from their insistent attempts to extract assurances from us it might also be supposed that we were the guilty party.'[150] The Foreign Office were also slow to amend their over-all approach in the light of the efforts being made by the Free Siamese Movement: as the same official (Sterndale Bennett) confessed in the middle of May, 'Up till quite recently we have been considering policy towards Siam from the angle of the terms which we might want to impose upon her as an enemy.'[151]

If the Foreign Office tended to be inflexible over Siam, the Cabinet, as already observed in the preceding period, were worse still—slow, insensitive and unrealistic—and set the tone for Whitehall to emulate. At the end of September 1944, they approved S.O.E. operations into Siam, but warned that no commitments could be entered into regarding 'the ultimate regime and organization' of the country.[152] Events then forced a further look at the subject when it was learned in the following February that Luang Pradit was secretly sending to S.E.A.C. Headquarters a mission which included a former Siamese Foreign Minister, Nai Direk. Again, however, London responded in the most cautious manner, insisting that the talks must be confined to military matters and that nothing must be said which might by implication rule out alterations in Siam's boundaries after the war. Mountbatten, too, decided to leave the interview with Nai Direk and his companions to Dening, an interview at which, the Foreign Office noted with relief, the visitors, unlike Free Siamese messages that were reaching Washington, at least did not ask for the setting up and recognition by the Allies of a Provisional Government in exile.[153]

Despite this grain of comfort, however, it was apparent that the Americans, even though they turned down the provisional-government proposal, were ready to welcome the establishment of a Free Siamese Liberation Committee in Washington (an idea that the Foreign Office judged 'premature and unwise'), and that, in Eden's words, they appeared to be seeking 'to take the lead in a question where we have the primary interest as being the neighbour of Siam and at war with her.' Therefore, a full reassessment of Britain's own policy had reluctantly to be undertaken in the latter part of April, the task being passed on from the Cabinet to the Far Eastern Committee. Even then, the Committee were told that the opinion of the Foreign Secretary was that 'the position created by Siam herself must be radically altered by the Siamese before our old friendly relations with them can be restored.'[154]

During the months that followed—and the Far Eastern Committee were not to present their report until the middle of July—a wide variety of factors had to be taken into consideration. One which pointed in the direction of helping to strengthen, rather than weaken, Siam was fear of the pressure which China might seek to exert upon that country through the three million Chinese (nearly one-fifth of the population) living there, a development which might in the long run bring Siam 'under China's political sway' and would certainly have 'immediate repercussions on the analogous problem in Malaya and Burma.' The thought also arose that the United States might encourage China to act in this way over Siam in order to offset Chungking's resentment at the failure of her mentor to stand up to Soviet claims in the north.[155] On the other side of the equation, however, there lay the need to recover from Siam the Malay territories that she had been given by Japan since 1941 (we have seen already that Amery among others wanted to take additional areas in the same region);[156] and as a lesser matter, there was also the desirability of avoiding a misunderstanding with France, between whom and Siam there had long existed tension, now exacerbated by Japan's award to Siam in 1941 of parts of Indochina.[157]

At the same time it was widely agreed in Whitehall that pressure would have to be exerted upon Siam to ensure that use could be made of her surplus rice supplies immediately after the war, in order to help feed India and Ceylon, together with Malaya and various other territories liberated from the Japanese. The idea was also put forward that the rice in question might be obtained free of charge, as part of the reparations that Siam should pay, or at least at a price less than the one prevailing on the world market.[158]*

Two other major desiderata, this time long-term ones, were among those advanced by officials and politicians in London who advocated a forceful approach to the Siamese question.[159] One was the need to restore Britain's trading position in that country. The other, and most weighty one of all, was the need to ensure that Siam did not remain what it had proved to be in 1941, a weak and obstructive element in the defence of British territories in Southeast Asia. The Post Hostilities Planning Staff had been working for some time on this last subject. Siam, they declared, was of vital importance as a result of its position as a link with Indochina, which was itself the key to the defence of Burma and Malaya. In addition, if Indochina were to fall to an enemy, Britain might want to fight a delaying action across Siam before taking up defensive positions on the approaches to her own colonies. A list of requirements was therefore drafted, whereby Siam's Government would agree to act in peacetime on British advice as regards defence matters, and to grant Britain special rights in the Kra Isthmus and in the Siam–Burma border areas; in war-time, or when 'the threat of war' arose, Siam was to make available to Britain full transit facilities and to allow her to deploy her forces and take whatever defence measures she deemed necessary within Siamese territory. (Such war-time rights, it was hoped, would also be granted by Bangkok to the U.S.A., France and the Netherlands.) In the same, bullish spirit, the First Sea Lord, Admiral of the Fleet Sir Andrew Cunningham, observed towards the end of March that 'since we were at war with Siam and the United States were not, we should be in a position to insist that our special claims were satisfied', possibly, he suggested, by means of an Anglo-Siamese treaty akin to the one governing relations between Britain and Egypt.[160]

It was taking London a long time to arrive at a comprehensive policy, endorsed by the Cabinet. There was of course a great deal of other business for officials to attend to, by the side of which Siamese affairs often appeared unimportant, while the Chiefs of Staff for their part were not expecting major operations into Siam to take place until December 1945 at the

* The Foreign Office, in opposition to the Ministry of Food, did accept, however, that if the United States wished to do so, she should participate in the rice-control unit that would have to be set up to administer the procurement and distribution of supplies.

earliest.[161] It was estimated, moreover, that at least three months would be required to train and equip the Free Siamese who were waiting to rise against the Japanese in their country, and the Chiefs of Staff felt bound to await a Cabinet policy decision before authorizing Mountbatten to make such assistance available. Meanwhile S.E.A.C. Headquarters continued to the end of the war to urge the Siamese resistance not to take action before Allied troops were also ready to move.[162]

Nevertheless, although a sense of urgency was thus lacking in a good many quarters in London, as the summer of 1945 went by circumstances began to force some officials to have second thoughts as far as Siam was concerned. For one thing, the Free Siamese Movement, it seemed, had now to be taken more seriously. Thus, a Foreign Office minute on a report from Brigadier V. Jacques (who, from the end of April onwards, was operating almost openly in and around Bangkok, under the noses of the Japanese, as liaison officer with the F.S.M.) admitted: 'We are likely to obtain far more practical assistance in Siam than could [have been] anticipated. There is no doubt that Ruth [the code name for Luang Pradit] and his friends possess a con-siderable degree of organising and administrative ability.'[163] At the same time the Foreign Office were alerting others in Whitehall to the modifications which might have to be made to British policy in the light of the international situation. For example, they pointed out to Cunningham and his fellow Chiefs of Staff that the United States, and perhaps even France, would be likely to object to exclusive rights being obtained by Britain in Siam, and that the Siamese themselves were unlikely to cooperate in this respect without first obtaining from London a guarantee of their territorial integrity and of financial assistance.[164]

Thereafter, the promulgation of the United Nations Charter and further representations over Siam that were made by Washington prompted an even greater degree of caution. Thus, although the Far Eastern Committee continued to hope that Bangkok would agree 'to act [militarily] in time of peace on British advice', and to provide Britain in the event or threat of war with 'such facilities as are normally granted by an Ally', the Joint Planning Staff now advised the Chiefs of Staff in July that a unilateral approach to Siam over these matters would be unwise, that prior discussions should be held with the United States, and that a United Nations framework was what should be envisaged for Siam's defence arrangements.[165] In a similar vein, the Far Eastern Committee, in its final report dated 14 July, warned that

'if we go beyond mere restitution and seek to impose some form of reparation or some form of control . . . over Siam in the post-war period, it must be realised that we shall possibly meet with great difficulty in achieving these ends . . . The United States Government are at present in a position . . . to block or hinder military operations into Siam. As to non-military measures [to bring pressure to bear on Bangkok], . . . the facilities which Siam required could no doubt be easily forthcoming from the United States.'

The Committee's own proposal, that compensation should be demanded from Siam for the work done by British prisoners-of-war on the Siam–Burma railway, was itself discarded by a Cabinet Committee examining the question.

Other conditions to be presented to Siam were still being discussed in London when the war ended (the change of Government and the need to consult the Dominions had also helped to delay matters), and it was thus not until 17 August that a new Far Eastern Ministerial Committee under Bevin agreed on their outline. British territory obtained during the war was to be returned, and one and a half million tons of rice were to be made available, as Siam's contribution to the Allied war effort; militarily, she was to 'carry out such measures for the preservation of peace and security as the United Nations Organisation may require' (gone, in other words, were Britain's own demands for special facilities, although Bangkok was still to be required to undertake not to build a canal across the Kra Isthmus, and to recognize Siam's importance for the defence of Burma, Malaya, Indochina, the Indian Ocean and the Southwest Pacific); in the commercial sphere, Siam was to take all possible steps to restore her pre-war trade with neighbouring British territories and, pending the signing of a new treaty that would cover such matters, was not to exclude British commercial, industrial or professional interests from participating in her trade and economy; Bangkok should also agree to abide by post-war arrangements for the trade in tin and rubber, on the same basis as other producers.[166]

On these terms, a draft of which was to be shown to the Americans, Britain would agree to make peace with Siam. Yet even now, scaled down though they had been, the conditions were to prove too stern for the Siamese readily to accept, and above all were to arouse hostility and resentment on the part of the United States. From the moment that Britain had declared war on Siam while the U.S.A. had refrained from doing so, the two countries had failed to coordinate their policies in that part of Southeast Asia, and were to continue in this state for the remainder of 1945. Not every American suspicion of British intentions was, in fact, justified, while Washington had ambitions of its own in Siam; conversely, Britain's concern over the future of the Kra Isthmus was as understandable as the United States preoccupation with the fate of Japan's Pacific islands. Nevertheless, and in contrast to most Far Eastern issues, the responsibility for Anglo-American disharmony in the case of Siam lay more with London than with Washington.

Indeed, there are times when it is hard to avoid the impression that British Ministers and officials were viewing Siamese affairs, not in a detached and careful manner, but with an underlying resentment which arose from the humiliation that had been suffered in 1941–42. The treatment of Japan, who had been responsible for that irreparable blow to Britain's prestige, had to be approached with great circumspection and in any case was primarily a matter for the United States. To aim a few kicks at Japan's erstwhile jackal, however, may have helped some in London to relieve their feelings, at the same time as fostering the illusion that Britain was once more going to be able to exercise a dominating influence over the affairs of Southeast Asia. Siamese issues, in short, showed London's Far Eastern policies at their worst.

The war came to an end before full-scale military operations could be carried out in Siam and thus influence the arrangements that were made for that country. Similarly, it was of great significance that the American advance upon Japan was passing Indochina by as well. Unlike the case of Siam, however, fighting did break out within Indochina itself before Tokyo surrendered, when, on 9 March 1945, the Japanese turned upon the French forces that still remained there.[167] Militarily, the outcome of this sudden outbreak of violence was a disaster for the French, with those units that survived being forced to flee into China. Politically, however, the episode enabled the Government in Paris—whose growing stature, internationally, has been noted in an earlier chapter—to claim that France was shedding blood in the liberation of her own territory. Thus the Minister of Colonies was better placed to affirm, as he did on 24 March, that 'Indochina is called to a special place in the French community . . . The Indochinese Federation will form, together with France and other parts of the Community, a French Union whose interests abroad will be represented by France.' De Gaulle himself had already and imaginatively declared that 'in the suffering of all and in the blood of the soldiers a solemn pact is at this moment being sealed between France and the peoples of the Indochinese Union.'

The French Provisional Government also attempted to rally support among the traditional Vietnamese ruling class for a restoration of French sovereignty by offering some form of local autonomy on a federal basis (although the actual political structure that would be involved was not clarified). Paris sought in addition to preserve the allegiance of the Kings of Laos and Cambodia, and to head off attempts by nationalists to bring Tonkin, Annam and Cochin China together to form an independent state.[168] The need for some such forestalling action was increasingly apparent as the Viet Minh, led by Ho Chi Minh and now more significant than the multiparty League of Vietnamese Revolutionary Parties (Dong Minh Hoi) which had been founded in 1942, consolidated their position within Vietnam itself. The Japanese, too, were contributing to future trouble for the French by allowing their puppet emperor, Bao Dai, to extend his nominal authority from Annam to Tonkin in March, and then to Cochin China as well, early in August.[169]

Meanwhile de Gaulle's Government also sought to ward off any interference on the part of the United States, formally declaring that France 'could not admit any discussion about the principle of her establishment in Indochina', even though she was ready to examine measures aimed at achieving international security in the area and to permit other states to compete for a share in Indochina's economic development. When de Gaulle learned that American forces were under orders not to send aid to the

French units that were fighting for their lives in Indochina in March, he added for Washington's benefit a somewhat far-fetched warning of the possible consequences for the United States as regards her interests in Europe:

'What are you driving at?', he asked the American Ambassador in Paris. 'Do you want us to become, for example, one of the federated states under the Russian aegis? The Russians are advancing apace as you know. When Germany falls they will be upon us. If the public here comes to realize that you are against us in Indochina there will be terrific disappointment and nobody knows to what that will lead. We do not want to become Communist; we do not want to fall into the Russian orbit, but I hope that you will not push us into it.'[170]

As for the British, they were recognized by the French authorities as being in favour of a restoration of the sovereignty of France in Indochina. At the same time, however, they were seen as being limited in the extent to which they could go in opposing the will of the United States over a matter such as this. General Sabattier, formerly commander of the French forces in the Hanoi region, thus reported to the Ministry of Defence in Paris in June:

'Dès les premières negotiations, il apparut que les Anglais étaient favorables à nos projets, mais qu'ils ne voulaient rien faire sans avoir l'accord des Américains.' [Sabattier therefore advocated that France should keep a foot in the camp of each of the two Allies:] 'Dans la conjoncture présente, entre le mauvais vouloir des Américains ... et l'esprit de compréhension, intéressé cela va de soi des Anglais, il serait semble-t-il logique de s'arrêter à la solution qui consisterait à appliquer nos forces militaires, partie avec les Anglais sur le sud de l'Indochine, partie avec les Sino-Américains sur le nord.'[171]

British policy was indeed still in favour of the return of France to Indochina, albeit with the introduction of some form of United Nations security system there. The Foreign Office did not waver from the line which the Cabinet had already approved, and briefed Churchill in this sense before Hurley paid his unhelpful visit to London in April:

'What is most likely to be lacking in the Far East after the defeat of Japan', ran the paper sent to the Prime Minister, 'is stability, and it is in our interest to support those elements of stability in the Far East which are capable of preserving law and order. So far as Indochina is concerned we do not believe that there is any satisfactory alternative to the French as a stabilising element. We just do not understand the President's attitude when the United States Government have committed themselves up to the hilt to the contrary.'[172]

A similar briefing paper had been prepared before the Yalta Conference, emphasizing the strategic significance of Indochina, the resentment which France would direct against Britain if the latter tried to interfere with her position there, and the uncertainty which would be cast over the future of all Southeast Asian colonies overrun by the Japanese if Roosevelt were allowed to put what Cadogan called his 'sinister intentions' over Indochina into practice.

As for the wider setting, a member of the Western Department of the Foreign Office summarized the reasons why a 'strong and friendly' France was essential for Britian's own post-war security:

'1. because it is vital that her northern ports should be in strong and friendly hands; 2. because we must rely on France to play the major role in containing Germany from the West; 3. because with the many European and imperial interests which she has in common with us, France should prove a useful ally on occasions in the counsels of the Great Powers . . . In trying to strengthen France we also bear in mind her usefulness as a counterweight to Russian influence in Europe.'[173]

Meanwhile the Government of India—for security, anti-Chinese and pro-imperialist reasons—also let it be known that it desired to see the return of France to Indochina.[174] So, too, as we have already seen in an earlier period, did Australia, a surprising attitude on Canberra's part for which Evatt received the warm thanks of Bidault at San Francisco.[175]

Senior British officers and officials in S.E.A.C. itself were by now keen to establish a basis for full cooperation with the French, and were anxious to forestall what the Foreign Office in London also feared, namely an impatient decision on the part of Paris to throw in their lot with the United States after all, and to work into Indochina from Chungking rather than from S.E.A.C. in the south.[176] Mountbatten himself instructed the Commander of S.O.E.'s Force 136 and others to assist in bringing French personnel out to S.E.A.C. from Europe 'with the minimum of fuss', and in this way help to present the Americans with a fait accompli. 'Surely', he wrote to Eden in March, 'in view of what one imagines to be the U.S. plans for French Indochina, it is essential on political grounds alone to implicate the French in this Theatre, and ourselves with them, as much as possible . . .'[177]

Force 136 had in fact been working with French agents since the end of 1944, so that by the beginning of 1945 François de Langlade, de Gaulle's representative on the spot, had got at least a dozen parties into Indochina; the Direction Générale des Études et Recherches (the French equivalent of S.O.E. and S.I.S.) also set up its own headquarters in Calcutta.[178] In addition, arrangements were made in the spring to train French civil administrators in India or Ceylon, in preparation for their return to Indochina, although a formal civil-affairs agreement with the French had not been signed by the time Japan surrendered.[179]

London, meanwhile, had been pressing Washington for a reply to the proposal to send out to S.E.A.C. a French military mission under General Blaizot and troops of the Corps Léger d'Intervention. (It will be recalled that Roosevelt had prevented the Joint Chiefs of Staff from making a favourable response in August 1944.)[180] Mountbatten was urging that something should be done to clear this matter up, warning at the end of September 1944 that 'these interminable delays will, if they result in General Stilwell obtaining concentrated control of Indochina, have a disastrous effect not only on the future operational prospects of this Command but on the whole British position in the Far East.' The Foreign Office, too, thought that the American attitude might be part of a plan 'to assign to us a purely minor role in the war with Japan.' At the beginning of October, therefore, without waiting any longer for Washington's approval, the Foreign Office informed the French that General Blaizot could proceed to S.E.A.C. temporarily; before the end of the month, Churchill went further still, and agreed that the mission could now stay with Mountbatten on a permanent basis. (It needs to be emphasized that no attempt was or could be made to conceal what had occurred from American officers on Mountbatten's staff, who were, indeed, consulted on the Command's use of French agents in Indochina. 'The Americans have known what we are doing', reported Dening to London, 'and will continue to be kept completely informed of our intentions.')[181]

It was not surprising then, that when fighting broke out in March between Japanese and French forces in Indochina itself, the British attitude was one of sympathy and anxiety to help in some way. Bearing in mind the value of any disruption that could be caused to Japanese supply lines running through Indochina to Burma, the Joint Intelligence Committee in London recommended to the Chiefs of Staff that S.E.A.C. should provide what assistance it could to the beleaguered French units, that the Americans should be urged to do the same, and that thought should again be given to the possibility of moving the Corps Léger out to the East from North Africa. Early in April, Churchill agreed that the Joint Chiefs in Washington should be told that Britain proposed to despatch the Corps Léger to Ceylon as an interim measure, even though Marshall and his colleagues were insisting that there must be no commitment as to the actual employment of that body in Indochina. Meanwhile S.E.A.C. was flying in supplies to that country, the Prime Minister taking the view 'that it will look very bad in history if we were to let the French force in Indochina be cut to pieces by the Japanese through shortage of ammunition if there is anything we can do to save them.' In addition, and at the prompting of the Foreign Office, British supplies were subsequently made available to those French units (about 7,000 men in all) which were forced to retreat across the border into China.[182]

As the summer advanced, so de Gaulle's representatives increased their attempts to have, not simply the Corps Léger, but substantial French land forces, together with naval units, sent out to take part in the war against Japan. Again, as was the case over similar Dutch demands, the Chiefs of Staff, the Foreign Office and the Prime Minister himself were sympathetic, and agreement in principle over the employment of French naval forces east of Suez was reached in Anglo-French staff talks held in Paris in June. As for the military role that de Gaulle's army could play, Brooke's idea, as he outlined it on the eve of the Japanese surrender, was that French troops should be used to occupy all of Indochina apart from Saigon (which S.E.A.C. would initially take), and that the entire territory should be recognized as constituting a French theatre of operations.[183]

Amid these developments, as we have seen to have been the case in the preceding period, British officials showed little awareness of, and no sympathy for, the growing force of nationalism among the Vietnamese. Aside from the hostility of Roosevelt, the main threat to a resumption of French rule was still seen as being likely to come from Chinese ambitions in the area; thus, 'the Annamite nationalist party (or Annamite Kuomintang)', as it was referred to, was assumed to be a creature of the Chinese, while towards the end of May it was also described as being 'more numerous and active than the communists.'[184] Whatever the state of native opinion, however, London remained convinced that the French should return to their Far Eastern possessions, and in the middle of April, in a briefing paper prepared in the Foreign Office for use by the British delegation to the San Francisco U.N. Conference, the possibility was even envisaged of having openly to oppose the Americans over this issue. 'We should profoundly regret a Franco-American controversy', ran the document, '. . . since we might find ourselves forced to side against the United States, an eventuality we should naturally prefer to avoid.'[185]

Yet however strongly the Foreign Office felt about this issue, it is by no means certain that Churchill would have approved the taking up, in public, of an anti-American and pro-French stance had such a moment of choice arrived where the future of Indochina was concerned. Not only did the Prime Minister place his partnership with Roosevelt and the United States above all other considerations, but his relations with de Gaulle were still far from smooth; nor was he yet paying sustained attention to post-war Far Eastern affairs. It is also obvious that for him there were many other issues at this time that appeared to be of infinitely greater importance than the fate of Indochina. (One thinks, too, of his remark in 1953: ' "I have lived seventy-eight years without hearing of bloody places like Cambodia." ') Thus, when the fighting broke out there in March, he had to ask Ismay to tell him what had happened in Indochina since the war began: 'How is it', he wrote, 'that there are French troops and a Governor General there now? Are they survivors of the Vichy period? Have they not yet joined up with de Gaulle? I have not followed affairs in that country for some time.'[186] The Prime Minister's own response to French requests for a place within S.E.A.C. and on various bodies concerned with the Far Eastern war continued for much of this period to be one of procrastination. In October, he instructed the Foreign Office to leave the matter quiet; in November, it was: 'This can certainly wait' and 'Nothing doing while de Gaulle is master.' He also vetoed discussions with the Dominions on the subject.[187]

In conformity with Churchill's approach, therefore, the military planners and Chiefs of Staff left on one side political issues that might involve the U.S.A. when considering, in January, possible operations into Indochina.[188]

The Prime Minister did then, it is true, move closer to the Foreign Office view when the French and Japanese started fighting one another, and on the eve of Roosevelt's death he even went so far as to urge the President that it was essential 'not only that we should support the French by all the means in our power, but also that we should associate them with our operations into their country. It would look very bad in history', he added, 'if . . . we excluded the French from participation in our councils as regards Indochina.'[189]

Yet this was still far from being an open confrontation with Washington. And when, in the following months, serious friction arose with the French, as we have seen earlier, over the Levant and the Val d'Aosta,[190] Churchill angrily rejected the advice of Duff Cooper, now Ambassador in Paris, and others that Britain should not align herself with the United States against France or be distracted from building up the latter's strength. 'We have reached a point', he wrote to Cadogan on 17 June, 'where any decisive taking up of a position by the United States should, in nearly all cases, be supported by us, and we should not drag our feet in matters of passing importance.'[191]* A similar awareness of Britain's huge degree of dependence on the United States ensured that the Chiefs of Staff, however sympathetic they might be to French desires to increase their military presence in the Far East, would not be drawn into a confrontation with the Joint Chiefs over this question, and at Potsdam they duly accepted that shipping could not in any case be made available for such a purpose for some time to come.[192]

Meanwhile, however, a serious and lengthy dispute between Mountbatten and Wedemeyer had been pushing Brooke and his colleagues in London towards making a proposal—the incorporation of Indochina within S.E.A.C.—which, if carried out, would not only resolve Anglo-American military disagreements in this area, but, incidentally, strengthen the position of Britain, and hence of France, when it came to deciding Indochina's future. (The word 'incidentally' is included because it is clear that the operational aspect of putting an end to the trouble with Wedemeyer figured far more than did the political aspect in the discussions on the matter that took place in London.)

It will be recalled that, in 1943, Chiang Kai-shek and Mountbatten had arrived at their 'Gentleman's Agreement' over the future adjustment of operational boundaries between the China Theatre and S.E.A.C. in Indochina and Siam, and that in addition—as was recorded separately, not only by Mountbatten but in the files of the U.S. Army's planners in Washington —the Generalissimo had agreed that Mountbatten could conduct pre-operational, clandestine activities into those same two countries.[193] Now, however, when Mountbatten came to proceed with these under-cover

---

* In return, as a French historian has noted, 'La malheureuse affaire syrienne, en provoquant à Paris de violentes réactions, en arrivait à y faire oublier la solidarité fondamentale qui liait en Extrême-Orient les intérêts français et britanniques.' (P. Devilliers, *Histoire du Viêt-Nam, 1940–1952* (Paris, 1952), 148. See de Gaulle, *War Memoirs: Salvation, 1944–1946* (London, 1960), 180ff.)

missions into Indochina, Wedemeyer (who, as the Supreme Commander's Deputy, had been informed by him at the time of what had taken place with Chiang Kai-shek) denied any knowledge of this aspect of the 1943 agreement. In his new capacity as Chief of Staff to the Generalissimo and as the American Commander in China, whose Theatre included Indochina, he demanded that Mountbatten should not engage in any activities in Indochina without his permission. The latter, in return, refused to do more than keep Wedemeyer informed, and although the two men appeared for a brief while, early in April, to have reached a compromise arrangement, the dispute was quickly resumed, with Wedemeyer being encouraged by Hurley to seek to keep the British out of Indochina altogether. The Chiefs of Staff in London therefore called in the Prime Minister, who, shortly before Roosevelt's death, arrived at an understanding with the President that Wedemeyer (in what Roosevelt insisted must be a coordinating role) and Mountbatten would keep each other fully informed of what they were doing in that territory and of the intelligence that they obtained there.

Even now, however, differences of interpretation arose, especially when Truman, soon after becoming President, made the assumption that Mountbatten was to obtain Wedemeyer's prior approval for any pre-operational missions he wished to conduct. Mountbatten tried to ease matters by agreeing that Chiang Kai-shek and Wedemeyer could veto any proposed S.E.A.C. activity that threatened to interfere with their own operations in Indochina, but still Wedemeyer sought to extend this power of rejection to every S.E.A.C. activity there, whether or not there was a likelihood of interference with his own plans. The British Chiefs of Staff thereupon joined Mountbatten in concluding that the American was seeking to exercise 'unwarranted control' over S.E.A.C.'s affairs. The only solution, Brooke and his colleagues decided, was to bring Indochina formally within S.E.A.C., and they therefore proposed this to the Joint Chiefs of Staff as an addition to the latter's own scheme for the transfer to Mountbatten's Command of the greater part of MacArthur's South West Pacific Area.[194]

The response of Marshall, King and Arnold to this proposal has already been outlined in a previous chapter. Despite Wedemeyer's objections, they suggested, it will be recalled, that Indochina should be divided at the 15° North parallel, the southern part to go to S.E.A.C. while the north remained the responsibility of Chiang Kai-shek. The British Chiefs of Staff in return accepted the principle of division (although the Foreign Office were unhappy about the possible reactions to this of both the Generalissimo and the French), and, after they had put forward counter-proposals for the line to be drawn at 16° and then 17° North, the Combined Chiefs agreed upon 16°, with a rider that the transfer of the whole of Indochina to S.E.A.C. might later prove desirable. Attlee and Truman then each put the proposal to Chiang Kai-shek, who was in no position to reject it. Britain thus became closely involved in the early post-war turmoil that was about to begin Indochina's long period of strife.[195]

That London and Washington could, at the very end of the war, agree in this fashion over strategic matters concerning Indochina reflected a narrowing of the gap between their respective positions over the future of that territory—a process of convergence which we have already observed taking place as regards colonial issues generally. Even so, for much of this period hostility towards the cause of France in Indochina continued to be expressed by some American officials. From the latter part of 1944 onwards, for example, Max Bishop sent frequent and emphatic warnings to Washington from Colombo about the way in which General Blaizot and others were swelling the French element within S.E.A.C., and of how the United States was in danger of being duped by a conspiracy among the European colonial powers in Southeast Asia.[196] A summary of Bishop's reports, together with similar O.S.S. and O.W.I. material, was passed on to Roosevelt by Stettinius in November, and the State Department submitted to the President in the following January a further memorandum in which it was argued that there existed 'a substantial sentiment for independence or self-government among the Indochinese', and that 'American influence among Asiatic peoples will suffer if the status quo ante is reestablished in Indochina. The United States', the survey continued, 'as the dominant power in the Pacific war, cannot in their eyes escape a major responsibility for post-war arrangements in the Far East.'[197]

Roosevelt himself, now clearly in decline and with so many other problems pressing in upon him, was not entirely consistent in what he now had to say on the issue. His emphasis in late 1944 and early 1945 still lay clearly in an anti-French direction; like Churchill, however, he was tending to put the question aside for the time being. Thus, he informed Hull in October that 'on this date . . . we should do nothing in regard to resistance groups or in any other way in relation to Indochina', asking that the subject be brought up again 'when things are a little clearer.'[198] Again, in November, he told Hurley that 'United States policy with regard to French Indochina cannot be formulated until after consultation with Allies at a forthcoming Combined Staff conference', although in the same month he also made it clear to the State Department that he had not given his approval for General Blaizot to go out to S.E.A.C., that no decision had been taken on the future of Indochina, and that the United States expected to be consulted fully by her Allies on all such Southeast Asian matters.[199]

By January, the President appears to have been becoming somewhat muddled in his thinking. To Stettinius, for example, he wrote: 'I still do not want to get mixed up in any Indochina decision. It is a matter for post-war. By the same token I do not want to get mixed up in any military effort toward the liberation of Indochina from the Japanese . . . From both the military and civil point of view, action at this time is premature.' (Roosevelt added that he had made all this clear to Churchill at the Quebec Conference in September, although according to British records the subject had not been raised between the two men.)[200] Yet to the Joint Chiefs of Staff a few weeks later, he was declaring that 'any action in Indochina which resulted in damage to the Japanese was satisfactory to him. He had no objection to any

U.S. action which it was considered desirable to take in Indochina as long as it did not involve any alignments with the French.'[201] At least the President's basically anti-French inclination remained clear, as did his desire to see Indochina placed under international trusteeship. He outlined this trusteeship idea once more to Stalin at Yalta, for example, adding that Britain was opposed to it (Stalin, for his part, agreed that it was a good proposal), while, according to Hurley, he was still speaking in this sense in private as late as March.[202]

In accordance with the President's wishes, United States policies were shaped so as to avoid any involvement in the French cause over Indochina. For example, requests from Paris for representation on bodies dealing with the war against Japan were rejected, as was a French proposal that the two countries should sign a civil-affairs agreement covering the Far East.[203] When the French in Indochina became embroiled in their fight against the Japanese in March, moreover, the O.W.I. received what Stettinius described as 'quite rigid' orders, 'emanating from the most authoritative sources', to play down in its reporting the extent of French resistance involved.[204] Wedemeyer, for his part, having been instructed in this sense by a Roosevelt whom he later recalled as having been vague and even dazed, saw to it that, initially, no help was provided by U.S. forces under his command for those French units who were struggling to avoid being wiped out by the Japanese.[205]

Meanwhile the Joint Chiefs of Staff were refusing, on the grounds of operational priorities, to provide the shipping needed to transport French troops from Europe to the Far East, a position they continued to adopt after Roosevelt's death.[206] Also in that post-Roosevelt period, Hurley in China went on seeking from Washington a clear and anti-French directive where the future of Indochina was concerned. (It will be recalled that, when in London in April, he had nevertheless sought to ingratiate himself by giving the impression that he disapproved of Roosevelt's attitude over the question.)[207] As for the O.S.S., which had been developing its own contacts within Indochina since 1944, it began in the summer of 1945 to send liaison officers to work with the Viet Minh; thereafter, some of those O.S.S. representatives not only urged that the U.S.A. should support the cause of Ho Chi Minh, but openly sided with the Viet Minh in early clashes which took place between them and the French at the end of the war.[208]

Yet if Roosevelt had continued to set a generally anti-French tone for American policy, he had still not laid down instructions in such a way as to avoid confusion and uncertainty. Thus, the Army's representative on the State-War-Navy Coordinating Committee declared on the day after the President's death: 'The lack of a policy is a source of serious embarrassment to the military', and he was supported by the Committee as a whole when he urged that 'President Roosevelt's prohibition upon discussion of our Indochina policy must be reconsidered or reaffirmed promptly.'[209]* Hurley and

* That men in such important positions in Washington should have been given to believe that they were not even allowed to discuss this potentially significant aspect of U.S.

Wedemeyer likewise informed Truman in May that they lacked a written directive on Indochina, while Wheeler, as the senior American officer in S.E.A.C., found himself in an awkward position when dealing with Mountbatten over that territory without having been informed beforehand of Washington's latest thinking on the subject.[210]

This muddled state of affairs was due, not simply to the chaotic and at times secretive manner in which Roosevelt tended to conduct his foreign policies; it reflected also the President's own inability to see and pursue a clear way forward over Indochina. In fact, unknown to many of his officials and senior officers, he was already in the last months of his life beginning to modify the line he had been pursuing since at least 1942. In January 1945, for example, when informed by Halifax of Mountbatten's desire to send French agents into Indochina, he replied, in the Ambassador's words, 'that if we felt it was important we had better tell Mountbatten to do it and ask no questions.' (The President did take the opportunity to repeat his desire to avoid a return to the status quo; he failed, however, to inform either Wedemeyer or Wheeler of what he had said about the use of French agents, with the result that those Generals were left to oppose actions of Mountbatten's which their own Commander-in-Chief had secretly sanctioned.)[211]

In March, Roosevelt made further and more significant compromises. On the 18th, nine days after the fighting in Indochina had broken out, he at last agreed that United States forces in China could fly in aid to the French units involved, providing that this did not interfere with other, planned operations. (Chennault, as commander of the Fourteenth Air Force, was already anxious to supply what help he could. Some American assistance was also provided subsequently for the French who were driven to seek refuge in Yunnan.)[212] Three days earlier, moreover, on the 15th, the President had made an even greater concession, during a conversation with Charles Taussig:

'I asked [him]', recorded Taussig, 'if he had changed his ideas on French Indochina as he had expressed them to us at the luncheon with Stanley. He said no, . . . that French Indochina and New Caledonia should be taken from France and put under a trusteeship. The President hesitated a moment and then said—well, if we can get the proper pledge from France to assume for herself the obligations of a trustee, then I would agree to France retaining these colonies with the proviso that independence was the ultimate goal. I asked the President if he would settle for self-government. He said no. I asked him if he would settle for dominion status. He said no—it must be independence. He said that is to be the policy and you can quote me in the State Department.'[213]

policies not only foreshadows attitudes that were to be adopted during the Vietnam war, but provides an echo of the situation within totalitarian regimes. Of course, there was still some way to go before the position was reached that had obtained in Berlin, after 1937 especially, when Ribbentrop threatened personally to shoot any diplomat who was heard to question the correctness of the Fuehrer's policies. (See C. Thorne, *The Approach of War, 1938-1939*, 27.)

With Roosevelt himself thus becoming somewhat more restrained, it is not surprising to find that others in Washington, where, as we have seen, some officials had always lagged well behind the President over Indochina, were by 1945 arguing in an essentially pro-French sense. This development was fostered by the revival of France herself, by the continuation of chaos in China, and by the marked changes, noted above, in the thinking of various American organisations and individuals about the future of Western colonies generally. The refusal of Britain to identify herself with Roosevelt's ideas on Indochina was another contributing factor. Thus, at a meeting with Stimson, Forrestal and Stettinius early in January, Hopkins suggested, as the Secretary of State recorded it,

'that there was need for a complete revision not only of the Indochina situation but of our entire French approach. In this connection he referred to instances in the past where we had held back on certain French matters, but on which we had finally, because of British pressure and other reasons, changed our position. He expressed the opinion that this had resulted in the French feeling that we were opposed to their regrowth.

The feeling seemed to be that with the British position what it is that [sic] our policy of deferring a decision on Indochina until some general peace settlement would probably be doomed to failure.'[214]

Nor, apparently, were the Joint Chiefs of Staff politically opposed to the French in Southeast Asia, despite their refusal to make early and special arrangements for the transfer of de Gaulle's forces to the Far East. At the end of March, the head of the British naval delegation in Washington, Admiral Somerville, wrote to Mountbatten: 'As a result of a talk, very strictly personal and therefore "eyes only",* that I had with Ernie King yesterday, it seems to me that the U.S. Chiefs of Staff are by no means in favour of the President's policy of keeping the French out of Indochina.'[215] As for the State Department, individual officials were making it known in Allied circles that the trend towards a soft line over this issue was continuing. George Blakeslee, for example, Special Assistant to the Director of the Office of Far Eastern Affairs, told the Australian Minister, Eggleston, in February that 'he saw no alternative but France taking [Indochina] over.'[216] Similarly, the Deputy Director of the Office of European Affairs, John Hickerson, informed a member of the Foreign Office team attending the San Francisco Conference

'that the American proposal at Yalta in connection with trusteeship had been partly phrased by the State Department in order to permit a climb-down from the position that President Roosevelt had taken in conversation as regards Indochina. The third category of territories suitable for inclusion in the trusteeship pool, that is Category C, would enable but not compel the French voluntarily to entrust Indochina to the trusteeship

* 'Eyes only' was a classification placed upon official messages that were to be read by the addressee and no one else.

pool. I do not imagine', the British official concluded, 'that Mr Hickerson expected the French to do this, but he made it clear that the State Department felt that President Roosevelt had gone too far and that Category C was a useful face-saver.'[217]

Within the State Department, in fact, the future of Indochina continued to be a source of disagreement between officials primarily concerned with European affairs and a group within the Far Eastern Office. Even 'F.E.' was ready to accept, in April, the proposition put forward by 'Eur.' that 'the Government of the United States should neither oppose the restoration of Indochina to France, with or without a programme of international accountability, nor take any action toward French overseas possessions which it is not prepared to take or suggest with regard to the colonial possessions of our other Allies.' 'F.E.', however, did wish to stress 'that for the protection of American interests* it is essential that French policies in Indochina follow a pattern more liberal than heretofore announced', and that the U.S.A. should therefore insist upon 'adequate assurances as to the implementing of policies in Indochina which we consider essential to assure peace and stability in the Far East.'

This last proposal by 'F.E.' was in turn strongly opposed by James Dunn (an Assistant Secretary of State), who cited French fears of being dominated by the Soviet Union and declared that the U.S.A. had 'no right to dictate to France nor to take away her territory.'[218] Nevertheless, the State Department did draw up a list of suggested reforms which Truman, if he wished, could put to de Gaulle. The document echoed past and more radical approaches to the question when it asserted that 'this Government will not assist the French to reestablish their control over Indochina by force, and . . . our willingness to see their control reestablished is predicated on the assumption that their claim to have the support of the population of Indochina is borne out by future events.' At the same time, however, the compromise nature of the paper was evident in its emphasis that the United States had 'no thought of opposing the reestablishment of French control in Indochina', while the goal it envisaged was not independence but an Indochina that was 'fully self-governing and autonomous except in matters of common concern to the contemplated French Union, and that in those matters Indochina may have a reasonable voice.'[219]

Clearly, there were still those officials for whom a great deal depended on the state of opinion within Indochina and the strength of the nationalist movement there, and one survey, written in June, did foresee considerable trouble for the French in that connection. Even 'F.E.', however, had to admit (as the O.S.S. research department were to do as late as October 1945) that adequate information on the subject was still lacking. Interestingly

---

* The emphasis upon American interests (and upon 'stability'), as in the case of U.S. policies towards China, rather than on the interests of the peoples directly concerned, is worth noting. There is nothing surprising in it, of course; but it does not accord with some of the more mythical versions of their country's record in the Far East which numerous Americans appear to entertain to this day.

enough, 'F.E.', even then, defined the dangers which could result from 'serious resistance to restoration of French control' in terms of 'a situation ... which might not only alienate American public opinion but affect adversely the position of all Western powers, including the United States, in the Far East, as well as weaken French prestige in world affairs.'[220]

Meanwhile the decision of the Truman Administration not to insist upon a trusteeship for Indochina was made clear both to Hurley in the Far East and to the Government in Paris.[221] Stettinius even went so far as to assure Bidault, the French Foreign Minister, that 'the record was entirely innocent of any official statement of this Government questioning, even by implication, French sovereignty over Indochina.'[222] In the field, an element of confusion still remained, with Wedemeyer, for example, ordering American arms to be supplied to both French and Vietnamese resistance groups alike; the Vietnamese, however, were instructed not to use these weapons against the French, while the O.S.S. came to an agreement with the Direction Générale des Études et Recherches over intelligence activities in the area.[223] Truman himself approved in principle the movement of French forces to the Far East,[224] and when de Gaulle visited Washington in August the President again made clear the absence of American opposition to the restoration of French rule in her Eastern Empire. To Madame Chiang Kai-shek, who raised the subject of Indochina with him a few days later, Truman reported that de Gaulle, for his part, had responded satisfactorily to the idea of eventual independence for that territory (can this really have been so, one wonders?), but that 'there had been no discussion of a trusteeship ... as far as he [the President] was concerned.'[225]

It was, indeed, a far cry from the assertive approach over Indochina that had manifested itself throughout Washington in 1942. And something of a similar contrast was present also, in this period, over the case of India.

Notes to Chapter Twenty-Seven

1 Mountbatten to WSC, 11 Oct. 1944, PREM 3, 149/8.
2 SEAC War Diary, 21 and 25 Oct. 1944.
3 WSC to Ismay, 11 Oct. 1944, and Cairo minutes, 20 Oct. 1944, PREM 3, 149/8; WSC to Ismay, 28 Nov. 1944, PREM 3, 149/9; COS, 7 April 1945, CAB 79/31.
4 Mountbatten to WSC, 22 Jan. 1945, PREM 3, 149/11; FO 371, F1365/12/10.
5 FRUS, 1945, VII, 48. See in general *Romanus and Sutherland*, III, cap. IV and Anders, *The Ledo Road*, 235ff. The Ledo Road cost $148 million to build and eventually absorbed a force of over 17,000 military engineers. During 1945 it was used to deliver only 147,000 tons of supplies, while the Hump air route carried 555,000 tons.
6 Ehrman, *Grand Strategy*, VI, 169, 181.
7 CCS to Mountbatten, 2 Feb. 1945, PREM 3, 149/11.
8 Material in PREM 3, 149/3 and 11; Ehrman, *Grand Strategy*, VI, cap. V; *Roskill*, III, part 2, 201.
9 Material in PREM 3, 149/10; Ehrman, *Grand Strategy*, VI, cap. VIII; SEAC War Diary, 27 July 1945; Slim, *Defeat Into Victory*, passim; *Bryant*, II, 464.
10 See CCS directive, 2 Feb. 1945, PREM 3, 149/11; Dening to Sterndale Bennett, 2

March 1945, FO 371, F1498/47/23; Wheeler to Marshall, 24 March 1945, OPD, Exec. file 17, item 26.

11 See also *Churchill*, VI, 639.

12 Material in PREM 3, 142/7, 149/2, 3, 4; Mountbatten to WSC, 11 March 1945, PREM 3, 159/14; SEAC War Diary, 7–11 March 1945; Ehrman, *Grand Strategy*, VI, 174ff.; *Kirby*, IV, 418ff.; *Mountbatten*, 104ff., 132ff.; *Romanus and Sutherland*, III, 143ff., 225ff.

13 Bishop to Grew, 5 Dec. 1944, DS, 123, Bishop file.

14 Wheeler to Marshall, 24 March 1945, OPD, Exec. file 17, item 26.

15 Sultan to Marshall, 13 Feb. 1945, Roosevelt Papers, PSF box 36.

16 SEAC War Diary, 18 June 1945.

17 *Wavell*, 22 Sept. 1945; FO 371, F5694/100/23.

18 Stimson Diary, 3 Oct. 1944; FRUS, 1945, VII, 2ff.

19 FO 371, F5702/34/10.

20 E.g. ibid, F4541/47/23; F3590 and 5394/69/23.

21 Mountbatten to Somerville, 14 Nov. 1944, Somerville Papers, box 9/2.

22 See above, 536.

23 FO 371, F5103/100/23.

24 Taylor, *Richer By Asia*, 372.

25 SEAC War Diary, 15 June 1945.

26 Ibid, 30 March 1945; Hansard, HC Deb, 411. col. 1493.

27 E.g. FO 371, F4928 and 5766/1/61; F1502, 1738, 1844, 2012 and 4011/16/61.

28 Ibid, F4563/1/61.

29 Ibid, material in file 46355.

30 FRUS, 1945, VI, 1264. See e.g. DS, 740.0011P.W./7–1945. For Mountbatten's attempts to coordinate clandestine activities, see SEAC War Diary, 18 Jan. 1945.

31 DS, 740.0011P.W./5–945.

32 Ibid, 1–945.

33 Stettinius to FDR, 10 Jan. 1945, Roosevelt Papers, PSF box 53.

34 *Chicago Tribune*, 7 Feb. 1945.

35 FO 371, AN1608/109/10.

36 *Chicago Tribune*, 1 April 1945.

37 FO 371, AN935/4/45.

38 Ibid, AN548/109/45.

39 Ibid, AN468/4/45; AN1793/4/45.

40 *Washington Post*, 8 Aug. 1945.

41 Hull to FDR, 5 Oct. 1944, Roosevelt Papers, MR box 166.

42 Hurley to FDR, 26 Nov. 1944, ibid, MR box 11.

43 Wedemeyer to Marshall, 15 Nov. 1944; ibid, MR box 11.

44 See above, 484, 547.

45 DS, 740.0011P.W./11–1744.

46 Donovan to FDR, 27 Oct. 1944, Roosevelt Papers, PSF box 167. An OSS survey of April 1944 (R and A 1398) observed that British statements concerning colonial policy 'do not of necessity indicate willingness to loosen imperial bonds.' On the American side, it acknowledged, there was much ignorance about the British Empire and a great deal of 'myth and doctrine' in that regard. It shrewdly concluded, however, that 'Ultimately it will be the character and popular conception of American and British interests in the colonial zones that will determine the degree of Anglo-American cooperation, and not success or failure in convincing American public opinion of the righteousness of British imperial ideas.'

47 Roosevelt to Hurley, 16 Nov. 1944, ibid, MR box 11.

48 FRUS, 1944, V, 1285; FO 371, F5868/168/61.

49 E.g. FRUS, Malta and Yalta, 56.

50 E.g. Taussig memo., 16 Jan. 1945, Taussig Papers, box 48.

51 E.g. *Roosevelt Letters*, 3 April 1945; Hassett, *Off The Record With F.D.R.*, 330.

52 FO 371, AN1748/4/45.

53 Taussig memo., 15 March 1945, Taussig Papers, box 49.
54 Rosenman, *Working With Roosevelt*, 478; see Hassett, *Off The Record*, entry for 22 Jan. 1945.
55 Roosevelt, *As He Saw It*, 223.
56 *Burns*, 593.
57 Taussig memo., 16 Jan. 1945, Taussig Papers, box 49.
58 Dulles and Ridinger, *Political Science Quarterly*, March 1955.
59 Taussig memos., 16 and 18 Jan. 1945, Taussig Papers box 48; Taussig memo., 15 March 1945, ibid, box 49; Frankfurter to Lippmann, 18 Jan. 1945, Frankfurter Papers, box 78; FRUS, Malta and Yalta, 81; memo. of 18 Jan. 1945, DS, Notter files, box 130; memo. of 4 Jan. 1945, SC-21, DS, Secretary's Staff Cttee., box 88E; Secretary's Staff Cttee., 19 Jan. 1945, box 88G; FO 371, U632/191/70.
60 FO 371, F247/91/61; AN1198/4/45.
61 Eggleston to Evatt, 15 Jan. 1945, ADEA, A1066/P45/153/2, pt. 1; Eggleston to Evatt, 20 Feb. 1945, Evatt Papers, Eggleston file, Washington; Eggleston Diary, 26 March 1945.
62 FO 371, U1047/191/70; Eden to WSC, 5 Feb. 1945, PREM 4, 31/4.
63 FRUS, Malta and Yalta, 975.
64 See FRUS, 1945, I, 93, 135, 140, 198, 204, 209, 211, 281, 290, 311, 330, 351, 459; Dependent Areas Cttee., DS, Notter files, box 131; DS, Secretary's Staff Cttee., box 88H; *Notter*, 387ff. and appendix 63; U.N. Charter, articles 82 and 84.
65 Minutes of 28 Oct. 1944, IPR Papers, box 362.
66 Taussig memo., 12 April 1945, Taussig Papers, box 49.
67 Taussig memo., 27 Aug. 1945, ibid, box 48.
68 *Washington Post*, 20 March 1945.
69 See above, 241, 358.
70 FRUS, 1945, I, 311ff., 445ff., 790ff., 954ff.
71 FO 371, files 50809–11.
72 Record, 12 May 1945, Grew Papers, vol. 7; FRUS, 1945, VI, 556ff.
73 OSS memo., 2 April 1945, Truman Papers, White House Central Files, OSS. See above, 353, note 75.
74 Hansard, HC Deb, 407, col. 31.
75 Minutes of 9 Feb. 1945, CAB 99/31, and for a more colourful version, Stettinius, *Roosevelt and the Russians*, 211.
76 FO 371, F5868/168/61; F1428/11/61.
77 Ibid, material in files 46463, 46465.
78 Eden and WSC minutes, 29 March 1945, PREM 4, 31/7.
79 FO 371, U2665/191/70. For the British draft as eventually put forward at San Francisco, see ibid, U3449/19/70.
80 Ibid, material in file 50807; material in PREM 4, 31/4; Cab, 19 March 1945 (CAB 65/49), 12 and 14 April 1945 (CAB 65/50); WP(45)200 (CAB 66/63), WP(45)208 (CAB 66/64), WP(45)300 (CAB 66/65); APW memos., CAB 87/69.
81 See *Hasluck*, II, 496ff.
82 WP(44)630, 641, CAB 66/57; Cabs, 13 and 24 Nov. 1944, CAB 65/44; material in PREM 4, 50/13.
83 WP(45)228, CAB 66/64; Cab, 12 April 1945, CAB 65/50; minutes, 4–13 April 1945, CAB 99/30.
84 Eggleston to Officer, 5 July 1945; Eggleston to Bruce, 9 July 1945, Eggleston Papers, 423/10/74 and 85 respectively; *Hasluck*, II, 503ff.; *Cadogan Diaries*, 23 May 1945.
85 Eden to WSC, 30 April 1945, PREM 4, 31/7.
86 van Kleffens memo., 27 Feb. 1945, and van Kleffens–Bidault conversation, 19 March 1945, NFM, DZ. El. 18(18).
87 *Louis*.
88 Cranborne to Stanley, 14 May 1945, PREM 4, 31/7; material in PREM 4, 31/4; FO 371, U3813/191/70.
89 APW, 5 and 26 March 1945, CAB 87/69.

90 APW, 14 Dec. 1944 (CAB 87/66) and 26 March 1945 (CAB 87/69); APW(44)124 (CAB 87/68); WP(44)738 (CAB 66/59); material in PREM 4, 31/4.

91 WP(44)643 (CAB 66/57) and 753 (CAB 66/60); Cab, 21 Dec. 1944 (CAB 65/44).

92 FO 371, F5868/168/61.

93 Material in ibid, files 45651–6, 45717, 45741.

94 See above, 459.

95 FEC, 29 Nov. 1944, CAB 96/5; Malaya and Borneo Cttee., 19 Dec. 1944, CAB 98/41; WP(44)762 (CAB 66/60), WP(45)287 (CAB 66/65); Cabs, 9 Jan. 1945 (CAB 65/49) and 15 June 1945 (CAB 65/53).

96 See above, 460, and Sweet-Escott, *Baker Street Irregular*, 242 and 256–7; Kennedy, *A History of Malaya*, 261; Purcell, *Memoirs*, 349.

97 Mountbatten to COS, 11 and 12 May 1945, PREM 3, 149/5; SEAC War Diary, 25 April and 11 May 1945.

98 SEAC War Diary, 7 June and 8 Aug. 1945; *Donnison*, 382ff.

99 See above, 459.

100 FO 371, F5031/4760/61.

101 Ibid, F129/129/61.

102 SEAC War Diary, 7 Feb. 1945.

103 Dorman-Smith to Amery, 16 and 17 Oct. 1944, IO, Private Office Papers, L/PO/238; Dorman-Smith to Amery, 13 Nov. 1944, Dorman-Smith Papers, E215/3. The Governor did envisage a treaty between Britain and Burma, however, 'concerning matters in which H.M.G. will have an abiding interest.'

104 Dorman-Smith to Amery, 25 July 1945, Dorman-Smith Papers, E215/59.

105 FEC, 15 Nov. 1944, CAB 96/5.

106 Amery to Dorman-Smith, 11 Oct. 1944, Dorman-Smith Papers, E215/39; material in IO, Private Office Papers, L/PO/238 and in PREM 4, 50/3; Hansard, HC Deb, 406, cols. 1076ff.; *Times*, 15 Nov. 1944.

107 *Cadogan Diaries*, 6 Nov. 1944.

108 WSC to Stewart, 3 Dec. 1944, PREM 4, 50/3.

109 Amery to WSC, 23 Nov. 1944, PREM 4, 50/3; Cab, 4 Dec. 1944, CAB 65/44.

110 India Cttee., 6 Dec. 1944 onwards, CAB 91/2–3, and memos., CAB 91/4; WP(45)275, 280, 290, CAB 66/65; Cab, 4 May 1945, CAB 65/50.

111 Hansard, HC Deb, 411, cols. 495ff.; White Paper, Cmd. 6635, in PREM 4, 50/3; Amery to Dorman-Smith, 4 June 1945, Dorman-Smith Papers, E215/3, and 10 May 1945, ibid, E215/39.

112 Dorman-Smith to Monteath, 17 June 1945, Dorman-Smith Papers, E215/39. On the planning of relief supplies and the transfer of power from military to civil control, see *Donnison*, 123ff. and cap. XIII.

113 SEAC War Diary, 25 Oct. 1944, 19 July 1945. On Mountbatten's ideas, see *Donnison*, 322ff. and Rose, *Britain and Southeast Asia*, 106.

114 For an outline of what follows, see *Donnison*, 353ff.; *Mountbatten*, 144ff.; Allen, *The End of the War in Asia*, 17ff.; *Kirby*, IV, 333ff. and ibid, V, 52ff.

115 SEAC War Diary, 27 and 28 March, 2 April 1945.

116 FO 371, F1036/169/61.

117 Peterson to Dorman-Smith, 7 Nov. 1944, Dorman-Smith Papers, E215/29; interview with Alec Peterson.

118 India Cttee., 29 March 1945, CAB 91/3; SEAC War Diary, 30 March 1945; Wise to BO, 30 March 1945, CAB 91/4.

119 MacDougall report, B(P)645, BO.

120 Eden to WSC, 31 March 1945; WSC minute, 2 April 1945, PREM 3, 149/5.

121 Mountbatten to COS, 15 and 16 May 1945; WSC minute, 20 May 1945; COS to Mountbatten, 22 May 1945, PREM 3, 149/5; material in India Cttee. docs., CAB 91/4; SEAC War Diary, 11, 16 and 26 May 1945.

122 E.g. Mountbatten to Dorman-Smith, 18 May 1945; Dorman-Smith to Mountbatten, 20 May 1945, CAB 91/4; Amery to Dorman-Smith, 24 May 1945, Dorman-Smith Papers, E215/3.

123 SEAC War Diary, 15 July 1945.

124 Dorman-Smith to Amery, 25 June 1945, CAB 91/4; SEAC War Diary, 30 May, 16 and 20 June, 15 and 17 July 1945; Mountbatten to COS, 5 and 19 June 1945, PREM 3, 149/5.
125 Interview with Dr. van Hoogstraten; FRUS, 1945, VI, 556ff.
126 *New York Times*, 11 July 1945; *New York Herald Tribune*, 25 March 1945.
127 Leahy Diary, 26 June 1945; FRUS, 1944, V, 1286.
128 NCM, 6 April 1945; e.g. Grew–van Mook conversation, 26 May 1945, Grew Papers, vol. 7; DS, 740.0011P.W./1–2645.
129 FO 371, F2413/52/61.
130 Ibid, F2319/52/61; F3340/3340/61.
131 COS, 10 April (CAB 79/31), 21 April (CAB 79/32), 11 July (CAB 79/36), 16 July (CAB 99/39), 10 Aug. 1945 (CAB 79/37).
132 FO 371, F1705/2/61; F5951/2/61. See *Donnison*, cap. XXII.
133 COS, 18 July 1945; JPS draft, 18 July 1945; CCS report, 23 July 1945, CAB 99/39; FO 371, F4463/52/61.
134 FO to Potsdam, 20 July 1945; Eden to van Kleffens, 25 July 1945, PREM 4, 80/1; FRUS, Berlin, II, 1341.
135 COS, 13 Aug. 1945, CAB 79/37.
136 FO 371, F5574/5501/10; FO to Potsdam, 17 July 1945, PREM 4, 80/1.
137 FRUS, 1945, VI, 556ff.; DS, 892.00/1–1045; see *O.S.S.*, 295.
138 Donovan to FDR, 23 March 1945, Roosevelt Papers, PSF box 169; Grew to FDR, 6 Feb. 1945, ibid, MR box 11.
139 See above, 462.
140 DS, 892.01/2–1645.
141 Ibid, 892.01/1–1045, 1–1345, 2–245; DS, 740.0011P.W./4–1945; SWNCC, Project I, SWNCC 5; FRUS, 1945, VI, 1242; Eggleston Diary, 30 Jan. 1945.
142 SWNCC, Project I, paper of 9 Feb. 1945; SWNCC 109 series 091 Thailand, minutes of 12 July 1945.
143 DS, 892.01/3–2345; DS, 740.0011P.W./12–2944; Donovan to FDR, 15 Dec. 1944, Roosevelt Papers, PSF box 168; Donovan to FDR, 22 Feb., 5 and 23 March 1945, ibid, PSF box 169; FO 371, material in file 46560; *O.S.S.*, 298, 305ff.; Gilchrist, *Bangkok Top Secret*, 188ff.
144 FRUS, 1945, VI, 1249.
145 Ibid, 1244, 1267; FO 371, F4053/738/40.
146 FO 371, F6160/1/61; F1497/47/23; F4574 and 4831/296/40.
147 Ibid, F269/54/40; Gilchrist, *Bangkok*, 86ff.; Ehrman, *Grand Strategy*, VI, 252ff.
148 FO 371, F2694/738/40; F3103/3103/40; FEC, 2 May 1945, CAB 96/5.
149 FO 371, material in files 46545 and 46560; FRUS, 1944, V, 1318–9; FRUS, 1945, VI, 1249ff.
150 FO 371, F3804/296/40.
151 Ibid, F2815/1349/40.
152 Cab, 25 Sept. 1944, CAB 65/43.
153 WP(45)102, CAB 66/62; Cab, 19 Feb. 1945, CAB 65/51; FO 371, F1229/738/40; Gilchrist, *Bangkok*, 125. London was also in contact with Luang Pradit via Stockholm. FO 371, F5244/23/40.
154 WP(45)249, CAB 66/64. Cab, 23 April 1945, CAB 65/52.
155 FE(45)22, CAB 96/5; FO 371, F6005/1599/40. It was decided on security grounds not to inform Chungking of the mission sent to Kandy by Luang Pradit. Material in PREM 3, 159/6. China and Siam had not declared war on each other.
156 See above, 347, 462.
157 FE(45)24, CAB 96/5.
158 FE(45)5; FEC, 2 May 1945, CAB 96/5; APW, 17 May 1945, CAB 87/69; APW(45)64, CAB 87/69; FO 371, file 46568. A Siamese surplus rice crop of about 800,000 tons was anticipated. Pre-war, 40 per cent of Siam's surplus had gone to Singapore, 25 per cent to Hongkong and 10 per cent to Ceylon.
159 For the approach of G. F. Hudson, for example, see FO 371, F5550/1599/40.

160 Series of PHP drafts in ibid, file 46544; FE(45)18, CAB 96/5; COS, 22 March 1945, CAB 79/30.
161 FO 371, F4053/738/40.
162 Ibid, F4831/296/40; Mountbatten to COS, 13 June 1945, PREM 3, 149/10; COS, 14 and 27 June 1945, CAB 79/35. There was a brief flurry at the beginning of July when a report suggested that the Japanese might be about to take over entirely in Siam. FO 371, F3942/738/40.
163 FO 371, F3490/738/40; Gilchrist, *Bangkok*, 100ff.
164 COS, 4 April 1945, CAB 79/31.
165 COS, 20 July 1945, CAB 79/36; FO 371, F4620/296/40; FEC, 13 July 1945, and FE(45)29, CAB 96/5. The F.E. Cttee. and Planners also wished Siam to pledge not to construct a canal across the Kra Isthmus without British approval.
166 FE(45)29, CAB 96/5; FO 371, material in files 46594–5, 46562, 50923; FE(M)C, 17 Aug. 1945, CAB 96/9. Other terms included ones dealing with currency for the payment of Allied troops, and also post-war civil-aviation arrangements.
167 See e.g. Allen, *The End of the War in Asia*, cap. 4.
168 Marshall, *The French Colonial Myth*, 134ff.
169 See Lancaster, *The Emancipation of French Indochina*, 107ff., and Elsbree, *Japan's Role in Southeast Asian Nationalist Movements*, 97.
170 FRUS, 1945, VI, 295, 300.
171 G. Sabattier, *Le Destin de l'Indochine* (Paris, 1952), 263ff., 284.
172 Briefing paper, 30 March 1945, PREM 3, 159/12, and e.g. FO 371, F1524/47/23.
173 FO 371, F668, 1269 and 1271/11/61.
174 E.g. ibid, F7957/7957/61.
175 Summary of Paris to Canberra telegram, 10 April 1945, ADEA, A1066/P45/153/2, pt. 2; Evatt–Bidault conversation, 3 May 1945, Evatt Papers.
176 E.g. FO 371, F4682/66/61; F86/11/61.
177 Ibid, F741/11/61; F3404/69/23.
178 Ibid, F6160/1/61; F4973/9/61; Sweet-Escott, *Baker Street Irregular*, 238.
179 *Donnison*, 404–5; FO 371, material in files 46296 and 46299.
180 See above, 468, and FRUS, 1944, III, 781–3.
181 FO 371, material in file 41720 and F163/11/61; material in PREM 3, 180/7; SEAC War Diary, 6 Nov. 1944.
182 COS, 19 March (CAB 79/30), 30 March and 5 April (CAB 79/31), 21 and 23 April 1945 (CAB 79/32); FO 371, material in file 46272; SEAC War Diary, 20 March 1945; material in PREM 3, 178/3.
183 COS, 11 July (CAB 79/36), 10 and 13 Aug. 1945 (CAB 79/37); FO 371, material in files 41721, 46304, 46321–2. The French were proposing to send out 2 colonial divisions and 1 brigade, together with 4 naval-air squadrons; the naval units envisaged were at least 1 light fleet carrier and 2 destroyers.
184 FO 371, F1271, 1470 and 3091/11/61.
185 Ibid, F2431/11/61.
186 *Moran*, 28 April 1953; FO 371, F1648/11/61.
187 WSC minutes, 16 and 22 Oct., 19 and 25 Nov. 1944, PREM 3, 180/7.
188 COS, 18 Jan. (CAB 79/28), 25 Jan. 1945 (CAB 79/29).
189 FO 371, F1829/11/61.
190 See above, 501.
191 FO 371, UE2435, 2528, 2588, 2710 and 2711/2/53.
192 COS, 17 April (CAB 79/32) and 18 July 1945 (CAB 99/39); CCS report, 23 July 1945, CAB 99/39.
193 See above, 301.
194 COS, 5 and 12 March (CAB 79/30), 16, 17 and 19 April (CAB 79/32), 30 May and 11 June (CAB 79/34), 21 and 26 June 1945 (CAB 79/35); FO 371, F586, 888, 1113, 1271, 1829, 2140, 2230, 2234, 2358, 2523, and 3492/11/61; F4106/47/23; material in PREM 3, 178/3 and 180/7; HST to WSC, 14 April 1945, PREM 3, 473; FRUS, Berlin, I, 915; SEAC War Diary, 14 Sept. 1944, 7 Feb., 8, 20 and 21 April, 28 and

29 May 1945.
195 COS, FO and CCS material, Potsdam, CAB 99/39; Sargent to Cadogan, 31 July and FO to Potsdam, 17 July 1945; WSC to Chiang Kai-shek, 1 Aug. 1945, PREM 4, 80/1; FRUS, Berlin, II, 1319–21.
196 DS, 740.0011P.W./10–2444, 10–2844, 12–3044, 1–945, 3–545; Bishop to Sec. of State, 22 March 1945, Roosevelt Papers, PSF box 53.
197 FRUS, 1944, III, 778; DS, 740.0011P.W./1–1245.
198 FRUS, 1944, III, 777.
199 FDR to Hurley, 16 Nov. 1945, Roosevelt Papers, MR box 11; FRUS, 1944, III, 780.
200 FRUS, 1945, VI, 293.
201 FRUS, Malta and Yalta, 564.
202 Ibid, 766 and FRUS, Berlin, I, 915.
203 DS, 740.0011P.W./3–2645.
204 DS, 851G.00/3–2145.
205 SEAC War Diary, 11 March 1945; Sabattier, *Le Destin de l'Indochine*, 206; Wedemeyer, *Wedemeyer Reports!*, 340.
206 See e.g. *Leahy*, 336.
207 FRUS, Berlin, I, 915; *Buhite*, 244ff.; Chiang Kai-shek–Hurley–Wedemeyer conversation, 28 May 1945, Wedemeyer Papers, box 7.
208 *O.S.S.*, 330ff.; P. Kemp, *Alms For Oblivion* (London, 1961), 46.
209 SWNCC, 13 April 1945 (SWNCC 35/7).
210 FRUS, Berlin, I, 915; Wheeler to Marshall, 22 March 1945, OPD, Exec. file 17, item 26.
211 FO 371, F190/11/61.
212 DS, 740.0011P.W./3–1945; Leahy Diary, 18 March 1945; *Stettinius*, 16 March 1945; J. Sainteny, *Histoire D'Une Paix Manquée* (Paris, 1953), 30; Chennault, *Way Of A Fighter*, 342; FRUS, 1945, VII, 99.
213 FRUS, 1945, I, 121; memo., 15 March 1945, Taussig Papers, box 49.
214 DS, 851G.00/1–445.
215 Somerville to Mountbatten, 27 March 1945, Somerville Papers, box 9/2.
216 Eggleston to Evatt, 13 Feb. 1945 ADEA, A1066/P45/153/2, pt. 1.
217 FO 371, F4240/11/61.
218 DS, 851G.00/4–2045, 4–2145, 4–2345.
219 Memo., 1945 (n.d.), DS, Matthews-Hickerson files, box 13. Other proposals were for a free port at Haiphong and tax-free transit from there to China; equal economic opportunity for all states; a peaceful settlement of Indochina's frontier disputes, and sympathetic consideration of any recommendations made by the U.N. Security Council over security arrangements.
220 FRUS, 1945, VI, 556ff.; DS, 851G.00/7–1445; OSS R. and A. 3336, 25 Oct. 1945.
221 DS, 851G.00/6–745.
222 FRUS, 1945, VI, 312.
223 DS, 851G.00/6–445; China Theater surveys, April and June 1945, Wedemeyer Papers, box 1.
224 FRUS, 1945, VI, 309; DS, 740.0011P.W./5–1645; CCS, 16 July 1945, CAB 99/39.
225 de Gaulle, *War Memoirs: Salvation, 1944–46*, 210; FRUS, 1945, VII, 540.

CHAPTER TWENTY-EIGHT

BRITAIN, THE UNITED STATES AND INDIA

IN THE opinion of the Viceroy, Wavell, as we noted earlier, Britain's entire position in Asia depended upon her ability to ensure that India became 'a friendly partner in the . . . Commonwealth', and to this end it was a matter of urgency for her to make further and imaginative efforts to secure agreement with India's political parties and communities on the vital subject of constitutional reform.[1] Nor was Wavell entirely without support in London on this issue, with Eden, for one, coming to find the former's arguments convincing; Amery, too, produced a scheme of his own early in 1945 (the Viceroy, like Attlee, Cripps and others, thought it well-meant but unworkable)* whereby India would immediately be declared free of control from London and obtain Dominion status.[2]

Churchill, however, remained instinctively opposed to any further initiative on Britain's part while the war lasted, and the Cabinet as a whole, its India Committee divided over the matter, displayed little enthusiasm for what Wavell had to propose. Attlee, who might have been expected to press for reform, was wary, rather, of any move which might 'substitute for the present government . . . a brown oligarchy subject to no control either from Parliament or the electorate', while Grigg, true to form, proposed to the Committee that Britain should not think of leaving India until the Indianization of the latter's Army had been completed, which he believed would take twenty years.[3]

Eventually, at the end of May 1945, it was reluctantly agreed that the Viceroy could summon a conference of the leaders of various Indian political parties and religious groups, with a view to having names put

---

* The scheme was what Wavell and many of Amery's Cabinet colleagues might have expected from him: a highly intelligent and sincere politician who nevertheless had what Wavell described as 'a curious capacity for getting hold of the right stick but practically always the wrong end of it.' (*Wavell*, 20 Jan. 1945.) Amery also tended to bore his colleagues by speaking at excessive length. This made it all the easier for Churchill to bully him. Thus, over Indian affairs, on which Amery, in Dalton's words, was 'always, in Cabinet, the warmest advocate of a "sympathetic" and "constructive" policy . . . —as many outside would be surprised to find', he was usually 'overborne by the P.M. and others', Churchill, for example, jeering on one occasion that he was 'more Indian than the Indians.' (Dalton Diary, 3 and 4 Aug. 1944.)

forward from which he himself could select a new Executive Council.* Even the Prime Minister allowed this proposal to go forward, provided that it was put to the Indians on a take-it-or-leave-it basis; his reason for this unwonted mildness, as he later admitted to Wavell, was that 'the India Committee had all told him [the idea] was bound to fail.'[4] And indeed, the moment that the news of the scheme got out in India it seemed that the Committee's pessimism had been justified—whereupon the Cabinet hastily and pusillanimously instructed Amery to 'amend any passages in his draft statement to Parliament which might imply that we thought the proposals had a good chance of success.' The ensuing Simla Conference duly failed as prophesied. While Congress believed Wavell to be biased in favour of the Muslim League, Jinnah, as leader of the League, refused to cooperate unless all Muslims present were members of that party, and unless special safe-guards were written in to ensure that it could block any proposals to which it objected.[5] The Viceroy rejected these demands, and his hopes thus came to nothing.

If the Government in London were lukewarm over Indian political reform, they also continued to respond with caution, to say the least, to Wavell's urgent demands for an increased supply of foodstuffs to be sent to that country. Thus, the Viceroy, attending a meeting of the Cabinet Com-mittee that was dealing with this matter, found Lord Leathers (Minister of War Transport) apparently 'indifferent to the possibility of famine', while Cherwell made what to Wavell seemed 'fatuous calculations' to show that India already had sufficient food.[6]† Wavell was equally concerned at the hard line taken by the India Committee when, against Amery's advice, it refused to revise those sections of the Government of India Act which protected the position of British businessmen in that country, and which thus inhibited the development of a domestically-based industry there. (Grigg went so far as to assert that 'industrialization would aggravate rather than cure India's troubles.')[7] Such an attitude scarcely squared with the hope expressed in the Far Eastern Committee that India, 'standing at the gate of a new era of potential export trade', could take over the markets for cheap goods which Japan had supplied before the war.[8] Nor did it suggest that Britain would take swift measures to enable India to play the role which Sir Firoz Khan Noon, attending Cabinet meetings in London as representa-tive of the Government in New Delhi, envisaged for her: that of the leading post-war Asian power, taking the place that others had expected to see filled by China.[9]

India did, however, possess one asset that could not be ignored: her ever-

* Wavell had in mind a Council composed of himself and the Commander-in-Chief, four Congress and one non-Congress Hindus, four Muslim League and one non-Muslim League Muslims, one representative of the scheduled castes, one Sikh and perhaps one other.

† In April 1945 Wavell called for imports of 1 million tons of foodstuffs annually. Leathers responded by suggesting a target of 40,000 tons monthly, which he later increased to 70,000 tons. Finally, at the end of July, the Government announced that it would ship 100,000 tons per month for the remainder of the year.

growing sterling balances. So great a problem had this become for London by the end of 1944 that Keynes believed it might be necessary to seek help in solving it from the United States, perhaps in the form of an additional loan to Britain, or some arrangement that would enable India to purchase goods in the U.S.A. The difficulty was, as Keynes himself acknowledged, 'that the Americans might wish to impose conditions affecting our relations with the sterling area countries.' Grigg and Beaverbrook, not surprisingly, were two Ministers who expressed great alarm at what this might mean as far as a political settlement with India was concerned: in the latter's words, 'it would be better to pay India a considerable tribute rather than permit the United States to intrude into the affairs of that country.'[10]

Those who resented American interference over India had particular reason in this period to dislike the continuing activities of the columnist Drew Pearson, whose embarrassing disclosures of British and American official documents in 1944 have been noted earlier. The source of the leaks to Pearson from within the Indian Agency General in Washington had now been traced; nevertheless he continued to obtain and publish writings by United States officials which reflected badly on the New Delhi Administration and on the attitude of the Government in London.[11] Louis Fischer was another correspondent who still sought to arouse the American public on India's behalf, as did the India League in the U.S.A.[12] Nehru's sister, Mrs V. L. Pandit, also spoke out vigorously for a free India at the I.P.R. Hot Springs Conference, and although she failed in her subsequent attempt to have the official Indian delegation to the U.N. gathering at San Francisco unseated, on the grounds that it was unrepresentative, she did secure considerable publicity for herself and her cause.[13]

Concern over India's future was also expressed during the discussions held within the United States' own delegation to the I.P.R. meeting. One of those present, for example, feared that sympathy aroused among the American public on behalf of India could be used 'not only as a stick to beat Britain with, but to beat the peace settlement [as a whole] with.' Owen Lattimore, for his part, envisaged the need for Britain to resort to what was in fact to be her eventual solution to the problem—the setting of a date for independence, 'say, 1950', so that (and here, of course, he proved to be mistaken)* contending groups within India 'would have to settle their differences before that time.'[14] Moreover, for some Americans on the spot in South and Southeast Asia, the situation that prevailed in India remained a cause for not simply apprehension but disgust. Thus, one fairly senior U.S. staff officer in S.E.A.C. wrote privately at the end of 1944: 'If we really believe our own propaganda, we would have to declare war on the British, for they have set themselves up as the master-race in India. British rule in India is fascism, there is no dodging that.'[15]

It was a view which did far less than justice to the attitude and efforts of

* In his own retrospective view, Lattimore's mistaken expectation that Hindus and Muslims would settle their differences under such circumstances was based on an underestimation of the drive for power by Jinnah. (Interview with Professor Lattimore.)

Wavell, for example, and of a good many lesser British officials serving in the sub-continent. And in wider terms, the present study has on many occasions pointed out how ill-informed and flimsily-based were many American suppositions and interpretations concerning Britain's imperial role and policies in general. Nevertheless, the manner in which the Government in London handled Indian affairs throughout the war was often deserving of the strongest criticism. It was not simply that these affairs showed up a side of Churchill that was ignorant, ugly and at times vicious (his observation that the natives 'needed the sjambok' will be recalled, for example), or that they revealed something of the way in which Cherwell approached the sufferings of the coloured peoples whom he found so distasteful. The Cabinet as a whole, with obvious exceptions such as Bevin, were wont to discuss India's problems, be they starvation, communal strife, or the country's economic structure, in a manner which, as we have seen, Wavell for one found appalling in its insouciance. This alone provides sufficient grounds for saying that American suspicions were by no means unwarranted.

Meanwhile, as noted in the previous chapter,[16] Roosevelt himself continued to dwell on the need to avoid hostility towards the white man on the part of the 'brown peoples' of Asia, Indians included, while William Phillips and other American officials also sought to warn Britain against unwittingly encouraging India to join the ranks of a pan-Asian movement. And yet, during this final phase of the war, India did not figure at all prominently as an issue between Washington and London. The American Administration, for example, did not risk a confrontation by attempting to send Phillips back to New Delhi, and its representation there was eventually regularized by the appointment of George Merrill, who was already on the spot, as United States Commissioner, with the rank of Minister.[17] Nor did Indian affairs any longer command headlines in the American press; commentators did, however, accord widespread approval to the new British offer made in June 1945, and tended to blame the failure of the ensuing Simla Conference on the Muslim League rather than on Wavell or London—the Viceroy, indeed, coming in for considerable praise.[18]

As for any practical display of American sympathy for Indians as individuals, little was forthcoming.* Thus, a naturalization and immigration bill that would have permitted a mere one hundred Indians a year to move to the United States, being opposed by the American Federation of Labor among other bodies, was defeated in Congress, despite support for it from the President and State Department. (The quota of one hundred was eventually brought in in July 1946.)[19] As with American attitudes towards China, rhetoric about freedom for Asia was one thing; having Asians on one's own doorstep was quite another.

---

* There were celebrated tales of how much-decorated Indian Army officers were refused admission to certain hotels or restaurants in Washington, D.C., when seeking to enter in company with white colleagues.

Notes to Chapter Twenty-Eight

1 *Wavell*, 24 Oct. 1944; Cab, 3 April 1945, CAB 65/52.
2 *Avon*, 540; *Wavell*, 20 Jan. 1945; India Cttee., 28 Feb. 1945, CAB 91/3.
3 *Wavell*, 29 March and 31 May 1945; Cab, 18 Dec. 1944 (CAB 65/44), 1 May 1945 (CAB 65/50), 30 and 31 May (CAB 65/53); WP(45)274 (CAB 66/65); India Cttee. 26 March 1945 and following (CAB 91/3).
4 Cab, 31 May and 8 June 1945, CAB 65/53.
5 CP(45)97, CAB 66/67; Cabs, 10, 12 and 19 July 1945, CAB 65/53; Gopal, *Nehru*, I, 304.
6 See WP(44)562, CAB 66/56; Cab. Cttee. on Indian Food and Grain Requirements, 22 Feb. 1945 and following, CAB 91/6; *Wavell*, 4 April 1945.
7 WP(45)317, CAB 66/65; India Cttee., 7 and 14 May 1945, CAB 91/3; *Wavell*, 11 May 1945. The question hinged upon sections 111–121 of the Government of India Act.
8 FD(E)(44)3, CAB 96/8.
9 Cab, 3 April 1945, CAB 65/50.
10 Cab. Cttee. on Indian Financial Questions, 20 Dec. 1944 and 16 Jan. 1945, CAB 91/5.
11 FO 371, AN4070 and 4170/121/45; AN4446/34/45.
12 Ibid, AN1561/24/45.
13 Dennett report, n.d., IPR Papers, box 362; Hess, *America Encounters India*, 152–4.
14 Minutes of 28 Oct. 1944, IPR Papers, box 362.
15 Taylor, *Richer By Asia*, 232.
16 See above, 594.
17 WP(45)285, CAB 66/65.
18 FO 371, AN1561, 2241 and 2287/24/45; AN2273/109/45; Hess, *America Encounters India*, 162; e.g. *New York Times*, 12 July 1945.
19 FO 371, AN1372/24/45; FRUS, 1945, VI, 281ff.; Hess, *America Encounters India*, 151, 159. Hornbeck, in a memo. of 10 June 1943 to Berle, had argued that there was an urgent need to modify American immigration restrictions in favour of the Chinese, who, 'by virtue of the showing which they have made in resistance to Japan over a period of six years, stand high at present in public favor.' In contrast, he continued, 'the people of India have a comparatively "sorry" record in relation to the war effort and do not stand high in favor; and China is important as one of the big four among the United Nations, whereas India is little if at all thought of in either the war effort or the peace effort context.' He concluded: 'It is going to be hard enough, if at all possible, to get done even a little that will be helpful in relation to the Chinese. . . . We therefore are more or less concentrating on the problem of just [that] one people and country. . . .' Hornbeck Papers, box 81.

CHAPTER TWENTY-NINE

AUSTRALASIA AND THE SOUTHWEST PACIFIC

BOTH AUSTRALIA and New Zealand continued to be faced with serious manpower problems during this final phase of the war, problems that were increased by such developments as the need to create a major base in Australia for the Royal Navy's Pacific Fleet, and the growing role of the two Dominions as suppliers of foodstuffs and manufactured goods for the Allied war effort in the Pacific.[1] Concern was also being expressed, both within Australian official circles and in public, lest the country's contribution in this field of supply should unduly diminish her military achievements. General Blamey, for example, the Australian C. in C., urged upon his Government that for political reasons their own forces, and not those of the United States, should be responsible for defeating those Japanese who remained in territories belonging to Australia. Canberra also chafed at the way in which American plans were preventing the early reoccupation of Ocean and Nauru Islands, where there were major phosphate deposits which both Pacific Dominions badly needed.[2]

Moreover, Curtin and the Secretary of the Australian War Cabinet, F. G. Shedden, felt obliged in this period to convey to MacArthur their country's regret that greater publicity was not being accorded to the work of Australian forces under his command, even though, in June, for example, it was those troops who recaptured Brunei and Sarawak; Curtin also indicated his disappointment that the Australians were not being employed in the early stages of the attack upon the Philippines.[3] MacArthur in turn blamed the Australian press for being 'incorrigible' over publicity matters, and Blamey for imposing such conditions that the use of his troops in the Philippines had proved impossible. The proposed transfer to S.E.A.C. and to Australia herself of much of MacArthur's South West Pacific Area, noted earlier, promised to provide its own solution to tensions and difficulties of this kind, although considerable problems would be involved for Canberra in finding the resources required to fulfil their part of the scheme.[4] Even before this change came about, however, Curtin's death early in July removed what had been a vital element in the relationship between MacArthur and the Australians.

As had been the case during the preceding period, warm sentiments towards Britain were again forthcoming from the two Pacific Dominions,

New Zealand in particular, despite her war-time dependence upon American protection, appearing to look forward to the resumption of an overriding relationship with the Mother Country.[5] In Australia, too, the arrival of the British Pacific Fleet was welcomed as a significant moment in the strengthening of imperial ties,[6] while even Evatt was going out of his way in private to assure Churchill of his personal friendship and of his desire for close relations within the Commonwealth in the future.[7]* Meanwhile, in both Australia and New Zealand, there were manifestations of anti-American feeling, which, according to one correspondent, writing to a leading American student of Australian affairs, was 'running very high.'[8]

Nevertheless, the closer ties with the United States that the war had brought about for the two Dominions were clearly not going to be abandoned entirely. As Evatt put it in a speech he delivered in California in March 1945, 'the plain fact is that the people, both of Australia and New Zealand, regard continued cooperation and comradeship, not only with the United Kingdom but also with the United States, as basic to the post-war security and welfare of all peoples of the Pacific.'[9] Privately, indeed, Evatt went further still, telling American diplomats and others that 'more and more [Australians] were coming to the realization that their political future as a people was cast in the Pacific', that 'they found little sympathy for their point of view in London', and that, as he wrote to his friend Frankfurter, 'we recognise U.S. leadership' in Pacific affairs. To Hopkins, Evatt forecast 'all sorts of trouble' if British Conservatives continued to ignore, as he held they did, the views of the Dominions. 'My own view of the future of Australia and New Zealand', he wrote at the end of March, 'is that they will quickly develop the fullest autonomy in international affairs without prejudicing the only legal tie that unites them with the United Kingdom—that is kinship. This will mean in practice', he continued, 'a close relationship with the United States . . .'[10]

Even where New Zealand was concerned, the retiring British High Commissioner to that country, Sir Harry Batterbee, felt the need to warn London in July 1945:

> 'If we do not make it plain by both deeds and words that Britain still leads the world,† there is the danger that New Zealand may eventually feel in too great a degree the increasing attraction of the United States as a great and progressive world Power, democratic and English-speaking like New Zealand herself, with, she may feel, perhaps a greater stake in the Pacific even than the United Kingdom . . . The Americans occupy a place closer to the hearts of the New Zealanders than before. Nor do the United States authorities lose any effort to improve their advantage by propaganda, some of it injudicious, but much of it subtle and effective.'[11]

* Canada, however, continued to oppose any possibility of a Commonwealth bloc which could appear unfriendly in American eyes. (MacDonald to DO, 18 May 1945, DO 35/1119.)

† Batterbee was a shrewd observer. It is thus all the more significant to find that, at his post in Wellington, he apparently failed to appreciate the extent of Britain's relative decline vis-à-vis the U.S.A.

What Australia and New Zealand sought above all, now as during earlier phases of the war, was to have their views heeded in the councils of the Allies. One manifestation of this desire, noted above in the context of colonial issues, was the November conference and announcement by the two Governments.[12] Evatt in particular strove—notably at San Francisco—to play a major role on the world stage, although it is difficult to say whether personal ambition or concern for Australia's position came first with him.[13] One subject over which Canberra and Wellington were especially anxious to be consulted was the future treatment of Japan—the surrender terms to be accorded her, occupation arrangements, the nature of a possible peace treaty, and so forth. This particular wish was made clear by Evatt and others in both Washington and London.[14] Yet although the Dominions Office and, somewhat more cautiously, Churchill, responded sympathetically (the Prime Minister, at a meeting of Commonwealth representatives in April, observed that he was 'not opposed' to the idea of Australia and New Zealand participating as principals in the making of a Far Eastern armistice), the rush with which the Pacific war came to an end proved to be a major handicap for the two Dominions.

Moreover, it was now the Americans who were firmly in the driving seat, and Evatt found that his efforts to develop a special partnership with Washington produced few tangible benefits during the dramatic events of July and August 1945. Thus, both the Potsdam ultimatum to Japan and the final shaping of the surrender terms were decided upon without Australia or New Zealand being consulted. Evatt, for his part, was furious, and registered his protest in public. Privately, he cabled to Eden after Potsdam: 'The Foreign Office talks about Dominion rights, but in practice does its best to evade them.' (The Dominions Office in London thought that he had a case in the light of Churchill's earlier remarks, cited above; on the other hand this interpretation rather overlooked the predominant role of the United States at Potsdam and the insistence of its representatives there on the need for the greatest speed.)[15] New Zealand, too, conveyed her disappointment at what had occurred.[16] Further outbursts—mainly by Evatt—were to continue into August and beyond, when it appeared that the American treatment of Japan was going to be less than draconian.[17]

In short, Evatt's many demands for a new status to be accorded to Australia, a campaign that he had waged since the very beginning of the Pacific war and even earlier, had met with little success. Meanwhile, the Netherlands remained in a weaker position still regarding the fate of their East Indies colony. The differing views of senior Dutch officials and Ministers over the question of whether to rely upon close collaboration with Britain or with the United States in this connection have been noted in the previous chapter.[18] Within a purely Southwest Pacific context, there also remained fears that Australia might be entertaining predatory thoughts about the East Indies, and the Netherlands Minister for Foreign Affairs raised the matter with his Cabinet colleagues in June, for example.[19] It was for this reason that Dutch officials who were negotiating with their opposite numbers in Australia itself were seeking a declaration on Canberra's part regarding the territorial integrity of the colony.[20] In addition, the Government in The Hague was becoming increasingly impatient to secure Australia's agreement (she had accepted the idea, but in principle only, in September 1944) to receive around 30,000 Dutch troops and civil servants who would then go on to the East Indies when the time came. Claiming that adequate facilities had been found to be lacking, however, Canberra eventually withdrew its original offer, a reversal that provoked angry accusations against the new Prime Minister, J. B. Chifley, by Menzies and other members of the Australian Opposition.[21]

Where Britain was concerned, Evatt's continuing outspokenness was but one reminder of an entire series of questions that would soon have to be faced, relating to the nature and functioning of the post-war Commonwealth as a whole. For example, would and should the trend be towards a greater degree of integration in policy-making, as Curtin and Halifax (the latter, notably, in a speech he had delivered in Toronto early in 1944) had suggested? Or would the emphasis be upon increased devolution, as Evatt—within the limits set by the need to keep roughly in line with Curtin—and to some extent Smuts anticipated?[22] Then again there was the issue—already put before the Cabinet in London—of the place to be occupied by the Dominions within the United Nations Organization, a matter that was complicated by differences between, for example, Canada and Britain regarding the powers of the U.N.'s Security Council.[23]

At least it was by now clear to most British politicians and officials (the case involving Australia, New Zealand and colonial policies has already been outlined)[24] that the Dominions were becoming more self-assertive. Thus, a survey drawn up by the Dominions Office in August 1945 anticipated that they would 'express their views on many more international questions, and more fully, than they have done in the past, that they will be anxious to obtain United Kindom support for these views, and that they will resent anything which can be considered as backsliding by the United Kingdom from conclusions reached jointly with the Dominions.'[25] (If there remained any doubts in London over this matter, they were to be diminished further during that same month of August, when the Australian press launched a strong attack on Britain, rather than on the U.S.A., over the Potsdam and Far Eastern-armistice episodes.)[26]

At the same time it was increasingly appreciated that, without the Commonwealth, Britain's own post-war position would be all the more overshadowed by the power of the United States and the Soviet Union. Only by 'enrolling [the Dominions] as collaborators with us', together with France and other West European states, wrote Sir Orme Sargent in July, 'shall we be able in the long run to compel our two big partners to treat us as an equal.' Sir Ronald Campbell likewise envisaged an especially vital role for individual Dominions and the Commonwealth as a whole as providing the basis on which to secure lasting collaboration with the United States—hitherto, he believed, too exclusively a United Kingdom affair.[27] As

Churchill himself summarized the situation, 'In material resources we could not hope to equal either [the U.S.A. or the U.S.S.R.]. We could hold our own only by our superior statecraft and experience, and, above all, by the unity of the British Commonwealth of Nations.'[28]

At least London could derive some comfort from the various expressions of loyalty to the Commonwealth which continued to be forthcoming from Australia, as if to ensure that the bitterness of 1942 was now completely buried. In addition, F. M. Forde, Canberra's Deputy Prime Minister, assured a meeting of Commonwealth representatives in April that 'the tendency towards isolationism which had at one time shown itself in Australia had now passed.'[29] Moreover, reports were again coming in of strains within Australian–American relations: thus, for example, MacArthur bluntly informed Lt. General Gairdner (Churchill's new representative on the S.W.P.A. staff) of his dislike and distrust of General Blamey (Gairdner himself put the blame on Blamey), and of the extent to which he missed Curtin. Chifley, Curtin's successor, was, said MacArthur, 'very ignorant of military matters and completely dominated by General Blamey.'[30] On the other side, and in less personal terms, the Dominions Office in London believed that 'the Australians were [becoming] restive because they feared the spread of U.S. influence in the area.'[31]

Britain meanwhile had problems of her own arising from the presence of the United States in the Southwest Pacific. For example, there was a sense in which American forces there, with their high calorific consumption level per capita, were competitors with Britain for supplies of Australian and New Zealand meat.[32] It was also known that MacArthur was opposing the transfer to S.E.A.C. of the greater part of his South West Pacific Area, an issue that has been outlined above.[33] Even so, MacArthur was going out of his way to be cordial to British representatives, and made a profound impression on Mountbatten when the latter was at last permitted by Churchill to visit the S.W.P.A. in July.[34] 'I fully admit I am completely under his spell', wrote Mountbatten privately after listening to 'a fascinating monologue' by the General. 'He is one of the most charming and remarkable characters I have ever met, and so sympathetic towards the Southeast Asia Command.'[35]*

MacArthur also again expressed on several occasions his support for the cause of the British Empire in the Far East. In October 1944, for example, he told General Lumsden that he fully appreciated the need for British forces to recapture Hongkong, as well as Singapore, while in the following May he again spoke of the important prestige factor that would be involved in such a Singapore operation. In addition, he repeated his desire to have units of the Royal Navy working under him, where they would have 'ample opportunities of gaining great renown for themselves and great credit to the British Empire.'[36] Not surprisingly, therefore, General Gairdner in the

---

* In London, Brooke, the C.I.G.S., continued to believe that MacArthur was 'the greatest general and best strategist that the war produced.' (*Bryant*, II, 513.)

summer of 1945 was expressing for his part a belief very similar to the one that Colonel Wilkinson had put forward in 1942:[37]

'General MacArthur', he wrote to Ismay (who passed the letter on to Churchill), 'in my opinion stands head and shoulders above any other officer I have met here, in the breadth of his views, in the lucidity of his arguments, and in the unerring way he puts his finger on the essentials of a problem . . . [He is] a sincere friend of the British Commonwealth. I think that it would pay a very good dividend to back him whenever it is possible without imperilling paramount interest . . .'[38]

As for MacArthur's private views, although he disliked the prospect of losing the southern areas of his Command—a scheme, it must again be emphasized, that emanated from Washington, not London, and which Marshall had put forward as early as January 1945[39]—his eyes were now turned northwards above all, to the Philippines and, beyond them, to Japan itself. For him, as we have seen, the recovery of the Philippines was vital to the entire future of the United States presence in the Far East. 'The Filipinos are reacting splendidly', he reported to Roosevelt in October, 'and I feel that a successful campaign of liberation, if promptly followed by a dramatic granting to them of independence, will place American prestige in the Far East at the highest pinnacle of all times. Once more', he continued, '(on the highest plane of statesmanship) I venture to urge that this great ceremony be presided over by you in person.'[40] In the same vein he strongly opposed the idea of appointing a new United States High Commissioner to the islands, a move which he believed would cast doubt on the American intention to grant early independence.[41] (Even so, Mountbatten among others observed how completely subordinate and in some ways humiliating a position was forced upon President Osmena* of the Philippines during MacArthur's military control of the colony.)[42] This emphasis of Mac-Arthur's upon speed troubled some people in Washington, notably Stimson, who feared that the outcome might be the casting loose of the Filipinos before they were adequately prepared, and that the American people themselves might 'lose interest in the Philippines.'[43]

As far as the British Commonwealth was concerned, State Department officials were aware of some of the problems that were having to be faced by London, observing, for example, that the divergent interests of the member states were 'apparent at every international gathering at which they are represented.' It was also, and correctly, noted in Washington that 'Mr. Churchill often offends the susceptibilities of the Dominions by forgetting that the British Empire has changed since Kipling's day.' Nevertheless, American officials concluded, for example in a briefing paper that was drawn up before the Potsdam Conference, that 'these very real divergencies among members of the British Commonwealth must not be allowed to hide from

* Manuel Quezon had died.

view those unwritten conventions and customs which give vitality to a unique political association possessing far more cohesion than any other grouping of separate nations in this disturbed and unsettled world.'[44] In short, the Commonwealth was seen as a body that would constitute a post-war asset for the United States in the latter's search for a stable international order, and there was no intention in Washington to try to draw Australia, for example, away from that connection. This was consistent with the attitude that Roosevelt, it will be recalled, had adopted during the difficult days of 1942.[45]

Australia herself, or more particularly Evatt's ambitions on her behalf, were still regarded with some wariness in American official circles. Thus, in a State Department survey of June 1945 it was recorded that 'the United States desires chiefly to prevent the somewhat expansionist tendencies which have their roots mainly in Australia rather than in New Zealand from unduly complicating the relations of the United States with the United Kingdom, France and the Netherlands.'[46] Evatt's aggressive tactics at San Francisco, concerning, for example, United Nations voting formulae, aroused particularly strong resentment among U.S. representatives. The Australian Minister for External Affairs, Stettinius reported by telephone to Washington, 'seemed determined to break up the Conference', while the Under Secretary of State, Grew, described Evatt as 'acting like a bull in a china shop' and 'following obstructionist tactics all along the line.' President Truman therefore raised the matter with Forde, Australia's Deputy Prime Minister, when the latter visited Washington, observing that 'Australia and the United States must be friends, and that this uncooperative attitude on the part of Mr. Evatt would clearly not conduce to future cooperative relations.' Forde in turn, as we have seen Curtin do earlier with Roosevelt,[47] went some way towards disowning Evatt. 'He would like to speak very frankly within the four walls of the President's study', he said, and then, in the words of Grew, who was present, proceeded to tell Truman 'several things about Mr. Evatt's personality and the methods he had followed at the San Francisco Conference, which he himself clearly disapproved.'[48]

Forde also promised on this occasion that he would try to bring his Minister for External Affairs into line, but so far as the Americans could see he was unable to do so. In general, Evatt's twin desires, for close collaboration with the United States and for a more prominent role for Australia, were not running easily together. His own methods were obviously responsible in part for this state of affairs. So, too, however, was the continuing determination on the part of the United States that, when it came to shaping the Far Eastern peace and the future of the Pacific region as a whole, it was for Washington to lead and for others, Australia included, to follow.

Notes to Chapter Twenty-Nine

1 *Hasluck*, II, 550ff., 621–4; AWC, 6 March 1945, A2673, vol. XV. Australia received £A466 million ($1,500,000,000) in Lend Lease from the U.S.A. during the war, and supplied reciprocal aid totalling £A285 million.
2 *Hasluck*, II, 569ff.; material in PREM 3, 159/13.
3 Curtin–MacArthur and Shedden–MacArthur correspondence, 12 Feb. 1945 and following, MacArthur Papers, RG 4.
4 See COS, 25 July 1945, CAB 99/39.
5 See Lussington, *New Zealand and the United States*, 97.
6 Cross to DO, 20 Feb. 1945, DO 35/1119, G579/38. On the excellent relations between British and Australian diplomats in Washington, see Eggleston Papers, 423/10/845.
7 Evatt to WSC, 6 May 1945, PREM 4, 42/2.
8 Hartley Grattan to Evatt, 1945, n.d., Evatt Papers, Grattan file. And see note of 29 Nov. 1944, Evatt Papers, External Affairs file, New Zealand.
9 H. V. Evatt, *Australia in World Affairs* (Sydney, 1946), 3.
10 FRUS, 1944, III, 198; Evatt to Frankfurter, 3 July 1945, Frankfurter Papers, box 53; Evatt to Hopkins, 30 March 1945, Hopkins Papers, box 338.
11 Batterbee report, 20 July 1945, DO 35/1119, G580/1/4.
12 See above, 601.
13 E.g. Hankinson to DO, 27 Aug. 1945, DO 35/1119, G579/52; *Hasluck*, II, 503ff.; Watt, *Australian Diplomat*, 62.
14 E.g. Evatt to Washington, 19 Dec. 1944, ADEA, A989/44/655/36; FO 371, F3766, 4114, 4310, 4401, 4762/364/23; F3047/584/61.
15 Material in PREM 4, 31/6; FO 371, F4673, 4706 and 4785/584/61; Edwards, *Bruce of Melbourne*; *Times*, 30 July 1945.
16 FO 371, F4885/364/23.
17 W. Levi, *American–Australian Relations* (Minneapolis, 1947), cap. XII; e.g. *New York Times*, 13 and 14 Aug. 1945.
18 See above, 481, 613.
19 NCM, 18 June 1945.
20 Hood memo., 22 Sept. 1944, ADEA, A989/44/600/5/1/7.
21 ADEA, material in files A816/19/305/114 and A989/735/306; 'George Ph.D.', 51.
22 See e.g. Thornton, *The Imperial Idea And Its Enemies*, 322–4.
23 Cab, 3 April 1945, CAB 65/50; WP(45)209, CAB 66/64.
24 See above, 601.
25 FO 371, U6491/5471/G.
26 Hankinson to DO, 27 Aug. 1945, DO 35/1119, G579/52.
27 FO 371, U5471/5471/G.
28 Cab, 3 April 1945, CAB 65/52.
29 Ibid.
30 Gairdner to Ismay, 30 May 1945, PREM 3, 159/14.
31 FEC, 15 Nov. 1944, CAB 96/5.
32 See Cab, 14 March 1945, CAB 65/49.
33 Gairdner to WSC, 12 May 1945, PREM 3, 159/7, and see above, 522.
34 Material in PREM 3, 53/14; COS, 5 June 1945, CAB 79/34. WSC still insisted that Mountbatten must not visit Australia 'or give press conferences anywhere.'
35 SEAC War Diary, 12 and 14 July 1945.
36 Lumsden notes, 4 Oct. 1944, PREM 3, 159/5; Gairdner to WSC, 12 May 1945, PREM 3, 159/7; Lumsden to Ismay, 30 Dec. 1944, PREM 3, 164/4.
37 See above, 266.
38 Gairdner to Ismay, 30 May 1945, PREM 3, 159/14.
39 Marshall to MacArthur, 2 Jan. 1945, MacArthur Papers, RG 4.
40 MacArthur to FDR, 20 Oct. 1944, ibid, RG 10.
41 MacArthur to Stimson, 7 Feb. 1945, ibid, RG 4.

42 SEAC War Diary, 12 July 1945.
43 Stimson to Crossman, 16 March 1945, Stimson Papers, box 148.
44 FRUS, Berlin, I, 253.
45 See above, 265.
46 FRUS, 1945, VI, 556ff.
47 See above, 486.
48 Grew conversations, 12 and 13 June 1945, Grew Papers, vol. 7.

CHAPTER THIRTY

JAPAN AND THE POST-WAR ORDER IN THE FAR EAST

WHEN IT came to the question of how Japan should be treated at the end of the war, Australia's attitude was a decidedly stern one. In a preliminary survey of the subject sent to London at the beginning of August, the Government in Canberra argued that no immunity should be granted to the Emperor for his part in Japan's acts of aggression and her war crimes, 'which in evidence before us are shown to have been of a most barbarious [sic] character.' The economic disarmament of Japan, the survey continued, should embrace all industries, and not merely those producing instruments of war; the entire Japanese merchant fleet should be handed over to the Allies, and the whole country should be occupied until a democratic and genuinely popular regime had been fully established.[1]

In Britain, too, the press was tending to advocate the imposition of severe measures once Tokyo had surrendered. *The Times*, for example, insisted that 'Japan's characteristic system of government', including the imperial prerogatives, must be rooted out, while the *Daily Telegraph* described the Emperor as 'a very convenient shield behind which the militants could build up their strength again.' During August 1945, newspapers ranging across the political spectrum were at one in warning that, if Hirohito was to be retained for the moment for the convenience of the Allies, great care must be taken to guard against trickery on his and Japan's part; unease was expressed in particular, as it was within the Foreign Office, over the Emperor's failure, in his announcement of his country's surrender, to acknowledge in any way its responsibility for the Pacific war.[2]

Where this and many other, and wider, aspects of the post-war scene in the Far East were concerned, however, the Foreign Office in London were far less advanced than were their opposite numbers in Washington in the preparation of exploratory studies. This was especially the case as regards Japan:[3] to take one of the smaller examples, when the fighting came to an end no policy had yet been arrived at concerning the treatment of the enemy's war criminals.[4] As for the question of the future of the Emperor and the Throne, opinion in British official circles continued to be more moderate than were the views expressed in the press, even though care was taken, as we have seen earlier, not to take any initiative in this connection and thereby give Washington the opportunity of subsequently saddling

Britain with the blame for the retention of the institution, if not the man.[5] Bevin did nevertheless tell Forrestal at Potsdam that he thought 'there was no sense in destroying an instrument through which one might have to deal in order to effectively control Japan', and he suggested that the absence of the Kaiser from Germany after the First World War might have helped to open the way for Hitler.[6]

As Foreign Secretary, Bevin repeated this view on 10 August when consulted by Winant about the surrender proposal that had just been put forward by Tokyo, and on the following day he let it be known that he and Attlee doubted the wisdom of demanding that the Emperor himself should sign the instrument of capitulation. Churchill, now of course out of office, also telephoned the American Ambassador to add his support to what Bevin had said, suggesting that 'using the Mikado will save lives in outlying areas.'[7] Meanwhile the Foreign Office's specialists in Japanese affairs continued to indicate that they, too, believed that it would be unwise to 'interfere with the structure of government in Japan—which means the Imperial structure—... the only one which the Japanese have any experience of obeying.'[8]

The Foreign Office were also extremely anxious to see Britain participating in the occupation of Japan, 'and certainly', as the Head of the Far Eastern Department put it, 'in the formulation of policy for the ultimate control of Japan. Our non-participation', he added, 'would affect our whole position in the Far East and with it our position in the world generally.'[9] At the same time, however, it was by now apparent in London that the American Government, in Sansom's words, 'expect to take the lead and run the show.' Indeed, it was even thought unlikely that Washington would stand for the setting up of an inter-Allied Far Eastern advisory commission on the lines of the one already established for Europe.[10]

When it came to considering what was known of the State Department's own plans and ambitions regarding the treatment of Japan and the complete reshaping of Japanese politics and attitudes, British officials tended to become mantled in scepticism. It was only late in the day, at the end of May, in fact, that sufficient information was extracted from Washington to make any kind of judgment possible. On Grew's insistence, Sansom was then shown an outline of the State Department's schemes, his immediate reaction being to question both the need for a total and prolonged occupation of Japan (the loss of her armed forces, armaments industry and empire, he believed, would render her too weak to make trouble), and the American expectations of what indoctrination could achieve there. 'It is extremely doubtful', he wrote, 'whether, even if the Allies had at their disposal a host of erudite archangels, the Japanese people would respond to their teaching.'[11]

L. H. Foulds of the Far Eastern Department in London was more scathing still, describing Washington's ideas as 'the production of a group of doctrinaires who have been planning a new Japan in accordance with pet theories without any regard for the realities of the situation which is likely to exist at the end of the war.' He, Sansom, Dening and Sterndale Bennett then, somewhat belatedly, drew up their own proposals which, they believed, 'offered a more hopeful line of approach than the academic American plan', and which received the general approval of the Chiefs of Staff Committee. Instead of undertaking a prolonged occupation and prescribing specific institutions for Japan, the Allies should guide developments by controlling her trade and, if necessary, withholding the treaties that she would require in order to resume the status of an independent state; by these means, it was argued, 'the Allies should be able, if they remain united, to induce Japan herself to introduce such reforms in her institutions and her working thereof as will justify confidence in her future good behaviour.' Sufficient material relief should be provided to prevent widespread unemployment and discontent in the country, thus again avoiding the need for a prolonged occupation as well as the alternative danger of a 'violent revolution'. In the meantime, the occupation of certain key areas, plus the presence of Allied naval units and 'occasional demonstration flights of massed aircraft' would suffice, and even these measures could be relaxed 'after a short interval.' Working through the existing structure of Japan's administration and applying economic sanctions if necessary, the Allies could at the same time ensure 'the repeal of obnoxious laws, the dissolution of political societies, the reform of education, freedom of speech and worship etc.'[12]*

These observations and suggestions on the part of the Foreign Office were put to Washington in a studiedly informal way early in August, and were found by the U.S. War Department to be closer to its own approach to the question than were the proposals that had been drawn up by the State Department.[13] By this time, however, American officials were preoccupied with arriving at their own decisions about Japan as the war rushed to a close. In this situation, what London might be thinking did not count for a great deal. We have seen earlier that some British effort was made to have the formula of unconditional surrender qualified, but that, like Stimson's endeavours in the same direction within Washington itself, this had only a limited effect. We have also observed how, at Potsdam, the British representatives were content to secure no more than a few amendments to the American draft ultimatum to Tokyo, that the use of the atomic bomb had already been approved by London without discussion, and that the handling of Japan's surrender was undertaken almost entirely by Washington.[14] 'The Americans are going ahead on surrender terms etc. without showing much disposition to consult us', noted Cadogan on 14 August. 'We must accept this, and if Dominions complain we can say that we, too, were not consulted.'[15]

The document that had been drawn up within the Foreign Office on the post-war treatment of the country's Far Eastern enemy would, no doubt,

* In an earlier Foreign Office draft of surrender terms for Japan, the requirements had been included that all heavy-industrial plant, including iron, steel and synthetic oil, must be dismantled, that all merchant shipping must be surrendered, and that reparations should be paid. (FO 371, F6162/208/23.) During the months that followed, however, the emphasis became less severe.

had it become publicly known, have been taken by numerous Americans as confirmation of their suspicions that, in the words of the diplomat, John Service, 'many British . . . favor a soft peace toward Japan.'[16] Certainly, spurred on by further revelations of Japanese atrocities against prisoners-of-war,[17] a substantial portion of the people of the United States still felt what one student of the subject has called 'an intense hatred' towards the enemy. Asked at the end of 1944 by Gallup Poll what should be done with the Japanese after the war, no less than 13 per cent of those responding suggested that they should all be exterminated. Similarly, when, in September 1945, another poll sought people's reactions to the use of atomic bombs on Japanese cities during the previous month, 54 per cent were to approve what had been done, while on top of that figure, an additional 23 per cent were to answer that 'we should have quickly used many more of [such bombs] before Japan had a chance to surrender.'[18] Many, it seems, shared Admiral Halsey's publicly-expressed opinion that the Japanese were in fact less than human, 'rats' and 'barbarians' as he called them.[19]*

American opinions regarding the fate of the Emperor were likewise generally fierce: in polls taken during July and August, roughly one-third opted for his immediate execution, about one-fifth for imprisonment or exile, one-sixth for a trial, and only between three and four per cent for his employment by the Allies.[20] Congressmen and the press were both divided on this issue, but they, too, clearly inclined towards severity. The view of the *New York Times*, that 'the strictest control of the Japanese people, even for one hundred years, would not be enough', also commanded wide support, as did the same newspaper's assertion that 'the Japanese Emperor is the keystone of the whole Japanese religious, social, political and economic structure . . . and the symbol of Japanese expansion which precipitated the war. By word and deed and every act of his he has publicly supported the worst that Japan has done, and has cloaked its savagery with religious sanctions.'[21]†

Within official circles in Washington, strong differences of opinion continued to exist over this question of the future of Japan's Emperor and Throne. Grew, for example, remained prominent among those who argued

* A more perceptive and balanced view from the battlefront was formed by Major John Masters of the Chindits. 'The Japanese', he wrote later, 'are the bravest people I have ever met. In our armies, any of them, nearly every Japanese would have had a Congressional Medal or a Victoria Cross. It is the fashion to dismiss their courage as fanaticism, but this only begs the question. They believed in something, and they were willing to die for it, for any smallest detail that would help to achieve it. What else is bravery? . . .

For the rest, they wrote beautiful little poems in their diaries, and practised bayonet work on their prisoners. Frugal and bestial, barbarous and brave, artistic and brutal, they were [the enemy] . . .' (Masters, *The Road Past Mandalay*, 162–3.)

† There were lively differences of opinion on this issue among members of the American delegation to the I.P.R. Hot Springs Conference, as there were over the question of whether Japan should be allowed to retain any heavy industry. Admiral Yarnell, for his part, anticipated Bevin's argument that after the First World War 'we succeeded in deposing Wilhelm only to get Hitler.' (Minutes of 28 Oct. 1944, IPR Papers, box 362.)

for the retention of the institution, while he was still opposed by men like Hopkins and one of the Assistant Secretaries of State, Archibald MacLeish.[22] The formal advice of the State Department, however, as conveyed to the War Department early in August, followed Grew's line. Stimson, too, wished to see the Emperor retained, while, as noted above, his views on the post-war treatment of Japan as a whole were closer to those of the British Foreign Office than to those of Stettinius' officials, in that he did not wish to see the Allies take over responsibility for the government of the entire country, as was being done in Germany. Instead, Stimson proposed that 'our occupation should be limited to that necessary to (a) impress the Japanese, and the Orient as a whole, with the fact of Japanese defeat, (b) demilitarize the country, and (c) punish the war criminals . . .'[23] (It seems also that the Secretary of War, in a remarkable change from the beliefs he had strongly held in the 1930s, came at this time to agree with Grew that Japan in the inter-war years had at first made an effort to abide by the intentions of the Washington Conference of 1921–22; had suffered thereafter from Chinese intransigence; and had been clumsily treated by the Western powers.)[24]

Meanwhile, groups within the State Department, and finally the State–War–Navy Coordinating Committee, had been preparing plans for the occupation and treatment of Japan which entailed a paternalist reorientation of her people, and a far greater degree of involvement in the life and affairs of the country than either Stimson or London wished to embark upon. As we noted in the preceding period, three stages were envisaged: one of total occupation, during which the Japanese would undergo 'stern discipline'; then one of 'close surveillance', when military government might be replaced by some other form of supervision; and finally one in which the ultimate aim of a free and responsible Japan would be realized. As for the programme to be followed during the period of military government, the last of many drafts of this was to be approved by S.W.N.C.C. at the end of August and endorsed by Truman early in September. Under the terms of this document, Japan would be disarmed and 'economically demilitarized'; her educational system would be controlled in such a way as to eliminate militarism and ultranationalism and to foster democratic ideas ('The Japanese people shall be afforded opportunity and encouraged to become familiar with the history, institutions, culture and accomplishments of the United States and other democracies'); in order to achieve 'a wide distribution of income and the ownership of the means of production and trade', the United States would favour 'the dissolution of the large industrial and banking combinations', while there should also be equality of opportunity for foreign enterprises that wished to operate in Japan.

Where the country's politics were concerned, the aim would be to bring about eventually a regime 'conforming as closely as may be to the principles of democratic self-government', but one that would also meet the freely-expressed wishes of the Japanese people themselves; meanwhile the Allied Supreme Commander would govern Japan as a single unit (there being no question of designating separate zones for individual Allied powers, as in Germany) and would 'exercise his authority through Japanese governmental machinery and agencies, including the Emperor, to the extent that this satisfactorily furthers United States objectives' and provided that 'evolutionary changes' were not ruled out.[25]

In retrospect, it appears that in certain ways British Foreign Office officials had not, in fact, entirely understood the nature of the plans which were being developed in Washington, in that they tended to exaggerate the extent to which their opposite numbers were intending that the United States (with other Allies playing a minor role) should directly assume the functions of government in Japan. It is evident, indeed, that there existed a considerable area of common ground between Grew, Borton and others on the American side and British specialists like Sansom and Foulds. Nevertheless, Washington was going much further than London in its plans for military occupation; it was also far more idealistic in its approach which, as we have observed in respect of an earlier period and will do so again after the war, represented in part an evangelical desire to see Japan Americanized. Nor was the Foreign Office mistaken in concluding that the United States had every intention of 'running the show' in Japan. Officials in the State Department did argue that Allied forces should participate in the occupation and that Allied governments should be consulted over such matters.[26] Both the armed forces and civilian agencies, however, were determined that the United States should nominate the Commander-in-Chief for that country, and retain what S.W.N.C.C., with Truman's subsequent approval, called 'a controlling voice' in the occupation. The U.S.A., the President informed his Cabinet, 'would run this particular business.'[27]

The U.S. Navy, backed by the Army, were particularly outspoken against the setting up of any kind of Allied commission for the Far East which might seek to interfere with occupation plans or the establishment and conduct of American security arrangements in the Pacific. The S.W.N.C.C. sub-committee for the Far East, however, prompted by its State Department members, believed that, in the light of the 1943 Moscow Four-Power Declaration, some such commission would have to be created. Possibilities were therefore explored whereby the competence of such a body could be restricted geographically to Japan alone, with its functions even there being strictly advisory and in no way executive. A proposal along these lines was eventually approved by S.W.N.C.C. and the Joint Chiefs of Staff in May; Truman, too, endorsed it early in June, but even then it was decided not to take any initiative over the matter, but to keep the scheme in reserve in case an Allied government should insist upon formal consultations regarding the treatment of Japan.

As it was, Evatt's cries in this sense went largely unheeded, while, to Washington's relief, Stalin for his part chose at Potsdam not to press the issue of how to control the territory of his forthcoming Far Eastern enemy. Trouble was then briefly experienced with Molotov shortly before Tokyo's surrender, when he suggested that the Soviet Union should share with the

United States in the High Command that was to be set up in Japan; Stalin, however, quickly made his Foreign Minister climb down in the face of prompt and fierce American resistance. It was not, in fact, until the end of August that Washington chose to outline its proposals for a Far Eastern Advisory Commission whereby the Allies could be associated with the management of Japanese affairs. And despite this gesture, as we shall see, those Allies were thereafter to find the role allotted to them an exasperatingly subordinate and ineffectual one.[28]

Amid all these various schemes for controlling and re-educating Japan, and with so many of those involved being concerned above all to ensure that there could be no repetition of Pearl Harbour, it was only occasionally that the question was asked, whether a revived Japan might not be needed as a counterweight to the growing Soviet presence in East Asia. Forrestal, for one, much preoccupied as he was with what he saw as a mounting threat to the West from the U.S.S.R., did raise the subject at a State–War–Navy meeting in May, while Stimson followed suit in a talk with Truman in July.[29] And in London, where the idea again was seldom mentioned, G. F. Hudson did surmise that, given the continuing weakness of China and the increasing power of the Soviet Union, the United States might in the long run be driven to favour a rebuilding of Japan's military (as distinct from her naval) forces; he emphasized, however, that such a notion was 'political dynamite', and that 'it should never be urged by Britain, because America already had an ineradicable suspicion that we stand for a soft peace for Japan and are lukewarm about the Pacific war.'[30]

Far more common among British officials was the fear, first of a revived Japan, and secondly of a Soviet–American clash over China. 'It seems almost inevitable', wrote Orme Sargent in July, 'that the United States and the Soviet Union will eventually struggle for the body and soul of China, unless the latter can acquire in time such a degree of national unity as is necessary to enable her to develop her latent resources in man-power and economic resources in defence of her national independence.' Gladwyn Jebb, among others, likewise foresaw Moscow establishing its control over Manchuria and Korea, thereafter quite probably clashing with the Americans, with Britain 'being drawn into such a dispute.'[31] Not that there was any wish to become involved: the emphasis, rather, was on steering clear of such trouble as far as possible. Over the future of Korea, for example, London did not hold any very decided views, and certainly did not see a sufficient British interest in that territory to warrant becoming embroiled in a contest for its possession. 'Korea', wrote Foulds, 'is not worth the bones of a single British grenadier.'[32] Manchuria, it was accepted, should return to China, but even here it was felt—and the degree of similarity with Roosevelt's approach to the question at Yalta will be noted—that the Soviet Union had a 'legitimate claim' to an ice-free Pacific port and that to this end she would require a share in the running of the main Manchurian railways.[33] In this context, too, the hope had to be, as Sargent emphasized in the memorandum cited above, that cooperation between the United States, the U.S.S.R. and

Britain could be established and maintained, as being the decisive factor in the Far Eastern situation as a whole.

As for Britain's own security requirements on a global scale, the Post Hostilities Planners eventually concluded in July that 'the defence of the Pacific area should be accorded lower priority than that of Western Europe, the Indian Ocean area or the Middle East, since a threat in the Pacific would be comparatively remote.' 'The strategic interests of the British Empire', the report continued, 'demand the continued suppression of Japan . . . The threat from the U.S.S.R. to British interests in Southeast Asia and the Pacific would be comparatively remote. Moreover, we can expect immediate reaction from the U.S.A. to Soviet aggression in this area.' China herself was not expected to be a menace, any more than she had been when the question was examined during the preceding stage of the war, but, the Planners suggested, Britain should 'endeavour to ensure that [her] great potential resources . . ., particularly in man-power, should be made available to the U.S.A. and ourselves, rather than to the U.S.S.R.'[34] (Again, in other words, China was being seen as an object, to be influenced and used by others, rather than as an independent actor on the world scene.)

When it came to preparing two more detailed studies, however, of the Indian Ocean region and of the Pacific and Southeast Asia, the work of the Post Hostilities Planning Committee continued to bring out considerable differences of opinion and attitude within Whitehall, as we have seen happening earlier in 1944. Where both regions were concerned, there remained disagreement between the Services and the Foreign Office over the former's wish to place considerable emphasis upon a potential threat from the Soviet Union. Thus, in the Indian Ocean case, the only likely attack foreseen by the Committee was a Soviet one, via Persia, Afghanistan or China—possibly assisted by the Germans or the Japanese. At the same time the assumptions were made that the defence of India, as of Burma, would continue to be an Imperial responsibility, that 'the future government of India would be prepared to cooperate in the general scheme of Imperial strategy', and that the same authority would allow Britain 'to station an Imperial strategic reserve in India.' In other words, were a newly-independent India to secede from the Commonwealth or to adopt a neutralist policy, the shock in London and the consequences for British defence planning would alike be considerable.[35]

An agreed paper on future defence requirements in Southeast Asia and the Pacific proved even more difficult to obtain, with draft succeeding draft through the latter part of 1944 and the early months of 1945. Again, the Foreign Office continued to react strongly against the emphasis placed by the Services on a potential Soviet threat, believing that the only possibility of trouble from that direction would arise from Britain's involvement in a Soviet-American conflict. There were, however, certain basic points that were less contentious: for example, that cooperation with the U.S.A. in the area would be vital, and 'the cornerstone of our policy'—even though some officials again went on to stress that care should be taken not to make the

Soviet Union feel threatened thereby, and that Britain should not, when partnered by the Americans, neglect her own, individual interests and role. It was also common ground that the full cooperation of Australia, New Zealand and, once more, India would be required as well, and that 'stable and friendly regimes' were needed in Indochina, Siam and China, with 'settled conditions' prevailing in other territories such as Malaya. In addition, the need continued to be envisaged for a chain of United Nations or Allied bases along a line from the Marshalls, via the Carolines, the Philippines and Formosa, to the coast of China. Should China fail to cooperate in this respect or the United States prove tardy in its own preparations, then an alternative series of bases would be required, running from Indochina through Borneo, Celebes and the Admiralty and Solomon Islands to Fiji.

A measure of progress was made towards drafting a version of this paper on defence arrangements in Southeast Asia and the Pacific that would be acceptable to all concerned. The Services, for example, toned down a little their phrases regarding a possible threat from the U.S.S.R., while remaining able to observe with satisfaction that cover against trouble from that quarter would in any case be provided by the bases that would be required to guard against a revived Japan.[36] The Foreign Office, however, were scarcely any happier, fearing, as a member of the Northern Department put it, that it would still be 'all too obvious to the Russians that our preparations are primarily directed against them.' (Jebb was in a minority among his colleagues when he argued, for his part, that 'the stronger we are in general the more likely the Soviet Government is to work in with us.') Other members of the Office believed that the entire scheme, as drafted, was too ambitious for Britain, given the extent to which her resources would be over-taxed after the war.

Eventually, therefore, the entire issue was placed before the Assistant Under Secretary of State concerned, Nigel Ronald. His response, however, instead of being to facilitate a clear and thorough arguing-out of the vital questions involved, was to decide, weakly, that 'this had much better be put away.' The most that was achieved, therefore, was that the Chiefs of Staff gave their approval to a version of the paper which the Post Hostilities Planners submitted to them; Brooke and his colleagues, too, however, emphasized that they did this only on the understanding that the document was a staff study, without Ministerial authorization, and that it was not to be taken as a basis for action of any kind.[37]

Planning for post-war defence in the Far East was thus far from being an example of Whitehall at its best. Differences were observed rather than resolved, and the whole problem suffered, as we have seen in earlier cases, from Cadogan's aversion to anything in the way of an attempt by the Foreign Office to predict possible international developments over the following ten years or so. There also existed a marked tendency to underrate the extent to which nationalist movements, together with Britain's response to them, would change the setting in South and Southeast Asia, and to view matters in terms of a possible repetition of the events of 1941–42. One complicating factor, of course, was the growing uncertainty over the financial, economic and military resources that Britain would have at her disposal after the war. Another was the absence of joint planning with the Americans; indeed, even now major questions surrounded the role which the United States would play in the Far East after Japan had been defeated.

Moreover, although London remained extremely anxious to see the U.S.A. fully committed in the Pacific and (as we have seen above in terms of Indochina) in Southeast Asia as well, difficulties might arise where some British territories were concerned. For instance, only 10 per cent of those Americans polled on the subject in this period were aware that Guadalcanal had belonged to the U.K. before the Japanese arrived there, while 60 per cent of those who had known this, together with 86 per cent of those who had not, declared that, notwithstanding the fact, the United States should refuse to hand the island back to its former owners.[38] One gesture in this connection that was proposed by Halifax was for Britain to give to the United States Tarawa atoll, in the Gilberts, where American marines had suffered severe casualties. Bevin and other Ministers looked favourably on the idea when it came before them in August 1945, but it ran into narrow-minded opposition from the Colonial Office, and also from Australia and New Zealand, who were already uneasy over American claims for a base on Manus Island (an Australian mandate in the Admiralties), and who feared that to hand over Tarawa would only encourage further United States demands.[39]

At least where American desires to obtain Japan's mandated groups of islands were concerned, there was no problem from a British point of view—only a certain cynicism regarding Washington's trusteeship proposals which were seen as 'a decent garment to conceal the nakedness of their control.' ('The so-called idealism of the U.S.A. is not for home consumption', wrote the Australian Minister in Washington, 'but only to provide a standard by which to judge other people.')[40] The Chiefs of Staff in London, together with the Post Hostilities Planning Staff, would indeed have been quite content to see an outright American annexation in this instance, and believed that 'in view of the close cooperation we have assumed will exist between the U.S.A. and ourselves . . ., it [is not] necessary that any specific "rights" should be reserved to us [there] in peace.'[41] Foreign Office opinion lay in the same direction, although more emphasis was placed by diplomats on the need to 'dovetail . . . U.S. control . . . into a system of international security and of collaboration in economic and other spheres under the World Organiza-tion.'[42] Churchill, too, as noted already, was anxious to see the United States obtain the Carolines, Marshalls and Marianas, if necessary under their 'strategic-areas' proposal that was put forward at San Francisco. 'You can take the whole Pacific Ocean', he told Baruch. 'Whatever America wants there will satisfy us.'[43]*

.   .   .

* Some senior Americans were even now wary of such a forthcoming attitude on the

The trouble that was meanwhile being caused among officials and Government agencies in Washington by the mandated-islands question, and the eventual compromise formula for placing certain trusteeship areas in a special, 'strategic' category, have already been indicated in outline in connection with the colonial issue generally.[44] A certain amount of significant detail remains to be added, however. It is important to note, for example, how great was the pressure from the press and from Congress for the United States to obtain outright not only the Carolines, Marshalls and Marianas, but other Pacific territories which might be needed in order to ensure that Pearl Harbour would never occur again. We have seen this movement of opinion beginning to build up during earlier stages of the war. Now, in 1944–45, it reached extensive proportions, stretching well beyond such familiar, America-first and Pacific-first organs as the *Chicago Tribune* and *San Francisco Examiner*, though needless to say they and those like them made a loud contribution.[45] The *New York Herald Tribune*, for instance, argued that the principle of self-determination was irrelevant when 'the security of the United States and the stability of the Pacific world' were at stake, and the paper applauded the efforts of Representative Carl Vinson, Chairman of the House Naval Affairs Committee, to ensure American control of the Japanese-held islands.[46] Some, it is true, did continue to express a measure of uneasiness—the *New York Times*, for example, noted that the people of Guam under United States rule before the war had had 'less autonomy than they had under the Spanish'[47]—but a far more common view was the one proclaimed by the *Chicago Daily News*:

> 'Manifest destiny is bigger than we are . . . It has us in its grip . . . Destiny has cast us in the role of protecting others too weak to protect themselves. If we are to accept the responsibilities destiny has thrust upon us, we must have those naval and air bases.'[48]

Not surprisingly, senior officers of the American armed services were as insistent as the press over this matter; nor did they deem it necessary to conceal their opinions from the public, as might have been expected of those wearing the uniform of forces who were wont to insist (and to be upheld in this by numerous American historians) that they were apolitical. Thus, Admiral King and General Arnold, together with officials like Artemis Gates, Assistant Secretary of the Navy, were openly calling for the retention of bases 'paid for', in King's emotive words, 'by the sacrifice of American blood.' Arnold, for his part, playing the 'simple soldier-man' (which on the whole he was), added in June that he did not understand what trusteeship meant, and went on to list a string of islands that the U.S.A. would need, including some that were then under British sovereignty.[49] Likewise a subcommittee of the House Naval Affairs Committee produced in August a

part of the Prime Minister. Hopkins, for example, told the Australian Minister in Washington 'that Churchill is always suggesting to [Roosevelt] that he take [the islands] over, [but] . . . the President would not be caught by this.' (Eggleston to Evatt, 5 Dec. 1944, Evatt Papers, Eggleston file, Washington.)

report which, it seemed, had strong Congressional backing, and which announced that the United States, having 'restored peace in the Pacific almost single-handedly', must now 'be given the authority and the means' to maintain that state of international tranquillity. There followed the naming of territories that would be required outright (for example the Japanese mandates, the Bonins and Ryukyus), of bases in areas belonging to others but for which full American title must be obtained (on Manus, Noumea, Espiritu Santo and Guadalcanal among other islands), and of the main defence line involved (Hawaii–Micronesia–Philippines), together with its flanking fortifications (in the Admiralties, New Hebrides, New Caledonia and Samoa).[50]

In private, too, the Army and Navy were adopting a tone every bit as insistent as this in the discussions that were taking place in Washington before the San Francisco Conference. Having first sought to have any international debates on the colonial/trusteeship issue postponed lest such talks should interfere with their own plans, the Services went on to ensure that no agreements would be entered into which could do the same.[51] The Marshalls, Carolines and Marianas, argued Stimson, which 'must belong to the United States with absolute power to rule and fortify them', would not be colonial possessions but 'outposts'; like Forrestal, he greatly feared that Roosevelt's trusteeship ideas would 'end up by having us make the only sacrifice while the others [that is, Britain, France, etc.] refuse to follow the President's example.' To the San Francisco delegation, the Secretary of War bluntly declared, in an echo of the views he had formulated during the 1930s, that absolute control of those islands was vital 'if the road to the Philippines and to China is to be kept open in the future.'[52] In reply, as noted in an earlier chapter, Vandenberg assured both Stimson and Forrestal that Congressional opinion was 'totally in sympathy with [their] position', while even Pasvolsky, a major architect of the State Department's schemes for a new world order, reassuringly (and revealingly) announced that under the proposals which were being submitted to the Conference 'it would be entirely possible for the United States to control any territory it might need.' Only Taussig among the delegates, as we have seen, maintained a moderate position over the whole issue embracing colonies, trusteeships and security.[53]

Nevertheless, by the time the proceedings at San Francisco were opened, the War and Navy Departments had been obliged to agree to a compromise with State, which had continued to oppose outright annexation of the Japanese mandates on the grounds that such an action would undermine the entire trusteeship system. Roosevelt himself had come down in favour of obtaining those islands under trusteeship, even though, typically, he was not prepared to argue the matter out face to face with Stimson, and despite the fact that at one time, back in November 1944, he had told Taussig that he liked a scheme thought up by the latter whereby the option would be kept open of 'altering our position . . . if we desire to maintain full sovereignty in the conquered Japanese islands.'[54] (Was this merely a meaningless piece of Rooseveltian flattery for an underling? Or was it a glimpse of the old Adam of the Assistant Secretary of the Navy?) 'What is the Navy's attitude in regard to territories?', the President asked Taussig in March. 'Are they trying to grab everything?'; and a few days before his death he clearly indicated that he would endorse the position taken up by the State Department.[55] Thereupon, during the week following Roosevelt's funeral, Stimson, Forrestal and a wavering Stettinius reached agreement on the proposal to declare certain trusteeship areas to be strategically vital, and hence to be removed from the jurisdiction of the U.N. Assembly. In this happy fashion, Stettinius informed his colleagues, the United States could 'maintain [its] strategic bases in the Pacific and at the same time not be charged with annexation and expansionist policies.'[56]

This American proposal was duly accepted by the other states at San Francisco. Meanwhile various officials in Washington, like the members of Congress and newspapers cited above, had also been casting their eyes at a number of other Pacific and Asian territories, besides the Marshalls, Carolines and Marianas, that is. At a Cabinet meeting in March, for example, the thought was expressed that the United States might wish to make special arrangements of a military kind in Malaya, Borneo and the Netherlands East Indies.[57] More firmly and specifically, Stimson, Forrestal and their Departments were determined that, before the Filipinos were granted their independence, they would have to agree to hand over all the base facilities in their islands which the U.S. might require.[58] (In a similar spirit, and with a delightful turn of phrase, the Joint Chiefs of Staff observed that, should the time ever come for Puerto Rico to be given its freedom, its inhabitants would first have to 'voluntarily and under no duress acknowledge the facts'—they would receive an offer that they could not refuse, presumably—and grant the United States unshakable defence rights there.)[59]

Nor did Roosevelt stand aloof from this process of hunting for acquisitions in the Pacific. An island towards which he had long directed his attention was Clipperton, strategically placed on the approaches to the Panama Canal and also in relation to potential trans-Pacific air routes. Disputed between France and Mexico before the war, it had been awarded by an international decision to the former—an outcome, moreover, by which the Mexicans themselves agreed to abide. By 1944, some British air-force officers were taking an interest in the use that could be made of this island, but they were easily outdistanced by the American Service Departments and the President himself. Thus, in November, having been advised that the existence of European interests in the area could constitute a threat to the United States and would mean 'surrender[ing] our present control of Pacific air routes through Honolulu', Roosevelt asked Churchill outright to cancel any British plans that might exist for making a survey of Clipperton.[60] The Prime Minister, who may well have been unaware even of the island's existence, readily agreed to suspend all such activities, whereupon the President promptly ordered that, in 'the utmost secrecy', American forces should themselves examine the possibility of setting up in the first instance a weather-reporting group on Clipperton.

A meteorological station, appropriately guarded by an armed detachment of U.S. troops, was duly established there. The French Government not unnaturally felt bound to protest—'This is very humiliating to us', declared Bidault to an American diplomat. 'We are anxious to cooperate with you, but sometimes you do not make it easy'—but the President was unconcerned. His own plans, indeed, were more ambitious still, much to the concern of the State Department, which realized that they were in flagrant disregard of the legal situation in respect of Clipperton that had been established before the war. 'Mexico has long contested the claim of France to this island', wrote Roosevelt blandly in January 1945, 'and the Mexican argument has not been without substance. It would be to our advantage that the United States, in the absence of direct ownership, should obtain base rights on Clipperton island on long-term lease through Mexican ownership.' The episode is a revealing one in terms of the President's approach to international relations, even at this late and internationally-acclaimed stage of his career. Nevertheless, S.W.N.C.C. followed the State Department in arguing that the United States must accept the fact of French sovereignty in this particular case, and that any base requirements would therefore have to be negotiated with Paris. In any event, Roosevelt's death put an end to his own high-handedness over the matter.[61]

Another island whose fate was threatening to give rise to trouble, as briefly mentioned earlier, was Manus, one of Australia's mandated Admiralty Islands, where an important war-time base had been established by United States forces. MacArthur, King, Forrestal and Roosevelt himself were all of the opinion that they should retain control of that base, King and Roosevelt adding that Noumea, in New Caledonia, might also be required.* Australian resistance to this proposal, however, was to be made clear even before the Japanese surrendered.[62] Meanwhile the Joint Chiefs of Staff, acting upon a directive from the President, also requested the State Department to see to it that the pre-war dispute with Britain over the sovereignty of the islands of Canton, Christmas and Penrhyn was now settled in favour of the United States, with exclusive American rights to be obtained in addition for the establishment of various facilities within the Phoenix, Ellice and other groups.[63]

Such, then, were the main American plans involving Pacific territories after the war. As for the international order that would then obtain, it was hoped, on the mainland of Asia, Washington's intentions concerning the Southeast Asian colonial area, Siam, China and Manchuria have already been examined. Over Korea, meanwhile, a somewhat desultory exchange of ideas between American, Chinese and British officials had taken place; the State Department, for its part, refused to grant official recognition to the self-styled 'Korean Provisional Government' of Syngman Rhee—

---

* Here, perhaps, is one clue to why Evatt, so zealous for the establishment of trusteeships, nevertheless argued strongly in favour of the right of France to repossess New Caledonia and her other Far Eastern and Pacific colonies.

subsequently to be cast as a champion of Western values in the fight against international Communism—and continued to think in terms of a four-power trusteeship (of the U.S.A., the U.S.S.R., Britain and China) for that territory during the immediate post-war period.[64] Roosevelt at Yalta, as already noted in passing, observed to Stalin that he could see no reason why the British should be brought into such an arrangement, which, he estimated, would last for twenty to thirty years; Stalin, however, warned the President that Churchill might 'kill us' if he got to hear of this: therefore, Britain should be included.[65]

This remark of Roosevelt's, though not in itself of any great consequence, did, nevertheless, reflect the extent to which, by the time the Yalta gathering took place, he had come to build his hopes for a stable post-war order in the Far East upon the basis of a Soviet-American understanding. The State Department, it is true, continued to suggest, even so, that three-power collaboration would be required—that is, bringing in Britain and the Commonwealth; some hopeful souls in Washington went further still, and continued to include China in the same context. Yet as the Pacific war came to an end, China appeared to be in greater chaos than ever. As for Britain, although she had managed to recover from her humiliating defeats of 1941–42 to the extent of retrieving some at least of her Asian territory, it was becoming evident, as we have seen in an earlier chapter, how weakened and overstretched she was going to be in the post-war world. Churchill himself had recognized before Pearl Harbour that it was for the United States to take the lead in the Far East, and had done so again once the Japanese had launched their attack. Now, too, it seemed that Britain must continue to accept the role of a decidedly junior partner, not only in that part of the world but in almost every aspect of the Anglo-American relationship.

For Roosevelt among others, therefore, it was Washington's links with Moscow that in 1945 were seen as holding the key to the future in the Far East. But would the Yalta system, if that is not too tidy a word for what he had envisaged, endure? If the political divisions within China led to a full-scale civil war there, would the Soviet Union continue to abide by its declared intention to work only with the Government of Chiang Kai-shek? And what might be the consequences in Asia of worsening Soviet-Western relations in Europe? In the colonial area of Southeast Asia, too, there remained unanswered questions which could become entangled with these broader issues involving the role of the Soviet Union and the developing attraction of Communism. The Japanese had been unable to maintain control over separate Asian nationalisms and had ultimately failed to identify the interests of Southeast Asian peoples with their own. The basic contradiction contained within their policies—between their appeal to nationalist sentiment and their determination to erect a system that would smother true national self-expression—had by 1944–45 become apparent. Nevertheless, they had heightened nationalist fervour in a way which not only strengthened the resolve of dependent peoples to be free of their former Western rulers, but which often exacerbated the tensions that existed between the various Asian populations living together within a single territory.[66]

What would happen, then, when the simplistic notion, entertained by many Americans, that there was a single Malayan or Burmese or Indonesian 'people' waiting to welcome their independence proved to be unfounded? What of the Chinese in Malaya, or the Indians, Karens, Kachins and others in Burma? What of the Communist movements in the area? How, in short, was one to reconcile American anticolonialism and 'populism'[67] with the ethnographic and political complexities that in fact existed throughout Southeast Asia? How, above all, to reconcile those same anti-imperialist and 'populist' beliefs with the accompanying concern of the United States for stability, open markets, the prestige and position of the white man in Asia, and the triumph of the American way—political, social and economic—over that of Communism?

When the Japanese at last surrendered under the double blows of nuclear bombardment and attack from the Red Army, it was evident that the United States had won in the Pacific the mightiest victory in its history. For all the rejoicing that followed, however, the country's long-standing dilemma in the Far East—its aspirations so high and yet its willingness and in some ways its ability to become embroiled on the mainland of Asia so restricted—remained unresolved. For the Europeans, their time in Asia was rapidly coming to an end. In disregard of Churchill's profound and reactionary imperialism, Britain would commence her departure voluntarily and almost at once; France and the Netherlands only after a final, armed struggle.* For the United States, however, conscious as never before of power, opportunities and responsibilities, the lesson that even she, for all her unparalleled resources, could not now impose her will upon the East was still to be learned through painful experience: painful, that is, to Americans and Asians alike; but the more so for Asians, on whose behalf, it had seemed, the United States had been solicitous to a greater degree than any other Western power during the war of 1941–1945.

---

* A senior Dutch colonial administrator has recalled, in conversation with the author, how much he admired the way in which Britain left India, in contrast to the bitter struggles that continued to the very end of his country's rule in the East Indies. (Interview with Dr. van Hoogstraten.)

Notes to Chapter Thirty

1 FO 371, F4762/364/23.
2 E.g. *Times*, 20 July, 1, 9, 11, 13 and 15 Aug., 3 Sept. 1945; *Daily Telegraph*, 30 July and 11 Aug. 1945; *Manchester Guardian*, 13 Aug. and 3 Sept. 1945; *News Chronicle*, 13 Aug. 1945; *Daily Mail*, 20 Aug. 1945; *Daily Express*, 19 Aug. 1945; FO 371, F5160 and 5458/630/23.
3 FO 371, F1274/127/61.
4 Ibid, material in file 51048.
5 See above, 532.

6 *Forrestal*, 29 July 1945.
7 FRUS, 1945, VI, 625, 628.
8 FO 371, F5090/364/23.
9 Ibid, F1834/364/23.
10 Ibid, F2774 and 3768/364/23; F584, 713 and 2574/584/61.
11 Ibid, F4052/584/61.
12 Ibid, F3238, 3768 and 4230/364/23.
13 FRUS, 1945, VI, 582 and 585; FO 371, F4310/364/23.
14 See above, 532. Sansom was not included in the British delegation to Potsdam, which he rightly thought a mistake. Sansom, *Sir George Sansom*, 141.
15 *Cadogan Diaries*, 14 Aug. 1945.
16 FRUS, 1945, VII, 52.
17 On American refusals to accept a proportional basis between the Allies for possible exchanges of prisoners with Japan during hostilities, see FRUS, 1945, VI, 316ff.; Cab, 17 Nov. 1944, CAB 65/44.
18 Mueller, *War, Presidents And Public Opinion*, 172–3; FO 371, AN 4/4/45.
19 *New York Times*, 13 Aug. 1945.
20 FO 371, AN 2035/4/45; FRUS, 1945, VI, 587; *Chicago Daily News*, 29 June 1945.
21 E.g. *New York Times*, 28 and 31 July, 11, 13, 14 and 15 Aug. 1945; *New York Herald Tribune*, 11 Aug. 1945; *Chicago Daily News*, 11 Aug. 1945; *Christian Science Monitor*, 28 July 1945.
22 E.g. FRUS, Berlin, I, 900; FRUS, 1945, VI, 545; H. Feis, *Japan Subdued* (Princeton, 1961), 23ff., 64.
23 FRUS, 1945, VI, 585, 587; Stimson Diary, 10 Aug. 1945; Stimson to Truman, 16 July 1945, Stimson Papers, box 149.
24 Grew to Stimson, 26 June 1945, ibid, box 149.
25 FRUS, 1945, VI, 549; SWNCC papers, Sub-Cttee. FE, SWNCC 150, SFE 107 and 110; DS, Secretary's Staff Cttee., SC-5A, RG 353, box 88E; SC-138A, RG 353, box 88F.
26 E.g. FRUS, 1944, V, 202, 1275.
27 E.g. FRUS, 1945, VI, 603; SWNCC, 12 Aug. 1945, box 121; *Forrestal*, 10 Aug. 1945.
28 FRUS, 1945, VI, 529, 629–30; SWNCC, 12 and 13 April 1945, box 121; SWNCC, 65 series 334, Pacific–Far Eastern Commission file; SWNCC FE Sub-Cttee., 27 Feb., 14 March, 2 April 1945.
29 *Forrestal*, 1 May 1945; Stimson Diary, 24 July 1945.
30 FO 371, F1334/127/61.
31 Ibid, U5471/5471/G; U1080/36/G; see U2885 and 3390/36/G.
32 E.g. ibid, material in files 41801, 46468 and 50806.
33 Ibid, F6162/208/23; F4812/587/23; F2664/2426/10.
34 PHP(45)29, COS, 12 July 1945, CAB 79/36.
35 FO 371, U1216, 1951, 3142 and 3922/36/G.
36 Ibid, U8166, 8292 and 8583/748/G; U36 and 890/36/G.
37 Ibid, U890, 3390, 4024, 4753, 4969 and 5363/36/G.
38 Ibid, AN3037/109/45.
39 Ibid, material in file 44623.
40 Ibid, F2099/327/23; Eggleston Papers, 423/10/1253.
41 COS, 27 March 1945, CAB 79/31.
42 E.g. FO 371, F1034 and 1648/327/23; FEC, 14 March 1945, CAB 96/5; APW(45)48, CAB 87/69.
43 Cab, 14 May 1945, CAB 65/50; Baruch, *The Public Years*, 321.
44 See above, 579.
45 E.g. *Chicago Tribune*, 1 April 1945; *San Francisco Examiner*, 2 and 10 Aug. 1945.
46 *New York Herald Tribune*, 24 and 25 Jan. 1945.
47 *New York Times*, 28 Jan. 1945; see also 22 April 1945.
48 *Chicago Daily News*, 9 April 1945.
49 *New York Times*, 31 Jan. and 25 June 1945; *New York Herald Tribune*, 5 April 1945.
50 *New York Herald Tribune*, 19 Aug. 1945; *Christian Science Monitor*, 20 Aug. 1945.

51 E.g. FRUS, 1945, I, 93.
52 FRUS, Malta and Yalta, 78; Stimson Diary, 23 Jan., 3 and 30 March, 3, 16 and 17 April 1945; Forrestal Diary, 13 and 17 April 1945; see Richard, *United States Naval Administration of The Trust Territory of the Pacific Islands*, 69ff.
53 FRUS, 1945, I, 311ff., 790ff., 1273.
54 Stimson Diary, 3 March 1945; Taussig memo., 13 Nov. 1944, Taussig Papers, box 47.
55 Taussig memo., 15 March 1945, Taussig Papers, box 49; DS, Secretary's Staff Cttee. 10 April 1945, box 88H.
56 Minutes of April 1945, passim, DS, Dependent Areas Cttee., Notter files, box 131; Secretary's Staff Cttee., April 1945, passim, box 88H; Forrestal Diary, 18 April 1945; *Stettinius*, 18 April 1945.
57 *Forrestal*, 10 March 1945.
58 E.g. FRUS, 1945, VI, 1203ff.; Forrestal Diary, 8 May 1945; Stimson Diary, 8 Feb. and 14 May 1945.
59 JCS memo., 12 June 1945, Leahy files, JCS correspondence, USNOA.
60 Forrestal Diary, 31 Dec. 1944 and 9 Jan. 1945; memos. in Roosevelt Papers, MR box 162.
61 Memos. in Roosevelt Papers, MR box 162; DS, Stettinius Diary, 1–6 Jan., 7–23 Jan. and 11–17 March 1945, Notter files, box 29; SWNCC 106, 091, Clipperton Island file.
62 Forrestal Diary, 28 Feb., 9 and 10 March 1945; Stimson Diary, 3 March 1945.
63 SWNCC 38/1, South Pacific Base Rights file.
64 FRUS, 1944, V, 1290ff.; FRUS, 1945, VI, 1028ff.; FRUS, Berlin, I, 314.
65 FRUS, Malta and Yalta, 766.
66 See Elsbree, *Japan's Role in Southeast Asian Nationalist Movements*, caps. 5 and 6.
67 See D. C. Watt, 'American Anti-Colonialist Policies and the End of the European Colonial Empires, 1941–1962', in A. N. J. Den Hollander, (ed.), *Contagious Conflict* (Leiden, 1973).

PART SIX

Aftermath and Conclusions

CHAPTER THIRTY-ONE

AFTERMATH

THE YEARS following the Second World War witnessed a swiftly increasing contrast between the immense wealth and might of the United States on the one hand, and on the other the decline of Britain as she made her way (no salvation being found, after all, in a Commonwealth grouping that was itself changing and ultimately withering)[1] towards the status of a second- and then even a third-rate power. For Churchill, who had striven so hard during the war to maintain his country's place among the world's leading states, it was a melancholy experience.[2]

Even before 1945 was out, the extent of the United Kingdom's dependence on America, which Keynes had been spelling out within the confines of Whitehall, had become far more apparent. In August, when London underwent the shock of the abrupt ending of Lend Lease, the new Chancellor of the Exchequer, Dalton, estimated that the country required financial assistance from the U.S.A. to the tune of about $5 billion (£1,250 million).[3] There followed, in December, a settlement of the Lend Lease account which was sufficiently generous on the American side to come near to the principle of war-time 'equality of sacrifice.'* The best that Keynes could obtain in the way of a loan, however, was $3·75 billion—and that at two per cent, rather than on the interest-free basis that had been hoped for.[4] At the same time Britain had to ratify at last the Bretton Woods agreement, and was also pushed in the direction of convertibility (to come into force a year after the American loan had begun) and non-discrimination (no quantitative restrictions could be placed upon U.S. exports to the U.K. after the end of 1946) at a pace which her enfeebled economy and trading situation could not sustain. Thus, one month after convertibility had duly been introduced in 1947, it had to be suspended. Meanwhile, Anglo-American wartime differences of these financial, economic and commercial aspects of international relations had been continued in the shape of Washington's emphasis on the need for multilateral trade as compared to London's prior concern for the maintenance of full employment.

* The war-time Lend Lease account, on which the U.S.A. was a net creditor by over $20 billion, was wiped out. $6 billion-worth of surplus U.S. property and Lend Lease goods located in the U.K. were transferred to the latter for $532 million, while the cost of Lend Lease material that was in the pipeline was settled at $118 million. The total of $650 million thus owing by Britain was to be paid on terms of two per cent interest.

Further, essential assistance from the United States was forthcoming for Britain thereafter, notably in the form of Marshall Aid in 1947, and, where military security was concerned, the enunciation of the Truman Doctrine in the same year (following London's admission that a protector's role in Greece and Turkey could no longer be sustained), and the formation of N.A.T.O. in 1949. What the Churchill and Attlee Governments had desired so ardently during the war, a full involvement on the part of the U.S.A. in peacetime international relations, had thus come about. There was a great deal, it seemed, to be thankful for, and much talk of the 'special relationship' that still bound the two countries closely together.[5]

Yet there was never any possibility of Churchill's war-time dreams of some form of Anglo-American 'reunification', perhaps by means of a common citizenship, being realized. These glowingly-depicted visions of the Prime Minister's had been based on an understandable but complete misreading both of the situation at the time and of the future. Britain and the United States were, and would remain, separate countries, each with its very distinct identity and interests. Those two sets of interests might in some spheres and at certain times overlap or even coincide; they could also conflict, however, even sharply so.[6] To declare, as Churchill had done to the Commonwealth Prime Ministers in 1944, that such conflict could not and would not occur was emotive nonsense.

As it was, N.A.T.O. was not an Anglo-American alliance but a wider, anti-Communist coalition. There were still, it is true, significant ways during these early years of the Cold War in which the connection between Washington and London—concerning strategic matters, for example—did stand out from the remainder of America's overseas ties. However, as the war-time partnership—itself, as we have seen, a diminished affair by 1945—receded into the past, transatlantic strains became more marked, notably during the Eisenhower–Dulles years, and again after the death of Kennedy.[7] (Even earlier, indeed, Britain had discovered that a war-time pledge given by Roosevelt, such as the one concerning the collaboration of the two countries in the nuclear field, could quickly come to count for very little.) Thus, despite the many connections that remained between them, the notion of a 'special relationship' binding the United Kingdom and the U.S.A. together became increasingly difficult to sustain. 'For one thing', Henry Kissinger was writing by 1964, 'the "special relationship" has never had the same psychological significance for the United States that it did for Britain. The memory of Britain's war-time effort, despite the very great prestige gained by it, has diminished with time. As the postwar period progressed, many influential Americans have come to believe that Britain has been claiming influence out of proportion to its power.'[8]

At the same time as Americans subjected the performance of the United Kingdom to a cool appraisal, a flow of resentment in the reverse direction was much in evidence, especially from the left and right wings of British politics. Even Churchill had been surprised and angered by Washington's insistence on interest being paid on the 1945 loan—another indication, it has already been suggested, of his failure to appreciate some of the significant realities of the American domestic political scene. Among other episodes, the behaviour of the United States Government during the Suez crisis of 1956 was particularly galling to the right wing of the Conservative Party; conversely, the affair demonstrated the continuing vigour of what we have encountered so often during the years 1941 to 1945: deep-seated American suspicions of and hostility towards Britain's imperial role. (The events of 1956 can in this regard be coupled with the pressure brought to bear on the Dutch by the United States after 1945, aimed at getting them out of Indonesia, pressure which culminated in a threat to cut off Marshall Aid and military supplies; similarly, they can be linked with American anti-colonial strictures directed against the French in Indochina, which were still to be heard even when the U.S.A. had begun sustaining the military efforts of France in that territory.)

This colonial issue was among the factors that lay behind another postwar feature of Anglo-American relations, and one that comes as no surprise in the light of what has been observed during the war-time years. In contrast to their considerable degree of closeness over many European questions, the two countries were frequently to be found standing well apart from one another in the Far East. 'In Asia', as one student of the subject has observed, 'the war created and the peace stimulated two quite different sets of attitudes, interests and expectations.'[9] Some of the tension that developed in this context immediately following the Japanese surrender—for instance, over Siam—will be illustrated below. Examples of later episodes can briefly be mentioned here, however. One such case arose as a result of the Communist accession to power in China in 1949, Britain's response to this dramatic development, in keeping with her own war-time pragmatism as well as with the attitude of independent India, being to accord formal recognition to the new Government. To the United States, this was a betrayal of the anti-Communist cause, a reaction that prompted Attlee to ask, in turn: 'Are we to refuse to recognise facts, however unpleasant they may be? Are we to cut ourselves off from all contact with one-sixth of the inhabitants of the world . . . ?'[10]

It followed that the growing American commitment to Chiang Kai-shek's regime on Taiwan (Formosa) was regarded with unease in London as constituting a potential cause of trouble with Peking. Even during the Korean war, moreover, when British and U.S. forces once more fought side by side (though with Britain again very much the junior partner), it tended to be accepted in London that China had become involved in that conflict for reasons of self-defence rather than as a result of her aggressive designs, as Washington maintained. The British Government also continued to advocate giving the Chinese People's Republic a seat in the United Nations, and, as is well known, responded with alarm when it was indicated that the Americans might be about to use nuclear weapons in order to bring the war on the Korean peninsula to an end.

During the years that followed, Britain, despite her own anti-Communist campaign in Malaya, was far less zealous than the United States in the cause of 'containment' in the Far East as a whole, emphasizing, rather, the need to retain the good-will of the countries of Asia. She also desired to see Mao Tse-tung's China brought into the negotiations that were to lead to a peace-treaty with Japan, a proposal that was swept aside by Washington, which was now bent upon securing Japan's place within the American security and economic systems. Likewise, a serious rift developed between Eden and Dulles in 1954 over what, in British eyes, was the latter's bellicose and uncooperative approach to the explosive affairs of Indochina, centring upon the seige of Dien Bien Phu and the Geneva Conference. Nor did the setting up of the South East Asia Treaty Organization in 1954 herald a closer Anglo-American partnership in the area, as Britain's dissociation from American policy in Laos between 1958 and 1961 and her refusal to join the United States in the Vietnam war—much to the disgust of Dean Rusk and others in Washington—was subsequently to underline. By 1971, indeed, so little had the 'special relationship' come to mean that the Nixon Administration did not even trouble to inform London in advance of its impending and dramatic change of policy over China.

Britain's own policies in the Far East had, in fact, run into difficulties with the Americans from the moment Japan surrendered. (This was also the case for Australia, which was soon involved in a dispute with the United States over the base on Manus, for example, and opinion in which regarded the moderate treatment of Japan decided upon by Truman's Government—an attitude eventually embodied in the 1951 peace treaty—as dangerously unwise.)[11] Washington's entire approach to the problems of that part of the world—which included, in November 1945, what was tantamount to a demand that all the twenty-five Pacific islands disputed before the war between Britain and New Zealand on the one hand and the U.S.A. on the other should now be acknowledged to belong to the latter[12]—appeared from London to be heavy-handed and at times arrogant. Ironically, in the light of America's war-time hostility towards Britain's apparent predilection for 'power politics' and Hull's campaign on behalf of a powerful international organization, Bevin and the Chiefs of Staff Committee were concerned at the way in which, in advance of any arrangements that the United Nations Security Council might decide to make, the Secretary of State, Byrnes, was demanding in November 1945 that Britain should provide or assist the United States to lay her hands on various bases around the world: in Iceland and the Portuguese Atlantic islands; on Manus, Canton Island, Tarawa, Guadalcanal, Espiritu Santo and various other Pacific territories.[13]

As for the treatment and control of Japan, Washington's proposals concerning the establishment of an obviously subordinate, inter-Allied Far Eastern Advisory Commission and an accompanying Allied Council caused indignation in Canberra and London as well as Moscow. Moreover, Foreign Office officials were soon exasperated by the extent to which MacArthur was dictating affairs in Tokyo. 'We are quite willing to let [the

Americans] take the lead in controlling Japan', wrote Foulds at the beginning of September 1945, '[but] . . . H.M.G. surely cannot accept the assumption which the Americans appear to be making that we have given them un-limited power of attorney in all matters relating to Japan.'[14] The United States Government, added Sterndale Bennett, were behaving as though Britain 'had acquiesced in General MacArthur acting as a dictator in Japan and in [Washington] acting on behalf of the "Big Four" in certain matters without any prior consultation at all.' When Bevin took the matter up with Byrnes, the latter explained it away by indicating that American plans were above all aimed at ensuring that the Soviet Union did not obtain a zone of occupation in Japan.[15*]

Meanwhile, during these early post-war months, Britain's own actions in other parts of the Far East were themselves helping to keep London and Washington apart. Too often, they appeared in American eyes to bear out the warning that U.S. officials on the spot had been uttering during the war years, that the restoration of British prestige and influence was being given priority over other considerations—even to the extent, so Max Bishop now thought, that London's agents were trying to prevent Asians from becoming aware of 'the preponderant contribution made by the U.S. to the defeat of Japan.'[16] Hongkong, inevitably, was one of the territories involved, and when the British Government, rejecting Chiang Kai-shek's claim that the colony lay 'within China', sent units of its Pacific Fleet hurrying to receive the Japanese surrender and take over there,† Washington found itself placed in a somewhat uncomfortable position.[17]

In this instance, an Anglo-American confrontation was in fact avoided. This was far from being so where Siam was concerned, however. We have seen earlier how, in the light of American suspicions and of the promulga-tion of the U.N. Charter, Britain had toned down the terms on which she was prepared to make peace with that country.[18] Even so, the State Department strongly disapproved of the conditions that London presented to the Siamese, regarding them, together with the manner in which they were put forward, as clear evidence that Attlee's Government intended to establish its domination over whatever regime emerged in Bangkok. This was especially so as regards those items in the British list of terms that dealt with military arrangements, opportunities for United Kingdom commercial interests, an agreement over the marketing of tin and rubber, and the provision of rice supplies. Thus, from the end of the war until the eventual

* On the subject of possible reparations from Japan, no proposals had been formulated in the Foreign Office before the autumn of 1945. The Far Eastern Department were now opposed to American and Australian arguments that the *zaibatsu*—the major Japanese financial and industrial concerns—should be broken up, fearing that if this were done the result might be 'chaos and widespread starvation', or, alternatively, the survival of these powerful combines 'in another and perhaps more formidable guise such as state-owned enterprises on the Russian model.' (FO 371, material in files 46514 and 46521.)

† The Commander in Chief of the Pacific Fleet was also informed, in an echo from a bygone age, that it was important 'that we should show the British flag in the main Chinese ports.'

signing of an agreement between London and Bangkok on 1 January 1946, Washington backed the Siamese in the latter's successful insistence on a revision of what Britain was proposing. In return, this American behaviour and the 'constant impugning of our motives' by U.S. officials gave rise to great resentment within the Foreign Office, as Sterndale Bennett made clear to John Carter Vincent of the State Department. 'We had no ulterior motives as regards Siam', he insisted, '. . . and the attitude of the State Department has tended to produce on our side suspicion as to what the real American motives were . . . When the Americans were seeking bases all over the world', he added pointedly, 'we could not understand their suspicion.'[19]

Privately, Sterndale Bennett, who remained Head of the Far Eastern Department in London, saw Britain's policies in that part of the globe during this immediate post-war period as labouring under a double handicap: 'The apparent inability of the Americans to realise that we have played an appreciable part in the Far Eastern war, and the comparative lack of interest and understanding in this country (as compared with regions nearer home) of our position and responsibilities in the Far East.'[20] In other words, plus ça change . . .

Sterndale Bennett might also have added other restricting factors. One was the severely overstretched position in which the British forces on the spot found themselves when Mountbatten, as instructed, had taken over responsibility for a vastly extended area, his Command now embracing the Netherlands East Indies, Borneo, Siam and Southern Indochina as well as the original S.E.A.C. territories—one and a half million square miles in all, containing over 128 million people, three-quarters of a million Japanese, and 123,000 Allied prisoners-of-war and internees; an area already in political turmoil and facing an economic crisis.[21]

A further problem again arose from this very extension of Britain's responsibilities in Southeast Asia (a development, it must be remembered, that was the result of an Anglo-American and not a purely British decision, with Washington, indeed, having supplied its full share of the original initiative). The dilemma now facing London was how to reconcile on the one hand the desire of its Labour Government (and, even more, Labour Party) to react positively to the forces of nationalism that were sweeping the area and on the other the accompanying wish to preserve order and to remain on good terms with Britain's European neighbours, France and the Netherlands.[22] The difficulty involved was summarized by a Foreign Office official towards the end of September 1945, with particular reference to Indochina:

'It is clear', he wrote, 'that we shall have to proceed with the greatest care [there]. As a colonial Power it is in our interest to see that evolution towards "progressive self-government" is smooth and gradual and is not accompanied by revolutionary outbreaks which could but have an unsettling effect on the native populations of our own territories in

Southeast Asia and in the meanwhile might also affect the quantity of rice available for export to the famine areas ... [Yet] if the British forces endeavour to suppress anti-French revolutionary activities we shall open ourselves to attacks from American anti-imperialist quarters and no doubt from the Chinese, whereas a policy of complete non-intervention would no doubt be interpreted by the French as a further step towards our long-term objective of pushing the French out of their colonial territories ... Our immediate object, it would seem [and this was the line that was agreed upon in the Foreign Office] must be to get French troops into southern Indochina with the utmost despatch, and after turning over to them to withdraw our own forces as soon as possible.'[23]

In the event, the British and Indian troops, under Major General D. D. Gracey, who arrived in Saigon on 13 September became deeply involved in enforcing order, not only in that city but in other parts of Indochina, and in actions against the Viet Minh, who had by now proclaimed an Independent Republic of Vietnam, centred upon Hanoi in the north. French forces, and even some of the Japanese who remained in the area, also took part in these operations, and eventually, in January 1946, the French themselves assumed responsibility for Southern Indochina, which was finally removed from S.E.A.C. in the following March. Paris, for its part, was able to negotiate agreements with Cambodia and Laos whereby those states became autonomous units within an Indo-Chinese Federation, itself part of the French Union. With Ho Chi Minh's regime, however, which was insisting that Cochin-China, as well as Tonkin and Annam, should be included within Vietnam, the French embarked upon a long and bitter struggle, the outcomes of which are well known: the breakdown of the *modus vivendi* that was negotiated by Ho Chi Minh in France in 1946; the French use of Bao Dai (proclaimed head of a new state of Vietnam in 1949); and the merging of the French colonial war against the Viet Minh into the Cold War in 1950, when China and the Soviet Union recognized Ho's Government, and the United States, on its side, began to supply the French with extensive economic and military aid.[24] Despite this American assistance, however, defeat and withdrawal were then forced upon France in 1954.

Meanwhile Mountbatten and London had had to face a similar dilemma in Indonesia, as the present writer has indicated in more detail elsewhere.[25] No warning had been given to S.E.A.C.'s Supreme Commander of the extent to which the nationalist movement under Soekarno, fostered as it had been by the Japanese, had grown and gained control of vital areas of Java. Thus, when a small advance party of British officers arrived there on 8 September 1945 (the delay in sending a more substantial force was due to MacArthur's insistence that the surrender of Japanese in outlying areas should not take place until after he himself had signed the main instrument of capitulation off Tokyo on 2 September, and even then Mountbatten had to give priority to resuming control in Singapore), they found that an Indonesian Republic had already been proclaimed on 17 August. Moreover, with Soekarno as its President, that Republic, which was functioning administratively, was clearly prepared to fight for its existence if necessary. Thereafter, not possessing adequate forces with which to conduct full-scale operations against the nationalist guerillas, even had he wished to do so, Mountbatten strongly urged the returning Dutch officials under van Mook to negotiate with Soekarno some form of agreement which would grant the colony a degree of autonomy sufficient to bring Indonesian armed resistance to an end.

During the tense and complicated exchanges that ensued, the Supreme Commander and Dening (who remained his political adviser) both became extremely critical of what they regarded as the short-sighted obstinacy of the Dutch Government in The Hague, and as the heavy-handed behaviour of its officials on the spot. The Foreign Office in London, on the other hand, believed that Mountbatten was going too far in his desire to propitiate the nationalists, and that the Dutch case was not being given adequate consideration within S.E.A.C. Bevin himself felt obliged to remind Dening that 'from the political angle, the arguments in favour of non-intervention . . . must be balanced against the very harmful effect on Anglo-Dutch relations which may be produced . . . Our action must be conditioned by the forces available. But I feel that no recognition should be given to any authorities not approved by the Netherlands Government.'[26] Attlee, too, although he was anxious to see the Dutch negotiate with Soekarno, resisted suggestions made by the Australian Prime Minister that other states should intervene in the East Indies and enforce a settlement there.

'Further concessions now', Attlee wrote in November, 'might only encourage [the] extremists to open their mouths wider still . . . We have need for good relations with a neighbour in Europe, and it would be wrong of us to take advantage of the accident that has placed us in temporary military control of Java to go any further in intervening in the domestic affairs of our Ally than is strictly necessary. We should indeed be most reluctant to do anything to suggest that sovereignty is a factor which can be lightly set aside . . . [and] we have to be careful to do nothing which could be construed as an attempt to impede resumption of Dutch control.'[27]

Attlee's moderation did not, even so, prevent bad feelings from developing between The Hague and London. Yet within Britain itself, members of the left wing of the Labour Party were openly critical of their Government's actions in an opposite sense, that is as being too friendly to the Dutch and stupidly repressive towards the cause of nationalism in Asia. The British press, too, having tended at first to be sympathetic towards the Dutch and hostile to Soekarno as a 'quisling' who had collaborated with the Japanese, now, as the armed struggle in Java continued, began to call for the withdrawal of British and Imperial forces.

Those troops were, indeed, becoming involved in increasingly severe actions against the nationalists. Yet under the Anglo-Dutch civil-affairs agreement concluded earlier, Britain was pledged only to hand over responsibility for the East Indies to their former owners, not to help impose Dutch rule against the wishes of the local population. Moreover, although it was decided in London at the end of 1945 that Mountbatten's forces would take stronger measures in order to impose their control over certain vital areas of Java, the Government's military advisers remained adamant that, even if it were thought desirable to do so, the units available to Mountbatten were far too small to conduct an all-out campaign against the nationalist guerillas.

Meanwhile the United States Government, although explicitly recognizing Dutch sovereignty in the East Indies, was content to sit on the sidelines, and some parts of the American press began to move in a strongly anti-Dutch and anti-British direction over the issue. British diplomatic attempts to bring about a settlement on the spot continued into 1946, but failed. It was with much relief, therefore, that S.E.A.C. handed over responsibility for the territory to the Dutch, the transfer being completed by November 1946. The Hague then proceeded to negotiate with the nationalists various agreements which promptly broke down and were followed by Dutch 'police action'. Eventually, with the United Nations now involved in the issue, the Netherlands were obliged to accept the independence of an Indonesian Federal Republic within a voluntary Dutch-Indonesian Union. In turn, that Union soon came to have little meaning, while the Soekarno regime transformed its federal state into a unitary one and set about the long task of enforcing its rule upon various minorities in the area.

Quite apart from thus becoming embroiled in the affairs of other colonial powers in Southeast Asia, Britain meanwhile had difficulties enough to face in her own territories there. In Malaya, for example, although the returning British forces were generally welcomed throughout the peninsula, and although an agreement was eventually reached for the disbandment of the Malayan People's Anti-Japanese Army, the Chinese guerilla organization, with its associated political activities, did not disappear, but became embodied in a People's Democratic Movement which embarked upon a campaign of anti-imperialist propaganda. Tension between Chinese and Malays had also been heightened, and when in 1946 Britain attempted to set up a Malayan Union, with a common citizenship, strong protests arose from the Malays and the Sultans, as well as from some former members of the Malayan Civil Service in Britain itself.

The response of the Attlee Government was to give way, and in 1948 it established instead a Federation of Malaya, with a Federal citizenship that gave an increased measure of protection to the Malays and restored much of the authority of the Malay rulers. The country's Communist Party, for its part, having extended its influence within the labour movement, used remnants of the M.P.A.J.A. as a nucleus around which to build up, from 1948 onwards, a full-scale guerilla campaign. The struggle that ensued lasted throughout the 1950s and, at its height, involved the employment of 40,000 regular troops and 70,000 police.[28] Nor, to this day, has the problem of Communist Chinese guerillas disappeared from the peninsula.*

In Burma, too, nationalist opposition to the return of British rule was quick to manifest itself. Before the country's Anti-Fascist People's Freedom League would accept places on the Governor's Advisory Council, it posed various conditions which Dorman-Smith found unacceptable; standing aloof from the latter's endeavours to get Burma on its feet again, therefore, the League worked for its own accession to power. Above all, the position of Aung San became a critical issue, especially when he was accused by the widow of the man involved of having murdered a village headman in 1942, a deed he readily admitted to the Governor that he had committed.[29] To the Burmese, however, in the words of the official historian of the subject, 'Aung San was a patriot, whatever his shortcomings and his admixture of motives.' The Government in London therefore vacillated over whether he should be arrested, eventually, in the spring of 1946, having shortly before ordered the Governor to carry this out, countermanding the instruction and deciding not to risk such a move; soon afterwards it dismissed Dorman-Smith in the shabbiest of fashions.†

* See, for example, the article in *The Times*, 16 Sept. 1976, on the continuing activities of Chin Peng, leader of Malaysia's underground Communist Party, who fought against the Japanese during the Second World War and then played a leading role in the internal struggle from 1948 onwards.

† When the Labour Government came into office in 1945, Dorman-Smith offered his resignation, having received no support in the preceding period from Attlee as Chairman of the Cabinet Committee dealing with Burma. His offer was declined, but during the winter of 1945–6 strain between the Governor and London increased, the former holding that the Government were seeking to run things without sufficient reference to himself, the man on the spot. (It should also be remembered that Dorman-Smith had by now fallen out with Mountbatten, whose influence with Attlee appears to have been considerable.)

Shortly after the Aung San-arrest episode, related above, a senior member of the Indian Civil Service arrived in Rangoon and informed Dorman-Smith, who had heard nothing from London, that he had been instructed to take over as Governor ad interim. The Governor's Secretary also revealed that senior officials had been forbidden to show him (Dorman-Smith) any more official documents. When the newcomer proposed that Dorman-Smith and his family should move out of Government House into a hotel, however, the latter refused. He did accept the strong suggestion that he should take ship for London, where it was announced that Sir Reginald was coming home for consultations. When the vessel reached Suez, the Governor (as he still was, as far as the public knew) offered by cable to fly the rest of the way in order to be available for consultations all the sooner. He was told that this would not be necessary.

When Dorman-Smith reported to the Secretary of State, Pethick-Lawrence, the latter's first remark was: 'You're ill aren't you.' His visitor replied that he was in good health (he had fully recovered from a bout of dysentery) but was told that it would be best if he gave out that he was ill. Pethick-Lawrence, without any questions on the situation in Burma, then announced that there was no more to say. He bade Dorman-Smith farewell, but did not offer his hand.

A few weeks later, Dorman-Smith received a demand from the Burma Office for the repayment of his final month's salary since, unknown to him or the public, his successor, Major General Sir Hubert Rance (formerly Mountbatten's commander of the occupying force in Burma) had already been appointed at that time, and of course the Treasury could not pay for two Governors of Burma at once. Dorman-Smith refused, and suggested that

The Governor, for his part, had been in an unenviable position ever since resuming control of the country. He had remained as anxious as ever, as he wrote to the new Secretary of State, 'to enable Burma to attain full self-government within the Commonwealth literally in as short a time as possible.'[30] The problem was, as he soon found, that it was 'still a matter of considerable difficulty to persuade many Burmans that there is not some awful catch in the programme which has been laid down. The main trouble is', he continued correctly, '. . . that [Burma] does not really want to be "helped" along the right road. As represented by her youth in A.F.P.F.L., she wants to gallop down the road without any help.'[31]

As for the case of Aung San, Dorman-Smith was actually urged in October 1945 by the Secretary of State, Pethick Lawrence—who was later to leave him in the lurch—to adopt a stern approach to the A.F.P.F.L. leaders if necessary:

'It is obvious', wrote Pethick Lawrence, 'that we must be very careful to avoid taking [these people] at their own valuation . . . The effect of doing so would be merely to hand over the future of Burma to a single party with marked Fascist leanings and to kill any hope of the emergence of a party system, or of a broad-based Government . . . Even if it means taking a rather tough line . . . if they are not prepared to pipe down a little, I have no doubt myself that that is the sound and healthy course to follow . . . We shall make no progress with the very astute politicians with whom we have to negotiate by playing the hand from weakness.'[32]

Dorman-Smith himself admired some of the characteristics of Aung San, who was pre-eminent among these 'astute politicians', but, like the Secretary of State before he slunk away, sought to encourage more moderate Burmese to whom power could be transferred. In retrospect, this may not have been a feasible policy, given the prevailing circumstances. Where Aung San, a self-confessed murderer, was concerned, however, the Governor was also greatly influenced by the belief that, as long as Britain bore the responsibility for such matters, it was essential that the rule of law must be upheld. Nor could he forget that Aung San had gone over to the Japanese when they first appeared.

One of the handicaps under which Dorman-Smith was having to perform his duties in Burma was a situation which was also affecting Mountbatten's approach to operations in Indochina and Indonesia as well as in British territories: that is, the sizeable proportion of the S.E.A.C. forces available in the area that consisted of Indians, and this at a time when the Congress Party was protesting loudly against the use of its countrymen to suppress the independence movements of fellow-Asians. Where the Indonesian struggles

the Government might like to bring an action against him to recover its money. He heard no more of the matter. (Interview with Sir Reginald Dorman-Smith, and signed account by him in the author's possession.) As Viceroy at the time, Wavell was treated little better by the Attlee Government. (See *Wavell*, 1945 onwards.)

were concerned, for example, Wavell, as Viceroy, had called on Mount-batten to send Indian troops back from there as quickly as possible, and thus '[increase] our chances of preventing widespread disorder in India and preserving the morale of the Indian Army.'[33] Likewise, in Burma, Mount-batten himself visited the Governor in January 1946 and warned him, as Dorman-Smith recorded later, that 'in the event of Aung San raising the flag of "Freedom" and starting an armed rising such as the Indonesians had staged against the Dutch, under no circumstances would I be allowed to use Indian troops to suppress the rising.' The G.O.C. Burma later confirmed that his orders were 'to withdraw Indian troops to their quarters if a "freedom" rising were to start.'[34] (There were few British forces in Burma at the time.)

Wavell was indeed facing a serious situation in India in 1945–46, with the conflict between Congress and the Muslim League becoming more acute, and the former Party making much anti-British capital out of the trial of members of Subhas Chandra Bose's Indian National Army.[35] The sub-sequent and troubled path to independence and partition need not be followed in any detail here, passing as it did through the visit of an all-party delegation from Britain, the increase in communal strife, London's announcement that power would be transferred not later than June 1948, the arrival in March 1947 of Mountbatten in the new role of Viceroy, the shortening of the deadline for withdrawal to August 1947, and the final failure to reconcile the claims of Jinnah and his followers on the one hand and of Nehru and his on the other.

Britain's granting of independence to India in 1947,* significantly affecting as it did her entire position as a world power as well as her strategic plans and capabilities,† marked the beginning of that withdrawal from Asia which in some ways had been foreshadowed, and certainly had been greatly hastened, by the Far Eastern war itself.[36] Ceylon, too, received its freedom in 1947, as did Burma (led by men of the A.F.P.F.L. after all) in January 1949, the latter, unlike India, choosing not even to join the Commonwealth. Malaya, in turn, became independent in 1957 and Singapore in the following year, the two of them, plus British Borneo, coming together to form a Federation in 1963, although this split up two years later. Only some scattered territories such as various Pacific islands, together with the anachronism of Hongkong, remained under the British flag.

In the years that followed, the defence of even these remnants of the Eastern Empire proved burdensome, as did the need to help protect

---

* On the extent to which independent India inherited from the Raj attitudes towards her northern borders—involving, eventually, war with China, see N. Maxwell, *India's China War* (London, 1970).

† When Mountbatten was back in London after presiding over the end of British rule in India, he encountered Churchill for the first time since his return at a reception, and advanced across the room to greet his former leader. Churchill, however, held up his hands, as if physically to ward off the last of the Viceroys. 'What you have just done in India', he declared, 'is as though you had struck me across the face with a riding whip.' Thereafter he ignored Mountbatten until early in 1955, when he offered him the post of First Sea Lord. (Interview with Lord Mountbatten and letter from him to the author, 27 Sept. 1976.)

Malaysia from a campaign launched against her by Soekarno's Indonesia. Yet although defence planning was not coordinated with the political process of decolonization (thereby perpetuating a weakness in Whitehall that we have observed during the period 1944–45), Britain did eventually embark upon a course of reducing her forces and bases east of Suez. Moreover, the issue then belatedly became the subject of major political debate, as a result of which it quickly emerged, not merely that the country's resources were greatly over-stretched, but that the British people were unwilling to make the economic sacrifices necessary to sustain even a flimsy pretence to a world role.

In 1968, therefore, only four years after Harold Wilson had fatuously repeated the old refrain: 'We are a world power and a world influence, or we are *nothing*',* the Government announced that British forces would be withdrawn from the Far East and the Persian Gulf by the end of 1971, and that no special capability for use in the area would be retained thereafter. Certain adjustments were to be made to this decision in the following few years, but essentially it was the end of an era. 1968 had become a date to set alongside the Anglo-Japanese treaty of 1902 and the withdrawal of the Royal Navy's battleships from the China station three years later as landmarks in a long process of decline. Britain had thus ceased to be, or even to pretend to be, a Far Eastern power.[37]

Against this background, it is not surprising to find that, despite their strong differences of opinion with the U.S.A. over base arrangements and the treatment of Japan, Australia and New Zealand had continued after the war to look to the United States above all to ensure their future security. Thus, in 1951, as something of a quid pro quo on America's part for the reluctant acceptance by the two Dominions of a Japanese peace treaty which they believed did not guard sufficiently against a revival of that country's militarism, Washington joined Canberra and Wellington in the ANZUS defence pact.[38] In London, Churchill was one of those who was greatly put out by the exclusion of Britain from this arrangement[39]—yet another demonstration of his failure adequately to comprehend international politics in the Far East—but in effect it had been in the making ever since Australia's dependence upon the United States had been made

* Cf. Harold Macmillan's remark, made in private during the Suez crisis, that if Britain failed to topple Nasser she would become 'another Netherlands.' The Britain of the 1970s could wish for many a less happy fate. It is interesting to observe that both Macmillan and Wilson, for all their differences of background and age, were a generation out in their underlying attitude towards Britain's place in the international order of the time. Perhaps the necessary mental (and emotional?) leap was too much to ask of most of those who had experienced as adults survival and eventual triumph during the Second World War. The rash of 'Dunkirk' metaphors (like the 'Munichs' and 'Manchurias' of Lyndon Johnson and Dean Rusk among others, or Eden's tired 'Rhineland' parallel over Suez) that are flourished when Ministers exhort the British to climb from economic decrepitude may point in the same direction. Churchill, rejected by the electorate in 1945 and his public usefulness then past, remains in the 1970s mighty yet. On balance, this is probably not to the advantage of the country whose life he, more than any other individual, had helped to save.

apparent in 1941–42. Facts were stronger than sentiment, and indeed the Commonwealth as a whole was on its way to adopting a looser structure and to assuming a dwindling significance.

Britain's own entry in 1973 into the European Economic Community (where her failing economy and tired, insular attitudes meant that even there she was something of a liability to her new associates) symbolized both the diminishing importance of Commonwealth connections and, above all, the ending of Britain's centuries-old role as a world power. In a mere thirty years —it will be recalled that 1943 had witnessed the beginnings of the strongly-marked decline in her war-time status vis-à-vis the United States—she had undergone a revolution in her international position. The extensive revision of attitudes required in consequence is still awaited at the time of writing.

As the British and European presence in the Far East began to wither away immediately following the war against Japan, it appeared that the United States would now not only dominate the Pacific for the foreseeable future, but could, if she chose, exercise a decisive influence upon the shaping of events in East and Southeast Asia in addition. (Hence, incidentally, the bitterness of American radicals, then and subsequently, over what they saw as a failure to bring about a total end to colonialism,[40]* as well as the shocked rage of their domestic enemies, on the American right, when the latter's expectations, too, were frustrated.) Militarily and economically, the European colonial powers were beholden to the U.S.A. for their survival. Siam sought her aid against the British; the Viet Minh hoped for her blessing for their struggle against the French; Australia and New Zealand needed her protection. Meanwhile, the Marshalls, Carolines and Marianas duly came under Washington's rule, while in the Philippines (where many of those who had collaborated with the Japanese now prospered)[41] the arrival of independence in 1946 was accompanied by a guarantee of base facilities for U.S. forces, the tying of the islands' finances to the dollar, and the signing, at America's insistence, of a Trade Act which ensured United States business interests virtually the same, privileged position which they had enjoyed before the war.[42]

The experiences undergone by the Philippines during these post-war years are worthy of note in other respects, as well. For example, American servicemen there who were charged with crimes committed either on or off their base-areas were tried, not by the Filipinos, but by U.S. military courts. As a subsequent United States Ambassador to the Philippines was to observe, 'there seemed to be an almost hysterical fear, particularly in Congress, of letting Americans be tried by systems not in conformity with ours.' It was thus with suitable restrictions of an extraterritorial kind fastened upon it by its former owners that the brave new Republic, so long held up by Americans to the rest of the world as a model colony that was being treated in ideal fashion, embarked upon its freedom.

* In October 1945, for example, Dean Acheson affirmed that the United States recognized the sovereignty of France, the Netherlands and Britain over their Southeast Asian colonies.

Similarly, not many years afterwards, the same U.S. Ambassador quoted above found that the American-style institutions with which the Philippines had also been saddled were proving to be quite unsuitable, and that, 'the Filipinos [having] been oversold by us on the virtues of free enterprise, corruption was rampant . . . Virtually no one's ethical standards put duty to country first.'[43] Indeed, a complete breakdown of the new Republic's political system lay not far ahead, and at the time of writing a situation of fragmented dictatorship by rival war-lords has for some years been succeeded by a single dictatorship sustained by martial law. Moreover, this country which was so prized by Stimson and others as a vital base from which American politics, religion and economics could spread out into East Asia is now to be found, in the mid-1970s, 'attempting to cast off the alien influences of its long association with the West and to reassert its essential character as an Asian nation.'[44]

In 1945, however, this repudiation of the American legacy lay out of sight in the future, and the United States' own interests in the Philippines appeared to have been thoroughly secured. In Japan too, meanwhile, MacArthur, ensconced within a set of arrangements which ensured that American rather than Allied policies were decisive, not only ruled but appeared virtually to reign. (When George Kennan was sent out by the State Department to see MacArthur early in 1948, his mission, he recorded later, 'was like nothing more than that of an envoy charged with opening up communications with a hostile and suspicious foreign government.')[45]

The General also approached his task overflowing with an evangelical spirit and with a determination to establish in Japan the American way of life, to find in that country the protégé his own had so long been seeking on the far side of the Pacific. 'The Japanese', he informed Kennan, 'were thirsty for guidance and inspiration, [and] it was his aim to bring to them both democracy and Christianity.'[46] Nor, apparently, did this greatly talented yet frailly egocentric man doubt his success. He had had thousands of Bibles distributed to the Japanese, he was to recall in his memoirs; he had built up sturdy new democratic institutions; he had, in short, brought about 'a spiritual revolution' which 'almost overnight tore assunder a theory and practice of life built upon 2,000 years of history and tradition and legend.'[47] Happy, indeed, the commander who can win not only his battles but the hearts and minds of his defeated but grateful foes.

Yet even as MacArthur pursued his triumphant course in Japan, the entire structure that Roosevelt had attempted to create for the Far East at Yalta was already crumbling away.[48] A major element in this process was the worsening of Soviet-American relations elsewhere in the world, as reflected, for example, in the enunciation of the Truman Doctrine in 1947. Meanwhile in China, the presence of Soviet forces in Manchuria had helped Mao Tse-tung's Chinese Communist troops, too, to establish themselves in that territory, an alignment which was to be given formal expression in 1950 in the treaty of alliance and friendship that was then signed by Moscow and the new Chinese People's Republic. Yet what is striking in retrospect is the degree to which Stalin did in fact keep aloof from the civil war in China between 1945 and 1949. The outside interference, indeed, came overwhelmingly from the side of the United States, with a Communist victory, which had been imminent, being forestalled in 1945 only by an American airlift of Chinese Nationalist armies into Shanghai, Nanking, Peking and other vital areas; in addition, U.S. marines themselves occupied Peking, Tientsin and essential economic and communications centres.[49]

Thereafter, the United States continued to supply extensive aid to the Chiang Kai-shek regime. At the same time, however, Washington's efforts to bring about a settlement of the civil war in China (efforts that centred upon the special mission there of General Marshall between December 1945 and January 1947, followed by the visit of General Wedemeyer in the summer of 1947) were a total failure. The reasons for this come as no surprise in the light of what has been observed of American policies during the Pacific war. After August 1945, the United States continued to hope for the formation of some kind of coalition government in China—seeking to promote this happy outcome by advocating the establishment there of essentially Western political institutions. Yet, as had been the case between 1941 and 1945, Chiang Kai-shek was regarded by those who determined American policy as being the one man who could lead the new China whose emergence they impatiently awaited. As before, in other words, Washington tied itself to what even Wedemeyer felt obliged to describe as 'the presently corrupt, reactionary and inefficient Chinese National Government', the behaviour of whose officials alienated potential supporters wherever they went. And as before, the United States Government drew back from coercing the Generalissimo (whose one solution to the extensive and complex problems facing him in China was to resort to force) by attaching stern political conditions to the continuance of American aid on his behalf.

Yet in addition—and again we are on familiar ground—there were marked limits to how far Washington would go in its attempt to realize its aims in China. Over-all, indeed, it was the affairs of Western Europe that were given priority in these post-war years, and, within the Far East itself, the occupation of Japan and the defence of the Pacific. Above all, neither the Truman Administration nor its Republican and 'China-lobby' critics were prepared to see American ground-forces committed on the mainland of Asia in an attempt to impose a solution of the China problem. Likewise, Wedemeyer's recommendations for a new and extensive programme of aid to the Nationalists were rejected and his report was suppressed.

Even before the Communists moved in for their final victories of 1948–49, indeed, the State Department had begun to write off not only mainland China but Formosa as well.[50] The resounding defeats suffered by the Kuomintang Government, together with the intransigence it displayed to the last, encouraged officials in Washington to follow this train of thought; so, too, did the belief that, even under a new regime, China could not pose a threat to the United States for a very long time. As Marshall put it:

'China does not itself possess the raw materials and industrial resources which would enable it to become a first-class military power within the foreseeable future. The country is at present in the midst of a social and political revolution. Until this revolution is completed—and it will take a long time—there is no prospect that sufficient stability and order can be established to permit China's early development into a strong state.'[51]

When Acheson succeeded Marshall as Secretary of State, the State Department attempted both to justify the policy which the Administration had been following and to embark on the long-overdue task of educating the American public in the realities of the situation in China, one of the means chosen being the publication of an annotated collection of documents in 1949.[52] The Joint Chiefs of Staff, for their part, reaffirmed their view that overt American military action to prevent the Chinese Communists from taking Formosa would not be justified, while Acheson himself, in a speech delivered in January 1950, argued that the United States should not deflect Chinese nationalist sentiments on to herself when they were likely to turn against the Soviet Union. The Secretary of State then went on to sketch a vital defence perimeter for the U.S.A. to hold in the Far East, the line he drew excluding from such a zone both Formosa and South Korea as well as Southeast Asia.

Even in this attempt to bring home the realities of the situation, however, the American Administration failed in its purpose. True, 50 per cent of those questioned in 1949 agreed that the country should withhold further aid from the Chinese Nationalists.[53] Yet, unlike the situation which existed where European affairs were concerned, no bipartisan basis had been created within the American body-politic on which to develop stable policies in a Far Eastern context. The Republicans, desperate for office after their long period in the political wilderness since 1932, were thus ready to seize upon the issue of China as a flail with which to attempt to drive the Democrats from the centre of power; in addition, they were all the more eager to take up their political weapons on this occasion in that they had within their ranks a good many former 'Pacific-firsters', together with various individuals and groups who had continued after 1945 to see in Chiang Kai-shek a symbol of a China ready to ape, thank and follow the United States.[54]

To such people, what they liked to term the 'loss' of China in 1949 came as a great shock, appearing not only as a product of Democratic ineptitude, if not worse, but in part as a monstrous act of ingratitude on the part of the Chinese themselves in return for America's paternalist benevolence over the years. To those who, like MacArthur, believed that it was 'to our western horizon [that] we must look both for the hope of a better life through yet untapped opportunities for trade and commerce in the advance of Asiatic races, and [for] threat against the life with which we are even now endowed', the triumph of Mao Tse-tung and his comrades was a setback of seemingly vast proportions. As the General himself was to put it later, 'at one fell blow, everything that had been so laboriously built up since the days of John Hay was lost.'[55] To many Americans, moreover, the Chinese, divested now of their well-nigh angelic qualities of 1941–42, came to assume a sinister and menacing aspect.[56]

For those who had continued to believe in America's ability to mould China to her wishes, there was one convenient and emotionally-satisfying explanation close at hand for what had occurred. As we have noted briefly in an earlier chapter, the conclusion was drawn that the cause of the United States must have been betrayed from within, for else, indeed, how could she have failed? On resigning from his post as Ambassador to China at the end of 1945, it will be recalled, Hurley had blamed his inability to settle the internal conflicts of that country on career diplomats who, he declared, had 'sided with the Chinese Communist armed party.' Growing fears of a world-wide Communist 'conspiracy', developments in Europe and the alarm caused by the apparent betrayal to the Soviet Union of American nuclear secrets all helped to ensure that, during the years following Hurley's accusations, the approach he had adopted and the suspicions he had helped arouse became all the stronger.

Thus, the shock of events in China in 1949 exploded within an already highly-charged atmosphere, and in turn did much to provide a well-nigh ideal environment in which Senators McCarthy and McCarran and others could develop their witch-hunt,[57] with the Institute of Pacific Relations and individuals like John S. Service and Owen Lattimore numbered among their quarry. Careers were destroyed, and along with them almost all of the State Department's expertise on Chinese affairs.[58] And although some of those involved, including Service and John Davies, were completely cleared by subsequent investigations, it was not until the sharp change of direction in American policy towards the People's Republic in 1971 that the potential value of what these men had tried to contribute during the war began to be appreciated.

The magnitude of this change in 1971 arose in part from the fact that in 1949, when the new regime took over in Peking, the Truman Administration had declined to accord it recognition—an echo of Stimson's non-recognition doctrine of 1932, and, like that earlier policy declaration, a desperate attempt to reconcile an unwillingness to abandon America's aspirations in the Far East with a refusal and inability to take sufficient measures to realize them. Hostility towards the People's Republic had then been reinforced by the Korean war. Growing criticism over the 'loss' of China was one factor which prompted Truman in June 1950 to reverse previous official judgments to the effect that the U.S.A. should not get involved in any struggle for control of that peninsula, and to order a swift military response to the North Korean attack. Other elements lying behind the decision included the Administration's over-all anti-Communist stance, the belief that America's allies would lose faith in her should she fail to act on this occasion, and above all the conviction on the part of Truman himself, Dean Rusk and others that history was repeating itself: that this was Manchuria again in

1931 or the Rhineland crisis of 1936, and that now was therefore the time to take firm action that would avert a slide into a third world war.[59]

'Containment' was thus extended to the Far East in 1950, which entailed, in a major change of United States policy, the commitment of U.S. forces on a large scale to a ground war on the Asian mainland. For MacArthur, himself conducting the campaign, nominally under the auspices of the United Nations, the conflict provided a vital opportunity to reestablish the American position in Asia as a whole. 'The prestige of the Western world hangs in the balance', he declared to those who doubted the wisdom of his Inchon landing. 'Oriental millions are watching the outcome.'[60] And when, thereafter, his advance towards the Yalu river brought the forces of the Chinese People's Republic into the war, the chance to make good the disasters of 1945–49 appeared all the greater. To his intense frustration, together with that of many Americans to whom the very concept of 'limited' war was alien, MacArthur was not permitted to fight with every possible weapon and in the cause of total victory.

The United States did, however, incur as a consequence of the Korean conflict new responsibilities towards Chiang Kai-shek's refugee regime on Formosa (Taiwan), while Japan's value to her as a strategically-placed and potentially powerful satellite became all the greater. Moreover, the very fact that, contrary to the deep-seated belief that the country drew the sword only in just and godly causes against evil (and therefore, by definition, sheathed it only after complete victory had been obtained), Washington accepted a compromise peace in Korea, meant that the perception of China as a major threat and a part of a world-wide Communist assault remained to the fore in many American minds. And this, in turn, helped to increase the involvement of the United States in another war on the Asian mainland, a war that was to end this time not with a compromise but with what amounted to defeat.

This is not the place to rehearse in any detail the rise and fall of the American role in the Vietnam war. It has in any case become familiar enough, from the supplying of aid to the French in 1950, through the growing involvement under Kennedy, the Gulf of Tonkin resolution in 1964, the massive air attacks on North Vietnam in 1965 and the abandonment in the same year of the transparent fiction that American troops were not taking part, to the Tet offensive of 1968, the fall of Johnson in that year, and—vainly screened by the bombs and words of Nixon and Kissinger—the eventual U.S. evacuation and fall of South Vietnam. Like the Korean war, Vietnam involved a break with America's past policies in that it meant a major commitment to a land war in Asia. As in the Korean case, too, images of past events played a significant part in shaping Washington's decisions, this time in the form of memories of what tough, no-nonsense Harry Truman had done over Korea itself and of the furore that had followed the 'loss' of China, as well as of what Johnson was wont to describe as the lessons of Munich.[61]

Of greater interest still in the context of our present study, certain aspects of the American involvement in Vietnam can also be seen to have had their antecedents before 1950, during the Pacific war and sometimes earlier still. Here, for example, in the futile devastation of Vietnam, was one outcome of a feature of the Washington scene that we have observed in 1945: a growing emphasis upon the need for stability in Southeast Asian colonial territories and for resistance to the spread of Communism there, as distinct from (although still accompanied by) the earlier prominence of hostility towards European colonial regimes. Or again, there was a direct connection between that confusion over America's aims and their relationship to the means employed which we have seen had been a feature of her Far Eastern policies both before and during the Pacific war, and the similar state of affairs that existed where Vietnam was concerned. 'I have asked a great number of Americans what their aim was in Vietnam', wrote Sir Robert Thompson, a British adviser to the U.S. Government on counter-insurgency in that country, in 1968, 'and have never yet received the same answer.'[62] (Joseph Grew's similar experience during the 1932 Far Eastern crisis, and Washington's state of confusion in 1940–41 will be recalled.)[63]

Other links between Vietnam and the Pacific war earlier years need emphasizing. There are, for instance, certain obvious similarities between the way in which the United States now committed herself to a corrupt, right-wing regime in Saigon, however much she might disapprove of some of its features (the case of Syngman Rhee in South Korea is also relevant), and the policy she had pursued to its futile end in this respect in terms of Chiang Kai-shek's war-time Government in Chungking. In both the South Vietnamese and Nationalist Chinese instances, moreover, Washington stopped short of using the well-nigh total dependence of each of those regimes on U.S. support in order to insist upon the enactment of radical domestic reforms—including an end to brutal repression of non-Communist opponents—on their parts.

In wider terms still, the United States in the 1950s and '60s also tended to approach Vietnamese affairs in a manner similar to the one it had manifested as regards those of China during the Pacific war: that is, relying upon assumptions that were based to a considerable extent on a projection of American values, experiences and self-images, this being coupled with a failure to appreciate the nature of the very different civilization and political culture that was involved on the far side of the Pacific. ('Part of the tragedy of the American experience in Vietnam', wrote Professor Ralph Smith in 1968, 'has been that a great deal in the political culture of the country and its people is not readily intelligible to the Western mind.')[64] Likewise, the failure to anticipate the strength of the historical factors in China which lay behind, for example, the strong anti-Western attitude embodied in Chiang Kai-shek's *China's Destiny* was followed in the case of Vietnam by Washington's serious inability to appreciate the extent to which the people of that territory, who from around A.D. 900 had staunchly defended their independence from China, would continue to stand apart from their huge neighbour to the north.

A further, and more obvious, connection between the Vietnam war and its Pacific predecessor lies in the fact that the arrogance of American power in the 1950s and '60s, involving the determination to enforce a Pax Americana in the Pacific and to establish there and in the Far East an open door for United States commercial enterprise, had been fostered by the manner and extent of the country's victory over Japan. What is more, post-war confidence on the part of Americans in these respects was accompanied by another feature whose presence we have observed between 1941 and 1945, and the continuation of which helped arouse resentment against them among their South Vietnamese allies just as it had done among the Nationalist Chinese. This feature, in short, was the deep-seated sense of racial superiority that formed an important part of the mental and emotional baggage of many (most?) white Americans.

The belief widely entertained in the United States of 1941–1945 that the Japanese enemy—'the Japs'—were essentially sub-human, 'rats' who seemed not to value life and for whom no treatment could be too harsh; Roosevelt's musings on the inferiority of Japanese skull patterns; the open contempt of American troops for the Chinese 'slopeys' among whom they found themselves after 1941;[65] the conviction in the 1960s that Vietnamese were 'gooks' and that they, too, as General Westmoreland carefully explained to the world, reacted to suffering and death in a non-Western manner (he did not actually use the term 'sub-human')—a conviction that lay behind not only an individual atrocity like My Lai but also much of the tactics adopted by U.S. forces:* the degree of continuity is evident.

Moreover, the Vietnam war in its turn helped to exacerbate racial tension within the United States itself, as black militancy was fed by the return of embittered Negro G.I.s, who had been used in undue proportions in the fighting on land, while a far higher percentage of young whites had escaped the draft on educational grounds. Again, there are links here with movements of opinion that we have observed taking place among American blacks during and with regard to the war against Japan.[66] And just as the Japanese victories of 1941–42 had made the white man appear newly-vulnerable in Asian and some Negro eyes, so, too, did the triumph of the North Vietnamese and Vietcong.

In the West itself, assumptions (implicit or explicit) about innate white superiority were far from being at an end. Nevertheless, developments in Vietnam helped inflict upon the United States a faltering of confidence which had been experienced by the European imperial powers earlier in the

---

* According to one estimate, for example, 55 per cent of the South Vietnamese population were refugees by the end of the war. Also relevant are the use of 'free-fire zones', the destruction of hamlets and crops, and the use of defoliants and certain sophisticated anti-personnel weapons. At a different level, the habit of an appreciable number of American troops of collecting about their persons the skulls of Vietnamese will also be recalled. (It is worth speculating what the reaction in the U.S. would have been had Asians practised this on American dead.) Thus were freedom, free enterprise and the blessings of a higher civilization brought to Indochina. That the North Vietnamese and Vietcong were themselves frequently ruthless is beside the point.

century. For some Western youth, indeed, it was not now their own countries and civilization that constituted the wave of the future; that role, it seemed to them, belonged to the China of Mao Tse-tung and the Third World of Che Guevara. For them, at least, and perhaps sub-consciously for others in the West, too, there was a feeling that, in the words of Jean-Paul Sartre, 'in the past we made history and now it is being made of us.'[67]

The United States did not, as a result of failure in Vietnam, abandon its position of predominance in the Pacific. Marked by such statements as the one made on Guam by Nixon in 1969, however, there did take place a clear retreat towards resuming the pre-Korean policy of avoiding any major commitment of American forces on the Asian mainland, and this against a domestic background which included the reassertion of a significant degree of Congressional influence (even if of a largely negative kind) on the country's foreign relations, and an international one which featured the decline of the once-supreme dollar. Moreover, the Nixon visit to China (accompanied as it was by a revival of those age-old dreams of a great market there for American commerce) represented a belated and tacit acceptance of the fact that Washington could not impose its will upon that part of the world.

Despite the magnitude of her power, in other words, it had taken only about twenty-five years since her triumph over Japan for the United States to follow her European allies of the Second World War in learning that the age of Western dominance in Asia was indeed at an end.

Notes to Chapter Thirty-One

1 See e.g. J. Frankel, *British Foreign Policy, 1945–1973* (London, 1975), 221ff.
2 E.g. *Moran*, 7 Jan. 1952.
3 FO 371, UE3762 and 3837/32/71.
4 Gardner, *Sterling-Dollar Diplomacy*, cap. X; Hall, *North American Supply*, 477ff.
5 See Nicholas, *The United States and Britain*, cap. 11. In general, see I. S. McDonald, *Anglo-American Relations Since The Second World War* (Newton Abbot, 1974).
6 See e.g. Wheeler-Bennett, *Action This Day*, 132.
7 See Nicholas, *The United States and Britain*, 13, 4, and e.g. C. Bell, *The Debatable Alliance* (London, 1964).
8 H. Kissinger, *The Troubled Partnership* (New York, 1964).
9 Nicholas, *The U.S. and Britain*, cap. 12.
10 McDonald, *Anglo-American Relations*, 86. In general see R. Boardman, *Britain and the People's Republic of China, 1949–1974* (London, 1976).
11 E.g. Reese, *Australia, New Zealand and the United States*, 50ff.; Watt, *The Evolution of Australian Foreign Policy*, 100, 131.
12 FRUS, 1945, VI, 206; FO 371, AN3853/35/45.
13 Bevin memo., 29 Nov. 1945, and Washington to Foreign Office, 8 Nov. 1945, IO, Private Office Papers, L/PO/393.
14 FO 371, F6131/584/61.
15 Ibid, material in files 46448–9 and 46524.
16 Bishop to State Dpt., 14 Aug. 1945, OPD Exec. file 17, item 26.
17 FO 371, files 46252–4; FRUS, 1945, VII, 500ff.; *Donnison*, 150ff.
18 See above, 619–20, and FE(M)C, 17 Aug. 1945, CAB 96/9.
19 FRUS, 1945, VI, 1296ff.; FO 371, files 46555–7.

20 FO 371, F6966/16/61.
21 See *Donnison*, passim; *Kirby*, V, 230, 307ff.; Mountbatten, unpublished section 'D' of his *Report*.
22 On the post-war scene in general, see B. N. Pandey, *Problems of Independence in South and Southeast Asia* (forthcoming).
23 FO 371, F7161/11/61.
24 See *Donnison*, cap. XXI; Lancaster, *The Emancipation of French Indochina*; Mountbatten, section 'D' of his *Report*; E. Hammer, *The Struggle For Indochina* (Stanford, 1954).
25 C. Thorne, 'Engeland, Australië en Nederlands Indië, 1941–1945', *Internationale Spectator* (The Hague), Aug. 1975. See also *Donnison*, cap. XXII; section 'D' of Mountbatten *Report*; FO 371, files 46392–46409; van der Waal (ed.), *Officiële Bescheiden Betreffende de Nederlands–Indonesische Betrekkingen, 1945–50, vol. I* (The Hague, 1971); H. van Mook, *Indonesië, Nederland En De Wereld* (Amsterdam, 1949), and van Mook, *The Status of Democracy In Southeast Asia* (New York, 1950).
26 FO 371, F7649/6398/61.
27 Ibid, F9294/6398/61.
28 *Donnison*, 383ff.; Section 'D' of Mountbatten *Report*; Rose, *Britain and Southeast Asia*, 126ff.; Kennedy, *A History of Malaya*, 261ff.; T. E. Smith and J. Bastin, *Malaysia* (London, 1967). In Borneo, as planned, the Rajah of Sarawak and the North Borneo Chartered Company surrendered their rights to the Crown, and the country passed under the administration of a British Governor.
29 *Donnison*, 383ff.; Collis, *First and Last in Burma*; interview with Sir R. Dorman-Smith.
30 Dorman-Smith to Pethick-Lawrence, 4 Aug. 1945, Dorman-Smith Papers, E215/3.
31 Dorman-Smith to Pethick-Lawrence, 22 Jan. 1946, ibid, E215/1.
32 Pethick-Lawrence to Dorman-Smith, 28 Oct. 1945, ibid, E215/3.
33 FO 371, F11065/6398/61.
34 Dorman-Smith notes, 7 June 1946, Dorman-Smith Papers, E215/2; interviews with Sir R. Dorman-Smith and Lord Mountbatten.
35 See Allen, *The End of the War in Asia*, 145ff.
36 One consequence of the transfer of power in India, of course, was that the affairs of Tibet now became a matter of concern to Nehru's Government, rather than to Britain. This was notably the case when the Chinese invaded Tibet in 1950 and crushed a rebellion there in 1959. There followed the Sino-Indian border war in 1962.
37 See P. Darby, *Britain's Defence Policy East of Suez, 1947–1968* (London, 1973); Frankel, *British Foreign Policy, 1945–1973*, cap. 12.
38 See Watt, *The Evolution of Australian Foreign Policy*, 131.
39 Darby, *Britain's Defence Policy East of Suez*, 23.
40 See e.g. Isaacs, *No Peace For Asia*, introduction to 1967 edn.
41 See FRUS, 1945, VI, 1233; Friend, *Between Two Empires*, 250.
42 Friend, *Between Two Empires*, 259ff.; Gardner, *Economic Aspects*, 181.
43 Bohlen, *Witness To History*, 452. See above, 231, note 115.
44 See *Times*, 3 Aug. and 22 Sept. 1976.
45 G. Kennan, *Memoirs, 1925–1950* (London, 1968), 382.
46 Ibid, 384.
47 MacArthur, *Reminiscences*, 310–11. On post-war Japanese reactions against excessive 'Americanization', and an emphasizing of Japanese qualities and traditions, see e.g. Kahn, *The Emerging Japanese Superstate*, 62, 77, 103.
48 See e.g. Iriye, *The Cold War In Asia*, 98ff.; *Tang Tsou*, parts three and four.
49 *Tang Tsou*, 308.
50 See ibid, 486ff.
51 Quoted in ibid, 394.
52 *United States Relations With China* (Dpt. of State, 1949).
53 Steele, *The American People and China*, 47.
54 See *Tang Tsou*, 447ff.
55 MacArthur, *Reminiscences*, 320. See Kubeck, *How The Far East Was Lost*, passim.

56 See Isaacs, *Scratches On Our Minds*, 209ff.
57 The 'China lobby' included men such as Senators Bridges and Knowland, General Chennault, William Bullitt, Alfred Kohlberg and Henry and Clare Booth Luce. See Stecle, *The American People and China*, 239; R. Y. Koen, *The China Lobby in American Politics* (New York, 1974); Kahn, *The China Hands*.
58 See e.g. *Shewmaker*, 269ff.
59 See G. D. Paige, *The Korean Decision* (New York, 1968); May, *'Lessons' of The Past*, cap. III.
60 MacArthur, *Reminiscences*, 350.
61 See May, *'Lessons' of The Past*, cap. IV. On the relationship between U.S. policy towards Japan and the Vietnamese war, see Lake, *The Legacy of Vietnam*, 5. SEATO was finally buried in 1977, having long been moribund.
62 R. Thompson, *No Exit From Vietnam* (London, 1969), 112. The point is amply illustrated in PP, vols. 1–4. See Lake, *The Legacy of Vietnam*, 314.
63 See above, 84. Similarly, contradictory explanations of the 'Nixon Doctrine' (first enunciated in 1969, and entailing a less ambitious American strategy in the Far East) were given by various senior members of the Washington Administration. See L. H. Brown, 'American Security Policy in Asia', *Adelphi Papers*, No. 132 (International Institute for Strategic Studies, London, 1977).
64 R. Smith, *Vietnam and the West* (Ithica, N.Y., 1971), 5.
65 E.g. Taylor, *Richer By Asia*, 89; Isaacs, *Scratches On Our Minds*, 17ff.
66 And see below, 726–7.
67 Introduction to F. Fanon, *The Wretched of the Earth* (Harmondsworth, 1967).

CHAPTER THIRTY-TWO

CONCLUSIONS

THROUGHOUT THE present study, it has been emphasized that any enquiry into Anglo-American relations during the Second World War must surely lead in the first place to a recognition of the remarkable nature of the partnership that was then achieved: 'a fusion of national identities', in the words of Professor Nicholas, 'if not of sovereignties, hitherto unprecedented.' Whether the particular subject for examination is grand strategy, the economic substructure on which the war-effort was based, or an inter-Allied Command in the field like that of Eisenhowever in Europe, what stands out initially is the attainment of 'a much higher degree of cooperation and unforced fusion than had ever before existed between two sovereign states.'[1]

Moreover, this outcome was not simply the work of those who held official positions on one or other side of the Atlantic. In an important sense it reflected also a readiness on the part of the two peoples, for all their differences and mutual ignorance and suspicions, to come together to this extent in the face of a common peril. The result in 1940–41, as we have seen, was a 'common-law alliance' which helped sustain Britain in her lone fight, and from 1941 to 1945 a combination which made certain the eventual defeat of Japan, and, thanks also to the crucial land power of the Soviet Union, of Nazi Germany as well.

At the same time, however, we have also observed how, with the growing imbalance between the respective strengths of the two Allies, the nature of their relationship underwent changes in a manner that was bound to produce considerable strain between them. What is more, this occurred against a background of war-time circumstances that did much to inhibit the kind of drastic rethinking about the nature and future of that relationship that Lippmann and Keynes, for example, believed was urgently required, with the result that many of those involved lacked, by the middle of the war, an adequate perspective within which to place specific issues and events.

On the part of Britain, morally and in some ways even materially an equal partner in 1941–42, there was the need to readjust to a status which by the end of 1944 was a decidedly junior one, and to a degree of dependence on the U.S.A. that outran the comprehension of a good many people in Whitehall and Westminster, let alone among the general public. For the United States, increasingly conscious of her vast strength, actual and potential, there was the question of how to balance a desire to make that strength tell—strategically, politically, and in virtually dictating to Britain a version of the post-war economic order which, like the prospective United Nations, would clearly centre upon American power and interests—against the importance of maintaining a satisfactory level of inter-Allied trust and cooperation.

It is not surprising, therefore, to find that in consequence there existed widespread suspicions on both sides of the Atlantic, sometimes involving mirror-like images of each other. Thus, within the U.S.A., not only Roosevelt's opponents but members of the Administration and senior officers like Marshall and King frequently believed that Churchill and his smoothly-operating advisers were manipulating, or seeking to do so, America's military strategy and political intentions. In London, meanwhile (where there did indeed exist the hope that after the war, as well as during it, Britain could exercise subtle but considerable guidance over her mighty friend), there were those in high places who were quick to suspect the United States of attempting to use her financial and material superiority to coerce Britain over certain major political issues (such as the future of India), or strategically (in Southeast Asia, for example), or in order to win for herself an undue share of, say, Middle East oil resources or post-war civil aviation.

Tension thus arose in connection with some of the means that each side was employing, or was thought by the other to be employing, in the pursuit of its own, distinct aims. Where the Americans were concerned, as we have seen, suspicions extended to a belief that Britain's entire approach to international affairs could be summed up and denounced as 'power politics', a method of proceeding that was not only creating trouble during the war itself for innocent Uncle Sam—fighting, as he was held to be, quite simply in order to defeat the powers of darkness in the shortest possible time—but that would jeopardize the creation thereafter of a new and healthier international order.

Already, however, we have moved from the realm of means to that of the ends for which they were to be deployed. And here, too, despite their joint endorsement of, for example, the Atlantic Charter and the Moscow Declaration of 1943, the United States and Britain more than occasionally looked with concern at one another, as they had done, indeed, during the First World War.[2] How far, Americans asked, would Britain now go in practice in order to achieve the goals embodied in that Atlantic Charter—emphasized by Roosevelt to be of universal significance—within the confines of her own Empire? Or again, was she not seeking to carve out for herself a sphere of influence in the Mediterranean and to set up on the European continent a power bloc with which to confront the Soviet Union? Might she not undermine Hull's long-cherished plans for a multilateral trading structure for the post-war world by clinging to imperial preference and bilateral tariff arrangements?

Conversely, there were those in Britain and parts of the Commonwealth who demanded of individuals like Law who wished to meet Washington's desires in this field whether multilateralism, coming on top of the formidable status now being acquired by the ubiquitous dollar, would not merely help to realize the aims of American economic imperialism. And did not the United States also intend to dictate a peace settlement that would be based in part upon hostility towards European colonialism? Did it not begin to appear already, indeed, that Roosevelt, in his war-time dealings with Stalin, was prepared to devalue the standing and overlook the interests of his British ally?

The existence of such strains—and there were of course others, involving, for example, the relations between London and Washington respectively and the Gaullist movement and Government—does not invalidate our initial emphasis upon the remarkable degree of Anglo-American collabora-tion that was achieved, notwithstanding. It is, nevertheless, a necessary reminder that, however close they might come to one another, Britain and the United States inevitably remained separate, sovereign states (in Britain's case, one should perhaps say 'would-be sovereign' in the context of her degree of dependence on the U.S.A. by 1944–45) whose interests, contrary to Churchill's assertion, could and did differ and conflict as well as coincide.[3]

Nor was there lacking at the end, as well as at the outset, of their war-time partnership the kind of mutual ignorance which was referred to in the early chapters of this study, and which, despite ties of ancestry, language and democratic institutions, helped exacerbate genuine differences and foster suspicions that were based upon misunderstanding or on a stereotyped image of the other nation. The complexity of each other's domestic political situation and the ways in which it could affect policy-making were not always well understood, even among officials who should have known better. In London, for example, the tendency of his colleagues in the Government to think of Washington in terms of Whitehall was frequently lamented by Richard Law; or, to view matters in a wider perspective, there was the habit of many Americans to take it for granted that 'Britain' meant 'Churchill', and that her imperial attitudes were epitomized by those of the Prime Minister, regardless of the beliefs of an Ernest Bevin, a Leonard Woolf, or a Margery Perham, and regardless of the strong swing to the left that was taking place within the country as a whole.

It is also apparent that individual, face-to-face encounters between Britons and Americans around the war-time world, although often har-monious, could reinforce the stereotyped images referred to above, together with the assumptions and suspicions that accompanied them, thus facilitat-ing the making of assertions about the other's policies that bore no relation whatever to the actual position in terms of the Government or even society concerned. In this fashion, for example, the reactionary pronouncements of a minor British official in India can be found being taken by his American listeners as substantiating their belief that the entire Government in London and even the country as a whole were incorrigibly Kiplingesque.

There is an added reason why it is necessary to recall these over-all Anglo-American strains when one comes to study in particular the partner-ship in action in the war against Japan. That is, that of all the parts of the world in which the alliance (or tacit alliance, one should say) was operating, it was very probably South and Southeast Asia and the Far East that constituted the most fertile area for the growth of friction, suspicion and resentment; it was here, in other words, that difficult aspects of the relationship as a whole were most likely to make their mark on the local situation. This is not to overlook the fact that considerable troubles between the two countries arose in other theatres, for example in the Mediterranean and over the treatment of France. Nor is it to suggest that in the Far East itself positive aspects of the over-all partnership did not play a significant part. For example, it was only the very existence of that partnership that gave Britain any hope of stemming the Japanese advance before it entered India, of seeing Australia and New Zealand adequately defended, and of eventually winning back in battle at least some of her lost Asian possessions. Without the United States at her side, in short, the United Kingdom could never have sustained the war on a global scale.

At the same time, despite considerable domestic pulls in the opposite direction, Roosevelt did continue to adhere to the strategy of 'Germany first', a deployment of Allied effort that again depended on American power being sufficient to hold the Japanese meanwhile, and which was very much in accordance with Britain's desires and needs. (It is worth recalling also at this point the extent to which, for Washington as well as London, Far Eastern affairs and policies could be greatly influenced by European considerations: before Pearl Harbour, for example, in the decision then taken to put increasing pressure on Japan, or again in 1945 in the softening attitude adopted during that final stage of the war towards European colonial rule in Southeast Asia.)

In addition, Roosevelt sought to avoid embarrassing Britain in regard to Australia and New Zealand, and to ensure that the vital American presence in those Dominions did not jeopardize the very existence of Commonwealth ties. Meanwhile, in return, Churchill for his part acknowledged both before and after Pearl Harbour America's leadership in the Far Eastern conflict, her special role in handling relations between the Western Allies and China, and the predominant position that she should establish in the Pacific after Japan's defeat.

If these were some of the obvious ways in which the positive aspects of the Anglo-American partnership were reflected in the Far Eastern context (and at a more detailed level one could also cite, for example, the excellent relations established between, say, Mountbatten and Wheeler, or the British Pacific Fleet and Nimitz's forces, or even Stilwell and Slim), one must go on to say, nevertheless, that it was the troubled and unsettling features of that partnership that left a more noticeable mark still on the Far Eastern scene. It was here, in the war against Japan, for instance, that the dwarfing of Britain by the increasing power of the United States was most apparent. Among the consequences of this situation that we have observed were American beliefs that Britain was not pulling her weight against the Japanese and that she was relying on the U.S. to make possible the recovery of her imperial possessions; that she was substituting selfish guile for honest, apolitical endeavour, and that she could therefore have no grounds for complaint if and when it was Washington that dictated the shape of the peace in that part of the world.

On the British side, meanwhile, there was keen resentment over the apparent refusal on the part of Americans to recognize the efforts that, within the limits set by her strained resources, the country was making in Burma, and over the use made by the United States of its control of vital resources to place what amounted to a veto on some of Mountbatten's plans. Matters were made worse by the way in which the U.S. Joint Chiefs of Staff permitted the Combined Chiefs to exercise only a very restricted role in the Far Eastern war, and by what, in London, appeared to be threats emanating from Washington concerning the benevolence or otherwise of American public and Congressional opinion towards Britain (with implications for the continuance of Lend Lease and the granting of post-war aid) in connection with the treatment of India or the future of colonial territories in Southeast Asia.

It is true, of course, that considerations relating to the preservation and functioning of the partnership as a whole did help to set a limit to strains of this kind east of Suez. During the Indian crisis of 1942, for example, Roosevelt, rather than bring about a total confrontation with Churchill, eventually backed down in the face of the latter's fierce refusal to be coerced and his dramatic—if, in retrospect, highly dubious—threat to resign. Conversely, the need to secure American understanding and to build the basis for a close post-war association between the two countries helped to push on the rethinking and planning over colonial matters which, despite the Prime Minister's own reactionary stance, was proceeding among British officials.

Nevertheless, when it came to the question of war aims it was in the setting of the fight against Japan, more than in any other, that the differences and suspicions outlined above in terms of Anglo-American relations in their entirety stood out—a state of affairs that owed not a little to Churchill's role as Britain's spokesman. Thus, it was over India and the Southeast Asian colonies above all (far more than over British colonial territories in Africa, for example, which the war had largely passed by) that there hung those questions concerning the applicability of the Atlantic Charter; it was over Southeast Asian raw materials like tin and rubber that there existed strong differences between the respective approaches of London and Washington to the issue of how far the control of a commodity should be vested in its producers; and it was over the shaping of the post-war order in the Far East, more so than in Europe, that Britain came to find herself cast in a subordinate role as Roosevelt set out to create a structure based on American–Soviet understanding and cooperation above all, and with anti-colonialism as one of its features.

Even where war aims as such were not involved, and where differences between the two Allies were largely avoided, there could still remain unanswered questions of a broad kind that had a particularly Far Eastern focus: to take one example, uncertainties about the nature of Commonwealth relations after the war and about the role that the United States might then play in the affairs of individual Dominions centred upon Australia above all. And while Britain was clear that she desperately desired to see a full American involvement in international politics and economics after the fighting had ended, the United States on her side, partly as a result of the colonial issue, had still to frame a clear and comprehensive answer to the question which had been posed by her Ambassador in London as long before as 1913: what was she 'going to do with this England and this Empire, presently, when economic forces unmistakably put the leadership of the race in our hands?'[4]

Such, then, were some of the main ways in which Anglo-American relations in the war against Japan were affected, both positively and negatively, by various aspects of the entire association of the two states. In order to arrive at a summary of the converse process—that is, the effects of Far Eastern affairs upon that partnership as a whole—it is helpful to make certain initial comparisons, both between the pre-war years and the period 1941–1945, and between British and United States policies, reactions and achievements in different areas of the struggle in Asia and the Pacific.

One of the most striking changes that was brought about by the war, for example, was the decline of Britain from the position she had occupied, even in the 1930s, as the leading Western power in China to one of near-impotence, together with the overwhelming superiority now established among those outsiders in China by the United States. This contrast was accompanied by another one, between on the one hand the high hopes regarding China's role in the war that were entertained by the American Administration, and on the other the more modest and realistic expectations that were to be found in London. We have seen, it is true, that this difference was not in fact as absolute as has often been assumed: Churchill, it will be recalled, placed great emphasis in 1941–42 on the current and potential value of the Chinese military contribution, while conversely the U.S. Army's planners, for their part, were by 1944 putting little reliance on this element in the Allied effort against Japan. And as for the belief among Western publics in the need to sustain China, this appears to have been widespread in Britain as well as in the United States. Nevertheless, British approaches to Chinese affairs did tend to be cooler, less emotional, than was the case on the American side, a feature that was reinforced by the limited extent to which the United Kingdom was now involved on the ground in China. Thus, when the true nature of Chiang Kai-shek's regime and its disinclination to fight began to filter through to the West as the war went on, less of a shock and less bitter reactions were produced in Britain than in the U.S.A. Similarly, the merits and potential of Mao Tse-tung's rival movement in Yenan, together with the problems that its existence could create in China, were also treated by British officials in calmer fashion than was frequently the case among

their American counterparts—this, despite the fact that serious misjudge-
ments as to the nature of that Chinese Communist movement, as well as
correct forecasts of its eventual triumph on the part of a few individuals,
were to be found on both sides of the Atlantic.

At the same time, American assumptions about the nature of Britain's
policies towards China were often seriously at fault, being based in many
instances on a stereotyped image of her as the leading treaty-port power,
and on the long-standing and flattering belief that the United States had
always stood apart from other foreign states in China by virtue of the lofty
and disinterested nature of her aims and behaviour. Hence the false notion—
endlessly repeated—that an unwilling London had had to be pushed by
Washington into grudgingly agreeing to put an end to extraterritoriality.
Nor was it true, as Hurley, Davies, Wedemeyer, Roosevelt and many others
believed, that the British Government and Foreign Office were hoping to see
China emerge from the war weak and divided. Indeed, a peaceful and united
China had an important place in London's plans for ensuring the security of
the region, as well as being desired as the best setting within which to
reestablish and develop commercial relations there.

To emphasize the incorrectness of such American assumptions is not to
dismiss the further differences that did, nevertheless, exist between the
attitudes towards China of the two Western Allies. Over Hongkong, for
example, Roosevelt's eagerness to see the colony handed over to Chiang
Kai-shek's Government stood in complete contrast to the defiant position
adopted by Churchill and, especially in 1944–45, the Colonial Office. Meanwhile, in certain British official quarters, notably in the Government of
India and the India Office, the fear existed that China could become a
menace after the war, either by seeking direct expansion or by making use
of Chinese communities living in various parts of Southeast Asia. This
concern in New Delhi above all over the disruptive potential of China was a
long way from Roosevelt's hope of giving that country a major role in the
establishment of a new, non-colonial order in the region.* In turn, this
constituted only one aspect of the contrast between the President's determination to build up and treat China as a great power and Churchill's scorn
for such a line of policy. In retrospect, it can be said in this connection that
it was the Prime Minister who was being by far the more realistic of the two
men in the immediate, war-time context; it was Roosevelt, nevertheless, for
all the weaknesses of his handling of foreign affairs where China was concerned, who correctly apprehended that, within the not-too-distant future,
China could unite and become a major force to be reckoned with in world
politics.

As for the respective aspirations of the British and Americans over China,
meanwhile, those of the latter were not only more 'bullish' as regards the

---

* Even in this context, however, it should be recalled that we have observed some
prominent Americans expressing in private their alarm at the thought of the Chinese
forming the nucleus of a new, 'Genghis Khan' threat to Western civilization.

development of extensive financial, industrial and commercial ties with that country after the war, but were more high-flown and evangelical (as we saw had been the case before the war also) in terms of guiding her politically and even, in a broad sense, spiritually; of conveying to her the benefits of the American way of life and expecting to receive in return her gratitude and full cooperation. Britain, on the other hand, and more particularly the British officials concerned, was far less inclined—though it was sometimes done—to project on to China her own values and self-images. The Chinese were not always understood in London, but they were at least assumed to be Chinese and not nascent Britons.

Moreover, although the Foreign Office were anxious to see the country's standing and influence restored in China, there existed in Whitehall far less of an expectation than in Washington that, for example, the Communist–Kuomintang conflict there could be brought to an end by means of outside influence and interference, or that Chinese politics generally could be shaped in the same manner. Perhaps if it had been the British, rather than the Americans, who were the more deeply involved in war-time China, the contrast might have been less marked. It was, nevertheless, in keeping with the differences between the approaches of the two countries to Chinese affairs that had existed for a long time before 1941. As it was, what emerged above all between Pearl Harbour and the Japanese surrender was the gulf separating American aspirations, assumptions and strength on the one hand and the inability of the United States on the other significantly to affect in practice the course of events in China.

There was a further, and fundamental contrast between the two Western Allies where China was concerned. In general, there existed on the British side a strong hope, shared by a body like the China Association as well as by most of the officials concerned, that both during and after the war the United States and the United Kingdom could collaborate closely over their dealings with that country. In part, this attitude can be attributed to the fact that for Britain, now by far the weaker of the two Western states within China, it was only by such collaboration that she could hope to regain something of her former position there. Yet at the same time there was among British officials in London and Chungking a genuine belief that the interests in China of their own country and of the United States were basically similar; that there was room for both of them to develop their commercial activities there; and that a policy of cooperation would produce the best results for all concerned. (The Chinese, who in such circumstances would have been prevented from playing off Britons and Americans against each other, might well have doubted whether the benefits accruing to them would, on balance, be substantial.)

Towards the end of the war, something of this idea of London and Washington collaborating over China, at least in the political sphere, did begin to make its appearance in State Department surveys of the Far Eastern scene. There never existed, however, a settled policy of this kind in Washington or anything approaching a consensus over it among American officials on which London could rely when anticipating U.S. reactions in regard to a particular issue. For the most part, indeed, American Government departments, military leaders like Stilwell and Wedemeyer, and businessmen as well, preferred either to ignore the British interest in China, dealing with that country on a strictly bilateral basis, or, indeed, to view the British as rivals there: rivals over China's war-time status and role; rivals over the kind of China that was to emerge from the war; and, not least, rivals over the great China market of the future.

Something of this fundamental contrast was present also where Southeast Asia was concerned, the American presence and interest in that region again greatly increasing during the war years (though to a lesser extent than in China), and the fortunes and standing of Britain and her fellow European colonial powers having received a severe blow in 1941–42. As in the case of China, there are certain qualifications that need to be made at the outset. For example, towards the end of the war the line taken by Washington over the future of colonial territories and the European presence in Southeast Asia was modified to a significant degree. Also, in the opposite direction, there were a number of British politicians and officials who not only resented the American tendency to put the United Kingdom in the dock on a charge of colonial exploitation and neglect (that, indeed, was a widespread feeling in London), but who continued throughout the war to deny that the U.S.A. had any right to take an interest in this imperial aspect of Britain's affairs in the first place.

Nevertheless, many other British officials did recognize, again, partly as a matter of necessity, but also, in some cases, as something that was worthwhile for its own sake, that such an American concern over the future of Southeast Asia must be accepted. Even Churchill occasionally brought himself to acknowledge this. For a time, indeed, there existed, as we have seen, considerable hope in London of getting Washington's agreement to a joint statement of colonial principles, while the idea was also raised of encouraging American investment in Britain's colonial territories. Within S.E.A.C., meanwhile, Mountbatten strove to create a truly integrated Command, proposing, for example, that he should be sent a political adviser from the State Department to match the one he had from the Foreign Office, and that political warfare and clandestine operations in the region should be organized on a combined, Anglo-American basis. Or again, in connection with the affairs of this part of the world, there was the acceptance on London's part that, as a matter of necessity, no future arrangements should be made among the rubber-producing states of Southeast Asia without first having reached some agreement with the U.S.A. —the major consumer of that commodity in its natural state, and now, in addition, a producer of synthetic rubber on a vast scale.

On the United States side, however, the overriding concern in regard to Southeast Asia was to avoid becoming contaminated in the eyes of both the American and Asian peoples by being in any way associated with Britain's attempts to recover her colonial territories there or with her suspected

intention to extend her influence over Siam and possibly even the Netherlands East Indies as well. Thus, U.S. political warfare activities within
S.E.A.C., for example, were maintained on a separate basis, while the idea
of attaching a State Department adviser to Mountbatten was rejected out of
hand. As for the future of the region, most Americans, from Roosevelt
downwards, viewed Britain's intentions with the greatest of suspicion, an
attitude that was strengthened by the accompanying belief that London was
secretly conspiring with the French and Dutch authorities in this regard.

Again, in this Southeast Asian context, as in that of Chinese affairs,
significant misperceptions and inaccurate assumptions were involved on the
part of the Americans when they emphasized in this fashion how far apart
they and the British were. There was not, for instance, any secret coordination of British, French and Dutch plans regarding their colonial territories,
as Hurley and others were insisting in 1944–45. In Whitehall, moreover,
there was a greater degree of awareness of the nationalist factor where
British colonies (not those of their European neighbours) were concerned,
and of the need to make some positive response in this respect, than most
Americans realized.* On the spot, too, a more radical approach still was
adopted by Mountbatten and some of his staff, together with representatives of S.O.E.'s Force 136, while the fact that someone like the Governor of
Burma, Sir Reginald Dorman-Smith, appeared on the surface to be very
much the Conservative ex-Cabinet Minister, and that he punctiliously
refrained from airing in public internal British differences over policy,
concealed from an American official like John Davies the extent to which,
in private, he was urging the quickest possible transfer of power to the
Burmese after the war, together with the establishment of special arrangements to ensure that the people of that country derived a clear benefit from
the activities of British firms there. Nor, in more general terms, did Americans appreciate the extent to which the war itself was helping to bring
about an increase in British concern for the welfare and development of the
colonies, a concern reflected in the raising of the sum allocated by the
Government for such purposes, and described by Professor Louis in his
forthcoming study of the subject as amounting to 'a moral regeneration of
British purpose in the colonial world.'[5]

And yet, misperceptions apart, genuine and strong Anglo-American
differences concerning colonial territories certainly existed. Churchill, for
example, did set severe limits to the development and enunciation of new
colonial policies in London, while on the other side Roosevelt's hostile
attitude to the British Empire represented a deep-seated American anti-
colonialism for which Britain tended to be the principal target, even if, in the
President's case, it was the French ownership of Indochina that bore the
brunt of his attacks. Moreover, even if the Prime Minister is left aside, one
finds, still, a broad measure of agreement among politicians and officials in

---

* As regards the colonial field in general, something of an exception must be made of the
case of Hongkong, over which attitudes in Whitehall actually became less imaginative and
flexible in 1944–5, as compared to 1942.

war-time Britain (and it must be remembered that Labour backbenchers like Shinwell, as well as Labour Ministers such as Attlee, took a fierce pride in many of the country's imperial achievements and were essentially paternalistic in their approach to the subject) that it would be irresponsible folly to rush towards a programme of granting independence to all colonies and that 'self-government' was in many instances a more realistic aim. The great variety of conditions that obtained among the country's colonies as a whole was, not surprisingly, far better appreciated in London than in Washington, as was, say, the problem of minorities living within a specific territory. This awareness contrasted with a somewhat crude and 'populist' American approach to the subject, and again, as over China, with a stronger tendency within the United States to project on to the foreign scene in question assumptions and expectations derived from America's own political culture and historical experience.

One must go on to add, however, that, just as Roosevelt was able to perceive an important long-term development in the case of China, so, notwithstanding the superficiality of some of his thinking where a specific imperial territory was concerned (and India provides a supreme example of this), he was far more aware than Churchill of the need to recognize and come to terms with the rapid growth of nationalisms in Asia. In Whitehall as a whole, moreover, remarkably little attention was paid to the signs that the development of nationalism in Indochina could well present the French with a greatly-changed and challenging situation when they returned there. Siam, too, which had already become a sovereign state, was treated by Britain with a heavy-handedness that was bound to help confirm American suspicions regarding her ineradicable acquisitive instincts. And although Ministers and officials in London did greatly desire to see the United States become involved in Southeast Asia after the war, and thus help to ensure the region's security (the establishment of American bases in Indochina, for example, being among the means envisaged), there existed also a contrary inclination to resist Washington's anti-imperialist designs by drawing closer to France and the Netherlands over this issue. In the specific case of Indochina, for example, Roosevelt's designs received no support from Britain.

Political issues such as these were interwoven with a fundamental difference of orientation between the United States and the United Kingdom where strategy in Southeast Asia was concerned, and this within circumstances whereby, although the area lay within Britain's sphere of responsibility for conducting the war, the U.S.A., too, had a major interest there and contributed to it not only forces but essential supplies and aeroplanes. (There thus existed a marked contrast between the way in which Southeast Asian strategy had to be hammered out on a combined basis, and the relative freedom of action that MacArthur possessed in the South West Pacific Area.) British military thinking, in so far as the Chiefs of Staff accepted that it was desirable to develop activities within the Theatre at all, was directed southwards from Burma towards Singapore; for the United States, on the other hand, the raison d'être of their own presence there lay in the perceived need to move northwards in order to open up an overland route to China.

With regard to the quarrels and suspicions that surrounded the ensuing strategic debates, we have observed that the Americans were correct in assuming that Churchill, Eden and Mountbatten himself were concerned to see Britain's forces recover her own, colonial territories from the enemy before the peace was signed. Yet the Prime Minister was at the same time eager to assault the Japanese as a direct contribution towards winning the war, while the Chiefs of Staff (although, again, political considerations were not lacking here) came to argue in favour of making the major British effort in the Pacific rather than in the Southeast Asian, colonial area. Mountbatten, too, besides being keen to get to Singapore, was looking beyond this to a possible advance northwards towards Japan.

As for the preoccupation of the United States' authorities with the overland route to China, the many Americans who believed, as an article of faith, that, like all of their country's military campaigns, this one was devoid of the kind of impure, political considerations beloved of the Europeans, were deceiving themselves. And although, in strictly practical terms, American drive and technology proved able to open the Ledo route more speedily than the British had thought possible, in regarding the undertaking as a waste of time, resources and effort, Mountbatten and the British Chiefs of Staff (their view, incidentally, being shared not only by MacArthur, but even by several senior Chinese officials) were proved entirely correct.

The desire of the United States to keep apart from the British politically in Southeast Asia extended also to the neighbouring sub-continent of India. Here, above all, an anti-British focus was supplied for American anti-imperial sentiments, even though public interest in and concern for the fate of the people of India was spasmodic. Once more, a striking degree of ignorance within the U.S.A. was involved, not least as manifested by Roosevelt himself in his facile attempt in 1942 to draw a parallel between the political situation in the sub-continent and the experiences of the American colonies in the late eighteenth century. Nor was United States concern for the future of India an entirely disinterested one, some Americans seeing in that country a 'new frontier' for their own to conquer commercially. At the same time, the sympathy for the Indian cause that existed on the left of British politics, or the efforts made on behalf of the people of India by Wavell as Viceroy and Amery as Secretary of State, were generally not appreciated in the U.S.A.; in addition, it is clear that British troops arriving in India for the first time could be every bit as shocked by the conditions they found there as were G.I.s.[6] As for the belief in Washington that the potential contribution Indian manpower could make to the war effort against Japan was far from being realized, that view, ironically, was shared by Churchill himself, whose castigations of what he regarded as the idleness of the Indian Army were intemperate and frequent.

The involvement of the United States in Indian affairs, including matters of finance and supply as well as military developments, was, of course, greatly increased as a result of the coming of the Pacific War. Yet just as the Government of India successfully suppressed nationalist agitation there after the summer of 1942, so Churchill, by yielding to the extent of permitting the Cripps mission to take place and then by standing fast once more and turning the issue, in effect, into a vote of confidence between Roosevelt and himself, managed to ward off the President's attempt (centred upon the visits of Johnson and, later, Phillips) to exert a significant degree of influence upon Britain's handling of the Indian constitutional question. Within British official circles, the Foreign Office was notable for its readiness to accept, and even to some extent welcome, an American interest in Indian affairs. Elsewhere, however, and especially where the Prime Minister himself, the India Office and the Government of India under Linlithgow were concerned, much alarm and resentment was aroused.

When it came to the attitudes towards India that were adopted within the British Government itself, individuals like Bevin and Cripps were obviously set far apart from reactionaries such as Grigg. Even among Labour Ministers, however, there existed hostility towards Gandhi in particular for his attempts to hinder the war effort in India, coupled with considerable suspicion of the machinations of Indian industrialists—Attlee's 'brown oligarchy'—within the Congress Party. In general, as Wavell found, even such matters as the threat of famine in India tended to be treated in London in a remarkably casual fashion. Finally, where Churchill himself was concerned, Indian nationalists and their American sympathizers were entirely correct when they saw in him a racially arrogant reactionary, completely out of touch and out of sympathy with the India of the 1940s. In private, indeed, the Prime Minister was quite prepared to give vent to his scorn for the Hindus of the Congress Party, his contempt for the performance of the Indian Army, and his belief that the 'baboos' could do with a taste of the whip; in addition, he was determined that, however unwilling Indians might be to remain under British rule, they should pay the entire cost of the privilege of being defended by their imperial masters. Quick to emphasize (and correctly so) the magnitude of the Communal problem as an obstacle to constitutional reform, be nevertheless welcomed conflict between Hindu and Muslim as a condition that would facilitate the continuation of British sovereignty.

At the same time, though to a less glaring degree, Churchill also displayed an inadequate awareness of and response to the changing attitudes and expectations of those people who were involved in the fight against Japan on the farther side of the latter's ring of conquests, in Australasia. Thus, we have observed Menzies, for example, an Australian politician noted for his loyalty to the Commonwealth connection, reporting to his colleagues in Canberra on his return from London in 1941 that the British Prime Minister had 'no conception of the . . . Dominions as separate entities', and that the more distant a Dominion was from the heart of the Empire, 'the less he thought of it.' Or again, when Curtin, the open clashes between him and

London of 1942 now well past, brought to the meeting of Commonwealth Prime Ministers in 1944 proposals for strengthening that body's consultative procedures, Churchill displayed remarkably little interest, and appears to have been quite content to accept the desire of the Canadian Government to avoid any developments that could be construed by the United States as the formation of a Commonwealth 'bloc' which could oppose her interests. Nevertheless, the Prime Minister obviously had difficulty in ridding himself of a tendency to assume that the Dominions would duly fall into line once a decision had been made in London—which implied the existence of a 'bloc' of a rather different kind. As for individual Commonwealth politicians, the only one to whom he paid marked attention was Smuts.

Elsewhere in British official circles, however (for example on the part of Cranborne and Attlee and within the Dominions and Foreign Offices), there was a growing awareness of the need to recognize and accept that the Dominions by now required a greater say in affairs. That this demand existed was amply demonstrated, not only during the storms of 1942 over Mediterranean affairs and Far Eastern military and consultative arrangements, when defeat and danger could be said to have created an untypically tense atmosphere, but also during the calmer years that followed—for example over the post-war arrangements to be made concerning the defeated Japanese and colonial territories. Evatt, above all, forcefully and frequently expressed this desire that the voice of Australia—and, by association, of New Zealand—should be heeded in the counsels of the Americans as well as of the British, seeking also to make full use of the United Nations forum when it became available to him in 1945.

For all Evatt's endeavours, however, Australia's aims in this connection were far from being realized. Having in 1941–42 felt neglected by London, Canberra discovered thereafter that it likewise had little say in the making of decisions in Washington—a state of affairs symbolized by the rapid decline of the Pacific War Council into a vehicle for jovial Rooseveltian ramblings. In personal terms, too, Evatt, by his blustering approach, made more enemies than friends in official circles in the U.S.A., as well as being disowned behind his back there by both Curtin and Forde.

In several respects, indeed, American–Australian relations came under some strain as the war progressed, and, to the muted satisfaction of British politicians and officials, it seemed that the initial enthusiasm displayed in the two Pacific Dominions for their rescuers from the United States was cooling. Curtin, for one, despite the excellent relationship he had established with MacArthur, was by 1944 making it plain in London that he was greatly concerned lest the position of Britain and the Commonwealth in the Far East should be completely overshadowed by the burgeoning power and self-regard of the Americans. Nevertheless, the rapid increase in the U.S. military presence in Australasia from the end of 1941 onwards, against a background of shocks and defeats that had exposed the hollowness of pre-war British assurances regarding the defence of the two Dominions,*

* When observing Britain's failures in respect of the defence of Australia and New

constituted for the latter a means of protection that clearly would remain indispensable even after the Japanese had been driven back to their home islands and finally defeated. In short, the ANZUS Pact of 1951, in which Britain was to be left aside, was being foreshadowed.

From Washington's point of view, Australia was of value, first as providing a fall-back position from the Philippines and then as a base from which to return to the offensive. In addition, it was seen as a matter of great importance that these 'white-men's territories' in the South Pacific must be protected from the ravages of the yellow barbarians from the north. Even so, the special position that the United States acquired in the area in 1942 presented her policy-makers with a delicate problem as regards the Commonwealth ties between the two Dominions and Britain. In this situation, it is evident, there were those Americans who began to think in terms of major new commercial opportunities which they could open up in Australasia as soon as the war was over, and who would have shed no tears had the Commonwealth broken apart. Both Roosevelt and the State Department, however, were anxious not to jeopardize relations with Britain in this context, and made clear their wish to see the public quarrels that were developing between Canberra and London settled as speedily as possible. Churchill in turn recognized that a substantial American presence in this part of the Commonwealth was essential, and went out of his way thereafter to maintain cordial relations with MacArthur himself.

In American plans, Australia and New Zealand were to play an important but strictly subordinate role in the post-war security system in the Pacific, and were dutifully to make available to U.S. forces a base like Manus or various islands whose ownership had till then been in dispute. The extent to which Washington was determined to secure whatever territory it required in order to ensure its permanent control of the Pacific was a mark, both of the shock which had been experienced at the time of Pearl Harbour and Corregidor, and of the knowledge that it was the United States which had been largely responsible for the defeat of the Japanese thereafter. One consequence of this demanding attitude on the part of the U.S. authorities was the development of friction between Washington and Canberra. In London, however, although there was no intention of surrendering any of the Empire in the Far East, the prospect of a lasting American involvement in and control of the Pacific was welcomed, with the additional hope that this would also entail the continuation of Anglo-American collaboration, including the sharing of defence facilities.

At the same time, and especially in the light of the many lectures that they had had to endure from across the Atlantic on the subject of the evils of European colonial empires, British officials tended to look somewhat sardonically at what were seen as manifestations of expansionist or imperialist

Zealand, together with the attitude displayed towards her by Evatt and the Australian Government during the period of defeat and extreme danger, the isolationism and opposition to defence expenditure that adorned the record of the Australian Labour Party—now in office—before the war should not be overlooked.

tendencies on the part of the United States herself. (To a Stimson, of course, the establishment of American sovereignty over Japan's mandated islands would have been in an entirely different category from the acquisition of colonies. Similarly, a Sumner Welles experienced no difficulty in asserting that, while the British must get out of Singapore, there must be no questioning of the United States presence in the Panama Canal zone, or Hawaii, or Puerto Rico.) Foreign Office specialists likewise rejected with some scorn the conviction and claim of Americans that their own record in the Philippines—whose history and circumstances, it was pointed out time and again in London, were quite different from those of British possessions in Southeast Asia—provided, in Roosevelt's words, 'a pattern for the future of other small nations' which European colonial powers would do well to copy. Collaboration by Filipinos with the Japanese thus afforded some satisfaction in Whitehall, where similar actions on the part of Burmese, for example, had had to be acknowledged. British observers also anticipated, and correctly so, that independence for the Philippines would in practice be greatly qualified by the continued presence there of American military bases and economic privileges.

The ability to point a finger in return at the United States, while affording London a degree of passing pleasure, did not, however, do anything to alter the fact that it was American opinions and decisions which had come to predominate in the Far East well before the end of the war. Nowhere was this more evident than in regard to Japan herself. Both Britain and the U.S.A. had had to learn a new respect for the fighting prowess of that nation in 1942, and both were determined to render her harmless once she had been defeated. In both countries, too, as in Australia and New Zealand, there were many who wished to see the Japanese severely punished, not only for their aggression but for the terrible atrocities which they had committed at the same time. (Churchill, it will be recalled, spoke of the need to bomb Japan to ashes.) Yet there existed differences between the British and the American approaches to this question. In the U.S.A., a substantial number of the population regarded Japan, rather than Germany, as the principal enemy, a view which was not to be found in Britain; it would also seem that among Americans in general (the poll figures in respect of the need to exterminate all Japanese and the desirability of subjecting them to extensive nuclear bombardment will be recalled in this context)[7] there flourished a greater degree of hatred for the Far Eastern foe than was the case on the other side of the Atlantic.

Paradoxically, however, it was in American rather than in British official circles that ambitious plans were developed which looked towards a wholesale re-education and re-shaping of Japanese society after the war and which, as put into practice by MacArthur, cast Japan in the role of a new Far Eastern protégé for the United States, not only to be rendered harmless for the future but to be accorded the blessings of the American way of life. Again, in other words, as we have seen was the case over China and Southeast Asia, there existed a greater tendency on the American than on the

British part to project one's own values, ambitions and self-images upon people whose political culture and civilization were in fact very different.[8]

This projection of American values formed a part of the belief, shared, as we have seen, by Stimson, MacArthur and many others, that the Far East was an area which had a special part to play in the destiny of the United States and which presented her with both a civilizing mission and vast commercial opportunities. Ideas of this kind had of course manifested themselves long before Pearl Harbour, having helped guide the conduct of Stimson, for example, during the 1931–33 crisis over Manchuria. Now, however, with the immense growth of U.S. power in the Pacific and with the achievement of a crushing victory over Japan (a country which had also, from around the turn of the century, developed a belief in her special mission in East Asia), it seemed that the United States was about to come into her own in what Stimson called 'her part of the world.' Now, more than ever, it appeared to make sense to declare, as Pearl Buck had done in 1942, that 'if the American way of life is to prevail in the world it must prevail in Asia.'

Thus, the United States could look forward to fostering freedom, democracy, and possibly even Christianity as well among the peoples of the region. At the same time she would open the doors to markets which her great war-time expansion of productive capacity now made more essential than ever; she would help to preserve stability and forestall any pan-Asian movement against all white men that might otherwise arise; she would establish, as part of a new world order, a Pax Americana in the Pacific and, with the help of China, in East Asia as well. Even when setbacks occurred and new dangers arose—when China failed to take on the attributes of a major power, for example, or when the potential influence of the Soviet Union in the area became apparent—it did not mean that these American aspirations were abandoned. Rather, adjustments were made which centred upon the understanding with Stalin that Roosevelt believed he had achieved at Yalta.

To summarize American hopes and aims in this fashion could, however, be misleading if it were taken to mean that the country's policies in the Far East during the war were carefully formulated, coordinated, and related to the means that were to be employed. For it has been one of the themes of this study that the confusion and ambiguity which had surrounded U.S. Far Eastern policies before 1941 did not disappear after Pearl Harbour, and indeed were now increased, amid the swirl of war, by the highly personal and shambolic manner in which Roosevelt conducted most of his war-time foreign relations. We have noted, for example, the gap between the lofty intention to build up China as a great power and the limited means that Washington in the event was prepared to employ in that connection; the confusion over whether the main aim was to support the cause of China or of Chiang Kai-shek's regime there in particular; the failure to exert the full degree of America's potential influence over Chungking; the contrast between Roosevelt's political designs for China and the diminishing role which that country played in the strategic plans developed by the U.S. armed forces. The President's anti-colonial sentiments also failed to become embodied within a coherent and workable policy, even in the case of Indochina, and the accompanying dilemma of how to pursue an anti-colonial line while at the same time maintaining good relations with the United States' European allies was never fully resolved.

In general, it can be said that the American official policy-making and executing machinery was in a sorry condition during these war-time years: the President given to secretiveness and the throwing out of random pronouncements; the State Department under Hull left for the most part on the sidelines; ambassadors ignored and (notably in the cases of London and Chungking) overshadowed by a succession of special emissaries sent out by Roosevelt; even relations between the President and the Joint Chiefs of Staff being maintained on an essentially ad hoc basis. In almost all such respects, the formulation, coordination and execution of Britain's overseas policies were superior.

Yet important qualifications have to be made to this last, simple comparison. On the American side, for example, matters were improved around the end of 1944 by the institution of the State-War-Navy Coordinating Committee and of regular meetings between Stettinius, Stimson and Forrestal. Moreover, for all its relative unimportance during the war, the State Department itself, with the aid of a network of advisory committees, explored ideas and prepared plans in regard to various post-war aspects of Far Eastern policy, especially where Japan was concerned, to an extent that was well in advance of the similar work that was only belatedly undertaken by the Foreign Office in London. On the British side, meanwhile, we have seen how Churchill formed a major obstacle to the development and approval of plans concerning imperial territories after the war, one consequence of this situation being the reinforcing of American suspicions as to what London's silence over such matters might portend. There also existed a tendency on the part of bodies such as the Ministry of Information, the India Office, and the Colonial and Foreign Offices to go their separate ways and to regard each other with a degree of wariness or even (notably as between the Foreign Office and the Government of India under Linlithgow) scorn.

More specific examples can briefly be given of this last feature of the British scene. Both the then-Governor of Burma and the then-Secretary of New Delhi's External Affairs Department have commented to the present writer on how, when they came back to visit London while the war was in progress, the Foreign Office appeared to have little or no interest in discussing with them either immediately relevant or wider aspects of British policy.⁹* Or again, we have seen above how, in 1944–45, the Foreign Office

* Of course there was nothing new in tension between, say, the Foreign Office on the one hand and the Indian or Colonial Offices on the other. Such a situation had been a feature of the early years of the century, for example. (See Thornton, *The Imperial Idea And Its Enemies*, 112.) Or again, to look ahead rather than backwards, during the years following

and Service Deparments were unable to push through to a clear and firm conclusion their discussions over defence plans for the Far East after the war. Here, again, one of the unfortunate features involved was to continue into the post-war years: that is, the disinclination of the Foreign Office to provide the Services, or anyone else, with long-term estimates of how the international situation might develop.[10] As a senior member of the Office was to admit in 1960, his organization tended to 'live from day to day, deciding questions as they came up sensibly enough, but never foreseeing what questions will come up or considering where they ultimately want to go.'[11]

An additional reason for this failure in London over defence planning during the closing stages of the war was the great number of uncertainties that by then had come to surround Britain's future east of Suez. At the hands of the Japanese in 1941–42, the country had sustained an enormous blow to her international standing in that part of the world, a blow from which, despite the ultimate success of her military efforts in Burma, she had never fully recovered. Indeed, those dramatic events following Pearl Harbour continued to affect Britain's relations with both Americans and Asians in the sense that neither were likely to forget the ease with which Japan had exposed the apparent rottenness of Britain's Eastern Empire. Thereafter, the contribution to the war against the Japanese which the United Kingdom had managed to scrape together had been completely overshadowed by that of the United States. In terms of the priorities that London had no choice but to set and enforce, Britain's commanders in the field in India and Southeast Asia had had to be content to receive whatever forces and matériel were left over after the demands of the Mediterranean and European Theatres had been met, while the general public, for its part, did not appear to be greatly interested either in the Far Eastern struggle as a whole or in the Burma campaign in particular.

Now, as the defeat of Japan at last came in sight in 1944–45, Whitehall, it is true, was not without its hopes with regard to the country's position and interests east of Suez: the hope, for example, that a close partnership with the U.S.A. would ensure adequate protection for British and Commonwealth territories in the Pacific and Southeast Asia; the hope that means could be found to reestablish Britain's commercial presence and standing in China; that the inhabitants of the country's colonies would welcome the restoration of British rule, suitably modified in the direction of, say, speedier self-government or citizenship for all; and that India, even when given her independence, would continue to play a vital role in Commonwealth defence arrangements between Aden and Singapore.

Yet the questions remained, and by 1945 had in some cases grown more formidable than ever. Where for instance, was the money to be found with which to grant China and other potential customers in the Far East the

the Second World War the shaping of Britain's defence policies east of Suez was to be severely handicapped by the separate existence and interests of the Foreign, Commonwealth and Colonial Offices, and of the Service Departments. (See Darby, *British Defence Policy East of Suez, 1947–1968*, 139–40.)

credits without which British trade in the area might not be given a new lease of life? Or would Britain be able to find the men and money with which to meet her defence commitments on a world-wide scale? Would the Americans collaborate as partners in the Far East, or would they rush to compete with Britain there, commercially, and seek to dictate both the politics and defence arrangements of the region? How was London to respond to such armed and newly-assertive bodies as the Anti-Fascist People's Freedom League in Burma and the Malayan People's Anti-Japanese Union?

Where Americans now saw not only grave new responsibilities but boundless opportunities, British Ministers and officials—their public apparently lacking interest in the matter—had to face up to another stage in the country's decline in the Far East, a decline whose early stages had been marked, over forty years before, by the need to form an alliance with Japan, and which was to reach its conclusion twenty-three years later, with the 1968 announcement that British forces would be gone from the Far East and Persian Gulf by the end of 1971.

What, then, can be said in over-all terms of Anglo-American relations in the context of the war against Japan, and of their effects, in turn, upon the two states' partnership as a whole? Certainly, not everything lay on the debit side of the ledger. At the local level, for example, just as the positive aspects of that entire partnership made it all the easier for, say, Mountbatten and Wheeler to work together in Southeast Asia, so there was a reverse process by which the harmony achieved by them and others on the spot east of Suez contributed something to the strength of the links joining Britain and the United States to one another. It can also be said that officials of the two countries came to share certain perceptions regarding the Far East, even when they had at first been far apart in this respect. For instance, by the end of 1944 the view was common to both London and Washington that little was to be expected from the Chinese in military terms, and that the Chungking regime was in a weak position, due partly to its own serious shortcomings. With each partner having moved some way towards the other's policy preferences, even if less far towards his over-all standpoint, there was also by the time the U.N. Conference assembled in San Francisco a significant measure of agreement between them over the handling of the colonial trusteeship issue—a far cry from the situation that had existed in 1942, when it had proved impossible to reconcile the opposing ideas and attitudes of Washington and London on that subject.

Moreover, even from the very first days of the Pacific war, the two countries had had certain interests in common within that context: to see Australia and New Zealand survive, for example, and above all to see Japan completely crushed. (Despite the suspicions of some Americans over the last question, there was never any likelihood that Britain would fail to see the Far Eastern war through to its conclusion.) As for some of the possible consequences of that conflict, by 1944–45 the State Department were beginning to emphasize the desirability of including Britain, as well as the Soviet Union and China, in the development of a new pattern of international relations that could bring lasting peace to the Pacific and Far East. In return, London had for some time accepted that the United States would take the lead in that respect, and although there existed British and Commonwealth fears that she might take advantage of her greatly-increased power there to develop some form of economic imperialism, even an American involvement in world affairs of such an overbearing and expansive kind was held to be infinitely preferable to a renewal of isolationism on her part.*

And yet, for all these instances of shared interests, cooperation and even understanding, the war that was conducted by the two countries against Japan did place a very considerable strain upon Anglo-American relations. In terms of grand strategy, for example, the decision to concentrate upon defeating Germany first, although initially it had been arrived at by the American planners on their own and before the U.S.A. became a belligerent, and although it was sustained by Roosevelt thereafter, from the 'Arcadia' Conference onwards, was irksome, to say the least, to Admiral King and the U.S. Navy, as it was to the many Republicans, ex-isolationists and China-admirers who became 'Pacific-firsters' after Pearl Harbour. Even General Marshall at one point proposed that, if Britain would not agree to embark upon a more direct and urgent strategy in Europe, the United States should turn her attention to the Far Eastern war above all. Moreover, despite the fact that the Germany-first principle was maintained officially, much to the relief of Churchill and his Chiefs of Staff, Washington's distribution of its forces modified it considerably in practice. (The level-headed General Ismay even went so far as to write, at the end of 1944: 'I am afraid that our American friends—much as I like them—have only paid lip service to the fundamental principle that Germany is public enemy No. 1, and that they have already committed far too much a proportion of their available resources to the Pacific.')[12]

It was also within the area covered by the war against Japan that there occurred the greatest degree of strain between the two Western Allies— strain reflected, for example, in the field of political warfare—regarding their proclaimed, implicit and perceived war aims. So long as Britain held on to India and made no declaration that envisaged the early independence of her Asian colonies, a large number of Americans, from Roosevelt downwards, regarded her as standing far apart from the United States in terms of the new world order that they desired to see created at the end of the war. The assumptions made by U.S. officials in Washington and in the Far East itself concerning Britain's aims in China again carried with them the suggestion that here, too, there existed a fundamental divergence: one

---

* There was nothing new in Britain's making such a choice. In the 1890s, for example, despite London's concern over American expansionist tendencies as manifested during the Venezuelan dispute between the two countries, it was accepted that concessions would have to be made to Washington in this respect, and that collaboration, not rivalry, must remain the goal.

which, as was also the case over Britain's imperial territories, had to it a commercial as well as a political side. Furthermore, there were fears among some Americans that Britain was ready to conclude a 'soft' peace with Japan, or even to make only a token effort against her beforehand, such suspicions having no parallels where the war against Germany was concerned.

The elements, not only of suspicion but of serious misperception, that were entailed in these Anglo-American strains, especially on the part of the United States, have been illustrated at length. They involved, it will be recalled, Britain's supposed wish to see China enfeebled and divided, her alleged designs on the Netherlands East Indies, the extent to which, it was believed, she was in league with her fellow European colonial powers concerning the future of Southeast Asia, and her apparent disinclination to fight vigorously against the enemy in Burma. Even in cases where Washington and London had in fact come closer to each other, as over their estimates of Nationalist China or their approach to the trusteeship question, the strength of the myths and the stereotyping process that surrounded such subjects helped to preserve the belief—and again, this was on the American side far more than on the British—that a significant degree of difference remained. Thus, even a clear worsening of Sino-American relations failed to remove the assumption that the U.S.A. would always stand out from the other foreign powers involved with China as a result of her sympathy, disinterest and understanding; thus, regardless of the earnest professions to the contrary by the Foreign Office and others, Britain, in American eyes, would always remain a rapacious treaty-port power, quintessentially imperialist, commercially ruthless and politically devious.

Assumptions of this kind were sometimes reinforced by the apparent nature of representatives of the other state who were encountered on the spot in Asia: reactionary or bumbling British administrators, loud-mouthed Americans with a quick, home-grown recipe for each of the world's troubles, and so on. Relations at this local level were indeed quite often poor—much more so than tended to be the case between officials in Washington and their counterparts in London. We have seen, for example, the extent of the troubles that surrounded Stilwell's sojourn in Southeast Asia, the mutual distrust and dislike between many Americans serving in the C.B.I. Theatre and various officials and officers of the Indian Government and Army, and the observations of Australian diplomats on mutual Anglo-American coolness in China. Nor did it help when Americans could see that, among the British now dealing with Chinese affairs in an official capacity, there were numbered individuals who had had, and presumably would seek to resume, a substantial commercial interest in that country, or when the British, Australians and New Zealanders, for their part, came across American officers who in private life had been connected with business concerns that could well be thinking now of extending their operations in the areas in which their former-employees were serving.

There existed, in addition, a further difficulty which once again appears to have been more prominent on the United States side of the relationship.

Often, it seems, an individual officer or official could feel obliged, whatever he might say to or think of the British privately, to conform to an 'us versus them' pattern when talking or writing within an essentially American context. Obviously, this was not always so—one thinks, for example, of that most upright of men, George Marshall, or of General Wheeler. But we have seen how thoroughly two-faced General Hurley could be in this respect, deprecating Roosevelt's Indochina policy when in London and assuring officials there that no differences existed between Britain and the U.S.A. where the future of China was concerned, while crying out to Washington for a radical line to be followed over Indochina and declaring it to be a fact that Britain was seeking to bring China down.

Or again, at a somewhat lower level, one can cite the experience of a British official who was serving in India at the time, and who heard a fairly senior U.S. officer, a personal friend of his, endorse in local staff talks a British appreciation of the amount of supplies that could be transported to the Assam front, and of the military consequences of this situation. Soon afterwards, both men were members of a high-level conference in Washington which studied the aforesaid appreciation among other subjects, and, to the great surprise of the British official from India, his friend joined in a violent onslaught on the document and the thinking behind it that was launched by the Americans present. Asked afterwards why he had so drastically changed his attitude, the U.S. officer explained that, in a gathering such as the one they had just attended, he would always feel obliged, whatever his private views, to follow the national line (as set in this case by Stilwell among others).[13]

Meanwhile, tension over the ends for which the Far Eastern war was being fought was reinforced by suspicion and resentment concerning some of the means that each country was perceived by the other to be employing in this connection. Thus, the huge disparity between the amount of resources which Britain and the United States respectively were able to devote to that part of the global conflict created a situation in which it was easy for the British to feel (not always without reason) that their Allies were not only dictating the over-all strategy being employed against Japan, but were seeking to use their control of essential supplies to thwart Britain's own designs and to minimize the role she could play. The hostility towards the Royal Navy of Admiral King and his desire to exclude it from the main operations in the Pacific was an outstanding example of the kind of thing that made British officials and officers feel that the Americans wished to have it both ways: to accuse their Ally of failing to pull her weight against Japan, but also to deny her a significant share in the glory of finally defeating that enemy.

Conversely, the paucity of British resources that could be deployed east of Suez before the defeat of Germany facilitated the widespread American belief—shared even by Marshall and by an Anglophile like William Phillips—that London and New Delhi alike had no desire to exert themselves in Southeast Asia. It must be added that the disinclination on

Churchill's part to get bogged down in a jungle campaign against the Japanese (correct though he may have been, and accompanied as this attitude was by his genuine desire to attack the enemy with ferocity somewhere else) also helped to increase American suspicions. So, too, did the coolness with which Brooke and his fellow Chiefs of Staff tended to look upon the Southeast Asian Theatre, the somewhat weary caution with which British commanders, until the arrival of Mountbatten, were wont to approach the difficulties confronting them, and the general British disbelief in the value of the North Burma campaign.

The zeal of Mountbatten, the daring of Wingate and above all—a far greater contribution than Wingate's—the achievements with his Fourteenth Army of that fine soldier and man, General Slim, did help to make some Americans revise their previous opinions. Yet even British successes in the drive down towards Rangoon and beyond served only to reinforce in the United States, and among her servicemen and officials on the spot, a widespread conviction that could encompass both idleness and effort on the part of their Allies: the conviction, voiced time and again, that Britain was fighting an essentially 'political' war in the Far East (as also in the Mediterranean), in complete contrast to the straightforward, even, some felt, downright naïve preoccupation of the U.S.A. with defeating the enemy as quickly as possible.

What truth was there in this last accusation? In part, the evidence would appear to sustain it. Thus, on the British side there was, indeed, a strong desire to recover territories such as Burma, Malaya, and, if possible, even Hongkong, in battle. In addition, mainly as a result of Churchill's close, if sometimes strained, association with the Chiefs of Staff Committee, there was a far better coordination in London of strategic and political considerations than was the case in Washington, the disjointed nature of whose military and political approaches to Chinese issues has been emphasized above.

In other respects, however, the evidence does not sustain the simple dichotomy that lay behind the American belief and charge against the British over this aspect of the conduct of the war. Few Americans apparently appreciated, for example, that their Ally's very lack of resources meant that she had little room for manoeuvre when it came to adjusting her Far Eastern strategies to suit political considerations. Rather, she was obliged to confront the enemy where he already appeared directly before her own forces— which happened to be on British territory. Nor was it sufficiently appreciated in the United States that Churchill was genuinely eager to kill large numbers of Japanese as speedily as possible, and thus do something to offset the humiliation that those hitherto-despised 'yellow dwarf-slaves' had inflicted on the British Empire at the outset of the war. Or again, Americans, even in official positions, could not know that, when, for example, Amery and the Government of India raised political objections to an increase being made in the number of Chinese troops to be brought to Ramgarh for their training, Eden and the Foreign Office, who carried the day in Cabinet, insisted that the sole criterion must be to adopt whatever course would best help in the defeat of Japan, and that if this meant more Chinese arriving in India, so be it. Likewise, it was the Foreign Office in London who argued, in the kind of 'apolitical' terms thought by Americans to be peculiar to them, that 'assistance to China should only be a primary consideration if it is in the interests of strategy', and that it should not be undertaken 'at the expense of prolonging the war against Japan.'

Conversely, moreover, was there not a significant political element, in the widest sense, in America's own determination to open up an overland route to China and to build her up into a major power who would become the influential friend and follower of the United States in East Asia? Were there no political considerations lying behind King's determination to keep the Royal Navy out of the Central Pacific, or behind MacArthur's insistence that the Philippines must not be by-passed by U.S. forces but must be liberated and thus reimbued with faith in their owners and mentors? To view MacArthur, for example, probably the most celebrated American commander of the Far Eastern war, solely in terms of the image he himself liked to project—as a simple fighting man, bent only upon defeating the foes of the Great Republic—was and remains absurd. His subsequent mission to bring to Japan 'democracy and Christianity', and his concern over the outcome at Inchon in terms of the 'Oriental millions' who were watching, were merely continuing, post-war manifestations of a set of political assumptions and convictions that had played no small part in shaping his approach to and strategies in the conflict of 1941 to 1945.

It has been suggested already that Anglo-American relations in the context of that Far Eastern war were adversely affected by the considerable difference which existed during those years between the great concern of the United States public over the fight against the Japanese, and the low level of attention which was given to that part of the world struggle by the majority of the British. (It was a feature which, as we have seen, caused concern among officials in London who were dealing with Far Eastern affairs, and aroused some resentment among British forces who, 'forgotten men', so it seemed for much of the time, were fighting the Japanese in Burma.) Nor, at the highest level, was the pairing of Roosevelt and Churchill, so invaluable in various other respects, a happy one where Asian affairs were concerned, for it was in this Eastern context that the former's fundamental anti-colonialism and the latter's equally deep-seated imperialist instincts came most directly into conflict.

Each man, while leaving no room for doubt as to the nature of his views and refusing to accommodate the other beyond a certain point, did sometimes temper what he had to say in direct exchanges between the two of them, or sought to sidestep and postpone consideration of a particular issue which threatened to bring about a dangerous confrontation. (There were moments, indeed, over the question of Indochina's future, for example, when a greater degree of plain-speaking might have helped to avoid much confusion.) The two leaders (Churchill more so than the President during the later stages of the war) valued their over-all relationship too highly to risk a major breakdown being precipitated by, say, the colonial issue; similarly, of course, it is evidence of the strength of the Anglo-American war-time partnership in its entirety that it was able to withstand, to at least an adequate degree, the severe strains placed upon it during the struggle against Japan.

In respect of the roles of the President and the Prime Minister, it must be added that neither was at his best over Far Eastern affairs. Each, it is true, had something to contribute in that field: in Roosevelt's case, a sense of the long-term significance of the stirrings within China and of the need to come to terms with the growing force of nationalism throughout Asia; where Churchill was concerned, a fierce determination to recover from the disasters of the *Prince of Wales* and *Repulse*, of Singapore and Burma, and a readiness to acknowledge the necessity—the inevitability, one should add—of United States war-time leadership. Nevertheless, the President's own vague, irresponsible and ultimately weak handling of American policy towards China, his distorted image of Chiang Kai-shek's achievements and the nature of his regime, together with his facile approach to the complex problems of India, were matched by his willingness to accept from in-adequate men like Hurley completely incorrect versions of Britain's Far Eastern policies, and by his readiness to indulge in private in deep scorn for his Prime Ministerial partner and for Britain's supposed motives and behaviour east of Suez.

As for Churchill, having thoroughly misjudged the outlook and intentions of the Japanese before December 1941, he went on mistakenly to believe that such a lesser breed could be suitably deterred by the presence in the South-western Pacific area of the *Prince of Wales* and *Repulse*.* And, in the military sphere again, his must be the ultimate responsibility for the failure to prepare Britain's defences in Southeast Asia with greater urgency and realism before Pearl Harbour, just as the long and damaging delay in deciding upon the country's Far Eastern strategy in 1944 must also in the final instance be attributed to his stubborn and somewhat slippery behaviour over the matter. In addition, some of his suggestions regarding specific courses of action and operations in Southeast Asia were, in the words of an official historian, 'pure cigar-butt strategy.'[14]

Politically, too, the Prime Minister's relative indifference to Australian and New Zealand views, together with his ignorance of many important aspects of the Far Eastern scene, represented a considerable handicap to the conduct of Britain's affairs in that part of the world. More serious still were his reactionary imperialism and his opposition to the formulation and presentation of new approaches to and policies for, say, Burma; his patent disbelief in the applicability (and in this he was at odds, not only with Roosevelt, but with British officials in the Foreign Office, for example) of

---

* It was of course originally intended that an aircraft carrier should accompany the two capital ships. But it was Churchill, not the Admiralty, who decided to let them proceed to Singapore notwithstanding the enforced absence of that third warship.

the principles underlying the Atlantic Charter to the non-European world; and, not least, his malignant racism.

In all, therefore, it can be said that Anglo-American relations in the context of the war against Japan were in many respects extremely poor, and that this in turn placed a considerable strain upon their war-time alliance as a whole, as well as foreshadowing serious differences to come. Indeed, there is much truth in Professor Kolko's observation that 'the Anglo-American alliance was essentially a European coalition.'[15] Neither militarily nor politically (in so far as it is possible to separate the two for the years in question) did there exist as regards the Far East anything like the degree of collaboration between the two states that was achieved elsewhere. Here, if nowhere else, they were only allies of a kind.

The responsibility for this state of affairs clearly did not lie entirely on one side alone. It can be said, however, that in general it was Britain which, not only out of necessity but also from conviction, believed that the two countries had significant interests in common in the Far East, and which sought to bring about closer collaboration and a greater degree of mutual understanding in that respect. In the eyes of many Americans, on the other hand—politicians, officials, military men and members of the public at large —the United States and Britain were, in the words of Adolf Berle, 'miles apart in Asia.' Their interests, attitudes, aims and methods, it was held, were fundamentally different, their collaboration a threat to the U.S.A.'s image and intentions alike, and their relationship in that part of the world after the war likely to be that of major commercial rivals.

The ensuing strains and difficulties amounted to more than just a minor flaw in the Anglo-American war-time partnership. They were, indeed, of sufficient significance to require something over and above a passing qualification to be made to that 'hands-across-the-sea' version of their entire relationship, whereby their 'whole course . . . from 1783 to the present day' is deemed to consist of 'persistent, even steady progress from mistrust to cordiality'; a version which proclaims that, in terms of the twentieth century, the association of the two countries with one another has been 'solidly based . . . on a foundation of similar, even common policies.'[16] The fact that the relationship between the United States and Britain has been, in many respects, sui generis, and that at times, above all during the Second World War, it has been a remarkably close one, can be established without the need to wander off, however well-meaningly, into the realms of mythology.

Anglo-American differences during the Far Eastern war serve as a reminder that that conflict was not fought on a basis of complete Western solidarity on one side and a similar Asian solidarity on the other. Among the white countries that were involved, indeed, there existed significant divergencies and even hostility (for example between Washington and the French over the future of Indochina). Meanwhile, where Asian peoples were concerned, both China and India fought the war as part of an alliance led by

Western states, against a Japan that was aligned with Germany and Italy. In addition, there were other Asian and Pacific peoples who, whether their territory had been overrun by the Japanese or not, remained loyal to their original Western rulers: some Burmese, for example; a portion of the Filipinos; the Fijians, who proved to be formidable fighters in the Allied cause.

Moreover, there were also those Asians who, even when opposed to the return of their former colonial masters, placed at least some of their hopes in the possibility of obtaining assistance from another Western power, the United States—as did Mao Tse-tung, even. And despite Japan's endeavours to create a feeling of solidarity within her Great East Asian Coprosperity Sphere, little cohesion was achieved in practice, with individual nationalist movements in the end turning against their Japanese patrons yet suppressors.[17] Standing back further still, one major aspect of the war of 1941–45 could be described quite legitimately in terms of a power struggle for the mastery of East and Southeast Asia and the Western Pacific, without having even to refer to the colour of the skins of those who were taking part.

And yet, as suggested at the outset of the present study, the Pacific war did have its strong racial aspects, and was seen in this light by many of those involved. In the West, for example, the danger of a Pan-Asian movement developing against the white man, partly as a result of his conflict with the Japanese—a danger that could still exist, even if Tokyo was eventually forced to surrender—formed a subject to which attention was occasionally given in London (Churchill talked in these terms in 1942, it will be recalled), but which was of very great concern to United States officials and indeed to Roosevelt himself. Nor is it hard to find evidence of similar thinking among the American public and press—such as the description of China by the *Chicago Daily News* as being the '"white hope" [of the United States] in the East'. No doubt Washington's higher level of anxiety in this connection owed much to the prominence of the race question domestically. Quite apart from the growing demands of American blacks during the war for equal rights, disturbing evidence was reaching the President that their attitude towards the war was in general one of 'frustration, pessimism, cynicism and insecurity.' More to the point still, there were also indications that the initial defeats suffered by the white powers at the hands of a 'coloured' people, the Japanese, had not passed unnoticed, and that, as we have seen Gunnar Myrdal observing at the time, 'even unsophisticated Negroes began to see vaguely a colour scheme in world events.'[18]

Not that this last danger prompted white Americans as a whole to embrace their black compatriots, as a study of what occurred during various war-time race riots in Detroit and elsewhere is enough to make clear. (It will be remembered, also, that the O.W.I. reported to Roosevelt that 'large numbers of [white] people in all regions' were displaying 'an illiberal attitude toward Negroes' and 'opposing . . . rights which have long since been granted to them.') Likewise, although United States officials were eager to see China sustained and India given her freedom as important steps towards forestalling the development of a Pan-Asian movement, opinion in America as a whole, as expressed in Congress, for example, was not at all keen to see either Chinese or Indians coming to live in the U.S.A. Related to this were the observations of some Americans on the spot that men of their own Army who arrived in India were wont to refer to the natives of that country as 'wogs' more frequently than did British troops, while in China the contempt of many G.I.s for the 'slopeys' they encountered there was soon apparent.[19] The extent to which General Hurley himself appeared to Michael Lindsay to entertain an underlying scorn for the Chinese should also be recalled in this context. Meanwhile, American soldiers and civilians alike had quickly come to regard the Japanese as 'barbarians' and 'rats', as Admiral Halsey put it, to be treated as befitted such species of sub-humans. The links between such attitudes and subsequent views of the Vietnamese as 'gooks' have already been suggested.[20]

If racial consciousness, then, was often present on the Western side, even more so was this the case among Asians. Again, this was the case even where Allied peoples were concerned. Thus, instances of American heavy-handedness and scorn when dealing with the Chinese, for example, were answered by signs of a growing resentment in official circles in Chungking and among the people at large.[21] (Again, similar post-war developments in South Vietnam also came to mind.) There were Indians, too, who not only longed to see the back of their British masters (and in Lichtheim's words, 'British rule in India had become the paradigm of Western imperialism in Asia. So had the racial animosity it created'),[22] but came to view both the British and the Americans as representatives of a single, white order of things, and who at times expressed their alarm at the prospect of a new, American imperialism of an economic kind replacing the British variety. It was Gandhi, it will be recalled, who in 1942 reminded Roosevelt of the suppression of the blacks in the United States in the same breath as attacking the imperial rule of the United Kingdom, while the belief that the Pacific war was essentially a racial one was asserted by Nehru's sister, Mrs Pandit, when she visited the U.S.A. in 1945.

In India, indeed, as elsewhere in South and Southeast Asia, the initial, sweeping victories of the Japanese in 1941–42 had made a considerable impression. Edgar Snow, for example, when talking to Nehru himself in 1942, found that even the latter shared the widespread 'emotional sympathy' for Japan's struggle that existed in his country.[23] One could cite, also, the example of those Burmese who turned out with a genuine welcome for the invader, or the Indian member of the Malayan Civil Service who admitted that, 'although his reason utterly rebelled against it, his sympathies instinctively ranged themselves with the Japanese in their fight against the Anglo-Saxons.'[24] Thereafter, Tokyo, notwithstanding its failure to win for Japan the loyalty of her new Asian subjects, greatly encouraged the development of nationalist self-consciousness and corresponding political movements which were directed above all against the reimposition of white rule. Hence the opinion (quoted earlier in this study) of a Frenchman who had spent the war in the East Indies, that, despite her ultimate defeat in the field, Japan had by that time already won a lasting victory in that part of the world.[25]

It is also significant that, when the moment arrived for those Japanese accused of being war-criminals to be tried, it was an Asian member of the court established by the Allies in Tokyo for that purpose, Mr Justice Pal of India, who insisted on setting the events of 1941–45, and even of 1931–45, in a far wider context, which included the existence of what he termed 'an Anglo-American economic world order' when Japan had emerged on to the international scene; the earlier examples of beliefs on the part of other nations in their 'manifest destiny' or 'the white man's burden'; the preservation by Western states of their control over areas of 'vital interest' that lay beyond their own borders; and the refusal of those states to relinquish the fruits which they were able to enjoy as the result of acts of aggression committed by previous generations. ('Perhaps it is right to say', observed Pal, 'that "the man of violence cannot both genuinely repent of his violence and permanently profit by it."')[26]

Pal's contention that all the defendants at Tokyo should be found not guilty is not one that the present writer—legally unqualified as he is—would accept, even though the entire basis and conduct of those trials do give rise to some disquieting questions.[27] Nor are all of Pal's historical judgments borne out by the evidence that has since come to light. Nevertheless, his attempt—and it proved to be a vain one—to establish a wider perspective, discomforting as it was for the victorious white powers, not least the Soviet Union, was entirely justified. In part, he was suggesting that it was the West that had set an aggressive and acquisitive example in Asia. At the same time, he was pointing to the deep sense of superiority that, despite, or indeed as a result of, this record of aggression, was deeply embedded in many Western minds. To recall Dr. Needham's comment again: 'Many people in Western Europe and European America . . . are firmly convinced that their own form of civilization is the only universal form . . . The basic fallacy of Europocentrism [however] is . . . the tacit assumption that because modern science and technology are universal, everything else European is universal also.'[28]

As it was, what Japan had achieved during the war of 1941–45, to an even greater extent than she had done by her defeat of a white state, Russia, in 1904–5, was above all a hastening of the decline of the West in Asia.[29] The European powers were now essentially finished there, although there were a few death-throes to come. Indeed, as suggested earlier, Japan had in a sense done them a service by quickening the end of their over-stretched empires, and thus obliging them to come to terms more speedily with the rise of Asian nationalisms, which in turn allowed them to concentrate their attention and resources more fully on domestic reforms and the creation of a new framework for international relations within Western Europe.* The

* Roosevelt had expressed a similar thought in 1942. 'It almost seems', he observed to Edgar Snow, 'that the Japs were a necessary evil in order to break down the old colonial system . . .' (Snow, *Journey To The Beginning*, 255.)

vacuum left by the ensuing departure of the Europeans, and even more by the defeat of Japan herself, did of course open the way for a great extension of power in the region on the part of another white power, the United States. But Asian nationalisms could turn against her, too, and she, too, would soon be obliged, after much Asian and American suffering, to come to terms with her inability to enforce her will on the far side of the Pacific. As argued above, this brief period of close involvement on the part of the United States in the affairs of East and Southeast Asia, extensive and dramatic though that involvement was, and with remnants of it still existing at the time of writing, constituted no more than a coda to an era of Western dominance that had lasted from the end of the fifteenth century to the middle of the twentieth.

For all their differences over the Far East, the United States and Britain had represented, in terms of the war of 1941–45, an essentially Western and white order, political and economic. Both were 'haves' rather than 'have-nots' and were 'imperial' states;[30] both, indeed, were prominent among what Mao Tse-tung termed the 'imperial cities' of the world as opposed to its 'revolutionary countryside', while both brought with them to Asia a Western political culture which Chiang Kai-shek, for example, as revealed in his book, *China's Destiny*, rejected as being alien to and destructive of the true, historic civilization of his own country.* In this context, it is worth recalling what the Japanese ultra-nationalist, Okawa Shumei, had written in 1925 in his book, *Asia, Europe, Japan*:

> 'The coming war between East and West', he had declared, '. . . between Asia and Europe, will be . . . the dawn of a new day in world history, when all mankind will be awakened from their slumber . . . The strong power representing Asia and the other strong power representing Europe will be chosen by Heaven as champions of the East and the West . . . The strongest country in Asia is Japan, *and the strongest country that represents Europe is America* . . . These two countries were destined to fight against each other as Greece and Persia, or Rome and Carthage had to . . .'[31]

Moreover, both Great Britain and the United States themselves, while waging the war of 1941–45, entertained various hopes and ambitions, the fulfilment of which would entail the preservation of an important place for the white man in the life of Asia, not least in the economic and commercial

---

* Owen Lattimore has recalled in conversation with the author a vivid illustration of Chinese views in this respect. During a Japanese air-raid on Chungking in 1941 or 1942, he found himself sharing a bomb shelter with a number of prominent Kuomintang officials and supporters. The generator which was providing light for the shelter then failed, and in the darkness, as a considerable time went by, the Chinese began to talk among themselves. Their subject was the dangers that would face the country after the war from the direction of the Western, imperialist powers. By far the greatest threat, they were agreed, would be the one posed by the United States, whose imperialist qualities and capabilities amounted (as Professor Lattimore paraphrased the opinions of his unseen Chinese neighbours in recollection) to an attack 'on the jugular.'

field. The British recognized this underlying community of interest far more clearly than did the Americans at the time; they were not alone, however, in their concern for the white cause as such. It was the Chief of the State Department's Far Eastern Division, for example, who, early in 1942, desired to see Singapore successfully defended in order to uphold 'the prestige of the white race and particularly of the British Empire and the United States.' It was Admiral King, no friend to the British, who argued that Australia and New Zealand had to be defended because they were '"white men's countries" which it is essential that we shall not allow to be overrun by Japan because of the repercussion among the non-white races of the world.' It was the State Department that was insisting in 1945 that American policies in Asia must exclude any measures that would 'undermine the influence of the West' there. Indeed, during the later stages of the war the concern in Washington that had been so pronounced in 1942–3, to secure the freedom and win the friendship of the various Asian peoples in the area overrun or threatened by Japan, was increasingly overshadowed by the desire to ensure, in Southeast Asia for example, 'order', 'stability', guaranteed commercial opportunities, and resistance to the spread of Communism.

At the same time, and as one of the binding elements in their partnership in arms, there existed among both British and Americans what a leading student of their relationship has called 'a kind of paranationalism which, however much given to internal rivalries, has yet often felt itself superior to "lesser breeds" and non Anglo-Saxon culture.' Henry Stimson, for one, had voiced just such a belief during the earlier Far Eastern crisis of 1931–33.[32] Now, in 1943, Churchill talked in the same terms to Stimson and others over lunch in the White House. As one of those who was present recorded it, 'He said why be apologetic about Anglo-Saxon superiority; that we were superior . . .'[33]

The Prime Minister, of course, was in some ways not typical even of the fellow-countrymen he had left behind in Britain. Nor, in the days when men spoke earnestly of the hopes enshrined in the Atlantic Charter and when Willkie's *One World* sold in its millions, was it done for either the British or the Americans to air in public sentiments such as his. Yet there were many in both countries who instinctively shared them, just as, in return, there were many Asians who saw all Westerners as essentially one. In this sense, too, the United States and Britain had fought the Far Eastern war as allies of a kind.

Notes to Chapter Thirty-Two

1 Nicholas, *The United States and Britain*, 98, 101.
2 See e.g. ibid, cap. 7.
3 See above, 384.
4 Quoted in Thornton, *The Imperial Idea And Its Enemies*, 146.
5 *Louis* (forthcoming).

6 E.g. Gilchrist, *Bangkok Top Secret*, 143.
7 See above, 657.
8 In the light of these W.W.II—and earlier—examples of American cross-cultural assumptions, it is remarkable to find former Vice-President Hubert Humphrey, writing in the mid-1970s, expressing surprise, as well as regret, that he and others had thought in a similar fashion over Vietnam. Likewise, Humphrey fails to recall how America's support for Chiang Kai-shek had foreshadowed her post-war reliance on other Asian reactionaries. Lake, *The Legacy of Vietnam*, 359, 362.
9 Interviews with Sir Reginald Dorman-Smith and Sir Olaf Caroe.
10 Darby, *British Defence Policy East of Suez*, 142.
11 W. Hayter, *The Diplomacy Of The Great Powers* (London, 1960), 45.
12 Ismay to Auchinleck, 8 Dec. 1944, Ismay Papers, IV/Con/1/1H.
13 Interview with Philip Mason.
14 Howard, *Grand Strategy*, IV, 85, 572.
15 *Kolko*, 200.
16 Allen, *Great Britain and the United States*, 27, 207.
17 E.g. Iriye, *The Cold War In Asia*, 58ff.; Elsbree, *Japan's Role In Southeast Asian Nationalist Movements*, passim.
18 See above, 9.
19 Isaacs, *No Peace For Asia*, 10ff., 17ff.; Taylor, *Richer By Asia*, 89.
20 On American public attitudes to foreign policy and the accompanying instability of mood, see G. A. Almond, *The American People And Foreign Policy* (New York, 1965).
21 In 1948, the U.S. China Aid Act was to help create a widespread and outspoken anti-American movement in China.
22 G. Lichtheim, *Imperialism* (Harmondsworth, 1974), 83.
23 Snow, *Journey To The Beginning*, 269.
24 See above, 206.
25 See above, 12.
26 See *Thorne*, 5, 418–9, and IMTFE, Judgment, vols., 157–8.
27 See R. H. Minear, *Victor's Justice* (Princeton, 1971).
28 Needham, *Within The Four Seas*, 11ff., 163ff.
29 A volume in the series, 'The Making of the Twentieth Century', which is edited by the present writer, is forthcoming from Richard Storry on this subject of 'Japan and the Decline of the West in Asia.'
30 See e.g. Lichtheim, *Imperialism*, 61 and 127; G. Liska, *Imperial America* (Baltimore, 1967), 23ff.; R. Aron, *The Imperial Republic* (London, 1974), passim. For a discussion of the economic aspects involved, see e.g. Lichtheim, 114.
31 IMTFE, Doc. No. 684, Exhib. 2179A; emphasis added.
32 *Thorne*, passim.
33 See above, 277. And note, for example, the warning (and underlying assumption) contained in a booklet, *Our Chinese Wall*, produced in the U.S. in 1943 by the Citizens Committee to Repeal Chinese Exclusion—i.e., a pro-Chinese body. 'The Japanese know', argued the Committee, calling for the admission of immigrants from China, 'that we have not treated the Chinese with the ordinary consideration granted to people from any other country. . . . One could not blame China if she should decide, some day after all, that Japan, and not America, can offer her better cooperation. Without China's goodwill, we shall incur the risk of another war *in which white supremacy may be openly challenged by the Oriental races*.' Hornbeck Papers, box 19; emphasis added.

BIBLIOGRAPHY

A. *Unpublished Material*

1. Official documents

(a) *International*
International Military Tribunal for the Far East, Proceedings, Exhibits and Judgement. (Imperial War Museum, London.)

(b) *Australia.*
War Cabinet, A2673.
Advisory War Council, A2682.
Prime Minister's Department.
Department of Defence.
Department of External Affairs. (All Commonwealth Archives, Canberra.)

(c) *Great Britain*
Prime Ministers' Office files, PREM 1, 3, 4.
Cabinet conclusions, CAB 65.
Cabinet memoranda, CAB 66.
Cabinet Committees and documents: Defence Committee (Operations), CAB 69; Armistice and Post-War Committee, CAB 87; Committees on India, Indian Financial Questions, and Indian Food Grain Requirements, CAB 91; Committee on Malaya and Borneo, CAB 98.
Far Eastern Committee and Far Eastern (Ministerial) Committee, CAB 96.
Pacific War Council (London), CAB 99.
Cabinet Office documents on arrangements in event of war with Japan, CAB 107.
Hankey, official files, CAB 63.
Chiefs of Staff Committee, CAB 79.
Chiefs of Staff Committee, inter-Allied conferences, CAB 99.
Joint Planning Sub-Committee, CAB 84.
Combined Chiefs of Staff, and Combined Staff Planners, CAB 88.
Foreign Office: Economic and Reconstruction Department; Economic Department; Reconstruction Department; Far Eastern Department; French Department; General Department; North American Department: all FO 371.
Dominions Office, DO 35.
Colonial Office, CO 865, 967. (All to here, Public Record Office, London.)
Burma Office. (India Office Library, London.)
India Office, Private Office papers. (India Office Library.)

(d) *Netherlands*
Council of Ministers (Notulen Ministerraad, 1940–1945). (Algemeen Rijksarchief, The Hague.)
Ministry of Warfare (Ministerie van Algemene Oorlogvoering). (Algemeen Rijksarchief, The Hague.)
Ministry of Foreign Affairs (Ministerie van Buitenlandse Zaken): Londens archief: Political Reports, Chungking and Washington; French files; I.P.R.

files. Washington Embassy files. Van Kleffens and Bylandt files. (Bureau Der Rijkscommissie Voor Vaderlandse Geschiedenis, The Hague.)
Colonial Ministry (Ministerie van Koloniën). (Ministerie van Binnenlandse Zaken, The Hague.)

(e) *United States*
Department of State: files 123/Bishop, Davies; 740.0011P.W.; 740.00119P.W.; 790.00; 790.00/5; 793.003; 811.20200; 841.248; 845.00; 845.24; 846C.00; 851G.00; 851G.01; 890.01; 892.00; 892.01; Liaison Staff; Matthews-Hickerson files; Notter files; Pasvolsky files; Secretary's Staff Committee.
State–War–Navy Coordinating Committee and Sub-Committees, minutes and studies, SWNCC.
Joint Chiefs of Staff, minutes, RG 218.
U.S. Army, Operational Plans Division, Executive files 1, 5, 10, 17, RG 165.
Office of Strategic Services, Research and Analysis reports. (All to here, National Archives, Washington, D.C.)
U.S. Navy: Double Zero files; Leahy files; China files; Naval Group China files; War Plans Division files; General Board Studies; report on Franco-American relations in New Caledonia. (Operational Archives, Naval Dockyard, Washington, D.C.)
China Theater, Wedemeyer files. (Federal Archives, Suitland, Maryland.)
South East Asia Command, War Diary. (Federal Archives, Suitland.)

2. Private papers. (Titles, etc., as in 1941–45.)

(a) *Australia*
Eggleston, Sir Frederick (Australian National Library, Canberra).
Evatt, H. V. (Flinders University, Adelaide).
Latham, Sir John (Australian National Library).
Officer, Keith (Australian National Library).
Page, Sir Earle (Australian National Library).
Watt, Alan (Australian National Library).

(b) *Great Britain*
Alexander, A. V. (Churchill College, Cambridge).
Attlee, C. R. (Churchill College, and University College, Oxford).
Beaverbrook, Lord (Beaverbrook Library; now transferred to House of Lords Library, London).
Bevin, Ernest (Churchill College).
Brooke-Popham, Air Chief Marshal Sir Robert (King's College, London).
Chatfield, Admiral of the Fleet Lord (National Maritime Museum, Greenwich).
Cherwell, Lord (Nuffield College, Oxford).
China Association (China Association, London).
Clark Kerr, Sir Archibald (FO 800, Public Record Office).
Cripps, Sir Stafford (Nuffield College).
Crozier, W. P. (Beaverbrook Library, now House of Lords Library).
Cunningham, Admiral of the Fleet Sir Andrew (British Museum).
Dalton, Hugh (London School of Economics and Political Science).
Dorman-Smith, Sir Reginald (India Office Library, London).
Grigg, Sir P. J. (Churchill College).
Halifax, Lord (FO 800, Public Record Office).
Halifax, Lord (Hickleton Papers, York, and Churchill College).
Hankey, Lord (Churchill College).
Ismay, General Sir Hastings (King's College, London).
Linlithgow, Lord (India Office Library).
Martin, Kingsley (University of Sussex).

Royal Institute of International Affairs (Chatham House, London).
Somerville, Admiral of the Fleet Sir James (Churchill College).
Wilkinson, Lt. Col. G. W. (Churchill College).
Woolf, Leonard (University of Sussex).

(c) *United States*
Alsop, Joseph (Library of Congress, Washington, D.C.).
Arnold, General of the Army H. H. (Library of Congress).
Ballantine, Joseph W. (Hoover Institute, Stanford University).
Barrett, Col. David D. (Hoover Institute).
Baruch, Bernard (Princeton University Library).
Chennault, Maj. Gen. Claire L. (Hoover Institute).
Connally, Tom (Library of Congress).
Dulles, John Foster (Princeton University Library).
Forrestal, J. V. (Princeton University Library).
Frankfurter, Felix (Library of Congress).
Goodfellow, Col. Preston (Hoover Institute).
Grew, Joseph C. (Houghton Library, Harvard University).
Hamilton, Maxwell M. (Hoover Institute).
Hopkins, Harry (Roosevelt Memorial Library, Hyde Park, N.Y.).
Hornbeck, Stanley K. (Hoover Institute).
Hull, Cordell (Library of Congress).
Institute of Pacific Relations (Columbia University).
Johnson, Nelson T. (Library of Congress).
King, Fleet Admiral Ernest J. (U.S. Navy Operational Archives, Washington, D.C.).
Knox, Frank (Library of Congress).
Leahy, Fleet Admiral William D. (Library of Congress).
Long, Breckenridge (Library of Congress).
MacArthur, General of the Army Douglas (MacArthur Library, Norfolk, Virginia).
Morgenthau, Henry Jr. (Roosevelt Library).
Phillips, William (Houghton Library, Harvard).
Roosevelt, President Franklin D. (Roosevelt Library).
Rosenman, Samuel I. (Roosevelt Library).
Sevareid, Eric (Library of Congress).
Stilwell, General Joseph W. (Hoover Institute).
Stimson, Henry L. (Sterling Memorial Library, Yale University).
Taussig, Charles W. (Roosevelt Library).
Truman, President Harry S. (Truman Memorial Library, Independence, Missouri).
United China Relief, Inc. (Princeton University Library).
Wallace, Henry A. (Roosevelt Library).
Wedemeyer, Albert C.: see 'China Theater' entry under 1e above.
White, Harry Dexter (Princeton University Library).

B. *Published Official Documents*

1. Germany
   Documents on German Foreign Policy, 1918–1945, Series D:
   vol. *VIII* (Washington, D.C., 1954).
   vol. *IX*   (London, 1956).
   vol. *X*   (London, 1957).
   vol. *XI*   (London, 1961).
   vol. *XII* (London, 1962).
   vol. *XIII* (London, 1964).

2. Great Britain

    Documents on British Foreign Policy, 1919–1939, second series:
        vol. *XIII* (London, 1973).
    Documents on British Foreign Policy, 1919–1939, third series:
        vol. *VIII* (London, 1955).
        vol. *IX*   (London, 1955).
    Mansergh, N. (ed.), *The Transfer of Power, 1942–7: vol. I, The Cripps Mission* (London, 1970).
    Mountbatten, Earl, *Report to the Combined Chiefs of Staff by the Supreme Commander, South East Asia, 1943–1945* (London, 1951).

3. Netherlands

    van der Wal, S. L. (ed.), *Officiële Bescheiden Betreffende de Nederlands–Indonesische Betrekkingen, 1945–50, vol. I* (The Hague, 1971).

4. New Zealand

    Documents Relating to New Zealand's Participation in the Second World War:
        vol. *I*   (Wellington, 1949).
        vol. *II*   (Wellington, 1951).
        vol. *III* (Wellington, 1963).

5. United States

    Esherwick, J. W. (ed.), *Lost Chance in China: The World War II Despatches of John S. Service* (New York, 1974).
    Gravel, M. (ed.), *The Pentagon Papers, vols. 1–4* (Boston, 1971).
    Notter, H. A. (ed.), *Post-war Foreign Policy Preparation* (Washington, D.C., 1949).
    van Slyke, L. (ed.), *The Chinese Communist Movement: A Report of the United States War Department, July 1945* (Stanford, 1968).

    Foreign Relations of the United States:

    Japan, 1931–1941, vol. II (Washington, D.C., 1943).
    United States Relations With China (Washington, 1949).
    1941, vol. IV (Washington, 1956).
    Conferences at Washington and Casablanca (Washington, 1968).
    1942, vol. I (Washington, 1960).
    1942, China (Washington, 1956).
    Conferences at Washington and Quebec, 1943 (Washington, 1970).
    1943, China (Washington, 1957).
    1943, vol. III (Washington, 1963).
    1943, vol. IV (Washington, 1964).
    Conferences at Cairo and Tehran, 1943 (Washington, 1961).
    Conference at Quebec, 1944 (Washington, 1972).
    1944, vol. III (Washington, 1965).
    1944, vol. V (Washington, 1965).
    1944, vol. VI (Washington, 1967).
    Conferences at Malta and Yalta, 1945 (Washington, 1955).
    1945, vol. I (Washington, 1967).
    1945, vol. VI (Washington, 1969).
    1945, vol. VII (Washington, 1969).
    Conference at Berlin, vol. I (Washington, 1960).
    Conference at Berlin, vol. II (Washington, 1960).

C. *Parliamentary Debates, etc.*

    Congressional Record, June 1948, Chennault Testimony (Washington, 1948).
    Hansard, House of Commons Debates, 5th series, vols. 374–411 (London, 1942–45).

D. *Press*

British Museum Newspaper Library, Colindale, London: various files of *Daily Express, Spectator, Times.*
Library of Congress, Washington, D.C.: Press Library microfilms of *Chicago Tribune, Christian Science Monitor, New York Herald Tribune, New York Times, San Francisco Examiner, Washington Post.*
Royal Institute of International Affairs, London: Press-cuttings Library: Far Eastern, Anglo-American and United States boxes, 1941–1945.
Stone, I. F., *The Truman Era* (New York, 1973).

E. *Other Primary Sources*

Cantril, H. and Strunk, M., *Public Opinion, 1935–1946* (Princeton, 1951).
China Association, *Annual Reports: 1941–2, 1942–3, 1943–4, 1944–5, 1945–6* (London, 1942–1946).
Directorate of Army Education, *The British Way and Purpose*, Nos. 1–18 (London, 1944).
Gallup Poll Archives, London.

F. *Memoirs, Collected Letters, Published Diaries, etc.*

1. Australia and New Zealand
Bertram, J., *The Shadow of a War* (London, 1947).
Casey, Lord, *Personal Experience, 1939–46* (London, 1962).
Evatt, H. V., *Australia in World Affairs* (Sydney, 1946).
Menzies, R. G., *Afternoon Light* (London, 1967).
Watt, A., *Australian Diplomat* (Sydney, 1972).

2. Burma
Ba Maw, *Breakthrough in Burma* (New Haven, Conn., 1968).
Thakin Nu, *Burma Under The Japanese* (London, 1954).

3. China
Chiang Kai-shek, *China's Destiny and Chinese Economic Theory* (ed. P. Jaffe, New York, 1947).
Schram, S. (ed.), *The Political Thought of Mao Tse-tung* (Harmondsworth, 1969).
Schurmann, H. F. and Schell, O. (eds.), *Republican China* (Harmondsworth, 1968).

4. France
de Gaulle, C., *War Memoirs: Unity, 1942–1944* (London, 1960).
　　　　　War Memoirs: Salvation, 1944–1946 (London, 1960).
Sabattier, G., *Le Destin de l'Indochine* (Paris, 1952).
Wavrin, A. de, *Souvenirs, vol. I* (Monte Carlo, 1947).

5. Great Britain
Adamson, I., *The Forgotten Men* (London, 1965).
Amery, J., *Approach March* (London, 1973).
Amery, L. S., *My Political Life, vol. III* (London, 1955).
Arnold, R., *A Very Quiet War* (London, 1962).
Attlee, C. R., *As It Happened* (London, 1954).
Avon, Lord, *Memoirs: The Reckoning* (London, 1965).
Band, C. and W., *Dragon Fangs* (London, 1947).
Bond, B. (ed.), *Chief of Staff. The Diaries of Lt. General Sir Henry Pownall, vol. II* (London, 1974).
Bryant, A., *The Turn of The Tide, 1939–1943* (London, 1957).
　　　　　Triumph In The West, 1943–1946 (London, 1959).
Butler, R. A., *The Art Of The Possible* (London, 1971).
Chandos, Lord, *Memoirs* (London, 1962).

Chapman, F. S., *The Jungle Is Neutral* (London, 1949).
Churchill, W. S., *The Second World War*, *vol. I* (London, 1948); *vol. II* (London, 1949); *vol. III* (London, 1950); *vol. IV* (London, 1951); *vol. V* (London, 1952); *vol. VI* (London, 1954).
Craigie, R., *Behind The Japanese Mask* (London, 1946).
Cunningham, Lord, *A Sailor's Odyssey* (London, 1951).
Dalton, H., *Memoirs, 1931–1945: The Fateful Years* (London, 1957).
Dilks, D. (ed.), *The Diaries of Sir Alexander Cadogan* (London, 1971).
Dixon, P. (ed.), *Double Diploma: The Life of Sir Pierson Dixon* (London, 1968).
Gilchrist, A., *Bangkok Top Secret* (London, 1970).
Gladwyn, Lord, *Memoirs* (London, 1972).
Gore-Booth, P., *With Great Truth And Respect* (London, 1974).
Harvey, J. (ed.), *The Diplomatic Diaries of Oliver Harvey, 1937–1940* (London, 1970).
Hayter, Sir W., *A Double Life* (London, 1974).
Ismay, Lord, *Memoirs* (London, 1960).
Kemp, P., *Alms For Oblivion* (London, 1961).
Kennedy, J., *The Business Of War* (London, 1957).
Lapwood, R. and N., *Through The Chinese Revolution* (London, 1954).
Lindsay, M., *The Unknown War: North China, 1937–1945* (London, 1975).
Macmillan, H., *The Blast of War, 1939–1945* (London, 1967).
Masters, J., *The Road Past Mandalay* (London, 1961).
Moon, P. (ed.), *Wavell: The Viceroy's Journal* (London, 1973).
Moran, Lord, *Winston Churchill: The Struggle For Survival, 1940–1965* (London, 1966).
Morrison, I., *Malayan Postscript* (London, 1942).
Needham, J., *Chinese Science* (London, 1945).
     Science Outpost (London, 1948).
Perham, M., *Colonial Sequence, 1930–1949* (London, 1967).
Peterson, M., *Both Sides of the Curtain* (London, 1950).
Purcell, V., *The Memoirs of a Malayan Official* (London, 1965).
Sansom, K., *Sir George Sansom and Japan: A Memoir* (Tallahassee, Florida, 1972).
Slim, W., *Defeat Into Victory* (London, 1960).
Stein, G., *The Challenge of Red China* (London, 1945).
Strang, Lord, *At Home and Abroad* (London, 1956).
Sweet-Escott, B., *Baker Street Irregular* (London, 1965).
Tedder, Lord, *With Prejudice* (London, 1966).
Thompson, R. W. (ed.), *Churchill and Morton* (London, 1976).
van der Poel, J. (ed.), *Selections From The Smuts Papers*, *vol. VI* (Cambridge, 1973).
van der Post, L., *The Night of the New Moon* (London, 1970).
Wheeler-Bennett, J. (ed.), *Action This Day: Working With Churchill* (London, 1968).
     Special Relationships (London, 1975).
Wiart, C. de, *Happy Odyssey* (London, 1950).
Williams, F., *A Prime Minister Remembers* (London, 1961).

6. Japan
  Shigemitsu, M., *Japan And Her Destiny* (London, 1958).

7. Netherlands
  van Mook, H. J., *Indonesië Nederland En De Wereld* (Amsterdam, 1949).
     The Status of Democracy in Southeast Asia (New York, 1950).

8. United States
  Acheson, D., *Present At The Creation* (London, 1970).
  Arnold, H. H., *Global Mission* (London, 1951).

Barrett, D. D., *The Dixie Mission* (Berkeley, California, 1970).
Barrett, N. H., *Chinghpaw* (New York, 1962).
Baruch, B., *The Public Years* (London, 1961).
Berle, B. and Jacobs, T. (eds.), *Navigating The Rapids: From The Papers of Adolf A. Berle* (New York, 1973).
Blum, J. M., *Roosevelt and Morgenthau* (Boston, 1970).
        From The Morgenthau Diaries: Years of War, 1941–45 (Boston, 1967).
        The Price of Vision: The Diary of Henry A. Wallace, 1942–1946 (Boston, 1973).
Bohlen, C. E., *Witness To History* (London, 1973).
Brown, C., *Suez to Singapore* (New York, 1943).
Byrnes, J. F., *Speaking Frankly* (London, 1948).
Campbell, T. and Herring, G. (eds.), *The Diaries of Edward R. Stettinius Jr., 1943–1946* (New York, 1975).
Chennault, C. L., *Way of a Fighter* (New York, 1949).
Davies, J. P., *Dragon By The Tail* (New York, 1972).
Deane, J. R., *The Strange Alliance* (London, 1947).
Eichelberger, R. L., *Our Jungle Road To Tokyo* (New York, 1950).
Eldridge, F., *Wrath In Burma* (New York, 1946).
Feis, H., *Seen From E. A.* (New York, 1947).
Freedman, M. (ed.), *Roosevelt and Frankfurter* (London, 1967).
Grew, J. C., *Ten Years In Japan* (London, 1945).
        Turbulent Era, vol. 2 (London, 1953).
Harriman, W. A. and Abel, E., *Special Envoy to Churchill And Stalin, 1941–1946* (London, 1976).
Hassett, W. D., *Off The Record With F.D.R.* (New Brunswick, N. J., 1958).
Hull, C., *Memoirs, vol. II* (London, 1948).
Ickes, H. L., *The Secret Diary of Harold L. Ickes, vol. III* (London, 1955).
Israel, F. L. (ed.), *The War Diary of Breckenridge Long* (Lincoln, Nebraska, 1966).
Kennan, G., *Memoirs, 1925–1950* (London, 1968).
King, E. J. and Whitehill, W., *Fleet Admiral King* (London, 1953).
Leahy, W. D., *I Was There* (London, 1950).
Leutze, J. (ed.), *The London Observer: The Journal of General Raymond E. Lee* (London, 1972).
Luvaas, J. (ed.), *Dear Miss Em.* (Westport, Conn., 1972).
MacArthur, D., *Reminiscences* (London, 1964).
Miles, M. E., *A Different Kind of War* (New York, 1967).
Millis, W. (ed.), *The Forrestal Diaries* (London, 1952).
Morgenthau, H. Jr., *Diary, China, vols. I and II* (Washington, D.C., 1965).
Peers, W. and Brelis, D., *Behind The Burma Road* (London, 1964).
Phillips, W., *Ventures In Diplomacy* (London, 1955).
Roosevelt, E., *As He Saw It* (New York, 1946).
        (ed.), *F.D.R.: His Personal Letters, 1928–1945, vol. 2* (New York, 1950).
Rosenman, S. I., *Working With Roosevelt* (London, 1952).
Service, J. S., *The Amerasia Papers* (Berkeley, California, 1971).
Smedley, A., *Battle Hymn of China* (London, 1943).
Snow, E., *Red Star Over China* (London, 1968).
        Journey To The Beginning (London, 1959).
Stettinius, E. R., *Roosevelt And The Russians* (London, 1950).
Stimson, H. L. and Bundy, M., *On Active Service In Peace And War* (New York, 1948).
Taylor, E., *Richer By Asia* (London, 1948).
        Awakening From History (London, 1971).
Truman, H. S., *Year Of Decisions, 1945* (London, 1955).

Vandenberg, A. (ed.), *The Private Papers of Senator Arthur Vandenberg* (London, 1953).
Wedemeyer, A. C., *Wedemeyer Reports!* (New York, 1958).
Welles, S., *A Time For Decision* (London, 1944).
White, T. H. and Jacoby, A., *Thunder Out Of China* (London, 1947).
White, T. H. (ed.), *The Stilwell Papers* (New York, 1948).
Winant, J. G., *A Letter From Grosvenor Square* (London, 1947).

G. *Secondary Works*
Addison, P., *The Road To 1945* (London, 1975).
Adler, S., *The Isolationist Impulse* (New York, 1960).
Allen, H. C., *Great Britain and the United States* (London, 1954).
Allen, L., *The End of the War in Asia* (London, 1976).
         Singapore, 1941–1942 (London, 1977).
Almond, G. A., *The American People and Foreign Policy* (New York, 1965).
Anders, L., *The Ledo Road* (Norman, Oklahoma, 1965).
Aron, R., *Peace And War: A Theory of International Relations* (London, 1966).
         The Imperial Republic (London, 1975).

Barnard, E., *Wendell Willkie: Fighter For Freedom* (Marquette, Michigan, 1966).
Barnett, C., *The Collapse of British Power* (London, 1972).
Beitzell, R., *The Uneasy Alliance: America, Britain and Russia, 1941–1943* (New York, 1972).
Beloff, M., *Imperial Sunset, vol. I* (London, 1969).
Berlin, I., *Mr. Churchill in 1940* (London, 1950).
Birkenhead, Lord, *The Prof. In Two Worlds* (London, 1961).
         Halifax (London, 1965).
Bishop, J., *F.D.R.'s Last Year* (New York, 1974).
Boardman, R., *Britain and the People's Republic of China, 1949–1974* (London, 1976).
Borg, D., *The United States and the Far Eastern Crisis of 1933–1938* (Cambridge, Mass., 1964).
         Historians and American Far Eastern Policy (New York, 1966).
Borg, D., and Okamoto, S., (eds.), *Pearl Harbor As History* (New York, 1973).
Bowle, J., *The Imperial Achievement: The Rise and Transformation of the British Empire* (London, 1974).
Boyle, A., *Poor, Dear Brendan* (London, 1974).
Boyle, J. H., *China and Japan At War, 1937–1945* (Stanford, 1972).
Brecher, M., *The Foreign Policy System of Israel* (London, 1972).
Buhite, R. D., *Patrick Hurley And American Foreign Policy* (Ithica, N.Y., 1973).
Bullock, A., *The Life and Times of Ernest Bevin, vol. II* (London, 1967).
Burns, J. M., *Roosevelt: The Soldier of Freedom, 1940–1945* (London, 1971).
Butler, J. R. M., *Grand Strategy, vol. II* (London, 1957).
         Grand Strategy, vol. III pt. II (London, 1964).
Butow, R. J., *Japan's Decision To Surrender* (Stanford, 1954).
         Tojo and the Coming of War (Princeton, 1961).

Calder, A., *The People's War. Britain, 1939–45* (London, 1969).
Calvocoressi, P., and Wint, G., *Total War* (London, 1972).
Castles, F. G., *Pressure Groups and Political Culture* (London, 1967).
Charlesworth, J. C., *Contemporary Political Analysis* (New York, 1968).
Clemens, D., *Yalta* (New York, 1970).
Cohen, B. C., *The Press And Foreign Policy* (Princeton, 1963).
Cohen, W., *America's Response To China* (New York, 1971).
Collis, M., *First And Last In Burma* (London, 1956).
Connell, J., *Wavell, Scholar and Soldier: to June 1941* (London, 1964).

Cooke, C., *The Life of Richard Stafford Cripps* (London, 1957).
Cosgrave, P., *Churchill At War, vol. I* (London, 1974).
Craig, A. and Shively, D. (eds.), *Personality In Japanese History* (Berkeley, 1970).
Crowley, J., *Japan's Quest For Autonomy* (Princeton, 1966).

Darby, P., *British Defence Policy East of Suez, 1947–1968* (London, 1974).
De Conde, A. (ed.), *Isolation and Security* (Durham, N. Carolina, 1957).
Devilliers, P., *Histoire du Viêt-Nam, 1940–1952* (Paris, 1952).
Divine, R., *Second Chance: The Triumph Of Internationalism in America During World War II* (New York, 1967).
           Roosevelt and World War II (Baltimore, 1969).
Donnison, F. S., *British Military Administration In The Far East, 1943–46* (London, 1956).
Drachman, E. R., *United States Policy Toward Vietnam, 1940–1945* (Rutherford, N.J., 1970).
Dunn, F. S., *Peacemaking And The Settlement With Japan* (Princeton, 1963).
Duroselle, J-B., *La Politique Extérieure de la France, 1914 à 1945* (Paris, 1965).

Edwardes, M., *Asia In The European Age* (London, 1961).
Edwards, C., *Bruce of Melbourne,* (London, 1965).
Ehrman, J., *Grand Strategy, vol. V* (London, 1956).
           Grand Strategy, vol. VI (London, 1956).
Elsbree, W. H., *Japan's Role In Southeast Asian Nationalist Movements, 1940–1945* (Cambridge, Mass., 1953).
Endicott, S. C., *Diplomacy And Enterprise: British China Policy, 1933–37* (Manchester, 1975).
Erickson, J., *The Soviet High Command* (London, 1962).

Farley, M., *America's Stake In The Far East* (New York, 1936).
Feis, H., *The Road To Pearl Harbor* (Princeton, 1971).
           Churchill, Roosevelt and Stalin (Princeton, 1967).
           The China Tangle (Princeton, 1972).
           Between War And Peace (Princeton, 1960).
           Japan Subdued (Princeton, 1961).
Fifield, R. H., *Southeast Asia In United States Policy* (New York, 1963).
Fishel, W. R., *The End of Extraterritoriality in China* (Berkeley, 1952).
Fitzgerald, C. P., *The Chinese View of Their Place In The World* (London, 1964).
           The Birth of Communist China (Harmondsworth, 1964).
Freidel, F., *Franklin D. Roosevelt: The Apprenticeship* (Boston, 1952).
           Franklin D. Roosevelt: The Ordeal (Boston, 1954).
           Franklin D. Roosevelt: The Triumph (Boston, 1956).
           Franklin D. Roosevelt: Launching The New Deal (Boston, 1973).
Friend, T., *Between Two Empires* (New Haven, 1965).

Gaddis, J. L., *The United States And The Origins of the Cold War* (New York, 1972).
Gardner, L. C., *Economic Aspects of New Deal Diplomacy* (Boston, 1971).
           Architects of Illusion (Chicago, 1972).
Gardner, R. N., *Sterling-Dollar Diplomacy* (Oxford, 1956).
Gibbs, N., *Grand Strategy, vol. I* (London, 1976).
Gilbert, M., *Winston S. Churchill, vol. V* (London, 1976).
Girdner, A., and Loftis, A., *The Great Betrayal: The Evacuation of the Japanese-Americans During World War II* (Toronto, 1969).
Gittings, J., *China And The World, 1922–1972* (London, 1974).
Goodspeed, S. S., *The Nature and Function of International Organization* (New York, 1967).
Gopal, S., *Jawaharlal Nehru, vol. I* (London, 1975).
Gowing, M., *Britain and Atomic Energy, 1939–1945* (London, 1964).

Grattan, C. H., *The United States and the Southwest Pacific* (Cambridge, Mass., 1961).
Greenfield, K. R., *Command Decisions* (London, 1960).
Gull, E. M., *British Economic Interests In The Far East* (London, 1943).
Gupta, P. S., *Imperialism and the British Labour Movement, 1914–1964* (London, 1975).
Gwyer, J. M. A., *Grand Strategy, vol. III, pt. I* (London, 1964).

Hall, W. H. D., *North American Supply* (London, 1955).
Hammer, E., *The Struggle For Indochina* (Stanford, 1954).
Hancock, W., *Smuts: The Fields of Force, 1919–1950* (Cambridge, 1968).
Hancock, W. and Gowing, M., *British War Economy* (London, 1949).
Harrod, R. F., *The Life of John Maynard Keynes* (London, 1951).
Hasluck, P., *The Government And The People: vol. I, 1939–41* (Canberra, 1952).
    The Government And The People, vol. II, 1942–45 (Canberra, 1972).
Heinrichs, W. H., *American Ambassador* (Boston, 1965).
Hess, G. R., *America Encounters India, 1941–1947* (Baltimore, 1971).
Hetherington, J., *Blamey* (Melbourne, 1954).
Hoffmann, S., *Gulliver's Troubles* (New York, 1968).
Hofstadter, R., *The American Political Tradition* (London, 1967).
    The Paranoid Style In American Politics (New York, 1964).
    Anti-Intellectualism in American Life (New York, 1963).
Holland, W. L. (ed.), *Asian Nationalism And The West* (New York, 1953).
Hornbeck, S. K., *The United States In The Far East* (Boston, 1942).
Horowitz, D., *From Yalta to Vietnam* (Harmondsworth, 1967).
Howard, M., *Grand Strategy, vol. IV* (London, 1972).
    The Continental Commitment (London, 1972).
Hudson, G. F., *The Far East In World Politics* (London, 1939).
Hunt, M., *Frontier Defense and the Open Door* (New Haven, 1973).
Huntington, S. P., *The Soldier and the State* (New York, 1957).
Hyde, H. M., *The Quiet Canadian* (London, 1962).

Ike, N. (ed.), *Japan's Decision For War* (Stanford, 1967).
Institute of Pacific Relations, *War And Peace In The Pacific* (New York, 1943).
Institute of Pacific Relations, *Security In The Pacific* (New York, 1945).
Iriye, A., *Pacific Estrangement* (Cambridge, Mass., 1972).
    Across The Pacific (New York, 1967).
    After Imperialism (Cambridge, Mass., 1965).
    The Cold War In Asia (Englewood Cliffs, N.J., 1974).
Isaacs, H. R., *Scratches On Our Minds* (New York, 1963).
    No Peace For Asia (Cambridge, Mass., 1967).

James, R. R., *Churchill, A Study In Failure, 1900–1939* (London, 1970).

Kahn, E. J., *The China Hands* (New York, 1975).
Kelman, H. C., *International Behavior* (New York, 1966).
Kennan, G., *American Diplomacy, 1900–1950* (New York, 1951).
Kennedy, J., *A History of Malaya* (London, 1970).
Kennedy, M. D., *The Estrangement of Great Britain and Japan* (Manchester, 1969).
Kiernan, V. G., *The Lords of Human Kind* (London, 1969).
Kimball, W. (ed.), *Franklin D. Roosevelt and the World Crisis, 1937–1945* (Lexington, Mass., 1973).
    The Most Unsordid Thing (Baltimore, 1969).
Kirby, S. W., *The War Against Japan, vol. I* (London, 1957).
    The War Against Japan, vol. II (London, 1958).
    The War Against Japan, vol. III (London, 1961).
    The War Against Japan, vol. IV (London, 1965).

Kirby, S. W., *The War Against Japan, vol. V* (London, 1969).
    Singapore: The Chain of Disaster (London, 1971).
Knapp, W., *A History of War and Peace, 1939–1965* (London, 1967).
Koen, R. Y., *The China Lobby In American Politics* (New York, 1974).
Kolko, G., *The Politics of War* (London, 1968).
Kubek, A., *How The Far East Was Lost* (Chicago, 1953).

Lake, A. (ed.), *The Legacy of Vietnam* (New York, 1976).
Lancaster, D., *The Emancipation of French Indochina* (London, 1961).
Langer, W., *Our Vichy Gamble* (New York, 1947).
Lash, J. P., *Roosevelt and Churchill, 1939–41* (London, 1977).
Lattimore, O., *Solution In Asia* (London, 1945).
Lee, B. A., *Britain and the Sino-Japanese War, 1937–1939* (Stanford, 1973).
Levi, W., *American–Australian Relations* (Minneapolis, 1947).
Lewin, R., *Churchill As Warlord* (London, 1973).
    Slim: The Standardbearer (London, 1976).
Lichtheim, G., *Imperialism* (London, 1971).
Lingeman, R., *Don't You Know There's A War On?* (New York, 1970).
Lippmann, W., *United States War Aims* (London, 1944).
Liska, G., *Imperial America* (Baltimore, 1967).
    Nations In Alliance (Baltimore, 1962).
Lissington, M. P., *New Zealand and the United States, 1840–1944* (Wellington, N.Z., 1972).
Lohbeck, D., *Patrick J. Hurley* (Chicago, 1956).
Louis, W. R., *British Strategy In The Far East, 1919–1939* (Oxford, 1971).
    Imperialism at Bay (Oxford, 1977).
Lovell, J. P., *Foreign Policy In Perspective* (New York, 1970).
Lowe, P., *Great Britain and Japan, 1911–1915* (London, 1969).
    Great Britain and the Origins of the Pacific War (Oxford, 1977).

MacDonald, I. S., *Anglo-American Relations Since The Second World War* (Newton Abbot, 1974).
MacFarquhar, R., *Sino-American Relations, 1949–1971* (Newton Abbott, 1972).
Marshall, D. B., *The French Colonial Myth And Constitution-Making In The Fourth Republic* (New Haven, 1973).
Maruyama, M., *Thought And Behaviour In Modern Japanese Politics* (London, 1963).
Marwick, A., *Britain In The Century Of Total War* (London, 1968).
Mason, P., *Prospero's Magic* (London, 1962).
    A Matter of Honour (London, 1974).
    Patterns of Dominance (London, 1971).
Matloff, M. and Snell, E., *Strategic Planning For Coalition Warfare, 1941–1942* (Washington, D.C., 1953).
Matloff, M., *Strategic Planning For Coalition Warfare, 1943–1944* (Washington, 1959).
Maxwell, N., *India's China War* (London, 1970).
May, E., *'Lessons' Of The Past* (London, 1975).
May, E. and Thomson, J., *American–East Asia Relations* (Cambridge, Mass., 1972).
Milward, A. S., *War, Economy and Society, 1939–1945* (London, 1977).
Minear, R. H., *Victor's Justice* (Princeton, 1971).
Morison, E. E., *Turmoil and Tradition* (Boston, 1960).
Morison, S. E., *The Two-Ocean War* (Boston, 1963).
Morley, J. W. (ed.), *Dilemmas Of Growth In Pre-War Japan* (Princeton, 1972).
    Deterrent Diplomacy: Japan, Germany, and The U.S.S.R., 1935–1940 (New York, 1977).

Morton, L., *Strategy and Command: The First Two Years* (Washington, D.C., 1962).
Mueller, J. E., *War, Presidents And Public Opinion* (New York, 1973).
Myrdal, G., *An American Dilemma, vol. II* (New York, 1944).

Nagai, Y. and Iriye, A. (eds.), *The Origins of the Cold War in Asia* (Tokyo, 1977).
Needham, J., *Within The Four Seas* (London, 1969).
Neumann, W. L., *America Encounters Japan* (Baltimore, 1963).
Nicholas, H. G., *The United States and Britain* (Chicago, 1975).
Nish, I., *The Anglo-Japanese Alliance* (London, 1966).
          Alliance In Decline (London, 1972).

Offner, A., *American Appeasement* (Cambridge, Mass., 1969).
Osgood, R. E., *Ideals And Self-Interest In America's Foreign Policy* (Chicago, 1953).
          Alliances And American Foreign Policy (Baltimore, 1971).

Paige, G., *The Korean Decision* (New York, 1968).
Pandey, B. N., *The Break-Up of British India* (London, 1969).
Panikkar, K. M., *Asia And Western Dominance* (London, 1953).
Paxton, R. O., *Vichy France: Old Guard And New Order, 1940–1944* (New York, 1972).
Pelling, H., *Winston Churchill* (London, 1974).
Perry, H. D., *The Panay Incident* (New York, 1969).
Pogue, F. C., *George C. Marshall: Ordeal and Hope, 1939–1942* (New York, 1966).
          George C. Marshall: Organizer of Victory, 1943–1945 (New York, 1973).
Potter, D. M., *The People of Plenty* (Chicago, 1968).
Purcell, V., *The Chinese in Southeast Asia* (Oxford, 1965).

Range, W., *Franklin D. Roosevelt's World Order* (Athens, Georgia, 1959).
Reese, T. R., *Australia, New Zealand and the United States* (London, 1969).
Reischauer, E., Fairbank, J. K., and Craig, A., *East Asia: The Modern Transformation* (London, 1965).
Richard, D. E., *United States Naval Administration of the Trust Territory of the Pacific Islands* (Washington, D.C., 1957).
Rolph, C. H., *Kingsley* (London, 1973).
Romanus, C. and Sutherland, R., *Stilwell's Mission To China* (Washington, D.C., 1953).
          Stilwell's Command Problems (Washington, 1956).
          Time Runs Out in C.B.I. (Washington, 1959).
Rose, S., *Britain And Southeast Asia* (London, 1962).
Rosenau, J. N., *International Politics And Foreign Policy* (New York, 1961).
          The Scientific Study of Foreign Policy (New York, 1971).
          Public Opinion and Foreign Policy (New York, 1961).
          Domestic Sources of Foreign Policy (New York, 1967).
Roskill, S. W., *The War At Sea, vol. I* (London, 1954).
          The War At Sea, vol. II (London, 1956).
          The War At Sea, vol. III, part I (London, 1960).
          The War At Sea, vol. III, part II (London, 1961).
          Hankey, Man of Secrets, vol. III (London, 1974).
          Naval Policy Between The Wars, vol. I (London, 1968).
          Naval Policy Between The Wars, vol. II (London, 1976).
Royal Institute of International Affairs, *The Colonial Problem* (London, 1937).

Sainteny, J., *Histoire D'Une Paix Manquée* (Paris, 1953).
Sapin, B. M., *The Making of United States Foreign Policy* (New York, 1966).

Scalapino, R. A., *Democracy And The Party Movement In Pre-War Japan* (Berkeley, 1962).

Schelling, T. C., *Arms And Influence* (New Haven, 1966).

Schlesinger, A. M., *The Imperial Presidency* (London, 1974).

Schram, S., *Mao Tse-tung* (London, 1967).

Shai, A., *Origins of the War in the East* (London, 1976).

Sherwood, R. G., *Roosevelt and Hopkins* (New York, 1948).

Shewmaker, K. E., *Americans and Chinese Communists, 1927–1945* (Ithica, N.Y., 1971).

Smith, G., *American Diplomacy During The Second World War* (New York, 1965).

Smith, R., *Vietnam and the West* (Ithaca, N.Y., 1971).

Smith, R. H., *O.S.S.* (Berkeley, 1972).

Smith, T. and Bastin, J., *Malaysia* (London, 1967).

Snyder, L., *The War: A Concise History, 1939–1945* (London, 1962).

Sorensen, T. C., *Decision-Making In The White House* (New York, 1963).

Steele, A. T., *The American People and China* (New York, 1966).

Stevenson, W., *A Man Called Intrepid* (New York, 1976).

Storry, G. R., *A History of Modern Japan* (London, 1962).
                 The Double Patriots (London, 1957).

Sykes, C., *Orde Wingate* (London, 1959).

Taiheiyo senso e no michi: kaisen gaiko-shi (Tokyo, 1962–3).

Tang, P. S., *Russia and Soviet Policy In Manchuria and Outer Mongolia, 1911–1931* (Durham, N.C., 1959).

Tang Tsou, *America's Failure In China, 1941–50* (Chicago, 1962).

Taylor, A. J. P., et al., *Churchill: Four Faces And The Man* (London, 1969).
                 English History, 1914–1945 (Oxford, 1965).
                 Beaverbrook (London, 1972).

Thomas, J. N., *The Institute of Pacific Relations* (Seattle, 1974).

Thompson, R., *No Exit From Vietnam* (London, 1969).

Thorne, C., *The Limits Of Foreign Policy* (London, 1972).

Thornton, A. P., *The Imperial Idea And Its Enemies* (London, 1966).

Tinker, H., *Race, Conflict and the International Order* (London, 1977).

Trotter, A., *Britain And East Asia, 1933–1937* (Cambridge, 1975).

Tuchman, B., *Sand Against The Wind: Stilwell And The American Experience of China, 1911–1945* (London, 1971).

Tugwell, R., *In Search of Roosevelt* (Cambridge, Mass., 1972).

Varg, P., *Missionaries, Chinese and Diplomats* (Princeton, 1958).
                 The Making of a Myth: The United States and China, 1897–1912 (East Lansing, Michigan, 1968).

Viorst, M., *Hostile Allies: F.D.R. and Charles de Gaulle* (New York, 1975).

Walker, R. and Curry, G., *The American Secretaries of State And Their Diplomacy, vol. XIV* (New York, 1965).

Watt, A., *The Evolution Of Australian Foreign Policy* (Cambridge, 1967).

Watt, D. C., *Personalities and Policies* (London, 1965).

Westerfield, H. B., *Foreign Policy And Party Politics* (New Haven, 1955).

Weston, R. F., *Racism in U.S. Imperialism* (Columbia, South Carolina, 1972).

Wheeler, G. E., *Prelude To Pearl Harbor* (Columbia, Missouri, 1963).

Wheeler-Bennett, J., *King George VI* (London, 1958).
                 John Anderson, Viscount Waverley (London, 1962).

Williams, W. A., *The Roots of the Modern American Empire* (New York, 1969).
                 From Colony To Empire (New York, 1972).

Wint, G., *The British In Asia* (New York, 1954).

Winterbotham, F. W., *The Ultra Secret* (London, 1974).

Wiseman, H. V., *Political Systems: Some Sociological Approaches* (London, 1966).

Wohlstetter, R., *Pearl Harbor: Warning and Decision* (Stanford, 1962).

Wolfers, A., *Discord And Collaboration* (Baltimore, 1965).

Woodward, L., *British Foreign Policy In The Second World War* (single volume, London, 1962).

        British Foreign Policy In The Second World War, vol. I (London, 1970).

        British Foreign Policy In The Second World War, vol. II (London, 1971).

        British Foreign Policy In The Second World War, vol. III (London, 1971).

        British Foreign Policy In The Second World War, vol. IV (London, 1975).

        British Foreign Policy In The Second World War, vol. V (London, 1976).

Wright, Q., *A Study Of War* (Chicago, 1942).

Young, A. N., *China And The Helping Hand, 1937–1945* (Cambridge, Mass., 1963).

H. Articles

Chan Lau Kit-Ching, 'The Hong Kong Question During The Pacific War', *Journal of Imperial and Commonwealth History*, vol. 2, no. 1, 1973.

Dallek, R., 'Franklin Roosevelt As World Leader', *American Historical Review*, vol. 76, no. 5, 1971.

Dulles, F. and Ridinger, G., 'The Anti-Colonial Policies of Franklin D. Roosevelt', *Political Science Quarterly*, March 1955.

Fairbank, J. K., '"American China Policy" to 1898: A Misconception', *Pacific Historical Review*, Nov. 1970.

Kimball, W., 'Churchill and Roosevelt: The Personal Equation', *Prologue*, Fall 1974.

Lawry, J., 'A Catch On The Boundary: Australia and the Free French Movement in 1940', *Journal of Pacific History*, vol. 10, 1975.

Lafeber, W., 'Roosevelt, Churchill and Indochina, 1942–45', *American Historical Review*, LXXX, 1975.

Lowe, P., 'Great Britain And The Coming Of The Pacific War, 1939–1941', *Transactions of the Royal Historical Society*, 5th series, vol. 24, 1974.

Morton, L., 'War Plan Orange: Evolution of a Strategy', *World Politics*, Jan. 1959.

Peterson, A., 'Britain And Siam: The Latest Phase', *Pacific Affairs*, Dec. 1946.

Pritchard, R. J., 'The Far East As An Influence On The Chamberlain Government's Pre-War European Policies', *Millennium*, vol. 1, no. 3.

Rosinger, L. K., 'Independence For Colonial Asia: The Cost To The Western World', *Foreign Affairs Reports*, Feb. 1944.

Shai, A., 'Le conflit anglo-japonais de Tientsin, 1939', *Revue d'Histoire Moderne et Contemporaine*, April–June, 1975.

        'Was There A Far-Eastern Munich?', *Journal of Contemporary History*, vol. 9, no. 3, 1974.

Sherwin, M. J., 'The Atomic Bomb And The Origins Of The Cold War', *American Historical Review*, vol. 78, no. 4, 1973.

Thorne, C., 'Britain And The Black G.I.s: Racial Issues And Anglo-American Relations In 1942', *New Community*, vol. III, no. 3, 1974.

        'Australia and the Americans: Letters From The Minister', *The Age* (Melbourne), 8 and 9 Jan. 1975.

        'Evatt, Curtin and the United States', *The Age* (Melbourne), 30 June and 1 July 1974.

        'MacArthur, Australia and the British', *Australian Outlook*, April and August, 1975.

        'Engeland, Australië en Nederlands Indië, 1941–1945', *Internationale Spectator* (The Hague), August 1975.

'The Indochina Issue Between Britain and the United States, 1942–1945', *Pacific Historical Review*, Feb. 1976.

'Chatham House, Whitehall and Far Eastern Issues, 1941–1945', *International Affairs*, January 1978.

Tinker, H., 'A Forgotten Long March: The Indian Exodus From Burma, 1942', *Journal of Southeast Asian Studies*, March 1975.

Venkataramani, M., and Shrivastava, B., 'The Unified States and the Cripps Mission', *India Quarterly*, vol. XIX, no. 3.

Watt, D. C., 'American Anti-Colonial Policies And The End of European Colonial Empires', in A. N. Den Hollander (ed.), *Contagious Conflict* (Leiden, 1973).

Williams, J. E., 'The Joint Declaration on the Colonies', *British Journal of International Studies*, 2, 1976.

Wynn, N. A., 'The Impact of the Second World War on the American Negro', *Journal of Contemporary History*, vol. 6, no. 2, 1971.

I. *Unpublished Paper*

George, M. L., 'Australian Attitudes And Policies Towards the Netherlands East Indies and Indonesian Independence. 1942–49' (Unpublished Ph.D. dissertation, 1973, A.N.U., Canberra).

INDEX*

* Compiled by Beryl and Christopher Thorne. Names, titles, etc. as in 1941–45.